THE MEDIEVAL WORLD

BY

LOREN CAREY MacKINNEY

PROFESSOR OF MEDIEVAL HISTORY
THE UNIVERSITY OF NORTH CAROLINA

FARRAR & RINEHART, INC.

PUBLISHERS   NEW YORK

PREFACE

WITHIN the past half-century the work of many scholars has led to a new understanding of the Middle Ages. I have therefore sought in this volume to present a history of the Middle Ages in terms of the findings of recent historical scholarship for students in general courses which survey the history of Western civilization as well as for those who specialize in the medieval period. My view of the place of the Middle Ages in European history and of the nature of the Middle Ages is both implicit and explicit in the volume and needs no further discussion here.

Throughout the volume I have endeavored to strike a rough balance between extremes of political narrative and institutional or cultural description. If our forefathers erred in viewing the past largely in terms of political and military history, our own age may perhaps go too far in its stress on institutional forms and cultural developments. I have tried, therefore, to give proper weight to the religious, socio-economic and cultural factors, as well as to present a solid core of political narrative.

In the preparation of this volume I have been fully aware of my indebtedness to many men and books. Among the individuals who have inspired me in countless ways Professor James Westfall Thompson is foremost. His brilliant lectures and dynamic personality made an unforgettable impression upon me during my student days at the University of Chicago.

I am indebted to Dr. Henry David of the College of the City of New York for his aid in the preparation of this volume. His critical sense and sympathetic understanding were helpful at all times. I have relied often, too, upon the advice of my friend and colleague, Professor Wallace E. Caldwell. Mr. Benjamin Nelson of the College of the City of New York gave me the benefit of his searching knowledge of many phases of medieval history. Professor Frank K. Cameron of the University of North Carolina and Professor J. A. Corbett of Notre Dame University were good enough to read and comment on the section on the Catholic Church. Others who have been helpful are Professors H. M. Wagstaff, Fred B. McCall, H. R. Huse, C. B. Robson, C. H. Pegg, and U. T. Holmes of the University of North Carolina, Professor Geneva Drinkwater of Vassar College, and the Reverend A. S. Lawrence of Chapel Hill. Among my students who have aided in the checking of details are Arnold Borden, Barnaby Keeney, Alexander McGeachy, and Edward Gibson. None of these, of course, is responsible for possible misstatements of fact or for expressions of opinion that appear in the volume.

By no means least is the debt I owe to my wife and son, who have so willingly accepted those tasks which a professor imposes upon the members of his immediate family.

L. C. M.

Chapel Hill, N. C.
May, 1938

CONTENTS

PART II

CIVILIZATION DURING THE LATE MIDDLE AGES

ILLUSTRATIONS

MAPS

AN INTRODUCTION TO THE ANCIENT WORLD

By

Wallace E. Caldwell

THE ANCIENT ORIENT

FROM the very beginning of human history man has been faced with two fundamental problems—material existence and the explanation of his presence in and relationship with the universe. In the making of tools, in food gathering, hunting, the domestication of plants and animals, in the manufacture of cloth and pottery, and in the building of homes, early man provided a solution to the first problem. Together with the development of these activities, and related to them, there came changes in social and political and religious institutions. Early man apparently discovered in the supernatural a way of getting in touch with, explaining, and controlling the world in which he found himself. It is thus entirely understandable that religion and magic entered into every phase of the life of primitive man. What we now call science and philosophy are but later attempts to solve these same difficulties. Inextricably bound up with all these developments are man's activities in literature and the arts.

Man has always lived in social groups. And every social group possesses in addition to its people, its technical practices, its economic, social, political, and religious institutions, its customs and tradition, its ideas and ideals, and a great deal more. These many interrelated elements constitute what is called *civilization*. These institutions, habits, traditions, ideals, and the like, tend to acquire a fixed pattern and to resist change. They are, however, always potentially subject to forces which make for change, transformation, or abandonment. History studies civilizations and the changes they undergo.

No written records exist for the early unnumbered centuries of human history, and this period is spoken of as preliterary history. Material objects, such as tools, weapons, pottery, the remains of dwellings, tombs, and monuments, and animal and human skeletons, enable us to reconstruct the history of this period. On the basis of techniques of tool production, types of tools and the basic material used in their manufacture, the cultural divisions of these early ages have been made. The major divisions are the Palaeolithic or Old Stone Age, the Neolithic or New Stone Age, and the Age of Metals, divided into the

Bronze and Iron Ages. The last two, however, bring us in many regions into the range of recorded history.

PRELITERARY HISTORY

THE OLD
STONE AGE

During the period when ice covered much of Europe and North America, men were living in many parts of Europe, Asia, and Africa. These men, finding shelter in grottoes, under overhanging rocks, or in caves, gathered wild grains, fruits, herbs, and roots, and hunted and fished for game. Their weapons and tools were made of flint and included fist hatchets, knives, and scrapers. In addition to the family the most important social groups were those that rested on kinship. There apparently was some measure of division of labor in primitive society as well as some trade between primitive communities.

The earliest skeletons which have been found definitely associated with tools of the Palaeolithic period belonged to what is called the Neanderthal race. The Neanderthals, who lived about sixty thousand years ago, had not attained full human development. Nevertheless they were skilled hunters and tool-makers and knew the use of fire. They were succeeded by Cro-Magnon man, who was much like ourselves. The Cro-Magnon peoples made a wide variety of tools from stone, bone and horn. Their skilled artists—probably for magical purposes—incised and painted striking likenesses of the animals they hunted on their tools and on the walls of caves in southern France and northern Spain. These early modern men apparently believed in an afterlife and worshiped deities. A changing climate, the retreat of the reindeer, and the disappearance of other animals brought an end to the Old Stone Age in Western Europe.

THE NEW
STONE AGE

While Old Stone Age men were still hunting reindeer in Western Europe, in the East men were making those notable advances which characterize the New Stone Age and also made possible the great achievements of later ages. Foremost among the contributions of the Neolithic period were the domestication of animals and the development of agriculture. Men also learned to bake clay and make pottery in addition to producing storage receptacles of baskets and skins. The weaving of flax and wool led to the substitution of clothing for skins, and the appearance of the first textile industry. While chipped flint was still used for tools, it was also polished, and hard stones were used to make axes with fine edges. At the same time man became a house builder. The domestication of plants and animals resulted in the development of village communities.

All these changes brought about a veritable revolution in the mode of life of early man, and were reflected in the appearance of larger and more complex social and political groupings. Society, however, still rested upon a kinship basis. The development of agriculture was reflected in religion, and every effort was made to secure the good will of the divine beings who ruled the elements and gave grain to man.

THE AGE OF METALS With the use of metals—first copper, then bronze and, much later, iron—men were able to reach greater heights in material civilization, the arts, and the technique of warfare. During the New Stone Age there had been numerous movements of peoples. Nomads wandering with their herds or flocks had penetrated into river valley areas and farmers had pushed on in search of fertile land when their old fields had become exhausted. The shifting of population was further intensified during the Metal Age by the development of superior weapons which insured easy conquest to their possessors. It is no wonder, then, that the Bronze Age was marked by migrations and produced epic tales of war, conquest, and heroes.

Comparable to the discovery of metals were other achievements of this age. The use of the wheel in the making of pottery and for transportation had revolutionary significance. In response to the needs of agriculture, the movements of the sun, moon, and stars were studied more intensively, calendars of months and years were worked out, and the development of systems of chronology was made possible. At the same time, when the increasing complexity of life made necessary the keeping of records, there appeared methods of writing. With the development of writing the preliterary age comes to an end.

WRITING Writing began with the drawing of pictures to represent objects. Then some of the pictures were used to represent sounds—that is, groups of letters. Egyptian writing, which the Greeks called *hieroglyphics,* contained pictures of objects, of sounds, and single letters. Though the Egyptians eventually simplified their pictures greatly, they never developed a phonetic alphabet. The Egyptians wrote on the walls of temples and tombs, and had an equivalent for our paper in papyrus, which they made from a river reed. In Babylonia, the Sumerians employed the pictures to represent syllables. These were drawn with blunt-ended reeds on clay tablets which were later baked. The wedge-shaped lines thus produced give this writing its name, *cuneiform.* This syllabic form of writing was adapted to other languages, and was widely used throughout the Near East for many centuries. Sometime before 1500 B.C. the Phoenicians learned the advantage of having each sign represent a single letter, and drew a picture which signified not the object but the first sound of the name of the object. These signs, taken over with some changes bv the Greeks, and from them by the Romans, have been transmitted to us as our alphabet.

ORIENTAL HISTORY

Even before the Age of Metals, important civilizations developed in the fertile valleys of the Nile, the Tigris-Euphrates and the rivers of India and China. Of these only the first two materially affected the formation of European culture.

EGYPT   The Nile River flows north to the Mediterranean from the heart of Africa through a gorge cut into a desert plateau, overflowing its banks every spring and depositing a film of black soil over a narrow strip of land. At its mouth a fertile area has been built up from the silt of the river. The periodic overflow of the Nile thus made possible the remarkable agricultural development of the valley. Strict control over the use of the water was and is necessary in order that no one section may receive more than its share. Egypt was most prosperous under a strong government which exercised such control. In the Nile Valley accumulation of wealth was possible; at the same time the transmission of acquired techniques to succeeding generations made for continuity and advance in culture.

Egyptian history is commonly divided into five periods: the pre-dynastic period, the Old Kingdom, the Middle Kingdom, the empire, and the period of decline. In the predynastic period, the land was divided into independent sections called *nomes*. Each of these had its own chieftain and its own gods. These nomes were eventually united into two kingdoms—Upper Egypt, comprising the valley from the first cataract to the delta, and Lower Egypt, the delta area. The Old Kingdom was established about 3400 B.C. when, after a series of wars, one ruler united all Egypt. The succeeding kings, called *pharaohs,* controlled the life of Egypt from their capital at Memphis, and built for their tombs great pyramids of stone.

About 2500 B.C. provincial governors and other powerful lords became independent of the central power, and Egypt suffered a decline until 2000 B.C., when the princes of Thebes in southern Egypt established the Middle Kingdom. In this period the nome governors regulated the affairs of their own districts, but paid due allegiance and obedience to the king. He was recognized as the source of all power and prosperity and as controller of the life-giving waters of the Nile. Some two hundred and fifty years later, invaders from Syria, the Hyksos, conquered Egypt. When they were driven out in 1580 B.C., the empire was established. Employing horse-drawn chariots, a contribution of the Hyksos, great conquerors like Thutmose III annexed Syria and the Upper Nile, and wealth poured into the land as booty

and tribute. Following the appearance of several notable rulers, a long
period of decline began in the twelfth century. Weak kings were followed by priestly rulers, Libyan and Ethiopian usurpers, and then by
Assyrian conquerors. A native dynasty won independence from Assyria, and then fell before Persia, which in turn was overcome by
Alexander of Macedon.

During the Old Kingdom, Egypt became unified, acquired great
power, and suffered disunity once again. In the course of this its rulers
developed a highly centralized and efficiently organized kingdom, in
which the king dominated the governmental structure. The pharaoh
was chief priest of all Egypt, and was regarded as a god. He owned
all the land, regulated the water supply, operated the quarries and
mines, supervised the workshops, and directed the building of temples.
When the valley was inundated he called out the people to work on
his buildings or fight his wars. The bureaucratic machine which administered affairs was supported by a complex financial system. Taxes
or rents, paid in kind or service, were levied on land, trees, produce,
cattle, products of industry and persons. The labor service rendered
made possible the extended works of the king, while payments in kind
maintained his servants, dependents, and laborers. Aiding the king in
carrying out his many duties were royal princes, nobles, and scribes.
Each of the nomes was governed by a prince or noble appointed by the
pharaoh. Still lower in the governmental machine were the scribes,
whose chief task was the keeping of records and who acted as administrative agents.

At the time of the Middle Kingdom the structure of government
underwent slight changes. While the pharaoh was still recognized as
divine and regarded as the source of all power, the nomes were now
governed by hereditary nobles. Miniature pharaohs in their own districts, they controlled the land, exacted forced labor services, settled disputes and collected taxes, a part of which went to the king. When the
empire was established, after the expulsion of the Hyksos, Egypt became a military state ruled by an emperor who claimed the land by
right of conquest as a royal possession. The administration was now
organized on a military basis, and the officials were officers of a king-
general.

Throughout all Egyptian history, the bulk of the Egyptians were
peasants whose existence in the villages of mud-brick houses was in
strong contrast with the comfortable, and at times luxurious, life of the
upper classes. During the Old Kingdom, the king, who owned the
land, granted it to subjects, and the temples and nobles held large
tracts. The great bulk of the peasantry were serfs on the landed estates.
They scratched the ground with crude plows, broke clods with hoes,
and used goats or cattle to tread in the seeds. After the planting they

were occupied with the handling of water in the irrigation ditches, and during the period of inundation they labored upon the works of the king. In the Middle Kingdom, the condition of the lower classes improved. Many peasants were free and owned or rented lands. Though in theory all the land belonged to the king under the empire, it was held by grant or lease by Egyptians, who were able to transfer it freely. The peasants—both serf and free—lived and worked as they had in former times, but there was a steady increase in serfdom. With the passage of time, the temples increased their great wealth in land and cattle, and ultimately most of the wealth of Egypt was concentrated in the hands of the priests and the temples.

Although agriculture was always primary in Egyptian life, industry and commerce were not unimportant. Artisans worked in the towns and in the great workshops attached to the palaces and temples. The great skill which they attained is displayed in the clay, stone, wood, metal, glass, and textile products they manufactured. The Egyptian objects which have been found offer evidence not only of great skill but also of a marked sense of beauty. Merchants carrying goods up and down the Nile engaged in active trade in the town markets, where exchange was carried on both by barter and by means of established weights of gold and silver. Even in the early period traders went overland to Syria and up the Nile to Nubia. Egyptian boats touched at Syrian ports and Crete and voyaged down the Red Sea to Punt for incense and spices. As a result of the conquests which followed the establishment of the empire, industry and especially commerce experienced a marked expansion. Both a flourishing trade and an enterprising industry, however, later suffered together with the general decline of the empire.

The Egyptians worshiped many deities, and all phases of their life were permeated with religion. The sun, represented by many divinities of whom Re (later called Amon Re) and the Nile (Osiris) became the foci of religious thought. Re, creator and ruler of the earth, was the father of the king and the divine source of law and justice. Osiris and his sister-wife, Isis, the chief divinities of immortality, were the central figures of a beautiful legend. Osiris worship at its best required men to be guiltless of murder, theft, deceit, or mistreatment of the poor and needy, if they were to gain entrance into "the Western world," where the dead gathered for eternity. The Egyptians also believed that a vital principle called the *ka,* or spiritual double, continued to live in the body after death. This belief provided the basis for the development of mummification and the building of the massive tombs for the protection of the body. The dead of the royal family and upper classes and, in the later periods, scribes and even workmen, were mummified and buried in the great pyramids, chamber tombs, or benchlike tombs (called *mastabas*). From the objects placed in the tombs and the pictures painted on their walls is derived most of our information about Egyptian life. An exceptional development in Egyptian religion came with the attack of Ikhnaton (1375-1358 B.C.) upon the traditional religious beliefs and the priesthood of Amon. He attempted to introduce the worship of one god under the symbol and name of the sun disk, Aton. He failed, however, and after his death the old priesthood regained its strength. Finally the chief priest of Amon acquired sufficient wealth to become the greatest landlord in Egypt, and enough power to make himself king.

In art and literature Egypt reached its height during the Old and Middle Kingdoms. To architecture the Egyptians contributed the pillar and column, and, though marked by a certain stiffness, their wooden, copper, and stone statuary offers proof of high artistic skill. This same artistic equipment is displayed in the tomb reliefs and paintings which, though dominated by religious convention and lacking in modern perspective, have vitality and reality. Further evidence of the skill of Egyptian craftsmen and of the aesthetic taste of the different periods is found in the objects of industrial art which have survived.

The papyri contain fragments of literature embracing hymns, prayers, poems, stories, records of kings, sage proverbs, and technical treatises on mathematics and medicine. Though Egyptian medicine was shot through with magic, the doctors knew much about drugs and performed delicate operations. In mathematics the Egyptians learned to solve relatively difficult problems in arithmetic and geometry such as the measurement of a piece of land or the determination of the number of bushels in a granary. Considerable knowledge and skill in mechanics were essential for the construction of the temples and pyramids. The calendar, based on the rising of the star Sothis, or Sirius, called for a knowledge of astronomy.

The achievements of Egypt were carried by conquest and trade to the people of Syria and the Aegean, where they played a great part in the development of other cultures.

BABYLONIA The Tigris and Euphrates rivers flow down from the mountains of Armenia into the plain called Mesopotamia, enriching and watering their banks by annual inundations; and pushing their delta into the Persian Gulf. Today the two rivers join before they reach the gulf, and the ancient coast line lies far inland. The canals, which are necessary to draw off the water after the inundation and to provide irrigation during the long dry summer, tend to fill up with the silt deposited by the waters, and must be watched and cleaned with great care. Unity of irrigation control, though desirable, is not essential, and separate canal systems were developed for the support of the many independent communities. In ancient times the fertility of the land was widely celebrated.

The rivers offered a natural highway for trade, which also went by water to India or overland to Syria. Trade enriched the cities of Mesopotamia, and many wars were fought for control of the routes of commerce. The people, exporting surplus foodstuffs and manufactured goods, took in exchange metals, stones, and wood, which were lacking in their region. The valley lay open to the hill folk of the plateaus of Armenia and Iran and to the nomads of the grasslands of Arabia. Invasion was easy and frequent.

The earliest inhabitants of the valley were the Neolithic "Painted Pottery Folk," a farming people. About 5000 B.C., the Sumerians, a people of unknown origin who already had a high culture, entered the valley and overwhelmed the earlier inhabitants. Among their earliest achievements were the use of copper, the potter's wheel and the wheeled vehicle, as well as the development of cuneiform writing and a calendar based on lunar months. After a great deluge which occurred before 4500 B.C., the Sumerians developed a number of important cities. Such independent communities, city-states, were ruled by priest-kings called *patesi* who controlled the land and looked after agriculture and the canals. These walled cities, with their temples and towers (ziggurats), prospered as a result of agriculture, industry, and trade. Short-lived empires appeared in the plain between the two rivers as one city after another established a brief supremacy through warfare.

In the course of the third millennium the Sumerians were overcome by Semitic-speaking peoples who moved out from the grasslands into the valley. The first of them were the Accadians, who under their leader, Sargon of Accad (ca. 2650 B.C.), established an empire which lasted but a few generations. The Accadian empire was succeeded by the brief rule of a hill people, the Guti, and then by a Sumerian revival. Finally, the Amorites, under Hammurabi of Babylon, completed the union of the land of the two rivers, thereafter called Babylonia (2000 B.C.). Later Babylonia (after 1780 B.C.) was conquered and governed by another hill folk, the Kassites.

The center of all activities in Babylonia, from the time of the Sumerians to the achievement of unity by Hammurabi, was the city with its surrounding farm land. The unification of the plain meant that the city-states were ruled as subject cities through the *patesi*. The king or emperor was assisted by a vizier and a host of subordinate officials. His chief duties were the maintenance of order, the administration of justice, gradually taken over from the temple priests, the supervision of the canals and the command of the army. In early times the army was composed of citizens; after the first Semitic conquest it came to be made up of professional troops.

Hammurabi is particularly famous for his code of laws—the oldest in the world—based on Sumerian and Semitic customs. It contains a highly developed body of laws relating to land ownership and tenantry, trade and industry, family affairs, slavery, and to civil and criminal procedure. Though the basis of the criminal law was the principle of retaliation, payments for injuries operated in place of the primitive concept of "an eye for an eye and a tooth for a tooth." The law distinguished between nobles, common people and slaves, providing different penalties and privileges for the different social classes. The family was the basis of society; consequently the code provided for marriage contracts, breach of promise suits, concubinage, divorce, and in general for the rights of women, which were well protected. The code offered protection for the lower classes and provided that slaves could own property, marry, will their possessions, and obtain freedom.

Agriculture was the chief basis of economic life. Most of the land came into the possession of the state or the temples, but, as the code indicates, there was some private ownership. Property was rented on shares or for a fixed rent. Barley, wheat, spelt, and many varieties of fruits and vegetables were grown, and the raising of cattle and sheep was important. Taxes were levied on the land, and forced labor was required on the canals and roads. Even after the Kassites had introduced the horse, the donkey was the chief beast of burden.

Industry was well developed in the valley, and organized on a craft basis with associations of craftsmen and apprentices. Apprenticeship and wages were fixed by law, and workmen were responsible for bad workmanship. Babylonia had a flourishing business life. There was active commerce between cities and along the trade routes which led to India, China, or the Mediterranean. The law provided for partnerships, associations, and agencies for carrying on trade; signed and witnessed agreements were common. Heavy penalties were inflicted for dishonest practices. The law recognized loans of grain and of silver and fixed rates of interest. In the absence of coinage, exchange was carried on by fixed weights of silver (the talent, mina, and shekel), which served for purposes of exchange. Wages and the prices of many products were regulated by the establishment of maximum and minimum limits. Grains, olives, dates, bricks, porcelain, gems, tapestries, and rugs were the major exports, and stone, wood, and metals were imported.

Religious beliefs and practices in Babylonia were chiefly concerned with securing prosperity and long life in this world. If the gods, who had created men out of clay for their own service, were properly served, they brought happiness. When angered by men's sins, the greatest of which was neglect, they withdrew their presence and protection, exposing men to agents of evil, who brought sorrow and disease. Magic

charms, and in the case of sickness, simple drugs, expelled these demons, and prayer and sacrifice served to win the favor of the gods.
Temple rituals, huge sacrifices, and elaborate festivals secured the blessings of the god for the king and his city. After death—the lot of all
mankind—the shades, if properly buried, found rest in a colorless
nether world. The Babylonians had no strong interest in a future life.

The great Babylonian contribution to ancient religion lay in the
field of divination. All natural phenomena and the movement of the
stars were carefully observed and interpreted. Meanings were assigned
to dreams; soothsayers learned about the future from the action of oil
dropped on water; and priests studied the liver and gall of freshly
killed sheep, which were thought to reveal the will of gods to men.
The priests, who acquired great wealth and power, were scribes, scientists, teachers, judges, bankers, and businessmen, as well as interces-
sors, liturgists, magicians and seers.

Babylonia made significant contributions in other fields to the civilization of the ancient world. The literature of the region, much of it
inherited from the Sumerians, included religious epics, some of which
dealt with the creation of the world, legends of early heroes and of the
flood, histories recording the deeds of kings, liturgies and prayers, laws
and letters. The study of the stars, which later developed into Chaldaean astrology, was actively pursued. Time divisions of years, lunar
months, and the day consisting of two sets of twelve hours were
worked out. The Babylonians used sixty as a unit of measure, providing the basis for our sixty-minute hour and the 360° circle.

Babylonian low-relief work and engravings on gems and seals
were outstanding in an art which never attained unusual heights, perhaps because of the lack of stone. The chief architectural material was
kiln-dried brick with which fine structures employing the column,
arch, vault, and dome were erected. The most distinctive feature of
their temple architecture was the tower or ziggurat, a series of terraces
of brick. It was mounted by elaborate stairs, and on top stood the temple residence of the god.

Babylonian achievements were spread abroad by trade and conquest and by the migrations of peoples into Syria and Asia Minor,
where they profoundly influenced the newly developing cultures of
the native groups.

INDO-EUROPEAN-
SPEAKING
PEOPLES

During the third millennium, peoples living in the
plains of Eastern Europe and speaking Indo-European tongues were developing and expanding. They
were nomads who had domesticated the horse, had
learned the use of the wheeled cart, and had developed an elementary
agriculture. Moving from the plains of Eastern Europe, they carried
with them their greatest contribution, their language, which spread

perhaps even beyond the borders of the migration of the folk, from India to Britain. Sanskrit, Persian, Greek, Latin, and most modern European tongues are Indo-European languages. At the end of the third millennium B.C., the Indo-European-speaking Hittites invaded Asia Minor and established there an empire which, after many vicissitudes, was able to contend on equal terms with that of Egypt by 1400 B.C. Federally organized, this empire had a king, a bureaucracy, a general assembly, and a written code of laws. The Hittites' outstanding contribution to civilization was the use of iron, which they were probably the first to mine and work on any significant scale. They also were in touch with the cultures of the Mesopotamian and Egyptian regions, and borrowed from both.

THE AEGEAN
WORLD

Before the rise of the Hittite empire there developed a maritime culture in the Aegean with Cnossus in Crete as its center. This brilliant civilization, influenced by both Babylonia and Egypt, reached its height in the fifteenth century B.C. when the rulers of Cnossus established control over the island of Crete and the Aegean basin. In the city of Cnossus a ruler, whose title or name may have been Minos, built a magnificent four-story palace consisting of many rooms around a central court. The Cretans, originally farmers and herdsmen, became the first commercial people of the Mediterranean, carrying wares to Egypt and the East and throughout the Aegean and Mediterranean basins. Skilled Cretan artisans made fine metal cups, daggers, and other utensils and pottery adorned with varicolored pictures. Their religion centered in the worship of the mother-goddess and her divine son, and their dead were buried in elaborate chamber tombs.

Their culture spread to the mainland, where it was taken up by northern invaders who were ancestors of the Greeks. Remains of powerful fortresses and fine palaces at Mycenae, Tiryns, and Athens furnish information about them, and the Greek legends of Heracles, Theseus, and Achilles are later memories of their deeds. These northern invaders succeeded in destroying Cnossus about 1400 B.C. This conquest marks the beginning of the Mycenaean Age which came to an end about 1100 B.C., and during which the expedition against Troy, controlling the entrance to the Hellespont, occurred.

SYRIA

The decline of Egypt, together with the collapse of Cretan sea power and of the Hittite empire at the end of the second millennium B.C., made possible the brief emergence of the little states of Syria. The Phoenicians of Tyre and Sidon, living on the seacoast, took over from the Cretans the sea trade of the Mediterranean. They carried the goods, which they secured from Egypt or Babylon or which they themselves produced, into the Aegean, throughout the Mediterranean, and even into the western Atlantic Ocean.

They became famous for their maritime skill, and established many colonies, the most famous of which were Carthage in Northern Africa and Gades (Cadiz) in Spain. Their chief industrial products were woolens, colored with the purple dye obtained from a shellfish, and glassware. Their wide-flung commerce made them active disseminators of culture traits, especially of the alphabet.

The overland trade of Asia Minor passed into the hands of a northern Semitic-speaking people, the Aramaeans, whose city of Damascus, which still exists, controlled the caravan route to Babylon. The Aramaic dialect became the common language of the Near East and was universally spoken throughout the Levant as late as the time of Christ.

In Canaan, southern Syria, were many little communities which had been ruled and influenced by both Babylonians and Egyptians. During the last century of the second millennium they suffered invasion from two sides. The civilized and warlike Philistines, who probably came from the Aegean, speedily gained possession of the littoral. From the interior came the Hebrews, who gradually conquered and blended with the Canaanites. After a brief period of subjection, the Hebrews, under their first kings, Saul and David, defeated the Philistines and established a united kingdom. The renowned Solomon, who organized his state in the tenth century B.C., entered into commercial relations with the Phoenicians and adorned Jerusalem with a temple for Jahweh. After his reign the kingdom split in two. The northern half was eventually overthrown by the Assyrians; the southern, a little later, by the Chaldaeans.

The Hebrews had brought with them into Canaan a tribal religion of spiritual beauty and moral power. During their short period of independence their prophets, resisting surrender to Canaanitish gods and religious practices, developed from the religion and laws of Moses, a belief in one God, Maker and Ruler of all Mankind, who demanded good behavior, economic and social justice, and true humility from all His worshipers. In their monotheistic religion and the books of the Old Testament the Hebrews made their greatest single contribution to civilization.

THE NEW ORIENT

In the ninth century B.C. the Assyrians, a martial folk who entered the Tigris Valley a thousand years earlier, established a great empire. Expanding under successive conquerors, it finally comprised Babylonia, Syria, and Egypt. Their contributions were essentially in the art of war and imperial administration and organization. The Assyrian army consisted of corps of infantry, chariotry, and engineers, with a well-directed service of supply. Their imperial government was marked by provinces with appointed governors, garrisons, and regularly collected tribute, and client kingdoms along the frontier. Colonization and deportation were used to unify the empire and break down local feeling; better control and easier communication were secured by a system of military roads. Their palaces and temples adorned with sculptures, reliefs, and inscriptions testify to their artistic ability. Scribes studied and copied ancient Babylonian texts and also produced accounts of the royal campaigns and other works of literature. Their astronomers continued the study of the stars, and their priests used the Babylonian methods of divination.

Continuous war and the growth of wealth destroyed the peasantry upon which Assyria's power rested. Finally, in 612 B.C., Nineveh, the capital, fell, and Assyria was conquered by the Chaldaeans. After the overthrow of the Assyrians, Egypt experienced a brief revival, and the little state of Lydia gained pre-eminence in Asia Minor. Lydia's rise was due to the wealth it secured from gold in its streams and from the trade which passed overland from the Greek cities. With Chaldaean rule, Babylon again assumed importance. Nebuchadnezzar, who rebuilt the ancient city with great walls, palaces, and the famous Hanging Gardens, also conquered Syria, including the southern kingdom of the Hebrews. The last of the Chaldaean rulers set scholars to work collecting old texts and studying the Sumerian language. The Chaldaeans thoroughly assimilated the ancient culture, and the Greeks and Romans attributed to them the entire Babylonian systems of astrology and divination.

THE PERSIAN EMPIRE   In the sixth and early fifth centuries B.C., Egypt, Asia Minor, Syria, and Babylon were all embraced in the empire of the Medes and the Persians, mountaineers from the Iranian plateau. The Persian kings, Cyrus, Cambyses, and Darius, were stopped only when they met the Greeks on the western side of the Aegean. Their roads and imperial government with its satrapies (provinces), governors, inspectors, and postal couriers was based upon the Assyrian imperial system. Peace and order brought prosperity to the empire, and the introduction of gold and silver coins facilitated the expansion of trade.

Shortly before the time of Darius there lived Zoroaster, the great Persian religious teacher who developed a theology of monotheistic character which is called Zoroastrianism. Under Darius the worship of Ahura Mazda, god of light who created the world and placed man upon it, was apparently established as the official religion. Ahura Mazda, demanding obedience, morality, and truth from his followers, waged constant war against the forces of evil and darkness led by Ahriman. To those who died fighting for him, he offered reward in

Paradise; to the world he held out the hope of the ultimate victory of truth over falsehood. Since the Persian king was the earthly representative of the god, dedicated to practice justice and establish law in the light of Ahura Mazda, the Persian empire became a state with a divine mission of world conquest in the name of religion.

— II —

THE HELLENES

THE achievements of the Greeks of antiquity are still an important influence in the civilization of the Western world. In a small land poorly endowed with natural resources, with a material culture which never attained a high level, they developed the arts, literature, philosophy, political theory, and science to extraordinary heights. The techniques which they borrowed from the Orient they transformed with their own genius, and they gave to their contributions an original and distinctive stamp.

The Greeks called themselves Hellenes, and to the lands in which they lived (the basin of the Aegean and later the littoral of the Mediterranean and Black seas), they gave the name Hellas. The Aegean Sea, dotted with islands and bordered on either side by mountainous Greece and Asia Minor, was the center of their activities. It provided fish and salt for food and served in addition as a highway for travel and trade. Greece itself, a land of mountains separated by little valleys, is not rich in natural resources. Scanty forests provided lumber; the hillsides, containing small deposits of gold, silver, copper, and iron, furnished wildflowers for the bees and pasturage for sheep and goats. Of marble there was a rich supply, and around the bases of the hills lay a fine deposit of clay. There are few significant rivers, none of which are navigable. Perennial springs, however, water the land. Barely a fifth of the land is cultivable, and the thin soil is easily exhausted and eroded. Yet with proper care the plains became fertile in the production of grains, fruits, vegetables, and olives. Though the land was intensively worked in antiquity there never was enough food, and this fact turned moderation into a primary virtue. The climate of Greece is mild and equable and the air clear. Many of the islands possessed little plains and became the site of flourishing communities. Along the coast of Asia Minor were rich valleys connected with the interior plateau by rivers which furnished highways for trade.

THE RISE OF THE HELLENES The Aegean area had already witnessed the rise of a flourishing civilization when the invasions which marked its end brought pressure on the older inhabitants and caused a general migration eastward across the Aegean. Our knowledge of the period of confusion which ensued, called the Greek Middle Age, is derived largely from the Homeric poems. In this age men were passing from cattle raising to agriculture. Some industrial techniques survived from Mycenaean times, and there were advances in the art of navigation, though trade was mostly in the hands of the Phoenicians. Government rested upon a tribal basis, and the king, who was leader in war, chief priest, and judge, was simply the most powerful noble. The aristocratic council which advised the king was gradually reducing his powers and also overriding or ignoring the tribal assembly.

Later there appeared the characteristic political institution of the Greek world, the city-state, called by the Greeks *polis,* which originally meant citadel. A group of people living around a conveniently located and easily fortified hilltop employed it as a common religious, political, and economic center. On it were built the temples of the gods; around it clustered the houses of the nobles, the market place and the shops and residences of the merchants and artisans. Under favoring circumstances a physical city in the modern sense of the term would appear. This, however, was not essential to the Greek idea of the *polis.* To the Greek, the city-state was essentially an aggregate of citizens, held together by a tradition of common descent and by a strong allegiance to their *polis.* Membership in the group (i.e., citizenship) depended on birth and not on residence; it could not be obtained except by gift of the community. Each city-state, except when conquered, was politically autonomous, and no matter how small, claimed complete freedom in local government and in its relations with other states.

POLITICAL AND ECONOMIC EVOLUTION

At the time when the economy of the city-states was dominantly agricultural, they were governed by aristocrats who were large holders of land. Claiming a god-given right to rule, these men overthrew the king and destroyed the popular tribal assembly. Wealth and superior armament contributed to their power. Many of the poorer class were meanwhile reduced to tenantry and serfdom or were forced out to work the waste lands and the rocky hillsides. The corruption of these noble rulers and the hardships of the small farmers are fully indicated in the writings of the poet Hesiod (ca. 750 B.C.). Scarcity of room for expansion and a growing Oriental demand for Greek wines and olive oil combined to bring about an agricultural revolution. The aristocrats dispossessed their tenants and serfs, and turned their land over to an intensive culture of grapes and olives, relying upon imported supplies for food. This resulted in the appearance of a large group of landless individuals. Political and social factions among the nobility added to the disturbed conditions, and the Aegean world virtually boiled over.

COLONIAL EXPANSION Some of the discontented went to the East as mercenary warriors, but the great majority, pressed by land hunger, went off to found colonies. When, after a while, these colonies became commercially profitable, others were founded primarily for purposes of trade. Colonial settlements were made along the northern coast of the Aegean, in the Black Sea region, in southern Italy and Sicily, and even on the coasts of Gaul and Spain. These colonies were recognized as new city-states and, though bound to the mother city by ties of blood and friendship, they were politically independent. The colonial expansion diffused Greek culture around the Mediterranean and also produced great industrial and commercial changes. In many of the cities, particularly in Asia Minor, textiles, pottery, and metal goods were produced for export. New techniques were developed; specialization appeared; and industrial slavery was introduced. There was a great quantitative growth in the commerce between the Greek cities and colonies, and with the Asiatic states and Egypt. One consequence of this was the introduction of coinage either by the Lydians or the Greek cities in Asia Minor.

POLITICAL CHANGES Economic developments brought political changes. When the complexity of business made written laws necessary, one of the chief sources of power of the aristocracy was removed. Money as well as land was now a source of wealth, and men rose from below to force their way into the ruling class. Oligarchies (rule of the few) appeared in the city-states, in which wealth gained from any source and not solely from landed estates became the chief requirement for the holding of office. When increased prosperity, cheaper metals, and improved methods of production brought armor within the reach of the average man, most states, following the example of Sparta, organized from among their well-to-do citizens the phalanx (solid body) of heavy-armed infantry. With this development, governmental control fell into the hands of those who were able to equip themselves with heavy armor, and normally resulted in the formation of an assembly and in the creation of an administrative council drawn from the well to do.

These economic and political changes were marked by many crises, and sharp struggles were waged between classes. The position of the debtor class was made worse by the growth of a monetary economy. Many of them were sold into slavery for debt, and their condition was a constant source of trouble. Economic or political troubles and civil strife created a situation where able men could

seize control of the state and make themselves monarchs. Such unconstitutional rulers were termed *tyrants* by the Greeks. Almost invariably the tyrants were popular champions. They broke the power
of the aristocrats, fostered trade by founding commercial colonies and
making treaties, and promoted the welfare of the artisan and farming
classes. They were patrons of the arts, and beautified their cities. The
tyrants played an important role in the development of industry,
trade, and culture, and also, in the end, in the growth of democracy.
Nevertheless they were always regarded by the Greeks as usurpers,
and none of them was able to perpetuate his rule.

IONIAN CITIES   The leadership during this period of rapid change
                       was taken by the Greek cities on the coast of Asia
Minor. Their rich fields and the supply of wool from the interior, of
metals from Asia Minor, and of clay, all brought these Ionian cities,
as they are called, wealth. Situated at the ends of the overland routes
of trade with Asia and in easy reach of Syria and Egypt by sea, they
enjoyed a favored commercial position. The strongest among them
was Miletus. A number of causes weakened them, however, and they
fell first into the hands of the Lydians, whose king, in the middle
of the sixth century, was the famous Croesus. Shortly afterward they
were easily reduced to subjection by the armies of the Persian conqueror Cyrus. An abortive revolt against Darius led to the destruction of Miletus and the end of Ionian supremacy early in the fifth
century.

SPARTA AND ATHENS

SPARTA   On the mainland two states, Sparta and Athens,
                   were meanwhile emerging to a position of dominance.
In Sparta, a Dorian agricultural state in southern Peloponnesus, the
Spartans ruled over a subject population of state serfs called *helots,*
who worked the land, and a group of conquered communities whose
people were called *perioeci* ("dwellers around"), engaged almost entirely in industry and trade. The Spartan ruling class of citizens
(Spartiates) was itself divided into nobles and commons with the
aristocracy in control. The land was divided among the Spartiates in
inalienable and indivisible lots, and the Spartan nobility held large
estates. For several reasons the Spartiates later declined in numbers,
and there arose a class of Inferiors whose status was not clearly
defined.

All citizens passed through a rigorous system of training as boys
and then spent their manhood in continual drill and preparation for
war. Girls likewise were trained to make them fit mothers of soldiers.
Family life was reduced to a minimum; boys were sent to live in bar-

racks at the age of seven; and the men took their evening meal at public tables to which they contributed. This system was shaped by the fact that the Spartiates lived in the midst of a subject population which heavily outnumbered them. While it produced a hardy people whose phalanx was well-nigh unbeatable for generations, it discouraged achievement in virtually all other fields. The Spartiates were dominated by a few of their own number. At the head of the state, and in command of the army was a dual kingship, hereditary in two families. The chief civil magistrates, called ephors (overseers), were elected annually and were advised by a council of twenty-eight men over sixty and the two kings. The assembly, composed of all Spartans over thirty, was a passive body electing the magistrates and voting on measures submitted to it by the council. During the sixth century the Spartans organized most of the neighboring states under their leadership into the Peloponnesian League.

ATHENS   Athens, at first a small agricultural state ruled by kings, became eventually the economic and cultural center of the Hellenic world. By the beginning of the seventh century the landed aristocracy had risen to power and the kingship had disappeared. Far behind the Ionian cities and even its neighbors Megara and Corinth in economic growth, Athens had no share in the colonial movement and in the early development of trade. Its aristocrats learned, however, to devote their lands to the growth of grapes and olives and began to engage in commerce. During the seventh century the need of a phalanx for purposes of defense placed governmental power in the hands of those who could provide themselves with heavy armor. At the same time the lower classes were becoming depressed tenants and debtors, many of whom were sold into slavery for failure to meet their loans. Among the leading families there were constant struggles for wealth and power. The situation called for reform, and the first step taken was the writing down of the laws by Draco (621 B.C.). This made possible a clearer conception of the laws and a more equitable justice for the lower classes.

Not until Solon (594 B.C.) was elected chief civil magistrate (archon) and given full power was there an attempt to solve the pressing economic problems. Solon canceled debts on security of the land or the person and forbade slavery for debt. He encouraged industry, reorganized the system of coinage and weights and measures to promote trade, and forbade the exportation of foodstuffs. He prepared the way for the later democracy by admitting all citizens to the assembly and by founding a Popular Supreme Court which limited the power of the magistrates. When, after his reforms, strife broke out afresh, Peisistratus, supported by the small farmers, charcoal burners, and miners of the back country, made himself tyrant (560 B.C.). He and his son Hippias redivided much of the land, contributed greatly to the growth of Athenian industry and trade, and beautified the city.

Two years after the tyranny was overthrown, Cleisthenes was elected chief magistrate (508 B.C.). Undertaking to break the political power of great families and to bring to an end the local party and class conflicts of the city, he remade the Athenian constitution. He established local government in the villages of Attica, united the Athenians into ten tribes (based upon territorial divisions) for political and military units, established a council with five hundred members and a board of ten generals who soon became the chief executives of Athens. These reforms laid the foundation for the democracy.

The years between 500 and 338 B.C. constitute the great age of Greek history. The first important event of the period was the war with Persia. Darius, king of Persia and ruler of the Asiatic Greeks, determined upon the conquest of the balance of the Aegean area. His army was defeated at Marathon in 490 B.C. by the Athenians. The forces of his son and successor, Xerxes, after triumphing over the Spartans in the celebrated Pass of Thermopylae and taking and sacking Athens, were defeated by the Greek fleet at Salamis (480 B.C.) and by an allied army commanded by Sparta at Plataea in the following year. Following these triumphs the Greeks under Athenian leadership freed the Ionian cities and drove the Persians out of the Aegean. These victories over Persia were a potent source of inspiration for the great products of the Greek genius in these classic years. In the postwar period Athens advanced to Hellenic leadership under the guidance of three great men, Themistocles, Aristeides, and Cimon. Through their efforts a maritime league, the Confederacy of Delos, composed of the island and Asiatic cities, was organized under Athenian control with its prime purpose the protection of the Aegean against Persia.

In 461 B.C. Pericles was elected general in Athens. During the Age of Pericles Athens became the richest and most powerful city of the Greeks. The Confederacy of Delos was transformed into an empire with most of the states subject and paying tribute to Athens. Though Pericles failed in his endeavors to control Greek trade with Egypt and the West, he succeeded in keeping Persia at bay and in bringing into Athenian hands the commerce of the Black Sea region, which was vital to Athens's food supply. Goods and travelers from the entire civilized world poured into Athens. With the wealth acquired from trade and tribute the city was adorned with temples and statuary. At the same time literature, science, and philosophy flourished to such an extent that Athenian culture became synonymous with Greek.

The great Age of Athens was brought to an end by the Pelopennesian War (431-404 B.C.) when Sparta, incited by Corinth and in the late years of the conflict supported by Persia, encompassed the downfall of Athens.

This freeing of the Greeks led to untold confusion during the fourth century. For a period (404-371 B.C.) Sparta maintained her ascendancy as leader of the cities against the constant hostility of Athens and Thebes. In 371 B.C. Epaminondas of Thebes defeated the Spartan phalanx at Leuctra and for nine years thereafter Thebes held the position of leadership. Following the death of Epaminondas, Philip of Macedon capitalized upon the confused situation to win power for himself in the Greek world. Demosthenes of Athens thundered against him in the famous Philippics, but Philip could not be checked. The Macedonian victory at Chaeronea in 338 B.C. marks not only the triumph of Macedon but also the close of the classic period of Greek history.

ATHENIAN DEMOCRACY
The Greek world in the classical period presented great diversity in its political, economic, and cultural life. The northern and western Greeks were still in a tribal and pastoral stage; in Macedon kingship survived; Thessaly, Elis, and Sparta were governed by landholding aristocracies; Corinth and many other commercial states were ruled by their wealthy merchants; in the West tyranny prevailed, and in Athens democracy had been established. Athenian democracy, therefore, was not typical of Greek government, but its achievements and its later influence make it worthy of special attention.

The Athenian population of about 315,500 in 431 B.C. consisted of 172,000 citizens, 28,500 resident aliens, and 115,000 slaves. Of this number about half lived in the urban area and the balance in the country villages of Attica. There was a long-time tendency of the rural population to shift to the city. Only children of parents who were both citizens were classed as citizens. A fourfold classification of citizens on the basis of wealth was maintained primarily for the assessment of financial and military burdens. The basic political unit was the deme, and each of the villages of Attica and the wards of Athens had a definite organization with local officials who kept the citizen lists and directed local affairs.

The demes were grouped into "thirds," and through these into the ten tribes, each of which had an assembly and leaders. War taxes were apportioned and levies were made for the army through the tribes. Fifty men from each tribe were chosen annually to serve on the Council of Five Hundred. This body examined the qualifications of magistrates, supervised the execution of the decrees of the people, the management of public property, the collection and expenditure of public money, the erection of public works, and the condition of the army and navy. In unimportant administrative matters it could pass decrees binding upon the people for a year. Here bills dealing with important matters were discussed and prepared for submission to the people in the assembly. The assembly, which held regular and special meetings, was composed of all citizens over eighteen. In this body everyone had an equal vote and the right to speak and to initiate or amend legislation. New proposals were first referred to the council for consideration and report, and an individual was held responsible for his proposals. If, wtihin a year, a measure was found to be unconstitutional or contrary to the best interests of Athens, its proposer was punished.

After the monarchy had given way to the aristocracy the chief magistrates were nine archons drawn from the upper class. After their term of office, which they could hold for only one year, they became life members of the Council of the Areopagus, then the most powerful body of the state. With the development of the democracy the Areopagus lost its power to the new council, and the archons became religious officials and clerks in the law courts. During the age of Athenian greatness the important executives were the ten generals who commanded the army and navy and directed the public policy of the state. This office was open to all Athenian citizens possessing land, and re-election was permitted. Pericles held the office of general for over thirty years. The law courts were a unique feature of Athenian democracy. Six thousand jurors over thirty years of age were annually chosen by lot from those who wished to be enrolled for service. Divided into juries varying in number, usually five hundred and one, they decided all cases of civil and criminal law and heard charges against magistrates and against the proposers of illegal or harmful measures. While the Athenian empire existed they also judged important cases appealed from the subject cities.

The strength of the Athenian democracy rested in part upon payment for services. Most magistrates, the councilors, and the jurors received salaries, and, in the fourth century, attendance at the assembly was paid for. This made it theoretically possible for every man to serve the state regardless of his economic condition.

Income from public properties (especially the silver mines at Laurium), tariffs, dues, fees, and fines were all major sources of state revenue. The rich were called upon regularly to provide out of their own means for certain expenses of the fleet and of the religious festivals (that is, to perform liturgies). Though opposed to direct taxation, the Athenians submitted to a special war tax which the citizens paid according to their means. In the Age of Pericles, the tribute from the subject cities of the empire was the greatest source of income. Frequent wars and the introduction of doles for the poor and pensions for the disabled materially increased the expenses of the state in the fourth century. Consequently, after the loss of the empire, the war tax was resorted to more frequently, and special measures were devised for its collection. The finances of Athens were generally in bad shape, even though there were attempts to work out a budget.

ATHENIAN ECONOMIC LIFE   The majority of the Athenian citizens were engaged in agriculture. Most of the farms were small, but the aristocrats maintained large estates in the country. The peasantry of the hillsides raised goats and cattle, cut and dressed wood or made it into charcoal, kept bees, and terraced the hillsides for the planting of vineyards. In the olive orchards of the valleys grain was raised between the rows of trees. Near the city, truck gardens supplied fruits, vegetables, and flowers. Implements were still primitive and the two-field system was regularly employed. On the large estates in the later period there was considerable improvement in farming methods.

Though many farmers lived in the city and went out to work their lands by day, the bulk of the city population was engaged in industry and commerce. Men of wealth invested in shops, commercial ventures, the purchase of slaves for hire, and money lending. In addition to the citizens, metics and slaves were important in the life of the city. The metics were aliens who, attracted to Athens by business opportunities, made it their permanent residence. As resident aliens they were not allowed to own land, were represented in the law courts by an Athenian patron, and paid a small tax for the privilege of living in Athens. All metics were required to serve in the army or the fleet, and the wealthier ones performed liturgies. The metics were found in every field of endeavor and many were as loyal to the state as Athenian citizens.

The slave population, which made up the lowest class, was recruited in various ways. There were those who were born slaves; some were obtained by piratical raids on the barbarians; others were prisoners of war or were sold into slavery for debt in states which still allowed that practice. Dealers also raised and trained unwanted children who had been exposed by their parents. The state owned slaves who were employed as heralds, clerks, and police, or who labored on public works. While many slaves were household servants of wealthy families, by far the greatest number, both unskilled and skilled, were employed in industry. Those who worked in the mines at Laurium were the most oppressed group. Athenian law protected the slaves from mistreatment to a certain extent, and many of them had opportunities to save small sums and eventually to purchase their

freedom. Despite the size of the slave population, the major portion
of the work of Athens was done by its citizens and metics.

Industry in Athens, and in all the Greek cities, was small in scale.
Many articles were made to order, the purchaser sometimes furnishing the raw material. The increasing demand for Athenian goods,
however, led to their manufacture for sale to retailers or for export.
Pottery, the finest product of the shops, was in great demand wherever
Athenian merchants traded. A shop somewhat larger than the average
would comprise the owner, his family, an apprentice or two, and a
few slaves. By the fifth century specialization between crafts and even
within crafts had become general. There was also some division of
labor within the shop.

Increased volume and a tendency toward specialization marked
trade as well as industry during this period. Peddlers went about the
Greek countryside; some merchants followed the great roads to
Delphia and Olympia to participate in the fairs held during the religious festivals. Some goods from neighboring cities came to the
Athenian market by overland routes. Most of the traffic, however,
followed the sea and was aided by improvements in boats and the
growth of geographic knowledge and skill in navigation. During the
trading season, ships went to the Black Sea, Syria, Egypt, and to the
West, carrying wine, oil, pottery, and other manufactured goods.
They returned with slaves, grain, drugs, tapestries, linen, papyrus, and
many other products. The government showed a constant interest in
trade and aided it in many ways. Athens became the focal center of
Mediterranean trade as a result of peace with Persia, an expedition
to the Black Sea, the activities of Athenian agents in that region,
Egypt, and Italy, the work of the navy in suppressing piracy and in
opening new markets, and a network of commercial treaties. The
maintenance of the value of Athenian coins—known as "owls"—by
the state facilitated commercial transactions. The grain trade was of
vital concern to Athens: it meant food for the people, and was a major
cause of Athens's wars. The state sought to develop and control the
sources of grain supply and passed regulatory laws. All grain ships
under Athenian control were compelled to stop at Peiraeus. Two-
thirds of all the grain they carried had to be sold in Athens, and the
remainder could be exported only after local needs were satisfied.
Trade in lumber was subject to similar regulations.

Trading methods were simple. Single merchants, or a group of
merchants united for a voyage, would buy up a supply of local goods,
often on borrowed money, rent a ship, and set forth. At a port town,
the goods would be displayed and bargained for by the local purchasers. With the money secured from these sales goods which could

be sold at home were purchased. Once home and the cargo disposed of, debts were paid off and profits divided. In fifth-century Athens men of wealth made loans on such voyages; later banking as a source of profit developed. Money changers first accepted deposits of money and valuables for safekeeping without interest. The next step was the payment of sums on order to the creditors of the depositors and the transfer of credits on their books from one customer to another. Finally, credits were transferred between various financial centers. Money deposited with the bankers was loaned on interest to the state or to businessmen for commercial transactions.

GREEK CULTURE

GREEK
RELIGION
Religion played a significant part in the everyday life and in the cultural achievements of the Greeks. For them, all nature was divine, and all the daily acts of man—his work and his play—also had their religious significance. The family was conscious of its supernatural protectors, and at the larger political and social gatherings the gods were deemed always present. Certain divinities connected with the larger aspects of nature and of life were universal and were recognized as the great gods, the dwellers on Olympus. Countless local deities were worshiped at shrines, and the spirits of great men were believed to continue to protect those interests which they had served in life. With the development of the city-state the gods were considered the protectors and heavenly rulers of the communities. The immortality cults of Demeter and Dionysus offered emotional release to the poor and oppressed and became rallying points for the democracy in its struggle with aristocracy. Finally the city itself became an object of devotion which seemed to involve religious elements. "I would have you fix your eyes upon the greatness of Athens," said Pericles, "until you become filled with the love of her." Like the Orientals, the Greeks sought to know the will of the gods and to peer into the future. They learned and practiced all the methods of divination which the East had developed, and they visited oracles where they believed that the gods communicated with them.

The sole essential to worship was an altar in the open air and a ritual prescribed by ancestral tradition. Prayers, hymns, choruses, processions, and sacrifices were employed to win the favor of the gods. From the choruses developed forms of poetry and finally the drama. The competitive element present in these festivals was more sharply displayed in the athletic contests, which also had their religious aspects. Almost every state had its local games, and four, the greatest of which were the Olympic games, attained the rank of national meets. Truces were declared for these occasions, and they became centers of diplomacy and trade.

Greek mythology made of the gods attractive and powerful beings with distinct human personalities and lives. This anthropomorphism is related to the development of architecture and sculpture, for the gods needed houses in which to dwell and statues to represent them. ARCHITECTURE The temples of the gods, modeled after the palaces of the early kings, consisted usually of a single room, with a porch on the front and sometimes another at the rear. Later, a row of columns, called a peristyle, was erected around the entire building for adornment. In the early period the Greeks developed two orders or styles of architecture—the simple and severe Doric, on the Greek mainland, and the more ornate Ionic, in Asia Minor. A search for more luxurious building led to the development of the Corinthian order which grew out of the Ionic, in which a flowered capital was substituted for the scroll capital.

From the beginning the Greek architects sought for grace and proportion. The temples of the early period may be regarded as experiments which prepared the way for the triumph of the Greek genius in a building such as the Parthenon at Athens. The old temples at Athens had been destroyed by the Persians, and after Athens had become the center of a wealthy empire, Pericles and his advisers were free to rebuild the sacred area on the Acropolis. At the crest of the hill the Propylaea, a monumental gateway with Doric porches, was erected. On the right of this on a steep corner stood the little Ionic temple of Athena, goddess of Victory. In the center of the area the Parthenon was built as a residence for Athena. Around the outside of the structure ran a peristyle of Doric columns, and at each end within the peristyle was another row of six Doric columns. The interior contained two rooms: a small room was the treasury of Athena, and the main room was the shrine which contained a gold and ivory statue of the goddess. The building was adorned with sculptures which pictured wars of the period of the heroic legends, the birth of Athena, the struggle between Athena and Poseidon for the possession of the city, and the procession at the festival of Athena. During the Peloponnesian War the Athenians erected another building on the Acropolis: the Erechtheum, an Ionic temple, adorned on one side by the Porch of the Maidens, in which sculptured statues served as columns.

SCULPTURE The history of Greek sculpture displays the same search for perfection of beauty so characteristic of architecture. In its development the games played a large part, since the athletes served as models as well as subjects for the sculptors. In the early statues Egyptian influence was strong, and they were rigid and ill proportioned. Gradually the artists learned the lessons of proportion and acquired unusual technical skill in work in marble.

The early sculptors prepared the way for Phidias, the sculptor of the Parthenon. Not only was he a master of technique and proportion, but he gave such religious feeling to his statues that he was said to have added something to traditional religion. In the fourth century there was a growth of individualism and a lessening of classic restraint. Praxiteles (fl. 360 B.C.), the greatest of all masters of the chisel, produced a series of portraits of divinities, the most celebrated of which is the Hermes found at Olympia.

LITERATURE   The earliest surviving works of Greek literature are the epic poems ascribed to Homer, the *Iliad* and the *Odyssey,* which apparently mark the culmination of a long series of epic poems which have been lost. In form and content, in music of language and brilliance of story, in a meter designed for the telling of heroic tales, these poems are outstanding. In a later generation, Hesiod used the same form to instruct men about the gods and about farming. Colonization, the advance of trade and commerce, political strife, new wealth, and new classes in the seventh and sixth centuries called forth new mediums. These were found in lyric and choral songs. In meters varied to suit the subject, poets sang the praises of their states or their party leaders and vilified their opponents. They praised victorious athletes, and wrote of love and wine and nature, or, in sterner tone, they rallied their countrymen to defend their native land. Some composed choral hymns for youths and maidens to sing in concert in honor of the gods or battle songs to rouse the warriors. Archilochus of Paros was the first of these poets. Alcaeus and Sappho of Mytilene in Lesbos, and Anacreon of Teos were also outstanding among the lyric poets, but the greatest of them was Pindar, who lived during the Persian Wars.

Civic life and religious ideas and practices combined to make the drama the most characteristic literary form of the fifth century. Out of the choral performances in honor of Dionysus the Athenians evolved the dramatic forms of tragedy and comedy. The fact that Greek tragedy sprang from the worship of Dionysus and was always performed at his festivals shaped both its form and choice of subjects. The tragedy was always composed in poetry, and the chorus with which it began remained a fixed element in the performance even when it no longer played an important part in the action. The masks and heavy costumes used made facial expressions and rapid or violent action impossible and account for the emphasis upon the speeches of the characters and the lyrics of the chorus. The tragedies dealt always with gods or with great personages and with epic themes of struggle and suffering, these traditional stories being employed as vehicles for the discussion of the ethical and social problems of the day.

Aeschylus, veteran of the Persian Wars, attacked the problem of divine justice and of the supremacy of divine law in his plays. Sophocles, product of the Age of Pericles, expressed pride in his city and confidence in the ability of man the citizen, under the gods, to achieve the highest ends. Euripides, who lived during the Peloponnesian War, was the spokesman of the poor, the humble, and the oppressed. In his plays the gods were reduced to psychological forces. He was the most popular of the Greek tragedians in later generations. Comedy, best represented by Aristophanes, who lived during the fifth and early fourth centuries, was not bound by the strict rules of tragedy and permitted sharp caricature and ridicule. Aristophanes's boisterous comedies dealt with the current scene and made fun of the foibles of the Athenians.

A significant body of prose literature first appeared in the sixth century in the writings of philosophers, genealogists, and geographers. Prose became the medium of later historians, orators, scientists, and philosophers. The chief of the historians were Herodotus, the "father of history," Thucydides, the first "scientific historian," and Xenophon, chronicler of the fourth century. Herodotus, an inimitable storyteller, wrote the history of the Persian Wars to preserve "the great and marvelous deeds of the Hellenes and the Barbarians." Thucydides, who critically weighed the sources for his history of the Peloponnesian War, in which he had participated for a brief period, also possessed a sense of dramatic values and a mastery of style. Xenophon, exiled from Athens, continued Thucydides' history to the end of Theban supremacy, and also wrote memoirs of Socrates, his teacher, and essays on a wide variety of subjects.

Oratory, a characteristic consequence of Greek democracy, was a product of the national gatherings of the Greeks, the democratic assemblies, and the law courts. Of the many Greek orators two, Isocrates and Demosthenes, merit attention. Isocrates set himself up as a teacher of practical wisdom and wrote speeches as pamphlets to be read by other men. His rules of style became the basis for later generations of orators and writers. Athenian oratory reached its culmination in the speeches of Demosthenes, who became the champion of Greek democracy against the advance of Macedon. Master of his art, his Philippics are marvels of invective and his oration "On the Crown" is regarded as outstanding in oratorical literature in terms of effective argument and organization.

PHILOSOPHY
AND SCIENCE
It is no exaggeration to say that the Greeks laid the basis for subsequent philosophical inquiry. From the Near East they acquired, however, a rich store of ideas and information concerning the universe. At first Greek philosophers sought to reduce the universe itself to a single principle. Thales of Miletus (ca. 585 B.C.) held that all things came from water. The importance of Thales and his followers lies not in their conclusions, but in their willingness to put aside old beliefs and examine the origin, form, and purpose of the world. Pythagoras in the late sixth century offered a view of the cosmos in terms of mathematical relationships. The search for an underlying principle of the universe brought diverse conclusions. The Eleatics held that it was stability, while Heraclitus argued that it was constant change. Two Greek philosophers, Democritus and Leucippus, even developed a crude atomic theory. Meanwhile Hippocrates, who lived in the late fifth century, put aside older ideas about disease and magic cures, and laid the foundation of medical science on careful observation and experience.

From a consideration of the physical universe and speculation in related problems other thinkers turned to the individual. The Sophists, representing this tendency, established schools to instruct the youth in oratory and in the practical workings of government. Their work led to the establishment of the studies of grammar and rhetoric, and they began those examinations into the practices of men in society which anticipate modern inquiry in political science, economics, and sociology. In education their utilitarianism professed to make better men and citizens, but their stress on individual success produced a scepticism toward established traditions of both gods and state. Emphasizing those things which are practical, possible, and contributory to success, they rejected the conception of right or wrong in any absolute sense. In the eyes of the Sophists each individual man was "the measure of all things."

The greatest intellectual figure of fifth-century Athens was Socrates. Believing that the admission of ignorance is the foundation of true knowledge, he set himself to search after the truth. He turned from disputes about the nature of the universe and sophistic practical interests to discover what is true, noble, just, and pious. His dialectic method sought by question and answer, by argument in analysis of a situation, to find proper definitions of such terms. The victim of a reaction which followed the Peloponnesian War, he was accused of denying the gods and corrupting the youth of Athens, and was forced to drink poison. Plato's "Apology of Socrates," a record of the speech which Socrates made in his defense, is a masterly exposition of his whole career and purpose.

After the death of Socrates, his disciple Plato established a school in the Grove of Academus. He and his students discussed and developed philosophic concepts, employing the Socratic method and principles. These discussions were recorded in dialogue form, with Socrates as the chief speaker. The dialogues, which are poetic in language and remarkable for their dramatic form, contain a wide range of discussion in the whole field of philosophy. Basic in Plato's philosophy was his theory of "ideas," which holds the reality of universal concepts or ideas of which actual objects are but shadows. The *Republic,* a description of the ideal state, is Plato's most popularly known dialogue. Plato's utopian city-state, made up of about five thousand citizens, was small enough to allow all to participate in its activities. Self-sufficient, politically, socially, and economically, it maintained at the same time "the moral character of the state" and the code of social ethics which Plato emphasized. His view of the state was fundamentally aristocratic, for its rulers constituted an intellectual aristocracy. Arguing that the members of the city-state should occupy that place in the social order where they could best serve for the good of all, he divided the citizens into three classes. The mass of the people were to be producers, the warrior class was to provide defense, and the intelligent, by virtue of their special training and comprehension of realities, were to rule. Plato's influence on subsequent philosophic thought has been remarkable.

Aristotle (born in 384 B.C.), too, stands pre-eminent in the intellectual world. After studying under Plato and serving as tutor for the youthful Alexander, he established a school in Athens in a garden called the Lyceum. Aristotle's work embraced the whole domain of knowledge, and he did much to establish the foundations of scientific method and the divisions of knowledge. Aristotle's interests ranged from plants, animals, and the heavenly bodies, to politics. He wrote, for example, the constitutional history of one hundred and fifty-eight Greek states. In the course of his work he created a system of formal logic and developed a theory of causation. Aristotelian philosophy had a tremendous influence during the Middle Ages, especially in science and logic. It may be pointed out that this influence was not always a fortunate one for the development of European thought because Aristotle came to be regarded as an authority that was rarely questioned.

≡ III ≡

THE HELLENISTIC AGE

WITH the battle of Chaeronea the classical period of Greek history comes to a close. The conquests of Philip of Macedon and his son Alexander the Great (336-323 B.C.) ushered in a new era and a new culture.

Philip, who had planned a war with Persia for the conquest of Asia Minor, was assassinated before he could put his plans into effect. He was succeeded by his son Alexander, who went far beyond his father's ideas. Driving the Persians out of Asia Minor, he captured Tyre and the whole coast of Syria, invaded and took possession of Egypt, overthrew the Persian empire and finally ended his advance to the east on the borders of India. Over the empire he created Alexander ruled as a god-king, even insisting that the Greek city-states enroll him among their gods. Following the Persian imperial organization he placed Macedonians, Greeks, and Persians in charge of satrapies. To bring about cultural unity and provide an outlet for the dispossessed elements among the Greeks, he founded Greek cities throughout his empire, the most famous being Alexandria in Egypt.

HELLENISTIC KINGDOMS After Alexander's death of a fever at the age of thirty-three his generals engaged in a long series of wars for possession of the empire. When the struggle ended there were three large kingdoms ruled by descendants of the generals: Egypt under the heirs of Ptolemy; Asia, under Seleucus and his descendants, and Macedon, in the hands of Antigonus, grandson of the ablest of the commanders. Athens, desperately struggling for freedom, was brought under the control of Macedon, and Sparta, after a revolutionary attempt at economic reform, was utterly ruined by the Macedonians. The other states of the Greek mainland were united into two federal leagues, the Achaean in the Peloponnesus, and the Aetolian in northern Greece, governed by elected generals and representative councils. While the cities retained autonomy in local affairs, interchange of citizenship was allowed. There was also established the small but wealthy kingdom of Pergamum in Asia Minor, which became renowned for its art, letters, and philosophic schools. Because there was a shift of trade to the east, the island cities of Rhodes and Delos were important ports of call along the trade routes and became wealthy and influential. Rivalry between the great powers—Macedon, Asia, and Egypt—enabled these smaller states to maintain a measure of independence.

MEANING OF
HELLENISTIC

The developments of this entire period led to the appearance of new cultures which are called Hellenistic. The period which runs from Alexander to the time of Christ is called the Hellenistic Age. In a sense Hellenistic means less purely Greek, and the Hellenistic cultures may be regarded as hybrids in which Hellenic and non-Hellenic cultural strains are mingled. The conquests, the movements of the Greek armies, and the founding of Greek colonies resulted in the penetration of Greek culture into the Eastern world to varying degrees in different regions. At the same time in Greece proper, Oriental cultural influences became very marked. The various Hellenistic cultures—Graeco-Persian, Graeco-Syrian, Graeco-Egyptian and the like—had many common elements. In the Hellenistic period older distinctions between Hellenes and non-Hellenes disappeared. The cosmopolitan character of the Hellenistic world is implied in such popular expressions of the time as "There are many cities, but they are all one Hellas," and "Above all nations is humanity." The spread of a common spoken language and of religious cults, the development of legal uniformity and of a recognized body of commercial law, and the widespread celebration of Greek festivals both reflected and contributed to the idea of world unity.

HELLENISTIC
ECONOMIC
DEVELOPMENT

A growing commerce and local specialization in agricultural and industrial production marked the Hellenistic Age. Trade expanded north and west, throughout the Mediterranean, along the routes from Alexandria and Antioch. Egypt, Asia, and Macedon struggled to control these routes, while Rhodes, to protect her interests, attempted to preserve freedom of trade and to suppress piracy. Trade contracts with Egypt enabled Syracuse to add to its wealth and Corinth to regain its earlier importance as a port of transshipment for westbound cargoes. In the western Mediterranean trade was still in the hands of Carthage. The Ptolemies, rulers of Egypt, and the kings of Asia, turned their attention to the East. The Seleucids established a fleet in the Persian Gulf and sent envoys to India, with which a prosperous trade flourished. The Ptolemies reopened the canal from the Nile to the Red Sea, renewed the caravan route from Coptos to the coast, established several ports on the Red Sea, and controlled an active trade in its waters with southern Arabia. Until the last century B.C. the commerce from the Red Sea with India was in the hands of Arab merchants. Then with the discovery of the monsoons, Mediterranean ships sailed straight from Egypt to India. In the last quarter of the second century A.D. direct contact was also made between the Mediterranean and China.

To the Mediterranean there came silk, pepper, and spices from the Far East, ivory and fine woods from Africa, frankincense and myrrh from Arabia, and gold from India, Nubia, and Spain. Macedon and Spain produced silver, and Cyprus continued to supply copper. Egypt and the Black Sea were the granaries of the Hellenistic world, and Tyre and the Anatolian cities prospered because of wool and the purple dye.

Industrial expansion and specialization came with the development of trade. Small shops supplied local needs in all the cities, and in the great cities there were establishments of larger size. In Egypt and Pergamum many industries were government monopolies. In the former, banking and the manufacture of paper, perfumes, leather goods, and oils were in the possession of the Ptolemies. Farmed out under careful supervision, they were organized for large-scale production and distribution. In Pergamum the kings owned and directed the manufacture of textiles, pitch, and parchment. Regional specialization is illustrated in Egyptian production of linen goods, paper, glassware, and vegetable oils, and in the control of the Mediterranean market for olive oil by Athens.

There were no fundamental changes in the types of slavery and in the employment of slaves during the Hellenistic Age. Increased wealth added to the number of slaves in domestic service, and the growth of great estates in Sicily and Italy led to the expansion of agricultural slavery in the West. In Egypt and Asia, however, the native systems of serfdom were an effective bar to the extension of agricultural slavery. As the slave trade became international in scope, with Delos as its chief center, the creation of new markets in Italy and Sicily later led to a westward shift in the traffic.

Gold and silver money was plentiful after Alexander had turned loose the flood of Persian treasure. The world-wide character of trade led to an enlargement of banks and an extension of banking transactions. The records of the state-owned banks of Egypt disclose the use of drafts, loans, and letters of credit. Many private banks in the Greek cities had international connections and carried on a widely diversified business. In spite of this development of financial and credit instruments, public finance in the cities reached a low ebb. Spending far beyond their income, they borrowed continually from temples or from bankers, pledging their revenues and the property of their citizens. Most of them were on the verge of bankruptcy, and were constantly calling upon wealthy citizens and friends for aid.

The economic activity of the period brought prosperity to many and enabled some to build fortunes far beyond the dreams of earlier times. Yet untold suffering was the lot of the poor. Wages, instead of keeping up with prices, fell. The competition of slaves and of the flooded labor market kept free labor at a subsistence level. Wages became so low that it was cheaper to hire freemen than to own slaves. The widespread poverty is reflected in the distribution of grain to the indigent by some states, particularly Rhodes and Samos, and in the endeavors of others to lighten the debt burden.

POLITICAL INSTITUTIONS — The political institutions of the states of the Hellenistic world were varied. In the eastern kingdoms, god-kings ruled. The Ptolemies in Egypt were successors to the pharaohs; the Seleucids to the Persian emperors; the king of Pergamum was also worshiped by his subjects. In Macedon, however, the king was a general who ruled by consent of the army. In Egypt and Asia local government followed ancient patterns somewhat improved by able Greeks. The Ptolemies were assisted by a bureaucracy with financial and military affairs in the hands of Greeks and Macedonians; native officials ruled over the nomes. The Seleucids maintained the Persian system of satrapies with local government in the hands of native rulers.

Wherever there were Greeks the city-states, or smaller organizations patterned after them, were units of government. Now, however, the individual cities were controlled by agents of the kings or by the federal leagues. While the city-states had lost their independence, the number and size of cities were increasing. Great centers of trade and industry like Alexandria and Antioch approached or surpassed the half-million mark in population. Many cities hired doctors to tend the sick, and state aid or private benefaction brought help to the very poor. Religious associations, social and athletic clubs, trade and industrial federations provided companionship for people in all walks of life and gave individuals a sense of dignity in a greater world.

LAW — The political and the economic structure of the Hellenistic world contributed to the development of uniformity in law. The kings rendered decisions for the peoples under their control; the leagues fostered conformity among their members; and the great extension of commercial transactions made the formation of a recognized, if unwritten, body of contractual law an absolute necessity. The request of states for outside commissioners to adjudicate suits created a rather large group of lawyers who made it their business to study legal systems. The informal method which these men used in their courts led substantially to a common system of equity and to a general understanding of obligations. This body of law became the basis of the *jus gentium* ("law of all nations") of the Roman law.

HELLENISTIC CULTURE

The universalism, specialization, and individualism which are apparent in the life of the Hellenistic Age generally are also to be found in its art, literature, science, and philosophy.

ARCHITECTURE AND ART The architecture and art of the Hellenistic period were essentially secular. Hellenistic cities were carefully planned, and adorned with market places, theaters, stadia, baths, and temples. The temples of the age were large and elaborately decorated, and private houses were lavish and elegant. Their walls were adorned with pictures, and their courtyard floors with mosaics.

In sculpture the artists demonstrated a complete mastery of technique and of subject. They strove for colossal effect, for the portrayal of emotions, for idealized portraiture, and for realism. The extremely realistic statues of the Gauls, the "Aphrodite of Melos," the "Apollo Belvedere," and the noble "Victory of Samothrace" are among the celebrated works of the period. Scenes of daily life, with backgrounds of natural scenery or of buildings, were popular subjects for house decoration.

LITERATURE In the Hellenistic Age books were produced cheaply and in quantity. This led to a broadening of the reading public and to the formation of libraries, among which the famous collection at Alexandria was the most notable. While literature displayed great versatility in form, technique, and subject matter, it lacked a great deal in originality and substance. Comedies of manners, mimes, and sketches of daily life were extremely popular. The Hellenistic tragedies were of little consequence, and audiences preferred the plays of the great Hellenic dramatists. Poets employed all the old forms and meters and experimented with a wide variety of new ones. Idylls— short, graceful pictures of life—were in vogue; the master of this form was Theocritus. The poetry of the period was more notable for its versification, wording, and erudition, than for its emotional power and content.

Prose flourished under the stimulus of rhetoric and science. Books of history and geography, travel accounts and memoirs, pamphlets, letters, stories, and philosophic and scientific treatises made their appearance. In most of these works contact with reality was frequently sacrificed to literary style, and the manner in which a fact was stated was more important than the fact itself.

The most important branch of prose was history. Memoirs were written by many of Alexander's followers; writers composed literary histories of their own and earlier periods and scientific historians made careful studies of the antiquities of their own states. Polybius of Mega-lopolis, among the greatest of the historians, recorded the history of Rome and of the Greek leagues during the period of the Punic Wars and the Roman conquest of the East. Of the forty books which he wrote, only the first five and fragments of the others have survived. He held with Thucydides that history was useful for the instruction of future generals and statesmen. In his earlier pages Polybius alluded to "chance" as a dominant force. His ideas of causation grew to such an extent, however, that he realized the importance of geographic and climatic elements, the significance of men and of institutions, and even declared that nothing happened without a natural cause. He was most specific in his statements of the obligations of the historian. The first object of the historian's search, declared Polybius, must be truth. To arrive at the truth, he said, the first requisite is a careful study and criticism of all sources; the second is knowledge based on travel and examination of the sites of the events described; the third is the prac-tical experience of politics and warfare which alone makes possible the understanding and explanation of history.

SCIENCE   The advance in science in the Hellenistic period, par-ticularly in Alexandria, is especially notable. In Alex-andria the first Ptolemy founded the famous museum as a home for scholars who were subsidized by the government. A zoological garden contributed to the study of natural science. The great library provided a workshop for scholars, who issued texts of the great masters and established canons of literary criticism. Significant strides were taken in medicine during this period. Herophilus of Chalcedon (fl. 300 B.C.), for example, learned that the arteries carried blood, not air, ascertained the significance of the pulse in disease, and discovered the nervous system. He practiced dissection and performed major operations. Other physicians made advances in treatment by dieting, massage, exercise, and baths. Popular medicine, however, was still dominated by magical cures effected in the temples of the gods.

Alexander's march to the East stimulated an interest in geography, and one result was the exploration of the route to India. A voyage by Pythias of Marseilles led to the discovery of the Arctic Ocean. The greatest of the geographers, Eratosthenes of Cyrene (275-200 B.C.), who lived and worked in Alexandria, drew a map of the known world in which he utilized parallels of latitude and longitude. Holding that the earth was round, he made a remarkably accurate estimate of its cir-cumference.

Aristarchus of Samos (ca. 310-230 B.C.), leading astronomer, learned from earlier scholars that the earth turned on its axis, and developed the heliocentric theory of the solar system. Last in the suc-cession of geographers and astronomers before the Roman Empire was

Poseidonius of Rhodes (135-51 B.C.), who journeyed to Gades to study the tides, attributing their cause to the wind and their variations to the phases of the moon. He calculated the size and distance of the sun and the circumference of the earth, and he argued that a man sailing west could reach India.

Mathematics kept pace with and made possible many of these studies. Euclid collected geometric theorems and prepared the textbook of geometry which is the basis of all modern handbooks of the subject. Other men began the study of trigonometry and conic sections. Archimedes (ca. 287-212 B.C.), who towers over all the Greeks in mathematics and mechanics, advanced the study of geometry, calculated the value of π, and began the study of calculus. He formulated the law of floating bodies, based on his discovery of specific gravity, and invented the double pulley and the water screw. He also understood the principle of the lever. After his death some progress was made in hydraulics. Clocks, mills, and organs worked by water were invented; a catapult operated by compressed air was produced; and Hero of Alexandria (fl. 100 B.C.) discovered the expansive power of steam.

These scientific achievements were not put to practical use. They were made by men who regarded themselves as philosophers, and who thought it beneath them to apply their discoveries practically. Furthermore, labor was so cheap and plentiful that machinery was unnecessary and even undesirable.

PHILOSOPHY   Hellenistic philosophy dealt largely with the problems of the individual. The old moral sanctions of the family and the state had gone. In a disturbed and overwhelming universe men everywhere, rich and poor alike, felt the helplessness of the individual. To the question: "What must I do to be saved?" which men were asking, philosophy and religion endeavored to give an answer.

Under such conditions philosophy dealt chiefly with ethics, using their explanations of the universe to justify their ethical theories. Philosophers were in agreement that the aim of living is the good life, which may be termed happiness or virtue. On the definition of these terms, however, and on the method of attaining the good life there was much disagreement among the different Hellenistic schools of philosophy. The three most important schools were the Epicurean, the Cynic, and the Stoic, and these dominated philosophic thought even beyond the close of ancient civilization.

The founder of the first, Epicurus, set up his school in Athens in 306 B.C. To him the world was a soulless atomic mechanism. Atoms flying through space swerve and meet to create life; they fly apart to cause death. Men have always believed in gods, and they may well exist. But they live apart in perfect happiness and have nothing to do with men. All human hopes and fears, all prayers, charms, and magic arts are therefore idle fancy. Man, once convinced of this, and freed from the weight of superstition, may see the earth and himself for what they are—simply mechanisms. To Epicurus the chief end of life was indeed happiness, not measured in sensual pleasure, but negatively conceived. It was the avoidance of pain, an escape into a gentle quiet world of the intellect. Appealing to the few of strong intellect, Epicureanism, however, furnished no salvation for the masses.

It was the Cynics who reached the masses to a greater degree. They taught that the end of life is virtue; that virtue is knowledge; and that knowledge concerns oneself alone. All the conventions of society, all the ties of state and family are as nothing to the free individual. The cares and worries about friends, fortunes, reputation, and even daily living must be laid aside. Since whatever is, is right, man therefore must take what comes. Until late in Roman imperial times, the Cynics traveled, usually in pairs, carrying a message of endurance to the poor and simple. Their disregard of the amenities of life offended the rich and the intellectual, few of whom became Cynics.

Stoicism, first taught by Zeno in Athens in 302 B.C., embraced the best elements in Cynicism, and, developed by its founder's followers, became a philosophy which swept the Graeco-Roman world. From Zeno, Stoicism received a religious tinge and a missionary fervor. It taught that the world of inert matter is animated by a divine fire which is God, and that all living and moving things therefore partake of the divine. God has established for the world a perfect universal law, and virtue and hence happiness depend upon obedience to that law. Life is thus a struggle toward virtue by means of knowledge in which the flesh must be overcome. To the truly wise man who knows the law, said the Stoics, affairs of the body and the problems of daily life will be of no importance when compared with matters of the mind and soul. He will be sincerely happy, understanding that whatever comes must be endured as a part of the divine plan. The Stoics also argued that all men are brothers, since they all partake of the same divine element. All men are parts of one divine and universal state. Each individual, therefore, has his obligations to his fellow men and his duties to this ideal fatherland. Whatever part a man is given to play on the world's stage, he must play it, and when his time comes to leave the stage, he must go cheerfully. Stoicism's appeal was essentially intellectual, for the Stoic was trying to save himself by the powers of his own reason. The great mass of the people, however, sought salvation not in Stoicism and its rival schools, but in religious faith and ritual.

RELIGION   The old gods of Greece had been divinities of the city-state. Philosophy and criticism had weakened their position, and they did not offer a sufficiently personal religion to men of the Hellenistic Age. With charms and amulets many sought the favors of Tyche, Fortune, Lady Luck, or tried to learn her will by attending oracles, practicing divination, or reading the stars. Charlatans peddled amulets and books of magic charms, and astrology was widely practiced.

While the worship of the god-king provided a hope of economic salvation, at the same time a flood of Oriental divinities whose appeal and promise of help were more personal and satisfying came into the Greek world. Greeks in the Eastern lands, identifying the local divinities with those of Olympus, accepted them and their rites. Those who remained at home learned as readily to worship the gods whom the Orientals brought with them. In every Greek community many little religious associations appeared in which men found brotherhood and dignity under the protection of a friendly deity.

The so-called "mystery religions" which based their dogma and ritual upon ancient myth and by their initiatory rites awakened in their converts a sense of sin and of purification, had the widest appeal. With their order of elaborate ceremonials and codes of ethics, they promised the reward of a glorious immortality to the faithful. The old mystery religions of Demeter and Dionysus flourished widely. The legend of Dionysus' earthly life, death, and resurrection was dramatized, furnishing to his worshipers the magic words by which they might escape the ever-turning wheel of life and enter the Elysian Fields of eternity. In Egypt, Ptolemy I created a god of healing and protection—Serapis— out of a combination of Osiris, Apis, and elements of Zeus and Dionysus, associated him with Isis and Anubis, and set him up as the god of the Greeks in Egypt.

Among the host of goddesses of the Hellenistic world, the most beloved were the mother-goddesses. In Anatolia men and women prostrated themselves before Cybele, or Ma, and her divine son, Attis. The greatest and most widely worshiped of the goddesses, however, was Isis. Faithful wife and mother, she presided over marriage and childbirth. To the weary and worn she extended a mother's arms. "I am all that is, all that has been, and all that shall be," said Isis in her ritual. Rome, too, fell under the spell that she cast over the Mediterranean world.

CONCLUSION Greek history draws to an end with the close of the Hellenistic Age. In the classic period the Greeks, achieving greatness in their city-states, had taught the world the lessons of democratic government and the worth of man as a citizen and an individual. After the decline of the city-states the leagues demonstrated the advantages of federalism, and men, abandoning local feelings of city and of race, developed concepts of cosmopolitanism and of world culture. In art, architecture, literature, philosophy, and science, striking achievements were recorded. Nor did the story of Hellenic culture end with the Hellenistic Age. Greek architects, artists, scientists, and men of letters of great ability played their part in the history of the Roman Empire. Greek influence on the development of the Christian Church was strong, and a genuine revival of Hellenism took place in the Byzantine world. Mingling with other cultural currents in the Western world from the time of the Romans to the present, the Hellenic stream is still a recognizable element in our own culture.

⚌ IV ⚌

THE RISE OF ROME

THE ROMAN CONQUEST

THE meteorlike rise of Rome introduced a new element into the Hellenistic world. Alexander and his generals had served to bring about a measure of cultural unity in the East. Rome, already dominant in the West, conquered the East in the last two centuries B.C. and united the Mediterranean world into the Roman Empire. Absorbing and transforming Hellenistic culture, Rome carried its civilizing force to the Western world.

The geography of the Italian peninsula is important in Roman history. The long narrow boot-shaped peninsula, lying northwest and southeast with the Alps on the north and Sicily at the toe, is dominated by the single long range of the Apennines. To its north lies the fertile valley of the Po, not considered a part of Italy in classical times. On the east the mountains approach close to the sea, leaving a sandy shore and an area fit only for the raising of cattle. While the whole peninsula may be said to face west, southern Italy and Sicily face the east. Their history was bound up from early times with that of the Aegean. The heart of Italy is the coastal plain to the west of the mountains, where the fertile soil and fine rivers made possible the development of agriculture. The scarcity of harbors and of raw materials for industry combined with the fertile soil to make the Italian tribes communities of farmers.

THE PEOPLES OF ITALY   In the Neolithic period Italy was occupied by farmers and herdsmen of Mediterranean stock. In the Bronze Age southern Italy and Sicily were invaded from Crete, and after them Greeks and Phoenicians came into the area. Peoples speaking an Indo-European language entered from the north, occupying first the Po Valley. Moving south, they blended with the older inhabitants. They left definite evidence of their presence in the pile-village remains of the Po region. These people were competent farmers, used bronze and later iron, and burned their dead. From the blend of these folk with those of Mediterranean stock the later Italian tribes were descended.

The first highly civilized people with whom the Italians of the western plain came in contact were the Etruscans. Coming from the East, in the eleventh century B.C., these invaders settled in the valley of the Arno, where they founded fortified cities combined into a league. Later they expanded into Campania to the south and the Po Valley to the north.

For a period, the Etruscans dominated western and northern Italy and were able to stop the Greek advance, but they failed to perpetuate their power. Within many of the cities they were only a small ruling class surrounded by retainers and supported by serfs. The Greeks drove them out of Campania, and the Celts occupied the Po Valley in the fifth century B.C. Native rebellions cost them many Italian communities. Finally the Romans conquered and overwhelmed them.

THE ETRUSCANS   The Romans were profoundly influenced by the Etruscans in many ways. Etruscan kings established themselves in Rome, and Etruscan domination influenced the political organization of the city. From the Etruscans the Romans learned to plan and fortify cities, to build temples and erect statues, and to employ the arch and the vault in architecture. From the Etruscan craftsmen the Romans acquired the knowledge of many industrial arts. Advanced agricultural techniques were also borrowed from the Etruscans by the Romans. Many Greek elements entered Roman culture by way of the Etruscans, who carried on an active trade with the Carthaginians and Greeks. From the latter the Etruscans had adopted the alphabet, the phalanx, principles of art, and many traits of private life. Much of Roman religion was Etruscan in origin. Central in the religion of the Etruscans was the triad Jupiter, Juno, and Minerva. Their books of sacred lore contained the rules of ritual according to which they carried on all important activities and learned the will of the gods from the lightning, the thunder, the flight of birds, and the condition of the entrails of sacrificial animals. These practices the Romans also adopted.

On the hilltops south of the Tiber River lived the Latin tribes, united by the worship of Jupiter and by a league centering in the temple of Diana. When many of their fortified towns were seized by Etruscan nobles in the seventh and sixth centuries B.C., they were brought into the current of Italian commercial life. About the end of the sixth century B.C. the Latins threw off the Etruscan yoke and began a vigorous independent development. The leader in this movement was Rome.

ROME   The legendary history of Rome ascribes the founding of the city to Romulus, descendant of Aeneas, in 753 B.C. Actually it seems that in the twelfth or eleventh century B.C. a village was established on Palatine Hill which was expanded by additions until it occupied the seven hills of classic Rome. These early Romans were united into family groups (*gentes*), and the leaders of the more powerful of these were aristocrats called *patricians*. The rest of the people were termed *plebs* or *plebeians*. The patricians were great landowners, and many of the plebeians were attached to them as retainers, or clients. The ruler was an elected king who served as general, priest, and judge, and was advised by a senate composed of the great patricians. The citizen assembly voted by wards, *curiae,* of which there were thirty.

The early Romans seem to have been pastoral people. Under Etruscan dominion, they advanced in agriculture, trade and industry, and gradually extended the power of the city over the Latin League. The Etruscans were probably overthrown by a combination of the landowning farmers under patrician leadership.

THE CONQUEST OF ITALY   Conquest and expansion are primary in Roman history. After the expulsion of the Etruscan kings the Latins were bound to Rome by treaty. Then the peoples in the hills to the south and west of Rome were made subject, and in 396 B.C. the Etruscan city of Veii was taken. This led to the conquest of northern Italy, and control over the hills to the south involved the Romans in Campania. Here they came into conflict with the southern mountaineers, the Samnites, and an alliance of Samnites, Umbrians, Etruscans, and Gauls failed to check the Roman advance. New Roman interests in the south led to trouble with the Italian Greeks, who called in Pyrrhus of Epirus to aid them. Although Pyrrhus won two costly victories over Roman armies, he was finally defeated, and in 272 B.C. Rome was mistress of Italy.

Much Italian land was confiscated during the course of the conquest and given to Roman citizens or to Latins. Some of the Italian communities annexed to Rome received from the senate municipal charters for self-government; others were garrisoned by Romans and Latins and acquired the status of a colony. Most of them were bound to Rome by separate treaties which allowed them self-government and freedom from tribute but required them to supply troops for the Roman army.

PATRICIANS AND PLEBS   During the years while Rome was extending its control over Italy, its citizens were engaged in a bitter class struggle. After the expulsion of the kings, the patricians had monopolized the offices of the new republic and membership in the powerful senate. The plebeians desired a share in the government and adjustment of other inequalities. Since plebeian man power was needed for the army during this period, the plebs won significant concessions. They obtained the right to organize an assembly, to pass measures binding on themselves, and to elect four—later ten—tribunes, protectors with a right of veto over the magistrates. In 451-449 B.C. they secured the recording of the laws in the Twelve Tables. Following these victories they gained admission to the magistracies and the senate and power of legislation for all the people. In response to their demands, laws lightened the debt burden and forbade enslavement for debt. Because the patricians took a large share of the confiscated lands in conquered territory, the plebeians secured a measure limiting the amount of public land any one man might occupy.

These plebeian victories, however, did not mean the establishment of democracy in Rome. No office carried pay, and only the well to do could afford an official career. Power passed into the hands of a hundred or so wealthy families, patrician and plebeian, who constituted an office-holding nobility. This wealthy class controlled the election machinery, and consequently the offices, and conveniently failed to enforce the restrictions on the holding of public lands.

CONQUEST OF
THE MEDITER-
RANEAN

Shortly after conquering Italy, Rome launched upon an expansion which made it supreme in the Mediterranean world. Rivalry in Sicily involved Rome in several wars with Carthage, the first of which began in 264 and ended in 241 B.C. As a result of its victory in the First Punic War, Rome acquired Sicily. Shortly afterward a new Gallic raid led to Roman control of the Po Valley. Strife between the Carthaginians and their mercenary troops enabled Rome to add Sardinia and Corsica to its holdings. Carthage had been defeated but not destroyed. To compensate for its losses Hamilcar, hero of the First Punic War, turned to Spain. In 218 B.C. his son Hannibal launched a war of revenge upon Rome from Spain. Swiftly crossing the Pyrenees, Gaul, and the Alps, he entered the Italian peninsula, where he brilliantly defeated the Roman armies. At Cannae he destroyed the largest force ever put into the field by Rome. Final victory in the Second Punic War, however, lay with Rome, and in 202 B.C. Hannibal was defeated at Zama in Northern Africa by Scipio, the Roman commander. In 201 Carthage surrendered supremacy in the West to Rome. In 146 B.C., after a third war provoked by Roman greed, Carthage was destroyed and its territory was made into a Roman province.

At the close of the Second Punic War, Rome was drawn into the rivalries of the powers over the East, when it answered an appeal of the Greeks for aid with a declaration of war upon Macedon (200-197 B.C.). Victory in this was followed by a successful campaign against Antiochus III of Asia (191-190 B.C.), and another war with Perseus of Macedon (171-168 B.C.) also ended victoriously for Rome. Thus far

Rome had annexed no territory in the East, but its will was supreme there. Control without possession did not work, however, and in 146 B.C. Macedon was annexed, Corinth was sacked, and the Greek leagues were dissolved. The king of Pergamum willed his kingdom to Rome in 133 B.C. In the course of the next century Bithynia came into Roman hands likewise by will; wars resulted in the conquest of the rest of Asia Minor, except the eastern portion; and Syria and Judaea (in 63 B.C.) were conquered by Pompey. In 30 B.C. Egypt also fell into the grasp of Rome, now mistress of the civilized world.

ROMAN INSTITUTIONS   The Greek historian Polybius observed that Rome's rise to power was due to her institutions, which, he said, combined the best features of monarchy, aristocracy, and democracy, all checking one another. The monarchical element was found in the magisterial system, which gave great power to the higher magistrates. The Roman who pursued a political career passed through a regular sequence of offices. He served first as a junior officer in the army. Then, if a plebeian, he was elected to the board of ten tribunes, who at first enjoyed only the right of veto but finally acquired power to preside over the assembly and the senate. Next in rank were the four aediles, in charge of buildings, markets, and games, and the eight quaestors, to whom fell care of the treasury and the management of funds. In 367 B.C. the praetorship was established to assist the consuls in military affairs and to take charge of the courts. In 242 B.C. a second praetor was added to deal with legal cases involving non-Romans. Shortly thereafter four more praetors were added to serve as governors of Rome's first provinces. The consuls, two in number, were chief executives and commanders of the army. Their power was in theory autocratic; actually it was limited because they held office only for a year and had the power of veto upon each other. In addition, custom decreed that they follow the advice of the senate, while their civil power in the city was limited by the veto of the tribunes. In times of great emergency a dictator with unlimited power was chosen for six months. After the Hannibalic War, the office fell into disuse.

When it was necessary to secure additional commanders or to obtain continuity of command for more than a year, the senate, with the consent of the people, prolonged the command of a consul or a praetor or appointed ex-magistrates. Such officials were called proconsuls or propraetors, and after the development of the provincial system they were regularly assigned to provincial command. The crowning honor of an official career was the censorship. Two censors, elected every five years for eighteen months, took the census, assigned each man to his tribe and class, let and supervised public contracts, and drew up the list of the senators.

The senate was a body of three hundred men, chosen for life, and drawn primarily from the ranks of ex-magistrates of the grade of quaestor or above. It had no responsibility to the people, and its powers depended upon custom more than upon law. It advised the consuls, appointed proconsuls, and assigned commands; it supervised legislation, approved contracts, provided for the levy of armies, the raising of taxes, and the allocation of funds. Foreign affairs were in its hands, and in dangerous times it declared martial law by its "final decree."

The people acted politically through the assemblies, of which the most powerful in the early republic was the centuriate assembly. It was made up of 193 centuries in which the people were organized on the basis of wealth. Of this number the wealthy, composing the cavalry and the first class—there were five classes in all—controlled 98, a clear majority. This assembly elected magistrates, voted on peace and war and on laws submitted to it by the magistrates. In the more democratic tribal assembly the people voted in the tribes or wards in which they were listed as landowners, the landless being enrolled in the four city tribes. Normally this assembly met under the presidency of a tribune and passed plebiscites. It was most active in a legislative sense in the later years of the republic. All measures and nominations were presented to the assemblies by the presiding officer and no debate was allowed. Even at the less formal meetings held for purposes of discussion no one might speak without the consent of the magistrate in charge.

During the period of conquest Rome developed a provincial system. At the time of conquest a "law of the province" was drawn up describing the status of the communities in the territory. Some, like Athens and Rhodes, were made allies; others were granted freedom from taxation; most paid taxes to Rome. Subject to the supervision of the governor and to Roman control over foreign affairs, these communities were allowed to govern themselves. The governor, whose right of command was limited to the borders of his province, was virtually independent during his term of office. He protected the frontier, kept order, saw that taxes were paid, and judged cases involving Roman citizens. The lack of a central control in this system had disastrous results in the end.

Among the elements which contributed to Roman success were their army, road system, and law. During the Samnite Wars the Romans abandoned the phalanx borrowed from the Etruscans and adopted the open order of the legion. The legion was composed of thirty companies arranged in three lines and deployed in checkerboard fashion. The first-line soldiers were recruits, the second experienced men, and the third, or reserve, veterans. Equipped with body armor, a shield, two darts, and a short sword, the men, as they advanced spaced eight feet apart, threw their darts and closed in with drawn swords. At this close fighting the Romans were supreme. Training was rigid and discipline absolute. Wherever the Romans conquered they built roads celebrated for their directness and durability. Built for military purposes, they were used by travelers and merchants and helped to bind first Italy and then the Mediterranean world together.

The civil law, which was Rome's greatest and most enduring contribution, had its beginnings in the regal period under the authority of the king, assisted by the pontiffs, his advisers on legal matters. With the establishment of the republic, the consuls replaced the king, and later control over the law was entrusted to the praetors. The rules of procedure and the principles of private law, *jus civile,* developed by decisions, were written down in the famous Twelve Tables. They contained principles of family and property law, of injuries and remedies and some provisions of public law. Procedure was rigidly regulated. The plaintiff, who was given the authority to summon the defendant to court, made a formal charge, and lost his case if he employed the wrong formula. A private judge appointed by the magistrate determined the facts, and the law was strictly applied. Interpretation, procedural reform and expansion all served to bring these rules and laws into accord with the needs of economic and intellectual growth.

After the first plebeian pontiff had published the pontifical interpretations of the law, there appeared a number of lay private jurists who made knowledge of the law their specialty and gave interpretations freely to all. Procedural reform and expansion were the work of the praetors. The necessity of dealing with foreigners who did not know Latin led to changes in procedure. In such cases the praetor, calling the litigants before him, drew up a formula stating the nature of the case and the principle of law to be applied. This approach extending to the civil law enabled the praetors to evolve new rules of law to meet new situations, and there grew what was termed the *jus honorarium* ("official law"), which received sanction in the praetor's edicts. On assuming office, the praetor issued an edict stating what formulas he would accept in legal actions. Normally he took over the edict of the preceding year with changes made necessary by experience. Thus the law was kept up to date without losing its continuity and tradition. The *praetor peregrinus* who dealt primarily with foreigners made a further contribution in the *jus gentium,* "law of all nations." During the Hellenistic period certain principles of commercial relations were recognized as binding on all peoples. The Roman praetors opening their courts to foreigners discovered these principles and embodied them in the *jus gentium.* Never more than a body of principles, its provisions acquired the force of law only when they were recognized in the courts and embodied in the praetor's edicts. They did much, nevertheless, to broaden the foundations of the Roman law.

Basic in Roman life and in shaping Roman character was the family, over which the *pater familias* (the father of the family) presided. He had power to inflict punishment for disobedience even on grown sons; and his wife, unmarried daughters, and his sons' and grandsons' wives were in his charge. He controlled all clients and slaves and the family estate. Also of utmost importance in Roman civilization were the *mores maiorum*—the customs of the ancestors—for tradition prevailed in every aspect of life. While discipline and conservatism were the keynotes of custom, they did not prevent necessary changes. The emphasis of tradition was laid rather on qualities of constancy, diligence, faith, and pre-eminently on valor, steadfastness, and loyalty.

THE CONSEQUENCES OF ROMAN IMPERIALISM

Roman institutions and traditions met a severe test as a result of the conquests which led to the development of empire. In the century which followed the expansion, the Roman Empire was an almost unmitigated calamity for the world. Whatever their virtues, the Romans were rapacious. Land hunger and the desire for booty lay in the background of most Roman wars. The conquests meant land confiscation. The covetousness of the Roman landed class was probably the chief cause of the destruction of Carthage into whose possession its rich fields passed. Commanders and soldiers plundered at the time of conquest. Tax collectors, operating on contract, seized more than was their due, while Roman businessmen exploited the provincial resources and loaned money to cities at exorbitant rates of interest. Most of the governors levied exactions to enrich themselves. The tribute which poured into Rome was squandered, the provinces failing to receive in return the protection which was their due.

Italy, as well as the Hellenistic world, suffered as a result of the expansion of Rome. Its fields, ravaged by Hannibal, in some areas never recovered. Its small farmers suffered at the hands of the great Roman landowners; its merchants were overwhelmed by the business class in Rome. The Romans, treating the Italians as subjects, interfered in their local affairs, and rejected their demand for Roman citizenship.

The economy, government, and society of Rome were all vitally affected by the conquests. The early Romans were farmers who maintained themselves on relatively small farms. While the conquest of Italy had led to the growth of large estates, the wealth which the empire brought aided in an agricultural revolution. Forbidden by law to engage in trade, the senatorial class invested their means in land which was worked for profit. In northern and central Italy cattle or sheep were primarily raised on the large estates; in the south the growing of grapes and olives predominated. Olive and grape culture spread with the Romans to Sicily and Africa. Available for the working of these estates were great numbers of slaves acquired from war or piracy, many of whom were skilled in the culture of the olive tree and the vine. Gangs of slaves also tended the herds of cattle and sheep. A slave revolt in Sicily in 134-132 B.C., which was brutally suppressed, gave evidence of the menace of the slave system, but no measures were taken to improve the conditions which had led to the outbreak.

The competition of the large estates brought about a decline in the number of small farmers. Many of them, returning from years of foreign war, had no desire to return to farming; others found their farms destroyed, or eroded, or exhausted. The presence of Sicilian grain in the market made grain-farming less lucrative than previously. The pressure to sell the small holdings to the aristocracy was constant. Some clung to their farms; others remained as free laborers on the great estates; but many drifted into the city to form a landless and poor proletariat.

As a result of these developments the population of Rome was being divided into a city mob and an upper class of landowners. The latter derived their income from great estates which they managed for profit, monopolized the offices and affairs of government, and increased their wealth at the expense of the provincials. This in turn led to a departure from the traditions of their ancestors and an earlier simplicity of life. Though they called themselves *Optimates,* "best men," they replaced loyalty to the best interests of the state with devotion to their own interests, and they failed to manage successfully the affairs of Rome and the empire.

Challenging their power was a third group, the businessmen, called *Equites,* "knights." While commerce and industry remained relatively undeveloped at Rome, the needs of war and imperial administration led to the growth of a class of contractors who executed public works, managed expeditions, and collected taxes. The influx of mobile wealth led to the appearance of a banking group. Since industry was not a field of productive investment, this group lent their money to senators or to provincial cities, and used it in the collection of taxes by contract and the exploitation of provincial resources. These capitalists did not hold office and had no social standing with the *Optimates.* Their sole measure of success was money. In the provinces, however, they came into competition with equally rapacious governors who belonged to the ruling class. The struggle between the *Optimates* and the *Equites* for imperial control marks the period before the appearance of Caesar and Augustus.

The period of conquest saw the triumph of the senate in government. The need for consistent direction in war and in the management of the provinces made it possible for that body to take over the direction of affairs. The authority of the consuls was restricted to Italy; the senate assigned the provincial governors and defined their powers. Through influences and bribes the ruling class easily controlled the assemblies, composed largely of the city proletariat. Aspirants to office found their paths blocked unless they belonged to the ruling class and were entirely amenable to the will of the senatorial leaders.

In the test, however, the senate failed. It was found necessary in military emergencies to displace regularly chosen consuls with proconsuls of experience and ability. Under the pressure of circumstance the strong man became greater than the constitution. Graft and corruption could not be prevented, and provincial governors were not adequately directed and checked. The knights were offended by the senate's refusal to admit them to a share in imperial control. All attempts to solve the problems of the proletariat, of the slaves, and of the Italian allies were sharply rebuffed by the ruling class.

THE ROMAN REVOLUTION

Out of the failure of the senate came a series of events known as the Roman Revolution. Beginning with an attempt at agrarian reform, there ensued bitter struggles for control between the classes, a series of economic crises, rioting in the city streets, threatened revolts, foreign disasters, the formation of professional armies ready to follow their leaders even against the state, and the rise of great personalities who destroyed the constitution. Finally the contest was resolved into a struggle not between the senate and the great man, but between leaders for power.

In 133 B.C. Tiberius Gracchus, a young man of noble origin, endeavored as tribune to restore the public land to the people. Charged with unconstitutional procedure, he was assassinated. Ten years later his brother Gaius revived his policy, and added a program of public works and commercial colonies. He also tried to secure political support with which to challenge the senate by giving power to the knights and proposing citizenship for the Italians. His program precipitated a riot, and he committed suicide. A few years later, when the senate failed to deal properly with the Jugurthine War, the business class secured the election of a "new man" of marked ability, Gaius Marius. After Marius accomplished the end for which he had been elected, a new danger arose in the invasion of Germans into Gaul. To meet this Marius, illegally re-elected, established a professional army (enrolling volunteers for a term of sixteen years), with which he triumphed over the barbarians. Marius's attempts at democratic reform in 100 B.C. failed dismally.

The refusal of the conservatives in 91 B.C. to grant citizenship to the Italians was followed by an Italian revolt called the Social War. The Romans were forced to yield the coveted privilege after a bloody war in which a senatorial champion, Sulla, was the hero. To him the senate assigned charge of the war with Mithradates of Pontus who had secured control of the Aegean and occupied Athens. The business leaders, however, desiring to share in what promised to be a lucrative campaign, secured his deposition and the election of Marius. Sulla then led his army against Rome to reaffirm his own appointment. After victory in the East, he returned to Rome and drove out his opponents in the First Civil War, and as dictator restored the government to the senate.

The senate, however, proved to be utterly incompetent, and new leaders competed for political and military control. Pompey, gaining renown by military success in Spain, by suppressing piracy in the Mediterranean, and by a brilliant campaign against Mithradates, vainly sought recognition from the senate as the first citizen of Rome. Crassus, wealthiest man in Rome, who had suppressed the Spartacan revolt (73-71 B.C.), contended for political power and the booty of empire. Caesar, nephew of Marius and shrewd politician, also strove to secure position for himself. Cicero, rising to the consulship as champion of law and order, vainly worked to persuade the senate to adopt a program to save the republic.

In 60 B.C. Caesar, Crassus, and Pompey formed an informal alliance known as the "first triumvirate." Caesar, as consul for the year 59, flaunted constitutional safeguards in the passing of legislation and went as governor to Gaul the following year. There he gained rich territory for Rome, and wealth, glory, and a loyal army for himself. In 53 B.C. Crassus was killed fighting against the Parthians. Disorders in Rome and fear of Caesar forced the senate to turn to Pompey. But it was too late. Caesar was victorious in the Second Civil War, which followed, and emerged as dictator of the Roman world. He nominated magistrates, appointed governors, and directed the administration of the empire. He was granted a number of honors which emphasized his divine ancestry and, bestowing upon him divine attributes, placed him in the succession of Hellenistic monarchs. He unified the imperial government under central control, enrolled knights and provincials, settled the proletariat on Italian and provincial lands, and carried out or planned many other reforms, including a revision of the calendar.

Caesar's position and program were offensive to the senatorial class and violated Roman tradition. In 44 B.C. he was assassinated by a band of conspirators. After Caesar's death Cicero fought for the restoration of the republic without success, Antony, Caesar's lieutenant, Octavian, his grandnephew and adopted son, and Lepidus, his general, united to establish the second triumvirate. Those who had conspired against Caesar were defeated, and when Lepidus was shorn of his power, Octavian in the West and Antony in the East strove with each other for possession of the Roman world. Octavian emerged victorious after Antony's defeat at Actium in 31 B.C., became Augustus, the ruler of the Mediterranean world, the first of the Roman emperors.

THE AGE OF AUGUSTUS (31 B.C.-14 A.D.) Once in power, Octavian organized a new imperial government, re-established peace and order, rehabilitated the Roman ruling class, and rebuilt the city. He assumed both the tribunician power, which gave him the direction of civil affairs, and the proconsular power, which made him governor in those provinces which required an army and the right of supervision over the others. He took charge of the grain supply and of the police and fire departments of Rome. The titles he acquired reflected his pre-eminence in the state. As *princeps* he was consulted first on all nominations and questions of policy. His military glory was expressed by the word *imperator* "victorious general." "Augustus," a name conferred on him by the senate, signified "consecrated," and carried with it the implication of divinity. Throughout the East he was worshiped as a god, and in Italy, the *Genius Augusti* received worship. Hailed as a *pater patriae,* "father of his country" in 2 B.C. by the senate, he was formally deified and listed among the gods of Rome after his death.

The senate was reduced to an advisory body and the chief agency which Augustus used for registering his desires. The control over legislation which the senate possessed meant little more than that it ratified the wishes of Augustus. The republican magistrates who were still elected were overshadowed by the imperial appointees. Members of the senatorial order served as officers of the army and governors of the provinces. A high property qualification for membership in the senate was established, and measures were taken to reawaken the old patriotic and religious loyalties of the class.

Augustus established a civil service consisting of procurators and prefects who had charge of financial and administrative matters. Knights were appointed to these offices, and the *Equites* thus reaped the reward of their long struggle with the senate. For the lower posts of the service freedmen were widely used. A standing army of three hundred thousand men, twenty-five legions with their auxiliaries, was established, while a select body of men drawn from Italy formed the praetorian cohort, bodyguard of the emperor. Soldiers enlisted for a term of years and received bonuses or lands at the end of their term. A permanent fleet was organized to keep down piracy.

Augustus divided the provinces between himself and the senate. The older provinces retained by the senate were governed by promagistrates as before; the others belonged to Augustus and were governed by his lieutenants—*legati*—of senatorial rank. Disorder and corruption were checked by the power of supervision which Augustus retained. Collection of taxes by imperial agents ended the evils of the tax-farming system. Egypt, Augustus' personal possession, was administered by a prefect of equestrian rank. The Roman Caesar was recognized as pharaoh by the Egyptians.

The frontier was wisely regulated by Augustus. On the East, peace was made with the Parthians, and the annexation of Judaea and Galatia completed Roman control. The northern frontier was extended to the Danube. An attempt to conquer to the Elbe, however, was abandoned, and the line of the Rhine was strongly fortified. The problems which had beset the late republic were thus settled. The affairs of the empire were put in order. With the restoration of peace by Augustus and the decline of corruption, industry revived, trade began to flow freely, Italian agriculture was rehabilitated, and prosperity returned. Together with these developments, under the patronage of Augustus and his ministers, Agrippa and Maecenas, Rome was rebuilt and arts and letters flourished.

ROMAN CULTURE To understand the cultural developments of the Augustan Age it is necessary to deal briefly with the early Roman culture. The early Romans were practical and unimaginative. Their gods were formless powers inherent in objects and in the processes of life and nature. Notable among them were the Genius, guardian spirit of the family, the Lar, who took care of the farm, the Penates, guardians of the storehouse, and Vesta, spirit of the hearth fire. Jupiter and Mars protected and extended the state, while other divinities guarded the harvests and the herds. The only art of these early Romans was the making of wax images from death masks of their great men, and their literature consisted of rough hymns and prayers, crude and ribald verses, and puppet shows. Under Etruscan influences and that of the expansion their religion underwent change. Gods of conquered states were brought to Rome; deities of trade and industry were added, and new divinities were created to meet new needs.

Contact with the Greeks resulted in the first bloom of Roman culture. From them the Romans learned much in architecture and sculpture. Statues plundered from the Greek cities were placed in the temples, and Romans became proud possessors of Greek objects of art. After the First Punic War a Greek freedman, Andronicus, translated the *Odyssey* into Latin and produced plays taken from the Greek. Naevius made similar translations and wrote an epic poem on the war.

Plautus and Terence in the second century wrote comedies based on Hellenistic works, and Ennius composed a great epic, the *Annals of Rome*. When the Romans found it necessary to explain themselves to the Greeks several annalists, notably Fabius Pictor, wrote histories of Rome in Greek. Cato, conservative champion of things Latin, composed the first Latin history of Rome and wrote a textbook on agriculture. At the same time Greek rhetoricians, philosophers, and teachers, many of them brought to Rome as hostages or as slaves, introduced Hellenistic philosophic and religious ideas. Stoicism, the principles of which coincided with the Roman traditions of valor and endurance, became the dominant Roman philosophy. Many of the younger generation, however, turned to Epicureanism and misinterpreted it to claim freedom, on the authority of intellectualism, from the restraint of ancient sanctions.

The effect of Greek influence on Roman religion was to destroy much of its simple spirituality. Thereafter Roman and Greek gods were identified with each other, and the whole gorgeous imagery of mythology was handed over to the literal-minded Romans. Greek philosophy punctured the faith of the educated classes in the ancestral religion, and the Punic Wars also wrought untold havoc when, in the crisis of the second war, it seemed as if the gods themselves had deserted the Romans. The people turned to such barbaric practices as human sacrifice, and finally brought the Great Mother of Pessinus to Rome. In southern Italy, in Sicily, and in the East, Roman soldiers became aware of other emotional cults. The secret worship of Dionysus—whom the Romans called Bacchus, and his festivals, Bacchanalia—spread widely in Rome until it was suppressed by the senate. It was impossible, however, to prevent the penetration of Eastern religions into Rome.

To this period belong the development of games, circuses, and the growth of gladiatorial combats introduced from Etruria in 264 B.C. The gladiators were usually slaves, trained in special schools and offered for hire. Until the close of the republic they were presented almost exclusively by private persons, but in the imperial period the combats became great public spectacles.

The finest products of Latin literature appeared in the Ciceronian and Augustan periods. The outstanding poets of the first were Catullus and Lucretius. Catullus, master of the Alexandrian meters, composed many lyrics as well as other poems, and his fame rests on a group of short poems which reveal him as one of the appealing poets of love. Equally under Greek influence, Lucretius differed sharply from the passionate Catullus. In the first successfully written Latin hexameter he brought to the Romans the Epicurean message of *quietude*. In the

De Rerum Natura, "On the Nature of Things," he appealed to men
to lay aside their troubles and worries and find peace in Epicureanism.
He praised Epicurus for first freeing men from the weight of superstition, and explained the atomic and mechanistic universe which
Epicurus had portrayed. Describing the evolutionary growth of the
world and of man and explaining the processes of nature, he tried to
free the Romans from those fears which were then driving them to
the emotional religions of the East.

Handling words and phrases like cohorts on the field of battle
Caesar recounted in terse and clear prose his deeds in Gaul and in the
civil wars. Though his *Commentaries* were campaign documents, explaining and justifying his own actions, they are apparently detached
and impersonal and it is difficult to separate propaganda from fact.
Of his other writings, nothing has survived. Sallust (86-35 B.C.),
quaestor, proconsul of Numidia, and follower of Caesar, devoted the
closing years of his life to the writings of readable, but not always
accurate, histories in which he abandoned the annalistic method of
composition.

Statesman, orator, and philosopher, Cicero looms large in the history of the period. He was a master of Latin prose and of rhetorical
form. His orations disclose the crosscurrents of Roman politics and
society. Though not a profound thinker, he carried the message of the
Greek philosophers to his own generation through his essays, and
created a vocabulary for philosophy in Latin which has descended
through the medieval schools to our own time. He was an inveterate
letter writer, and his correspondence, preserved and published by his
freedman secretary, Tiro, and his friend, Atticus, offers a revealing
portrait of the man, at the same time providing a most illuminating
body of source material for the historian.

With the confusion of city life during the revolution, art and
architecture in Rome lagged far behind literature. Augustus remedied
this by rebuilding Rome to make it a worthy capital of an empire.
Eighty-two temples were repaired; the Capitoline Temple of Jupiter
and the Senate House were rebuilt. Near the spot where Caesar's body
had been burned, a temple to the "Deified Julius" was erected. The
Forum of Julius Caesar was completed and a new Forum of Augustus
constructed which served as the Hall of Fame for imperial Rome.
On the Palatine, near the home of Augustus, temples to Apollo, to
the Great Mother, and to Vesta were erected. Most beautiful of the
monuments and symbolic of the new order was the Altar of the
Augustan Peace, ornamented with carvings symbolizing peace, prosperity, and plenty.

Latin literature reached its greatest height under Augustus. Livy

(59 B.C.-17 A.D.), a native of Padua, wrote a magnificent history of Rome, from the founding of the city, designed to call the Romans back from the vices of the day to ancient virtues by a recital of Rome's glorious deeds. Primarily a literary artist interested in the telling of a great story, Livy was also an able historian. He used and criticized his sources intelligently, and recognized the lack of accurate information for the earlier period and the weakness of the family traditions upon which the annalists depended. When he found varying opinions, he chose that which seemed best founded. With a clear and vivid historical imagination, he wove a striking tapestry of the history of Rome from earlier and contemporary strands of information. No ancient historian ever again attempted the task, and those who wrote later of republican Rome leaned heavily upon his vigorous and eloquent narrative. His work remains our chief source, at times our only source, for the early history of Rome. The disappearance of all but thirty-five books of his history and a late epitome is an irreparable loss.

Vergil (70-19 B.C.) was an epic poet of the first rank. Born in Mantua of a peasant father, he went to Rome to secure an education. There his group of pastoral poems called *Eclogues* attracted the attention of Maecenas, friend of Augustus and patron of letters. Maecenas, securing means of support for Vergil, encouraged him to compose the *Georgics,* a poetic treatise on farming. Inspired by the Augustan Age and prompted by Augustus himself, he wrote the *Aeneid,* which, though dealing with the story of the trials of Aeneas, was really the epic of Rome itself. Lauding that "devotion to duty" which had made Rome great, it declared Rome's mission to conquer and organize the world. "In no other poetry," it has been said, "are the chords of human sympathy so delicately touched, its tones so subtly interfused. In none is there so deep a sense of beauty and sorrow of life, of keen remembrance and shadowy hope, and, enfolding all, of infinite pity."

Horace (65-8 B.C.), Vergil's friend, was the son of a freedman, and was also supported by Maecenas. A skilled writer of lyrics, he was an urbane interpreter of his own age and of the art of living. In matchless verse he portrayed the pleasures of the simple life, trifled with mild affairs of the heart, glorified the civic virtues, and sang the praises of Augustus.

Among a number of youths of wealth who amused themselves and delighted their friends by writing polite love songs in the elegiac meter were Tibullus, Propertius, and Ovid (43 B.C.-18 A.D.), of whom the last was the most brilliant and versatile. Belonging to the younger set, who rejected the strict standards of Augustus, he composed a series of verses on love affairs and on the art and remedy of love itself. In the *Fasti* he wrote an account of Roman festivals to please Augustus, and in his celebrated poem, the *Metamorphoses,* he presented the greatest myths of the ancient Greeks.

The age to which Augustus gave his name not only saw the greatest development in literature and art, it also marked the beginning of a new era in the history of Rome and the Mediterranean world.

THE GREATNESS AND FALL OF THE ROMAN EMPIRE (14-180 A.D.)

THE JULIAN-CLAUDIAN EMPERORS
During the years following the death of Augustus, there was general extension of the power of the princeps. In the reign of Tiberius (14-37 A.D.), Augustus' stepson, there was a crystallization of the Augustan system of government and frontier control. By placing control over finance and the administrative business of the empire in the hands of his own freedmen responsible to himself alone, Claudius (41-54 B.C.) advanced the power of the princeps. After Nero's reign (54-68 A.D.) ended disastrously with his own deposition and death, the senate, the praetorian guard, and the armies of the empire contended for a year for the right to name the emperor. Ultimately the Eastern armies placed their general Vespasian on the throne.

THE FLAVIAN DYNASTY (69-96 A.D.)
During the period of the Flavian emperors, the monarchical principle of the imperial government was greatly expanded. The military foundation of the ruling family, the principle of dynastic inheritance and imperial policies reflect the mastery of the emperor. Vespasian emphasized the imperial as against the Roman character of his regime by enrolling Gauls and Spaniards in the senate, and his son Domitian was a thoroughgoing autocrat. His merciless punishment of criticism produced a reign of terror in Rome which ended in his assassination.

THE AGE OF THE ANTONINES (96-180)
The accession of Nerva, chosen by the senate to succeed Domitian, ushered in the Age of the Antonines, sometimes called the Age of the Good Emperors. The superior power of the princeps, already strengthened by the Flavian rulers, was definitely recognized by the senate. Under Trajan (98-117), the first non-Italian emperor, the Roman Empire reached its greatest bounds with the annexation of Dacia, the west coast of Arabia, Armenia, and Mesopotamia. He was followed by Hadrian (117-138), a great administrator who gave up Trajan's program of expansion. Abandoning Armenia and Mesopotamia, he promoted the defense and consolidation of the frontier. To the tribes outside the border and around the Black Sea, Hadrian assigned native

rulers educated in Rome. He also changed the complexion of the army by stationing contingents in permanent camps and recruiting their numbers from the surrounding regions. In administration he organized a permanent bureaucracy, and filled official posts with knights. The civil law received a form of codification and was brought definitely under imperial control. The uneventful reign of Antoninus Pius (138-161) marks the climax of the prosperity of the empire. Marcus Aurelius (161-180), the philosopher-emperor, spent much of his life on campaigns and repulsed a Germanic invasion of Italy. His famous *Meditations* are a record of his thoughts on life and its meaning. With his death, the great age of the Roman Empire came to an end. In succeeding generations the empire was transformed into an undisguised military autocracy.

INSTITUTIONS OF THE EMPIRE

The Roman Empire was an aggregate of communities united in provinces and ruled by the Roman emperors and their officials. Centering in the Mediterranean, it extended from the Arabian Desert on the east to the Atlantic Ocean on the west, from the Sahara Desert on the south to the Rhine, the Danube, and the Carpathian Mountains on the north, and reached across the channel to include Britain. Within its frontiers were Syrians, Jews, Phoenicians, Egyptians, Greeks, Iberians, Celts, Germans, and numerous other peoples, united by the bond of a common allegiance to a princeps, held to be source of all law, fountain of all wisdom and power, united with divinity when alive and god after death.

THE PRINCEPS The emperors bore the names *imperator* and *Caesar* and the title *princeps,* emblematic of their power. They became imperator by acclamation of the army and Caesar and princeps by act of the senate. They were commanders in chief of the army and navy and supreme judges in all matters of law. The tribunician power gave them direction of civil affairs and the office of Pontifex Maximus direction over religious practices and laws. Controlling all nominations for offices in Rome, they also appointed the prefects, curators, and officers in the provinces, the army and the administration. Their commands, speeches, letters, and decisions had the full force of law. The senate had been transformed into an advisory and assisting body. The overwhelming power of the princeps made freedom of political action by the individual impossible. Independently minded provincials were sternly checked by the ever-watchful agents of the emperor. Men of ability were drawn into the imperial circle so that sycophancy took the place of courageous thought. Emperor-worship made loyalty to the emperors and obedience to their will a matter of religious duty. Many of the emperors throttled all free expression of opinion and, at times, instituted reigns of terror.

THE
MAGISTRATES
The chief assistants of the emperor were drawn from the senatorial and equestrian orders according to the nature of their duties. Military and political positions were still held by senators who, in accordance with tradition, served as junior officers in the army, as judges in the lower courts, passed through the republican offices from quaestor to consul, and became proconsuls in the senatorial provinces. In the imperial service they were appointed lieutenants of Caesar to govern his provinces, commanders of the legions, and curators in charge of some of the services in Rome. On the whole, the senators were faithful and competent imperial servants.

The civil administration, originally in the hands of the secretariat organized under Claudius, was transformed into a civil service of equestrian rank by Hadrian. There were five great bureaus—finance, correspondence, petitions, investigations, and records. Under the secretaries were the procurators and their assistants, who had charge of tax collections, the government of minor provinces, or the management of imperial lands and other properties. The great prizes of the equestrian career were the prefectures, the most powerful official positions in the Roman Empire. The praetorian prefect, commander of the bodyguard, became the emperor's personal representative and acquired by custom great judicial authority. The prefect of the city was in charge of the urban government of Rome, assisted by the prefect of the watch and the prefect of the grain supply.

FINANCES
Imperial revenues were derived from port duties and tolls, income and rents from state lands, mines and quarries. A 5 per cent inheritance tax was collected from Roman citizens; there were also taxes on auction sales and on the sale and manumission of slaves. These taxes, at first levied in Italy, were later extended to the provinces. The provincials paid the land tax, usually a tithe, the poll tax on all noncitizens, and a tax on the income of artisans and small tradesmen. For the purpose of levying these taxes a census was taken first every five years, and every fifteen years after Hadrian, in which all persons and properties were recorded. The collection was in the hands of procurators who at some times and in some places collected directly. Elsewhere the taxes were farmed locally. In many cases the municipalities were made responsible, and the collection was carried out by local officials, who often advanced the revenue themselves before collection. Most of the money was spent in the provinces on roads, public works, supplies for the army, and on the defense of the frontier.

LAW   The greatest and most enduring achievement of the
empire was the law, both administrative and civil.
With the passage of time administrative legislation came into the
hands of the princeps and the senate, and finally into those of the
emperor alone. After the time of Hadrian the emperor's edicts, commands, decrees, and letters came to have the force of law by themselves. Civil law also came under the control of the emperor. The *jus
honorarium* developed by the republican magistrates through their
edicts, was fully recognized by the imperial officials, and throughout
the early empire the praetors continued to issue edicts, doubtless controlled and supplemented by the edicts and the decisions of the
emperor.

One point of conflict between the senate and the earlier emperors
had been the interference of the princeps in the courts. By Hadrian's
time it had been definitely established that the princeps, usually represented by the praetorian prefect, was the highest court of appeal. Since
the power of legislation inherent in the praetor's edict was inconsonant
with the principle of autocracy, Hadrian removed it. With the assistance of Salvius Julianus he codified the edictal law and issued the
Perpetual Edict. Thereafter changes were made by imperial order
alone.

The emperors also licensed and thus controlled the jurists, who
influenced the interpretation of the law by their advice. The writing
of the jurists were carefully preserved and selections from them appear
as definitive law in the Digest of Justinian. Of them and of the many
legal commentaries composed during the empire, only the *Institutiones*
("Principles of the Civil Law") by Gaius, written about the middle
of the second century A.D., and fragments of the writings of Paul and
Ulpian, who lived in a later period, have survived apart from the
Digest.

THE ARMY   While the law accompanied Roman citizenship and
Roman governors into every corner of the empire,
the most evident symbol of empire was the army, which had undergone a striking change since the days of the republic. Recruits from
Italy barely filled the ranks of the imperial guard of the city, and
provincials, usually citizens of towns, were drawn in under a system
of voluntary enlistment. They were at least partially Latinized and
were either Roman citizens or received citizenship upon enlistment.
The Latin language used in the legions and their distinctly Roman
traditions speedily completed the process of Romanization. During
their twenty-year period of enlistment, the men kept order in the
provinces, executed many public works, and defended the frontier.
Their enlistment over, they were entitled to retirement with a grant
of land or a pension. Other provincials were enlisted in the auxiliary

forces organized in cohorts. These served for twenty-five years and received citizenship and a bonus on retirement.

The frontier was defended by a long series of walls of stone or earth on the north, and elsewhere by forts and watch towers with connecting roads and permanent legionary camps at strategic points. Around the great camps clustered the *canabae,* or huts of camp followers. Many of the camps developed into permanent communities, some of which have survived to the present. The camps exerted a Romanizing influence over the surrounding territory, and did much to disseminate prosperity among the provincials through the purchase of supplies, particularly of grain and meat.

THE PROVINCES   In the time of Hadrian the eleven senatorial provinces were governed by promagistrates who held office for a year, but imperial interference and the presence of imperial procurators made senatorial control merely nominal. The remaining thirty-four provinces were imperial; their governors were chosen by the emperor and held office at his will. Smaller provinces were governed by procurators who performed military and judicial as well as financial duties. Provincial conditions had improved over those of the late republic, but there was still some corruption and extortion. At times discontent led to provincial uprisings. In many regions local feelings or racial antagonisms led to clashes between elements of the populace. Local councils existed in most of the provinces which eventually acquired some political importance, although their original purpose was religious.

The preferred unit of local government was the municipality. In the East, where city life was already flourishing, Rome, recognizing the existing order, continued the traditional methods of government. In the West the cities were drawn into the Roman system, and efforts were made to develop urban organizations in country districts. The villages around the great camps received a city form of government, and colonies of Roman veterans were settled in the provinces. Thus urban centers multiplied in the West, and those cities which were sufficiently Latinized were granted a charter prescribing the form of government and conferring special rights. Their government was modeled on that of Rome, having two magistrates elected by an assembly of property holders and a senate or *curia* drawn from ex-officeholders. Members of the upper class were called *curiales*. The active urban political life passed with declining income, the mismanagement of public finance, and imperial interference. Financial difficulties brought such heavy burdens on the magistrates in the second century that they sought to avoid office, and the emperors found it necessary to appoint curators to look after finances.

THE JEWS IN
THE EMPIRE
Its role in the Roman Empire and its significance in the development of Christianity give the Jewish question special importance. When the Persians allowed the re-establishment of Jerusalem, Judaea became a small, theocratic state governed by its priests. The temple was reconstructed and the Law, center of Judaism, was codified and sworn to by all of the people in a great covenant with Jahweh. Since it was necessary that the people should know the Law, synagogues, "houses of the Law," were established in the cities and villages to teach the all-important law to the people. In them the Law and the prophets were read, and liturgies of prayer and praise were developed for the Sabbath gatherings. Scribes, often laymen, learned the Law and began to interpret it in the schools of the synagogues and to apply it to specific cases. A body of traditional unwritten law grew from the teachings of the scribes developing out of, but distinguished from, the Torah or Law of the Pentateuch.

Jewish teaching was narrow in its emphasis upon its own people and its insistence on their strict adherence to the Law. Nevertheless it bore the prophetic assurance that Jahweh was a universal deity whose name would become great among the Gentiles and who would raise His chosen people to dominion with Him. The Jews dreamed of a Messiah who would re-establish their independence, make Jerusalem the spiritual capital of the world, and therewith bring about a Golden Age. This dream found expression in the apocalyptic writers.

The events of the second century B.C. promised fulfillments of their hopes. When as spoils of war the Jews passed into the possession of Antiochus III of Asia in 199 B.C., the question of Hellenization became acute. Many wealthy and cultured Jews had come under the influence of the Greek manner of life. They knew and admired Greek literature, art, and architecture. The work of the scribes, however, had been well done, and there was also a vigorous reaction against Hellenization. When Antiochus IV of Asia, to establish cultural unity, enjoined acceptance of the Greek way of life, there was a revolt led by the Maccabean family. Aided by Rome, the Jews established an independent kingdom of Judaea in 143 B.C. after twenty-five years of struggle. Judaea, after experiencing different relationships with Rome, finally became a procuratorial province after 6 A.D. During the rule of the Maccabean kings, a religious crisis developed which produced two famous sects, the Pharisees and the Sadducees. The latter, chiefly members of the upper class associated with the priests in the temple, were believers in ritual and in a strict adherence to the Mosaic Law. They denied the validity of the scribal tradition and of the growing belief in immortality. The Pharisees, followed by the great mass of the people, supported the scribes, and were progressive and liberal in their interpretations of the Law to meet the changing needs of the time. In contradistinction to the Sadducees, they believed in a future life; their work survived to be the foundation of later Judaism.

Meanwhile there had taken place the great *diaspora,* the scattering of the Jews throughout the civilized world. There were many in Babylonia, descendants of exiles who had not returned to the homeland, and during the Hellenistic period great numbers moved into the cities of Syria, Asia Minor, Greece, and Egypt. Under the aegis of Rome they migrated to Africa, Spain, and Gaul, and a large colony settled in Rome. In many cities they lived in special quarters, and in some, certainly in Alexandria, they were governed by their own officials. Carrying with them their religion, their sacred writings, and the synagogue, wherever they went they resisted Hellenization or Romanization. The Jews presented a problem to the Roman government not only because of their religion but because of the quarrels which arose between them and the other peoples of the provinces. Caesar and Augustus, confirming the status which the Hellenistic rulers had conferred upon them, tolerated their presence in Rome. Their ancestral pride and exclusiveness, their devotion to their own God, their refusal to conform to the religious and social customs of their neighbors made them derided and suspected. At the same time their special privileges inspired jealousy. Freed from obeisance to the imperial cult and from attendance upon the public festivals on the ground of religious scruple, the Jews were permitted to substitute prayers for the well-being of the emperor. They were even allowed to collect a small temple tax and send it to Jerusalem. Proselytizing, however, was frowned upon.

In Judaea, however, where Roman rule bore hard upon them, the Jews were discontented. Leaders appeared who claimed to be the Messiah and caused a constant ferment. Finally in 66 A.D. war broke out against the Roman governor as the result of a quarrel over the desecration of a synagogue in Caesarea. Vespasian, sent against them by Nero, methodically set about to reduce their strongholds. At Jotapata he captured a young priest, Joseph, who became his client. The latter, henceforth called Flavius Josephus, later wrote a history of the war and a book on Jewish antiquities. The conquest was completed after Vespasian became emperor, and in 70 A.D. Jerusalem and the temple were destroyed. Thousands were sold into slavery, and the ornaments of the Holy of Holies were carried to Rome. Troubles between Jew and Greek and general hatred of the Romans involved the Jews in revolt against Trajan (115-117). Again when Hadrian settled Romans in Jerusalem and built a temple to Jupiter on the site of the temple, a great uprising took place led by a priest, Eleazar, and a popular hero.

Simon, called Bar Kochba. Hadrian pitilessly suppressed the revolt and forbade the Jews entrance into the temple area.

From that time Judaism, though preserving memories of past glories, and never giving up hope of a restoration of Israel to its homeland, centered its devotions in the Law and its interpretations. The legal teaching of the scribes, codified into the Mishna, and the expositions and tales of later authorities were gathered together into the collections known as the Talmud. This was the source of the law and of the strength of medieval and modern Judaism. The destruction of Jerusalem served to free Christianity from attachment to its place of origin, and made it more easily adaptable into a religion for the Gentiles.

ECONOMIC LIFE   The *Pax Romana* created unity in the civilized world. A common code of laws and a uniform system of weights, measures, and coins made trade between distant points easy. Greek remained the language of the East, and the spread of Latin in the West established a two-language system for the empire. The system of roads begun in Italy was extended throughout the empire, with all important roads maintained at imperial expense and inns built at convenient points. The roads and seas were policed, and travelers were provided with maps and road-books.

Provincial prosperity ultimately led to the decentralization of trade, and the consequent decline in the importance of Rome. New municipal centers of provincial trade appeared, rivaling Rome in size and wealth. Most business activities were carried on by single individuals, though there were partnerships or associations for single enterprises. There is no evidence of any large-scale corporations engaged in trade or industry. Except for small regional tolls and constant concern with the grain trade, there was no governmental interference in commercial affairs. The former royal monopolies in trade, banking, and industry in Egypt and Pergamum were abolished. Commerce was not limited to the confines of the empire. Roman merchants ranged the Atlantic coasts of Europe and Africa, penetrated Germany and even reached the markets of Turkestan in search of Chinese goods. The canal from the Nile to the Red Sea was kept open; trade flourished on the Red Sea, and Roman ships traveled to and from India. A Roman embassy even reached China in the reign of Marcus Aurelius. The spices and silks which came from the Far East were paid for with coins.

Industry, like commerce, profited from the prosperity of the provinces and became decentralized. For a period the already industrialized East kept its pre-eminence, particularly in textiles, glassware, and metal goods, and the West was primarily a source of raw materials. In time transportation costs and difficulties made the growth of local industries profitable in the West. Gallic clothing and Spanish metal and leather goods appeared, and many skilled Greeks and Syrians established shops in the West for the production of silk and glassware. Industry remained small-shop in size, and business employed free or slave labor, depending on the local supply. Slavery, a bountiful supply of cheap free labor, and the absence of industrial organization combined to hold the laboring class to very low levels of subsistence.

Agriculture remained the basic source of wealth and the chief occupation of the greater part of the population. The growth of cities and the presence of great army camps provided markets, and the cost of transportation protected the local farmers from world competition. While many small farmers still remained, the growth of great estates begun during the republic continued with increasing force. The management of these estates underwent a marked change. First on the imperial estates—the emperor was the largest landowner—and later on the private ones, a system of tenant farming began to develop due to the uneconomical character of slave labor and the increasing cost of slaves. The tenant, called *colonus,* renting a lot for a fixed term on a renewable lease, paid a quota of his produce and a small sum per head for his cattle, and in addition worked a fixed number of days for the imperial manager or the estate owner. In the second century tenantry became prevalent everywhere as freemen sank and slaves rose into this status. Still later the *coloni* became fixed in their status and were tied to the soil. Many of the large estates seeking self-sufficiency developed industrial establishments to supply their own needs.

SOCIAL LIFE   Public service, agriculture, industry, and commerce brought prosperity to the upper and middle classes of the empire. Below them, however, the great multitude in the cities and the tenant farmers in the country were miserably paid, wretchedly housed, overtaxed, and continually exploited. Often dependent at least in part on charity, they were unhappy and hopeless in the midst of plenty. Rome itself was the focus of all eyes, the goal of every ambitious provincial, the hub of all activities. Its population, composed of elements from every corner of the empire, had spread far beyond the republican wall. Estimates of its number vary from 260,000 to 800,000. Temples, theaters, and baths dotted the city. The fine and comfortable houses of the wealthy, adorned with paintings, mosaics and statuary, were erected on the hills. The huge tenements, where the poor lived, stood on the lower ground. Aqueducts supplied the city with water which overflowed in fountains or was carried into the houses of the rich in pipes.

One consequence of the imperial expansion and the great increase in wealth had been to weaken the traditional social values and customs and to diminish the power of the *pater familias.* Women in high society enjoyed greater freedom than in earlier periods, the strict laws placing women under male control having been relaxed. Ladies of wealth now controlled their property and moved freely in society. Divorce was easy and there was much moral laxity. The moralists inveighed against the luxury and corruption of Roman society, and stories of orgies, expensive feasts, and luxurious appointments were ever current. Those engaged in business activities—and this includes freedmen—found great opportunities for amassing wealth in commerce and industry and in the offices in the civil administration. Aping the social life of the senatorial society, they often engaged in vulgar and ostentatious display of their wealth.

Juvenal portrayed the Roman populace as a mob in which all elements of the Roman Empire met and mingled and which sought only "bread and circuses." Yet the city populace was far from being an idle and pampered mob. Two hundred thousand people received from the state a grant of grain, which assisted them to live but did not provide entire sustenance. Some received gifts of money or of food from men of wealth. For the most part they were employed in the industries, the small shops, the tasks of transport and all the other varied activities of a busy metropolis. They lived in huge tenements, sometimes five stories in height, and always in danger of fire or collapse. For amusement the state provided regular festivals, with chariot races, wild-beast shows, gladiatorial combats, and even naval contests in the Colosseum and the Circus. Plays were produced in the theaters, and puppet shows were frequently presented on the street corners.

The common man in Rome and in the provincial cities found companionship, a sense of security and a small opportunity for distinction in the *collegia* or clubs. These performed no economic functions, and were primarily social, religious, or burial societies. They secured for those in the lower walks of life companionship and a measure of recognition from their fellow men, and gave dignity and meaning to their life. Secret meetings and unlicensed associations were strictly forbidden, and all *collegia* had to have legal charters with the permission of the senate.

Slavery existed under changing conditions in the empire. The decrease in the number of slaves, with the drying up of war and piracy as sources of supply, resulted in an increase of the price of slaves. They were still used in the households of the wealthy, in industry, and on the cattle and sheep ranches. Cheap free labor, however, caused a decline in industrial slavery, and agricultural slavery was yielding to the tenant system. Manumission was secured by purchase, gift, or will. Freedmen, however, were always attached to their former owners, who acted as patrons. Despite this dependence, the world of business and the lower branches of the imperial service were open to them and the priesthoods of the imperial cult were reserved for them. Many achieved

great wealth and power and some even renown as scholars and philosophers.

The provincial communities appeared to be small-scale replicas of
Rome. On the surface their life was prosperous and happy, but there
was much discontent and misery underneath. The ever-watchful imperial agents hindered freedom of thought and expression and independence of action. Fear of confiscation, the load of taxation, and the
expenses of public careers limited the acquisition of wealth by the middle class. For the poor the burden of living was almost more than they
could bear.

THE PROVINCES   The Roman system of provincial administration pro-
                 duced considerable political diversity. Not only did
the Romans willingly recognize and perpetuate local forms of government, but the variations among the charters granted to the colonies
and municipalities produced still further variety. The concessions to
traditional practices fostered local pride and patriotism, causing jealousy between neighboring communities which resulted in disturbances.
The beginning of imperial interference in the second century presaged
the later end of local independence and the triumph of centralization. Differences arising from local characteristics of race, language, or
religion, and the varying degrees of influence of Roman culture existed
in all sections of the empire. The division between the eastern and
western halves of the empire was most striking, for while the West
was Romanized, the East remained Hellenistic. There Greek was the
language of daily life and literature; architecture and art preserved
their Hellenistic character; classical plays were produced in the theaters; and the great games and the historic festivals of classical times
were still celebrated. In the first and second centuries there was even
a distinct revival of Greek culture, and Athens continued to be the
center of philosophic studies.

While the Greek motherland was declining in population and
wealth, the cities of Asia Minor thrived because of their fertile lands
and industry and the trade which still flowed overland from Asia.
Even though the Roman government fostered the Hellenization of the
peoples of Asia Minor and Syria, particularistic elements were nevertheless strong. Native languages persisted, and contemporary religious
tendencies brought the Eastern religions into prominence. In Egypt
the institutions which had developed under the Ptolemies continued
almost unchanged under Roman domination. The Egyptian language,
writing, methods of work, and religion persisted. All property was
carefully registered, and the status of every individual inhabitant was
recorded. The overworked and heavily taxed natives, bound to the
soil, still clung to their ancient practices and beliefs. The cults of the

gods continued, though deprived of much of their property, and Isis-worship spread throughout the Roman world.

In the West, too, there was local variation amid general uniformity. Sicily remained predominantly Greek, but elsewhere the Latin language and Roman culture spread. The provinces provided their share of imperial rulers. Trajan and Hadrian came from Spain, and Antoninus and Marcus Aurelius were of Gallic descent. Nevertheless the local cultures and traditions continued in the use of local tongues and in the persistence of local gods. Of all the Western lands, Gaul was most thoroughly Romanized. The Roman policy of urbanization was especially effective, and the presence of army cantonments on the Northern frontier, with their incessant demands for the products of the fields and workshops of Gaul, brought prosperity to the people.

Along the Rhine and the Danube and in Dacia, camps and colonies provided centers from which Roman influence spread among the provincials within and to the Germanic peoples beyond the frontier. These newly conquered regions were often troublesome for the imperial administrators. The restless barbarian tribes proved a constant menace, and became a positive danger in the reign of Marcus Aurelius. Nevertheless by the end of the fourth century, when the Germanic tribes began to pour in across the frontier, they had secured a veneer of Roman culture and an appreciation of the institutions and customs of the Romans.

THE CULTURE OF THE ROMAN EMPIRE

Throughout the territory of the empire the symbols of its prosperity and greatness still stand: the ruins of Ostia, Herculaneum, and Pompeii, in Italy; of Carthage and Timgad (Temesa) in Africa; the temples and arenas and aqueducts at Nîmes, Arles, and Orange in southern France the remains of towns and villas and the great wall in Britain; traces of the limes across the Northern frontier; the buildings of Roman times in Athens, Eleusis, and Corinth, in Asia Minor and at Baalbek in Syria; hieroglyphs of the Roman emperors in the temples of Egypt. Everywhere remains of roads and bridges and thousands of inscriptions convey the message of the imperial majesty of Rome.

ARCHITECTURE AND ART The achievements of Rome in architecture are displayed in the many structures which have survived and in the traditions which have influenced the architects of the Middle Ages. Learning the basic elements—the column, the arch, the vault, and the dome—from their Oriental, Greek, and Etruscan predecessors, the Romans developed and combined them in the great works of the empire. These borrowed elements were transformed and given characteristic Roman expression. The arch, for example, was used in the construction of bridges and then in the erection of aqueducts like the Claudian at Rome and the celebrated Pont du Gard near Nîmes in southern France. The great memorial arches of imperial triumphs were a Roman creation. The barrel vault was also essentially a Roman contribution. Groined or cross-vaulting, employed to great effect in the ceilings of the great halls of the baths and the basilicas, was produced by the intersection of two barrel vaults at right angles. The dome as a roofing device was likewise first developed on a magnificent scale by the Romans. Roman achievements in the use of the dome and the vault made possible the development of the Byzantine and Romanesque styles of the Middle Ages. Thus were achieved buildings with great vaults or lofty domes massive in size and magnificent in appearance.

Typical Roman structures included the basilica, the bath, the amphitheater, and the great *insula* or apartment house. The basic building materials were bricks and concrete, the surfaces of which were covered with a veneer of tiles or, in the finer buildings, with slabs of granite or marble.

A few words may be devoted to the *insulae*—the huge apartment houses of many stories which marked city building. The first floor contained shops or business offices. In front of these, arches supported the façade of the upper stories and provided a sheltering arcade. The higher levels contained apartments of varied size and elegance. The early inner supports of wood or cheap stone, which resulted in many fires and collapses, gave way later to brick or better materials.

In sculpture, as in architecture, the Romans learned their fundamental lessons of technique from the Greeks and infused it with their own spirit. Their reliefs portrayed historic scenes and processions decorated with elaborate floral ornaments. The memorial column covered with bands of relief in spiral, like those of Trajan and of Marcus Aurelius, was a Roman creation. Portrait sculpture, which was distinctively Roman in its realistic faithfulness to life, had its origin in the wax death masks of great men. From these masks sculpture acquired naturalness and adherence to the details of appearance, even to the furrowed lines of the face.

LITERATURE With reference to its literature, the post-Augustan period is spoken of as the Silver Age. In this period there was an unusual development of rhetoric which can be ascribed to patronage and to fear of the tyrannic power of the princeps and his informers. Free expression of opinion was discouraged, and writers in general paid greater attention to the words and the forms they employed than to the substance of what they wrote. Little remains of the voluminous writings of the period, but there have survived the compositions of Seneca, of Petronius, whose *Satyricon* created the Latin novel, and of Lucan, who wrote an historical epic of the Civil War. Vespasian's friend and helper, the erudite elder Pliny, was the author of a history of the German Wars, no longer extant, and of an encyclopedia of miscellaneous information called the *Natural History.*

After the tyranny of Domitian brought about a temporary silence, a new group of literary men appeared in the period of the Antonines, led by Pliny the Younger, Tacitus, Suetonius, Martial, and Juvenal. Pliny, servant and loyal supporter of Trajan, regarded himself as a second Cicero and composed orations, most of them now lost, and letters, which have been preserved. Pliny's correspondence is of particular value for the letters between himself and Trajan which deal with provincial and municipal problems and policies.

A considerable portion of the works of Tacitus (ca. 55-120 A.D.), one of the great figures in the history of history, has survived. In matchless style and with an extraordinary gift for epigrammatic terseness, he wrote the *Annals,* a history of Rome from the death of Augustus to the death of Nero, the *Histories,* on the events from Galba to Domitian, a treatise on Germany, a biography of his father-in-law, Agricola, and an essay on oratory. History, in the opinion of Tacitus, had a moral purpose. "This, I regard as history's highest function," he wrote, "to rescue merit from oblivion and to hold out the reprobation of posterity as a terror to evil words and deeds." To this end he devoted some of his most brilliant epigrams with which he characterized the deeds of the Romans, and his pages reflect bitter indignation at the tyranny of the rulers and the luxury and vices of the aristocracy.

Suetonius (ca. 75-150 A.D.) was a biographer rather than an historian; of his many works only the *Lives of the Caesars,* from Julius to Domitian, and scattered fragments have survived. His biographies are primarily character studies filled with gossip and episodic materials, and pay little attention to chronology or to the great affairs of state. Nevertheless his work is a valuable source for the history of the first century of the empire, and his manner of writing became the pattern for later Roman and medieval biographers.

The Greeks had developed the epigram; Martial (ca. 40-102 A.D.) established it as a Latin form and gave to it the content of pungent Roman satire. In a series of brilliant verses he described the many-faceted life of Rome of his day. His younger friend Juvenal (ca. 55-130 A.D.) employed the satire for the same purpose that Tacitus used history and Martial the epigram. The noise and confusion of the city streets, the crime, the self-seeking, the graft, the favoritism and corruption of the imperial city were the themes of his poems. His famous tenth satire on "The Vanity of Human Wishes" mocked the desire of men for power, eloquence, beauty, wealth, and fame.

The specialized treatises by other writers which have survived from this period dealt with a wide range of subjects, and include Quintilian's study on oratory. Quintilian gave to the world the ancient literary canon when he composed his *De Institutione Oratorica,* a complete survey of rhetoric in twelve books which contains educational principles still of some value.

GREEK
LITERATURE

Greek literature during and after the first century B.C. boasts many famous names. The *Library of History,* an annalistic collection of excerpts and comments, was composed by Diodorus, the Sicilian, during the revolutionary period. In the Augustan Age, Dionysius of Halicarnassus wrote on rhetoric and composed a book on the antiquities of Rome which is one of our chief sources for the early period of Roman history. His contemporary Strabo provided a mine of information in a descriptive geography of the Mediterranean world. Ptolemy's *Geography* and Galen's treatise on medicine, both composed in the period of the Antonines, were used as texts during the Middle Ages. During Hadrian's reign a civil servant, Appian, composed histories of Rome's foreign and civil wars, and Arrian wrote a life of Alexander the Great and an account of a voyage around the Black Sea.

Of the Greek men of letters in the Roman period two are pre-eminent—Plutarch and Lucian. Plutarch (ca. 50-125 A.D.), who dealt with historical and moral problems, sought the secret of greatness in biographies of illustrious Greeks and Romans. These he arranged in pairs and made comparisons for purposes of elucidation. Lucian, a Syrian born about 125 A.D., was more a product of his own generation than was Plutarch. His dialogues are one-act plays in which gods and men discuss every sort of problem, natural and supernatural. In them the religious and philosophic thought of the age is reviewed and dissected with keen and brilliant sarcasm, and the conclusions are reached that human life and ambition are alike worthless and that virtue must be its own reward.

MORALITY AND
RELIGION

In this imperial age morality absorbed the interest of most of the Latin and Greek men of letters. Despotism, the restraint on intellectual discussions about questions of public policy, and the lack of political activity or opportunity for social service, all served to make men introspective. Luxury and wickedness in high society and abject poverty and slavery at the base aroused in thoughtful minds considerations of the problems of humanity. In the midst of prosperity the wealthy became afflicted with an abnormal consciousness of sin, a "weariness with life." The poor and enslaved, with little hope of economic betterment, on the other hand, sought every means of escape from reality. In answer to the cries from all strata of society, moralists, philosophers, and missionaries of a multitude of religions went from one end of the empire to the other and found eager audiences for their messages.

Out of this setting came great moral preachers like Dio Chrysostom, who went about teaching temperance and justice, the reality of virtue, and the freedom of the individual who gives himself over to simple pleasures, confidently reliant upon the fatherhood of God. Epicureans brought contentment through the messages of Epicurus and Lucretius, which taught release from vain desires and superstitious fears through the acceptance of a materialistic universe. Hated and feared by the populace as atheists, they made headway only among the intellectuals. At the same time, pairs of Cynic philosophers, often sincere though sometimes obscene and corrupt, carried to the poor the message of the renunciation of vain desire, liberation from evil, and the search for a life according to nature. The dominant philosophy of the empire, however, was a Roman version of Stoicism. This focused attention fully upon the position and duties of man and the power and character of that "Pantheon," the all-divine world god. The great spokesmen of Roman Stoicism were Seneca, Epictetus, and Marcus Aurelius. The first, whose own life contradicted all he wrote, taught the Stoic doctrines of self-control, moral self-discipline, obedience to a "rational law of conduct," and of social obligations to the jaded members of Nero's court. The influence of Seneca and of Epictetus appears in the *Meditations* of Marcus Aurelius, who was confident that man's inner will was free, though he believed life was but a play whose lines were written and whose limit was set. He felt that man alone could do himself injury, and that a full and suitable life meant service of one's fellow men.

Many of the philosophers had embraced within their systems religious elements and dependence upon a Divine Being, but their message was still intellectual. It showed men how to save themselves by the power of thought. Once again, as in the Hellenistic Age, men turned to religion, seeking salvation by faith. The great gods of old, destroyed by the skepticism of the philosophers and by the failure of the civic institutions they had once served, were no longer vital forces. Emperor-worship was more real and gave a deeper sense of hope and satisfaction than did the festivals of Jupiter himself. The provincial prayed to the god-emperor for economic betterment, and participation in that worship carried with it a sense of patriotism, of community in a civilized world. As earlier, men and women sought charms to secure good luck or to avoid evil, thronged the wonder-working shrines of Asclepius in search of health, visited the oracles, and poured money into the hands of fortunetellers. The belief in miracles was widespread, and only when philosophy compromised itself by alliance with magic was it acceptable to the people.

Though many turned for contentment to the deities of early times, most people sought salvation in the mystery religions. With their initiatory ceremonies, their ecstatic rituals, their calls to service, and their promises of immortality, they spread throughout the empire. Among them the worship of Isis, whose maternal loveliness captured the hearts of men and women, and the soldier religion of Mithras were pre-eminent. In Mithraism, an adaptation of the Zoroastrian worship of Ahura Mazda, Mithras was the general of the forces of the great god of light. In the third century Mithraism became the chief rival of Christianity.

CHRISTIANITY   In scattered places in the empire, particularly in the East, there began to appear groups of people called Christians, who attributed the foundation of their religion to Jesus of Nazareth, who was crucified during the reign of Tiberius. His message and the belief in the divinity of the risen Christ were spread and firmly planted in the Roman world by Paul and the apostles. In the struggle with the pagan cults, Christianity had certain advantages. In place of the nature myths on which most of them were based, it had as its background the fine creation story of Genesis and the grand theological concepts of the Hebrew prophets. Its code of morals, with its greater emphasis on behavior than on ritual, was of a higher order than those of its rivals. It claimed fulfillment of the Jewish Messianic hope, and gave definite promises of immortality in a glorious Paradise. Finally, in place of a mythical founder, it looked back to a personality who remained vivid and living. Freed from the burden of Jewish law by Paul, it made a universal appeal. The poor and oppressed flocked to it, and even members of the imperial family of the Flavians became converts. For a period the Roman government ignored the Christians. Those caught in Nero's persecution in Rome were punished as incendiaries, not as Christians. Domitian's religiosity led him to punish a Christian member of his own family on the charge of "leading a Jewish life."

In the provinces, however, the Christians were in constant trouble. They took no part in festivities; they failed to worship the gods; and they refused to sacrifice to the emperor. Such persons were regarded as certainly guilty of the "hatred of the human race," which Tacitus imputed to them. In addition, in the regions where they were strong, the sale of sacrificial animals and votive offerings of silver declined and business suffered. Accordingly there were sporadic outbreaks and some executions. Charges against them were brought before Pliny, who wrote to Trajan for a ruling. The emperor declared that if accusations were properly made (no anonymous charges were to be heard), the governor should investigate and punish in accordance with the offense. This ruling was confirmed by Hadrian. All Christians violated the law by belonging to associations for an unlicensed religion, by holding secret meetings, and by offending the majesty of the emperor. For these offenses they were tried and punished. The imperial administration, however, was little interested in them, and no concerted effort was made to destroy them.

The Christians of the early church were organized into groups under bishops (i.e., overseers), and elders or presbyters. Finances and the care of the poor and sick were in the hands of deacons. The Christians at Rome buried their dead, as did other societies, in the underground catacombs, and they probably held meetings in the chambers where lay the bones of their martyrs. It was not until after the second century that Christianity underwent its period of trial and ultimate triumph.

THE THIRD CENTURY OF THE ROMAN EMPIRE

After the reign of Marcus Aurelius the dream of universal peace and prosperity of the Antonine Age came to an end, and those forces of disruption which had always been present in the imperial structure triumphed. To a greater degree than before, rule rested in the hands of those controlling the military power. The armies, localized on the frontiers, rose to claim the imperial purple for their commanders and to secure for themselves the rewards of booty. Civil wars wracked the empire, and for the greater part of the third century the throne was the prize of victorious generals. This situation made it possible for the barbarians to break through the frontier and lay waste the border provinces. Political disorder, civil war, the advance of economic decentralization, an increase in the number of self-sufficient estates, and the overwhelming burdens of taxation and of exactions by generals and their armies, were accompanied by municipal and general economic decline. Intellectual life became sterile, and religious controversies and persecutions brought confusion and dismay.

THE EMPERORS   A succession of worthless emperors followed the death of Marcus Aurelius until in 193 the throne became the possession of the Severi. Septimius Severus (193-211) and his son Caracalla (211-217) made the empire a military institution. The senatorial class was disregarded as knights were given high office in the army. The pay of the soldiers was increased, and the men were allowed to contract legal marriages. Caracalla in 212 issued an edict conferring Roman citizenship on all freemen in the empire.

Shortly after their rule anarchy descended upon the empire.

Claimants to the throne were established in the provinces as the peasant armies, learning their power and desiring booty and high office, hailed their commanders as emperors. Amid the civil wars which followed the German tribes crossed the Rhine, the Goths entered Dacia, and defeated and killed the Roman emperor Decius; a newly revived Persian Empire fell upon the eastern border of the Roman Empire. In the midst of these troubles pestilence decimated the populace. The emperors debased the coinage until it became utterly worthless, commerce almost ceased, and the Roman world was threatened with collapse.

At the close of the third century the period of anarchy was brought to an end. Claudius Gothicus (268-270) defeated the Goths, and Aurelian (270-275) re-established the unity of the Roman world and the defense of the frontier. Though he endeavored to strengthen his own position by proclaiming himself the earthly incarnation of the sun god, whose worship he established as the official religion of Rome, he was murdered in 275. Four emperors followed Aurelian in quick succession until in 285 Diocletian was elevated to the throne by the Eastern army and entered upon a program of reform which gave new life to the Roman Empire.

DIOCLETIAN   Diocletian, a Dalmatian soldier who had risen to the
(285-305)   imperial purple, determined to carry out a reorgan-
              ization of the imperial structure which would remedy
the manifest political and economic evils. His initial reforms were a logical extension of the militarization of the empire by the Severi and its orientalization by Aurelian. Recognizing the army as the basis of his power and providing a coherent structure for the military rule of the empire, he nevertheless endeavored to break down the control which the soldiers had exercised over the imperial office. He expanded Aurelian's policy and set up an Oriental court with himself as a divine ruler surrounded by a host of palace officials. In the interest of a more efficient direction of military affairs, and realizing that one man could not hope to defend the entire frontier, he associated with himself Maximian, to whom he gave the title Augustus. Without making a formal division of the empire, he entrusted the West to his colleague, while he himself resided in and looked after the East. With this he maintained his own pre-eminence. To secure further assistance and to prevent wars of succession he appointed two assistant emperors, called Caesars, who after a period of years would replace the Augusti, and would in turn be replaced by new Caesars.

Along the frontier Diocletian established in permanent stations small bodies of border troops, called *limitanei,* who had lands for their support and were recruited locally. This, completing the process of the preceding century, made the army definitely peasant in composition and virtually hereditary. In place of the praetorian cohort, the emperor and his assistants maintained imperial guards of young men drawn chiefly from the upper class and trained to be future officers. The frontier forces were thus no longer able to continue the third-century practice of elevating their commanders to the purple or of establishing local kingdoms. The commanders of the larger armies were placed in such a secure line of succession that, it was hoped, their rivalries and ambitions could be satisfied without recourse to war.

The administration of the empire was rebuilt on a civil basis entirely distinct from the military. The provincial system was completely revised. The division between senatorial and imperial provinces had disappeared during the preceding century, and Diocletian proceeded to wipe out the older provinces themselves. The empire was redivided into more than a hundred small provinces, grouped into thirteen dioceses, ruled by *vicarii,* and these in turn were divided into four prefectures, each under a praetorian prefect. The duties of these magistrates were judicial and administrative, including general supervision of finance and, in the case of the provincial governors, control over municipal affairs. They were, however, without military authority. The bureaus of the central administration were reorganized to accord with this new system. Many agents and spies were employed to keep check on local administrators and on one another. From the highest group of imperial officials and nobles was drawn the consistory, a body of twenty men who formed the supreme council of advisers to the emperor.

The city of Rome was governed by the city prefect with the assistance of the senate, which continued to meet as the local governing body. The senatorial order was now spread over the entire empire as great landowners and higher officials received the title *clarissimi,* which signified membership in the order. Local government, both municipal and rural, had undergone changes. The cities still maintained their local *curiae* and their magistrates, but actual government was in the hands of imperially appointed curators, who had supervision of public finance. In the country districts the senators had secured immunity from municipal control and were allowed to act as magistrates and tax collectors on their own estates.

A large and steady income was needed to support this tremendous system of officials. Taxes in money were levied upon tradesmen, municipal aristocrats, and senators. Their value varied greatly because of the debasement of coinage and the wide fluctuation of prices, and Diocletian collected payments in kind from the landowning class. Land, capital, labor, and livestock were all assessed. Each region of the empire bore its share of the amount to be raised. In addition, communities were compelled to render services in support of the imperial post and of the army, and merchants were forced to transport without payment the taxes in kind. These taxes assured the army and bureaucracy of a steady income of fixed value. Though giving considerable power to the senatorial landowners, whose produce was essential to imperial well-being, they also constituted a heavy burden on this class. At the same time they wrought even greater hardships upon the small landowners and upon the municipal councilors, the *curiales*. Many of the small farmers surrendered their farms to near-by senators to evade the exactions. The *curiales,* however, compelled to pay taxes on their own property, to render governmental services, and to be responsible for the collection of taxes in their own communities, were allowed no relief. When they endeavored to escape by resigning or by moving to another city, the government interfered and by the law of *origo* (origin) compelled them to stay in their native city and to hold office as long as they possessed sufficient property. On the same principle of *origo,* which involved the performance of service to the community, merchants and artisans were forced to remain members of their *collegia,* pay the taxes, and render the required labors. To such burdens was added the further expense caused by graft and corruption, which continued everywhere in spite of spies and those who spied upon the spies.

In an era when coinage was debased and the state was resorting to collections and payments in kind, prices varied greatly between regions and fluctuated widely within them. In 301, to secure stabilization, Diocletian issued the celebrated Edict of Prices which fixed the maximum cost of goods and labor under penalty of death but which proved impossible to enforce.

Possibly to restore imperial unity and to magnify his own claim to divinity, Diocletian, on the persuasion of Galerius, opened warfare upon the Christians. In 302 Diocletian ordered the confiscation of all church property and the enforcement of imperial worship. This edict was vigorously enforced in the East, but not in Gaul. The persecution came to an end with the Edict of Toleration of Galerius in 311 and Constantine's Edict of Milan in 313, which placed Christianity on a level with the other religions.

Diocletian succeeded in restoring order throughout the empire, in re-establishing the northern frontier in Britain, on the Rhine and the Danube, and in defeating the Persians. When he retired in 305, however, his system of succession proved a failure. Rivalries arose over the appointment of the new Caesars, and wars broke out afresh. From these, Constantine (306-337), son of Constantius, emerged triumphant. The recognition of Christianity and the establishment of an eastern capital, Constantinople, both of which took place under his reign, made it the beginning of a new era. The renewed life which Diocletian's reforms had given the Roman Empire enabled it to continue as a powerful force in succeeding centuries. It was, however, an empire in a world very different from that of Augustus' day. Not only the imperial structure but all phases of government, economic life, culture, and religious outlook had been transformed during the dark years of the third century.

PART I

*THE CIVILIZATION OF THE EARLY
MIDDLE AGES*

PROLOGUE

THE idea that history is divided into three grand divisions—ancient, medieval, and modern—is comparatively recent. The Italian humanists of the fifteenth and sixteenth centuries, misunderstanding the period from the decline of the Roman Empire in the West to their own time, assumed that those centuries constituted an interlude of cultural darkness and barbarism. The humanists gave to this period the name "Middle Ages," and to the term "medieval," the sense of a long dark period of barbarism and ignorance in sharp contrast to the highly developed civilization of the ancient world and of their own "modern" age.

Most people still accept the humanistic dictum and believe that the Middle Ages are synonymous with the Dark Ages. This view holds that Rome, after having reached the peak of her development during the first and second centuries, experienced a marked political, economic, and cultural decline; that during the fourth and fifth centuries, with the triumph of Christianity and of the barbarians, Roman civilization rapidly disintegrated, especially in the West. In terms of this viewpoint, the first five centuries A.D. witnessed the decline, fall, and extinction of classical civilization, and the appearance of a Christian-Germanic society characterized by unintelligent piety and primitive barbarism. Many people still think that Western civilization was submerged in almost hopeless darkness for ten centuries more (500-1500).

In recent years, however, the entire medieval period has been viewed as an age of active reconstruction. Even during the early centuries of conflict and invasion the West was a crucible in which Roman, Christian, and Germanic elements interacted to form the basis of a new and distinctively Western civilization. From this point of view these early centuries not merely are regarded as the twilight of a dying Roman society, but also as the dawn of the modern occidental world.

There is justification, however, for making a distinction between the *late* Middle Ages (1000-1500) and the preceding period. The first ten centuries of the Christian era, which saw the disintegration of classical civilization and the rise of the new Western civilization, we shall

3

call the *early* Middle Ages, distinguishing it from the later era of rapid expansion of the West. For several centuries (from about 300 to 600 A.D.) Western history was dominated by the interaction of Roman, Christian, and Germanic elements. Although there were other factors, notably the Moslem and Byzantine (or East-Roman), it was the inter-play of these three which provided the foundations for medieval civili-zation.

It is, of course, impossible to set an exact date for the beginning of medieval history. While the new civilization was well established by the age of Charles the Great, we cannot ascertain just when the West crossed the line from ancient to medieval times. The Middle Ages have no clear-cut and fixed characteristics that always unmistakably distin-guish them from ancient or modern times. Some scholars "doubt the validity of the very conception of any definite medieval period."

If there is reason for not insisting upon exact characteristics and chronological limits of the Middle Ages, we can, nevertheless, trace (within the limits of the first ten centuries A.D.) the gradual changes that came over Roman, Christian, and Germanic life in the West, and their eventual fusion to form what is customarily called medieval civili-zation. In Part II of this volume we shall consider the changes by which this civilization became increasingly modern during the late Middle Ages.

$$=\text{I}=$$

THE ROMAN EMPIRE

ROME'S expansion from a city-state in central Italy to a world empire in the five hundred years preceding the opening of the Christian era is one of the most notable developments in all history. The next five hundred years, equally important for Rome and the Mediterranean world, saw the climax and decline of this vast empire, its division into an Eastern and a Western section, and the disintegration of the latter into a group of Germanic states. This period of five centuries marks the most glorious period of Roman history, also the passing of ancient civilization in Western Europe and the beginnings of an era that is commonly designated as the Middle Ages. During this half of a millennium, Roman civilization reached its climax and began a long process of decline. The eventual fusion of the civilization of the Roman world with Germanic and Christian elements produced the new medieval civilization of the West. For an understanding of this development it is first necessary to examine those institutions of the Roman world upon which it was based.[1]

The first two centuries A.D. were the most peaceful and prosperous of all Roman history. The third century, or, to be more accurate, the period from the death of Emperor Marcus Aurelius in 180 to the accession of Diocletian in 284, was a period of recurring civil wars, barbarian invasions, and general economic hardship. Throughout most of the fourth century, order, security, and freedom from foreign invasion prevailed in most parts of the empire. Diocletian, Constantine, Julian, and Theodosius were outstandingly competent rulers. The death of Theodosius in 395 opened a new era of internal and external disorder. Under his inefficient sons, Arcadius and Honorius, the Eastern and Western parts of the empire rapidly drifted

---

[1] See Caldwell, *The Ancient World*, which comprises Volume I of this series for a detailed account of Roman civilization, and for much of the material on which this brief survey of Roman civilization is based.

apart, eventually becoming separate units. Both regions were afflicted
with internal troubles and barbarian invasions. Only in the East was
an effective governmental regime maintained. In the West the imperial administration weakened, lost its provinces to Germanic conquerors, and finally came to an end at the close of the fifth century.

    This brief sketch of imperial history reveals the fact that before
the third century the empire was strong and that, in general, the
Mediterranean world was prosperous. Afterwards, in spite of able
emperors and temporary successes, ancient civilization deteriorated
rapidly. In the West it passed away within two centuries, leaving
certain of its institutions as a heritage for the new Christian-Germanic world. Our immediate task is to show how this flourishing
civilization weakened and gave way to the new order.

THE ROMAN CIVILIZATION OF THE EARLY EMPIRE

IMPERIAL
FRONTIERS
         The empire attained its greatest extent and its most
         effective organization during the second century. By
         this time it had expanded to its ultimate natural
boundaries: to the deserts of Arabia and Northern Africa, and to a
system of easily defended rivers on the north and east. New provinces had been added in Northern Africa and Syria. For a time
Roman rule extended northward even beyond the line of the Rhine
and Danube rivers and the Black Sea, but these boundaries eventually
became the northern frontier. Beyond these waterways no permanent acquisitions were made, except in Britain, where the wall of
Hadrian was built as a defense against the raids of the Picts and
Scots. This rampart, with its near-by military road, stretched like a
great serpent, over the hills and through the valleys of southern
Scotland. At various strategic points were the block houses of the
frontier patrols. On the Continent there were even more effective
defenses. Garrison posts were established along the Rhine and Danube
rivers to check wandering bands of Germanic or Asiatic barbarians,
and naval guards patrolled the Black Sea and certain navigable
streams. The frontier provinces of Asia Minor were strongly fortified
against the dangerous Parthian forces of Persia, and further south,
where Roman rule extended to the edge of the Arabian desert,
frontier posts defended Syria against Bedouin raiders. The cities and
the grain lands of the most profitable of all the provinces, Egypt, were

protected by imperial galleys and legionnaires. The prosperous provinces of the coastal region of Northern Africa, including the territories of modern Libya, Tripoli, Tunis, Algeria, and Morocco were defended from the attacks of desert tribesmen by a line of garrison towns on the edge of the Sahara.

The coastal regions of the empire which faced the Atlantic Ocean needed no defense save from pirates. Everywhere throughout the Mediterranean and on navigable rivers, there were naval galleys which protected commerce from marauders. With a surprisingly small force of naval and frontier guards the Roman world was made secure from barbarian attacks. The efficiency of the military and administrative forces accounts for the empire's relative freedom from invasion from the time of Augustus to that of Marcus Aurelius toward the end of the second century A.D.

Within the circle of these defenses was the immense domain over which the emperors ruled. It encircled the Mediterranean Sea and included peoples of varied races, cultures, classes, and interests. There were the Celtic inhabitants of Britain and Gaul, the Iberians of Spain, the swarthy natives of Northern Africa, the remnants of the ancient Carthaginians, and the hardy farmer settlers along the Rhine and Danube rivers. In the East were the peasants and the teeming city populations of Greece, Asia Minor, Syria, and Egypt.

IMPERIAL GOVERNMENT: THE EMPEROR

All of these regions and peoples were subject to the will of the emperor, who symbolized the power and glory of Rome. In theory his authority was granted by the senate, but as a matter of fact the support of the army was the essential factor in the making, and at times in the unmaking, of emperors. Even during the peaceful second century the emperors were careful to select as their successors men who were acceptable to the soldiery. On the death of an emperor his successor was acclaimed by the armies as *imperator* and voted the titles *princeps* (first citizen) and *Caesar* by the senate. As *imperator,* an emperor controlled the military forces and exercised supreme judicial powers. The tribunician power gave him control over civil affairs, and the office of *Pontifex Maximus* made him the master of the religious priesthoods and ceremonies. The emperor's decisions on all public affairs were supreme, and through his power of appointment he controlled all officers in the city of Rome and all members of the imperial bureaucracy.

THE IMPERIAL The traditional positions of honor in the capital city
BUREAUCRACY   and in the provinces were still held by senators and
equestrians, or "knights." Among these officers were
the consuls, praetors, aediles, and quaestors—ancient republican functions which had become mere honorary appointments. None but the
praetors (who served as judges), and the proconsuls in the senatorial
provinces had any important governmental duties. From the senatorial class the emperor also selected commissioners of finance and
poor relief, and curators of roads, grain supply, and public works in
and about Rome. From the class of "knights" were selected the prefects of the imperial provinces, of the praetorian guard at Rome, of
the government of the city, and of its grain supply. "Knights" also
headed the great bureaucracy of civil servants who carried on the real
business of provincial government. This imperial civil service was
co-ordinated under five departments: finance, correspondence, petitions, investigation, and intelligence and records. In the various provinces affairs were administered by procurators and lesser posts were
filled by freedmen and slaves. Broadly speaking, the imperial officials seem to have comprised a well-trained, energetic, and faithful
class of administrators with good pay and opportunity for promo-
tion.

FINANCES   The finances necessary for carrying on the gigantic
imperial government were derived from various
sources. There were sales taxes, taxes on industry and trade, an inheritance tax, a tax on land paid only by the provincials, and a poll
tax which fell heaviest on the lower classes. The collection of taxes was
supervised by the procurators, the actual collecting being done usually
through private agencies of tax "farmers" or, in some regions, through
the municipal officials. There was comparatively little corruption or
extortion, and in return for their taxes the citizenry had defense, security, roads, and other public works. The government also realized
a substantial income from state-operated mines and from the emperor's private domains. By gifts, inheritances, seizures, and the like,
the emperor accumulated untold wealth, much of which was used
for public purposes.

IMPERIAL LAW Among the services rendered to the people of the
empire, two were outstanding—justice and defense.
The Romans considered it their destiny to conquer and rule. Wherever Roman rule went, the general principle of fair trials by judicial
methods was introduced. Litigants were compelled to appear before

a judge, present their case in person, and accept his decision. One of the most satisfactory characteristics of Roman law was its practical adaptation of general legal principles to existing conditions. Since legal processes were based on custom, in conquered regions the provincial governors judged cases according to the customary law of the locality rather than by Rome's legal code. Imperial law merely co-ordinated and supplemented local law. As the powers of the emperors increased, their edicts, decrees, orders, and rescripts took the place of senatorial legislation as the co-ordinating law of the empire. Theoretically the emperor presided over important cases, but his representative, the praetorian prefect, came to be recognized as the highest court of appeal. The decisions of the praetorian prefect, of the lesser praetors, and of other judges were recorded, as were also the opinions given by the jurists. In the second century, legal procedure was regularized by the Perpetual Edict of Hadrian and his praetorian prefect. Centuries later comprehensive codifications of Roman law were made by Theodosius II (408-450) and Justinian (527-565).

IMPERIAL DEFENSE Imperial law and order depended in the last analysis on armed force. Here the early empire rendered a more efficient service than that provided by most of the modern rulers of this region. An area now defended, policed, and fought over by millions of armed men was made peaceful and secure, within and without, by a comparatively small armed force. As time went on the soldiers were drawn more and more from the provinces. They usually enlisted for a period of twenty years, most of which time was spent in some frontier garrison. On retirement each legionnaire was granted citizenship and a bonus of land. During the second century it became customary to recruit soldiers from the region in which their legion was to be stationed. The duties of the recruits were simple and the discipline was strict. When not engaged in patrol duty on dangerous frontiers, they were often employed in building roads, bridges, or other public works. There were naval forces in the Mediterranean and on large rivers such as the Rhine and Danube. Piracy on the seas and brigandage on land were much reduced, and throughout most of the first and second centuries there was no major war or invasion.

LOCAL ADMINIS-
TRATION: MU-
NICIPALITIES
Internally the empire was organized into provinces, under proconsuls or imperial legates.[2] Each was assisted by the local military commander and by imperial agents called *procurators*. In most of the provinces there were annual assemblies composed of representatives from the local municipalities. Although virtually without power, they celebrated certain religious rites in honor of the emperor and discussed provincial affairs. The actual government was carried on by cities, towns, or rural communities. In most regions municipal government was encouraged and cities grew rapidly, many being granted charters which gave them special governmental rights. By the second century practically every province was dotted with such settlements.

It has been suggested that the empire may be conceived of as a gigantic federation of city-states, closely bound together and regulated by imperial administrators. Although purely local matters were often left to the municipal officials, the provincial governor might interfere directly in the affairs of any city. During Trajan's reign an imperial official in Bithynia refused to allow the people of a large city to organize a volunteer fire department for fear of encouraging secret societies. In order to check municipal extravagance and financial corruption, imperial curators and "correctors" were appointed to oversee the local authorities. There were also innumerable special agents of the central government who spied on individuals and had power to interfere in municipal policies. In theory, and to a considerable degree in practice as well, local affairs were subject to the arbitrary will of the emperor.

For the most part, however, local government was carried on by the local citizenry. They elected their own officials, usually two head magistrates (called *duumvirs*), quaestors, aediles, and so on.[3] Property qualifications tended to restrict the vote to the middle and upper classes, and office-holding to the wealthier citizens. All ex-officials automatically became members of the local senate, or *curia*. Thus most municipal governments followed the model of that of the city of Rome in republican times.

[2] The provinces administered by the senate were headed by proconsuls, appointed by the senate. Most of the provinces were under imperially appointed legates.

[3] We are dealing principally with the cities of the Western regions. In the East, municipal government followed the forms, official titles, and so on, of the ancient Greek *polis* (city).

URBAN SOCIAL
AND ECONOMIC
LIFE
The most energetic members of the empire's population lived in the cities, and their business activities provided a considerable portion of the governmental revenues. Not only commerce and industry but agriculture as well contributed to civic prosperity, and since municipal wealth was an important factor in the imperial revenues, city life was encouraged. Cities had long flourished in the East and they sprang up rapidly in the West, even in outlying regions. Frontier garrison posts and intersections of important roads often gave rise to thriving settlements which eventually received municipal charters and other privileges from the government.

THE CITY
OF ROME
Rome, the imperial capital, was the most prosperous of all cities, although its own commercial and industrial activities were of secondary importance. Its political position gave it considerable social and economic dominance. On the city's seven hills were the palaces of the emperors and of the wealthy nobles. Near by, in the Forum and in the numerous public buildings of the city were the headquarters of the imperial bureaucracy. Governmental officials, senatorial aristocrats, and enterprising businessmen made Rome the center of their activities. Its broad streets were thronged with important personages from all parts of the empire and from all regions of the civilized world. In its palaces and gardens banquets of fabulous splendor were given. To tempt the appetites of revelers delicacies from distant regions were imported. Guests were amused by troops of singers, dancing girls, jugglers, dicing, and other forms of gambling. In the homes of the newly rich, especially, there was much vulgar display. Morals were lax, divorce was common, and among certain groups private life was hopelessly corrupt.

THE
ARISTOCRACY
In contrast with this there was the example of simple living and cultural interests set by emperors such as Vespasian, Hadrian, and Marcus Aurelius. Many a Roman banquet was accompanied by academic discussion rather than by bacchanalian orgies, and many Romans spent their leisure hours in literary and philosophical pursuits. As time passed the senatorial nobility took less interest in governmental affairs, and concerned itself almost wholly with cultural or social activities. Many of its members retired to the country estates whence they drew most of their incomes, and where they could lead lives of leisure, since the care of their estates was in the hands of overseers and stewards. By the end of the

second century the senatorial nobility, whether at Rome or elsewhere, had been forced into a parasitical existence. The typical Roman gentleman rose early in the morning, received callers, attended to a few business affairs, lunched, took his siesta, and spent the rest of the day with his friends at the baths, which served as club houses, and at dinners, which occupied the entire evening.

The active class of inhabitants of the capital was the middle class of governmental officials and businessmen. Those in the imperial service were well provided for and had ample opportunity for advancement. Those in private business were sometimes able to amass fortunes in banking, the collection of taxes, or the manufacture of brick, pottery, metal products and the like. Importers of luxury goods found Rome an unusually good market. There are cases on record of men whose business ventures brought them wealth and social position. For the majority, however, profits and risks were small.

THE ROMAN POPULACE The masses in the capital are often represented as a shiftless depraved proletariat whose vices were encouraged by the government's provision of free food and entertainment in the Colosseum and the Circus. As a matter of fact, poor relief was a necessity, because there was not sufficient industrial activity in the city to employ its immense population. The employment problem was accentuated by the fact that secretarial tasks, certain kinds of manufacturing, and menial labor were performed by slaves, of which Rome had a comparatively large number. Some members of the lower classes lived in fairly comfortable tenement houses; others barely existed, in squalor and poverty. But even the unemployed and the poor laboring classes had their social life. There were *collegia,* associations organized primarily for mutual benefits, such as burial service. The members paid dues, attended banquets in the club house, and took part in the religious services which were a prominent feature of the organization's activities. The government supervised all such organizations, prohibiting secret meetings or propagandistic activities. Religious festivals, horse races at the Circus Maximus, theatrical exhibitions, and the games of the Colosseum also contributed to recreational life in the city.

PROVINCIAL CITIES The average city dweller of the empire lived in a provincial center which bore only a superficial resemblance to Rome. It had its forum, temples, schools, perhaps a hospital, a theater, and an amphitheater. But here the similarity ends. The municipal government, commerce, industry, and social life were dominated by the middle-class ideals of practical businessmen. They held the offices, became members of the local burgher aristocracy of ex-officials, and frequently endowed the municipality with libraries, aqueducts, bridges, or other such public works. They set the social standards of the community, controlled its economic life, and in general were the backbone of imperial society. They managed the industries which gave employment to the lower classes. They provided subsistence and amusement (bread and circuses) for the proletariat, and they exploited the agricultural resources of the vicinity. During the first and second centuries the energetic business class increased in wealth and influence and gave stability to Roman civilization.

PROVINCIAL IN-
DUSTRY AND
COMMERCE
From the economic standpoint, the provincial cities were the vital centers of the empire's commerce and industry. In the course of the first century, industrial life became more localized, and flourishing industries developed in various provincial centers. Ancient cities whose business life had been ruined by the early Roman conquest, recovered their prosperity. New industrial centers arose at strategic points on land or sea, along the frontiers, and in regions that produced valuable raw products. The absence of tariffs and other restrictions made it possible for many a locality to exploit its own natural resources and to sell its goods in neighboring regions. Thus Rome and Italy gradually lost their favored position and the various regions of the empire tended to develop their own mercantile centers.

With the exception of grain supplies for the largest cities, most of the necessities of life were produced, exchanged, and consumed within the sphere of activity of each locality. Grain, livestock, olive oil, wine, meat, fish, and other bulky or perishable products were both difficult and expensive to transport. Since most of them could be produced in most regions of the empire, they were usually raised, bought, and sold in the same locality. Much of the business in the average city was concerned with local products for local consumption and was carried on by small shop owners and merchants. As a result of the prevailing order and security of the imperial regime, such activities flourished and through the various provinces the standard of living rose rapidly.

INDUSTRIAL AND
COMMERCIAL
ACTIVITIES
Even with the expansion of economic activities, industry and commerce in the empire never reached what we today regard as large-scale proportions. It is true, however, that specialized products were manufactured in huge quantities in regions favorable for such operations, and then shipped to all parts of the empire to be sold. For a time, ancient Eastern cities such as Sidon, because of secret processes of manufacture, monopolized the trade in certain types of fine textiles and glassware. The control of important clay deposits in southern Italy enabled the industrialists of that region to make immense profits on pottery and clay lamps. Even with comparable concentrations of resources in the metal, leather, and woolen industries, the general tendency was in the direction of economic decentralization. New Western centers vied with the eastern textile cities, particularly in the production of the cheaper varieties of woolen cloth. Southern Gaul exploited its own clay pits and competed with the pottery industry of southern Italy. Spain developed flourishing centers of iron and leather manufacture.

SMALL-SCALE
INDUSTRY AND
COMMERCE
With the exception of certain monopolistic characteristics most Roman business life was unlike that of our day. To be sure, there were "factories" in which a hundred or more slaves might be employed, but most industries were carried on in small home shops in which the owner worked along with a few employees. Some industrialists might produce goods on a large scale and ship them to distant points by means of seagoing vessels, river barges, pack trains, and the like, but the average man played for smaller stakes. There were doubtless many men in actual life like Trimalchio, the millionaire freedman of Petronius's *Satyricon,* who boasted that he had lost a fleet of ships, repeated the venture, and eventually made a fortune. Imports of foreign materials such as the much-prized goods of the Orient and the furs, amber, and timber of the Baltic regions, necessitated considerable outlay of capital and great risks. But to every merchant who engaged in distant commerce, there were thousands of small-town merchants who limited their financial dealings to the local market. Banking practices and credit instruments were common in the large cities. Most businessmen, however, operated without complicated financial transactions. Partnerships were common, but there were no business organizations similar to our modern corporations. Usually the individual handled his own business in his own way.

GOVERNMENTAL CONTROL

There were a few exceptions to the general pattern of small-scale local and individual economic activity. The emperors, due to their tremendous accumulations of landed estates (such as the great Egyptian domain), controlled immense resources in mines, quarries, and forests, to say nothing of agricultural products. These were handled on a large scale, in some regions approximating a local monopoly. Then too there was the rigidly centralized transportation service. Uninterrupted supplies of grain and other public necessities for the armies, for Rome, and for other large cities were assured by careful supervision and regulation of private shipping. As time went on, governmental control of seagoing commerce increased. The transportation of bulky products by land was comparatively unimportant and continued as a local function under private initiative.

AGRICULTURE

Since the days of the Republic the Roman nobility had organized its landed estates for the effective production and sale of grain, wine, oil, and livestock. During the early empire the business classes followed their example with the result that throughout the Mediterranean area agriculture came more and more under the influence of the wealthy city folk. Landed estates were the chief form of wealth in ancient times, and businessmen bought them not only as investments but also for social prestige, since the ownership of farm lands peopled with slaves and tenants marked the aristocrat. Thus the small rural estates and free farms in the vicinity of the cities tended to drift into the hands of wealthy citizens who operated them for profit, and sometimes used them as country residences. Although the members of the nobility continued to own and operate great landed estates, the successful businessmen of the cities sought the same goal. Thus there came into being a new nobility of wealthy landlords. This resulted in a closer relationship between agricultural and business interests. Through their investments in land, the wealthy city classes furnished additional capital for agriculture, while the needs of the population of the cities provided markets for rural products.

The relationship was one in which the city tended to dominate and exploit the rural sections. With a view to increased profits, marked improvements were made in marketing and scientific farming. Not only grain, wine, and oil, but meat, vegetables, and other foods were produced for the city markets. In regions in which there were army posts, enterprising men profited by the raising of herds of pack animals. Quality and quantity of products were improved by scientific breeding and by the fertilizing of the soil, by rotation of crops, clearing of forests, and draining of swamps.

TENANCY   There were also marked changes in methods of management and labor. The slave-gang system of republican days slowly gave way to tenant farming, a form of labor that had been employed on a large scale in the East. It was adopted first by the emperors for their immense estates, and later by private landowners throughout the West. Tenancy was produced largely by the dwindling supply of slaves with the cessation of wars in the early empire, and by the increase in the number of landless farmers, as wealthy men bought up the better farm lands. A dispossessed debtor, instead of moving to the poorer upland regions to eke out a scanty living, or to the city to swell the ranks of the poverty-stricken populace, might remain on the estate of the new owner as a tenant. During the second century, as the trend toward large estates continued, tenancy also grew. Freed slaves and barbarian immigrants often became tenants. Such tenant-populated estates were called villas.

The fact that tenancy had advantages for both the owner and the tenant was also responsible for its increase. Each tenant had a house in the village and a plot of land somewhere on the estate, which he held by lease for a given length of time. It was customary to renew leases, which came to be recognized as hereditary rights. The tenants (called *coloni*) paid rental fees in produce and in work on the owner's fields. They could use his mill, wine press, ovens, looms, and other mechanical conveniences on the payment of certain fees. He was their legal protector, and defender against physical violence. So far as the landlord was concerned, the tenant system was a simple and reasonably effective means of handling the problem of agricultural labor. Extensive lands, well populated and effectively supervised, not only provided financial profits but social prestige.

Though popular with the great landlords and with many tenants, the tenant system was not universal. Thanks to the attempts of certain emperors to aid the small farmer, there were peasant owners who stubbornly maintained their independence. Ex-soldiers received farms as pensions, and occasionally city folk took up small farms in the country. In general, however, the poorer inhabitants of the rural regions sank to tenancy as they came under the domination of the wealthy classes of the neighboring cities. So long as city life prospered, this had its compensations, for flourishing cities furnished dependable markets for agricultural products. Later, with the decline of city life and the increase of the independent rural villa, we shall find Roman agriculture taking on more of the characteristics of the manorial and semiservile regime of the Middle Ages.

SIGNS OF
DECLINE
In the course of the third century conditions in all lines took a decided turn for the worse. The history of the empire during this century was marked by constant internal wars of succession, devastating barbaric invasions and recurring periods of economic chaos, panic, and depression.

We must not, however, take it for granted that the empire was swept by a storm of unforeseen disasters from which the preceding period had been entirely free. The predominantly optimistic picture we have given of the first and second centuries has its shadows; there was political disaster and economic suffering. The peace and security of the citizenry and particularly of the upper classes in Rome, might be temporarily upset by a reign of terror, in which a mad or tyrannical emperor such as Caligula, Nero, or Domitian employed espionage, treachery, confiscation, and assassination to wreak vengeance on those whom he feared or hated. In such times it was fatal for a citizen to be wealthy or to speak his mind.

Even the lesser folk in the provinces suffered occasionally at the hands of grasping or arbitrary local officials. There were civil wars, due chiefly to Augustus' failure to establish a definite method of succession to the imperial office. When an emperor was removed suddenly by assassination the imperial guard was likely to set up a successor whose authority might be disputed by other military or political forces. The year 68 saw three soldier emperors set up only to be overthrown by rival armies in a welter of civil warfare. Some of the outlying provinces experienced local revolts. In Syria there were two serious uprisings of the Jews. Beginning in the reign of Marcus Aurelius a plague ravaged the empire.

At times economic conditions were so difficult that the provincials protested, all too often in vain. Severe governmental restrictions were placed on the *collegia* and on any secret organizations that might encourage treasonable propaganda. Nevertheless, the outcroppings of protest in literature indicate a steady undercurrent of discontent among the lower classes. The populace turned in ever-increasing numbers to the mysteries of Oriental religions for solace.

THE DISASTERS OF THE THIRD CENTURY

As a matter of fact, in many respects the desperate conditions of the third century seem to have been merely the accentuation of a downward trend that had been long in evidence. This is particularly true of the economic situation. During the second century there were ominous signs of declining prosperity in many regions. Large-scale commerce gradually gave way to local production for local consumption. Export industries tended to decline and production sank to a lower level as markets became more limited. The increase of self-supporting villas, on which peasant artisans manufactured all of the necessities of life, restricted the sale of the products of the city industries. For reasons that are still not entirely clear to the historian, Mediterranean civilization during the second century had begun to revert to a more primitive economic regime characterized by restricted markets, barter, localized production and consumption, and subsistence farming. Meanwhile as private initiative and prosperity decreased, governmental regulation and taxation increased. To this already weakened economy, the political disorders of the third century dealt a heavy blow.

GOVERNMENTAL DEMORALIZATION   In the third century, there was a decided breakdown in the efficiency of the central administration which in turn contributed much to the general decline of peace and prosperity. The chief political difficulties arose out of the increasing domination of the military in governmental affairs. This was exemplified most vividly in the selection of emperors. For a century, the will of the soldiery was supreme in both the choice of emperors and their continuance in power. This was not the first time that the military had exerted an influence in such matters. Several times in the first century the imperial guard had taken a hand in the overthrow of an emperor and the setting up of his successor. But on the whole the soldiery was the servant of the early imperial government. Usually the emperors, with the approval of the senate, selected their own successors. During the second century the emperors selected able men as their associates and trained them for the imperial office. Trajan, Hadrian, Antoninus Pius, and Marcus Aurelius were brought to imperial power by this means.

With Marcus Aurelius the regime of peaceful successions ended. He chose for the succession his inefficient and wayward son, Commodus, who was assassinated by the imperial guard after a few years of hopelessly misguided rule. This was the beginning of a century of chaos during which the imperial office was almost constantly subjected to the will of the armies. The death of an emperor invariably led to an unseemly scramble for his position. Army after army would proclaim its general as *imperator*. At one time there were nineteen rival candidates.

For long periods of time the empire was torn by devastating internal wars. Except for a few short reigns of strong rulers, such as Septimius Severus (193-211), Caracalla (211-217), and Alexander Severus (222-235), these conditions prevailed until late in the 'third century. Anarchy and civil strife, formerly the exception in imperial government, now became common. The military, once the servant of the central administration, was now its master. Rough military men determined not only the selection of emperors but also their policies and even their overthrow. A general who had been raised to the imperial office by his legions was likely to remain in power only as long as they were satisfied with his government. Increased pay and privileges and easy garrison duty in the capital tended to insure their loyalty. A single unpopular act might lead to assassination and the setting up of a new emperor.

A MILITARY GOVERNMENT

Under such conditions none but ruthless fighting men could succeed in imperial affairs. Thus it was that the more orderly regime of the first and second centuries gave way to either anarchy or military despotism. During most of the period from Marcus Aurelius to Diocletian, the destinies of the Roman world were in the hands of "barracks" emperors and their legions. To make matters worse, the personnel of the armies had deteriorated. In the early days of the republic, Rome's militia armies were composed of citizen farmers who had a patriotic interest in their government. Later the legions were filled with men drawn largely from the provinces but officered and disciplined by Romans of the upper classes. This provided an effective army of professional soldiers. By the third century the legions were recruited largely from the ignorant semibarbaric peasantry of the rural or frontier regions.

Thus, long before the Germanic barbarians became a serious menace to the empire, her own soldiery had begun the process of barbarizing a civilized government. These rough fighting men had little respect for Roman governmental methods and little sympathy with the prosperous city folk, whom they felt were exploiting the

lower classes. With such men in power, Roman institutions disintegrated rapidly. When the armies deserted their frontier posts to fight
for the imperial prize, the borders were left unguarded and barbarian
invaders found easy access to the empire. Scottish clansmen, Germans,
Parthians, Arabs, and tribes from the African deserts raided the
frontier provinces at will during most of this troubled period. In
desperation the provincials sometimes turned to local leaders and set
up independent governments.

ECONOMIC
DECLINE

The unsettled political conditions dealt a serious blow
to municipal prosperity. Throughout much of the
third century, the business life of cities in all parts of
the empire was insecure. Many centers were either pillaged or taxed
into a state of permanent economic depression. Shortsighted policies
of ever-changing imperial administrations added to the economic confusion. The coinage was debased to such a degree as to cause hoard-
ing, dangerous fluctuations in prices, and the temporary disruption
of commerce. Constant warfare not only interfered with economic
activities, it also brought a tremendous increase in governmental expenses. Military necessities forced each new emperor to turn to the
already impoverished cities for additional revenues. Military requisi-
tions and forced contributions were levied recklessly. Thus economic
ruin threatened an empire of once flourishing cities.

Some historians argue that the fate of ancient civilization was
sealed in the first half of the third century by the destruction of the
middle class of wealth-producing folk in many parts of the empire.
This portion of the population was not only the backbone of local
culture and political administration, it was also the chief source of the
wealth by which the imperial and city governments existed. By permitting or perpetrating the ruin of municipal prosperity, the imperial
rulers and their warring armies brought about an economic crisis
from which Rome never fully recovered.

ROMAN CIVILIZATION OF THE FOURTH AND FIFTH CENTURIES

In general, the disasters of the third century were so destructive of
the political and economic institutions of the empire that many historians consider this period as the final epoch of ancient civilization.
This does not mean, however, that imperial institutions were completely undermined and deprived of all recuperative power. There

were third century emperors who succeeded in restoring order for
short periods and who made honest efforts to preserve the prosperity
of the taxpaying citizenry. But the periods of peace were short-lived
and economic conditions showed little improvement until the end of
the century. The latter half of the century, however, saw the beginnings of an imperial recovery that is of great importance in the history
of medieval and modern Europe. Much of the Roman influence exerted on succeeding centuries was that of the new imperial institutions
of this age of reconstruction.

POLITICAL RE-
CONSTRUCTION
The empire reached the height of its military chaos
during the second and third quarters of the third century. Decius, one of the "barracks" emperors of this
period, was defeated and killed by barbarian invaders in the year 251.
External disaster was accompanied by internal catastrophe. Ten years
after Decius' downfall a score of rival candidates were fighting for the
imperial throne. But thereafter, and to the end of the century, conditions showed a marked improvement. In the year 269 Emperor
Claudius defeated his rivals and drove out the Gothic tribes who had
been ravaging the Balkan regions. Shortly afterward Emperor Aurelian (270-275) won the title "Restorer of the World" by his exploits.
He not only fought his way to the imperial crown, but forced rebellious provinces to renew their allegiance, and made the frontiers secure
against barbarian attacks. Ten years after his death another soldier,
Diocletian, who had risen from the ranks, undertook the task of re-
organizing the empire.

DIOCLETIAN
(284-305)
Like Aurelian and other energetic rulers of this
troubled century, Diocletian's chief aim was the restoration of order. He solved the problem, but unfor-
tunately his success was attained only by sacrificing political and economic flexibility. Security and stability for a devastated and war-
ravaged world demanded a strong central power that could control
the frontiers, the provinces, and the armies. Accordingly, in soldier-
like fashion, Diocletian set up a rigid military system of government,
organized and disciplined like an army. The area of the empire was
regrouped into over a hundred small provinces, each of which was
controlled by a civil governor, appointed by the emperor. The provinces in turn were grouped into dioceses, thirteen in number. Each
provincial governor was responsible to the vicar of his diocese. The
thirteen dioceses were grouped into four prefectures, each ruled by an
imperial prefect who was the lieutenant of Diocletian or one of his

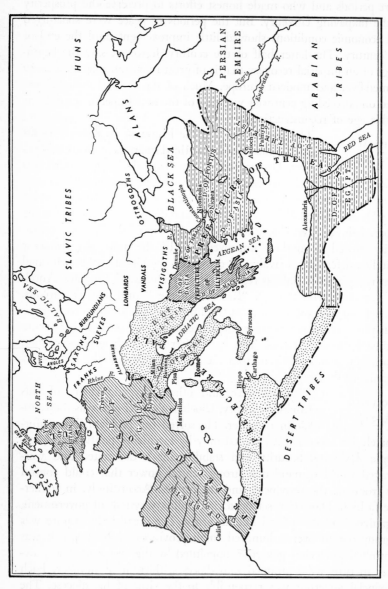

THE ROMAN AND BARBARIAN WORLDS IN THE FOURTH CENTURY

Shadings indicate the four prefectures of the Empire. D. indicates diocese. The provinces, over a hundred in number, are not indicated.

assistants. None of these local officials had armed forces, and from bottom to top all were directly responsible to their immediate superiors, the final authority resting with the emperor himself, who kept in touch with local problems and checked overly ambitious officials by means of special agents who acted as supervisors and spies. Thus the danger of local rebellions was eliminated and a centralized administration re-established. At the imperial capital were the headquarters of the various bureaus of the civil service, of the emperor's legal staff, his finance ministers, and the inner council of advisers, called the Consistory. The emperor himself lived amid the splendors of an Oriental court, a divine monarch whose power was absolute and whose person was sacred. By such means Diocletian and his successors endeavored to strengthen the emperor's authority and to unify the empire.

The least permanent of Diocletian's innovations was the setting up of four administrative divisions with four emperors, himself and his friend Maximian as Augusti, their two assistants and successors, as Caesars. Each of the rulers had direct supervision of one of the four prefectures, thus insuring effective control of a restricted region. The two Caesars were assigned to the more dangerous military prefectures, along the Rhine and Danube. Diocletian took the Near East under his personal supervision, with Nicomedia near the Straits of the Bosporus as a capital. Maximian's headquarters were at Milan. After a certain number of years the two Augusti were to retire in favor of their Caesars, who would then choose two more Caesars to train for the imperial office. It was, in theory, an admirable plan for the elimination of wars of succession and for the division of responsibility. We shall see, however, that in practice it broke down, once Diocletian's authority was removed.

BUREAUCRACY, ECONOMICS, AND MILITARISM
Diocletian's governmental system was a marked improvement over the disorderly regime of the earlier decades of the century. In many respects it was a return to the bureaucratic centralization of the first and second centuries. The chief differences were Diocletian's emphasis on Oriental absolutism and military power. He established a highly regimented government with all authority rigidly centralized in a divine emperor, assisted by military and civil servants. The splendid imperial court and the civil service, with its graded series of officials controlled from imperial headquarters, continued as dominant factors in the government of the Eastern Empire, and persisted to some de-

gree in the West during the Middle Ages. This system provided a class of professional imperial servants and perpetuated effective methods of centralized administration. On the other hand the imperial officials tended to become a bureaucracy with special privileges. A governmental caste of this sort, once in operation, could carry on with little supervision, but it soon became rigid and unprogressive. It crushed what little spirit of independence and initiative remained in the local municipal government. Thus local freedom and flexibility were sacrificed for centralization and unity.

Furthermore, the cost of maintenance was overwhelming: the number of tax collectors and "tax eaters" increased, while the taxpayers steadily diminished in numbers and wealth. Meanwhile economic life showed little recuperative power. As we shall see presently, Diocletian and his successors instituted a regime of peace and order that gave industry and commerce a new lease on life. They checked the depreciation of the coinage and made honest efforts to stabilize financial conditions. But economic prosperity never returned to the businessmen and middle-class city folk of the empire.

The military policies of the new imperial government were more successful. For frontier defense Diocletian and his successors relied more and more on troops recruited from the local peasantry, many of them barbarian immigrants. They were assigned to definite frontier posts with lands upon which they lived as a sort of frontier militia. This gave them an additional incentive to check invaders. In times of invasion they were reinforced by mobile units of professional soldiery which were concentrated at strategic points. Each of these units was under the control of one of the four emperors. In addition to these forces, each of the imperial rulers had his own guard with which to reinforce the frontier troops and, if need be, to check the power of ambitious generals. Such a military system, when directed by able emperors, could keep the frontiers secure and also prevent civil warfare.

THE NEW EMPIRE   The reorganized military and political regime of Diocletian, his predecessors, and successors, which continued without fundamental change for two centuries in the West, and even longer in the East, was very different from the early Roman Empire. The emperors reigned amid an Oriental splendor unknown to the *princeps* of the first and second centuries. For the first time in Roman history the ruler was crowned god-king

with divinely absolute rights over the lives and property of his people.
Under Diocletian the empire crossed the threshold of the fourth
century, into an age fraught with even more momentous changes.
With the reign of Constantine the Great (306-337) the student of history begins to feel that he is in a different world—a world that is less
pagan and more Christian, less Roman and more Germanic, less civilized and more barbaric. We begin our survey of this century—sometimes referred to as the period of the birth of the Middle Ages—
with an account of the rise of Constantine the Great.

THE RISE OF
CONSTANTINE

According to Diocletian's plan of succession, he and
Maximian, the Western emperor, retired in 305. Thus
their assistants were automatically promoted to imperial power, and proceeded to choose two new assistants. But here
the neatly regimented system of Diocletian broke down, chiefly because of the ambitions of the various underlings. Several men sought
the assistantships, and soon a civil war broke out which eventually
wrecked Diocletian's program of succession. In the West there was a
bitter rivalry which finally resolved itself into a life-and-death struggle
between Constantine, son of the Western Caesar, and Maxentius, son
of the former emperor, Maximian. Young Constantine fought his
way to Italy from Britain and Gaul, where his father had served as
assistant emperor. Outside the gates of Rome, near the Milvian bridge
(312), he won a decisive battle, and with it the undisputed title to the
Western part of the empire. According to Christian writers of the
time, Constantine, on this occasion, having seen in the skies a cross
with the emblem, *in hoc signo vinces* ("By this sign, conquer"), had
his soldiers march into battle with Christian standards.[4]

Constantine, having become master of the West, made terms
with the Eastern emperor, and they ruled jointly over a peaceful empire for ten years. In 323, however, after they had developed irrecon-
cilable differences of opinion, the two emperors met on the battlefield
and Constantine became sole ruler of a reunited empire.

CIVILIZATION
SHIFTS EAST-
WARD

Although Constantine's victory ended Diocletian's
system of divided administration and selective succession, it crystallized certain other tendencies that
had been in evidence for some time. One of the most
notable of these was the eastward shift of imperial interests. In earlier
days many a Roman general and emperor had felt that imperial

[4] See below, p. 64.

destiny lay in that direction. Diocletian, perhaps realizing that the East was the most important, strategic, and productive region of the empire, had chosen it as his administrative division and had set up his headquarters at Nicomedia in Asia Minor. Constantine went a step further. In the same region, at Byzantium on the straits leading from the Black Sea to the Aegean, he built a new capital city, Constantinople (Constantine's city). This became the "New Rome," the center of imperial government and civilization for over a thousand years.

It was a magnificent location for the imperial capital. On a long promontory easily defended from land attacks, and provided with a marvelous harbor, Constantinople was impregnable as long as she controlled the seas. Within easy marching or sailing distance from the danger points on the Danube and Euphrates frontiers, and close to the great seaports of the eastern Mediterranean, the city had an unusual strategic position for military and commercial activities. Its long and brilliant career as mistress of the Mediterranean justified the wisdom of Constantine's choice. The selection of Constantinople as the capital of the reunited empire also marks the declining influence of Italy in the Mediterranean world. Thanks to Rome's early military and political expansion, Italy had been for centuries the metropolis of the entire Mediterranean. But the East still had the greater population, the larger cities, and most of the industrial resources of the civilized world. In the second and third centuries the weaknesses of Rome and Italy were revealed. Constantine gave tacit recognition to the new conditions by removing his capital to the region which was the chief producer of the empire's wealth. Gradually Italy and the Western provinces faded into the background, and throughout the Middle Ages, as in the early centuries before Rome's imperial conquests, the eastern Mediterranean was the center of civilized life.

In other respects, also, the age of Diocletian and Constantine marks a decided change in imperial history. They and the other emperors of this period rescued the empire from anarchy, and reconstructed its political and economic institutions, at least in part, according to new principles. Most prominent among these was the militaristic and Orientally despotic nature of the central government. These characteristics became firmly established during the reigns of the soldier-emperors who succeeded Diocletian, and had important effects on the political, economic, and social institutions of the fourth and fifth centuries.

IMPERIAL
DESPOTISM

Constantine took over Diocletian's entire governmental system with the exception of one major element: he abolished the system of double emperors and assistants. He reunited the empire, and under his absolute authority it became a more perfectly integrated mechanism than in the days of Diocletian. With the advice of a council, composed of the heads of the great governmental bureaus, he made decisions, issued edicts and gave orders to be carried out by the various ranks of civil and military officials. His power was absolute, his word was law, and his decisions irrevocable. He was, in fact, a god-king, before whom all subjects, high and low, bowed in humble submission. Court ceremonial was pompous, glittering, and filled with the mysterious pageantry that had always been associated with sacred royalty in the Orient. The ruler was surrounded with the trappings of Oriental despotism: with the diadem, scepter, and throne, and with throngs of courtiers who prostrated themselves before his divine majesty. This new emphasis on the divinity of the Roman emperor, in marked contrast to the vague ideas of deity associated with the "princeps-imperator" of the earlier period, was an outgrowth of the third century. It had been adopted by Aurelian and permanently established by Diocletian as a means of strengthening the emperor and ending the chaos of civil wars and assassinations. The emperor was clothed with extraordinary honor and sanctity by being raised to the pedestal of deity. Rough soldiers and peasants who might strike down a self-made emperor-general would be likely to give military and financial support to a ruler who was officially recognized as divine at his accession to the throne. The source of this political fiction was the East, where there had been god-kings since the days of the Egyptian pharaohs. As early as Augustus, emperors were recognized as divine *after* death. The idea of the living emperor as a god was permanently and universally recognized in the third century, at a time when the imperial headquarters were being shifted to the eastern Mediterranean, the region in which this idea had originated. The Oriental influences prevailing in this region, along with the strong militaristic tendencies everywhere prevalent during the third century, became the dominating factors in the imperial government of the succeeding period. In the East they continued for centuries. In the West they were less firmly rooted and gradually disappeared with the decay of imperial government and the rising influences of Christianity and the Germanic invaders.

TAXATION   The economic-social aspects of the new governmental regime can be seen most clearly by considering the problems of imperial taxation. Governmental expenses were constantly increasing, an inevitable result of the expansion of the military and civil service. Since the ever-increasing body of government officials must be supported, obviously an increase in taxation was necessary. There were customs duties, municipal tolls, sales taxes, a levy on inheritances, the poll tax, the land tax, and other minor levies; but these yielded insufficient revenue because of the fact that the economic life of the empire, badly depressed during the third century, had never recovered. Consequently those economic enterprises which still existed were oppressed with additional burdens. Diocletian went so far as to subject Italy to levies from which this region had formerly been exempt.

Everywhere, in order to assure the collection of much-needed revenues, the curials (members of the town council, or *curia*) were made personally responsible for the payment of all taxes due from their municipality. When they sought to avoid this public office (once considered a high honor), the government applied force. By the law of *origo,* they were prevented from leaving their native city (place of origin). Eventually all citizens of a certain income were forced automatically to become curials and fulfill the duties of that office. This insured the state revenues, that is, as long as there were wealthy curials. Constantine went so far as to rule that the sons of curials must inherit their fathers' office. In similar fashion, the members of the guilds of merchants and artisans were made responsible for industrial taxes. By such efficient method tax evasion was reduced to a minimum.

But there was one loophole which could not be stopped—bankruptcy. The government could collect its taxes only as long as the curials and businessmen were prosperous. Many of them were ruined by the combination of decreased income and increasing taxation. Slowly but surely the tax mill, in grinding revenues for the government, ground down the leading class of wealth-producers in the municipalities. One of the most disastrous burdens was the gold-silver tax (*chrysargyrum*) on industrial products, payable only in coin. In order to enforce payment, the guilds and their officials were held responsible and brought under strict governmental control. Those who attempted to evade the burden by deserting the organization were prevented by law. Thus artisans and businessmen, like curials, were chained to their task of producing revenue for the state. As cash collections dwindled, the government was forced to rely upon produce and the confiscated property of bankrupt citizens. Taxation gradually shifted to land and agricultural products and the government became a collector of food as well as of manufactured goods and coined money. Private organizations were forced to transport such goods for the government.

GOVERNMENTAL CONTROL OF BUSINESS

Meanwhile the imperial government was forced more and more into business. It was necessary to regulate and maintain the industrial and transport service which provided military supplies for the armies and food, clothing, and other necessities for the city populace. When private enterprises in these lines broke down, they were taken over and operated by the government. Gradually transportation by land and sea, mining, and the handling of food and military supplies came under governmental control. Diocletian went so far as to fix maximum prices for foodstuffs, military supplies, and for wages in certain industries.

In general these policies provided a dependable income for the army, the governmental officials, and the city mobs, but they accentuated the already sad plight of private business. The problem was one that most governments have found insoluble: to provide revenue for an increasingly expensive administration in a period of declining business prosperity. The emperors and their assistants secured a steady income with which to carry on the government, but in so doing they dried up the sources of their income. As commercial and industrial revenues dwindled, heavier pressure was applied to the taxpayers, and they became the slaves of a gigantic machine which made them less and less prosperous and ambitious. Commerce, industry, and city life carried on, but with decreasing returns for all concerned except the government.

TAXES AND AGRICULTURE

In agriculture, likewise, the imperial government showed more resourcefulness as a revenue seeker than as a protector of the prosperity of the citizenry. The empire possessed great agricultural resources upon which there had been levied a general land tax, payable in agricultural produce. As city revenues declined, this became the mainstay of the imperial treasury. Diocletian did away with Italy's exemption from the tax and changed the method of assessment. Henceforth the tax was applied universally throughout the empire in a more effective manner. It was levied by local units with payments adjusted according to productiveness so that each district paid in proportion to its ability. From time to time there were reassessments. Inasmuch as the tax was paid in produce, the government had an unfailing supply of agricultural products, such as grain, oil, and meat, with which to service the army, the civil service, and the masses in the great cities. This was all very well for governmental dependents: regardless of price fluctuations, their living was secure. But, as in the case of private business, the farmers suffered. The more agricultural products the government collected in taxes, the less market there was for such goods. With city life on the decline the market for agricultural produce was dwindling. As a result the average landholder produced less and less. Agriculture for profit tended to deteriorate into subsistence farming, and free agriculturalists were forced into tenancy. Unable to maintain their economic independence in the face of diminishing incomes and increasing taxation, many free farmers deliberately gave up their individual freedom and their property. It became customary for freemen to place themselves and their lands under the protection and control of a local nobleman. As tenant-clients they enjoyed the use of the land and security of life under a powerful protector.

The noble landowners prospered. Those who enjoyed the favor of the government were sometimes able to make considerable profit from the sale of military supplies. Their influence also secured for them exemption from certain taxes and immunity from the jurisdiction of local officials. Thus they, and their clients also to a certain degree, were comparatively prosperous.

While the government held them responsible for certain revenues and services, these might be lightened, if not entirely evaded, through the influence of powerful friends. The prominent landholder occupied a position of political, social, and economic independence that was far superior to that of the city dweller. A rural estate, or villa, could be made secure and self-sufficient, with adequate supplies of food and also of industrial products, manufactured by skilled artisans. Many a villa owner enjoyed all of the luxuries of city life without any of its disadvantages. Even the industrial and agricultural population, although subject to the will of their landlords, were likely to be happier and more comfortable than the majority of city folk. As the pressure of governmental exactions fell with increasing weight on the free peasants and less wealthy landowners, more and more of them abandoned their lands and freedom to become tenant-clients of villa owners. From the latter they received a measure of the security and protection that the imperial government failed to provide.

SERFDOM
As with the business classes in the cities, the government took drastic measures to keep its tax-producing citizens in the country. By means of the law of *origo,* tenants and even freeholders were forbidden to leave their farms: they must produce food in order that the responsible head of the village or villa might collect the all-important governmental revenues. One of the results of this situation was the development of serfdom. In times of unusual economic stress the poorer classes tended to desert their farms. However, since the government held the local officials and landlords responsible for all local taxes, it was impelled to assist them in keeping the soil populated. Therefore the law of *origo* was invoked to keep the peasants on their lands. In 332 Constantine issued an edict ordering that runaway farmers be restored to the domain on which they had been born, with payment of an indemnity to the landlord. Persistent runaways were to be "put in chains like slaves." While it was impossible to enforce such laws strictly, they nevertheless operated to bind a considerable portion of the rural population to the land.

Thus the fourth century saw the emergence of a semiservile system as a part of the emperors' efforts to stabilize rural society and enforce a rigid policy of land taxation. It should be noted, however, that the system worked both ways. The tenants might not run away; neither could they legally be evicted, nor could their rents be increased arbitrarily. Of course, powerful landlords could evade the law, and as time went on, they tended to become more and more independent. Many a great rural villa, far removed from the eye of the central government, became a miniature state in which the proprietor was a virtual king. His domain was economically self-sufficient, and he had armed retainers whom he might use to defend it from trespassers and even, perhaps, to defy the imperial officials. Thus, in many rural regions a semifeudal society began to emerge during the fourth and fifth centuries. This was particularly true of the West, where the imperial government was weak and life was predominantly agricultural. Everywhere the loss of independence of the average citizen was apparent. In the West he tended more often to become the subject of a local landlord. In the East he was likely to be subjected to the will of the imperial bureaucracy. The more efficient the landlords and the governmental officials, the more restricted were the liberties of the citizens.

SOCIAL AND
ECONOMIC
REGIMENTATION
So far as social conditions were concerned, the eventual outcome of the imperial policies was a gradual reconstruction of society in which economic and social as well as political affairs came under rigid governmental control. All classes became parts of an immense hierarchy of social castes, headed by an imperial bureaucracy whose major purpose was financial exploitation. Little by little the revenue policies of the empire transformed honored municipal officials into the bankrupt tax collectors of an insatiable treasury. Those rural nobles who were unable to evade or defy the regulations of the central government became the local agents of an oppressive bureaucracy. From the wealthiest courtier in Constantinople or Rome to the poorest provincial peasant, all citizens were servants of the state and under orders from its dictator, the emperor. The lives of merchants and artisans, as well as of soldiers and taxgatherers, were subject to the absolute control of a centralized bureaucracy. Even the unborn were caught in the toils of this great machine. The sons of curials, of soldiers, of commercial and industrial workers, of farmers, and of other citizens were compelled by law to follow in their fathers' professions. Thus free competitive business degenerated into forced labor, and the mass of the citizenry became little more than cogs in a vast governmental machine chiefly concerned with tax collecting.

We must not, however, imagine that the majority of citizens felt that the imperial government was merely a harsh taskmaster. In its struggle for existence the empire was following a policy similar to that of certain rigidly organized states of our own day. The individual citizen and his private welfare were subordinated to the needs of the state. It was considered necessary for every citizen to do his part without question in order that the empire might carry on. Had it not been for the governmental regimentation of society in the late third and early fourth century, conditions might have been much worse. As it was, civilized institutions continued, and in some regions they flourished. But the foundations shifted and many of them crumbled. As the prosperity of the middle class of city dwellers was sacrificed to political necessities, civilization lost its flexibility and vitality. In the cities, economic and social ambition gave way to passive indifference. Few people outside the official bureaucracy and the privileged senatorial aristocracy enjoyed security and prosperity. Members of these classes lived on rural estates or in administrative centers (such as Constantinople) where there was wealth and luxury. Their clients and servants were often well cared for. Even the proletariat in a provincial or imperial metropolis could count on obtaining the means for subsistence from the governmental dole. While the great cities, particularly in the East, enjoyed a superficial prosperity, on the whole the economic and social life of the provinces reverted steadily to the primitive and localized existence that characterized the early Middle Ages.

There was little incentive for the average citizen to produce a surplus of goods: the taxgatherers would seize it. Mere subsistence was simpler. It was in these centuries of declining prosperity that many city folk, finding it impossible to attain success in material affairs, turned to religion. The people of the lower classes, in particular, found comfort and inspiration in Christianity. Occasionally there were outbursts of rebellious discontent. In the outlying provinces the inhabitants were sometimes impelled to set up independent governments or to welcome the invading barbarians as liberators from bondage to an oppressive central government. It is apparent that imperial civilization was losing its inner vitality even as it assumed a more despotic and rigidly centralized form of organization. Underneath the shell of empire there was a steady increase in independent local units of government, under the control of a rural aristocracy, and supported by a villa system of agriculture.

II

THE DISINTEGRATION OF THE EMPIRE

IN spite of economic decline and social stratification, the imperial government carried on for a while without serious disasters. The administrative machinery set up by Diocletian and Constantine weathered occasional invasions and civil wars with little difficulty. As long as Constantine lived (until 337) the empire was governed as a unit, and the frontiers were secure. There were few internal disorders, and the centralization of the imperial administration progressed along the lines laid down by Diocletian. Difficulties developed later in the century, but the centralized governmental system survived every crisis.

After Constantine's death a three-cornered rivalry ensued between his sons, Constantine II, Constans, and Constantius. His brothers having died, from 350 to 361 Constantius was sole emperor. His rule was weak and tyrannical, and he was in constant fear of rivals. He sent his young nephew, Julian, to the Rhine frontier, where the barbarians were threatening the Gallic provinces. Here Julian made an enviable reputation for himself by driving the invaders out of Gaul and making secure the Rhine frontier. His exploits against the Alamannians read like those of Julius Caesar in this same region four centuries earlier. When Constantius suddenly recalled a portion of the popular young general's army, his disappointed legions promptly proclaimed him emperor. As he was marching eastward to win the throne, Constantius died, leaving him undisputed emperor. For three busy years (361-363), he worked hard to restore governmental efficiency by reforming the tax system and eliminating corruption. Meanwhile he tried in vain to crush Christianity.[1] A defensive war against the Persians also took a great deal of his attention, and he was mortally wounded while campaigning along the Euphrates.

Julian's successor ruled for one year, after which the empire once more fell into its two natural divisions, East and West. While Valentinian I (364-375) administered the affairs of the West, Valens (364-

[1] See below, p. 70.

378) struggled with the difficult problems of the East. There were corrupt and inefficient officials to control; economic crises threatened; there were religious quarrels between the various Christian sects; and, finally, troublesome barbarian tribes threatened the frontiers. The busy career of a fourth-century emperor is well illustrated by the events amid which Valens met his death. While in Syria planning the reconstruction of cities destroyed by an earthquake, he was summoned posthaste back to the capital to meet a serious military crisis. The Visigoths, admitted to the empire as refugees from the savage Huns, had revolted; Valens fell at Adrianople (378) in one of the most disastrous defeat ever suffered by Roman arms.[2] Still the empire survived.

THE EMPIRE DRIFTS APART
Order was restored by Theodosius (379-395), another general who—like Constantine and Julian—had won his spurs in the West. For about three years after the death of the Western emperor, Valentinian II, Theodosius was sole emperor—the last to rule over the entire empire. Henceforth, although still one empire in theory, the East and West were separately administered and steadily drew apart. Thus Diocletian's plan of permanent Eastern and Western divisions of the imperial administration, though overthrown by Constantine, proved to be the only possible method of ruling the empire. Meanwhile, victorious Christianity was made the state religion (381).[3] Theodosius' sons, Honorius (395-423) in the West and Arcadius (395-408) in the East, proved to be weaklings, and the government fell more and more into the hands of their councilors. In the East, however, the government was strengthened internally and was able to weather a storm of barbarian invasion and to hold in check the rival sects of Christians. Nothing perhaps constitutes such a lasting tribute to the effectiveness of the work of Diocletian, Constantine, Julian, and Theodosius as the success with which the East carried on, even though elsewhere the empire was in process of disruption.

DISINTEGRATION OF THE WESTERN EMPIRE
In the West, Honorius and his successors were as unsuccessful as their Eastern contemporaries were successful. Honorius showed neither ability nor good intentions. He turned over the military defense of the realm to a German general, Stilicho by name, and although Stilicho was successful in holding off the Visigothic invaders,[4] ordered his

---

[2] See below, Chapter V, concerning the Germanic invasions.
[3] See below, Chapter III, concerning the rise of Christianity.
[4] See below, Chapter V, for a detailed account of the Visigoths.

assassination because of the jealousy of the anti-German element at
court. When Alaric's Visigoths overran Italy, Honorius refused to
come to terms until too late. His successor was little better: he assassinated his best general and administrator, Aetius, shortly after the
latter had checked the Huns at Chalons.[5] He was himself assassinated
by an ambitious senator, who in turn was overthrown by another
usurper.

It is apparent that the imperial administration in the West was
rapidly weakening, even inviting invasion by striking down its own
best defenders. All the while, the barbarian Germans were waxing
stronger and stronger. Some of them were the mainstay of Rome's
armies; others were the invaders of her fairest provinces. Their conquests will be considered in detail in a later section. Meanwhile the
empire drifted from bad to worse.

During the next twenty years (455-476) the imperial office received the disrespectful treatment which its record of incompetence
merited. The so-called emperors of this period were mere puppets in
the hands of Germanic generals and soldiery. One sturdy German
(Ricimer) set up and overthrew half a dozen emperors between the
years 455 and 472. The next power behind the throne was a former
secretary of Attila named Orestes. Having married a wealthy Roman
lady he finally ventured to raise their son Romulus to the imperial
throne. A year later, when Orestes refused the demand of the Germanic soldiery for Italian lands, he was killed. His place was taken by
Odoacer who allowed the "Little Emperor Romulus" (Romulus Augustulus) to retire unharmed, in 476, to a villa. No victorious Roman could have been more liberal to a defeated emperor. Odoacer
also respected the imperial office. Unwilling or afraid to take it for
himself, he had the senate transmit to the emperor at Constantinople
the request that he be appointed to rule Italy. Thus the "barbarians"
ended the imperial farce and put an end to the line of puppet emperors in the West.[6]

THE "FALL OF ROME"   It is apparent to the student who has followed the
fortunes of Rome during the first five centuries of
the Christian era that the "Fall of Rome" in 476 was
merely "the mythical fall of a hypothetical empire." The spectacular

---

    [5] See below, Chapter V, for a detailed account of the Huns.
    [6] See below, Chapter VI, for an account of the role of the Germans during this
period.

events of that year affected only a small section of the Western division, and only in a superficial way. The great majority of the people of the Mediterranean area were unaware that anything important had happened, and their lives were in no sense affected. The city of Rome, the Western provinces, the eastern section of the empire, and imperial civilization continued after 476 and with no break in continuity.

As a matter of fact, most of the changes which people still refer to as the Fall of Rome had taken place gradually during the preceding centuries. The early empire, established by Augustus, was almost completely destroyed by the civil wars of the third century, to be succeeded by the new imperial system of Aurelian, Diocletian, and Constantine. This new empire had a twofold history. In the East, in spite of obvious defects and unsolved economic problems, it achieved noteworthy successes. The Eastern emperors "muddled through" the political, military, and economic crises of the fourth and fifth centuries, and maintained imperial institutions without serious interruptions. In fact, as time went on, the Eastern Empire grew stronger and more influential. From Zeno (475-491) to the great sixth-century emperor, Justinian (527-565), Constantinople became, even more than before, the political, economic, and cultural center of the civilized Mediterranean world. In a later chapter we shall trace the history of this brilliant East-Roman, or Byzantine, civilization.[7]

LOCALISM IN THE WEST   Meanwhile, Roman imperial government in the West had been gradually falling to pieces. Ever since the third century, the Western provinces had experienced a regime of disorder, civil war, and disunity that contrasts with the more centralized and smooth-working government of the East. It was in the West that Diocletian's system of divided administration and automatic imperial succession first gave way to the violence of rival claimants. It was in the West that the legions continued to set up their generals as emperors. Here also the barbaric invaders found it easy to penetrate the frontiers and conquer the outlying provinces.

The reason for the rapid disintegration of the West is twofold. In the first place, imperial administration and defense were less efficient than in the East. Of greater importance was the fact that the West had fewer natural bonds of unity. The West was predominantly agricultural in its economy. Commercial activities were restricted in scope and the great industrial cities quickly gave way to small towns, self-

[7] Chapter VII.

supporting rural estates, and subsistence farming. From the third century onward, the tide of human existence flowed in the general direction of a decentralized rural economy. Even all-powerful emperors such as Constantine were unable to reverse these tendencies. After the removal of the imperial capital to Constantinople, Italy and the other regions of the West became more and more provincial.

Government followed the same trend of decentralization as it was forced to adapt itself to the developments in economic and social life. Imperial administration became more and more localized. As the imperial systems of communication deteriorated, local officials far removed from Rome looked more and more to their own regional interests. The frontier legions, recruited chiefly from the near-by provinces, tended to disregard their allegiance to the emperor and to follow local leaders. A central government that paid little attention to the needs of its distant subjects could not hope to retain their fidelity.

From the imperial point of view such developments were disastrous. But, as far as the inhabitants of the West were concerned, localized control was more satisfactory than a rigidly centralized but inefficient Roman imperialism. The underlying forces of social and economic decentralization paved the way for the rapid disintegration of the Western Empire. The weak central government of Constantine's successors was incapable of checking the development of localism in the West. In fact, it encouraged such tendencies by its neglect of the outlying regions. Long before the year 476 the inhabitants of the Western provinces found that they were dependent on their own resources. In some cases they came under the control of local landlords, provincial generals, or even of barbarian chieftains. Usually this was better than the arbitrary authority of a decadent imperial administration. By 476 the emperors of the West had forfeited all rights of government in Britain, Gaul, Spain, and northern Africa. Even in Italy they proved their incapacity to rule. The West had become a group of regional units, as disorganized and independent as in the early centuries before Rome had forcibly annexed them to her world empire.

ROMAN CULTURE[8]

THE GOLDEN
AGE OF LITERA-
TURE
The cultural life of the empire, like its governmental and economic-social institutions, reached a high peak of achievement during the first and second centuries. Then, after suffering an apparent eclipse during the third century, it experienced a temporary revival during the fourth. In general, from the third century on, Roman culture was transformed and merged with Christian culture. These two formed the basic element in the culture of the Middle Ages.

The literature, learning, and arts of the early empire, and particularly of the Age of Augustus (31 B.C. to 14 A.D.), were glorified by the works of some of the greatest geniuses ever known to Roman civilization. During this period the capital city served as a magnet that drew literary talent from other centers. The wealth and unlimited opportunities that Rome provided attracted outstanding people from outlying parts of Italy and, later, from more distant provinces. Amid the cosmopolitan atmosphere of wealth, luxury, ambition, and Hellenic intellectualism that pervaded the Eternal City many and varied works of great literary merit were created. Before the Augustan Age republican Rome had produced the lyric poetry of Catullus, the orations and philosophical essays of Cicero, the scientific-philosophical treatise of Lucretius, Varro's encyclopedias [9] and the commentaries of Julius Caesar. Of this group of writers, Cicero exercised an abiding influence over men of intellectual interests, from his own days throughout the Middle Ages, and even to modern times. But this was only a foretaste of the achievements of the period of Augustus. Thanks to the generous patronage of the government and of the many wealthy aristocrats who followed Augustus' example, writers and artists flourished in Rome as never before. Three of them were superlative poets. Ovid, one of the gay and socially prominent young men of the capital, wrote of love, of Roman mythology, and of the great Roman festivals. His *Art of Love* and *Remedy of Love* were known and cited by many of the clerical scholars of the Middle Ages. Horace, a poor boy from southern Italy who was befriended by the wealthy

---

[8] We shall use the term culture, throughout this section and the entire volume, to denote the intellectual and artistic aspects of civilization, in distinction from the political and economic-social aspects. Roman religion, which has a definite relationship with culture, will be treated in connection with the backgrounds of Christianity (Chapter III).

[9] We shall consider, later in this section, Varro's influence on medieval education.

Maecenas, composed short masterpieces of poetry, ranging from verses concerning a jug of mellow wine to stately odes commemorating the patriotic achievements of Augustus. Greatest of all the poets was the immortal Vergil, another of Maecenas' protégés. He depicted Italian rural life in his shorter poems and in the *Aeneid* glorified Rome's early history by relating the wanderings of Aeneas and the legendary beginnings of Rome. Throughout medieval times Vergil's poems and Cicero's prose works were highly prized as supreme examples of secular literature. The Augustan Age also produced eminent writers of prose, second only to Cicero in their influence on later writers. Among the most outstanding were Livy, the greatest of Roman historians, and Vitruvius and Celsus, compilers of encyclopedic works on agriculture, architecture, medicine, and other scholarly subjects. Not only literature but all aspects of civilized life attained such heights of grandeur during this period that contemporaries—and modern commentators after them—have called it the "Golden Age."

THE SILVER AGE   After the Augustan Age the provincial cities began to share more fully in the prosperity and culture of the empire. At Rome the period comprising the greater part of the first and second centuries is marked by the wider diffusion of cultural life rather than the higher development of genius. In the cities of Gaul, Spain, Asia Minor, Egypt, and other provinces, schools, writers, and artists flourished. In general, both at Rome and elsewhere, quantity seemed to be more sought after than quality, and the title "Silver Age" has been given to this period to distinguish it from the more brilliant "Golden Age."

The decline in literary ability at the imperial court is apparent when one calls the roll of the writers of the Silver Age. There were men such as Pliny the Elder, scientist and encyclopedist, Quintilian, the educator-rhetorician, Martial and Juvenal, composers of witty epigrams and satires, Suetonius, the biographer of the emperors, and Tacitus, the last great Roman historian. A comparison of these names with those of the Augustan Age reveals a marked decline of literary genius, particularly in poetry. To be sure, Martial has been called "the world's greatest epigrammatist," and his brilliant bits of sparkling verse give us glimpses of Rome's life that are not only fascinatingly human but also of great value for an understanding of the age in which Rome began to show the first signs of decline. But aside from Martial, there is no poet of this period who can compare with the great Augustan trio—Vergil, Horace, and Ovid. In learned writings the decline is not so apparent. Tacitus, for example, is ranked with Livy as one of Rome's greatest historians. There were scientific writings in Greek by Easterners such as the astronomer Ptolemy and the physician Galen. They contained original contributions to human knowledge as well as excellent summaries of earlier scientific ideas. Works of this sort, in Latin translations, were popular in the West not only during imperial times, but throughout the Middle Ages.

THE DECLINE
IN LITERARY
GENIUS
In general, however, a spirit of cynicism, pessimism, and superficiality began to take possession of Latin literature. There was an increasing emphasis on moral philosophy. As thinkers found it unsafe to express themselves freely on governmental policies, they became introspective. Some exercised their talents in scholarly researches or literary studies that had little bearing on public affairs and therefore were safe from governmental interference. Many writers sought merely to imitate the style of Cicero, Vergil, or Horace. Others, such as the biographer Suetonius, and the satirist Juvenal, condemned the failings of their own generation and looked back with hopeless longing to the days before Rome had become corrupt and decadent. Such ideas became increasingly prominent in the second century. In the provinces, cultural life continued to flourish in a small way, but as local centers of culture arose fewer writers and artists gravitated to the imperial capital. This was in keeping with the general tendencies in economic and social life. The far-reaching effects of economic prosperity in the provinces enabled more people in more cities to enjoy the benefits of civilization. Imperial culture became more provincial and less Roman.

Under such conditions literature and art became more popular—and also less inspired—than they had been in the Golden Age. Fewer men of surpassing genius appeared. In literature, mere compiling from earlier works, or imitations of the stylistic effects of the past, became more common. Original scholarship found little encouragement. For serious information, even the educated classes resorted to condensed handbooks. Most people preferred light entertaining reading such as the *Satyricon* of Petronius and the *Golden Ass* of Apuleius. A world which had become accustomed to prosperity and the luxuries of city life took less and less interest in original research and serious studies. To the general picture of decline we must make one marked exception: the book of philosophical thoughts and proverbs, called *Meditations* or *Thoughts,* written by Emperor Marcus Aurelius, whose influence on later ages is comparable to that of Cicero. Alfred the Great considered the *Meditations* worthy to be translated into Anglo-Saxon, the language of the people. It should be noted, however, that the *Meditations* were Hellenistic, rather than Roman, in spirit, and were written in Greek.

THE ARTS OF THE GOLDEN AGE

Imperial art, like literature, had its greatest achievements in the first century. The artistic accomplishments of the Golden Age are often illustrated by Augustus' own words to the effect that he found Rome a city of brick and left it marble. Although this is an exaggeration, it does vividly indicate the transformation of the imperial capital that took place during his generation and the primary position which architecture held among the arts in Rome. The Roman engineers of late republican times had proved their ability in the building of roads, aqueducts, bridges, harbors, and in city planning.

ARCHITECTURE

During the Age of Augustus the same practical types of construction were carried to still greater heights of achievement. One of Augustus' advisors, Agrippa, directed the work on innumerable public edifices. In the great civic center of Rome —the republican Forum—new buildings were erected, among them the Forum of Augustus, comprising arcades where businessmen and politicians met, law courts, and a splendid rectangular temple built in the traditional pillared style of the Greek Parthenon. Elsewhere in the capital city temples were built or restored, most of them in this same Greek style. During the Augustan Age, temples and religious observances were considered important: they gave dignity and stability to the new imperial regime.

For the amusement of the populace there were even more imposing edifices: theaters, the great amphitheater, public baths, and the immense Circus Maximus which could accommodate more than a hundred thousand sports enthusiasts. However much Augustus might lavish funds on public buildings which served the needs of the populace and helped to impress upon the world the greatness of the empire, his own private wants were few. On the Palatine Hill, overlooking the Forum, a rather simple residence was built for the emperor. It was the nobles and the later emperors who built luxurious palaces with splendid courtyards, gardens, and spectacular decorative effects.

SCULPTURE

The decorative arts of the Augustan Age were not as splendid or original as the architecture. As formerly, much statuary was imported from the Hellenistic East. The Romans of this period sent to the older regions of the East for works of sculpture in much the same manner in which wealthy Americans of the nineteenth century imported *objêts d'art* from Italy for the adornment of their palatial residences and gardens. It also became the fashion for Roman sculptors to make copies of famous Greek statues.

There was, however, something of sculptural originality in the Roman portrait statues and busts. During the Golden Age, and for some time afterwards, statues of statesmen, generals, emperors, and wealthy citizens were done in a detailed and naturalistic style that approximates the realism of individual portraiture. Excellent examples of this type of sculpture are to be found in the numerous statues of Augustus. The best known of them represents him clad in full armor and toga, in the act of addressing his soldiers, with arm outstretched in a characteristic Roman gesture of authority.

Roman artists, or sculptors imported from the East, also did a good deal of "flat sculpture," called *relief*. Outstanding in this field was the great outdoor "Altar of Peace," erected at Rome in commemoration of the end of the civil wars. It was decorated with long sculptured reliefs portraying a procession including members of Augustus' family, officials, priests, and citizens coming to pay homage to the gods who had brought peace to the empire. No finer work of the sculptor's art was produced in Roman times.

THE SILVER AGE   Strange to say, the Silver Age was much more splendid and luxurious than the Golden Age in its artistic achievements. At Rome, Augustus' successors erected the Colosseum, the imposing ruins of which still astonish tourists. Nero built for himself a "Golden Palace," with wondrous conveniences and luxuries, including a revolving banquet hall. At Tivoli, in a marvelous natural setting, Emperor Hadrian laid out a villa of splendid proportions and had it decorated with all the artistic refinements that could be furnished by Hellenistic artists. Not only at Rome, but in many a provincial city, there were baths, forums, theaters, arenas, temples, and other public buildings. To commemorate their victories over frontier tribes, emperors such as Titus, Trajan, and Marcus Aurelius set up triumphal arches or columns of victory on which were sculptured realistic scenes of battle and processions of soldiers and captives. To the present day, victorious nations glorify their wars by erecting triumphal columns and arches modeled after those of imperial Rome.

In constructing private buildings, also, there was increased artistic activity. The ruins of the palaces at Pompeii, with their open courts, statuesque fountains, mosaic floors, and mural decorations reveal some-

thing of the artistic ability that was lavished upon the homes of
wealthy Romans in prosperous provincial cities. The walls of banquet
halls were often decorated with dainty flower designs and Greek
mythological scenes. Others were done with remarkably realistic effects: an entire wall might be painted to represent an outdoor scene
so natural that the diners seemed to be looking out over a field or a
wooded landscape. There were also obscene murals and carvings which
indicate a lower level of taste and morals.

The dominant impression derived from a survey of imperial art
in the first and second centuries is the practical-mindedness of the
Romans. Their architects used economical but substantial materials:
brick, native volcanic or lime stone, and concrete. These they covered
with a surface veneer of stucco or marble. Their public works were
carefully planned. Not only at Rome, but in most provincial cities,
the streets were laid out in straight lines, intersecting at right angles
and concentrating in a civic center usually called the forum. In addition to the palaces and estates of the wealthy, there were in the larger
cities immense apartment houses for the poorer classes. Many dwellings had glass windows, central heating (by means of hot-air con-
duits), and lead or tile plumbing for drainage and running water.
The numerous aqueducts of the city of Rome provided her population
with a generous supply of cool fresh water from the mountains. Portions of the arched supports of one of these aqueducts can still be
seen on the plain west of the city. Many of the provincial centers had
systems of water supply that compare favorably with those of modern
European cities.

Although most of Rome's arts were borrowed from other peoples,
in architecture and engineering she made remarkable improvements.
Many structural features acquired from earlier civilizations were perfected and handed on to later generations to become important influences in medieval and modern architecture. For example, the
Romans used the arch—an Eastern invention—with such success that
it replaced the Greek lintel and pillar as the fundamental element in
construction. This new principle, which involved the curved rather
than the straight line, led to three remarkable developments in stone
ceilings: the barrel vault, the groined vault, and the dome. The semi-
cylindrical barrel vault, borrowed from the Etruscans, was applied
to the problem of roofing buildings with stone instead of wood (a
great advantage from the standpoint of fire hazard). By the end of the

THE COLOSSEUM, INTERIOR (I C)

Both Courtesy of the University Prints

THE ARCH OF CONSTANTINE (IV C)

ROMAN ARCHITECTURE

(See pp. 42 f.)

THE GOOD SHEPHERD AND OTHER CHRISTIAN SYMBOLS

Both Courtesy of the University Prints

VINTAGE SCENE AND OTHER CLASSICAL THEMES

EARLY CHRISTIAN MURALS

(From the Catacombs)

(See p. 328.)

first century, Roman architects had learned how to build tremendous vaulted ceilings of stone or concrete over spaces a hundred feet or more in width.[10] For intersecting vaults, they developed the groined vault, a feature that eventually led to the Romanesque and Gothic ribbed vaulting of the medieval cathedrals.[11] More spectacular than the vault was the dome, a half-sphere of concrete built over a circular or square space. The Pantheon, a second-century example of this type of building, is still standing in Rome. It is an excellent illustration of the sturdy lasting qualities of Roman architecture. The Roman dome, with certain modifications that were made during the Middle Ages,[12] has become one of the most popular types of construction in modern public buildings.

The Romans were not nearly so successful in the art of decoration. Their engineers could erect immense and substantial structures, but they devised no better style of decoration than an overlay of Greek pillars and slabs of marble. The result was often a confusing combination of Roman arches, Corinthian pillars, and other bits of ornate foreign decoration. One is reminded of the manner in which modern American architects have built marvelous skyscrapers of structural steel and concrete, only to camouflage them with combinations of Greek pillars, Roman arches, or Gothic pinnacles.

Late Roman sculpture manifested little more originality. The portrait statues and busts showed a tendency to stiff, formal poses, copies of earlier styles, sometimes even to the facial expressions. For centuries emperors were represented in the famous Augustan pose: armor, toga, and outstretched arm. The second century produced one sculptural type that had marked originality, the equestrian statue, of which the best example is that of Emperor Marcus Aurelius. This form of statuary, the mounted general, was revived centuries later in Italy[13] to become an important influence in modern sculpture. Napoleon, Bismarck, Washington, Sherman, and Robert E. Lee are but a few of the military heroes whose figures, mounted on horseback, adorn public places in Europe and America.

[10] One of the best existing examples of vault-construction is the baths of Caracalla, at Rome, built in the third century. Sometimes, for greater security, architects covered a space with several *cross vaults,* instead of one longitudinal vault. The ruins of the fourth-century basilica of Maxentius (or Constantine) in Rome show the method of construction of such a structure.

[11] See below, Chapter XXXIV.

[12] See below, pp. 727 ff.

[13] See below, p. 731.

CULTURAL
DECLINE IN THE
THIRD CENTURY
Toward the end of the second century, Roman culture began to show a marked downward trend. In the period following the reign of Marcus Aurelius (d. 180), the civil wars and invasions, the destruction of the prosperity of many provincial cities, and the prevailing economic disorder were reflected in the decline of intellectual and artistic interests. When one recalls that the imperial court of this period was dominated by the armies made up largely of provincials from backward rural regions, it is easy to see why Roman civilization produced so little of merit. To be sure, there was architectural activity, including public works of a spectacular and grandiose character. At Rome the emperors, eager to impress the world with their power, built magnificent structures. Among the remains still to be seen are the triumphal arch of Septimius Severus and the immense public baths erected by Caracalla. In many of the provinces, also, there was noteworthy activity. One of the most imposing architectural works of Roman times, the temple of Jupiter-Baal at Baalbek in Syria, was completed during this period. In general, however, there was little that can compare with earlier productions.

From the West during this period there comes almost no classical literature that is worthy of mention. The only noteworthy historians of the third century (Dio Cassius and Herodian) and the founders of the Neoplatonic philosophical system (Plotinus and Porphyry) were Easterners. Their writings—in Greek—were products of Hellenistic rather than of Roman thought. The most popular Latin work of the century seems to have been Solinus' historical geography, which was little more than a reworking of the subject matter of the *Natural History* of Pliny. There is one bright spot in the prevailingly pessimistic picture—the jurists. Until the middle of the third century we have a line of great Roman jurists: Julian, Gaius, and Salvius Julianus in the second century; Ulpian, Papinian, and Paulus in the third. Thereafter little was done until the sixth century, when Tribonian and his assistants compiled a digest of juristic works for the Code of Emperor Justinian. There was, however, constant change in legal statutes, and in the fifth century Emperor Theodosius II brought forth a statutory code. In law, as in other aspects of intellectual life, the *late* empire saw little creative work except the compilation of earlier materials into more practical and usable form.

Many scholars see in the third century the death of ancient Roman culture. The truth seems to be that the political and economic anarchy of the century dealt such a blow to the flourishing city life of the empire that the downward trend, already in evidence, was rapidly accelerated. Later, when order was restored, it was accompanied by a rigidly despotic form of government that stifled independent effort in literature and the arts. Roman civilization never had the opportunity to recover. In the meantime other cultural forces were appearing. As pagan Roman culture declined, Christian and Germanic influences were able to expand within the empire relatively unchecked. The Germanic tribes that invaded the frontier provinces during the third century were uncivilized and made no constructive contribution at this time. The Christians, however, after two centuries of struggle for existence, had evolved a distinctive culture. In literature and in certain forms of church building and decoration, they displayed vigor and originality.[14] Writings in defense of Christianity, such as that of the converted Roman lawyer, Minucius Felix, late in the second century, and those by Tertullian and Cyprian of Carthage in the third, show that men of outstanding intellect were arising within the ranks of the Western Christians. The East produced even greater Christian thinkers, notably the Alexandrian philosopher, Origen.

THE FOURTH-CENTURY REVIV-AL OF ART
Toward the end of the third century, as we have already seen, emperors such as Diocletian succeeded in restoring order to the empire, and a semblance of prosperity to certain of the governmental centers of the Roman world. This was accompanied by a revival of cultural life which was most apparent in architecture. Diocletian repaired roads and bridges and provided for extensive public works. One of the most remarkable examples of the increased activity in building was Constantine's construction of a new imperial capital at Constantinople. This city, at the outlet of the Black Sea, soon became the chief center of the culture of the empire. Henceforth Rome, Italy, and the West played a minor role in all phases of imperial civilization.

Constantine, from the start, lavished upon his Eastern capital imposing works of architecture. Palaces and churches, temples and theaters richly decorated with sculptures and mosaics, rose like magic. From all parts of the empire, it was said, works of ancient art were carried to Constantinople to adorn the new imperial buildings. From the temple of Apollo at Delphi, for instance, was brought the famous bronze tripod which had been placed there eight centuries earlier as

14 See below, Chapters XIII-XVII.

a thank offering by the victorious Greeks, who had captured it from the invading Persians at the battle of Platea. This treasure of early art graced the Hippodrome (the race track) in Constantinople throughout the Middle Ages; and there it can still be seen.

Much of the art of the new city was ornate, splendid, and massive, rather than refined, and its best works of sculpture were pieces taken from structures of the Golden or Silver Age. Everywhere the new art of this age was characterized by size and a spectacular striving for effect. This is evident in both architecture and sculpture. The immense baths at Rome, the basilica of Constantine (or, more accurately, of Maxentius), and the Circus of Maxentius, to say nothing of innumerable temples, palaces, and arenas in the smaller cities, reflect the grandeur, if not the refinement, of late imperial architecture. Of the statues, reliefs, and sarcophagi (stone coffins) of this era, a modern writer remarked that by Constantine's day the sculptors of the earlier centuries had been replaced by mere "stone-cutters."

There were, however, certain arts that showed originality and refinement of technique. Beautifully carved ivories and gems, enamel work, mosaics, and all sorts of small *objêts d'art* were produced in considerable quantity. Nevertheless, in its general course, late Roman art seems to have turned from the aims and ideals of ancient art (which was distinctly plastic) and to have become formal and decorative. Not only in the new Eastern capital, moreover, but everywhere in the empire, Christian and Oriental influences were increasing.

REVIVED CLASSI-   In literature the recovery that came with Diocletian
CAL LITERATURE   and Constantine was so marked that the fourth century has been called "the Indian summer" of Roman literature. Although most of the intellectual leaders of this period show the influence of Christianity, many of them were so predominantly classical in spirit that their best works could pass for writings of the Golden or Silver Age.

Among those who illustrate the purely classical literature of this century is Claudian a young Easterner who, in the year 400, was living and writing at the court of the Western emperor, Honorius. Like Vergil, Claudian lauded in stately classical verse the glories of Eternal Rome, of her consuls and of her victorious generals. Like the poets of the Golden and Silver ages, he wrote on mythological subjects: "The Rape of Proserpina" is one of his best-known works. He also wrote informally amusing verse on everyday subjects such as "French

Mules," "The Lobster," "The Nile," "The Magnet," and "The Old Man of Verona" who never left his home town.[15]

Another who exemplifies the continuance of Roman literary ideals is Ausonius (d. 393). Born and educated in the university town of Bordeaux in Gaul, he became professor of rhetoric there, and for a time tutored the emperor's son at Rome. Besides teaching rhetoric and writing scholarly works, Ausonius composed lyric poems that have a remarkably human appeal. Years after the death of his beloved young wife, he paid her a beautiful tribute in verse. In a lighter moment he wrote a ditty concerning Vergil's unhappy heroine:

> Poor Dido found but little rest,
> By neither of her spouses blest;
> She flies, because the first is dead,
> And dies, because the second fled.

Another aspect of the poet is revealed in his descriptions of roses, or of the beauties of nature along the Moselle River, its ridges "crowned with the vine's odoriferous clusters," and its meadows "clothed by the grass with an emerald verdure."

There are modern critics who see in such nature poetry a new emotional expressiveness that was destined to "fill the old bottles" of classical poetry with a more vital spirit. Often the poets of the fourth century displayed a humanism, romanticism, and an appreciation of the beauties of nature that is perhaps more modern than classical or medieval in spirit. To one of them is attributed a "Woodland Scene," a poem in which classical allusions are mingled with "brooklets flowing over pebbles," "flowers bright," "verdant laurel trees," and other such references to the beauties of nature. The same poet is thought by some to have written the famous "Vigil of Venus," with its recurring refrain:

> Knowest thou not love's joy and sorrow?
> Thou shalt learn of love tomorrow.

The titles themselves of other works from this period suggest the extent of this romantic element. There is "Cupid Crucified," "Invitation to the Dance," "Prayer to Venus," "Painted Passion," and "The Eunuch's Delight." These poems have an "ecstasy of emotion" that was new in classical literature. On a more plebeian level of popularity

---

[15] Excerpts from the writings of Claudian and the other writers mentioned in this section can be found in the histories and anthologies of Roman literature given in the bibliography. The quotations given below are from Showerman's anthology.

were the boating songs, barracks ballads, peasant poems, and other forms of folk song. But it is evident that the poetry which flourished in the fourth century, in spite of its vigorous expressiveness and human interest, was not the poetry of great genius. The muse of the Golden Age seems to have descended to the level of mediocrity and to the tastes of the common man.

DEVELOPMENTS IN EDUCATION Turning from poetry to more scholarly pursuits we find similar tendencies. Late in the fourth century, an old soldier named Ammianus Marcellinus wrote a history of his day. It was not a literary masterpiece, but modern scholars have high respect for the author's simple style and straightforward dependable narrative of the military and political events of the century. There is also ample evidence of a revived interest in classical learning. Public schools and colleges flourished throughout the West. Excellent educational institutions existed in Gaul at such cities as Bordeaux, Autun, Lyons, and Treves, as well as in Spain, Northern Africa, and at Rome. On the other hand, it was increasingly difficult to maintain high standards of scholarship. For instance, an imperial edict ordered that "a teacher of Greek be secured for the city of Treves, *if a worthy one can be found.*" Apparently, even in a Western provincial center, although there were students who were eager to study that "dead language," trained linguists were hard to find.

At this time the classical educational system was still in force, operating with more or less effectiveness along the lines that had prevailed for centuries. The average youth from the better-class family, after being tutored at home, attended a grammar school, which resembled a modern "prep" or high school. Here he studied Greek and Roman literature. In this process he learned a smattering of grammar, logic, rhetoric, arithmetic, geometry, astronomy, music, and history. Then he went to a more advanced school of rhetoric, for special training in the speaking and writing of Latin. By such means the young aristocrat was prepared for a life of refined leisure or for a public career in the governmental service. A few students specialized in oratory, medicine, law, philosophy, or some other learned profession. In the higher institutions of learning, instruction was carried on chiefly by lectures, the professor reading and commenting on some classical work. As in the succeeding medieval centuries, all books were handwritten (*manu-script*); therefore they were so rare and expensive that few people owned copies. But there were public libraries (the city of Rome had twenty-eight in the fourth century); consequently learning was available to those of the upper and middle classes who desired it. There was, of course, no free public education for the masses. The books, like the subject matter of the courses, were largely classical. Yet there was an increasing tendency to rely, not on the original works of great Roman writers, but on brief summaries or condensations comparable to the textbooks of modern times.

TEXTBOOKS:
VARRO
The fourth-century student still depended on classical handbooks such as the *Disciplines* of Varro, a Roman compiler of the Golden Age. Following the general method of Aristotle, Cicero, and other ancient men of learning, Varro had organized all usable knowledge into nine subjects; three of them were literary (grammar, rhetoric, and logic); three were mathematical (arithmetic, geometry, and astronomy); and three were specialized studies (music, medicine, and architecture). In general, this ancient Roman program of education continued throughout the Middle Ages with little fundamental change. Medicine and architecture dropped out of the regular curriculum, leaving seven major subjects. By the time of Charles the Great (the ninth century), these seven had fallen into two groups; (1) three literary subjects (grammar, rhetoric, and logic) which were called the "triple way" (*tri-vium*); and (2) four mathematical subjects (arithmetic, geometry, astronomy, and music),[16] which were called the "quadruple way" (*quadri-vium*). In actual practice these courses involved much more than the titles suggest; in the literary subjects, for example, the students read and discussed works of history, general literature, mythology, government, philosophy, and religion. On the other hand, they also involved much less than the titles suggest, especially the subjects of the *quadrivium*. A fourth-century course in astronomy taught little mathematics and comprised more mythology and mysticism than science.

From Cicero's day on, these subjects had been considered the best training for a free gentleman (*liberus homo*); therefore they came to be called the "liberal arts." In the fourth century they were still the major educational prerequisite for either a professional or nonprofessional career. Their importance and popularity are shown by the large output of textbooks. One of the most influential was that written in the fifth century by Martianus Capella entitled *The Marriage of Philology and Mercury*. Notwithstanding its romantic title, this volume was a handbook of information on the seven liberal arts. Throughout the

16 The study of music in ancient and medieval times emphasized the philosophical and physical aspects; it involved much more of mathematics than it does in our day.

entire work academic subject matter was presented (in both prose and poetry) on a framework of allegorical fantasy concerning the mythological marriage of the god, Mercury. Seven slave girls, given by the bridegroom to his bride as wedding presents, personify the seven liberal arts; each in turn, as she is presented to her mistress, relates the details of the subject which she represents. The book was designed to allow the student to imbibe learning without effort as a part of an interesting story. It was so successful that it was used throughout the Middle Ages. In a later section we shall consider the more serious fashion in which classical scholars such as Boethius and Christian writers such as Cassiodorus, Isidore of Seville, and Bede presented the subject matter of the liberal arts to medieval students. It will suffice for the present to say that they helped to perpetuate the seven liberal arts as the fundamental basis of both secular and religious education throughout the Middle Ages.

These subjects prevailed in Western schools well into modern times, and in a modified form they still exert a strong influence on college curricula in the United States. Today the liberal arts (expanded to include the physical and social sciences and modern foreign languages) are generally accepted as the highest type of educational training, and a necessary foundation for specialized professions such as law, medicine, teaching, and the ministry.

Another of Varro's compilations, an encyclopedia of *Antiquities Human and Divine,* also exerted a great influence on medieval education. Like the liberal arts, this twofold division of knowledge (human and divine) was taken over by late Roman and medieval educators. It appears constantly in the writings of Christian scholars such as Augustine and Cassiodorus. There were also other classical handbooks, more specialized than Varro's, that were more common during the fourth and succeeding centuries. The *Natural History* of Pliny, an immense collection of fact (and fancy) concerning man, animals, plants, minerals, and so on, was so popular during late Roman times that in the third century it was used by Solinus as the basis for a condensed "book of facts" entitled *Wonders of the World.*

In the literary realm, there was a first-century work by Verrius Flaccus *On the Significance of Words.* This had a handy alphabetical arrangement, and contained such a mass of general information that it was abridged for popular use by a fourth-century compiler, Festus. Four centuries later, Paul the Deacon made a condensed version of Festus's condensed version. By such processes, which were becoming more and more prevalent, the original subject matter of classical writings tended to be reduced to the vanishing point, and, in the process of successive condensings, the facts were often twisted beyond recognition. Another popular type of textbook was the glossary, or dictionary, an alphabetical handbook of definitions and short comments on the meanings of words.

In general the learning of these centuries was derived from brief handbooks of condensed classical knowledge. Some few literary scholars wrote dull and learned commentaries on the works of the ancient writers, but there was a much greater demand for brief textbooks on grammar, rhetoric, and the other liberal arts. Donatus, a popular teacher at Rome in the fourth century, wrote a long and also a short textbook of grammar. His short grammar (*Ars Minor*), dealing with the parts of speech in simple question and answer form, was widely used by children and adults from his day until the sixteenth century. It gave rise to innumerable commentaries and collections of illustrative excerpts. Priscian, a late fifth-century scholar, wrote a much more detailed grammar. Because of its generous supply of illustrative quotations from both Greek and Latin writers, it provided a mine of classical information for those whose access to the originals was limited and, in fact, served as a handbook of classical quotations for students and teachers throughout the Middle Ages.

THE DECLINE OF CLASSICAL CULTURE — Our survey of Roman culture indicates the slow but sure decline of earlier classical standards. The underlying reason for this trend seems to be the fact that the old Roman cultural ideals were outworn, impractical, and unfitted for the new age. Classical education, literature, and learning were suited to a leisure class of prosperous city people. The mark of an educated Roman gentleman was a knowledge of the ancient classics, an appreciation of Greek art, and the ability to speak and write in a refined manner which impresses modern people as exceedingly affected. Polished style was preferred to a clear and direct presentation of subject matter. As city life and the leisure class declined, such cultural accomplishments became less and less important. To the average Westerner of the later centuries a knowledge of Greek and Roman classical literature and rhetoric was no more important than a knowledge of Latin and other strictly cultural subjects is to a modern laboring man. Therefore the classics languished and even educated people demanded brief textbooks of secondhand information, condensed in form and written down to a lower mental level.

Ancient classical art, education, learning, and literature were no longer suited to the existing conditions of life. Therefore they declined in popularity and were constantly modified to meet changing conditions.

The classical culture that continued to exist was of necessity adapted to the less sophisticated mentality of a more religious and rural age. From the standpoint of ancient culture, this is the catastrophe of decline. Christianity and Germanic or provincial barbarism seemed to be triumphing over the finest products of Greek and Roman civilization. To those who considered Roman culture the acme of perfection, any change must necessarily have seemed to be for the worse. Thus it was with our own fathers and grandfathers who saw the classical education of their youthful days slowly giving way before the unrefined materialism of a more scientific and businesslike age. In the case of Roman classicism, the destructive forces were more primitive: Christian religiousness and Germanic barbarism.

In the West the transition from Roman to Christian-Germanic domination was well under way by the beginning of the fourth century; it was pretty well completed by the year 500. By that time, triumphant Christianity had modified Roman literature, architecture, art, and music to suit its own purposes. The conquering Germans, likewise, were rapidly assimilating many of the elements of imperial civilization. The result of this mingling of influences was a culture so unlike that of the Golden and Silver ages that it no longer can be called Roman or classical. Although Western culture still had many of the external characteristics of Roman classicism, after the fifth century it was distinctive enough in character to warrant the name *medieval*. The development of this mingled Roman, Christian, and Germanic culture (which we call medieval) is the subject of later treatment.[17]

[17] See below, Chapters XIII-XVII

III

THE RISE OF CHRISTIANITY

IF one views the beginnings of early medieval civilization in terms of declining Roman institutions, it seems, in general, as if all the institutions and ideals which had taken mankind centuries to produce were either dying or being ruthlessly destroyed by the forces of barbarism. There is, however, even in the West, a brighter side to this tragic picture. With the disintegration of the ineffective Western Empire and the decline of classical culture during the fourth and fifth centuries, new forces were arising to replace them. Over this "outworn civilization," an eminent modern scholar has remarked, "swept two great waves—Christianity from the east, Germanic invasion from the north."[1]

To these apparently destructive, yet eventually constructive, forces we now turn our attention. They were destined to replace the declining Roman civilization of the West and to build a new Roman-German-Christian world. Christianity and migrating Germans had both been troublesome elements in the history of the early empire. By the third century both were of outstanding significance; during the fourth and fifth centuries they had become so influential that they threatened to overwhelm imperial institutions. By the year 500 Christianity and Germanic barbarism had vanquished Roman imperialism in the West. In the East, on the contrary, the empire maintained its control over both.

For the first two centuries of its history Christianity was merely one of many struggling religious sects. During the third century, the chaotic conditions in the empire encouraged the rapid expansion of Christianity. In the fourth century it proved its superiority to all other religions, and by the year 500 was a powerful organization, prepared to match its strength with the ruling powers, both Roman and Germanic. The rise of Christianity from weakness and obscurity

[1] Gummere, *Germanic Origins,* p. 8.

to a position of dominance is one of the most important factors in the making of medieval and modern Europe.

RELIGIONS OF THE ROMAN EMPIRE When Christ began his program of reform among the Jewish peoples of Palestine, a great many religions were current in the Roman world. Among them only one, the worship of the emperor, was universally enforced upon all citizens as the state religion. But emperor-worship, more a patriotic duty than a religious faith, was primarily the citizen's formal recognition of the unity of the empire and the sovereignty of its head. There was also the ancient Roman religion of Jupiter and his divine family. Like its Greek forerunner, this had once been widespread, but eventually it degenerated into a dead ritualism carried on in splendid temples by stately priests and priestesses and had no great hold upon the people.

The more intelligent Roman of the early centuries was more interested in Greek philosophy. Stoicism, combining stern moral principles and rational idealism, attracted many of the upper classes. Under its influence Seneca in the first century urged his fellow nobles to live lives that would be worthy of the benefits God had bestowed on them. A century and a half later, the Stoic emperor, Marcus Aurelius, by both word and deed, encouraged every good citizen to do his duty like a man and a Roman. Stoicism was an admirable working philosophy for sturdy souls, but it furnished little comfort or inspiration to the mass of humanity.

Intellectuals of a more imaginative and emotional temperament found greater attraction in Neoplatonism. This revival and exaggeration of certain of Plato's ideas became very popular because it taught that every human soul could emancipate itself from material things and attain harmony with the supreme spirit of the universe by contemplation. Neoplatonism thus became a sort of universal religion of mystical revelation to which anyone might aspire. For the majority, however, it was too vaguely abstract. The masses turned more and more to Oriental cults which had a strong emotional appeal. As a result of the political and commercial unity which Rome had brought to the Mediterranean world, the ancient religions of Egypt, Syria, and Asia Minor had spread westward where they were eagerly accepted by all classes. Their mystical and sometimes sensual rites, their dramatic ritual, their promises of purification from sin and of attainment of eternal salvation, and their legends of divine death and resurrection attracted rich and poor alike. Thus it was that the religion of the Egyptian Osiris and Isis, of the Syrian Baal and Astarte, of the Phrygian Attys and Cybele, and other similar cults were known in all regions of the empire. Most of the Oriental religions emphasized the feminine element: Isis, Astarte, and Cybele were goddesses of love, motherhood, and fertility.

With men, particularly with the more practical-minded, the Persian cult of Mithra was popular. Mithra was a young hero who brought salvation to mankind by descending to earth and fighting against the powers of evil. Those initiated into the ranks of his followers went through an elaborate ceremony in which, among other things, they were purified by the blood of a sacrificed bull (bull baptism, or *taurobolium*). They were thus consecrated to fight for Mithra and Ahura Mazda, the God of Light, against the powers of evil in their own lives and in this world. Mithraism found special favor among soldiers, and ruins of its sacred chapels are found on the frontiers, even along the great wall in faraway Britain.

In the first and second centuries Christianity was overshadowed by these more popular Eastern religions. Very slowly did Christianity and Judaism, of which it was an offshoot, penetrate the great cities of the West.

JEWISH CHRISTIANITY Not only was Christianity one of many sects in the great Roman world, but it was itself composed of several sects or denominations. In the beginning it comprised a small group of reformers who were opposed to the formalism and narrow conservatism of Judaism. Their chief opponents were the Jewish clergy: the pharisees and sadducees of the New Testament narrative. John the Baptist, a more radical reformer than Christ, assailed them as "whited sepulchres of corruption." His outspoken criticism of corruption in high places lost him his head and put an end to one of several minor sects of Jews. Christ and his group were more conservative. The story of Christ's life, as told in the Gospels, pictures a small band of zealous but law-abiding folk, drawn largely from humble walks of life. To them Christ preached the blessings of poverty and submission. "Render unto Caesar the things that are Caesar's," he said. Even to the dramatic close of his career, when condemned to death by prejudiced judges, he continued to be a peaceful reformer who strove to keep his followers from acts of violence. His was to be a peaceful reform which would make men orderly citizens and good neighbors. His own example of ministering to the sick and needy, his precepts urging every individual to "love God and thy neighbor as thyself," and his loosely organized group of adherents offered no threat to imperial institutions. Christ came into the life of a distant Roman province, and left there a small band of followers who at the outset made scarcely a ripple on the surface of imperial civilization. No contemporary historian even mentioned him, and a half century later, the Roman historian, Tacitus, merely referred to a certain "Christus who suffered death under Pontius Pilate, the procurator of Judea."

GENTILE
CHRISTIANITY
It has been said that Christ's real importance was the influence of his life on succeeding generations of followers. Certainly the history of Christianity begins after Christ. Here again from the very beginning there were independent groups and leaders, each of which put a different interpretation or emphasis on certain aspects of Christ's teachings. The most important differences of opinion were between the Jewish and the Gentile Christians. At the outset the strict constructionists at Jerusalem, including some of the twelve disciples, insisted that Christian converts should abide by the old Jewish law. Paul, Barnabas, and a younger group of leaders who had never belonged to the inner circle of the twelve disciples, were interested in carrying the faith to Gentiles as well as to Jews. Jewish hostility forced them more and more to turn to the Gentiles.[2]

Eventually Paul organized independent groups of converts at Colossae, Ephesus, Philippi, Thessalonica, Corinth, and other cities of Asia Minor and Greece. The books of the New Testament which bear the names of these cities,[3] were Paul's letters of advice and exhortation written to his churches. He was, in fact, the founder of a new sect or denomination, composed principally of Gentile Christians. Through the labors of Paul, Barnabas, and other independent missionaries, many groups of Gentile believers came into existence in various cities of the Roman world. As a result of such developments, first-century Christianity was far from a unified religious organization. Each leader, and to a certain extent, each church, was independent. Rome, Corinth, Alexandria, and Antioch, which were Gentile centers, became more influential than Jerusalem. In fact, the word *Christian* was first applied to a group of converts at Antioch.[4]

As time went on the Christians of various regions developed their

[2] Acts 15-17 and 21:18 ff.
[3] Corinthians, Galatians, Ephesians, Philippians, Colossians, and Thessalonians.
[4] Acts 11:26.

own religious peculiarities. Alexandria came to be known for her group of Christian intellectuals who wrote learned treatises in which they worked out a rational interpretation of Christ's teachings. One group of Christian philosophers, called Gnostics, developed a system of thought which emphasized the contrast between the materialistic (or visible) and the spiritual (or invisible) aspects of the universe. By ignoring the material things of life one might attain the spiritual perfection which brought salvation. Montanus, another leader, insisted upon returning to the first principles of Christianity by eliminating all formalities, doctrines, and organization, and living as simply as Christ and his disciples had lived.

CHRISTIAN
BELIEFS
While the Christianity or—to be more accurate—the Christianities of the first two centuries manifested infinite variations, there were also certain distinctive features which tended to unify all Christians into a single spiritual brotherhood. The inspiring story of Christ's life and death for the redemption of mankind from sin was a vital reality to Christians. The Master's glorification of poverty and suffering created a strong bond of sympathy among the lower classes, who comprised the great majority of believers. This teaching found active expression in the Christian practice of charity, and in each community the poor, the widows, and the orphans were provided for by their more fortunate brethren. In Jerusalem the converts actually organized a system of Christian communism.[5] In times of famine or unusual distress the Christian communities sent aid to "the brethren" in distant cities.[6]

The simple morality of right and honest living was an important principle among Christians everywhere. To this was added an insistence on the mystical importance of Christ's resurrection. This was Paul's special contribution to Christian thought. Although he had never belonged to Christ's group of personal followers, he had seen his risen Lord in a blinding flash of light at the time of his conversion. This risen Christ, and a mystical faith in his power over human lives, was the constant theme of Paul's preaching and writing. From the great Augustine in the fourth century to modern times, this doctrine has been uppermost in the thinking of many Christian leaders. Such was the inspiring Christian faith that Paul, more than any other individual, gave to the Roman world. For this service and for his ex-

[5] Acts 2:44-46; 4:32 ff.
[6] Acts 11:29-30.

tensive missionary work among the Gentiles, he is sometimes referred to as the real founder of Roman Christianity. But, with due regard to the able leadership of men such as Paul in the early Christian communities, the success of the faith was very largely a result of the zealous spirit and morality of simple folk of the lower classes who were inspired by the life and teachings of the Christ.

EXPANSION AND OPPOSITION — Once Christianity had become a Gentile religion, it began to spread rapidly among the cities of the Mediterranean world. Most of the converts were from the laboring classes of the industrial centers. From city to city along the great trade routes of the empire Christianity advanced westward. Self-appointed Christian missionaries traveled from place to place, holding services, organizing their converts, and in this way establishing new centers of expansion.

Because of the great number of independent religions in the Roman world, and the imperial policy of toleration, Christianity's development went on with little governmental interference. At about the middle of the first century Nero, in order to shift the blame for a disastrous fire, is said to have cruelly tortured "a number of Christians." But this atrocity, often referred to as the first persecution, was not directed against the Christian religion. Furthermore, it was restricted to the city of Rome. Later in the century, Domitian executed several individuals suspected of treason among whom there were both pagan philosophers and Christians.

Through the first and second centuries the Christians suffered more from the hatred of the populace than from the government. Disliked for their unsocial intolerant attitude, they suffered at times from anti-Christian riots. To say the least, all true Christians were unpatriotic pacifists. They refused to hold public office, since theirs was the Kingdom of Heaven. They would not serve in the army, for warfare was sinful. Most serious of all, for fear of committing idolatry, they refused even formal adherence to the official worship of the emperor. This was treason and prevented the Christians from enjoying the toleration and protection which the government extended to all law-abiding religions. Nevertheless, the emperors were willing to give the Christians the benefit of the doubt. Even when brought to judgment, they sometimes went unpunished.

During the reign of Trajan, Pliny, a provincial official in Asia Minor, reported that he had been forced to deal with many cases in his province. The Christians were increasing rapidly, and their secret meetings were of a suspicious character. Under torture, certain of the members admitted that they met before dawn, but merely to sing songs in honor of Christ and to take oaths not to commit criminal deeds. The governor, after putting all of them to the test of "denying the name of Christ" and sacrificing to the emperor's statue, executed those who refused and set the rest free. To this the emperor gave his full approval and ordered the governor not to hunt out the Christians nor to pay any attention to anonymous accusations.

Throughout the second century this semitolerant policy prevailed. When convicted of violating imperial regulations, Christians were *prosecuted* to the full extent of the law. But there was no effort at *persecution,* that is, to hunt down all Christians and feed them to the hungry lions of the amphitheater. On the contrary, there are edicts (by Hadrian) ordering provincial governors to protect Christians from hostile mobs.

PERSECUTION For two centuries the general attitude of the imperial government was simply that of strict enforcement of the law. During the third century this lenient policy was abruptly replaced by one of drastic persecution. This was due to the rapid growth of Christianity during the chaotic early years of the century and to the new type of imperial government that arose later in the century. Under the rule of military despots such as Decius, Aurelian, and Diocletian, Christians could no longer expect lenient treatment. It is significant that the first strong emperor after the period of imperial anarchy inaugurated the new policy of drastic persecution. Decius instituted the first general empire-wide persecution of Christians. Practically every able and efficient emperor during the remaining years of the century outlawed all Christians everywhere and ordered that they be hunted down. Decius, Valerian, Aurelian, Galerius, and Diocletian deliberately set about to destroy Christianity.

There were valid reasons for this new and drastic policy. By the middle of the third century Christianity had not only spread widely but was effectively organized. Its activities among the city populace throughout the empire could no longer be ignored. The suspicious nature of the secret gatherings of Christians and the close bonds of unity between their widely scattered communities were interpreted by governmental officials as evidences of a dangerously treasonable organization. This attitude was especially noticeable during the age of strict imperial regimentation which followed the disorder of the early third century. A Christian organization which had been generally undisturbed under the tolerant imperial regime of earlier days was sure to be repressed by the military despots of the late empire. The pacifistic beliefs of the Christians, their strange practices, and, above all, their undercover organization marked them as opponents of the imperial regime.

The third-century emperors who set out to crush Christianity met with stubborn resistance. From this period comes much of the tradition of Christian martyrdom. There are legends concerning the brutal execution of leaders such as bishops Cyprian and Sixtus and Deacon Laurentius, who was said to have been roasted alive over a slow fire. Less heroic but perhaps more truly representative of the average Christian are the evidences concerning those called *lapsi,* who "backslid." Some claimed like Peter that they were not Christians, others submitted and made sacrifice before the image of the emperor. Indications of such relapses are found in the many certificates that were issued to those who proved their outward loyalty to Roman paganism by performing certain ritualistic acts. Some Christians went so far as to purchase these certificates in order to avoid suspicion.

DIOCLETIAN'S
PERSECUTION

The most severe epidemic of persecution came in the reign of Diocletian (284-305), after a short period during which the law against Christians had been practically unenforced. At the suggestion of his assistant, Galerius, Diocletian adopted drastic measures for the uprooting of Christianity. His program of centralized government could not tolerate the existence of an independent organization such as that of the Christians. All soldiers were subjected to the test of sacrificing to pagan gods. Christians were excluded from public office, from holding religious meetings, and from possessing Christian writings. Christian places of worship throughout the East were raided and destroyed; Christians were hounded out of public positions and driven from their homes. Many submitted and many were killed, but the religion of Christ stood the test. Legend has it that the emperor, on learning that his own wife and daughters were secretly Christians, went mad. Better evidence of the strength of Christianity is found in the fact that in some parts of the empire, particularly in the West, the provincial officials refused to enforce the imperial decree. With Diocletian's retirement in 305 and Constantine's rise to power in the West, persecution lagged.

TOLERATION
RESTORED
Even in the East, in 311, after eight years of vain effort, persecution ceased. Galerius, who had become the Eastern emperor, submitted to the opinions of his colleagues and issued an edict of toleration for his half of the empire.

At Milan two years after Galerius's edict, Constantine and the new Eastern emperor, Licinius, decided to issue a decree of broader scope, for the entire empire.[7]

THE EDICT OF
MILAN-NICO-
MEDIA (313)
The only existing account of the provisions of the edict is the description by a Christian named Lactantius of an edict sent out from Nicomedia by Licinius. Similar decrees were doubtless promulgated at Rome or Milan for the Western part of the empire, but nothing definite is known concerning them. Thus it appears that the so-called Edict of Milan was merely planned at Milan; it was promulgated separately at Nicomedia and probably at other imperial centers.[8] The Nicomedia edict provided that "Christians and *all others*" should have liberty to follow their chosen religion, "in order that *whatever deity there is* on the heavenly throne may be propitiated." It also provided that "all restrictions contained in former instructions concerning the Christians . . . are entirely canceled." The same freedom as to religious observances was "granted to others."[9] The edict also contained detailed instructions concerning the restoration of churches and church property to Christians, but this was due to the fact that they had been the only sufferers from the recent persecution. The Edict of Milan did not give Christianity a favored position; it merely extended to Christians those generally recognized rights enjoyed for centuries by all law-abiding religions.

CONSTANTINE
AND CHRIS-
TIANITY
Nor was the attitude of Constantine in this matter particularly new or epoch-making. It was the natural outcome of his own father's policy as prefect of Gaul and Britain. The elder Constantine had never approved the Diocletian program of persecution and had refused to

[7] It should be noted that this was neither the first nor the last edict of toleration. Gallienus (260-268) had ended the persecutions of Valerian's reign by the Edict of Nicomedia, freeing all Christians from prison and permitting Christian worship.

[8] Some modern scholars believe that since the so-called Edict of Milan was merely an extension of Galerius's edict and since it was promulgated at Nicomedia, it should be called the Edict of Nicomedia.

[9] The complete translation of Lactantius's description of the edict can be found in most source books of medieval history. See, for instance, Scott, Hyma, and Noyes, *Readings in Medieval History,* p. 50.

put it into effect in his prefecture. He and his son after him were favorably disposed toward Christianity, even though they were officially pagan. Like many of the emperors of earlier times, Constantine's father was tolerant in his attitude toward all religions.

Constantine appears to have been of similar mind. For a time, while busy with political and military matters and the problem of becoming ruler of the West, he showed no special interest in religion. This disinterested attitude continued until the Edict of Milan. According to a contemporary Christian account which some historians accept, Constantine was converted about a year before the promulgation of the edict, at the battle of the Milvian Bridge, in which he defeated a rival ruler and became emperor of the West. He is said to have seen in the sky a cross with the words "By this sign, conquer" (*In hoc signo vinces*), and to have accepted Christianity. The Christian symbol was then placed on the shields and standards of his soldiers. If this event actually happened, Constantine apparently became a secret Christian, for it is known that he was not baptized until late in life.

So far as Constantine's official acts are concerned, it is clear that there was no sudden change at this time in his public policy. Like his father and many former Roman rulers, he continued for a time to be officially neutral toward all religions. To be sure, there were soldiers in his army who carried the Christian symbol on their shields and standards. But, until late in his reign, Constantine used *pagan* as well as Christian symbols on the military insignia and on imperial coins. Furthermore, as we have seen, the Edict of Milan was couched in decidedly nonpartisan language. Up to this time (313) and for some time thereafter, Constantine's public acts appear to be those of an enlightened pagan who sought religious peace and harmony. He realized the *political* value of organized religious supporters and for a time worked for the aid of both pagans and Christians.

Ten years later, after his conquest of the entire empire (323), he seems to have decided that Christianity was the most influential religion, and henceforth Christians were given special favors. By imperial decree, wills in favor of Christian churches were legalized and the Christian clergy was given special judicial powers. Magnificent churches were erected at Jerusalem and at Constantinople, the new imperial capital. The clergy was assisted in its task of collecting Biblical manuscripts. If in every way Christianity enjoyed the favor of the court, Constantine enjoyed, in return, the favor and support of the Christians.

THE COUNCIL
OF NICÆA (325)

One of the most significant of Constantine's pro-Christian acts was the calling of the Council of Nicæa (325) at a time when he was not himself a professed Christian. Officially he was still connected with the imperial pagan worship. Political motives, however, led him to interfere in a theological conflict in order to restore religious peace among an important group of his supporters. When Constantine, after defeating a rival emperor, came East in 323 to reorganize the imperial government, an intense controversy was raging among the Christian clergy in Egypt and Palestine. Arius, a priest of Alexandria, criticizing his bishop's ideas concerning the divinity of Christ, insisted that Christ, having been created by God, was of a different substance and, therefore, was an inferior deity. In short, he denied the doctrine of the absolute divinity of Christ, which, he said, encouraged polytheism. This rationalistic, unitarian position infuriated Athanasius, a conservatively minded deacon. Athanasius championed the bishop's cause, and eventually organized that clergyman's rather jumbled theology into a set of dogmas that finally became the orthodox Trinitarian belief.

In an effort to end the factional strife, several local councils were held, but matters grew steadily worse. Constantine's clerical representative, when sent from the West to investigate, reported that in the course of these theological conflicts "more than one person has been killed by having his skull split." To settle this and other religious problems, Constantine summoned representative clergymen from all parts of the empire to meet in council at Nicæa. The result was the first of a number of councils at which representatives from all parts of Christendom met to legislate on church affairs.

THE CREED
OF 325

An important factor in the Council of Nicæa was the influence of the government. Although not yet a full-fledged Christian, Constantine called the council, acted as its official president, and exerted governmental pressure at various times during the deliberations. He appears never to have realized what the religious argument was about, but he knew that factional strife impeded the smooth workings of the imperial government, and he was determined to have harmony at any price.

After two months of deliberation on the theological problem, the three hundred bishops seem to have fallen into three general groups.

The great majority were mildly conservative in their views; the rest were violently Athanasian or Arian. Eventually, in accordance with the emperor's insistence on unity, the majority of the conservatives acceded to the Athanasian demands and condemned Arianism. Thus Christianity's first great parliament decreed that Christ was "begotten and not created" and that "those who say that . . . the Son of God was of a different substance or being [from the Father], or that he was a created being capable of change or alteration; these the Catholic Church anathematizes." Thus early in Christian history conservatism triumphed and branded as heretical all who believed in unitarianism or denied the absolute divinity of Christ.

THE AMENDED
NICENE CREED
OF 381

This creed and attitude were not genuine expressions of the desires of lay Christendom, of the entire Christian clergy, or even of the majority of the bishops of the church. There were about eighteen hundred bishops in the entire empire, of which three hundred, or about one-sixth, were at Nicæa. Of these three hundred, the majority would have preferred a more tolerant attitude. The emperor, however, swung his support to what he considered the best settlement, and by means of governmental pressure the creed insisted upon by the Athanasian minority of one-sixth of the bishops of the entire church was adopted as the official creed for all Christendom. Arius and two of his supporters were exiled. This settlement was too drastic to last, however, and before his death (337) Constantine found it expedient to reverse the council's decision. He recalled Arius and exiled Athanasius. Later in the century, after a series of long and bitter theological controversies, a more tolerant statement of the Athanasian faith was adopted; it is this, rather than the Creed of 325, that is commonly known today as the "Nicene Creed."

IMPORTANCE OF
THE COUNCIL
OF NICÆA

In addition to its decision concerning creeds, the Council of Nicæa legislated upon other religious matters. Its twenty "canons," or decrees, regulated the elections of bishops and the holding of provincial synods, condemned various abuses among the clergy, and provided that the bishops of Rome, Alexandria, and other prominent churches should be allowed to exercise a certain jurisdiction over their neighboring bishops. Finally, after a formal banquet, which was provided by the government, the attending bishops and their retinues started homeward. Traveling expenses were also furnished by the government.

Constantine was largely responsible for bringing Christianity into the realm of imperial politics. His motive seems to have been to insure religious solidarity and thus to strengthen the political unity of the empire. The result was a greater unity in church beliefs and organization. This not only led to Christian persecutions of heretics, as a fixed policy of both church and state, but increased the bitterness of the existing spirit of intolerance among opposing factions of Christians. On the other hand, the scattered Christian communities were welded together into more workable units, and both church and state became more effective in their influence on pagan society. The church became a more powerful instrument both for good and ill. It became more influential and also more deeply involved in governmental intrigues.

The Council of Nicæa indicates in a small way the tremendous influence that church and state were to exert upon each other during the succeeding centuries. The close interrelation between the Christian Church and the empire is apparent in the history of the later councils. Until the ninth century the Eastern emperors called and controlled the great councils that were held at or near Constantinople. In the West throughout the Middle Ages, in similar fashion Germanic chieftains, feudal princes, and Holy Roman emperors took an active part in the settlement of church affairs. Even to the present day in some countries church and state work hand in hand.

CONSTANTINE "THE GREAT" Although Christianity did not become the state religion until late in the fourth century, by the end of Constantine's reign it had obtained a favored position among the competing religions of the Roman world. His support enabled it to make great progress. It advanced from outlawry to imperial favor; it became conscious of its strength, and finally won the complete allegiance of the great emperor. On his deathbed he is said to have accepted Christian baptism with the remark, "Let us cast aside all duplicity." This event is a significant commentary on the career of Constantine the Great. With notable success he employed religion, both pagan and Christian, as an aid to his political program. Realizing the strength of Christianity, he made it a primary factor in his imperial system. He was greater as a manipulator of religion for political purposes than as an adherent of the Christian faith.

THE VICTORY OF CHRISTIANITY

EARLY
CHRISTIAN
HERESIES
The reign of Constantine paved the way for the ultimate triumph of Christianity during the next half century. Victory was not easily won, for there were two dangerous adversaries—disunity within and paganism without. Long before the Council of Nicæa Christianity had been troubled by factional strife. In the first century the Judaizers had bitterly opposed Paul and his non-Jewish converts. In the second century the puritanical ideas of the Montanists met with widespread opposition from the conservative clergy. Throughout these early centuries the simpler believers had struggled constantly against such philosophical groups as the Gnostics. After the Council of Nicæa the battle between the Arians and Athanasians held the center of the stage.

ARIANS VERSUS
ATHANASIANS
From 335, when a pro-Arian council reversed the decision of the Council of Nicæa, until the Council of Constantinople in 381, Arianism was in the ascendancy. The emperors were Arian in belief, and orthodox; Athanasians consequently suffered almost constant persecution. This was particularly true in the East. On five different occasions Athanasius and his close followers were exiled. Emperor Constantius (337-361) went so far as to incite pagan mobs to violence against the Athanasians in Alexandria. In defense and retaliation the Athanasian leaders called in from the neighboring deserts armies of fanatical hermits. These wild and uncouth men, carrying candles and crucifixes, struck terror to the opposition. Emperor Julian the Apostate (361-363) encouraged the rivalry of the two factions, hoping by this means to bring about a revival of paganism. Later, Emperor Valens of the East ordered the massacre of Athanasians who resisted his will.

In the West the Athanasians were more popular. After 379, when the Spanish general, Theodosius, became emperor, troops were used to defend them against the attacks of Arian mobs. It was at the summons of this new "Constantine" from the West that Christendom's representatives met in council at Constantinople (381) and condemned Arianism and re-established the Athanasian doctrine as Christianity's orthodox belief. Henceforth governmental influence was everywhere vigorously exerted, not only against the Arians but also against other minority groups whose beliefs were held to be unorthodox or heretical. Among those who stubbornly held their ground in spite of persecution were the Donatists, Circumcellions, Montanists, Priscillians, Manicheans, Novatians, Meletians, Nestorians, Monophysites, and Pelagians.[10]

THE SUPPRES-
SION OF
HERESY

From the standpoint of the church authorities repression of such groups was necessary in order to unify Christianity and to prevent it from sinking to the level of the pagan religions and philosophies. In some cases it was even considered necessary to condemn those enthusiasts who insisted on reviving the simplicity and poverty of the early apostles. Inasmuch as the clergy had become a powerful organization with extensive propertied interests, such a development was unthinkable. The leaders of Christendom thus strengthened their own position by avoiding dangerous extremes of any kind, and by condemning as heretical those who differed from the conservative opinions of the majority. By such means the various denominations of earlier days were welded into the more unified organization and faith known as the Christian *Church.*

From the standpoint of the government, also, it was expedient to repress religious radicalism. The most stubborn heretical movements were supported by the dissatisfied populations of regions which had steadily resisted Roman conquest. Egypt, Syria, and Carthaginian Africa were inhabited by people who were imbued with a strong spirit of racial and political, as well as religious, independence. In Northern Africa, the hatred of the Carthaginians for the Romans had persisted long after the region had been conquered. It was amid such a hotbed of sectionalism that the Donatist sect arose. The people of this region supported Donatus' claim that sacred ceremonies were useless when performed by evil, or illegally chosen, clergymen. Even after the doctrine was condemned as heretical (in 314) Donatism persisted in Northern Africa and in other localities of the West.

It was natural for church and state to join hands in crushing radical minorities which obstructed the smooth workings of centralized political and religious administration. There was no place for either religious or political tolerance in the unsettled centuries of the late empire. The orthodox church and the new imperial regime, work-

---

[10] We have already noted (p. 59) the Montanist heresy, and shall have occasion to refer to the Donatists, Manicheans, Nestorians, and Monophysites. The other groups mentioned were minor sects.

ing together for the unity and stability of society, sacrificed freedom
and flexibility for uniformity and centralization. In the West the
church was so successful in its regimentation of religious institutions
that it eventually replaced the empire as the unifying force in Western
civilization.

CHRISTIANITY
AND PAGANISM

While Christianity was struggling to achieve some
sort of internal unity, it was also waging constant
warfare against paganism, which was a real menace
to Christianity until the middle of the fourth century. Constantine
until late in life was officially neutral in the conflict between Christianity and paganism. If he bestowed many favors upon the Christians, he did not revoke the rights of the pagan sects. In 356, Constantine's successor, Emperor Constantius, prohibited the worship of idols
and attendance at pagan sacrifices on pain of death, but this law was
not enforced. From the succeeding years come many evidences of
the persistence of paganism: accounts of sacrifices on altars at Rome,
of innumerable temples in Alexandria, and of pagan schools of philosophy. It was reported that in the very next year after his prohibi-
tory edict, Constantius reconfirmed the privileges of the temple and
the virgins of Vesta in Rome. To be sure, he had the pagan altar
of Victory removed from the entrance to the senate house because
of the protests of Christian senators, but it was subsequently restored
and became a storm center during the later years of the century.

JULIAN THE
APOSTATE

The existence of paganism is well exemplified by
the career of Emperor Julian the Apostate (361-363),
who was responsible for the last serious effort to
crush Christianity and restore paganism. As a youth he had received
a thorough Christian training, but turned away in disgust from the
Scriptures and the arguments of the theologians. He found real satisfaction in the pagan classics, mysticism, and Neoplatonism. Afraid of
the jealous suspicions of the imperial court, he outwardly conformed
to Christianity but secretly attended magical séances and was eventually initiated into the mysteries of the popular pagan cult of Mithra.
Later, as emperor, he decided to crush Christianity and restore paganism. Unlike Constantine, Julian "cast aside all duplicity" at the beginning of his reign and frankly announced himself a pagan. For three
years he struggled to introduce throughout the empire a revived and
improved religion comprising the good points of the various pagan
sects and also of Christianity. This new religion, to be carried to the

people by means of a hierarchy of pontiffs, priests, and ministers, was to have the intellectual and philosophical tolerance of paganism and the vigorous group spirit of Christianity. The sturdy elements of Stoic philosophy were to be combined with Neoplatonic mysticism and with Christian asceticism, sacramentalism, hymn-singing, and charitable practices.

Julian's method of action was somewhat like that of Constantine: though officially neutral he extended favors to his chosen religion. But to the Christians, Julian's toleration seemed to be an empty form, for he ousted Christians from public office and abolished most of the Christian symbols from the imperial coins and standards. Christian education was hampered by various restrictions, and persecution of Christians by pagan mobs or heretical factions was permitted and even encouraged. Such tactics tended to hurt rather than help Julian's cause. By the end of his reign it was evident that paganism as a state religion was doomed. Its priests were self-satisfied officeholders; its membership was a cultured aristocratic minority. It continued solely as the private religion of many members of the old aristocracy. In only a few regions were pagan customs publicly observed after Julian's reign.

CHRISTIANITY THE STATE RELIGION
Gratian (375-383) and Theodosius (379-395) threw the entire weight of governmental authority into the balance in favor of Christianity. They forbade all pagan worship and withdrew the government's support of the ancient priesthoods. In Alexandria mobs of fanatical Christians stormed the temples of Mithra and Serapis. In the West the crisis came in the latter part of the reign of Theodosius, when influential pagans petitioned for the restoration of the senatorial altar of Victory and of the incomes of the pagan priesthood. Today their appeal strikes one as a reasonable, dignified, and convincing request for religious toleration. To Bishop Ambrose of Milan, however, it represented the fading light of a decadent pagan world. His vigorous counterappeal strengthened the emperor in his decision to stamp out paganism. By the end of Theodosius' reign, even the Olympic games had been discontinued and there was a growing demand for the prohibition of gladiatorial contests and chariot racing, especially on Sundays. Christianity was now the state religion; non-Christians were barred from public office and the law courts; and Christians who reverted to paganism were severely punished.

PAGANISM
PERSISTS

Although paganism was officially dead by the end of the fourth century, its festivals and semireligious observances persisted. At one time during the reign of Theodosius, when a pagan usurper gained temporary control of the city of Rome, the ancient priesthoods, sacrifices, processions, and even the senatorial altar of Victory were temporarily restored. During the early years of the fifth century pagan banquets and festivals were still celebrated. A monk who tried to stop the performance of gladiatorial games in Rome in 404 was killed by an enraged mob. In Corsica a Christian was crucified for refusing to take part in a pagan sacrifice. Bishop Augustine of Hippo bewailed the fact that in his day the churches were empty while theaters and other spectacles of a worldly pagan character were well attended. His motive in writing *The City of God* indicates that he was aware of the strength of pagan ideas. It is recorded that at the time of the Visigothic invasion (410) there were three thousand dancing girls from pagan theaters among the fugitives who fled from Rome. In 416, Alexandrians of cultured interests sat at the feet of Hypatia, the daughter of a pagan philosopher, and the Christians so feared the influence of her teachings that their fanatical leaders incited the rabble to murder her. She was the noblest of the *pagan* martyrs.

PAGAN SURVIVALS
IN CHRISTIANITY

To a certain extent, paganism was taken over by Christianity. Christian ritual bears abundant evidence of the persistence of pagan observances and of Christianity's tactful adoption of prevailing religious practices. Altars, halos, bells, holy water, candles, incense, and the sign of the cross were common to both Christianity and paganism. Many elements in the clerical hierarchy and in the priestly vestments were adaptations from Roman practices. It has been asserted that "pagan gods and goddesses were discreetly made over into Christian saints . . . Their relics were sold far and wide . . . as fetishes guaranteed to ward off evil, and their ancient festive days were made part of the Christian calendar." [11] It has been suggested that the rising cult of the Virgin Mary, called "Mother of God" at least as early as the fourth century, indicates that Catholic Christianity was strongly influenced by the goddess religions of the Orient.

It is likely that the similarities in practice between paganism and Christianity were a result of Christianity's policy of bringing all the

[11] Browne, *This Believing World*, p. 294.

activities of its converts under the protecting wing of the church. Pagans who turned to Christianity might continue to enjoy their traditional days of festival, but in a different way and under new auspices. The church authorities were very strict in the matter of essential beliefs, but they borrowed many minor practices from rival religions and consecrated them to Christian uses. Thus the Roman festivals of late December—the Saturnalian revels, the gift-giving Sigilaria, and the Birthday of the Unconquerable Sun—were merged with the birthday of the Christ child. Likewise, the Spring mysteries symbolizing the death and rebirth of various gods assumed the Christian forms of Lent and Easter. Similar relationships can be seen in the pagan Parilia (April festival) and the feast of St. George; Diana's Holy Day in August and the feast of the Assumption of the Virgin; the Feast of the Dead and All Souls' and Halloween. Throughout its twenty centuries of existence Christianity has manifested a remarkable adaptability to varied human conditions and an unusual power of assimilation.

THE BEGINNINGS OF THE MEDIEVAL CHURCH While Christianity was fighting its way to victory and forging a set of orthodox doctrines on the anvil of religious controversy, a permanent administrative organization was taking shape. Out of the early centuries of struggle emerged certain distinctive institutions such as the papacy and monasticism, which are still influential in the lives of millions of Christians. The church organization grew gradually along with the evolving beliefs and practices of the early centuries. The papacy, monasticism, the sacraments—in fact, the Christian Church in its entirety—comprised an immense structure that took shape slowly as a result of the labors of thousands of people through generations of effort.

EARLY CHURCH ORGANIZATION In its organizational aspects the Christian Church moved from loosely federated and democratically governed units of laboring people to a complex centralized organization directed by clergymen. The average Christian community of the first century was in keeping with the economic-social character of its membership. It was made up of simple working folk, "those who labor and are heavy laden." The affairs of each church were directed by the older members (called elders), assisted by deacons. There was little emphasis on organization, ritual, or material surroundings. Church services were often merely prayer meetings, held in private homes. Each church was a self-governing unit, very loosely bound to the other churches which had been founded by the same missionary bishop or apostle. The Epistles of Paul to the Galatians, Ephesians, and other city churches indicate something of the problems of these early Christian communities and the influence exerted by their founders.

CHANGES IN CHURCH ORGAN- IZATION By the fourth century great changes had taken place. Christianity, like the Roman world of which it had become such an important part, was now an intricate economic-social organism. It was a gigantic federation of city churches, instead of scattered communities of poor folk. Many of the city churches were great religious corporations with immense incomes and important property rights. The most influential members of society attended the services and gave their financial support. In the larger churches the religious rites were resplendent with ornate vestments, gilded altars, candles, and embroidered banners. The simple religious functions of the elders and deacons of apostolic times had become a complicated ritual performed by a hierarchy [12] of clergymen. Every city had its bishop whose manifold activities demanded a small army of clerical assistants. A third-century bishop of Rome mentioned the fact that he had under his control forty-six priests, seven deacons, seven subdeacons, forty-two acolytes, fifty-two exorcists, readers, and doorkeepers, and fifteen hundred widows, orphans, and cripples.[13] A century later, the church at Constantinople boasted, in addition to clergymen, nine hundred grave diggers and six hundred sick attendants.

THE BISHOPS The city and its bishop were the principal unit of Christian society. The bishops, considered the spiritual heirs and successors of the twelve disciples, were clothed with a

[12] A hierarchy is, strictly speaking, a sacred government, but it usually refers to the graded system of officials in a highly regimented organization.

[13] The priests were the bishop's assistants in purely spiritual matters such as preaching and the performing of sacred ceremonies. The deacons and subdeacons, originally designated to handle charitable funds and functions, later came to assist the bishop in most of the religious ceremonies and in many purely administrative functions. The acolytes were minor attendants at the altar ceremonies. Exorcists had charge of those possessed with demons, which they drove out by prayers and other religious observances. The readers (lectors) not only read certain portions of the service, but had custody of the sacred books. In the larger churches there were also catechists who instructed the new church members (catechumens), cantors or chanters for the musical portions of the service, doorkeepers (called janitors), and deaconesses who cared for the women catechumens and women of the church who were old, sick, or in trouble.

definite religious authority. When Constantine decided to hold a council at Nicæa, it was the bishops who were summoned to represent the entire Christian population of the empire. By this time the bishop had become the responsible religious official of each city and its surrounding regions. No longer were they merely traveling evangelists like Paul or Timothy. They had acquired narrower but more absolute jurisdictions. A fourth-century bishop ruled with an authority and lived in a splendor unknown to first-century Christianity. As a lineal spiritual descendant of the original disciples, he was the religious supervisor of the diocese, which comprised the parishes of his city and vicinity. He was also recognized by the imperial government as the local judge for religious affairs. Such a position was attended by great honor and influence. In fact, it was so desirable that unprincipled candidates sometimes resorted to political intrigue and even to violence to win the coveted office. In their external relations, also, the bishops found themselves in a competitive world. Like the heads of nonreligious organizations, they must be ever-watchful for opportunities of gaining religious, economic, and social advantages for their churches. As a result, church councils sometimes took on the characteristics of political conventions, with conflicts and compromises between rival bishops.

THE ARCHBISHOP To complicate matters further, there were various grades of bishops. The bishop of a large and wealthy church, or of the political headquarters of the province, came to exercise jurisdiction over the lesser bishops. Such superbishops were called archbishops or metropolitans. Among the archbishops, also, there were some who acquired superior authority by reason of the importance of their church or city. The archbishops of outstanding centers such as Jerusalem, Antioch, and Alexandria in the East, and Carthage, Lyons, Milan, Ravenna, and Rome in the West, were held in especially high esteem. The pre-eminence of some of these archbishops, such as those of Jerusalem and Antioch, for instance, was due chiefly to the religious reputation of their church. In most cases, however, it seems to have been a result of the economic or administrative importance of the city. Among the superarchbishops also, there were differences in authority. By 300, the bishop (or patriarch) of Alexandria had become pre-eminent in the East, and the bishop (or pope) of Rome dominated in the West. It is apparent that Christianity's expanding organization was gradually crystallizing into provincial units and these in turn into Eastern and Western hierarchies, quite similar to those of the empire during the age of Diocletian and his successors. The trend of Christian organization followed the natural economic and political evolution of imperial institutions.

EARLY BISHOPS OF ROME

The bishop and church at Rome went through the same general evolution as the other churches of the empire. In the first century there was a simple group of believers at Rome under the leadership of such men as Paul and Peter. Although these officials were called bishops or elders, they were the ministers, rather than the masters, of the local church. During this period, for instance, letters from the congregation at Rome were written in the name of the *church,* not of the bishop. By the opening of the third century, however, the bishop of Rome had acquired extensive religious powers. A pope named Victor asserted his right to excommunicate certain bishops of Asia Minor. Other churchmen of the West, especially the bishops of Lyons and Carthage, protested against this procedure as an unwarranted assumption of authority over the pope's fellow bishops. Nevertheless, within a decade, Pope Calixtus laid claim to supreme judicial authority over all Christians on the grounds that Christ had bestowed upon Peter the "keys," and the power "of binding and loosing." [14]

Before the end of the third century the bishops of Carthage were protesting against the increase of appeals to Rome from distant churches. When these objections were presented at the Council of Nicæa (325) the assembled bishops recognized Rome's right to supervise the neighboring bishops, but also decreed that the bishop of Alexandria should exercise similar authority over the regions around Alexandria. Furthermore it decreed that "similarly, in Antioch and in other provinces the [metropolitan] churches shall retain their prerogatives." The intention of this decree was to keep all bishops closely within their respective provincial jurisdictions, and to prevent any of them from interfering in distant regions. Within twenty years, however, a Western council at Sardica (ca. 342) had definitely recognized the right of the bishop of Rome to receive appeals from bishops throughout the West, and to order retrials of cases. It is evident that, in the West, religious authority was being concentrated at Rome, the age-old center of economic and political life.

[14] Matthew 16:18-19.

THE GREEK
CATHOLIC
CHURCH

The relationship between governmental and religious centralization goes a step further. Both church and state developed double organizations with separate administrations and capitals in the East and West. Late in the third century Diocletian, realizing the impossibility of effectively controlling the empire as one unit, had set up separate emperors and administrations for the East and West. Henceforth each region tended to go its own way. The Hellenic-Oriental East, with its highly industrialized life, slowly drifted away from the more rural West. The same is true of the Christian Church; Eastern Christianity came more and more under the domination of Constantinople, while the Westerners looked to the Roman church for leadership. Although the bishops of Rome *claimed* that they were the successors of Peter and therefore superior to all other churchmen, they were never able to enforce their will upon the Easterners. Eventually the bishop (or patriarch) of Constantinople, with the aid of the Eastern emperor, brought most of the churches of the East under his control.

This gave rise to the Greek or Orthodox Catholic Church, which was never permanently joined to the Western Church. During the Middle Ages its interests were so closely associated with those of the Eastern Empire that we shall consider its later history as a part of that of the empire. For the present it may be noted that, although the Greek Catholic Church suffered from imperial domination, it enjoyed imperial protection and flourished. It still exists as a separate church with its own patriarchs, lesser clergy, creed, language (Greek), and a splendid ritual particularly noted for its impressive music. As far as medieval church history is concerned, the most important developments took place in the West, where numerous regional churches were gradually merged into the unified organization that we know as the Roman Catholic Church.

═ IV ═

THE PAPACY AND MONASTICISM

THE PAPACY

WHILE the emperors and patriarchs at Constantinople were bringing the Eastern churches under their control, Western Christianity was building its own religious system. In this process there were three outstanding elements: (1) the intellectual influence of the Church Fathers [1] of the West; (2) the rise of the papacy as the administrative center of Western Christianity; and (3) the activities of the monks in extending Roman Christianity in the West.

INTELLECTUAL INFLUENCE The history of the Eastern Church during the age of the great councils is characterized by theological and political dissension. During the same period the West was laying a remarkably substantial foundation for its Christianity. We have already noted the rising influence of the church at Rome in the early centuries; later we shall consider the importance of the papal administrative organization as a rallying point for Western Christianity. Meanwhile during the fourth century the religious leadership of the West came into the hands of men of an unusual type. Their field of action was intellectual rather than administrative. The chief result was a system of Christian theology that is still the basis of the Roman Catholic faith. The beginnings of Roman Catholic theology are an essential factor in the development of Christianity in the West.

Before the time of Ambrose, Augustine, and Jerome, Easterners had monopolized Christian theology. The papacy had not yet risen to a position of dominating influence. The great church councils were held in the East and were attended by few Westerners. Most of the literature of Christianity had originated in the East and was written

[1] Church Fathers is a term applied to the outstanding leaders of the church in early times.

in Greek with which most Westerners were not familiar. The version of the Old Testament taking shape at this time and still current in the Greek Orthodox Church was the Greek Septuagint. The Latin West was distinctly on the frontier of Christianity. Up to the time of the Council of Nicæa, Minucius Felix, Lactantius of Gaul, and Cyprian and Tertullian of Carthage were the only Westerners who had attained any prominence in Christian thought.[2] Within a century the West had produced three leaders of such surpassing merit that they (along with one of their successors, Pope Gregory I) are ranked as the four "Fathers" of the Roman Catholic Church. Ambrose, Augustine, and Jerome contributed much to the Western Church during its first great century of independent growth. Each of them was a prominent member of the clergy and actively interested in ecclesiastical administration, monasticism, Christian education, and theology. A medieval commentator said that "they were most learned in both human and divine knowledge," but that they laid chief emphasis on the divine. In spite of similarities, each exemplifies in a special way certain outstanding characteristics of the expanding life of Western Christianity. Ambrose won unusual fame as a bishop-administrator, Augustine as a theologian, and Jerome as a scholar.

AMBROSE OF
MILAN

Ambrose of Milan (d. 397) was perhaps the most practical-minded of the three. His father was a high imperial official, and Ambrose received a typically Roman education in the liberal arts and law. Then, like many a young noble, he entered the government service. After making a fine record as governor of northern Italy, he rather suddenly turned from political to religious administration. Christian legend has it that, while supervising a disputed church election, he was miraculously nominated as bishop by a little child, and elected unanimously by an awe-struck congregation. As bishop of Milan he was no less energetic than he had been as governor. He set a rare example of simple Christian living: he studied theology, preached regularly, and took a close personal interest in his flock. Among the many who were won over to Christianity by his inspiring influence was the young professor, Augustine. Ambrose's writings are not outstanding, although he wrote many letters of practical advice, as well as eloquent sermons, theological treatises, hymns,[3] and a noteworthy exposition of *The Functions of Ministers* which bears a striking resemblance to one of

[2] See above, p. 47.
[3] See below, p. 304.

Cicero's works. Ambrose was well versed in Greek and in pagan literature, but his life and writings were dominated by religion. The
crowning events of his life were in the realm of Christian politics.
He won a great victory when he forced Emperor Theodosius [4] to do
penance, like any other Christian, for massacring an unruly mob at
Thessalonica, and another when he prevented the Roman aristocrats
from restoring the pagan altar of Victory to the senate house. These,
more than his writings, exemplify the sturdy fighting spirit of this
great leader who strengthened Western Christianity by insisting that
the church was greater than pagan senators or Roman emperors.

AUGUSTINE OF
HIPPO

Augustine of Hippo (d. 430) was a leader of higher
intellect and also of greater tolerance. In contrast
with Ambrose, he was educated for a life of scholarship, and specialized in the Latin classics and philosophy. For
years he dabbled in religion and philosophy, especially in Neoplatonism. Suddenly at about the age of thirty-two, after having
been a teacher of rhetoric at Carthage, Rome, and Milan, he dedicated himself to a career of Christian priesthood and scholarship.
Thenceforth he produced innumerable letters, philosophical treatises,
treatises against heresies, theological works, and a series of textbooks
on the liberal arts. His theological writings, however, are outstanding
in both quantity and quality, and have exerted the greatest influence
on medieval and modern Catholic faith. In them all of the problems
of Christian faith are clearly analyzed and systematized. Protestant
leaders such as Luther and Calvin owe much to Augustine's analyses
of the problems of sin, salvation, and predestination. No other writer
since Paul has so completely dominated Christian thinking.

Most famous of all his works are the *Confessions* and *The City of
God*. Although the *Confessions* contain many ridiculously trivial descriptions of youthful sins, and a morbid emphasis on sex as the
root of human evil, in general they are the sincere expression of a
great experience. Having vainly sought contentment in pagan worldliness, Augustine finally found perfect peace in the Christian way of
life. It is as the heartfelt expression of this great change that the
Confessions have taken their place among the world's literary masterpieces. Many of the most intelligent men of Augustine's age seem to
have been making this same transition from sophisticated classical
intellectualism to the simple dynamic faith of Christianity.

[4] See below, p. 109.

"THE CITY OF GOD"

The City of God, likewise, reflects the power of Christian ideas in the early fifth century. Written for the express purpose of combating the pagan charge that Rome's disasters, particularly the Gothic invasion of 410,[5] were due to her desertion of the ancient gods for Christianity, it was strongly pro-Christian and actively propagandistic. Augustine asserted that *pagan* Rome, "the city of the world," had suffered worse tribulations than *Christian* Rome, "the city of God," and that the recent disasters were a justly merited punishment for man's sinfulness. Furthermore, he viewed all history as a conflict between the worldly and heavenly cities. Throughout this drama he saw the hand of God in human affairs. This became (and still is) the orthodox Christian philosophy of history. At Augustine's request, one of his pupils, a young Spaniard named Orosius, wrote a world history to illustrate this theory. Such a reassuring interpretation of history was exactly suited to the rising Christian faith, and the "City of God" ideal became the guiding light of medieval thought in the West. Likewise, Augustine's philosophy of a divine program of human existence from the Creation to the Judgment Day, is still an essential element of Christian faith for most Catholics and Protestants. Augustine's success in explaining life's problems in a convincing, as well as orthodox, manner made him the most influential thinker of his day. His fusion of the pious viewpoint of early Christianity with the intellectual demands of his day was well-nigh perfect. It was he, more than any other single individual, who won the thinking people of the Western world to the fundamental beliefs of Catholic Christianity.

Augustine's writings were not only pious, they were also remarkably clear in thought and eloquent in expression. He is said to have written more beautiful proverbs than any other churchman and to have wielded the keenest argumentative pen ever known to Christian thought. These unrivaled talents were enhanced by a sincerity of purpose that carried conviction. Toward the end of his life he wrote a book entitled *Retractions,* in which he frankly confessed his mistakes. Among other things, he said: "I disapprove of the emphasis I once laid on the liberal arts; of these many saints are very ignorant and some who know them are not saints." This exemplifies another dominant trait of medieval thought, a strong distrust of secular learning and a tendency to subordinate reason to faith. Such were the

[5] See below, pp. 113 f.

conservative religious ideals which Augustine popularized among thinking Christians of the West. They were to continue well into modern times as the prevailing religious concepts of Christendom.

JEROME   Jerome (d. 420) was less pious and philosophical than Augustine, but more scholarly. He is an outstanding example of the blending of classical and Christian ideas in the fourth and fifth centuries. Although Jerome's life and writings were strongly influenced by the pagan classics, he was a prominent churchman and zealously interested in monasticism. Educated in the Latin liberal arts, he became proficient in Greek and Hebrew as well. His allegiance to classical scholarship faltered at one time in middle life, when he was under strong monastic influences. As a result of a dream in which he was condemned at the judgment seat of God for being a "Ciceronian" rather than a Christian, he resolved to give up all pagan studies. Thereafter, for a few years his writings showed a considerably smaller proportion of classical quotations and references. Nevertheless, even after he had retired to Palestine and dedicated himself to the monastic life, Jerome continued his secular studies and trained his followers in the liberal arts. While in Palestine he also prepared the famous Vulgate translation of the Bible, an immense task which involved the use of both Greek and Hebrew. In a later revised form, the Vulgate is still the official Roman Catholic Bible.

Jerome also wrote theological treatises, church history, and biography, and innumerable letters. His letters are a strange mixture of theology, scholarly thought, monastic propaganda, bitter personal invective, and keen ironical comment on the worldliness of his fellow Christians, particularly women and clergymen.[6] As uncompromising as the other Church Fathers on matters that involved the Christian faith, Jerome surpassed all of them in the vigor, violence, and almost un-Christian invective with which he condemned heretics.

Although the succeeding centuries were to find many intelligent men dedicating their lives to the service of the Roman Church, none of them performed a greater task nor with greater success than the three Fathers who laid the foundations of Catholic theology in the fourth and fifth centuries. Whatever minor variations there might be in Christian beliefs, henceforth there was a recognized body of doctrine that the majority of Westerners could look to as the orthodox faith. This constituted a strong unifying bond during the early period in which papal supremacy was not widely accepted. Unity of faith was also a powerful influence in the extension of papal control.

PAPAL LEADER-
SHIP IN THE
WEST

The Western Church, having worked out its own system of theology, continued the evolution of a centralized administrative system. The development in church government led to the formation of a hierarchy of churchmen similar to the imperial bureaucracy. The outstanding development in the West during the fifth century was the rapid rise of the bishop of Rome to a position of administrative supremacy. At the beginning of this period there were men of greater influence than the pope, or bishop, of Rome. Augustine and Jerome were outstanding in the realm of the intellect, and in political affairs Bishop Ambrose of Milan spoke with an authority greater than that of the bishop of Rome. A century later the church at Rome had assumed the position of leadership in the West.

The success achieved by the papacy in the fifth century was not achieved suddenly. For centuries various types of human activity had concentrated the attention of Westerners on Rome. Even during periods of decline, civil warfare, and barbaric invasion Rome had continued to be a great metropolis, the chief cultural, economic, and political center of the West. This position of importance, together with Rome's former reputation as the mistress of the civilized world, carried over into the ecclesiastical realm. Rome therefore came to be considered as the natural religious center of Western Christendom. Furthermore, the bishop of Rome was generally acknowledged to be the outstanding clergyman of the West, if not of the entire Christian world, on the ground that he was the successor of Peter, chief of the apostles.[7] As the bishops of the church at Rome continued, century after century, to assert their right to supreme authority over all Christians, the idea gradually became prevalent in the West.

The greatness of the Roman church, however, did not depend solely on past reputation. During the fourth and fifth centuries her bishops were men of unusual administrative ability. This was due in

[7] By the beginning of the third century, as we have seen above, the bishops of Rome claimed to be the successors of Peter, who was said to have assisted Paul in establishing Christianity in Rome. According to tradition he was the first bishop of Rome and was martyred there during the reign of Nero.

part to the fact that the papacy was a position of such importance that it attracted able men. In the fourth century, for instance, the bishop of Rome had under his direct control forty branch churches with all their clerical officials. In addition to this, he had great influence in church councils and over the other bishops of the West. Consequently able (if not always pious) men sought the office. In 366 two rival candidates waged such a strenuous campaign that about two hundred people were killed in a pre-election riot. Pagan Romans such as Emperor Julian and the historian Ammianus Marcellinus remarked that the papacy was a prize well worth the efforts of any ambitious man. At any rate, the men who became popes, by means of their effective leadership, won the confidence of Western Christendom. Even those who were personally ambitious magnified their position, and as a result the papacy prospered.

POPE LEO I
(440-461)

The fifth century saw the bishops of Rome leading the West and attempting to extend their authority eastward. Leo I vigorously asserted universal jurisdiction over all the bishops of Christendom on the ground that he was the successor of Peter, the chief of the twelve disciples. But mere assertion did not mean achievement. Eastern councils received his recommendations concerning beliefs but denied his claim of supreme authority by recognizing the equally high rank of the bishops of Constantinople. Pope Leo's denial of the validity of this conciliar decision marks the first definite rift between the Eastern and Western churches.

In the West, thanks to the absence of any other outstanding church, and to the weakness of the imperial power, Leo was able to assert his claims with some degree of success. He not only insisted that the bishops of Rome were the heirs of Peter's authority, but he won formal acknowledgment of these claims in an imperial decree of the Western emperor Valentinian III (425-455). But a weak emperor's assertion of papal supremacy did not necessarily enforce it. At this time the emperor had little influence outside of Italy; consequently the pope exercised only that control which his own abilities warranted. Leo's importance in Rome and its vicinity is shown by the fact that he carried on diplomatic negotiations with the invading Huns (452) and Vandals (455).[8] Throughout Italy, and to some extent beyond the peninsula, he asserted his authority in ecclesiastical affairs. On

[8] See below, pp. 118, 121.

the whole, Leo claimed and exercised broad powers in the West; in the East, although his advice was accepted, his commands were disregarded.

THE CLIMAX OF
THE EARLY ME-
DIEVAL PAPACY
After Pope Leo, the progress of the Roman Catholic Church continued to be influenced by the trend of civil affairs. The disintegration of the West in the fifth century brought the papacy face to face with new problems. In one respect conditions were better. The passing of the dynasty of Western emperors freed the popes from imperial domination. At a time when the patriarchs of Constantinople were mere puppets of the Eastern emperors, the empire in the West completely disintegrated, leaving the popes masters of their own destinies. This independent position, however, had its disadvantages. By 500 the Western Empire had passed entirely into the hands of Germanic rulers and throughout the entire sixth century the bishops of Rome were compelled to struggle for the recognition of their authority. For a time they seemed to be in a more difficult position than before, for the new Germanic rulers were Arian heretics and little inclined to respect the rights of Athanasian popes. Theodoric, the Ostrogothic king of Italy (493-526),[9] constantly disregarded the pope's wishes. When the Ostrogoths were overthrown by the Eastern emperor, Justinian,[10] the popes found themselves in a worse predicament. Now they were forced to take orders from the emperor and his patriarch at Constantinople. The domination of the orthodox emperor and the Greek Catholic clergy was harsher than that of the Arian Ostrogoths. Justinian and his empress, Theodora, deposed and set up popes, arbitrarily imprisoning any who resisted their will. The popes of the sixth century could merely assert their independence and await better times. They were finally saved from Eastern despotism by the coming of the Lombards (568).[11] But this new barbarian power which had brought deliverance from imperial control in turn threatened to overwhelm the papacy. Fortunately a remarkable pope appeared, and by his energetic and skillful leadership papal prestige was saved. The career of Gregory I serves as an excellent and vivid illustration of the difficulties which were encountered by the rising papacy and also of the characteristics of successful papal leadership which developed during this critical period.

[9] See below, p. 124.
[10] See below, p. 124.

[11] See below, p. 124.

GREGORY THE
GREAT: EARLY
CAREER
Gregory I (590-604) came from a noble Christian family. Educated for the legal profession, he, as a young man, became prefect (mayor) of Rome. He did not remain long in the service of the state, however. Religious influences were strong in that day, and at the death of Gregory's father, his mother became a nun. Soon Gregory gave away the family inheritance and turned the ancestral mansion into a monastery. He then engaged in ascetic practices and strenuous religious activities which threatened his health. Besides founding six monasteries in Sicily and managing the home establishment, he planned a missionary journey to England. But the church authorities had better uses for the converted lawyer-prefect. He was made a deacon of the Roman church, then sent to Constantinople as a papal ambassador for six years, and finally elected pope, much against his own wishes.

Gregory's accomplishments as pope were remarkable. He began his pontificate in the midst of a raging pestilence which (according to tradition) he ended by means of a sacred procession. As the clergy and penitent populace marched through the streets of the city, the avenging archangel was seen sheathing his sword over the tomb of Hadrian, which, in commemoration of the event, has ever since been called the Castle of the Holy Angel (*Castello Sant'Angelo*). Throughout his pontificate Gregory emphasized the religious functions of his office. He preached regularly at various churches in Rome, and forty of his sermons (called *homilies*) have come down to the present day. They reflect the practical yet mystical attitude of the typical medieval theologian. In order to impress moral truths it was customary to expound as actual fact superstitious ideas and incredible occurrences. Each of Gregory's sermons was a simple explanation of a Biblical text with special emphasis on the moral lesson involved. This was driven home by an illustration taken from some event of everyday life which proved the miraculous power of religion. In every age, such pious anecdotes have been popular with uneducated listeners. Throughout the Middle Ages, the stories from Gregory's *Homilies* enjoyed the greatest popularity.

GREGORY AS A
WRITER
Gregory also composed formal religious treatises which had a universal appeal. He wrote so clearly and simply that his theological works were among the most popular of the entire medieval period. The writings of Augustine, Ambrose, and Jerome were more profound, but those of Greg-

ory were read, quoted, and loved by pious folk everywhere. In his
Moralia, a commentary on the book of Job, he interpreted the Scripture in a fashion that seems very strange today, but was characteristic
of his time. In every passage he found a mysterious allegorical meaning. The word *oxen,* for instance, meant more than the animals usually
indicated by the term. It might signify stupidity, or patience, or the laboring men. Wherever numbers appeared, they had a mysterious sacred
significance. Fifty (according to Gregory) indicated rest, since it was
formed from seven times seven, plus one. Five hundred, which is ten
times fifty, represented perfect rest. In every age there are people who
are fascinated by the mystical interpretation of numbers or other portions of Biblical passages. The practice, popularized by Gregory, of
finding in the Bible a hidden meaning which threw light on contemporary conditions or events, continued throughout the Middle Ages,
and is still prevalent among certain types of zealous Christians.

Gregory's *Dialogues,* so called because they were written in the
traditional Greek form of a dialogue, related pious tales concerning
the lives of various Italian saints, and especially of the monk, St. Benedict.[12] In them Gregory told of miraculous occurrences connected with
purgatory, the mass, penance, relics, and other matters of church ritual
which were prevalent in his day. As in the *Homilies* and *Moralia,* he
accepted without question strange tales of divine intervention, of sa-
tanic influences, visions, spirits, demons, saints, and magic. The average Christian of that day believed in such things, and Gregory was
writing for the average Christian. Furthermore, he was a practical
churchman who was convinced that such pious beliefs would help to
make people better Christians—the supreme aim of the church.

Of greater modern appeal than the works already mentioned is the
Pastoral Rule, a handbook of instructions for bishops. It was sensible
and practical and showed a real understanding of human psychology.
After the manner of a skillful physician Gregory advised different
kinds of spiritual treatment for different types of individuals. For
instance, he advocated a sympathetic and tolerant attitude toward the
heathen shrines and pagan customs of the newly converted Germanic
peoples. Toward heretics, however, and in relation to the corrupting
influences of worldly society, bishops must display a strict and uncompromising zeal. Above all they must remember to set an example of
high moral conduct and spiritual integrity.

[12] See below, p. 98.

GREGORY'S
BUSINESS
LETTERS

Still more in keeping with the character of the states-manlike pope are his letters. Most of them were concerned with religious matters, but many dealt with the business affairs of the Roman church in an amazingly practical fashion. It has been estimated that, in Gregory's day, the church at Rome owned some eighteen hundred square miles of land in various parts of Italy, Sicily, Illyria, and southern Gaul. These estates brought in from one to two million dollars' worth of revenue annually, from grain, olive oil, slate, marble, lead, and timber. The letters concerned with the management of these estates reveal activities that one seldom associates with a medieval pope. The scores of letters which Gregory wrote to the clerical overseers who managed the estates reveal a knowledge of the practical details of agriculture and business that is astounding. To a subdeacon in charge of certain Sicilian estates he wrote: "The herds of mares which are utterly unprofitable to us, I wish to be sold in lots and only four hundred of the younger ones kept for breeding . . . As for the herdsmen, place them on the different farms that they may be of some use in the cultivation of the land. All the brazen vessels and utensils, the property of the Church at Syracuse and Palermo, should be sold before they are entirely destroyed from age." [13]

The letters also indicate Gregory's insistence upon justice for the lowliest peasants on the papal domains. To one of his agents he wrote: "I have frequently charged you not so much to promote the worldly interests of the church as to relieve the poor in their distress and especially to protect them from oppression." In another letter he gave orders for the distribution of "cows, sheep, and swine . . . to each according to his degree of poverty." Gregory's concern for the welfare of the common man in no way affected his insistence upon absolute spiritual obedience. A letter to a Sardinian bishop suggested that if any *pagan* peasant "be so obstinate as to refuse to come to the Lord God, he must be heavily burdened with taxes so that he will hasten to the right way."

GREGORY AS A
DIPLOMAT

Throughout Gregory's correspondence one meets with a many-sided pope. Perhaps the most difficult of his duties was that of upholding the rights of the papacy and the church in a world of ruthless and powerful monarchs.

---

[13] Dudden, *Gregory the Great,* I, 314 ff., gives the text of several of the pope's business letters.

Here the pope displayed rare, and sometimes disappointingly diplomatic, shrewdness. On one occasion he sent congratulations to a cruel usurper who had murdered the Eastern emperor, extending greetings to his "Imperial Benignity and Piety." This was followed by an exhortation to suppress the patriarch of Constantinople who, with the support of the previous emperor, had encroached upon the rights of the pope in the East. A similar tone characterizes certain of Gregory's letters to the Frankish queen, Brunhilde of Austrasia, a ruthlessly ambitious woman who was too powerful a personage to antagonize; besides she might be of great assistance to the missionaries whom Gregory was sending to England by way of Gaul. But he could clash with monarchs when the occasion demanded. He courageously defied the Eastern emperor on matters concerning the freedom of the church. In Italy he led in the fight against the Lombards. When they began to push southward into papal territory, Gregory allied with the East Roman governor of Ravenna in order to stop them. Papal money and man power provided for the erection of a series of forts between Rome and Ravenna to serve as a frontier defense against the enemy.[14]

GREGORY AND THE EASTERN CHURCH

Gregory's greatest contribution to succeeding ages was his firm insistence on the pope's right to rule the entire church. It was this claim that eventually made the papacy a great international power. In the East such claims led to sharp conflicts with the patriarch of Constantinople and his patron, the emperor. In spite of rebuffs Gregory held his ground thereby strengthening the reputation, if not the actual influence, of the papacy in the East. On one occasion the emperor attempted to force him to recognize a newly elected Dalmatian archbishop who was a man of unsavory reputation. Gregory refused, insisting that "if the affairs of the bishops committed to my charge are to be settled by patronage at the court . . . woe is me."

Gregory also sought to increase the powers of the papacy at the expense of the patriarch of Constantinople. When that prelate assumed the title "Bishop of Bishops," Gregory countered with the deceptively modest title "Servant of the Servants of God," and refused to admit the patriarch's authority even in the Eastern Church. Although Gregory won little recognition in the East, his firm stand strengthened the position of the papacy at home.

[14] See below, p. 124 concerning the Lombard invasion.

GREGORY AND
THE WESTERN
CHURCH

In the West, Gregory's claims were more favorably received, and in most regions the local bishops and monarchs acknowledged his right to intervene in their affairs. In Spain the Visigothic king accepted the orthodox faith and recognized Gregory as "the superior of all other bishops." In return, Gregory recognized the authority of the local archbishop of Seville, and sent a gift of sacred relics for the king. This exchange paved the way for papal letters of advice, and, down to the Moslem conquest (711), the Spanish church was subject to papal control. Gregory also asserted his unrestricted right to supervise the bishops of the imperial territories in southeastern Spain and Northern Africa. On one occasion he insisted that there was "no bishop who is not subject to the Holy See." [15] Even though Gregory's claims were not always enforced or recognized, he asserted them so confidently that the West came to think of the pope as one who possessed universal authority in religious affairs. For the first time in its history, the papacy was a world power.

GREGORY
"THE GREAT"

Gregory was the greatest pope of the early Middle Ages and one of the outstanding ecclesiastical figures of all time. He represented some of the most important forces in the building of medieval Christianity. As a writer he brought the doctrines and practices of the church to the attention of the masses in a marvelously effective manner. As bishop of Rome he had greater success than any of his predecessors—and many of his successors—in welding the various Western churches into a united whole. It was he who started the Benedictine monks on a great missionary enterprise that eventually brought England, Scotland, and Ireland into the Roman church. A century and a half later, the same impulse was transmitted from this region to the Rhinelands by the monk Boniface, who thus laid the foundation for papal control over the Germanies. Had it been possible for the Eastern emperors to work in harmony with the Benedictine monks and Roman popes, Christendom would have been brought to a glorious unity during the Gregorian age.

As it was, Gregory can be called the builder of the Western or Roman Catholic Church. His achievements as an administrator appear more remarkable when one remembers that he was a sick, pain-racked monk who by sheer will power organized and directed the

15 The "Holy See" is the papacy.

forces that were destined eventually to bring order to a disunited Christian world. At his accession most of the Western churches were independent or were grouped in small regional units controlled and exploited by Germanic rulers. By the end of his pontificate, innumerable bonds of unity with the Roman church had been established and all Western Europe recognized, even if it did not follow, the leadership of the bishops of Rome.

In spite of the achievements of a pope such as Gregory, the rise of the papacy was neither the work of one man, nor of several. It was the culmination of underlying forces that had been in operation for centuries. The most prominent of these were (1) the political, economic, cultural, and historical prestige of the city of Rome; (2) the religious prestige of Paul and Peter as founders of the Roman church; (3) the absence of any other outstanding church in the West; (4) the absence of a strong imperial power in the West; and (5) the religious orthodoxy and political ability of bishops such as Leo and Gregory. As a result of this fortunate combination of circumstances the Roman church assumed the leadership of Western Christianity during the early period of Christian expansion. By 300 A.D., Christianity, having won the right to exist, had proceeded to conquer the Roman world. During the three centuries from Constantine to Gregory, paganism was overcome, the Germanic barbarians were converted, and Christendom was organized into an Eastern and a Western Church. It was in this process that the church in general, and the papacy in particular, found a valuable ally in monasticism, a new Christian institution.

EARLY CHRISTIAN MONASTICISM

Second only to the papacy among the organized forces of Western Christendom was monasticism. Like many other Christian institutions, monasticism was not Christian in origin. Wherever and whenever religious fervor abounds, certain pious individuals withdraw from their fellows to seek peace of soul through communion with God. Such people usually believe that perfect peace and communion are best attained through ascetic practices—those bodily hardships by which natural human desires are repressed so as to leave the spirit pure and free from distracting earthly influences. Poverty and physical affliction are highly prized by ascetics because of their disciplinary effect.

Six centuries before Christ, Buddha, in India, not only lauded poverty and self-denial but set an example of asceticism which led thousands of Hindus to adopt that ideal as a means of attaining spiritual perfection. In Greece and Rome, during the later centuries, there were similar types, among them the luxury-hating Cynics. Among the Jews there were at least two sects of ascetics, the Nazarenes and the Essenes. Samson, John the Baptist, and Christ himself at times, devoted themselves to ascetic practices. It will be remembered that Christ once told a rich young ruler: "If thou wilt be perfect, go and sell that thou hast and give to the poor, . . . and follow me." [16]

In all ages, religious fervor tends to produce mystical ascetics who seek peace of mind through isolation, purity of soul through unattractive surroundings, salvation through suffering, and happiness in the world to come through unhappiness on earth. Monasticism is the organized institutional life assumed by such religious groups.

MONASTICISM IN THE EAST

For three centuries Christianity showed little trace of asceticism. Christ's life was not primarily ascetic. His followers, and most of the early Christians, came from the lower ranks of society in which poverty and suffering were normal conditions of life. Among minority groups such as the Gnostics, the Manicheans, and the puritanical Montanists, however, the ascetic ideal was emphasized.

Asceticism came into prominence first among the Christians of the East. There, during the fourth century, it began with hermits, or lone ascetics. The severe persecutions of the third century had driven many Christians into the wilds, where some of them had learned the joys as well as the discomforts of solitude. After the persecutions ended, individual Christians continued to withdraw to uninhabited places, not so much for safety as for prayer and meditation. Some Christians seem to have adopted ascetic practices in imitation (or perhaps rivalry) of the hermit followers of the pagan Egyptian god Serapis. Nonreligious conditions also contributed to the popularity of monastic life. Economic depressions, heavy imperial taxation, and the increasing uncertainties of city life led many people to desert their homes for a simple free existence in the wilderness.

Essentially, however, monasticism was a religious movement. It is probable that the cessation of persecutions and soul-inspiring martyrdoms was the chief influence in the popularization of this new type of religious suffering. As Professor Randall has expressed it in his *Making of the Modern Mind:*

[16] Matthew 19:21.

So long as the persecutions lasted, no man needed to seek the crucifixion of the flesh; soldiers and athletes of Christ found their discipline in training for the martyr's crown. But when Christianity became respectable, the universal laxity of morals, particularly that bane of the fathers, sexual promiscuity, crept into the fold with the new "converts." Then it was that multitudes turned away from such a world in quiet disdain and sought out for themselves a purer and more temperate life. Those whom death had not daunted now fled from luxury and looseness.[17]

Monasticism was primarily a protest against the increasing worldliness of organized Christianity. The fourth-century Christian zealot substituted self-inflicted exile for the martyrdom of earlier days. Public opinion came to laud the suffering hermit as it had venerated the Christian martyr. The ardent faith and frugal lives of the holy men of the deserts were an ever-present indictment of the ceremonial pretenses and pagan worldliness of nominal Christians and unspiritual clergymen.[18] Thus it was that both hermitism and the organized monasticism that developed from it became symbols of Christlike poverty and suffering in the increasingly sophisticated Christian world of the fourth century.

THE HERMITS OF THE EAST   By the end of the fourth century the Egyptian deserts along the Nile were peopled with Christians who had forsaken the world in order to attain true spirituality. The popularity of hermit life and its rapid development are vividly illustrated by the legend of St. Anthony, the patron saint of Eastern monasticism. At about twenty years of age, so it was said,

---

[17] P. 64.

[18] A vivid picture of the disgust of genuine Christians for their worldly fellows and for unspiritual clergymen is to be found in the letters of Jerome. With biting irony he commented on the lives of Christian women "who wear a fresh frock every day . . . while Christ [i.e., Christ's poor] lies naked and starving at their very doors." He vented his pious spite especially on gay widows, with "their red lips and plump sleek skins . . . with belladonna in their eyes . . . their faces so covered with powder and so disfigured by excessive whiteness that they look like idols. If a tear falls, it makes a wet furrow on their skin. . . ." The extremes in which clergymen indulged in worldly pleasures is suggested by Jerome's warning: "Keep your tongue, as well as your eyes, chaste; never discuss a woman's figure." To those clerics who yielded to the temptation of drinking, he also directed a warning: "Never let your breath smell of wine . . . or shechar. Now every intoxicating drink is called shechar in the Hebrew language; whether it is made of grain or the juice of apples . . . or distilled from honeycomb (a rude sort of mead) . . . or by squeezing dates or straining a thick syrup from a decoction of grain." Apparently as pious a clergyman as Jerome knew a great deal about liquors, rich foods, and women; and all such influences he considered dangerous for the true Christian. See *Select Letters of St. Jerome,* translated by F. A. Wright, Putnam, 1933; and *Nicene and post-Nicene Fathers,* 2nd series, 1890, Vol. VI, *passim.*

he sold his property, gave all to charity, placed his sister in a *parthenon* (a young girls' home), and settled in a tiny hut to live a life of prayer and service for wayfarers. Later he retired to a cave and became a solitary hermit. But the fame of his moral struggles in fighting off the Devil inspired so many others to join him that he moved farther into the desert. Even here there was no escape from his zealous followers. For twenty years he lived in a solitary cell, surrounded by the dwellings of the fellow hermits over whom he was forced to assume a vague jurisdiction.

There are many curious tales which illustrate the ardent Christian asceticism of this period. One pious hermit was said to have gone without bread for eighty years; another reveled in such filth that he was covered with vermin; another, in order to escape all worldly influences, resolved never to look at his own body, and refused even to take off his clothes. All of the holiest of the hermits resorted to drastic physical tortures in order to fight off the temptations of the Devil, who appeared most often in the form of an alluringly beautiful woman. By standing in ice cold water, rolling in thorns, or lashing themselves with whips, the true soldiers of Christ were usually able to defeat the wiles of the Evil One. To many Christians the fanatical hermit was one of God's saints, and no miracle was too great for him to accomplish. However fanciful the stories of the hermits of the desert, they illustrate the high religious idealism and stern courage that animated thousands of men and women in Egypt, Syria, Asia Minor, and Greece in the early centuries of the Christian Church.

THE MONKS
OF THE EAST

Once hermitism had taken root, it began to change to a more normal type of life. As soon as a hermit became famous, other hermits settled near by; thus he was no longer a true hermit, but the leader of a *group* of hermits. As a result of the inevitable tendency of men to live in groups, hermitism quickly evolved into monasticism. So far as is known, the first organized community of hermit-monks was that of Pachomius, a younger contemporary of St. Anthony. Before his death (at about 350) Pachomius had established nine monasteries. One of them was located in an old pagan monastery of Serapis, on an island in the Nile; another was in the ancient Egyptian temple at Karnak. In these communities, most of the monks lived in the same building, but in separate cells. They had their meals and religious services together. Eventually Pachomius drew up a set of regulations which provided for the testing of all new members, a period of probation, and a systematic schedule of living, including manual labor of various kinds. Before long the Nile Valley and the neighboring oases were dotted with monastic settlements of a similar nature. Many of them became prosperous well-organized communities, endowed with valuable landed estates by wealthy Christians.

The activities of Basil (d. 379), a clergyman of Asia Minor, were also significant in the development of monasticism. Unlike Anthony and Pachomius, Basil was a bishop and an intellectual man, well trained in the pagan classics and in Christian theology. He realized that Christians, even those who were dedicated to the ascetic life, must associate with their fellows and must have some sort of mental and physical development. Therefore his monastic rule provided for study and teaching, for industrial and agricultural tasks, and for. works of charity. Throughout the East, and later in the West, the rule, and also the career of this famous bishop-abbot had a wide influence.

Basil was, however, only one of the many Eastern churchmen who labored to make monasticism a practical and constructive influence in religious life. Gradually monasticism became more closely associated with the other institutions of the church. Women, as well as clergymen, came under the monastic spell. In many places nunneries were established, often by the wives or sisters of the founders of monasteries. The well-known tale of Thais, the popular Alexandrian dancer who deserted the stage to enter a nunnery, illustrates the manner in which the monastic movement attracted people of various classes. There were many types of monks.

The occasional extremes to which some individuals were carried by their fanatical piety is shown by the spectacular careers of the pillar saints of whom St. Simeon Stylites was the most famous. He was reputed to have lived for years on the top of a sixty-foot pillar. He attained such popularity and influence that even the Bedouin tribes of the Arabian Desert venerated him. The pillar saints and other extremists, such as the grass-eating hermits of Syria, have given to Eastern monasticism a reputation for uncontrolled fanaticism. Although some Eastern monks tended toward the excessive mysticism and emotionalism of the Orient, others made notable advances in practical Christian service and in economic organization. In all regions there were monasteries in which religious life was carefully regulated. The Greek peninsula of Mount Athos still has several communities which were known throughout the Middle Ages for their well-organized life and cultural achievements.

MONASTICISM
IN THE WEST

Western monasticism, which was an adaptation from the East, went through the same general evolution from independent hermit life to organized communities of monks, from local self-regulation to regimented centralization, and from primitive ideals of poverty to the struggle for power and prestige. In Western monasticism one finds considerably less of individualism and fanaticism than in the East; also a more rapid development toward efficient organization and regulation. There were fewer hermits and more well-regulated communities in the West. This was in keeping with the more practical and disciplined type of mind of the people of the Latin regions of the Mediterranean.

In 339 Athanasius of Alexandria, during one of his many periods of exile, took refuge in Rome. With him were two hermits from the Egyptian desert. Their enthusiasm for St. Anthony and the ascetic way of life won many Westerners to the monastic ideal, but there was little of hermitism and fanatical asceticism in Italy. A Roman senator made over his palace into what is usually considered as the first monastery in the West. This aristocratic type of monasticism was quite different from the unregulated hermitism of the East. Even so, the moderate monasticism practiced by a few of the upper-class Italians was unpopular with the majority of the clergy and the people of Rome. When the great Christian scholar, Jerome, after his return from the East, induced several noble ladies to found nunneries in their villas, he and his protégés became subjects of scandalous gossip and public derision. When a young nun died as a result of excessive fasting, angry mobs threatened violence, and Jerome, followed later by several pious ladies, retired to Bethlehem where they founded a number of monasteries and nunneries. Here, in the East, Jerome lived and worked until his death. Thither he invited some of his less enthusiastic Roman friends, urging them to desert "the roofs and smoky dungeons of the cities" for "the desert where the flowers of Christ are blooming." The mingled attractions of religion and "nature in the rough" apparently met with little response among the Romans.

Meanwhile in other parts of the West a more practical form of monasticism was taking root. At Vercelli in northern Italy the local bishop had his clergy live together like monks. Bishop Ambrose founded a similar institution at Milan, and in Northern Africa Bishop

Augustine of Hippo organized the clergy of his cathedral into a semi-monastic group of regular (i.e., regulated) canons.[19] He also drew up an informal rule for nuns. By the end of the fifth century it was evident that Western monasticism was destined to become strictly regulated and closely allied with the priesthood of secular clergymen.[20]

GALLIC
MONASTICISM

In some regions of the West the more individualistic type of monasticism flourished for a time. In Gaul, for instance, the evolution of monasticism resembles that in Egypt. It began with hermitism and progressed to organized community life. The "Anthony of the West" was Martin of Tours, a conscientious objector who, after refusing to fight in the imperial army, entered a monastery at Poitiers, and finally (at about 362) established a hermitage on the banks of the Loire River. As in the case of St. Anthony, his fame spread and within ten years at Marmoutier there were eighty hermit-monks, each living in his own cave, but under the general supervision of Martin. Eventually the colony numbered two thousand persons who lived in separate cells but ate and worshipped together. In other parts of Gaul, especially amid the volcanic mountains of Auvergne, unorganized hermitism flourished. For a while the city of Treves tolerated a pillar saint similar to Simeon Stylites. But, for the most part, Western monasticism was well regulated. At Marseilles early in the fifth century John Cassian, "the Pachomius of the West," established two monasteries and drew up a set of regulations called the "Institutions" which were modeled after the rules of the Easterners, Pachomius and Basil.

By the year 500 the West had many communities of monks, monastic canons, and nuns. The unsettled conditions that accompanied the disintegration of the Western Empire and the coming of the Germanic tribes during the fifth century strengthened monasticism. Not only people of pious ambitions, but also scholars, widows, orphans, and those who had lost positions, property, and homes, flocked to these refuges. Such conditions also placed a greater emphasis on the practical type of monasticism. Both the conditions of life in the fifth century

[19] The clergy of a cathedral church were called canons, a rather confusing word also used of conciliar decrees and of church law (i.e., canon law). *Regular* canons were canons who lived according to a monastic *regula* or rule.

[20] Inasmuch as the growth of monasticism created a new and distinctive type of clergy, called *regulars,* the members of the ordinary clergy (the bishops, priests, deacons, and so on) were called *seculars.* They continued to live and work in the world (*saeculum*) of everyday people instead of withdrawing to the regulated and secluded life of a monastery. See below, p. 419, for further discussion of the two types of clergy.

and the fundamental Roman characteristics of the people of the West tended to make its monastic institutions practical and conservative.

BENEDICT
OF NURSIA

During the sixth century Western monasticism took on still more of the practical characteristics of the Roman West. In Italy Benedict of Nursia (ca. 480-ca. 550) established a "systematized form of perfect Christian life" which, under the name of Benedictine monasticism, soon spread throughout most of the Christian world. Benedict, like his younger contemporary, the famous Pope Gregory I, came from a noble Italian family. While pursuing his education in the secular schools of Rome he became so disgusted with the licentious lives of the members of polite society that he abandoned his studies and became a hermit, living in a cave in the mountains near Subiaco. Other hermits joined him, and the inevitable evolution from hermitism to monasticism followed. He founded several monasteries, finally establishing a community in the Campanian plain south of Rome, on a high hill called Monte Cassino. Here he drew up the Benedictine rule for the monks among whom he lived and worked. Although the monastic rules of Pachomius, Basil, and of Westerners such as Augustine and Cassian, had long been known in Italy, Benedict's rule eventually supplanted them all. This was due to its simple practical character. The "Little Rule for Beginners," as Benedict himself called it, reduced fanatical asceticism to common-sense religious living. Although the rule was little used in Benedict's day, in succeeding centuries it was introduced into distant regions as missionary monks were sent out by the popes. Eventually it was so widely adopted that it has been referred to as "The Magna Carta of Western Monasticism."

THE BENEDIC-
TINE RULE

The rule, providing for well-organized communities of monks, safeguarded them from excesses. New members went through a one-year "novitiate" of instruction and training. During this period they might withdraw in case they could not sincerely continue the monastic regime. Those who decided to become monks took solemn written vows in which they promised to forsake the world, to continue steadfast in the monastic life, and to obey the abbot in all things. Besides these, they were expected to dedicate themselves to a life of poverty and celibacy.[21]

The routine of the monks was strictly but sensibly regulated. Their daily schedule included approximately eight hours of rest, eight

---

[21] Celibacy is abstinence from marriage, usually for religious reasons.

hours of manual labor, and eight hours for religious services, reading, and eating. The chief monastic duty was the celebration of the seven religious services, beginning with vigil-matin, before daybreak, and ending with vespers and compline, just before dark. Most of the morning and the latter part of the afternoon were spent in manual labor in the gardens and fields or in the monastic workshops. After the first meal of the day, which came at noon, there was a siesta and a period of reading. Monastic meals consisted of wine, bread, and vegetables—simple food in a limited quantity. Even today, guests at Monte Cassino are told that "our monastic fare is simple, but such as it is, you are welcome." After the evening meal came the final religious service; then until dark the monks read religious books. Sleep was interrupted by the early morning service; like the others this consisted of prayers and the chanting of several psalms. All monks, rich and poor alike, arose at the regular hours, took part in the religious services, worked in the kitchens and gardens, and strictly obeyed the orders of the abbot.

In a remarkably democratic as well as efficient manner, the rule provided that the abbot should be elected by the monks; but, once elected, his authority was absolute. Under his control were the other officers, all of them appointed by him; the prior, or vice-abbot, the chamberlain who had charge of the treasure chamber, the cellarer who cared for the food and drink, the sacristan who kept the holy relics and vestments, the cantor who trained the singers and often had charge of the library, the infirmarian who kept the sick ward, the hospitaler who took care of the guest house, the almoner or dispenser of alms, and the scholastic who conducted the school.

The rule of St. Benedict consists of short chapters concerning the duties of monks, miscellaneous affairs, religious services, internal administration, and discipline. So effective was this brief set of regulations that it was eventually adopted by monasteries in all parts of Western Europe. Pope Gregory (himself a monk) used his influence in extending the sphere of Benedictine activities. His missionary assistant, Augustine of Canterbury, introduced the rule into England, whence it spread to Scotland and Ireland. Later, missionary monks from England carried it to Germany and to Frankish Gaul, where it soon replaced the older monastic systems of that region. As the Benedictine rule spread throughout Western Europe, monastic life became standardized and its contribution to medieval society became more effective. Its influence is still widespread in the Roman Catholic Church.

WHY MONASTI-
CISM GREW
The expansion of Benedictine monasticism was due to the essentially workable character of its rule and organization. Monasticism as a whole grew because it served both the religious and secular needs of an age of declining security and prosperity. In the earlier centuries, the monastic life was the mark of an exceptionally pious inclination. Later, as monasticism became an established institution of Western society, it offered a variety of opportunities, both religious and secular, that attracted varied types of people. In ever-increasing numbers men and women of ambition and intelligence sought in monasticism an escape from a world that offered less and less hope of material advancement. Ever since the second century, the Roman world had tended to a psychology of pessimism and had turned from the realities of life to mysticism. As the empire crumbled and the Germanic invaders triumphed, despairing men and women took refuge in monasticism.

Intellectuals found in the monastic environment an opportunity for contemplation, reading, and writing, untroubled by economic or political problems. Even though the mental horizon might be restricted by pious fanatics, and intellectual activities interrupted by religious duties, the learned monk found it possible to delve deeply into classical and Christian literature. A man of pedagogical inclinations might find ample exercise for his talents in the monastic school. Young boys, of either noble or peasant birth, who showed a bent for intellectual pursuits, could be dedicated to a monastery, there to be trained for a position of importance in the church. A man or boy of cultural instincts, who in our day plans an intellectual career in a university, in that day would have entered a monastery.

Monasteries also had material attractions. They provided a relatively high degree of security from warfare, robbery, and deeds of violence. Their extensive lands and efficient methods of cultivation and craftsmanship furnished interesting activities and comfortable living for the members of the order. Monasticism offered attractions to people of all ranks. Noblemen and noblewomen, even royal princesses, sometimes founded monastic establishments, over which they presided, living amid the luxuries of court life but with none of its disadvantages. For many a peasant boy, the monastic life was the gateway to advancement from serfdom to a religious and administrative career that might lead to an abbacy, bishopric, or even to the papacy. Monasticism also provided an escape from intolerable conditions; from an unendurable marriage, from the intrigues of aristocratic society, from shameful associates, from failure in a political career, or merely from insecurity and poverty.

It is well to bear in mind that the monastery aimed, first and foremost, to provide a highly organized form of religious training for those who, with singleness of purpose, placed the salvation of their souls above earthly glory. But with all its religious functions, a monastery was something more than a church. It was a social institution, a little world in itself within which there was a place for any person of peaceful and righteous intentions. There a king, warrior, merchant, artisan, agriculturalist, or homeless wanderer could find the solace of religion and the co-operative relationships of true community life. A monastery might take on the appearance of a school, a model farm, or an old folks' home, in addition to serving as a religious refuge.

THE INFLUENCE OF MONASTICISM　Monasticism, and, for a time, Benedictine monasticism, was the spiritual dynamo of Western Christianity. Even in centuries and regions of marked corruption in church and state, there were many monks who put spiritual values first. Obedience, humility, and the worship of God were dominant forces in monastic life. To be sure, the emphasis on personal salvation, self-control, and religious ceremonial made for a self-centered religion, but the monastic ideal also expressed itself in acts of charity for mankind. The monks cared for the poor, for travelers, and, in times of famine, for entire communities. During most of the Middle Ages the monasteries were the chief agencies for social service and charity. Last, but not least, Benedictine monks, such as Augustine of Canterbury and Boniface, were successful in converting the heathen, not only to Christianity, but also to Roman civilization.

ECONOMIC INFLUENCES　Of great importance was the economic leadership of the monks. Most monasteries acquired immense endowments from wealthy patrons. Inasmuch as Roman civilization was steadily drifting toward a rural economy, this wealth was chiefly landed property, valuable for its agricultural products. This forced the monks into agriculture on a large scale, and every well-organized monastery became a model farm-community which tended to set a high standard of agricultural efficiency. The monks studied Roman methods of scientific farming, improved the breeds of cattle, developed varied fruits and grain crops, employed fertilizers, and worked out many other improvements in farming. In many respects the medieval monastery functioned as a sort of agricultural experiment station. Since many monasteries were established in the wilderness, the monks also served as pioneers, draining swamps, clearing forests, and converting the heathen to settled agricultural pursuits as well as to Christianity.

As a secondary form of economic activity most monasteries also developed important home industries. Beer, wine, cordials such as Benedictine and Chartreuse, iron work, leather goods, and the like, were produced by skilled monastic artisans. Celtic monasteries were famous for bell casting; monks in certain parts of Gaul specialized in the manufacture of gloves and certain kinds of cloth; in other places the production of lead pipe was almost a monastic monopoly. It is little wonder that, in the later centuries, industrial communities sometimes grew up about monasteries, and that tradesmen settled in such places. By encouraging the settlement of artisan and merchant colonies under the shelter of their protecting walls, monasteries often became trading centers of great importance. It was not by mere chance that some of the great fairs of medieval Europe were held on or near monastic domains, and that monastic settlements gave rise to towns in the later centuries.

INTELLECTUAL
INFLUENCES
Not the least of the contributions of monasticism to medieval civilization was the encouragement of intellectual activities. Cassiodorus (490-585),[22] one of the enlightened ministers of Theodoric the Ostrogoth, gave a great impetus to such tendencies by founding on his own estates in southern Italy a monastic "university" in which literary and other educational activities were emphasized. His ideal, like that of Jerome in his Bethlehem retreat, was to work out a fusion of religious and intellectual interests, and to harmonize sacred and secular learning. By the light of mechanical self-feeding lamps and to the time of water clocks, Cassiodorus' monks studied not only the Scriptures and Church Fathers but also classical works and his own handbooks on the seven liberal arts. They also copied both sacred and secular (i.e., classical) writings.

Such activities were in marked contrast to the life at Benedict's monastic "military academies." Benedict and his immediate successors manifested little interest in secular studies. Their rule called for little mental labor, and even during reading periods, it provided only for

---

[22] See below, p. 263.

the use of *religious* books. Each Benedictine monastery had a school, but the monks acquired only the rudiments of secular learning. During the sixth and seventh centuries it was the rival organizations of the Irish monks [23] that kept the torch of learning burning brightly, not only in the British Isles but in many places on the Continent. Greek was studied and taught in their schools and they made great progress in the art of illustrating manuscripts.[24] Only with the coming of such English scholars as Bede and Alcuin in the eighth century did Benedictine monasticism take a prominent place in the field of learning. In later centuries, such scholars and scientists as Roger Bacon, Albertus Magnus, and Thomas Aquinas were to bring deserved glory to the monastic order.

During the early medieval centuries monasticism, like other church institutions, followed the general trend of civilization. In the East the monasteries were more wealthy, industrial, and cultured. In the West intellectual activities were subordinated to less advanced religious and agricultural activities, since most monasteries were rural centers. With the disintegration of the empire in the West and the supremacy of the Germanic invaders Western Europe became ever more agrarian in character. Thus monasticism was a vital factor in the economic and social life, as well as in the religion of the medieval West. It also served as a valuable ally of the papacy in the difficult task of Christianizing and civilizing the Germanic people and bringing them under the sway of the Roman Church.

[23] See below, p. 269.
[24] See below, p. 332.

$$\equiv V \equiv$$

THE GERMANIC PEOPLES

BARBARIAN INVADERS AND IMMIGRANTS

FROM early times the Roman Empire had been bounded on the north by a troubled sea of Celtic, Germanic, and Slavic peoples whose migrations kept these waters in constant agitation. Before the days of Julius Caesar, Celtic folk had dominated the regions of Northwestern Europe, and once in the second century B.C. the frontier defenses had been broken by the Cimbri and the Teutons. Within a century the pressure of Asiatic and Slavic people had driven numerous Germanic tribes southwestward into the territories of the Celts, some of whom in turn began to encroach on the Roman province in southern Gaul. Julius Caesar won enduring fame by subduing the Celts, driving the invading Germans out of Gaul, and establishing the Rhine as the Roman frontier. Half a century later, Augustus Caesar's legions failed in their attempt to push the Germans back to the line of the Elbe River. For the next two centuries all was comparatively quiet.

THE CHANGING GERMANS
If we are to trust the accounts of Roman writers, the Germans of this early period were a sturdy warlike people, primitive in their habits but capable of advancement. About a half century before Christ, Julius Caesar wrote a very brief account of the Germans with whom he had fought along the Rhine. He pictured them as fierce nomads who lived on meat, milk, cheese, and whatever they could get by fishing and hunting. They made frequent raids upon the more civilized Celtic inhabitants of Gaul. For over a century after Caesar the Romans had peaceful as well as warlike relations with the Germans. Occasionally small groups were employed as mercenary soldiers or guardsmen, and one emperor (Tiberius) allowed 40,000 of them to settle on farmlands in Gaul.

From the end of the first century A.D. comes a detailed account which shows that Germanic life had changed since the time of Julius Caesar. Tacitus, a Roman historian, wrote a book called *Germania* in which the Germans were pictured as a settled agricultural people, very different from those of whom Julius Caesar wrote. They lived in timber huts, wore clothes made of skins, and had both pasture land and plowed fields. Every year "they changed their fields," probably so as to prevent exhaustion of the soil. They used soap, boats, and the products made by wheelwrights and blacksmiths, and they traded furs, amber, and slaves to the Roman merchants who visited them. In economic, social, political, and religious institutions they were well advanced on the road to civilization. The gods worshipped by these Germans were much like those of the early Greeks and Romans. Their political assemblies, which comprised all of the fighting men, also resembled Greek and Roman assemblies, although they did little more than give assent to the proposals of the tribal chieftains and of the principal chief, who was their leader in war. Such was the civilization of the more advanced Germanic tribes late in the first century A.D. For about a century thereafter we have little evidence concerning them. Then, suddenly, during the reign of Marcus Aurelius, they began to play an important role in imperial affairs.

THE GERMANS OF THE RHINE-DANUBE FRONTIER   The period from the reign of Marcus Aurelius late in the second century to that of Diocletian late in the third century was another era of violent shifts of populations in North and Central Europe. As a result, various barbaric German tribes were pushed southward as far as the weakly garrisoned Rhine-Danube defenses, which quickly gave way. Thus it was that, during the third century, Rome's serious internal disorders were complicated by barbarian invasions.[1] Saxon pirates raided the English Channel, Frankish tribes ravaged Gaul even to the borders of Spain, and the Alamannians crossed the Rhine and plundered near-by Gallic cities. Some modern scholars believe that these devastating ravages struck such a blow to the Celtic-Roman civilization of Gaul that it never fully recovered. Further east, the Goths who were already in control of the Black Sea surged across the frontier and, in 251 at Abrittus near the mouth of the Danube, defeated and killed Emperor Decius. This disaster was the first barbarian victory over an imperial army *inside the borders of the empire,* and after it the Goths ravaged at will, penetrating as far south as Athens. Eventually

[1] See above, p. 19, for details concerning the internal condition of the empire during the third century.

they were defeated at Nish in the Balkans and forced back across the Danube by Claudius "Gothicus" (268-270). During the reign of Aurelian (270-275) they were allowed to occupy the outer province of Dacia. For a century thereafter the Goths were quiet and the Danube frontier was secure.

Several conclusions may be drawn concerning Rome's frontier troubles during the third century. First, they were caused by a vast tribal movement in the North European plain, a region which a later historian called "the womb of nations." Second, these movements brought about dangerous disturbances all along Rome's northern frontier. Third, in spite of internal disorders and temporary defeats, the empire recovered from the shock and solved the difficulty in a satisfactory manner. By the end of the critical third century it was evident that Rome could handle even an unusual wave of barbarian invaders. The fact that the same empire a century later failed to withstand a similar shock is probably to be accounted for in two ways: first, in the meantime Rome had been weakened by internal troubles; second, during the fourth century the Germans had learned much of Roman civilization, including military tactics and were consequently more formidable foes.

THE ROMANIZING OF THE GERMANS During the first three quarters of the fourth century Rome's frontiers were relatively quiet. Along the British wall, the Channel, and the Rhine the legions were able to hold in check the Picts and the Scots, the Saxons, the Franks, Vandals, Thuringians, and Alamannians with comparative ease. Further east, the Visigoths had settled in Dacia while their kinsfolk, the Ostrogoths, occupied the northern shores of the Black Sea.

Roman civilization exerted a strong influence on these and other Germanic people who dwelt along the frontiers of the empire. There was a great deal of peaceful activity between the two peoples. Roman traders exchanged manufactured articles for such raw products as furs, amber, soap, and vegetables. There was also a thriving trade in slaves, for the Germans sold their own less fortunate kinsmen and war captives for profit when the occasion presented itself. Other Germans, in small groups or as individuals, migrated into imperial territory and found lucrative employment. For centuries the Roman emperors had been hiring sturdy barbarian warriors as mercenary soldiers, not only for the frontier legions but even for the imperial guard. Some of these fighting men worked their way up to positions of importance in the

Roman army. Other Germans, sometimes as many as 40,000 at a time, were allowed to settle in outlying regions as peasant farmers. The Romans saw the advantage of having a buffer of sturdy warrior settlers in certain frontier provinces where they might bear the brunt of any invasion. Thus the mutual needs and advantages of the two races brought about permanently peaceful relations along the frontiers.

GERMANIC
IMMIGRANTS

Until the end of the fourth century, most of the Germans, most of the time, were at peace with their Roman neighbors. Constant migration brought into the empire individuals and small groups of Germans who quickly learned the ways of civilization and thus became an element of strength. Most of the Germans were simple sturdy folk eager to make a living, either in the army or on farms. Inasmuch as the native Romans cared little for such activities, German immigrants were welcome. There was also constant intermarriage with the lower-class Romans, and the distinction between Roman and German thus tended to vanish. In the gigantic melting pot of Roman civilization the Germans were merely one of many diverse elements, but one which contributed much to the strengthening of the empire. In Constantine's day one might well have imagined that Rome was destined to go on forever in her imperial task of receiving and assimilating Germans, as well as other foreign races, and making them an integral part of Mediterranean civilization.

A GERMANIC
DELUGE

These peaceful and constructive relationships came to an end, however, late in the fourth century. The change was due in a large measure to the invasion of the Huns, a ferocious people who swept across the Asiatic steppes and into the Crimean regions north of the Black Sea. This upset the existing situation, and for a generation masses of Germans, many of them wild savages from backward regions, were forced into the empire. Some came in peacefully as migrating nations of settlers or as warrior allies. Others invaded the provinces and roved about like brigands or conquering hosts. Either peacefully or as destructive raiders, nation after nation came into the empire. Rome could handle barbarians in moderate numbers, but this was a deluge which could not be held back by the imperial defenses nor assimilated by the imperial civilization. It was as if a great river, with a system of dams and levees that could take care of the normal flow of water, was suddenly flooded with unusual rains. Rome's frontier levees gave way before the unusual flood of Germans that was precipitated by this new pressure. The history of the Visigoths vividly illustrates this situation.

THE VISIGOTHS

THE VISIGOTHS
OUTSIDE THE
EMPIRE
Scanty information from later centuries, notably that contained in Jordanes's *History* [2] makes it possible to trace the evolution of the Goths from savagery to civilization and their part in the stirring events of this era. During the nomadic stage of their existence (the first and second centuries) they had apparently wandered southward from their homes in Baltic lands. In the third century they invaded the empire but were driven out and settled along the Danube River and the Black Sea. The Dacian group, called Visigoths, were much influenced by Roman civilization. During the fourth century many of them became Arian Christians as a result of the missionary labors of Bishop Ulfilas, a Roman, who after having been brought up among the Goths, undertook their conversion. His translation of the Bible into Gothic is our earliest example of any written Germanic language. The Visigoths were also influenced by the political institutions of the Romans, and exhibited a decided trend from the older tribal organization toward centralized royal government.

THE VISIGOTHS
ADMITTED INTO
THE EMPIRE
By the last quarter of the fourth century, after a century of peaceful contact with Roman-Christian society, the Visigoths had reached a stage of advancement that was relatively civilized. Their actions during the next few years were not those of a ruthless and destructive nation of savages. When they entered the empire it was as friendly allies seeking refuge from the savage Huns.

About the middle of the fourth century the Huns, wandering westward from Asia, reached the Crimea. After conquering the Ostrogoths they attacked the outlying settlements of the Visigoths, driving the terror-stricken population southward to the Danube. It is understandable why Emperor Valens, feeling the need of strengthening his frontier defenses, allowed the Visigoths to come into the empire as soldier-settlers. This had been an accepted policy of imperial diplomacy and defense since the third century, and was to become more prevalent in the next century. But Valens's intention of temporarily dis-

---

[2] Jordanes was a sixth-century Italian bishop of Gothic ancestry.

arming them was not carried out, and soon great numbers of Visigoths, and other barbarians, among them thousands of armed men, crossed the Danube. Thus it was that, in the year 376, a strong Germanic tribe found itself inside the imperial frontiers.

VISIGOTHIC REVOLT: ADRIANOPLE (378)

Aside from minor disorders, all was peaceful for two years. But the destitute refugees who crossed the Danube were mercilessly exploited by corrupt Roman officials. Finally in desperation the Visigoths revolted. They were joined by renegade Romans and other wandering bands of barbarians. Emperor Valens, hurrying back from Syria, found Constantinople and the vicinity in turmoil. After an attempt at negotiations he decided to employ the old Roman policy of stern repression. The result was a terrible disaster at Adrianople, to the west of Constantinople. The imperial army was routed, the emperor killed, and soon the Balkan peninsula was at the mercy of a victorious marauding enemy.

Adrianople was a decisive defeat, though perhaps not so epoch-making as is popularly supposed. This was not the first defeat of a Roman army by Germanic forces; in the days of Augustus the legions of Varus had been annihilated in the Teutoberg Forest. Nor was Adrianople the first occasion on which the Germans had defeated a Roman army on Roman soil; a century before, Emperor Decius had suffered defeat and death at the hands of the Goths. Nor did the defeat at Adrianople cause the downfall of the empire. Order was restored after this disaster, as it had been a century earlier. Although the Visigoths made a dash for Constantinople, they were driven off, thanks to the walled defenses and the faithful mercenary forces. They did, however, take cruel revenge for the months of exploitation at the hands of the Romans by mercilessly ravaging the regions near Constantinople.

THEODOSIUS PACIFIES THE VISIGOTHS

By 382, an energetic Roman from the West, who became emperor Theodosius, had pacified the rebels, and they once more settled down as allies of the empire and defenders of the frontier. Throughout this period Rome's relations with the Visigoths indicate the willingness of the latter to accept reasonable terms and their loyalty to emperors who treated them well. Theodosius made effective use of his Visigoth allies. In Thessalonica, when a Roman mob murdered a governor who had refused to release from prison their favorite charioteer,

Theodosius sent a detachment of his Visigoths who killed thousands of Roman rioters in restoring order. In the West, also, Theodosius used German generals and troops against his enemies. The Visigoths remained faithful to him throughout a series of struggles to maintain the authority of the empire not only against dangerous barbarians along the borders but also against ambitious generals who attempted to seize the imperial throne. It is significant that during the reign of his son, Honorius, in the West, a German general, Stilicho, was the power behind the throne.

THE VISIGOTHS MOVE WEST The renewed outbreak of trouble after Theodosius' death was due chiefly to the inefficiency of the Eastern emperor, Arcadius, and to the ambitions of a new Gothic leader named Alaric. The entire situation bears eloquent witness to the fact that often the troubles of the empire were due to the corruption and inefficiency of its own government. In the absence of a strong ruler, Roman political intrigue and Germanic military power ran rampant. The German chieftains soon learned how to use their positions to force the hand of weak emperors. As in the third century, the armies constantly interfered in governmental affairs. But now the armies were largely German; the regular troops were often commanded by German generals, and the auxiliary forces were composed of allied nations such as the Goths. Thus the Germanic leaders were able to take advantage of the situation to their own profit and occasionally to the benefit of the Roman citizenry. Their followers were rough and primitive, but often they proved to be better defenders of the empire than the Romans themselves.

Shortly after the death of their friend, Emperor Theodosius (d. 395), the Goths once more revolted, this time as a result of the weak and vacillating policy of the Eastern emperor, Ârcadius. Under the leadership of Alaric, they ravaged Macedonia, threatened Athens, sacked Corinth, and devastated the Peloponnesus. At one time Stilicho, the German commander of the Western imperial forces, came from Italy with an army, but due to disagreements with the Eastern emperor, failed to crush the rebels. Consequently the Visigoths continued their depredations. Unable to control the situation, Emperor Arcadius finally granted Alaric a commission as military governor of Illyria, a province along the Adriatic Sea. Thus the Goths were temporarily pacified and removed to a safe distance from Constantinople. For ten years Alaric and his fellow countrymen occupied the mountainous

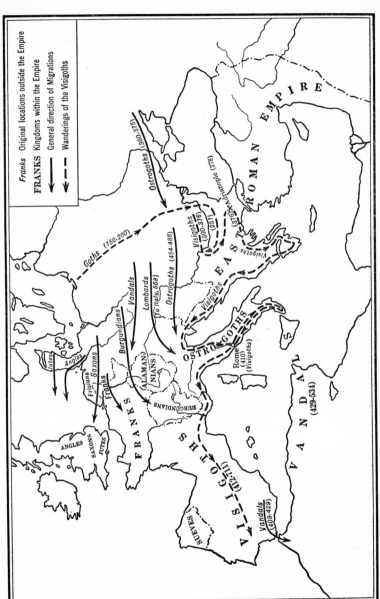

Legend:
Franks Original locations outside the Empire
FRANKS Kingdoms within the Empire
General direction of Migrations
Wanderings of the Visigoths

Ostrogoths (300-375)

Visigoths (378) Adrianople

Visigoths (300-376)

(251)

(376)

Visigoths

Goths (150-200)

Vandals

Lombards (To Italy, 568)

Burgundians

Ostrogoths (454-488)

ALAMAN-NIANS

BURGUNDIANS

Frisians

Saxons

Franks

Jutes

Angles

ANGLES

SAXONS

JUTES

FRANKS

EAST ROMAN EMPIRE

OSTROGOTHS

Rome (410) (Visigoths)

Visigoths (412-711)

SUEVES

VISIGOTHS

Vandals (409-429)

VANDALS (429-534)

EUROPE AFTER THE GERMANIC MIGRATIONS, AT ABOUT 500

Balkan province, ready to swoop down at any time on either Constantinople or Rome. Once they entered northern Italy but were checked by Stilicho, who was the veritable "shield of Rome" during this period. While Emperor Honorius lived in the safety and security of marsh-encircled Ravenna, his great general fought off all assailants. One nondescript mob of barbarians managed to cross the Alps into the Po Valley, only to be completely outmaneuvered and overwhelmed by Stilicho with a small Roman army. This did not, however, solve the problem of the barbaric nations who were assailing the northern frontiers.

We have seen that Rome was at first able to handle the Germans under normal circumstances, and that the empire could recover from a minor invasion of barbarians. Then we noted the influence of the Huns in upsetting the peaceful relations of Romans and Germans. Once the frontier defenses were broken, the Visigoths and other bands of Germans wandered at will through the provinces. The empire was not destroyed; in the East it continued for ten centuries. On the other hand, it never completely recovered. The incoming Germans, even where they gained complete control, were much affected by their contact with Christian Roman civilization. The Visigoths present one of the best examples of a conquering Germanic people who adopted much of the civilization of the conquered Romans.

BARBARIANS IN BRITAIN, SPAIN, AND GAUL

Although Alaric's Visigoths and other would-be invaders were kept from overrunning Italy, Rome lost control of Britain, Spain, and Gaul, whence legions had been recalled by Stilicho to reinforce his Italian defenses. To make matters worse, Roman soldiers in Britain proclaimed their general, emperor, and when he departed for Gaul to fight his way to the crown, this island province was left defenseless. Barbaric Picts and Scots soon began to ravage, invading from the north across the wall of Hadrian. Tradition has it that this led the Britons to call in the Angles, Saxons, and Jutes, and that after helping the Britons out of their predicament, they helped themselves to the territory they had defended. The truth seems to be that the Angles, Saxons, and Jutes came as barbaric invaders rather than as kindly rescuers. At any rate, by mid-century the east coast of Britain was peopled by Germanic tribes from across the Channel. Northumbria, East

Anglia, Essex (East-Saxony), Sussex (South-Saxony), Wessex (West-Saxony), and Kent soon became tribal centers from which the Angles, Saxons, and Jutes pushed westward to occupy the lands of the helpless Britons.

In Gaul, also, Roman government broke down completely. Since the frontier garrisons had been weakened by withdrawals, there was no defense against invaders. Germanic allies of Rome, among them the Franks, occupied regions along the frontiers. In the winter of 406, thousands of Vandals, Sueves, and Alans crossed over unopposed into the inner province. For three years the Gallic countryside and cities as far south as the Pyrenees were ravaged without mercy by these barbaric hordes. It is apparent that so far as the northwestern provinces are concerned, Roman imperial power had collapsed. Meanwhile the Vandals pushed on into Spain, whence they were eventually (429) driven into Northern Africa by the Visigoths. The opening years of the fifth century had left the Western Empire in a serious state of weakness.

THE VISIGOTHS
CAPTURE
ROME (410)

Returning to Italy and the Visigoths, we find that disaster had come upon the imperial capital primarily because of the weakness of Honorius, and the selfishly misguided patriotism of his Roman advisers. Many high imperial officials were jealous of Stilicho's increasing influence. Eventually they persuaded Honorius that he was plotting with hostile Germans, among them Alaric, to seize the imperial throne. Accordingly the order was given for Stilicho's assassination, and he and many of his fellow Germans in the imperial service were put to death on charges of treason. Thus at one stroke Rome removed her only sure defender and opened the way for Alaric's march on the defenseless capital. Even in this crisis Honorius continued a ruinous, do-nothing policy. Safe in his impregnable stronghold at Ravenna, he refused to come to terms with the Visigoths, and Rome was left to its own resources. Made desperate by starvation as Alaric cut off all supplies of food, the citizens bought off the besiegers with an immense ransom.[3] Alaric withdrew his forces but demanded imperial recognition as a Roman military governor. With incomprehensible stubbornness, Honorius refused to avail himself of a settlement similar to those by which his father and brother had successfully pacified the Visigoths. Consequently Alaric moved on Rome a second time

[3] The ransom included three thousand pounds of pepper, an interesting commentary on the civilized tastes of the Visigoths.

and finally set up a Roman senator named Attalus as emperor. Honorius, after resuming negotiations broke them off again, and Alaric, having fallen out with his newly made emperor, advanced on Rome for the third time.

This resulted in what is sometimes called "the Fall of Rome" in 410. It is probable that the gates were opened to the Visigoths by slaves within the city. Several days of pillage followed, during which the lower-class Romans wreaked vengeance upon their aristocratic oppressors. Alaric ordered his men to spare the Christian clergy and churches, and there was little wanton destruction. Emperor Honorius apparently was not greatly troubled by the disaster. In its physical effects, the sack of Rome by the Visigoths was much less destructive than many of the ravages during the succeeding centuries by more civilized soldiery. But the events of 410 were a serious blow to Roman morale. Not since the early republic had a foreign army entered the city.

There were many fugitives who fled to escape real or anticipated horrors, and their tales of disaster grew more and more hysterical in the telling. The news that reached Jerome in his monastic retreat in faraway Bethlehem made him despair of Gaul, Rome, and the empire. In Africa, Bishop Augustine of Hippo was so impressed by the pagan charges that Christianity had brought this disaster upon the Eternal City that he wrote his famous *City of God* to refute them. Later, Orosius, one of his pupils, wrote a *History against the Pagans* in similar vein, proving to the satisfaction of his Christian readers that in former times many a pagan city had fared worse than Christian Rome.

Although the psychological effects of the capture of Rome were far reaching, the "Eternal City" seems to have quickly recovered. An imperial edict, two years later, ordered certain provincial governors to send back all fugitives, including hundreds of actresses (the populace must be amused). At about the same time, a poet who was leaving Rome for his devastated Gallic estates expressed his regret at leaving "the fair queen of the world," of whose continued triumph he was confident. Orosius, also, in his history, insisted that Christian Rome showed every promise of a future more glorious than anything in the brilliant past of the former pagan city. All evidence seems to indicate that the citizens of Rome in 410, though temporarily upset, had no idea that their city or empire had permanently fallen.

THE VISIGOTHS
IN SOUTHERN
GAUL AND SPAIN

Meanwhile Alaric and the Visigoths had moved southward. The lack of food supplies in and about Rome necessitated this, and it is probable that Alaric hoped to settle his people in the grain-growing regions of Sicily and Northern Africa. The venture failed, and Alaric died. Alaric's brother-in-law Ataulf succeeded him and led the Visigoths back to northern Italy by way of Rome. Finally he was commissioned by Honorius to govern Gaul. Shortly after the emperor's change of heart, Ataulf married the imperial princess, Galla Placidia, who had been held by the Visigoths as a hostage. Ataulf, his Roman bride, and the Visigoths were soon on their way to a permanent home in southern Gaul and Spain. Vandals and other barbarian plunderers were driven out, and under Ataulf's successors, a firm and orderly government was established.

Thus ended not only forty years of Visigothic wandering in the empire, but also a cycle of development: the barbaric Goths who invaded the empire in the third century were now Romanized Germans restoring order to the provinces of the West which had been ravaged by more barbaric tribes. Later they became so fused with their provincial subjects that there was no perceptible difference save that the Goths, like all Germans, were Arian Christians. Visigothic law, codified after the manner of the Romans, was set forth in the *Antiqua*. The life and language of the court took on Roman imperial forms. Within a century, however, the Germanic ruling class had sunk into the same decadence as their Roman predecessors, and the Arab invaders in 711 found the Visigothic government of Spain unpopular, disorganized, and impotent. A Germanic nation, which had wandered through the empire for a generation and had conquered a Roman province, itself finally succumbed to the influences which had weakened the people it conquered. This phase of Germanic history makes it evident that the empire had lost its former defensive and recuperative strength. This was particularly true of the West, where the Asiatic Huns and their Germanic allies were proving to be a serious menace to imperial civilization.

THE HUNS

The story of the Huns is a sharp contrast to that of the Visigoths. It should be remembered that the Huns were an Asiatic people similar to the Hungarians, Tartars, and other savage hordes that have periodically descended upon the West from the great steppes. While the Visigoths were moving from place to place inside the empire, the pagan and barbaric Huns remained for the most part beyond the Rhine-Danube frontier, whence they brought terror to Romans and Germans alike. Originally they came from Eastern Asia, arriving in the Crimean region during the fourth century. They subjugated the Ostrogoths and, as we have seen, forced the more civilized Visigoths in a panic of fear to enter the empire. At this stage of their existence the Huns were, according to a contemporary Roman historian, "a race savage beyond all parallel"; beardless, with scarred faces, closely knit and of great size, thick-necked and inhumanly ugly. They ate, bought and sold, even slept on horseback; they seemed to be "almost welded to their horses." Their food consisted of roots and half-raw meat, "merely warmed between their thighs and the backs of their horses."

ATTILA   Three-quarters of a century after their encounter with the Goths, the Huns and their Germanic allies were in the region now known as Hungary. Their leader, the famous Attila, was known as "the scourge of God," and it is still popularly believed that "where his horse's hoofs trod, no grass ever grew." He was a ruthless and wily despot; otherwise he could neither have won, nor held for twenty-five years, the allegiance of the Huns and their barbaric allies. He was not, however, an unrestrained savage. As a youth he had seen service in the Roman armies, as had many of his countrymen. As a matter of fact, Attila and his entire army were for a time enrolled as Roman allies and given appropriate titles and rewards by the Eastern emperor, Theodosius II (408-450). In their Danubian homes, Attila and his chieftains lived in luxury. Priscus, an ambassador from Constantinople, noted that one of Attila's lieutenants lived in a splendid house which had a large bath built of imported stone. Attila's palace, which was within a large enclosure, was constructed of beautifully carved beams, and furnished with rugs, chairs, tables, soft couches, and beds with linen sheets and embroidered coverlets. Guests were served with wines, meats, bread, and other viands on gold and silver plate. Attila himself was frugal and clean in his food and dress.

The ambassador was very much surprised to find, among the lesser officials of Attila's court, a Greek-speaking Roman. He had been a rich Danubian merchant who, after living as a captive among the Huns, decided to cast in his lot with them. He had a barbarian wife and children, and had served in campaigns against his former countrymen. He insisted upon the wisdom of his choice by citing the universal sufferings of the Roman citizenry at the hands of corrupt

officials and ruthless taxgatherers. Such cases were doubtless exceptional, but the story as a whole illustrates the fact that a half-century
of settled life on Rome's borders had exerted a civilizing influence on
the Huns and their barbaric Germanic allies.

THE HUNS IN
THE WEST
With the accession of Marcian (450-457) to the im-
perial throne at Constantinople payments to the
rapacious Huns abruptly ceased. Forced to fight by
this new policy they attacked the West instead of the East. The reasons are obvious. Constantinople was strongly defended; Gaul, since
Stilicho's day, had been helpless. Furthermore, there was a pretext.
Honoria, Honorius's niece and namesake, daughter of the princess
Galla Placidia who had married Ataulf, invited Attila to invade the
West. It was said that Honoria, already in disgrace because of a romantic escapade, was being forced into an obnoxious marriage; rather
than submit, on a sudden impulse she offered herself to Attila, sending him a ring as a pledge of their betrothal. Tradition has it that the
Hun demanded half of the Western Empire as a dowry and, on the
emperor's refusal, invaded Gaul. As a result Treves, Metz, Paris,
Amiens, and other smaller cities of the North suffered ravages similar
to those inflicted by the Vandals in 406. At Orleans, however, Attila's
advance was checked and he withdrew to the Seine River where in
June, 451, the famous battle of Châlons-Troyes was fought. His opponent, Aetius, advanced to the attack with an army of Romans, Visigoths, Burgundians, Alamannians, and Franks. With Attila were other
Frankish tribes, Ostrogoths, and many of the more barbaric Germans.

In a sense this was a conflict between the settled Romanized
Germans from within the empire and the less civilized nomadic forces
from without. The actual battle was doubtless neither so terrible nor
so decisive as is often represented. It was not a crushing victory for
Aetius, nor did it save Europe from barbarism. Attila's forces were
not so destructive as to have wrecked a healthy civilization. Roman
civilization in Gaul had already been pretty thoroughly shaken by
internal disorders, Roman misrule, and earlier Germanic ravages. So
far as the Huns are concerned, Attila made an undisturbed and
strategic retreat from the Seine-Marne Valley.

THE HUNS
IN ITALY
The next year saw him in Italy, where he had little
better success, although Aquileia and other cities were
plundered or forced to pay tribute. Refugees fled
before the Huns, some of them to sandy islets off the Adriatic coast.
Thus, it is said, the foundations were laid for the later city of Venice.

Rome was spared, apparently through the efforts of Pope Leo and the civil officials who went with him to meet the advancing Huns. Christian tradition from subsequent centuries and a fresco by Raphael in the Vatican represent Attila as having been frightened off by the pope and two protecting saints, Peter and Paul. It is more probable that the decision of Attila was influenced by liberal bribes, the anticipated approach of Aetius's army, and fear of the devastating fevers of the Roman plain. At any rate, Rome was spared and the Huns retreated to the Danube. The very next year (453) saw the death of Attila, and soon his tribal federation fell to pieces.

⸻ VI ⸻

THE GERMANIC KINGDOMS OF THE WEST

WHILE the Visigoths were extending their power on both sides of the Pyrenees and while Attila's Danubian federation was being welded together, the Vandal ravagers of Gaul and Spain were taking to a settled existence in Africa. They had crossed the Straits of Gibraltar in 429 because of the pressure exerted by the Visigoths, who had recently arrived in Spain. This, together with the growing weakness of Roman rule in Africa, led them to seek homes and fortunes in that province. Under the leadership of

THE VANDALS
IN AFRICA

Gaiseric, an energetic chieftain, they rapidly conquered the regions now known as Algeria and Tunis. As in many of the Roman provinces, here also the citizens were so dissatisfied with the imperial government that they made little resistance to the invaders. Taxes were intolerable and the heretical sects of Christians were so cruelly persecuted that they welcomed the Vandals. Some of the wild native tribes actually joined in the invasion. Since Count Boniface, the provincial governor, was at swords' points with the emperor and Aetius, there was no hope of assistance from Rome. One Roman fortress after another fell before the attack of the Vandals. By 430 they had reached Hippo, where the famous Bishop Augustine died during the long siege. Ten years after they had crossed the Straits, the Vandals captured Carthage, and the emperor was forced to recognize them as masters of the province.

Gaiseric's harsh but effective rule led to the arbitrary seizure of lands and the imposition of heavy taxes, particularly on the wealthy. It is probable that the poorer citizen was as well off as under Roman rule, except for the fact that orthodox Christians were severely persecuted by the Arian conquerors. By the middle of the century the Vandals had taken to the sea, and were systematically raiding the neighboring islands. In 455 they surprised Rome and plundered the city for two weeks, carrying away not only much treasure but also the

119

Empress Eudoxia and her daughters, one of whom married Gaiseric's son.

Gaiseric's rule, which lasted until his death in 477, may be said to have been the climax of Vandal history. Under his leadership his followers had transformed themselves from a tribe of ravaging nomads into vigorous builders of a land and maritime empire. After Gaiseric's death the enervating effects of the African climate and the luxuries of Roman civilization began to take their toll. The history of Vandal wanderings, raids, conquests, and ultimate decline seems to be typical of the history of all Germans who settled in the midst of a decadent Roman civilization. In their case the decay was very rapid.

THE FALL OF THE WESTERN PROVINCES

The much-used expression "the Fall of Rome" has many possible interpretations. At least two of the most prevalent can be dismissed as grossly inaccurate. Neither the empire nor the city of Rome was suddenly hurled to destruction by the barbarian invaders, like a great building overwhelmed by an earthquake or a deluge. The facts are that the imperial government had shown its inability to handle an external emergency. By the middle of the fifth century it had broken down completely in Britain, Gaul, Spain, Africa, and, to a considerable degree, in Italy. Britain by 450 had fallen into the hands of the invading Angles, Saxons, and Jutes; northern Gaul also had been conquered, first by an usurping Roman general, then in 486 by neighboring tribes of Franks. Similarly the Rhone Valley had been conquered by the Burgundians, while the Visigoths had taken southwestern Gaul and Spain. Meanwhile, Africa had succumbed to the Vandals. Thus by the middle of the fifth century most of the Western provinces had already fallen. But Roman *civilization,* even though it was declining, still existed and everywhere exerted a tremendous influence upon the Germanic conquerors.

IMPERIAL ITALY

In Italy, neither Roman government nor Roman civilization had passed away. To be sure, since the days of the great Theodosius, both had shown signs of serious weakness. In the West, his successors had manifested such incompetence that the emperor had become a mere figurehead. Because of the incomprehensible folly of Honorius (395-423), his father's allies, the Visigoths, had overrun Italy. As a result in 410 the city of Rome fell into the hands of the Visigoths for a few months. But the Eternal City and the imperial government in Italy went on much the same after 410 as they had before that all too-famous date. Fifteen years later Honorius was succeeded by Valentinian III (425-455), an emperor as long-lived and almost as incapable as his predecessor. Stilicho's place was filled by Aetius, who had at first given his support to an unsuccessful rival of the emperor. Because of his great influence with the Huns and Germans, however, Valentinian not only pardoned him but entrusted him with high military and political powers. Aetius, nevertheless, remained under suspicion, even after he had checked the invading Huns. The emperor thought that after the battle of Châlons-Troyes he had failed to follow up his advantage and had deliberately allowed the Huns to enter Italy. Some time later, fearing a treasonable plot, he summoned Aetius to Ravenna and struck him down with his own hand. Within a few months the emperor-murderer was himself killed by revengeful Huns who had been members of Aetius's guard. By such mismanagement the Western Empire weakened itself and invited destruction.

THE END OF THE WESTERN EMPIRE

Valentinian's successor in imperial folly was a former senator named Maximus, who forced the Empress Eudoxia to marry him. This brought further tribulation to the hapless city of Rome. It is said that in desperation she called on Gaiseric the Vandal to avenge her, and in 455 he descended upon Rome. Pope Leo I, who had interceded with Attila three years earlier, was able to save the citizens from indiscriminate massacre and the city from destruction by fire. But for two weeks the Vandals plundered Rome of its art treasures and gold. Although this visitation was much worse than that of the Visigoths in 410, there was little wanton destruction, for by this time the Vandals had acquired some appreciation of Roman civilization. Much of the loot was lost in a storm at sea, but the remainder was brought safely to Carthage. One of the most interesting of the stolen treasures was the famous seven-branched golden candlestick which Emperor Titus had brought to Rome from the Temple of Solomon, after the sack of Jerusalem (70 A.D.). On the Arch of Titus at Rome can still be seen a sculptured relief showing Roman soldiers carrying the candelabra in Titus's triumphal procession. From 455 to 533 it was in the possession of the Vandals in Africa. Then it was carried to Constantinople by Justinian's conquering armies. The pious emperor soon sent it back to Jerusalem, its original home, whence it later disappeared, never to be recovered.

Many people still believe that the invading Germanic barbarians were solely responsible for the fall of Rome, an event which is variously thought to have occurred in 410, 455, 476, or 486. It is clear that Rome's existence did not end with the Visigothic capture and plundering of the city in 410. The Vandal raid of 455, though far more destructive, did not wipe out either the city, the government, or the civilization of Rome. In 476, after twenty years of confusion, during which a series of emperors were set up and overthrown by the barbarian guardsmen, a famous but relatively unimportant event occurred. A German general named Odoacer deposed the puppet emperor, Romulus Augustulus, and took over directly the reins of government. Thus ended a line of emperors who had already in effect destroyed themselves. The sole importance of the year 476 lies in the fact that at this time a line of Western emperors whose power had already completely disintegrated was definitely brought to an end. Henceforth the Eastern emperors considered Italy as one of the administrative provinces of their empire, although actually Italy, like the rest of the West, soon came under the control of Germanic invaders. This occurred as a result of internal difficulties in the Eastern Empire.

THE OSTROGOTHS   Emperor Zeno (475-491), to whose authority Odoacer made formal submission, used the Italian situation as a means of saving Constantinople from a new Germanic menace. Like his predecessors a century earlier, Zeno was endangered by a troublesome ally, the Ostrogoths, who for a time had been subject to the Huns. Attila's death and the disintegration of his federation left the Ostrogoths in about the same situation and region in which the Visigoths had been a century earlier. In fact, the experiences of the two Gothic peoples in the Eastern Empire are strikingly similar. Both nations proved to be rather troublesome allies. When dissatisfied with governmental policies they were prone to take matters in their own hands and plunder neighboring provinces. It was during this period of mutual suspicion between the Ostrogoths and the emperor that one of their young princes named Theodoric spent ten years as a hostage at Constantinople. He was a favorite of the court and received many offices and honors. Meanwhile he developed a marked appreciation for Roman civilization, though, strange to say, he never learned to read or write. On returning to his people, the young chieftain sought to improve their condition. Angered at the evasive policies of the imperial government, he led a revolt which resulted in his being granted a commission to replace Odoacer as imperial governor of Italy. Thus did Zeno, after the fashion of his predecessor, Arcadius, shelve a troublesome Gothic ally upon Italy.

THEODORIC   Like Alaric the Visigoth, Theodoric attained his objective with great difficulty. A march of some nine hundred miles with the entire nation of the Ostrogoths during the winter of 488-489, four years of hard fighting, and Theodoric was master of the situation. After agreeing to share the power with Odoacer, Theodoric murdered him. The new regime in Italy was established with little violence and with almost no change in governmental institutions. The Ostrogoths occupied certain Italian lands, probably those which Odoacer's Germans had already confiscated. Thus most of the inhabitants were left relatively undisturbed. The Romans were governed according to existing Roman laws, and by the same sort of officials as in former times (consuls, praetors, and so on). There was no change in the dole of free bread and games. Although military power was concentrated in the hands of the Goths (weapons were prohibited to all others), civil affairs were carried on almost entirely as formerly. Every effort was made to preserve Roman civilization. Literature, the arts, and public works were encouraged and carried on by means of governmental patronage. Some of the buildings still to be seen in Ravenna were erected during the Ostrogothic regime.[1]

Theodoric's efforts to restore agriculture and industrial prosperity were so effective that the Italy of his age is said to have been better off economically than it had been for several centuries. In religious toleration, Theodoric was far ahead of his age. Himself an Arian Christian, he insisted that "no one be forced to believe against his own will," and he put this maxim into practice by stopping the persecution of the Jews and by preventing unfair discrimination against fellow Arians who had turned orthodox. Theodoric's foreign relations were so successful that he seemed about to become the leader of a league of Germanic nations. The Franks, Visigoths, and Burgundians were closely bound to him by marriage alliances. So far as the Eastern Empire was concerned, Gothic Italy was practically independent, though the authority of the emperor was accepted in theory, and given nominal recognition on coins, in public proclamations, and in official letters.

[1] See below, p. 325.

THEODORIC AND
THE CHURCH
It was only toward the end of his reign, when beset by the plots of the very Romans and orthodox churchmen who enjoyed his favors, that Theodoric exhibited despotic tendencies which had unfortunate consequences. Trouble began when Theodoric learned that his orthodox subjects approved of the Eastern emperor's policy of persecuting Arians. When Theodoric threatened in turn to persecute the orthodox Christians of Italy, religious hostility developed among his subjects. Moreover many Roman nobles ardently hoped that the emperor might overthrow Theodoric and re-establish Roman rule in Italy. Theodoric finally brought charges against a number of senators. Boethius, a trusted Roman adviser, vigorously defended his fellow Romans. As a result he himself was tortured, convicted, and eventually executed for treason, along with several other prominent Romans.[2]

THE FALL OF THE
OSTROGOTHIC
KINGDOM
When Theodoric died in 526, he left to a daughter the unenviable task of maintaining harmony among the discordant elements of the Italian kingdom. There was strife, not only between the Arians and Athanasians, and the Germans and Romans, but also among the Goths themselves. Encouraged by these internal difficulties, Justinian, the Eastern emperor,[3] decided to regain control of Italy. After twenty years of devastating warfare, the imperial generals destroyed the last Gothic army and Italy became a part of the Eastern Roman Empire (553). Vandal Africa and the southeast corner of Visigothic Spain were also conquered. It seemed, for a time, that Justinian was destined to re-establish Roman supremacy over the entire Mediterranean. But the wars between the Eastern emperors and the Germans of the West weakened both, and paved the way for new disasters.

THE LOMBARDS
CONQUER
ITALY
Shortly after Justinian's victory the Lombards, former barbarian allies of the Eastern Empire, descended from the upper Danube bringing new woes to war-ridden Italy. Of all the Germans, this last invading nation is said to have been the most savage. According to the *History of the Lombards,* written in the eighth century by Paul the Deacon, their king, Alboin, had a drinking cup made from the skull of a defeated opponent whose daughter was forced, not only to marry him, but also to drink from her father's skull.

---

[2] See below, p. 261, concerning Boethius's literary works, one of which, *The Consolation of Philosophy,* was written in prison.

[3] See below, p. 149.

There are, however, more credible records of Alboin's activities. Somewhat after the manner of Attila, he headed a Danubian federation consisting of various tribes, not only Germans such as the Saxons and Gepids, but also Asiatic Sarmatians and Avars. Some of these people, notably the Saxons, joined in the invasion of Italy. This increased the disorders of the conquest, for the Lombard kings had great difficulty even in controlling their own tribal subordinates. Consequently most of central and southern Italy came to be occupied by independent "dukes." From the Lombard capital at Pavia, the successors of Alboin dominated the rich Po Valley, and as the invaders took on the settled ways of civilization, they became so completely identified with this region that it still bears the name of Lombardy.

THE TWILIGHT OF ROMAN ITALY Thus, within the space of one century (476-565), imperial Italy had disintegrated into a conglomeration of barbaric Italies. An impotent line of emperors had given way to the enlightened rule of a Romanized Goth, whose regime had been shattered by the imperial forces of the East. And then anarchy descended upon the once proud mistress of the civilized world. To be sure, the city of Rome and Roman civilization lived on in spite of the ravages of warfare and invasion. But the Eternal City was becoming less Roman and more Christian, less imperial and more papal as time rolled on. By the year 600, Lombard barbarians and medieval churchmen had become dominant in Italy. Unfortunately the Lombard kings, the popes, and the Eastern emperors fought and intrigued for control of the peninsula. As a result, the forces of disunity ran rampant and Italy soon disintegrated into numerous principalities whose rivalries for centuries prevented any successful national movement.

GERMANIC KINGDOMS OF THE WEST Within the space of seventy-five years—from Stilicho to Odoacer—Germanic chieftains and their warriors had replaced emperors and provincial governors throughout the West. The general mass of the population in city and country remained relatively unchanged, but the governmental machinery was very different. There was no longer any emperor in the West. The emperor at Constantinople was theoretically the ruler of the West, but he exerted no effective influence. The former provinces of the Western Empire had given way to Germanic tribal kingdoms. Many of the city-states continued as self-governing units, but their importance steadily diminished.

In England several kingdoms of Anglo-Saxon people were taking shape. Meanwhile the Romanized Celtic population of Britain was either enslaved or pushed into the western regions of Cornwall and Wales. These sections of England, like Scotland and Ireland, still show Celtic characteristics that are very different from those of England proper. Because of the weakness of Roman civilization in England and because the conquerors had come direct from their Germanic homeland, the Anglo-Saxon kingdoms were for a time almost untouched by Latin influences. As a result, English institutions and civilization from the start showed characteristics very different from those across the Channel. For instance, the Anglo-Saxon language was used even by literary men in spite of the fact that Latin was introduced by Christian missionaries in the seventh century. English laws and methods of carrying on local government also continued to be strongly Germanic in character.

THE KINGDOM OF THE FRANKS

THE FRANKS   On the Continent, where Roman civilization had been more firmly established, the Germanic kingdoms took on more of the characteristics of the former imperial government. The only invading people who retained much of their primitive Germanic character were the Franks. Among the Germanic tribes on the Continent, their history is unique. Most of their fellow Germans crossed the Roman frontiers, wandered about, and finally settled down, only to be assimilated by the people whom they had conquered. The Franks, on the contrary, kept in close contact with their Germanic homeland, maintained their military strength, and eventually conquered most of the West. No other Germanic people except the Anglo-Saxons was so successful in maintaining its native characteristics and extending its conquests.

As early as the first century A.D., according to Tacitus, there were along the lower Rhine two Frankish tribes, the Chatti and Sygambri. In the third century Diocletian fought against the barbaric Franks of this region, but eventually employed many of them as defenders of the Rhine frontier. In the fourth century when Julian restored order in Gaul he settled the more peaceful Franks as allies in what is now known as Belgium and drove the rest back across the Rhine. During the fifth century, disorders along the Gallic frontier tended to weld

the scattered Frankish tribes into two federations—the Salians, who
lived toward the mouth of the Rhine, and the Ripuarians, who occupied both sides of the river as far eastward as Cologne. From the first
to the fifth century, therefore, it appears that the Franks had been in
approximately the same region. Though at times some of them had
been allies of the Romans, they often ravaged the neighboring imperial territories. For instance, during the invasion of the Huns (451),
some of the Franks fought for Aetius and the Romans, while others
fought in Attila's army. Of greater importance is the fact that they
never separated themselves from the Germanic North, but merely expanded southward into the regions of Gaul from which the Romans
were receding. Thus they had little contact with Roman civilization
and their sturdy barbarian ways were relatively unchanged. As late
as the time of Clovis (Chlodweg or Louis), they were still in the
tribal stage. The Salians, for example, had four separate chieftains selected from the princes of the ruling families and controlled by councils of elders. Most of the Franks were still barbaric pagans who
fought on foot and half naked.

THE REIGN OF
CLOVIS (481-511)
Clovis's career marks the beginnings of real Frankish expansion and political development. Two notable
advances were made during his reign and under his
leadership. For one thing, the Franks became a united people with a
strong monarch. By the rankest of treachery Clovis eliminated the
other Salian and Ripuarian rulers and made himself sole king of the
Franks. He overthrew his former ally, the king of the Ripuarians, by
persuading the son to kill the father and take the throne. Then, when
the crime had been committed, Clovis had the son executed for the
murder and took the kingship to himself. Similarly ruthless methods
mark Clovis's exploits in territorial expansion. At the time of his accession (481) there were four distinct ruling powers in Gaul. The
Franks occupied the extreme north; Syagrius, the last imperial commander of the West, held the Seine basin; the Burgundians dominated the Rhone Valley; and southwest Gaul belonged to the kingdom of the Visigoths.

In 486 Clovis began his career of conquest by defeating Syagrius
at Soissons, thus destroying the last remnant of Roman rule in Gaul
and in the West. As a result of this victory all the region north of the
Loire River was opened to Frankish domination. Ten years later, near
Strassburg, Clovis, with the assistance of the Ripuarians, defeated the

Alamannians, thus bringing the entire Rhineland under his sway. Next the Burgundians, who had established themselves in the Rhone Valley, first as allies of the emperor and then as rulers, were defeated and made tributary. Their territories were not actually annexed until the reign of Clovis's sons. In 507, barely twenty years after his first great victory, Clovis overwhelmed the Visigothic forces and burned Toulouse, their principal Gallic stronghold. Three Frankish armies, led by Clovis, his son, and Gundobald, the allied Burgundian king, then swept the Visigoths from southern Gaul. It was only through the intervention of Theodoric, the Ostrogothic ruler of Italy, that Clovis was prevented from occupying Arles and the coastal towns of Provence along the Mediterranean.

CLOVIS'S GOVERNMENT: CHRISTIANITY   Within the space of twenty-five years Clovis succeeded in consolidating the Frankish tribes and bringing all Gaul under their domination. This remarkable feat seems to have been due to several unusual conditions. As already noted, the Franks had maintained a rugged Germanic spirit which facilitated their conquest of the less virile Romans, Germans, and Celts of Gaul. The personal genius and ruthless methods of Clovis were also important factors. Whether dealing with fellow Franks, civilized Burgundians, or Christian bishops, his vigorous policies were universally successful.

Perhaps one of the most notable of his decisions was the choice of orthodox (i.e., Athanasian) rather than Arian Christianity for himself and his people. Of all the Germanic conquerors of the West, the Franks alone were of the same religious faith as their subjects. This of itself is a factor of considerable importance in accounting for the success and permanence of their regime. It will be noted by way of contrast that every *Arian* German kingdom in the West fell. It is probable that Clovis's acceptance of orthodox Christianity was a deliberate political move, similar to Constantine's. Neither was a true spiritual conversion. Bishop Gregory of Tours, the sixth-century historian of the Franks, told how Clovis's wife had "unceasingly urged him to acknowledge the true God and to forsake idols," but in vain. Finally, in the midst of a terrible battle, "his heart was stirred, he was moved to tears," and having "won the victory by calling on the name of Christ," he and over three thousand of his men were baptized. This tale, so similar in spirit to the legendary account of Constantine's vision of the cross, is probably a pious exaggeration. By becoming orthodox Christians the Franks won the support of the clergy and laity of their newly conquered lands.

The favorable attitude of the clergy toward the converted king is admirably reflected in a passage from Bishop Gregory's history. "Henceforth [he wrote] God each day delivered his [Clovis's] enemies into his hands and increased his realms because he walked with a perfect heart before him and did what was right in his sight." Such an interpretation of the treacherous deeds that marked the king's later career merely indicates that formal acceptance of the orthodox type of Christianity covered a multitude of sins in sixth-century Gaul. That the converted monarch was fully aware of the advantages of his religious position is shown by the pretext given for attacking the Visigoths. As Bishop Gregory reported it, the king and his bishops thought it "unendurable that Arians should possess any part of Gaul." So, "with God's aid" the Franks went forth to smite the unbelievers, and their southwestward expansion took on somewhat of the nature of a crusade. Even though the Franks were Christians in name only, the Christian bishops and people of Gaul, and to all appearances a gracious Providence as well, looked with favor upon Clovis's regime. In accomplishments, Clovis, like Constantine, ranks high among the world's great rulers. In each case, the support of the Christian populace and the active assistance of the clergy were important factors in the monarch's political success.

FRANKISH
GOVERNMENT

Clovis left to his successors a realm that comprised most of the old Roman provinces of Gaul. In the north and northeast it extended to, and in some places beyond, the Rhine. To the south, there were regions along the Mediterranean and the Rhone held by other Germanic powers. The successors of Clovis rounded out his conquests in this direction. In government, also, the kingdom bore some resemblance to the older Roman realm. The rulers considered themselves the successors of the imperial officials. Clovis himself at times appeared in purple robes and scattered coins to the populace, after the fashion of the emperors. His court, though composed chiefly of Germans, followed the forms of the courts of the Caesars. The officials bore Roman titles, and much of the administrative business followed the ancient formalities. Even the old imperial taxes were collected as long as it was profitable to do so.

For the most part, however, the court ceremonial was a sham.

The real government was carried on in a more practical manner. Money was scarce; therefore officials were few and inefficient. The king had to depend on his loyal followers in each locality to keep order and give military support when it was needed. In return for such services he granted them great tracts of land—his chief source of wealth. In each district a count was appointed to act as the king's representative. He was governor, general, and judge. As governor he transmitted the king's orders to the local leaders and reported to the king concerning local conditions. As general, he mobilized the fighting men when summoned for warfare. Since each warrior provided his own weapons and provisions, it was a difficult task to organize and maintain a fighting force. But in case of victory, there was plunder. As judge, the count followed the local customs which were codified in separate codes for the Germanic and Roman populations. Under the existing conditions, with little money, poor communications, and an unruly set of nobles, government became more and more localized. Only a king of outstanding ability and powers of leadership could make royal government a reality. There were few such, after the time of Clovis, and Frankland drifted steadily toward the condition known later as feudalism.[4]

OTHER GERMANIC KINGDOMS
Within the ancient province of Gaul there were, before the conquests of Clovis, three Germanic kingdoms whose governments somewhat resembled that of the Frankish kingdom. They were the kingdoms of the Alamannians along the middle Rhine, the Burgundians in the Rhone Valley, and the Visigoths of southern Gaul and Spain. Each of these peoples had taken possession of well-populated Roman provinces which contained cities of considerable size and importance. The Rhineland region of the Alamannians, having been ravaged by constant invasions, tended to revert to barbarism. The Burgundian and Visigothic kingdoms were much more civilized. The Roman populations of these regions were well protected by their Germanic rulers. They had their own municipal institutions and separate codes of law. For instance, the Italians were judged according to an edict or code promulgated by Theodoric; the Spaniards according to the *Breviary* of Alaric; and the Roman inhabitants of the Rhone Valley according to the so-called Code of King Gundobald. These codes were composed of excerpts from the earlier codes of Roman law, chiefly that of Emperor Theodosius II.

[4] See below, Chapter XI.

Like the Visigoths, the Burgundians and the other Germanic people had their own laws. These were written codes of tribal customs, particularly regulations concerning the adjustment of quarrels and deeds of violence. The most famous of these collections are the Salic Code of the Franks and the Visigothic *Antiqua.*

In the more northerly regions the Germanic people held strongly to their own native customs, dress, and speech. They avoided the cities, which were already declining in prosperity. Inasmuch as the Germans were the ruling race, imperial civilization gave way rapidly to the Germanic type of rural life. There were, of course, a few large centers where the royal court or governmental headquarters preserved a somewhat more cosmopolitan type of life. But everywhere in the West there was a marked drift from the urban centers which were characteristic of Roman civilization to the isolated rural estates that mark the appearance of feudal manorial life.[5]

THE EFFECTS OF THE INVASIONS The prevailing opinion of bygone days to the effect that the Germanic invasions obliterated Roman civilization in the West has undergone much revision in recent times. It is obvious to anyone who is familiar with the general course of events during the Germanic conquest of the Western provinces, that the invaders themselves were strongly influenced by their contacts with imperial civilization. In the mutual exchange of ideas and customs that took place, it is impossible to estimate the exact proportion of influence exerted by each race, but scholars of our day are inclined to emphasize the influence of Roman civilization upon the Germans. It seems that the Germanic conquerors of the West were themselves pretty thoroughly conquered by the institutions of the conquered peoples.

This was more apparent in the highly Romanized regions of the South. In southern Gaul, Visigothic Spain, Vandal Africa, and Italy, Roman civilization persisted much more strongly than in the North. In the South there were great masses of Roman people among whom the institutions of civilized life were deeply rooted. Great cities, many of them relatively undisturbed by invasion, carried on the economic, political, and cultural traditions of imperial times. The majority of the people were Romans, even in regions that were under the immediate control of the invaders. In Italy, Spain, and the other southern regions, the Germans comprised less than 10 per cent of the popula-

[5] See below, Chapters XI-XII.

tion. Even in Britain and northern Gaul, the population was largely non-Germanic.

POLITICAL
INSTITUTIONS
The underlying strength of Roman institutions is evident when one considers governmental changes. At the outset it seems that the conquerors, being supreme in the realm of government, introduced certain of their own political customs, but not to the exclusion of existing Roman institutions. This double system of government is clearly illustrated by the legal codes. Roman judicial methods, as they had evolved throughout the centuries of imperial rule,[6] continued in force for the great mass of the population. Romans were tried by lay or clerical judges, by methods that involved an inquiry into the factual evidence pertaining to the case. One type of Roman procedure, the inquisition, or inquiry on oath, persisted in a modified form throughout the medieval centuries and exerted a considerable influence on methods of trial for heresy and on the English jury system.

GERMANIC LEGAL
CUSTOMS
On the other hand, the legal procedure of the Germanic ruling classes also had its effect. Although Germanic in origin and applicable only to the Germanic element of the population, these regulations were codified after the Roman manner. The resulting Burgundian, Visigothic, Alamannian, and Salic (Frankish) codes contain brief but enlightening descriptions of certain of the institutions of the conquering race. In general they reveal a crude and primitive system of justice. An accused German cleared himself of charges by compurgation, ordeal, or combat. He might present a certain number of compurgators to swear to his honesty and thus to support his oath of innocence. He might submit to the ordeal of carrying a hot iron, or thrusting his arm into boiling water, or being thrown into a stream. If he was unharmed by the hot iron or hot water, or if he sank beneath the surface of the stream, he was considered innocent by divine judgment. In the trial by combat the defendant was adjudged innocent if victorious. Such methods of trial illustrate the Germanic emphasis on a man's personal honor and on divine interposition in matters of justice. The accused was expected to defend his honor rather than to present evidence. God would strike down the man who swore falsely.

Less fantastic, to the modern mind, is the Germanic system of fines for personal injuries. In order to preserve man power for foreign

[6] See above, pp. 8 f.

wars, the early tribal law of blood revenge, which demanded "an eye for an eye" and "a life for a life," was replaced by a system of money payments. Thus the family of a wounded or murdered man was compelled to accept *wergeld* (i.e., "man-money," or the value set upon a man's life) from the assailant, instead of waging a destructive war of revenge. Payments varied, not only according to the nature of the injury, but also according to the rank of the person injured. In short, it cost more to kill or wound a noble than a serf. The penalty of harming a childbearing woman, the source of the nation's future warriors, was very severe. Such efforts at the adjustment of human relationships, though crude in form, persisted in many regions and had a marked influence on the development of legal institutions in the West.

As time passed and the races lost their identity, both Germanic and Roman methods of government were intermingled and adapted to the varied problems of an ever-changing society. Although Germanic customs are discernible in certain aspects of feudalism, in the long run in the shaping of medieval and modern law, the legal institutions of the Roman Empire and the Christian Church exerted a more lasting influence than did those of the Germanic conquerors.

GOVERNMENTAL ADMINISTRATION In governmental administration, likewise, Roman methods persisted, despite the military triumph of the Germans. To be sure, in governmental administration, as in legal procedure, the ruling class of Germans introduced certain of their own characteristic institutions, but the average citizen was affected little by the change. Local government was allowed to continue in the timeworn channels which had been followed for centuries by Roman provincial administrators. Like them, the Germanic rulers governed each locality according to established custom.

In the great provincial centers of administration, Germanic influence was strong. The Germanic methods of fighting and governing were dominated by personal relationships between individuals rather than by legal status in highly organized groups. The Germanic king, like his predecessor, the ancient tribal chieftain, was assisted in battle and in government by noble retainers who were bound to him by the sacred ties of personal fidelity. His advisers were personal attendants of noble lineage. The army was composed of warriors who provided their own equipment, served as a matter of personal duty, and had strong ideas as to individual rights. The Germanic spirit of personal honor and the loyalty of individuals in warfare and government exercised a strong influence on feudal institutions and other aspects of medieval government. The functions of the ruler, even of a king, were viewed as personal rights and duties which might be allotted to his sons or to trusted retainers.

In the more practical aspects of administrative organization, however, Roman imperial forms and methods prevailed. When they came to rule Roman provinces, most Germanic chieftains took over much of the existing framework of government. The Roman methods of local administration and taxation continued. Former provincial officials and Christian bishops continued to function in their own localities. Even at the royal headquarters, the Germanic king's personal retainers were supplemented by a staff of experienced Roman administrators. Boethius, Cassiodorus, and other eminent Romans served as secretaries of various departments in Theodoric's Ostrogothic state. Often a Germanic court employed the formal dress and ceremony of imperial times. Many German kings considered themselves as the representatives of the emperors. Clovis, king of the Franks, issued edicts in the Roman manner, dressed in royal purple, and assumed the imperial titles of proconsul and Augustus. In such fashion the conquering Germans adapted their rule to the customs and governmental institutions of the Romans. There was little attempt to force their subjects into the mold of Germanic life.

This does not mean, however, that Roman imperial government was revived or even preserved without change. Under a regime of separate Germanic states, with a steady increase in the independence of local leaders, with numerous wars of aggrandizement, and with diminishing financial resources, the centralized governmental system of the Roman Empire continued to disintegrate. Prominent nobles, either Germanic or Roman, lay or clerical, administered the affairs of their respective localities in an independent manner. Some of them made use of the provincial and municipal institutions of imperial times. Others did not, and, as time passed, Roman methods of taxation, justice, and local administration were adapted to new conditions. Government, along with other aspects of civilization, was becoming more and more localized, rural, and primitive and was moving in the direction of feudalism.

ECONOMIC
AND SOCIAL
INSTITUTIONS
The economic and social conditions at the close of the age of invasions indicate the continuance of much of Roman civilization, though in a greatly modified form. The social and economic institutions of the late empire seem to have suffered no sudden or catastrophic destruc-

tion, but merely a natural process of evolution. This was due in part to the fact that the invaders were relatively few in numbers and could not have changed the habits of the mass of inhabitants, even had they so desired. Furthermore they were more eager to appropriate than to destroy the fruits of Roman civilization. Recognizing the superiority of the Roman methods of agricultural and industrial production, they took over the institutions, along with the lands and peoples of the imperial provinces.

This procedure is particularly evident in relation to agriculture. In most regions the conquerors seized a large portion (usually about one-third) of the productive lands, but without upsetting the existing system of landholding, cultivation, or social organization. Germanic nobles merely replaced Roman nobles as the proprietary exploiters to whom certain amounts of the products were due. The great mass of peasant freeholders, tenants, and servile or slave laborers continued to work their plots of land as formerly. There was little immediate change in their status, either for better or for worse. In most of the territories that had belonged to the empire, the German landlords left intact the systems of tenancy and property holding of the former owners. But inasmuch as the newcomers were inexperienced in the management of large agricultural estates, the German-controlled lands were operated with less efficiency, and agriculture drifted to more primitive levels.

There were certain sections of the West in which Roman agricultural methods had never gained a foothold, or in which they had been destroyed by the continued disorder of invasions and wars. In such regions the lands were occupied by Germanic settlers who followed the freeholding system of their ancestors. They lived in rural villages and worked the land according to democratic and co-operative methods by which all members of the community were adequately provided with the means of subsistence. But even in the more northerly regions where the population was largely Germanic, and where the type of agricultural community called the *mark* is thought to have been prevalent, the much-vaunted democracy and freedom of traditional Germanic society were not permanent. The inevitable conditions that accompany the occupation and exploitation of land soon created a stratified social and economic regime which resembled that of the Roman villa estates. It was controlled by a relatively small group of noble landowners who dominated the mass of free farmers, tenants, serfs, and slaves. Thus the process of conquest and settlement changed a rather primitive society of free Germanic warriors into a caste of exploiting landowners and agricultural peasants.

Meanwhile the Roman agricultural regime was also undergoing marked changes. The regime of villa estates, which had become widely prevalent in the empire before the coming of the Germans, was extended still further as a result of the invasions. During the interim between the breakdown of the imperial administration in the West and the organization of effective Germanic governments, the owners of great estates were forced to protect and govern, not only their own lands, but also those of their clients and neighbors. Their power and prestige was greatly increased as they came to dominate the lesser landowners of their localities. Most freeholders were forced into a position of dependence in order to obtain protection. As the middle class of independent freemen dwindled in numbers and influence, society became more and more unbalanced with its two sharp extremes, a small group of powerful nobles and a mass of dependent peasants. Although the trend was most apparent on the Roman villa estates, the same tendency was present among the conquering Germans. These developments indicate the coming of the medieval regime; an inflexible social organization and an unprogressive agricultural economy which lacked (at least until the later centuries) the energy and ambition which are characteristic of a free middle class.

INDUSTRIAL AND COMMERCIAL DECLINE The effect of the invasions upon industry and commerce was, as might be expected, exceedingly detrimental. The already noticeable decline in such activities was greatly accelerated by the disorder and ravages of warfare and by the increase of great agricultural estates. As Roman landowners concentrated their economic resources and political activities on the rural villas, and as the Germanic ruling class settled down to an agrarian life which suited their native temperament, city life, commerce, and industry languished. To be sure there were still many populous administrative centers, episcopal cities of considerable clerical and lay population, and a few flourishing seaports. As long as the Mediterranean was open to Western commerce, Marseilles and other ports carried on a substantial trade in Oriental luxury products. But such transactions were restricted to a small portion of the population, the upper classes, and in general industrial and commercial activities dwindled to the small-scale exchange of local products at market places.

The existing industrial and commercial life of the West had little vitality, and even the most enlightened Germanic rulers were unable to revive its former prosperity. As the means of subsistence for urban populations of artisans and tradesmen decreased, city life declined. Large cities shrank in size, many of them retreating to the protecting circle of their innermost defensive walls. At Arles, in southern France, the ancient Roman arena was large enough to shelter the meager population. Small cities became rural villages dependent almost entirely on agricultural economy. Industry, reduced to a primitive type, producing only enough for local needs, continued to exist in small towns and on the villas of the nobility or in the more populous cathedral and monastic centers. There was, however, less and less manufacture for export. Communications, coined money, and purchasers were so uncertain that there was little incentive to trade. The unsettled conditions of the late Roman Empire and the age of invasions, with its increasingly agricultural trend of life, made it impossible for industry, commerce, and cities to flourish. Roman emperors had been unable to check the drift from urban to rural life. Obviously the new race of Germanic rulers, with their more primitive rural tastes, had neither the incentive nor the ability to reverse the trend of social and economic development.

THE GERMANS
AND THE
CHURCH

So far as the Christian church was concerned, the coming of the Germans had a double effect: it was both strengthened and weakened. The church was already firmly established in the Roman Empire, and in the West the papacy was acquiring a position of great influence. Inasmuch as the majority of the Germanic invaders were heretical Arian Christians, their successes gave a decided setback to the papacy and the orthodox Athanasian faith of the West. For a time there was sharp conflict between the Arian Germanic rulers and their orthodox Roman Catholic subjects. In Ostrogothic Italy, as we have seen, this struggle was one of the factors that weakened Theodoric's regime. In the end, everywhere in the West, Roman orthodoxy overcame Germanic Arianism. By the close of the sixth century the Visigothic and Burgundian monarchs had forsaken the Arian heresy. In England and France, the pagan Anglo-Saxons and Franks were converted directly to the Athanasian faith, and became valuable allies of the papacy in its later efforts to Christianize the outlying Germanic peoples of the North.

Eventually the church won all of the Germanic rulers to the orthodox faith and became their allies in governing the West. One of the less desirable results of this partnership was the subjection of the church to the policies of the Germanic states. Even the popes were forced to follow the dictates of lay rulers during most of the early medieval centuries. As in the time of Constantine the Great, the church, by its close associations with lay rulers, gained for the time being considerable influence, landed property, and prestige, but it lost much of its freedom of action and purity of spiritual leadership.

CULTURAL
INFLUENCES
The Germanic invasions resulted in a temporary set-back for culture. Most of the invaders were not equipped to appreciate or keep alive Roman art and literature. For centuries, Roman culture was little appreciated outside the monastic and cathedral centers. As time passed, however, the Germanic element of the population developed a cultural life which contributed much of lasting value to the civilization of the West. From it came the basic languages of most of the peoples of Northwestern Europe. The Anglo-Saxon, Scandinavian, and German languages have played an important part in the life and literature of the West in both medieval and modern times.

The literary treasures of these languages include *Beowulf,* the Norse sagas and eddas, and innumerable masterpieces of German poetry in which the traditional legends of ancient heroes and gods were handed on from generation to generation throughout the medieval centuries. The *Song of the Nibelungs* provided Wagner, in modern times, with the basic plot for much of his opera; Siegfried, Brunhilde, Lohengrin, the Valkyrie, and Valhalla are merely the most familiar names from this rich storehouse of early Germanic literature. In the less literary phases of modern life there are also evidences of the strength of Germanic institutions. Several of the days of the week (Wodens-day, Thors-day, and Freyas-day) bear the names of primitive Germanic deities. In many of our holiday observances—for example, the Easter rabbit and the Christmas tree—there are traces of Germanic folk custom. The primitive but vigorously expressive arts of the early Germans will be given separate treatment in a later section.[7]

From the viewpoint of Western Europe's political, social-economic, and cultural development, the coming of the Germans cannot be interpreted as the catastrophe which destroyed ancient civilization. The invasions occurred when ancient civilization was in process of decline; they did not initially cause that development. The Germanic invasions

[7] See below, pp. 330 f.

mark the appearance of a vigorous new element in the stream of Western civilization. The invaders took over and adapted to their own needs many Roman and Christian institutions, but they gave to them the imprint of their native character. Furthermore they contributed much of their own civilization, primitive though it was, and molded Western institutions in innumerable ways.

Not only during the age of the great invasions (the fifth century) but throughout the early Middle Ages, the West received fresh infusions of Germanic blood. Among the late comers were the Norse, one of the most progressive and constructive peoples of medieval times. All told, the Germanic influences on medieval and modern civilization constitute one of the major elements in the making of Western Europe. Three of these we have considered in relation to the beginnings of the Middle Ages. After the passing of the Roman Empire of the West and the coming of the Germans, the European world was a melting pot in which Roman, Germanic, and Christian institutions interacted with one another to form a new civilization. It was crude, rural, and barbaric, in contrast to the declining civilization of the Roman Empire, but it had strength and virility, and gave promise of unlimited future growth.

═ VII ═

BYZANTINE CIVILIZATION

B Y the year 500 the unity of the ancient Mediterranean world had passed away. The empire in the West had disintegrated into a confused group of Germanic kingdoms. The empire in the East, though badly shaken, was intact, and for this realm the future held much of glory and achievement. During the next five centuries (from 500 to 1000) the Mediterranean world was still further divided as a result of the expansion of the Moslems (i.e., Mohammedans). If a line were drawn from east to west through the Mediterranean, dividing the civilized world of that day into two sections, it would be found that the southern half (comprising the North African lands) and the lands at either end of the Mediterranean (Syria and Spain) were in Moslem hands. The northern half (comprising European lands for the most part) was Christian. It was divided into a western section consisting of the various Germanic kingdoms and an eastern section, the East-Roman or Byzantine Empire. In the following sections we shall consider these three regions: Byzantine, Moslem, and Germanic.

THE ROMAN EMPIRE IN THE EAST
The East-Roman or Byzantine Empire was the one political unit of the ancient Mediterranean world that had an unbroken existence during the first ten centuries of the Christian era. Constantinople, which was also called "New Rome" and "Byzantium" (its ancient Greek name), continued till the end of the Middle Ages as the capital of an empire and a civilization that was essentially ancient and classical. In certain respects its culture was more Greek than Roman, and as the centuries rolled onward it was influenced by new elements: Oriental, Christian, Germanic, Slavic, and Moslem. But its connection with the Roman Empire was unbroken and since it was essentially a continuation of the institutional life of the eastern part of the empire, it is permissible to call it the Eastern, or East-Roman Empire, and its

140

civilization East-Roman. The traditional name, Byzantine, is, however, more common.

The history of the East, as a separate empire, begins during the troubled third century when Diocletian turned over to his co-emperor the administration of the West. In theory at least the empire continued to be one unit, but with separate administrative divisions. About a century later, during the reigns of the two sons of Theodosius (Honorius and Arcadius), it was evident that the East and West, in spite of their theoretical unity, were drifting apart. During the fifth century, with its complex of barbarian invasions and political intrigues, neither emperor could pay much attention to the problems of his colleague. In general, Constantinople and Rome went their own ways.

THE EASTERN EMPIRE SURVIVES
During the troubled fifth century their ways diverged more and more, until by the close of the century the Western Empire had come to a fitting end. It had not the strength to survive the vigorous new forces of Christianity and Germanic barbarism. The Eastern Empire, although exposed to the same influences, emerged victorious. Though badly battered by the shock of invasion, the imperial government at Constantinople continued to dominate both the Christian Church and the Germanic tribes along the northern frontiers. We have already noted the outcome of the invasions of the early centuries: how the Eastern Empire, in spite of disasters such as the defeat of Decius (251) and the battle of Adrianople (378), weathered the storm and maintained its political stability.

Though shot through with corruption and intrigue the governmental bureaucracy at Constantinople survived both the plots of ambitious courtiers and the attacks of Visigoths, Huns, and Ostrogoths. The Eastern Empire was also swept by wave after wave of Christian conflict. During the fourth century there was the long struggle between the Christians and pagans, and between the Athanasians and Arians. Later there was strife between the orthodox believers in the Incarnation and their Nestorian critics, and between the Monophysites and Diophysites as to whether Christ's human and divine natures were united (*mono*) or double (*dio*). There were also the conflicts of rival churches and churchmen; the archbishop of Alexandria against the patriarch of Constantinople, and at times either or both of them against the pope of Rome. Through all this conflict, the empire stood unshaken, and in the sixth century it rose to great heights of splendor and power.

ELEMENTS OF
STRENGTH
The student of history is justified in demanding an explanation of the contrast in the history of the East and the West. One factor may be dismissed at the outset: the emperors of the East were not *personally* superior to those of the West. Both regions had able emperors, and also endured the rule of inefficient rulers. The Eastern emperors of the fifth century were no better men than those under whom the Western Empire came to a disastrous end. Theodosius II (408-450) paid tribute for years to the Huns. His successor, Marcian, was a courageous general but he ruled for only seven years. Zeno (474-491), the emperor who reigned during the period when the Western Empire finally succumbed, was a barbaric soldier whose success in imperial government seems to have depended more often on good luck than on good sense.

But a government with a poor executive head often succeeds by virtue of an efficient administrative organization. In this respect, the Eastern emperors were well endowed. The bureaucracy established by Diocletian and his successors, though corrupt and extravagant, continued to function. Even under weak emperors, so long as there was financial support for the army of imperial officials, they could be depended upon to keep the wheels of government moving. At the capital were the heads of the various departments of state, each bearing a high-sounding title; Praetorian Prefect, Master of Offices, Count of the Private Estate, and Quaestor of the Sacred Palace. Each was the head of a staff of trained administrators and clerks whose control extended to the most distant provinces. This highly centralized bureaucracy kept the imperial government in close touch with the outlying parts of the empire, maintained a unity that was effective though artificial, and brought in a substantial revenue.

In the matter of finances, also, the Eastern Empire had an immense advantage over the regions of the West. It possessed populous cities of industrious artisans and prosperous merchants. Most of these municipal centers were surrounded by thriving agricultural districts. So long as business flourished, the imperial government had a dependable income and could support the civil and military forces on which its power and the imperial security rested. At a time when the Germanic rulers of the West were forced to grant landed estates to their noble retainers in order to secure military and administrative assistance, the Eastern Empire carried on as a great tax-collecting machine. Its bureaucracy functioned almost automatically, whether headed by a

royal moron or by an able and ambitious emperor. Peasants and artisans were ground down by crushing financial burdens in order that
their protector, the state, might have ample revenues.

Commerce and industry were carefully regulated in the interests
of the imperial treasury. All corporations and labor organizations
were forced to perform certain public services, in addition to their
payments of taxes, tariffs, and fees. Certain important industries, notably mining, the minting of coins, and the manufacture of military
supplies, were carried on by the government as state monopolies.
Everywhere the economic welfare of the individual citizen was subordinated to that of the government in much the same fashion as it
is in modern totalitarian states. But inasmuch as the welfare of the
state depended on the welfare of the citizen, measures were taken to
assure his prosperity. Here it was that the imperial mechanism proved
its worth. With all its corruption, the bureaucracy was remarkably successful in preserving the security and prosperity on which its own
existence depended.

From the standpoint of administrative and financial centralization, the Eastern Empire had a remarkable capital city from which to
exercise its co-ordinating activities. Constantinople was also strategi-
cally located for the control of commerce. The wealth of the world was
brought thither by land and sea. Cargoes or pack trains came from
the Balkans, Asia Minor, the Black Sea, the Mediterranean, and even
from the Far East, laden with raw and manufactured goods. Only
Alexandria could compete with Constantinople in commercial prosperity. From the standpoint of military strategy the capital was even
better situated. Its location gave the imperial army convenient access
to the strategic frontiers along the Danube and the Euphrates. In case
of a surprise attack, whether by land or sea, it was equally strong. In
many a critical situation it was shown that a small naval and military
force could make Constantinople impregnable against invaders. Natural location, economic advantage, and a well-organized governmental
machine combined to give the Eastern Empire security and permanence. Its long record of successful defense against formidable foes
can best be accounted for on the basis of this unusual combination
of economic and military advantages.

It was such advantages that enabled the Eastern Empire to survive the centuries of Germanic invasions and later, under more favorable circumstances, to make great accomplishments in all lines. The

climax of this era of recovery and achievement came during the sixth century under Emperor Justinian.

THE AGE OF JUSTINIAN

EMPEROR
JUSTINIAN

Justinian (527-565) was of Illyrian peasant stock, well educated, and an earnest supporter of the church. Before his accession he had gained a good deal of experience in governmental affairs as the nephew and associate of Justin I (518-527), a soldier who had come to the imperial throne as a result of a series of court intrigues. Justinian, said to have been virtuous, a tenacious worker, and a man of high ideals, was also vain, suspicious, and in times of crisis likely to vacillate. During the last eighteen years of his reign, after the death of his beloved empress, Theodora, he became morose and morbidly religious. It is evident that the imperial successes of Justinian's reign were not due primarily to his own personal ability, but rather to the effective governmental system of which he was the head.

There are two outstanding factors which, on several occasions, worked together to bring the Eastern Empire unusual success. One concerned the mechanism of government; the other the personnel of the imperial office. In spite of the bureaucratic organization, new men were able to work their way upwards from the lowest ranks of society to positions of leadership. Often such a rise was by way of the army, and sometimes it was accompanied by brutality and cruel massacres. Nevertheless, many a decadent ruler was overthrown and new blood brought in to invigorate the imperial office. Such was the effect of Justinian's accession.

In the second place, once a man attained the position of emperor, thanks to the mechanism of centralized government, his will was absolute and he had an opportunity of effectively exerting his influence. Ever since the governmental reforms of Diocletian, the emperor had been vested with a supreme and majestic divinity. He was a god-king of the despotic Oriental type, whose authority was religious as well as political. He headed not only the political bureaucracy, but also the religious hierarchy. He was God's vicar on earth, a priest-king, the defender and ruler of the church. With such authority over church and state, and with a realm closely knit by political, economic, and religious ties which centered in Constantinople and in the person of his divine majesty, an able emperor might well succeed in any imperial program. Such was the situation in Justinian's day. He was the supreme head of a governmental organization which provided him with able advisers and experienced public servants.

EMPRESS
THEODORA

One of the most valuable of Justinian's advisers was the Empress Theodora. Like her royal husband, she was of lowly origin. According to the *Secret History* of Procopius, a cynical courtier who set forth all of the sensational gossip he could lay hands on, she was of the lowest moral character. If it be true that her father was one of the animal keepers at the Hippodrome, and that she grew up amid degrading influences and companions, her rise to power is all the more remarkable. If, as was rumored, she actually had lived a disreputable youth as an actress and dancer, it is a still greater tribute to the fair-mindedness of Eastern society and the courage of Justinian that she was raised to the highest position in the empire by merit of her ability and personality. Whatever her former life may have been, Empress Theodora amply justified the expectations and trust of Justinian. He was wont to speak of her as "a gift from God," and after her death he paid her memory the tribute of remaining unmarried for the eighteen years he survived her. Theodora was undoubtedly beautiful: a mosaic in a church at Ravenna bears out the contemporary descriptions of her faultless figure, delicate and regular features, marble-white complexion, and brilliantly alert eyes. She was also, as might be expected, an imperiously proud beauty, with violent hates.

Her influence in the government, however, was anything but destructive. At one of the most critical points in Justinian's career, the famous Nika riot, it was Theodora's courage and intelligence that saved him from ruin. Again, by her influence the emperor issued decrees by means of which young girls were protected from corrupting influences, and by which their less fortunate sisters were enabled to escape from degrading bondage. An old palace was provided as a refuge for ex-prostitutes, many of whom, however, were said to have returned to their former manner of life.

JUSTINIAN'S
ADMINISTRATIVE
REFORMS

Among Justinian's advisers there were also several outstanding men: the generals Belisarius, Narses, and Mundus; the architects Anthemius and Isidore of Miletus; a great lawyer named Tribonian; and a clever but unscrupulous minister of finance, John of Cappadocia. With the help of able assistants, the emperor was able to make the existing administrative bureaucracy into a more efficient governing body, with a carefully supervised civil service. The widespread sale of offices was prohibited and salaries were increased so as to reduce temptations to dishonesty on the part of the lesser officials. Courts of appeal were established for the speeding up of justice. By ousting corrupt officials, by consolidating local governmental units, and by eliminating various sources of waste and duplication, great economies were effected. Unfortunately these reforms did not lighten the burden of taxes. Much money was expended on the extravagant imperial court, on extensive building projects in Constantinople, Antioch, and other cities, on doles to the city mob, on payments to barbarian allies, and on unending wars of aggrandizement. As a result, the taxpayers experienced little permanent relief. To be sure, there were economic reforms, but they merely brought increased revenues to the luxury industries and the governmental monopolies on cloth, salt, and minerals.

Strenuous efforts were made to maintain trade routes to the Far East, particularly those by way of Russia and the Red Sea, both of which were being threatened by the Persians. By smuggling Chinese silk worms into the empire, an effort was also made to develop an independent silk industry. Eventually, however, Constantinople was forced to depend on Persian middlemen for most of the Oriental products which were necessary for the luxury industries of the capital city. In Constantinople, Egypt, and elsewhere within the empire, the governmentally controlled corporations carried on extensive enterprises, but it cannot be said that the majority of the citizens were prosperous. The vast city mobs dependent on governmental doles and the masses of tax-ridden peasants came to be danger points in a glamorous but top-heavy social structure.

THE HIPPO-
DROME
The Hippodrome at Constantinople was a center at which Byzantine society expressed itself without restraint. It has been said that the scenes enacted there mirrored the worst in the life of the people of Constantinople. Its ample seating space (370 by 70 yards) accommodated 30,000 people. In addition to horse races, it was used for such entertainments as acrobatics, dancing, the Gothic games at Christmas, and a rose festival every spring. The chariot races were the surpassing amusement of the citizenry. Only men attended, but the empress and her ladies were allowed to occupy a box high up at one side, next to the palace. The races were the occasion for many public activities. Here prizes were awarded to the winning charioteers, who were held in higher esteem than any other civic heroes save perhaps the monastic

preachers. Here also, in celebration of military triumphs, the people were given doles of bread, oil, wine, and fish. Imperial decrees and public petitions were proclaimed in the Hippodrome, and political agitators found it an admirable place for their propaganda. The associations of people who supported the respective colors of the charioteers extended beyond the mere winning or losing of a race. The "Blues" and "Greens" were also powerful political factions, with officials, financial organizations, and militia forces.

THE NIKA RIOT

On one occasion the hostility of the Hippodrome organizations almost wrecked Justinian's career. In 532, when he seized and executed some trouble makers, all factions suddenly broke forth in a furious revolt. The angry populace hissed the emperor, stormed his box, and when troops were sent against them, set fire to the buildings. To make matters worse, the descendants of one of the former imperial families encouraged the revolt in the hope of overthrowing Justinian. For a time it seemed that the rallying cry of the rebels, *Nika* ("Victory") was about to be realized. Justinian shut himself up in the palace, and on hearing of the election of a rival emperor, prepared to flee. His councilors approved, but Theodora asserted that she would rather perish than give up the crown, and that "the imperial purple is a suitable shroud." Encouraged by her example, Justinian decided to fight it out. A band of mercenaries was sent to make a surprise attack on the populace, who were gathered in the Hippodrome to greet the new emperor. After a terrible massacre, in which thousands of people were killed, order was restored and Justinian recovered control. For six years the activities of the Hippodrome were discontinued. Never again was Justinian's rule threatened.

ST. SOPHIA

The latter part of Justinian's reign was rendered glorious by two great achievements. One was the Church of St. Sophia, a triumph of architectural skill that has been called "one of the noblest buildings ever erected by the hand of man." The other, the Justinian Code, marks an epoch in the development of Roman law.

St. Sophia, the Church of the Holy Wisdom, was in a way quite as important as the Hippodrome in the life of the capital city, for religious life centered in the great imperial church. Here the members of the court and the people met to pray, to listen to the exhortations of the clergy, and to see society on parade. On great feast days a service at St. Sophia could furnish emotional ecstasies quite as thrilling as those provided at the Hippodrome. On one such occasion, a visiting ambassador was so impressed by the clouds of incense, the glowing candles, the chanting choirs and ornately garbed ecclesiastics that he claimed to have seen "angels descending from Heaven to assist in the service." A historian of Justinian's day, describing the spaciousness and sumptuous splendor of St. Sophia, wrote that the domed interior seemed to be suspended from Heaven by golden chains so that whoever entered felt that God, rather than man, had constructed it. Always, he said, its mystical beauty and majesty tended to lift the soul of the beholder on high. It might be added that modern tourists are similarly awed by the grandeur of the interior of the great church.

In its construction Justinian's architects not only lavished an untold magnificence of varicolored pillars and decorative ornamentation, but they erected the first great aerial or raised dome known to history. This dome, which was of the wide, shallow Roman type, measured over one hundred feet across and almost fifty feet in height. It rested on four huge pendentives[1] and arches which were supported in turn by gigantic pillars, arches, and buttressing domes in such a manner that the top of the central dome towered one hundred and eighty feet above the ground. As an architectural feat this was a noteworthy step in the age-long evolution of the dome from its original low-lying Roman form to the spectacularly high domes which have characterized modern buildings.[2] In the perspective of time the importance of St. Sophia is quite as notable as it was in Justinian's day. Even in his lifetime it was copied in church buildings throughout the empire, and was considered one of the wonders of the world.

THE JUSTIN-
IAN CODE

The Hippodrome, imperial palaces, and religious edifices of Constantinople, great and important though they may have been, called for a tremendous outlay of money without adequate returns. The Justinian Code is not subject to this criticism. It was accomplished by a small commission of legal experts under the direction of the eminent lawyer, Tribonian. In about a year's time they collected and condensed the accumulated mass of Roman legal writings into a code that far outshone the codifications that had been effected by earlier emperors such as Hadrian and Theodosius II. Justinian's commissioners performed a tremendous fourfold task with very few mistakes and in an incredibly short time.

[1] Pendentives are spherical triangles of masonry.
[2] See below, pp. 727 ff.

CHURCH OF ST. SOPHIA, CONSTANTINOPLE (VI C)
(See pp. 146, 326.)

IVORY CARVING — A TRIPTYCH (X C)

BYZANTINE ART

Christ and the Apostles
ST. PUDENZIANA, ROME (IV C)

Christ and the Virgin Mary Enthroned
SANTA MARIA IN TRASTEVERE, ROME (XII C)

MOSAIC

(See p. 319.)

One committee examined all the imperial edicts (*constitutiones*) of preceding centuries and, after discarding obsolete material, published a one-volume *Code* containing all usable laws. To this were added, later, over a hundred and fifty new ordinances called the *Novels*. Thus, the best of Rome's law was condensed and put at the disposal of legalists. Meanwhile another committee examined and "digested" the great mass of existing judicial commentaries on legal problems. From the writings of eminent jurists of earlier centuries they sifted out a volume of the most useful legal opinions. This was called the *Digest* or *Pandects*. It is said that in this work about 3,000,000 lines were condensed into about 150,000, thus providing lawyers and judges with an admirable handbook of legal opinions. Further practical aid for lawyers was provided by a textbook of law, called the *Institutes,* written by Tribonian. The fourfold reorganization and condensation of Roman law outlasted all of Justinian's other governmental reforms. Throughout the later Middle Ages it exerted a powerful influence in the West, and its effect on modern law is comparable to that of the English common law.[3]

JUSTINIAN'S WESTERN WARS The political and military accomplishments of Justinian and his successors were, for the most part, of negative significance. Under former rulers in the fifth century the Eastern Empire had weathered the storm of German and Hun invasions. On the heels of this successful defensive, Justinian decided to take the offensive. His major aim was to recover the Western regions that had recently fallen under Germanic sway, and thus to re-establish a united Roman Empire. In 533 an armada set sail for the conquest of Vandal Africa. Under the skillful leadership of Belisarius, imperial rule was restored along the southeastern shores of the Mediterranean. The islands of Sicily, Sardinia, Corsica, and the Balearics and the southeastern corner of Visigothic Spain were also recovered.

In Italy the imperial cause met with a serious check. The Ostrogothic successors of Theodoric put up a stubborn resistance. It took twenty years of warfare and two of Justinian's best generals (Belisarius and Narses) to crush the Ostrogoths. Worse yet, by 552 when the imperial forces triumphed, Italy had been so devastated by warfare, famine, and pestilence that the victory was barren of gain. By the end of Justinian's reign, imperial taxation had added further bur-

---

[3] See below, pp. 460 f.

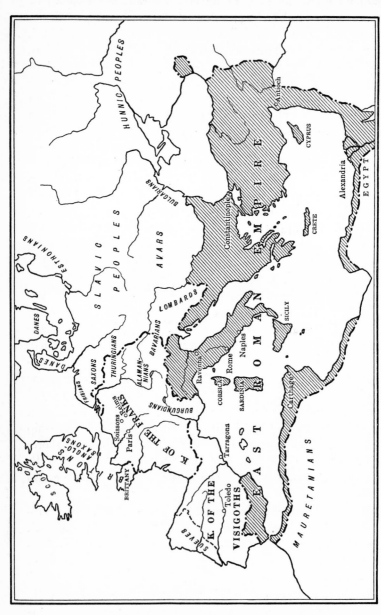

EUROPE AT THE DEATH OF JUSTINIAN (565)

Shading indicates extent of the East-Roman or Byzantine Empire

Adapted from Ault, *Europe in the Middle Ages*.
By permission of D. C. Heath & Co., publishers.

dens. Roman Italy's ruin was completed when the barbarian Lombards, descending from the Danube frontier, overran the peninsula. An Eastern governor, called the Exarch, continued at Ravenna, and the popes maintained a precarious position in Rome, but not until the nineteenth century was Italy again united. After Justinian's day imperial control in the other Western provinces gradually dwindled, and in the eighth century, when the conquering Moslem hosts swept westward, they met with little resistance. It must be obvious to the modern student that Justinian's Western conquests were merely a magnificent gesture of imperialism.

THE BALKAN FRONTIER

Justinian's Eastern campaigns, particularly those in the Balkans, brought more permanent success. The security of the Danube frontier was all-important for Constantinople, and the defensive policy adopted by the emperor was not only well chosen but ably executed. Walls were built at strategic points, and along the Danube eighty castles were established as bases for frontier garrisons. There was also a mobile army of mercenaries, chiefly heavy-armed cavalrymen who could readily be concentrated at any danger point. This army of shock troops was used chiefly for offensive operations. The ordinary defense of the frontier was carried on by means of farmer militia (called *limitanei*) of the sort which had been employed along the borders since the days of Diocletian. Beyond the frontier these defenses were supplemented by barbarian allies.

Justinian was particularly successful in his policy of playing off one group of barbarians against another. By bestowing official titles and funds upon those who were accepted as allies, he kept bands of Huns, Avars, Lombards, and others in imperial employ. Throughout his reign, the Danube frontier was kept free from serious danger, and with little expenditure. This was a marked improvement over the preceding century when, on several occasions, ravaging bands of Huns had broken through the border defenses and thrown Constantinople into a panic of fear. Later, the Avars, an Asiatic people akin to the Huns, began to press southward, and from the sixth to the eighth century they were a constant menace along the Danube. To these perils was added the increasing pressure of the Slavs and Bulgars, who had been at the frontiers of the empire since the fifth century and who were eventually to occupy great stretches of Balkan territory. Justinian was able to hold these forces in check and to concentrate his military resources elsewhere.

WARS ON
THE PERSIAN
FRONTIER

Had it not been for the long Gothic war in Italy Justinian might have been able to solve the critical problem of the Persian-Euphrates frontier in a manner that would have saved the empire from many later difficulties. Since the third and fourth centuries, when two emperors had perished while campaigning against the Persians, the Euphrates frontier had been constantly endangered. During the fifth century, the pressure was relieved, because Asiatic peoples from the northern steppes occupied the attention of the Persians. But in the sixth century, Persia once more took the offensive against the empire. During the early years of Justinian's reign, his generals won several battles, but failed to follow up their victories. Then, in order to concentrate his forces for the reconquest of Italy, Justinian decided on a policy of peace at any price in the East. For twenty-five years there was no offensive, and not even a vigorous defense against the Persians. Frontier cities were lost without a struggle, and it became the custom to pay tribute to the enemy. By the time the imperial armies were free from their Western campaigns, it was too late to check the Persians. Justinian's successor ceased paying them tribute, and made an alliance with the Asiatic Turks in order to hold Persia in check. This was not permanently effective, and both Armenia and Syria were eventually lost.

THE EMPIRE
DECLINES

The century following Justinian was as disastrous for the empire as his reign had been glorious. External attacks and internal disturbances threatened to tear it asunder. On one occasion an usurper named Phocas (602-610) overthrew the reigning emperor and slaughtered every relative of the monarch he could lay hands on. Then, in order to win support, he acceded to Pope Gregory's request and temporarily subjected the Eastern Church to the supreme control of the Roman papacy. Soon he was overthrown by a soldier named Heraclius (610-641), who became the outstanding emperor of this troubled century.

HERACLIUS,
SAVIOR OF
THE EMPIRE

Although assailed on all sides by apparently insuperable foes, Heraclius kept the empire together. The fierce Avars and Slavs had crossed the Danube and were ravaging the Balkans. A small region around Constantinople was safe from their attacks, thanks to the defensive walls which had been built across the peninsula west of the city. Meanwhile the Persians, having occupied portions of Syria (including Jerusalem), invaded Asia Minor and threatened Constantinople from the east.

Heraclius' tactics in warding off this double threat were masterful. He bought off the Avars and obtained a respite in order to deliver the eastern provinces from the Persians. Inasmuch as the Sacred Cross, which had been captured at Jerusalem, was in the hands of the enemy, he was able to inject into this expedition the religious fervor of a crusade. Churches donated their treasures, the people joined wholeheartedly in the cause, and the small imperial army marched forth with sacred banners and emblems. In a series of brilliant campaigns, Heraclius forced the Persians to restore the Cross and the captured provinces. The East was safe. Meanwhile, Constantinople had been assailed on land and sea by combined Avar and Persian forces. The attack failed, thanks to the walls, the fleet, and the heroism of the defenders, and in 629 Constantinople was able to celebrate one of the most remarkable triumphs in her entire history. For the time being, at least, the empire was saved.

THE RISING TIDE OF ISLAM

Before the death of the heroic emperor in 641, new troubles arose. Heraclius lived to see the Moslems in possession of both Syria and Egypt, and in full tide of conquest elsewhere. Under his successors the imperial fleet was destroyed by this new enemy (655), and soon the victors were attacking Constantinople. Its marvelous defensive position and recuperative powers, and the use of Greek fire [4] enabled the capital city and the heart of the empire to withstand repeated shocks. No more strange or more heroic story can be found in history than the hairbreadth escapes of the Eastern Empire from annihilation during these centuries. Having come through a particularly trying ordeal during Heraclius' reign, it seemed that Constantinople was invulnerable.

LEO III, THE MOSLEMS, AND ICONOCLASM

One of the most important and successful emperors of this period was Leo III (717-741). At the beginning of his reign the Moslems made a desperate attempt to capture Constantinople, but the city withstood a year's siege until Leo's forces succeeded in driving the enemy off. He also reformed the imperial administration and restored a meas-

---

[4] Greek fire was similar to the liquid fire used in modern warfare; it was a liquid composition which was ejected from tubes (called *siphons*) onto the ships of the enemy in order to set them on fire. Greek fire seems to have been invented, or at least perfected, by Kallinikos, an architect from Syria. It was first used against the Moslem fleets in the latter half of the seventh century. N. D. Cheronis, "Chemical Warfare in the Middle Ages," *Journal of Chemical Education*, XIV (1937), 360-365.

ure of prosperity. During his reign another of the perennial religious controversies of the Eastern Church came to a head. Like the Moslems, certain Christians had come to the conclusion that the excessive use of icons, or images, encouraged idolatry. Because of their violent reform measures, they were called *iconoclasts* (image breakers). Led by Emperor Leo III the reformers endeavored to remove all images from the churches. For over a century the iconoclasts had the advantage over the *iconodules,* or image worshippers. Later, however (843), images were restored with a strict injunction against making them objects of idolatry.

In the West, the popes refused to enforce the prohibition against icons, even to the point of resisting imperial edicts and officials. Fortunately for the rebellious Italians, the fleet which had been sent to punish them was wrecked, and in the West the unrestricted use of images continued. This is still apparent in the appearance of the interior of Roman Catholic churches, as contrasted with the unsculptured adornment of Greek Catholic edifices. As in the case of the earlier theological controversies, the struggle over icons indicates the gradually widening rift between Eastern and Western Christendom. It was evident that the two Christian churches were to continue as separate organizations.

RENEWED
DISASTERS

For half a century or more after the vigorous reign of Leo III, the empire held its own not only against internal disturbers, but also against Moslems, Slavs, and the Bulgars, who were now the chief danger along the Danube frontier. In the ninth century, however, new disasters troubled Constantinople. In 814, the city barely escaped capture by the Bulgars, and just fifty years later (in 865) a band of Swedish pirates,[5] called Varangians, swept down from the Black Sea, almost succeeding in taking the city by surprise. To make matters still worse, the threat of Moslem naval attacks was so constant that the emperors sought aid from the West. Although the successors of Charles the Great were unable, or unwilling, to give aid, the Italian city of Venice placed her fleet at the disposal of the Easterners. In return for such favors the Venetians received commercial concessions which bound them closely to the empire.

During this time of trial, internal conditions were also unsettled and able leadership was lacking. At one time the imperial power was

[5] See below, p. 205.

wielded by a cruel and ambitious woman named Irene (d. 802), who, after murdering her husband and son, is said to have sought a marriage alliance with Charles the Great. The inefficient reigning dynasty was brought to an inglorious end by Michael III, appropriately nicknamed "the Drunkard," who was finally murdered by one of his favorites, a former charioteer. The latter then ascended the throne as Basil I.

RECOVERY   Basil I (867-886) and his successors of the Macedonian dynasty brought the empire to a new era of prosperity and expansion. Through the influence of the church, as well as by force of arms, near-by peoples were brought under imperial control. During Basil I's reign, the king of the Bulgars formally accepted Christianity and entered into peaceful relations with the empire. Over a century later, in the time of Basil II (976-1025), Tsar Vladimir of Russia did likewise. It was also during this reign that the dangerous Bulgar kingdom in the Balkans was attacked and defeated. So decisive were Basil's victories that thousands of Bulgar prisoners were captured, blinded, tied together by hundreds, and with one leader for each group, sent home as an example to their fellow tribesmen.

Meanwhile the imperial armies took up the offensive against the Moslems on the eastern frontier and for a time the empire seemed likely to recover all of her lost possessions in Asia. During the reigns of Nicephoras Phocas, John Zimisces, and Basil II, from about 950 to 1025, imperial forces wrested from the Moslems Asia Minor, Crete, and Syria, including such great cities as Damascus and Antioch. But the full tide of success was checked by the coming of the Seljuk Turks in the eleventh century. The consequences of this new crisis will be considered later, in connection with the crusades.

BYZANTINE   Whatever the failures and defects of Byzantine civilization, during five critical centuries, from the age of
CIVILIZATION   Justinian to the crusades, it endured the test of time. There are certain noteworthy characteristics that stand out prominently amid the disasters of Moslem, Persian, and Bulgar attacks—the heroic defensive efforts of the emperors and people of Constantinople, and the remarkable era of recovery toward the end of the tenth century. Among the elements of lasting strength that were manifested during this five-hundred-year period, is the effective governmental organization. Whatever the cruelty and corruption of the imperial rulers, their centralized civil and military service functioned with success in

times of crisis. Formidable attacking forces were beaten back time after time by the military and naval defenses. Revolts and disorders among the restive city populace were invariably quelled. Taxes were collected with such regularity and in such amounts that the varied forms of public service were maintained without serious interruptions. Throughout most of the period there was a continuous and well-organized regime of law and order which made possible an unbroken development of highly specialized urban life. The empire and civilization of the Byzantine East was a closely integrated organism of political, economic, and social elements, the control of which was centralized at Constantinople.

BYZANTINE
AND WESTERN
CIVILIZATION

The superiority of this civilization is revealed not only by its success in surviving the attacks of its barbaric and predatory neighbors, but by a comparison with the civilization of the West during the same period. In contrast to the centralized urban society of the East, with its flourishing commercial and industrial economy, was the disorganized, sectional spirit of the rural and agricultural West. While the disunited and mutually hostile regions of Western Christendom were falling piecemeal into the hands of Norse, Moslem, Hungarian, and Slavic invaders, or at best making only local efforts at resistance, the forces of the Eastern Empire were parts of one unified organism which survived an unprecedented series of formidable invasions. The explanation of this contrast lies in the difference in the underlying social and economic conditions in the two regions.

In contrast to the rural localism prevailing throughout the West, conditions in the East made possible—in fact, demanded—a highly integrated economic and governmental regime. Artisans, tradesmen, merchants, soldiers, nobles, and imperial officials were directed, dominated, and regimented by the central bureaucracy at Constantinople. Thus the activities of the various classes of the population could be readily adjusted to the needs of society as a whole, and to the administrative necessities of the state, notably to the need for revenues. So rigid was the governmental control of economic activities that there was little individual freedom for the citizens. But the Byzantine statesmen saw to it that industry, commerce, and even agriculture, prospered. This was necessary in order to assure ample revenues for the immense governmental bureaucracy.

The demands of the tax collectors rested heavily on the serfs and free farmers, but they were not crushed out of existence. The populous cities provided dependable markets for agricultural products and, in spite of rapacious landlords and insistent tax collectors, the peasantry lived comfortably (although on a lower standard than city dwellers) and with considerable security. The imperial armies were usually able to protect the most important agricultural regions from the devastation of internal warfare and invasion. Great estates flourished in certain favored sections of Asia Minor and the Balkans. Some were operated as state farms. In most regions there were many small freeholders, but the majority of the agricultural lands were controlled by the wealthy nobility.

AN URBAN CIVILIZATION

Byzantine civilization was essentially urban. Through the early centuries of internal disorder and barbarian invasion, and during the later era of Moslem and Persian wars, industry, commerce, and wealth continued to flourish in the eastern sections of the Roman Empire. In fact, the financial resources provided by prosperous industrial cities was an important factor in the success with which the Eastern Empire withstood its enemies. Even after the loss of the outlying provinces to the Persians and Moslems, the imperial capital, Constantinople, was still the metropolis of the Mediterranean and the wealthiest city of the Occidental world. Thanks to the imperial navy which guarded her commercial routes in the Black Sea, the Aegean, Syria, and portions of the West, Constantinople continued to exploit much of the trade of the Mediterranean. As long as the imperial capital was a commercial metropolis, her citizenry prospered, the government was able to carry on, and Byzantine civilization flourished.

THE METROPOLIS OF THE MEDITERRANEAN

The commercial and administrative position of Constantinople made it the center of a society that was wealthy, refined, luxurious, and cosmopolitan. Here was concentrated the income of the empire's industry and trade. Here the immense revenues of the imperial government were controlled and disposed of. People as well as wealth were drawn to Constantinople in such numbers that it became a miniature world of varied races and classes. The population, estimated at from 500,000 to 1,000,000 people, exceeded that of imperial Rome or Moslem Cordova, the greatest of Spanish cities. Among the upper ranks of society were to be found the privileged governmental officials, aristocratic courtiers, and higher clergy. At the other end of the scale was a poverty-stricken and corrupt rabble, dependent on the government for food and amusement. The city had its dens of vice and sections of habitations scarcely fit for human beings; on the other hand there were beautiful streets, luxurious palaces, and ornately decorated churches. Only Bagdad in the Moslem East could rival Constantinople in material splendor.

In its varied manifestations of squalor and sophistication, corruption and refinement, Constantinople is to be compared with the Babylon and Rome of antiquity and with a modern London, Paris, or New York. It had contrasts of fanatical piety and vicious immorality, indescribable luxury and hopeless poverty, intellectualism and barbaric ignorance. The strange mingling of such varied characteristics was due to the fact that Byzantine civilization was derived from equally strong Greek, Oriental, and Roman influences. It had the fine intellectual qualities of ancient Greece, the efficient organization of imperial Rome, and the lavish material splendor of the Orient.

A modern writer has expressed something of the glamorous superficiality not only of the capital city but also of the empire as a whole, by describing Constantinople as "the Golden City." Everywhere along its grand avenues could be seen golden statues of emperors, saints, and the Holy Virgin. Courtyards, colonnades, porticoes, and baths were decorated with "gay, garish, gaudy, glaring gold." But the Golden City also used other metals for her adornment. At the Hippodrome, on the *spina* about which the charioteers guided their four-horse teams, was a "chariot of Corinthian brass" with four bronze horses, reputed to have been "the horses of Constantine brought from Rome." [6] Constantinople was also a city of color; there were the bright hues of enameled tile, of mosaics, and of pillars of porphyry, marble, and other rare stones. Above all rose the "white and rose-colored walls of St. Sophia."

CONTRIBUTIONS
TO THE WEST

In all the Christian West, throughout the Middle Ages, there was no such display of material wealth. Only Venice, thanks to her maritime activities and contacts with Byzantine civilization, was able to establish a miniature

---

[6] Amy Lowell is the author of the quoted phrases in this paragraph. See "The Bronze Horses," in her *Can Grande's Castle,* Houghton Mifflin, 1921, pp. 141 ff. As a matter of fact, the four horses are thought to have been sculptured by a Roman artist to adorn Nero's triumphal arch in Rome, whence they were removed in the second century to the arch of Trajan, whence they were again removed by Constantine to adorn his new city. In 1204, the Venetian "crusaders" who sacked Constantinople took them to Venice to adorn the façade of St. Mark's. Napoleon in 1797 carried them to Paris for his triumphal arch in the Place du Carrousel. In 1814, when he was sent to Elba, the horses were returned to St. Mark's where they still stand, "trampling upon space, facing out to sea on the currents of the morning breeze."

of this Eastern life in her island city on the Adriatic. With this exception, Westerners had little contact with Constantinople until the age of the crusades. During the eleventh and twelfth centuries Western pilgrims, merchants, and crusaders in ever-increasing numbers traveled from their towns, castles, and rural hamlets to the East. To those who passed through Constantinople, the great capital was an experience as awe-inspiring in many respects as the Holy City itself. In addition to its wondrous churches and treasures of gold and silver, Constantinople had riches of classical literature, science, and art. Unfortunately for Western scholars, after the time of Justinian most Byzantine literature was in Greek. Thus they had little knowledge of the Greek versions of the medical science of Hippocrates, Galen, Alexander of Tralles, Paul of Aegina, and other eminent scientists. The learned compilations of Easterners such as Suidas, a tenth-century encyclopedist, and Michael Psellus, a century later, were likewise closed books to most Westerners.

The arts of the Byzantine Empire, however, were widely copied in the West from the time of Justinian until the late medieval centuries. In a later section we shall consider the Eastern styles of domed architecture, mosaic decoration, and mural painting as they appeared in Italy and other parts of the West. Industrial and military techniques, likewise, were carried westward from Constantinople, especially during the crusading period. In fact, until the late Middle Ages in most branches of civilization the Easterners were the teachers of the West. The Byzantine Empire served as an immense storehouse in which the economic, political, and cultural lore of antiquity, with later modifications and additions, was preserved until such time as the more primitive peoples of the West were able to appropriate and assimilate it.

Nevertheless, important as Byzantine civilization was in its contributions to the West, the history of Constantinople has an importance of its own. Apart from its relations with the West, the capital city and the empire had a long, adventuresome, and glorious career. By the end of the tenth century, the Eastern Empire had passed the halfway mark of its span of life. As in the days of Constantine, Constantinople was the most prosperous, cultured, and cosmopolitan city of the Mediterranean world. Her harbor sheltered merchant ships from distant ports. Her Hippodrome offered the greatest thrills to the greatest crowds that assembled in any land. St. Sophia, the church dedicated to the "Holy Wisdom," if not the most holy, was certainly the largest and most ornate of Christian temples. Nowhere in Europe were there palaces so grand, luxurious, and fascinating. Here it was that an Empress Theophano could help her husband to the purple by the murder of his own father, then poison him to marry a victorious general, and finally assist in the latter's assassination. With all its crimes, intrigues, and enemies, the empire had a military and governmental machinery, and a wealth of economic resources that enabled it to carry on through many more critical centuries. Not until the fifteenth century was the proud city of the Bosporus brought to its knees.

$=$ VIII $=$

THE MOSLEM WORLD

THE RISE OF THE MOSLEMS

AMONG the most formidable of the peoples that attacked the East-Roman Empire after the age of Justinian were the Moslems.[1] They were a constant and increasing source of danger from the seventh century, when they attacked the provinces of Egypt and Syria, until the fifteenth century, when the Turkish Sultan, Mohammed II, captured Constantinople and ended the long career of the Eastern Empire.

Ever since the beginnings of their expansion during the age of the prophet Mohammed, Moslem peoples have had a marked effect on Western Europe. Arab Moslems in the East, Moorish Moslems in Sicily and Spain, and Turkish Moslems in crusading lands and in the Balkans from the fifteenth century to our own day, have been important factors in European history. The Moslems have been not only a grave danger to the West, but also one of the great constructive forces in the advancement of mankind. Throughout most of the Middle Ages their civilization surpassed that of Western Europe. Of no little importance is the fact that their religion (Mohammedanism or Islam) has been one of the most dangerous rivals of Christianity.

THE ARABIAN BACKGROUND — The Moslem civilization, which was spread by the peoples of Arabia, was a combination of various cultures, both Occidental and Oriental. The Arabian peninsula, which is in reality a small continent equal in size to Western Europe, can be divided into two distinct regions: the arid interior, and the fertile external rim. Both are important in Moslem history. The great arid interior, still unexplored, has always been inhabited by

[1] The term Moslem is used as the equivalent of Mohammedan or Saracen, and includes (1) the original Arabs, (2) the Moors (who were a combination of Arabs and North African Berbers), and (3) the Turkish, Egyptian, and Persian Mohammedans. We use the term Moslem rather than Mohammedan because of the fact that Mohammedan has come to be thought of as restricted to religion.

nomadic tribes of Semitic people. Before Mohammed's day their rather primitive religion and society was dominated by a crude polytheism which included the worship of idols of various kinds. Economic life was (and still is) backward. Existence depended on flocks and herds, whose subsistence depended, in turn, on the grass produced by a scanty and uncertain rainfall. As a consequence, rival tribes waged fierce wars over the choice water holes and the neighboring grass lands.

It is probable that a prolonged dry cycle which culminated at about 600 A.D. intensified the struggle for existence and forced many tribesmen to seek new homes. At any rate, during this period the men of the desert carried on unceasing raids along the Persian and Byzantine frontiers in much the same manner in which their Semitic ancestors in ancient times had troubled the civilized peoples of the Tigris-Euphrates Valley. As the struggle for existence had affected the nomads of the Asiatic steppes, so it often drove the desert sheiks and their followers into the settled regions of outer Arabia and the surrounding countries. Throughout history such hordes of hungry nomads have invariably proved to be an invincible enemy and a fearsome scourge to their more civilized neighbors. The conquests of the Arabs during the seventh century may be thought of as merely one of the successive swarmings of Semitic tribes from the foodless Arabian deserts into neighboring lands of greater fertility.

There was, however, another Arabia, with a more civilized and less nomadic population. This region, the exterior rim of the peninsula, was better watered than the interior and supported a settled population of agriculturists and traders. Along the Red Sea, in the vicinity of Mecca and Medina, there were many Jews, Christian heretics, Hindus, and Persian Zoroastrians. It is significant that the reformer-leader of Arabia came from this region of higher civilization, whereas his conquering hosts of nomadic warriors were recruited very largely from the arid interior. It was the union of the desert fighters with the Mecca reformers that started the Moslem religion and Arabic civilization on their remarkable expansion.

MOHAMMED
THE PROPHET

Mohammed came from an unimportant Meccan family, and grew to manhood as a poor orphan. At twenty-five he became the commercial agent of a rich widow, whom he eventually married. It was after his marriage that Mohammed began to have heavenly visions, somewhat similar to those experienced by Joan of Arc and many such mystic spirits. His wife described these experiences in terms that have led some commentators to insist that he was merely a misguided epileptic; they came (so she said) during attacks of fever, and he "became red in the face, rolled on the ground, and roared like a camel." For a time Mohammed feared that these were visitations from the Devil, but became convinced that he was the medium for divine revelations.

Thenceforth his inspired words were recorded and subsequently gathered together to make up the Koran, the sacred scripture of the Moslems. This strange collection contains varied materials: prayers, short proverbs, poetical passages of rare beauty, moral precepts, and instructions on social and political affairs. Mohammed came to be lauded by his followers as a messiah who was not only the successor but also the superior of Moses, the Hebrew prophets, and even Christ.

Like many another religious leader, he seems to have been an unusually emotional mystic who considered himself and his visions to be divinely inspired. He was described as having a large head, black eyes, long beard and hair, and delicate hands. In the matter of tastes and smells, he was very sensitive and, as one of his several wives put it, "he was as bashful as a veiled virgin." It was perhaps inevitable that a spirit such as his would find the primitive religious practices of the Arabian tribes unbearable.

THE MOSLEM RELIGION   When he was forty, Mohammed found himself financially independent and in a position to devote himself to the realization of his rather vague ideas of religious reform. Many points of this program seem to have been picked up in the course of his business contacts with Christians or Jews. For instance, Mohammed's insistence on "One God, the Merciful and Compassionate," is strongly Christian in spirit. The same is true of his reverence for the Hebrew prophets and for Christ, and of his teaching concerning the "Day of Judgment," the "Fires of Hell," and the "Joys of Heaven." To be sure, Mohammed's Heaven was quite different from that pictured in the Revelation of St. John. It was, in fact, a sort of super-oasis where Moslem saints and soldier martyrs "quaff from inexhaustible rivers of wine; each waited on by seventy dark-eyed, deep-breasted houris who, befitting this Garden of Delights, dwell in enormous hollow pearls." Throughout Mohammed's teachings are to be found similar examples of the sensitive imagination of the Oriental mind as it clothed Christian or Hebrew ideas in Arabic language.

There was also a great deal of practical common sense in Mohammedanism. The moral code, much like that of the Hebrews and the Christians, condemned idolatry, adultery, witchcraft, murder, perjury, usury, and fraud or cruelty against orphans, women, and slaves. Cleanliness and abstinence from strong drink were emphasized and quite rigorously practiced. The Koran also enjoined individual prayers five times a day, daily fasts during the sacred month of Ramadan, and pilgrimages to holy places, especially to Mecca. All in all, Mohammed upheld high moral and spiritual ideals. He emphasized two supreme ideas: there is one God and Mohammed is his prophet; man's supreme duty is to submit to God's will and live an honest life. These comprised Islam, the central theme of Mohammedanism.

MOHAMMED
THE WARRIOR

Few prophets are honored in their own country. After three years of preaching, Mohammed had only a handful of converts, chiefly from his own household. Persecutions followed, and in 622 he fled to Medina at the invitation of the more cosmopolitan and tolerant inhabitants of that city. This event, which is called the Hegira, or "Flight," marks the first year in the Moslem era. It is also important because it brought about a noteworthy change in Mohammed's policy. Up to this time his career of courageous but peaceful preaching strongly resembled that of Christ.

After the Hegira, he ceased to be a persecuted prophet and became a persecutor; he turned abruptly from peaceful preaching to warfare and plunder, and from idealistic reform to organized conquest. Jewish opponents in Medina were exiled; at one time an obstinate group of six hundred citizens were massacred, their wives and children being sold as slaves. When Mohammed's followers began to plunder the caravans of the Meccans, war broke out, and the desert tribesmen were soon drawn to the banner of the militant prophet. By the year 630 he was able to enter Mecca in triumph. The conqueror treated his former persecutors with laudable kindness. Most of them were pardoned, and their city replaced Medina as the center of the new religion. Thereafter the faithful were urged to make annual pilgrimages to the Kaaba (a shrine at Mecca) where they kissed a black stone meteorite that had long been held in veneration by the inhabitants of the region. All other idols were destroyed. The reformed Arabian religion spread rapidly. It was accepted by most of the tribes of the interior who had been accustomed to worship at Mecca. By 632, when

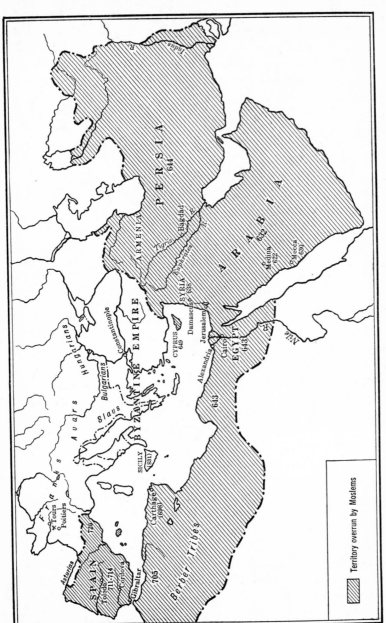

MOSLEM EXPANSION (622-732)

Dates of conquests are approximate

Territory overrun by Moslems

Mohammed died, not only Medina and Mecca, but much of inner Arabia was under his sway.

MOSLEM
EXPANSION

Mohammed's successors set out to realize his dying command, "Preach Islam [i.e., the Moslem faith] to all; those who refuse shall be humbled." Thus began the most rapid political and religious expansion known to history. The tribes along the northern border of Arabia joined Mohammed's father-in-law and successor, Caliph [2] Abu Bekr, when they heard that the unbelievers in the neighboring Persian and Byzantine lands were to be conquered. The time was favorable, for the Byzantines and the Persians had weakened themselves by a long series of wars. Furthermore this was the period during which the empire of Heraclius was beset on all sides by dangerous foes. Before the middle of the century, the Tigris-Euphrates Valley and Syria (including the city of Jerusalem) had fallen before the Moslem attack. Eastward into Asia, armies of conquerors swept, occupying Persia and portions of western India. Meanwhile their forces had taken to the sea. They captured Cyprus (649), Rhodes (653), and after defeating the imperial fleet, began a series of unsuccessful naval attacks on Constantinople.

To the south in the Nile Valley success was even more rapid. The tax-burdened populace and the heretical Christians who had been harshly treated by imperial officials actually welcomed the invaders. After the conquest of Egypt (640-643), the victorious Moslems concentrated their efforts on Asia Minor and Constantinople. Here they were checked by land and sea. This was due to two factors: the defensive strength of Constantinople, and the rivalries which had developed among the Moslems themselves. There was constant strife, and at times assassination and open warfare among the ambitious relatives of Mohammed. Not until late in the century was there a renewal of Moslem expansion under the Ommiad caliphs of Damascus, whose greatest successes were in Northern Africa. In 670 a powerful army reinforced by hordes of Libyan tribesmen pushed westward from Egypt, through Tripoli, and on toward Carthage. Civil wars and the opposition of the Berber tribes of the northern Sahara delayed the conquest, but before 700 the city of Carthage and the Byzantine province of Africa had fallen.

From this base of operations the warriors of Islam invaded West-

[2] Caliph is a Moslem title which means successor (of Mohammed). As the head of the Moslem religion the caliph's position is somewhat similar to that of the Roman Catholic pope.

ern Europe by land and sea. Sicily and southern Italy, under their Byzantine and Lombard rulers, held out until the ninth century. Visigothic Spain was an easier and more willing victim. In 711, General Tarik, with an army of North African Moslems, crossed the narrow straits and landed in Spain near the promontory which has been called, ever since, "Gibraltar" or *Gebel-Tarik* (that is, the "Hill of Tarik"). General Tarik quickly overwhelmed the Visigothic forces, and soon most of Spain was under Moslem control.

Within ten years, southern Gaul was being used as a base from which raiding parties penetrated all parts of Aquitaine. The all too-famous battle of Tours, or Poitiers (732), merely prevented one of the largest of these raiding armies from capturing Tours with its rich monastic and ecclesiastical treasures. It did not keep the Moslems out of Gaul, nor did it drive them south of the Pyrenees. It did check their advance, and doubtless prevented further raids and the temporary occupation of central Gaul, but it was not primarily this battle that saved the West from Mohammedanism. Frankish power was too deeply intrenched in Gaul to be overthrown by a single defeat. Even in the parts of the South which the invaders occupied and held for over a generation, Christian civilization continued with relatively little change. The Pyrenees were the natural Moorish frontier [3] and the existence of Christian institutions in Gaul was never seriously endangered. Incidentally, the Christian Frankish civilization of Gaul was much less progressive than that of the Moslem regions in the West.

The year 732 is, however, important in that it marked the end of the first, and most remarkable, century of Moslem history. Within a hundred years after the death of Mohammed (632), his religious faith and Arabian arms had expanded into three continents and had conquered a realm that extended from Delhi in India to Granada in Spain, and from the Sahara deserts to the steppes of Central Asia.

REASONS FOR MOSLEM EXPANSION The unusual rapidity and permanence of Moslem expansion can be accounted for not only by the strength of the conquerors, but also by the weakness of those whom they attacked. The Arabs were a hardy courageous people trained to rapid movement and fierce fighting. The Moslem faith developed these traits by its zealous fatalism. Moslems were taught that they should "fear not the heat of conflict;

---

[3] Strictly speaking the Moors were one of several North African tribes who adopted Mohammedanism. The term is, however, commonly used of the Moslems who invaded Spain, and of all Western Moslems.

Hell's flames are hotter," and that a paradise of pleasure awaited the hero who died in battle. Furthermore, the expanding population of Arabia (possibly a result of polygamy), coupled with the pressure of reduced pastures and herds, furnished an effective economic impetus for conquest. To the hard-pressed Arabian tribesmen, the rich cities and fertile lands of Persia and Byzantine Christendom were an irresistible attraction. Had not the prophet Mohammed commanded the faithful to humble the unbelievers? Thus religious motives served as a pretext for satisfying an irrepressible urge for warfare and expansion. Islam was a religion that welded many fierce and often hostile tribes into a formidable conquering force.

If the Arabs were willing and anxious to conquer, many of the inhabitants of the invaded regions were willing, if not anxious, to be conquered. The Persian and the Byzantine governments were so unpopular with their tax-ridden populations and persecuted heretics that few of the citizens would fight in defense of the existing regime. The invaders were often welcomed by the people, once the defending armies had been defeated. Heretical groups found Moslem rule more tolerant than that of Christian emperors. The Jews who (like the invaders) were Semites, found life more attractive and profitable under Arab than under Christian rule. In Jerusalem, which is the holy city of three religions, Arabs, Christians, and Jews worshipped in comparative harmony, save for the fact that the Christians urged the Arabian rulers to persecute the Jews. Some churches in Arab-controlled Palestine were used by both Christians and Moslems.

There is no basis for the popular belief that the Moslems forced people to choose either Islam or death—the Koran or the sword. As a matter of fact, they had three choices: (1) they might accept the Koran, and with it all the privileges enjoyed by Moslems; (2) they might keep their own religious faith and pay tribute, which often was equivalent to a graduated income tax; or (3) they might refuse these terms, and be put to the sword. Many oppressed people in both the Byzantine and the Persian empires welcomed the change of masters, and some of them accepted the Moslem faith. One of the most interesting and convincing evidences of the popularity of the Moslem regime is the fact that the new rulers found it necessary to revise their tax system because of the decrease in tribute caused by great numbers of Christian subjects turning Moslem. Converts found excellent opportunities in trade or the governmental service. The general conclusion seems to be that many of the regions overrun by the Moslem armies were better off religiously and economically than they had been formerly. The number of cities that were surrendered to the invaders by traitors within their gates speaks eloquently of the discontent of the inhabitants and helps to account for the remarkable ease and rapidity of Moslem expansion.

THE INFLUENCE OF MOSLEM CIVILIZATION

POLITICAL DECLINE

Within a short time the loosely organized Moslem empire began to disintegrate. In fact, it can scarcely be said that there ever was a permanently consolidated empire. Within thirty years after the death of Mohammed (632), wars of succession were raging among the leaders of the Mecca dynasty. By the end of the century, the Ommiads of Damascus had wrested the control from the older Meccan dynasty, only to be supplanted in turn by the Abbasids of Bagdad, who made a clean sweep of their rivals by massacring ninety Ommiad leaders. One prince, Abd-er-Rahman, escaped to faraway Spain where, at Cordova, he set himself up as emir (emperor), of all Western Moslems. Still later, at Cairo, in Egypt, there was established another independent dynasty, with a caliph who claimed descent from Fatima, one of Mohammed's daughters. Farther to the east, also, Moslem political power decayed. Everywhere the sultans of the various regions eventually became the actual rulers. In time, these regional kingdoms tended to disintegrate or reorganize into new combinations.

From the religious standpoint, Islam manifested similar tendencies. Quite early the Meccans had split into Shiite and Sunnite factions. The conservatively minded Shiites favored the restriction of the office of caliph to members of Mohammed's family, whereas the Sunnites insisted on a wider selective basis. The Shiites also restricted the authoritative religious law of Islam to the Koran, whereas their opponents accepted other traditional teachings as well. These fundamental differences created serious rifts among the Moslems and accentuated their bitter political rivalries. The disintegrating effects of religious and political factionalism were most apparent after the first great era of expansion which began in the seventh century. It was not until the eleventh century, when the Seljuk Turks infused a new militant vigor into the Moslems of the Near East, that they launched upon a second era of aggressive expansion, the threat of which stirred Western Christendom to crusading enthusiasm.[4]

ECONOMIC
PROGRESS

Despite religious and political differences, the Moslem world developed a civilization that manifested remarkable unity and progressiveness of spirit. The early Arabian conquerors preserved the older civilizations of the Near East, encouraged further developments, and during the later medieval centuries gave to Western Europe a great wealth of Hindu, Persian, and Greek-Roman culture.

From the economic standpoint, the Arabian Empire introduced a renewed period of commercial prosperity, not only in the Near East, but also in the South-Mediterranean lands and in Spain. This was due in large measure to the fact that the Moslem conquests brought into being an economic world of greater extent than any of ancient times. Thanks to the prevailing tolerance of the Moslem religious and political regime, and to the unifying bonds of the Mohammedan faith and the Arabic language, there was a remarkably free flow of commerce and culture, throughout the regions stretching from Spain in the West to India and the Far East. Moslem merchants penetrated even beyond these limits: into Egypt and the Sahara, far down the east coast of Africa, and past the Straits of Malacca to Canton in China. The commerce of the Moslem world brought regions as far distant as China and Spain, Egypt and the Baltic Sea into closer contact than ever before. The numerous Arabic coins found by modern excavators along the Varangian route in Russia, in Baltic lands, and in India bear silent witness to the far-reaching activities of Moslem merchants.

Although the commercial activities of the Moslems were in many ways a continuation of those of classical times, under their enlightened regime great advances were made. Constant travel, even to distant lands, was encouraged by the universal custom of making pilgrimages to Mecca, and by the excellent facilities for transportation by both land and sea. Roads, bridges, and ports were improved, and water transport was developed by canals and by seagoing ships. Merchant craft, both large and small, plied the Mediterranean, the Persian Gulf, the Red Sea, and even the Indian Ocean. It is not by chance that the Western world inherited from the Moslems such terms as admiral, sloop, barque, traffic, and tariff. In their maritime achieve-

⁴ See below, Chapter XXV.

ments, the various Moslem peoples proved themselves a remarkably adaptable people.

Overland, caravans carried products from seaport towns to inland centers, and also across great stretches of foreign territory. From Bagdad on the Tigris River there were permanent land routes leading to Egypt, the Sahara and Arabia, to Kiev and other Russian centers, and to India and faraway China. This was long before the day of Marco Polo. From the North European world of the Baltic and North seas, enterprising merchants brought raw materials such as furs, wax and honey, amber, fish products, special kinds of wood, and slaves. From the Orient they imported spices, gems, gold and silver, silks, and various kinds of luxury products. Standard types of coined money and a variety of credit operations were employed in commercial transactions.

INDUSTRY   Moslem industrial centers produced ample supplies of goods for exchange. In their early era of expansion, when the nomadic Arabs conquered the cities of the Persian and Byzantine empires, they took over practically unchanged the existing systems of industry and local government. Under a practical and enlightened Moslem administration, native merchants and craftsmen were free to exploit the wider markets offered by an expanding empire. Older cities prospered and great industrial centers developed, especially at the Moslem capitals. Thus Cairo in Egypt, Damascus in Syria, and Bagdad on the Tigris River, became immense commercial and industrial cities. Cordova, the capital of Moslem Spain, was a city of over half a million inhabitants, and in population, wealth, and splendor Bagdad rivaled the greatest cities, not only of its own day, but also of ancient times.

Even the fanciful tales of *The Arabian Nights* can scarcely exaggerate the material resources of this metropolis. In the tenth century it covered an area five miles in diameter. There were streets and quarters for Christians, Jews, Persians, Chinese, and other foreigners; industrial sections were also set aside for the shops of the perfumers, silk merchants, weavers of woolens, cottons, and other textiles, workers in gold and metals, dealers in paper, leather workers, armorers, bankers, and hundreds of merchants who sold the necessities or luxuries of life. Here one could buy needles or elephants, embroidery or hay and grain. The bazaars, mosques, and palaces of Bagdad presented civilized life in all its extremes of economic and political activity.

Most Moslem cities produced quantities of textiles of wool, cotton, linen, and silk. The Moslem names, muslin (Mosul), damask (Damascus), gauze, and satin suggest a few of the many varieties of cloth that were made and marketed in large quantities. There were also cloaks and blankets of wool or camel's hair, brocaded and embroidered silks, tapestries, and beautiful rugs of fascinating colors and designs. Moslem metal workers were famous throughout the world for their fine articles of gold and silver, and especially for coats of mail and swords. Everywhere Damascus and Toledo blades were known and admired. In all Moslem lands leather was produced, but two Western centers, Morocco and Cordova, gave their names to the finest of leather, often brightly colored. Luxury goods were prominent in the bazaars of the larger cities. These included gems, jewelry, perfumes such as the famous attar of roses, glass, fine pottery, and musical instruments.

As early as the ninth century, paper, originally a Chinese product, was made from cotton. Its use, however, was limited. Drugs of all kinds, sirups (a word of Moslem origin) and sugar (not common enough to be used as a food), were also made in small quantities. Hundreds of other articles were produced, exported, and sold in hundreds of Moslem cities. Throughout the Moslem world the general standards of industry, commerce, and therefore of living, were equal to those of the Byzantine realm, and far superior to those of the Christian West. They were comparable in many respects to those of Roman imperial times. This high degree of material prosperity was brought about not so much by the superior ability of the Moslem conquerors, as by their preservation and encouragement of the already existing achievements of urban civilizations that had been deep rooted in the Near East since the early days of Oriental, Greek, and Roman antiquity. The relative peace and unity that Moslem rule brought to a great expanse of the civilized world made possible the acceleration and extension of economic exchange on a scale seldom known until modern times.

AGRICULTURE   Agriculture, though apparently of secondary importance in this urban civilization, was highly developed by the Moslems. The agricultural institutions of the conquered regions were not destroyed, and in the course of time they were much improved as a result of the scientific methods introduced by intelligent Moslem rulers. This was particularly true in irrigation, horticulture, and the terracing of hilly slopes. In the West, especially in certain parts of southern Spain, regions deserted since the Roman imperial regime were made fertile and productive by means of irrigation and the introduction of new varieties of crops, vegetables, fruit trees, and flowers. Among the agricultural and horticultural products whose growth and use the West learned from the Moslems, are flax, hemp, rice, asparagus, spinach, artichokes, olives, lemons, melons, saffron (for dyes), and the mulberry.

SCIENCE The wide extent of Moslem conquests and trade relations bore fruit in a remarkable development of learning, literature, and the arts. The conquering Arabs were more anxious to possess than to destroy, and under their enlightened rule many of the cultural achievements of the Hindus, the Persians, the ancient Greeks, and the Romans were made available to scholars of the East and West. Hindu mathematics, including algebra, trigonometry, and in particular the decimal system of numbering, were adopted, improved, and spread westward, eventually to be assimilated by Christian Europe. The most notable contributions of the Moslems to mathematics were the sciences of algebra and trigonometry, but they also made marked improvements in geometry and astronomy. They used the astrolabe and sextant, they figured degrees of latitude and longitude, made maps, and listed the known stars and planets. Many stars, for example, still bear Moslem names. Their physicists carried on experiments in optics, using prisms, lenses, and curved mirrors. Along with the various aspects of mathematical science which were passed on to the West, were transmitted technical Moslem terms; some of these, algebra, zenith, nadir, zero, and cipher, are still in common use. One of the greatest of Moslem mathematicians was the Persian, Omar Khayyám, better known for his poetry.

MEDICINE The Moslems were also the channel through which much of classical philosophy and medical science reached the West. The works of Euclid and Ptolemy on geometry and astronomy, of Dioscorides, Hippocrates, and Galen on medicine, and the writings of Plato, Aristotle, and many less famous thinkers were translated into Arabic, whence they were later retranslated into Latin by Western scholars. Once the Moslem scientists and philosophers had acquired the learning of classical antiquity, they began to write commentaries and, eventually, original works in which there were revealed a keenness of observation and a brilliancy of reasoning that have seldom been surpassed.

Physicians wrote learned studies on surgery (even concerning operations on the eye), on pharmacy, diet, and specific diseases, and also comprehensive handbooks of general medicine. The most noted of these physician-philosophers were Razis and Avicenna. In the late Middle Ages many of the Arabic medical works were translated into Latin and used in the West along with the medical writings of Hippocrates, Dioscorides, and Galen. In the West after the eleventh century, Avicenna's encyclopedic work, *The Canon,* rivaled the older classical writings. At a time when Western medicine was just beginning to emerge from an atmosphere of superstition and reliance on divine intercession, scientific physicians and a tradition of intelligent medical learning flourished in the Moslem world.

ALCHEMY   The Moslems were also responsible for much of Western Europe's knowledge of alchemy, a science that they had acquired from earlier classical and Oriental civilizations. Although concerned chiefly with efforts to change the less valuable metals into gold and silver, the alchemists discovered many hitherto unknown substances; among them, carbonate of soda, sal ammoniac, borax, and cream of tartar. The study of alchemy also encouraged experimentation and eventually led to modern chemistry. Whereas modern chemical terms such as sal, oxide, and precipitate reveal a classical heritage, terms such as alchemy, alkali, and alcohol indicate the importance of the Moslems in the evolution of chemical science.

PHILOSOPHY   In philosophy, most clearly of all, the Moslems manifested their ability to assimilate the cultural contributions of other civilizations. Moslem philosophy was a curious but effective combination of the thought of the Greeks (particularly that of Aristotle), the Hindus, the Hebrews, and various Semitic peoples. The Moslems not only combined the varying philosophies of other peoples into a homogeneous system, they also made progress in the difficult task of reconciling science with religious faith. In most of their philosophical syntheses, Aristotelian and Hindu rationalism was dominant. This tendency eventually precipitated a critical struggle between the liberal scientific thinkers and the conservative exponents of divinely revealed religion based on faith. From the tenth century onward, Moslem scholars wrote extensively concerning the essential harmony of religious faith and scientific rationalism. Although their rationalized scheme of religious thought was not accepted by the ruling class and by conservative Moslems, it became widely prevalent among the intelligentsia. Its chief exponent was Averroës, a twelfth-century Spanish Moslem. His commentaries on Aristotle, in which the prob-

GIRALDA TOWER (XII C) AND CHRISTIAN CATHEDRAL, SEVILLE

Both Courtesy of the University Prints
INTERIOR OF MOSQUE, CORDOVA (VIII C)

MOSLEM ART

(See p. 176.)

COURT OF THE LIONS, THE ALHAMBRA, GRANADA (XIV C)

Both Courtesy of the University Prints

COURT OF THE MYRTLES, THE ALHAMBRA, GRANADA (XIV C)

MOSLEM ART

(See p. 176.)

lem was thoroughly analyzed, became the basic influence on European thought in the succeeding period, when Western theologians were struggling to harmonize the Christian faith with Aristotelian rationalism and science. The scholastics of the West [5] seem to have followed closely in the footsteps of earlier Moslem thinkers, save for the fact that the Moslems were more objective and less subservient to theology.

LITERATURE   The literature of the Moslems was somewhat less imposing than their scientific and philosophical achievements. Nevertheless they produced notable works in most of the literary forms common to highly developed civilizations. In addition to collections of the early folk poetry of the nomadic Arabs, there were epic poems, especially those concerning the popular hero Rustam, lyric and romantic verse on a variety of subjects, and even learned or philosophical poems of unusual merit. It is noteworthy that many of the prominent Moslem poets were Persians, among them Omar Khayyám, composer of the immortal *Rubáiyát*. In the field of prose literature, there was, as has been mentioned, a remarkable body of scientific and philosophical writing; also a considerable array of encyclopedias, histories, romances, short stories, and so on. In contrast to the literature of the West, not only of the same period, but even through the later medieval centuries, Moslem interests ran strongly to secular subjects. There is perhaps no better example of this characteristic than the famous collection of fanciful and erotic stories which comprise *The Thousand and One Nights,* commonly called *The Arabian Nights.*

THE ARTS   In the arts, as in literature and learning, the Moslems were superior to their contemporaries in Western Europe, and on a par with the Byzantines. There are, however, two notable exceptions—the pictorial arts, and especially sculpture. Mohammed's strict prohibition of all forms of idolatry forbade any representation of human or animal forms. This restricted Moslem sculptors, painters, and decorators to conventionalized designs. Fortunately this resulted in a marked development of formal types of decoration. Varieties of intricate patterns were used for exteriors and mural decoration, sometimes with alternating strips of contrasting stone, or variegated tiles, mosaics, wood and metal work, handled with such richness of detail as to give a sumptuous though refined effect. This

[5] See below, p. 665.

characteristic of Moslem art is excellently illustrated in the interiors
of the mosques and in palaces such as the Alhambra at Granada, and
in the so-called arabesque type of decoration, with its highly complicated patterns based on geometrical designs and conventionalized trees,
shrubs, and flowers.

THE MOSQUE   Moslem architecture was dominated by the mosque,
in which are to be seen three outstanding features:
the minaret, the dome, and the open courtyard. From the distance,
the most impressive feature of a mosque is the tall, graceful, turreted
minaret. In purpose and architectural effect it is comparable to the
Italian campanile and the Gothic cathedral spire save for the fact
that it has no bells, the Moslem faithful being called to prayer by the
voice of the muezzin, the one who cries the hour of prayer. Of similar prominence is the high bulbous dome, a structure somewhat reminiscent of the uplifted Byzantine dome, but characteristically Oriental
in that it is more than a half sphere. The horseshoe-shaped arches of
the doorways and windows are, likewise, more than a half circle. A
third architectural feature of the Moslem mosque architecture is the
open court with a central fountain (originally for ritual ablutions)
and arcaded or colonnaded walks around the four sides. Although
similar to the monastic cloister and the inner court of the ancient
Roman home, the Moslem courtyard was distinguished by the delicacy
of its decorative effects and the atmosphere of luxurious worldliness.
The courtyards of palaces such as the Alhambra at Granada or of
mosques such as that at Cordova reveal this feature of Moslem architecture in its most refined splendor. The inner sanctuary of the
mosque, in contrast to that of the Christian church, is simple and un-
adorned save for passages from the Koran inscribed on the walls.

In the more practical phases of architecture, such as military forti-
fication, and in the industrial arts already mentioned, the Moslems
also achieved great success. There are hints of their architectural contributions to the modern age in words such as alcove, cupola, and
arabesque. More direct influences can be seen in the imitations of
mosques and palaces that are found in modern motion-picture theaters and in "Shriners'" temples. The tower of the Giralda, an ancient
mosque in Seville, is said to have been the architectural inspiration for
the tower of the old Madison Square Garden building in New York
City. At the opposite extreme of the Moslem realm from Seville
stands another architectural masterpiece that is much admired: the

unsurpassed Taj Mahal, which was built by a Moslem ruler of seventeenth-century India.

The Moslem world was dotted with splendid cities, provided with public baths and libraries, with mosques and palaces, with bazaars and universities. The inhabitants of such cities lived at a much higher level of material comfort and cultural advancement than their contemporaries in Western Europe. Only in Constantinople and Venice could one have found standards of living comparable to those that prevailed in hundreds of Moslem cities. Not until the tenth and eleventh centuries was the West sufficiently advanced in culture to appreciate fully the achievements of her civilized neighbors in Byzantine and Moslem lands. Not until the thirteenth, fourteenth, and fifteenth centuries could Western civilization compare or compete with that of Byzantium and the Moslems in Spain and the Near East. When the West did finally create a civilization equal to that of neighboring peoples, it incorporated many of the achievements of the Moslem world.

⟹ IX ⟸

THE FRANKISH EMPIRE

W E have already observed that the civilized world of the early Middle Ages may be considered in terms of three rather distinct regions: Byzantine, Moslem, and Germanic. Having dealt with the first two we now return to the Germanic kingdoms in the West. Here, too, we may make a rather distinct threefold division. Far to the northwest, in the British Isles, was a group of Anglo-Saxon tribal kingdoms; across the Channel in Gaul was the rapidly expanding Frankish kingdom; to the south, in Italy, was a combination of three powers. In Italy, by the end of the sixth century, the Ostrogoths had given way to the armies of the Byzantine Empire and the invading Lombards. For two centuries thereafter there were three Italies: that of the Lombards, that claimed by the Eastern emperors, and that controlled by the popes. Of the three Italian powers only the papacy was destined to survive; in time it became one of the dominant powers in Western Europe. In the West at large, the region controlled by the Franks expanded until it dominated all others on the Continent. To this important development we now turn our attention.

THE MEROVINGIAN FRANKS

POLITICAL
CONFUSION
The southward movement of the Franks under Clovis and the establishment of their kingdom in Gaul have already been considered in detail. This period of military and political expansion was followed by two centuries of confusion, violence, and decadence. The descendants of Clovis displayed considerable vigor, but most of their energies were woefully misdirected. The century following his death (511) was marked by civil wars and by successive divisions of the Frankish realms. Nevertheless, for a while external expansion continued. To the south, Burgundy was annexed (in 534) and by 567 the conquest of

Auvergne, Provence, and Gascony had carried Frankland's frontiers to the Alps, the Mediterranean, and the Pyrenees. Meanwhile to the east, in the Germanic regions beyond the Rhine, Thuringia was conquered and an opening wedge was driven into Frisia to the north, and into Bavaria to the south. For the most part, the Frankish realm was confined to the regions of ancient Gaul; beyond these limits little permanent conquest was made until the period of the Carolingian monarchy in the eighth century.

Internal affairs, the chief concern of Clovis's successors, were marked by constant confusion and warfare. This was due chiefly to what has been called "the fatal Frankish custom" of dividing the realm, as though it were a private estate, equally among the king's sons. Usually their quarrels, murders, and family feuds made it impossible to maintain a strong monarchy. During most of the sixth century the kingdom seemed on the point of complete disintegration. A brief survey of the reigns of Clovis's descendants will make this point clear.

After his death in 511 his four sons exercised a supposedly joint control, though in separate regions. There was unending rivalry and intrigue among them. Chlotar of Soissons outlived all three of his brothers, and for three years controlled the entire realm. At his death in 561 there was another fourfold division among his four sons. After six years one of them died, leaving three rival kings. From the confusion and conflict of this period there emerges the fact that the realm was gradually breaking up into three kingdoms. The least important of the three was Burgundy in the Rhone Valley. Its king merely tried to maintain his independence by playing the role of mediator between his more warlike brothers of Neustria and Austrasia, which were the active centers of Frankish life at this time. Austrasia, the old homeland of the Salians and Ripuarians, comprised the lower Rhine Valley, from Metz and Mayence northward to the North Sea. It was a rich agricultural land, almost purely Germanic in population. Neustria, to the southwest, was a region more recently occupied. It comprised the fertile Seine basin with its Roman cities and civilized Celtic-Roman inhabitants. Here and to the south there were fewer Germanic settlers and the remnants of imperial civilization continued to flourish for some time.

EARLY FRANKISH
CIVILIZATION
The *History of the Franks* written by Bishop Gregory of Tours (d. 594) [1] gives us a vivid and detailed record of the state of civilization in the Frankish realm. This is important because it enables us to see rather clearly the manner in which the new Roman-Christian-Germanic civilization took shape during the early centuries. In central Gaul, the region in which Gregory lived and wrote, the mingling of Germanic customs with the elements of Christian and Roman civilization went on more naturally than elsewhere. Further south the Germanic invaders were absorbed into the remnants of the civilization of the empire. In England and other more northerly regions the Germans overwhelmed and dominated all other peoples and institutions. In contrast to such extremes, Gregory's picture of Frankland in the sixth century reveals much of Germanic barbarism, something of imperial civilization, and a vigorous but rather primitive type of Christianity.

To begin with, there was no distinction between Romans and Germans, Christians and non-Christians. All inhabitants of the realm were members of one church and state. Life was far from refined, but it was by no means the life of primitive savages. There were the class distinctions that usually mark a well-developed society. The chief social classes noted in Gregory's account are slaves, serfs, free peasants, clergymen, and nobles. There were a few merchants, but the middle class of business folk was conspicuously unimportant. The actions of the individuals described by Gregory indicate sharp extremes of brutal repression and equality of opportunity. Often the lower classes were cruelly treated: a slave could be tortured at his master's pleasure, and the fine for killing one was the same as that for killing a horse. Gregory of Tours tells of two slaves who were buried alive for marrying without their master's consent. On the other hand, there were instances of marriage between serfs and nobles; by marriage, a girl of low birth might even become queen. The condition of the free peasants and the middle classes was comfortable but insecure. In this rough age life among the nobility was violent and, according to modern standards, immoral. Both men and women committed crimes of brutal violence.

Economic life, as revealed by Gregory, was chiefly agricultural. Kings, nobles, and clergymen relied principally on the income from their rural estates (called villas). Each estate was to a large extent

---

[1] See below, p. 267.

self-supporting. There were a few towns with markets and shops at which imported luxury goods and simple local products could be purchased, but there was little large-scale trade or industry. Syrians or Jews imported small amounts of silk, spices, and other Oriental goods. Most of the trade at the local markets and fairs was the barter of simple home products made by the artisans on monastic or royal estates. To an ever-increasing degree the life of the vast mass of the people during this age came to be absorbed by the rural estates.

Churches, monasteries, and clergymen were found everywhere. Religious practices and beliefs, however, reflected a low level of intelligence, and religious life was marked by gross superstition. Relics of saints were relied on for all sorts of wonders. Gregory was particularly eloquent concerning the marvelous cures that were brought about by taking a sacred drink containing dust from the tomb of St. Martin of Tours. The blind, deaf, and dumb were healed by such means. Gregory himself, so he wrote, was miraculously healed of stomach trouble at this shrine. On the other hand, he also told of physicians who performed difficult surgical operations, and interestingly enough the son of a poor laborer became the chief physician to one of the kings. As one reads the records of life in this early age he is constantly impressed with its marked contrasts and violent contradictions. Gross barbarism went hand in hand with intelligence and civilization. A few incidents from the lives of the ruling dynasty will serve to illustrate this point and also to indicate the trend of Frankish political life.

CHILPERIC
AND
BRUNHILD

Chilperic of Neustria, though a cruel despot, was intelligent and cultured. He was addicted to the writing of books and poems. Gregory reported, however, that the meter of his poetry "limped." Nevertheless, he was a patron of culture and a thinker of such independence that he denied the orthodox doctrine of the Trinity. Chilperic's theological interests, however, had no bearing upon his morality. For political reasons he married a young Visigothic princess from Spain, but soon had her assassinated, doubtless at the behest of his mistress, Fredegund, a woman of the lower class who later became his queen. Further east, at Metz in the Rhine Valley, lived his brother Sigebert, king of Austrasia. His queen, Brunhild, was a younger sister of the murdered queen of Neustria. The two brothers were already rivals and it was easy for Brunhild to stir her husband to warfare against the Neustrians. Thus Brunhild's determination to avenge her sister's death added fuel to the already smoldering fires of political jealousy, and the feud between Brunhild and Chilperic soon became a civil war. In spite of the efforts of the king of Burgundy to reconcile his brothers, both Neustria and Austrasia were ravaged by invasion and counterinvasion. At one time treachery among the subjects of Chilperic so undermined his power that Sigebert and Brunhild seemed about to triumph. But a sudden turn of the wheel of fortune and a poisoned dagger were fatal to the victorious Sigebert. Disputes as to his successor prolonged the trouble, and permitted the nobles of both kingdoms to increase their power and lands at the expense of the monarchs.

Brunhild with her five-year-old son somehow managed to escape death, and eventually her fortunes began to look up. She married Chilperic's son, and when the jealous Fredegund plotted her death, she fled to Austrasia where her own son was now king. Henceforth Brunhild's star of destiny rose to unparalleled heights. She assumed control in Austrasia and, until her death in 613, dominated the kingdom. She made an alliance with the Burgundian king according to which her son Childebert II, and his two sons after him, ruled both kingdoms. Finally Brunhild, still burning with ambition and revenge, persuaded her grandsons to make war on Neustria where the son of Chilperic and the hated Fredegund reigned. By 613 both grandsons had died, but Brunhild, now a great-grandmother, eighty years of age, still endeavored to control the destinies of the Franks. The tragic consequences of this ambition finally overtook her. The jealous nobles rose in revolt and turned her over to King Chlotar II of Neustria who had her dragged to her death, bound by her own hair to the tail of a wild horse. As a result of the fall of Brunhild, Chlotar became ruler of an apparently reunited Frankland.

The defeat of Brunhild was also the defeat of the monarchical cause, for the rebellious aristocracy emerged the real victor. Its predominant position was assured by the Pact of Paris (614) in which Chlotar gave to the lay and clerical nobles innumerable royal lands and political rights. Henceforth the Merovingian kings merely reigned; it was the aristocracy that actually ruled. Many modern scholars see this as an important step in the development of feudalism in France. Chlotar II (614-629) and his son Dagobert I (629-639) were theoretically kings of all Frankland, but in reality each of the three units was under the control of the mayor of the palace who represented the interests of the local aristocracy.

The mayor of the palace was originally merely a major-domo who supervised the servants and officials of the palace. Later he became chief administrator of the royal estates, which constituted the chief source of the king's wealth. Eventually the mayor became a sort of secretary of the treasury, prime minister, and commander in chief, combined. In Austrasia this office was held by Pepin (I) of Landen, the leader of the nobles in their revolt against Brunhild. One of Pepin's successors was so influential that he began to take over the functions of the monarch. But when he attempted to depose the child-king in favor of his own son the nobles turned against him, called in the kings of Neustria and Burgundy, and put both father and son to death. Apparently the nobles could be counted on to overthrow any mayor of unusual ambition and power. They preferred a weak monarch whom they could easily control. In the other Frankish kingdoms also the government was in the hands of the aristocracy. During the chaotic seventh century the kings were mere pawns in the struggles between nobles and ambitious mayors, or between rival mayors. Quite accurately, therefore, the weak, inefficient, and degenerate successors of Chilperic, Sigebert, Brunhild, and Dagobert have been called "do-nothing" kings. They lived practically as prisoners on their country estates. Once a year they rode in state (on an ox cart) to meet their subjects and read an address that had been prepared by the mayor of the palace.

Of all the mayors those of Austrasia were the most powerful. They finally gained control over the mayors of the other kingdoms as a result of the battle of Tertry (687) in which Mayor Pepin (II) of Heristal with an army of Austrasian nobles decisively defeated the Neustrians. This event assured (1) the domination of Pepin's family in Austrasian affairs, (2) Austrasian control over all Frankland, and (3) the eventual replacement of the "do-nothing" Merovingian kings by the energetic Carolingian mayors of Austrasia.

Pepin during his twenty-seven years of rule (687-714) maintained order and concentrated his efforts on the expansion of Austrasia's eastern frontiers. Beyond the Rhine, in Frisia, Thuringia, Alemannia, and Bavaria, Frankish influence was extended through the efforts of monastic missionaries and governmental officials.

In 714 Mayor Pepin died and it seemed that Frankland was once more to be torn asunder by civil wars. Fortunately he had a son, illegitimate Charles Martel (the Hammer), who led the Austrasians to a second victory over the Neustrians and assumed his father's position as mayor of all the Franks. Thenceforth, for almost thirty years (714-741), Charles was busy "hammering" at the Frisians, Saxons, and other peoples who threatened the peace of the realm. In order to strengthen Frankish influence among the fierce border tribes beyond the Rhine, he encouraged the missionary work of the famous English monk, Boniface.[2]

At about the middle of his career Charles was called to the south to meet a formidable menace. The Moslems, after conquering Spain (711-720), invaded southwestern Gaul. Aquitaine was overwhelmed, Burgundy was ravaged, and in 732 Bordeaux was captured. In desperation the Duke of Aquitaine called on Charles for assistance. Later in the same year the army of the Franks met the advancing Moslems somewhere between Tours and Poitiers, and a fierce battle ensued. Although the infantry phalanx of the Franks successfully withstood the cavalry charges of the light-armed Moslems and checked their advance on the city of Tours, the invaders were able to retire unmolested. It has often been asserted that this battle saved European civilization. But it was not solely the battle of Tours-Poitiers that kept Western Europe from becoming Moslem. The sturdiness of existing Frankish-Christian institutions and the limitations of Moslem expansive power were also of importance. Not even a series of Moslem military victories could have destroyed Germanic-Christian civilization in Frankland, England, and Italy. Even in those portions of southern Gaul over which the Moslems kept control throughout the first half of the century, the life of the Christian populace went on relatively unchanged.

FEUDALIZED
CAVALRY

On the other hand, the battle of Tours-Poitiers did bring about a change in Frankish institutions. After the victory, Charles Martel found that his self-equipped infantry forces were unable to carry on successful offensive operations against the swift-moving cavalry of the invaders. Consequently he modified his military system by developing mounted soldiery. Since this involved expensive equipment, it was found necessary to compensate those who incurred the additional burden by giving them extensive grants of land (the chief form of wealth in those days). Inasmuch as the royal lands were insufficient for this purpose, Charles appropriated vast stretches of church land and parceled them

2 See below, p. 274.

out to his new cavalrymen. Theoretically, the government merely had the *use* of this land, and paid a nominal rental fee to the clerical *owners*. Charles's noble vassals, in turn, held their portions of land solely on condition that they furnish him with certain specified military services. Thus, mounted military service came to be associated with landholding, and the old-time Frankish infantry-militia was eventually replaced by an aristocratic array of landholding cavalrymen, called *equites,* or knights. This marks an important stage in the evolution of feudalism.[3]

MARTEL, THE
UNCROWNED
KING

One of the unfortunate consequences of this change was that the clergy was disgruntled over what amounted to the confiscation of its lands. Charles still further antagonized the church by refusing the pope's plea for assistance against the encroachments of the Lombard king. At this time the Lombards were assisting Charles in driving the Moslems out of southern Gaul, and he could not afford to alienate them. It was in part the hostility of the clergy that prevented Charles from making himself king in 737, when the weak Merovingian monarch died. Nevertheless, for the remaining four years of his life, he ruled as though he were king. Before his death, in truly royal fashion, Charles Martel allotted the kingdom to his sons Carloman and Pepin (III) the Short. During the reign of Pepin the "do-nothing" Merovingian dynasty finally came to an end, and the Carolingians assumed their rightful place as monarchs of the Frankish realm.

MAYOR PEPIN
BECOMES KING

Fortunately for the peace and unity of the kingdom, Carloman, the weaker of Martel's two sons, soon retired to a monastery, leaving Pepin in undisputed control. During his twenty-seven-year reign (741-768) Pepin continued two of the major policies of his father: (1) strict control of the local nobility and clergy, and (2) a vigorous offensive against the Frisians, Saxons, and Moslems. In other respects he made notable innovations. The most important of these were his close alliance with the papacy and his appropriation of the royal title. These two developments were closely related, and arose out of the mutual needs of Pepin and the popes, who needed each other's aid. The pope sought for protection against his Lombard enemies. Pepin was looking for advice and assistance in the important problem of getting rid of the useless Merovingian kings. Both Pepin and the pope were in a position to furnish

[3] See below, Chapter XI.

what the other needed. Pepin, it seems, took the initiative when in 751 he sent an embassy to ask the pope's advice concerning the Frankish kingship. The pope's reply was: "He who exercises royal power should be called king." With such clerical approval Pepin was able to persuade the nobles to elect him, and in 751 he was *raised* to kingship (according to the old Germanic custom) by being carried on the shields of the nobility. He was also *anointed* after the fashion of the early Hebrew kings. Thus the Carolingian mayors became kings not only by the choice of their nobles but also by the grace of God. This is the first hint of the divine right of kings in the West. The religious sanction was symbolized by a coronation ceremony in which Archbishop Boniface anointed the king with sacred oil. Meanwhile the last Merovingian monarch had been deposed and sent to a monastery.

PEPIN AND THE PAPACY   The pope, having helped Pepin solve his difficulty, was in a position to ask favors, and he was shortly in desperate need of assistance. Ever since Charles Martel's day the Lombards had become increasingly dangerous to the papacy. They had extended their power southward at the expense of papal and Byzantine possessions. To make matters worse, the pope had openly broken with the Eastern emperor and could no longer hope for his aid. Soon the Lombards had captured the Byzantine stronghold of Ravenna and were besieging the city of Rome. This situation came to a climax shortly after Pepin had received papal support for his seizure of the royal power. Little wonder that the pope turned to him for aid, and little wonder that the pope was welcomed to the Frankish realm. Pepin promised to deliver him from "the son of iniquity" who was besieging Rome. The pope then gave his official blessing to Pepin's kingship by anointing him and his two sons.

Pepin did more than keep his promise. He made two expeditions against the Lombards, forcing them to give up all conquered territories. These lands, including extensive domains that had been taken from the Eastern emperors, were formally donated to the papacy. In this manner were founded the Papal States, a small dominion in central Italy comprising Rome, Ravenna, and certain intervening territories. For the pope and the Frankish monarchs these events resulted in a mutually profitable alliance between the two chief powers of Western Europe: the Frankish political empire and the papal spiritual empire. The reign of Charles the Great, Pepin's son, saw the culmination of this union and its effective influence for a revival of religious and political unity in the West.

THE CAROLINGIAN EMPIRE

CHARLES THE
GREAT
In 768 Pepin died, leaving two sons, Charles (or Charlemagne) [4] and Carloman. After three years of joint rule, Carloman died and Charles took over the entire kingdom. For over forty years (771-814) the destinies of Frankland were directed with remarkable success by this tall, good-natured, and remarkably efficient German king. According to his friend, secretary, and biographer, Einhard, Charles was an attractive personality,

. . . large and robust, of commanding stature and excellent proportions . . . in height seven times the length of his own foot.[5] The top of his head was round, his eyes large and animated, his nose somewhat long. He had a fine head of gray hair and his face was bright and pleasant; so that whether standing or sitting he showed great presence and dignity. Although his neck was thick and rather short, and his belly too prominent, still the good proportions of his limbs concealed these defects. His walk was firm and the whole carriage of his body was manly. His voice was clear but not so strong as his frame would have led one to expect. . . . He took constant exercise in riding and hunting. . . . He also delighted in natural warm baths, frequently exercising himself in swimming in which he was very skillful, no one being able to outstrip him. . . . In his eating and drinking he was temperate; more particularly in his drinking, for he had the greatest abhorrence of drunkenness. . . . He partook very sparingly of wine and other drinks, rarely taking at meals more than three draughts.[6] In summer, after the midday repast he would take some fruit and one draught, and then . . . would repose for two or three hours.[7]

Like most of his ancestors, Charles was a ruthless warrior, but he was also an intelligent statesman whose firm and just rule over both Franks and conquered peoples brought order, peace, and security to

[4] Charlemagne is the modern French form of his name. Charles himself neither knew nor heard it. In his own day he was called Karl (German) or Carolus Magnus (Latin). We shall use the Anglicized form, Charles the Great.

[5] Charles was not, as is often asserted, seven feet (i.e., eighty-four inches) tall, unless, perchance, his foot was twelve inches long, and this is most unlikely.

[6] A "draught" was a cup or flagon; therefore Charles was not what would be called temperate in modern times.

[7] Einhard, *The Life of Charles the Great,* Chaps. XXII, XXIV; translation from Robinson, *Readings in European History,* Ginn and Company, I, 126-7.

much of Western Europe. Although unable to write with ease, he was a patron of education, literature, and the arts. All in all, his title "the Great" seems more completely justified than in the case of many better-known heroes of modern history.

AQUITANIAN, BAVARIAN, AND AVAR WARS

First and foremost, Charles was a military man. His success in warfare has given him a place among the great generals of history. At his accession, Frankland comprised Gaul and certain territories beyond the Rhine; at his death much of Western Europe was under Frankish control or influence. Every year of his reign, save one, was marked by campaigns against internal or external foes. At the outset he found it necessary to reduce Aquitaine to submission. Later, the Bavarians revolted, at the instigation of their anti-Roman Catholic clergy and under the leadership of a native duke named Tassilo. On this occasion Charles displayed his characteristic energy and effectiveness. Three armies were sent into the rebellious region: one from Italy, another from the north, while a third under Charles himself marched down the Danube. When Tassilo surrendered he was imprisoned for life and Bavaria was annexed to the Frankish kingdom. This victory soon led to a war with the Avars, an Asiatic people with whom Tassilo had allied himself. For years these nomadic warriors had ravaged the Danube frontier, somewhat after the manner of Attila and his Huns in earlier centuries. After several campaigns they were crushed and their accumulated plunder was carried off to Frankland.

THE SAXON WAR

Further north, between the Elbe and the Rhine, Charles had a more formidable problem, one, in fact, which occupied him for thirty years. In this region dwelt the Saxons, an uncivilized pagan Germanic people with whom Charles's predecessors had been waging border wars for over a century. Neither Martel nor Pepin the Short had attempted seriously either the conversion or the conquest of these fierce pagans. For Charles they constituted an unavoidable problem, since they threatened the security of his entire northern and eastern frontier. The fact that the Saxons resisted all efforts at Christianization as well as conquest made matters still more difficult. In the end Charles found it necessary to force Christianity upon them in order to assure their submission. Thus the conquest of the Saxons was a crusade for the extension of Christian-Frankish civilization.

For several years after Charles's accession there were border skir-

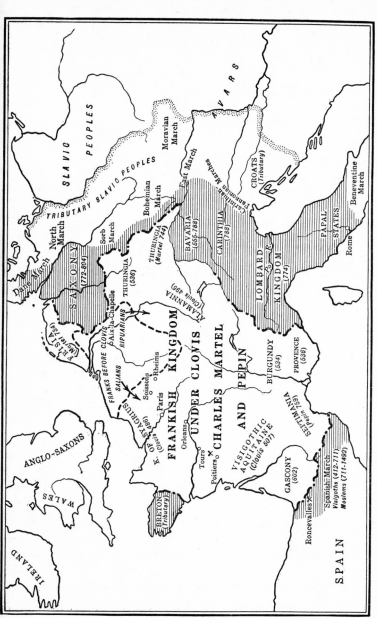

FRANKISH EXPANSION FROM CLOVIS TO CHARLES THE GREAT

Shading indicates the conquests of Charles the Great

mishes. During a summer campaign Charles ravaged the Saxon frontier, among other things capturing and destroying an important pagan shrine, the Irminsul. The following year the Saxons retaliated by devastating villages and churches in Frankish territory. Two years later Charles made a punitive expedition, forcing the conquered Saxons to grant hostages and to receive baptism as a symbol of their submission. Scarcely had he left for Italy when revolt and disorder broke out once more. Year after year, he repeated the process of re-conquest and re-Christianization with increasing severity. Thousands of conquered Saxons were deported to Frankland and the rebellious regions were divided into bishoprics and placed under the strict regulations of martial and ecclesiastical law. The death penalty was invoked against all who persisted in practicing pagan rites or who did violence to Christian churches and clergymen. Such measures seem to indicate Charles's faith in Christianity as an aid to government rather than his zeal for the conversion of the heathen.

Finally, after another revolt, the worst in all Saxon history, the king gave way to what was perhaps an excusable outburst of vengeance; he had forty-five hundred helpless prisoners massacred in cold blood. But this act engendered fury rather than submission. Under a great leader named Widukind, the Saxons carried death and destruction to the missionaries, churches, and Christian settlements along the frontier. Charles now mobilized all of his available resources and throughout the winter of 784 kept his entire army in the field. In the following year Widukind agreed to surrender and his submission led the Saxons to accept Christianity and Frankish rule. Soon by dint of military action, strict governmental regulation, Christian missions, and church schools, the entire region from the Rhine to the Elbe was pacified. The yoke of Frankish-Christian rule was not easy, and the burden of tithes and military service was by no means light. In the course of time, however, Christian Saxony became the greatest state of northern Germany, and a center of Christian civilization.

SLAVIC AND
SPANISH WARS
Having moved the Frankish frontier to the Elbe, Charles found it necessary to fight the Slavic tribes beyond that river. With the assistance of Frisian and Saxon troops he established, near Magdeburg, a defensive border state which was called the Altmark. Soon he made the entire eastern frontier secure against the attacks of the Slavs and Avars by extending this system of border provinces (called *marches,* or *marks*) all the way

from the Baltic to the Adriatic. Each march had a permanent military force under the command of a military governor.

During this period, Charles was also engaged in other wars. In 777 while he was in Saxony an embassy of Spanish Moslems offered to assist him in a war against the emir of Cordova if he would lead his army into Spain. Attracted by the glamor of an easy conquest, Charles accepted, and the following year saw him forcing his way through Gascony and the western Pyrenees. But Charles, like Napoleon and many another invader, found Spain a difficult country to conquer. He was welcomed by only a few of the Christians and Moslems of northern Spain. The Christian population of Saragossa, on the Ebro River, repudiated the alliance made by its own rulers and resisted the advance of the Christian army. Soon Charles found it expedient to return to Frankland. En route he met with a serious disaster at the hands of the Christian Basques (or Gascons), whose enmity he had aroused during his passage through the Pyrenees. A contemporary, Charles's own secretary, Einhard, recorded that at the pass of Roncesvalles "the Gascons who were in ambush at the crest of the mountain . . . suddenly fell on the baggage train and on the troops of the rear guard . . . a fight took place in which the Franks were killed, to a man. . . . In this engagement fell Eggihard master of the king's household, Anselm count of the palace, and *Roland prefect of Brittany.*" [8] Einhard wrote this brief account shortly after the event occurred, explaining also that the traitorous Christian Duke of Gascony was responsible for the ambush at Roncevalles, and that Charles put him to death for his treasonable act.

Three centuries later the story had assumed astounding proportions in the *Song of Roland,* a gloriously patriotic but unhistorical epic poem.[9] In this famous *Chanson de Geste* the wounded hero was represented as having died at the close of a terrific battle with Moslem infidels; his little band of heroes was finally wiped out by the countless hosts of the "paynim" in spite of prodigious deeds of valor in which scores of the greatest warriors of the enemy were slain. As for Charles's conquests in Spain, it was with considerable difficulty that he established even the small Spanish march which hardly extended to the Ebro River. It was merely a defensive province similar to those set up on the borders of Brittany, Denmark, Slavic Germany, and southern Italy.

[8] Einhard, *Life of Charles the Great,* Chap. IX. The italics are mine.
[9] See below, p. 689.

THE LOMBARD WAR

Second only to Saxony in importance was Charles's conquest of Lombard Italy, a region which had caused much trouble for his father. Ever since the days of Gregory the Great, Lombard encroachments on the territories of the popes had compelled them to seek outside aid. Charles Martel, it will be remembered, had refused to take action against the Lombard king because he was his ally. Pepin the Short, being in debt to the pope for supporting his usurption of the Frankish crown, saw fit to defend the papacy.

He donated to the pope, as we have seen, all the territories that had been recovered from the Lombards. For a time, Charles the Great maintained friendly relations with the Lombards. Early in his reign he married a Lombard princess, in spite of papal protests against such a "diabolical union." But when the Lombard king Desiderius took up the claim of the widow and sons of Charles's brother to a share in the Frankish government, a rift developed. Charles sent his Lombard wife back to her father and accepted the pope's well-timed exhortation that he follow his father's example and defend the Holy Church against the wicked Lombards. Charles easily overcame the forces of King Desiderius, sent him to a monastery, and took possession of Lombardy. At the pope's request he renewed Pepin's gift of confiscated Lombard lands, and granted additional Italian territories to the Papal States. Charles increased the pope's domains, but he himself was recognized as the protector of the Papal States, and throughout his reign he treated the pope as a political subordinate.

THE REVIVED WESTERN EMPIRE

In 800 Charles was summoned once more to Rome. Pope Leo III was unable to keep order even in his own city. In the midst of a religious procession he had been set upon by some of the Roman populace and so roughly handled that he fled to the court of Charles. Charles immediately sent armed forces to restore the pope, and in December of the same year he came to Rome in person. On Christmas Day, while he was at prayer in St. Peter's Church, the pope placed a crown on his head and in the presence of the assembled people hailed him as "Emperor of the Romans."

Einhard, in his *Life of Charles,* reports that the king was completely taken by surprise and would not have permitted it had he known of the pope's intention. Many modern scholars accept this version at its face value, and point to the fact that at this time Charles was considering a marriage with Empress Irene of Constantinople which the pope might well have wished to forestall by making Charles emperor of the West. Some historians, however, doubt that Charles could have been kept in ignorance of a plan of such importance as a coronation. Nor was Leo the sort of pope to take the initiative, especially with a monarch of Charles's dominating character. When one recollects that Charles's own father, Pepin, had asked the pope for a royal anointing, it seems probable that Charles might have arranged things so that he would receive the imperial crown from the pope. His surprise could well have been a modest pretense.

Whatever the truth of the matter or the motives involved, the fact remains that the event brought about a closer relationship between Charles and the Roman Church. Eventually this was to strengthen the position of the popes, for the coronation ceremony tended to give them a certain control over the selection of emperors. For the time being, however, Charles's position as emperor added considerable prestige to his already great reputation. It revived the Empire of the West, under the rule of a Germanic chieftain who had the energy and ambition to magnify his office. It is thought by some scholars that Charles's projected marriage with Empress Irene of Constantinople was for the purpose of becoming emperor of the East as well as of the West. Meanwhile, in the West, Charles played the role of a ruler invested with unlimited authority. He followed the precedents set by Constantine and his successors in both the East and West, and assumed supreme responsibility over religious as well as temporal affairs. Like the late Roman emperors, Charles presided over clerical councils, and asserted his God-given authority over clergy and laity alike. Even the popes were forced to obey him. He was a firm believer in Augustine's ideal of a Christian society ruled according to Divine will. *The City of God* was one of his favorite books, but in its practical application to imperial conditions he, and not the pope, was the supreme representative of God's government on earth.

CAROLINGIAN GOVERNMENT
As conquering king of the Franks, Charles had already expanded the former system of government into a more effective administrative machine. After becoming emperor he developed it still further. He maintained his control over the many parts of the realm by means of centrally appointed officials called *counts*. In places such as Aquitaine and Bavaria, where revolts had been frequent, the local dukes were replaced by counts. Eventually every section of the empire was under the control of a count. In order to manage more effectively the

numerous counties, Charles grouped them into districts through which each year a pair of supervisors (one a clergyman, the other a layman) made a tour of inspection, holding court, hearing complaints, and correcting injustices. This was an extension of the governmental institutions that had been worked out on a smaller scale by earlier rulers. These officials were called *missi dominici,* or "messengers of the lord king." The border provinces were governed by military counts called *margraves,* or *counts of the marches.*

It was Charles's function to see that these various officials were faithful and efficient. This was a tremendous task, for there were hundreds of counts, many of them located in out-of-the-way places, difficult of access. Some were ambitious for personal power; others were inefficient. On the frontiers the counts of the marches, with their military forces, created danger points of revolt. As long as Charles lived, his intelligent statesmanship and driving energy kept the governmental machine working smoothly. He himself made secret tours of inspection. Often when he was supposed to be on a hunting expedition, he turned up unexpectedly at the headquarters of some local official. Inefficient counts were ruthlessly eliminated.

CAPITULARIES: ECONOMIC POLICIES

Charles was also an able legislator. In a very practical, though rather dictatorial, fashion, he issued decrees concerning military, administrative, religious, and cultural matters. Often these regulations were his own arbitrary decisions, influenced perhaps by the advice of his councilors. These capitularies, or laws, were publicly proclaimed at local or general assemblies of the clergy, nobility, and commoners. By such means Charles carefully regulated the lives of his people. He presided at church councils and actively supported the work of the clergy. As a result the church was reorganized, expanded, and reformed. The clergy was warned to live strictly according to its religious vows, and to avoid such worldly interests as the keeping of dogs, horses, and hawks for hunting. With his lay subjects, also, Charles was strict but just. All men were forced to take an oath of fidelity to the emperor. Every freeman was expected to attend the judicial assemblies of his locality and to serve at his own expense in the army. Due, however, to the constant burden of military service upon the poorer farmers, these rules were modified so that only one soldier was summoned from every four units of land. Thus the smaller farmers might pool their resources and send only one of their group at a time to do military service.

Charles seems to have been genuinely interested in the economic welfare of his people. The capitularies contained many regulations for the benefit of the oppressed populace. Like Pope Gregory two centuries earlier, he realized that in a predominantly agricultural era the prosperity of the realm depended on the prosperity of the peasantry. Charles's officials were warned against forcing the populace to labor at plowing, sowing, harvesting, stubbing up trees, loading wagons and the like. In some places the people were said to have been so grievously abused that they were unable to bear it and had fled to the forests. As a result good land lapsed into wilderness. In another capitulary (of the year 811) attention was called to the fact that

the poor complain that they are being evicted from their property. . . . If a poor man will not give up his property to the bishop, abbot, or count [who desires it], these influential men use some pretext to get him involved in the courts, or compel him to do military service until the wretched man, quite impoverished, has to mortgage or sell his property, which they then snap up at a low price.

It is evident that at this time Frankish life was tending to center in large-scale, noblemen's estates which tended to engulf the small free farmer, as had happened in Rome during the warlike age of the republic. Charles, realizing that a free peasantry would strengthen his regime and serve as a check on the nobility, did his best to stem the tide. During the terrible period of civil wars and invasions after his death, however, the free peasantry practically disappeared. Most freemen were only too glad to associate themselves with some powerful noble who would not only control but also protect them.

Charles was more successful with his own economic affairs. One of the most noteworthy of his capitularies concerned itself with the businesslike management of the royal villas or estates. His insistence on biennial reports from the stewards reminds one of the efficient methods of Pope Gregory the Great as revealed in his letters to the overseers of the papal estates.[10] Charles insisted on inventories of the pigs, chickens, colts, vegetables, fruits, honey, vinegar, mead, beer, perry, wine, fish, and so on, at each villa. His instructions as to the care of the royal peacocks, swans, bedclothes, counterpanes, andirons, and various tools, are also interesting indications as to the surroundings in which Franks of the upper class lived. If this "capitulary concerning the villas" is an accurate indication of Charles's efficiency in

10 See above, p. 88.

administrative affairs, it is not difficult to understand how he managed to control so successfully an extensive empire.

CHARLES'S
RURAL-MINDED-
NESS

At this point we take occasion to mention a phase of economic life in which Charles brought about no marked improvement—commerce and industry. Charles has often been falsely credited with having revived the business life of the West. Recent studies in economic history have shown clearly that he did not even attempt it. Intelligent statesman that he was, Charles concentrated his attention on an activity that was more vital to his age—the increase of agricultural prosperity. The absence of commercial and industrial interests in Charles's day illustrates the outstanding characteristic of early medieval society. It was predominantly a rural society, and centered largely in the *villa,* or manor.

The disintegration of the Roman Empire of the West hastened the already declining life of Western urban centers. Industry and trade became more and more localized as invasions and civil wars continued. The Germanic conquerors, like the Roman nobility of the later centuries, were farm-minded and preferred to live on rural estates. As distant markets for manufactured products dwindled, industry and commerce, and with them city life, slowly died. In short, the West "went rural." So far as the Frankish realms are concerned this tendency was especially marked during the three centuries from Clovis to Charles the Great. The lowest ebb of business and city life in the West probably came during the Carolingian age.

In spite of the rapid growth of the Carolingian Empire and its effective governmental organization, economic life continued to drift to the scattered agricultural estates. Commercial and industrial life flourished in the Mediterranean regions controlled by the Moslems and the Byzantines, but the Franks had little contact with these urban civilizations. With the exception of a few Italian cities which had commercial relations with Constantinople, Western civilization continued to be rural; consequently it was backward in its cultural development.

Although Charles won his greatest reputation in military and governmental affairs, neither his conquests nor his empire was permanent. Soon after his death the Carolingian Empire was assailed by internal and external forces of disintegration somewhat similar to those that had wrecked the Roman Empire of the West. Such, it seems, is the usual fate of political institutions which run counter to the normal current of social and economic life. Whether for better or for worse, after the passing of the city life of the Roman Empire, the West was destined never again to be united under one supreme governmental organization. In economic as well as political lines localism continued to be dominant in the West until the later medieval centuries.

CAROLINGIAN
CULTURE
Charles had more permanent success in his efforts at the centralization of cultural life. He brought about such notable improvements that his age has been called the Carolingian "Renascence," and is often represented as a period of intellectual brilliance in the midst of a long dark age. This is an exaggeration. Under Charles's enlightened rule, the Frankish court became the center to which artists, writers, and teachers gravitated from all parts of the West. In previous centuries Anglo-Saxon England, Ireland, Visigothic Spain, and Ostrogothic Italy had surpassed Frankland in culture. Charles merely outdid his Germanic predecessors in patronizing men of learning. In Carolingian times, the greatest intellects of the West were found at the court of Charles, and throughout his realm education, literature, and the arts flourished as never before. But this was merely a concentration and speeding up of the cultural life that had continued to exist in various regional centers after the disintegration of the Western Empire.[11]

Long before Charles's day, in isolated monasteries and cathedrals and at many of the Germanic courts, encouragement had been given to men of culture and learning, to educational activities, and to artists and architects. With his customary energy Charles surpassed former patrons. He appropriated the existing cultural life and centralized it at the imperial court. It was as if a thousand candles lighting a thousand homes were brought into a great mirrored hall to illuminate a royal banquet. Here they shone with greatly enhanced brightness. Furthermore, the emperor's patronage of learning encouraged similar activities in outlying regions. Thanks to Charles, culture flourished as never before in the Frankish realm. But it was neither a new nor a very brilliant culture.[12] It was the remnants of a declining Roman civilization mingled with the rather primitive rural culture of the new Christian-Germanic West. It was inferior to the civilizations of Moslem Spain, of certain parts of Italy, and of Constantinople. The best that can be said is that it was sturdy and progressive. In the church

[11] See Chapter XIV, for a detailed treatment of Carolingian culture.
[12] For a full treatment of Carolingian culture and "renascence" see pp. 274 ff.

schools it continued long after Charles had passed away, eventually coming to full bloom in the cities and universities of later centuries.

In cultural, as in political, lines Charles's achievements depended upon his remarkable ability for organization and consolidation on a large scale. In warfare, government, education, and the arts he expanded and organized forces already in existence, bringing them for a time to a high degree of effectiveness. The age of Charles should be thought of, not as a renascence or revival of a dead civilization, but as a centralization and vitalization of existing institutions. Charles's empire might have become a permanent state had conditions been more favorable and his successors more energetic. Unfortunately, Western Europe was not ready for a unified regime, and within a generation most of his imperial ideals and institutions had given way before the prevailing forces of decentralization.[13] The energy and ability of a Charles the Great could not reverse the current of human life. Western civilization was to develop very slowly from the small-scale units of the Germanic and feudal era to the national states which still control its destinies.

[13] See pp. 200 ff.

$$\equiv \text{X} \equiv$$

THE DISRUPTION OF THE FRANKISH EMPIRE

IN 814 Charles the Great died, leaving the fortunes of the empire and of Western civilization in the hands of an only son, Louis the Pious (814-840). Louis, a well-meaning person, was incapable of administering government on the large scale set up by his father. It seems unlikely that anyone but a superman could have successfully maintained, in a disintegrated world of isolated regional units, so complex and far reaching an organization as the empire of Charles. In many ways it is surprising that the Carolingian Empire held together at all after Charles's death.

INTERNAL WEAKNESSES On the surface it was the old Frankish custom of dividing the realm among all of the king's sons that led to the disintegration of the empire. Early in the reign of Louis the Pious a tentative allotment of territories was made to his three sons. This was merely the first of a series of partitions which undermined the power of the emperor. The uncertainty of the situation was aggravated by a rebellion led by a nephew of the king and also by the death of the queen. Additional tribulations came when Louis selected as his new queen a woman who proved to be as troublesome as she was beautiful. With the birth of their son Charles, she began to urge upon Louis the creation of a separate inheritance for the child. As a consequence, the remainder of the reign was marked by a succession of territorial reallotments which satisfied none of the royal princes. There were innumerable rebellions, plots, and counterplots. At one time Louis himself was captured and temporarily imprisoned by his rebellious sons.

CIVIL WARFARE When the pious but troubled life of the unhappy Louis finally dragged to a close in 840, the inevitable disintegration occurred. While the jealous heirs fought over the royal domains, the Carolingian system of imperial government went to pieces. The two younger brothers, Charles the Bald and Louis the

German, made common cause against their elder brother, Lothaire, who had inherited the imperial title and the more desirable sections of the realm. The contemporary records of this alliance throw interesting light on two aspects of the civilization of the period.

After a bloody but indecisive battle with Lothaire at Fontenay, Charles and Louis met at Strassburg (842) to assure one another and their followers of their determination to continue the struggle. Each swore an oath of loyalty to his brother. Charles took the oath in German, the language of Louis's men. Louis, however, repeated it in the old French (*lingua romana*) which would be understood by Charles's West Frankish followers. These "Strassburg Oaths" are our earliest examples of the early German and French languages as they developed in the eastern and western sections of Frankland. They also indicate the political disunity of the empire. The landed nobility, whose forces comprised the fighting men of both armies, was so powerful that the two princes were forced to swear their alliance in public and to state therein the right of their followers to revolt in case the agreement was violated. These oaths indicate the early development of the basic feudal principle of the right of the nobles to limit the power of their king. The same principle appears later in such documents as the Great Charter of England.

A DIVIDED
EMPIRE

A year after the Strassburg alliance Lothaire came to terms at Verdun (843), and the three brothers proceeded to divide the inheritance. This consisted of royal estates, monasteries, bishoprics, and various rights of overlordship. Lothaire was permitted to retain the imperial title and a long central strip of territory stretching from the mouth of the Rhine along the valleys of the Rhine and the Rhone rivers to Rome. Louis the German received most of the lands east of the Rhine; Charles the Bald, most of Gaul. This was the first recognized division of the Carolingian Empire. Never again was there any real political unity, and, during the years that followed, each of these three kingdoms was further subdivided. By the end of the century the disintegration was so complete that Western Europe soon became a hodgepodge of large and small regional units. As a contemporary chronicler put it: "Once we had a king, now we have kinglets; once we had an empire, now we have fragments of kingdoms."

The central kingdom was the first to disintegrate. In the first place, it was not a natural geographical or political unit, for it comprised a portion of the German Rhinelands, the Burgundian Rhonelands, the Lombard regions of the Po Valley, and the Papal States. In the second place, there was the fatal Frankish custom of dividing a realm among all the sons of the king. At Lothaire's death (855), the Rhinelands went to one son, the Rhonelands to another, and the Italies to a third. Eight years later (863), the king of the Rhonelands died without heirs and his lands were allotted to his two brothers. Several years later both the Rhinelands and Rhonelands were seized by the ambitious uncles, Louis of Germany and Charles of France. One of these aggressions was consecrated by the Treaty of Mersen (870), which marks the beginning of an agelong struggle between German and French rulers for the Rhineland regions. This is particularly notice-able in the history of the territory known as Lorraine. At that time it was called Lotharingia (Lothaire's *regnum,* or kingdom). In mod-ern times German and French successors of Charles and Louis have waged many wars and drawn up many treaties over this same region, a portion of which is still called Lorraine (i.e., Lo[tha]ringia).

INDEPENDENT
STATES

By 870 the Carolingian Empire had apparently fallen into three grand divisions comprising somewhat the same territories as modern France, Germany, and Italy. It was in reality, however, merely a mass of independent princi-palities of all sizes and types. A brief sketch of the outstanding princi-palities will indicate the extent to which local self-government had re-placed the centralized administration of the Carolingian Empire. In north central Spain, for instance, by the opening of the tenth century, a powerful nobleman named Sancho had established himself as king of Navarre. To the eastward, the remainder of the old Spanish march of Charles the Great had disintegrated into several independent coun-ties, the most important of which was Aragon. Each of these states consisted of a variety of smaller units. Meanwhile, a baron named Bozo had himself proclaimed king of southern Burgundy; shortly thereafter another powerful noble became king of northern Bur-gundy.

In France proper independent rulers appeared in Gascony, Aqui-taine, Brittany, and in the Seine Valley. In and about Paris, Count Robert the Strong and his son, Odo, were laying the foundations for a new French dynasty, that of the Capetians. In the meantime Ger-many, under the weak successors of Louis the German, tended to revert to its ancient tribal units. Independent native dukes rose to power in Saxony, Thuringia, Franconia (a portion of old Austrasia), Swabia (formerly called Alemannia), and Bavaria. Along the eastern frontier, the counts of the marches (called margraves) became independent. Everywhere counts, abbots, and bishops ruled like local monarchs.

Similar conditions existed in Italy, where the successors of Lothaire found it impossible to maintain any real authority. Independent dukes governed Friuli, Spoleto, Tuscany, and Benevento. The popes were virtual sovereigns of the Papal States, and many cities in Lombardy became independent. Even in these small kingdoms, duchies, and counties there was no real government. The actual rulers were the local landholding nobles, on whom the kings, dukes, or counts relied for troops, and on whom the populace depended for protection. As time went on this sort of localized government became universal. It is known as feudalism.

INTERNAL CAUSES OF DISINTEGRATION The causes for the disintegration of the empire are twofold—internal and external. From the internal standpoint alone it seems inevitable that the local units would become independent once the strong hand of Charles the Great was removed. As in the case of the Roman Empire, and many another large group of sectional and racial units, only an unusually strong central power could hope to maintain unity. The Carolingian Empire had an unusually weak central government. The Frankish custom of plural inheritance of royal power, as we have seen, invariably led to rival governments, factional strife, and devastating civil wars. This in turn encouraged the appropriation of governmental powers and resources by the local clergy and aristocracy. Thus many abbots, bishops, counts, margraves, dukes, and even the *missi dominici* became independent rulers in their own localities.

Difficulties in communications and the lack of ready money with which to equip royal armies prevented the central authorities from counteracting these tendencies. Meanwhile the church took advantage of the situation; the popes were politically ambitious and, by means of their functions in the royal coronation ceremony, they assumed more and more authority in governmental affairs. At the same time, there was a marked inferiority in the personal character of the emperors. Although the late Carolingians were by no means "do-nothing" kings, they certainly lacked the forcefulness of Charles the Great and his predecessors. This personal element should not, however, be stressed, for it seems probable that only a miracle worker could have stemmed the rising tide of decentralization that assailed Western Christendom during the ninth and tenth centuries. Both the personnel and the machinery of the central government were incapable of maintaining unity. While the jealous successors of Charles weakened themselves by civil wars, the local aristocracy became more and more powerful. Then, as the West became increasingly decentralized in its political and economic life, invaders from outside the empire took advantage of the confusion and disunity to ravage and conquer.

NEW FORCES IN WESTERN CIVILIZATION

MOSLEM
INVASIONS
As in the case of the Roman Empire of the fifth century, the already weakened Carolingian realm was overrun by barbarian invaders who contributed important elements to the new civilization that was taking shape in the West. There were Scandinavian sea rovers from the north, Slavs and Hungarians from the east, and Moslems from the south.

Southern France and Italy bore the brunt of the renewed Moslem invasions, the chief impetus of which came by sea from Northern Africa. Sicily, and southern Italy were the first to suffer. Palermo was captured in 831, and soon all the important coastal towns of Italy were threatened with destruction. The monastery of Monte Cassino, miles inland, was sacked and plundered. In 846 a raiding party penetrated thirteen miles up the Tiber and devastated the suburbs of Rome, including the Church of St. Peter. After this raid walls were built so as to encircle this region which now comprises the Vatican City. Stirred to action by the disaster, the pope and emperor mobilized the independent dukes of southern Italy and joined forces with the Byzantine Empire in an effort to check the ravages. They not only defeated the Moslems by sea but eventually drove them from their strongholds along the Italian coasts and carried the war into infidel territory.

Until the eleventh century, however, the Moslems retained their control of Sicily and the other islands of the western Mediterranean. Southern Gaul likewise was troubled by their ravages. As late as the tenth century Moslem strongholds in the western Alps greatly hampered pilgrim travel from France to Italy.

HUNGARIAN
INVASIONS
Scarcely had Italy been delivered from the worst of the Moslem peril when it was subjected to another danger—from the north. In 898 bands of Hungarians crossed the Alps and ravaged the Po Valley. Until the middle of the

tenth century, Lombardy, central Italy, and even Apulia at the foot of the peninsula were constantly threatened.

The principal ravages of the Hungarians, however, were in Germany. They appeared here late in the ninth century, having drifted westward from their original homes in Asia in much the same fashion as had the Huns, Bulgars, and Avars of earlier centuries. In 892 a German emperor employed bands of Hungarians as allies. Within ten years they began raiding northern Italy and southern Germany. Soon they were ravaging far up the Danube and into the Rhinelands. Saxony was temporarily overrun, but within ten years King Henry I, the Fowler (919-936), managed to erect a military system that checked the Hungarian menace in north Germany. Throughout Saxony, Henry established fortified "burghs," with peasant garrisons for defense. For offensive warfare he organized an army with a strong force of heavy-armed cavalry. In 933 Henry decisively defeated the Hungarians on the Unstrutt River in southern Saxony. Henceforth northern Germany was free from the menace of invasion. The people of the Danube Valley continued to suffer, and it was not until 955, after a terrible Hungarian raid, that Henry's son, Otto the Great, seriously took the offensive against "the heathen." Near Augsburg he met the invaders with a great army of Germans and overwhelmed them. Never again was Germany seriously threatened, for Otto's successors established a buffer state on the Danube between Bavaria and the Hungarians. It was known then as the Ostmark (i.e., East March); today it is Austria. Its modern metropolis, Vienna, was originally an outpost on the Hungarian frontier. By the year 1000 the Hungarians had formally accepted Christianity, their converted king, Waik, assuming at baptism the Biblical name of Stephen.

THE SLAVS   On the northeastern frontier of Germany during this same period the Saxons were fighting battles of Christendom against the heathen Slavs. It is interesting to note the short interval between Charles the Great's forcible conversion of the Saxons and their forcible conversion of the Slavs. It was King Henry I, the Fowler, who took the initiative. In 929 he led his army across the Elbe, captured a Slav stronghold at Brunabor, renamed it Brandenburg, and there established the chief outpost of his frontier province, the Nordmark (North March). Like the Danubian Ostmark, this was eventually to become one of the leading German states of modern times; it gave birth to Berlin, the capital of modern Prussia.

For centuries the destiny of both Saxony and Brandenburg was bound up with the task of driving the heathen Slavs still further eastward.

To the south, on the upper Elbe, the Bohemian Slavs also succumbed to the advancing Germans. Their ruler, "good King Wenceslaus" of the old Christmas carol, adopted Christianity and agreed to pay tribute to King Henry. From the tenth century onward, even to the twentieth century, much of the history of the northern German states has been bound up with the ever-present Slavic problem on their eastern frontier. Throughout most of this thousand-year period the Germans have steadily pressed forward from the Elbe to the Oder, thence to the Vistula, and even into the regions of East Prussia on the borders of the Russian Baltic.

SCANDINAVIAN INVASIONS

More violent than the Slavs, and therefore a graver menace, were the invasions of the Scandinavian Vikings, or Norsemen, a people of Germanic origin, better organized than the Hungarians or Slavs, and more virile than the Moslems. Their invasions were inspired both by the weakness of the defensive forces, and by the expansive power of the people of Scandinavia. During the earlier period other Germanic peoples had served as a buffer between Frankish Europe and the Norsemen. But after the death of Charles the Great the tide of the Carolingian Empire's northward advance ebbed, and once more Western Christendom was on the defensive. At the same time, an unusual era of expansion throughout the area of the Baltic Sea let loose a flood of northern invaders upon Western Europe. This Scandinavian expansion was due in part to the failure of agriculture and the other resources of the region to keep pace with the needs of a rapidly increasing population. Furthermore, during the late ninth century, the rise of strong rulers in the North led many dissatisfied nobles to take to the seaways in search of freedom, adventure, and fortunes.

By 861 Norsemen had explored and settled Iceland; shortly thereafter Greenland was colonized. At about 1000, other adventurous spirits discovered the coasts of North America and settled in "Vinland the Good." Meanwhile, far to the east, the Scandinavians from Sweden were pushing up the rivers of Russia and conquering the native Slavs. In the ninth century Rurik the Swede and his *Rus* (i.e., "Rowers") gained control of Novgorod on the Neva River. A century later Scandinavian fleets were ravaging the Black Sea, even threatening Constantinople, the capital of the Eastern Empire. Throughout the tenth century Norsemen (called Varangians) con-

Iceland 874
Greenland 986
Vinland 1000

NORSEMEN

SWEDES

Novgorod
(862)

Dublin
(820)

THE DANELAW
(835-)

(787)

DANES

SLAVS

Varangian
Route

Kiev
(864)

NORMANDY
(911)

Siege of
Paris (885)

Defeat at
Unstrut
(933)

Defeat at
Augsburg
(955)

HUNGARIANS
King Stephen
(1000)

MOSLEMS

(890)

MOSLEMS

Rome
(846)

Constantinople

SICILY
(831-)

MOSLEMS

MOSLEMS

Routes of Norsemen
Routes of Hungarians
Routes of Moslems

NINTH- AND TENTH-CENTURY INVADERS

Dates indicate important battles and conquests

trolled the rivers and trade routes that connected the Baltic and Black seas. Many of them served in the imperial guard at Constantinople. Commerce and government from the Baltic to the Black Sea came under their control, and they laid the foundations for the Russian kingdom of later times.

THE NORSEMEN IN ENGLAND

Western Europe, particularly England and France, however, bore the brunt of the Scandinavian raids. During the age of Charles the Great, Norsemen had ravaged the shores of Scotland and Ireland. Northern Ireland was constantly threatened, and by the end of the ninth century there were Norse kingdoms at Dublin and on the Isle of Man. Meanwhile, in England also, raids had given way to systematic conquests. At about 850 the Danes (as the Norsemen were called by the Anglo-Saxon annalists) began to establish permanent bases of operations along the eastern coast. York became a Danish center, and northeastern England fell under their control.

Throughout the second half of the ninth century, Alfred the Great and his predecessors in Wessex fought bravely to save southern England from the invaders. Their defensive warfare was successful. After the battle of Edington (878), the treaties of Wedmore (878) and of London (885) provided that the invaders should withdraw from Alfred's realm. But the Danish king Guthrum, on accepting Christianity, was recognized as ruler of the Danelaw, which comprised most of northeastern England and parts of Scotland. Alfred's successors were even more effective than he, for they carried on a vigorous offensive by means of which all of the English Danelaw was eventually recovered.[1]

THE NORSEMEN IN FRANCE

Meanwhile, France also felt the force of Norse invasion. As early as Charles the Great's reign, the Norsemen of Denmark had given shelter to his Saxon opponents, and Norse fleets had raided the Channel coasts. Later, they ravaged the shores of the Continent all the way from the North Sea to Gibraltar. Dorestadt, near the mouth of the Rhine, was raided four times before 840, and at one time the invaders stabled their horses in the chapel that had been built by Charles the Great near his palace at Aix-la-Chapelle. In 845 and 856 the long black ships of the Vikings sailed up the Seine River as far as Paris. Similar ravages occurred along the Loire and Garonne. In Moslem Spain, Lisbon,

[1] See below, p. 452.

Cadiz, Seville, and Cordova were attacked, and at least one band of daring raiders sailed through the Straits of Gibraltar and raided the north coast of the Mediterranean as far as Pisa. At times during this period Italy was threatened with triple invasion: by Hungarians from the Danube, by Moslems from Africa, and by Norsemen from the Atlantic Ocean.

Until about 880, the Norse raids in France were sporadic. Thereafter, it seems, Alfred's peace treaty with the Danes in England resulted in shunting the main stream of northern invaders to the coasts of France. The first year after the English treaty of 878 a powerful Norse fleet attacked the lower Rhinelands and the adjoining regions of France. Weak and ineffective resistance encouraged further invasions. The emperor, Charles the Fat, bought off the raiders with large sums of money and grants of land. Such tactics were not effective and in 885 Paris was beleaguered for months by a large force. Count Odo and other local leaders fought off the besiegers for over a year, but the emperor, after a tardy arrival, once more bought them off. Little wonder that two years later the people of the Seine Valley deposed him and elected Count Odo as their king. After the failure of the Norse at Paris they suffered a disastrous defeat at the hands of the German king, Arnulf, at the River Dyle near Louvain in the Netherlands (891). This, together with Alfred's victory at Edington (878), marked the beginning of the end of Norse invasions.

EFFECTS OF THE NORSE INVASIONS

Like their kinsmen, the Danes, in England, the Norse on the Continent quickly adopted the civilized ways of Frankish life. In 911 the king of France granted the regions now known as Normandy to Duke Rollo and his Norsemen on condition that they accept Christianity and render him homage for their holdings. Thus France purchased her peace with the invaders and established a "Norselaw" along the lower Seine just thirty years after Alfred's creation of the English Danelaw. Once the disorder of raids and war had ceased, the Norsemen in England, France, and elsewhere made valuable contributions to European civilization. Their ability in warfare and seamanship was exceeded only by their genius for government. As conquerors they organized remarkably efficient states everywhere. Iceland, Russia, Norman England, Normandy, and Sicily bore witness in later centuries to the effectiveness of their rule.

The rough but vigorous Norse culture also contributed to medieval civilization. The sagas and eddas, poetical tales of gods and heroic warriors, reveal a literature rich in Germanic mythology and in the simple art of epic narrative. However, one of the most important of Norse contributions to the development of the West was in economic life. We hear much concerning the disorganization which the invasions brought to trade, industry, and agriculture. It is true that for a time, and in certain regions, there was cruel devastation. In the Netherlands, for example, the lucrative cloth trade of the native Frisian merchants, extending up the Rhine as far as Cologne and Mainz, was badly disorganized. But although the Norse were violent and destructive in warfare, it is not true that wherever they appeared commerce permanently ceased. As a matter of fact, many Norsemen were interested in trade. Like the Elizabethan seamen of the sixteenth century, they were merchants as well as piratical adventurers. When Rollo and his followers landed in Normandy in 911, he was reported to have said: "We seek trade, and a profitable peace." There were also Danish invaders in northern Germany who insisted that they wished "to make peace so that the merchants of both kingdoms might buy and sell."

More convincing than these words are the actual careers of traders whose business pursuits led them to both Norse and Christian realms. One of these international merchants in seeking trade visited points as far apart as Iceland, Ireland, England, Norway, Schleswig, and Novgorod in Russia. At a *Baltic* seaport town a certain *Icelander* was reported to have purchased an *Irish* slave girl from a *Russian* merchant. The economic interrelations of this great northern trade world extended from the American settlements of Leif Ericson across the north Atlantic, the Baltic, and the Russian plains to the Black Sea and beyond. It had contacts with the Moslem world of Bagdad and Egypt. Oriental goods from the Far and the Near East, and from Byzantine Constantinople, were carried by way of Kiev and Novgorod to the Baltic ports, whence they were sold to Western merchants. In similar manner, the raw products of Greenland, Iceland, and Northern Europe (fish, furs, and the like) found their way to Western Europe or to the Near East. It has been said that the Varangian and Baltic trade routes provided a means of international exchange comparable to that of the Mediterranean in Roman imperial times. At various points along this artery of commerce there have been found evidences of its far-reaching contacts: Eastern coins from Bagdad, Arabia, Egypt, Constantinople, and even India; and Western coins from Germany, France, and England. In the tenth century, a

EXPANSION OF WESTERN CHRISTENDOM BEFORE THE
CRUSADES

Arrows indicate general lines of expansion; dates, the approximate time of
Christian conquest

German emperor received a gift of a camel which came from the Orient by way of Kiev in Russia. Thus it was that Western Europe, having lost control of the Mediterranean routes, maintained indirect contacts with the Orient by means of the arteries of Norse trade along her northern frontiers. This was of great importance in the early development of town life in north Germany and the Netherlands. For every year of Norse invasion and destruction there were decades of constructive interchange of material goods and ideas.

During most of the latter half of the ninth century the impact of the Norsemen on Western civilization was destructive; but even this helped to sweep away the shattered fragments of the Carolingian Empire. Thereafter, once the Norse had established permanent contacts with the people of the West, they contributed valuable elements to the new civilization that was taking shape. In short, these late Germanic invaders not only accelerated the decline and disappearance of the Frankish Empire, but contributed vigorous elements to the new European civilization which was emerging from the wreckage of Carolingian times.

AN AGE OF RECONSTRUCTION   When considered from the viewpoint of declining Carolingian institutions, this confused period shows little promise of achievements. Politically it was an age of disorder and disunity. Religiously it was marked by clerical corruption and papal impotence. Economic life was much hampered by civil wars and invasion. Cultural life was so unimpressive that the period has been called a second dark age.[2] In spite of the essential truth of these generalizations, there is another brighter side to the picture. A centralized regimented system such as the Carolingian Empire was unsuited to the conditions in the West and therefore could not hope to continue. The sooner it was abandoned for a more workable set of institutions, the more permanent would be the progress of Western civilization. The future was with the smaller states and localized institutions which emerged out of the ruin of the Carolingian Empire. Once we realize this fact, we can look with more understanding upon the destructive changes that took place in this unsettled period.

Furthermore, as we have seen, constructive developments were taking place. There was much of importance for modern European history in the ninth and tenth centuries. The foundations of the

[2] Some writers consider the periods *before* and *after* Charles the Great as the true "Dark Ages" of medieval culture. See below, p. 301, on this subject.

national monarchies of the West are to be found in the small, but vigorous states established by Alfred in England, the Capetians in France, and the princes of Aragon and Castile in Spain. Out of this age also came the Holy Roman Empire of Otto the Great and the revived papacy of Gregory VII. Monasteries and churches flourished during these dark centuries and within their cloistered walls art and literature were taking root.

INCREASING
COMMERCE

Most noteworthy of all was the steady increase of industry and commerce. Charles the Great's regime had marked a low point in the industrial life of the West. After his reign business activities increased steadily in volume. Even though this was an era of almost unending foreign and civil wars, there was constant trade, especially in luxuries. Throughout the period of Norse and Moslem invasions, the upper classes in the West were supplied with Oriental spices, incense, silks, gems, Tyrian purple garments, and fine leather goods from Eastern centers. In 973, at Mainz on the Rhine River, an Arab visitor found all sorts of spices for sale. In the same century, at a market controlled by a German monastery, twenty-five varieties of spices were listed, in amounts running from two to one hundred pounds. In faraway London, foreign merchants were allowed to carry on their trade on condition that they pay the king a tax in *pepper* and *cloth*. In addition to the luxuries which were imported from the East, merchants purchased a variety of articles in Moslem Spain; among these were olive oil, nuts, mantles, and Cordova leather. As in the earlier medieval centuries, most of the import trade was for the upper classes and was carried on by foreigners, chiefly Syrians and Jews.

The Jews, in particular, seem to have prospered, especially under Charles the Great and his immediate successors. They possessed farms, vineyards, mills, and had their own synagogues. The export of wine to the East was almost completely in their hands, and they did a thriving trade in slaves. Verdun was the chief center for this traffic; here were assembled gangs of Slavic prisoners captured in the Germanic frontier wars. Thence they were driven southward to be sold to the peoples of the Mediterranean lands. The harem and the bodyguard of the Spanish caliph were said to have been made up almost entirely of Slavic slaves. It was doubtless the wealth, the shrewd financial practices, and the slave trading of the Jews that caused them to be so intensely hated. From seventh-century Italy, Spain, and Frankland came our earliest examples of Jewish "pogroms." In the late ninth century they were expelled from Italy. Earlier in the century Bishop Agobard of Lyons wrote a treatise *Concerning the Insolence of the Jews*. This is the first example of anti-Jewish literature in the Middle Ages. In France and other northern lands the Jews fared rather well up to the time of the crusades.

A noteworthy factor in the development of economic activities during this period was the increase in the native merchant class. In 877 certain "Christian merchants" were sufficiently important to be included in a tax of 10 per cent which was levied on all tradesmen in France. It is possible that these merchants were natives of the region around Paris, or perhaps "Italian merchants" such as were mentioned by contemporary writers. At any rate, business was beginning to flourish in many Frankish centers during the ninth and tenth centuries. Paris, a half century after Charles the Great, was described as "a popular emporium, full of people and commerce." Nantes, at the mouth of the Loire River, and Rouen, at the mouth of the Seine, were active in seafaring commerce. In 841 King Charles the Bald made use of twenty-eight merchant vessels from Rouen. Still further north, in the Netherlands, Frisian cloth merchants, though much hampered for a time by Norse invaders, carried on a lucrative business. Their wares and their coined money (bearing a ship insignia) circulated throughout this region and far up the Rhine to Cologne and Mayence.

The clergy also began to take an active part in commerce. Monasteries often served as trading posts. Usually they had their own special agents who handled the monastic business affairs. As time passed, groups of peasant artisans settled in villages on the monastic estates. At some of the flourishing monasteries in northern France there were saddlers, bakers, cobblers, winemakers, furriers, and dyers, all living under the protection and control of the monastery. Such workmen produced more goods than they themselves and the monks could use. These goods were sold or bartered either to neighboring people or to foreign merchants. In this way a monastery might become a producer and distributor of industrial goods. Just how far the monks of this early period carried on mercantile enterprises is not known, but it is certain that many monasteries had warehouses, market rights, port privileges on rivers, and immunities from tolls.

In concluding our survey of economic life in the Frankish realms, it is well to caution against extremes of opinion. The theory that Roman business life continued, unaffected by the Germanic invasions, is impossible of proof. Equally unsatisfactory is the opposite view which presents the gloomy picture of an age of barbaric economy. From the fifth to the eleventh century, most of Western Europe was primitive in its economic life. Industry and commerce, much depressed, continued, but on a small scale. In the ninth and tenth centuries they began to expand in certain regions and thereafter Europe began to be increasingly industrial and commercial. By the year 1000, a century before the first crusade, Western Europe had started on the road to economic recovery, and was already employing certain types of business organization on a small scale. There were markets, fairs, guilds, and towns in many places. The industrial and commercial classes, however, still comprised a very small portion of the population.

For centuries to come, rural ideals were to dominate the life of the West; and agriculture, as compared with business activities, was primitive and unprogressive. Very few of the great rural estates were run with any high degree of efficiency, and the lot of the majority of the peasantry was hard. At worst, the sufferings of the populace during periods of invasion and warfare were terrible. A ninth-century writer asserted that in various parts of Gaul, men were forced to eat bread made of dirt with a little flour mixed in, and bemoaned the abominable crime of reducing men to eating dirt while the horses of those who were devastating the land were plentifully supplied with fodder.

Naturally famine stalked on the heels of the warring armies. Ninth-century Saxony suffered so much that "many were forced to live on horse meat," and at times cannibalism seems to have been resorted to. Occasionally the peasantry, goaded by suffering, rose in savage but vain revolts. Even the sturdy German farmers of Saxony were crushed beneath the weight of economic and military exploitation, as the process of consolidation of free lands into large estates went on. In Frisia and Normandy likewise there were uprisings. Many peasants fled for refuge to the mountains, islands, or even to the camps of the barbarian invaders. One of the Norse chieftains, Hastings by name, was said to have been a runaway Frankish serf. There is considerable evidence to support the contention that the lower classes suffered less from the ravages of the invaders than from the rivalries of their own rulers and the economic pressure exerted by grasping landlords. At any rate, the two centuries after the death of Charles the Great saw hard times for the small free farmers. It

was during these centuries that most of the free agricultural population succumbed to the inevitable and sought security by becoming
servile dependents of the feudal nobility.

In surveying the rise of feudalism and the manor, we shall see
further evidence of the new political, economic, and social institutions that arose out of the wreck of the Carolingian Empire.

FEUDAL SOCIETY

THE NATURE OF FEUDALISM

FEUDALISM is a term that has been used since the eighteenth century to denote the type of government and social organization that existed in Western Europe during the Middle Ages. The word was derived from *feudum* (fief) which means the rights pertaining to an estate, usually of landed property. Often the word *fief* is used for the estate itself. The fief was not only landed wealth, the basis of agricultural income; it was also the unit of government and the symbol of membership in an aristocratic caste of nobles. Since the fief was the basis of the economic income, the governmental power, and the social rank of the nobility, it was a fundamental factor in medieval society. The sum total of customs pertaining to it comprised feudalism. Thus, from the economic standpoint, feudalism involved the agricultural regime of the manor; politically it concerned the localization of government in the hands of the landholding nobility, and socially it represented an aristocratic warrior class of rulers.

Although some historians still apply the term *feudalism,* in a restricted sense, merely to certain political institutions of certain regions, in general it is used to denote the complex of political, economic, and social institutions in the West during several centuries of the Middle Ages. We shall follow this broader usage, but with certain cautions and reservations. First, it is now generally recognized that the feudal type of social organization was not a peculiarly medieval institution. It has occurred in many ages and is recognized as a rather normal stage of human development. In the second place, at no time did medieval men have a fixed set of institutions called feudalism. In fact, the term feudalism was neither known nor used in the Middle Ages. Finally, the economic, political, and social customs of the Middle Ages were never regimented into any *system,* feudal or otherwise. Medieval methods of social organization varied from region to region and from century to century according to existing conditions. There were feudal states, city-states, papal states, kingdoms, and even empires.

Nevertheless, when viewed as a whole, medieval Europe manifested certain *tendencies* which were very different from those of the same regions in ancient and modern times, and which can be called feudal. These tendencies were (1) a marked decentralization of government which led to the dispersion of political power among many local rulers; (2) the breakdown of city life and a reversion to self-sustaining agricultural units; and (3) the association of political functions with landholding and personal relationships involving honor and fidelity. These trends became so powerful in the West that, for a time, in many regions they left their mark on all phases of civilization. We shall use the term feudalism to denote these general tendencies and the complex of institutions to which they gave rise in certain parts of Western Europe from about the tenth to the thirteenth centuries.

THE BEGINNINGS OF WESTERN FEUDALISM

It is to be noted that we consider feudalism as a somewhat indefinite and intangible set of customs, not as a complete system of government that was forced upon a people like a new constitution. As a matter of fact feudal institutions evolved in Western Europe in much the same manner as they have in other parts of the world under similar conditions. The feudal type of social organization developed in varying degrees in ancient Egypt, in the states of the Eastern Mediterranean after the death of Alexander the Great, in the late Roman Empire, among the Turks of Asia Minor, and in modern Japan. Feudal tendencies first appeared in the West during the closing centuries of the Roman Empire. As in the other regions mentioned, the most noticeable symptom of the change was the assumption of governmental powers by the noble owners of great country estates. This began when they were made responsible for the taxes, the administration of justice, and the enforcement of law and order in their localities. Often the central government was glad to shelve such responsibilities. If not, perhaps the noble landowner was powerful enough to defy the imperial officials. At any rate, by one means or another, the rural nobility in outlying regions came to exercise governmental authority. During the troubled centuries of the late empire these conditions became more and more prevalent until prac-

tically all great landlords enjoyed immunity or exemption from interference on the part of the officials of the central government.

In these confused centuries political, social, economic, religious,
and cultural life tended to become localized on great rural estates or
villas controlled by nobles. In most regions the powerful landlords
became the actual rulers. They defended the populace from invasion,
taxed them, settled disputes, and directed most of their activities.
Whether the landlords were Germanic or Roman nobles, whether they
usurped such functions or were assigned them by the central authorities, the fact remains that most of the population came under the
control of the noble owners of great estates. This tendency, brought
on by the granting of immunities which strengthened the landholding nobility at the expense of the central government, laid the foundation for feudalism.

Meanwhile the political powers of the landed nobility were also
being strengthened from below. The people themselves saw the advantages of independent local rule. As the central imperial government proved incapable of doing anything except overburden them
with taxes, the lesser folk voluntarily placed themselves and their
property under the protection and control of the local nobility. They
ceased to be owners of the land but were allowed to use it as tenant-
clients of the new owner. Such a transaction was advantageous to
all concerned. The noble landlord obtained both land and faithful
supporters to swell the ranks of his retainers. The tenant-client lost
the title to his land but retained possession and gained a powerful
protector. The landholding aspects of this relationship were called
precarium; the personal bond between protector and client was called
patrocinium. In later times the terms *beneficium* and *feudum* (fief)
were applied to similar landed relationships, while *commendatio*
and *vassalage* were used for the personal relations. Although there
were technical distinctions in the use of the various terms, so far
as landholding and personal fidelity were concerned, the fundamental
character of the feudal relationship continued with little change.

As a result of immunities and the *patrocinium-precarium* relationship there came into being in the rural sections of the West a new
social and political order based on landholding and personal loyalty.
The great majority of the population became peasants who tilled
the soil as tenants or serfs. The aristocratic landlords became a virtual caste of warriors who ruled in their respective localities. This
combination of political rights with landholding is the essential factor

that marks the beginning of feudalism. As the conditions suitable to such methods of government continued, feudalism took deeper root and eventually became the dominant factor in medieval political life.

GERMANIC
FEUDALISM

When the Germanic invaders settled in the Roman Empire, they took over the existing organization or developed similar customs of landholding and government. Great landed possessions were granted to the nobility by their chiefs or kings as rewards for military and governmental assistance. Meanwhile, the majority of the population, both Roman and German, gradually sank to a position of economic and political subordination. The Germanic chieftains who became great landholders assumed governmental powers similar to those of the Roman nobles in earlier times. They ruled with the assistance of dependents who were bound to them by strong personal ties that resembled the Roman *patrocinium* and also certain of the ancient customs of their Germanic forefathers.

One of these was the oath of fidelity sworn by the young warriors who were members of the *comitatus* (*gefolge* in German), or retinue, of a chieftain. The Romans and the Celtic inhabitants of Gaul had similar customs, but historians tend to emphasize the influence of the *comitatus* relationship, particularly in the development of the feudal oath of homage.[1] It is our belief that everywhere feudalism was more strongly influenced by conditions prevailing at the time than by the ancient customs of any particular race or nation. By the time feudalism began to take definite form, the distinctions between Germans, Romans, and Celts had passed away. Therefore the resemblance of certain feudal institutions to those of the Germans or Romans of earlier centuries may not be so much an evidence of a direct inheritance as of the universality of certain problems and of man's tendency to solve them in much the same fashion in various ages.

CAROLINGIAN
FEUDALISM

In the Germanic West it became increasingly difficult to maintain a centralized government with a highly organized bureaucracy. The localized rural type of life that prevailed called for a decentralized, local government based on the personal leadership of the landlord class.

As time went on, government became more and more a matter of personal relationships between landholders. Even powerful rulers

---

[1] See below, p. 223, for a further discussion of homage and of other early practices of a similar nature.

such as the early Carolingians were forced by circumstances to associate governmental functions with landholding. In the absence of ready money, land, which was plentiful, could be used to purchase the services that the ruler needed. Charles Martel, for example, assigned lands to his noble followers with the understanding that they were to be used to maintain a force of mounted soldiers. Charles the Great's counts and other officials were rewarded for their services by grants of land. Great landholders came to be looked upon as potential if not actual rulers.

With the disintegration of the Carolingian Empire, and the accompanying invasions, conditions similar to those of late Roman times became universal. Local government was left in the hands of the local nobility, and every great landowner was forced to look out for himself and his dependents. Emperors and kings assigned governmental duties to the landowning nobles, and lands to their faithful officials. They granted immunities to local nobles and sometimes encouraged them to build fortified castles with which to defend their domains. A powerful landlord who succeeded in governing and defending his neighborhood during a period of invasion was likely to become the virtual ruler of the region. Not only peasants and small farmers but even great landowners were eager to safeguard their property by associating themselves with him. A wealthy man who had valuable holdings which he could not defend against barbaric invaders or unscrupulous neighbors, might gladly become the dependent of a powerful local noble in order to have security. Again, he might build up his own defensive forces by giving over portions of his land to warrior noblemen on condition that they render him military service. This relationship, so similar in character to the earlier Roman and Germanic customs, was called *commendatio* and *beneficium*. The landowner bestowed upon his noble dependent the *beneficium* (benefit) of the use of property in return for commendation and promises of loyalty and faithful service.

In a period of local disorder and invasion such as the late Carolingian era, such relationships expanded rapidly. At first it was customary to make grants of land and promises of service for limited periods, usually for the lifetime of the one to whom the grant was made. Eventually, however, the hereditary possession of benefices came to be recognized; usually a man's son had the right to retain the benefice so long as he performed the required services. This made for political as well as economic stability, since landholding carried with it the right of local government. As feudalism developed it was also recognized that a benefice should go to the oldest son of the deceased holder; otherwise it was likely to be divided and subdivided. This custom came to be known as *primogeniture.* Everywhere in the West, after the breakdown of the Carolingian Empire, government drifted more or less into the hands of the landholding nobility, and personal relationships of man to man tended to replace obedience to kings and states.

In northern France such feudal conditions were almost universal by the end of the tenth century. In England, southern France, Germany, Spain, and Italy they developed more slowly and with less universality. In these regions there were many men of both high and low rank who owned their lands as *allods,* without any feudal conditions or entanglements. Sooner or later, however, the close bonds of landholding and personal fidelity that had been evolving slowly for centuries became the chief basis for government in the West. Except in regions or periods in which there chanced to be a strong central government, men looked to their immediate landlords for protection and leadership. These leaders, in turn, looked to their dependents for revenues and military service, and government thus became an integral part of the local landholding system.

From the time of Charles the Great (800) to the end of the crusades (1300), this sort of localized, noble-controlled government was prevalent throughout most of Western Europe. Even where there were kings who had been crowned and anointed and who claimed to rule by hereditary right, the actual process of governing was predominantly feudal. Many kings were merely powerful feudal lords who clothed their regime with some of the formalities of monarchy. The majority of the populace lived under a regime that was dominated by the local feudal nobility and the ideals of the landowning aristocracy.

FEUDAL RELATIONSHIPS The interlocking feudal relationships which grew up among the landholding nobility after the functions of local government came into their hands constitute a complex structure which may not be readily understood. They came into being slowly and often imperceptibly without governmental decrees and sometimes—to our modern way of thinking—without much purpose. Naturally the relationships of kings with their nobles and of nobles with nobles were unlike those of Roman or modern times. Landholding was associated with governing, and therefore exchanges of land had a political significance.

When a king granted certain political rights to one of his followers, he also granted certain lands, in order to provide the revenue necessary for the performance of the duties of the office. The reverse was also true. A grant of land carried certain political responsibilities. The receiver of the office and lands pledged his personal loyalty; he promised to furnish troops when needed, to do justice and to maintain peace and order. But these political functions might be passed on to others by a process that is called *subinfeudation*. If the nobleman who received a tract of land needed to build up his following, he might assign or subinfeudate a portion of it to some other noble, on condition that he render fidelity and military assistance. Thus a great lord might parcel out his lands to a number of fellow nobles, each one pledged to be faithful to him, to govern properly the land he had received, and to furnish the required number of fighting men and other specified services. All such pledged followers were called *vassals*. The one to whom they were pledged was their lord or *seigneur*. The lands or privileges granted were called either a *benefice* (beneficium) or a *fief* (feudum). These were of various kinds, from great landed estates to the right to certain fees, concessions, or other types of income.

An individual landlord might have a number of vassals, and he might also become the vassal of a number of lords. Thus he might hold several fiefs from several lords. He might also regrant portions of these fiefs to other nobles, thus becoming a lord as well as a vassal. Strictly speaking, a noble owed to one lord, his *liege* lord, a fidelity that took precedence over all others. In addition to this he might have varying types of feudal relationships with other nobles. To some he owed military service. To others he might be bound to furnish some lesser services, perhaps merely a ceremonial act of some kind.

Feudal relationships also extended downward even to nonnoble functions. A simple freeman might serve as a hunter or stable keeper in return for a lesser grant of some kind. The grant might not even consist of landed property: often it was the right to a certain income. Still lower in the scale of feudal relationships were the free peasants and serfs who had the use of their lord's lands in return for manual labor and other menial services. There was, to be sure, a sharp distinction between noble vassals, who performed honorable services, and the peasantry whose functions were ignoble. In general, however, all feudal society from kings to peasants was based on grants of land (or the income from lands) in return for specified services. With the lands went certain rights and duties.

ENTERING THE FEUDAL RELA- TIONS
The ceremonial customs by which men entered into these all-important feudal relationships seem very strange to modern folk. In some respects, however, they resemble the arrangements by which men in any age come to an agreement. If, for instance, the Count of Blois agreed to become the vassal of the Duke of Normandy, the affair was handled as a *contract*. Having arranged the terms, the two nobles went through the ceremonies of *homage, fealty,* and *investiture* to seal the bargain. First the Count went down on his knees before the Duke, placed his hands in the Duke's, and promised to be his "man," for such and such a fief.[2] Thereupon the Duke raised him to his feet, gave him the "kiss of peace," and led him to the altar where he swore fealty (i.e., fidelity). Then the Duke "invested" (or inaugurated) him by presenting a clod of earth, a banner, or some other article that symbolized the fief. Thereafter the Count had possession of the fief, while the Duke had a right to certain specified services from his new vassal. Like any modern contract this agreement continued as long as both parties held to the terms.

THE FEUDAL CONTRACT
The lord, like the vassal, was bound to perform certain services. As one medieval writer put it, "he was quite as much bound to be faithful to his vassal, as the latter to him." Although there was much variation in feudal contracts, they usually provided that the lord should guarantee two things: (1) *protection* of the vassal from foreign aggressors, and, in case he died without a mature heir, protection of the interests of the widow and children; and (2) *justice* according to "due process" and "the law of the land." In the Middle Ages, this meant a trial before a feudal court composed of his fellow vassals or "peers" (*pares,* i.e., equals). Cases were decided according to the customs of the region; these, as interpreted by the assembled vassals, were "the law of the land." Incidentally, the lord's motives were not entirely unselfish in rendering such services. He realized a considerable revenue from

---

[2] The ceremony was called homage, from the Latin word for man (*homo*). It was quite similar to commendation, which term was derived from *con-manus,* referring to the clasping of the hand (*manus*). It was also akin to the ancient Germanic ceremony in which a member of the *comitatus* pledged himself to his chief.

the fines and fees levied in his feudal court. His guardianship of widows and orphans was also lucrative inasmuch as he enjoyed the income from their estates. In addition to such privileges and duties, it was also generally understood that the lord guaranteed to the vassal the hereditary possession of the fief, and that he would reward him with gifts of land and revenue for special services rendered.

The vassal, in turn, was expected to render *counsel* and *aid*. The lord needed *counsel* especially at the three great festival seasons (Christmas, Easter, and Pentecost) when he held court and was expected to settle disputes among his vassals. In an age of uncertain and varying local customs, legal counsel was important. *Aid* was rendered in several ways. First and foremost, was military aid, which consisted of (1) guarding the lord's castle for certain specified periods; (2) putting his own castle at the lord's disposal; and (3) accompanying him on expeditions, with a certain number of knights. Expeditionary aid, or knight service, as it was called, was customarily limited to forty days a year, within the realm. Even King Edward I was unable to force his English barons to do military service overseas in Normandy.

Almost as important as military aid was financial aid. Vassals were not taxed, but they were expected to render financial assistance in times of emergency. The medieval lord's most important financial emergencies seem to have included the raising of ransom if he was made prisoner, the knighting of his eldest son, and the marriage of his eldest daughter. Sometimes a farsighted vassal would make an agreement by which marriage aids were limited to the *first* marriage of the daughter. Often in the later feudal contracts a fourth aid was mentioned: namely, a contribution when the lord went on a crusade. One of the heaviest financial burdens was the relief, a sort of inheritance tax paid by the holder of a fief whenever death led to the accession of either a new lord or vassal, and the renewal of the feudal relationship. This payment sometimes amounted to a year's revenue from the fief. It was also customary for the vassal to furnish food and lodging whenever the lord and his retinue paid a visit, a formidable outlay in case the lord brought a large company and stayed a long time. In some contracts there were sections providing for fantastic services, such, for instance, as presenting the lord with two candles at Christmas, or holding his head while he was seasick on an ocean voyage.

THE COM-
PLEXITY OF
FEUDALISM
The complexities of feudal life may seem to modern folk like a labyrinth of confused interrelationships. Like all social organizations it had its advantages and its disadvantages. In the earlier centuries, for the civilized people of cities which were formerly parts of the Roman Empire, it represented the reversion to a more primitive type of life. In place of the standardized public service of imperial civilization there was the uncertain authority of noble landlords who might defend their subjects from outside dangers but who might also exploit them mercilessly. Then, too, feudalism encouraged localism in such an extreme form that it tends to shock moderns who are accustomed to centralized government. Every duke, baron, count, margrave, bishop, and abbot was practically an independent ruler in his own little realm. Thus there arose a complicated mass of feudal dominions large and small.

An accurate map of all the separate realms of feudal Europe would look like a crazy quilt. The territorial states of Germany, Italy, Spain, England, and France did not exist. In the tenth and eleventh centuries what is now known as France consisted of over a hundred independent units, each under a feudal ruler who violently resented any encroachment on the "integrity" or "honor" of his realms. Each of these units was likewise composed of smaller states, or estates, the noble owners of which had certain inalienable rights.

THE IMAGINARY
FEUDAL
PYRAMID
One can perhaps visualize this situation by imagining the conditions in the United States if each of the forty-eight states were an independent nation, and if each county, township, and city within each state had independent rights in all local affairs, and if each landowner exercised full governmental authority on his own estate. It should be remembered, however, that the feudal units of medieval times were not usually organized into successively larger and larger groupings, such as our counties and states. Often a feudal state such as France or Germany is represented as a group of fiefs systematically mobilized in a sort of military hierarchy in which the king, as supreme lord, parceled out all of the realm in large tracts to the greater nobles, each of whom in turn dealt out portions to the lesser nobles, and so on down to the humblest subject. This beautifully logical scheme of arrangement does not represent any real situation, for no such feudal pyramid ever actually existed. In England, Normandy, and the crusading state of Jerusalem, feudalism was more systematic than else-

where, but at best it had no such regular organization as this. No feudal regime was ever founded by issuing blocks of land in successively smaller portions to successively lesser folk. The feudal structure took shape slowly and the actual drift of affairs was in the opposite direction. Great feudal lords tended to amass more and more territory by the long and difficult process of conquest, inheritance, and marriage alliances. An unusually successful feudal noble might become king. But as soon as any ruler gained direct control of a large portion of the lands, revenues, and powers of the realm, feudalism was doomed. Its place was taken by national monarchical absolutism.

CONSTRUCTIVE ASPECTS OF FEUDALISM

In spite of the fact that feudalism tended to encourage local independence, and was the antithesis of centralized monarchy, it should not be inferred that it was a condition of anarchy. On the contrary, feudalism came into being as a result of the anarchy caused by the disintegration of the late Roman imperial government, and it tended to mitigate the disorder of those troubled times. By encouraging the nobility to organize and administer local affairs, it provided a practical method of preserving law and order. In many cases it seemed to be the only available system by which men might get on together. For the more primitive Germanic people who had formerly lived as nomads or migrant farmers, this was a distinctly progressive move toward civilized life. Even for the civilized populations of imperial regions, vigorous local administration was better than the corrupt remnants of Roman rule.

As time went on, governmental units tended to become larger and more efficient in their workings. Thus there arose large feudal states such as England and France. Furthermore, even the roughest of feudal barons made some effort to keep his subjects contented and prosperous—for his own if not for their benefit. Even the most independent of rulers could not avoid some sort of co-operation with his fellow rulers, and thus interfeudal relations and common feudal customs were strengthened.

BROKEN FEUDAL CONTRACTS

Feudal contracts, even when made in good faith, did not enforce themselves automatically. The unavoidable complexities of feudal interrelationships led to dissatisfaction, hostility, and broken promises. A noble, whether lord or vassal, who violated his feudal duty was usually summoned to the court of the overlord who, with the fellow vassals (peers) of the defendant, gave judgment. Often an independent spirited noble refused to accept the decision, or perhaps failed even to appear before his overlord to answer the charges. In such cases, he was formally condemned as a false vassal and ordered to surrender all fiefs held from the overlord.

This meant war, for the defending noble had all the means of resistance. Many a vassal, disgusted with a certain relationship, deliberately broke his feudal pledge in order to end the hated vassalage. So far the procedure was likely to be the rational application of legal principles, based on definite contracts or upon the generally recognized duties of vassals and lords, as recorded in the written codes of feudal custom. But as far as enforcement was concerned, there was no recognized group of neutral officials who could be called upon to carry out the court's decision. If the defendant refused the judgment, the wronged parties must make war on him. The enforcement of feudal law was more like the enforcement of modern international treaties than of modern legal statutes by a police force. It was warfare, and it prevailed constantly and widely. Due to the fact that most noblemen held several fiefs and from various lords, everyone was involved in many contracts. Since conflicting interests and changing conditions were sure to upset some of these arrangements, most of the time some lord or other was at war.

This situation is often interpreted as an evidence of the anarchical and brutal life of the Middle Ages. For instance, the expression "War was the law of the feudal world" has led many people to imagine that medieval folk did nothing but vent their warlike hatred upon one another in a sort of jungle world in which "might made right" and only the brutally fit survived. In the light of recent international conflicts, we can realize that war is quite as much the law of the modern as it was of the medieval world. It is resorted to commonly when vital interests are at stake or agreements are violated. Since medieval Europe had many more political and economic units than modern Europe, there were many more conflicts of interests; therefore more wars. Medieval Europe had many more wars per century than modern Europe has, but a medieval war was a mere "tempest in a teapot" compared with one of the devastating conflicts of our day. A comparatively small proportion of society—the feudal nobility—took part, and only for short summer campaigns. Most medieval "battles" were mere skirmishes and few lives were lost. The greater part of the praying and working population—the clergy and common folk—continued their appointed tasks. Conditions for noncombatants were also improved by the Peace and Truce of God.

MEDIEVAL WARFARE

Nevertheless the medieval nobles were no weaklings at their major occupation. While wars lasted, they were waged with a right good will and with lusty strokes. The author of the *Song of Roland* believed that, to be a warrior, one must be strong and brave; "otherwise let him be a monk in a monastery." Even more of an enthusiast for the game of warfare was the troubadour who, after describing the horrors of a battlefield, the calls for help and the shrieks of the dying, said: "I love the melee of shields, pennants, the splintering of lances, the riddled shields, the split helmets, and the give and take of blows." Still another wrote:

> Peace delights me not; war, be thou my lot.
> Law I do not know, save a right good blow.

But there was a less spectacular, more brutal, and better organized aspect of feudal warfare. Since the chief wealth of the enemy was his landed estates, one devastated the fields of the subjects of his opponent. After a raid by Hugh Capet it was said that "not a peasant hut was left in the region." Often feudal armies had special forces of *insangeries,* "burners," who set fire to the crops and buildings of the peasantry. All the chivalrous ideals of knighthood and the penalties of the Peace of God could not prevent such atrocities. On the same brutal plane was the practice of torturing and mutilating captured soldiers of the lower ranks of society. During the Hundred Years' War, the captors of bowmen (who, being poor men, were worthless for ransoms) would cut off the fingers that were used to draw the bowstring, and then set the captives free, so as to save the cost of feeding them.

Sometimes even noncombatants were massacred. A French count once mutilated over a hundred defenseless people. William the Conqueror, in quelling a revolt, left behind him a trail of helpless persons whose arms, hands, or feet had been chopped off as a lesson to other rebels. Even the Black Prince, England's "mirror of chivalry," after capturing a French city that had shown a stiff resistance, put to the sword over three thousand children, women, and old men. The comment of the historian Froissart was: "There was no pity taken of the poor people who had wrought no treason, yet they paid dearer than the great personages such as had done the evil . . . God have mercy on their souls, for I trow that they were martyrs." One can well understand why medieval preachers condemned as "hellish crews of human wolves" the armies of invading soldiery.

HUMANE AS-
PECTS OF WAR-
FARE
In all fairness, however, it must be said that such atrocities were exceptional, and they occur in all ages when man's beastlier instincts are unleashed in the inhuman business of warfare. The wonder is that there was not much more horror and much less humanity in an age which educated every noble lad for the profession of warfare. But here it was that chivalric ideals and the influence of the church exerted something of a restraining influence. The young noble, during his five-year apprenticeship as squire or shield-bearer to a warrior, was taught courtesy, proper speech, and knightly honor, as well as the tricks of fighting. The ceremony of knighting, which came at the end of this training period, gave the church an opportunity to emphasize the restraints of religion. At this time the young knight might spend an entire night in prayer at the altar of the cathedral, dedicating his newly acquired weapons to the service of God, honor, justice, and the church. Then, having been "dubbed" knight with a stroke across the shoulder by an older knight, and with a priestly blessing, he set forth to "win his spurs." At its best, feudalism sent young men into the world with some ideals of honor, courage, and protection of the helpless. At its worst, it produced brutal soldiers of fortune.

THE TOURNA-
MENT
There was one means by which the Middle Ages "let off the steam" of its warlike population with somewhat less damage. This was the tournament, or mock war. During the eleventh century, when the Peace and Truce of God were placing limitations on regular warfare, a Frenchman is said to have "invented *torneamenta*." In spite of clerical opposition this game of warfare became very popular. In the earlier centuries of its existence the tournament was a series of actual combats, but carried on according to strict regulations. Often such tournaments were as dangerous as real battles, for the contestants fought with all the equipment of regular warfare. Not until the late medieval centuries were blunted or wooden weapons used. Occasionally a tournament would close with a group combat which reproduced all of the conditions of actual warfare, the winners being rewarded with ransoms and the equipment of the vanquished. Lives as well as fortunes and reputations were lost in these contests. With all its destruc-

tiveness and brutality the tournament flourished, and it was of real military value as a training school for warfare under realistic conditions. It also seems to have satisfied the craving of both fighters and spectators for "red-blooded" excitement in a manner that reminds one of the Roman gladiatorial games, the Spanish bullfight, the rougher aspects of American football, and prize fighting.

Like many such sports, tourneying became commercialized. Professional men-at-arms made the rounds of the local tournaments, winning immense prizes, chiefly of armor and horses. A certain William the Marshall of Normandy was said to have captured ten knights and twelve horses at a single tournament. In the course of one season he and a professional companion captured three hundred knights, for each of whom they received a ransom. But such business was dangerous as well as profitable. After one fight William had to be taken to a smith to have his battered armor removed. In time, as civilization developed, the tournament became a gentleman's sport, with more pageantry and less bloodshed.

The medieval knight usually fought on horseback—
ARMS AND at least he started the fight on his horse. The two
ARMOR opponents charged at each other at full speed, each endeavoring to unseat the other with a long lance which was poised somewhat as a vaulter does his pole. After the impact and the splintering of lances or the unhorsing of the opponent, if there was any fight left in either, they resorted to swords, battle axes, or maces (iron-studded clubs). These heavy weapons, swung with a two-handed grip, could inflict smashing blows.

Protection was provided by means of armor which in earlier times consisted of leather studded with small metal buttons or rings. Later chain mail was used, and still later solid metal breastplates, leg guards, and helmets. In the late Middle Ages even the horses were iron-plated at vulnerable points. A fully armed knight and charger were about as formidable looking and as cumbersome in action as a modern tank. It was only for a short time, during the later medieval centuries, that knights wore the iron-plated armor and vizored helmets with which modern artists usually clothe them. Throughout most of the Middle Ages helmets were rather simple affairs: iron caps (somewhat like those used in trench warfare) with metal guards in front and rear to protect the nose and the back of the neck.

The poorer knights and foot soldiers were, of course, very simply armed, often merely with leather or quilted cloth jackets. Furthermore, the "picture-book" armor began to go out of use shortly after it came in. It was discovered that many a heavy-armed knight and horse died, not from wounds, but from the weight of the armor. Fighting men were found without a cut or bruise on their bodies —dead from suffocation or the shock of falling from the horse. Finally the development of the crossbow, the English longbow,[3] and the Swiss pike[4] sounded the death knell of the knightly warrior. By the end of the Middle Ages all the European world was relying upon cheap but effective mercenary infantrymen who could stand off many times their own number of knights.

These developments also mark the passing of the castle. Artillery began to supersede tunneling operations, the catapult, battering ram, movable tower, blazing arrow, and other such spectacular methods of siege warfare. As a result the nobility lost their position of military predominance.

THE FEUDAL NOBLE AT HOME
Much as the medieval noble loved weapons and warfare, he did not spend his entire lifetime in a suit of armor swinging a battle axe. Feudal barons ate, dressed, slept, and played games much as people of all ages have done. At banquets, for instance, they ate meats such as haunch of venison, boar's head, pork, beef, and all kinds of fowl, including peacocks; fish, crabs, eels either broiled or in pies, and many other variations of meats, fowls, and eggs. They had various kinds of bread, and most of the vegetables with which we are familiar, though they used them less. There were apples, pears, cherries, and other fruits; and for desserts, cakes, custards, "jelly royal," raisins and spiced foods such as "rice with milk of almonds and powdered cinnamon." For drinks there were wines, ale, and beer. The medieval menu of the upper classes was far from primitive. They were hearty eaters, and doubtless many of them "dug their graves with their teeth."

Table etiquette was not very refined according to our standards. Contrary to modern popular opinion, forks were used to some extent in Italy as early as the eleventh century, and in England long before Elizabethan times. Nevertheless the practices regarded as proper in those days shock the sensibilities of our day. All drank from a common cup, for example, and there was point in the compliment paid by Chaucer to his Prioress for her neatness in having an

[3] See below, pp. 584 f.
[4] See below, p. 613.

upper lip so clean that no grease was left on the rim of the cup. *Babees Book* of about the same period warned diners against sipping with much sound, picking teeth with knives, spitting across, or on, the table, and blowing their noses on the table cloth!

For outdoor amusement, medieval noblemen and their ladies hunted with dogs and trained hawks or falcons. "Falconry" was extremely popular, and no less a personage than Emperor Frederick II wrote a carefully illustrated book on the care of falcons. Indoors the time was whiled away by playing backgammon and chess, or by listening to the ballads of minstrels. There was, of course, little reading. The women busied themselves with the management of the castle, with spinning, and weaving. Church festivals, fairs, and tournaments relieved the monotony somewhat, and occasionally troops of wandering jongleurs stopped at the castle to pick up a scanty sum by amusing the people with their tricks.

Even at its best, the life of the nobility in the real feudal age was rather primitive. Castles were damp and chilly in winter. The furniture, rugs, and hangings were simple. The average laboring man of today has more comfortable chairs, tables, and beds than many medieval nobles had. Seldom was there running water, and the toilet facilities were about like those of European country folk today.

EARLY MEDI-
EVAL CASTLES
The feudal noble's home was a castle. There has been much romanticizing concerning the medieval castle. Fairy tales, the "Knighthood in Flower" type of moving picture, illustrated books for children, and even Rhineland tourist guidebooks have contributed to the concept of a medieval castle as a maze of dungeons, high towers and turrets, moats, and drawbridges. As a matter of fact, medieval nobles enjoyed very few of these imaginary splendors. To be sure, most of the castles still standing in Europe are of this type, but they date from the later centuries of declining feudalism when castles were built for show rather than for defense. Such châteaux are not characteristic of the real feudal age. The castle evolved slowly along with feudalism, and in its changing aspects we can trace the rise, climax, and decline of the feudal nobility.

Castles became common in Western Europe during the post-Carolingian age when each nobleman became responsible for the defense of his locality. Like the feudal noble of this age, the castle

From Hudson, France, Harrap
FORTIFIED MANOR HOUSE
MEROVINGIAN AGE

CASTLE OF FOUGÈRES

From the Royal Library, Brussels
ATTACK ON A CASTLE (XV C)

FEUDAL LIFE

(See pp. 227 ff.)

From Steinhausen, *Geschichte der Deutschen Kultur*,
Courtesy of the Bibliographisches Institut, Leipzig.

MONKS BUILDING A MONASTERY (XV C)

(See pp. 706 f.)

was crude and primitive. Originally most castles were merely forti-fied manor houses or wooden blockhouses. Many of them were little more than a tower built on a large mound and surrounded by a wooden palisade. For centuries the feudal castle consisted essentially of an inner wooden tower (called a "dungeon" or "donjon"), usually set on a hill or mound, and an outer courtyard, or corral, enclosed by a wooden wall and protected by a moat. The courtyard con-tained stables, sheds, and buildings to accommodate the servants and retainers. The dungeon was usually three stories high, and was entered by means of an outside stairway which opened into the second or third story, and which was removable so as to make the place more easily defensible. The living quarters were on the third floor. Thence a trap door and ladder or inside stairway led down to the second story, which was used as a storeroom. From there another trap door opened into the windowless first story where prisoners (if there were any) were kept. Thus, it is the dark first floor of the medieval dungeon-tower that has given the word "dun-geon" its unpleasant connotation in modern times.

These early castles had none of the sophisticated refinements of picture-book castles. They were mostly of wood, with the top covered with skins. The palisaded courtyard was used as a corral, and in time of invasion it sheltered the neighboring peasantry and their animals. From it all sorts of barnyard and garbage odors arose even in normal times.

STONE CASTLES   With the increase of wealth and engineering ability, the feudal castle improved. In the eleventh cen-tury, just before the crusades, stone castles began to come in. They were, however, single-towered affairs of simple square design, and often only partially of stone. Famous medieval castles such as the original Tower of London, the real Kennilworth (not Sir Walter Scott's fictitious castle), Rouen and Falaise in Normandy, and Wart-burg in Germany were of this rather simple type. Not until the late crusading era (the thirteenth century), after warriors such as Philip II and Richard the Lion-Hearted had brought home new archi-tectural ideas from the East, was the many-turreted, round-towered castle introduced. Of this type was the defensive line of castles built by Richard along the frontier between Normandy and France. Be-hind these was a second, reserve line, with connecting roads, ferries, and even routes of communication to and from the Channel ports.

After Viollet Le Duc, from Thatcher and McNeal,
Europe in the Middle Age, Charles Scribner's Sons.

THE NORMAN CASTLE OF ARQUES

Certain of these Norman castles, and some of the counter defenses built by Philip II, were complicated structures, consisting of
an immense round dungeon and several smaller ones all connected by
a line of stout walls. Outside of the inner circuit there might be a
second and third ring of defenses. Such an arrangement of walls
within walls is known as a concentric castle. At Les Andelys on
the Seine one can still see the ruins of Gaillard, Richard's finest
castle, which was built in this fashion. Up to the time of the World
War tourists could see an even more spectacular example in the
Castle of Coucy north of Paris, built in the thirteenth century. This
castle had concentric circles of walls dotted with round towers and
bastions, and a central dungeon about a hundred feet in diameter
and twice that in height. The curved outer surface of round towers
withstood battering rams very successfully and by the fourteenth century this type was universal in the West.

Bastions (i.e., towers that jutted out from the accompanying
wall) were built so as to give the defenders a clear view and a
cross fire along the entire wall. The towers of Coucy and other
castles, also, had *crenelated* tops which provided the archers with
open spaces for shooting, and alternate sections of wall for protection. The huge walls of Coucy, which enclosed a space of about
thirty acres, were so thick (about twenty-four feet) that several horsemen could ride abreast along the top. Coucy also had a rather unusual feature in a subterranean passage three miles long. Large
castles also had many minor mechanisms such as the *portcullis* (a
gateway grill), a drawbridge with creaking chains and wheels, wind-
ing staircases, and slimy underground dungeon-prisons. Such castles
were, however, the exception. Most nobles lived less magnificently.

The greater nobles continued to build structures of this sort
until the effective application of gunpowder to warfare in the sixteenth century. Then the heavy concentric castle was abandoned and
defensive walls were scattered to more distant outer works by means
of which attackers might be kept at a safe distance. With this change
the residence of the nobles tended to become less defensible but more
livable. By the sixteenth century the castle had given way to the
picturesque country residence commonly called the château. The
famous Rhineland castles and many late French structures, such as
Chambord and Chenonceaux, are of this type.[5]

[5] See below, p. 720.

KINGS AND
FEUDALISM

Although feudalism with its complex of governmental functions, warfare, tournaments, and castle life was an institution especially adapted to the needs of the nobility, it affected all classes of society, from the greatest monarch to the poorest serf. The position of the king in the feudal world was a peculiar one. Since feudalism was a decentralized type of government in which each noble landlord was ruler of his own domain, what place was there for a king and how is it that there were kingdoms? As a matter of fact, feudalism did not sweep away all traces of earlier forms of government. It was merely a practical substitute for the increasingly ineffective kingships of the successors of Charles the Great. Although weak Carolingian kings continued to reign in most parts of the West, the local feudal nobility actually ruled. In the region of Paris, a Charles the Simple, or a Hugh Capet might be elected, crowned, and anointed as the divinely appointed king of the Franks, Bretons, Normans, Gascons, and so on, but the inhabitants of these sections looked to the local feudal nobles as their actual rulers. The inhabitants of Paris obeyed Hugh Capet, not so much for his kingship as for the fact that he was the feudal count of Paris.

The same situation existed elsewhere. In the Germanies, Conrad of Franconia might be nominally both king and emperor, but the dukes, counts, margraves, and noble landlords considered this an empty formality as far as their domains were concerned. In short, royal titles remained, but the realities of central power had given way to feudalism. Kings and emperors who continued in power were forced to rule in the feudal manner, as members of the feudality. Every king, like every other great noble, was a feudal lord, and he might even be a feudal vassal. The king of England was overlord of various dukes, counts, and lesser nobles; as Duke of Normandy he was also vassal to the king of France. All kings were involved in the network of feudal relationships. Only by such means could they exist in a feudal world.

But the king was something more than a feudal noble. He was also God's anointed and theoretically the superior of all other nobles. As soon as conditions developed which called for centralized governmental institutions, feudalism gave way to national monarchy, and the theory of the divine right of kings gained ground.[6] In later

[6] See below, p. 680.

chapters we shall consider the decline of feudalism and the development of royal power in several of the Western states. Meanwhile,
until the twelfth century, feudalism was in the ascendancy in most
of them. In spite of its decentralized system of government it did
the Western world a valuable service by maintaining local order and
security until such time as advancing civilization could form larger
units of government.

THE CLERGY
AND FEUDALISM
The members of the higher clergy (bishops and abbots), most of whom were descended from noble
families, were also drawn into the network of feudal
relationships.[7] Indeed the members of the clergy, despite the fact that
their vows prohibited them from taking part in warfare, were a very
important element in the feudal system. The church possessed about
a third of the landed property of Western Europe. Inasmuch as landed
possessions carried with them governmental responsibilities, the clergy
was of necessity drawn into feudal relationships. For one thing, its
members needed the protection that powerful lords and warrior vassals offered. On the other hand, the ruling powers needed the income
and services that prosperous church estates could provide. Bishops
and abbots could contribute generous financial aids, and as advisers
at the lord's court they were much more valuable than unlettered
laymen. Even though they could not bear arms in person, they could
—and did—send their quotas of knights to fight the battles of their
overlords. Many a churchman who loved the excitement of warfare
went into battle swinging a mace, with which he might smash heads
without committing the sin of shedding blood.

In most parts of Western Europe the clergy performed their part
in feudal government with success. As administrators they were so
much more efficient than the average layman that great lords came
to rely on them as their governmental assistants. Since the religious and
the political duties of the feudalized clergy frequently conflicted, this
led to serious difficulties. The church, however, could not do without
the feudality any more than the feudality could do without the church.
Under the circumstances the clergy had no other choice but to play
a double role. Its members lived in a feudal world and they had
to be a part of it or perish. But as a result their religious functions

[7] Due to the custom of primogeniture in the inheriting of fiefs, younger sons had
to look elsewhere for careers. Many of them became bishops or abbots.

suffered and this precipitated serious problems which will be considered later.[8]

THE PEASANTRY
AND FEUDALISM

The mass of common folk who comprised the great majority of the population during the feudal age occupied a somewhat illogical position. Their legal position in the feudal system of government was in no way related to their numbers, nor to the fact that, as agriculturists, they provided the economic basis for the system's very existence. Due to their economic activities, they were one of the most important factors in the feudal system. Yet they had no part in the government. Noble landlords who would have found it impossible to exist without the peasantry gave them no voice in their feudal assemblies.

In the Middle Ages the farm population was of much greater importance than it is in modern life. In a rural age where the everyday necessities of life came from the lord's own estates, agricultural labor was a vital necessity. Every member of the feudal nobility was constantly and directly dependent on the products of his estates. It is this condition that made the peasants and agriculture so important in the feudal economy. When one considers the importance of agriculture in the Middle Ages, it is obvious that there were two outstanding phases of feudalism: (1) upper-class feudalism which concerned the nobility and their governmental functions, and (2) manorialism which dealt with the productive labor of the peasantry and their relationships with one another and with their lord. To use modern terminology, the feudal system depended on two equally important functions: management (by the nobility) and manual labor (by the peasants). In the preceding pages we have considered the life of the nobility as they organized, defended, and governed their landed estates. In the succeeding section we shall concern ourselves with the activities of the peasantry and the agricultural institutions upon which feudal society rested. In this process we shall also shift our attention from the fief, which was the chief governmental unit, to the manorial village which was the prevailing unit of agricultural life.

[8] See below, pp. 380 f.

══ XII ══

THE MANOR

THE peasants, although they took no active part in feudal government, were the chief economic support of the ruling class; therefore they are essential to any description of feudalism. The rural peasantry comprised almost the entire working class in the early Middle Ages, and the workers comprised about 95 per cent of the total population. They were the "third estate" in a trinity of classes which consisted of the clergy, the nobility, and the workers. A tenth-century bishop wrote that "the house of God [i.e., Christian society], which is thought to be one, is triple; one class pray, others fight, others work." Another writer of the same period asserted that "every just throne rests on three props . . . the prayers, the fighters, the laborers." Two centuries later, medieval scholars were referring to society as an organism similar to the human body: "The clergy are the eyes that see and point out the road to salvation; the nobles are the hands and arms which protect society, enforce justice, and defend the realm; the lesser folk, like the lower parts of the body, support the upper parts." [1]

THE PEASANTRY During the early Middle Ages, while town life was unimportant, almost all of the common folk lived in rural communities and gained their living from agriculture. Before the eleventh century, doubtless 90 per cent of Western Europeans were born, grew up, married, and died in rural peasant villages. It was these communities that provided the feudal nobility with its economic resources. They furnished the man power, not only for agriculture, but also for the handicrafts by means of which rich and poor were fed, housed, and clothed. Gangs of peasants built roads, bridges, and castles for the lords. Peasant women wove the cloth out of which everyday clothing was made. Furniture, armor, shoes, and a hundred and one other things were made by peasant artisans in manorial work-

[1] See below, p. 683, on medieval social theory. The third estate comprised not only the peasantry, but also the burghers, who became more important during the later Middle Ages.

shops. Most important of all, every castle depended on its own farm laborers for food. In a primitive agricultural era such as the early Middle Ages, the chief wealth of the nobility consisted of landed property. Furthermore, in such a machineless age, land was absolutely useless without plenty of laborers. It was therefore the peasantry that cultivated the land and gave it economic value. Not merely land, but land populated with peasants, was the necessary economic foundation of feudal life.

If the peasant was indispensable to the noble, the noble was likewise indispensable to the peasant. The peasants were protected from brigands and invaders by their noble lords. The courtyard of a castle served as a refuge for peasant families and their flocks during times of invasion. Thus the lives of the nobles and peasants were closely bound together, despite their differences in social rank. They formed a sort of political-economic partnership. Political and military activities were monopolized by the nobles. The production of economic resources by manual labor was the function of the peasants. To this realm of agricultural production, in which the peasant was pre-eminent, we now turn our attention.

THE LATE ROMAN VILLA — Medieval agriculture had two outstanding characteristics that differentiate it sharply from that of modern times. It was machineless, and it was co-operative. The first of these characteristics has been common to most ages, for until comparatively recent years, agriculturists have been forced to depend almost entirely on animal and man power. In this respect the Middle Ages were similar to other early periods of social evolution. The methods of plowing, planting, and reaping were essentially the same in ancient Rome, medieval Europe, and early America.

More distinctive was the co-operative nature of medieval agriculture. Peasants lived and worked, not on individual home-farms, but in rural communities on large estates called villas, villes, or manors. This was necessary for two reasons. In a machineless age, co-operative labor was essential in those agricultural activities which demanded more man power than one family could provide. Furthermore, the needs of defense in a lawless age of ineffective governmental action forced men to live in large groups. As in the case of the political aspects of feudalism, this co-operative type of community life was not a medieval invention. Under similar conditions it has existed in many ages. It arose in the West as a result of the decentralization of Roman civilization during late imperial times, and was the inevitable method of economic organization under such conditions.

Whenever a highly developed society marked by bureaucratic government and urban centers breaks down, government and economic activities tend to become localized and rural. Without an efficient central government, the commercial and industrial life of large cities gives way to agricultural life in co-operative communities. It was tendencies of this kind that produced the great rural estates of the Roman Empire during the third, fourth, and fifth centuries.

We have already noted that the independent rural villas of the nobility of the late Roman Empire arose as a result of the decline of a centralized system of economic and political life. A self-supporting self-governing villa, with its noble proprietor and his community of dependent tenants and serfs, could flourish even amid the unsettled conditions of the age. It was compact, easy to defend, and simple to operate. It was unaffected by invasions and civil wars in neighboring regions, by interruption of communications, and by lack of transportation facilities. So long as such conditions continued, villa life continued. It stood the test of the barbarian invasions and was taken over in more or less modified form by the Germanic conquerors.

GERMANIC
INFLUENCES

The barbarian invasions of the Western provinces did not destroy the Roman villa. When the conquering Germans occupied Roman villas, they made little change in the economic organization. In many cases, the Roman proprietors and their estates were left intact, save for the acknowledgment by the Romans of the overlordship of the new rulers. This was particularly true in the southern provinces. From southern Gaul after the Germanic conquest of the fifth century we have glimpses of the undisturbed villa life of the Roman nobility. The letters of Sidonius, a former imperial official who became bishop of Auvergne, give a surprising and delightful picture of aristocratic life on the Roman villas in this German-controlled territory. These country gentlemen had all the comforts that could be desired: games, boating, baths, sun rooms, expansive views, banquets with music and dancing, and well-stocked libraries where one could dip into the writings of classical authors. Each villa was a self-supporting estate with a community of semifree artisans, servants, and agricultural laborers. Obviously such luxuries were not universal, nor could they continue for long in an age of war and invasion.

In backward regions, and further north, as Roman influences

weakened, rural life became more primitive. In his *History of the Franks,* written just about a century after Sidonius, Gregory of Tours (in central Gaul), gives a very different picture. Life among the Frankish nobility was less luxurious, and members of the lower classes were treated with extreme brutality. But the organization of agricultural economy was essentially the same as in earlier times in the Roman regions of the South. The ruling class still lived on rural estates, worked by a dependent peasantry. Throughout the early Middle Ages this same general system of rural economy continued with only minor modifications.

The Germanic peoples before their settlement in the Roman Empire had lived as freemen in democratic communities, but in the process of settling conquered territory they developed agricultural institutions that were quite similar to those of the late Roman villa. It seems that the primitive and localized conditions of existence in this age forced Romans and Germans to adopt the same general type of agricultural economy—large estates controlled by a noble aristocracy and worked by communities of semifree peasant tenants. Within a century after the Germanic invasions there was little distinction between the two races and the differences that developed in economic institutions were due to variations in local conditions rather than in racial inheritance.

THE MEDIEVAL
VILLA-MANOR
Throughout the Merovingian and Carolingian periods the trend of Western life was the same. Society came to be organized more and more around the self-supporting agricultural community, which was still referred to as a villa. Interesting and important evidence of this tendency is to be found in the records of the age of Charles the Great. Even though Charles was able to counteract the decentralization of political life, he made no effort to modify existing economic institutions. His own revenues consisted for the most part of the products of rural villas. His capitulary "concerning the villas" (*de villis*) gives a vivid picture of the manner in which an enterprising landlord was forced to organize his agricultural resources in order to have a constant and adequate income. Everything from wine, grain, and livestock to tools and counterpanes was carefully recorded and reported by the overseers.

During the period of anarchy and invasion that accompanied the disintegration of the Carolingian Empire, the villa system became almost universal. As in the case of political feudalism, it had long been in the making. Now the conditions were ripe for it to dominate the economic life of the West. By the ninth century the villa had become a distinctly medieval institution, neither Roman nor German in character. It had attained the general character which it was to maintain throughout most of the Middle Ages. In some regions it had even taken on a new name, *manor,* which is still commonly used to differentiate the medieval from the Roman villa.[2] In order to understand something of the nature of this most important of economic institutions of the early Middle Ages, we turn now to a detailed description of the manor as it existed from this period well into modern times. There were so many local variations in custom and organization and the existing evidence is so uncertain that we can do little more than establish a general pattern which roughly illustrates the probable situation in most regions and centuries.

THE TYPICAL MANOR   Though no two manors were exactly alike, the following features were doubtless present in the majority of cases. The center was a farm village where the noble lord, or his overseer, and the peasants lived. Here was the lord's private demesne, consisting of (1) an enclosure of some kind containing a manor house, barns, granaries, bake houses, and so on, and (2) the lord's private fields.

The manor house of a large estate on which the lord himself resided was usually a well-equipped, fortified building, sometimes a wooden castle on a small scale. On a small manor managed by a steward it might be a simple farmhouse such as is described in an early English manuscript:

[there is] a sufficient and handsome hall [i.e., house] well ceiled with oak. On the western side is a worthy bed, on the ground a stone chimney, a wardrobe, and a certain other small chamber; at the eastern end is a pantry and a buttery. Between the hall and the chapel is a side room. There is a decent chapel covered with tiles, a portable altar, and a small cross. In the hall are four tables on trestles. There are likewise a good kitchen well covered with tiles, with a furnace and ovens, one large, the other small, for cakes, two tables, and alongside the kitchen a small house for baking. Also a new granary covered with oak shingles, and a . . . dairy. . . . Likewise a chamber suited for clergymen and a necessary chamber. Also a henhouse. These are within the inner gate.[3]

2 The Latin word *villa* still persists in the French term for manor (*ville*) and in the name *villein,* used of certain classes of peasants. We shall use the term *manor* for all such institutions after the Carolingian age.

3 Robinson, *Readings in European History,* Ginn and Company, I, 404.

As indicated in this account, near the manor house were barns, granaries, a garden, an orchard, and buildings for spinning, weaving, baking, brewing, winemaking, and blacksmithing. Near by, on a stream of running water, there might be a mill. Not until the age of the crusades did Westerners use wind mills. All such apparatus was the lord's property and for the use of his equipment the peasants paid him a portion of the bread, wine, or meal that they made. The lord's private fields and pasture lands were usually enclosed by hedges, or a palisade (there was no such thing as barbed wire, or even rail fencing, in those days). He also had portions of the common fields and meadows. On or near the lord's demesne there might be a parish church or chapel with a house and fields for the support of the priest.

The peasants lived in small cottages, usually clustered together into a sort of village somewhere near the lord's demesne. This gave them the protection of his enclosure and the use of his ovens and other such mechanical equipment, when needed. Thus they had not only defense, but also the advantage of co-operative labor and sociability. Many of the peasant houses had garden plots and perhaps rough shelters for pigs, chickens, and other animals. There was considerable variation in the appearance of the homes of the peasantry. Many of them were wretched one-roomed huts with thatched roofs, dirt floors, no windows or chimneys, and little furniture. On the other hand, some of the better-class peasants might live as did a German farmer named Helmbrecht who could boast of a house in which there was a stove and a "soft bed" with a "bolster and a soft pillow."

THE LAND OF
THE MANOR
The lands of the peasants were grouped together into co-operative units in which each was a shareholder in accordance with his tenure rights. Pastureland and some wasteland were held in common, and all the cattle, sheep, and pigs ran at large thereon. Each peasant had his proportional share of pasturage, firewood, and other rights. The meadows were also a unit, though individual portions were usually allotted to the various peasants until the hay had been cut. The cultivated land was also arranged in group units. In each field, each peasant had one or more portions, usually long narrow strips, separated by double furrows or by unplowed sod. Generally the lord and the priest also had strips in the various fields. The farming on a given field was done co-operatively, all who had crops working together, usually at the same time. This was necessary because no one peasant had enough oxen and equipment to complete his plowing or harvesting at the ap-

propriate time. On a small manor there might be only one plow, a heavy wooden affair with an iron point. It might take several yoke of oxen, hitched together, for heavy plowing. Often the plow and plow-

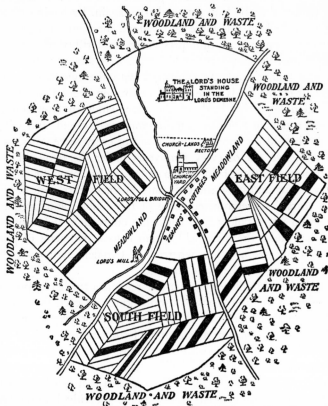

From Allson, *Introduction to English Industrial History,* Macmillan and G. Bell and Sons.

PLAN OF A MANORIAL VILLAGE SHOWING THE STRIP-FIELD SYSTEM

oxen were owned jointly by several peasants. Furthermore, in harvesting the crops, joint activity was a protection against thievery by the shiftless peasant who might be tempted to help himself to the produce on neighboring strips of land.

In the early Middle Ages the average manor had two distinct sets of fields: one in crops, the other lying fallow so as to recover its fertility. Later, an important improvement, the three-field system, came into common use. A given field was planted with a spring crop, such as oats or barley. After harvest it would be left uncropped for the following year so that the cattle could feed on it and fertilize it with manure. The next fall it would be planted with a winter crop such as rye or wheat; then back to oats or barley again. By having three sets of fields worked on this three-shift system, the crop on a given field was changed every year, thus preserving the fertility of the soil. At the same time, the peasants would always have summer crops, winter crops, and fallow land. As compared with the two-field system in which half of the fields were out of cultivation every year, the three-field system kept two-thirds of the plow lands in crop constantly. This was a double advantage; more crops were raised, and with less work. Each field produced crops two out of every *three* years, as compared with two out of every *four* years under the two-field system. Furthermore, the three-field system called for less plowing, since each field lay fallow and grew sod only once in three years, instead of once in two years. This eliminated some of the double plowing that was necessary to put a fallow field back into cultivation. It has been estimated that under the three-field system it took two acres of plowing to produce an acre of crops, whereas the two-field system took three acres of plowing for the same amount.

Late in the Middle Ages, in a few regions a further improvement was made: by rotating crops of various kinds on each field, the land was kept in cultivation all of the time without ever lying fallow. There was also some improvement in fertilization, especially by the use of materials such as marl. For the most part, however, except for the introduction of the three-field system, medieval agriculture was primitive and progress was slow. The very fact that fields were usually worked in common tended to discourage individual initiative and new ideas. This was particularly true with respect to improvements in breeds of animals. All were pastured together, on the tilled fields after harvest, on the fallow fields, on the meadows after the hay had been cut, and on the common pasture which consisted of wasteland such as marshes and woods. Inasmuch as all the flocks and herds ran at large, there was little inducement for any individual to improve the breed of his stock.

THE PEOPLE
OF THE MANOR
    The variety of people on the average manor was quite as complex as the variety of lands. Although there were many classes of peasants, depending on the amount of land they held and the terms of tenure, they can be

grouped into two general divisions, the so-called "freeman" and the serfs. The standard amount of land worked by a given freeman or serf was called a virgate and approximated thirty acres, scattered in strips in the various fields. A peasant might, however, hold only a half-virgate, or a quarter, and so on. He had rights to meadow land and pasturage, and likewise obligations in proportion. His virgate determined his economic position as a shareholder in the community. His quality of tenure determined his social position, as a freeman or serf.

The "freemen," comprising the lord's manorial officials, the free holders and the free tenants, were not free from all dues, services, and other manorial restrictions. They were merely peasants of free status whose dues and services were restricted by a definite contract which in theory at least was enforceable at law. Most freemen had lighter burdens than the serfs, but they were bound to perform certain services and were subject to the lord's authority. Freedom on a medieval manor was a relative matter. Very few even of the freeholders were entirely free to do as they pleased with their holdings. The lord's steward (the bailiff) and some of the higher class of peasants, such as the miller, the smith, and other skilled artisans, were free from all or a part of the ordinary servile dues and restrictions. Some of these freemen might even own their farm lands. Others might be free *tenants* who occupied portions of the lord's land on a rental or crop-sharing basis. By the fourteenth century most of the peasants in France and England had become free tenants, but they were still subject to many burdensome payments and restrictions.

In earlier times the majority of the inhabitants of most manors were semifree serfs, or villeins.[4] The serf had no free status and was held in absolute subjection to the lord. The villein, in theory at least, was free as to his person. Both held land from which they could not be evicted as long as they paid the customary dues and services. Thus in spite of his lowly position and restricted rights, even the serf enjoyed a measure of security. The lord of the manor was bound by unwritten custom, as well as by self-interest, to protect his peasants from ravages, to provide certain kinds of manorial equipment, to assure them their proper use of the common meadow and pasture land, and to guarantee their holdings to their legal heirs. In

4 In England *villein* and *serf* were practically synonymous. In France the villein was of slightly higher rank. Technically the serf was the property of the lord, whereas the villein was legally free as to his person.

addition to the villeins and serfs, most manors had groups of folk called borderers, cotters, or crofters, who lived like squatters on the borders of the village and eked out an existence by doing odd jobs or working small plots of land.

Each manor had a court to which any peasant could appeal for the enforcement of the customs of the manor against his fellows. On the other hand, the peasantry could not enforce their rights against the lord in the same fashion as the noble vassal could in a feudal court. The lord of a manor might, if he chose, violate most servile rights. In actual practice, however, in his own interests the lord was likely to see to it that his tenants were well treated in order that they might remain with him to till the soil and provide him with the necessities of life. His problem was to exploit them as much as possible without destroying their efficiency. As it was, the free tenants, serfs, and various other ranks of peasants paid such burdensome dues and services that many of them had little more for themselves than a bare subsistence.

PEASANT OBLIGATIONS So far as payments were concerned, the free peasants and serfs were subject to poll taxes, rents for their strips of land, fines for infractions of manorial custom, fees for the use of the lord's ovens, wine presses, and so on, tolls for market privileges, and worst of all, a general tax, called the *taille* (*tallagium*). The *taille* was particularly burdensome because it was not a fixed payment. For certain classes of peasants, payments were restricted by the terms of their tenure, but most serfs were "tallageable at the lord's will." For them it was an unlimited tax. Until the later Middle Ages all such dues were paid in produce (pigs, chickens, grain, and the like).

In addition to payments of produce, the serfs were compelled to work for the lord. Two or three days a week (and sometimes as many as five) they labored on his private fields, plowing or harrowing; at harvest time they did extra "boon" work. Then there were the hated "corvees," mass labor for the repair of roads, the digging of ditches, or even the building of castles. The serf was also bound down by other burdensome restrictions. He could not marry without the lord's permission and, in case the girl was from another manor, he must pay a fee, the *maritagium,* or *merchet*. The removal of a serf from an estate was an economic loss and must be paid for.

When a serf died, his son inherited his property, but only after

OVERSEER AND REAPERS

Both from Mss. in the British Museum

PLOWING

From Dorez, Les manuscrits à peinture de Lord Leicester, *Leroux*

HERDSMEN

From Steinhausen

HARVESTING GRAIN

MANOR LIFE

(See pp. 243 ff.)

MANOR YARD, SHOWING VARIOUS AGRICULTURAL ACTIVITIES

MANOR LIFE

(See pp. 243 ff.)

the payment of heavy inheritance taxes, the *heriot* for the personal property, and the *relief* for the lands. An English manorial record summarizes the obligations of a group of its serfs as follows:

And it is to be noted that none of the above-named villeins can give their daughters in marriage, nor cause their sons to be tonsured [i.e., become clergymen], nor can they cut down timber growing on the lands they hold. . . . And after the death of any one of the aforesaid villeins, the lord shall have as a heriot his best animal, if he had any; if however, he have no living beast, the lord shall have no heriot, as they say. The sons or daughters of the aforesaid villeins shall give, for entrance into the holding . . . , as much as they give of rent per year.[5]

PEASANT LIFE   Much has been written and spoken concerning the harsh and cruel conditions of peasant life. Modern writers have described in vivid detail the "damp forests" frequented by "packs of wolves" who struck terror to inhabitants even of cities such as Paris, to say nothing of the lonely herdsmen who slept in the open with their flocks. Caterpillars, grasshoppers, tidal waves, drought, incessant rains, and the ravages of warfare also added to the hardships of rural people. Of all these catastrophes, famine is the one most commonly referred to in the contemporary records. To make matters worse, barons and merchants often exploited such situations mercilessly. For instance, at the time of the first crusade the peasants were said to have been forced to eat roots, wild herbs, and (according to some accounts) even human flesh. This was not solely because of local famines, but through the actions of "avaricious merchants who, *according to their custom,* speculated upon the misery of all." In times of warfare, also, the defenseless peasantry suffered more than the rest of the population. It is well to note that the Peace of God aimed at the betterment of this condition.[6] One modern French writer has asserted that "the peasant was merely a creature to exploit at home and to destroy abroad."

To a certain extent this pessimistic view of medieval peasant life is supported by much of the contemporary evidence from pictorial and written sources. The sculpturing and stained glass windows of the churches, and the illustrations in most medieval manuscripts portray the serf as a low and brutish type of human being. An eleventh-

[5] Robinson, *Readings in European History,* Ginn and Company, I, 402.
[6] See below, p. 498.

century French writer described the Bretons as "dwellers in pastures who live on milk, keep cattle, and smell like them; who have ten wives and forty children apiece, and whose tribal chieftains have coarse uncombed hair." In French romantic literature, such for instance as *Aucassin and Nicolette,* the peasant was pictured as "tall, marvellously ugly and hideous. His huge head was black as charcoal, his eyes set a handbreadth apart. He had big cheeks, a broad flat nose, thick lips redder than a collop, and ugly yellow teeth. He wore leggings and shoes of bull's hide, bound around with cords of bark, and leaned on a big club."

A German poet wrote of a certain peasant "a brutish fellow named Ber, tall and broad-shouldered" who went about "snarling like a bear. . . . Whoever you are, keep out of his way." A thirteenth-century Englishman mentioned "the ugly boorish laborers who moved with great din and heavy trampling, their coarse eyes twinkling and looking and staring about." As late as Chaucer's day, English peasants, even of the better sort, were pictured in uncomplimentary terms. One of his characters was "a dangerous fellow, his skull as bald as an ape's, his face round, and his nose a pug"; another was a great strong man "a loud prater, a ribald jester, who knew well how to steal corn." As for the reeve, he was "a slender bilious man" with "legs full long and lean like a stick."

But there are illustrated manuscripts and written accounts that present other types of peasant: serfs who feasted, danced, sang, and played games. The brutish creature driven to despair by baronial tyranny does not tell the whole story.

There were famines throughout the Middle Ages, but most of the time most of the peasantry had plenty of plain food. Contemporary accounts mention porridge, meats such as bacon, fowl, salt pork, and fish; vegetables such as cabbage, sauerkraut, peas, beans, onions, and various fruits; cheeses, black rye bread, honey, butter, and drinks such as ale, beer, cider, and wine. Peasants were scorned for their habit of loosening their belts at meals, or blowing the foam off their beer. *Piers the Plowman,* in the fourteenth century, complained because he had no pullets, geese, pigs, salt bacon, or eggs; but he had "cheese, curds, cream, an oat cake, two loaves of beans and bran baked for the children"; also "parsley, leeks, and many cabbages." Evidently there were English peasants who had plenty of vegetables but little meat. One twelfth-century manorial record, listing the extra labor rendered by certain peasants, reveals that the work done by several of the peasants was actually worth less than the meals furnished them by the lord.

Even at work the peasant was seldom a persecuted bond servant driven by a merciless taskmaster. Illustrated medieval calendars, portraying scenes of plowing, sowing, and harvesting, often show one or two serfs at work, with several eating or resting in the shade. It seems that the co-operative nature of manorial agriculture tended to make peasant labor more or less of a sociable affair like the old-fashioned American "barn raising" or "corn shucking."

The medieval peasant worked from sunup to sundown, but not every day of the year. In addition to fifty-two Sundays, on which it was forbidden to do manual labor, there were about as many more holy days (which meant holidays), to say nothing of prolonged merrymaking at Christmas and Easter. Attendance at church, as in modern rural communities, was also a social occasion—a time for gossip, courting, and the like. Many a clergyman was blamed for joining with his parishioners, as did a certain priest, "in celebrating the day of Saints Peter and Paul with music and dance." The annual pilgrimages of parishioners to their bishop's church, like the early American camp meetings, were often more of a gay excursion than a deep religious experience. Such constantly recurring religious activities lightened the drab routine of peasant life.

Then there were distinctly nonreligious activities, village festivities, market days, fairs, courting, and Maypole dances. A thirteenth-century Bavarian poem gives several interesting glimpses of the frolicsome side of peasant life. One of the popular sports seems to have been "passing ball," a game in which one of the rustic lads

darts here and there, flying and chasing and playing tricks with the ball. . . . What pretty speeches the girls make to him; how they shriek, how wild they get . . . they stretch out their hands . . . [saying] "now throw it to me." . . . In the scrimmage some of them get pushed down. . . . Eppe, the prettiest one, . . . picks herself up, tosses the ball into the air, everybody screams, "catch it! catch it"; but no girl can play better than she; she judges the ball so well, and is so sure at catching it.

In the dance, however, the poet pictures the peasants, especially the rustic swains, of whom he was evidently jealous, as awkward upstarts.

Look at Engelmar [he wrote] how high he holds his head . . . he is a poor gawk with a rough head; he puffs himself out like a stuffed pigeon

. . . how proud he is of his new jacket with its four and twenty small pieces of cloth and the sleeves coming down over his hand. . . . There are two other peasants wearing coats of Austrian cloth of court style. [Others of the overdressed rustics roused the poet to even bitterer scorn.] . . . Their cloaks are superior to their social rank. They wear small coats and small cloaks; red hoods, shoes with buckles, and black hose. They have on silk pouches in which they carry pieces of ginger, so as to make themselves popular with the girls. They wear their hair long, a privilege of the well born; they put on gloves that come up to their elbows. One had a fustian jacket, green as grass; another flaunts it in red. Still another carries a sword as long as a hemp flail . . . and the knob of its hilt has a mirror in which he makes the girls look at themselves. . . . Poor clumsy louts, how can the girls endure them? One tears his partner's veil. . . . Their awkward feet tread on the girls' skirts, and even drag them off. But they are more than clumsy. They have an offensive horseplay, a kind of pleasantry that is positively insulting. They put their hands in wrong places, and one of them tries to get a maiden's ring, actually wrenching it from her finger.[7]

Such accounts, along with the manuscript illustrations of frolicsome peasant life, lead one to conclude that medieval farm folk had fun and frolic as well as work and suffering.

THE PLACE OF THE MANOR IN MEDIEVAL LIFE
The chief advantages of the manorial system were its suitability to the disorganized conditions of the feudal age. Each manor tended to be a self-supporting unit providing the bulk of the necessities of life for its population. A lord could hold many or few manors, and could add to his possessions or diminish them with no difficulty since each was a self-supporting unit. Management also was simple: a resident steward could supervise the manor, since all that was necessary was to see to it that the lord's income was collected. The routine of agriculture was so primitive that it practically regulated itself. The court of the manor handled the allotment of lands and settled all minor differences among the local peasantry.

The disadvantages appeared when the needs of the nobility transcended the primitive standards of rural life. The products of the manor were simple and limited in amount. It was difficult to concentrate the produce from all of a lord's manors at one point, such as his central castle. Often great landlords with extensive retinues of followers found it necessary to move from manor to manor, remaining at

[7] Adapted from McLaughlin, *Studies in Medieval Life and Literature,* G. P. Putnam's Sons, p. 75.

one estate only as long as the provisions held out. A certain French lord was considered extremely wealthy because he possessed so many castles and estates that, if he chose, he had one for each day in the year. Transportation of agricultural products, at best, was cumbersome, and usually means of communication were bad. A crop failure in a restricted region meant famine, even though neighboring regions were plentifully supplied.

Finally the very simplicity and self-sufficiency of the manor made it unprogressive. It was suitable only to a small-scale localized type of life. It tended to perpetuate the backwardness of rural communities, and until Western Europe evolved a business economy to supplement that of the manor, and a nonservile type of agriculture, civilization's advancement was slow and painful. The business economy of the towns, which began to develop late in the tenth century, will be described in a later chapter. The rise of the peasantry from serfdom followed the rise of the towns and was dependent on the rapid development of industry and trade in the twelfth and thirteenth centuries. Industry, trade, and towns meant expanding markets for agricultural produce. In Italy, England, and France, as we shall see later, the medieval system of agriculture gave way rapidly. In other parts of Europe, notably the Germanies and Russia, it continued with little modification well into the nineteenth century.

⸺ XIII ⸺

LEARNING AND LITERATURE TO THE NINTH CENTURY

BACKGROUNDS OF MEDIEVAL CULTURE

THE history of medieval culture[1] is marked by strong prejudices and sharp controversies. Until comparatively recent times the great majority of scholars have inclined to a very derogatory point of view concerning the intellectual and artistic achievements of the Middle Ages. They held that the entire Middle Ages were conspicuous for cultural backwardness, and they called them the "Dark Ages." Within the past century, however, a more realistic appreciation of Gothic art, medieval romantic literature, the poetry of the troubadours, and the intellectual achievements of the university men has changed this attitude considerably. Yet all of these cultural contributions are products of the *later* medieval centuries (after 1000), and as a result the reputed backwardness of the period has come to be limited to the *early* Middle Ages. Many scholars, however, believe that as painstaking researches reveal more information the present conception of the early centuries as a Dark Age will undergo change.

It will be our endeavor to interpret early medieval culture as an expression of the life of a growing people. We shall consider it as one of the many aspects of the new Roman-Christian-Germanic society, and not as an isolated phenomenon to be condemned or praised as it compares favorably or unfavorably with ancient or modern standards. Even to those who insist on the essential darkness of early medieval culture, it must be evident that such comparisons are not very fruitful. The Franks of Charles the Great's day, as compared with their nomadic ancestors in the swamps and forests of Germany, were highly civilized and had made great cultural progress. On the other hand, in comparison with the inhabitants of the Byzantine Empire and the Moslem realms, they had an inferior culture. Our primary purpose

[1] In this discussion we use the term *culture* with reference to the nonmaterial aspects of civilization—literature, learning, education, and the fine arts.

is not to compare Western culture with that of other peoples, but to analyze its growth in such a manner as to show how it developed its distinctive characteristics.

THE ELEMENTS OF MEDIEVAL CULTURE   Early medieval civilization took shape in the West during the same five centuries (500 to 1000) in which Constantinople became the center of East-Roman or Byzantine life, and in which the Moslems established themselves at both ends of the Mediterranean, with Cordova in Spain rivaling Bagdad and Cairo in artistic and literary achievements. In comparison with the brilliant Moslem and Byzantine civilizations, the culture of the West during this period was insignificant. At the outset, it consisted of three elements of cultural importance: (1) the remnants of declining *Roman* civilization; (2) the religious enthusiasm of a *Christianity* that was opposed to purely intellectual influences; and (3) the vigorous but primitive cultures of various *Germanic* peoples. It was these three elements, rather than the more highly developed cultures of contemporary Islam and Constantinople, that dominated the West during the early Middle Ages.

Western cultural inferiority was due not so much to its heredity as to the conditions of life under which it grew up. Isolation and ruralism are the keys to the history of the early Middle Ages. After the fifth century, the West had no large cities and none of the far-reaching political, economic, and social relationships which make for the unity and progress of civilization. Along with the steady decline of political unity and the means of economic exchange, all phases of life became rural, rustic, and unprogressive. The laity took little interest in literature and the arts; the nobility were busied with military and political problems, the peasantry were burdened with the unending labor of the manor. Even cultured men living in the country villas or monasteries of the West lacked the stimulation and competition that goes with cosmopolitan city life. For centuries almost all cultural life was sponsored and carried on by the monastic clergy in isolated rural retreats. During periods of invasion and civil warfare, many of these centers of intellectual life were destroyed. Even under favorable conditions they were few and far between.

For at least five centuries (from about 500-1000), culture was on the defensive in the West. But it did not disappear, and in isolated centers it took deep root. Meanwhile under clerical domination and royal patronage, Western culture developed a sturdy unity of purpose that made for stability and strength, even though it discouraged individual initiative. Finally, in the last five centuries of the Middle Ages, as expanding commerce, town life, and monarchical government provided favorable opportunities, this typically Western culture made remarkable progress. The early medieval period, therefore, is apparently unproductive but it constitutes at the same time a very important stage in the history of Western culture. In it three types of cultural life (Roman, Christian, and Germanic) were welded into one, and were tempered by the fires of adversity for the task of laying the foundations of modern civilization.

We shall now survey briefly each of the three major elements that went into the making of early medieval culture, and then trace the process by which they were blended into the distinctive type of thought and expression which we call medieval.

THE CLASSICAL
ELEMENT
From what has been said in another connection [2] it is clear that the roots of Western culture were diverse and lay buried deep in Europe's past. We have already discussed Roman culture and the decline in intellectual and artistic attainment from the Golden Age through the third century and to the downfall of the Western Empire. In the East, classical culture continued with a splendor that was reminiscent of old Roman days, but this Greek-Oriental culture belongs to the history of the East-Roman or Byzantine Empire. In the West, by the year 500, classical literature, learning, and art, along with other aspects of civilization, were in a state of decline. The Western Empire had given way to a group of independent regional units ruled by Germanic kings, local landlords, and Christian bishops. The comparatively sudden change from imperial to local government was a severe blow to the cultural as well as the political life of the West.

The barbarian rulers and the Christian clergy did not destroy classical culture; neither did they provide conditions that were favorable to its continued prosperity. Roman culture was the product of flourishing cities, and the disintegration of imperial government in the West was a crowning disaster to an already declining city life. As time passed there were fewer and fewer centers of population, wealth, and cultural inspiration, and those centers which existed were dominated by new interests, Germanic and Christian. At the court of a Germanic ruler there was little demand for classical literature and art. The Germans had their own native culture, which asserted itself vigorously. In like manner, Christian monasteries and episcopal cen-

[2] See above, pp. 38-54.

ters emphasized new nonpagan ideals, which were opposed to the antique culture of Ciceronian or Vergilian days. Even though the Christianized Romans and the Romanized Germans assimilated and preserved much of classical culture, henceforth it was bound to be a minor factor. To those modern scholars who consider classical ideals the highest standard of culture, this trend spells deep tragedy. But there were other cultural influences which were more important to the people of that day than the poetry of a Vergil or the sculpture of a Phidias.

THE GERMANIC ELEMENT   We turn now to these new and more vital forces that were destined to dominate the feeble and superficial classicism of the late empire. The energetic spirit of Christianity and Germanic barbarism, though crude and primitive in contrast with the sophisticated ideals of the ancient world, eventually produced a progressive culture. Out of it have come many permanent elements of modern civilization.

We have already noted certain literary and artistic productions of the early Germanic tribes.[3] Until the end of the period of warfare and conquest, Germanic culture had little permanence, and when the Germanic tribes settled in the Roman Empire their culture was overshadowed by the better-established cultures of the imperial centers. Only in the Northern regions, where the Germans predominated, were their native arts and their poetical literature able to take permanent root. We shall later find that rulers of these regions, such as Charles the Great and Alfred the Great, collected some of the remnants of the literature of their Germanic ancestors. The modern languages of Germany, of the Rhineland, and of England still bear evidence of the strength of Germanic influences. Up to the time of the Norman Conquest, the language of England was Anglo-Saxon, a purely Germanic tongue. Further south, particularly in the lands bordering the Mediterranean, the Germanic peoples were in the minority. Here they consequently took on the language and culture of their Roman subjects. The Romance (Roman) languages of Spain, France, and Italy bear witness to this fact. There are also many instances of early Germanic rulers who showed their appreciation of classical culture by patronizing Roman writers and artists. In most of the Southern regions of the West the culture of the original Germanic invaders was lost in the dominant classical-Christian civilization of the late empire.

[3] See above, p. 138.

THE CHRISTIAN ELEMENT
Of the three outstanding cultural elements in the West at the end of the fifth century, that of Christianity was the most vital. Its influence so overshadowed all others that we must consider it in detail. From the beginning the Christians had their own cultural standards, which were strongly anticlassical. In a manual for Christian clergymen, from the early centuries we find the following instructions:

Abstain from all the heathen [pagan] books. . . . If thou hast a mind to read history thou hast the books of the Kings; if books of wisdom or poetry thou hast those of the prophets, or Job, and the Proverbs, in which thou wilt find greater depths of sagacity than in all the heathen poets and sophisters, because these are the words of the Lord the only wise God. If thou desirest something to sing thou hast the Psalms; if the origin of things thou hast Genesis; if laws and statutes, thou hast the glorious law of the Lord God.[4]

But because Christianity grew up in the Roman Empire it was strongly influenced by the literature and art of classical antiquity. The architecture and much of the decoration of the Christian churches were classical.

The first great leaders of Christian thought in the West (Lactantius, Cyprian, Tertullian, Ambrose, Augustine, and Jerome)[5] were trained in Roman schools according to classical educational standards. These "Fathers" of Roman Catholic theology, even though they were sworn enemies of paganism, could not escape their classical heritage. In spite of Jerome's determination to be a Christian rather than a "Ciceronian," his writings were generously spiced with quoted fragments from pagan literature.

CHRISTIAN POETRY
It was in the outward forms of learning and literature that classical influences persisted most strongly. The subject matter revealed unmistakably the rising tide of Christianity. This is clearly shown in the field of epic poetry. From the fourth century onward, poetical narrative was almost entirely dedicated to Biblical history and to tales of Christian martyrs; the mythological heroes of classical antiquity were relegated to the background. The most popular portions of the Old and New Testament were done over into poetical form again and again. A fourth-century noblewoman went so far as to compile a patchwork poem

[4] *The Apostolical Constitutions*, I, 6; in Cubberley, *Readings in the History of Education*, Houghton Mifflin Company, pp. 54 f.
[5] See above, pp. 68 ff.

of Bible history out of excerpts from Vergil. A century later the Biblical story of the creation and the fall of man, arranged according to the
"Paradise Lost" theme, was set forth in poetical form. Other Bible
themes were likewise used, often with a success more pious than
poetical. Such was the "Paschal Hymn" of Sedulius, an allegorical
poem concerning miracles, particularly those of Christ's passion.

PAULINUS   In much the same way the saintly martyrs of the
early Christian centuries were glorified in epics and
ballads. Often this was done by some cleric poet of the church which
had adopted the martyr as its patron saint. Thus the life, festivals, and
miracles of St. Felix of Nola in southern Italy were commemorated
by the songs of Paulinus (d. 431), a wealthy Roman who, on accepting Christianity, retired from public life to serve as priest of this
small parish church.

Paulinus had been one of the favorite pupils of Ausonius, the
famous Roman professor of Bordeaux, and Ausonius never quite for-
gave him for deserting the world of cultured Roman aristocrats for
a rural Christian priesthood. The correspondence exchanged by them
as they drifted apart—much of it in poetical form—is not only an
interesting example of Christian and pagan poetry but a vivid commentary on the clash between classical and Christian ideals in this
era of rapid transition. Paulinus, for all his desertion of the cultured
Roman world, continued to write poetry that is rated even higher than
that of Ausonius and the other pagan classicists of his day. To Ausonius he wrote:

> In words of anger and love you rebuke me
> For being away from my native land for three long years,
> For choosing another part of the world . . .
> Forgetful of the life of refinement
> Spent with you in former days . . .
>
> Cease, I beg you, to wound your friend. . . .
> Even though time and space may separate us,
> Yet in mind and heart I shall ever be with you;
> Sooner will life itself depart from this body
> Than your image from my heart.[6]

His simple piety of spirit was harmoniously combined with unusual
beauty of expression. Among the poets of his age Paulinus is ranked

[6] Adapted from a prose translation, in Kuhnmuench, *Early Christian Latin Poets*,
Loyola University, pp. 214 ff.

second only to Prudentius, whose work we shall consider in greater detail.

PRUDENTIUS

Prudentius (d. ca. 410), the "Vergil and Horace combined" of early Christian poetry, was a Spaniard who wrote epic, lyric, and didactic poems with equal facility. Like Paulinus, he was a man of classical training. As an epic poet he is best known for his *Crowns of the Martyrs,* commemorating the deaths of fourteen famous martyrs. Although the subject matter was strictly Christian, the poetical framework was classical, with distinct traces of the style of the Augustan Age. Prudentius merely took the current martyr tales and clothed them in classical poetical form. In every story the Roman officials are cruel tormentors; the martyrs are high-minded long-suffering heroes, unmoved by the taunts of the persecutors. One of them banters with the men who are roasting him over a slow fire; another argues with the judge even after his tongue has been torn out. St. Eulalia, when urged to sacrifice to a pagan deity, spits in the official's face and knocks the idol to the ground. As she suffers death by fire, her soul mounts to Heaven in the form of a dove, and falling snow covers her mortal remains. Such tales, set forth in graceful classical form, took the place of the epics of pagan mythology.

In the realm of learned poetry Prudentius wrote several theological works in which he proved himself an able philosopher and a vigorous defender of the Christian faith, but he attained greater fame by his Christian lyrics. His *Daily Hymnal* is a collection of songs for various types of religious service—matins, vespers, burial services, and the like. In them the deepest religious sentiments were expressed in a style so graceful that at least one modern critic considers them more perfect in form than anything written since Vergil. Several of these hymns are still used in the Catholic service. The following verses suggest something of the emotional intensity and flowing style of his poetry:

> The toil of day is ebbing, The quiet comes again
> In slumber deep relaxing The limbs of tired men.
> And minds with anguish shaken, And spirits racked with grief
> The cup of all forgetting Have drunk and found relief.
> The still Lethean waters Now steal through the vein
> And men no more remember The meaning of their pain.

> Let, Let the weary body Lie sunk in slumber deep
> The heart shall still remember Christ in its very sleep.[7]

The Latin reads as follows:

> Fluxit labor diei, Redit et quietis hora,
> Blandus sopor vicissim Fessos relaxat artus.
> Mens aestuans procellis Curisque sauciata
> Totis bibit medullis Obliviale poclum.
> Serpit per omne corpus Lethaea vis, nec ullum
> Miseris doloris aegri Patitur manere sensum.

.   .   .   .   .   .

> Corpus licet fatiscens Jaceat recline paullum
> Christum tamen sub ipso Meditabimur sopore.

CLASSICAL AND CHRISTIAN LEARNING FUSED   The fusion (and sometimes confusion) that was brought about by the blending of Christianity and Roman classicism is illustrated in the careers of many men of the fourth and fifth centuries. There were classical scholars, such as Jerome, Augustine, Prudentius, and Paulinus, who, abandoning their earlier classical interests and attitudes, adopted a viewpoint completely Christian. Others, such as the Christian bishop, Apollinaris Sidonius of Auvergne (about 450), continued to live and write like Roman gentlemen of leisure.[8] Still more interesting is the manner in which certain of the invading Germanic chieftains adopted both the Christian and the classical elements of culture. An outstanding example is Theodoric "the Civilizer," Ostrogothic ruler of Italy after the downfall of the Western Empire. Under his generous patronage the arts and literature of both pagan and Christian Rome flourished. Classical learning, in particular, enjoyed a brief period of such vigor that it has been referred to as a "classical renascence."

BOETHIUS   Theodoric's reign was enlightened by such learned men as the classicist Boethius and the Christian scholar Cassiodorus. Boethius (d. 524) was a master of Greek and so thoroughly classical in his ideas that he has been called "the final flicker of ancient learning in the West." But this statement is more vivid than accurate. To be sure, his treatises on philosophy, logic, arithmetic, geometry, and music are reminiscent of the Roman literature of earlier centuries, but he represents more than "the decline and

---

[7] Waddell, *Mediaeval Latin Lyrics,* Constable, p. 43.
[8] See above, p. 241.

fall" of classical learning. Like his age, Boethius was a complex of
many characteristics. He represents not only the fading influence of
classical thought but also the rise of a new spirit and organization in
philosophical thought.

It has been said that he aimed at "nothing less than the transmission to his countrymen of all the works of Plato and Aristotle, and
the reconciliation of their apparently divergent views." Because of his
early and tragic death the task fell far short of accomplishment. He
translated most of Aristotle's works concerning logic, adding commentaries to several of them. But this material had less influence in
succeeding centuries than his translation of a commentary on Aristotle, written by the Neoplatonic philosopher Porphyry. Had Boethius
lived to complete his program of synthesizing Aristotelian and Platonic philosophy, he might have prevented much unintelligent theological repression of rationalistic thought during the early Middle
Ages. As it was, he put into circulation several substantial philosophical concepts, and suggested a rationalistic approach to the problems
of theology that was quite different from that of the Church Fathers.

During the early medieval centuries a few independent thinkers
followed in Boethius's footsteps. For the most part, however, their
intellectual position was too radical for a world of rough Germanic
rulers, pious Christian clergymen, and ignorant laymen. But the concepts persisted and finally, in the universities of the thirteenth century,
the scholastic thinkers carried the Boethian program to its logical
conclusion.[9]

"THE CONSOLA-
TION OF
PHILOSOPHY"
More famous than Boethius's translations of Aristotle
is his last work, *The Consolation of Philosophy,*
composed in a prison cell while its author awaited
execution for alleged treason against Theodoric's government. The *Consolation* is a curious assemblage of reflections, classical and original, in both prose and poetry, concerning the uncertainties of human life, especially as exemplified by his own tragic career.
Along with Socrates's last words, Marco Polo's *Travels, Pilgrim's
Progress,* More's *Utopia,* and Sir Walter Raleigh's *History of the
World,* it is a noteworthy example of "prison literature." It is also a
philosophical work that, according to modern classicists, "admits
Boethius to the company of Cicero" and warrants the title "the last
of the Roman philosophers." But the Middle Ages enrolled Boethius

[9] See below, p. 283, on John the Scot, and p. 665, on scholasticism.

among the Christian saints who had suffered martyrdom. Thus could medieval Christianity appropriate the heroes as well as the fruits of pagan philosophy.

CASSIODORUS   Contemporary with Boethius and, like him, an official at Theodoric's court, was Cassiodorus (d. ca. 585). He was, however, more fortunate in his public career: for over forty years he served the Gothic government, outliving both Boethius and Theodoric. He was also less of a pagan than Boethius. More than any other scholar of the early Middle Ages, Cassiodorus exemplifies the full blending of classical and Christian thought. While secretary of state to Theodoric, he wrote letters that were as stiltedly classical as those of any pagan Latinist of late Roman times. It was he who once asserted that "[literary] adornment alone distinguishes the learned from the unlearned." It was he who, after Theodoric's death, retired to his private estates and established a monastic retreat in which both secular and sacred, classical and Christian books were copied, preserved, and studied.[10]

THE BEGINNINGS OF MEDIEVAL CULTURE

Cassiodorus and his contemporaries of the sixth century, with all of their classicism, usher in a new cultural world. Not only had the hollow shell of imperial government disappeared, but the purely classical culture of Rome had gone, never to return. With the passing of Boethius, Christian ideals dominated Western culture. For a time it appeared as though classical influences might be entirely uprooted. Ever since the end of the fourth century, when Christianity became the state religion, certain of the more pious churchmen had urged the abolition of all classical learning, lest the minds of the rising generation of Christians be polluted by paganism.

This tendency has led certain modern scholars to see in the sixth century nothing but cultural decline. Here, they insist, are to be found not only "the eclipse of ancient literature," and "the graveyard of Latin literature," but also "the twilight of culture." The beginning of the century has been called "a plunge downward, its middle a ditch, its consummation a bottomless pit." Such opinions have a certain validity if restricted to classical culture and to certain regions, such as Italy, but they were not true of sixth-century culture as a whole. This age, like every other century of the Middle Ages, produced intelligent

[10] See above, p. 102.

scholars. They did not have the intellectual standards of earlier days, but many of them were familiar with Latin classical literature, and some were acquainted with Greek and Hebrew. Even among the churchmen of the West there were men who believed that Christian education demanded mentality as well as spirituality, and that secular classical studies tended to produce intelligent (and therefore good) Christians. Consequently secular classical subjects continued, even in the church schools. The seven liberal arts were studied as an integral though subordinate part of the education of Christian clergymen, and churchmen such as Cassiodorus and Isidore of Seville wrote textbooks for these subjects.

NEW CULTURAL STANDARDS The fact remains, however, that sixth-century culture was very different from that of the preceding century. The change, though not sudden, was very evident, especially in the aims and ideals of writers and artists. The chief reason for the change in intellectual standards was the fact that the West had ceased to be Roman, pagan, and cosmopolitan. The Roman imperial government had been replaced by Germanic kingdoms or tribal states; classical paganism had been overcome by the vigorous energy of Christianity; and the cosmopolitan life of flourishing cities had slowly given way to the rustic simplicity of rural villages.

Along with political and economic life, cultural activities followed the general trend; little was accomplished except in isolated centers and on a small scale. While Roman municipal schools, deprived of imperial support, were passing out of existence, centers of Christian education were arising in hundreds of monastic centers. Meanwhile Germanic kings, courtiers, and local landlords were replacing the Roman officials and aristocrats of imperial times as patrons of culture. The new culture, of necessity, followed the standards of the new patrons. In England, northern Gaul, and the Rhinelands, these standards were strongly Germanic. In southern Gaul, Italy, and Spain the classical influence was more prevalent. Everywhere, however, Christianity replaced Roman classicism as the dominating influence.

It is this distinctive change from imperial Roman to Christian-German domination that makes it possible for us to speak of the new culture of the West as medieval rather than ancient. For a millennium or more Western cultural life was to be shaped by the all-pervading influence of the Christian Church. Churchmen created the Christian-Germanic-classical culture which emerged during the fifth and sixth centuries, and thenceforth practically every writer, educator, and artist in the West was a member of the Christian clergy.

ITALIAN CUL-
TURAL DECLINE
For centuries the contrast in achievements between the old classical world and the struggling Germanic-Christian peoples of the West was strongly marked. In Italy, the former center of Mediterranean civilization, conditions were particularly bad. This was due very largely to the devastating warfare between Emperor Justinian's armies and the Ostrogoths, and to the subsequent inroads of the barbarous Lombards. Despite Cassiodorus' example of Christian intellectualism, most of the monasteries of this period forbade the reading of classical literature. Benedict of Nursia [11] drew up a monastic rule that permitted only religious reading, and very little of that.

Late in the same century, Pope Gregory I, one of the greatest intellects of the age, deliberately turned his back upon the liberal arts and reviled the classical works that he had studied in his youth. He sent a strict warning to one of his bishops forbidding the pollution of the minds of Christian students by the reading of classical poetry. "The same mouth [he asserted] cannot sing the praises of Jupiter and Christ." Gregory took the narrow principles of the orthodox Christian faith as his supreme intellectual guide. We have already considered in detail the writings by which he popularized this viewpoint.[12] Little wonder that his Italian contemporaries, and conscientious churchmen for centuries thereafter, tended to subordinate intelligence to piety and the classics to the Scriptures. Few Italians of this period wrote anything but works of pious erudition.

POETRY:
VENANTIUS
FORTUNATUS
It was not strange, then, that Venantius Fortunatus (d. ca. 600), an accomplished young Italian classicist of this era, deserted his native Ravenna for Gaul, where the Frankish court was already patronizing artists and writers. After a visit to the shrine of St. Martin of Tours in gratitude for a miracle of healing, he remained in Gaul. Here he became a sort of Frankish poet laureate, for he had remarkable success in adapting his talents to the rather crude intellectual standards of the Germanic courtiers. He wrote marriage hymns for royalty, panegyrics in praise of the living, and epitaphs for the dead. The following lines, taken from his verses written in praise of an influential patron, illustrate the manner in which he employed his poetical ability:

[11] See above, pp. 98 f.
[12] See above, pp. 86 f.

> Duke Bodegiset's presence is ravishing,
> His wife is like the Morning Star.

More sincere àre the occasional verses he dedicated to his friend and neighbor, ex-Queen Radegunde, who had retired from the intrigues of court life to a comfortable convent at Poitiers where Fortunatus was a priest, and later bishop.

The most famous of Fortunatus' compositions were hymns. Like Ambrose and Prudentius, he contributed several which have become permanent additions to the ritual of the church. One of these, entitled "The Banners of the King Advance" (*Vexilla regis prodeunt*), was written to commemorate the arrival from Constantinople of a relic comprising wood from the True Cross. Another, entitled "Extol O Tongue" (*Pange lingua gloriosa*), likewise glorifies the Cross of Christ in language that is filled with a warmth of religious emotion unlike that in any classical poetry. It reads (in part) as follows:

> Faithful Cross! above all other,
> One and only noble tree!
> None in foliage, none in blossom,
> None in fruit thy peers may be;
> Sweetest Wood and sweetest Iron!
> Sweetest Weight is hung on thee.

> Crux fidelis, inter omnes arbor una nobilis,
> Nulla talem silva profert flore, fronde, germine,
> Dulce lignum dulce clavo dulce pondus sustinens.[13]

Fortunatus is often called "the last of the classic poets," but the emotional fervor of his hymns and other religious poems marks him as a true representative of the dawning Middle Ages. Like many medieval men, he used classical modes of expression, but he filled the wine skins of classical poetry with the vigorous new wine of the Germanic-Christian West. The surprising thing is that a poet of his literary polish was appreciated by the Franks, a people who had so recently been converted from pagan barbarism.

HISTORY:
GREGORY OF
TOURS

Further evidence of the rapid development of the new culture in Frankish Gaul is found in the fact that during the sixth century this region produced a historian of note, Bishop Gregory of Tours (d. 594). His work, though somewhat primitive in form, is a pleasant contrast

---

[13] Kuhnmuench, *op. cit.*, p. 404.

to the propagandistic histories of Augustine and Orosius written more than a century before,[14] and to the crude *History of the Lombards,* written by a contemporary Italian bishop (Jordanes). Gregory's *History of the Franks* was an artlessly sincere narrative, dramatically interesting and intensely personal in viewpoint. Although he was prejudiced in his attitude toward religion, his fearless criticisms of the Frankish monarchs win our admiration. Most of the work dealt with Gregory's own century, for which it is a valuable source of information. He also wrote several religious biographies, among them a life of St. Martin of Tours, and an excellent treatise on astronomy.

Although Gregory enjoyed a great reputation in his own day, modern critics have tended to discount his intellect and that of his contemporaries. The pages of his history are filled with superstition and stories of violence and intrigue. The Latin in which he wrote is unclassical, and he expresses regret over his own errors in grammar, his "rustic style," and the conviction that "the love of learning has perished from among us." Such statements should not be taken too seriously, for, in spite of his modest pose, it is evident that Gregory was well educated and familiar with classical literature. Naturally he used the popular spoken Latin, which would be easily understood by his readers, rather than the Latin of classical times.

Of greater importance to our survey is the fact that he reflects clearly and with sincerity the spirit of the new Christian-Germanic culture. He and his age were superstitiously religious, enthusiastic to the point of violent prejudice, and disarmingly frank. The rustic qualities of strength, vigor, and even brutality were outstanding in that day. Frankish Gaul was still in a rough but vigorous stage of cultural progress. Roman classicism had given way before Christian influences and the primitive virility of a young race. As yet, the Franks did not have a highly developed culture, but they were making a start.

ENCYCLOPEDIAS:
ISIDORE
The outstanding Western scholar of the sixth century came from Spain, where Christian scholarship flourished under the patronage of the Visigothic kings. Isidore of Seville (d. 636) was only one of a long line of Spanish bishops who were intelligent as well as pious. He was well trained in the liberal arts, and the list of his writings is a noteworthy commentary on the sacred and secular learning of the day. In addition to numerous and varied religious works, he wrote several biographies,

---

[14] See above, p. 114.

two histories, a grammatical study, a scientific treatise *On the Nature of Things,* and the *Etymologies.*

The *Etymologies* was a medieval encyclopedia containing (as the author expressed it) "everything that ought to be known." It was the crowning glory of his, and of Spanish, scholarship, and was used in all parts of the West throughout the Middle Ages. The *Etymologies* contained a mass of information collected from Roman encyclopedias, classical authors, and Christian writings. It was rather loosely organized into sections that dealt with each of the seven liberal arts, with medicine, law, and theology, and with miscellaneous topics such as alphabets, man, animals, metals, and so on. The amazing thing about the work is the emphasis placed on classical learning. As one contemporary wrote, "he adapted his words to both the ignorant and the learned. . . . God raised him up . . . to revive the *works of the ancients* so that we might not grow duller from boorish rusticity." Thus, at a time when Pope Gregory the Great was turning his back on classical literature, scholars such as Isidore were eagerly collecting bits of learning from the past.

The information in Isidore's works is very superficial and inaccurate, but often this was quite as much the fault of the originals as of Isidore. Many of his most ludicrous passages were taken from classical works such as Pliny's *Natural History.*[15] On the other hand, it cannot be said that Isidore showed a very critical attitude toward the material from which he compiled his "scrapbook of information." There were many unnoticed contradictions, and often the explanations were superficial to the point of unintelligibility. In the *Etymologies,* so called because each item was explained by means of the origin or etymology of its name, there are passages that seem ridiculous to us. For example, the reader is told that

Man is called *homo* because he was made of earth (*humus*), as is told in Genesis . . . Bees (*apes*) are so called . . . because they are born without feet (*pes*) . . . The cat is called *catus* by the common folk because it captures (*captus*) mice. Others say because it sees (*catat*) . . . in the dark.[16]

Isidore's scientific information was characteristically medieval. He recognized in a vague way the sphericity of the earth, the movements

15 See above, p. 40.

16 Author's translation. For an abstract of the entire work, with translated excerpts, see Brehaut, "An Encyclopedist of the Dark Ages," *Studies in History, Economics, and Public Law,* Columbia University, 1912, XLVIII, especially pp. 215, 226.

of the planets, and the cause of eclipses. But he accepted without question the ancient idea of the earth as a fixed body about which the sun and the seven spheres of stars revolved. Like most medieval scholars he accepted as true all scriptural passages on scientific phenomena. On the other hand, he was surprisingly open-minded. Concerning the sky he wrote:

As to its shape, whether it covers the earth from above like a plate, or like an egg-shell shuts the whole creation in on every side, thinkers take opposite views . . . the mention the psalmist makes . . . [Psalms 104:2] does not conflict with either.[17]

Although Isidore was inaccurate in many of his views, he was a diligent scholar, eager for information, and broad-minded in his outlook on life. Yet his works are pitifully simple and inadequate when considered as examples of "everything that ought to be known" by intelligent people.

IRISH LEARNING: COLUMBAN There was one center of sixth-century learning that is often overlooked. It was in faraway Ireland, a comparative newcomer to civilization. Since this land had been spared the ravages of Germanic invasion, Christian scholarship developed there with great rapidity. As early as the fifth century, such men as St. Patrick, born in England and educated in a Gallic monastery, had carried Christianity and learning to Ireland. Soon the Irish were famous for their centers of learning and mission stations. The Irish monks were also priests and carried on the religious work of the surrounding parishes. Less than two centuries after Patrick's journey to Ireland, St. Columban (d. 615) and twelve companions were carrying back to Gaul the ripe fruit of Irish religion and scholarship. The monasteries established by St. Columban, St. Gall, and other Irishmen in Gaul, Switzerland, Italy, and the Rhinelands, soon became centers of religious as well as cultural reform. The strict clerical discipline and brilliant learning of these priest-monks were in marked contrast to that of the lax Continental clergy.

When he was exiled from Gaul because of the enmity of the Frankish clergy and of Queen Brunhild, Columban found a refuge at Bobbio in Italy, where he spent his last days collecting a library of Greek and Latin manuscripts. He typifies the best Irish scholarship of these early centuries. Stern as a John the Baptist in moral principles, he was nevertheless a cultured man. He wrote beautiful religious

[17] *Ibid.*, p. 54.

poetry in the ancient classical style. Like many of his countrymen he could both read and write Greek. Little wonder that the Western Europe of his day is said to have "gone to school" to the Irish. For a while their scholarship overshadowed that of the English, and for centuries many of the most brilliant scholars of the Continent were "Scots" (Irishmen) or their pupils.

A century which produced such men as Venantius Fortunatus, Gregory of Tours, Isidore of Seville, and Columban may claim consideration for something more than cultural darkness. To be sure, the torch of classical Roman literature burned feebly, and Christian scholarship tended to emphasize piety rather than intellectuality. Throughout the West, however, there were local centers of learning, and in many places this slowly emerging culture gave promise of worthy achievements.

ANGLO-SAXON LEARNING

By the year 600 the leading centers of the new Western culture were the Spain of Isidore of Seville, the Italy of Pope Gregory, and the Irish monasteries scattered about through the British Isles and the Continent. Two centuries later, Charles the Great began to draw the best scholars from all of these regions to Frankland, where he established a great new rallying point for learning. The two intervening centuries are usually considered the darkest period of the entire Middle Ages. Spanish and Irish scholarship continued to flourish, but elsewhere in the West learning was relatively unproductive. It was an era of transition during which many old centers declined or were destroyed by invaders. The new centers arose very slowly. Only toward the end of the seventh century did the English monasteries begin to produce the first fruits of a brilliant new scholarship which was destined to outshine that of all other regions.

Christian learning in medieval England was originally transplanted from Rome. At about the year 600 an Italian monk named Augustine, who had been sent out as a special agent of Pope Gregory, brought the papal and Benedictine form of Christianity and education to the Anglo-Saxons. Canterbury, where Augustine established himself, soon became an active frontier post from which Roman Catholicism distributed missionaries, teachers, books, and even building materials to the Germanic world of the north. Under Archbishop Theodore of Tarsus (d. 690), the Anglo-Saxon church was effectively organized, and the school of Canterbury began to rival those of the

Irish monks. The historian Bede, a generation later, paid tribute to the teaching of Theodore and his assistants, writing that

They transmitted to their hearers a knowledge of metrics [the writing of poetry], and of astronomy and ecclesiastical arithmetic [for computing the church calendar], along with volumes of sacred writings. As evidence, even today [731 A.D.], there are some of their pupils who know Latin and Greek as well as their native tongue [Anglo-Saxon].[18]

From Canterbury, in turn, this learning spread elsewhere. One of Theodore's assistants, Benedict Biscop, founded monasteries near by at Jarrow and Wearmouth, where many famous scholars were trained.

THE VENERABLE
BEDE
The most prominent of these scholars, and one of the greatest of the early Middle Ages, was the Venerable Bede (d. 735). Dedicated to religion as a boy, he spent his entire life at the monastery of Jarrow, where he was educated in religious subjects and in the liberal arts. He learned Hebrew and Greek, as well as Latin, and was familiar with classical authors such as Vergil, Ovid, and Horace. Throughout his life, it was said, "he always took delight in learning, teaching, and writing." It was the last, however, which won him everlasting fame. Besides numerous theological works, he wrote textbooks on the liberal arts, several biographies, and a treatise *On the Nature of Things* which, although based on Isidore's treatise of the same title, was more scientifically accurate. From various classical works and from Isidore he compiled studies concerning the seasons, astronomy, and spelling, as well as a treatise on the art of poetry that was much used as a textbook. It was he who made practically universal the method of dating events from the birth of Christ (*Anno Domini*, or A.D.). He also wrote epigrams, hymns, and religious poems.

Most noteworthy of all was his *Ecclesiastical History of England* (to the year 731 A.D.). Outstanding among medieval historical writings, this work was so comprehensive, accurate, fair-minded, and well organized that its author has been called "the father of modern history." Truly he was the first Westerner who showed critical intelligence in the collection and presentation of historical information. He used, and sometimes quoted, ancient Roman documents, native chronicles, contemporary writings, and oral information. Questionable points, based on uncertain evidence, were so designated. He pre-

[18] Bede, *Ecclesiastical History of England*, IV, 2; author's translation. See *Baedae Opera Historica with an English Translation by J. E. King*, Putnam, 1930, II, 10 ff.

sented his material with accuracy, simplicity, dramatic power, and literary charm. The one notably unmodern element was his sincere belief in miracles, but this was universal in his day. Compared with the feeble chronicles and annals of his monastic contemporaries, or with the piously propagandistic works of Augustine and Orosius, Bede's history was a marvel of research and historical scholarship. He is one of the best examples of a monastic scholar who combined sincere religious piety with common sense and intelligence.

ALCUIN OF YORK A twelfth-century English historian wrote that "Bede's grave was the grave of English scholarship." But these words were more flattering to Bede than accurately descriptive of literary conditions after his death. This was the period in which Anglo-Saxon was making a place for itself as a literary language. The national epic, *Beowulf,* was already in existence and written copies were being made. There were also Anglo-Saxon poems by Caedmon and Cynewulf, a poetical version of the Bible, and noteworthy anonymous poems such as "The Seafarer," "The Wanderer," and "The Phoenix." By the end of the ninth century, thanks to Alfred the Great's efforts, many prose works had been translated into Anglo-Saxon.[19] Much of this literature was popular and religious rather than learned, and during the eighth century *Latin* scholarship declined, particularly in the region of Canterbury and Jarrow where Bede had lived. Elsewhere, however, English scholars were winning fame. On the Continent Boniface and his monastic successors rivaled the Irish in their zeal for missions and learning.[20] In certain parts of England also scholarship flourished. In the north, the cathedral school of York acquired a notable reputation.

Alcuin (d. 804) was a product of this new intellectual center. On the Continent, the fame of York and Alcuin soon eclipsed that of Jarrow and Bede. During the late eighth century, when Alcuin was studying there, York had an excellent library, renowned teachers, and well-organized courses; there were classes in reading, writing, singing, and the like. Of Master Albert, who taught grammar and rhetoric, arithmetic, and geometry, geography, law, and theology, Alcuin wrote:

The learned Albert gave drink to thirsty minds from the streams of the sciences. On some he poured forth the art and rules of grammar; on others,

---

[19] See below, p. 287.
[20] See below, p. 274.

rivers of rhetoric. Some he exercised in law, others he taught to chant the songs of Adonia [i.e., to recite poetry] or to play the Castalian flute and to trip with lyric feet the hills of Parnassus [i.e., to compose poetry]; to others he made known the harmony of the Heavens, the courses of the sun and moon, the five zones of the sky, the seven planets, the laws of the stars, and their rising and setting; also the movements of the sea, earthquakes, the nature of men, of cattle, of birds, and of beasts. He taught the different qualities and combinations of numbers, the method of calculating the date of Easter and above all the mysteries of the Holy Scriptures.[21]

In the study of these subjects, classical works, as well as the standard textbooks, were used. Alcuin, who served for a time as librarian at York, made a partial list of the books in the library. Among them were works by Vergil, Cicero, Ovid, Horace, Terence, Statius, Lucan, and the like.[22] To Alcuin's dying day he quoted from these writers. But, as he himself expressed it, "above all" were the Scriptures, and he exhorted a clerical friend to "put the four gospels ahead of the twelve Aeneids." Alcuin became so famous as a scholar that in 782 Charles the Great persuaded him to come to Frankland to help raise the intellectual standards in that realm. Still he kept in touch with York, sending occasionally to have books copied for his monastic library at Tours. It is apparent that English scholarship was so active during the century after Bede's death that it furnished Charles the Great's realm with its greatest intellectual leader, Alcuin. With the passing of Alcuin from York to Tours it may be said that the center of Western culture shifted back once more to the Continent, where the light of learning had been dimmed for about two centuries.

21 *Concerning the Saints of the Church at York;* author's translation. See also translation in Cubberley, *Readings*, p. 85 f.

22 The full list includes Jerome, Ambrose, Hilary, Athanasius, Augustine, Orosius, Leo, Gregory the Great, Basil, Fulgentius, Cassiodorus, Chrysostom, Bede, Aldhelm, Victorinus, *Boethius, Pliny,* Pompeius, *Aristotle, Cicero,* Sedulius, Juvencus, Albinus, Clement, Prosper, Paulinus, Arator, Lactantius, Fortunatus, *Vergil, Statius, Lucan,* Donatus, Priscian, Probus, Phocas, Eutychius, Servius, Pompey, Comminian. Of a total of forty authors mentioned, seven (those in italics) were pagan classics. In conclusion Alcuin mentioned the fact that "there, O reader you will find many more masters of ancient lore." See Cubberley, *Readings*, pp. 86 f.

☰ XIV ☰

NINTH AND TENTH CENTURY LEARNING AND LITERATURE

CAROLINGIAN CULTURE

O N the Continent, the period from about 600 to 800, in contrast to the age of Charles, is often called "the darkest of the Dark Ages." It has even been said that Gregory the Great, Gregory of Tours, Isidore of Seville, and Fortunatus "took Latin letters to the grave with them." There is no solid basis for this judgment. Continental learning continued, its light dim but still burning. Due to devastating wars, however, Italy and Gaul produced no scholars comparable to Bede and the gifted Irishmen who migrated to the Continent during this period.

With the eighth century new light appeared from foreign lands. In 711 Spain was conquered by the Moslems, who later developed a brilliant civilization in that peninsula. Meanwhile, Boniface (d. 754), an English monastic missionary, had begun to convert and civilize the heathen Germans along the Rhineland frontiers of Gaul. From Frisia on the North Sea to Bavaria on the Danube River, monastic mission stations, schools, and libraries were established. Boniface once sent home to England for books written "in large letters" (so as to preserve his failing eyesight). In the library at Fulda, his favorite monastery, there were, among other items, several medical books and a Greek psalter interlineated with Latin. Here also were compiled the annals of the Frankish kings. By the time Charles came into power, Christian-Germanic culture was already making headway on the Continent.

SCHOLARS AT
CHARLES'
COURT

In the light of these conditions it is clear that Charles was not a miracle worker who started a "renascence" which revived the culture of Western Europe from barbaric darkness to brilliant splendor. For Gaul, it is true, he did wonders. The writers of his day asserted, somewhat pessimistically, that "before Charles there was scarcely a trace of the liberal arts in Gaul," that "there could scarcely be found in Gaul anyone sufficiently educated in grammar to write a biography," and that "the study of literature was well-nigh extinguished." Even granting the somewhat doubtful truth of these opinions, it is clear that there was scholarship in many other regions of the Continent. What Charles actually did was to bring learned men from neighboring lands and concentrate them at his court. Thus he appropriated an already flourishing foreign scholarship to make it more effective and to glorify his own realm.

In the words of one of his contemporaries, he was "most eager in searching for wise men and giving them such a living that they might pursue learning in all comfort." This kind of subsidizing of learning had been done on a minor scale by his predecessors and was to be carried on with great success in succeeding centuries by Alfred in England and Otto the Great in the Rhinelands. Like a magnet Charles drew scholars from all parts of the West. From Italy came a witty grammarian named Peter of Pisa, also Archbishop Paulinus of Aquileia, and the Lombard historian, Paul the Deacon of Monte Cassino. Several brilliant Irish poets, grammarians, and scientists were brought to the court, much to the jealous disgust of the other scholars. From England came Alcuin, and it is possible that Theodulf, the bishop-poet and scientist of Orleans, came originally from Moslem Spain. There were only two prominent Franks among the literary men at court—Angilbert, an epic poet, and Einhard, the secretary, friend, son-in-law, and biographer of the emperor.

THE
BIOGRAPHER
EINHARD

Of this circle of learned men, only two, Einhard and Alcuin, can be considered in detail. Einhard exemplifies the secular classical element in the literature of the day. His brief but famous *Life of Charles* was closely modeled after Suetonius's *Lives of the* [*Roman*] *Emperors.* Nevertheless it was an excellent first-hand account of the great Frankish ruler. It recounts in simple unaffected style many intimate details of the life of Charles and his court. The following description of Charles's intellectual interests is typical:

He was ready and fluent in speaking, and able to express himself with great clearness. He did not confine himself to his native tongue [German], but took pains to learn foreign languages, acquiring such knowledge of Latin that he could make an address in that language as well as his own. Greek he could better understand than speak. Indeed he was so polished in speech that he might have passed for a learned man. He was an ardent admirer of the liberal arts, and greatly revered their professors, whom he promoted to high honors. In order to learn grammar, he attended the lectures of the aged Peter of Pisa, a deacon; and for other branches he chose as his preceptor Albinus, otherwise called Alcuin. . . . The king spent much time learning rhetoric and logic, and more especially astronomy. He learned the art of determining the dates upon which the movable festivals of the church fall, and with deep thought and skill most carefully calculated the courses of the planets. Charles also tried to learn to write, and used to keep his tablets and writing book under the pillow of his couch . . . he made little progress in this task, too long deferred. . . . While he was dining he listened to music or reading. History and the deeds of men of old were most often read. He derived much pleasure from the works of St. Augustine, especially from his book called *The City of God*.[1]

THE THEOLO-
GIAN ALCUIN

Unlike Einhard, Alcuin, the leading scholar of the court, was a confirmed theologue. Though trained at the English cathedral school of York in the liberal arts including the classics, he asserted that "the mysteries of the Holy Scriptures" were the most important of all studies. According to one of his medieval biographers, he himself had been "nourished in youth on the writings of Vergil and other wise men of antiquity." Nevertheless "in later life he thought best to prohibit them to his students. He told them that the *Christian* poets were sufficient and that they must not let themselves be corrupted by Vergil's dangerously smooth style."[2] Some of the less "dangerous" classics were used, but with caution. As Alcuin himself wrote to the emperor: "To some [students] I impart the honey of the Holy Scriptures, to others the old wine of ancient learning . . . to some the apples of subtle grammar, to others a knowledge of astronomy." His own works illustrate clearly the dominance of theology and religious interests in both his life and that of his age. To Charles he once sent "a gift of the Sacred Books . . . in one noble volume carefully emended." Doubtless this was his revision of the Vulgate Bible of Jerome.

He also wrote numerous theological treatises and Biblical commentaries, composed (as he put it) "by culling beautiful flowers from the patristic gardens"—from Augustine, Jerome, Bede, and others.

[1] Einhard, *Life of Charles the Great,* Chaps. XXIV, XXV; translation from Robinson, *op. cit.,* I, 127 f.

[2] From an anonymous life of Alcuin (in Jaffe, *Monumenta Alcuina*); author's translation.

Like most clerical scholars he also composed diatribes against the heretical sects of his day, and wrote voluminous letters which reveal the characteristic religious dignity of a Carolingian intellectual leader. Alcuin's nonreligious works were those of a scholar who seems to have been more interested in the "apples of subtle grammar" than in "the old wine of ancient learning." He wrote textbooks on grammar, rhetoric, and logic, and also dabbled a bit in the sciences, particularly in medicine and astronomy. At one time he advocated a minor change in the calendar. All in all, his scholarship had neither the breadth nor the depth of that of his predecessors, Cassiodorus, Isidore of Seville, and Bede.

CAROLINGIAN
POETRY

Religion permeated Alcuin's poetry as well as his prose. He wrote a beautiful poem, "To the Nightingale," in which he paid the following tribute:

> You were not sad. From out your little throat
> Your voice poured forth an endless happy note.

But, pious cleric that he was, he must needs add a moral:

> And ever from your mouth God's praise went ringing.
> .   .   .   .
> Man has no joy
> Such as he knows who makes it his employ
> By day and night, to praise like this, the Lord.[3]

In similarly orthodox fashion he ended a description of his monastic retreat:

> And all the cloisters of thy gardens are
> Fragrant with branches bearing fruit, and with
> White lilies mixing with the crimson rose.
> And birds chant matins every morning there,
> Praising their maker, in the face of God.

Even more vigorously moral was his comparison of the poems of Vergil with Solomon's Song of Songs.

> The song of [Vergilius] Maro's sweeter but with falsehood very rife,
> And frivolous and vain it is, and evil to your hearing;
> While *these* [Solomon's] are precepts unto truth, and to perennial life!

In one lyric passage, "To the Cuckoo," Alcuin either forgot or chose not to moralize. It begins with the springtime refrain, "Now from the

---

[3] This, and the following passages from Alcuin, are from Allen and Jones, *The Romanesque Lyric,* University of North Carolina, pp. 149, 229, 240.

topmost boughs resounds the song of the cuckoo," and ends with the gracious lines:

> And now in the golden land the nightingale never-tiring,
> Pours its melody forth, uplifting our ears to its music.

Most of Alcuin's learned contemporaries likewise wrote poetry that was conspicuous for its theological moralizing. The Italian monk, Paul the Deacon, inserted dull religious verses in his *History of the Lombards*. He produced a poetical *History of the World* for his Italian patroness, a Lombard princess, a set of verses in honor of Charles, and one really beautiful description of the "scent of myrtles and the everlasting spring" that hovered over Lake Como in Lombardy.

The most human of all the Carolingian poets was Bishop Theodulf of Orleans. With him the sunshine of poetry really breaks through the clouds of theological conservatism. Like Venantius Fortunatus two centuries earlier, he was an ardent classicist. He knew the works of the Christian poets but he loved those of Vergil and Ovid and modeled his own poems after the poetry of the pagan Romans. With a sense of humor as keen as that of Martial he wrote the following epigram:

> Here Hincmar lies, a thief by Avarice fired
> His only noble deed, that finally he expired.

It is interesting to note that the writer of this epigram also penned the inspiring hymn "Glory, Laud and Honor," which is still sung in Roman Catholic churches for the Palm Sunday processional. But for the most part religion, not witticism, was the life work of Theodulf and other Carolingian clergymen.

EDUCATION: THE "PALACE SCHOOL" Above all else Charles the Great emphasized the educational duties of the clergy. Alcuin was not only the greatest scholar of the court, he was also the leader of Charles's educational reforms. These centered in the "palace school" and the regional cathedral and monastic schools. The palace school was the most famous but not the most important of Charles's educational institutions. It was not, as is often supposed, a university; it was merely an expansion of the court school of former times in which the young princes and nobles were taught the rudiments of the seven liberal arts. During the reign of Charles it attained unusual fame because of the outstanding scholars who were members of the court circle.

There were also informal meetings of the intellectually minded people of the court, in which Charles himself took an active interest. In the discussion at these meetings Charles was called "David," and some of the other members were known by classical names: Alcuin, for example, was known as Flaccus, and Prince Pepin as Julius. The predominance of Biblical names indicates, however, the prevailing interest of Charles and his scholars in religious subjects.

Perhaps the most important contribution of the palace school was its influence in encouraging scholarship not only at the court but throughout the realm. Everywhere Charles was generous in giving financial rewards to men of learning. Choice positions, bishoprics and abbacies in important centers, were given to able scholars. Thus in many localities an interest in learning was revived or expanded.

MONASTIC AND CATHEDRAL SCHOOLS   The most constructive phase of Carolingian culture was the reform of the local educational institutions. Charles set out to create an intelligent clergy at all costs. In an official governmental document to the priests of the realm he urged "the study of the liberal arts," explaining that "we constantly seek to improve the conditions of the churches, and have endeavored to advance the cause of learning." In similar fashion he wrote to the abbots of the monasteries, as well as to the other clergy, calling attention to the fact that their letters contained "awkward expressions."

> Therefore [he continued], we began to fear lest unskillful writing might be accompanied by a lack of wisdom in understanding the Holy Scriptures. . . . Since images and other figures of speech are found in the Scriptures, one gets the spiritual sense better if he has been well trained in literature. Choose men for this work who have the will and ability to learn and also the ability to teach others.[4]

His capitularies (proclamations) also emphasized the importance of churchmen's knowing reading, writing, singing, secretarial work, and even "the art of medicine." He provided for rigid enforcement of his educational program, including the suspension of ignorant priests. In order to provide training schools for the local clergy,

---

[4] Author's translation. For longer quotations from Charles's proclamations see Cubberley, *Readings*, pp. 89 ff., and Robinson, *Readings*, I, pp. 144 ff.

the existing system of monastic and cathedral schools was improved in both extent and efficiency. St. Riquier, a monastery in northern France, was said to have expanded until it had a hundred students, a tremendous enrollment for that day. Reichenau, in the Alps, had four hundred volumes in its library. St. Gall and Metz had special courses in music; Orleans specialized in the liberal arts. Most notable of all was the monastic school of St. Martin at Tours, where Alcuin worked hard to develop a school like that at York from which he had come. The results were disappointing except in one respect: the training of copyists. His monastic scribes developed a beautifully clear style of handwriting (*manu scriptum*) which soon set the standard for copyists throughout the realm. The "lower case" type used in modern printing (in which these words appear) is modeled after the Carolingian hand which was perfected and popularized by Alcuin's monks at Tours.

THE LOWER
SCHOOLS
In addition to his extension of the existing system of monastic and cathedral training schools Charles has sometimes been credited with having established a system of free public education. This is not true, for, like those of previous centuries, all of the schools were controlled by and organized for clergymen. To be sure he ordered that *every bishopric and monastery* should have a school, and even went so far as to provide that young men "from the servile class, as well as the sons of freemen" might enroll as students. But these schools were primarily for the training of monks and priests. They were more like religious teachers' colleges than public schools.

The only hint of a system of free primary education is to be found in the local village schools, in which, as formerly, the children were given instruction in reading, writing, singing, and religion by the parish priests. These schools were open to the general public, but, like modern parochial schools, they were clerically controlled. One of the local councils of Charles's day made the following democratic ruling: "Let every man send his son to learn letters, and let him remain until he is well instructed." This suggests that Charles may have intended to enforce attendance at the parish schools. There is, however, no evidence that this ideal was carried out. Whatever the extent to which Charles's plans were or were not put in force, he is one of the few statesmen in the annals of history who have made education a vital factor in their governmental program.

EDUCATION
AFTER CHARLES

With the passing of Charles (814) his imperial system rapidly disintegrated, but intellectual life continued to flourish. In fact there seem to have been more eminent scholars after his reign than during it. The palace school continued. For a time, to be sure, during the reign of Louis the Pious (814-840), the court was noted more for pious than for intellectual interests, and narrow-minded monastic theologians were dominant. But Louis was no ignoramus (he knew Greek), and he kept a number of learned Irishmen at his court. During the next reign, an Irish philosopher, John the Scot (also called Erigena) was as much of a favorite of Charles the Bald as Alcuin had been of Charles the Great.

Local schools also continued to flourish. Boys of all classes attended the "outer" schools of the monasteries. One abbot was said to have had "a public school for monks . . . with many auditors, even laymen." At another monastery, it was reported, "dukes, counts, sons of dukes and counts, and even kings' sons are educated." In some cases girls who had no intention of becoming nuns were educated in convent schools, and in at least one such school handicraft arts were taught. Although the schools were under clerical management, the laity was taking advantage of its opportunity to obtain an education.

Though the monastic schools were most prominent in educational affairs, many bishops also displayed an active interest in education. At one time the bishops of Louis the Pious's realm urged him to provide "two or three public schools so that every man . . . in any rank of the Church may attend . . . in order that the work of your father [Charles] and yourself shall not perish." Eventually nine new educational centers were established. In Italy the pope, after commenting on the lack of teachers and the absence of interest in the study of letters, ordered that "in all bishoprics and parishes . . . teachers and persons learned . . . in the liberal arts and sacred theology shall be appointed to teach these subjects." Apparently there were in the period after Charles the Great three categories of educational institutions—palace schools, monastic and cathedral schools, and parish schools.

THEOLOGICAL
INFLUENCES

Theological interests were, of course, predominant. Alcuin had emphasized the supremacy of the Bible and faith over the liberal arts and reason. Even more strongly was this attitude stressed by his monastic successors. Paschasius Radbertus, abbot of Corbie, wrote *Concerning the Body and Blood,* one of the first treatises in which it was asserted that "Christ's body and blood actually come into existence in the ceremony of the mass." This doctrine was to be a storm center of medieval theology,[5] and *transubstantiation* (the transformation of the "elements") is still an important article of Roman Catholic faith.

A learned contemporary, Rabanus Maurus, abbot, archbishop, and teacher, at Fulda and Mainz, wrote a series of textbooks on the liberal arts, all with a piously religious interpretation. He also worked over parts of Isidore of Seville's *Etymologies* for his own encyclopedia, giving it a strong theological emphasis so as to provide proper reading matter. He was a firm believer in the use of human reason, but only as the handmaid of theology. When a radical young monk named Gottschalk asserted that if one followed Augustine's theology to its logical conclusion, men were predestined to hell as well as to heaven, Rabanus led the conservative theologians in an attempt to force him, even by torture, to give up his heretical views. Gottschalk was made of stubborn stuff, and although condemned to life imprisonment in a monastery, he defied his persecutors.

RATIONALISM IN THEOLOGY   Gottschalk was only the most tactless and radical of the rationalistic scholars who attacked the dogmatism of conservative theologians. Ratramnus, a monk of Corbie, vigorously opposed the "Body and Blood" ideas of Paschasius Radbertus, insisting, like many Protestants of later centuries, that ·the "elements" used in the mass remained merely bread and wine. Bishop Claudius of Turin criticized the worship of images and relics in the churches, and Bishop Agobard of Lyons wielded a liberal pen in condemning superstitions, and trials by combat and ordeal, which he declared were unjust.

In these ninth-century theologians one can see the unending struggle between radicalism and conservatism in religion. Gottschalk and Ratramnus, like the moderns of our day, emphasized reason; Paschasius and Rabanus, like present-day fundamentalists, made faith and religious authority supreme. And John the Scot, greatest of them all, like Boethius, Abelard, Erasmus, and many other intellectuals, took a liberal middle ground in which his rationalism was tactfully veiled.

[5] See below, p. 402, for the final settlement of the question.

JOHN THE SCOT John the Scot (d. ca. 880) was a second Boethius. Facing both the past and the future, he appreciated classical philosophy as well as Christian theology. This dual interest makes Boethius and John important landmarks in the transition from Roman philosophy to medieval scholasticism. Boethius, in the sixth century, introduced Western Christendom to Aristotelian thought and contributed much to the rationalization of Christian ideas. John, living three centuries later in a world of conservative theologians, was less philosophical in his thinking.

Nevertheless, like Boethius, he turned to the Hellenistic East for his inspiration. He translated into Latin the works of pseudo-Dionysius, a Greek-Roman philosopher who was believed to have been converted by St. Paul and sent West, where he founded the monastery of St. Denis (Dionysius) near Paris. Dionysius' writings were Neoplatonic, and John the Scot adopted much of this spirit, along with certain of the Aristotelian concepts that had been emphasized by Boethius. These pagan philosophical ideas he blended with the theology of Augustine and other early churchmen to form a complete system of Christian thought. Rationalistic ideas, as the oneness of God and Nature, the oneness of philosophy and religion, the superiority of reason over faith and religious authority, and the allegorical nature of certain portions of the Bible (such, for instance, as the account of the Creation) were strongly emphasized in his work. John's orthodoxy was not doubted by his contemporaries (probably because they did not fully comprehend his works), but certain of his ideas were later branded as heretical. He had a great influence on some of the most advanced thinkers of the later Middle Ages, and in the thirteenth century many of his concepts were adopted by the scholastic theologians.[6]

HISTORY In historical writing, there were only faint traces of genius after the days of Bede and Einhard. A *Chronicle,* now sometimes referred to as the first French-produced history of the world, was compiled by Bishop Freculf of Lisieux. More noteworthy is the history of the civil wars following the death of Charles the Great, written by Nithard, son of one of Charles's daughters. This, "the first *layman's* history" of medieval times, was a clear-cut but somewhat prejudiced account of events that the author had actually seen during his career as a general and diplomat in the

6 See below, p. 665.

service of Charles's grandson. For the second half of the ninth century there is little historical writing of merit. Only meager monastic annals, such as those of St. Bertin, St. Vaast, Lorsch, and Fulda, have come down to us.

THE CLASSICS   In other phases of secular scholarship, this age was more active. Bishop Lupus of Ferrières was a more remarkable classicist than any of the men of Charles the Great's court. Although educated at Rabanus' monastic school, he showed more interest in classical than in religious books. He begged several of his friends—Einhard, the pope, and certain scholars at York— to lend him Cicero's works on oratory and rhetoric, Quintilian's *Oratory,* and Aulus Gellius's *Attic Nights* in order to correct and "complete those copies of which we have parts." One of his students (the bishop of Auxerre) knew Greek and lectured on the Roman satirical poets. Many of the contemporary Irish scholars in various European centers knew and quoted classical writings. Most of the educated men of that day were familiar with Cicero, Sallust, Vergil, and Ovid. They quoted from them, cited them, and wrote their poems in the classical meters. A learned German bishop of this period reflected the attitude of Christian scholars toward the pagan classics when he quoted Cassiodorus' line, "The classics are like manure in which one searches for gold," and added, "and manure fertilizes the land."

POETRY   Practically all the scholars of this age, even conservative theologians, dabbled in poetry. Rabanus Maurus wrote staid and serious poems, hymns, poetical letters, and prayers. Gottschalk, the young radical, composed verse that had a strain of melancholy genius. John the Scot, philosopher and scholar that he was, wrote verse *in Greek.* Another Irishman, Sedulius the Scot, living at Liége, showed the best poetical ability of the period, and that was not of a very high order. He wrote playful odes, one of which described the dilapidated house, "dark as Caccus' cave or the Cretan labyrinth," in which he and his fellow clerics lived. This poem ended with a request that the luxuriously housed bishop send them some good wine for consolation. Concerning his own worthless life, he mused as follows:

> I read or write, I teach or search after learning,
> Day and night I implore the heavenly throne in prayer,
> I eat, I drink freely, in my rhyming I invoke the Muses,

> I snore as I sleep, I stay awake to pray,
> With burdened soul I weep over my sins,
> Have mercy, Christ and Mary, on a poor sinner.[7]

Some of the doggerel verses which he wrote involved dialogues between animals, after the fashion of Aesop's fables. His "Debate between the Rose and the Lily" is on only a slightly higher plane. More sincere and serious were his Easter hymns, and an ode concerning the defeat and slaughter of a band of raiding Northmen. In Sedulius's poetry the ponderosity of medieval theology was lightened by a wealth of classical allusion and by that indefinable touch that is characteristic of Irish literature. Walafrid Strabo, abbot of Reichenau, is the only contemporary poet who can compare with him in ability. Most of Strabo's work was monastically serious—hymns, visions of hell and heaven, and odes to royalty. In a few poems he showed the sensitivity of a true lover of nature. In verses dedicated to "The Flowers in the Monastery Garden," he wrote:

> Thou dost bear me the beauty of a purple flower,
> In early summer bringing a gift like to the sweet dark hued violet,
> Or like the hyacinth new grown under Apollo's high table. . . .[8]

In the poetry devoted to religious subjects, the modern reader finds little to admire. The occasional human and classical touches seem out of place in such a setting. It was not considered incongruous, however, in that day to set the Scriptures, hymns, prayers, and condemnations of paganism and heresy to formal classical meter with interspersed classicisms such as "Castalian rills," "Apollo's laurel," "Parnassus," and the like. The medieval theologian had no qualms at mixing religion with poetry and classicism. He could rise to heights of lyrical emotionalism in glorifying the Virgin Mary as "the fountain of pure water, the holy source of Salvation and of honesty, the essence of myrrh, of balsam, and of nard; the gem of onyx, crystal, and beryl." One well-meaning versifier composed in her honor a hundred lines, because this signified the number of the Ten Commandments multiplied by ten, "by which is signified eternal life."

Even moral treatises were written in verse. In a long poem, "On Sobriety," Milo of St. Amand roundly condemned the drunkenness of Noah, Lot, and Esau, in contrast to the temperance of Sam-

---

[7] Author's translation. See also Waddell, *The Wandering Scholars,* p. 62.
[8] Laistner, *Thought and Letters in Western Europe: A.D. 500 to 900,* p. 329.

son, Daniel, Judith, and Esther. Although poetry of a serious sort was the rule in the ninth century, there was an occasional effort of an entirely different kind. One of the most startling products of the period is the following ditty in praise of "The Monk of Angers," who seems to have violated every principle of sobriety:

> They say   each day   he cries out for wine to drink;
> Daylight   nor night   sees him pause or makes him shrink;
> That sot   does not   cease until he staggers by,
> Like a   tree that's
> wheeling   reeling   underneath a blowing sky.
>
> Praise him, praise him, praise him, praise him!
> Sing we Bacchus' praises now!
>
> I swear   he'll bear   his carcase to eternity
> So stained   and grained   with life-preserving wine is he;
> He'll keep!   Don't steep   his body with embalmer's myrrh—
> No spice   so nice   as alcohol, I do aver!
>
> Praise him, praise him, praise him, praise him!
> Sing we Bacchus' praises now! [9]

If it is evident that the poetry of this period lacked the touch of genius, it is equally true that Germanic barbarism and Christian religiousness were developing an emotional expressiveness and a feeling for the beautiful in literature. In time these progressive influences were to produce works of real merit.

TENTH-CENTURY LEARNING

FROM ALCUIN
TO ALFRED

The ninth century opened with Charles the Great's court leading the Western world in culture. By the end of the century the glories of the "Carolingian Renascence" had waned. Cultural leadership shifted once more to England, which had been the center of European intellectual life before the coming of Charles. As we have seen, at about 800, Charles robbed England of her best scholar, and soon the school of York was reduced to a secondary importance. Even more disturbing for English learning in the hundred years between Alcuin and Alfred was the cruel ravaging of the country by the Danes during this century. In 866 York itself was captured and the school destroyed.

[9] Allen and Jones, *op. cit.,* p. 239.

Out of the ashes of destruction, however, there arose a new intellectual impulse. Alfred's "renascence," like that of Charles the Great in Frankland a century earlier, was more nearly a reconstruction than a revival or rebirth. Learning had not died out in England with the passing of Bede, or Alcuin, or the school of York; there was merely a shift in cultural centers.

As the Danish menace abated in southern England during the last quarter of the ninth century, Alfred undertook to reconstruct cultural as well as economic and political life. In a manner similar to that employed by Charles the Great, he called in the best leaders he could find, whatever their race or origin. From Frankland came a monk named Grimbald; from Saxony, John of Corbie; from Mercia in north central England, Plegmund. Most famous of all the members of this English "palace school" was Bishop Asser of St. David's in Wales. Among other things, he wrote *The Life of Alfred,* a quaint biography in which one can read the legend of the burnt cakes, and accounts of the boy-king's love of learning, of his time-marker candle, and of the quarrelsome scholars of the palace school.

ALFRED: SCHOLAR AND TRANSLATOR

Charles the Great had hunted and warred while his men of learning studied. Alfred wielded not only the sword of defense against the Danes but also the pen of scholarship. Asser wrote that "amid the various manifold worldly cares that oft trouble both mind and body," Alfred took time to collect a scrapbook of proverbs "about the size of a psalter," and to translate entire books from Latin into English. Among these books were a portion of the *Psalms,* Gregory the Great's *Pastoral Rule* and *Dialogues,* Orosius' *History against the Pagans,* Bede's *Ecclesiastical History,* Marcus Aurelius's *Meditations,* and Boethius's *Consolation of Philosophy.* As a translator, Alfred took liberties with the originals, omitting, condensing, paraphrasing, or adding passages. He Christianized some of Boethius's pagan ideas, and added to Marcus Aurelius's proverbs some pious platitudes of his own concerning riches, adversity, and the joys of giving. His program of translation was a curious combination of religious and intellectual reconstruction. The aims and methods that motivated it were set forth as follows in his translation of the *Pastoral Rule:*

So general became the decay of learning in England [during the Danish invasions] that there were very few . . . who could understand the rituals in English or translate a letter from Latin into English. . . . I re-

membered also how I saw the country before it had been ravaged and
burned; how the churches throughout the whole of England stood filled
with treasures and books. There was also a great multitude of God's
servants, but they had very little knowledge of the books, for they could
not understand anything of them because they were not written in their
own language. . . . Therefore it seems better . . . for us also to translate
some of the books into the language which we can all understand.[10]

Like Charles the Great, Alfred was convinced of the importance of
education in the lives of his people, and of the importance of the
clergy in the progress of education. But he went a step further: he
resolved to translate Latin learning into the language of the nation.

ANGLO-SAXON
LITERATURE

Alfred's greatest contribution to medieval culture
was neither religious nor educational: it was the establishment of Anglo-Saxon as a recognized literary
language. This was accomplished without deliberate intent, as a by-
product of his other aims. One of these was his interest in ancient
Germanic poetry. Like Charles the Great, he had the traditional
epics of his people collected and preserved. Unfortunately *Beowulf*
is the only one that has come down to us intact. In another respect,
however, Alfred's work contributed not only to the pre-eminence
of the Anglo-Saxon tongue, but also to historical knowledge. He established a national co-operative history, the *Anglo-Saxon Chronicle*.
By having various monasteries collect, organize, and copy the earlier
existing chronicles of the kingdom, he preserved much historical information that would otherwise have been lost. He also saw to it
that the monastic chroniclers kept their records up to date by noting
contemporary events. Thus Canterbury, Abingdon, Worcester, Peter-
boro, and other monasteries had similar records of Anglo-Saxon history in the Anglo-Saxon language. One of these chronicles was continued to the middle of the twelfth century.

It was by such efficient methods of organization that Alfred carried on one of the most remarkable intellectual reconstructions in
English history. He planned to have "all of the free [i.e., noble]
youth . . . to be able to read Anglo-Saxon . . . and those whom it
is proposed to educate further and promote to higher office should
be taught Latin." This ideal was not completely realized, but, thanks
to his efforts, Anglo-Saxon literature—the first vernacular literature in
Europe—was firmly established. Even though renewed disorders set

[10] Cubberley, *op. cit.,* pp. 94 f.

in during the tenth century, and Continental centers again took the lead, the impulses set in motion by Alfred never completely died in England. As we shall see presently, Dunstan and other churchmen kept the torch of learning burning during the trying period of the late tenth century. In cultural reforms, as in other fields, Alfred worked so kindly and understandingly that his name is synonymous with constructive reform. It has been said—with considerable historical validity—that he was a victorious warrior who left no sting of defeat, a saint without superstition and intolerance, a king without cruelty, and a national hero of military, intellectual, spiritual, and moral force.

THE TENTH
CENTURY

The tenth century, according to a keen modern observer, "has a bad name," equaled only by that of the seventh century with which it shares the reputation of being the nadir of European culture.[11] Other modern writers have called this century "barren," "the wastest place of Western civilization and of the human mind," and "an epoch of evil" during which the Western world "suffered a veritable mental anemia." Medieval chroniclers wrote that "by the year 1000 A.D. there was scarcely a personage of real worth in all Europe," and that in that day "a writer of a true poem could not be found." But the truth is that, at its worst, the tenth century was by no means a total loss to civilization. Miss Waddell, in *The Wandering Scholars,* asserts that the tenth century saw the passing of an impotent Carolingian dynasty in France; but in Germany it witnessed the reigns of three great emperors. It saw St. Denis and St. Martin of Tours sacked by the Northmen, while wolves hunted in Auvergne; "but before the century was out the same Northmen were peaceful citizens among the apple-orchards of Normandy." The Hungarians burned the library of St. Gall and "spared the cellar, yet enough of both vintages was left to make the tenth century the Golden Age of the monastery." It saw a succession of Italian popes "as short-lived and wanton as May flies," but in England there was Dunstan's reform of the church, and in France, the founding of Cluny, the monastery that produced the great reforming popes of the next century. From the same century "dates the beginning of modern music," and of modern love lyrics.[12]

For two reasons it is advisable to examine with special care cul-

11 Waddell, *The Wandering Scholars,* p. 64.
12 *Ibid.,* p. 64 f.

tural conditions during the tenth century. In the first place, it is reputed to have been one of the darkest eras of the Middle Ages. It is worth our while to know something of medieval culture at its worst. Secondly, the tenth century marks the close of the first five centuries of the independent growth of Western culture. By this time the West had developed its own standards and types of literature and learning. It is important for us to know in some detail the nature of medieval culture after it had begun to take firm root. In general we shall find considerable *quantity* of production in all fields of endeavor. The *quality* of achievement, however, according to both ancient and modern standards, is disappointing. Medieval civilization was still in a primitive and rustic state of development. Furthermore, at the beginning of the century Western Europe was still beset by Norse, Hungarian, and Moslem invaders. The wonder is that letters, philosophy, and learning were able to survive and to make such rapid progress in the succeeding centuries.

HISTORICAL
WRITING
The century produced a number of historical writings of merit. At the opening of the period, Regino of Prum (d. 915) was writing a noteworthy German chronicle, and Notker the Stammerer of St. Gall (d. 912) was compiling the simple annals of his monastery. At the mid-century, Widukind, a monk of Corvey, was setting forth the glorious deeds of his fellow Saxons in a historical work that was well written, convincingly frank, and filled with thrilling tales of battle. It was he who told the story of Otto the Great's defeat of the Hungarians at the Lech River near Augsburg.[13] Meanwhile at Rheims a French monk named Flodoard (d. 966) had produced a *History of the Church of Rheims* and a set of *Annals.* Thirty years later another French monk, Richer of Rheims (d. 996), completed a more literary but less reliable history that was closely modeled after that of the Roman historian Sallust.

At the same time, in Italy, Bishop Liutprand of Cremona (d. 972) was producing a smart, vivid, but quite untrustworthy brand of history. His *Deeds of Otto I* was fairly accurate, but the account of his embassy to Constantinople is a series of spiteful snapshots of Byzantine life and intrigue. Similarly, his *Antapodosis,* or *Book of Retributions* (*Tit for Tat,* as a recent translator has called it), is highly interesting, chiefly because of its violent prejudices. It is filled with

[13] See below, p. 373.

bitter reproaches against the Italian enemies of his patron, Emperor Otto, and with vivid accounts of the Saracen and Hungarian invasions. The author's versatility is shown by the classical quotations, Greek expressions and occasional poems (fifteen in all) with which he flavored his account.

In faraway England, at about the same time, Ethelward completed his *Chronicle of World History* (to 975). None of these, nor the many lesser histories of this era, was a real work of erudition comparable to the *Ecclesiastical History* of Bede. Yet they illustrate the fact that in all parts of the West throughout this century, historical literature flourished. Every monastery kept annals—yearbooks in which important local events were briefly recorded in somewhat the manner in which a diary is kept. Often the record for an entire year fills less than a half page of modern print, and contains little more than a reference to the death of an abbot, the coronation of a king, famine, invasions, and miraculous events of various kinds. Even so, these annals were the seeds from which real histories grew. The chronicles were more comprehensive. Usually they covered a longer period of time and a larger territory. Most of them commenced with a sketch of world history beginning with the Creation. This was copied outright from some early Christian chronicle such as that of Jerome or Isidore. The portions dealing with contemporary events were more detailed and more original; in fact, they were often a combination of material gleaned from a number of local annals. Some of the better chronicles, written by intelligent and diligent monks, tended to become regional or national histories that reflected the individuality and interpretative ability of their authors. But, at its best, tenth-century historical writing was much restricted by the narrow bounds of religion and localism.

POETRY DURING THE TENTH CENTURY — Poetry was less closely bound by religious ties. Early in the century Abbo of St. Germain, inspired by the successful resistance of the Parisians to the Norse siege of 885,[14] wrote an epic poem concerning "The Wars of the City of Paris." It was a vivid account full of picturesque detail. Poetry of all kinds seems to have been popular in the tenth century. Even boys wrote verse. At St. Gall, on one occasion, the students in the monastic school rhymed so well that the abbot gave them a triple holiday. Some of their teachers were famous for poeti-

[14] See above, p. 208.

cal compositions; notable among them were a flute player named
Totilo, Ratpert, a scholarly poet, and Notker the Stammerer, author
not only of lyrics but also of hymns and histories.

Later in the century, another monk of St. Gall, Ekkehard by
name, wrote the "Epic of Walthari." This noble poem is an interesting blend of three influences. It was originally a *Germanic* ballad
concerning heroic German valor during the invasion of the Huns.
Notker, however, retold it with a strong *Christian* emphasis and in
verse that had a pronounced *classical* Vergilian meter. In such fashion,
a tenth-century monk could combine Christian, pagan Roman, and
heathen Germanic elements. Another such combination is to be found
in the works of a *German* nun named Roswitha, who was both pious
and classical in her poetry. In a long epic poem she celebrated the
achievements of Otto the Great, applying to him the ancient title,
"Imperator Caesar Augustus Otto." She also composed six comedies
after the manner of the classical Roman writer Terence, but with
subject matter of a pious Christian character which would be proper
for nuns to read.

The poetry of this period constantly reflects the varied types of
thought and expression of early medieval writers. Solemn churchmen and professors in monastic schools, along with their young
students, knew and used the classical forms of metrical poetry. They
produced epic poems on secular subjects, and dramas that often
showed pagan tendencies. On occasion they wrote irreligious and
even profane ditties in the newer accented and rhymed styles of
informal nonclassical verse. Outstanding, however, are the overwhelm-
ingly religious ideals of the age and the stubborn persistence of classical materials and Roman metrical forms. As usual the Germanic-
Christian mind was more eager to assimilate and preserve the elements of ancient civilization than to develop its own modes of expression. Unfortunately the glamor of the classics tended to encourage
superficiality of style and delayed the development of a truly medieval
poetry. Often the dead hand of classical antiquity was as much of a
drawback to the progress of medieval literature as was the dogmatic
conservatism of the Christian clergy.

MONASTIC OP-
POSITION TO
THE CLASSICS
In the more learned pursuits similar trends are noticeable. There was much activity, but of mediocre
or inferior quality. Of particular importance are the
increasing interest in the ancient classics and the
sharp opposition which this aroused among the more conservative

monastic leaders. Pagan Roman authors were read by most educated men, even by those who were trained in monastic schools.

One of the most notable examples of the conflict between classical and religious interests is found in the order of Cluniac monks which was established in 910 for the purpose of religious reform.[15] For a time the Cluniacs seemed to favor the suppression of all classical studies. It was Abbot Odo, one of the founders of the order, who was reported to have had a dream (somewhat like that of Jerome) in which the classics were likened to a serpent lurking in a beautiful vase. The Cluniac rule discouraged the reading of the ancient pagan writings. A monk who wished to get a book from the librarian during the silent hour went through the motions of turning pages, and if a classical author was desired, he scratched his ear "even as a dog does when itching, since unbelievers [i.e., classical pagans] are not unjustly likened to such an animal." Evidently, however, many a Cluniac monk "scratched his ear." Odo himself, writing in his *Collations* concerning the luxury and vanity of the higher clergy, went out of his way to cite from a classical poet the metaphor, "Venus would be cold if Bacchus and Ceres did not produce an abundance."

It is clear that not only Odo but many another Cluniac monk knew the classics. Late in the tenth century we find Odo's successor carrying classical as well as sacred books with him on his travels. He was said, however, to have cut out of them "with a sharp implement" all offending passages. Thus early did clerical conservatives resort to the expurgation of dangerous portions of useful books. Interestingly enough, the same abbot, so it was reported, "in his youth having read the philosophers of old and the lies of Vergil, [in old age] no longer desired to read them *nor to let others do so.*"

The fear of, and bitter opposition to, the classics manifested by some of the more conservative churchmen suggest the wide extent and popularity of such studies. Many pious men felt that the classics threatened to destroy all religion and morality. Toward the end of the tenth century a papal legate asserted that the popes were not interested in "Plato, Vergil, Terence, and the other troops of [classical] philosophers." God's servants, he continued, were "unlettered rustics, not orators and philosophers." In Italy a grammarian of Ravenna was actually burned as a heretic for accepting the classi-

15 See below, p. 382.

cal poems as articles of religious faith and for claiming that Vergil, Horace, and Juvenal had appeared to him in a vision and promised him a part in their Paradise. Many clergymen, after having been led astray, repented of their allegiance to the classics. A Flemish abbot confessed that at the cathedral school of Rheims he had studied "the ancient poets, who tell only of passions satisfied and how we may satisfy ours." But realizing that "while learning literature one might strangle his soul" he tore himself "from the embraces and kisses of these crime-inciting mistresses," and was saved. Late in life he gave to the monastic library thirty-six volumes, all of them religious books.

There is little doubt that at the end of the tenth century the conservative anticlassicists were strongly intrenched, particularly in monastic centers. The Cluniac reform was in full swing. Many church leaders were determined to crush sin and heresy, to eliminate warfare and vice, and to purify the clergy at all costs. For every classicist there was a score of stern reformers such as Odo of Cluny, Abbo of Fleury, and Dunstan of Canterbury. In England, for a time, the reforming abbot Dunstan was second only to the king in influence. To be sure, these conservative leaders were cultured men. Dunstan himself decorated manuscripts, worked at handicraft arts, and played the organ. But he and most of his contemporaries subordinated secular learning and the classics to theology and the spiritual welfare of mankind.

Under the domination of such ideals and such leaders the progress of classical and other secular studies was bound to be slow. But it was constant. Even in the strictest monastic centers of learning, the classics were available and were used. Monastic scholars such as the famous Abbot Abbo of Fleury (d. 1004) knew the classics and on occasion cited Vergil, Horace, Terence, Juvenal, Persius, Lucan, and other pagan writers. Evidently some of the reforming Cluniacs who publicly favored the absolute prohibition of "the wine of ancient learning" to the younger generation were themselves familiar with the taste of the forbidden liquor.

CLASSICISM IN THE CATHEDRAL SCHOOLS   In the cathedral centers the classics were used more freely. At Liége, which had one of the most progressive cathedral schools of the tenth century, a history of the local bishops was compiled in which Horace was mentioned twenty-four times, Cicero thirteen, and Vergil, Sallust, and others, several times each. There is abundant evidence that the students of the cathedral schools of the tenth century were well versed in the classics; they were certainly more familiar with them than is the average college student or professor of our day.

Although in certain respects the tenth century resembles a dreary night of violence and unintelligent piety, it also manifests some of the signs of a cultural dawn. During the latter half of the century a broader interest in learning was noticeable in the cathedral schools. These schools, located in the more populous episcopal centers and somewhat removed from the strict religious influences of monastic life, developed a progressive cosmopolitan spirit. Here secular interests and classical studies found a more sympathetic reception.

GERBERT   One of the most influential schools of the late tenth century was that of the archbishop of Rheims, and its headmaster, Gerbert, was by all odds the most versatile intellect of the era.

Gerbert, among other things, was an out-and-out classicist. His interest in Roman literature has led a modern scholar to assert that he was "a humanist nourished on Vergil, Horace, Lucan, and other Latin poets, a writer whose Ciceronian letters have a poignant charm." More convincing proof of Gerbert's interest in the classics can be found in his letters requesting the assistance of friends in obtaining copies of classical works. To one acquaintance he wrote:

> I am eagerly collecting a library; and as formerly at Rome and elsewhere in Italy, so likewise in Germany and Belgium I have obtained copyists and manuscripts with a mass of money. . . . [After requesting assistance, he continued] We will append at the end of this letter a list of those writers we wish copied. We have sent for your disposal parchment for the scribes and money to defray the cost.[16]

Unfortunately the list of writers whose works he wished to have copied has not come down to us. Gerbert's deep appreciation of the classics is shown by his remarks to a neighboring abbot to whom he was writing concerning the greatness of Julius Caesar. "The knowledge of great men," he said, "written in volumes of books . . . and the writings of M. Tullius Cicero *console me amid my cares."* Here we have, five hundred years after Boethius, a cleric-scholar who, in the "age of iron," knew "the consolation of the classics."

[16] Taylor, *The Medieval Mind,* Macmillan, I, 287.

Education, like scholarship, during the tenth century was for the most part serious, religious, and practical. It differed somewhat from that of the Carolingian age, but, in spite of the intervening period of devastating wars and invasions, the same types of educational institutions, courses, and methods existed. There were, as earlier, three general types of schools (palace, monastic and cathedral, and parish). Otto the Great and his sons maintained their circle of learned men at the imperial court in much the same manner as Charles the Great had done at Aix-la-Chapelle a century and a half earlier. At Otto III's court, Gerbert (recently exiled from Rheims) occupied a position comparable to that of Alcuin at Charles the Great's palace school. There were also monastic and cathedral schools, of which we shall say more later. Finally, there were the lesser schools in each parish, in which the local priests instructed the children in religion and the rudiments of grammar, arithmetic, and music.

A set of tenth-century instructions for the English clergy contains a passage which illustrates the simple religious objectives of education in the parish schools. Priests were expected to conduct schools in their homes for the instruction of children, and they were not to take pay from the relatives "except what they might give of their own free will." They were to teach the people diligently "for those well versed in book learning can teach others to avoid evil, to do good, and to seek peace."

The continuity of education during the early Middle Ages and the regional characteristics of educational institutions are illustrated by Mr. Taylor's summary of the situation in Italy:

There was no break between her antique civilization and her mediaeval development, but only a period of depression and decay. Notwithstanding the change from paganism to Christianity and the influx of barbarians, both a race-continuity and a continuity of culture persisted. . . .

In Italy, as in no other country, the currents of antique education, disturbed yet unbroken, carried clear across that long period of invasions, catastrophes, and reconstructions which began with the time of Alaric. . . . In the seventh and eighth centuries the grade of instruction was very low; but there is evidence of the unintermitted existence of lay schools, private or municipal, in all the important towns, from the eighth century to the tenth, the eleventh, and so on . . . in Italy there never ceased to be schools conducted by laymen for laymen, where instruction in matters profane and secular was imparted . . . without regard to its utility for the saving of souls.[17]

Elsewhere in the West, however, there was no trace of *lay* schools, and even in Italy most of the schools were controlled by the clergy.

The most marked trend in tenth-century education was the shift of leadership from monastic to cathedral schools. About mid-century the school of the bishops of Liége was outstanding. It even rivaled the monastic schools of Cluny and St. Gall. During the second half of the century Gerbert's school at Rheims was pre-eminent, and drew students from all lands. After Gerbert was exiled from Rheims in 982, Bishop Fulbert's school at Chartres took the lead. In both monastic and cathedral schools the subjects of study and the texts used were much the same as in previous centuries. Ever since the Church Fathers had adopted the Roman liberal arts as a basis for Christian education,[18] the fundamentals of grammar, rhetoric, logic, arithmetic, geometry, astronomy, and music had been taught. It was during the Carolingian age that the first three were grouped together into the trivium and the last four into the quadrivium.

EDUCATIONAL AIMS AND METHODS

These subjects were taught to tenth-century students by lectures, the professors reading from the classics or more often from the handbooks that had been compiled by Roman authors such as Donatus, Priscian, Martianus Capella, and Boethius, or by churchmen such as Augustine, Cassiodorus, Isidore, Bede, and Alcuin.[19] All of these secular subjects, however, were subordinated to theology, for which there were innumerable texts, notably the Scriptures and commentaries and treatises of various kinds written by the Church Fathers. Even in the study of the liberal arts, constant emphasis was placed upon religion and morals. The building of Christian character was the supreme aim in most of the church schools.

The methods of most teachers of that day were formal and strictly disciplinary. Like the schoolmasters of a century ago in the United States, they advocated and practiced the use of the rod, especially for the younger students. They insisted that "it is necessary to teach youths with severity; to coddle them is to undermine discipline."

[17] *Ibid.*, I, 249-250.
[18] See above, pp. 51 f.
[19] See above, p. 258.

Ratherius, bishop and head of the school of Liege, thought it best "to correct errors with strokes as well as with words." Another teacher, "enraged when a student would not learn, applied the rod to his back so effectively that the suffering skin was broken by the fervent flagellation." In sculptures on the cathedral at Chartres, grammar was personified as a harsh-faced teacher brandishing a rod over two children. On the other hand, there were schoolmasters who believed in educating students by kindlier means than back-beating, or even browbeating. Egbert of Liége wrote the following in condemnation of the "rod wielders":

> They strike the body and care nothing about correcting the spirit. Radamanthe is less implacable than certain masters; Eaque torments less cruelly the spirits of the damned; the Furies wreathed with serpents demean themselves with less fury. Some of these teachers want their students to know more than they do themselves. It is not strokes of a stick that impart knowledge; it is the inner work of the spirit. You may break a whole forest on the backs of your unhappy pupils, but you will not get anywhere in the developing of their intelligence. . . . You maltreat equally him who is capable of learning, and him who is not. It is by gentleness that one makes children learn. The unhappy little one whom you belabor will go away as little educated as when he came.[20]

Egbert was not the only enlightened educator. In England, Elfric wrote a book called *The Colloquy* in which he upheld a high and intelligent ideal of education. In an imaginary dialogue between teacher and pupils, Elfric represents the latter as saying: "We would rather be flogged while learning than remain ignorant; but we know that you will be kind to us and not flog us unless you are obliged." This is followed by a series of dialogues between the master and various of the pupils. Each, in turn (plowman, shepherd, cowherd, hunter, merchant, shoemaker, baker, and so on) describes his profession. After this it is urged that "each of them should do his work as well as he can. . . . Whether you are a priest or a monk, a layman or a soldier, apply yourself to that, and be what you are." In conclusion, all of the pupils are exhorted "to keep the commandments of God, and behave properly everywhere. Walk quietly when you hear the church bells and go into church, and bow to the holy altars, and stand

[20] Author's translation from G. Kurth, *Notger de Liége et la Civilization au Xe Siècle*, Picard, pp. 293 f.

quietly, and sing in unison, and ask pardon for your sins, and go out again without playing, to the cloister or to the school." [21]

In the higher branches of learning there was little physical coercion. At Rheims, Master Gerbert used advanced methods in teaching the liberal arts. In the trivium, according to Richer, one of his former students

[Gerbert] put in practice his opinion that one cannot attain the art of oratory without a previous knowledge of the modes of diction which are to be learned from the [classical] poets . . . he read and explained the poets Virgil, Statius, and Terence, the satirists Juvenal and Persius and Horace, also Lucan the historiographer. When they were familiarized with these, and practiced in repeating them, he taught his pupils rhetoric. After they were instructed in this art, he brought in a sophist to give them practice in disputation, so that when trained in this art they might argue with ease. This he deemed to be the height of Oratory. [22]

It is apparent that Gerbert employed two methods of teaching—lecture and discussion (disputation).

In the mathematical subjects of the quadrivium, his instruction seems to have been less formal, and involved the use of mechanical apparatus for demonstrations.

With what pains [wrote Richer] he set forth the method of astronomy, it may be well to state, so that the reader may perceive the sagacity and skill of this great man. This difficult subject he explained by means of admirable instruments. First he illustrated the world's sphere by one of solid wood. . . . He fixed it obliquely as to the horizon with two poles, and near the upper pole set the northern constellations, and by the lower one, those of the south. . . . By his sphere thus fixed, he demonstrated the rising and setting of the stars, and taught his disciples to recognize them. And at night he followed their courses and marked the place of their rising and setting upon the different regions of his model. [23]

Such astronomical spheres, constructed according to descriptions in the works of the ancient Greek scholar, Ptolemy, were known and used in Moslem and Byzantine lands. In fact, it is probable that Gerbert learned this and other scientific ideas in Moslem Spain where he had studied for a while as a youth. In teaching arithmetic he introduced the counting board (abacus) and the Hindu-Arabic numerals

[21] A. Leach, *Educational Charters and Documents,* 598-1909, Cambridge University, pp. 37 ff.

[22] Richer, *Historia,* III, 47-48; translation adapted from Taylor, *op. cit.,* I, 289 f.

[23] From Richer, *Historia,* III, 48; translation by Taylor, *op. cit.,* I, 290.

(but without the use of the zero).[24] He also intimated, in a letter to a friend, that he had some "splendid geometrical diagrams." To the modern mind one of the most curious of Gerbert's methods was that used in music.[25]

It is little wonder that the cathedral school at Rheims attracted young priests, monks, and princes from all parts of the West, and that they returned to their homes enthusiastic over the wonders of science and the beauties of the classics. Gerbert's greatness was appreciated in his own lifetime and he exerted a wide influence in both the lay and clerical world. As expressed by a modern writer,

the year 1000 saw the inscrutable master of all sciences, Gerbert, in St. Peter's chair; his gallant and ill-fated scholar, Otto III, Emperor; Fulbert [another of his students] . . . teaching music and the humanities in the school of Chartres; and Robert, henpecked saint, poet and humourist, on the throne of France.[26]

In many other European centers less famous leaders carried on intellectual activities similar to those of the inspiring master of Rheims.

CONCLUSION

The existence of men of learning such as Gerbert—and there were many such—has convinced modern scholars that the post-Carolingian era was active in intellectual pursuits, and that Christendom during the years immediately preceding the year 1000 was by no means stupefied with religious terror and ignorant fanaticism. It is evident that the tenth century recovered much and made considerable progress in cultural lines. In many regions during the early part of the century, civil wars and invasions interrupted intellectual activities, but cultural life carried on. As old centers were destroyed, new and sometimes better ones arose to take their places. In somewhat the same manner in which cultural leadership had shifted from Charles the Great's Frankland to Alfred's England in the ninth century, so also in the tenth century it shifted from the monastic centers to the cathedral school of Rheims and finally to the German realm of the Ottos.

Those who prefer to emphasize contrasts can find in the tenth century evidence of both cultural darkness and "renascence." The same is true of the five medieval centuries (500-1000) which we have surveyed. By concentrating on the more backward periods and regions, it can be shown that the sixth, seventh, early eighth, late ninth, and early tenth centuries were "dark ages." On the other hand, a shift of viewpoint will disclose "renascences" at about the year 600 (Pope Gregory I, Isidore of Seville, and Gregory of Tours); at about 700 in Bede's England; at 800 in the realm of Charles the Great; a century later in Alfred's England; and just before 1000 at Gerbert's Rheims. Such generalizations, however, tend to obscure rather than clarify the history of culture. The truth is that throughout these centuries there were both cultural darkness and cultural light.

In summarizing the dark side of the picture we find several contributing factors. Cultural progress was certainly held back by the political and social-economic disorganization that prevailed. The period with which we are concerned saw the disintegration of two empires (Roman and Carolingian), and two ensuing periods of devastating civil wars and invasions (the Germans in the fifth century, the Moslems, Hungarians, and Norsemen in the ninth and tenth). Then, too, even in times of peace, society was disorganized. The early Middle Ages lacked the orderly large-scale institutions of human life under which intellectual and artistic geniuses flourish. As long as the monastery, the villa, the manor, and the feudal estate were the dominant units of medieval society, culture was bound to be localized and unprogressive. The limited industrial, commercial, and municipal life was the most serious drawback to cultural advance. Culture expands and thrives under the same conditions that create prosperous cities. Moslem and Byzantine civilizations had such conditions and, along with them, culture flourished during the very period in which Western Europe was most backward.

The one possible unifying element in the West was the church, but it had not yet consolidated its strength or achieved effective leadership in cultural affairs. The papacy itself was struggling for existence and was more often led than leader. The monasteries, in which the spirit of learning burned like a candle, sometimes brightly, sometimes dimly, were under the domination of orthodox theology. Therefore the freedom of thought and expression which makes for cultural progress, was badly hampered. There was no real scientific spirit and very little appreciation of the secular aspects of existence in this world. On the whole, the religiousness that pervaded the early Middle Ages like a heavy incense tended to stifle men's mentalities while it made their souls safe for eternity. Even the veneration for the classics, which was widespread among learned men, had very little humanizing influence. It was, for the most part, a blind adherence to stilted literary forms. The authority of the classics, like the domination of the church, could also have a deadening effect upon individual initiative.

On the other hand, there were encouraging signs. The monasteries performed an invaluable service in copying and preserving important literary works. Many of the Latin classics were transmitted to the modern world by means of manuscripts copied in monasteries of the early Middle Ages. The monastic schools taught young clergymen something of classical learning and occasionally provided an atmosphere in which intellectual genius might thrive.[27] More spectacular than the monasteries in the encouragement of culture were the palace schools of such monarchs as Charles, Alfred, and the Ottos. In their patronage of men of learning, these medieval rulers compare favorably with those of any period of history.

Toward the end of the early Middle Ages the cathedral schools provided the most potent and constant influence for cultural progress. In them can be seen the beginnings of an enlightened secular spirit which was to find fuller expression in the towns of the later medieval centuries. With the increase of royal power, city life, and commercial activities in the eleventh and twelfth centuries the culture that had emerged during the early Middle Ages entered into a period of accelerated expansion.

[27] Note, for instance, the career of Bede.

═ XV ═

EARLY MEDIEVAL MUSIC

I**N the artistic activities of the early medieval centuries, we find the
same broad developments noted in the intellectual and literary
history of the period: the decline of classical genius, a fusion of
Roman, Christian, and Germanic influences, and finally the slow emergence of characteristically Western arts. We shall trace in turn the
evolution of the musical, architectural, and decorative arts in Western
Europe to the end of the tenth century, by which time the West was
beginning to find itself culturally.[1]

EARLY CHRIS-
TIAN MUSIC

The history of medieval music centers in the church.
Like the other arts, it had its origins in the fusion of
declining classical culture and rising Christian-Germanic influences.

Our earliest records of church music, which are found in the New
Testament, suggest that from the beginning there were varied types
of Christian singing. At the Last Supper, the disciples "sang a hymn,"
and the Apostle Paul urged Christians to admonish one another "in
psalms and hymns, and spiritual songs."[2] Hymn singing was also
mentioned by a Roman provincial official, Pliny the Younger, who
wrote (about 112 A.D.) that the Christians in Asia Minor were accustomed to meet once a week "before daylight to sing by turns a hymn
to Christ." It seems, then, that the early Christians had two types of
singing: (1) *psalms,* which were probably chanted responsively by the
clergy and congregation, somewhat after the manner of the Jews in
their synagogues; and (2) *hymns* sung in unison by the congregation.
The chanted psalms, as in our own day, were little more than passages
of Scripture recited in slow stately measure with little attention to the
musical melody. The hymns were more musical and more popular.
This was doubtless due to the fact that they were derived from secu-

---

[1] The later development of the arts (from 1000 to 1500) will be treated in subsequent chapters.

[2] Ephesians 5:19; Colossians 3:16.

303

lar hymns of pagan origin worked over into Christian melodies that
had a greater appeal than the chanted psalms.

HYMN SINGING   Although there is little evidence concerning hymn
singing, it seems to have had a prominent place in
early church music. This element of public worship was less formal
than the chant, and in the East it was quite prevalent. As early as
the third century certain heretical sects were using popular tunes and
hymns as a means of winning followers. In retaliation, the orthodox
clergy passed conciliar decrees prohibiting all such "idiotic songs," and
at the same time set their own musicians to composing orthodox
hymns based on popular melodies with which to win the people back
to the true faith. In this type of Eastern church music many scholars
find traces of ancient pagan songs. If this be true—as seems likely—
Christian music had two parents, one Hebrew, the other classical.
The chanting was predominantly Hebrew; the hymn singing, classical,
an outgrowth of Graeco-Roman music.

HYMN SINGING   The earliest example we have of the popular congre-
IN THE WEST   gational hymn in the West was distinctly classical,
and very different from the Hebrew chant. It was a
novel type of rhythmic song which Bishop Ambrose of Milan introduced from the East late in the fourth century. The bishop's enemies
paid tribute to the popularity and effectiveness of such music when
they asserted that he used it "to cast a magic spell over the people."
So influential were the Ambrosian hymns that he has been called
"the pioneer of Western hymnology" and "the father of church singing." From contemporary sources we learn that the new type of music
made a deep impression on the hearers. One of Ambrose's friends,
Augustine of Hippo, "wept over the singing of hymns," and was con-·
cerned for fear that he might miss the religious message because of
the beauty of the melody. "When I am stirred more by the music than
by the words," he wrote in his *Confessions,* "I confess that I commit
a grievous sin, and I would prefer not to have heard it." At times
Augustine felt that it would be better if the reader of the psalms intoned "with little change of voice so as to be more like speaking than
singing," and if "all the sweet melody of singing with which the
psalms of David are frequently sung, were removed from the church."
But he also reflected how

in the early days of my conversion I wept over the songs of the church;
and when now I am moved, not by the music, but by the words sung with

a flowing voice and with suitable modulations, I realize the great usefulness of the custom . . . and am inclined to approve of church singing
. . . in order that weaker souls may be inspired to piety by the pleasures
of music.[3]

It should be noted that the music which inspired and also frightened Augustine was nothing like the religious singing in modern
churches. It was simple unharmonized melody sung in slow and
stately measure. There was little effort at polyphonic or harmonized
music until the later Middle Ages. All sang the same tune, the boys'
and women's voices in a falsetto register, an octave above those of
the men.

MUSICAL TECH-
NIQUE; CHURCH
SINGERS
Very little is known concerning the technical details
of early church music. Neither the late Romans nor
the early Christians had any effective system of notation. Tunes or melodies were preserved almost entirely by memory, and we therefore have no contemporary records
of the music as it was actually sung. The hymns were undoubtedly
sung with more spontaneity than the chants, since they were simple
popular tunes in which the entire congregation took part. In some
regions enthusiastic Christians clapped their hands rhythmically as
they sang, but this was condemned. Usually the words of the hymns
were given a strongly accented rhythm, and sometimes they had
rhymed syllables at the middle and ends of the lines. Thus the
rhythmic beat of the words helped to keep the singers in some sort of
unity. In all medieval church music, it will be noted, the chief interest was in the words.

So far as we know, even the trained choir singers had no musical
scores. At best there was a copy of the words with marks to indicate
accent, upward and downward shifts of the voices, and the like. Ordinarily the only copy was that used by the leader. This was sufficient,
for in the early church the singing was done almost entirely in a
"follow the leader" fashion. This was especially true of the chanted
music.

BEGINNING OF
PLAIN CHANT
Even though hymn singing was stirring and popular,
in the Western Church it gradually gave way to the
better-organized psalm chanting which became the
recognized form of Western church music. In a modified form it is

---

[3] Author's translation. For the Latin text and a translation by William Watts, see
St. Augustine's *Confessions,* Putnam, Book X, Chap. 33.

still widely used not only in Roman Catholic but also in Greek Catholic and Episcopalian services of our day. It is commonly referred to as plain chant, plain song, or Gregorian chant.

By the fourth century the responsive chant had become an established part of Christian worship. The chant leader (usually a priest or deacon) conducted this part of the service in somewhat the same alternating fashion in which the Psalms are read responsively in modern churches. This custom was probably taken over by the Christians from the service of the Jewish synagogue where the psalms were intoned by a cantor (chanter), with responses by the choir or congregation. One of our earliest references to this type of music in the West is found in the writings of Augustine of Hippo, who wrote (about the year 400) that at his mother's funeral a certain clergyman "took up the psalter and began to chant, the whole congregation responding."

CHURCH CHOIRS It is evident that at this time the lay public was accustomed to take part in the chanted responses. But the chants were usually integral parts of a complicated religious service which demanded careful organization and precision. This led, very early, to the development of trained choirs, which tended to discourage congregational singing. The church at Rome is thought to have had a choir in the fourth century, and a hundred years later Pope Leo I showed a great deal of interest in his chanters. Even in faraway Gaul, as early as the fifth and sixth centuries, there were trained choruses. A sixth-century writer mentioned a choir of men and boys at Paris whose "voices blended like various instruments of music, in fine harmony." Eventually, most of the larger churches had specially trained chanters directed by expert leaders. Thus church music came to be monopolized by the choirs.

Women were absolutely excluded from church choirs, and some churchmen would have prohibited them from all singing in public. Jerome insisted that "women should sing in the privacy of their own rooms, away from the company of men and crowded congregations." One of the popes urged that there be "no songs or choruses of women in church." The constantly recurring prohibitions against women singers, however, hint at the possibility of mixed choruses on special occasions. Undoubtedly women took some part in the congregational singing and in processions on festival days. A ninth-century pope complained that women were abusing their religious privileges by singing as they approached the altar on feast days. The objections to women singers came from several sources. According to Christian tradition, women, whether singers or not, were forbidden to approach the altar. Throughout the early centuries, females "on account of the *imbecillitas* of their sex," were strictly prohibited from violating with their presence the sanctity of the most sacred place in the church. To this was added the Christian abhorrence of pagan entertainments, in which women singers were prominent. In classical times female entertainers were women of bad reputation. Finally, among the Christians there was a vague feeling that music had a powerful effect which, if unguarded, tended to worldliness. Jerome reflected his suspicion of choir singers when he wrote that the chanters (all of whom were men) should "let their character, and not their clothes, be their adornment."

GREGORY I: WESTERN MUSIC — Meanwhile the technique of church music seems to have made progress. There were men who understood the theoretical aspects of classical as well as of Christian music. Augustine wrote a treatise *Concerning Music* at about 400 A.D. A century later Cassiodorus' *Institutions of Music* was written, and at about the same time his contemporary, Boethius, wrote a five-book treatise on the philosophical and mathematical aspects of music. To Pope Gregory I (590-604), however, fell the task of establishing the music of the Western Church on a practical basis.

Although Gregory has been called "the inventor of the Gregorian modes" (scales), "the founder of the Roman choir school," and "the father of Western church music," none of these designations is historically accurate. The "Gregorian modes" and chants were based chiefly on developments which had started before Gregory's time and culminated after his death. The Roman choir school, as we have already seen, existed over a century earlier, in the time of Pope Leo I. Gregory did, however, reorganize and reform it. Finally, the title the "Father of Western church music" rightfully belongs to Bishop Ambrose of Milan, Gregory's predecessor by two centuries. Nevertheless Gregory did have a definite influence upon music. His re-establishment of the choir school was a part of his reform of the entire clerical organization. His aim was not only to improve the singing by turning it over exclusively to trained choristers, but also to improve the religious character of the higher clergy by removing them from the supposedly contaminating influences of a musical career.

The development of choir schools had a discouraging effect upon congregational singing. The concentration of singing in specialized groups of singers tended to eliminate not only the priests and deacons

but also the populace from active participation in the musical parts of
the service. In the church at Rome this change seems to have come
about even before the time of Gregory the Great. In other churches,
notably at Milan, the more democratic custom of congregational singing persisted much longer. Eventually, however, church music,
whether the chanting of the psalms or the singing of hymns, came to
be monopolized by the choirs.

ROMAN OR
GREGORIAN
PLAIN CHANT

The development of the modes or scales employed in
chanting was likewise more of an evolution than an
invention by Gregory. Some of the so-called "Gregorian" modes, or scales, had been used long before
his day. He introduced notable changes, however, and further improvements were made during succeeding centuries. All of this was a
part of the gradual development of the plain chant at Rome. As in
many other fields, the leadership of the papal church was so effective
that the Roman form of chanting eventually became predominant
throughout the West.

Its introduction and subsequent success in England are characteristic of the general trend of expansion. Ever since the year 597,
when Augustine of Kent and his missionary monks entered Canterbury "singing a litany with harmonious voice," the clergy of Kent
had kept in touch with musical as well as other developments at
Rome. It was reported by Bede (about 700) that English monks had
been instructed in music "according to the Roman mode which had
been learned from the disciples of St. Gregory." According to the
same writer, "throughout all the churches of England men began to
learn to chant in the [Roman] manner hitherto known only in Kent."
In the eighth century a church council formally adopted the Roman
plain chant as England's official form of religious music.

Across the Channel in Frankland Roman plain chant was likewise
adopted. It is reported that Charles the Great had "authentic song
books made in order that the Roman method of singing should be
both taught and learned." He also asked the pope to send trained
singers to teach the Roman form of chanting to the Franks. Charles
also had two Frankish clerics go to Rome to learn plain chant in order
to teach it in Frankland. One of these Roman-trained singers was constantly at court, and at mealtimes Charles listened either to religious
reading or to singing. It was asserted that for a time he deserted the
old Frankish ballads and listened only to Latin religious chants. This

same pious musical tendency was also attributed to a Visigothic king who preceded Charles by two hundred years. He prohibited all organ playing and frivolous vocal music from this court and had only serious music with his meals.

Charles, like his predecessors and successors, was interested in new musical ideas. Once, while the members of a Byzantine embassy were celebrating their religious services in his private chapel, he had the royal chaplain copy the melodies used by the chanters of his guests, "taking special care to have a separate syllable written down for every note." This suggests the development of a crude system of musical notation in the West. Meanwhile the Roman Catholic methods of chanting were being taught throughout the Frankish realm. At St. Gall, Metz, and Lyons in the ninth century, there were flourishing choir schools for the training of clerical singers. Even more interesting are the regulations that were made during this period for the elimination of those tendencies which, in our own day, are sometimes referred to as "jazz" in church music. The clergy officially condemned and prohibited in church services "stagey or garrulous voices," those that were "sibilant, whinnying like a mule's bray, bellowing or bawling like cattle, and all falsetto or feminine voices," for the reason that "these breathe forth vanity and folly, rather than religion." Charles, during whose reign these clerical regulations were passed, was more tolerant. At his court he is said to have had "a cleric who was unsurpassed . . . in singing both ecclesiastical and festive music."

INDEPENDENT
MUSICAL STYLES
The Roman Catholic style of music was not, however, received with universal approbation. In Milan and many other places, the ancient Ambrosian service, with its congregational hymn singing, was still firmly entrenched in the hearts of the people. For centuries Europe witnessed a sort of musical warfare, with Roman plain chant waging a vigorous offensive against the popular Ambrosian hymn. Until the time of Charles the Great, the Ambrosian music and liturgy were prevalent in France. In seventh-century Spain a national church council at Toledo refused to prohibit the use of the Ambrosian hymns. Thereafter, and until the eleventh century, Spanish churches used the Mozarabic ritual which was a combination of the Eastern and the Gothic forms. Most bitter of all was the opposition of the people of Milan to the Roman ritual and music. They were so devoted to their Ambrosian liturgy and the stirring emotionalism of congregational hymns that they stubbornly

resisted even the slightest change. Outsiders (such as Charles the Great) and many of the popes of succeeding centuries tried in vain to popularize the more formal Roman ritual. Finally in the fifteenth century their efforts ceased. The Ambrosian liturgy is still used in Milan.

SECULAR MUSIC   We know even less of the nonreligious, or secular, music of the early Middle Ages than of church music. Almost all the writers of that day were churchmen and therefore uninterested in secular music. They mentioned irreligious music only to condemn it. But even such hostile evidence shows us something of the songs that were sung outside of the churches. The Christian leaders of the second and third centuries disapproved of all non-Christian music: they condemned "heathen hymns," and "the music of pipes [flutes] and trumpets," such as were used in the Roman amphitheaters and theaters. Christians were exhorted to "reject superfluous music which enervates men's souls and leads them to varieties of emotions; first mournful, then licentious and voluptuous, then frantic." "Burlesque singing [said Tertullian] is the boon companion of drunkenness; . . . liquid and chromatic harmonies are to be avoided." [4]

Such men, of course, frowned upon the playing of pagan stringed instruments and flutes and upon the "tragic vocal ravings" which seem to have been as much a part of Roman banquets as they are of modern night clubs. "Let the temperate meal resound with psalms," wrote Cyprian in the third century; "you will provide better entertainment for your friends if the sweetness of religious music charms their ears."

WESTERN FOLK   Whether the clergy approves or not, people will sing MUSIC   secular as well as religious songs. The populace of the Roman Empire had its folk music, and the singing of ballads was also popular among the Germanic tribesmen of that day, according to Tacitus, who wrote at the end of the first century. Although we have few examples of the folk songs of these early centuries, there is ample evidence of the fact that they were sung. In the writings of Augustine (about 400) there is a reference to "the boat songs" with which rowers "cheer their toil." At about the same time, Ausonius wrote about the peasants along the Moselle River in northern France who "move and work on the heights and along the slopes of the valley singing their country ditties."

---

[4] Compare this with the attitude of modern churchmen (and other conservatives) toward "jazz," "torch singers," "crooners," and the like.

Two centuries later in Spain, decrees were passed condemning the popular custom of "spending the night-vigils before solemn feast days in singing wicked songs." In all parts of Europe, however, folk songs continued to flourish.

GERMANIC
BALLADS

The most distinctive early medieval folk song was that of the Germans. They sang ballads to the accompaniment of a stringed instrument. This rather primitive form of entertainment bears some resemblance to our own American cowboy, "Cajun," and hillbilly music. Charles the Great and Alfred the Great, both of whom were interested in preserving the folk songs of their ancestors, had the ancient Germanic ballads collected and copied down. One of the secular songs of Alfred's day, "The Phoenix," in paying tribute to the various types of music enjoyed by the Anglo-Saxons, praises the singing of a famous minstrel in these words:

Never was trump, nor horn, nor thrill of harp, nor any voice of man on earth, nor organ, nor strain of melody, nor wing of swan, nor any of the harmonies which God hath created for the cheer of men in this sad world, like unto that descant.[5]

Much of this old English love of singing seems to have been associated with drinking songs. The most ancient English epic, *Beowulf,* fairly reeks of strong drink: the "swough of the harp" and the "ringing song of the minstrel" were invariably a part of "the hall joy invoked along the mead bench." The Venerable Bede told how the poet Caedmon as a youth was in despair because "at beer drinkings" he was unable to take his turn at playing the harp and singing; such performances were expected of all gentlemen in that day. It is said that in Wales, until late in the Middle Ages, three things were indispensable to a respectable man: his *harp,* his cloak, and his chessboard. There was another medieval proverb to the effect that a married man must have "a virtuous wife, a cushion for his chair, and a *harp in tune."* Even clergymen could, on occasion, sing popular ditties. According to legend, an eighth-century English bishop, on finding no congregation at his church one morning, took his harp, went to a near-by thoroughfare, and attracted a crowd by his playing and singing. For the youthful, however, the music of flute and lyre had

[5] Cook and Tinker, *Select Translations from Old English Poetry,* Ginn, pp. 147 f.

one supreme theme—love. The following tenth-century song suggests
the popularity of romantic music and poetry:

> There sound enchanting symphonies;
> The clear high notes of flutes arise;
> A singing girl and artful boy
> Are chanting for thee strains of joy;
> He touches with his quill the wire,
> She tunes her note unto the lyre.[6]

RELIGIOUS VS.
SECULAR MUSIC

Such frivolous songs met with stern disapproval
from the clergy and contributed to the eternal warfare between sacred and secular music. A ninth-century pope condemned "the diabolical songs with which the populace
are accustomed to while away the nocturnal hours of the deceased"
(evidently a reference to "wakes"). But folk singing was too deeply
rooted to be abolished by clerical legislation. It continued, with little
effective restriction, and we have from the ninth and tenth centuries
fragments of boating songs, harvest songs, marching songs, and songs
celebrating military victories. Of the last mentioned, there is an interesting ninth-century example which was sung in honor of a victory
over the Saxons. Contemporaries reported that "it floated from almost
every mouth, and a chorus of women danced and clapped their hands
to the popular rustic tune." Similar songs were sung in commemoration of victories over the Norsemen.

The most interesting phase of the struggle between religious and
secular music was the tune-borrowing practiced by the clergy. Unable
to destroy folk music, they set about to capture it for the church, and
provided popular airs with religious words. Many a secular tune was
thus transmitted to later ages, but under a religious title and with
pious words. Sometimes, however, the process was reversed, and a
popular folk poem was sung to a religious tune.

MUSICAL
INSTRUMENTS

Of the instruments used, we know very little. This
is due to the fact that all of them, except the organ,
were used for nonreligious purposes, and the clerical
writers were averse to mentioning such secular devices. It is certain,
however, that when the Germanic peoples settled in the West they
adopted some of the ancient Roman instruments. From earliest times
the Celtic and Germanic bards or minstrels had used some sort of
stringed instrument to furnish a musical accompaniment for the re-

---

[6] Symonds, *Wine, Women, and Song*, p. 15.

citing of ballads. The Roman lyre and zither also suited this purpose; therefore they were adopted and used along with the native instruments. It is not surprising, then, to hear that King Theodoric of Ostrogothic Italy sent to King Clovis of the Franks (about 500) "a lyre player able to delight the Franks with skill of hand and voice, and like a new Orpheus to tame their savage hearts." Among the other instruments in use in the northern regions were the flute, the harp, and a Breton stringed instrument called the *chrotta*. There is an account of two sixth-century kings of Frankland who, while sailing past Coblenz on the Rhine, enjoyed the rather unusual experience of hearing "organs and metal instruments [probably trumpets]." Thus, barbaric Frankland in the sixth century had Roman, Germanic, and Celtic musical instruments. In the ninth century, St. Gall in Switzerland was known for its musicians, among them a monk who was a famous flute player.

PIPE ORGANS   Of the musical instruments just mentioned, the organ was so important that it deserves further comment. It was the only pagan musical instrument with which the Christian Church made terms. The organ, invented by an Alexandrian barber in the second century B.C., was much used for secular entertainments. The fourth-century emperor Julian wrote the following description of a pipe organ, such as was common in the East:

A strange growth of reeds do I behold. Surely they sprang . . . from another brazen field, so wild are they. The winds that wave them are none of ours, but a blast leaps forth from a cavern of bull's hide and beneath the well-bored pipes travels to their roots. And a dignified person, with swift moving fingers of the hand, stands there and handles the keys that pass the word to the pipes; then the keys leap lightly, and press forth the melody.[7]

Pipe organs were also used in the West. We have already mentioned the sixth-century king of the Visigoths in Spain who considered organ playing a frivolous pastime. From the same period comes a description of the Western type of organ:

The organ is built like a tower out of divers pipes from which a very rich voice is produced by a blast from the bellows, and in order that a seemly modulation may order it, it is built with certain wooden tongues

[7] *The Works of the Emperor Julian,* with an English translation by W. C. Wright, Putnam, III, 305 f.

(protruding) from the interior which, when the trained fingers of the masters restrain them, produce a sublime sweet song.[8]

About a century later a chronicler described the organ which Charles the Great was said to have had built in imitation of one which the members of an embassy from the Eastern Empire had with them. It had "great chests of brass" and "bellows of ox hide which blew through pipes made of brass." Some of the notes were like the "roaring of thunder," and others as "sweet as the tinkling of a lyre or cymbal."

These organs, it should be noted, were small instruments which could be moved from place to place. As time went on, organs came into common use in churches. Tenth-century England had a large organ in Winchester Cathedral, and the noted churchman Dunstan not only played but also installed organs in churches. By the end of the tenth century they were in use in most of the great churches of the West, and treatises on organ construction were being written by clerical experts.

Meanwhile, however, there was little advance in the study of music. Music, as one of the four subjects of the quadrivium, was entirely divorced from singing or the playing of musical instruments. It was merely a superficial juggling of the ancient mathematical and philosophical theories of music which Boethius and other writers of textbooks had compiled from classical works. A brief quotation concerning Gerbert's knowledge of the subject will serve to illustrate the uselessness of such works for the average musician. According to one of his tenth-century contemporaries, Gerbert

demonstrated the origin of tones on the monochord; he also distinguished their consonances and symphonic relations in tones and semitones, and in di-tones and sharps. By classifications of the sounds in the different scales he gained a perfect understanding of the science [of music].[9]

Musical progress in the early Middle Ages, it seems, was almost entirely a matter of practical improvements worked out in the process of the training of church singers or the construction of church organs. By the end of the tenth century the general principles of the pipe organ and the music of the mass had been established, although both were

[8] From a work attributed to Bede, but actually written by Cassiodorus in the sixth century. Translation by Mrs. Bittermann, "The Organ in the Early Middle Ages," *Speculum*, IV (1929), 396.
[9] Richer, *Historia*, III, 49; author's translation.

still in a crude stage of development. Secular music, so far as is known, had changed little. As in early Germanic times, the chief form was the ballad, recited to the accompaniment of a stringed instrument. More remarkable developments in music were to be made in the later medieval centuries.[10]

[10] See below, Chapter XXXV.

═ XVI ═

EARLY MEDIEVAL ARCHITECTURE

OR many centuries the church was the social as well as the spiritual center of the lives of most people. Aesthetic experience was usually an outgrowth of religion and was associated with the cathedral or parish church. There the medieval man might hear inspiring music or gaze into vaulted expanses, the sight of which directed his thoughts heavenward; and there in silent wonder he could see Biblical scenes portrayed in sculptured stone, carved wood, painted murals, colorful mosaics, or stained glass. It has been said that the medieval church was not only a place of worship, but an illustrated Bible and an art museum as well.

ROMAN INFLU-
ENCES
The form of the early Christian churches was for the most part derived from the pagan buildings of imperial Rome. This was mainly the result of two factors. First, the Christian religion originated and developed during the most flourishing period of Roman building, the Golden and Silver ages. Even had they tried, the early Christians could not have escaped the influences of imperial architecture. Second, the eventual breakdown of pagan government and religion resulted in Christianity's appropriating for its own uses many imperial buildings. Most churches of the early centuries were either old Roman buildings or new edifices constructed after the Roman manner.

ROMAN HOME
CHAPELS
A brief sketch of Christian church building in Italy, where many of the ruins can still be seen, will illustrate these two factors. First let us mention some very early Christian meeting places which reflect pagan influences. These were usually private rather than public buildings. Like the early Christians at Jerusalem who "continued with one accord in prayer and supplication," "in an *upper room*"[1] the first-century Roman believers usually met in private homes. One of the most fa-

---

[1] Acts 1:13-14.

316

mous of these meeting places was the residence of a wealthy lady who is still venerated as St. Cecilia because of her martyrdom for the faith. It seems that many a prominent Roman who turned Christian during the first and second centuries established a chapel in his own home. The rectangular central hall of a Roman home, with slight alterations, could be used as a Christian chapel. These halls served as the model for the small-sized churches that took the place of private chapels after Christianity's recognition as the state religion. One of the best existing examples is the well-preserved Church of St. Clement, which was the rebuilt private chapel of a Roman citizen. There were also low-vaulted funeral chapels, built both inside the catacombs [2] and at the entrances. At the catacombs of St. Agnes in Rome one can still see examples of this type of church. The general plan of the smaller Roman churches of the first three centuries, and also of later churches of similar type, was derived from such rectangular chapels in private homes or in catacombs.

ROMAN BASILI-
CAN CHURCHES

Beginning with the age of Constantine, as Christianity gained public recognition, many large churches were erected. These were of two general types: the rectangular basilica and the circular domed rotunda. Both had a pagan Roman origin. The basilica was derived from the public court halls or basilicas of imperial times. In fact, during the later centuries of the empire, many unused court halls were turned over to the Christians, who adapted them to religious purposes. It was found that Roman basilicas could easily be put to Christian uses. The bishop and his assisting clergy merely took the place at the front of the hall previously occupied by the pagan judge and his clerical staff. The Christian altar replaced the Roman bar of justice and its pagan altar. Christian sacraments replaced imperial ceremonies. Thus, with little change, the assembly place for pagan legal affairs became the Christian church. Such seems to have been the origin of the famous Church of Santa Maria Maggiore (still to be seen in Rome), and also of the Lateran Church, which was originally a Roman basilica that Constantine gave to the Christians. There were also new churches built according to the basilican form: Santa Maria in Cosmedin, St. Paul's, and the old Church of St. Peter, to name a few.

[2] Catacombs were underground burial places. Pagans as well as Christians used this type of subterranean cemetery.

A TYPICAL
BASILICA
The Christian worshiper who attended one of the
basilicas of the age of Constantine would approach
the entrance by way of a cloister-like courtyard similar to the outer court of an ancient Jewish synagogue or the open
forum of a Roman civic center. The basilica courtyard was surrounded by a colonnade or arcade. In the center was a fountain or
receptacle for washing the hands. This may have been an early form
of the Roman Catholic custom of dipping the fingers in the font of
holy water on entering a church.

As seen from the center of the courtyard the front of the church
very much resembled a high barn with "lean-to" sections on both sides.
But let us imagine that we are fourth-century Christians entering the
church. Proceeding from the courtyard to the interior of the basilica
we pass through a porch or lobby (called the *narthex*).

This is reserved for the uninitiated Christians (or catechumens),
who are not allowed to enter the church proper. On entering the
basilica we see a vast rectangular hall, the main portion of which—
the nave—is separated from the side aisles by two rows of immense
columns. Many of these were taken from pagan temples. In some
churches most of the nave is reserved for the clergy; one of the side
aisles is occupied by women; the other by men.

As we walk down the nave we seem to be passing along a wide
corridor flanked by antique Roman pillars. High above us is the
gilded paneling of the wooden ceiling, or perhaps merely the naked
rafters of the roof. In either case, the roof rests on the clerestory, which
is merely the side walls of the upper portion of the nave, rising above
the aisles. The clerestory is pierced with narrow windows which furnish the only natural lighting for the church. The spaces between the
windows are beautifully decorated with scenes from the Bible or
from the lives of the saints and the patrons of the church.

Proceeding down the nave we approach the altar, which is in the
apse, the rounded front end of the church. The altar is a simple affair, perhaps only a large rectangular stone behind which the priest
says mass facing the congregation. At either side of the altar are the
pulpits, or lecterns, from which the lessons from the Gospels and the
Epistles are read. All of these, and the bishop's seat (called the
cathedra), are raised above the level of the rest of the church and are
set off by a series of steps, and perhaps by a marble railing.

MOSAIC
DECORATIONS

If we kneel here and raise our eyes we see above us in the semidomed ceiling of the apse a beautiful expanse of frescoed or mosaic pictures. Let us imagine that we are at the altar of the small but famous basilica of St. Pudenziana, which is said to have been built over the house of Senator Pudens, who entertained Peter on his arrival at Rome. The mosaics of this church, made from bits of colored glass or enamel fitted together in pictorial patterns, vividly portray religious scenes. The lower portion of this mosaic represents the apostles engaged in animated discussion. Senator Pudens and his daughters wait on them. All of the figures are in Roman garb; in fact the apostles resemble pagan philosophers rather than ex-fishermen missionaries destined for martyrdom. In their midst, seated on a raised throne, is Christ, holding a book in his hand. It is interesting to note that in this case the Christ has a bearded Oriental face. This is very different from the earlier beardless Christs of the murals in the catacombs. It is this bearded Oriental Christ, thoughtful, mature, and tender, that has become traditional in medieval and modern Christian art.

In the background of the mosaic of St. Pudenziana are the colonnades, domes, arched windows, and other structural details of a typically Roman city. It is thought that the artist intended to represent Jerusalem, or possibly the New Jerusalem where Christ and his faithful ones were to spend eternity. But, as in the case of the architectural structure of the basilicas, the early Christians could not forget their pagan Roman environment. Only in the upper background of the mosaic is the purely Christian element predominant. Resplendent against a background of white clouds is an immense jeweled cross. At the sides are allegorical figures symbolizing the four evangelists: the ox representing Matthew; the lion, Mark; the man with the book, Luke; and the eagle, John.

Similar pictures, either in mosaic or painted murals, adorn the apses of most of the early basilicas. For instance, in the Lateran Church there is a jeweled cross and a bearded Christ surrounded by angels, apostles, saints, and flocks of sheep (symbolizing the congregation). At the Church of Santa Maria Maggiore the central position in the apse is occupied by the Virgin Mary, about to be crowned by Christ. In Ravenna the Church of St. Apollinare in Classe (the port town) has a beautiful sixth-century mosaic featuring a great jeweled cross beneath which St. Apollinare stands in a field bedecked with flowers, shrubs, and trees. Before him are twelve sheep, symbolizing the apostles, and above are pictured twelve more sheep passing before Christ and the four evangelists. In some churches the crucifixion is the central theme of the decorations of the apse.

Quite early the subjects and types portrayed in mosaics became standardized, even to the point of determining in detail the relative positions of the figures and the garments, thrones, halos, and other habiliments of God, Christ, the Virgin Mary, the apostles, saints, and clergy respectively. Usually the laymen or clergymen under whose auspices the church was built were represented somewhere in the picture.

SECULAR SUBJECTS
The mosaics and murals on the side walls show more variety. There one finds Bible stories, tales of heretics who came to a bad end, and endless processions of saints, apostles, and martyrs. The non-Biblical was also represented. At Ravenna, for instance, the side mosaics of the Church of St. Apollinare Nuovo (the New) show processions of people facing the mosaic of the Madonna and Child which adorns the apse. On one side are men, among them saints, martyrs, and former bishops of Ravenna, headed by the three Wise Men. On the opposite wall are saintly women carrying crowns of baskets or fruit, while little lambs gambol about "amid the scarlet anemones and lilies at their feet in a field of living green."

Mosaics of great beauty are also to be seen in the octagonal rotunda of St. Vitale, still another of the Ravenna churches. Here the great personages of the Eastern court who contributed to the building of the edifice are portrayed in brilliant colors on a gold background. On one side is the royally clad Emperor Justinian, bearing a gift and accompanied by the bishop and lesser clergy (on his left), and by the civil and military officials (on his right). On the opposite wall stands Empress Theodora richly bejeweled and robed in regal splendor, carrying a precious chalice. Around her is a retinue of court ladies and eunuchs. All of the mosaics at Ravenna are resplendent with the brilliance and luxury of the court of Constantinople.

The mosaics and other mural decorations are easily the most striking and artistic features of the early basilicas; frequently they are the wonder and the despair of modern artists. The fine workmanship, vivid coloring, and intricate designs of birds, flowers, acanthus leaves, and other purely decorative elements are evidences of a classical art that continued long after the passing of the Western Empire and well into the early Middle Ages of Italian history. It is understandable why the Christian churches of this period were so rich in pictorial art, for in that age of short sermons and scanty reading material, pictures were one of the chief sources of popular information concerning the Bible and religious history.

BASILICAS OF RAVENNA

During the sixth century Ravenna and her Byzantine rulers took the lead in Western church building. The structural genius and decorative ability of the architects of Ravenna is well illustrated in two churches, dedicated to St. Apollinare, which are still standing. Both exemplify the prevailing Western type of three-aisled "lean-to" basilica, but they differ from most of the Roman basilicas in that they were built entirely from new materials, instead of from the spoils of pagan edifices. The interiors of St. Apollinare in Classe and St. Apollinare Nuovo, called "The Church of the Golden Ceiling," are still resplendent with brilliant ornamentation. From the outside, however, both churches with their high, pitch-roofed naves, buttressed on either side by lower, "lean-to" sections had the unattractive appearance of the typical basilica.

At the side of each church there is a structure that resembles a sturdy stone silo. These were built, so we are told, as watchtowers and storehouses. Only in far-off Ireland was there anything resembling them in the early Middle Ages. The round towers of Ravenna are the ancestors of such medieval Italian campaniles as the Leaning Tower of Pisa.[3]

MODIFICATIONS OF BASILICAN ARCHITECTURE

After the time of Constantine, modifications were made in the structure of the basilicas to suit the more complicated ritual. In keeping with the increasing formality of the service, the apse (the altar end of the church) was shut off from the nave by a railing so as to prevent the populace from crowding into the sacred place. The clergy was a distinct class and churches were constructed so as to separate them from the congregation. An additional space near the altar, called the choir, was set apart for them. Still another important change came about as a result of the popularity of saints. It became the custom to place the relics of some martyr in a crypt beneath the altar, or to build the choir of the church over the chapel of some venerated saint. Thus, many basilicas had high altars and choirs built over the

[3] See below, p. 727, note 2.

crypt or ancient chapel of the patron saint to whose memory the church was dedicated.

EARLY ROMAN-ESQUE ARCHITEC-TURE
The expression Romanesque is commonly applied to the architecture of the eleventh and twelfth centuries. Like so many of the epoch designations handed down to us by our predecessors, this term is open to serious objections. Romanesque means Roman-like. But the so-called Romanesque cathedrals of the eleventh and twelfth centuries were less Roman in structure and appearance than the basilican churches of earlier centuries, and the later Italian (Renascence) churches. The Romanesque cathedral, like its successor, the Gothic cathedral, was not copied from Roman structures. It was the result of an evolution motivated by the experimental efforts of architects who sought to adjust construction to existing needs, particularly to the necessity for larger churches with stone roofs. The name Romanesque might better be restricted to the Roman-like structures of the early Middle Ages (500-1000), but present-day usage precludes any such radical departure. We shall, however, refer to the architecture of the early Middle Ages (500-1000) as *early* Romanesque, with emphasis on the fact that it was more truly Roman than the so-called Romanesque architecture of later times.

The evolution from the Christian basilica to the early Romanesque church centered in Italy. This development went on in many regions of the West, but it can be traced most clearly in Lombardy. It illustrates not only a change in church structure, but also an interesting northward shift in Italian architecture. As we have seen, the building of basilicas centered in Rome during the earlier period. Then for about a century—the sixth—Ravenna, under East-Roman (Byzantine) control, was the scene of a remarkable building program. By 600 the Lombard conquest had cut short Ravenna's importance and soon a third architectural center came into prominence, in the Po Valley. Here, under the protection of the Lombard rulers, the so-called "Master Masons of Como" evolved the germ of the Romanesque cathedral.

The crucial point in this development was the stone ceiling, a problem which the basilica builders of Rome and Ravenna had never completely solved. From a knowledge of the groined vaults of ancient Roman buildings,[4] the Como architects learned to construct

4 See above, p. 45.

stone ceilings in square vaulted sections. Each section was crisscrossed with arched ribs of groined masonry which served as reinforcements, one for the other. The lower ends of these stone ribs were concentrated at the corners of the section in such a manner as to rest on clustered columns (or piers) of masonry. These were an improvement over the old-style Roman pillars in that they could be enlarged and strengthened at will to support a roof of any size and weight. The ancient churches of St. Ambrose at Milan and of St. Michael at Pavia are examples of this revolutionary change in Italian basilica structure. In another chapter more will be said concerning the later Romanesque style which grew out of this Lombard experiment.[5]

CHURCH BUILD-
ING IN NON-
ITALIAN LANDS

For centuries the development of the basilican form of church outside of Italy seems to have been slow and uneventful. This was apparently due to the setback caused by the Germanic migrations. There are only a few remains of the chapel-churches and basilicas of Anglo-Saxon England, Frankish Gaul, and Visigothic Spain. We know, however, that many churches were built in these regions. A contemporary Frankish poet, for instance, described a sixth-century church in Paris built with "columns and . . . lighted with windows filled with transparent glass. It was as though the hand of some skilled craftsman had imprisoned the light of day in the sanctuary," for it was lighted "as by the light of day even when the sun was not shining."

In similarly glowing terms, Bishop Gregory of Tours described the church which was built, during the same century, over the tomb of St. Martin of Tours. Evidently there was a great deal of architectural activity in France during the early centuries.

In Spain the remains of a sixth-century Visigothic church are still to be seen at St. Juan de Banos. The three square apses at one end of this church give a cross-shaped floor plan that is similar to that of the typical Latin cathedrals of later times. England seems to have had few large basilicas, but there were small parish churches of rectangular form, often with huge square towers. In such structures we see the evolution of pre-Romanesque architecture in non-Italian lands.

The most remarkable of the larger churches of this period was that built at the monastery of St. Gall, near Lake Constance, shortly after the reign of Charles the Great. This church, unusually large and well equipped for its time, had two apses: one at the altar end of the nave,

[5] See below, Chapter XXXIV.

the other, for the choir, at the opposite end. The monks entered and
left the church by way of side doors which opened into the cloister.
At one end of the church and slightly removed from it were two
watchtowers similar to those at Ravenna. Outside of Italy the development from basilican to Romanesque architecture lagged in general
until the late tenth century, when remarkable progress was made in
the regions of Burgundy and Normandy.[6]

DOMED ROTUN-
DA CHURCHES
Although the basilica was the prevailing type of
church in the West during the early Middle Ages, it
had a formidable rival in the circular (or octagonal)
domed structures that are often called rotundas. Italian church architecture during this period is marked by the contrast between the rectan-
gular-basilican and the circular-rotunda styles. The modern visitor to
an Italian city is presented with evidence of this when he sees, face
to face in the central plaza, a basilica and a domed rotunda (used as a
baptistry).[7] In some cities it is thought that the rotunda was originally
the main church, but was later replaced by the more spacious basilican
cathedral. Quite early the rotunda took a place of secondary importance.

ROMAN ORIGINS
Like the basilica, the rotunda was pagan in origin.
Some of the smaller rotundas seem originally to have
been Roman burial vaults which were made over into Christian baptistries or chapels. Among the many examples that still exist is the tomb
of Constantine's daughter (now the Lateran Baptistry). There were
also large rotunda churches in the West. Some of these were pagan rotundas that had been appropriated (like the Roman basilicas) for Christian uses. Of these dome-covered structures, built during the heyday
of imperial paganism and taken over by the triumphant Christians,
the Pantheon is the most famous. Today it stands, amid the hustle and
bustle of downtown Rome, much the same building that it was when
erected in the second century.[8] Its thick cylindrical wall, capped by a
low-lying dome, led a modern tourist to call it "a chopping bowl of
concrete, turned upside down as a lid for a squat stone jar." This
pagan temple, dedicated to "All Gods" (Pan-theon), was appropriated
by the Christians in the fifth century and rededicated as a church of
"All Saints."

[6] See below, pp. 708 f.
[7] See below, p. 727, concerning Pisa and Florence.
[8] See above, p. 45.

INTERIOR OF SANTA MARIA IN
COSMEDIN, ROME
(Restored)

BASILICA OF ST. APOLLINARE THE
NEW, RAVENNA (VI C)

Courtesy of the University Prints

RUINS OF BASILICA OF MAXENTIUS OR CONSTANTINE, ROME (IV C)

CHRISTIAN BASILICAS

(See pp. 318 ff.)

CHARLES THE GREAT'S CHAPEL,
AIX-LA-CHAPELLE (IX C)

TOMB OF THEODORIC, RAVENNA
(VI C)

CHURCH OF ST. VITALE, RAVENNA (VI C)

EARLY MEDIEVAL ARCHITECTURE — DOMED BUILDINGS

(See pp. 324 ff.)

CHRISTIAN
ROTUNDAS
Eventually the Christian West learned to build its own rotundas. Among the rather scanty and little-known examples of such buildings are St. Angeli at Perugia, St. Stephen's at Rome, and a small church at Nocera near Naples. In each of these churches the central rotunda is encircled with an outer section which serves as a circular lobby or ambulatory surrounding the main portion of the structure. The central dome-covered portion rises higher than the roof of the ambulatory, and the inner church is lighted by windows cut into this upper wall. The effect is that of a very tall domed church with high windows, around which has been built a low circular section. As in the case of the side aisles of the basilica, the ambulatory not only gave more room but also helped to buttress the inner structure, thus making it possible to erect a higher, wider, and heavier dome.

When the Christian Ostrogoths conquered Italy, they also adopted the rotunda, but due to their lack of architectural technique, they could not match the earlier Roman buildings. The architects of Theodoric the Ostrogoth lacked sufficient engineering skill to construct, out of masonry, a dome for his mausoleum at Ravenna in the sixth century. Instead they used a single block of stone, twenty-six feet in diameter, which was hollowed out into a flat, saucerlike dome.

ROTUNDA
CHURCHES AT
RAVENNA
During the Byzantine domination of the late sixth century, Ravenna produced the most noteworthy of Western rotunda churches. St. Vitale, built by the resident Italian officials of Justinian, is small (only 110 feet in diameter), octagonal in shape, and surmounted by an unimpressive dome, scarcely visible from the exterior. Although insignificant in external appearance, this church nevertheless has great beauty and is of interest and importance in the history of Western architecture. Most of all it symbolizes the influence of Byzantine methods of church building. There are the same glowing mosaics, marble pillars, and sculptured details so characteristic of the churches of Constantinople. St. Vitale also exemplifies the Eastern type of dome, uplifted on a series of supporting piers, pillars, and arches, and buttressed with a ring of semicircular recesses. Two centuries later when Charles the Great built his small royal chapel at Aix-la-Chapelle, it was done in the rotunda style of St. Vitale. He brought in Italian architects and even transported across the Alps classical pillars from Roman ruins.

THE DOME The Eastern Christians, having greater resources than their Western brethren, were more successful in the construction of domed structures. The great sixth-century Church of St. Sophia, built in Constantinople by Emperor Justinian, is an admirable example of the manner in which the dome was adapted to a church of grand proportions. The dome of St. Sophia does not rest, like that of the Pantheon, on a low circular wall, but on an uplifted circular drum, which rests in turn on a large square base supported by a series of pillars and arches.[9] Thus the spacious dome seems to float on high, far above the worshipers. With the erection of the Church of St. Sophia, the low-lying Roman dome began, as it were, to grow up.

In the West this development was delayed. From the sixth to the tenth century there are only two important examples of domed churches, the royal chapel of Charles the Great and St. Mark's in Venice. The latter was strongly influenced by Byzantine architecture. Throughout these centuries Venice maintained close commercial relations with Constantinople, and in many respects its buildings reflect its Eastern contacts.

Like many Eastern churches, St. Mark's was not a true rotunda. Its ground plan was, and still is, that of a Greek cross, with a large dome over the central intersection and smaller domes over the ends of the four transepts. This plan gave ample space inside the church without creating the difficult problem of building one gigantic dome to cover the entire structure. Another interesting feature of St. Mark's is the shape of the domes. Unlike those of the Pantheon, of St. Vitale, and of St. Sophia (each of which was less than half a sphere), the domes of St. Mark's are more than half a sphere. In fact, they resemble somewhat the bulbous domes of Russian churches and Moslem mosques.

By the end of the tenth century, when the old church of St. Mark's was built, Western Europe seems to have settled on the basilica as its favorite church style. Only in Italy was the rotunda form much in evidence, and this was chiefly restricted to baptistries or small churches built under Eastern influences. Later, as we shall see, notably in the cathedral of Florence and in St. Peter's at Rome, the dome attained a towering splendor, and was merged with the rectangular

[9] Like many Eastern churches, St. Sophia was built in the form of a Greek cross, with the dome erected over the square crossing of the arms of the cross. In the West the dome was more often used for circular or octagonal structures (rotundas).

church to form another architectural style, the so-called "Italian Renascence."[10]

Apart from the gradual evolution of domed churches and early Romanesque structures, there were few advances made in Western church building in the early Middle Ages. The general trend was toward smaller and simpler structures than those of imperial times. This was due chiefly to the localized rural type of life. Until commerce, wealth, and populous cities came into existence on a large scale, there could be few building projects of great importance.

HOUSES, VILLAS, PALACES　　But what of the nonreligious buildings of Western Europe? Obviously churches were not the only type of early medieval structure. Throughout this period the dwindling populations of the few existing cities continued to live in houses of Roman design: tenement houses for the poor, palaces for the rich. Public buildings tended to disappear along with the decline of imperial and municipal institutions.

In the country, a comparable decline can be observed. Until about the end of the fifth century there were Roman nobles who continued to live on magnificent estates, surrounded by servants and armed retainers. Bishop Apollinaris Sidonius, a nobleman of southern Gaul, has left us in his letters interesting descriptions of the porticos, dining halls, vaulted bathing rooms, and game courts of the villas in which many fifth-century Gallo-Roman gentlemen dwelt. Further north, however, after the Frankish conquest, living accommodations were not so pleasant. A contemporary writer recorded that a villa on the Moselle River had a defensive palisade, a single gate with castle-like towers, and a contrivance for raising water to turn mill wheels. Apparently the inhabitants of these regions had few, if any, Roman luxuries.

In most regions of the West, Roman villa life, like Roman city life, declined. The conquering Germans lived a relatively simple rural life. The common folk dwelt in crude wooden or thatched huts. The nobles had more pretentious country homes, but only kings and bishops built residences of any architectural merit. Not until later did the picturesque castles and town halls, so characteristic of medieval secular architecture, appear. Consequently, the history of nonreligious buildings in the early Middle Ages is largely the slow submergence of Roman architectural forms under a steadily increasing Germanic ruralism.

[10] See below, p. 727.

═ XVII ═

THE DECORATIVE ARTS OF THE EARLY
MIDDLE AGES

PAINTING, MOSAIC, AND SCULPTURE

IT has been said that architecture is the mother of painting, mosaic, and sculpture. This is particularly true of the Middle Ages, for practically all of these arts were employed originally for the purpose of decorating churches. They can be regarded, therefore, as decorative arts.

CHRISTIAN MURALS

We have already seen how the walls of the catacombs and churches of the early centuries were covered either with paintings or mosaics. The mural decorations in the Roman catacombs are particularly interesting because they are our earliest examples of Christian art in the West. Christianity came out of the East, and these paintings mainfest peculiarly Oriental characteristics. One of these is the tendency to employ symbolical figures. On the walls of the catacombs can be seen the fish and the lamb (both of which represented Christ), the dove representing the Holy Spirit, and the four figures (the ox, the lion, the man, and the eagle) which symbolized the evangelists (Matthew, Mark, Luke, and John).

The pictures dating from the earlier centuries also have marked pagan characteristics. For instance, there are classical designs consisting of birds, flowers, grapevines, and also seminude woodland sprites, and occasional representations of the Cupid-Psyche myth, or of Orpheus with his lyre. Soon, however, scenes from the Old Testament became more prominent, and by the third century, portrayals of actual events from the lives of Christ and the apostles were the principal theme of the catacomb decorations. This meant the triumph of the simple narrative and descriptive realism of Westernized Christianity over Oriental symbolism and classical paganism in art. Examples of this shift from pagan to Christian themes are found in the manner

328

in which the classical Greek representation of the winged victory came to be used for Christian angels, while the young man carrying a calf or lamb became the popular interpretation of Christ the Good Shepherd.

CHRISTIAN MOTIFS
In general, during the first five centuries of Christian history, the art of mosaic, like that of painting, showed the same trend toward the simple portrayal of Biblical events. We have already seen how apostles, saints, martyrs, bishops, and royal patrons became more and more prominent in the mosaics of Italian churches of the sixth and seventh centuries. Elsewhere similar tendencies are noticeable, save for the fact that outside of Italy mural *paintings* were more prevalent than mosaics. Everywhere in the West, Christian churches were richly decorated in glowing colors. In the sixth century, a church in France was decorated with pictures of animals and birds eating grapes. At another place, so a contemporary tells us, the wife of the bishop superintended the decoration of the church, "holding a book open upon her knees from which she read the tales of deeds done of old, and instructed the painters as to what scenes should be represented." From contemporary references to churches in Italy and England, as well as France, it appears that there was much church building and mural decoration during the centuries from Constantine to Charles the Great.

SCULPTURE
Early Western sculpture tended to follow the same lines of evolution as the other arts. The steady decline in Roman technique was accompanied by an increasing Christian influence especially in subject matter. In statuary, the decline in technique was marked. The Christian commandment prohibiting idols discouraged artists from sculpturing God or Christ, and the puritanical attitude toward sex led pious church members to turn in horror from the nude forms of classical statuary. The victory of Christianity thus sounded the death knell of pagan sculpture. One modern writer has gone so far as to say that in the West "statuary was forgotten from the fourth century on." However, fifth- and sixth-century statues of emperors and women have come down to us, and also many ivory or gold statuettes. We can, nevertheless, dismiss the art of sculpturing statues as relatively unimportant throughout the early Middle Ages.

RELIEFS
In contrast to "sculpture in the round," "sculpture in the flat," usually called relief, flourished. Inasmuch as reliefs are carved on walls, sarcophagi and pillars, in a crude sense

they are merely a sort of picture incised on stone rather than painted on plaster. In many ways they show the same trends as painting: a decline of Roman technique and subject matter, and the rise of a vigorous new art based on Christian themes and Germanic-Oriental symbolism.

By the end of the fourth century, pagan reliefs showed signs of decline. The classical sculptors had given away to mere stonecutters. In many cases, emperors (notably Constantine) used slabs of relief from earlier monuments for the decoration of triumphal arches, instead of depending on the inferior work of contemporary workmen. The Christian West, however, picked up the declining Roman art and gave it renewed life. This is best illustrated by the reliefs on sarcophagi (stone coffins). In Italy, southern Gaul, and the Rhinelands, there can be seen today many sarcophagi carved in a mingled pagan-Christian style. Traditional Christian themes, such as Bible stories and the Good Shepherd, were combined with pagan vintage scenes and border designs of grapevines, flowers, leaves, and curious symbolical figures. One of the strangest features of this new art is the absence of portrayals of the crucifixion until the fifth century. Apparently the early Christians preferred happier themes, particularly youthful Christs in the role of the Good Shepherd. The change to more solemn subjects was doubtless due to the increasing influence of monasticism and the ascetic spirit.

ENGRAVING AND JEWELRY   Similar contrasts between the classical Roman arts and those of the early medieval centuries are to be noted in the engraved gold and ivory chalices and reliquaries. Ravenna and Constantinople produced a much greater quantity and higher quality of such work than the West. But everywhere church portals, pillars, altars, choir screens, and woodwork were carved with scenes from sacred history. To be sure, with the decline of imperial and municipal influences in the West, such work was usually done in a crude manner. The figures were stiff and lifeless, often merely conventional suggestions of human or animal forms. The tendency toward symbolism was due in part to an important new influence, that of the Germans. These people, whose art is often considered worthless and barbaric, had produced, even during the nomadic stage of their existence, noteworthy works of art. These works, because of the nomadic life of the Germans, were of necessity the small portable objects produced by goldsmiths and engravers.

At various places in the great plains of Northern and Western Europe, modern excavators have discovered hoards of treasures that were hidden by the Germans during the period of their migrations toward the Roman frontiers. There are gold plaques, jeweled buckles, filigreed trays, bracelets, inlaid metal baskets, and beautifully ornamented swords. On some of these, the chief decorations are figures of men and weird animals such as serpents and dragons. Archeologists identify these as Oriental themes, doubtless acquired through Germanic contacts with peoples of the Black Sea region. It is also believed that, as the Germans moved westward, their art took on the more geometrical forms (straight lines and spirals) that were used by the natives of the Rhinelands. The Germans also seem to have become very fond of gold work with insets of gems and enamel. This tendency is admirably illustrated by the famous "iron crown of Lombardy," which is thought to have been produced by sixth- or seventh-century Lombard jewelers in northern Italy. The iron portion, which is supposed to be one of the nails from the Cross, is entirely concealed by a gem-encrusted golden circlet, typically German in workmanship. Similar jewel-studded crowns were manufactured in great quantities in Visigothic Spain, where pious donors frequently dedicated them as votive offerings at the altars of the churches.

All of this indicates that the Germanic peoples had a well-developed jewelers' art which, in earlier times, was devoted to the production of articles for personal adornment. In the course of their wanderings, they picked up new art forms and merged them with the classical and Christian arts of the people they conquered.

IRISH ART   One region of the West produced an exotic type of art during this period. Ireland, almost untouched by either Roman civilization or Germanic migrations, developed during the early Middle Ages fascinating art forms which seem to have been inspired partly by Eastern influences, and partly by the earlier native arts of the West. For instance, the Irish used the same spiral, interlaced, and knotted lines that were present in the gold work of the Germans after they had come to the West. In Ireland these designs were found on metal buckles, chalices, episcopal staffs, engraved Bible covers, and even on sculptured stone crosses and in manuscript illustrations. Some of the later Irish work indicates a mingling of these Western geometrical-spiral patterns with the older

Oriental themes of men and animals. This same combination of Oriental figures with Western designs appeared also in Scandinavia. Many a Norse ship has been found with wood carvings in similar patterns.

ILLUSTRATED
MANUSCRIPTS
But the most noteworthy example of Irish art is found in the illustrated manuscripts. The Lindisfarne Bible and the Book of Kells (seventh and eighth centuries) are famous for their full-page colored illustrations and capital letters. Although the figures are grotesquely distorted (somewhat like those of ultramodern art), the decorations and border designs are wondrously executed, with intricate lines, patterns, and color schemes done in such fine detail that they amaze the modern draftsman. Nowhere, until the late Middle Ages, did manuscript illumination attain the fascinating complexity of line and color that the Irish scribes and illustrators accomplished.

Other regions of Europe, however, also produced remarkable manuscripts. The artists and scribes of the Eastern Empire were noted for their lavish use of gold, silver, and brilliant colors in pictures and decorations. Most beautiful of all were the copies of the Gospels, the Psalms, and other portions of the Scriptures. Many of the manuscripts made for emperors and great churchmen were written in gold, silver, or purple on colored parchment, and bound in covers of wood, leather, metal, and ornately carved ivory with insets of gems. Due to the strict regulations of an all-powerful clergy, artists were forced to represent Biblical characters and religious personages in a set fashion. There was little opportunity for individuality of expression or realism.

The work of the Western artists was less splendid, but more progressive. In the Frankish realm, during the Carolingian and post-Carolingian era, there was a great deal of copying and illustrating of manuscripts. The decorations and illustrations of these manuscripts indicate varied outside influences. Designs were copied from Oriental rugs and textiles. Gold, silver, purple, and bright colors were employed, as by the Eastern artists. Intricate patterns, scrolls, and curious animal designs were frequently used in making large ornamented capital letters. The representations of humans were more lifelike than those of the Byzantine and Irish artists. Christ, the apostles, the evangelists, saints, clergymen, and kings were portrayed with vigor and realism. Occasionally an artist attempted a scene from the life of

Emperor Justinian and Attendants (VI C)
CHURCH OF ST. VITALE, RAVENNA

Mosaic Representing a Procession of Saints
BASILICA OF ST. APOLLINARE THE NEW, RAVENNA

MOSAIC

(See p. 320.)

Ornamented Initial Letters
THE BOOK OF KELLS (VIII C)

Christ Changing Water into Wine
A TENTH-CENTURY BIBLE

Both Courtesy of the University Prints

MANUSCRIPT ILLUMINATION

(See pp. 331 ff.)

Christ or even a battle from Biblical history. In the small-scale works of these miniaturists, as also in the murals on church walls, we see the germ of the Western art of painting which was to come to a magnificent climax in the later Middle Ages.[1]

[1] See below, p. 723, concerning the later illuminators, and p. 733, concerning painting in the late Middle Ages.

A RÉSUMÉ OF EARLY MEDIEVAL CULTURE

A GREAT historian has recently suggested that the history of civilization might be divided into alternating periods of stability and instability, rather than of decadence and renascence. The periods of instability apparently produce little; this is because they are busied with the task of working out new bases and forms of culture. Invariably they are followed by periods of stability which reap the fruit of the cultural reorganization. Thus it was that the early Middle Ages were apparently unproductive; they witnessed the sloughing off of much of the outworn and decadent civilization of antiquity and, at the same time, the merging of certain classical remnants with the primitive Christian and Germanic cultures. In the eastern part of the empire, classical antiquity was deep-rooted and the classical element always played a dominant role throughout the Middle Ages. In the West, Roman elements gave way rapidly. This was due to the complete disintegration of imperial government and prosperous municipal life, and to the subsequent expansion of Christian and Germanic institutions.

The new civilization of Western Europe did not develop as a unit, according to a set pattern. There were many regional variations. The civilization of the Southwest, including Italy, Spain, and much of Gaul, which had been thoroughly Romanized, was rather homogeneous. This fact is still evident in the linguistic unity (the Romance languages) of these regions. In the more northerly regions of the West, which had enjoyed little or no Roman influence and which were predominantly Germanic in population, the emerging culture was vigorous and primitive. It is usually classed as "barbaric." In a technical sense the term is accurate but it must not be taken too literally. In these regions—England, northern France, and the German Rhineland—there were significant independent cultural developments. Here, relatively uninfluenced by classical traditions, the native institutions of the West slowly advanced, subject to the interrupting effects and influences of invading Moslems, Norsemen, Slavs, and Hungarians.

Obviously, during these troubled centuries there was constant change. Centers of culture rose and fell, often with unusual rapidity. We have noted that from the fifth to the tenth century, leadership in learning and the arts shifted successively from Rome to Byzantine Ravenna, then to Visigothic Spain, to monastic Ireland and England, to Carolingian Frankland, and finally to the imperial Rhineland. The geography of these changes is significant. Slowly but surely the torch of civilization was passing from the old Roman regions of the Mediterranean to the more northerly and more Germanic regions. This fact, of itself, is indicative of a new age: that of a distinctly Western culture. To the ardent classicist, the passing of the glorious civilization of Greek-Roman antiquity spells only tragedy. To those who would turn their backs on the dead bones of the past, the vigorous iconoclastic spirit of Christian-Germanic Europe suggests something of the brutal progressiveness of the world of today. Whatever may be his sympathies or prejudices, the student of history can see in these early centuries both the old and the new mingling, interacting, and fusing to produce a new culture.

THE "DARK AGES"—A MISNOMER?
A realization of the vigorous cultural activity of Western Europe during the early Middle Ages often leads the discerning student to question certain concepts which are in common usage. This is true of the term "Dark Ages." It has been suggested that the term is "obsolete"; and that it is accurate only when it is used to indicate the fact that we moderns are very much "in the dark" as to many of the achievements of the early Middle Ages. Our survey of political, economic, religious, and cultural life in Europe from imperial times to about 1000 A.D. lends support to this view and we should be glad to see the term replaced by some other less open to objection. In the light of the growing modern understanding of the past, such terms as "Dark Ages," "medieval," "revival" or "rebirth" of learning, and the like often mislead rather than enlighten the student. But it is easier to abolish inaccurate expressions than to furnish adequate substitutes. We have therefore continued to use certain of these traditional titles, but insist that they should not be taken as absolute characterizations of the status of civilization in the periods referred to.

Thus we hold that the essential characteristic of the so-called "Dark Ages" was not cultural darkness. During this period there were highly complex and sophisticated civilizations in the Byzantine

15   10   5   0   5

KINGDOM
OF
SCOTLAND   Edinburgh

IRELAND
Dublin   Durham
York
ANGLO-
Chester
SAXON
WALES
Cork   KINGDOM   Norwich
50
Cardiff   Oxford   London   Utrecht
Canterbury   DY. OF
Hastings   CO. OF   Ghent   LOWER
FLANDERS   Agincourt   LOTHRINGEN
Boulogne   Arras   Cambrai
Creçy   Laon   Verdun
DY. OF   Rouen   CO. OF   Metz
DY. OF   NORMANDY   Seine   CHAMPAGNE   LOTHRINGEN
BRITTANY   Paris   R.   Toul
DY. OF   Orleans   Troyes   Strasb
Nantes   FRANCIA   DY. OF   Besancon
Loire   Tours   BURGUNDY
45
Poitiers   Bourges   Autun
F   R   A   N   C   E   Gene
DY. OF   Lyon
Limoges   AQUITAINE   Vienne
Bordeaux   CO. OF
Garonne   Nimes   Avignon   S
Oviedo   Bayonne   DY. OF   R.   Arles
ASTURIA   K. OF   GASCONY   TOULOUSE   Marseilles
Leon   KM. OF   Pamplona   Toulouse
Burgos   NAVARRE   Narbonne
KINGDOM   CASTILE   RIBA   CO. OF
OF   CORCA   BARCELONA
LEON   Zamora   Ebro   Lerida   Barcelona
40   Salamanca   Saragossa   R.
Tagus   Toledo   Cuenca
R.
Lisbon   CALIPHATE   M   O   S   L   E   M   P   O   S   S   E   S   S
OF   Valencia   BALEARIC ISLES
CORDOVA
Cordova   Murcia
Seville   Cartagena
Malaga
Strait of Gibraltar

5   0   5

EU

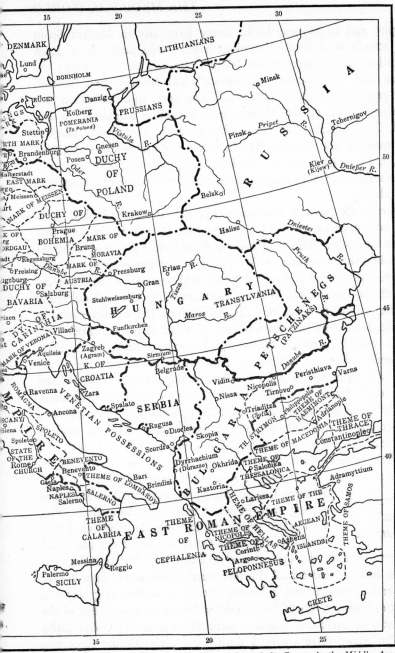

DENMARK
Lund
BORNHOLM
RÜGEN
Stettin
POMERANIA
Kolberg
Danzig
(To Poland)
PRUSSIANS
LITHUANIANS
Minsk
Pinsk
Pripet
R.
Tchernigov
RUSSIA
Brandenburg
Posen
Gnesen
Oder
R.
DUCHY
OF
POLAND
Belsk
Kiev
(Kijew)
Dnieper R.
50
EAST MARK
Meissen
MARK OF MEISSEN
DUCHY OF
Prague
Krakow
Halisc
Dniester
BOHEMIA
MARK OF
Brunn
MORAVIA
Regensburg
Danube
R.
Freising
MARK OF
AUSTRIA
Pressburg
Gran
Erlau
R.
Tisza
R.
Maros
R.
HUNGARY
TRANSYLVANIA
Proth
R.
45
Salzburg
Stuhlweissenburg
DUCHY OF
BAVARIA
DY. OF CARINTHIA
MARK OF VERONA
Villach
Funfkirchen
Zagreb
(Agram)
Sirmium
PETSCHENEGS
(PATZINAKS)
Danube
R.
Aquileia
Venice
K. OF
CROATIA
Belgrade
Zara
Vidin
Nissa
Nicopolis
Tirnovo
Peristhiava
Varna
Ravenna
VENETIAN POSSESSIONS
Spalato
SERBIA
Ragusa
Dioclea
THE STRYMON
Triaditza
(Sofia)
Philippopolis
THEME OF
HAEMIMONT
Ancona
SPOLETO
Skopia
Adrianople
THEME OF
THRACE
Siena
Spoleto
Scordra
THEME OF MACEDONIA
Constantinople
STATE
OF THE
CHURCH
Rome
BENEVENTO
Benevento
THEME OF LOMBARDY
Bari
Dyrrhachium
(Durazzo)
Okhrida
BULGARIA
THEME OF
SALONIKA
THEME OF
THESSALONICA
Adramyttium
Gaeta
Naples
NAPLES
Salerno
SALERNO
Brindisi
Kastoria
Larissa
THEME OF
SAMOS
THEME
OF
CALABRIA
THEME
OF
CEPHALENIA
EAST ROMAN EMPIRE
THEME OF
NICOPOLIS
THEME OF
HELLAS
Athens
THEME OF THE
AEGEAN
ISLANDS
Corinth
Messina
Reggio
Palermo
SICILY
Argos
PELOPONNESUS
CRETE
15
20
25
30
15
20
25

Adapted from Ault, *Europe in the Middle Ages.*
By permission of D. C. Heath & Co., publishers.

Empire and in Moslem lands. Every large city in Moslem Spain had schools, a university, luxurious bazaars, and public baths. Even Christian Europe during the "dark" centuries before Charles the Great and his so-called "renascence" had learned men, schools, and progressive cultural interests. To be sure, this civilization was inferior to that of the Moslem and Byzantine neighbors. In Ireland, England, and the Germanies, however, remarkable progress was made in several fields. The literature and arts of classical, Christian, and Germanic centers were interacting with new influences from Constantinople, from Moslem Spain, and even from the Scandinavian Northlands.

From the political standpoint, likewise, the early Middle Ages was an important epoch. Of outstanding interest is the fact that it was the age in which the Franks evolved from a group of barbarian tribes into the rulers of a civilized Christian empire which for a time dominated the West and won the respectful attention of the monarchs of both the Eastern and Western Mediterranean. Although culturally inferior to the Moslems and the Byzantines, the Franks played a significant role in the development of those Roman-Christian-Germanic institutions which were destined to emerge finally as the bases for modern Western civilization. Along with their allies, the popes, the Frankish monarchs were the outstanding political leaders of the West during an age which saw the birth of Western civilization. The later centuries of the early Middle Ages also saw stirring events, momentous in their influence on the development of certain modern European states. This was the age during which England, France, and the three Spains (Portugal, Castile, and Aragon) were born and attained a confused but vigorous start toward national unity.[1]

EVOLUTION OF WESTERN CIVILIZATION Western Europe during the early Middle Ages was stirring with impulses that were destined to affect the modern world. In the south the mingling of classical, Christian, and Germanic influences was eventually to produce the literature of a Dante and the marvelous art of the Italian "renascence." Further north there would later appear the germ of the modern university and such intellectual geniuses as Abelard, Chaucer, Wiclif, and François Villon as well as one of the most striking architectural achievements of all time—the Gothic cathedral. In music there emerged during the early Middle Ages two

[1] See below, Chapters XXIII-XXIV.

contrasting elements, the minstrelsy which was represented later by the troubadours of the twelfth century, and the Roman Catholic plain chant, which eventually developed into modern harmony and produced some of the most impressive music ever sung by mankind. To the later medieval centuries, which saw the flowering of many such impulses, we now turn our attention.

PART II

CIVILIZATION DURING THE LATE MIDDLE AGES

THE BEGINNINGS OF MODERN CIVILIZATION

THE *late* Middle Ages (from the eleventh century onward) present an increasingly different type of life from that of the *early* centuries of the Middle Ages. Its society is much closer to the early modern period than it is to the age of Charles the Great. The most progressive aspect of late medieval life centered in the towns, with their busy and ambitious burgher inhabitants. Here, rather than on the manor or in the feudal castle, are found the active forces which finally came to shape all phases of modern life. Town life more than anything else transformed medieval Europe into that which we call modern Europe.

Although small in numbers, the burghers were active, progressive, and, above all else, wealthy. They so increased in numbers and importance during the twelfth and thirteenth centuries that the highborn clergy and nobility were forced to take cognizance of them. First the kings took up with the lowly burghers, using them and their money to crush hostile nobles and to dominate the church. Eventually the merchant class came to control governments as well as trade and industry. Their unceasing ambition and purposeful activity eventually made them the masters of the modern European world. Modern civilization is very largely the product of the burgher ideals and energy that came into being during the late Middle Ages. Therefore we begin our survey of the late medieval (or early modern) age with a consideration of the rise and development of this all-important town influence.

THE RISE OF TOWNS

THE REVIVAL OF BUSINESS AND TOWN LIFE
IN THE WEST

IN an earlier chapter we have made it clear that from the disintegration of the Western Empire in the fifth century to the end of the Moslem, Norse, and Hungarian invasions in the tenth century towns and business life in the West were in a state of decline. The names, walled defenses, and some of the buildings of Roman cities such as Milan, Rome, Cologne, Paris, and London continued throughout these early centuries. But their civic life, municipal governments, and economic activities died out, or changed so decidedly that a citizen of ancient times would not have recognized his native city. Town population decreased, industry and commerce languished, municipal governments were taken over by feudal or ecclesiastical authorities. Grass literally grew in the streets and outlying sections of older urban centers. Whatever there was of town life during these early centuries had little vitality, and the great majority of the ancient cities (save for remnants of walls and buildings) had entirely disappeared.

Roman city life, which had begun to decline in the second and third centuries, was further depressed by the Germanic conquerors whose mode of life was rural. After the passing of the Empire of the West in the fifth century, economic and social life in this portion of the Roman world changed even more rapidly. Its character is summed up in terms of decentralization, localism, and ruralism. The larger cities continued to exist, but chiefly as centers of government. Their industrial and commercial activities were gradually reduced to a shadow of that of former times. These conditions obtained generally in most parts of the West until about the end of the tenth century.

COMMERCE IN THE WEST

It is an obvious fact that progress in civilization is associated with city life.[1] Likewise the decline of cities invariably marks the decline of civilization. The glory of ancient Greece and the grandeur of the Roman Empire disappeared when their flourishing city life gave way to an ever-increasing ruralism. The passing of the Western Empire and the Germanic invasions accentuated and prolonged this condition of affairs. Even after the establishment of Germanic kingdoms, there were constant wars and new barbaric invasions. There was little opportunity for peaceful activities and almost no encouragement of industry and trade. Even the orderly regime of Charles the Great was so limited in extent and had so brief an existence that it failed to restore any semblance of the vibrant city life of the ancient world. Some scholars attribute the long continuance of ruralism and localism to the fact that Western Europe's lines of communication with the great Eastern centers were permanently blocked—by Moslems in Northern Africa, Spain, and the western Mediterranean, and by Hungarians and other rather primitive peoples in the Balkan regions. In short, Western Europe was commercially isolated. For centuries there was little import trade save that of an occasional Syrian or Jewish peddler who brought in Oriental manufactured goods. All that men needed for existence was taken from the soil or produced by servile workmen in the manorial workshops, to be bartered at local markets.

The steady advance of town civilization from the tenth century onward is as difficult to account for as the decline of that same sort of life seven hundred years earlier. One fact is clear: as in all ages, the prosperity of business and the merchant class was absolutely necessary for the growth of cities. Just as civilization depends on cities, so cities depend on business. Therefore in tracing the rise of cities in the Middle Ages, we turn first to the revival of commerce and industry. Of these two activities, commerce seems to have been the more important in stirring the West to new life.

NORTHERN AND SOUTHERN SEA-WAYS

The revival of commerce was dependent on a decided change in both internal and external conditions. This began to be apparent during the tenth century. Externally, the Christian West came into contact with the Norsemen, a vigorous trading folk. Internally there was sufficient stability in governmental conditions to make it pos-

[1] The very word *civilization* is derived from a Latin word that means city-dweller (*civis*).

sible for foreign traders to penetrate certain of the inland regions. It is interesting to note that the first turn of the tide from a decentralized rural society to the commerce that eventually built up a flourishing city life, came at the end of a period of devastating invasions. Invasions always tend to interrupt commerce and industry. But often they furnish new impulses and opportunities for new types of economic exchange. Throughout the West the invasions forced the local rulers to establish military centers for defense against invasion. These burghs, boroughs, and castles became trading centers which later developed into towns. Even the ravages of the invaders might contribute to certain kinds of commercial activity. The Norsemen plundered many a church of its accumulated gold, silver, and gems, only to barter the treasure away to camp followers and traders who eventually put it into circulation. Thus the Norse ravages increased the income of many Western communities. Furthermore the invaders, once they were rulers of a region, contributed more than they had destroyed.

The Norsemen, though ferocious fighters in times of warfare, were also a commercial people. Their merchants traded from the shores of America and Iceland to Moscow and the Black Sea where they made contact with caravans of Oriental goods from Asia. After a comparatively short period of raiding and conquest[2] the Norsemen settled along the coasts of England and France. Thenceforth the North Sea and the English Channel became a part of the great northern world of seafaring trade. There was piracy as well as commerce along these waterways but the constant exchange of goods stirred neighboring Western folk to a realization of the advantages of trade and industry.

Further south, in Italy, similar activities were on the increase during the tenth and eleventh centuries. There were certain fortunate regions in which business life, having survived the ravages of civil wars and invasion, expanded very rapidly. Venice, for instance, because of her favored location, had escaped the worst of the Moslem and Hungarian raids. In Charles the Great's time, Venice already had commercial contacts with Constantinople, and long before the crusades she was a flourishing maritime city, well prepared for

---

[2] The Norse invasions, though terribly destructive, were intermittent and seldom continued for much more than a half century in any one region. There were few raids on the Continent before 840, and by the end of the century the worst was over and the invaders were settling down. See above, p. 208.

her great era of business expansion as the middleman between the eastern Mediterranean ports and Western Europe.[3] Other Mediterranean towns were not far behind Venice, and by the tenth century the seaports of Italy and southern France were hives of commercial activity. The weakening of Moslem power in the western Mediterranean during the tenth and eleventh centuries made it possible for Southern Europe once more to play her part in the economic world that extended from Gibraltar to Jerusalem. It was Western Europe's expansion in the Mediterranean and its new contacts with the trade routes of the North and the Baltic seas that ended her long economic isolation and paved the way for increased commercial and industrial activities. Contacts with the trading folk of the northern and southern seaways gave the West a new economic impulse. This change in external relationships was an important factor in the revival of commerce.

POLITICAL STABILITY — But commerce could make little headway as long as Europe was torn by internal strife and foreign invasion. At least a measure of peace, order, and settled existence was necessary if merchants were to penetrate the interior regions and carry on a profitable trade. Conditions improved very slowly during the tenth century. Early in the century the Norse invaders ceased to trouble the coastal regions and began to organize their own states. By the end of the century they had established themselves in England and Normandy. Under their vigorous rule, commerce flourished along the Channel and the North Sea and in the interior. Meanwhile, further east in the Italies and Germanies, the depredations of the Hungarians were brought to an end. After the year 1000, when they and their leader, King Stephen, accepted Christianity, the Danube River became more and more important as a highway for travel to and from Constantinople. Internal conditions in the Germanies were also improving. Otto the Great's unification of the German duchies under his sway as king and emperor[4] encouraged economic exchange along the Rhine and its tributaries.

Feudal lords also throughout the West began to solve the peacetime problems of local government. Some of them began actively to foster trade in order to increase their revenues. In France, Normandy, and the Rhinelands they joined with the clergy in enforcing the Peace and Truce of God, which protected merchants, as well as

---

[3] See below, Chapter XXXI.
[4] See below, p. 372.

peasants, travelers, clergymen, and other noncombatants, in regions where war was being waged.[5] Under such conditions, often without direct governmental assistance, economic life prospered. A significant innovation in farming methods, the adoption of the three-field system,[6] by increasing the prosperity of the rural population, provided favorable conditions for trade and industry. The general trend toward economic and political stability was accompanied by an increase in population and wealth. Such were the conditions under which commerce and industry began once more to thrive.

COMMERCE INSPIRES INDUSTRY

Against this background of changing internal and external conditions we are better able to visualize the manner in which the West began to waken to new economic impulses. From the great industrial centers of the eastern Mediterranean, and from the trading centers of the Baltic and North seas, products were brought in increasing amounts to the seaports of the West. From the northern regions furs and wax were imported. From Spain came ivory, finished leather, fine weapons, tropical birds, and lion and leopard skins imported from Africa. The eastern Mediterranean furnished Western Europe with Oriental spices, silken goods, and other luxury products. From coastal settlements enterprising merchants carried these and many other kinds of goods inland by rivers, by roads, and along bypaths which only pack animals could traverse. Foreign products in ever-increasing quantities began to trickle into the castles, monasteries, cathedral centers, crossroads markets, and manorial villages of the West. Even on the military frontiers merchants found opportunities for profitable trade. From the native peoples they obtained valuable raw products such as furs, amber, and wax. To the soldiers and officials of the garrison posts they sold their imported goods. Some of these forts (called burghs or boroughs) drew so many traders and other settlers that eventually they became flourishing towns. The late medieval cities of Magde-burg and Branden-burg in the region of the Elbe River originated as military outposts against the Slavs.

There was also a good deal of local exchange. Fish, salt, and other goods that were found in certain favored regions were transported elsewhere to be bartered for local products. More and more

[5] See below, p. 498.
[6] See above, pp. 245 f.

during the tenth and eleventh centuries rural Europe was impelled to produce a surplus in order to acquire imported articles. In this change of attitude from an economy of subsistence to one of exchange, from the desire for enough for mere existence to an insatiable ambition for more and more worldly goods, lies the origin of a capitalistic economy. Its beginnings can be clearly seen in Western Europe before the year 1000.

As yet the active factor in commerce was the foreign merchant. Usually a lone Syrian or Jew, he was constantly on the move. Not more than once a year, for a short time, could he visit each settlement on his route. Outlying rural centers therefore had very little commercial life; they saw only an occasional peddler. Even so, many a peasant was encouraged to produce a surplus in order to obtain attractive foreign wares when they were available. The artisans on a large manor were inspired to increased activity. A cobbler who made extra pairs of shoes could barter them for imported cloth, leather goods, or valuable tools. The lords of manors, likewise, saw the advantage of increased production and exchange. Thus it was that foreign importations, even on a small scale, were the inspiration for industrial expansion.

BUSINESS CENTERS

As time passed there was more demand for goods and local trade began to flourish. Local markets were usually held weekly. Importers took their goods to the junction points of inland routes or to strategic locations on rivers. Here at certain specified times fairs were held at which they sold to the local dealers who assembled from the surrounding regions. A fair was usually under the control of the outstanding lord of the region. At St. Denis, near Paris, the monks and their titular abbot, the Capetian king, were the proprietors. The lord patron of the fair guaranteed to the visiting merchants security from violence, freedom of exchange, special merchant courts for the settlement of their affairs, and other advantages. In return, he profited from the fees and the increased prosperity of his subjects. A fair might last from a few days to three or four weeks.

The upper Seine and Marne rivers provided such a convenient meeting place that regular annual fairs were held here as early as the ninth and tenth centuries. Later on a succession of fairs were held in Troyes and other cities of this region (Champagne) one after another throughout most of the year. The assembled merchants usually went the rounds of all of them, perhaps first attending a fair that specialized in woolens, then moving on to a silk fair at another place, and so on. Even though markets and fairs were intermittent, they were contributing factors of considerable importance in the development of foreign trade and of business settlements.

Permanent communities of businessmen developed most rapidly at the strategic points of this sort where merchants assembled to purchase or exchange goods. Seaport towns such as Venice, Genoa, Marseilles, Bordeaux, Rouen, London, Antwerp, and Hamburg from early times had settlements of tradesfolk. Inland centers such as Milan, Lyons, Paris, Cologne, and Augsburg, because of their importance as exchange points, also attracted permanent populations of merchants and artisans. During the tenth and eleventh centuries such settlements increased rapidly. Not only foreign merchants but also local tradesmen and artisans began to flock to centers where men could make a living by trade and industry.

HOW TOWNS GREW

By the year 1000, we find that settlements of traders were flourishing in all parts of Western Europe: at crossroads, at the fords and bridges of rivers, near monasteries, cathedrals, or castles, at important seaports. In short, in all sorts of favorable commercial locations, merchants and artisans congregated and formed permanent communities. From the late tenth century comes an interesting account of the beginnings of such a settlement at a bridge head just outside a protecting castle wall on a river in Flanders. Eventually this became the city of Bruges, one of the chief trading centers of the north. It seems that, after the castle was built, certain traders began to flock to the place in front of the gate of the bridge which led to the opposite side of the river. First merchants and tavern keepers, then other outsiders, drifted in to make money by providing food and shelter for those who might have business transactions with the count who lived in the castle. Houses and inns were erected for their accommodation, since there was not room for them within the château. These habitations increased so rapidly that a permanent settlement came into being. The people called it "Brugghe [Bruges] from the word for bridge." [7]

This description indicates the two outstanding prerequisites for a successful business community: (1) the opportunity for financial gain, and (2) adequate protection. Any location in which these were available was likely to attract business folk and eventually to de-

---

[7] See the detailed account in Professor Thompson's translation, *An Economic and Social History of the Middle Ages*, p. 772.

velop into a town. Protection was not restricted to the military defense furnished by a near-by castle or fort: it might be provided by a church, a monastery, a crossroads shrine, or some other religious institution, the sanctity of which was respected by all true Christians. As to the opportunity for financial gain, this was possible in any place at which large numbers of people lived or assembled regularly: a populous manorial village, a great castle or fortress, a famous church or monastery, important crossroads, a permanent market or fair, a good seaport, a ford or bridge on a much-traveled road.

The present name of many a European city reflects the original reason for a settlement at that point. Fords, for instance, furnished the names of Ox-*ford* and Stam-*ford;* bridges gave the suffix of Cam-*bridge* and Stour-*bridge,* to say nothing of the entire word *Bruges;* castles or forts are represented in New-*castle,* Ham-*burg,* Frei-*burg,* Magde-*burg, Bourg*os, and so on. Other town names such as *Abbe*-ville or *Ports*-mouth suggest fascinating historical origins.

EVOLUTION OF
A TYPICAL
TOWN

From the eleventh century on, the new economic interests became increasingly evident. We must remember, however, that a community of business folk did not immediately or automatically become a town. Practically every business community grew up on a feudal domain, some of the inhabitants of which were originally serfs or free tenants. Therefore most business settlements began their existence not as towns but as minor parts of a feudal estate. Increasing numbers, wealth, and power might enable them to secure the local independence that characterizes a town or city, but this advantage had to be won and usually it came after a long, hard fight.

Although each town has its own peculiar history, a general pattern for the development of medieval urban centers can be established. At a favored location which provided both protection and economic profit, a community of commercial and industrial folk came into existence. This population was composed of artisans from the neighboring manors of the feudal lord and the tradesmen who had made this place their headquarters. The lay or ecclesiastical lord allowed them to settle alongside the protecting wall of his castle, monastery, or cathedral enclosure (whichever it might be). In case the domain was the site of a very old town, the settlers might find themselves living in or near the walled defenses of an ancient Roman city. This happened at Cologne, Regensburg, London, and elsewhere. Such a community would attract the attention of passing merchants. Its wealthy nobles, soldiers, and lesser folk presented a possible market for the spices, leather work, silks, and other luxury goods which they peddled through the West. There were also other business opportunities. Inasmuch as the local craftsmen produced more than enough shoes, cloth, metalware, and the like, for the needs of the local population, there was a surplus for sale.

As soon as the local opportunity for purchase and sale of goods was sufficient, merchants settled in the community and a permanent market was set up. By this time there was a thriving settlement of craftsmen and merchants. For purposes of protection the community might be surrounded by a palisade or even a wall. This settlement was called a borough, burgh, or *faubourg*.[8]

The inhabitants, or the burghers, rapidly became conscious of their differentiation from the ordinary serf or peasant. They were wealthier, more important, and socially superior. Already freed from the agricultural duties of the manor, they sought to free themselves from other burdensome restrictions of feudal life. Sooner or later the entire group of burghers was likely to demand the right of regulating their own economic and political life. They had no place in the feudal or manorial structure, and their interests were in no way furthered by either of these essentially rural institutions. This situation involved readjustments with the feudal overlord. Usually the wealthy tradesmen took the initiative, acting as a unit through their merchant association (the guild).[9] By means of this or some other group organization the burghers bargained for privileges that involved local self-government. If fortunate, they might obtain in a single grant the fundamental privileges of townsfolk. These included freedom from servile obligations, the right to move at will, personal ownership of property, freedom to buy and sell in the local markets, the right of trial in the burgher court, and certain group privileges in the payment of financial obligations.

Some farseeing lords, in order to increase the prosperity of their

---

[8] Compare the medieval *faubourg* with the suburb or addition to a modern city. Suburb means literally "under the city," that is, under or near the city walls. The medieval *faubourg* was often built under the shadow of the walls of a castle, monastery, or ancient Roman city. Its inhabitants were called burghers. In its later French form, the word for burghers was "bourg-eoisie," which is used today for people of the middle class.

[9] In some cases the entire population formed an organization whose members were bound by an oath to support one another. Such an association was called a *commune*. See below, p. 483.

estates, took the initiative in founding towns and offering attractive terms to peasants and tradesmen. In most cases, however, the burghers met with considerable opposition. Bit by bit freedom from this or that vexatious regulation was gained: by purchase, by threats, and sometimes by actual revolt. The most important development was the recognition of the fact that the burghers were a distinct group which had secured a place in the feudal world. Once they learned how to negotiate with their feudal lord as an organized group, they had an immense advantage.

The recognition of the burghers of a community as a group meant that the settlement was a town. Their representatives formed the nucleus of an organization that had some privileges of self-government. At first this might be nothing more than the regulation of trade and industry. Eventually it might result in complete independence from interference on the part of feudal officials. Naturally feudal lords received ample compensation for all such grants: sometimes the remuneration was a sum of money paid outright, sometimes a permanent tax or fee, sometimes certain financial rights in the town.

CHARTERED
RIGHTS

Once granted, privileges were recorded in written documents called *charters*. One mutually profitable agreement usually led to another until a group of burghers had become completely self-governing. But chartered rights did not necessarily free the townspeople from all obligations to their feudal lord. A charter was likely to grant them freedom from direct interference in their internal affairs, but they were still responsible, as a group, for certain feudal services and payments. Overlords expected military service, tolls, rents, and other contributions from their subjects, whether rural or townsfolk. If these contributions were not in the form of personal service or produce, cash payments were expected. The chief advantage for the townspeople was the elimination of those customs that conflicted with their business activities and the right of handling their remaining obligations as a group, under their own officials, and without constant outside interference. It is important to remember that the burghers in a medieval town continued to be subjects of a baronial or royal state and therefore were still bound to observe feudal laws and customs and to render certain services. Royal or feudal officials had ultimate authority over the military, judicial, and tax policies of the towns. But the townsfolk, instead of being dealt with as individual serfs or freemen, were an incorporated group, a composite or collective vassal with definite chartered rights. In only a few cases, notably certain Italian and German city-states, were the towns entirely independent of their former lords. Ordinarily the burghers were satisfied to remain under the protection of an overlord, so long as he allowed them to run their own internal affairs. In short, they sought security and prosperity, not complete independence. The foregoing sketch indicates in a general way the manner in which a medieval town might come into being. There was much variation, and in some cases farseeing rulers took the initiative and granted generous charters in order to attract settlers. In other cases the struggle for rights was marked by violence and warfare.

COMMUNAL
REVOLTS

There were many conservative barons, abbots, and bishops to whom the idea of self-governing towns was synonymous with wicked rebellion against the God-given social order. To them burghers were servile upstarts who should be kept in place. "New and detestable name," said a clerical historian, speaking of the French communes. In France, particularly, during the early days of town growth this feeling led to desperate conflicts. The burghers were sometimes so insistent on their right to organize that when peaceful negotiations failed they used violence against obstinate and unjust lords. The people of Cambrai fought their lord bishop in 1024, 1064, and finally, in 1076, forced him to grant a charter. The history of Tours records a dozen or more revolts. Le Mans and Laon also had extended conflicts with their reactionary clerical masters. Medieval bishops, it seems, were not the most liberty-loving of masters.

The lay nobles were usually more reasonable than the clergy, but many of them had trouble with their townsfolk. The citizens of Avignon, early in the thirteenth century, boasted that they "obeyed none but God," and to prove it they captured and burned alive a hostile nobleman. Frederick Barbarossa, as we shall see,[10] resented what he considered the "insolence" of the upstart burghers of Rome and Milan. The latter town was destroyed for its presumptuousness in questioning his decisions and precipitating a revolt. Later, in alliance with other Lombard towns and with the pope, Milan was able to inflict upon him a decisive defeat at Legnano. Other medieval towns, preferring diplomacy to war, often won rights by allying with

[10] See below, p. 393.

one or the other side in a conflict. In the bitter struggles between the emperors and the popes, clever townspeople were sometimes able to sell their support for grants of chartered privileges.

KINGS AND
BURGHERS

Time, money, and intelligence were on the side of the townspeople as they steadily forged ahead both economically and politically. Kings, barons, bishops, and abbots came to realize that the towns were valuable allies—and dangerous enemies. The kings, in particular, were quick to see the advantages of allying with people who had business brains as well as ample moneybags. Many a king who ruled his own burghers with a rod of iron gave encouragement, if not active assistance, to other burghers who were fighting to gain recognition from feudal lords whose power he wished to weaken. But such encouragement was no gift: every king had his price, and the townsfolk paid well for royal assistance.

For similarly selfish reasons kings and feudal nobles sometimes founded towns on their own estates and offered generous inducements to settlers. At Lorris in France, King Louis VI laid out a town and invited colonists to come and take advantage of a very liberal charter. Each newcomer was promised a home at a nominal rental, market rights, freedom to come and go as he pleased, moderate taxes, tolls, and fines, protection from unjust trial, and exemption from military service, seizure of his property, and other unreasonable feudal burdens. Such "new towns" sprang up throughout the West, as enterprising rulers recognized that they were a good investment. The income from thriving towns was an important item in a world that was becoming conscious of the need and value of financial wealth.

TOWN LIFE: BURGHER POLITICS, BUSINESS, AND SOCIETY

TOWN
GOVERNMENT

As a group of business folk bought or fought its way out of the net of feudal and manorial life it was necessary to set up machinery for self-government. At first little was needed save representatives for collective bargaining and a few guild regulations for industry and commerce. But additional privileges created additional responsibilities. With an increasing population, complex civic problems arose. Markets must be regulated, guild rules enforced, commercial and industrial disputes settled. Separate courts were established for business cases, and special town officials were selected for the enforcement of internal order. External defense was a vital problem: stout walls and towers had to be built and defended. This called for military officials and a town militia. Such varied needs demanded an organized system of government, and as towns increased in size their government became rather complicated.

Medieval towns enjoyed a high degree of self-government but little of democratic government. As in early American days, so also in the Middle Ages, only property holders had a voice in governmental affairs. Usually a few wealthy guildsmen dominated the town council and the other governing bodies. This was due to the fact that the guildsmen were usually the ones who had taken the initiative in gaining chartered rights from the feudal lords. Naturally, having acquired the privileges, they employed them for their own special interests and opposed their extension. The mass of the populace, sometimes called plebs (plebeians), seldom had any political power. Only on rare occasions were they summoned to a sort of mass-meeting assembly in the market place or, in case of rain, in the cathedral. Even then, they were only asked to give assent to matters that had already been decided by the inner circle of officers and the wealthy members of the council. In some towns the assembly was little more than a meeting of the militia.

ARISTOCRATIC CONTROL
The active citizen body consisted of the "patricians," that is, those whose fathers (*patres*) had been voting citizens. Active citizenship was therefore an hereditary right. The patricians met occasionally in a large council (sometimes called an assembly). Although they exercised the controlling influence, the actual business of governing was usually carried on by a smaller council composed of a dozen or so executives called *aldermen, priors, scabini, jures, jurati, boni homines,* or *rathsherren.* In the case of a small town, these councilors might themselves administer all governmental affairs, but in large towns there were additional commissions or executive officials. Venice had a "Cabinet of Sages" and Florence a *podesta, capitano,* and *gonfalonier,*[11] to whom certain of the details of governmental action were entrusted. Such commissions and officials were usually responsible to the smaller council, which was in turn responsible to the large council of active

[11] See below, Chapter XXXI, for descriptions of the governments of Florence, Venice, and Milan.

citizens, which in turn might occasionally refer important matters to a mass meeting of the entire citizen body.

ADMINISTRA-
TION

In spite of its apparent complexities, medieval town government was essentially simple. Most towns were actually controlled by a rather small group of businessmen. The citizens as a whole met very seldom. Since their chief desire was to have business prosper, as long as public and private affairs flourished, there was little objection to the ruling oligarchy. Whether the councilors and officials were elected or appointed, whether the terms of office were for life or for one year, the main purpose of town government was to maintain security and prosperity for the dominant group of wealthy citizens. This very practical purpose explains why so few medieval towns were democratically governed. The ruling class could control a small group of councilors more effectively than a popular assembly; therefore governmental power was concentrated in the hands of the councilors, and the citizenry were seldom called together. The town officials and their policies were usually controlled to a certain extent by the small assembly of wealthier citizens, but this assembly in turn was dominated by a narrow oligarchy of guild members. Most towns won their charters, and established self-government under guild leadership; therefore it was natural for them to remain under the control of the guild. In many towns the guild government was the town government.

MERCHANT
GUILDS

What, then, was the nature of the guilds which exercised such a monopoly on town governments? Every town had various kinds of guilds or associations. Some were merely social organizations; others were more or less like mutual benefit societies. Of greatest importance were the merchant and crafts guilds. In most regions, especially in earlier times when shopkeepers sold their homemade goods direct to the consumer, businessmen belonged to the one general guild of merchants. The guild had one major purpose, the well-being of the entire group; therefore it subordinated the activities of the individual members to certain general principles of economic practice. Because the primary purpose was the prosperity of the members, the merchant guild aimed, first and foremost, to prevent outside competition—in short, to maintain a monopoly of all trade in the town. Nonmembers, whether natives or foreigners, were rigidly excluded from doing business or owning shops in the town. The merchant guild controlled the town market with great care so that no member might take unfair advantage of his fellow merchants. It established a scale of just prices for the more common goods and prohibited their sale at reduced or advanced prices or at irregular hours and places. Cornering the market, manipulating prices in any manner, and engaging in speculative activities were considered unfair trade practices and were strictly forbidden. The adulteration of goods and short measure or weight were severely punished. In the earlier period the guild also regulated the various industrial crafts in which its members engaged. It also levied dues, passed ordinances of various kinds, maintained an elaborate guild hall, and often built and kept up roads, bridges, docks, warehouses, and ships. Inasmuch as the merchant guild regulated all trade in the town, it performed many of the functions of governments. Its authority also extended to the actions of its members while abroad. They enjoyed the protection of the guild on their travels, and likewise they were responsible for their fellow guildsmen. A merchant could be held for the debts of another merchant of his home town. Naturally such varied functions demanded a staff of officers, usually consisting of a president or chairman, a board of governors (sometimes called aldermen), and certain lesser officials.

CRAFT OR ARTI-SAN GUILDS Craft guilds were narrower, more specialized, and later in point of time than merchant guilds. They came into being as a result of the development of separate crafts engaged in separate kinds of manufacture with special interests and needs. There were guilds of cobblers and shoemakers, of harness makers and also of saddlers, of old-clothes dealers and also of tailors of new clothes, to say nothing of guilds of spurriers, drapers, dyers, wool carders, and innumerable other artisans. Like the merchant guilds, each craft guild was a monopolistic organization, formed for the purpose of insuring profitable business conditions for a restricted group of shop owners. The owner, a master workman, with the assistance of one or more expert hired artisans (called journeymen), and several apprentices, manufactured his special product and sold it either in his own shop or in the town market. Thus the member of a craft guild was a merchant as well as an artisan.

The craft guilds operated in the interests of the comparatively small number of master workmen who were shop owners, and not for the journeymen and apprentices. The chief objective was security and equality of opportunity for the master workmen, in whose interests the well-being of the laboring class and the consuming public was often sacrificed.[12] If the journeymen and apprentices profited from the guild regulations, it was merely because their interests coincided with those of the masters. In their later stages of development craft guilds were essentially associations of employer-manufacturers.

CRAFT GUILD REGULATIONS

In general, guild regulations were restrictive of free competition and individual initiative. In most regions no outsiders were allowed to manufacture or sell goods in the town. As in the case of the merchant guild, the members were subject to innumerable regulations, the object of which was to prevent unfair practices and to maintain absolute equality of opportunity for all shop owners. Work must be done at certain hours and never at night, which was annoying to neighbors and might lead to inferior or fraudulent products. It was customary for artisans to work in plain sight of passers-by. Here the fellow artisans, the guild inspectors, and the prospective purchaser could see that they were doing honest as well as expert work. Deceitful practices were punished by fines and, in serious cases, by expulsion from the guild. The need for such measures is shown by the complaints that were made concerning spur makers who used inferior or "cracked" metal, concealing the defects by gilding; or upholsterers who used thistledown and the fluff from "cattails."

Although many of the guild regulations resulted in the protection of the purchaser, they were fundamentally in the interests of the guild members. It was for the good of the business that the guild insisted on sound materials, reasonable prices, and honest workmanship. For similar reasons hours, wages, and prices were carefully regulated. Each shop owner was restricted as to working hours, but this was for the purpose of facilitating inspection and checking inferior workmanship. The limitation of working hours was never for the purpose of relieving the laboring class. In fact, their welfare usually suffered as a result of the guild regulations. For instance, a shop owner could employ only a limited number of apprentices, whose length of service and remuneration were specified in detail by the guild. The number of apprentices that a master workman was allowed generally varied from one to five. The parents of an apprentice might pay the master a sum of money for the educa-

12 See below, p. 547.

tion of their son. He kept the apprentices in his home, provided food and lodging, taught them the trade, and saw to it that they learned proper conduct. The master was allowed to punish his apprentices; runaways, in particular, were harshly treated. Obstinate offenders might be excluded forever from the guild, for apprenticeship was an educational privilege. On the other hand, harsh and cruel masters might be punished by the guild. At the end of his period of apprenticeship, which might run from three to twelve years, the young man received a small sum of money; the lodging and training were, however, considered as an adequate remuneration for his services. The apprentice regulations were designed not only to teach the craft, but also to keep down the number of candidates for guild membership, and thus to limit competition and prevent overproduction.

After serving his apprenticeship, the young worker became a journeyman, or day laborer (from the Old French *journée,* meaning day). His wage scale was fixed by the guild and often it compared favorably with the income of a master workman. But he could not become a shop owner until he had worked for several years, accumulated some capital, and proved his skill in the craft by passing an examination before the masters. Until the later medieval centuries it was comparatively easy to gain admission to the guilds. If successful, the young master set up his own shop and became an employer of apprentices and journeymen.

In general there was little social distinction between the masters and their employees. The master workmen generally worked along with their apprentices and journeymen in the home shop. Most of them made only a comfortable living for themselves and their families. Life was simple and there were few wealthy craftsmen. There was little chance for even a shop owner to expand his business very rapidly, for the market was limited and the guilds were essentially tied to tradition. Once the craft was established, the masters tried to prevent any change that would upset existing conditions of equality and security. In the later Middle Ages, both merchant and craft guilds became more exclusive and unprogressive. No matter how skillful a worker became, he had little chance of becoming a master unless he was backed by influential guild members. The rift between employers and employees became more and more distinct until a sort of industrial caste system developed.[13]

13 See below, p. 547.

SOCIAL SERVICE   Almost as significant as their economic functions
                   were the social activities of the guilds. They cared for
their members when they were sick, gave them a decent burial when
they died, paid for prayers for their souls, and looked after their
widows and orphans. Some of them, like modern fraternal orders,
provided schools, orphanages, and hospitals for the unfortunate dependents of guild members. At festival times they presented miracle
plays, provided floats for processions, and contributed to community
charity. Each guild had its officers, treasury, guild hall, ordinances, and
organized social activities.

During the earlier period of their existence, the guilds were an
effective means for organizing and controlling the new economic
forces of town life. They unified the business classes and enabled
them to win a place in medieval society. They provided the organization for group action in gaining charters and establishing municipal
governments. Once the burghers and their civic institutions were
chartered, the guilds reaped the rewards of political power. The same
business leaders held the chief offices in both guild and town government. Often the guild hall served as a city hall, the center of government, as well as of business activities. Such close relationships were
natural and, to a certain degree, advantageous. Economic and governmental policies were co-ordinated, and the city had the benefit of
a practical and unified administration. But, on the other hand, public
affairs were run in the interests of the guildsmen. This tended to produce a narrowly aristocratic or (to be more accurate) plutocratic government which no longer served the needs of the majority of the
townsfolk. The result was discontent and bitter civic strife, particularly toward the end of the Middle Ages.

A SUMMARY OF   Although each town has its own distinctive history,
TOWN GROWTH   there are certain trends that characterize the rise of
                 town life in the West. The first stage of develop-
ment was the rapid growth of business activities and settlements of
business people. This led to the establishment of chartered communities which were free from the restrictions of the feudal system. A third
aspect of the movement was the formation of town governments and
guilds. Finally these organizations came to be run so exclusively for
the wealthy class that strife arose within towns and the old burgher
institutions began to weaken. This later period of internal conflict, particularly noticeable in the fourteenth and fifteenth centuries, ushered

in certain economic problems that are still dominant in modern life—
the conflict between wealth and poverty, capital and labor, *bourgeoisie*
and proletariat, plutocracy and true democracy.[14]

DRAWBACKS
TO TRADE

In certain of his problems and business methods the
medieval merchant was very unlike his modern successor. He had no such facilities for travel as those
of modern times. The roads were muddy, full of ruts, rough in dry
weather, and impassable much of the time. Pack animals were the
chief means of land transport until late in the Middle Ages, when
wagons came into common use. Bridges were few and widely scattered, and heavy tolls were charged for crossing them. Moreover, feudal lords charged fees and tolls for the use of the roads, bridges, ferries, fords, ports, and markets on their domains. According to feudal
law, a lord could claim the produce from a wrecked wagon or ship
that fell on or floated to his land. For this reason there was small incentive to improve the roads and waterways. In fact, false beacons
were sometimes used to lead ships astray. The famous tale of Inch-
cape Rock, though legendary, illustrates the manner in which ships
were deliberately wrecked by unscrupulous men.

In addition to such tribulations the lack of good maps and com-
passes, combined with unseaworthy ships and ever-present pirates,
made seafaring very dangerous. On land, brigands, mountain passes,
and innumerable tolls kept the merchant traveler in constant trouble.
On the other hand, there were hospices, such as that of the St. Bernard Pass (still famous for its St. Bernard dogs). Orders of bridge-
building and bridge-repairing monks also tended to improve conditions.

Even when the dangers of travel were overcome, the merchant
still had to struggle with the peculiar and very rigid regulations of the
various cities he visited. A man might be held in a distant town as a
hostage for the unpaid debts or transgressions of some fellow guild
member. Even in their own home towns, merchants were severely
punished for such offenses as buying up goods before they were put
on public sale (forestalling), or for cornering the market on a certain
product (engrossing), or for speculating on prices (regrating). The
modern merchant who resents governmental interference in his busi-

---

[14] At various points in the succeeding chapters we shall have occasion to refer to
this later stage of medieval economic development. See especially Chapter XXVII, pp.
547 ff.

ness would have been driven to distraction by one half the regulations of a medieval town. Then, too, there was the clerical prohibition against the taking of interest, and the general antipathy of the church to profit-making.[15]

THE SIZE OF MEDIEVAL TOWNS

Before passing on to other phases of medieval life, we should familiarize ourselves with the general character of urban life during the period of town expansion. There were all sorts of towns, differing according to each region and century. In the eleventh century, they were small and scattered. England at the time of the Norman Conquest, according to William's Domesday survey, had only about eighty "boroughs," and many of these were merely straggling hamlets. France had hundreds of chartered towns, but these were not large cities. The Rhinelands and northern Italy, due to their background of business activities (extending in some cases well into the early Middle Ages), had large cities such as Cologne, Regensburg (Ratisbon), Venice, Milan, and Rome. Few of these, however, exceeded a few thousand in population until after the crusading era. The Netherlands was another region of thriving trade and town life even before the eleventh century. Bruges, Utrecht, and Ghent were important but small towns.

INFLUENCE OF THE CRUSADES

Small in number and size though these eleventh-century towns were, they were vigorous and well on the road to prosperity before the crusades ushered Western Europe into an era of accelerated economic expansion.[16] To the towns, especially those in Italy, the crusades spelled commercial profit. In a later chapter we shall note in detail the manner in which the Venetians, Genoese, and Pisans profited by the assistance they gave to the first crusaders and how the Venetians joined in a crusade "for the love of God"—and a portion of the spoils, which turned out to be a goodly share of Constantinople and her economic resources. Meanwhile, outside of Italy, businessmen were cornering the markets on crusading supplies, lending money to crusaders at high rates of interest, and purchasing charters at bargain prices. Little wonder that in the twelfth and thirteenth centuries the economic life of the West was transformed and the townsfolk enjoyed unparalleled prosperity. Meanwhile, regions untouched by the crusades were developing in like manner. This was an age of rapidly expanding economic life.

[15] See below, p. 683.
[16] See below, Chapters XXV-XXVII.

CITY HALL, BRUSSELS (XV C)

MARKET PLACE AND BELL TOWER,
BRUGES (XII-XV C)

A FORTIFIED TOWN, CARCASSONNE (XIII C)

NORTH-EUROPEAN TOWNS
(See pp. 365 ff., 721.)

PALACE OF THE DOGE, VENICE (XIV C)

THE RICCARDI (MEDICI) PALACE,
FLORENCE (XV C)

TOWN HALL AND BELL TOWER,
SIENA (XIV C)

ITALIAN TOWN ARCHITECTURE

(See pp. 720 f.)

A TYPICAL MEDI-
EVAL TOWN
Let us take an imaginary visit to one of the medium-sized towns of this prosperous era. It is not a large populous metropolis; even as late as 1500 there were only a few cities, such as Paris, Milan, Venice, and Rome, with as many as 100,000 inhabitants; cities such as London, Ghent, Bruges, Cologne, Nuremberg, and Augsburg had scarcely 50,000. Our town is, let us say, one of about 10,000 population, in thirteenth-century France.

As we approach from the distance, the sky line reveals a stout wall, perhaps twenty feet high and ten feet broad. It has several gates with towers (Cologne, for instance, in the thirteenth century had thirteen gates and sixty-five towers). Above the wall can be seen a confused mass of sharp peaked roofs of colored tile, with chimney pots and dormer windows jutting out at all angles. High above these rise the sturdy square tower of the town hall, the graceful twin spires of the Gothic cathedral, and other smaller towers of parish churches, guild halls, and possibly of private mansions.[17] From a distance, in the dim glow of twilight the sky line might vaguely resemble that of a modern city, in miniature. There is a distinct impression of jumbled buildings of varied types, sizes, and heights, all struggling, as it were, to rise above their fellows in a mad scramble for wealth and success. Such was the moving spirit of the medieval town and its people.

As we approach the town we encounter first of all the castellated turreted wall before which the town guard stops all comers. Strangers, in particular, are compelled to prove their identity and peaceful intentions. Even neighboring peasant folk must stop to have their wagonloads of produce examined and to pay toll (*octroi* or town tariff) on all marketable goods. Finally we pass through the massive gate and find ourselves inside the walls.

STREETS AND
HOUSES
Once inside, we notice a marked contrast to the typical American city. The streets are crooked, narrow alleys, extending in every direction. Most medieval cities, it must be remembered, were not planned. Let us follow one of the less crooked and narrow streets which looks like a main thoroughfare leading toward the center of town. It is about twenty feet "narrow," paved with rough cobblestones, and lined with tall narrow buildings, for the most part rickety wooden affairs. Because of the limited amount (and high cost) of street frontage, the people build

---

[17] In Italy, especially, the aristocratic families built great towers. Bologna still has two of them; one is over a hundred feet high.

their shops and residences high, sometimes four or five stories. Furthermore, in order to get more space, they extend the upper portions out over the street. Instead of recessional skyscrapers, they have overhanging tenement houses. Thus, narrow though the street is, the jutting upper stories make it appear even narrower; in some places it resembles a canyon. There were towns in which an official rode through the streets once a year carrying a lance crosswise on his saddle. Any structure that the ends of the lance touched in passing had to be removed.

Let us enter one of the better class of shop-residences, that, for instance, of a master cobbler. The ground floor is the workshop and showroom. Shoes are hanging everywhere, even outside on the street. At night, of course, everything is taken inside and stout shutters are set up, like a barricade, before all doors and windows. But now the master with his journeymen and apprentices are hard at work, cobbling shoes. In the rear there may be a storeroom, a little courtyard, and perhaps a dirty alleyway. Upstairs are the living rooms of the master and his family. There is little furniture except beds, and what there is seems very primitive to us. The apprentices live in little cubbyholes in the garret, close under the roof. After a short tour of these dark smelly quarters we are glad to get out into the street again.

We notice now that the street slopes toward the middle where one lone gutter catches and carries onward all the accumulated refuse. These gutters are the sewers; consequently all garbage is dumped into the middle of the street. It has been said that the modern custom of a gentleman's walking on the outside, between his lady and the street, was originally very necessary. She walked in safety underneath the jutting upper stories; he took the outside position from which he might protect her by receiving the mud splashes of passing horsemen or carriages and any misdirected shower of refuse thrown from an upper window. Of course there were no sidewalks. At best, a medieval thoroughfare was a poor excuse for a street; at worst, it might be littered with filth which the pigs and chickens had not yet eaten or which had not been washed away by the rain. The unsanitary conditions of medieval towns undoubtedly intensified the ravages of medieval epidemics.

The side streets, as one can still see for himself in many a European town, were even narrower, crookeder, and darker than the main thoroughfares and were lairs for thugs and sneak thieves. There was no street lighting, and honest citizens hesitated to venture outside their homes, unattended, after curfew. Throughout the night the town watch made regular rounds with his lantern, sounding the cry of "all's well."

THE TOWN SQUARE

If we continue on our way down "Main Street" to the town square, we come upon a large open space about the size of a modern city block. Like the main streets it is paved with rough cobblestones; little grass grows under or around the feet of these townspeople, for space within the town is too precious to waste on parks. In the center of the square is a fountain, whence the womenfolk and children carry drinking water to their homes in tall jugs or pitchers. The square is surrounded by important civic, religious, and private buildings. On one side is the cathedral; it is the central church of the town and the pride and joy of the local clergy and citizens, most of whom have taken an active part in contributing towards and perhaps in actually working at its construction. Cathedrals were, and still are, an integral part of the architectural scheme and also of the life of European towns. The cathedral was not only the religious meeting place, but also the social center, the public museum, and the artistic masterpiece of the city—an everlasting witness to the unified spirit of townsfolk in an age in which faith as well as business flourished.[18]

THE TOWN HALL

Across from the church is the town hall,[19] surmounted with a bell tower, the symbol of civic self-government. This is the political center of the town. Here is the jail, the headquarters of the town guard and watchmen, and the city council. Inside its intricately carved but stout wooden portals are the luxurious tapestried chambers of the town officials. Here are the regally ornamented quarters of the mayor, or chairman of the council. Here is the council chamber where each alderman has his own richly upholstered chair and ornately furnished desk. Near by is the grand assembly hall where the voting citizens assemble occasionally, and where, more often, stately social functions are held. All of these chambers, and the long hallways, are lavishly decorated with mural paintings, tapestries, woodcarving, and inlaid work. In short, the appointments of the city hall reflect the aristocratic money power that dominates the government and the economic life of the town.

[18] See below, Chapter XXXIV, on cathedral building.
[19] See below, p. 721, concerning the building of town halls.

THE GUILD HALLS Since the guilds play an important role in the life of the town, their halls occupy prominent places on the square. At Ypres in Belgium, up to the time of the World War, the hall of the clothmakers' guild was the most splendid building in the town. The guild halls of the medieval town resemble the town hall, but on a smaller scale. Each has rooms for the guild officials, assembly halls, and banquet rooms. In fact, these buildings are a sort of businessman's club. Here the prominent bankers, merchants, and shop owners meet to talk, lounge, and make business deals. Here is the center of the economic life of the town, just as the town hall is the center of the political activities, and the cathedral of the religious and social affairs.

RESIDENCES In other places on or near the public square are to be seen the ornately decorated residences of the wealthier burghers. They have picturesque high-pitched roofs of various colored tiles, ornamented gables, paneled doors, and carved heads or figures along the door sills and cornices. But even the finest of these residences are not very comfortable. None have the running water and sanitary conveniences of modern homes. Only a few of them are built of stone. In the crowded side streets, the houses are flimsy, dingy, wooden affairs. These dark and rickety dens of disease and filth were fire traps more dangerous than our most neglected slum tenements in a modern crowded city. Fires often destroyed entire towns in those days. Little wonder that curfew, the "covering of fires" was enforced rigidly. Shortly after dark everyone was supposed to be at home and in bed, with all fires and lights out.

ATTRACTIONS OF TOWN LIFE Town life, though harsh and uncomfortable for many citizens, was much more interesting than life on a rural manor. There was plenty of social life. On market days friends and strangers crowded the town square, to buy or merely to see the wondrous things displayed by visiting merchants. Singers, jongleurs, and acrobats enlivened the scene. Church and civic festivals also provided much wholesome amusement. Christmas, Mardi gras, Easter, and Pentecost, occasions for fun and frolic as well as for religious ceremonies, were enjoyed by young and old. On these festal days the guilds often joined with the clergy in dramatic presentations of Biblical scenes. These might take the form of floats in a procession, or of scenes in a religious pageant. For instance, the shipbuilders might present the building of the ark; the carpenters, the erecting of

Haman's gallows; the fishermen, the miraculous draft of fishes, and so on.

For guild members there was also the annual banquet and drink-fest at which everyone ate and drank to the limit of his capacity. Perchance some had to be carried home in the drunk wagon provided by some town governments for the convenience of the more bibulous citizens. By and large, townsfolk enjoyed life. With all of their extremes of poverty and wealth, they represented the more active and progressive aspects of medieval life. In the towns ambitious men found opportunity, for here one might rise as fast and as far as his abilities could carry him.

XIX

EMPIRE AND PAPACY

DURING the period in which business life and towns were beginning to expand and to lay the foundations for future economic greatness, two outstanding institutions, the empire and the papacy, occupied the center of the European stage and engaged in a struggle which threatened to destroy both of them. This conflict had consequences and by-products that are of great importance for the Middle Ages and for modern civilization. As a background for the struggle it is necessary to trace the rise of each of these institutions and to analyze carefully the factors which brought them into such constant and destructive rivalry.

First we shall consider the rise to power of the German kings, their revival of the Carolingian imperial ideal, and the resulting interrelations with Italy and the papacy. In this process we shall see not only the revival of imperial ambitions in the West but also certain developments in early German history. We shall then follow the evolution of the papal power in Italy. Finally in the clash between these two regions and institutions we shall see the conflict of church and state, papacy and empire, Italy and Germany. We turn now to the Germanies during the period in which a new royal-imperial power was arising out of the wreck of the Carolingian Empire. Until this new state had become strong and unified there was no serious conflict with the church.

THE REVIVED EMPIRE

THE DECLINE OF THE CAROLINGIANS   The entire history of medieval Germany is dominated by the story of successive revivals and disintegrations of the royal (or imperial) power and its unending struggle with the local baronage and the Italian papacy. The rise of the Carolingian Franks during the seventh and eighth centuries, and the metamorphosis of Charles the Great

370

from king of Germans to "Emperor Ever August of the Romans" is the first instance of centralized royal power on a large scale among the German people. It also marks the first of several revivals of the Western Empire. The death of Charles, however, was followed by internal disunity and external invasions, in Germany as well as in the rest of Western Europe.

The successors of Charles were unable to maintain even a semblance of imperial power. Under Louis the German (843-876), Arnulf (887-899), and Louis the Child (899-911), the local bishops and barons of the East Frankish (or German) realm became practically independent. The result was at least *six* Germanies. In the south, along the Danube, were the two great duchies of Bavaria and Swabia (or Alamannia). North of Swabia, along the Rhine, were Franconia and Lorraine. To the northeast, between the Rhine and the Elbe rivers, were Thuringia and Saxony, regions inhabited by the sturdiest of all the German people.

Within, or attached to, these six major (or "stem") duchies, were many semidependent realms ruled by powerful bishops, counts, and margraves. Along the eastern frontier, for instance, stretched a series of marches, each under the control of a practically independent margrave. On the Danish border was the Dane mark (modern Schleswig); along the Elbe were the Saxon, Thuringian, and Bohemian marches; south of Bavaria, stretching to the Adriatic, was the Carinthian mark. Internal disunity, moreover, extended even deeper, pervading the realms of the dukes, margraves, counts, and bishops. Every local region had its feudal lord, and the entire realm was, in fact, a complex of feudal dependencies roughly grouped into great duchies. The royal power depended on the uncertain and constantly shifting fidelity of thousands of feudal nobles great and small.

THE NEW SAXON DYNASTY At the death of Louis the Child, the last of the German Carolingians, the dukes, great barons, and clergy selected Duke Conrad of Franconia as king. His power was, however, only vague and shadowy. Like Hugh Capet, who was elected king in France later in the same century, Conrad ruled only over his own duchy; elsewhere he merely reigned. He was, so to speak, the honorary president of the "Disunited States of the Germanies." Throughout his reign (911-918), Conrad made no real progress in gaining control of the other duchies. The strength of feudal interests is shown by the method in which his successor was chosen. According to a contemporary chronicler: "Duke Henry [of

Saxony] was chosen king by agreement of the Franconians, Allmen [Alamannians, or Swabians], Bavarians, Thuringians, and Saxons." The selection of a Saxon duke to succeed the rival duke of Franconia is also significant. For over a hundred years the kingship was to remain in the hands of Saxons. This dynasty magnified the royal office, developing a powerful monarchy and reviving, for the second time, the Empire of the West.

Henry I, the Fowler (919-936), not only defended Germany against Danes, Slavs, and Hungarians but also asserted some authority over the powerful dukes of Lorraine, Swabia, and Bavaria. For the most part, however, his control was restricted to his own duchy, Saxony. Elsewhere he depended on the friendship of the churchmen and on the willing co-operation of the dukes and feudal barons. Nevertheless, he laid the foundation for a stronger central government.

OTTO THE GREAT Of great importance is the fact that Henry had sufficient influence to designate his own successor. According to Widukind's *Chronicle:* "All the people of the Franks [Franconians] and Saxons chose as their chief Otto . . . whom his father had wished them to choose . . . and the dukes and chief counts and soldiers . . . gave him their hands promising fidelity." Thus early did the hereditary principle assert itself in the selection of a German king. Nevertheless, it is clear that the king was little more than a supreme feudal overlord to whom the great nobles "promised fidelity."

What would be their attitude if he played the role of king? The answer to this question came when Otto I (936-973) proceeded to assert with energy what he considered his rightful kingly powers. Two ambitious brothers who revolted against his authority were crushed. Eventually he subjected all of the duchies to his own direct or indirect control. Dukes who revolted were replaced by his relatives. Thus all of the great duchies were brought into Otto's hands or those of members of his family. He also took measures to maintain this control and to bind the German duchies to the Saxon dynasty. Like Charles the Great he had a personal vigor which made his rule effective. He wisely utilized churchmen in government, and all through Germany friendly bishops and abbots were given the rights of imperial counts in and about their monastic or episcopal centers. By such means the German church was made the ally and servant of the monarchy. As in Charles the Great's day, this relationship was mutually profitable. Clerical counts, since they had few family interests, were usually faithful to the king. In return, they received lavish gifts of lands and other favors. Thus Otto established a virtual partnership between the German clergy and their monarch. This relationship was destined to play an important role in the later struggles of the empire with the papacy and with the feudal powers. Throughout imperial history, most of the German clergy remained faithful to their king, even though at times it meant resistance to the pope.

OTTO'S ITALIAN EXPEDITIONS

Otto's governmental regime in Germany met with outstanding success and it seems probable that he would have left to his son a centralized monarchy and a consolidated Germany but for two factors. In the first place, his kingship was feudal in practice. He was the suzerain of a number of federated duchies, not sovereign of a united realm. No matter how extensive and effective his powers, he and his subjects recognized that the king was an elected monarch with limited authority. In the second place, Otto intervened in Italy, a region which had been and was to be for centuries the burial ground of many German ambitions, armies, and kings. The Germans, it is said, were particularly susceptible to the deadly marsh fever of the Italian plain, but it seems that the prevailing Italian malady of political disunity and intrigue may have had even more tragic influences on Germany.

In Otto's day, as always, the Italies consisted of hundreds of hostile units, variously combined, each one eager for favorable intervention by some foreign power. Already certain dukes of southern Germany had intervened on opposite sides of a feudal struggle in Lombardy. It was therefore quite natural for the Italians to call on Otto for assistance, and for him to respond. In 951 he took up the cause of Adelaide, the attractive young widow of a recently crowned "King of Italy." Otto's German troops easily overthrew her enemies and conquered Lombardy. He then married the queen-widow and was himself crowned "King of Italy." After having thus acquired a wife and a royal crown, Otto devoted himself to German affairs for ten years. It was during this decade that he put an end to the raids of the Hungarians, at the battle of the Lech, near Augsburg in Bavaria (955). In 962 he made a second trip to Italy, and at Rome he and Adelaide were crowned emperor and empress by the pope. Thus the Western Empire was once more revived by a German king and a Roman pope.[1]

[1] Note the fact that Charles the Great revived the empire in 800.

Idealists saw in this event the perfect co-operation of church and state for the accomplishment of God's will in civil and religious affairs. Eventually, in the twelfth century, this viewpoint gave to the revived empire the rather misleading title of "Holy Roman Empire." Centuries later, Voltaire, with rare wit and ample justification, remarked that "it was neither holy, nor Roman, nor even an empire." As a matter of fact, the name *German* Roman Empire is more accurately descriptive of both the Carolingian and Ottonian empires. It is noteworthy that, whereas the *ancient* Roman Empire comprised most of Western Europe, the *Carolingian* Empire comprised only France, Germany, and Italy; and the *Ottonian* Empire, only Germany and Italy. Otto's imperial sway was restricted, not only in extent, but also in strength. In most parts of his "empire" the actual government was in the hands of the local feudal lords.

Otto I's son and grandson, Otto II (973-983) and Otto III (983-1002), failed to uphold his governmental system in Germany. Both of them, and particularly Otto III (whose mother was a Byzantine princess), emphasized the imperial and Roman aspects of their government. Otto III established himself in a palace on the Aventine Hill and set up a court like that of the ancient Roman emperors. He and Pope Sylvester II (Gerbert) [2] spent much time planning the betterment of a church and a state that did not seem to be ready for reform. While Otto wasted his energies in Italy, Germany relapsed into disunity. By the time of his death, even the Romans were disgusted and on the verge of revolt.

THE END OF
THE SAXON
DYNASTY Since the days of Otto the Great, the revived imperial power had declined sharply. The reign of Henry II (1002-1024) ended a line of five Saxon emperors who had reigned over Germany for a century.

With the election of Conrad II of Franconia (1024-1039), the empire entered upon its second stage, a hundred-year era of centralization and expansion under the Franconian dynasty. Conrad, adopting a policy of "Germany first," made only one brief trip to Italy. He paid little attention, and gave no favors, to Italian popes or to German churchmen. In a ruthlessly practical fashion he set about to build up the power of the monarch by favoring the lesser feudality at the expense of the great barons and the clergy. One of his greatest successes

[2] See below, p. 379.

was the training and coronation of his son during his own lifetime. As a consequence Henry III (1039-1056) acquired not only a well-organized kingdom, but also an excellent preparation for the imperial office.

Thanks to his father's work and to his own energy, Henry was able to bring Germany once more to a high point of territorial expansion and administrative efficiency. He ruled over all the Germanies, the newly acquired realm of Burgundy, and northern and central Italy. Besides this the kings of Slavic Poland and Bohemia, and of Hungary acknowledged his suzerainty. Little wonder that a party of respectable Romans invited him to come to Rome and reform the corrupt and inefficient papacy. Inasmuch as this event involved Henry and his successors in unending conflicts with the popes, we must turn now to the history of the papacy during this period.

THE REVIVED PAPACY

CENTRALIZING AND DECENTRAL-IZING FORCES The entire history of the medieval church is dominated by the rise of the papal power, its fluctuations, and its eventual decline in the fifteenth century. We deal now with the period during which spiritual authority in the West was consolidating in the hands of the bishops of Rome. This development involved two inevitable and unending conflicts in the church: one between the forces of centralization and decentralization, and another between spiritual and secular interests. During the era of its most remarkable growth, the papacy became the rallying point for the forces of centralization; that is, for those who desired a unified Christian Church organized on an imperial scale similar to that of the ancient Roman Empire. In somewhat the same fashion, the papacy also became the representative of the highest spiritual interests of the church. If at times the papacy itself was by no means a purely spiritual force, the outstanding papal leaders nevertheless usually emphasized the supremacy of spiritual over secular interests.

During the early centuries of Christianity's growth in the Roman Empire, a number of forces led to the development of a centralized form of church government. This is illustrated by the rise of the clerical hierarchy and by the steady increase of papal power in the West to the time of Leo I (440-461) and, after a temporary setback, to the end of the pontificate of Gregory I (590-604).[3] The papal ideal of a great spiritual empire, however, found serious opposition; first, in the strong Germanic kingdoms which replaced the disintegrated Western Empire; second, in the feudal trend toward independent regional churches; and, much later, in the movement for national churches which led to the Protestant revolution. We turn now to the story of the long and difficult struggle of the early medieval papacy against the forces of decentralization and secularization.

THE DECLINE OF PAPAL POWER   We have already traced the growth of the papacy during the era of the decline of the Empire of the West. Even after the disintegration of the empire, thanks to the continuing influence of Roman civilization, the church maintained a centralized organization that enabled a pope such as Gregory I to exercise imperial sway in spiritual affairs. But during the next two centuries—the seventh and eighth—papal influence suffered a decided setback. This was due not so much to the inferior personal character of the popes as to the general situation in the West; internal confusion, invasions and lack of means of communication tended to disrupt any large-scale administration, whether papal or imperial.

The Germanic kingdoms of the Visigoths, Lombards, Franks, and Anglo-Saxons had by this time developed governmental organizations which tended to exercise control over religious as well as secular institutions. The native-born clergy of these kingdoms were more closely bound to their own rulers than to the bishops of Rome. Thus the churches in these realms became subject to secular and also sectional interests. Western Christendom was about to become a group of independent regional churches instead of one papally controlled Roman Catholic Church. The popes themselves, in spite of Gregory I's ideal of a Christian world under one supreme authority, were little more than local bishops of the city of Rome, compelled to beg for foreign protection against the encroachments of the neighboring Lombard rulers.

As we have already seen,[4] they were finally rescued by Pepin the Short and Charles the Great. The protecting friendship of the Frankish monarchs did not, however, restore papal prestige. Instead the relationship tended to become a rather strict, though wholesome, domi-

---

[3] For the events of *early* papal history mentioned here and in the succeeding paragraphs, see above, Chapter IV.

[4] See above, pp. 186 ff.

nation of the church by the state. After the disintegration of the Carolingian Empire, late in the ninth century, one pope, Nicholas I (858-
867), asserted with vigor the Gregorian ideal of papal authority and
spiritual leadership. He interfered in the domestic affairs of the
Lotharingian king, preventing him from divorcing the queen in favor
of a mistress. He also forced the independent French archbishop,
Hincmar of Rheims, to come to terms with a local bishop with whom
he had quarreled. Like Gregory I, he even tried, though in vain, to
exert papal authority over the Eastern Church.

FEUDAL
TENDENCIES

If Nicholas's efforts to restore the lost reputation and
influence of the papacy came to little more than a gesture, the fault was not his. During the ninth century
the West had disintegrated into that condition of extremely localized,
personal government which is called feudalism. The papacy could not
hope to exercise imperial sway, even in spiritual affairs, over a Western Europe that consisted of innumerable kingdoms and petty feudal
states. It had to contend not only with the opposition of local rulers
and people, jealous of outside interference, but also with the physical
difficulty of maintaining close communications between Rome and the
clergy of distant realms. For about two centuries (until 1050) the
papacy found itself submerged in a world of small, independent units.
Religious, as well as economic, social, and political institutions came
under the dominating influence of local feudal rulers. As Western
Europe became more and more feudal, the church was forced to follow the general trend. As the church became feudalized, the papacy
lost its position of leadership and was swept along with the tide.

THE PAPACY
IN LOCAL
POLITICS

The papacy of the tenth and early eleventh centuries
vividly illustrates the depths to which the clergy
could sink when subjected to the unspiritual and
factional influences of local politics. Within the eight
years from 896 to 904, eight popes were set up and overthrown by the
political factions of Rome and vicinity. The next half century was even
worse. An able but unscrupulous woman named Marozia dominated
the papacy for years through the influence of her relatives or para-
mours. Like her mother before her, she was the pope's mistress. Then,
chiefly for political purposes, she became the wife successively of the
Duke of Spoleto, of the Duke of Tuscany, and of "King Hugh of
Italy," with whom she finally became ruler of Rome. She was also
the mother of two local politicians who dominated papal affairs. By

Pope Sergius III she bore a son who became Pope John XI (931-936);
and, by the Duke of Spoleto, another son, Alberic, who ruled Rome
for almost a quarter of a century.

Alberic eventually became his mother's bitterest opponent and
leader of the faction which overthrew her regime. He attempted to
revive the ancient Roman Republic, instituted various reforms, and
subjected the papacy completely to the policies of his "Republic." The
religious situation was improved as a result of his interest in church
reforms, for, among other things, he fostered the adoption, in certain
Italian monasteries, of the Cluniac reform,[5] a program which was
destined eventually to free the papacy from lay interference such as
his. It is noteworthy, in the case of Alberic as of Charles the Great
and other high-minded monarchs, that lay domination of the papacy
sometimes worked for the improvement of spiritual conditions.

After Alberic's death, however, the papacy was worse
IMPERIAL off than ever. His own son, whom he had made
INTERVENTION pope, John XII (955-964), embarked upon a career
of vice and duplicity that shocked the Christian world. A French
writer of this era referred to Rome as "the seat of every iniquity . . .
a city sunk in ignorance and sin." Convinced that neither the papacy
nor the local laity could handle the situation, certain Romans called
in an able foreign monarch, Emperor Otto I of Germany. This invitation was the occasion for Otto's first visit to Rome and for the imperial coronation of 962. After receiving the imperial crown from
John XII, Otto called a church council which deposed the pope on
charges of "murder, sacrilege, and immorality," putting in his place
a respectable clergyman who had been nominated by the emperor.
Thus early, we find the new German Empire involved in papal and
Italian affairs. This interrelationship was to have long-standing and
momentous consequences for both parties.

No sooner had Otto left Rome than his appointee was overthrown,
and the papacy once more came under the control of local factions.
Conditions continued thus for almost a century, except for one more
vain effort at reform. This was attempted by Otto's grandson, the well-
meaning but hopelessly impractical idealist, Emperor Otto III (983-
1002). He had imperial ambitions, not only for himself, but also for
the papacy. He hoped that the emperor and pope, in close co-operation, might organize and administer both church and state as one

[5] See below, p. 382.

unified whole. For this purpose he called to the papacy his former tutor, Gerbert of Rheims, the most brilliant scholar of the age.[6] At Rome for a number of years he and Gerbert (as Pope Sylvester II) worked together to establish a united and reformed Christendom. But their program, somewhat similar to that which had been successfully employed by Charles the Great, was unworkable in the feudalized world of Otto's day.

PAPAL DEGRADATION The ensuing period presents a startling contrast between papal ideals and practice. Catholic scholars consider the first half of the eleventh century as one of the worst examples of papal corruption in the annals of the church. Matters came to a climax in the year 1046 with three rival popes, each supported by a local faction, each claiming to be God's sole representative on earth, and each condemning the other two popes as usurpers. One of the claimants was a young man who was accused of murder, robbery, adultery, and numerous other crimes. Another was a pious priest who admitted that he had deliberately bought his way to the sacred office in order to reform the papacy—a vivid commentary on the manner in which even the sincere clergymen of this age felt impelled to resort to the questionable practices of lay politics.

As formerly, the outrageous situation finally led certain Romans to seek aid from an outside source. Their choice was Henry III, who, as we have seen, had brought all Germany and parts of northern Italy under his imperial sway. He was urged to come and deliver the church from its own scandalous leaders. Henry responded. He was already deeply interested in the welfare of the church, and had encouraged the Cluniac reform movement among the German clergy. On arriving in the vicinity of Rome, he called a council (at Sutri in 1046) and all three of the rival popes were eliminated. For the next ten years Henry, like Otto I a century earlier, selected the popes and supported their efforts at clerical reform. In fact, he may be said to have pulled the papacy out of the mire of Roman politics, set it on its feet, and started it once and for all on the road to independence and spiritual leadership.

LEO IX The dawn of the new day in papal history is clearly indicated by the career of Leo IX (1048-1054), a noble Alsatian bishop, Henry's second appointee to the sacred office. In spite of the fact that Leo was a relative of the emperor, from the outset he asserted the spiritual independence of the papacy. Nomina-

[6] See above, p. 295.

tion by the emperor was equivalent to election, but Leo refused to assume office until he had been duly elected by the clergy and laity of Rome. He insisted on entering the city as a simple layman, in the garb of a humble pilgrim. It is said that he looked so much like other pious visitors to the Holy City that the welcoming delegation failed to recognize him as the pope-elect. After the formal election ceremonies, Leo immediately set about reforming the clergy. In church councils held at various places throughout the West, he not only condemned clerical immorality and political corruption, but dismissed clerics, both high and low, who were guilty of such offenses. In Italy and Germany, thanks to the hearty co-operation of the emperor, much was accomplished. In France, the king and his clerical appointees did all they dared to obstruct the papal reform program. But by the end of Leo's pontificate the papacy had won the respect of clergy and laity alike through the West.

ORIGINS OF THE REFORM MOVEMENT   The remarkable success of the pope's reform program was due not merely to a sincerely religious emperor and to the high personal ideals of his appointee. Underlying this was a century or more of gradual change in spiritual ideals and in the general condition of feudal society. By the middle of the eleventh century, a more orderly civilization based on larger political, social, and economic units had been achieved. Everywhere town life was developing rapidly, and national monarchies were taking shape in England, France, and northern Spain.[7] In the church these developments were paralleled by a movement to purify the clergy, strengthen the papacy, and centralize the clerical administration. For the beginnings of this reform program, we must go back to the tenth century, to the French monastery of Cluny, which took the lead in rousing the clergy to action.

THE FEUDALIZED CHURCH   The Cluniac reformation began as a protest against the conditions by which the clergy, and particularly the monks, were being despiritualized through their interrelations with the lay feudality. During the tenth century, not only the papacy, but also the lesser clergy throughout the West, had become entangled in a network of feudal relationships. In the light of the prevailing conditions, this was inevitable. The clergy could not avoid contact with lay society. The lesser members of the clergy were constantly associated with their lay parishioners, and were usually

---

[7] See below, Chapters XXIII-XXIV.

called upon to take an active part in governmental affairs. Furthermore, bishops and abbots as important landlords were compelled to enter into feudal relationships in order to protect church holdings. Economic interest, political expediency, and common safety demanded it. But there were serious spiritual disadvantages.

Feudal obligations consumed much of the time and interest of clergymen, who were supposed to devote themselves to spiritual affairs. Even at best, when the overlord was a sincere layman interested in the religious welfare of society, feudalism tended to infect the clergy with worldly ideals and practices. For instance, in most regions, the rulers had the right of appointing abbots; in fact many a king was ex-officio abbot of several monasteries. As a result the monasteries tended to come under the direct administration of the feudal laity. Hugh Capet is said to have controlled hundreds of monasteries in all parts of France. Under such lay administration, the monks lived worldly lives, forgetful of monastic ideals and regulations.

The bishops were in a similar situation. Since the time of Charles the Great, they had been endowed with great estates and had been considered officials of the government. In order to control these lands and officials, the lay rulers felt that they had a right to take part in the selection of the local bishops. As a matter of fact, they usually nominated bishops in much the same fashion in which the emperors named popes. As a result of such practices, church offices were filled with men of lay rather than of spiritual interests. It was common for feudal lords to place their sons or favorites in church positions. By such means they were able to control, and often to appropriate, church property. Thus the political methods prevailing in secular governments invaded the clerical administration. As in secular affairs, bribery became common, and church offices were bought and sold.

Priests and lesser clerics followed the example of the bishops and abbots, and from top to bottom the church took on the characteristics of the lay world. For instance, marriage was prevalent even among the higher clergy, and in consequence church property was often parceled out as inheritances to members of the family of the bishop or abbot. This practice threatened to establish an hereditary caste of parasitical clerics dominated by materialistic rather than spiritual interests. It is obvious that such conditions, if unchecked, would have destroyed not only the soul of religion, but also the political and economic structure of the church.

THE CLUNIAC
REFORMATION

Such were the conditions amid which the Cluniac reformers began their work. Founded in the year 910, this French monastery soon became the center of a movement for the rescue of monasticism from lay control and for the renewal of its spiritual life. The program was accompanied by a vigorous campaign for the elimination of external lay interference in monastic elections, for the abolition of lay abbots, and for the strict observance of the ancient Benedictine rule. Almost immediately the movement came under the sponsorship of the papacy, whose valuable ally it became in extending its influence over the local clergy. Of outstanding importance was the regulation which placed all Cluniac houses under the direct control of the pope and forbade any interference by local authorities. This applied even to bishops. Thus the Cluniac program broke the grip of the secular clergy and the lay feudality on monasticism. It also greatly increased the authority of the papacy. In every region of the West the Cluniacs served as rallying points for zealous groups of papal supporters and religious reformers.

So successful was the Cluniac campaign for monastic independence that almost immediately it spread to the secular clergy. If the monks could be freed from lay domination, why could not the priests and bishops be restored to their rightful allegiance to the papacy and to the spiritual life of the church? This hope, and the determination to bring it to pass, caught the attention of the revived papacy and inspired Leo IX and his successors. Thus it was that in the late eleventh century, the papacy, so recently the scandal of Christendom, became the leader in a program of reform. This movement was destined to revive the spiritual life of the clergy, to bring the church to the climax of its influence, and to make the papacy the greatest power in the Western world.

The Cluniac program, as it was adopted by the eleventh-century papacy, called for (1) the elimination of all forms of clerical worldliness, particularly immorality (which included marriage); and (2) the freeing of all clergymen from lay control. The campaign against clerical worldliness was launched by a series of decrees which provided for the rigid enforcement of *clerical celibacy*. To the age-old monastic antipathy for clerical marriage, there was added at this time a more practical motive, the weakening of self-perpetuating groups of clergymen whose local and secular interests clashed with papal plans for a centralized administration in the church. It was obvious that clergymen who remained unmarried would be more wholehearted in their service of

Christianity and the papacy; they would also be less likely to distribute church offices and property to members of their families. Celibacy thus tended to preserve the morals, the morale, and the wealth of the church. From the eleventh century onward, the papacy made slow but sure progress, especially in Italy, toward the enforcement of celibacy among the clergy.

THE PAPAL DECLARATION OF INDEPENDENCE
More immediate results were realized in the campaign for the liberation of the clergy from lay control. In this reform, the papacy started at home. It will be remembered that Emperor Henry III, having freed the Roman church from a three-headed papacy, and from the domination of local political factions, took over the selection and control of the popes. Thus the papacy, after having been rescued from Roman factions, found that it was subject to the German emperor. Even though this imperial influence was benevolent and was exerted in the interests of religious reform, it was inevitable that the papacy, as its strength and ambition increased, should seek complete independence.

The opportunity came, immediately after the death of Henry III, who died suddenly in 1056 leaving a six-year-old heir. During the nine-year regency that intervened before the accession of Henry IV, the papacy had ample time to establish itself as an independent power. Within three years of Henry III's death, at the Lateran (Roman) Council of 1059, it was decreed that the initiative in papal elections was to be taken not by the emperor but by the College of Cardinals— that is, by the cardinal bishops, priests, and deacons of the churches of the city of Rome. Their selection was to be ratified by the Roman people; the emperor, instead of nominating the candidate, merely gave his consent to the action already taken by the clergy and people. The Lateran decree has rightly been called the papacy's "declaration of independence." It marks the beginning of the end of domination by German emperors, as well as by local political factions. Henceforth the responsibility for the selection of popes was to rest primarily upon the Roman clergy. Although the new procedure was far from perfect and was often disregarded in practice, the general principle remained unchanged, and still exists with only minor modifications.[8] With this

[8] Over a century later (1179) the rule of a *two-thirds majority* was adopted. In the next century, due to deadlocks and delays in voting, the *conclave* was instituted; according to this arrangement the cardinals were kept, like a modern jury, under lock and key (the Latin word for key is *clavis*) until they came to a decision. Nowadays certain of the clergy of Rome and vicinity have complete control over the

declaration the papacy assumed once more a position of independent leadership in the religious affairs of the West.

Almost simultaneously with the Lateran decree, the papacy made another move which strengthened its power of resistance to imperial interference. Leo IX's successor recognized, as feudal vassals of the popes, two warlike Norman princes, Robert Guiscard, who had conquered most of southern Italy, and his brother Roger, who was setting forth to wrest Sicily from the Moslems.[9] Shortly thereafter Norman troops actually rescued one of the popes from the armies of the emperor. It was during this same period that another pope gave his approval to Duke William of Normandy's invasion of England. This resulted in a marked extension of papal influence on both sides of the English Channel. Thus, along with its reform program, the papacy launched upon a series of international alliances which made it a formidable political power.

GREGORY VII   It was not long before the revived and ambitious papacy was put to a severe test, in which the leading role was taken by Hildebrand, better known by his papal name of Gregory VII (1073-1085). Hildebrand was a man of humble birth, educated by the church, and strongly influenced by the Cluniac ideal. He had risen to a position of great influence under Leo IX and his successors. For years before his election, Hildebrand was the power behind the papal throne. Insignificant in appearance, he was a man of stern and puritanical character; he is said to have given up eating onions because he was so fond of them. He had been excellently trained in papal administrative affairs, was an experienced diplomat, and had the highest of ambitions for the papacy.

Although Hildebrand had been active in establishing the procedure of election by cardinals, he was raised to the papal office by popular acclamation before the cardinals had taken any action. He explained the inconsistency on the grounds that he was forced to submit to the will of the people. As a matter of fact, this was not the last time that he was to overstep precedents. Throughout his pontificate Gregory VII boldly asserted the unrestricted powers of the pope. In the famous *Dictatus,* composed by some member of the papal clergy, is to be found a list of the powers which Gregory and his as-

selection of popes. At the death of a pope the cardinals (all of whom, even those in America, are either actual or titular members of the Roman clergy) meet in conclave and continue thus until a selection is made.

[9] See below, p. 395.

sistants considered as the prerogatives of that high office. Among other things it was asserted that the pope "may depose emperors. . . . His decrees may be annulled by no one. . . . He alone may annul the decrees of all. . . . He may be judged by no one." Gregory appears to have believed implicitly in his right to exercise these unlimited powers. Such claims, if realized, would have made him the absolute ruler of all Christendom. Although he fell far short of this objective, his successors a century and a half later came very close to attaining it.

THE STRUGGLE OVER LAY INVESTITURE Having asserted the pope's independence of the empire, Gregory set about to free the entire clergy from imperial and feudal control. Hitherto lay rulers had been accustomed not only to nominate candidates for clerical positions, but also to invest or induct them into office. By this means they were able to control the procedure from start to finish. A sincerely religious ruler might thus prevent a group of misguided clerics from selecting an unworthy abbot or bishop, but on the other hand self-seeking lords often forced the selection of their own nominees by refusing to invest any other who might be chosen by the clergy. Then, too, conscienceless lords were encouraged to demand fees from candidates in return for their support. In order to end this sort of bribery (called *simony* [10] by the church authorities), and to establish the right of free clerical elections. Gregory prohibited *lay investiture*. He decreed that "no one of the clergy was to receive investiture to a bishopric or abbey or church from the hand of the emperor or king or of any lay person."

It is obvious that this was an epoch-making program. If enforced it would remove all churchmen from direct lay control and enable the pope to consolidate them into a centralized papal bureaucracy. It would at one stroke sever the ties between lay rulers and many of their most valuable clerical administrators. It would prevent the local feudality from controlling the appointment of parish priests on their own estates. Most serious of all from the materialistic standpoint, it would remove from lay control all church property. In most regions this comprised about a third of the land, much of which had been donated to the church by the laity. Thus Gregory's reform program threatened as drastic an economic change as does the modern de-

[10] See the Biblical story of Simon (Acts 8:18-19) from which this name originated. Although Simon's sin was the attempt to purchase the "gift of the Holy Spirit," in the Middle Ages, the term *simony* was applied to the act of purchasing church offices, and, in a loose sense, even to the receiving of lay investiture.

mand for governmental socialization of private property. In either case, those who had been enjoying extensive property rights would lose control of them.

THE CLASH BETWEEN POPE AND EMPEROR

GREGORY VS.
HENRY IV

The natural fears of the ruling class were increased by the determined manner in which the pope went about the enforcement of the new decrees. Clergy-men as well as lay rulers were alarmed. In Germany the reaction to the papal program was decidedly hostile, because of the fact that the bishops and abbots were the emperor's most effective governmental officials. He depended on them and they upon him as a defense against the encroachments of the feudality. At this time the young emperor, Henry IV (1056-1106), who had only recently taken over the reigns of government, had made remarkable progress in re-estab-lishing royal power over the feudal nobility. All parts of the German realm, except Saxony, were under his control, and he had hopes of quickly subduing the hardy rebels of that duchy. Meanwhile he had paid little attention to the papal reform program. In fact he deliber-ately disregarded it in the case of the important Italian city of Milan, which he felt it necessary to control by securing the election of a bishop of his own choosing. This violation of a papal decree in Italian territory could not be overlooked. If the pope was to reform and rule the church, he, and not the emperor, must control the bishops.

The issue was unavoidable, and Gregory brought matters to a head by sending legates to the imperial court with a letter of expostu-lation. The salutation of this letter clearly indicated that the pope ex-pected the emperor not only to reform, but to obey him in all matters. It read: "Bishop Gregory, servant of the servants of God, to King Henry, greeting and apostolic benediction:—that is, if he be obedient to the apostolic chair [i.e., the papacy] as beseems a Christian king." [11] In succeeding passages Gregory reminded Henry of his failings and of the fact that the pope was responsible before God for all of his ac-tions. He closed with an exhortation for him to imitate the humility of King David by submitting to papal guidance. When the papal legates added verbal threats to these written suggestions, Henry's tact-

[11] This and the succeeding quotations from Gregory and Henry follow the trans-lation in Robinson, *Readings in European History*, I, pp. 276 ff.

ful attitude gave way to anger, and the inevitable break came. Open warfare was declared between the empire and the papacy.

MUTUAL
CONDEMNATIONS
From this point, events marched swiftly. On Henry's invitation, his German clergy met in council at Worms (January, 1076) and deposed Gregory. Henry's letter of notification to the pope indicates not only the undercurrent of youthful courage and resentment by which he was swept into this momentous struggle, but also his viewpoint concerning his own God-given functions. In the opening sentences he flung down the gauntlet to the pope as follows: "Henry, King not by usurpation but by holy ordination of God, to Hildebrand, now no pope but false monk." This defiant announcement was followed by a vigorous defense of his position and actions. He condemned Gregory's claims to an "illegal and unscriptural" authority over the emperor. Henry insisted that Peter himself, "the true Pope," had exhorted all Christians to "fear God; honor the King . . . [with the warning] if anyone whether I or an angel from Heaven, shall preach any other gospel . . . he shall be damned." The emperor's letter closed with the audacious command: "I, Henry, king by the grace of God, together with all our bishops, say unto thee: Come down [from the papal throne], come down to be damned throughout all eternity."

When this letter was presented at a papal synod in Rome, those in attendance were so horrified at the insult to the pope that Gregory himself was forced to intervene in order to prevent them from mobbing the imperial ambassador.

Gregory shrewdly responded in a calm and dignified letter, couched in the form of a prayer invoking Peter's protection of his church against the attacks of ravagers. In his final words the pope struck the young emperor a telling blow: "For the honor and security of thy [i.e., Peter's] church, in the name of God Almighty, I prohibit Henry, the king . . . from ruling Germany and Italy. I release all Christians from the oaths of fealty they may have taken to him, and I order that no one shall obey him."

DEADLOCKED:
CANOSSA
Thus began the most dramatic episode in the agelong struggle between popes and emperors. For a time it seemed that Gregory would be completely victorious. In Germany the Saxons and the feudal nobles, who resented Henry's autocratic policies, took immediate advantage of his difficulties. The German diet (an assembly of feudal barons), after consultation with legates from the pope, decided to elect a new emperor un-

less Henry made his peace with the church. At this point Henry displayed masterly statesmanship. Accompanied by his wife and little son, he hurried across the Alps in the dead of winter and presented himself to the pope at Canossa in Tuscany. Here he assumed the guise of a humble penitent, and after three days' delay, Gregory, much against his will, granted absolution.

From the standpoint of papal diplomacy Gregory would have preferred that Henry remain unforgiven, an excommunicated and deposed monarch. As a clergyman, however, he could not refuse absolution to a repentant sinner. This dramatic incident, which has often been interpreted as a complete triumph for the papacy, was actually Henry's salvation. Although he was forced to humiliate himself outwardly, and to promise to "do justice according to the pope's judgment," in reality he stooped to conquer. He returned to Germany, secure in his rights as emperor. For the time being he had disarmed the pope of his most powerful weapon, excommunication, and from this point his fortunes began to improve.

HENRY GAINS GROUND   The favorable effect of the Canossa incident on Henry's cause is clearly shown by the reaction of the German feudality. Convinced that the pope had deserted them, they disregarded the settlement at Canossa and proceeded to elect a rival emperor. For the next three years (1077-1080) Gregory was in the difficult position of an arbiter who was besieged by appeals from each emperor to depose his rival. He could not afford to depose the emperor set up by his German allies; nor could he remove Henry for crimes which had been forgiven. Meanwhile Henry steadily gained ground. Finally he became so truculent that Gregory found grounds for redeposing him. Here Henry's cause proved its strength. The pope prophesied incorrectly that within a year Henry would be either dead or dethroned. In 1080, however, Henry's imperial rival was killed in battle, and soon the victorious emperor invaded Italy and set up one of his clerical supporters as a rival pope. The fidelity of the Romans and the military support provided by Duchess Mathilda of Tuscany and the Norman duke, Robert Guiscard of southern Italy, enabled Gregory to maintain himself in Rome for a few years.

In 1084, however, his cause was completely lost. His Norman allies sacked and plundered parts of the city of Rome in such a manner that Gregory found it wise to retire with them to Salerno, where he lived in exile for the remaining months of his life. "The Devil [so he wrote to a friend] has won no such victory since the days before Constantine; the day of Antichrist is approaching." It was reported that he died saying: "I have loved righteousness and hated iniquity; therefore I die in exile." To his followers this may have seemed an accurate explanation of the tragic fate of a heroic pope, but the Romans must have felt that it was a just retribution for having subjected the papal city to Norman ravagers. To Henry it may have seemed that at last "Hildebrand, false monk" had descended from his usurped papal throne "to be damned throughout eternity."

Whatever Gregory's failings, it is clear that he set for the papacy a high ideal of universal spiritual power. Furthermore, he vigorously sought to realize this program. Even though he himself failed, the papal cause was not lost. Henry might defeat a great pope, but he could not crush the papacy. For twenty years more he was to wage a losing fight against the combined forces of the German baronage and the papal successors of Gregory. Gregory had given the Christian world a magnificent example of the papacy functioning as the head of a spiritual empire.

HENRY IV'S DOWNFALL Within a year after Gregory's death a French Cluniac pope named Urban II (1088-1099) took up the struggle against Henry and his pope. Slowly but surely Urban's cause gained strength in Italy. By 1094 he had gained access to the city of Rome. The following year, at the Council of Piacenza, held in northern Italy, a region that strongly favored the imperialist cause, Henry and his pope were re-excommunicated. A year later, after the Council of Clermont, Urban made a tour through southern France preaching the crusade,[12] and incidentally strengthening his own cause.

Whatever Urban's motives in sponsoring the crusade—to rescue the Holy Land, or merely to counteract the tide of Henry's successes— the enthusiasm accompanying the first crusade tended to put the imperialists on the defensive and to win international support for Urban. The papal cause steadily advanced. Meanwhile Henry's expeditions into Italy gave his German enemies an opportunity to conspire against him. The last years of his life were as tragic as those of Gregory. Assailed on all sides by ambitious clerics and faithless barons, he died in 1106, defeated and deposed by his own son, excommunicated, and even deprived of Christian burial.

[12] See below, pp. 499 ff.

Scarcely had Henry's faithless son, Henry V, ascended the throne when he fell out with his papal ally. Soon he himself was upholding the imperial rights which had been so ably championed by his father. He was at swords' points with the popes until 1122, when a settlement was made which recognized the inescapable fact that both the emperor and the pope had a claim on the services of clergymen.

According to the Concordat of Worms, bishops and abbots were to be *elected* by the clergy. They were to be *invested* by clergymen so far as the *religious* insignia were concerned, but the emperor or his representative was to grant the *civil* insignia. In Germany, elections were to be held in the emperor's presence; this, of course, allowed him considerable influence over the selection. Although the settlement was a compromise which recognized the emperor's rights in clerical elections, it was clear that the Gregorian papacy had dealt staggering blows to the imperial system. In spite of the fact that the empire under the three Henrys (1039-1125) had attained its greatest extent since the days of Charles the Great, it had been checked by the papacy, and had suffered its first great defeat at the hands of the German feudality.

The Concordat of Worms, however, did not end the struggle. Conflict between papacy and empire was inevitable as long as each claimed that it was divinely ordained to exercise universal authority in its own realm—the papacy in spiritual affairs, the emperor in government. Trouble arose whenever ambitious popes extended their spiritual sway over matters which were a part of the political functions of the emperor. The same was true of the emperor. There was a zone in which both had important interests. Here they were bound to clash whenever it chanced that both the pope and the emperor were able and ambitious.

XX

THE TRIUMPH OF THE PAPACY

NEW PAPAL PROBLEMS

THE second quarter of the twelfth century saw comparative peace between the empire and the papacy. Both were headed by rather insignificant men who busied themselves with local problems. The reigns of the emperors Lothaire II (1125-1137) and Conrad III (1138-1152) were marked by a serious feud between two great families, the Welfs (or Guelfs) and the Hohenstaufen (or Ghibellines). Emperor Lothaire's son-in-law, the Welf duke, Henry the Proud, was so powerful that the feudality refused to make him emperor and chose Conrad of the rival Hohenstaufen family. Consequently Henry and his Welf adherents did all in their power to weaken Emperor Conrad and his Hohenstaufen successors.

Until the reign of the powerful Frederick Barbarossa, the Red-Bearded (1152-1190), the papacy had little to fear from Germany. But in Italy the popes had difficulties of their own. Innocent II (1130-1143) and Eugene III (1145-1153) had trouble with antipopes and rebellious Italian townsfolk. In 1143 the Romans ousted their papal lord and (as in the days of Alberic, two centuries earlier) set up a republic after the ancient Roman model. To make matters worse for the papacy, sometime later Arnold of Brescia, a brilliant and radical reformer, became the leader of the rebellious Romans. Arnold had studied under Abelard at Paris and had been exiled from Brescia, his home town, for heretical and revolutionary ideas. At Rome he seized the opportunity to put into practice some of his radical religious and political ideals. These included (1) the separation of church and state, (2) the divesting of the papacy of all civil power, (3) the confiscation of all clerical wealth, and (4) the placing of political power in the hands of the burgher class.

Such proposals naturally met with bitter opposition, and Bernard of Clairvaux, the leading churchman of the day, condemned Arnold's teaching as so "poisonous" that France repelled him, his home town, Brescia, "vomited him forth," and Italy as a whole refused to receive him. Both Emperor Conrad III and his young successor, Frederick the Red-Bearded, refused to have any dealings with Arnold or the Roman "Republic." Eventually the combined forces of the emperor and the pope crushed the rebels. Arnold was burned as a dangerous heretic, and imperial troops restored the pope to his former position as ruler of the city. Frederick, at this early stage in his career, failed to see the advantage of weakening the papacy by encouraging the rebellious Roman townsfolk. Soon he was to learn by bitter experience the strength and importance of Italian townspeople.

A NEW PAPAL-IMPERIAL STRUGGLE Within two years a new papal-imperial struggle broke out. It began with a misunderstanding concerning the pope's power in the coronation of the emperor. Although in itself a trifling incident, it illustrates the resentment of the imperialists at what they considered the papal tendency to encroach on the God-given rights of the emperor. A papal legate arrived at Besançon in 1158 with a letter from Pope Hadrian IV to Frederick. One portion of the letter referred to the *beneficia* which the pope had bestowed upon the emperor at his coronation. The German courtiers resented this expression since it inferred that the empire was a *benefice* or *fief* bestowed by the pope. When the papal legate gave his interpretation, with the bold assertion, "From whom, if not from the pope, does the emperor get his power?" the imperialists were furious. Frederick's response was that his imperial power was derived directly from God, with the consent of the German princes, and without the need of papal sanction.

Once more a clear-cut issue was drawn, with the empire challenging the papacy's assertion of superior authority and claiming the same divine origin for its power that had been asserted by Henry IV. Frederick was encouraged in his insistence upon unlimited royal authority by the legal experts of the day, who found in the ancient Roman law valid arguments in support of imperial absolutism.

FREDERICK: THE LOMBARD CITIES Although matters were temporarily patched up, the inevitable conflict could not be avoided. Hadrian's successor, Pope Alexander III (1159-1181), allied with the Lombard cities which were also bitterly hostile to the emperor. Many of the towns of northern Italy, made prosperous by industry and Mediterranean commerce, had become practically independent city-states whose intercity rivalries led to wars. These in turn led to the formation of rival leagues.

Early in the reign of Frederick, the Pavia-Cremona-Como League called on him for protection against the oppression of Milan and her league. The emperor, who had already (in 1155) taken sides against the citizens of the Roman "Republic," gladly availed himself of the opportunity of chastising the arrogant Milanese burghers. In 1158, at Roncaglia (in Lombardy) it was decreed that all cities must submit to direct imperial control. When Milan opposed the installation of an imperial governor (*podesta*), Frederick brought up his army and after a long, cruel siege completely destroyed the rebellious city.

This ruthless act of vengeance marks the beginning of Frederick's losses in Italy. A few years later the Lombard cities formed a defensive league which included Verona, Padua, Vicenza, Bologna, and other important cities of northern Italy. Milan was quickly rebuilt and a league-capital was set up at Alessandria, on the Po River. This new city was named after Pope Alexander III, whose active support had done much to assure the success of the federation.

THE LOMBARD WAR (1176-1183): LEGNANO Difficulties with his Welf enemies kept the emperor busy for several years, and by the time he had his forces organized for an Italian expedition the League was well prepared. In 1176 he invaded Lombardy, where he was decisively defeated by the forces of the League at Legnano. A year later, at Venice, he not only concluded a six-year truce with the League, but also made a humiliating submission to the pope. This latter event has been interpreted as a notable triumph for the papacy and an irretrievable blow to the empire. It is perhaps more accurate to view it as another "Canossa," at which Frederick submitted to the pope merely in order to divide the opposition in such a way that he might ultimately triumph. Frederick, however, was less successful in Italy than Henry IV had been. Although he was able to restore his authority in Germany, never again did he lead his armies across the Alps into Italy. In 1183, at Constance, he recognized the virtual independence of the Lombard cities, reserving to the empire only a vague suzerainty and certain minor privileges.[1]

[1] The years 1176 and 1183 are as noteworthy in the history of the Hohenstaufen empire and the Italian cities as 1776 and 1783 are in the history of the British Empire

Adapted from Thompson and Johnson, *An Introduction to Medieval Europe.*
By permission of W. W. Norton Company, publishers.

THE HOLY ROMAN EMPIRE UNDER THE HOHENSTAUFEN

Frederick's last years were remarkably successful. He crushed his Welf enemies in Germany, and more than offset his losses in Lombardy by the acquisition of a new realm in southern Italy. At this point it is necessary to trace the origin and development of this region. Under its Norman founders it played an important part in both papal and crusading history. In the thirteenth century, under a German ruler, Frederick II, it exerted a far-reaching influence on all phases of European civilization.

THE NORMANS OF SOUTHERN ITALY AND SICILY

The early history of the Normans in Italy is not only a fascinating story of adventure, but an important episode in papal, imperial, and crusading history. Popular legend has it that in 1016 a group of Norman pilgrims, after assisting the Prince of Salerno against a band of Moslem pirates, agreed to remain in his service as mercenaries. Soon other Norman adventurers came to southern Italy to fight for the Italian princes. Most of them eventually carved out for themselves feudal domains. Among the most successful were Robert Guiscard, who became Duke of Calabria in southern Italy, and his brother Roger, who conquered Sicily from the Moslems.[2] A few years later, Guiscard's son, Bohemond, went east with the baronial crusaders of 1097 and became ruler of Antioch,[3] while Roger's descendants wielded their swords against the Moslems of the West. Of the successors of these Norman adventurers, Roger II (1103-1154) was the most important. He was the builder of the Norman king-

and its American colonies. The similarities are striking, not only in dates, but also in the fundamental importance of the events. In each case the autocratic ruler of a great empire, by tactless insistence on certain legal rights, drove his subjects to revolution. In each case the assistance of an important third power (the papacy in 1176; France in 1776) encouraged the rebels and made it possible for them to win their independence. It is also noteworthy that in each case, the defeated empire weathered the storm and recovered in a large measure its prestige. In each case the result was the advance of an important new element in world politics: the city-states of Lombardy and the United States of America.

[2] After conquering Apulia and Calabria in southern Italy, Robert Guiscard appropriated the Byzantine territory of Bari in the heel of the peninsula. In 1081 he made an unsuccessful effort to seize the imperial port of Durazzo across the Adriatic in the Balkin peninsula. Henceforth the Normans and the Byzantine rulers were at swords' points. Meanwhile, as Robert's brother Roger set out to conquer Sicily, he announced that he was about to "win back to the worship of the true God a land [hitherto] given over to infidelity."

[3] See below, Chapter XXV.

dom of the south. Roger expanded his realm in all directions. In continuation of his father's "crusade" against the Moslems of Sicily,[4] he carried the warfare into Northern Africa and gained control of the coastal regions from Tunis to Tripoli. This was accomplished during the same period in which, far to the eastward, the Kingdom of Jerusalem was being established by the barons of the first crusade. Neither conquest was permanent. During the period of Saladin's first gains in Syria, the West was struck by a new tidal wave of African Moslems, the Almohades. Sweeping northward, they drove the Normans out of Africa and also recovered the southern half of Spain for Islam.

Roger II's exploits against his Christian neighbors were more permanently successful. He took possession of the south Italian realms of his brother Robert Guiscard, after the death of the latter's two heirs, and soon was encroaching on the Balkan territories of the Eastern Empire. These conquests laid the foundations for the united Norman realm of the south (known as Naples-Sicily). Over this state Roger assumed the title of king in 1130.

THE KINGDOM OF NAPLES-SICILY

Under Roger II's direction a centralized and efficient government was established. It was run by a staff of expert officials comprising native businessmen, Moslems, and other foreigners who were experienced in administrative affairs. The royal treasury was filled to overflowing by reason of their efficient management of the king's lands, by the careful collection of feudal dues, tolls, and other taxes, by the fostering of industry and commerce, and by the well-managed government monopolies on lumber, salt, and other necessities. As a consequence of his ample financial income, Roger was able to afford salaried officials and a mercenary army, thus freeing himself from reliance on the feudal nobility. In judicial affairs, likewise, royally controlled officials were supreme. The king's courts received appeals from all local and feudal courts, thus consolidating justice in the hands of the central government.

Roger's fostering of cultural life is also noteworthy. The kingdom was a melting pot of Italians, Greeks, Normans, and Moslems, and in consequence its art, literature, and religious thought and practice were unusually varied. Thanks to an enlightened policy of toleration, these cultural influences from many lands were permitted to

---

[4] See above, note 2.

interact freely with fortunate results. In some respects this resulted in strange combinations; for instance, the architecture of the period reveals the rugged square towers of the Norman Romanesque style,[5] along with the high arches and mosque-like domes of the Moslems and the classical lines and decorative effects of the Byzantines. Advancement was particularly noticeable in the sciences. Latin translations of the works of classical writers such as Aristotle, Euclid, and Galen were made from Greek and Moslem sources. Soon Western scholars had access to ancient treatises which had been unused for centuries. Here we find a genuine revival of classical learning in twelfth-century Italy. From Roger II's realm cultural influences and progressive ideas in government spread to other kingdoms. It is probable that Henry II of England and Philip II of France modeled their administrative reorganizations [6] after that of Norman Italy.

NAPLES-SICILY UNDER THE HOHENSTAUFEN

Roger II's inefficient sons, William I and II, were succeeded by a woman named Constance. It was a great triumph for Frederick the Red-Bearded when, in 1185, he secured for his son Henry the hand of Constance, and with it the right to rule the magnificent Norman realm. In 1188 when Frederick started on his famous crusading venture, he left to his son a reunited Germany, a semblance of authority over northern Italy, and (in the south) one of the most efficient and progressive kingdoms in all Europe. Thus the empire seemed on the way to recover its lost prestige in Italy.

Unfortunately, the reign of Henry VI (1190-1197) was disastrously short. Although he was able to take possession of his wife's inheritance, he did not have time to restore it to order and prosperity. To make matters still more difficult, Richard the Lion-Hearted, en route to the Holy Land, stopped in Sicily and assisted certain of the rebellious Norman nobles in their opposition to Henry. The young emperor died suddenly, at the age of thirty-two, in the midst of preparations for a crusade. He left the destinies of Naples-Sicily and the empire in the hands of (1) his three-year-old son, Frederick, (2) the child's mother, Constance, (3) two rival German princes, one of whom was the child's uncle (Philip of Hohenstaufen), and (4) last but by no means least, the little prince's overlord, Pope Innocent III. The outcome of this complex situation involved most of the outstanding personalities of Western Europe, and brought to

[5] See below, Chapter XXXIV.
[6] See below, Chapters XXIII-XXIV.

a spectacular climax the ever-recurring conflict between the empire and the papacy.

INNOCENT III AND THE DOWNFALL OF THE EMPIRE

Innocent III (1198-1216), the most powerful ruler ever to sit on the throne of St. Peter, came from a noble Italian family, seven members of which had already served the church in the capacity of pope. After a thorough education at Rome, Paris, and Bologna, he entered upon a clerical career. At twenty-nine he was a cardinal, and by his thirty-seventh year had won such an unusual reputation for practical statesmanship that, on the death of Celestine III, he was elected pope.

The youthful but brilliant and experienced pope instituted a vigorous and efficient administration. The time was ripe for a wide extension of papal power. Sponsorship of the crusades had brought the popes much prestige and as yet little criticism. The influence of the Holy Roman Empire in northern Italy had been weakened by the defeat of Frederick Barbarossa, and under his successor, Henry VI, imperial rule had become very unpopular in the south. By taking advantage of Italian resentment against the threat of German domination, Innocent was able to bring central Italy under his political control. His position was strengthened by the prevailing belief that this region had been given to the popes by Pepin and his son Charles the Great. Never, until Innocent's day, had the papacy held undisputed sway over the "States of the Church." With only a few of the larger cities of Tuscany refusing to recognize his lordship, Innocent was, in general, master of central Italy.

But the pope's ambitions were not satisfied with the control of central Italy. Innocent endeavored, and with remarkable success, to put into practice the portion of the papal coronation ceremony that read: "Thou art *the ruler of the world,* the vicar on earth of our Savior Jesus Christ." Many popes had insisted on being recognized as *spiritual* rulers of the world, but few had ever asserted *political* lordship. Innocent not only made this claim but proceeded to put it into practice. He constantly interfered in temporal affairs throughout Western Europe. In the kingdom of Naples-Sicily, where papal overlordship had been disregarded by Emperor Henry VI, he won a notable victory. Henry's widow, Constance, renewed the customary oaths of allegiance to the pope, who at her death became guardian of her little son, Frederick, the heir to the throne. As long as Innocent lived, papal influence over Naples-Sicily was secure.

INNOCENT III
AND THE
EMPIRE
The death of Emperor Henry VI and the selection of his successor gave Innocent an opportunity of extending papal influence in Germany. As a rule, a deceased emperor was succeeded by his son, but the imperial title was voted by the princes and was not considered an hereditary right. Many of the German princes had sworn to support the child Frederick as his father's successor, but on the unexpected death of Henry VI, the assembly of electors chose his uncle, Philip of Hohenstaufen, youngest son of Frederick the Red-Bearded. Philip's German opponents then held a rival assembly and selected Otto of Brunswick, whose rights were upheld by the princes of northwestern Germany. Thus Innocent III found a strangely complicated situation: three persons had claims to the imperial crown.

With his accustomed energy and diplomatic ability, the young pope took advantage of the unusual opportunity. First he assumed the supreme right of decision in the matter, and then kept Europe waiting three years for a verdict. He gave no consideration to the claims of his own ward, the young Frederick, whose accession would have created a dangerous merger of the two powerful realms of southern Italy and Germany under one ruler. Of the remaining candidates, he chose Otto, who had agreed to papal control in central Italy. The reasons given for the selection were superficial; apparently the pope was playing a shrewd diplomatic game.

INNOCENT III
AND
FREDERICK II
Once Otto had obtained the pope's approval and the imperial crown, he forgot his promises and began to interfere in Italian politics. Innocent then turned against him, claiming the right to change his mind as God had when he put David in Saul's place as king of Israel. Otto was excommunicated, and since Philip was dead, Innocent finally agreed to make young Frederick emperor. Meanwhile various European nations were drawn into the dispute. Otto's English uncles, Richard the Lion-Hearted and John, supported him and his north German allies. Philip II of France, the sworn enemy of England, joined the pope in supporting Frederick's cause. Thus the Welfs of north Germany with their English allies were arrayed against the Hohenstaufen of south Germany, the French, and the pope.

Frederick, now an ambitious young man, made a hasty trip to

southern Germany, where he was received with great enthusiasm. Matters came to a head in 1214, when Frederick's ally, King Philip II, won a decisive victory over the forces of John of England and Otto at the battle of Bouvines in France. Thus Frederick was assured of the imperial crown. But Innocent was too wise to allow the young monarch so complete a success. He insisted that as soon as Frederick was crowned emperor he must turn over to his young son the kingdom of Naples-Sicily. No pope could willingly permit the union of two great realms to the north and south of the Papal States. Under an ambitious ruler, such a combination might envelop and crush the papal dominions. Innocent's death, in 1216, before the imperial coronation had taken place, made it possible for Frederick to evade the fulfillment of his promise. This merely postponed for both Frederick and the papacy troubles of the greatest import which we shall consider directly.

INNOCENT III
AND FRANCE

Meanwhile Innocent had found other opportunities for the application of his policy of "ruling the world." An occasion for papal interference in France arose from the fact that King Philip II had persuaded the French clergy to let him put aside his Danish wife, Ingeborg. In matters which threaten the sanctity of marriage, the church has always taken a strong stand. As early as the ninth century, Pope Nicholas I had prevented a French royal divorce. The problem of Philip II's marriage was pending when Innocent III became pope. He immediately took a firm stand and not only ordered Philip to put away his new wife, but also to restore Ingeborg. On the king's refusal, he laid the entire realm under an interdict.[7] After eight months Philip yielded because he found that public opinion was opposed to his policy. His submission, however, was largely a pretense, for Philip continued to live with his new wife until her death. Ingeborg's restoration was merely an empty formality. Years later, however, Innocent secured the complete restoration of Ingeborg as a condition to his support of Philip's warfare against John of England.

INNOCENT III
AND ENGLAND

The French king was never as completely under the domination of the pope as was his English rival, John. The latter's tactlessness and unpopularity invited papal interference. The first opportunity came when John used the royal authority to force the election of his own candidate for the

---

[7] Interdict was a prohibition of all or a part of the church services and sacraments within the region concerned.

archbishopric of Canterbury. Innocent, to whom the rival candidate appealed, rejected both men and ordered the election of Stephen Langton, an English cleric of unusual merit and ability. John, now thoroughly aroused by what he considered outrageous interference on the part of the pope, forced his candidate into office and appropriated the revenues of the archbishopric and of all opposing clergymen. Innocent retaliated, laying an interdict upon England. This act, however, had little effect on John, and during the four years of the interdict, he ruthlessly confiscated church property and exiled all bishops who resisted. Finally, when the pope excommunicated him, many of the nobles showed a disposition to take advantage of his difficulties. Meanwhile he was becoming more and more unpopular with the people. In 1213, after the pope had called upon his bitterest enemy, Philip II of France, to invade and take possession of England, John came to terms. He received Langton as archbishop of Canterbury, restored all church property, and became the pope's vassal.

It is significant that this submission was of some advantage to John: henceforth the all-powerful Innocent was his ally. Two years later, when the barons forced John's approval of Magna Carta, it was the pope who obligingly released him from his sworn promises and condemned those who had "insolently, rebelliously, presumptuously, and with arms in hand, said things which should have been said humbly and submissively." Thus John's submission to the pope was somewhat like that of Henry IV at Canossa, Frederick I at Venice, and of other monarchs who have submitted to the papacy as a matter of political strategy.

INNOCENT III AND THE LESSER KINGDOMS

Elsewhere in Europe Innocent used every opportunity to increase his influence and to establish papal overlordship. He constantly interfered in the affairs of the Spanish kingdoms. The king of Leon was forced to break off a marriage with his cousin. The kings of Portugal and Aragon, like John of England, recognized the pope as their overlord. Peter II of Aragon even came to Rome in person to receive his kingdom as a fief from Innocent.

In Northern and Eastern Europe the pope had similar success. The kings of Denmark, Poland, Bohemia, and Hungary manifested no resentment at Innocent's interference. The kings of Serbia and Bulgaria brought their state churches into the papal fold and welcomed the participation of Innocent's representatives in their coronation ceremonies. For a while after the "fourth" crusade,[8] Innocent exercised considerable influence over the Eastern Empire and the Greek Church. By the end of his pontificate, most of the kingdoms of Western Europe, and many of those of the East, were under papal domination. Neither before that time nor since has the papacy ever exercised such far-reaching political influence.

INNOCENT AND THE CLERGY

We have considered in some detail Innocent III's success in extending papal control over kings and nations, for it is in this, the realm of secular politics, that he transcended the fondest hopes of his predecessors and successors. Just as significant was his work in controlling and directing the great ecclesiastical organization of which he was the supreme head. Realizing the importance of an honest priesthood in preventing the spread of heresy, Innocent strove to eliminate the flagrant corruption that existed everywhere among the clergy. In his sermons he called upon them to forsake their immoral and selfish ways, to imitate "Him who was meek and lowly in spirit," and thus to set an example for the lay populace.

Heresy and clerical corruption increased to such an alarming degree, however, that toward the end of his pontificate Innocent called a great religious council (the Fourth Lateran Council) for the express purpose of dealing with the "evil of the times" among both the clergy and the laity. Innocent's seventy canons providing for "the reconquest of the Holy Land and the reform of the church universal" were promptly adopted by the vast assemblage comprising twelve hundred bishops and abbots, together with lay representatives from most of the nations of Western Europe. Among the decrees adopted was one which made it compulsory for all Roman Catholics to believe in the *transubstantiation* of the bread and wine in the mass.

But it was not easy to carry out the papal program. Innocent's "Reconquest of the Holy Land" was a vain hope. Nothing could wipe out the disgrace of the sack of Constantinople by the crusaders in 1204 or of the children's crusade.[9] Few of the resolutions for clerical reform were ever actually put in force, although it is true that Innocent endeavored to eliminate bribery and to speed up justice in the papal courts. Perhaps the most successful action proposed by the council was that which was directed against non-Christians. All Jews

---

[8] See below, p. 520.
[9] See pp. 504, 520, for accounts of these crusades.

and Moslems residing in Christian realms were required to wear distinctive costumes, and Jews were prohibited from holding public office. Public opinion could be relied upon to make such ordinances self-enforcing in most regions. The decrees in condemnation of heretics were also effective. This, however, was due largely to the fact that the Albigensians and Waldensians had already been crushed by the devastating "crusade" of 1208, by the Inquisition, and to some extent also by the newly created orders of friars.[10]

THE FAILURE OF THE REFORM PROGRAM
Within a year after the great council, Innocent III died. Given a longer span of life, he might have brought about a real reformation in the church. As it was, he attained a higher reputation for political statesmanship than for ecclesiastical reform, and he has never been canonized by the church which he led to its greatest heights of political influence. In spite of the efforts of Innocent and the prohibitions of the Lateran Council, evil conditions continued practically unchecked. There were, to be sure, decrees forbidding priests to throw dice, drink to excess, and hand on their ecclesiastical offices to legitimate or illegitimate sons. But worldliness and political corruption appear to have been as prevalent as ever. Regulations prohibiting the acceptance of sacramental fees, the holding of more than one office simultaneously, and other such questionable practices were constantly violated. Interestingly enough, one of the canons approved by the Lateran Council provided for restrictions on indulgences,[11] the commercialization of which was one of the influences that wrecked Luther's loyalty to the papacy and the unity of the church three centuries later.

FREDERICK II'S AMBITIONS
Innocent III's leadership had raised the papacy to great heights of temporal and ecclesiastical authority. His successors endeavored to maintain this position in the face of the rising power of the brilliant young emperor, Frederick II. The result was a renewal of the agelong conflict between church and state, papacy and empire, priesthood and laity.

---

[10] See below, pp. 444 f.

[11] An indulgence was the remission (or canceling) of the penalty for sins which had been confessed and forgiven. A repentant Christian who did some unusually pious deed, such as going on a crusade, or contributing to a religious cause, was sometimes granted a full (plenary) indulgence. This freed him from *all* of the penance which must be performed either on earth or in purgatory for past sins. The granting of indulgences was often used by unscrupulous clergymen as a means of raising money. This abuse gave rise to the expression "the sale of indulgences."

This led to episodes similar to those which marked the struggles between Pope Gregory VII and Emperor Henry IV in the eleventh century and between Alexander III and Frederick Barbarossa in the twelfth century.

Encouraged by the favorable outcome of the battle of Bouvines (1214) and by his successes in Germany, Frederick II attempted to extend his power still further. Fortunately for Frederick, Honorius III (1216-1227), the successor of Innocent III, was a kindly soul who set no obstacles in the path of his former pupil's ambition. Even when Frederick's plans threatened serious consequences to papal prestige, Honorius made no serious objections. In 1220 he granted him the imperial crown, thus sanctioning a dangerous concentration of power which included the Germanies, northern Italy, and Naples-Sicily. Frederick promised to go on a crusade and to divide his realms with his son, but both promises were evaded.

FREDERICK II'S CRUSADE — In 1227 there came to the papal throne, under the significant name of Gregory IX, a foeman worthy of Frederick's steel. Concentrating upon Frederick's one vulnerable point, the fiery old pope demanded that the crusading oath be carried out immediately and unconditionally. When Frederick delayed, on the ostensible grounds of ill-health, Gregory excommunicated him. This was merely the first of a series of anathemas, for the pope repeatedly smote his clever opponent with the powerful weapon of spiritual outlawry. Frederick's every move was forestalled or nullified by the brilliant political tactics of the wily pontiff.

For instance, when Frederick, publicly protesting against the "unreasonable violence" of the pope, actually set forth on his crusade, Gregory re-excommunicated him for going "like a pirate" without first being released from the original excommunication. The pope was apparently determined to force the emperor to submit whether he went or stayed. It is equally clear that Frederick was employing every technicality in order to avoid submission. And so the struggle continued. The pope forbade the Christians of the Holy Land to give any assistance to the unrepentant emperor. Nevertheless, by clever diplomacy, Frederick made his crusade a brilliant success, winning once more for Christendom the sacred places of Jerusalem, Bethlehem, and Nazareth. But in return for these territories, he promised to assist the Egyptian caliph, even against his Christian enemies, to prevent for ten years any Christian attacks on Egypt, and to permit Moslem worship in Jerusalem. When the clergy in

Palestine refused to have anything to do with Frederick he crowned himself King of Jerusalem. Soon he was forced to return to Italy, where the pope had launched a crusade against him. The papal "crusade" against the returned crusader was a fiasco and the embittered rivals patched up a temporary truce.

DEADLOCKED Frederick, now released from excommunication, was able to reorganize his governments in Italy and Germany and to gather resources for future hostilities. In Germany he succeeded in crushing a rebellion led by his own son Henry, and in northern Italy he won a decisive victory over the Lombard League at Cortenuova. These brilliant successes, combined with his campaign of propaganda against the papacy, finally stirred Gregory to action. Frederick was once more excommunicated and, for good measure, deposed from his kingdom and empire. A desperate war of vilification ensued, with innumerable charges and countercharges. Frederick appealed to the princes of Europe for aid against the papal octopus which, he claimed, aimed at nothing less than the crushing of all civil power. Gregory, on the other hand, condemned the emperor as an unrepentant rebel and infidel. At one point in the struggle, Frederick prevented the assembling of a papal council by capturing several North European clerics, including three cardinals, who were en route from Genoa to Rome. In 1241 Gregory died, still breathing forth condemnations against Frederick, "the spawn of Satan."

DOWNFALL OF THE HOHEN-STAUFEN Two years later Innocent IV (1243-1254) came to the papal throne. In spite of the fact that he was an old friend of Frederick's, permanent peace between the pope and emperor was impossible. In Rome, the emperor's partisans were so powerful that Innocent finally removed to Lyons, where in 1245 he called a general council of all Christendom for the express purpose of putting an end to Frederick. Once more the emperor was excommunicated and deposed from the thrones of Germany and Naples-Sicily. A rival king was elected in Germany, and an interdict and crusade launched against Sicily. Undaunted, Frederick issued a manifesto condemning his "persecutors," and for five years fought it out with the enemy. In spite of reverses, he was about to make an expedition into Germany when death overtook him in 1250.

Four years later, and seven months after the death of Frederick's son Conrad, Innocent IV died. This left Conrad's infant son, Conradin, with his uncle Manfred to defend the hopelessly shattered Hohenstaufen realms. Nevertheless, it was not until 1266 that a French pope, with the assistance of an army of "crusading" Frenchmen led by Charles of Anjou, was able completely to crush Manfred and Conradin.[12] For a while France replaced Germany as the papacy's troublesome partner in Italian affairs.

FREDERICK II's
ATTAINMENTS

In many ways Frederick's career marks a turning point in history. With him the medieval empire (and within half a century the medieval papacy as well) lost its former position of importance. Frederick was not only the last great medieval emperor, but also the "first of the moderns," a man far ahead of his age in most lines of thought and action. He strove in vain to maintain the traditionally medieval authority of the empire in Germany and to extend it once more over northern Italy. Yet, at the same time, in Naples-Sicily he improved the administrative system of the Norman monarchs in a manner so unmedieval that it has been called the "first modern state." Law courts and codes, public works, taxes, and regulations for the encouragement of commerce and agriculture were rigidly and efficiently centralized in the hands of a well-organized royal bureaucracy. But Frederick's benevolent despotism in the south contrasted strangely with conditions in northern Italy, where he supported the ruthless tyrannies of his illegitimate son, Enzo, and his son-in-law, Ezzelin. Thus the career of the last Hohenstaufen emperor manifests curiously conflicting tendencies. He struggled to establish both imperial autocracy and "renascence" despotism in Italy.

In the intellectual realm Frederick's influence was equally important and even more "modern" in character. He spoke several languages and was a zealous student of the sciences. With much more efficiency than Charles the Great had displayed, he gathered about him learned men and directed their researches.[13] Thanks to his active interest and patronage, existing educational institutions were expanded. Frederick was a skeptic in religion, and his attitude toward religion is indicated by the remark attributed to him that, of the world's three great impostors (Moses, Christ, and Mohammed), only one suffered the punishment (crucifixion) that all three deserved. Because of the eunuch-guarded harem and the menagerie which often accompanied him on his travels, Frederick was sometimes called "the baptized sultan." He was physically unattractive: red-haired with

---

[12] See below, p. 619.
[13] See below, p. 675.

a tendency to baldness, nearsighted, short, and fat. An Arab once remarked that he would not have fetched even two hundred drachmas on the slave market. In European annals, however, his accomplishments won for him the title "Wonder of the World."

Nonetheless, in his major activities Frederick failed, and his career marks the downfall of the empire. Arrayed against him were the outstanding political, economic, and religious institutions of European life. A recent commentator has remarked that he was beaten by the stubbornness of the Lombard burghers, by the invincible arrogance of the popes, and by the shifting quicksands of feudalism. So complete was the disintegration of the Hohenstaufen imperial system after Frederick that for a generation there were no emperors at all. Two centuries later the Hapsburgs were to restore Germany's imperial pretensions by the brilliant exploits of Charles V, but this was not the *medieval* empire, and its strength soon waned. Meanwhile the triumphant papacy consolidated its position and brought the church to its highest peak of glory and power.

≡ XXI ≡

"THE CHURCH TRIUMPHANT"

FROM Innocent III to Boniface VIII, that is, during most of the thirteenth century, the Roman Catholic Church and its papal leaders were supreme in Western Europe. Never before nor since has organized religion been so effectively organized and so completely in control of the lives of human beings. We turn therefore to a consideration of the organization and government of the church during this period.

CLERICAL INFLUENCE OVER CHRISTIAN SOCIETY

The medieval clergy exercised a remarkable control over Christian society. A great Protestant historian, Charles H. Lea, once paid the medieval church a high tribute when he said:

History records no such triumph of intellect over brute strength as that which, in an age of turmoil and battle, was wrested from the fierce warriors of the time by priests who had no material force at their command, and whose power was based alone on the souls and consciences of men.[1]

There is much to be said in support of this assertion. Practically every human being in Western Europe (barring heretics, Jews, and Moslems) belonged to the Roman Catholic Church and was therefore subject to the influence of the clergy. This influence was direct, active, and constant. Its strength was in large measure due to two factors, ruralism and the sacraments. In rural communities, even today, religion and the clergy exercise a great influence. In the predominantly agrarian society of the Middle Ages, their influence was still more powerful. Of similar importance was the appeal of the sacraments, which comprised the principal part of the medieval church service and of the religious duties of the laity.

[1] Lea, *A History of the Inquisition of the Middle Ages,* I, 1.

THE PROBLEM
OF SALVATION
The emphasis of the medieval and modern church upon the sacraments is the result of an evolution in religious thought and practice which reaches back to the first century. It involved the all-important Christian problem of human salvation. Christ, and Paul after him, had emphasized the importance of each Christian's believing in the Savior's divine mission. But, with Paul, certain religious acts, particularly baptism and the Holy Supper, were given a mystical significance as means for bringing about that perfect union of the true Christian with his Savior, by which salvation was assured. During the early Middle Ages, and particularly during the age when the rude Germanic tribes were being converted to Christianity, there was an increased emphasis on sacred ceremonies as means of salvation. In the twelfth and thirteenth centuries, Christian faith and practice were thoroughly synthesized and rationalized through the efforts of the theologians and popes. Out of this movement came two developments which are of great importance in Roman Catholicism, the sacramental system and the doctrine of the late medieval and the modern church. In these two co-ordinate aspects of the way of salvation is to be found the interrelationship of faith and works which became such a vital problem for Martin Luther and the Protestant reformers.

Outwardly, and certainly in the minds of most of the laity, "works," as represented in the sacraments, were the most important aspect of religion.

THE
SACRAMENTS
Through the early Middle Ages the term *sacrament,* meaning a sacred act, was applied to a great many of the ceremonies of the church. Gradually certain observances came to be considered as particularly important aids to salvation. In the twelfth and thirteenth centuries the theologians emphasized at first twelve and later seven sacraments as essential for the welfare of the soul. By the middle of the fifteenth century the church had formally recognized the seven sacraments which are today observed by the Roman Catholic world. Three of these, as we shall see, baptism, penance, and the eucharist, were given special emphasis as early as the thirteenth century.

Normally all the sacraments were performed only by members of the clergy.[2] The laity, by attending and participating with genuine

2 Under exceptional circumstances, as at the time of the Black Death, laymen were permitted to receive confession. Technically, a priest did not have to perform the marriage ceremony. The key sacraments, however, were never performed by laymen.

piety, gave expression to their true faith and strengthened their souls against the wiles of Satan. The sacraments played an all-important part in the religious life of the average Christian, for at every crucial point in his development the importance of religion and the influence of the church were dramatized in some one of these impressive sacramental observances.

(1) Shortly after birth an infant was purified from hereditary sin and received into Christian society by the *baptismal* ceremony. At the same time he was given a "Christian" name; hence the term "christening." (2) Later the child was *confirmed*—that is, strengthened in the faith and made an active member of the church—by being anointed and blessed by the bishop. (3) The miracle of the *mass* (i.e., the *transubstantiation* of the bread and wine into Christ's body and blood) was the central feature in the re-enactment of the Last Supper. Closely connected with this sacred rite was the communion or eucharist, by means of which the clergy kept church members in direct contact with God's saving grace. (4) *Confessing* to a priest, being *absolved,* and doing penance comprised the sacrament of penance by which the individual was freed from the burden of his sins. No Christian could (5) *marry* or be (6) *ordained* to the priesthood without the ministrations of the clergy in a religious sacrament.[3] (7) Finally, at the approach of death, a priest administered *extreme unction* by anointing the dying person with sacred oil. The Roman Catholic theory was that the sacraments were the means through which God's saving grace reached mankind. Thus the clergy served as a sort of transmission line by which the mysterious current of salvation was transmitted to the Christian believer. Those who failed to attend church and the celebration of the sacraments were, so to speak, refusing to put themselves in touch with the means of salvation.

DOCTRINAL   Although the mere ritual of sacramental observances
DEVELOPMENTS   seems to have dominated the religion of the laity,
                        faith in certain dogmas played an important role in Roman Catholicism. From the early medieval centuries orthodoxy of belief had been stressed by the leaders of the church. Paul emphasized the necessity of faith in the divine Redeemer. At Nicæa in 325, and at later Christian councils, the clergy had struggled to maintain the purity of the faith. Augustine and others of the Church Fathers worked out the details of a system of religious belief that

---

[3] Ordination, like confirmation, could be administered only by a bishop.

is still held by the majority of Protestants and Catholics. Since Augustine's day, orthodox Christianity has been based on fundamental dogmas such as the omnipotence of God, the essential evil of human nature, the freedom of the human will, and the necessity of relying on Christ and His church for salvation.

THE CRYSTAL-
LIZATION OF
DOCTRINE

As in the case of the sacraments, the twelfth and thirteenth centuries were the age of co-ordination and, to a certain extent, of rationalization of the beliefs of Western Christendom. During this period famous theologians such as Albertus Magnus and Thomas Aquinas contributed much to the rationalization of Christian theology. It was chiefly the work of a great council, held at the Lateran Church in Rome in 1215 by Pope Innocent III, that brought about a formal pronouncement concerning Roman Catholic doctrine. The necessity for clarifying the doctrines of the church was made emphatic by the differences of opinion that had developed among the various schools of theologians, and, what was even more serious, by the inroads of heretical sects. In order to assist the clergy in holding the laity to the true faith it was necessary that the beliefs of Christendom be clarified. As in earlier times the papacy took the lead in the movement for a set of unified orthodox doctrines and practices.

THE LATERAN
CREED OF 1215

The result was promulgated in the decrees of the Lateran Council of 1215, which was headed by a concise confession of faith. With only one major change and several slight modifications, this statement has continued to the present day as the essential doctrine of both medieval and modern Catholicism. The orthodox Christian was hereby bound to believe in a Triune God, comprising the Father, Son, and Holy Spirit, all three equal, omnipotent, and eternal; God is the creator of all things, spiritual and material; Christ, the only begotten Son, conceived by the Virgin Mary, was born with two natures, divine and human; He suffered and died for the sins of mankind, which had fallen by reason of the temptations of the Devil; at the last judgment Christ will judge every man according to his works; there is no salvation outside the church, whose priests, ordained according to the powers granted by Christ to the apostles and their successors, perform the sacraments of baptism, penance, and "the sacrament of the altar"; in this last-mentioned sacrament the bread and wine are transubstantiated into the body and blood of Christ.

It will be noted that this statement of faith combined the fundamental principles laid down by the early church councils with those of Augustine, and that it made the church and its priesthood the sole medium of salvation. This salvation, however, depended not only upon orthodoxy of belief and the works according to which man was to be judged on the last day, but also upon the three sacraments mentioned. There were at this time, as heretofore, other sacraments which were not deemed essential for salvation. The provisions of the Lateran Council, both in regard to beliefs and practices, suggest something of the manner in which Roman Catholic institutions evolved during the early Middle Ages.

RELICS AND THE   In addition to the seven sacraments, there were in-
MIRACULOUS   numerable other sacred acts by means of which the lives of medieval people, from birth to death, were closely bound up with religion, the church, and the clergy.[4] Only clergymen could *exorcize*—drive demons out of houses, sick persons, and fields—by means of holy water, prayers, and the like. They alone could provide the people with sacred medals or badges, bits of parchment inscribed with religious formulas, pieces of holy wax stamped with the words *Agnus Dei* ("Lamb of God"), or bells engraved and dedicated "for chasing out demons." Then, too, the clergy had control of sacred relics. These souvenirs of holy men and women were supposed to have wondrous powers. If carried in a religious procession they would drive out plagues, and cripples were said to be healed by touching them. Every church had some such prized possession. Cologne claimed to have the skulls of the Three Wise Men. The cherished bones of St. Ursula and ten thousand martyred virgins were said to have been dug up in a German cemetery. The miraculous rod of Moses was treasured in a Roman church, and Marseilles claimed to have three skeletons of the fish with which Christ fed the five thousand. Feathers of the Archangel Michael were venerated at many shrines.

Difficulties arose, however, when it was found that there were several jawbones of James, arms of Andrew, and heads of John the Baptist in various churches, the clergy of each church insisting that their relic was the only genuine one. There were also, scattered through Europe, enough pieces of "the True Cross" to make several

---

[4] Originally the term *sacrament* was applied to a great many of the minor ceremonies of the church. During the late Middle Ages, seven of them were recognized as sacraments that had a special spiritual significance. Other sacred acts were (and are still) called *sacramentals*.

crosses. As a result of such conflicting claims, the papacy adopted a policy of investigating relics and registering those which it deemed authentic. The Roman Catholic Church has constantly exercised a restraining influence on all such excesses of clerical ambition and popular superstition.

CLERICAL CON-
TROL OVER THE
LAITY

To the clergy and to pious church members, sacramental observances were the outward signs of the inner grace, or faith, which bound all Christendom in one common spiritual unity. According to this religious ideal, all Christians were members of the mystical body of Christ, of which the church was the earthly manifestation. The beliefs, practices, and organization of medieval religion were dominated by this concept. It was this ideal, accepted by the great majority of Westerners throughout the Middle Ages, that gave the period its strongly religious character, a character that is reflected in the expression, "the Age of Faith."

To the clergy was assigned the duty of carrying out this ideal by organizing and controlling human society in accordance with the principles of Christianity. In a period so chaotic and confused as the Middle Ages, this task was very difficult. There were many warlike and godless men who refused to be bound by the standards of peaceful Christian society. With such persons, it was necessary to use mental coercion. By threatening excommunication, by capitalizing on the popular dread of being deprived of the sacraments, and by dwelling on the terrors of hell, the clergy could control not only the ignorant masses but even powerful princes. There were also more positive methods: by means of the catechism, short sermons, religious pageants, and the like, the clergy inspired men with moral ideals and checked dishonesty, immorality, and unbelief.

Moderns often lose sight of the fact that the formal sacramental services of the church were powerful forces for spiritual uplift. The ritualism of a solemn feast-day procession, with bishops, priests, deacons, altar boys, and choirs clad in sacred vestments, carrying crosses and lighted candles, could be an inspiring religious experience that touched the hearts of rough men. The beautiful altar with its gilded cross, brilliantly lighted with candles, the gorgeous vestments of the clergy, the chanting of the singers, the pealing organ, and the incense—all combined to make a profound impression. Such pageants appealed not only to man's spirit but to his eyes, ears, and even to his sense of smell. These minute mechanical factors were —and still are—of great religious importance. They helped to bind men together in Christian harmony.

A CATHEDRAL SERVICE Today, as in the twelfth or thirteenth centuries, one can attend a high mass in which there is an impressive harmony of solemn chanted music, Latin liturgy, clerical vestments, flaming candles, incense-laden air, and the sculptured figures with which the vaulted Gothic choir is peopled. Let us imagine ourselves attending a cathedral mass, say at Notre Dame in Paris, either today or in the Middle Ages; there would be little difference between the two services save in the dress of the people and in the fact that then the men and women occupied separate sections of the dimly lighted nave.

THE INTRODUC- TORY SERVICE Just before the service commences, an acolyte lights the candles in and about the main altar. With hundreds of reflecting points of flame, the chancel (the space about the altar) is ablaze with subdued but glorious splendor. At the sound of a bell the singers file into the choir and begin the *introit,* an introductory psalm, "Praise Ye the Lord" (Psalm 150). Meanwhile, from the opposite end of the church the procession of officiating clergymen, splendid in their embroidered vestments, moves slowly down the nave toward the altar. The acolytes carry lighted candles, and as the altar boys swing their censers, the pungent odor of incense blends with the solemn strains of the chanted psalm. On reaching the chancel, the acolytes, altar boys, and other assistants take their places at the sides while the celebrant (i.e., the officiating priest) and his assistants in their gold, scarlet, and white vestments, slowly approach the altar.[5]

"KYRIE ELEISON" Now the introductory portion of the mass begins. At a signal from the bishop the choir chants the "Kyrie eleison"—"Lord have mercy." Originally a Greek chant, this was sung by the entire congregation in a very simple manner in the early Middle Ages. One tenth-century example that has come down to us in manuscript form is merely a repetition of the words "Kyrie eleison" on about five prolonged notes. Later the plain-chant theme was much embellished, and in the sixteenth century, Palestrina composed a "Kyrie" of such harmonious beauty that it is still used.

[5] The color scheme of the vestments, and also certain chants, psalms, and other ritualistic details, might vary somewhat according to the type of service, the period, and the region concerned.

After the "Kyrie," the bishop begins to chant the "Angels' Song" (Luke 2:14)—*Gloria in Excelsis*. The choir picks up the strain and for several minutes it is developed and repeated in various musical forms.

THE SCRIPTURES, GRADUAL, AND SEQUENCE

Now, for the first time, the music is interrupted by the reading of the Scriptures. From a reading desk (*ambo*) at one side a deacon reads a lesson from the Epistles.[6] Then he moves across the chancel to another reading desk, where he reads from the Gospels. But, while the deacon is moving from one *ambo* to the other, the musical part of the service is resumed with a very interesting type of composition. It is called the *gradual* (from the Latin *gradus,* "steps"), because originally it was chanted from the *steps* of the *ambo*. This is immediately followed by the *sequence* (from the Latin *sequor,* to follow). Originally it was merely a series of "Alleluiahs" sung to fill in the interval while the deacon was moving from one *ambo* to the other.

In a large spacious cathedral, where this occupied some time, in order to avoid an awkward pause additional music was introduced, something after the manner of offertory music in a modern church. The sequences used for this purpose vary according to the occasion. For Pentecost it is customary to use the *Veni Creator Spiritus* ("Come Holy Spirit"), the words of which were written in the eleventh century; for a requiem mass, the famous *Dies Irae* ("Day of Wrath"); and for the festivals of the Virgin Mary the *Stabat Mater* ("There Stands the Mother"). In each age musicians have adapted these grand Latin hymns to their own type of music. A tenth-century monk of St. Gall named Notker Balbus was canonized for his remarkable sequences. The late medieval composers introduced such elaborate compositions that the sixteenth-century Council of Trent eliminated most of them. Modern musicians have therefore reverted to the more stately medieval forms; Rossini's *Stabat Mater* is an excellent example of the modernized medieval sequence.

THE "CREDO" AND OFFERTORY

After the Scripture reading comes the *Credo.* Having recited the creed ("I believe in God . . ."), the celebrant seats himself at one side while the choir sings the *Credo* in numerous musical variations. Today, the *Credo* music of Mozart's mass for St. Cecilia's Day is very popular. The

---

[6] Sometimes the Scripture is read from the altar steps.

sermon, which is usually a relatively unimportant part of the service, comes just before or after the *Credo*.[7]

With the *Credo,* the introductory part of the service gives way to the preparation for the main portion (or *canon*) of the mass. This is the solemn ceremony that has developed in the celebration of the "miracle of the mass," in which the bread and wine is transformed into the body and blood of Christ. The first step in the preparation is the *offertory*. In the early days this was a complicated musical chant, prolonged so as to allow the communicants to bring to the altar their offerings of bread and wine, which the priest then "offered" to God. In the later Middle Ages, when money contributions became common, the offerings were dropped into a box or collection plate. Thus the offertory was reduced to a mere intermission of incidental music, sung while the priest or bishop prepared and offered the bread and wine. This is the only place in the music of the mass in which an independent solo is permissible.[8]

THE "CANON OF THE MASS": THE "SANCTUS" — The *Sanctus* marks the transition to the "canon of the mass." This portion of the service begins with the ringing of a bell at the altar and the lighting of all the candles of the chancel. Thus, in an additional blaze of glory, with solemn prayers and the sound of the altar bell, the most sacred of Roman Catholic rites proceeds. Meanwhile the choir sings the *Sanctus* ("Holy, Holy, Holy"). Originally this was chanted by the entire congregation, but later it became a distinctive musical number rendered by the choir. In modern times some of our most inspiring religious compositions have been written for this part of the service; among these is Gounod's *Sanctus.*

While the *Sanctus* is being sung the bishop and his assistants prepare the receptacles and materials, and then proceed to the most solemn and sacred part of the entire cathedral ritual, the consecration of the bread and wine. This is performed without music, amid tense silence broken only by the bishop's intoning of the words *Hoc est enim corpus meum* ("This is my body . . ."). It is at this point in the ceremony that the "miracle of the mass" takes place, the transformation of the bread and wine into Christ's body and blood. For a moment the celebrant kneels in adoration of the sacred host, then, at the sound of the bell elevates it for the congregation to

[7] In some modern cathedrals it comes at the very end of the mass.
[8] Here sometimes in modern services is heard one of the beautiful "Ave Marias" of Gounod or Schubert.

adore. The same is done with the chalice of wine, after which there are other ritualistic observances and prayers. Meanwhile the choir sings the *Benedictus* (Psalm 103) and *O Salutaris Hostia* ("Saving Host").

COMMUNION   The next step in the service is the communion, or partaking of the newly consecrated elements. While the celebrant makes the preparations, the choir chants the quietly inspiring *Agnus Dei* ("Lamb of God . . .").

Following the communion by the celebrant and people, the *host* (i.e., the consecrated elements) is placed in the tabernacle for later use. Then in a solemn ritualistic manner the celebrant drinks the remainder of the wine, cleanses the chalice, and washes his hands. Finally, turning from the altar, he faces the congregation and pronounces the words of dismissal, *"Ite missa est"* ("Go, it is finished"), which have given the name *Missa,* or mass, to the entire service. After the reading of the opening words of the Gospel of John, the members of the clergy move slowly down the central aisle of the nave while the choir sings a recessional.

Until one has seen and heard a solemn high mass in a great cathedral he cannot realize the tremendous emotional intensity of this most sacred of all religious ceremonies. To the Roman Catholic it is the re-enactment of Christ's sacrifice on Calvary, and therefore an essential religious rite, the holiest symbol of "the faith of our fathers." In the Middle Ages, even more than in modern times, rough ignorant people who would have been oblivious to a spiritual sermon or to any sort of mental appeal were likely to be tremendously impressed by the dramatic solemnity of the mass. A priest who would have found it impossible to make an effective appeal concerning abstract righteousness or Christ's passion, could, by the use of crosses, images, and pictures, or the music and drama of the mass, instill into the hearts of his parishioners some sense of solemnity and reverence for god.

COERCIVE   The medieval clergy also found it necessary to employ the less admirable but very effective influences
MEASURES   of spiritual coercion. Many of the institutions of the church took shape in an age of barbaric warfare in which men must be controlled chiefly by fear of punishment. By such methods the clergy were often able to force their will upon violent or stubborn church members. Excommunication, which cut off the rebellious one from attendance at religious services and frequently from

all the privileges of and contacts with Christian society, was usually effective. Even powerful monarchs such as John of England, Philip II of France, and the emperors Henry IV and Frederick II were unable permanently to withstand a papal excommunication that solemnly warned all Christians to renounce their allegiance to the obstinate monarch. Excommunication was often accompanied by an interdict, which prohibited public services in the realms of an unrepentant ruler, thus tending to mobilize public resentment against him.

In an even more effective manner the clergy could dominate the lives of simple laymen. By reason of the popular fear of hell and the hope for heavenly rewards, the clergy swayed the minds of most men. The dread of being cut off from the saving sacraments, and the terror of hellish demons could be used to bring a man to repentance. Religious superstitions and fear made people so susceptible to mental terrorism that at times they were the victims of scheming clergymen.

CLERICAL CONTROL OVER EDUCATION
In addition to those we have considered, the clergy had other sources of influence. The church held what amounted to a monopoly of intellectual resources. Until late in the Middle Ages throughout most regions of the West, virtually all schools were conducted by and usually for the clergy.[9] The teachers in the universities, cathedral schools, monastic schools, and even parish schools, were clerics. Practically all of the great medieval scholars were clergymen. If ever there was a real "brain trust," it was the medieval clergy. The church and the clergy formed, in a broad sense, the whole pattern of medieval thought. It is impossible adequately to estimate the extent to which this educated clerical influence permeated society. Most kings and baronial rulers were clerically trained, and their counselors were very largely recruited from the clergy.

CLERICAL CONTROL OF CHARITY
In still another realm the churchmen wielded a tremendous influence: that of public charity. After the decline of the Western Roman Empire the duty of caring for the poor and the sick had almost entirely fallen to the church. Consequently the social services performed by the clergy gave them great power over the lower classes. Every church or monastery was an almshouse and a place of refuge for the desti-

---

[9] See below, p. 655. Italy was a notable exception. Here, in the cities, lay education was always prevalent.

tute and afflicted. Nunneries sheltered unfortunate girls. Entire communities were fed by the clergy in times of famine. Pilgrims and other travelers found lodging in monasteries, and in wild and deserted regions they were likely to find none but monastic refuges. There are still numerous Alpine monastic hospices.

With the increase of town life the church found an opportunity for service and influence among the lower classes and the unfortunates. The career of St. Francis and his friars is one of the most vivid illustrations of the way in which the church gave itself to suffering humanity, gaining thereby the heartfelt allegiance of the masses.

THE CLERICAL BUREAUCRACY

THE HIERARCHY OF SECULAR CLERGYMEN
    The spiritual, intellectual, and social influence of the clergy was made effective by a well-organized hierarchy of church officials. As we have already seen,[10] the church early developed a systematic organization. Like the Roman Empire, and also like a modern army, its clerical officers were sharply set off from the rank and file of laymen. Every ordained clergymen was a sort of commissioned officer in the "army of the Lord." Clerics were differentiated from laymen in their religious powers and, consequently, in social status. Even though an ordained cleric, as an individual, was less intelligent or less moral than other people, as a clergyman he bore an "indelible character," that made him forever different from all laymen. His clerical office, as symbolized by the clerical vestments and hair cut (tonsure), were to be respected regardless of his personal character. Thus, at the outset, every clergyman occupied a position of great responsibility and influence.

The clergy fell into two grand divisions, each of which had many gradations of rank within itself. The secular (i.e., of the world, *saeculum*), or priestly clergy, were set apart from the regular (regulated), or monastic clergy. The secular hierarchy ranged from lowly priests to the all-powerful pope.

THE PARISH PRIESTS
    From the beginning to the end of the Middle Ages the primary unity of spiritual life was the parish church. Each parish had a priest who was usually selected by the lord of the region and was installed by the bishop of the diocese or his representative. Regardless of their wishes, parishioners were forced to contribute to the priest's support. Their chief con-

[10] See Chapter III.

tribution was called the tithe although it varied from the theoretical 10 per cent. It was levied on everyone's income and was paid either in money or produce, usually the latter in rural districts. This income was supposed to be divided four ways: to the bishop, the priest, the repair of the parish church, and the relief of God's poor. Often, however, the bishop and the lord patron appropriated most of it. In that case God's poor and the church repairs went begging, and the priest might have to depend on fees received for performing the sacraments, or on the produce of the land reserved for the church, or on his own ingenuity in nonclerical occupations. Many a hard-pressed country priest was condemned by his well-fed bishop for running a tavern or for holding more than one parish appointment.

Far more justifiable than these were the accusations of priestly ignorance, neglect of duties, and immorality. Many a bishop and council condemned in vain those priests who "transform the house of God into a den of thieves," or who "take money for the sacrament of baptism, which should be the gift of the Holy Spirit," or who "eat and drink in taverns and visit shows." Worse yet was the priest who would "have commerce with women" or "have a woman live in his home" and have illegitimate sons to succeed him in his sacred office. Gregory VII, it will be remembered, made a strenuous effort to enforce clerical celibacy.

In general, the actual records that have come down through the ages indicate that few medieval clerics were so absorbed in preparing themselves for eternal life that they were completely uninterested in the pleasures of the world. Many of the clergy seem to have been keenly concerned with worldly delights, as the report of a thirteenth-century Norman bishop concerning the clergymen in his diocese reveals. In his annual tour of inspection this bishop discovered that at Rouen the clergymen

talked in the choir in violation of their rule. Clerks wandered about the church and chatted with women while the service was going on. They . . . chanted the psalms too fast without making the pauses . . . they failed to observe many other of the rules, and their temporalities [i.e., business affairs] were badly managed. As for the canons themselves, we found that Master Michael of Berciac was accused of incontinence, likewise Lord Benedict. Likewise Master William of Salmonville of incontinence, theft, and homicide . . . Likewise Master Alain of frequenting taverns, drunkenness, and gaming. Likewise Peter of Auleige of carrying on business. On the *nones* of May we visited the chapter of St. Firmat. . . . Morell, the choir clerk, is a rough fellow. Regnaud of Stampis is accused of incontinence and has a boy with him whom he supports. Bartholomew, the vicar of the cantor, sometimes gets drunk and then does not get up to matins . . . We accordingly admonished [them to reform] . . . else we should come down upon them with a heavy hand.[11]

It seems that this was no isolated case, no exception to prove that the rule was righteous living. An English university professor was so disgusted with scenes of priestly vice that he asked whether those clergymen are the Lord's servants who "frequent taverns and public places more freely than churches and who delight more in wanton ditties than in songs of devotion."

But the worldliness and corruption of individual priests must not obscure the valuable services for humanity that were performed by the priesthood. They baptized, married, and buried their parishioners. The priest also instructed the children in reading, writing, singing, and religion. He cared for the sick, kept records of births, marriages, and deaths, and administered wills. At church festivals he not only performed the sacraments and other religious duties, but also mingled with his parishioners in their games and dances. Incidentally, priests were sometimes severely reprimanded by their superiors for allowing "dancing in the churchyard."

In the Middle Ages the church was the social center of the common people and the priest was their leader. In general, parish priests corresponded to the level of life in their communities. In backward regions and centuries they were uncouth and ignorant. In growing towns they were likely to be more progressive. They were seldom worse, and usually not much better, than the average people of the parish. Obviously, the priesthood neither ruined society nor drastically reformed it. In *Piers Plowman* we read of a priest of thirty years' standing who frankly admitted that he could not read a Latin life of the saints, and that he was better at "following a hare in a field or furrow" than "explaining the first Psalm." Apparently in the Middle Ages, as always, the clerical influence tended to stabilize the life of the people rather than to change it very radically.

CHAPLAIN PRIESTS AND CATHEDRAL CANONS   In monastic churches and private chapels belonging to kings or nobles, the life and functions of the priests, or chaplains, as they were called, were quite different. A chaplain was usually the appointee and servant of the one who owned the chapel. Thus he was often little

---

[11] Robinson, *Readings*, I, 378. This and several other extracts in this section are quoted by permission of the publishers, Ginn and Company.

more than a priest-courtier, whose easy living depended on his ability to please the patron, his lady, and their influential counselors. A ninth-century bishop once complained that the chaplains of a certain lord were forced "to wait on his table, care for his dogs, and even dress his lady's hair."

Cathedrals and other large city churches had staffs of priests, deacons, lectors, readers, acolytes, and the like, who carried on the religious activities of the church. As early as the fourth century the church at Rome had 154 lesser clerics. Such assistant clergymen were of two types. There were the priests and their assistants, entrusted with strictly spiritual duties, such as performing the sacraments. Then there were the deacons and other assistant clergymen who also handled financial and administrative affairs. Among these administrative officials was the rural dea[co]n, who had the oversight of a portion of the rural parishes of the bishop's diocese. Often, too, there was a provost who had supervisory duties. Then there was the archdea[co]n, the active head of the cathedral clergy. The cathedral clergy as a whole were called canons, and were organized into a group called the cathedral chapter. Financially speaking, the canons were usually well provided for, and had comparatively few duties. Often they merely drew their ample incomes, spending their money and time elsewhere. Wealthy cathedral canons were probably the most envied, corrupt, and hated of all the lesser clergy.

THE BISHOPS   Obviously the priests, deacons, archdeacons, and canons of each region had to be controlled by some higher official. Early in Christian history, as we have already seen, the bishop became the responsible head of all the clergy in the parishes comprising his diocese. As time went on, the bishops became the key men in the church organization. Like the provincial governors of the Roman Empire, they supervised the lesser officials of their respective regions and were in turn responsible to the pope—their spiritual ruler —for the peace, order, and efficient working of the affairs of the diocese. In the early Middle Ages bishops were freer from papal control than in the days of a strong ruler like Innocent III. At all times, however, their problems and duties were of the same general nature.

SPIRITUAL   As *spiritual* supervisors (the name *episcopus,* or
FUNCTIONS   bishop, means overseer), it was their chief duty to see that the sacraments were properly administered. The bishop performed very few sacraments himself. In his own cathedral this was done by the canons; in the outlying parishes, by the

parish priests. But he alone could ordain priests and confirm members of the church. On his annual tours of inspection through the parishes of the diocese, he attended to these needs, and also preached to the assembled parishioners. At the same time he investigated religious conditions in the parishes. The magnitude of this last task is well illustrated by the memorandum made out by a certain bishop, who planned in each parish an investigation of drunken laymen, usurers, "those guilty of the seven sins," evil houses, wills, taxes, illiteracy, "the care of the sacred host," priests, concubines, simony, hereditary religious benefices, and the extortion of fees for the sacraments. In addition to these multiple duties, the bishops were also expected to supervise all monasteries in their dioceses, except those which were specifically exempted by papal decree. The need for investigation of monastic institutions is made clear by the following report of a bishop concerning a nunnery which he inspected.

We visited the nunnery of St. Savior. There were sixty-three nuns. They did not have books enough: we ordered that these should be procured. The rule of silence was not properly observed: we commanded that it should be. We admonished them to go to confession every month. We enjoined that they should not keep dogs, birds, or squirrels, and should send away those that they had . . . When they receive new gowns they do not return the old ones. We ordered that no nun should dare to give away her old gown without the permission of the abbess.[12]

Finally, every bishop held a council at least once a year at which the clergy of the entire diocese assembled to legislate on local ecclesiastical affairs and to settle other clerical matters.

POLITICAL FUNCTIONS   Apparently a conscientious bishop could be fully occupied in keeping his clergy functioning properly, but the spiritual duties were only half—and the lesser half—of his activities. He was also a feudal, and often a municipal, ruler, and therefore a political (as well as a spiritual) administrator. This was due to the fact that bishops were agents for the enforcement of law. As early as the reign of Constantine, they had been assigned special courts for the settlement of religious cases. With the passing of Roman imperial government and the rise of feudalism, these political duties increased. The bishops' courts had jurisdiction over all cases involving churchmen (including monks and university students) and

[12] Robinson, *op. cit.,* I, 378 f.

also church *affairs,* which embraced wills, marriages, widows, orphans, clerical property, and all contracts involving sacred oaths.

In addition to such semipolitical activities, every bishop was a feudal lord or vassal, or perhaps both. In order to survive in a feudal world the church was forced to enter into feudal relationships. Therefore bishops held and attended feudal courts. Furthermore, as feudal lords they had to fulfill certain obligations to their vassals. On the other hand, as feudal vassals they owed their overlords financial, judicial, and military services. These duties, if not performed in person, had to be provided through proxies. Although military service was usually by proxy, many a bishop accompanied his overlord on campaigns. In Germany especially, bishops swung their battle-axes and maces with a right good will. The chief assistance that bishops rendered their political lords was that of counsel, secretarial aid, and the like. In Germany ever since the days of Charles the Great's *missi,* the emperors had found it advantageous to use bishops as counts. They were far more efficient and trustworthy than laymen, who had family cares and political ambitions. In addition to such duties, many bishops were the rulers of large cities such as Milan, Mayence, and Cologne.

Few bishops could successfully handle both the spiritual and political tasks which society laid upon them. As a result spiritual matters were usually neglected. Naturally, the kings and feudal lords saw to it that the bishoprics in their territories were held by politically minded men. This could be done by manipulating the elections. Bishops were supposed to be selected by the clergy and people of the diocese, with the assent of the neighboring bishops and the pope. But the lay rulers asserted their influence in order to have bishops who would be efficient governmental officials. This led to a bitter rivalry between church and state as to which should dominate the elections, a rivalry that further complicated the problem of getting good bishops.

Although there were extenuating circumstances, it is difficult to absolve many bishops from the charge that they led completely worldly lives. A twelfth-century bishop of Bordeaux, for example, deserted his churchly functions for a life of debauchery and hunting with a gang of dissolute fellows and prostitutes. At about this same time a French council condemned bishops who had fur clothing, golden bits and decorated saddles for their horses, who hunted, swore, attended plays, danced, accepted money for ordaining priests, talked business during church services, and heard mass in bed.

On the other hand, of course, there were many bishops who strove manfully against great odds to perform their double duties. One might mention hundreds of men such as Gerbert of Rheims, Fulbert of Chartres, Stephen Langton and Thomas à Becket of Canterbury, who showed resourcefulness and courage in upholding spiritual ideals. Although the majority of bishops were wealthy aristocrats, many peasant boys worked their way, by sheer pluck and ability, to this high office and to a position of influence and service for Christian society. When judged according to strict spiritual standards, the average bishop presented a faulty record. According to political standards, he did much better. The greatest handicap for the medieval bishop was his double set of duties.

ARCHBISHOPS The problems and general situation of the metropolitan or archbishop (ruling bishop) were almost exactly like those of the bishop. He was merely a bishop who was given supervisory authority over the neighboring bishops because of the size or importance of his church. His only important function as archbishop was to call and preside over the councils of the bishops of his province, which comprised a group of dioceses. The greatest of the archbishops of a region (for example, the archbishop of Canterbury in England or of Rheims in France) was called the primate, or first archbishop. He was, so to speak, a superarchbishop. The special functions and authority of the archbishop were symbolized by a narrow woolen scarf bestowed on him by the pope.

THE POPE From the viewpoint of ecclesiastical rank and authority the archbishop was the bishop's superior, the primate was superior to the other archbishops, and the pope was supreme over all primates, archbishops, and bishops of Western Christendom. Of course, no such graded hierarchy actually existed throughout all the Middle Ages. The papacy was neither recognized nor obeyed to any extent outside of Italy during the early Middle Ages. Even in the early thirteenth century, Innocent III, most powerful of all popes, was unable to regiment the clergy into a perfect hierarchy. The widespread spiritual authority that the papacy exercises over Roman Catholics today did not exist throughout the majority of the medieval centuries. Nevertheless the full-grown papacy as it existed in the days of Innocent III exercised great authority, and we shall describe the papal institutions of this its greatest period of influence.

THE SPIRITUAL
POWERS OF THE
POPE

From the time of Gregory VII (late eleventh century), through the age of Innocent III, and that of Boniface VIII (late thirteenth century) there was a marked tendency toward papal absolutism. Like all bishops, the pope's duties and powers were twofold: spiritual and political. The papacy considered itself the spiritual leader of Christendom, and this came to be pretty generally recognized throughout the West. As such the pope was the supervisor of all the bishops and therefore responsible before God, whose supreme representative he was, for the other bishops and their flocks. Thus he claimed the right to control the appointment, and deposition if necessary, of any religious official.

As chief executive of the clergy he had a large staff of assistant administrators: committees (called congregations), secretaries, treasurers, chancellors, and ambassadors (called legates). The cardinals constituted his advisory cabinet, and since they were also the electors of popes, their influence was great. Occasionally the pope summoned representative clergymen from all parts of Christendom to a council which served as a sort of enlarged cabinet or religious parliament to assist in legislating for the entire church. Usually, however, church legislation took the form of papal decrees rather than of conciliar laws. The only time when councils dominated legislation was in the early centuries before the popes had gained power, and during the brief fifteenth-century period of reform councils.[13]

For the most part, therefore, church laws were merely papal orders or decrees. Since these were published in manuscript form stamped with the pope's leaden seal (*bulla*), they are commonly called papal *bulls*. Papal orders were transmitted to the clergy and brought to the attention of the lay princes by means of official messengers, usually called legates. The popes built up a sort of combined diplomatic and inspector service, somewhat like that of the lay kingdoms. This kept the papacy in close contact with the local clergy and tended to weld all churchmen into a centralized and papally controlled organization. Through the legates, papal headquarters at Rome could keep in touch with the bishops and through the bishops with every priest and parishioner in Christendom. An ambitious and efficient pope such as Innocent III could become a veritable emperor with kings and peasants, as well as bishops and priests under his sway.

---

[13] See below, pp. 568 ff.

THE PAPAL COURT
The pope was not only the supreme executive and legislator but also the supreme judge of Christendom. He and his staff of assistants constituted the papal *curia*, the church's supreme court of appeal. As in the bishops' courts, so also in the papal *curia*, almost any kind of civil or criminal case might come up. It might be a dispute over the selection of a bishop such, for instance, as that which occurred in King John's reign over the archbishop of Canterbury; it might be an attempt on the part of the relatives of a pious woman to break the will by which she had left her entire fortune to the church. It might be a plea for the annulment of a marriage, or an appeal by a clerical professor (such as Abelard) who had been accused of teaching heretical doctrines.

A staff of lawyers who knew the regulations of the church on all matters was absolutely essential. Church law, called canon law, consisted of a mass of papal edicts, conciliar laws, and legal opinions from earlier times. As in the case of the Roman law, the church was forced to codify its law from time to time. Constant revisions were made until the sixteenth century, when canon law was condensed into the immense code in use until our own day.[14] Naturally the application and enforcement of canon law were difficult tasks. Numberless technicalities and "red tape" served to delay action, and as in our day, justice often seemed to be rendered only to the man with political influence or with money enough to hire clever lawyers. In the late Middle Ages papal courts and canon lawyers came to be almost synonymous in the mind of the people with graft, favoritism, corruption, and the defeat of justice.

Most of the routine of legal cases was left to the pope's assistants, but he often interfered and asserted his supreme judicial authority. He had the power to set aside a penalty, and such a papal grant of exemption from a church regulation was called a "dispensation."[15]

PAPAL FINANCES
One other papal function deserves attention here. The pope was a temporal—that is, a political—ruler, and as such had many nonreligious duties. We have already discussed Pope Gregory I's handling of the papal estates. By Innocent III's time these estates had become states and were federated into a central Ital-

[14] In 1917 a new revision was made. This *Codex Juris Canonici* is now the official canon law.

[15] Today, as in the past, a Roman Catholic sometimes obtains a dispensation to marry a close relative, or to be relieved from some other such regulation. There must, of course, be sufficient reason for the dispensation.

ian political unit called "the States of the Church." Innocent, as we
have seen, not only ruled these states but was also overlord of such
distant realms as Naples-Sicily and England. Thus, like the other
bishops, the pope found himself enmeshed in a network of political
relationships. Innocent III was forced to devote himself quite as much
to political as to spiritual affairs. Three centuries later, popes such as
Alexander VI of Borgia seemed to be solely concerned with secular
activities and ambitions.[16]

One reason for this lamentable situation was the increasing demand for revenues with which to run the church. During the early
medieval period immense landed estates provided the church with its
income. With the shift to a town economy of industry and commerce,
the church found itself better supplied with landed wealth than with
money. That is, the clergy were "land poor." With an expanding bureaucracy, in an increasingly cosmopolitan world of cities and business affairs, the rising costs of administration and of living forced the
papacy to look to its financial resources. And, it must be said, the
clergy met the changing situation with remarkable success.

The Papal States in Italy and the vassal states elsewhere provided
a tremendous annual income. To this were added the fees and fines
from the papal court. Liberal contributions also came from annates,
provisorships, expectatives, and other such clerical appointments.[17]
From more purely spiritual sources came tithes, crusading contributions, gifts of land, the free will offerings of pilgrims (in centennial
years this was considerable),[18] Peter's pence, the annual papal tax
levied on every Christian family, and indulgence payments.

All in all the popes had the responsibility of collecting and ex-
pending a tremendous amount of money. For the most part the men
and methods employed were as justifiable as those used by the secular
rulers. But Christian society expected more of its religious leaders, and
the popes of the late Middle Ages acquired an unenviable and perhaps exaggerated reputation for financial misdeeds. The corruption
of the Borgia popes [19] and their contemporaries cannot be excused but
it can be understood. Wherever large amounts of money pass through
many human hands, there are bound to be worldly and dishonest individuals. Medieval churchmen, such as St. Bernard, Petrarch, and
Wiclif condemned these practices. Councils and occasionally even

[16] See below, pp. 624 f.   [18] See below, pp. 558 f.
[17] See below, p. 563.   [19] See below, pp. 623 ff.

popes (such as Innocent III) legislated against what we call "graft." Financial corruption and clerical profiteering increased, however, and there are many who insist that they were the chief causes for the rapid increase of heresy and eventually for the Protestant Revolt. Without question, financial necessity was "the root of many clerical evils" in the late Middle Ages.

═══ XXII ═══

CLERICAL REFORM AND HERETICAL
MOVEMENTS

THE REGULAR CLERGY

IN certain respects the Roman Catholic organization can be compared to an army. All Christians were, so to speak, members of the
militia of Christ: the laymen as privates, the priests as corporals
and sergeants, the bishops and archbishops as commissioned officers.
All of them were under the control of the pope as commander in
chief. But there was another important fighting force under the pope's
command which is comparable to the professional soldiery or "shock
troops" of an army. This was the *regular* clergy. We have already
traced the rise of monasticism and Pope Gregory I's use of the
Benedictine monks in winning England for the Roman Catholic
Church. We turn now to a description of the organization and activities of this branch of the clerical army during the later medieval
centuries.

WAVES OF
MONASTIC
REFORM

It has been said that in every great crisis of Roman
Catholic history monasticism has been the decisive
element in the church's defensive and offensive operations, and that when Christianity needs it most, a
wave of militant monastic zeal sweeps over the church, purifying it
from internal corruption and repelling external assailants. The concept of regularly recurring cycles of monastic zeal should not be over-
emphasized, but it is useful as an indication of the valuable services
that the monks rendered to the church at several critical periods. For
instance, it is clear that St. Martin's hermits and monks initiated a
wave of religious enthusiasm in fourth-century Gaul, and two centuries
later, when the papacy was badly disorganized, Benedict of Nursia
and his Italian monasteries served as a rallying point for the forces
of clerical righteousness.[1] It is also true that during the intervening

[1] See above, pp. 97 ff.

430

periods of clerical decline, monasticism itself sank into such a state of corruption that it too was badly in need of reform. To their credit it must be said that the monks usually took the lead in reforming, first themselves, then the rest of the clergy. We now turn to a consideration of some of the monastic reform movements of the late Middle Ages.

THE CLUNIAC
REFORM
The Cluniac movement of the tenth and eleventh centuries was first of all a reformation of the sadly disorganized and secularized Benedictine monasteries of the West. After the age of Gregory the Great there was a noticeable breakdown of Benedictine monasticism. Under Louis the Pious a vain effort was made to restore and enforce the strict old Benedictine regulations. But a century later, during the confusion of the Norse, Hungarian, and Moslem invasions and the uncertainties of early feudal government, monasticism was worse off than ever. Most monasteries had either been destroyed or had fallen into the hands of irreligious bishops and feudal lords.

In the year 910, at one of Christendom's darkest hours, a French nobleman set up five reformed monasteries in the region of Cluny, west of Lyons. A few years later Abbot Odo of Cluny (927-948), taking the lead in the movement, did for French monasticism what Benedict had done in Italy four centuries earlier. Odo and his zealous successors spread the reformation to other decadent monasteries in France. The reigning prince of central Italy (Alberic) called in Cluniacs to revive Roman monasticism, and even Monte Cassino, Benedict's ancient foundation, came under their inspiring influence. By the year 1000 the Cluniacs had become so powerful in France that kings and princes were giving immense estates to the order. Thus other monasteries and churches came to be affiliated with the mother monastery. The popes exempted all Cluniac monasteries from the control of the local bishops, and took them under their own special protection.

Meanwhile, liberal donations enabled Abbot Odilo (994-1049) to build a splendid marble church at the home monastery. This church was larger than any other in the West, and four hundred monks and crowds of visitors worshiped there daily. Cluny also boasted a flock of branch monasteries whose heads, called priors, were appointed and controlled by the superabbot at Cluny. During the eleventh century there were over fifty monasteries in the West that had adopted the Cluniac program and enrolled their monks in the steadily increasing "army that marched under Abbot Odilo's orders." Eventually all Cluniac monasteries were grouped into ten provinces, each of which had a supervising abbot who was subject to the head abbot at Cluny. Thus, unlike the earlier Benedictines, the Cluniacs formed a centralized bureaucratic organization under one administrative official.

So popular and effective was the Cluniac movement that priests, bishops, archbishops, and popes adopted its program. Cluny also began to train its own priests to go forth and reform the parish churches. Thus it became a movement for priestly as well as monastic reform. Zealous popes such as Gregory VII and Urban II used the Cluniacs as shock troops in the battle against graft, immorality, lay investiture, and other forms of clerical corruption. For the first time in Christian history, monasticism was regimented under a supreme abbot-commander, to be used by the popes for the reformation of monks, of priests, and even of the laity.

THE DECLINE OF THE CLUNIACS Unfortunately the Cluniacs, like their predecessors, the Benedictines, could not withstand popularity, prosperity, and power. Never as strict as that of Benedict, the Cluniac rule emphasized learning and culture; servants performed the kind of manual labor that Benedict's monks had been proud to do for themselves. By the twelfth century, Cluny had become an aristocratic and conservative fraternity. One clerical critic said: "Don't send a monk to Cluny; they will make a knight of him." St. Bernard, leader of the rival Cistercian order, suggested that the Cluniacs considered their magnificent festivals, furnishings, and buildings as evidences of monastic success, whereas they were signs of decay. He was disgusted at their great church "with its immense trees [candelabras] of brass, glittering with jewels," and the cloisters where the brothers' minds were distracted from religion by sculptures of "disgusting monkeys, spotted tigers, and fighting men." Furthermore, said he, their appetites are so finicky that "they must have their eggs sometimes fried, sometimes roasted, sometimes soft, hard, or chopped fine."

It is evident that, after two centuries of vigorous effectiveness, Cluny had ceased to be a reforming force. The order was characteristic of the feudal age: it was rural, militaristic, and aristocratic. In their day, the Cluniacs served the church well. They gave way to a new monasticism that was more serviceable in an age of towns, burgher ideals, and social service.

NEW MONASTIC ORDERS

For a time, in the eleventh century, there was an extreme puritanical reaction which gave rise to several orders of strict (even fanatical) monks such as those of Grammont and Chaise Dieu in Auvergne, Fontevrault in Poitou, and Romuald's Camaldolesian hermits in Italy. Soon a more practical type of monasticism appeared, that of the priest-monks. In England a priest named Gilbert organized an order called, after him, the Gilbertines; in Germany there was a similar organization called the Premonstratensians, whose ideal was to serve humanity rather than to save themselves by ascetic isolation from the lay world. The same ideal of practical service appeared in the Near East during the early crusades. Here there arose several fraternities of soldier-monks. The Knights Templars, the Hospitalers, and the Teutonic Knights were organized for the purpose of defending and nursing needy pilgrims.[2] For a time these social service orders satisfied a real need. With growing prosperity and diminishing crusades, however, they became self-centered fraternal orders of clever financiers or pleasure-loving aristocrats who had once fought the infidel. Their history serves to illustrate two important characteristics of monastic evolution: (1) its practical ideals of social service, so in keeping with the spirit of the age of towns and businessmen, and (2) the deteriorating effect of popularity and wealth on any order of monks.

The crusading orders, like the Benedictines and Cluniacs, succumbed to the enervating influences of prosperity. There was, however, this difference. The decay of the Hospitalers and the Templars was due to financial rather than to landed wealth. They flourished in an age of industrial and commercial revenues; therefore they went in for banking rather than for farming.[3] The eventual downfall of the Templars, who acquired as hateful a reputation for "high finance" as a modern Wall Street corporation, followed a series of financial scandals. In spite of temporary reversions to the early Christian ideal of poverty, monastic history was to be dominated more and more by financial interests.

CARTHUSIANS AND CISTERCIANS

In twelfth-century France there appeared two monastic movements that did much to revive the pious reputation of monasticism. Bruno of Cologne, head professor of the cathedral school at Rheims, disgusted at the worldliness of the clergy, founded a hermit retreat in the French Alps near Greno-

[2] See below, pp. 514 ff.
[3] See below, p. 537.

ble. At this "Grande Chartreuse" learned and pious men might study, read, and pray, far from the world, the flesh, and the Devil. Eventually, over a hundred branch monasteries of this order were founded. In all of them the monks lived like groups of hermits in separate cells. Italy, even today, has many Carthusian houses called Certosas. It is of interest to note that the Carthusians made a famous liqueur, called Chartreuse, which is still a favorite after-dinner liqueur.

St. Bernard's Cistercian order was less retiring and intellectual but more influential than the Carthusians. The Cistercians came into being as a protest against the worldliness of the Cluniacs, just as the Cluniacs had been organized in an effort to reform the decadent Benedictines. Early in the twelfth century a French nobleman turned from the worldliness of monastic and priestly life and established a community of twenty zealous monks at Citeaux near Dijon. Later an Englishman named Stephen Harding drew up a set of strict regulations and began the expansion of the order. Still later St. Bernard joined and popularized the movement. He established three more monasteries, one of them the famous Clairvaux (Clear Valley). Soon there were seventy branch communities of monks all living simple rural lives.

A visitor at Clairvaux in its earlier days was impressed with the fact that the monks, clad in rough garments, worked in the gardens with hoes, in the fields with forks and rakes and sickles, in the woods with axes. Nevertheless he felt that "God was in this place" for it had the genuine humility of the poor of Christ. "The silence of noon was . . . broken only by the chanting of the services and the sound of garden and field implements."

The Cistercians were the most puritanical of all twelfth-century monastic orders. Their ideal seems to have been a "back to nature," rural simplicity. In marked contrast to their bitter rivals, the Cluniacs, they had severely unornamented churches, simple living quarters, few guests, plain food, and rough woolen clothing. Stern strict religiousness was their highest ideal; culture and education were held in suspicion. To one runaway monk who could not stand the pioneer hardships of Cistercian life, Bernard wrote with biting irony: "What doest thou in the city, dainty soldier [of Christ]? While thy brothers are storming the battlements of Heaven thou ridest about the highways, clad in white linen."

With such scornful invective Bernard was accustomed to lash

MONTE CASSINO
(Today)
(See p. 98.)

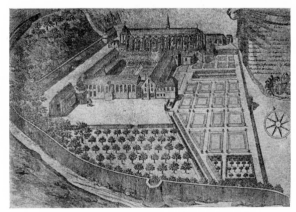

MONASTERY OF
ST. PÈRE,
CHARTRES

ISLE, TOWN, AND MONASTERY OF MONT ST. MICHEL
(Today)

MONASTERIES

(See p. 717.)

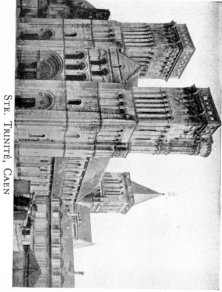

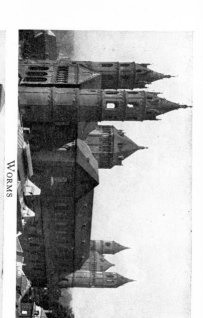

ST. SATURNIN, TOULOUSE

STE. TRINITÉ, CAEN

WORMS

ST. AMBROSE, MILAN

All Courtesy of the University Prints

ROMANESQUE CHURCHES (XI-XIII C)

(See pp. 708 f.)

both his fellow monks and the priesthood. His fearless condemnation of evil and his zeal for righteousness made him so popular that he was one of the most influential characters of his day. Popes feared him, yet sought his aid against opposing monarchs or clergymen, and the church relied on him for assistance in crushing corruption within and heresy without. Abelard, a brilliant young professor of the University of Paris, found out to his sorrow that it was disastrous to stir up the resentment of the fanatical old preacher-monk. Because of his wide influence and manifold activities, Bernard has been called "the uncrowned pope" of the twelfth century.

In spite of the work of men like Bernard, the Cistercians went the way of all monastic movements. Honors, popularity, and wealth were heaped upon them. With power and prosperity came worldliness. Bernard himself lived to lament the fact that his fellow Cistercians had ceased to live in "shepherds' huts thatched with straw," and "were beginning to live in palaces of stone set with all the stars of Heaven for adornment." A century after Bernard's death the Cistercians were better known for their success in capitalistic farming, wool trading, and money-making than in soul saving. Like all church institutions, they were affected by a world that was becoming more citified and money-conscious.

ST. FRANCIS OF ASSISI   Only one medieval monk, St. Francis of Assisi, has won greater approval and fame than St. Bernard. He and his order of Franciscan friars mark another effort to bring Christianity back to the simple unsophisticated ideal of its founder. It has been said that no one since Jesus has so clearly exemplified the simple Christian virtues as St. Francis.

He was the rather poetical son of a rich merchant, and at the age of twenty, after a severe illness and a term in prison, he was converted. Forsaking his friends, he wandered about dressed in rags, repairing dilapidated churches. This queer existence so scandalized his father that he disinherited him. Nothing daunted, this rich young man of Assisi not only gave all he had to the poor, but even turned over to his irate father the clothes from his back. It is possible that during this period Francis was mentally unbalanced. It is said that on meeting a band of robbers he announced that he was "the herald of a great king [Christ]"; they promptly stripped him of his meager belongings and threw him into a snow bank.

FRANCIS AND
SOCIAL SERVICE
Soon Francis turned from self-centered hermitism to a life of service for suffering humanity. After hearing a priest read the scriptural admonition: "And as ye go preach . . . heal the sick, cleanse the lepers . . . provide neither gold nor silver . . . ,"[4] Francis dedicated himself to a life of poverty, preaching, and ministering to the needy. His steadfast adherence to this purpose made him the greatest of Roman Catholic saints and his followers one of the most influential of all religious orders.

For a while Francis had only twelve followers; later others joined and were sent forth "two and two," like Christ's seventy apostles.[5] These simple men, who depended on the people for food and shelter, were called mendicant friars (begging brothers). Their unselfish lives of service soon won the hearts of the poverty-stricken populace of the crowded Italian cities. Francis himself set an example for all time by his care for the homeless, the crippled, and especially the lepers, whom all others avoided. Crowds flocked to hear his simple Gospel message and his praise of both the beauties of nature and the joys of religion. He may not have actually preached to the birds, as medieval legend relates, but he did love all of God's creatures, whether animals or human beings. He was equally ready to care, in a gentle kindly spirit, for a wounded bird or a diseased beggar. He spoke of himself and his followers as "God's troubadours," dedicated to the service of "Lady Poverty." The *Little Flowers of St. Francis,* a collection of legendary stories, illustrates his true character. He was a religious mystic who appreciated nature and "loved his neighbor as himself." Rarely have Christian idealism and practical social service been so perfectly combined in one personality.

THE FRANCISCAN
ORDER
Francis's idealism is best exemplified in his own words and deeds. His practical program of social service shows forth more clearly in his order of Franciscans, also called Friars Minor, Minorites, and Gray Friars (because of their gray garb). The original organization was tentatively approved by Pope Innocent III (1210), and a later pope recognized it as an international order (1220).

The Franciscans differed from most earlier monastic orders in that they sought, rather than shunned, the nonclerical world. Instead of shutting themselves up in monasteries, they wandered about, espe-

[4] Matthew 10:7-9.
[5] Luke 10:1 ff.

cially in the cities, seeking to serve mankind's physical as well as spiritual needs. Their houses were more often located in the slums of the cities than in the countryside or wilderness. At first no gifts were accepted unless they were for the poor or for food and clothing for the friars. Each brother had only two robes, often patched, and no shoes, unless necessitated by rough roads. It has been said that wherever "the people met together there could be found the friars preaching in homely and telling fashion, stirring the dulled religious instincts," and bringing men back to their rightful allegiance to the church.

The work of the Franciscans was twofold: (1) the care of the souls, and (2) the care of the bodies of suffering humanity. Their original program was to "go into all the world to seek and save the lost." At first they preached and ministered chiefly to the Italian city folk of the lower classes. Later they were found throughout the West. For instance, in 1224 nine friars landed in England. In a year they had five city chapters; in thirty years they had forty-nine houses and twelve hundred members. In London one of their chapter houses was a sort of Salvation Army rescue mission, located in "Stinking Lane." In plague-stricken regions, the Franciscans often did work similar to that performed by the modern Red Cross. Soon, however, they were employed in other, less Christlike activities. The popes sent them to preach crusades, to take charge of declining churches, to oppose hostile clergymen, and even to convert Moslem and Tartar peoples. Francis himself went on a mission to Egypt, only to be deported by the Moslem sultan. Franciscan foreign missionaries visited Armenia, Palestine, Northern Africa, Spain, Eastern Europe, and Asia. Centuries later, when Columbus set forth for America, he was accompanied by Franciscan friars.

THE DECLINE OF THE FRANCISCANS   At their best the Franciscans set a glorious example for Christian Europe. With remarkable success, they applied Christian ideals to the practical needs of their day. They were, however, rather loosely organized and with 200,000 friars scattered throughout Europe, laxness was bound to develop. The chief cause of the deterioration of the Franciscans lay in their acquisition of wealth. The poverty regulation was changed to allow contributions for the increasing needs of the order. Next, friars were sent out to raise funds for the pope as well as for their own treasury. When they were given the right to administer the priestly sacraments, and were exempted from the jurisdiction of the local bishops, bitter strife arose with the secular clergy. Further trouble broke out in the universities when the friars took up teaching. The formation of auxiliary orders, such as the "Poor Clares" (nuns), tended to expand and also to weaken the original Franciscan ideals. So many selfish and worldly men came into the order that scarcely a half century after its foundation Francis's successor was condemning the hypocrisy, greed, idleness, corruption, legacy hunting, and vagrancy of the brothers. They were reputed to be "begging like paupers while living in luxury."

A group of strict constructionists, called *Spiritual* Franciscans, attempted in vain to enforce the rule of poverty. In spite of their efforts, a program of financial expansion and administrative centralization was adopted. Symbolic of the change was the housing of the simple tomb of St. Francis at Assisi in a magnificent new church. Everywhere the friars began erecting expensive buildings, and within a century after the death of Francis, his followers were being reviled for their hypocritical self-seeking ways. Once more monasticism had succumbed to the forces of urban life.

THE DOMINICAN PREACHING FRIARS   Contemporaneously with the Franciscans a rival order of friars was attaining fame in the realm of learning and heresy hunting. The Dominican order was founded by Dominic, a Spanish theological student. As a result of a mission in southern France he was so impressed by the strength of the Albigensian heretics that he began to train young men as missionaries to convert them. Although Innocent III hesitated to approve the order, his successor recognized it, and within a few years there were sixty Dominican houses in Europe.

The "Black Friars," as they were called, went forth with much the same determination as the Franciscans, but they ministered to the souls of heretics rather than to the physical needs of poverty-stricken Christians. They held open-air meetings in heretical towns, they worked individually to convert unbelievers, and they supported orthodoxy in the universities. Even in foreign lands, these scholarly theologian-missionaries carried on a vigorous warfare against Christian unbelief and against Jews, Moslems, and other infidels. Eventually they adopted the Franciscan policy of poverty and social service in a modified form. From the start, they were a distinctly intellectual order and won their chief fame as such. Many of thirteenth-century

Europe's greatest scholars—notably Thomas Aquinas and Albertus Magnus—were Dominicans.

Much of the unpopularity of the Dominicans came from their zealous activity in the battle against heresy. Under their auspices the Inquisition won an unenviable reputation for cold-blooded efficiency. This activity, along with other natural causes, led to the decline of the Dominicans. Only the Jesuits of later Protestant times attained as great intellectual fame and as bitter popular disapproval as the Dominicans.

THE WEAKNESSES IN THE MEDIEVAL CHURCH

FINANCIAL AND POLITICAL EVILS

The failure of Benedictines, Cluniacs, Cistercians, Franciscans, and Dominicans to effect a lasting improvement in the church makes it clear that there were certain permanent factors that prevented a successful reform of the priesthood and the monastic orders. First and foremost, clerical wealth, even though necessary for the support of religious institutions, brought the church far more evil than good. The richer the church, the more completely its activities contrasted with the teachings and actions of its founder. Wealthy, luxury-loving, and immoral clergymen stirred the populace to resentment and revolt. But the church could not sacrifice its wealth.

Closely related with these financial evils were several grave political defects. The purchase and sale of clerical office, the close relations between church and state, and the accompanying conflicts between the two presented serious problems. For instance, the church claimed, at one and the same time, to be exempt from taxation and yet to have control over the coronation of kings. Many medieval writers pointed out that clergymen would be better off if they gave up their wealth and political functions. But the great majority of popes and bishops were either unwilling to do this or uncertain as to how it could be accomplished without ruining the church. Among the other political difficulties of the church were the papal claims to temporal power, the exemption of the clergy from civil trials, and the general failure of the priesthood to adapt its aims and methods to nationalism, autocratic monarchy, increasing town life, and other elements in the changing medieval scene. The financial and political ills of the church contributed to the emergence of a third evil—heresy.

HERESIES: THEO-
LOGICAL AND
ECONOMIC

Theological heresies, such as the Arianism of the early centuries, were based for the most part on rational-mindedness. They were not so great a danger to the church as the social-economic heresies of the later Middle Ages. It is a well-known fact that the heresies of the twelfth and thirteenth centuries were closely connected with town life. Certain heresies (notably that of the Albigensians) spread along the trade routes. Most heretical movements were strongest in regions of large cities: northern Italy, southern France, and the Netherlands. And finally, their chief supporters were the working classes in industrial centers. A noteworthy example of this is found in the heretical movements among the textile workers of the Netherlands and northern Italy.

The rapid development of town life produced a new mode of life and thought with which the church found it increasingly difficult to cope. When religious radicals not only criticized the theology of the church but also brought to public attention the immoral economic and social practices of the clergy, the church had good cause for alarm. It was difficult for it to disprove the charge that the members of the clergy were living in immorality and luxury on money extorted from poverty-stricken parishioners. For centuries the church responded to these charges by condemning and punishing its critics as heretics. This policy met with reasonable success until the growing populations of the cities showed signs of group resistance.

THE PATARINES
OF MILAN

One of the early examples of this combined social-economic and theological heresy occurred in eleventh-century Milan, one of the largest cities in the West. Here a young nobleman, assisted by a rural priest, started a violent agitation against the wealth and immorality of the local clergy. The populace were urged to seize the wealth of the clergy: "if they resist, let their houses be given over to pillage, and both they and their bastard children hounded out of town."

This proletarian propaganda was actually translated into action, and Milanese mobs invaded the homes of wealthy clerics, and driving them and their concubines out of town, took possession. A people's militia was organized. The name "Patarines," meaning ragpickers, applied by their enemies in derision, was adopted as a slogan. When Pope Gregory VII gave a tentative approval to their program of drastic clerical reform, the rebels seemed to be firmly established. But in time the forces of religious respectability and economic stability regained control. The Patarine leaders were executed, their doctrines condemned as heretical, and the movement crushed.

CLERICAL CRITICS   The church might crush proletarian heretics, but it could not suppress all criticism of its faults. At the same time as the Patarine revolt, Peter Damiani, himself a prominent clergyman, was telling the Christian world that there were corrupt clerics whose "bellies were filled with lust and drunkenness," and whose lives were "as rotten as Jeremiah's loin cloth." [6] In reference to a disputed election to the papacy he cried: "Woe is the papacy; once the glory of the world, now alas it is a place of simoniacs." He cursed the claimant of whom he disapproved as an "old dragon," "a preacher of the devil," "an apostle of antichrist," "a son of perdition," "a whirlpool of lust and shipwreck of chastity," "a disgrace to Christianity, and the priesthood," "a stench to the world," "a disgrace to the universe," "a slippery serpent," "dung of mankind, cesspool of crimes, abomination of Heaven, food for Hell, and the stubble for eternal fire." Damiani also wrote a book so packed with accounts of clerical scandals that one pope suppressed it. If eminent clerics could say such things concerning the priesthood, it is not strange that the common folk believed what religious radicals told them. During the eleventh century such heretics as Tanchelm in Flanders, Eon in Brittany, and Peter of Bruys and Henry of Lausanne in France reviled the corrupt clergy and preached a religion of simplicity and Christlike poverty. It is likely that the church would have had a serious revolt on its hands had not the Gregorian reforms, the struggle between church and state, and crusading enthusiasm directed popular attention elsewhere.

Criticism continued, however, and late in the twelfth century St. Bernard wrote to the pope as follows: "Could I but see the Church of God, as in the ancient days when the Apostles cast nets for souls rather than for gold and silver." Yet when Arnold of Brescia urged, as a solution of the problem, the drastic confiscation of all clerical wealth and the separation of church and state, he was ruthlessly crushed. Bernard himself joined with Emperor Frederick the Red-Bearded and the pope in condemning to death and eternal hell-fire such a fiendish heretic. At about the same time that Arnold's follow-

[6] Jeremiah 13:1-7.

ers, the Arnoldists, or "Poor Men," were being mercilessly persecuted, two new heretical movements began to spread rapidly in France.

THE WALDENSIAN "POOR MEN" — The Waldensians of southeastern France were probably related to earlier Alpine heretical groups, but their origin is usually attributed to Peter Waldo, a merchant of Lyons. His reading of the Bible led him to practice Christ's command to "go into all the world and preach." Somewhat like Francis of Assisi a generation later, he turned from a life of luxury and, selling all of his property, took up the apostolic ideal of poverty and preaching. He also translated portions of the Bible into the language of the people, and began to send forth his preaching comrades "two by two." The local bishop refused to allow the "Poor Men of Lyons" to spread their subversive teachings concerning the evils of wealth, and two popes to whom Waldo appealed refused their approval. When the simple, Bible-reading brothers insisted on "obeying God rather than man," they were branded as heretics. Thenceforth the Waldensians became more bitter in their denunciation of the papal "antichrist" and his clerical minions. Naturally the church classed them along with the Arnoldists and other "Poor Men," as dangerous radicals, betrayers of God and His church, and fit only for ruthless extermination.

It will be remembered that thirty years later Innocent III, recognizing the essentially constructive value of teachings similar to those of Peter Waldo, gave his approval to the program of Francis of Assisi. He even encouraged the formation of loyal Catholic associations of "Poor Men." But the Waldensians and Arnoldists, having tasted the bitterness of clerical intolerance, could neither be won over nor stifled. It is not improbable that had Innocent been pope when Waldo sought papal approval, his program, which was almost identical with that of Francis, would have been encouraged instead of repressed. Waldo might have become (like Francis) one of the great Roman Catholic saints, a loyal warrior in the ranks of the clergy, fighting against the enemies of Christianity. Why is it that Waldo, Arnold of Brescia, Wiclif, Hus, Luther, and innumerable other sincere reformers have been branded as heretics, while men such as Francis, Damiani, and Bernard, with programs of drastic reform, have been sainted? Was it merely the chance misfortune that they came into prominence during the time of reactionary popes? Is it that they were too far in advance of their times? Or did their reforms strike at certain vested interests in the church hierarchy?

HERESY AS
TREASON
Roman Catholic scholars have suggested that the difference between a heretic like Waldo and a saint like Francis is that Waldo deserted the church, whereas Francis remained loyal regardless of his own personal ideas. A man of the highest idealism who disobeys orders and fights against, rather than for, his mother church is guilty of religious treason. From this viewpoint it is possible to understand the attitude taken by the church toward heresy. Heretics were regarded with the same suspicion and treated with somewhat the same ruthlessness as are radical opponents of the established social and economic order in most modern countries.

THE ALBIGENSIAN
"PURE MEN"
Hostile though the Waldensians were to the clerical system, the church was forced to deal with a more formidable menace in the Albigensians of southwestern France and the Netherlands. So radical was their religious and social program that, to many people, they were not even Christians, but on a par with the infidel Moslems. Their ideas were derived from an old Persian-Manichean heresy that had spread westward by way of the Balkan regions. These new Manicheans are commonly known as Albigensians from the name of their chief center of influence in southern France. As a matter of fact, they called themselves Cathari ("the Pure"). They were really a sect of puritanical mystics who were dedicated to the task of purifying their own lives and the external world of all materialistic influences. Marriage, civil government, the taking of oaths, warfare, and all such institutions of organized society were condemned as creations of the Devil, whom they identified with the ancient Persian god of evil and of darkness and also with the Jehovah of the Old Testament. The church, the clergy, and their temporal allies seemed to them to be the earthly representatives of this antichrist. The simple God-fearing lives of the Cathari, especially of their missionary preachers (the "Perfected"), were in such startling contrast to the worldly lives of the higher clergy that their heretical teachings were widely accepted. Members of the nobility joined the sect, many of them with the hope that they might be on hand to despoil the clergy of their worldly goods. In many of the towns of France, and even to the northward in the textile regions of the Netherlands, the artisans and poorer classes became enthusiastic in their support of Cathari beliefs and bitter in their hatred of the clergy. Everywhere, among people who were eager for reform of the clergy, the Cathari found adherents and sympathizers. By the end of the twelfth century the Albigensian Cathari and the Waldensian Poor Men had become

such a menace to Roman Catholicism that Pope Innocent III took drastic steps to crush them.

THE ALBIGENSIAN CRUSADE

Since the local bishops were unwilling or unable to handle the situation, papal legates were sent to southern France. Innocent's agents, however, found it impossible to eliminate the Albigensian heresy by peaceful methods. After ten years of vain effort, the pope resorted to force. Some sort of action was justified by the fact that a papal ambassador had been murdered by the heretics, but the means by which the Albigensians were crushed were ruthless. An army of so-called crusaders, including adventurers and land-hungry nobles from northern France and other parts of the West, carried fire and the sword to innocent and guilty alike. For twenty years the most flourishing agricultural and industrial regions of southern France were ravaged by warfare. After the first bloody conquest carried out by the crusaders, there was a series of wars between the invaders and the local nobility. All who resisted were classed as allies of the heretics and therefore were subjected to crusading attacks. Count Raymond of Toulouse employed every device of defensive warfare and diplomacy in efforts to save his feudal domain. King Philip II of France, who for a time had observed strict neutrality, finally sent his son to lead the crusade, in order that the anarchy might be ended and the rights of the monarch preserved. For a time the south was ravaged by a second invasion. The Count of Toulouse, condemned by the pope and hard pressed by the royal army, managed to defend his territories in and about Toulouse, but the French king annexed a series of feudal domains in Languedoc stretching from the Pyrenees to the Rhone River. A half century later Toulouse itself came into the possession of the French crown as a result of a marriage alliance and an inheritance. Thus in the end the French monarchy profited much from the Albigensian Crusade.

Meanwhile heresy in southwestern France had been blotted out, but the destruction of human life and civilization was so terrible that the crusade brought much discredit to the church, as well as to the invading warriors. A modern commentator has remarked that "no Mongol conqueror ever wiped out a Christian community with greater savagery." Henceforth Lombardy surpassed Languedoc in culture and it was doubtless for this reason that Italy rather than France led in the remarkable developments which are usually spoken of as the Italian Renascence.

THE INQUISITION
AND HERESY
Less violent but more effective than crusades was the work of the Inquisition. Pope Innocent's successors decided that staffs of expert theological investigators were more successful than armies in handling heresy. When a group of Dominican inquisitors entered a community they served as father confessors for repentant heretics, as investigators and prosecutors of suspects, and as judges of the innocence or guilt of those who were accused. Their procedure was to begin by preaching and urging all heretics to confess voluntarily and to do penance. From those who confessed they secured information about others. Then, after a final call for voluntary repentance, they began to call in suspects for inquisition (i.e., quizzing). Here their methods were more like those of detectives conducting a "third degree" than of father confessors or judges in court.

Often a man was not allowed to know who the accusing witnesses were. Seldom were there any defense witnesses, for defenders of convicted heretics were severely punished. A prisoner might defend himself, but it was taken for granted that he was guilty until his innocence was clearly proved. On the other hand, the flimsiest rumors against a suspect were accepted as evidence of his guilt. If a suspect's testimony contradicted itself or that of others, he was tortured until he told the truth. If he persisted in asserting his innocence, even though there was no actual evidence of guilt, he was kept in prison with the expectation that he would eventually confess. Thus the prisoner had little chance. He was expected to talk, but only against himself or some other suspected heretic. The Inquisition worked on the principles that all suspects were guilty; that a guilty man will lie; and therefore that nothing favorable to him should be believed. This method of trial doubtless led to the apprehension of many guilty heretics, but it also made it possible for many an innocent man to be victimized by personal enemies or by people who coveted his wealth.

It should be noted that once a man admitted his guilt, he was absolved and sentenced merely to do penance, usually the performance of certain prayers or pilgrimages, fines, the wearing of penitents' garb, or light imprisonment. Only the heretic who refused to talk or who stubbornly insisted on his innocence was tortured or shut in a cell on bread and water, or, as a last resort, turned over to the civil government to be burned. Such harsh treatment was defended on the ground that heroic measures were justified in order to save souls from hell. What matter if a man's body were wracked, torn, and tortured for a few hours so long as it resulted in the salvation of his soul for eternity? And if he persisted in refusing salvation, he must be consigned to the flames here on earth so as to prevent others from being infected with his deadly heresy. This attitude is similar to that which led the Protestant fanatics of New England to torture and burn witches. In fairness to the medieval church it must be said that similarly harsh methods were used in the secular courts.

THE FAILURE OF REPRESSIVE MEASURES   Needless to say, the Inquisition was little more successful than the crusades in permanently solving the problem of heresy. As with Rome's failure to crush the early Christians, "the blood of the martyrs is the seed of the church," whether it be orthodox Christians of the fourth or heretical Christians of the thirteenth century. It seems that nothing could suppress heretical criticisms of a church, many of whose clergy continued to live selfish, corrupt, and worldly lives. Brutal methods of warfare and inquisition might blot out Waldensian and Albigensian communities, but many good Christians were so horrified that in the end the church lost more than it gained.

St. Francis's approach came closer than any other to solving the problems of heresy. Had his followers only continued to feed the bodies and the souls of the masses, their applied Christianity might have destroyed heresy by loving-kindness.

THE ROOTS OF THE PROTESTANT REVOLT   It is reasonable to suppose that a thoroughgoing reform of the clergy, such as was proposed by Innocent III, would have eliminated the criticisms of heretical propagandists. The clergy, however, was not ready to be reformed. Later we shall see how it condemned as heretics many of its own members when they insisted on drastic reform and how sincere reformers such as the Spiritual Franciscans, Wiclif, and Hus were crushed. When influential laymen, in church councils, tried to force certain changes on the clergy, shortsighted clerical politicians managed to forestall action. The Council of Constance (in the fifteenth century) [7] had an opportunity to initiate a Roman Catholic Reformation a century before that of Martin Luther. Instead, it burned as heretics three clerical radicals who insisted on drastic action. A reform of the financial and political evils of the church would have silenced the radical teachings of Hus and Wiclif far more effectively than did the fires of martyrdom.

[7] See below, pp. 571 f.

But instead of reforms, Christendom saw unrepentant, worldly, luxury-loving bishops and popes who preached crusades against heretics and Moslems instead of improving conditions within the church. Some of them, such, for instance, as the Borgia pope, Alexander VI,[8] were immoral despots. Others were wealthy aristocrats, with political and financial, rather than spiritual, ambitions. Thus, in the early sixteenth century, Leo X, scion of the Medici banking dynasty of Florence, basked in his Vatican palace and gardens, while far to the north an emaciated professor of theology at the University of Wittenberg wrestled with the problem of personal salvation. Luther might have lived and died, a faithful professor-monk, amid the theological tomes of his university library had the better clerical element been able to enforce but one of its long list of proposed reforms—the elimination of the commercialization of indulgences. As it was, national monarchs took advantage of the weakness of the clergy and eventually the entire church was afflicted with a series of terrific religious revolutions which shattered the religious unity of medieval Europe, and produced the religious disunity of modern times.

[8] See below, p. 624.

≡ XXIII ≡

THE BIRTH OF MODERN NATIONS: ENGLAND

IN preceding chapters we have had ample evidence of the fact that medieval Europe manifested certain tendencies that seem to be modern in character. There is no clear line of demarcation between medieval and modern history, for many modern institutions originated and developed during the so-called medieval centuries. One of the most vivid and tangible of these early modern tendencies is to be found in the political development of the nations of the westernmost regions of Europe. Since the tenth century the section of Europe comprising what we know as Spain, France, and England has shown continuous progress in its political and economic institutions. It has been suggested that almost every outstanding factor in the permanent advancement of modern civilization originated in the western part of Europe. Many of these developments began during the late Middle Ages. All of them have spread eastward to the more backward European states.

The trail of advancing nationalism, democracy, capitalism, and of the Industrial Revolution can be traced from their origins in the westernmost parts of Europe, across the Continent, to Eastern Europe, and thence even to the Far East, where in our own day they have become dominant forces in Japan.[1] When applied to nationalism, the outstanding political characteristic of modern times, the formula is unusually accurate. The first nations to take shape in Europe were the Spains, France, and England. While the Germanies and Italies were still under the hypnotic spell of the revived Roman Empire, their western neighbors were forging out of the raw materials of feudalism, town life, and Catholic Christianity a new type of social-political organization which we call the modern national state.

Nationalism has been defined and interpreted in many different

---

[1] One must, however, include in this formula—the West-to-East expansion of modern institutions—late medieval Italy, with its remarkable achievements in economic and cultural lines.

and sometimes contradictory ways. Some modern scholars refuse to admit the existence of true modern nationalism until the Hundred Years' War or the French Revolution, when the imagination of the English and French peoples was stirred to that high pitch of group consciousness which has been called the electric current of modern political life. Others, viewing the achievements of Alfred the Great in leading his people against the Danes and giving them a literature in their own native language, find the germs of national unity early in the Middle Ages. Some point to such epic poems as the *Cid* and the *Song of Roland* as evidence of a budding national consciousness in eleventh-century Spain and France.

More definite traces of the trend toward national institutions are to be found in the establishment of royal dynasties. By the year 1000, *Capetian* kings were wearing the French royal crown in Paris, where in 1793 their remote descendant "Citizen Louis [XVI] *Capet*" was guillotined by the Revolutionists. If one looks at a map of Western Europe during the late Middle Ages he finds national domains that bear a striking resemblance to modern France, England, Aragon, Castile, and Portugal. However one may define present-day nationalism, it is evident that certain regions now known as Portugal, Spain, England and France, with their distinctly modern institutions of government (kings, parliaments, councils, and the like) were taking shape in the late medieval centuries.

Therefore, without further theoretical speculation, we turn to the history of some of the most important of these regions. In every case we shall find a confused situation. Nations were not created, or even born, in a day. They grew out of the complex interrelationships of feudalism and evolved so slowly that it is difficult to determine exactly when the feudal groups in a given region became consolidated into one national state.

It is important to observe that national royal governments emerged during the same period in which towns and the Roman Catholic Church became strong. These factors—nationalism, Catholicism, and town life—all of which are characteristic of modern civilization, became prominent during the eleventh, twelfth, and thirteenth centuries. All three of them were predominantly antifeudal, and they tended to combine their resources in support of a centralized form of government which would make for a more peaceful, orderly, and commercial society. Churchmen were dissatisfied with the feudal regime which permitted local warfare with its destruction or seizure of church property and constant baronial interference in religious affairs. Townsfolk were desirous of centralized, large-scale units of government which would permit safer and less feudally hampered business activities. Both groups found that their interests were most often bound up with those of the king and nation. The West was outgrowing the small-scale rural type of life of which feudalism was the governmental counterpart. Larger units of activity and a more centralized type of government were needed. The national monarchy suited the needs of the new day.

We turn first to the British Isles because here national life began to develop earlier than elsewhere. In large part this was due to geographical influences. The islands are a distinct unit set off from the Continent by a formidable barrier, the English Channel.[2] England has been free from many of the distracting external influences that have tended to upset and disunite her Continental neighbors. Then, too, her population has been relatively homogeneous, Germanic peoples of Anglo-Saxon, Danish, and Norman stock.[3]

ANGLO-SAXON STATES   Among the other possible reasons for England's rapid advance toward nationalism was the early and complete disappearance of Roman imperial influences. By the end of the fifth century the imperial regime had passed away and Anglo-Saxon institutions were established throughout most of England.[4] Unlike the Continental regions, England never experienced a revival of the Roman Empire. Throughout the Middle Ages, the Germanies and Italies were haunted by their Roman past; by a revived empire which was only a ghostly shadow of the ancient imperial regime. Whatever the tribulations of the English, they had no Carolingian or Holy Roman Empire to interrupt the development of local institutions. The Anglo-Saxon tribal states that were established in fifth-century England steadily advanced, during the succeeding period, toward a sort of national unity. By the sixth century, the seven leading kingdoms—Northumbria, Mercia, East Anglia, Kent, Essex, Sussex, and Wessex—had become confederated into a loose union in the process of conquest and civil war. For a time (during the seventh and eighth centuries) the Angles of Northumbria and Mercia

---

[2] Down to the time of the Spanish Armada and even as late as the time of Napoleon, this "silver thread" of water, thirteen miles in width at the narrowest point, has often served as an impregnable line of defense against invaders from the Continent.

[3] The outstanding non-Germanic element, the Celtic, survives only in the extreme west and north.

[4] See above, p. 112.

dominated the federation. It was during this period that their tribal name became the name of the entire realm, Angle-land or England.[5]

Later, due in part to Norse (or Danish) ravages in the north, the balance of power shifted southward and, shortly after 800, Egbert the Saxon of Wessex (West-Saxony) became overlord of all the Saxons, Jutes, and Angles. He even subjugated certain of the Celtic tribes of Wales. Thus at the time when Charles the Great was uniting the Continental people under the emblem of a revived Roman Empire, the Anglo-Saxons were developing a more normal and permanent unity under their own Germanic institutions. In addition to the "great king" (called bretwalda), and the subkings or chieftains of the tribal units, there were smaller units, called shires, in which local self-government was combined with centralized administration through the supervision of royal officials.

CENTRALIZING AND DECENTRALIZING FORCES The evolution of Anglo-Saxon England is not merely the history of a series of kings, each of whom exercised more extensive powers over an increasingly unified realm. It is the story of constant struggles between inevitably hostile forces. Outstanding was the conflict between the forces of monarchical centralization and feudal decentralization. During the ninth century, from the death of Egbert (839) to that of Alfred the Great (899), England (like Carolingian Europe) seemed about to be overwhelmed by the two floods of foreign invasion and internal disorder. The Danes, as we have already seen,[6] occupied large portions of the realm and overran the rest, even threatening the existence of Wessex.

One of the darkest hours in English history was the period just before Alfred's accession (871). But, unlike the empire of Charles the Great, the kingdom of England survived. Alfred rallied his people, fought it out with the invaders, and saved the kingdom from annihilation. Even though he purchased peace from the invaders by granting them permanent possession of northeastern England (the Danelaw), he was able to consolidate his remaining territories in the south. Henceforth the English kings were actual monarchs of all the territory south and west of the Danelaw, the boundary of which ran from London to the site of modern Liverpool.

---

[5] We shall restrict the name England to the southern part of the island, exclusive of Scotland and Wales, which were distinctly Celtic.

[6] See above, p. 207.

Alfred ruled over a smaller England than his predecessors, but he was more of a ruler than any of them. By expanding the earlier system of shires, each controlled by a royally appointed officer called the shire reeve (sheriff), his influence was extended into outlying regions. Thanks to the solid foundation laid by Alfred, his successors were able to recover most of the Danelaw. His grandson, Ethelstan (924-940), called himself "King of All Britain." This designation was not accurate, but he and his successors were actually kings of all England and nominal overlords of the warring tribes and clans of Scotland and Wales. In the second half of the tenth century, during the era of the able "prime minister," Archbishop Dunstan, the unification of England progressed under a strong, though limited, monarchy.

The Anglo-Saxon kings of this period were advised and checked by the Witenagemot ("wise men's meeting"), composed of royal officials, nobles, and churchmen. In the government of the shires, the chief executive (the shire reeve, or sheriff) was assisted by a shire moot composed of officials and freemen. The subdivisions of the shire (called hundreds) had similar assemblies. In this manner, from top to bottom, English government was carried on by royal officials in co-operation with committees or assemblies of the people. This combination of local self-government with efficient supervision from above is one of the great contributions of the English people to the science of government.

DECLINE OF THE ANGLO-SAXON MONARCHY   Toward the end of the tenth century the kingship began to decline under the impact of decentralizing forces, both internal and external. For one thing, there was a renewal of Danish invasions. At the same time the greater nobles, influential churchmen, and royal officials increased their own landed estates and governmental powers at the expense of those of the monarch. As on the Continent, the forces of disunity and localism were bringing about conditions that are commonly called feudal. During the reign of Ethelred the "Reedless" (senseless) or "Unready" (978-1016), conditions became so chaotic that a Danish army was able to conquer England. In 1016 King Canute of Denmark took possession of England and made it a part of his Scandinavian empire.

English life and government was, however, little changed, for Canute ruled after the manner of the earlier Anglo-Saxon kings.

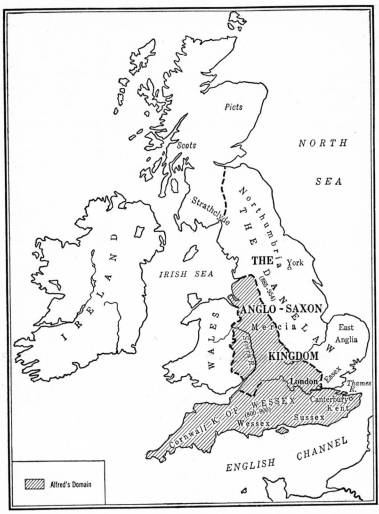

Key
▨ Alfred's Domain

EARLY MEDIEVAL ENGLAND UNDER ALFRED AND HIS
SUCCESSORS

Furthermore Danish rule was only temporary. Canute's two sons were succeeded by an English king, Edward the Confessor (1042-1066), who continued the weak governmental policies of former times. Before long it was evident that Edward was the helpless victim of two powerful feudal factions, one Norman, the other Anglo-Saxon. Edward had grown up in Normandy, and when he came to the English throne he brought with him many Norman courtiers, churchmen, and officials. In opposition to these Norman influences Earl Godwin of Wessex and his sons built up a party of native Englishmen. At the death of Godwin, his son Harold became the power behind the tottering English throne, only to be faced with a rival in the person of young Duke William of Normandy.

THE NORMAN CONQUEST At the death of Edward in 1066 the long impending storm burst. Harold managed to get himself elected king by the Witenagemot. Though he thus obtained a temporary advantage, he was compelled to fight against two formidable contenders. One of them, Harold of Norway, a descendant of Canute, was defeated decisively in northeastern England. Thence Harold rushed southward by forced marches, totaling some three hundred miles, to meet William, his other opponent, near the coast of the English Channel. William of Normandy had collected a large army of feudal vassals and military adventurers from various regions and had persuaded the pope to support his cause. Harold was charged with hostility to the Roman Church and with having broken the sacred oath by which he had promised to support William's candidacy for the English throne. In fighting to defend his throne, Harold lost not only the famous battle of Hastings (or Senlac), but also his life.

Although William was received as king he found it necessary to fight for the possession of the realm. There were ruthless campaigns into rebellious regions. In some places people were massacred or maimed in a heartless fashion. Once the revolts were crushed and castles with permanent garrisons had been established at strategic points, England was in many ways better off than before the conquest. Old local customs were little changed, and law and order were more strictly enforced. The shire system of local government was continued, and the functions of the Witenagemot were still carried on, after a fashion, in the Norman Great Council. William even retained the Anglo-Saxon *fyrd,* or militia—but with Norman modifications—so as not to be entirely dependent on his Norman feudality for military service.

CONSEQUENCES OF THE CONQUEST
Under William England became a much more highly centralized realm. So far as territory is concerned, the Conquest brought about the union of England and Normandy under one ruler. Henceforth, for four centuries, England had close contacts with the Continent. This led to the rapid development of trade along both sides of the Channel, to increased town life, and to the introduction of Continental culture.

The budding national language and literature of Anglo-Saxon times was supplanted by Norman-French. Until the time of Chaucer and Wiclif,[7] the use of Anglo-Saxon marked an Englishman as a member of the lower classes of society. But, on the other hand, England was enriched by the chivalric literature of France,[8] and Latin learning was invigorated by churchmen trained on the Continent. Even more apparent was the effect on English architecture. Anglo-Saxon churches were restored, and new stone cathedrals built after the sturdy Romanesque style that was developing in northern France and Normandy.[9] On the whole, the Conquest had significant cultural consequences for England. What was lost by the submersion of the native Anglo-Saxon culture was more than compensated for by the fact that the island became an integral part of the rapidly advancing civilization of the West.

NORMAN GOVERNMENT
In government the Conquest swung the pendulum sharply in the direction of strong royal power. William's reign marks a decided triumph for the forces of centralization. The ineffective disorganized regime of Ethelred and Edward became almost overnight a strong and efficient feudal monarchy. This was due to the fact that William reorganized England's central government along Norman lines. To be sure, Norman government was feudal, but it was a strongly integrated feudalism. In England William instituted an even better organized government, one so effective that it is said to have "permitted the growth of modern political institutions in England generations in advance of other parts of Europe."

At the outset, by reason of his complete conquest of all England, William became theoretical owner of all the land. This he re-

---

[7] See below, pp. 692 f.   [9] See below, p. 708.
[8] See below, p. 689.

granted to the faithful English possessors, or parceled out to his own
Norman barons, on terms that were suitable to him. As a result, every
landholder in England was either directly or indirectly the king's
vassal. As time passed Anglo-Norman feudalism, in turn, became less
feudalistic, and eventually evolved into a centralized monarchical state.
In spite of occasional revolts, William was able to subject all vassals
to his will. He prohibited private warfare, the erection of castles,
and the coinage of money by the feudal nobles. Eventually, in 1086,
at Salisbury, by William's command "all landowning men of substance . . . bowed down to him and became his men [i.e., vassals]
and swore to be faithful to him against all men." Even though these
oaths of fidelity may have been more or less empty forms, they illustrate the fact that English feudalism was subordinated to the power
of a monarch. Not since Charles the Great had royal power cut
across feudal lines in so distinct a fashion.

FINANCES AND
THE CHURCH
UNDER WILLIAM
William's emphasis on centralization in government
was also shown by the Domesday Book, a survey
made in 1086 by royal officials for the purpose of listing all taxable persons and property. The church, too,
felt the strong, but just, hand of the Conqueror. Although William
had made his expedition under papal sponsorship, he refused either
to acknowledge the pope's overlordship, or to allow him to interfere at will in English affairs. Except by royal permission no pope
might be recognized by the clergy of the realm, no royal baron might
be excommunicated by the pope, no English clergyman might go
to Rome, and no papal decrees be circulated in England. Thus it was
that Gregory VII's investiture decrees failed to reach England. On
the other hand, William showed a real interest in the welfare of the
English clergy. Although the high church positions were filled with
Normans, they were usually able men who worked for the betterment of the church. The most noteworthy of them was Lanfranc,
an Italian-Norman who was made archbishop of Canterbury. William's grant to churchmen of the right to try all spiritual cases in
the bishops' courts [10] indicates his desire to free the clergy from
worldly influences.

----

[10] This provision had momentous consequences. During the weak kingship of
Stephen (1135-1154), the clerical courts assumed jurisdiction not only of spiritual
cases, but also of all cases involving clergymen. Later when Henry II insisted that
clergymen accused of crimes must be tried in the royal courts, a critical struggle arose
between him and Archbishop Thomas à Becket. See below, p. 461.

THE ADVANCE
OF ROYAL
POWER

William's sons, William II, the Red (1087-1100), and Henry I, the Clerk (1100-1135), carried on the royal program of their father with such zeal and efficiency that they made themselves and the kingship unpopular, particularly with the feudal nobles and the church. The rights of the crown, especially in financial matters, were pressed to the limit. William the Red is said to have trebled his income from certain sources; and, by the same token, he stirred up bitter opposition. His chief financial expert was Bishop Ranulf, commonly referred to as "Flambard, the torch that licks up everything." Archbishop Anselm of Canterbury won not only the hatred of the red-haired king but eventual exile because of his courageous resistance to the extortionate royal levies on church property.

The reign of Henry I, who was more tactful than his brother, also saw the onward march of centralized royal power. At his accession he issued a charter in which he promised to do away with his brother's unpopular methods of government. The promises were soon forgotten, but the charter had an important bearing on the Great Charter of King John's reign, a century later. On one point of conflict, the royal control over church elections, Henry made an important compromise in order to end a longstanding dispute with the archbishop of Canterbury. Archbishop Anselm, who had been exiled by William II, refused to recognize clergymen who had received their investiture from the king. Since Henry I held to his brother's contention that lay investiture of churchmen was valid, England witnessed a struggle somewhat like that between Emperor Henry IV and Pope Gregory VII.[11]

Eventually, in 1107, Henry agreed to a compromise according to which churchmen were invested by churchmen. But the election of bishops was held in the king's presence and they took an oath of homage to the king for their lands. It is noteworthy that these same conditions were used in the compromise, made fifteen years later (in 1122), between the emperor and the pope at Worms.

This period witnessed great improvements in the machinery of royal government. The old *curia* (or council) of William the Conqueror, composed largely of feudal nobles, met less frequently. The business of government was being handled more efficiently by a group of experts—many of them clergymen trained in financial affairs.

[11] See above, pp. 385 ff.

Particular emphasis was laid on the administration of finances. The sheriffs were held strictly to account for the revenues from manors and towns. Many feudal vassals were allowed to make money payments in place of military services. The king realized that money was power, and his governmental bureaucracy was organized with that in view. In Anglo-Saxon times the royal revenue had been largely agricultural and the royal treasury was contained in a chest kept in the king's chamber. Now a specialized department of the treasury, called the Exchequer, was slowly emerging. In this, as in other respects, England's government reflected the rise of the businesslike methods of burgher society.

CIVIL WAR AND
A FEUDAL
REACTION

Feudalism, however, was far from dead. The very successes of the centralized royal bureaucracy made the feudality realize the danger and before long it found an opportunity of recovering its strength. This came about as a result of a dispute concerning Henry's successor. When his only son was drowned in a shipwreck, he insisted that his daughter Matilda should be recognized as his heir. But a nephew, Stephen of Blois (1135-1154) opposed Matilda's claims and obtained the crown. Stephen, a brave and chivalrous man, lacked kingly qualities. He was not only unable to fulfill the many rash promises by which he had won the throne, but was totally unfitted to deal with the feudal barons and with foreign invaders. Soon England learned by sad experience the chaos and disorder of unrestrained feudalism. When Matilda appeared on the scene from Normandy, she found plenty of willing supporters. The result was a long and devastating civil war.

For fifteen years the two factions fought. Eventually Matilda retired, but her energetic son, Henry, continued the fight. He had inherited most of northwestern France, including Maine, Anjou, and Normandy. To these he added an immense section of southwestern France (called Aquitaine), by a lucky marriage with Eleanor, Europe's most sought-for heiress, the divorced wife of Louis VII of France.[12] Thus when Henry invaded England in 1153 he was already ruler of most of western France. After a short struggle, Stephen agreed to recognize Henry as his successor. The fortunate young prince had not long to wait for Stephen died within a year, leaving him undisputed king of England. Henry was "heavy, bull-necked, sensual, with a square

---

[12] See below, p. 477.

jaw, freckled face, reddish hair, and fiery eyes that blazed in sudden paroxysms of anger." A man of tremendous energy and efficiency, he was a worthy descendant of William the Conqueror and the type of leader to restore the English royal power and to crush feudalism.

ADMINISTRA-
TION OF
HENRY II
When he was twenty-one Henry II (1154-1189) had possession of a realm which extended from Ireland to the Pyrenees and which presented serious problems as well as unlimited possibilities. His able and efficient handling of the situation in England gives him a high place among her kings. During the civil war the church had become independent and the great feudal barons lived like kings, each with his own castle, court, and armed retainers. Private warfare, murder, extortion and all the brutal practices of medieval gangsterism prevailed.

Henry's first task was to restore order and the royal authority. This was done by taking over all illegal (nonroyal) castles and disbanding the mercenary armies of the independent feudality. Then he set to work to rebuild the former system of bureaucratic royal administration which had been almost entirely swept away during Stephen's reign. Henry not only accomplished this but he also increased the efficiency of the central government to a point hitherto unknown in England. In order to handle the increasing volume of administrative business, the king's council (*Curia Regis*) was organized, as in Henry I's day, into special committees for special types of business. Financial affairs, for example, were assigned to a committee of financial experts. This group was known as the Exchequer because of the checkerboard table at which the members worked in checking accounts.[13] The chief of these officials was called the Chancellor of the Exchequer, a name still applied to the English secretary of the treasury.

Strictly judicial affairs were entrusted to the lawyer members of the council. Those to whom the most important cases were re-

[13] The Exchequer worked on the principle of the abacus (see above, p. 299). As the collectors turned in their revenues, the auditing officials placed counters in certain squares. These were checked against the amounts due. Even an illiterate collector could see at a glance how his account stood. For receipts, wooden sticks were notched to indicate the amounts received. Then the stick was split, one part going to the collector, the other to the checkers. This simple method was still in operation in the nineteenth century. Henry's treasurer, Richard Fitz Nigel, left to posterity and to modern historians a valuable description of medieval governmental finance, in his famous *Dialogue on the Exchequer*.

ferred were known as the Court of King's Bench, because of the official seat from which the king or his judges gave decisions. Other judges were assigned to other specialized duties, and in this manner arose the Court of Common Pleas, and the circuit justices. The circuit justices were assigned to certain circuits in which they made periodic visits to each shire for the purpose of assisting and checking the sheriffs. They settled cases that were too difficult for the sheriff, and referred matters of outstanding importance to the Court of King's Bench, the Court of Common Pleas, or the Exchequer. Thus the circuit justices functioned as connecting links between the central and the local government, much in the same manner as Charles the Great's *missi dominici*[14] and the French *bailli*.[15]

THE JURY SYS-
TEM AND THE
"COMMON LAW"

In this same connection there developed two other modern institutions: the grand and the petit jury. During Henry's reign it was the custom for the king's officials to call upon a group of dependable men in each locality to *present* (i.e., report) *upon oath,* the names of suspected criminals for trial. Therefore they were called *juries* (from the Latin, *juro,* "to take an oath") of *presentment.*[16] Today such bodies are called grand juries. As at present, the actual trial was conducted by others, usually the circuit justices. The *petit,* or *trial,* jury was a committee of jurors who told, on oath, what they knew about the case in question (usually matters of ownership of property). At first the petit jury was used only in civil cases; later it was applied to criminal cases as well. It is interesting to note that these early jurors gave the evidence, in addition to deciding the case, whereas modern jurors who have any evidence or opinion on the case are rejected.

Henry's system of royal justice was so cheap, efficient, and popular that it tended to overshadow the feudal, ecclesiastical, and local Anglo-Saxon systems of law. The people of England came to realize that they could secure a better brand of justice by appealing to the royal courts. The king, on his part, realized that courts brought in

[14] See above, p. 194.
[15] See below, p. 480.
[16] The procedure of using certain men to investigate and report on their honor concerning certain matters was an old custom, called the "sworn inquest" or "inquisition on oath." Traces of its use appear in the Theodosian code, the Carolingian *missi,* and the court procedure in William the Conqueror's Normandy and in Henry's Angevin possessions. The unique factor in Henry's England was its use for *criminal* cases. The sworn inquest also had an influence in later times on representation in parliament. See below, p. 468, note 22.

a steady stream of fees, fines, and other revenues. For this reason, rather than from any idealistic motives, Henry and his successors expanded the royal system of justice. They borrowed ideas from Anglo-Saxon law, from the new merchant courts, and from the revived Roman law that was being taught in the schools. The eventual result was a national system of law, *common* to all classes. Feudal and ecclesiastical law slowly faded into the background. So effective and progressive was the new legal system that its sphere of influence continued to expand, and a good portion of the modern legal world still relies heavily upon English *common law*.

CHURCH AND STATE

At only one point did Henry's judicial system fail: this was in his attempt to overrule the church courts. William the Conqueror had granted the clergy its own separate courts for the settlement of spiritual cases. During the civil war of Stephen's reign the church had extended its jurisdiction to the point where it denied the right of the royal courts to try or punish any clergyman even though he had violated the law of the land. Henry II, in his move for stricter law enforcement, found that "criminous clerks" (criminal clergymen) were escaping the punishment that was meted out to other criminals. He therefore demanded the right at least to supervise the trial and punishment of clergymen. But he met with obstinate resistance from Thomas à Becket, one of his former friends and courtiers whom he had made archbishop of Canterbury.

As in most of the disputes between the popes and emperors concerning the respective rights of church and state,[17] both parties stubbornly refused to yield. For six years the deadlock continued. But in 1170, during a fit of anger, Henry was heard to say, "My subjects are sluggards . . . they allow me to be made the laughing stock of a lowborn clerk." Stung by the remark, several courtiers hurried to Canterbury and, after a violent argument with Becket, murdered him in the cathedral. The unfortunate and unintended outcome of Henry's rash words defeated his cause, for Becket damaged his enemy more by his death than by his life. The king did public penance for the murder and gave up his efforts to control the clergy. For centuries thereafter English clergymen enjoyed "benefit of clergy," that is, the benefit of clerical immunity from royal justice. Meanwhile Becket had been canonized, and ever since, his grave

[17] See above, Chapter XIX.

has been the most popular miracle-working shrine in England. It was to this shrine that Chaucer's Canterbury pilgrims journeyed.

HENRY'S REBEL-
LIOUS SONS
Henry's later years were made unpopular by his efforts to extend the new royal system of government to his Continental possessions. There were revolts in Normandy and constant difficulties with his sons, Richard and John. Even Queen Eleanor took sides against Henry. His spirit was completely broken when, in 1188, Richard and John joined forces with his bitterest enemy, Philip II of France, and forced him to make humiliating concessions. He died shortly thereafter, muttering to himself, so it is said, "Shame, shame on a beaten king." Thus treacherously betrayed by his own children died one of England's greatest kings. Had he been succeeded by a son of equal ability, England might have become a unified nation and the leading state of thirteenth-century Europe. As it was, the efficient administrative machine built up by the two Henrys was used so ruthlessly and with such waste of revenues that once more the feudality took things into their own hands. This reaction, which led to the Great Charter, took place under Henry II's two sons, Richard and John.

RICHARD THE
LION-HEARTED
The romantically famous Richard the Lion-Hearted (1189-1199) played a negative role in the advancement of the English kingship. While the third crusade brought him glory, his subsequent imprisonment in Germany cost the English people a tremendous sum of money in payment of ransom. The best that can be said concerning his reign is that financial needs led him to sell innumerable charters to the rising towns of his realm, thus benefiting the English middle-class. An additional advantage was the fact that his prolonged absence (he spent only about half a year in England) left matters in the hands of his father's staff of well-trained administrators, who carried on England's government.

JOHN
John (1199-1216) was probably a man of greater political ability than Richard. His three great failures were due to his personal meanness, to bad fortune, and to the unusually formidable opponents he had to face. In personality, John had all of the vindictive cruelty and tyrannical traits of the Angevins, with none of the winning ways that saved a man like Richard from infamy. John also had the misfortune to inherit a realm that had been financially overburdened for ten years in an effort to satisfy Richard's spendthrift ways. Furthermore, in diplomatic affairs John

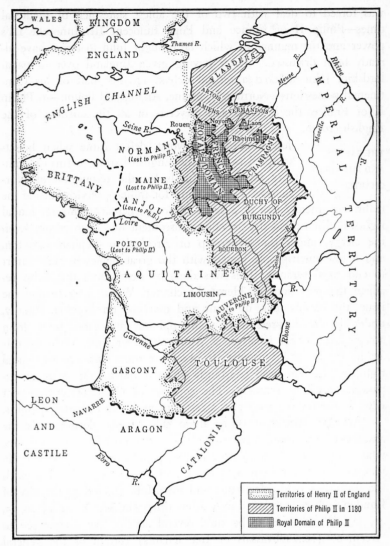

ENGLISH AND FRENCH DOMINIONS AT THE END OF THE
TWELFTH CENTURY

This was the greatest extent of English possessions on the Continent. Henry
also claimed Ireland, Scotland, and Wales as fiefs. Territories marked "Lost to
Philip II" were lost by Henry II's sons.

was forced to deal with two of the ablest statesmen of medieval times—Philip II of France and Pope Innocent III. Innocent III's power and the manner in which he brought John to terms have already been discussed.[18] After having given England over to papal lordship, John suffered a second defeat. He lost half of his Continental possessions—Normandy, Maine, Anjou, and Poitou—to Philip II of France, the bitterest and cleverest of all the enemies of the English crown.

THE BARONS
AND THE GREAT
CHARTER

John's third, and worst, defeat came when he attempted to force the English barons to furnish military forces and funds for the reconquest of Normandy. This demand for military service outside the realm was merely one of a series of royal encroachments on feudal rights, and it turned the prevailing discontent into open revolt. Even the clergy, under the leadership of Archbishop Stephen Langton, and a few townspeople joined with the great nobles in their effort to end royal tyranny. This was done by demanding that John reaffirm the provisions of Henry I's charter. When John evaded the issue, the barons took up arms and marched on London. Finally, under the double pressure of public opinion and armed force, John accepted the Great Charter, at Runnymede, in June, 1215. By this act he registered his promise to observe certain longstanding feudal rights which had been constantly violated during the years of expanding royal government. The contents of the Charter were not new. It was for the most part a restatement of older chartered rights.

Another significant thing about this famous document is the absence of provisions concerning the common folk. The peasants, who comprised the majority of the population, were specifically mentioned only once (in Article 20), and that was in connection with the fines they paid. Merchants and townsfolk (including the city of London) where mentioned only a few times (in Articles 12, 13, 20, 35, 41, 42). There were, to be sure, several articles that guaranteed to "freemen" (i.e., subvassals or free tenants) certain of the general rights that the feudal nobility enjoyed. The importance of these provisions should not, however, be overestimated. For instance, there is the all too-famous Article 39, which provided that "no freeman shall be arrested or imprisoned or deprived of his freehold, or outlawed . . . except by the legal judgment of his peers or by the law

[18] See above, pp. 400 f.

of the land." This clause did not guarantee jury trials. The "law of the land" specified other forms of criminal trial, and, furthermore, "freemen" did not include serfs. It appears that the barons insisted on this article so that they themselves might be tried in feudal rather than in royal courts. In fact, the great majority of the articles in the Charter relate to clerical and feudal rights. Prominent among these were provisions for church elections free from royal interference, for the limitation of royal exactions to a few recognized feudal payments, and so on.

The Great Charter was for the nobility, not for the common folk, and it was certainly not intended as a democratic document. It was rather an aristocratic constitution that was designed to subject the monarch to the recognized limitations of feudal government. One of its final sections (Article 61) provided for a commission of twenty-five barons who had the right to make war on the king if necessary in order to enforce the provisions of the Charter.

THE IMPOR-
TANCE OF THE
GREAT CHARTER
The Charter was, however, of tremendous importance. It was the first English charter that was extorted from an unwilling sovereign by his people. As such, it set a precedent for baronial (and later for popular) domination in government. Furthermore, it definitely established the theory that the king was not a law unto himself, but that he was subject to the law of the land. Therefore it set up the idea of a government based on constitutional authority in which the king's power was specifically limited. At that time the constitutional authority was aristocratic feudal law.

It was during the later modern era that the Charter attained its reputation as a "touchstone of *democracy*." So far as medieval England was concerned, it was the rallying point of the supporters of feudal limited monarchy in their struggle against rising royal absolutism. The Great Charter neither began nor closed the conflict between the forces of autocratic centralization and those of feudal decentralization. It did, however, mark a swing of the pendulum away from the more advanced monarchical ideal of such men as Henry II back toward the earlier regime of feudal limitations on the central government.

The immediate effects of the Charter were disappointing. It had been forced upon John, and he had no intention of observing it. Indeed many Englishmen disapproved of the revolutionary actions of the baronial leaders, who eventually went so far as to invite a

French prince to be their king when John violated the Charter. But Pope Innocent III, now John's overlord and protector, released him from the oath to uphold the Charter and excommunicated his opponents.[19] Had John not died suddenly he might have completely nullified the Charter. His son, Henry III (1216-1272), reissued it on seven different occasions, but each time in a modified form that was favorable to the royal cause. The chief effect of the Charter in the thirteenth century was the precedent it set. The feudality having once forced the king to submit to their demands would do so again if the occasion presented itself. And this is exactly what happened.

BARONIAL GOVERNMENT
Realizing that the Charter itself was becoming a dead letter, the barons set about to control the monarchy. Opportunity presented itself when Henry III's weakness and his subserviency to the pope and to foreign favorites precipitated another popular feudal revolt. Matters came to a head in 1258, when a council of barons, reinforced by representative knights from the shires, presented themselves before the king in full armor with demands for reform. The situation was less violent than that at Runnymede in 1215 but only because Henry III was a weaker king than John. He quickly agreed to allow a committee of twenty-four barons (half of whom were his appointees) to formulate a set of reform proposals.

The committee presented not only a list of grievances, but also a new scheme of central administration. A commission of fifteen barons, assisted by various other committees, was to control the entire government. This revolutionary plan, called the Provisions of Oxford, in effect overthrew royal control, substituting for it a commission form of government by the baronial oligarchy. When differences of opinion arose between the reformers—led by Simon de Montfort—and a hostile faction of conservatives, the king took immediate advantage of the situation. He allied with the conservatives and the pope. Once more a pope obligingly annulled the entire reform program, and the Montfort party was forced to fight for existence.

In an effort to win public support for his cause Montfort called in representatives from the towns, along with the knights of the shires, to deliberate with the council of barons. In 1265, however, Montfort was killed in battle and with him the baronial plan of

[19] See above, p. 401.

government collapsed. Until the death of Henry III, seven years later, Prince Edward was the dominating force in the government. The well-meant but unenforceable program of the Montfort reformers was set aside and royal control was restored. Fortunately, however, Edward had the wisdom to abide by the fundamental principles of the Great Charter and to do away with many of the grievances that had aroused the followers of Montfort.

EDWARD I AND PARLIAMENTARY GOVERNMENT
With the reign of Edward I (1272-1307) it can be said that England attained a happy medium between the extremes of royal autocracy and feudal oligarchy. The reign of John had witnessed the collapse of autocratic government. The experiment of Simon de Montfort and his feudal supporters showed the impracticability of a baronial commission government. In the course of his long reign, Edward I tended to a middle course, and his government, partaking of the best points of each, was in a sense a partnership of king and barons. To be sure, he extorted funds unjustly from his subjects at times, and on one occasion (1297) the barons came armed to parliament to insist on the "Confirmation of the Charters," with additional guarantees against irregular taxes "except by the common consent of the realm." [20] In general, however, Edward governed with the co-operation and approval of the nobles in parliament.

But, what was this institution (parliament) which acquired such sudden prominence? Although the name parliament was new,[21] the institution was in a sense an evolution from the ancient advisory bodies of the Anglo-Saxon and Norman kings. The Witenagemot and the Great Council were essentially feudal *curias,* consisting of the king's chief vassals, assembled to assist him in governmental

---

[20] It was during this crisis that a famous event occurred which vividly illustrates the clash of feudal and royal interests and the boldness of the English barons in defending their rights. A certain earl named Bigod had refused to do military service overseas (in France) on the ground that it was outside the English realm and therefore illegal. In a rage, Edward shouted, "By God, Sir Earl, you shall either go or hang," to which the Earl stoutly replied, "By God, O king, I shall neither go nor hang." The Earl was right, the law upheld his contention, and like most English kings of this period, Edward decided to observe the law of the land.

[21] The name *parliament* comes from the French word *parler* ("to talk"). All through the West during the thirteenth century it was used to designate conferences, discussions, assemblies, and, in a more restricted way, the general, open sessions of the king's court (*Curia*) or council. In France, for instance, *parlement* was the name for the judicial sessions of the king's court. In Italian cities, on the other hand, a mass meeting of the populace in the town square was called a *parlemento*. In England the name came to be used for the enlarged sessions of the royal council.

affairs. As such they were composed of the higher nobles, church-men, and royal officials. Later, with the addition of representatives of the lesser vassals, these advisory councils became "parleys." Parliament cannot be said to have actually come into being until the feudal council had become a national council or assembly which (1) was truly representative of the leading classes and sections of the realm (i.e., of the clergy, barons, knights, and townsfolk) and (2) which met with some regularity. The Anglo-Saxon and Norman councils met regularly, but they were not truly representative. The assemblies of the early thirteenth century had wider representation, but did not meet regularly. For instance, the meeting of barons, knights of the shire, and townsfolk called by Simon de Montfort in 1265 was merely a mass meeting of his partisans. It comprised, however, representatives from the various sections (shires) of the realm and it has been called "England's first parliament." Nevertheless it was merely one of many irregular forerunners of the actual parliamentary institution.

It seems that the first "parley" at which all of the important classes of society and all of the shires were represented was Edward's so-called "Model Parliament" of 1295.[22] Even though this "model," which included knights from the shires and townsmen, was often disregarded in the later assemblies of his reign, during the next few years Edward I established the custom of holding relatively representative meetings with relative regularity. Under his successors, parliament gradually divided into two houses: the feudal aristocracy, including the higher clergy and barons, in the House of Lords; the representatives of the shires and the towns, in the House of Commons. In general parliament was fairly well established by the end of the royal baronial struggles of the thirteenth and early fourteenth centuries. In succeeding centuries it was to extend its influence to an astonishing degree. It should be noted, however, that the parliament of medieval times was unlike its modern successor in many respects. The so-called House of *Commons* was neither composed nor representative of the *common people*. In fact, until the nineteenth century it was actually a house of lesser nobles and wealthy merchants.

Parliament marks the increased activity of the upper and mid-

---

[22] In the early days of parliament, the knights of the shire were very important. In fact, according to some modern scholars, parliament came into being as a result of the king's plan to mobilize the shire representatives at the meetings of his council, so as to avoid making separate inquests in each shire.

dle classes of English society in solving the problems of central government. By such processes the people of the various parts of the realm were welded into a national unit under a co-operative form of government. As we have seen, this was the culmination of centuries of experience in avoiding the opposite extremes of feudal anarchy and royal tyranny. William the Conqueror had an efficient centralized government in which feudalism was held in check by an unusually strong king. But his successors carried the ideal of contralized monarchy to excesses of personal tyranny. During the subsequent era of discontent, England went to the other extreme—baronial domination.

Finally, late in the thirteenth century, a compromise was effected. The institutions of centralized royal government continued to function, but they were supplemented by a parliament of churchmen, feudal nobles, shire representatives, and townsmen. This served not only as an effective aid to royal government but also as a check against tyranny. This fundamental principle of English government, and, along with it, the beginnings of the English nation of modern times, was apparent by the end of the age of Edward I, who has been called "England's first national monarch."

ENGLISH TERRITORIAL EXPANSION

The reign of Edward I saw not only the emergence of a national government but also a remarkable expansion of the English realm. Edward, the successor of a series of kings who had lost territory, spent a quarter of a century in wars which added territory and paved the way for further expansion in later centuries.

WALES
On the western frontier, the Welsh had taken advantage of the baronial revolts of the reigns of John and Henry III to make themselves practically independent. Edward put in five years (1277-1282) of active campaigning in that mountainous region, and, after the death of the native prince, Llywelyn, he was able to subjugate the Welsh people. Wales was eventually divided into shires and organized as an integral part of England. In 1284, when a royal prince was born at Carnarvon Castle in Wales, Edward christened him the "Prince of Wales," thus establishing the title that is still borne by the heir to the English throne.

SCOTLAND
Soon thereafter Edward found occasion to interfere in Scotch affairs. When King Alexander III died, Edward, as overlord of Scotland, assumed the right of deciding be-

ENGLAND IN THE AGE OF EDWARD I
With dates of important conquests

Within the map:

SCOTLAND
(Conquered 1296,
lost 1314)

NORTH

SEA

×Bannockburn
○Edinburgh

IRELAND
(1154-1172)

IRISH SEA

○Dublin

K. OF

WALES
(1277-1282)

ENGLAND

London

ENGLISH CHANNEL

Kingdom at begining of Edward I's reign

tween several claimants to the throne. But scarcely had the new Scotch king, John Baliol, been crowned when he began to resist the demands of his ambitious English overlord. When Edward proceeded to dethrone him and to annex Scotland, there ensued a fierce revolt which finally became a heroic war for Scotch independence. William Wallace, leader of the rebels, was defeated, captured, and executed as a traitor. His place was taken by the famous Robert Bruce, Scotland's "George Washington." Edward died in the midst of preparations for a campaign by which he hoped to crush once and for all the stubborn Scotch rebels. Seven years later, in 1314, his son Edward II with a formidable army invaded Scotland only to meet with a crushing defeat at Bannockburn.

Although Edward and his successors refused to recognize the independence of Scotland, they were never able to enforce their authority in that land. Throughout the Hundred Years' War,[23] and until the union of the two realms in the person of the Scotch king, James VI (in 1603), Scotland was an active ally of France, England's bitterest enemy.

In Ireland and Aquitaine, Edward I had better success. Although he made no territorial gains, these regions were kept closely under English control. In Flanders also, and along the Channel coasts, Edward's forces held their own against the French. Edward's reign ended with the English nation firmly united and well prepared for the renewal of warfare with France over England's Continental possessions.

ENGLISH NATIONALISM

In our brief survey of English history from Alfred to Edward we have seen the birth and early development of a nation. Through periods of fierce Danish invasion, through the Norman Conquest, feudal anarchy, and royal despotism, peoples of different races and cultures were gradually welded into a more or less homogeneous unit, proud of its king, its parliament, and of the fact that it was English. Edward I's England was not the feudal England of William the Conqueror's time. It was in process of becoming a modern nation with a centralized government and a consciousness of its identity.

[23] See below, Chapter XXIX.

$=$ XXIV $=$

THE BIRTH OF MODERN NATIONS: FRANCE, AND THE IBERIAN PENINSULA

FRANCE

ON the Continent the formation of national states began later than in England. In the Germanies and Italies and in France, national unification had two formidable obstacles. On the one hand, as in England, was the existing feudal structure. On the other, was the ghost of Roman imperial unity which haunted Continental Europe throughout medieval times. The attempts of the Carolingians, the German Ottos and the Hohenstaufen Fredericks to regiment the West into a revived Roman Empire were as hostile to nationalism as was the independent localism of the feudal lords. After the fifth century England was free from Roman imperial influences. The Germanies and Italies, on the contrary, were unable to shake off the dead weight of the Holy Roman Empire until modern times.

French nationalism was afflicted equally by imperial and feudal ambitions. Until late in the tenth century the descendants of Charles the Great sought to control the destinies of France by right of their Carolingian imperial inheritance. By the time they had passed from the scene the unity of Charles the Great's empire had vanished. France was a conglomeration of many independent warring feudal principalities. It has been estimated that in 900, just a century after Charles the Great was crowned emperor, there were six kings in various parts of France. In addition to the rival Carolingian and Capetian kings in the region of Paris, there was an independent king in Aquitaine, a King Sancho of Navarre in the Pyrenees, and King Bozo and King Rudolph of Lower and Upper Burgundy. In addition to these so-called kings, there were hundreds of feudal princes.

France, during the early Middle Ages, was caught between the hammer and the anvil. There was no opportunity for national unity to develop so long as the feudality was tearing to pieces the remnants of Charles the Great's empire. Moreover, for a time the Norse invaders brought fire and the sword to most of the coastal regions. Thus, within a century after the death of Charles, centralized government in France had completely disappeared.

FEUDAL DIS-
UNITY IN
FRANCE
Many scholars consider France to have been the most completely feudalized region in Europe. Throughout the tenth century the weak Carolingian successors of Charles the Great fought with their Capetian rivals—Count Odo of Paris and Duke Hugh of Francia—for the empty title of king. Meanwhile the outlying regions were following the trend of the times, and independent feudal kingdoms and duchies were taking shape. North of Paris, along the coast near the Strait of Dover, the counts of Flanders assumed control and built up a formidable feudal state. Baldwin Iron-Arm and his successors combined military ability with statesmanship and laid the foundation for the agricultural and industrial prosperity of the Netherlands.

Further to the south, by the year 911, Rollo the Norseman had taken possession of the Channel coast at the mouth of the Seine River and had forced the "King of France" to recognize him as duke of Normandy. So effective was the Norman government and so rapid the development of agriculture and commerce in this region that the duke was envied and feared by all his neighbors. In battle the stout Norman warriors defeated all who opposed them, even their overlord, the Capetian king of France. During the century and a half from Rollo to William, the conqueror of England, the dukes of Normandy became an outstanding feudal power on the Continent and a constant problem to the French kingship. South and west of Normandy was the rocky peninsula of Brittany, another practically independent feudal realm. Its Celtic people, many of them hardy fishermen, were rough and warlike. Not even the neighboring dukes of Normandy could subject them to their authority.

To the south of Normandy and Brittany across the Loire River was a series of three great feudal domains that were practically independent, despite the fact that they acknowledged the vague overlordship of the king of France. One who traveled from the Loire to the Pyrenees would pass through Poitou, Aquitaine, and Gascony. In the ninth century the duke of Aquitaine assumed the title of king in these regions. Later the three duchies and many lesser domains in the Garonne-Gironde valleys came under the control of the feudal rulers of Poitou. Throughout the Middle Ages this great stretch of fertile land, commonly referred to as Aquitaine and comprising most of southwestern France, was an important factor in French, and English, history.

Swinging round the circle to the east, one would traverse the county of Toulouse lying between Gascony and the Rhone River. The Rhone Valley, comprising several territories known as the Burgundies, was claimed by the German emperors, but the portion to the north was known as the French duchy of Burgundy. It controlled portions of the upper basins of three important French rivers—the Saône-Rhone, the Loire, and the Seine—and it touched on the southeastern frontier of Francia, the central domain of the Capetian kings. Because Burgundy dominated the royal gateway from Paris to the Rhone Valley and thence to Italy, the Capetians strove to keep it under control. The dukes of Burgundy were usually brothers or near relatives of the French king. With the county of Champagne, to the east and northeast of Francia, we complete our survey of the great feudal domains surrounding the Capetian kingdom of Paris. No further evidence than the foregoing is necessary to illustrate the backwardness of the royal power and the lack of national unity in "the Frances" at the accession of Hugh Capet in 987.

THE CAPETIAN FEUDAL CONFEDERATION

Hugh is often hailed as the first king of France, but in reality he was a great feudal lord, like his father before him, and like the neighboring dukes and counts. His reign is, however, of importance because of the fact that he bore the royal title. Furthermore his accession ended the Capetian-Carolingian contest over the kingship and started the dukes of Francia on the long upward climb from feudal to royal power. It took three centuries of struggle for the Capetian dukes to become real kings of France and for the many feudal domains to become welded into a centralized monarchical state. The process by which this was accomplished was similar to that which united England. The final outcome, however, was somewhat different.

At the outset, in the tenth and eleventh centuries, the slowly emerging town and church life of France called for modifications in the prevailingly feudal methods of government. Those rulers who were progressive, and improved their governmental administration in keeping with changing economic and social conditions, prospered.

Their governments became less feudal, more practical, and more centralized. This marks the first trend toward the modern national state. Among the most progressive of French rulers were the dukes of Normandy and the dukes of Francia. As a consequence of the Norman Conquest one of these dynasties came to rule England; the other became the dominant power in France. In discussing the Capetians and their evolution from dukes of Francia to kings of France we shall emphasize (1) the increasing extent of territory over which they ruled, and (2) the increasingly efficient methods of government by which they ruled.

SOURCES OF ROYAL POWER Hugh Capet, like his ancestor, Odo of Paris, enjoyed a slight advantage over the other French dukes in that he was the regularly elected and God-appointed "king of the Franks, Flemish, Bretons, Aquitanians, Burgundians, and Gascons." Even so, Hugh's kingship was far from real, and he was only king in name. He had no real power in the great duchies and counties. Over most of the realm now known as France he merely reigned. He actually ruled only in his own small Parisian duchy—Francia. Even here he ruled by reason of his strength as a feudal lord rather than because of his royal title. The history of medieval France was to see the extension of Capetian rule from this central duchy into all of the feudal regions that had joined in Hugh's election.

During his short reign of nine years, Hugh made little attempt to exert royal authority outside the duchy of Francia. He did, however, end all uncertainty as to the royal succession by having his son Robert crowned and associated with him as co-king. This custom was continued by the Capetians, and for three centuries there were no royal elections in France. The kingship passed automatically to the oldest son of the monarch, and not once did the dynasty lack a prince to inherit the crown. "The king is dead, long live the king" was a reality from Hugh's accession to the death of Philip IV in 1314. Thus the Capetians enjoyed the prestige that went with royalty. Of great importance also is the fact that they were long-lived. Not all of Hugh's successors were powerful, but most of them reigned for long periods of time. Hugh was king for only nine years, but the next ten Capetians ruled for thirty-five, twenty-nine, forty-eight, twenty-nine, forty-three, forty-three, three, forty-four, fifteen, and twenty-nine years respectively.

The first four Capetians—Hugh (987-996), Robert the Pious (996-1031), Henry I (1031-1060), and Philip I (1060-1108)—accomplished little either to increase their powers or to extend their domains. None of them had any real authority outside of the duchy of Francia. Great nobles, such as the dukes of Aquitaine, defied the king with impunity. On more than one occasion the dukes of Normandy took up arms and gave their lord king a sound drubbing. As a matter of necessity, the early Capetians allowed matters to take their own course in Flanders, Champagne, the Burgundies, Auvergne, Toulouse, Gascony, Aquitaine, Maine, Anjou, Brittany, Normandy, and the minor feudal domains.

An encouraging factor was the church's support of the dynasty. Hugh had been elected very largely by means of the influence of such friendly churchmen as the archbishop of Rheims. Recognizing the importance of clerical supporters, Hugh and his pious son Robert assiduously cultivated them. They also placed their friends in important church positions, and Hugh, it is said, came to control the appointment of about one-third of the bishops of France. He himself was ex officio abbot of the wealthy monastery of St. Denis, near Paris. In 1049, when Pope Leo IX came to France to reform clerical conditions,[1] King Henry I had sufficient influence over the local clergy to keep many of the bishops from attending the council called by the pope. The members of the French clergy worked hand in hand with their king—to the mutual profit of both. Not only troublesome barons but hostile popes were compelled to realize that the French churchmen would stand by their king. This in itself was an important factor in the expansion of Capetian royal power.

Another element of the French population that entered into a profitable union with the monarchy was the townsfolk. By the middle of the eleventh century the burgher class had begun to assume a position of financial importance. When clerical or baronial rulers refused to grant or sell rights to their townspeople, violent revolts sometimes occurred. Quite early the French kings took advantage of this situation. They not only granted charters to towns on their own domains; they even encouraged the revolts of townsfolk in the realms of the feudal lords. Obviously any weakening of baronial power increased the strength of the king. Gradually the kings came to use

[1] See above, p. 380.

townsmen, as well as churchmen, to undermine feudal government and to centralize authority in their own hands.

CAPETIAN
EXPANSION:
LOUIS VI

Louis VI (1108-1137) came to the throne with over a century of royal tradition behind him. Louis, who was called "the Fighter" in his younger days, and "the Fat" in his old age,[2] did very little to extend the royal domain, but he established the royal power within the duchy of Francia. He well earned his title "the Fighter" by his successful subjugation of the feudal nobles in the region around Paris. In only one of his projects was Louis destined to fail, and that through no fault of his own. Some time before his death he arranged for the marriage of his son, Prince Louis, to Eleanor, heiress of the extensive Aquitanian lands in southwestern France. Thus, without a blow, the Capetian dynasty might have gained permanent possession of a feudal domain many times as large as its own duchy.

Had the young Louis VII (1137-1180) retained this territory, the French kings would have been well on the way toward the territorial unification of France. But Louis, unable to get on with his frivolous young wife, divorced her. Eleanor's lands went with her hand, and soon she, and the great realm of Aquitaine, were wedded to Louis's most dangerous enemy—Henry II of Normandy and England.[3] Perhaps the best that can be said for Louis VII is that he had a remarkable son, Philip II.

PHILIP II "THE
CONQUEROR"
(1180-1223)

Philip is as important in the evolution of royal power in France as Henry II is in the rise of the English monarchy. Yet Philip and his burly rival were opposites in personality. Philip was not a heroic figure. Bald, physically weak, and nervously high-strung, nevertheless he worked wonders for France. He managed to win from Henry II, Richard, and John half of their French possessions and to create a real French monarchy. It was under him that the French monarchy made its first notable gains in territory and power. This was due, first to the solid foundations laid by Louis VI, and second to Philip's exceptional ability and constant application to the business of being king. For example, in an age of crusades he wasted little time crusading. Although forced by circumstances to accompany Richard the Lion-Hearted on the third crusade,[4] he returned home at the first op-

---

[2] Eventually Louis put on so much weight that he was unable to mount his horse.
[3] See above, p. 458.
[4] See below, p. 518 f.

WALES
KINGDOM
OF
ENGLAND
Thames R.

ENGLISH CHANNEL
FLANDERS
IMPERIAL TERRITORY
ARTOIS
AMIENS VERMANDOIS
Laon
Noyon
Rheims
NORMANDY
Paris
CHAMPAGNE
(1283)
BRITTANY
(Claimed by England)
MAINE
Loire R.
Orleans
BLOIS
ANJOU
BERRY
DUCHY OF
BURGUNDY
CO. OF BURGUNDY
(1300-1363)
POITOU
BOURBON
AUVERGNE
Garonne R.
Saône R.
ENGLISH
Dordogne
Bordeaux
AQUITAINE
Rhône
Moselle R.
Meuse R.
Rhine R.
TERRITORY
TOULOUSE
(1223-1271)
PROVENCE
GASCONY
LEON
NAVARRE
AND
ARAGON
CASTILE
CATALONIA
Ebro R.

Royal Domain at the accession
of Philip II, 1180

Regions annexed to Royal Domain
by Philip II and Louis VIII

THE GROWTH OF THE FRENCH ROYAL DOMAIN IN THE
THIRTEENTH CENTURY

Dates indicate feudal territories annexed before 1300

portunity to build up his own royal power by undermining that of Richard.

Philip's first successes were the acquisition of certain feudal territories—Artois, Amiens, Vermandois, and Valois—by means of which the Capetian realm was extended northward to the Flemish frontier. Later, by conquering Normandy and the Loire basin (including Anjou, Maine, Touraine, and Poitou), he extended his domains westward to the Atlantic.

The acquisition of these territories, which comprised over half of the English possessions on the Continent, was the culmination of long years of intrigue. It seems that during the later years of Henry II, Philip had encouraged and profited by the revolts of Richard and John against their father. After Richard had become king and had gone to the Holy Land, Philip plotted with John against his royal brother. When John came to the throne, Philip worked to undermine his power. Philip's opportunity came when John, who was his vassal, was summoned to appear before his feudal court to answer criminal charges. John's refusal gave Philip the legal right to confiscate all the fiefs which John held from him. As a consequence of this, and of John's growing unpopularity, Philip was able to take possession of practically all of northwestern France.

But the tale of international intrigue does not end here. John kept up the struggle. About ten years later, in alliance with two of Philip's Continental rivals—Emperor Otto of Brunswick and the Count of Flanders—he launched against France a double invasion, from the north and the south. At Bouvines, in 1214, Philip won a brilliant victory which has been called the most decisive battle of medieval history because of its consequences. It gave Philip permanent possession of his recent conquests and greatly enhanced his reputation throughout Europe. It is important to note that he relied heavily on the French townsmen for financial and military assistance in this critical battle. Elsewhere also, the victory had momentous consequences. The defeat of Otto of Brunswick led to the recognition of Philip's ally, Frederick II, as emperor.[5] As an indirect result of the battle, the English barons forced King John to sign the Great Charter.

[5] See above, p. 400.

THE INCREASE
OF ROYAL
POWER

Of equal importance with Philip's expansion of the royal domain was his expansion of the royal power. In order to control effectively a realm that had trebled in size, he developed a more centralized system of government. The French kings had already been accustomed to manage the outlying portions of their domain by means of royally appointed officials called *prévôts* (provosts).[6] During Philip's reign so many new territories were added that the number of *prévôts* had increased to seventy or more. In order to oversee the *prévôts* and keep them under effective royal supervision, Philip instituted a staff of salaried officials, called *bailli* (or bailiffs), each of whom controlled a group of *prévôts*. The *bailli*, much like the *missi* of Charles the Great and the circuit justices of Henry II, were royal inspectors and adjusters of judicial, financial, and other administrative affairs. They saw to it that the various revenues of the king were collected, and that the royal rights were enforced, especially with respect to the local feudality with whom the *prévôts* were inclined to be overly sympathetic. In matters of justice the *bailli* extended the jurisdiction of the king by encouraging appeals from the feudal courts to those of the king. They also had charge of the royal military levies from the feudal vassals and towns of the district, supervised roads and bridges, and forwarded the king's interests in innumerable other ways.

INSTITUTIONS OF
CENTRALIZED
GOVERNMENT

The *bailli*, and also the seneschals, who played a similar role in the southern territories that were acquired later, mark the evolution from localized government by the king's feudal vassals to a more closely integrated administration by royal officials. Under Philip and his successors steady progress was made in extending the royal authority into all parts of the realm, and in co-ordinating local government with the central administration. The consequent increase of the financial, judicial, and general administrative functions of the king's central court led to noteworthy changes in the central governmental institutions. At the royal court, as in the local administration, the feudal customs and functions of earlier days gave way to more efficient types of organization. The king's court became less of an assemblage of great feudal vassals and more of an administrative staff of trained and trusted royal officials.

Gradually the king surrounded himself with able clerical ad-

---

[6] Compare the *prévôts* with the English sheriffs, above, p. 452, and with the Carolingian counts, above, p. 193.

visers, faithful supporters from the lesser nobility, lawyers trained in the principles of Roman law, and burgher businessmen. Special kinds of business were assigned to those of the court who were familiar with such affairs; thus there developed groups of expert advisers and administrators. Among these was a special commission for financial matters, and another for cases at law. As in England, these commissions eventually became permanent departments of government, such as the *Parlement* (a supreme court of justice), the Chamber of Accounts (for finances), and an inner advisory group called the Royal or Privy Council. These later developments came under Philip's successors.

Although the first important steps in the administrative organization of local and central government seem to have come during the reign of Philip II, this development cannot be attributed to any one monarch. The new institutions of royal government evolved slowly, first out of the efforts of earlier kings to organize effectively their feudal resources. Later, under certain of Philip's successors whom we shall have occasion to mention, these institutions assumed more highly specialized forms and functions. In this administrative evolution the reign of Philip II is nevertheless of great importance because the unusual amount of territory added to the royal domain forced the rapid expansion of the machinery of central and local government. New territories created new fiscal opportunities and problems. There were increased feudal dues, fees and fines from courts, commercial and industrial revenues from towns, loans, gifts, and innumerable other types of income to be collected, audited, and expended. There was also the expanded royal coinage, which Philip made legal throughout all his realms, both old and new. Increased levies for the army, now composed of mercenary troops and town militias as well as mounted feudal vassals, necessitated a centralized military organization. These, and many other problems of similar import, forced the king and his counselors to concentrate their attention on the improvement of the royal administrative service. Henceforth the older methods and personnel of feudal government tended to give way rapidly to the more businesslike regime of centralized absolutism.

IMPORTANCE OF PHILIP'S REIGN

Philip II's successes in governmental administration were largely due to concentration of effort. Restricting his activities for the most part to northern France, he refused to be drawn into distant undertakings. He avoided crusades after one brief experience in 1189. He even rejected the tempting papal appeal to lead a crusade against the Albigensian heretics in southern France.[7] After the French barons, under the crusading banner of Simon de Montfort the Elder, had ravaged these regions, many of the inhabitants appealed to Philip for protection. Finally, in order to safeguard his royal interests in the south, he sent an army. Later his son, Louis VIII (1223-1226), reaped the harvest by annexing Auvergne and other territories in southeastern France.

Philip's long and effective reign started France on the high road to national unity and strength under royal leadership. With almost no setbacks he built up the territorial domain and bureaucratic power of the Capetian monarchy. Only once, when excommunicated by Innocent III for putting away his Danish wife, did Philip suffer defeat.[8] And in this case his submission was to the will of the nation rather than to the command of the pope.

LEGAL DEVEL-
OPMENTS:
LOUIS IX

After the three-year reign of Philip's son, Louis VIII, the destinies of France passed into the hands of Louis IX (1226-1270), often called "the Saint" because of his sincere piety. His achievements were unspectacular but marvelously effective in strengthening the kingship. During his minority (1226-1234), his mother, Blanche of Castile, broke up a formidable coalition of feudal barons, thus paving the way for his peaceful accession to the royal throne in 1234. For some time thereafter, the nobles caused trouble, but the young king's position was never seriously threatened. With the exception of two disastrous crusading ventures, Louis proved himself an able monarch.[9] His most noteworthy contribution to the Capetian royal power was in judicial affairs, and his legal ability and accomplishments won for him the title of "the French Justinian." Like the great English king, Henry II, and like his predecessor, Philip II, he worked constantly to bring the feudality under the jurisdiction of the royal courts. He forced the nobility to recognize the right of their own vassals to appeal to the royal courts in certain "royal cases." When his brother, the powerful Count of Anjou, objected to an appeal to the king's court, Louis replied, "I will have but one king in France."

[7] See above, p. 444.
[8] See above, p. 400.
[9] In 1248 Louis led an expedition to Egypt, for the recapture of the Holy Land. It ended in disaster, with the king held captive by the Moslems. An immense sum had to be raised to ransom him. Equally futile was his effort (in 1270) to win Tunis in Northern Africa. He died there, as a result of a plague. One of the most sincere crusaders, Louis was also one of the least successful.

In the long run the fair-mindedness of both Louis and his judges in deciding cases resulted in a tremendous increase in the reputation of the royal tribunals. The nation soon learned that these courts meted out justice even against the great feudal nobles. As a result of the number of cases which came before the king and his lawyers, a permanent committee of legal experts was established at Paris. This body, called the Parlement of Paris, became the supreme court of France. The influence of the Parlement and Louis's personal interest in justice resulted in further efforts at the extension of legal methods of procedure. Trials by combat were replaced by decisions based on evidence obtained by inquests.[10] The earlier prohibitions against private wars for the settlement of feudal rivalries were more rigorously enforced. Louis acquired such a reputation for justice that he was frequently called upon to arbitrate cases in foreign countries.[11]

In his dealings with the communes and with heretics Louis's fair-mindedness is not so evident. Although he was the soul of justice in dealing with his lowliest subjects, he insisted that laymen should not discuss religion with Jews and heretics but should rather "defend the Christian faith with a good sharp sword." Blasphemers were punished by having their tongues pierced with a hot iron. So far as the towns were concerned, the king kept them under close supervision, subjecting them rigorously to the jurisdiction of the royal courts. Free communes were to him as dangerous as independent nobles, and he put a stop to the process of enfranchisement of towns. But royal favor was extended to the good and obedient royal towns. Trade and industry were carefully regulated for their prosperity, and thus for the king's profit. In like manner, Louis took care of his own interests when he freed thousands of serfs on the royal domains. Their enfranchisement fees contributed a handsome sum to the king's treasury. Many of Louis's reforms indicate this same practical type of altruism. In keeping with the traditional Capetian policy, able clerics and businessmen found profitable employment in the governmental service. Like their English rivals, the Capetian kings were building a centralized bureaucracy that, by its sheer efficiency, soon eclipsed feudal government and strengthened the monarchy.

10 See above, p. 460, note 16.

11 During the struggle between King Henry III of England and the Montfort faction of baronial reformers, Louis was called upon to arbitrate a disputed point of law. Needless to say, he decided in favor of the king.

PHILIP III
AND IV

Louis's son, Philip III (1270-1285), reaped much of the fruit of his father's wise reign. As certain feudal dynasties died out, several territories (notably Toulouse) were added to the royal domain. Capetian France had now expanded southward to the Mediterranean and the Pyrenees. Of the major regions of France, only Aquitaine in the southwest, Provence in the southeast, Brittany in the west, and Flanders in the north were still outside the royal realm. Territorially France was rapidly becoming the modern state with which we are familiar today. At the same time entire regions were assigned to the younger princes of the royal family. These grants, called *appanages,* resulted in a new group of feudal states controlled by the king's relatives. In later times, after the monarchy had crushed the power of the older feudal lords, its security was endangered by the ambitions of the houses of Anjou, Orléans, and Burgundy, which had originated as royal appanages.

The reign of Philip IV (1285-1314) was a fitting climax to the first three centuries of Capetian rule. He had planned to round out the royal domain by attacking Aquitaine and Flanders. After several victories over Edward I, who was ruler of Aquitaine as well as of England, Philip made a compromise by which he acquired Flanders. Not until the end of the Hundred Years' War, a century and a half later,[12] was Aquitaine annexed to the French realm.

PHILIP IV'S
FINANCIAL
POLICIES

The internal affairs of Philip's reign reflect the power rather than the wisdom of French absolute monarchy. Constant wars, salaries for an ever-increasing civil service, higher standards of living, and outright extravagance kept the royal treasury in constant need. The effective governmental machinery, comprising *prévôts, bailli,* and central administrative officials, enabled Philip to increase his income almost at will, but in the long run the methods used brought unfortunate results.

Towns, guilds, and peasants were not only heavily taxed but were subjected to the exploitation of tax farmers—private individuals who bid for the right to collect the tax. Then there were heavy sales taxes (*gabelles*). These, it is thought by some scholars, ruined many legitimate business enterprises, such as the prosperous fairs of Champagne. Thus Philip destroyed revenue-producing institutions that had been fostered by wiser rulers. The wealth of the Jews and of Lombard money changers was practically confiscated, thus crippling trade and

[12] See below, Chapter XXIX.

banking. Constant debasing of the coinage upset commerce. Excessive taxes on the thriving textile towns of Flanders drove this newly acquired province to the point of revolt. The heavy duties levied on Flemish imports of wool from England brought on war with Edward I.[13]

As we shall see in another connection, Philip's efforts to extort money from the clergy led to a critical struggle with the pope.[14] His financial needs also led to the abolition of the order of Knights Templars, an incident which reflected little credit upon Philip's integrity.[15] More praiseworthy were his successes in standardizing feudal revenues. Irregular payments were regularized so as to become the equivalent of taxes. Where possible, feudal services were changed to payments of money. Everywhere the king's agents exploited new and old sources of financial income so as to provide unfailing streams of revenue for the insatiable royal treasury.

It should be remembered, however, that Philip's arbitrary financial policies were no different from those of other rulers of his day. Everywhere governmental activities and needs were increasing. Governments levied taxes right and left in order to increase their revenues. As in all eras of economic transition, experimentation was inevitable, and maladjustments could not be avoided. The autocratic nature of Capetian royal power, however, accentuated the financial evils in France.[16] The English, as we have seen, kept a more effective check on their kings.

FRANCE'S FIRST ABSOLUTE MONARCH The strength of French royal government lay in the well-organized machinery of the central administration. We have already noted that, as early as the reign of Philip II (1180-1223), the royal *curia* of feudal nobles had begun to give way to a group of expert administrators: businessmen, clergymen, and lawyers. By the time of Philip IV the *curia* had been replaced by three commissions of specialists. One section, called the *Chamber of Accounts* (like the English Exchequer), handled the royal finances. Another, called the *Parlement*, which resembled the English Court of King's Bench, handled the ever-increasing appeals from local or feudal courts. A third body, the *Privy*

---

[13] See below, p. 583.
[14] See below, p. 558.
[15] See below, p. 561.
[16] The same is true of the papal finances of this period. Boniface VIII and his autocratic successors had an unenviable record of ruthless financial exactions. See below, p. 563.

Council, which was much like the English Royal Council, gave the king counsel on affairs of state. Policies were proposed, decided, and carried out almost entirely by the king's administrative councils. These were composed of highly trained royal servants chosen from the ranks of the clergy, the legal profession, and the middle class of businessmen. The king was no longer dependent on the services of the feudal nobility in governmental administration.

Despot though he was, Philip was the creator of an important representative institution, the Estates-General, or national assembly. When he was in the midst of a struggle with the pope in 1302, he summoned representatives from the towns to join with the clergy and nobility in France's first Estates-General. Similar assemblies were held on two other occasions, one of them for the purpose of voting funds for a war. Like the English parliament, the Estates-General was an outgrowth of the feudal practice of calling together vassals for aid and counsel. The unique factor was the concentration of so many vassals, and the inclusion of town representatives. As in the case of the English parliaments, their presence can be explained by the fact that towns were royal vassals and therefore subject to a royal summons. Furthermore, at this time, because of their extensive financial resources, they were very important vassals. By contrast, the poor, unorganized peasants were unrepresented.

As for the townsfolk, Philip consulted with them separately, as well as in the Estates-General. Toward the end of his reign, when discontent over royal taxation had driven some of the burghers into an alliance with the nobility, he called together the representatives of the towns and promised to redress their grievances. It was on the petition of the townsfolk that he continued his prohibition of local coinage and other feudal practices.

It is obvious that, even though Philip was absolute, he was attentive to public opinion—clerical, noble, and burgher. The "third estate" of France, like the "commons" of England, was represented in both local and national assemblies. In many respects the French Estates-General of 1302 was quite similar to the English "Model Parliament" of 1295 and other such representative bodies of late medieval times. The difference lay in the fact that the French Estates-General became more and more subservient to the will of an autocratic king. Never did the French estates develop the unity, regularity of action, and aggressiveness of the English parliaments. The Estates-General met and adjourned at the command of a monarch who merely chose, on occasion, to consult it. Even though Philip called into being the Estates-General, it was his reign that marked the coming of absolute monarchy in France.

Thus, under somewhat similar circumstances, both the English and French monarchs triumphed over feudalism. In the meantime, however, they worked out different systems of national administration. The English nation supported a central government in which king and parliament were partners. The French people, throughout most of their history, have looked upon their kings as the undisputed masters of the central administration.

THE IBERIAN PENINSULA: PORTUGAL, CASTILE, AND ARAGON

Although the Spanish countries have never been one united nation, their history during the Middle Ages illustrates the development of royal government and nationalism. Unlike nationalism in England or France, that of Spain is the nationalism of several small nations. The beginnings of modern Portugal, Castilian Spain, and Catalonia-Aragon go back to medieval times just as surely as does French or English national history. Their history is, however, much more complex and intricate than that of France or England.

Modern Spain is usually considered to be a merger of two states: Castile, comprising the great central plateau and most of the southern part of the peninsula; and Aragon, comprising the triangular northeastern region along the Mediterranean. But historically each of these was itself a merger of several states. What we now think of as Castile was originally Asturias, or Leon, a north-Spanish mountain state. As the Spanish Christians expanded southward into Moslem territory, a frontier state filled with castles, and therefore called Castile, came into being. In the course of time it was united with Asturias-Leon. Thus Leon became Leon-Castile, and, after further conquests, became Leon-Castile-Toledo-Cordova-Seville, etc. The name Castile came to be used for the national state which eventually dominated the entire central portion of the peninsula.

The same is true of Aragon, which was originally an inland feudal state, one of the remnants of Charles the Great's Spanish march. Aragon united with another remnant of the Spanish march, Catalonia, on the Mediterranean coast. Catalonia was practically the same as the county of Barcelona, so called from its seaport town,

Barcelona. After the inland state of Aragon had combined with the coastal state of Catalonia-Barcelona, the Balearic Isles and the coastal state of Valencia were added. The entire realm (comprising Aragon-Catalonia-Barcelona-"Balearica"-Valencia, etc.) came to be known as Aragon.[17]

SPAIN'S CRUSAD-
ING FRONTIER
The evolution from feudalism to royal power and national unity in each of the three Spanish nations is bound up with the unending struggle between Christians and Moslems. From 711, when the first Moslem invaders landed at Gibraltar, until 1492, when Ferdinand of Aragon and Isabella of Castile captured Granada, Spanish history was an intermittent crusade. Portugal, Castile, and Aragon won territorial possessions and built their royal governments during the period in which the Christians of northern Spain were fighting, first for existence, and then for expansion, against the firmly entrenched Moslems. Thus Spain has a significant frontier history, for the expansion of the Spanish states in the Middle Ages depended upon successful drives to the southward against the Islamic frontier.

Charles the Great's famous expedition across the Pyrenees, although indecisive, marks the first notable southward advance of Christian Spain. By the end of the ninth century several little states (Aragon-Catalonia, Navarre, and Asturias-Leon) had taken shape and were beginning to push southward. But there were setbacks and inter-Christian conflicts. Meanwhile the Moslems took the offensive under such able leaders as Abd-er-Rahman III (912-961) and Almansor (978-1002). Christian cities as far north as Pampluna, Saragossa, Navarre, and Burgos were raided or captured. Almansor ravaged the frontier from Barcelona on the Mediterranean to Leon, even carrying off the bells from the famous shrine of St. James at Compostella. As late as the year 1000, Christian Spain was fighting desperately with its back to the wall of the Pyrenees and Cantabrian mountains.

Early in the eleventh century affairs took a turn for the better. The Moslems fell into disunity and the Christian states displayed unusual unanimity of action. Before 1035 most of the northern states had come under the sway of King Sancho the Great of Navarre (970-1035), and for a time there was a sort of United States of Christian Spain. With the exception of short periods of internal strife,

---

[17] We shall use the terms Leon-Castile (or Castile) and Catalonia-Aragon (or Aragon) for the two states whose early history we have sketched. The relatively simple origins of Portugal will be considered later.

the second half of the century saw his successors, Ferdinand I (1037-1065) and Alfonso VI (1065-1109), expanding their domains at the expense of the Moslems. The bitterly contested central portion of the peninsula was occupied by the Castilians, and Toledo became the headquarters of King Alfonso. To the eastward, on the Mediterranean coast, Valencia came under the control of the Cid, a famous Christian hero who became the subject of epic poems and ballads.

FRENCH "CRU-SADES" IN SPAIN   A noteworthy factor in these Spanish wars is the role played by the French. Ever since Charles Martel's defeat of the Moslems at Tours-Poitiers in 732, and Charles the Great's expedition across the Pyrenees, Frankish warriors had fought constantly against the Moslems along their southern border. Late in the tenth century, Hugh Capet promised to aid his hard-pressed fellow Christians in Spain. During the following century, expeditions were made into Spain by Normans (1018), Aquitanians (1068), and by French royal armies. For a time the count of Burgundy made annual expeditions into Spain. By 1095 Count Henry had married a Spanish princess, had captured Oporto on the Atlantic coast, and had won recognition as duke of the region, which later became the independent kingdom of Portugal.

Accompanying the periodical expeditions of feudal nobles into Spain was a continual influx of French pilgrims and monks. The Cluniac order came into possession of many Spanish monasteries and churches during this era of triumphant Christian warfare. Even the popes (especially Gregory VII) became interested in acquiring a part of the lands conquered from the Moslems. During the eleventh century, Spanish history manifested most of the religious and nonreligious characteristics of the later crusades to the Holy Land.[18]

THE DISASTER OF 1086   In 1086, when the Moslems secured reinforcements from Africa, the onward march of Spanish Christendom was rudely checked. Yusuf, leader of the fanatical Almoravids, brought into Spain a horde of warriors, and at Zalaca in 1086 won a decisive victory over the Christians. Soon the tables were turned: central Spain was once more in Moslem hands, and the Christians were again fighting desperately to save the remnants of their kingdoms.

If ever Spain had need of French assistance, it was in this crisis. Nevertheless, in 1095, at the Council of Clermont, only a short dis-

[18] See Chapter XXV.

tance north of the Spanish frontier, Pope Urban persuaded the enthusiastic warriors of France to set out for the faraway Holy Land
to rescue the Lord's sepulcher from the Moslem Turks and to bring
aid to the Eastern Christians.[19] Scarcely a voice was lifted in the interests of the hard-pressed Christians of Spain and the much-threatened
sepulcher of St. James at Compostella. Yet within the next two centuries thousands of lives were sacrificed in vain efforts at recovering
Jerusalem for Christendom.

THE RISING
SPANISH STATES
Had Urban II sent his crusaders to Spain rather than
to Palestine, the Spains might have been quickly delivered from Moslem domination and welded into a
united Christian state, closely bound to France. As it was, they were
left to work out their own salvation, with the result that innumerable
feudal states and several kingdoms were formed, instead of one united
Spain. For centuries each Christian state carried on its own independent warfare, not only against the Moslems, but often against its
Christian neighbors. There was (1) Catalonia-Aragon (including
Barcelona) on the east coast; (2) little Navarre in the Pyrenees; (3)
Leon-Castile, south of the Bay of Biscay; and (4) Portugal (on the
west coast). In spite of internal feudal strife and inter-Christian wars,
these states made remarkable strides in territorial and governmental
growth.

In territorial expansion, the achievements of Leon-Castile were
the most spectacular. During the twelfth century her kings gained
most of north-central Spain from the Moslems, and also a window
to the southeast on the Mediterranean. Meanwhile Catalonia-Aragon
acquired realms of lesser extent, but of greater commercial value, along
the Mediterranean coast. Among these were the Balearic Isles. On the
Atlantic coast, little Portugal pushed steadily southward, conquering Lisbon in 1147 with the help of crusaders from England.

At one time during the pontificate of Innocent III, all three of
these states combined with French and Italian crusaders in a concerted drive against the Spanish Moslems. The results were notable. In
1212 at Navas de Tolosa, less than a hundred miles north of Gibraltar,
the Moslems were so decisively beaten that Spain seemed about to be
rid of them, once and for all. Within half a century the last remaining Moslem state (at Granada) was hemmed in on three sides.
Portugal, to the westward, had attained its present boundaries. On the

[19] See below, p. 500.

Mediterranean, Aragon-Catalonia had occupied the principality of Valencia, once ruled over by the famous Cid. The Castilians held not only Cadiz on the Atlantic near Gibraltar, and Cartagena on the Mediterranean, but also the important inland cities of Seville, Cordova, and Toledo. They were in a position to crush Granada, the last Moslem stronghold in Europe.

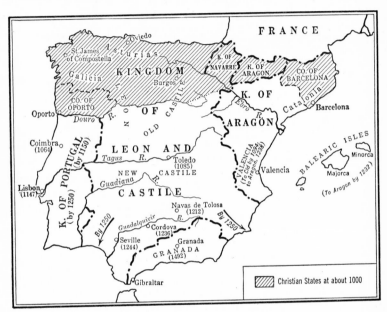

THE EXPANSION OF THE SPANISH STATES (1000-1500)

Dates indicate conquests of Moslem territory

But the last chapter in the history of the Spanish crusades was not to be written for another two centuries, when Ferdinand and Isabella finally captured Granada. One may well ask why Moslem Granada was permitted to linger on. The answer is simple. Her rulers paid a handsome tribute to the Christian monarchs; and medieval crusaders, whether in Spain or in the Holy Land, were not averse to sparing the Moslems when it was profitable to do so. Furthermore, the kings of Castile-Leon were occupied with organizing their already extensive domains and warring against the rival Christian states on either side. Consequently the Moslems retained their foothold in Spain, and the peninsula continued to witness the rivalry of three Christian states:

Portugal, Castile, and Aragon.[20] Even in the twentieth century, we find three Spains: Castile occupying the central plateau, flanked by two commercial states, Portugal on the Atlantic and Catalonia (Aragon) on the Mediterranean.

LIMITED MON-
ARCHY IN THE
SPAINS
During the period of crusades and territorial expansion, the Spanish kings worked out their political problems along lines that are strikingly similar to those of medieval England. In Leon-Castile, strong and energetic kings such as Ferdinand I (1037-1065) and Alfonso VI (1065-1109), did not rule autocratically. It seems that the Castilian feudality, clergy, and townsfolk were made partners with their kings in governmental affairs even before the English parliament came into prominence. In 1188, for instance, a quarter of a century before the Great Charter and over a century before the Model Parliament, the "Ordinances of Leon" provided for municipal privileges in local government; for the protection of freemen against arbitrary arrest; for royal pledges that local charters would be observed; for the enforcement of justice for all citizens; and for many other guarantees similar to those of England's Charter.

Representative bodies appeared earlier in Spain than in England. There was a parliament (called *Cortes*) in Leon-Castile as early as 1188, and in Aragon possibly by 1163. An Aragonese chronicle for the year 1218 describes a meeting of the *cortes* of Aragon which comprised archbishops, bishops, abbots, and nobles, "as well as the citizens of Catalonia." Each estate deliberated separately, but there was a general session at which "the nobles, clergy, and the city representatives spoke." Throughout Christian Spain in the twelfth and thirteenth centuries, the cities had elected representatives in the Cortes and also charters which provided for local self-government by the citizenry. Jews and serfs enjoyed many legal rights that were unknown in most parts of Western Europe. As for the nobles, there were ordinances that guaranteed their rights and—after the fashion of the Great Charter—authorized them to take action against the king or his officials in case the law of the land was violated.

The explanation for these advanced institutions seems to be twofold. Moslem civilization in Spain was centuries ahead of that in the rest of Europe and the Christian Spaniards profited from it. Furthermore, the ever-advancing Spanish frontier created conditions which

---

[20] Navarre in the central Pyrenees was blocked in its expansion by Castile and Aragon. Consequently it practically dropped out of Spanish history.

offered unusual opportunities for feudal nobles, townsfolk, and peasants. Special privileges were granted to warlike nobles and to peaceful settlers as inducements to conquer and exploit the new lands. Charters to towns and privileges to nobles were granted so freely that institutions of self-government became widely prevalent.

THE RISE OF ABSOLUTISM
    In the late Middle Ages, however, limited monarchy gave way, as in England and elsewhere, to absolutism. In Castile there was a series of disastrous civil wars, during which lawless nobles devastated the country. Order was finally restored, but at the expense of freedom.[21] Peace could be attained, it seems, only through autocratic monarchs such as Isabella (1474-1504) who, in spite of her well-known piety, was a ruthless tyrant. With her marriage to Ferdinand II of Aragon and the accession of their grandson, Charles V, to the throne of Spain,[22] the history of Castile merges with that of Aragon and of modern Europe. But there was no real union of the two nations. They were merely ruled by the same monarch.

    As for Aragon, from the time of James II (1291-1327) to Ferdinand II (1479-1516), territorial expansion and royal autocracy advanced steadily. Although foreign invasions (by the French and English) and disputed successions led to temporary feudal reactions, city life and royal power continued to expand. By the year 1500 Sardinia, Sicily, and southern Italy were coming under Aragon's commercial and political domination.[23] Meanwhile Portugal, under strong and intelligent monarchs, was becoming a great maritime power. With the career of Henry the Navigator and the voyage of Vasco da Gama around Africa,[24] Lisbon for a time became one of the great financial centers of the West. It was this group of thriving Spanish states that gave Charles V and his son Philip II much of the financial and military resources with which they dominated the sixteenth-century Western world.

21 Compare the situation in England; below, p. 602 f.
22 See below, p. 610.
23 See below, p. 621.
24 See below, p. 552.

═ XXV ═

THE CRUSADES AND THE EXPANSION OF
WESTERN EUROPE

IN the preceding chapters we have frequently spoken of crusades. The age of feudalism, of town growth, of papal-imperial rivalry, and of rising nationalism was also a crusading age. In the crusades it produced the most spectacular military and religious activities of the Middle Ages. But the crusades were something more than a series of exciting expeditions to the Holy Land. They were a significant phase of the expanding life of the West.

THE BACKGROUND OF THE CRUSADES

VARYING
VIEWPOINTS
There are two major contradictory viewpoints concerning the crusades. One holds that they were a sudden mass outburst of unselfish popular idealism— an example of the characteristically spiritual tendencies of medieval people. At the opposite extreme is the viewpoint that our own day seems to favor: that medieval people were not unlike those of modern times in their desire for lands, wealth, and power; and that most crusaders, therefore, were influenced more by material than by spiritual motives. From this point of view the crusades, in spite of their highly colored religious emotionalism, appear to have been essentially an episode in the political and economic expansion of the West during the Middle Ages.

We tend toward this latter viewpoint, and shall treat the crusades to the Holy Land as that phase of Western expansion during which there was a concentration of commercial and military ventures in the eastern Mediterranean. To be sure, the word *crusade* means an expedition of the cross—that is, a war for Christianity—but the cross was little more than a pious symbol for a war of aggression. As we have already seen,[1] religiously motivated wars of expansion had been going

[1] See above, pp. 203 ff.

on, after a fashion, for centuries on Christendom's Norse, Slavic, Hungarian, Bulgar, and Moslem frontiers. These wars continued as long as there was any serious opposition on the part of the "heathen." It was for less than two centuries (1096-1291) that Christendom's major efforts were directed toward a distant eastern frontier where the Seljuk Turks had made dangerous inroads. For a time this movement reflected a strongly religious impulse. Pilgrimages to the Holy Land, which were very popular just before the crusades and during the early period of expeditions to the East, injected a fanatically religious element into certain of the early expeditions. There were also a few spectacular mass movements of the lower classes and several colorful expeditions of kings and barons. Interesting though these may be as examples of the religious psychology or military prowess of medieval people, the essential importance of the crusades lies in its relationship to the expansion of the West. From this point of view, the only permanent successes of the movement were the achievements of the merchant classes in exploiting the commerce of the Near East. As military and political expansions, the crusades were only temporarily successful notwithstanding tremendous expenditures of lives and treasure. The earlier wars in the West against the Norse, Slavs, Hungarians, and Spanish Moslems for the recovery of England, northern France, the Netherlands, northern Germany, southern France, southern Italy, Spain, and the Balkans were successful, whereas the efforts in the far distant Holy Land were a failure.

WESTERN CHRIS-
TENDOM TURNS
EASTWARD
If the crusades are to be considered as a phase of Western expansion, an important question arises: Why did Western Christians suddenly turn from their home frontiers to rescue the Holy Sepulcher? In 1096, as in preceding centuries, Christian territory at home still needed protection. As early as the sixth century, the recently converted chieftain of the Franks, King Clovis, had assumed the orthodox Christian task of driving the Arian Visigoths out of Gaul. Three centuries later, Charles the Great, during thirty years of fierce warfare, had fought the pagan Saxons. After his death, Christendom was put on the defensive by the pagan invaders on all frontiers. Even after the tenth century, there were still Moslems to be conquered in Spain and Sicily, Slavs along the Elbe River, and Norsemen in the Baltic lands. Nevertheless, in 1095, at a time when the situation in Spain was still critical, Pope Urban II urged Western Christians to concentrate their military efforts in the East.

There are valid reasons for this development. An attack on the eastern front might draw the Moslem forces away from Spain and Sicily, thus relieving the pressure in the West. Doubtless of much greater importance was the fact that the papacy was in the midst of a desperate struggle with the empire and needed to make a spectacular appeal for the support of Christendom. A call for a crusade to the Holy Land would evoke a more enthusiastic response than a local war in the West. Furthermore powerful religious influences for over a century had tended to concentrate Christian attention on the Holy Land, thus making the recovery of the Holy Sepulcher a popular project.

RELICS AND PILGRIMAGES IN THE WEST

Long before the eleventh century Western Europe was interested in pilgrimages, not only to the Holy Sepulcher but also to local shrines. Every diocese had its local saint to whose sepulcher the populace flocked on holy days. There were also the more important centers to which crowds of pilgrims came from afar for healing or to do penance before the relics of some famous saint or martyr. In England there was the tomb of St. Edmund, a ninth-century king who had been tortured to death by Danish pirates. In France the shrine of St. Martin of Tours drew constant streams of eager pilgrims and hopeful cripples. So great was the popular reliance on the relics of such saints that religious frauds were perpetrated by unscrupulous men. Agents actually traveled about certain parts of France, taking orders for what they represented as the genuine remains of holy martyrs. Occasionally there was widespread suspicion of clerical fraud in connection with relics thus procured. For instance, in 1010 at St. Angely near Bordeaux, the local clergy claimed to have found the head of John the Baptist. So great was the popularity of the new shrine that the jealous proprietors of other pilgrimage centers charged fraud, but in the end a clerical investigating committee upheld the genuineness of the relics.

Important though the French shrines were, many people from the region north of the Pyrenees traveled to the distant sepulcher of St. James at Compostella, where the body of the apostle had been discovered in the eighth century. So popular was this pilgrimage that a regular route was established with hospices for the convenience of those making the journey. The most famous of all Western shrines was that of St. Peter at Rome. Each Easter, so it was said, noblemen from northern lands made the long and difficult journey over the Alps to worship at the church of the chief of the apostles. Often there were so many princes in attendance at special Roman festivals that the city took on the appearance of an international congress.

PILGRIMAGES
TO JERUSALEM

The most noteworthy factor in eleventh-century pilgrimages was the tremendous increase in both the number and size of the expeditions to Jerusalem. The Holy Land had been a favorite pilgrimage point as early as the fourth century, when Emperor Constantine's mother discovered the True Cross at Jerusalem. Jerome, writing at about 400 A.D., said, "Every man of importance in Gaul hastens thither." With the coming of the Moslems in the seventh century, conditions of travel in the East became somewhat more difficult for Christians, but through the succeeding centuries there was no cessation of pilgrimages. In fact during the century just preceding the crusades, there was a marked increase in Western pilgrimages to the Holy Land. This may be explained, in part, by the fact that at this time the Eastern Empire had control of Syria, and that in the year 1000 King Stephen of Hungary officially accepted Christianity, thus making the important Danube route safer and more attractive for pilgrims. It is important to note that, even after the coming of the Seljuk Turks in the eleventh century, Westerners continued to visit the Holy Sepulcher in ever-increasing numbers.

Some of these eleventh-century pilgrimages were so large and so well organized that they resembled crusades save for the fact that they were not military expeditions. In 1064 a band of seven thousand Germans set forth from the Rhinelands, but before reaching Jerusalem they had so much trouble with stray bands of marauders that they were forced to take up arms in order to save their lives. They were finally escorted to and from the Holy City by Moslem troops; apparently the Moslem authorities were not averse to pilgrimages. Many smaller groups, under the leadership of churchmen or of nobles such as Fulk of Anjou and Duke Robert of Normandy, made the perilous journey to Jerusalem, and returned home to tell of sufferings both real and imaginary.

These tales, doubtless much enhanced in the telling, laid the foundation for Western Europe's belief in Moslem atrocities, and fanned the flames of Christian fanaticism. By 1096 Westerners were more conscious than ever before of the glories and dangers of pilgrimages to the Holy Sepulcher. Atrocity tales not only appealed to the warrior's spirit of adventure but also fostered a vivid hatred of the Moslems. Such psychological developments prepared the way for a more warlike type of expedition, the crusade. Likewise they made it inevitable that the crusading objective would be the Holy Land rather than Spain or some other western frontier.

THE ELEVENTH-CENTURY PEACE MOVEMENT

While Western Christendom was developing a keen interest in the Holy Land and a burning resentment against the Turks, a popular peace movement was arising in France which was destined to contribute much to the crusading spirit. This eleventh-century peace movement paved the way for crusading councils such as that at Clermont in 1095, and for the special interest taken by the French in crusades. For over a century before the crusades, the clergy and laity of France had been co-operating in holding councils and in establishing organizations for the mobilization of public action in the interests of peace. Late in the tenth century, at Charroux in southwestern France, a council of bishops took united action against the longstanding evils of local warfare and brigandage in that region. The result was the "Peace of God," by which divine condemnation as well as excommunication from the church was directed against any Christian who attacked the persons or property of the church, and of women, unarmed travelers, or peasants. This was in effect a declaration of neutrality for all noncombatants; it was to be enforced by means of spiritual penalties.

Within a quarter of a century the idea had spread throughout France, and everywhere assemblies of nobles were promising to obey and enforce the Peace. Meanwhile the regulations were expanded to protect the domestic animals, vineyards, and orchards of the peasantry. The populace in general tended to support the movement. In 1033, at Limoges, a mass meeting was held at which even the common folk, "with hands upraised to Heaven and with shouts of 'peace, peace, peace,'" promised their support. Soon the clergy in many dioceses had enrolled their people in organizations pledged to march against peace breakers in mass formation, but armed only with the religious weapons of prayer, crosses, and sacred relics. Thus by the middle of the eleventh century, Christians in France were being mobilized by the clergy for a peaceful "crusade" to end local warfare.

As early as 1027 the peace movement had begun to assume still another form, called the *"Truce* of God." This was an extension of the "Peace of God" in that at all times noncombatants were declared to be immune from attack. In addition warfare among Christians was absolutely prohibited on holy days. At first this applied only to Sundays, but later it comprised the entire week end, from Thursday night to Monday morning, and also special holy seasons such as Lent. In some regions the "open season" for fighting was reduced to less than half the days of the year. If the Truce could have been enforced rigorously it would have been of great economic advantage. Planting and reaping usually came during the "closed season," and theoretically the produce of the peasant was protected.

Both the Truce and the Peace were too ideal to be effective. Since the chief economic resources of an opponent were his manors, a feudal warrior could not afford to leave them unravaged during a military campaign. Not until the national monarchs began to enforce law and order under the name of the "King's Peace" was the problem of local warfare solved. But the peace movement was significant in that it showed what could be done to mobilize public opinion in support of a public cause. This was its most important influence on the crusades. The members of the clergy had learned to direct public opinion against troublemakers at home and soon they were directing it against the Moslems. Furthermore, the very failure to enforce the Peace and Truce had a bearing on the crusading movement. Realizing the impossibility of suppressing the warlike tendencies of the feudality, the pope hit upon the expedient of diverting them into useful channels. The excess fighting power of the Christian West was turned against the Turks. In essence, this is what Urban II did at Clermont in 1095. His crusading program was a combination of two important projects: (1) the maintenance of peace at home; and (2) the waging of war against the infidel Turk in order to rescue the Holy Sepulcher and assist the hard-pressed Eastern Empire.

THE COUNCIL OF PIACENZA (1095) Urban's appeal for a crusade was by no means an innovation. Previous popes, notably John X (914-928), Sylvester II (999-1003), and Gregory VII (1073-1085), had urged Christians to take up the sword against the Moslems. Therefore Urban II was following papal precedents when he proposed a crusade. A little less than a year before the famous Council of Clermont, at Piacenza in northern Italy, he tried out the idea, perhaps for the purpose of feeling out public sentiment. The occasion was a mass meeting of Urban's adherents, assembled primarily to join him in condemning that bitter enemy of the papacy, Emperor Henry IV of Germany. Some 4,000 clergymen and 30,000 laymen were said to have attended the council. But the project of a crusade was apparently a minor issue. The only existing account of the event merely

mentions the fact that an embassy from the emperor at Constantinople asked for aid "against the pagans who had advanced even to
the walls of Constantinople," and that "the lord pope incited many so
that even by sworn oaths they promised to go." Here, it will be noted,
the initiative seems to have come from the Eastern emperor and the
objective was to rescue *Constantinople* from the threat of a Moslem
invasion.

THE COUNCIL
OF CLERMONT
(1095)
    Late in the same year (1095), at Clermont in France,
the crusading appeal was repeated in quite different
fashion, to a different group of people, and with
startlingly different results. In some respects the
Council of Clermont resembled the average church council. It took up
various matters of ecclesiastical policy, among them the re-enactment
of the Peace and the Truce of God. A contemporary chronicler reported that at the final session "all of those present, priests and people
alike, gave thanks, assuring him [the pope] that these [peace] decrees would be well kept." [2] The importance that was attached to this
matter is illustrated by the fact that similar Peace and Truce decrees
were promulgated at several other French councils during the ensuing
years.

    The crusading appeal was made in a final public session, held on
the ninth day of the council, in an open space outside the city, for
"there was no building large enough to hold all the people." Among
those who attended were 250 bishops and abbots, many of the lesser
clergy, and "persons without number from many regions." According
to accounts written by contemporaries, the papal exhortation was remarkably effective. It was directed particularly to the fighting class.
They were reminded that the Turks had taken possession of "the land
our Savior made illustrious by his birth, beautiful by his life, and sacred
by his suffering, the land he redeemed with his death and glorified
with his tomb." The "Christian soldiers" of France, "descendants of unconquered ancestors," were urged to cease striving against one another,
and to "set out for the Holy Sepulcher, to take that land from a wicked
people." In contrast to his appeal at Piacenza, the pope made little
reference to the plight of Constantinople. But the sufferings of pilgrims
to the Holy Land were emphasized by recounting Turkish atrocities,
with harrowing details concerning the disemboweling of innocent vic-

---

[2] See Krey, *The First Crusade*, pp. 24 ff., Robinson, *Readings in European History*,
I, 312 ff., and Thatcher and McNeal, *Source Book*, pp. 514 ff., for contemporary accounts such as are quoted here and below.

tims, the ravaging of women, and the desecration of churches. Those who died fighting for the cause were promised the complete remission of all penalties for past sins and immediate entrance into Paradise.

The pope also appealed to the more materialistic motives of his hearers. He may have had in mind the unprecedented famines from which the French had suffered when he urged them to leave their native land, a region "too thickly populated . . . with a soil scarcely yielding enough to support you," and to conquer "the land flowing with milk and honey . . . a second Paradise of delights." Urban's appeal, far more attractive than accurate, roused the mass of hearers to fanatical enthusiasm. It was reported that, when he had finished, "all who were present were moved to cry out with one accord: 'It is the will of God.'" Urban, feeling that "God had put the words into their hearts," announced that this was to be the battle cry of all who enlisted. Each crusader, as a symbol of his pledge, was to wear on his breast a cross. Hundreds immediately came forward to "take the cross" from the pope in person.

Even amid such stirring scenes, the more practical aspects were not neglected. Perhaps as a result of the overwhelming response, clergymen, women, and other noncombatants were discouraged from joining the expedition. Women, it was suggested, might go if accompanied by their husbands or brothers, and clergymen must have the consent of their bishops. The pope also urged the "rich to aid the poor and equip them for fighting, and take them along." It is evident that Urban was planning an orderly military expedition in which the crusading enthusiasm should be effectively controlled and directed. In a final session of the council, Bishop Ademar of Puy was selected as official leader of the crusade, and a date was set for departure late in the following summer. Thus ended the famous Council of Clermont. It was followed, however, by a widespread and uncontrollable campaign of crusade propaganda.

PETER THE HERMIT

Clermont marks neither the beginning nor the end of the preaching of the crusade. At Piacenza, almost a year earlier, the pope had seconded Emperor Alexius' appeal for aid. At Clermont a carefully planned program for the recovery of the Holy Land was launched by means of propaganda that appealed to a variety of human motives. After the council a supplementary campaign was conducted throughout the length and breadth of France in which distinctly new types of propaganda developed. Urban himself led in the campaign to spread abroad the enthusiasm that had been generated at Clermont. Before returning to Italy he visited Limoges, Angers, Tours, and Nîmes, ostensibly for the purpose of dedicating newly erected cathedrals, but at each place "he exhorted the people" concerning the crusade. Meanwhile, according to one chronicler, the bishops went about, "each in his own diocese eloquently heralding the expedition to Jerusalem." The news was also circulated by "pontifical letters." Thus "an immense multitude" aided in "rousing the Heavenly Host." It was reported that, sometime during the year 1096, at a tournament in Flanders three hundred knights took the cross.

Peter the Hermit, although he must be denied the major role in the launching of the crusade, was certainly the most important of the self-appointed exhorters who stirred the populace to action. Urban and his clerical assistants addressed their exhortations chiefly to the fighting nobility. Peter's fanatical eloquence, however, was focused on the common folk among whom the crusading movement took on an explosive popular character resulting in misdirected activities which had tragic consequences.

Everywhere Peter went the populace responded enthusiastically to his frenzied appeals. Many considered him a divinely inspired saint, and crowds of fanatical and ignorant folk followed him from place to place in central and northern France. Within three months after the adjournment of the Council of Clermont his followers were said to have numbered 15,000. Before summer several bands of these misguided enthusiasts started overland for Jerusalem. Oblivious of the pope's plans, of the appointed leader, and of the date set for the departure, thousands of poor folk, trusting implicitly in God's protection and in Peter's guidance, streamed eastward, intent on rescuing the Holy Sepulcher from the hated Turks.

CRUSADES BY THE COMMON PEOPLE AND FEUDAL BARONS, 1096-1110

PETER'S "CRUSADERS"   In March, 1096, four months after the Council of Clermont, Peter the Hermit and his enthusiastic followers were in the region of the Loire River. By mid-April they had reached the Rhinelands. At Cologne for a full week Peter exhorted the Germans to take up the crusading cause. Meanwhile a band of the French crusaders, impatient at the delay, pushed on ahead under the leadership of a knight who bore the picturesque name of Walter the Penniless. Down the Danube they hurried, through friendly Hungarian territory. In Bulgaria they had trouble with the local populace, but by July the straggling crowd had reached Constantinople. In spite of a rather dubious welcome from Emperor Alexius, they remained at Constantinople to await the arrival of Peter the Hermit.

Meanwhile Peter, with his motley array of French and Germans, had followed the same route. All went well until on arriving at the border between Hungary and Bulgaria, Peter heard that the natives had killed some of Walter's men and were lying in wait for his band. Without waiting to be attacked, the crusaders stormed a near-by city, and then "with wagonloads of spoils," hastened into Bulgarian territory to escape an avenging army of Hungarians. Like Walter's crusaders, they had trouble with the Bulgars, and in the ensuing hostilities many were killed. Further on, officials of the Eastern emperor received them kindly, made restitution for their losses, and escorted them to Constantinople. After camping outside the city for a week they were persuaded to cross the straits and join the army of Walter the Penniless.

The emperor, dismayed at having such masses of useless peasants descend upon his capital, evidently intended to shunt them on into Asia Minor where they could be housed and fed until the arrival of the fighting men of the West. But disaster came upon them when, contrary to Peter's wishes, some of the more daring crusaders attacked a Turkish fort near Nicæa. This precipitated a battle in which the Christians were completely defeated. Many were killed, and the remnant, including Peter, fled to Constantinople, where they remained until the arrival of the better-organized bands of crusaders in the fall.

Meanwhile, during the same summer, three other mobs of Christian pilgrims and warriors streamed eastward from Germany, down the Danube, and into Hungary, where they were cut to pieces by the revengeful natives. Thus the first crusading effort of Urban's age ended in tragic disaster. One of the most shameful aspects of the situation was the heartless manner in which the Jews of the Rhineland cities were plundered by several of these later bands. It is noteworthy that the unfortunate expeditions made during the summer of 1096 were the only crusades ever carried on spontaneously by the populace of the

West.[3] Whatever success attended the so-called first crusade was achieved later, not by uncontrolled crowds of common folk, but by armies organized and directed by the nobles who, in obedience to the papal instructions, had delayed their departure until the fall of 1096.

MOTIVES OF CRUSADERS

At this point we may pause to ask why it was that so many people, from so many regions and classes of society, engaged in crusading ventures. What was it that stirred alike Peter the Hermit's peasant bands and the armed fighting men who followed them during the ensuing months? Was it primarily the call of religion, or were materialistic motives uppermost? Obviously medieval people were influenced more deeply by religious factors than are most modern folk. Pilgrimages had focused the attention of Christendom on the Holy Land with such vividness that many pious Westerners were eager to visit the Holy Sepulcher as a supreme act of religious devotion. The spiritual rewards which Urban II and later popes decreed tended to encourage such activities. Even hardened sinners and criminals were urged to obtain full remission of the penalties for their sins by making the perilous venture in a spirit of genuine repentance.[4] Thus it was that the ranks of the crusading hosts were swelled by throngs of nonmilitary folk, intent on the salvation of their souls. As a matter of fact, many of the expeditions were more nearly mass pilgrimages than military crusades.

But even the most pious were impelled, whether consciously or not, by materialistic factors. Not only were the families and property of crusaders taken under the protection of the church, but a mora-

[3] In this connection, however, mention should be made of two expeditions which, though not actually launched for the recovery of the Holy Land, manifested the same sort of mass hysteria as the crusades of 1096. In 1212 Germany and France were swept by pious emotionalism. Stirred to action by two boy evangelists, bands of French and German children marched about singing and shouting. Frenzied mobs of children, accompanied by a few fanatical adults, soon started for the Holy Land, hoping that the Lord would open the Mediterranean so that they could march through it "dry shod," as the children of Israel had passed through the Red Sea. Most of the French mobs were dispersed by royal officials, but some 20,000 German children reached Italy. Some went as far as the port of Brindisi; others drifted westward to Marseilles, where many were lured onto ships and sold into slavery to the Moslems by unscrupulous merchants. Only a few returned home. Again in 1251 there was a popular rising, this time on the part of the French "shepherds" and peasants, who believed that their saintly king, Louis IX, while crusading, had been betrayed into Moslem captivity by treacherous Christians. With the slogan "It is for the poor to deliver him," crowds of common folk started off pell-mell for the East. When they became disorderly and began to pillage, government officials and members of the nobility hunted them down.

[4] Such a remission of the penalties (or penances) for past sins was called an indulgence. See above, p. 403, note 11.

torium was declared on certain taxes and on prosecution for debts. A contemporary writer pointed out that "some went to the East out of curiosity; others who had lived at home in pinching poverty, . . . to end their poverty; still others fled from their debts, from duties which they ought to have performed or from punishments which their crimes deserved." [5]

It seems clear that the economic pressure of poverty was unbearable for many French people at this time. According to a chronicler of the crusading period, "the French at this time suffered from famine; bad harvests . . . had raised the price of grain. . . . Avaricious merchants speculated according to their custom on the misery of all. There was little bread and it was very dear. The poor supplied the place of it by eating roots and herbs." [6] Not only famine, but poverty, debt, and other intolerable conditions impelled individuals, groups, and even entire communities to respond to the crusading call. Was not Jerusalem situated in "a land flowing with milk and honey"? Why, then, should not poor starving peasants respond to the appeal of men such as Urban II and Peter the Hermit? Many crusaders must have started for the Holy Land in much the same manner and with somewhat the same hopes as our forefathers who plodded westward at the side of their covered wagons to start life anew on the frontier.

Medieval historians reported that

Nothing was more touching than to see these poor people using their cattle like horses, dragging along the roads in two-wheeled peasant carts, upon which they had piled their sorry belongings and their little children. At every castle, at every town . . . the children stretched out their hands and asked if it were not Jerusalem. [7]

A German writer told how his fellow countrymen "laughed to scorn the many legions of knights . . . the many companies of foot soldiers, and the crowds of country people, women, and little ones who passed through their land."

It seems probable that most of the nobles and commoners expected to better their material conditions by taking the cross. Peasants who could see no chance for advancement as serfs on a manor eagerly set forth, perhaps under the banner of one of the many younger sons of a large noble family, or with an ambitious baron who hoped to

[5] Translation from Thompson, *An Economic and Social History of the Middle Ages*, p. 392.
[6] *Ibid.*
[7] *Ibid.*, p. 395.

carve out for himself a rich principality elsewhere. And what feudal warrior was not tempted by the thought of unending adventure, fighting, and plunder in the glamorous regions of the East! In short, there was everything to gain and nothing—save a humdrum life—to lose by crusading. By the actions of the fighting barons who met at Constantinople in the fall of 1096, we may be sure that the average crusader was thinking of something more than the defense of the Eastern Empire, the rescue of the Holy Sepulcher, and the salvation of his own soul as he set forth for Jerusalem. The practical, materialistic motives and reactions of the crusaders will be illustrated time and again as we follow in some detail the events of this most enthusiastic and successful of all the crusading expeditions.

THE BARONIAL CRUSADERS

According to the papal program adopted at Clermont, the various contingents of Western knights were to start for Constantinople, the meeting place, as soon as possible after the harvests of 1096. It is significant that no kings set forth on this crusade. Henry IV of Germany, Philip I of France, and William II (Rufus) of England were under sentences of excommunication, and the Spanish monarchs, since Yusuf's invasion in 1086,[8] had been busy defending their own realms from Moslem attacks. As a consequence, the expedition to the Holy Land was distinctly a barons' crusade. It was also predominantly French. There were, however, some exceptions. From the Netherlands and Lorraine came Godfrey of Bouillon and his two brothers, Baldwin and Eustace.

Although Godfrey was a subject of Emperor Henry IV, Pope Urban's bitterest opponent, he eagerly took the cross in order to make expiation for the crime of having killed a man within the sacred precincts of a church. He exemplifies the highest of crusading ideals, and was eventually to be selected as the ruler of Jerusalem. With an army of about 10,000 knights and 20,000 foot soldiers, Godfrey crossed southern Germany, marched down the Danube, and arrived at Constantinople late in the year 1096. Meanwhile several armies from northern France were starting eastward, by way of Italy. Under the leadership of King Philip's brother, the proud Count Hugh of Vermandois, a band of knights in shining armor had crossed the Alps, traversed the length of Italy, and taken ship from Bari to the Balkan port of Durazzo. Unfortunately they suffered shipwreck, and it was a bedraggled group that finally reached Constantinople. The emperor received

[8] See above, p. 489.

Hugh with courtesy, but detained him as a sort of hostage until his followers had taken an oath of allegiance.

One after another during the spring of 1097 other bands of French crusaders arrived at Constantinople. There were the forces of Robert of Flanders, a pious count who had already made a pilgrimage to the Holy Land and had furnished Emperor Alexius with mercenary soldiers several years before the call for the crusade. In addition to fighting men, he now brought with him his most prized relic, the arm of St. George. Count Robert, one of the most resolute of the crusaders, also brought to the enterprise an unusual aptitude for conciliating the rivalries of the various leaders. There was also another Robert, the reckless son of William the Conqueror. In order to raise money for his expedition, this Robert mortgaged his duchy of Normandy to his jealous brother, King William II (Rufus) of England, who is said to have wished him Godspeed with the secret hope that he would never return to reclaim his inheritance.

Wealthiest of all the crusaders was Count Stephen of Blois, who possessed as many castles as there were days in the year. His wife was a rich English princess, and their son later became King Stephen of England. From southern France came the papal representative, Bishop Ademar of Puy, and the one-eyed Count Raymond of Toulouse, a scarred veteran of the Spanish crusades, reputed to have been "as fanatical as a monk and as land-greedy as a Norman." After crossing the Alps and northern Italy, Raymond led his forces through the Balkans, where they had much difficulty with the imperial officials and the suspicious populace. At Constantinople, he stubbornly refused to take any oath to the emperor, but was finally persuaded to promise that he would "do nothing against the life or honor of his majesty."

From southern Italy came Count Bohemond, son of Robert Guiscard, with his nephew Tancred and an army of hard-fighting Norman adventurers. Inasmuch as his stepbrother had inherited most of the Guiscard dominions, Bohemond decided to seek other worlds to conquer. He was dangerously ambitious, and by all odds the ablest military commander of the entire crusading army. The imperial officials had good reason to suspect the motives of these, their former enemies,[9] now coming ostensibly as allies. En route to Constantinople the Normans ravaged the countryside and fought several battles with the troops of the emperor. Eventually, however, Bohemond took an

9 See above, p. 395, note 2.

oath or allegiance to Alexius and, like the other leaders, received rich gifts in return. By May, 1097, almost a year after the appearance of Peter the Hermit's peasant bands at Constantinople, all of the crusaders had arrived and the emperor had guaranteed them safe conduct and assistance in return for their promise to turn over to him all imperial lands that were recovered from the Turks. This agreement soon caused mutual dissatisfaction, and eventually bitter warfare between the crusaders and the imperialists.

FROM NICÆA
TO ANTIOCH

Soon the crusaders crossed the Bosporus and moved on to Nicæa, the closest Turkish stronghold. After a desultory siege of over a month the defenders surrendered, but to the troops of Alexius. When an imperial garrison secretly occupied the city, with the gates still closed to the expectant crusaders, there was violent dissatisfaction, for the crusaders resented the loss of their first opportunity to massacre and plunder the Turks. Rich gifts from the emperor to the crusading leaders and the distribution of brass coins to the common soldiers had only a slightly mollifying influence. When Alexius moved on southward along the Aegean coast to recover his former possessions, in the face of the crusaders' insistence upon taking a more direct and dangerous route across the interior of Asia Minor, the resentment of the latter grew. Henceforth many of them referred to Alexius scornfully as "the jackal that follows after the brave lion to devour the leavings of what he has killed."

The march through Asia Minor during the midsummer heat was disastrous. Water and other provisions ran out, pack animals died, and many of the horses had to be killed for food. En route, at Dorylaeum, the crusaders narrowly escaped annihilation at the hands of a belated Turkish army coming to the relief of Nicæa. The hard fighting of Godfrey and the military skill of the Norman, Bohemond, turned the engagement from a panic-stricken rout into a questionable victory. Struggling onward, the crusaders finally reached the Christian city of Tarsus in southern Armenia. Here, almost within sight of their goal, the selfish ambitions of the leaders began to assert themselves. Tancred, Bohemond's nephew, and Baldwin, brother of Godfrey, quarreled over the possession of the city. Both were finally forced to give up their demands, and soon thereafter Baldwin left the crusading host to seek his fortunes at Edessa, another Armenian city, on the Upper Euphrates. As a result of this ambitious venture, Edessa became a powerful outpost of Christian defense against the Turks of Asia Minor. This first desertion from the crusading ranks proved to be the beginning of a mad scramble for landed possessions. Before long the majority of the leaders seemed to have completely forgotten the Holy Sepulcher and their crusading vows.

THE SIEGE OF ANTIOCH (1097-1098) At Antioch the rivalries of ambitious leaders threatened to bring the crusade to a disastrous end. In the eyes of such practical men as Bohemond and Raymond, this immense city, located in a fertile plain, was a prize far more precious than the Holy City. At first the overwhelming difficulties of the siege eclipsed all other problems. For over a year the crusaders suffered not only from the attacks of the Turkish garrison, and of several relieving armies of Turks, but also from hunger, thirst, and the elements. One chronicler relates that there was much rain and "many poor wretches, having no change of clothing, died of cold since they could not get under cover." Tents and food were also lacking, but some "appeased their hunger by chewing sweet reeds called cannamel [sugar] or cane and honey." During this terrible year in which the besiegers suffered more than the besieged, a peasant soldier claimed to have found the sacred lance with which the Savior's side had been pierced. Many doubted his story, but after he had undergone a trial by the ordeal of fire, the rank and file of the crusaders were convinced. As for the leaders, they were willing to approve of anything which would restore the morale of the army.

Success finally came when hard fighting on the part of certain of the Christian forces beat off the attacking Turkish armies, and when materials obtained from a Genoese fleet made it possible to construct machines of war with which to press the siege. Soon, however, new difficulties assailed the crusaders. New Turkish armies besieged the besiegers so closely that many faint-hearted Christians began to desert. Among the so-called "rope danglers" who escaped by means of rope ladders and started homeward were Peter the Hermit and Count Stephen of Blois. More harmful than desertions were the rivalries among the crusading leaders. Bohemond, it seems, had set his heart on winning Antioch for himself, and had persuaded the crusaders to promise the city to the one who should capture it. The imperial general, who was present to see that the city was turned over to Emperor Alexius, was bribed by Bohemond to retire. By bribery Bohemond also persuaded an inhabitant of Antioch to open the gates, thus admitting the crusaders to the unconquered portions of the city. The long siege ended with an indiscriminate massacre of Turks and natives. But trouble was still brewing.

Although most of the crusaders accepted Bohemond's claim that he was the rightful ruler of Antioch, Count Raymond of Toulouse resisted so bitterly that actual warfare threatened. Henceforth Raymond supported the emperor's contention that, in accordance with the agreement at Constantinople, the city should be turned over to him. Bohemond retained control, however, and eventually the other leaders grudgingly moved on southward. Many of them hastened to capture neighboring cities and to settle down in their new domains. According to one of the crusaders, more than 165 Syrian towns were thus occupied.

ON TO JERU-
SALEM (1099)
It was not until the winter of 1099, almost two years after the beginning of the siege of Antioch, that the remnant of the Christian host moved on to Jerusalem. Few of the leaders seemed eager to rescue the Holy Sepulcher, and it was said that the rank and file of the army finally forced the issue by destroying their camps and threatening to go on alone. Eventually a force of about 20,000 men closed in on Jerusalem. After much suffering, an ineffective siege, and a final two weeks of hard fighting, the defenses were carried by storm. As at Antioch, the fleets of the Italian city-states furnished the necessary siege engines and supplies. This, plus the weakness of the Turkish defense, was more effective than any special merit of the crusaders. None the less, the victory was decisive and meant much to the faithful little army and to the entire Christian world. Godfrey of Bouillon's report to the pope indicates something of the frenzied exultation of the victors: "And if you desire to know what was done with the enemy . . . know that in Solomon's Porch and the Temple, our men rode in the blood of the Saracens up to the knees of their horses. . . . We call upon you to exult in the admirable bravery and devotion of your brethren."

Shortly after the victory, Godfrey was elected to rule the newly conquered region. He refused to be considered king of the Holy City, and instead assumed the modest title of "Baron and Defender of the Holy Sepulcher." For a year (until his death late in 1100) he ruled with marked success. After the small army of conquerors had defeated a Moslem force from Egypt at Ascalon, most of them paid their religious devotions at the sacred places in and about Jerusalem and then returned home. Among the unsatisfied crusaders who remained in the

East to seek their fortunes was Raymond of Toulouse. Disappointed at both Antioch and Jerusalem, he now turned to the region of Tripolis, midway between these two cities, where he eventually carved out a kingdom for himself.

MINOR EXPEDI-
TIONS (1100-
1110)

The capture of Jerusalem marks a decided change in crusading history. Henceforth the objectives were very different from those proclaimed by Urban II— to assist the Eastern Empire and rescue the Holy Sepulcher. The problem was now the far more practical one of holding and expanding the conquered territories. This presented serious difficulties. For instance, the rulers of the crusading states lacked warriors with which to reinforce their depleted armies. When Godfrey of Jerusalem found that his forces had dwindled to about 1300 men, he sent urgent calls for aid. Fortunately the news of the capture of Jerusalem had stimulated many Westerners with the desire to visit the Holy Land, and in response to Pope Paschal II's summons, new bands of pilgrims and crusaders began to stream eastward by way of Constantinople. As earlier, serious difficulties were encountered en route. One expedition, under the leadership of Raymond of Toulouse, which marched into the heart of Asia Minor, was cut to pieces by the Turks. One of the aims of this group of crusaders was to rescue Bohemond, who had fallen into the hands of the Moslems. Inasmuch as its leader, Raymond, was Bohemond's bitterest rival, he and Emperor Alexius were accused of having betrayed the expedition in order to keep Bohemond in captivity and to get possession of Antioch.

The events which followed lent an aspect of probability to this charge, for soon the Holy Land was a battleground of Christians fighting against Christians, often in alliance with the Eastern emperor or even with the Turks. At one time, Emperor Alexius persuaded Raymond to head an expedition for the conquest of Antioch from their mutual enemy, Bohemond. Thereupon Bohemond, who had escaped from his imprisonment with the Turks, returned to Italy to seek Christian aid against Alexius and Raymond. As a result of this state of affairs, during the years 1105-1106 Western Europe witnessed the strange spectacle of Bohemond and a papal legate touring Italy and France to preach a crusade against Alexius and his Christian accomplices. The "crusade" failed and Bohemond agreed to restore all imperial territory under his control, excepting Antioch, which he was to retain as an imperial fief.

After Bohemond's death the Normans and imperialists continued their rivalries in the East.

RESULTS OF
THE "FIRST"
CRUSADE

In spite of (1) the fanatical ineffectiveness of the peasant expeditions of 1096, (2) the disunity and self-ishness of the baronial crusaders, and (3) the cut-throat rivalry of imperialists and Normans, much was accomplished during this stirring period. The general success of the numerous expeditions that comprised the so-called first crusade was notable. The two major objectives of Urban II were accomplished. In the first place, not only was the Turkish peril removed from Constantinople, but the emperor was able to recover the western part of Asia Minor. Second, not only was the Holy Sepulcher rescued from Turkish hands but a bulwark of Christian states was established, stretching from Edessa on the Upper Euphrates, southward to Jerusalem and the frontiers of Moslem Egypt. Between these extreme outposts were two important crusading states: Antioch, which remained in the hands of Bohemond's Normans, and Tripoli, which was held by their bitter rival, Raymond of Toulouse. Edessa and Jerusalem were ruled by Godfrey of Bouillon's family.

When the latter died in 1100, Baldwin of Edessa took his place, and began at once to expand and organize the Kingdom of Jerusalem on a grand scale. Like the other Christian rulers, he applied to his realm the feudal principles that prevailed in the West; personal fidelity, military service, and baronial control of landed estates called fiefs. Inasmuch as the Holy Land continued in a state of warfare and disunity, the feudal system of government continued.[10] The Kingdom of Jerusalem was typically French in organization: a group of fiefs of various types, headed by a king whose powers were strictly limited in favor of his feudal vassals. Military service and separate feudal courts for the nobles, merchants, and native subjects were provided. Similar conditions prevailed in the other three crusading states which formed this miniature feudal Europe on the distant eastern frontier. This was Western Christendom's first experiment in foreign colonies, and the fact that the several states held their ground for over a century speaks well for the practical working value of feudal institutions in a disorganized warlike world. The outstanding defect was in internal administration. The natives, even the Christian Syrians, were harshly treated. Those who escaped the massacres and ravages of the initial

[10] The "Assizes of Jerusalem," a later collection of regulations, gives a detailed picture of the governmental institutions of the kingdom.

conquest were soon reduced to a serfdom or slavery more cruel than that of the former Moslem regime. Such conditions paved the way for the Turkish reconquest of the Holy Land.

Adapted from Robinson's *History of Western Europe*, Brief Edition. By permission of Ginn and Company.

CRUSADER STATES AND SEAPORTS IN THE EAST

ITALIAN COMMERCIAL EXPANSION

Much more significant than the feudal governments of the crusading barons was Italian commercial expansion in the Near East. The continued assistance of the fleets of the Genoese, Pisans, and Venetians, after the capture of Antioch and Jerusalem, was a vital factor in the existence of the crusading states. The fleets provided the line of communication for these faraway garrisons of Western Christendom. Besides bringing military supplies and new recruits, they provided active military assistance in the conquest of Syrian seaports such as Jaffa (near Jerusalem), Acre, Tyre, and Sidon. Commercial concessions were the principal rewards for such services, and soon the Christian merchants of the West were reaping a rich harvest. They not only transported crusaders, pilgrims, and supplies to the Holy Land; they carried back to the West cargoes of Eastern goods acquired from the Moslems. Many pious folk resented this trade with the infidel, but the keen Italian businessmen, like the modern merchants of munitions, made the most of their opportunities.

Each Italian city that took part in the capture of a town received as its part of the spoils a "quarter" which became an independent trading post. Here were established wharves, storehouses, offices, and homes for the resident merchants—all under the control of the home city. The Mediterranean coast of the Holy Land was dotted with commercial outposts of Western Europe's expanding mercantile cities. These outposts of economic life tapped the resources of the interior and also put the Christian merchants in contact with the Moslem commercial world. By this means they gained access to the untold resources of India and the Far East. Eventually the Italian city-states, in conjunction with the Moslems, became the commercial middlemen between the Orient and Western Europe. Together they monopolized this profitable trade in spices and other luxury goods until late in the fifteenth century.[11]

RELIGIOUS INSTI-
TUTIONS IN THE
HOLY LAND
The conquest of the Holy Land stimulated the formation of religious as well as political and economic institutions in the East. Permanent churches, monasteries, and clerical officials were established in the various states. Religious life flourished, due chiefly to the constant stream of pilgrims from the West. They came in such numbers at the holy seasons (Christmas and Easter) that the Italian and south French cities ran special excursion fleets to and from Jerusalem. At the same time the increased travel by land led to the formation of organizations for the care and protection of stray pilgrims. The "Poor Brethren of the *Hospital* of St. John at Jerusalem" began as a nursing fraternity caring for the sick. Later they took over the defense of pilgrims, and eventually established fortified stations all along the main routes, even

[11] See below, pp. 532 f.

in Western Europe. These "Hospitalers," as they were called, adopted as their insignia a red cross which is still known as the "Cross of Malta," from the name of the island to which their headquarters were later moved.

Even more famous and influential were the Knights Templars, a more militaristic order which is also still in existence. Originally this organization was composed of knights, squires, and chaplains who lived in the *Temple* of Solomon, from which they went forth under their white-cross banner to defend hapless pilgrims. Soon they set up branch chapters and built great fortresses, whose walls and towers can still be seen in the Holy Land. The "Temple-ers" became so popular that throughout the West they were endowed with fine chapter houses and landed estates. Their wealth was their undoing, for they came to be known as thrifty bankers, luxury-loving nobles, and corrupt politicians rather than as benefactors of the poor.[12] Nevertheless in the Holy Land their castles and their monastic-military organization were valuable elements in the unification and defense of the crusading states.

[12] See below, p. 561.

$=$ XXVI $=$

THE LATER CRUSADES

THE DEFENSE AND LOSS OF THE HOLY LAND

FOR almost a half century after the first crusades there were no expeditions to the Holy Land except those of pilgrims and small bands of warriors going out as reinforcements for the eastern armies. The Christians had attained their objectives, and the Moslems were disunited and incapable of effective counterattacks. An era of renewed crusading set in toward the middle of the twelfth century, when the Turks, having consolidated their forces, set about to recover the lost territories. The new crusades were therefore defensive. At first the objective was merely to retain control of the eastern conquests; later, after the Turkish capture of Jerusalem, there was a new effort for the recovery of the Holy Sepulcher. Although the crusades were increasingly unsuccessful, they continued as long as there were Christians who could be prevailed upon to "take the cross." In general, for two centuries, every generation of Westerners saw some sort of crusading expedition.

The Moslem counterattacks which brought on the new period of crusades can be viewed as a renewal of the exploits of the Turks, whose conquest of Asia Minor and the Holy Land had stirred the West to action in 1095. After building up a united Moslem power along the Euphrates, in 1144 one of the Turkish leaders captured Edessa, the Christian outpost in the North. For a time it seemed that history was about to repeat the story of the "first" crusade. A French pope, Eugene III, called upon the Christian world to take the cross, and a French monk, Bernard of Clairvaux, preached the crusade. This time, however, the populace did not respond, and the expeditions were led by kings rather than by barons.

The undertaking was a ludicrous failure. The German emperor, Conrad III, became ill en route; King Louis VII of France, accompanied by his dashing queen, Eleanor of Aquitaine, was amazingly in-

516

effective at every point; and a spectacular attack on Damascus brought
the so-called second crusade to an inglorious end. As the first of the
kings' crusades and also the first episode in the new period of crusading, it was prophetic of the future. Whether led by kings, nobles,
preachers, or merchants, the twelfth- and thirteenth-century expeditions to the Holy Land were outstandingly unsuccessful. Most of
them fell far short of their objectives and reflected little glory either
on the motives or on the efficiency of crusading Christendom.

THE MOSLEM
ADVANCE:
SALADIN

While the two Western kings were vainly attempting to restore Christian prestige in the Holy Land,
the Moslem forces were going from victory to victory.
Under a new Moslem leader, the Turkish empire expanded southward in such a manner as to envelop almost completely
the crusading states. The narrow band of Christian lands was hemmed
in between the sea and a line of threatening Moslem outposts. Edessa,
to the northwest, was now in Turkish hands. Directly west of Antioch was Aleppo, the chief Turkish stronghold. A short distance to
the south, on the frontiers of Tripoli and the Kingdom of Jerusalem,
lay Damascus, another Moslem center. Egypt, still further south, was
brought into the Turkish alliance as a result of the efforts of Saladin
(1174-1193), the future leader and hero of the Moslem world. Having
consolidated the Moslem realms that touched upon the crusading
states, Saladin took the offensive. Soon the westward extension of his
power between Antioch and Jerusalem threatened to cut the communications between the Christian states. When Saladin captured
Tiberias, on the Sea of Galilee, Jerusalem was seriously endangered.
Meanwhile the forces of the Eastern emperor had suffered a terrible
defeat in 1176 at the hands of Saladin's Turkish allies in Asia Minor.

The feudal warriors of the Kingdom of Jerusalem, whatever their
shortcomings, displayed remarkable courage in this critical situation.
Taking the offensive, they marched boldly against Saladin, carrying
the "True Cross" as their sacred emblem, and shouting with confidence the crusading battle cry, "Deus Volt." They were completely
routed, however, and the "True Cross" fell into the hands of the victorious infidel. Soon the crusading strongholds in Palestine and along
the coast fell before the invincible forces of Saladin. Jerusalem surrendered after a twelve-day siege, and the Christian West learned how
a despised infidel could spare his captured enemies. This was indeed

a sharp contrast to the Christian massacre of Moslem prisoners after their conquest of the Holy City in 1099.

THE "THREE-
KINGS' CRUSADE"
(1189)
News of Saladin's unparalleled success stirred the entire West to activity. At the pope's orders, fervent preachers exhorted the faithful to go once more to the rescue of the Holy Sepulcher. Not since the Council of Clermont had the pressure of religious propaganda and Christian public opinion been so strong. Never again was it to bring such a response. The greatest monarchs of Christendom were prevailed upon to cease plotting and warring, to mobilize their military resources, and to enroll under the banner of the cross. Frederick the Red-Bearded, the aged German emperor who had for years intrigued and fought against the papacy, now made his peace and started for the Holy Land. Henry II of England, Normandy, and Aquitaine, who had all his life schemed and fought against the clever French king, Philip II, came to terms with him, and both took the crusading pledge. When Henry died shortly after, a similar agreement was made by his son Richard. As a reward for displaying such a Christian spirit, the pope granted the English king the privilege of collecting from his subjects a "Saladin tithe" to defray the expenses of the Holy War. Long after Saladin's death the people of England continued to pay this tax. Similar contributions in other realms were authorized by the papal organizers of the crusade.

The auspicious beginning of the crusade was followed by constant difficulties and disasters. Frederick, with a carefully organized army of Germans, from which poor people and all women (except laundresses) had been excluded, followed the Danube route to Constantinople. There trouble broke out with the Eastern emperor, and in the course of the hostilities, Adrianople was sacked by the Germans. This was ominous evidence of the increasingly bitter feeling between Western and Eastern Christians. As the crusaders marched through Asia Minor, Frederick was accidentally drowned, and only a small remnant of his army ever reached the Holy Land.

RICHARD VERSUS
SALADIN
Meanwhile the forces of Philip II and Richard the Lion-Hearted, moving eastward by sea, had stopped at the island of Sicily for the winter (1189-1190). Here Richard incurred the deadly hostility of the new German emperor (Henry VI) by assisting the rebellious natives. He also quarreled violently with Philip, who soon went on to Palestine. While the

French and Germans were beginning the siege of the important sea-port of Acre, Richard turned aside and captured the island of Cyprus from its native Christian ruler. This was the only permanent success of the crusade, and for three centuries it remained in the hands of crusading rulers, serving as an important point for Western trade with the Near East. Eventually Richard joined the other crusaders in the siege of Acre, which held out for almost two years. The besiegers were themselves assailed by relieving forces led by Saladin, who, by means of swimmers, kept up communications with the beleaguered city. The crusaders countered by stretching great nets in the harbor. Prodigious deeds of valor, chiefly on the part of Richard, gradually turned the tide of conflict in favor of the Christians.

But there was constant strife between Richard and the other crusading leaders. It was out of hatred for Richard that the German leader, Duke Leopold of Austria, withdrew from the siege and re-turned home. Relations between the French and English became so strained that they were segregated and sent to the attack in separate sectors. Eventually Philip returned home to stir up trouble for Richard in France. This, however, did not hamper the Christian operations in the Holy Land. An Arab diplomat remarked that "the French king had always been a burden to Richard who, thanks be to Allah, was like a cat with a hammer tied to its tail" as long as Philip was present.

Richard's energy and military ability finally brought matters to a successful conclusion at Acre. The city surrendered, but the inex-cusable massacre of 3,000 Turkish prisoners who were to have been ransomed started fresh hostilities. In spite of such actions, Saladin came to admire the military courage and resourcefulness of his enemy and eventually agreed to a truce for "three years, three months, and three days" when Christian pilgrims would be allowed to visit Jeru-salem. Thus the end of the crusade found the Christians in posses-sion of only a few coast towns such as Acre. Jerusalem and most of the Holy Land were left in Turkish hands, in whose possession they remained until 1917.

A DISASTROUS
OUTCOME

The failure of the "third" crusade illustrates the out-come of the entire crusading movement. Against a united Moslem power, Western crusaders, due chiefly to their own disunity and petty jealousies, could do nothing. The events of this crusade also showed clearly the crudeness and bar-barous cruelty of the Christian warriors. The difference in the actions of Richard and Saladin adequately indicates the superiority of Moslem civilization over that of the West. Richard's peace treaty with Saladin did not put an end to his troubles. Shipwrecked on the Dalmatian coast of the Adriatic Sea en route for home, he was captured by his crusading enemy, Duke Leopold, and finally sold to another enemy, Emperor Henry VI, whom he had angered by his actions in Sicily. He was kept captive in a castle on the Danube until he did homage to the emperor and paid an immense ransom, the burden of which was felt by every inhabitant of the English realm.

Meanwhile Emperor Henry VI joined in another of the many vain efforts for the recovery of Jerusalem. A crusade was preached in Germany in 1195 and a large army prepared to set out for the Holy Land. The sudden death of the emperor put an end to any serious effort on the part of the Germans, and by the year 1200 Palestine seemed to be irrevocably lost. But the crusades continued for another century during which Europe was to witness events of unparalleled selfishness perpetrated in their name.

THE "FOURTH" CRUSADE Early in the thirteenth century occurred the most crassly commercial of all crusades, a merchant-controlled expedition that was diverted from its objective and directed against two Christian cities. The outcome was a travesty on the original crusading motives of Western Christendom and all sincere believers in the religion of the "Prince of Peace."

The newly elected pope, Innocent III (1198-1216), in his eagerness to guide aright the destinies of church and state, revived the idea of a crusade to recover the Holy Sepulcher. Inasmuch as the Germanies were in the throes of civil war, and the national monarchs were busied with internal affairs, there was little response. However, in 1199 a group of French nobles at a tournament in Champagne "took the cross." An embassy of barons, including the historian, Geoffrey of Villehardouin, was sent to Italy to arrange for transportation to Egypt, which was to serve as the crusaders' base of operations against the Holy Land. The obliging Venetians agreed to furnish food and passage at the rate of two marks per man and four marks per horse, and also to send fifty galleys "for the love of God" and *half of all the plunder*. By the summer of 1202 the crusaders were in Venice, camped on the Isle of Lido. Financial difficulties arose, and they were unable to pay the sum agreed upon. Since the Venetians refused transportation without some compensation, the crusaders agreed to pay off their debt by assisting in the conquest of Zara, a rival sea-port on the Adriatic belonging to Christian Hungary. In spite of the pope's threat to excommunicate any crusader who warred against Christian people, the Venetians and their allies captured, massacred, and plundered the unfortunate Zarans.

THE CRUSADE DIVERTED — Innocent III promptly excommunicated the Venetians and the wayward crusaders, but they appear to have paid little attention to him. It is possible that the Venetians already had a secret treaty with the Egyptian Moslems according to which they were to receive special commercial privileges in Alexandria on condition that they prevented the crusaders from attacking Egypt. At any rate, the actions of the Venetians indicate that they were determined to divert the expedition to some other point. Although some of the French crusaders left in disgust, most of the leaders were willing to combine religious duties with material profits. Out of this situation came the final plan for an attack on Constantinople.

The ground had been well prepared for a crusade against the Byzantine Empire. Venice, for centuries a valuable ally of the Eastern emperors, had been alienated by increasing opposition to her monopoly of commercial concessions. There had been anti-Venetian riots in Constantinople, and, to cap the climax, a bitter rival, Genoa, had been given important trading privileges in the empire. Thus disappointed, the Venetians easily found a pretext for attacking their former allies. The attack on Constantinople also found favor in the eyes of certain of the crusaders. It will be remembered that, from the beginning of the crusades, the Eastern emperors had been accused of treachery. Bohemond, Emperor Conrad of Germany, Frederick Barbarossa, and many another soldier of the cross had already come to blows with the Easterners. This century-old antagonism came to a head in 1202, when the son of an exiled Eastern emperor got in touch with the crusading leaders at Zara. He was supported by his German brother-in-law and other influential Westerners who had designs on Constantinople. The young prince promised that, once the crusaders had restored him to power at Constantinople, he would reward them richly, bring the Eastern Church under papal control, and join in the expedition for the rescue of the Holy Land. What could be more plausible? En route to Palestine, the crusaders would turn aside for a short time to restore an exile to his throne, to win treasures for themselves, to punish the detestable Easterners, and meanwhile gain an ally for their holy cause. Accordingly, in the spring of 1203 the Venetians and the main body of crusaders moved on to Constantinople.

ON TO CONSTAN-
TINOPLE (1203)

From the memoirs of Villehardouin,[1] one of the French leaders, we have a vivid account of the arrival at Constantinople and the subsequent events. As the crusaders approached the city they "gazed on it, wit ye well, for they had not dreamed there was in all the world so rich a city." And "the boldest of them trembled, for never was so great an undertaking since the world was created." At the first onslaught, the city fell, and the young prince was installed, with his father as co-emperor. But difficulties arose over the promised rewards, and the resentful populace broke out into such violent riots against the Westerners that they were forced either to retreat or to fight. In April, 1204, they attacked and stormed the city. After three terrible days of fire, slaughter, and plunder, the conquerors stopped to divide the spoils. Contemporary accounts vividly record both the inhuman ravages and marvelous acquisitions of the victors. The pope, in condemning the outrage, declared:

These defenders of Christ who should have turned their swords only against the infidels, have bathed [them] in Christian blood. They have respected neither religion, nor age, nor sex. They have committed in open day adultery, fornication, and incest. Matrons and virgins, even those vowed to God, were delivered to the ignominious brutality of the soldiery. And it was not enough for them to squander the treasures of the Empire and to rob private individuals, whether great or small. They have dared to lay their hands on the wealth of the churches . . . tearing from the altars the silver adornments, breaking them in fragments . . . violating the sanctuaries, carrying away the icons, crosses, and relics.[2]

Vivid as was the pope's account, he did not relate the full extent of the desecrations. The drunken plunderers trod underfoot sacred books and images, tore priestly ornaments from altars to give to courtesans, and, like Belshazzar's fellow revelers, drank from the consecrated vessels. In the Church of St. Sophia, a prostitute was raised to the patriarch's throne to sing a ribald song. Villehardouin, with no apparent shame at such outrages, wrote at length of the spoils of victory:

The booty gained was so great that none could tell you the end of it: gold and silver, and vessels and precious stones, and samite, and cloth

_____

[1] See below, p. 691.

[2] Charles Diehl's translation, *Cambridge Medieval History,* IV, 420; quoted by permission of The Macmillan Company and the Cambridge University Press.

of silk, and robes of vair and grey, and ermine, and every choicest thing found upon the earth . . . never, since the world was created, had so much booty been won in any city . . . those who before had been poor were now in wealth and luxury.[3]

In the annals of the crusades there is no more convincing account of the manner in which the soldiers of the cross could combine materialistic motives with supposedly religious undertakings.

EXPLOITATION OF THE CONQUERED EMPIRE

The plundering of the city of Constantinople was followed by a systematic dismembering of the empire. The Venetians received the most lucrative share: in addition to select portions of the city, including St. Sophia, the patriarch's palace, and ample harbor frontage, they were allotted valuable commercial locations such as Adrianople (on the land route to the Danube), port towns throughout the Aegean, and the strategic Ionian Isles and Corfu, at the mouth of the Adriatic Sea. As a result, Venice gained what amounted to a monopoly of the trade of the Mediterranean coast line from the Adriatic to the uttermost limits of the Black Sea. Meanwhile, the French barons contented themselves with princely estates in Greece and the Balkan peninsula. A joint commission of Venetians and crusaders selected an insignificant count, Baldwin of Flanders, to be ruler of the *"Latin Empire of Constantinople."* Baldwin was monarch in name only, for as in the former Kingdom of Jerusalem, the government was feudal in character.

So far as the religious settlement was concerned, the new patriarch, a Venetian, brought the Eastern Catholic Church under papal control as had been promised. In recognition of this fact, Pope Innocent III revoked his excommunications, recognized the *status quo,* and gave thanks for "the miracle wrought by God, to the glory of His name, to the honor and benefit of the Roman Church, and to the advantage of Christendom." Thus was the stamp of Christian respectability given to a merchant-controlled, baronial, commercial, and buccaneering expedition.

[3] *Memoirs of the Crusades,* translated by Sir Frank Marzials, p. 65. Among the spoils carried to Venice by the victors were the four bronze horses of St. Mark's, which had originally been brought to Constantinople from Rome by Constantine for the adornment of his new city. In later centuries, another conqueror, Napoleon, carried them from Venice to Paris to decorate his triumphal arch in the Tuileries Garden. Today a replica of them can be seen there; the originals were returned to Venice, at the fall of Napoleon, and are now on the façade of St. Mark's Church. See above, p. 158, note 6.

THE GREEK
RECOVERY OF
CONSTANTINOPLE
The Venetians, the French barons, and the pope were well satisfied with the outcome of the crusade, but in Constantinople and elsewhere in the empire anti-Western feeling ran high. At Nicæa and in the Balkan Epirus, Eastern Greek emperors still reigned. Further north, the Bulgars refused to submit to the new regime. Surrounded on all sides by enemies, Emperor Baldwin and his successors had little rest, and the Latin dynasty finally succumbed. Due to the absence of the Venetian fleet, which was engaged in a naval war with the Genoese, Constantinople was left with weak defenses. In 1261, the combined forces of the Genoese and the Greek emperor of Nicæa captured Constantinople and put an end to Venetian-French rule. Thus the Eastern Empire was restored to its rightful Eastern rulers, and Genoa took over the Venetian monopoly of the trade of the empire.

The general effects of the "fourth" crusade were perhaps more far reaching than those of any other, save the "first" crusade. But the crusade of 1097 won great glory for Christendom, whereas that of 1204 was so completely diverted from its original ideal that it marks the beginning of the end of the crusading movement. It also indicates clearly the new materialistic spirit that was coming to dominate the West.

THE CLOSE OF
THE CRUSADING
MOVEMENT
Except for the prominent personages who were involved and for the fact that they illustrate the strange willfulness by which generation after generation engaged in disastrous and ineffective warfare, the remaining crusades of the thirteenth century are hardly worthy of attention. Pope Innocent III persisted in his crusading efforts. The Children's Crusade of 1212 was more idealistic but even less successful than the expedition to Constantinople.[4] The pope also tried his hand at crusades in the West. King John of England was brought into subjection to the papacy by the threat of a crusade against his realm.[5] The Albigensian heresy in southwestern France was crushed after twenty years of cruel ravaging by north French "crusaders" (1208-1229).[6] The four crusades of Innocent III's era may have increased the political power of the papacy, but they destroyed the crusading ideals of Western Christendom. Henceforth most of the expeditions to the Holy Land were half-hearted efforts, devoid of genuine crusading zeal. The materialistic attitude of both popes and crusaders is best ex-

[4] See above, p. 504, note 3.   [6] See above, p. 444.
[5] See above, p. 401.

emplified by the experiences of Emperor Frederick II (1212-1250). Forced by a scheming pope to carry out his crusading vow, the young monarch won a startling success by means of diplomatic intrigues with Moslem rulers, only to find that the pope had excommunicated him and had launched a "crusade" against his Italian realms.[7] The one genuinely idealistic crusader of the century, Louis IX of France (1226-1270), was rewarded by the most disheartening failure.[8] Nevertheless, popes continued to preach crusades, kings and clerics collected funds for warfare against the Moslems, and occasionally an expedition set forth on another vain venture. Finally with the fall of Antioch (1268) and Acre (1291), the last Christian strongholds in the East were lost and serious efforts for the recovery of the Holy Land came to an end.

THE RESULTS OF THE CRUSADING MOVEMENT

RECOVERY OF
THE HOLY
SEPULCHER

In the opinion of the majority of earlier historians the crusades were spectacularly heroic expeditions, motivated chiefly by unselfish devotion to the cause of religion, and resulting in great advancement for Christendom. The present generation of scholars views the crusading movement primarily in terms of materialistic motivation, needless waste, and negative results of a so-called righteous war. Although neither extreme of opinion is valid for all aspects of the crusades, the latter viewpoint seems to be the more accurate analysis, especially in the light of the results of the movement. This is most apparent when we consider the two major objectives of the crusades as set forth originally by Urban II: the recovery of the Holy Sepulcher, and the rescue of the Eastern Empire from the menace of Turkish invasion.

So far as the recovery of the Holy Land is concerned, the net result of two centuries of crusading (1096-1291) was Christian control of Jerusalem and its vicinity for only about half of that period—from 1100 to 1189. Antioch and Acre held out against the Turks with difficulty for some time longer. This was a pitifully meager result. Throughout the entire medieval and modern era, both before and after the twelfth-century crusades, Palestine was in Moslem hands. The Arabian Moslems captured the Holy Land from the Byzantine Empire in the seventh century; 400 years later they were displaced by

[7] See above, p. 405.
[8] See above, p. 482.

the Seljuk Turks. After one century of crusading rule came Saladin, whose Moslem successors were eventually conquered by the hordes of Genghis and Kublai Khan in the thirteenth century. A century later the Ottoman Turks appeared, and it was not until the World War that they were driven from Jerusalem by the forces of General Allenby. Thus, for only one out of the thirteen centuries since Mohammed has the Holy Land been held by Christians. The crusades were therefore an ineffective effort of the Christian West to break the Moslem grip on Palestine and the strategic neighboring regions that comprise the "bridge of the continents."

THE "RESCUE OF THE EASTERN EMPIRE" No less ineffective were the crusading activities and results as they affected the Byzantine Empire. For ten centuries after the passing of the Roman Empire of the West, the Eastern Empire stood intact, a bulwark that protected Western Europe from Moslem attacks. In 1095, Pope Urban II called upon Christendom to rescue the Eastern Empire from the Turkish menace. From the outset this crusading objective was violated. Few crusaders even attempted to co-operate with the imperial forces, and eventually (1204) a crusading expedition sacked, plundered, and occupied Constantinople, the greatest Christian city of the Mediterranean. The net result of the crusades was therefore the destruction, rather than the rescue, of the Eastern Empire.

After 1261, when the Easterners forcibly expelled the "crusaders" and re-established their empire, Constantinople once more became a bulwark of defense for the West against the advancing Moslems. But the restored empire had little vitality and the Ottoman Turks soon took possession of Asia Minor. Early in the fourteenth century, internal troubles in Constantinople gave the Turks their first opportunity to set foot on European soil. By the end of that century they had conquered most of the Balkan peninsula, and in 1453 the city of Constantinople, the last remnant of the Byzantine realm, fell before the artillery and infantry attack of the Moslem. For over two centuries thereafter (until 1683) Western Europe was threatened with invasion and conquest at the hands of the Turks.

It is interesting to note that these Moslem invaders invariably followed the Danube route, along which so many crusading armies had marched to attack the Turks. In the outer walls of St. Stephen's Church at Vienna are still to be seen the marks of the Turkish cannonading of those desperate years. It is apparent that the "crusade" of 1204, by crippling the Eastern Empire, hastened the advance of the

Turks and helped to bring the Moslem menace to the very threshold
of Central Europe, where for centuries the presence of the Turks in
Europe gave rise to serious complications in the Near East and in
Western politics.

INFLUENCE OF
THE CRUSADES
ON THE WEST

During the crusading period the military, political,
economic, religious, and cultural structure of Western Europe experienced many changes. Most of these
changes, however, were under way before the crusades began and probably would have occurred even had there been
no such expeditions. Nevertheless, changes already begun were greatly
hastened by the crusading activities. For instance, warriors who had
been trained in Western methods of warfare adopted many of the
more advanced military tactics of the Byzantines and Moslems. Among
these were various kinds of siege machinery, improved types of castle
construction,[9] and the use of Greek fire [10] and the crossbow.

The size and complexity of crusading armies also led to a decided
increase in the use of family names (such, for instance, as Smith,
Weaver, Brown, John-son, Fitz-Patrick, von Weber, de Villehardouin,
and so on) as a means of distinguishing individuals bearing the same
given name. Heraldic devices on shields and helmets, like surnames,
were employed because of the necessity of personal identification in
large groups of warriors.

Politically the crusades are sometimes said to have hastened the
development of absolute monarchy, due to the fact that the troublesome feudal nobility was drained from the homeland by crusades.
But absolute monarchy established itself with remarkable effectiveness
in regions such as Norman Sicily, where the feudal nobility remained
at home. In England, on the other hand, just after Richard the Lion-
Hearted's crusade there was a marked decline in royal power. Influences other than the crusades were the determining factors in the
political development of the Western nations.

The same is true of the religious influences of the crusades. To
be sure, many people found in expeditions to the Holy Land an outlet and renewed inspiration for their piety. But this was less evident
in the crusades than in the pilgrimages, which had been going on for
centuries. Then, on the other hand, many people found in the crusades that disillusionment, cynicism, and distrust of mankind which
wars always engender in reflective minds. So far as the papacy was

[9] See above, p. 233.
[10] See above, p. 153, note 4.

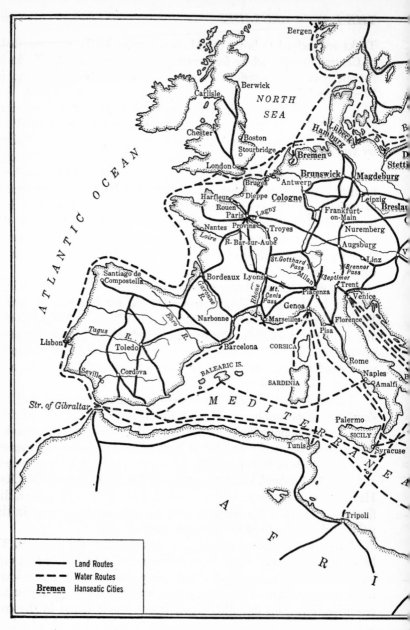

MEDIEVA

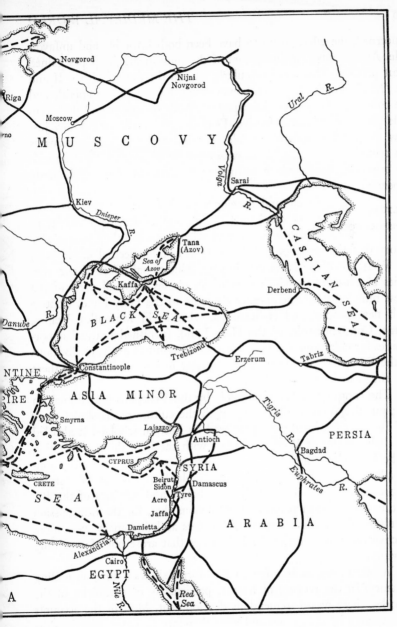

A

concerned, the effects seem to have been both favorable and unfavorable. At the outset, as instigators of the movement, the popes gained great prestige. This was particularly true in the case of Urban II and the "first" crusade. Later on, however, constant crusading appeals and the continued failures of the expeditions put the popes and their crusade preachers on the defensive. Doubtless we shall never know just how much Christendom's morale was shaken by such expeditions as the crusade of 1204, and how weary people became of papal appeals for crusading funds which seemed to be uselessly if not dishonestly expended.

CULTURAL CONSEQUENCES   In cultural developments it is evident that the crusades quickened an already advancing civilization. There is no ground whatsoever for the once-popular theory that the crusades ended a long era of intellectual darkness in the West. Yet there is no denying the educational effect of two centuries of crusades in which men of all classes from all parts of the West mingled with one another en route to the Holy Land. Contact with new peoples and civilizations, whether in Marseilles, Venice, Rome, Constantinople, or the Holy Land, furnished unusual opportunities for enlarging the mental horizon. Inasmuch as the civilizations of the East were at this time far superior to that of the West, there was much to learn.

The conquest of Constantinople by the Venetians and French in 1204 put the West in close touch with the culture of classical Greece and Rome, which had been preserved by Eastern scholars. It also led to a half-century of Western contact with the flourishing civilization of the East. Of even greater cultural influence, however, was the non-crusading realm of the Normans in Naples-Sicily, where Westerners were constantly associated with the scholars and writings of the Byzantine and Moslem realms.[11] It is obvious that, for the transmission of culture, the normal contacts of business and diplomacy were more effective than the occasional relationships that arose out of crusading activities.

Western progress in a few literary forms shows a direct crusading influence. In the writing of history, particularly of chronicles of the crusades, there was a tremendous development. Most of the accounts were written by clergymen and were therefore in Latin. But the thirteenth century brought forth a new type of crusade history which is

[11] See above, pp. 396 f.

nonclerical in character. Villehardouin and Joinville [12] were lay nobles who wrote concerning their own experiences, and in a vernacular tongue (French) which could be read by laymen. Geographical studies also made great strides during the crusades. Maps of the Mediterranean Sea became common and were much more accurate than formerly. Popular guide books were compiled for pilgrims, and thus travel-knowledge was brought to the lower ranks of society.

Western Europe, we may conclude, would have developed in much the same way, though perhaps much more slowly, had there been no crusades. During the period in which the crusades occurred there was remarkable progress in all phases of civilized life, but this was not due primarily to crusading activities. The age was one of unusual expansion. The crusades were one, and only one, of the symptoms of a rapidly changing civilization that was becoming more and more modern. This was particularly evident in the economic developments to which we now turn our attention.

[12] See below, p. 691.

═ XXVII ═

THE ECONOMIC EXPANSION OF
WESTERN EUROPE

ONE aspect of Western expansion which is clearly reflected in the crusades deserves special attention: the development of commerce. Commercial interests, as we have seen, tended to control the policies of the crusading states in the Holy Land and to dominate some of the later crusades. The commercial classes of the Italian, south French, and Spanish towns may not have made the major contribution to the crusading cause but they certainly derived most of the profits. As a result of the crusades, the growing commercial life of the West, particularly in the region of the Mediterranean, was given a tremendous impetus. It has been said that "the one lasting and essential result of the crusades was to give the Italian towns, and in less degree, those of Provence and Catalonia, the mastery of the Mediterranean." [1]

THE EASTWARD
EXPANSION OF
COMMERCE
Long before the crusades, the Italian townsfolk had been active in trade, both in the East and West. Nevertheless, because of Moslem control of Spain and the African coasts, this precrusading trade was restricted to the northern shores of the Mediterranean. In the East, most of the ancient routes of Oriental commerce were in the hands of the Byzantines and the Moslems. Of all the Westerners, only the Venetians had commercial concessions of much importance in the eastern Mediterranean, and most of these were in Constantinople.

The crusades did two things: they expanded Venetian commerce in the East, and they brought other cities into active trade relations with the Byzantines and the Moslems. The Genoese and other merchant folk who had confined their activities to the western Mediterranean, now began to compete with the Venetians for the Oriental carrying trade. With the siege of Antioch in 1097, Genoese and Pisan merchants began to co-operate with the crusaders and to extend their

---

[1] Pirenne, *Economic and Social History of Medieval Europe*, p. 33.

commercial activities into the East. Within a year after the arrival of the Genoese fleet with supplies, the crusaders had granted them valuable concessions. Soon enterprising traders from Marseilles and Barcelona, as well as from Genoa, Pisa, and Venice, were transporting crusaders, pilgrims, and provisions to the Holy Land. These merchants made double profits by *exporting* Western warriors (many of whom never returned) and by *importing* Eastern products purchased from the Moslems. Of the two kinds of cargo, the latter became the more profitable, for the crusades stimulated the Western demand for many products hitherto little used.

The West had always imported from the East small quantities of luxuries, such as spices. The crusades popularized these commodities and introduced new ones. Sugar, for instance, which had been used for centuries in the West as a drug, came into more common use after the crusaders learned its value as a food. Similarly, many Westerners developed a taste for novel articles such as rice, lemons, oranges, apricots (called "Damascus" plums), melons, and garlic (called "little onions of Ascalon"). There were also cotton, silks, new varieties of perfumes, and various kinds of cloth. Thus the rising standard of living of the West brought increased profits to enterprising merchant importers of the Mediterranean.

WESTERN EUROPE AND THE FAR EAST The crusading period was also marked by the eastward extension of Europe's trading posts and the establishment of distant points of contact which took the form of commercial colonies. For almost two centuries Western merchants held all of the important seaports of Syria, and controlled the commerce of the eastern Mediterranean. This enabled them to tap the Moslem trade routes leading to the Orient, and to import larger quantities of luxury products into Europe. Even after the Holy Land had been lost to the Turks (1189-1291), Westerners continued their trade with the advancing Moslems, and with Egypt and the Black Sea region.

The increasing interest in Oriental goods also inspired exploring expeditions, for the purpose of eliminating the Moslem middlemen by putting European merchants in direct contact with the Oriental producers. Of the Western missionaries, diplomats, and merchants who made their way eastward to the Orient the most famous were the Polos. At about 1271 two Venetian merchants, the Polo brothers, with their nephew and son, Marco, journeyed across Asia to the court of the Grand Khan at Peking. Marco remained there for almost twenty years, meanwhile serving as one of the Khan's officials. After his return to Italy, while a prisoner of war in Genoa, Marco wrote his *Travels,* an account of the wealth and wonders of the Orient: its great cities, beautiful parks and palaces, and, above all, its silks, gems, and lavish display of gold. The direct economic results of these expeditions was slight, but from books such as Marco's, Westerners became tremendously interested in the Orient.[2] This interest was an important factor in inspiring the later voyages of discovery.

THE WESTWARD
EXPANSION OF
COMMERCE

Meanwhile, efforts at commercial expansion not initiated by the crusades were under way in the West. In much the same manner in which the Venetians had been active in the eastern Mediterranean, the Genoese and Pisans had been exploring and exploiting the western Mediterranean long before the Council of Clermont. In 1087 a joint expedition captured Mahdia in Tunis, massacred "the priests of Mohammed," and forced the Moslems to sign a commercial treaty. The splendid cathedral of Pisa, built to celebrate this successful commercial "crusade," was adorned with Moslem spoils. During the period of crusading and merchandising in the East, the western Mediterranean, likewise, was being opened to Europeans. Italian merchants, Norman princes of Sicily, and Spanish kings carried on successful campaigns to make the coasts of Africa and Spain safe for Christian pilgrims and traders.

By the end of the thirteenth century, Genoese fleets were pushing past the Straits of Gibraltar and exploring the Atlantic coasts of Africa. But these enterprises had no permanent results and the commercial exploitation of the Atlantic was delayed until the explorations of the Portuguese in the fifteenth century and the subsequent voyages of Vasco da Gama and Columbus.

As in so many other phases of Western life, the crusades mark a rapid increase in economic activities already well under way. On the other hand, in some regions economic life suffered certain setbacks. The strenuous competition for Mediterranean trade led to bitter rivalries, such as that between Genoa and Venice. Genoese intervention in the East threatened Venetian trade, and the fleets of the two cities fought over commercial concessions in the Holy Land as fiercely as the Western crusaders contended for the spoils of Mos-

---

[2] Among other Westerners who visited the Orient and wrote of their travels were the French diplomat, William of Rubruk, and the missionaries, John of Plano Carpini, and John of Monte Corvino.

lem cities. Even the Eastern Empire was involved in the struggle. As we have seen, Genoese concessions in Constantinople so angered the Venetians that they began to plot against the empire, and eventually, in 1204, brought about its downfall. Half a century later, a Genoese expedition joined in overthrowing the Venetian-French regime and restoring the Eastern Empire. The reward was Genoese control of the trade of the empire.

Throughout the thirteenth century Venice and Genoa fought for supremacy in the East, in the West, in the Holy Land and even at their own harbor entrances. Long before they had exhausted themselves in this struggle for the monopoly of Mediterranean commerce, the prize had begun to slip from their hands into the grasp of a new Moslem power, the Ottoman Turks. Eventually all Italian traders were forced to make terms with the Turks, and by the end of the Middle Ages Italy's commercial prosperity was waning.

CHANGING METHODS OF COMMERCE
While the routes of Western trade were expanding during the crusading ages, methods of business were being revolutionized. It has been said that the crusades "enabled Western Europe not only to monopolise the whole trade from the Bosphorus and Syria to the Straits of Gibraltar, but to develop there an economic and *strictly capitalistic activity* which was gradually to communicate itself to all the lands north of the Alps."[3] In fact modern capitalism may be said to have been born during the age of the crusades. The word "capital" was actually used in thirteenth-century Italy for funds invested in business enterprises.[4]

By the end of the thirteenth century the ports of the Mediterranean, the English Channel, the North Sea, and the Baltic were filled with ships owned by clever merchants who employed most of the business methods that are associated with capitalistic commerce. It was the international carrying trade in Oriental goods that furnished the chief impetus for these early capitalistic activities. The Mediterranean trade in spices and other luxury goods provided an admirable opportunity for profits. These articles were light in weight, easy to transport, and found a ready sale, at high prices, in the West. The steady increase of prosperous towns and of the upper- and middle-class population broadened the European market for luxuries. The crusades and the reopening of the entire Mediterranean to West-

[3] Pirenne, *op. cit.,* p. 33. The italics are mine.
[4] *Ibid.,* p. 168.

ern commerce made it possible to acquire Oriental goods in larger quantities.

ITALIAN
COMMERCE

By the end of the crusading period the merchant importers of Italy, southern France, and Spain had made tremendous advances in economic technique. Contact with the Byzantines and the Moslems had taught them new business methods. They had fleets of ships, propelled by both oars and sails, which transported goods from their wharves and warehouses in the East to the home ports. Here these materials were reworked, packed, and sold to visiting merchant buyers, or reshipped to the markets of the West. By the fourteenth century the Genoese and Venetian importers of Oriental goods were reshipping them by way of Gibraltar and the Atlantic to Bruges in Flanders, where they were sold to North European buyers. Consignments were also sent by pack train to inland points in Italy or across the Alps to south German towns. In the thirteenth century, a suspension bridge, the earliest known in the West, was built across the gorge of the St. Gothard Pass in the Alps, to accommodate the increasing traffic.

NORTH EURO-
PEAN COM-
MERCE: BRUGES

Meanwhile, Northern Europe was developing its own mercantile life. The importation of attractive Oriental goods, by way of Italy, stimulated local industrial and commercial life. The townsfolk of the Netherlands found that their textiles could be exchanged for the goods brought by Italian importers, or could be sold to other northern countries. Before the middle of the fourteenth century Bruges, on the Scheldt (one of the mouths of the Rhine River), had become a great exchange center. Here the fine woolen cloth of Flanders was exchanged for luxury goods from Italy. To this port, likewise, came raw materials including timber, furs, honey, wax, and fish, from the Hanseatic cities of the Baltic [5] and long fine wool from the English countryside. The bustling economic life of such a port was reproduced on a small scale at innumerable trading centers elsewhere throughout the West.

FINANCIAL
TRANSACTIONS

Many merchants were chiefly wholesalers who served merely as distributors of goods to local dealers. Their transactions were carried on at seaport towns, large city markets, and fairs. They employed in some form or other most

_____
[5] See below, p. 615, concerning the Hanseatic League.

STREET SCENE

(Ca. 1500)

FISH MARKET (XIII C)

SHOPS (XV C)

JEWISH MONEYLENDER (XIV C)

BUSINESS LIFE

(See pp. 536 ff.)

HALLWAY OF JACQUES COEUR'S HOUSE, BOURGES (XV C)

Courtesy of the University Prints

COURTYARD OF JACQUES COEUR'S

HOUSE, BOURGES (XV C)

OLD HOUSE, ROUEN

BURGHER RESIDENCES

(See pp. 368, 720 f.)

of the methods of cash and credit payments known to modern business. Early in the era of town development there was an increased demand for coined money. For some time virtually the only *gold* coins in circulation were the East-Roman *bezants,* so called from Byzantium, the ancient name of the capital city, Constantinople. There were many silver coins, of innumerable and bewildering varieties and values. Every great baron coined his own money; in fact, often he recoined it so as to make a profit from the minting operation. Little wonder that Jewish and north Italian money changers and coin testers were in demand at markets and fairs. By the weight, ring, or bite of a coin they could estimate its approximate value; and they were ready to exchange it for the coinage needed, at a safe margin of personal profit.

By the end of the thirteenth century, Florence and Venice had established their currencies on a stable gold basis, and all Europe accepted the gold florin of Florence [6] and the ducat (named after the duke, or doge) of Venice at their face value. Eventually Florentine gold coinage became the standard of exchange and throughout the West other currencies, both gold and silver, were adjusted accordingly. In the course of time the various Western nations established their own gold coins, often calling in Florentine experts to assist in the establishment of their mints.

CREDIT
TRANSACTIONS
Meanwhile increasing trade, travel and the crusades had created a demand for credit. Many a royal crusader raised funds by mortgaging property to a monastery or the Knights Templars. From them he might receive what amounted to a letter of credit authorizing him to draw funds from any chapter of the Order in the Holy Land or en route there. Thus the danger of loss or robbery was eliminated. In like manner, a merchant, instead of carrying with him sufficient silver coin to finance a journey, could deposit his cash with a merchant-banker. The receipt that was given him could be presented at any other office of the same organization, in case he wished to draw funds. By the end of the Middle Ages travelers and merchants throughout the West were using bills of exchange and letters of credit in practically the

---

[6] England still has a silver coin called the florin. The Florentines began to mint gold florin in 1252. The Genoese had minted gold coins, perhaps even earlier, and in the early thirteenth century Frederick II minted gold augustals. Neither of these continued in use. The earliest ducats were minted by *Duke* Roger II of Sicily in 1140.

same manner in which they are used nowadays by Americans in Europe. Bank notes and checks were beginning to be used in some regions.

Merchants seldom paid cash for large purchases. Because of the danger and inconvenience of carrying large amounts of money, most payments were made by credit transactions. Papal bills of exchange were the commonest method. A buyer would give his written promise to pay the sum owed at a certain time and place. Most accounts of this kind were made payable at some trading point where merchants congregated—at the fairs of Champagne or, later on, at financial centers such as Bruges or Antwerp in Flanders. Quite early the financial agents at such places began to operate after the fashion of a clearing house, balancing each merchant's credits with his debts. Thus comparatively little cash changed hands, and much of Western commerce came to be handled on a credit basis. Money changers and other types of financial experts did a thriving business. Business records were kept according to scientific methods. Early in the thirteenth century an Italian wrote a book on accounting, and by the end of the century both single- and double-entry bookkeeping were in use.

BANKING

From the custom of extending credit to purchasers there developed regular loan banking.[7] For instance, at the Champagne fairs merchant bankers who had surplus capital made loans to monarchs. Both Edward I of England and Philip IV of France borrowed huge sums from the Italian bankers. Rates of interest varied from 5 to 40 per cent, according to the risks. Inasmuch as the taking of interest (usury) was forbidden by the church various methods of evasion were employed. Interest was paid in the form of labor, damages for delayed repayment, or by a fictitious sale and repurchase. Often a banker would merely withhold the percentage agreed on when he handed over the cash. Thus the borrower of a hundred shillings might actually receive only ninety; ten shillings were held back as the equivalent of 10 per cent interest. Some towns permitted the taking of interest openly.

By the end of the thirteenth century merchants with large capital surpluses were discovering that there was more profit in handling money than in dealing in merchandise. It was easy to evade

---

[7] The word "bank" was used in the thirteenth century for the tables (*banchi*) at which money was handled.

the religious prohibition against interest,[8] and banking became a lucrative side line for most wealthy merchants. It is interesting to note, however, that until rather recently the bankers were considered as usurious exploiters of their fellow men and deserving of ostracism from polite society. But when prosperity and money economy brought financial transactions into public favor, the bankers rose in the social scale and they have come to be rated with the upper classes in every modern town.

CAPITALISTIC FORTUNES

During the fourteenth and fifteenth centuries banking and capitalistic finance continued to develop throughout the West. In fourteenth-century Florence such financier families as the Peruzzi, the Franzoni, the Frescobaldi, and the Bardi handled international loans as well as imports, exports, and industrial enterprises. The Peruzzi are said to have amassed a fortune amounting to $800,000. Unfortunately, along with several other Florentine banks, they loaned Edward III of England funds with which to invade France. The expedition ended in disaster, the king repudiated the loan, and the bankers failed. Within a century the leadership in Florentine banking had come into the hands of the famous Medici family, who boasted a fortune approximating seven million dollars. Their chief income came from the handling of the papal finances. They also transmitted funds to Rome from various countries and made loans to the papacy. At one time they held the papal crown as security.

After the middle of the fifteenth century Northerners began to equal and even to surpass the Italians in financial activities. In the Netherlands, for instance, Antwerp and Ghent became important banking centers. Jacques Coeur of Bourges, in central France, at about 1450 operated an international banking and mercantile business with branch establishments in all important cities of the West. His wealth was comparable to that of a multimillionaire in our day, and his financial operations resembled those employed by the Rothschilds, Rockefellers, and Morgans in modern times. A century later, Augsburg in southern Germany was the headquarters of a still greater concern, that of the Fuggers. A modern writer has given the following vivid description of the far-reaching enterprises of this medieval corporation:

---

[8] A fourteenth-century Italian expressed the general attitude of businessmen when he wrote: "He who takes usury goes to hell; he who does not, goes to the workhouse." See below, p. 683, on the problem of usury in the Middle Ages.

Thanks to judicious loans to Maximilian, [they] had acquired enormous concessions of mineral property . . . silver and quicksilver mines in Spain, and controlled banking and commercial businesses in Italy, and above all, at Antwerp. They advanced the money which made Albrecht of Brandenburg archbishop of Mainz; repaid themselves by sending their agent to accompany Tetzel on his campaign to raise money by indulgences and taking half of the proceeds; provided the funds with which Charles V bought the imperial crown, after an election conducted with the publicity of an auction and the morals of a gambling hell; browbeat him, when the debt was not paid, in the tone of a pawnbroker rating a necessitous client; and found the money with which Charles raised troops to fight the Protestants in 1552. The head of the firm built a church and endowed an almshouse for the aged poor in his native town of Augsburg. [With a fortune of about $40,000,000] he died in the odor of sanctity, a good Catholic and a Count of the Empire, having seen his firm pay 54 per cent for the preceding sixteen years.[9]

Little wonder that sixteenth-century reformers condemned capitalists and their sharp practices as "usury and Fuggery." Such, in fact, were the capitalistic organizations and activities that had been developing in the West during the last five centuries of the Middle Ages.

TRADING COMPANIES — Among the many improvements in capitalistic methods during these centuries was the development of commercial organizations. As long as his business was conducted in a home shop, on a small scale, a merchant could operate as an individual. But foreign commerce demanded organized effort. Ordinarily one man could not carry on a big venture involving the sending of several ships to the Near East for spices. A partnership of two or more members might provide sufficient capital and administrative experience to handle extensive activities. Because of its simplicity of organization and operation, this was the prevailing form of business association until late in the Middle Ages. In Italy partnerships were common as early as the twelfth century; in the North they were about a century later in development. Many such associations, notably the great banking firms of Florence, were family affairs, or at least were under the domination of one family.

Another type of partnership was the *commenda,* or "sleeping partnership," an adaptation from Roman and Byzantine practice. The "sleeping" partners usually provided a certain amount of capital for an

---

[9] Tawney, *Religion and the Rise of Capitalism,* p. 79. Quoted by permission of Harcourt, Brace and Company.

enterprise which was managed by the active partners. Often such arrangements were made merely for one business venture. Rather similar to the "sleeping partnership" was the arrangement by which funds were merely loaned to those engaged actively in a specific enterprise. In such a case the lender played a role resembling that of the "sleeping" partner.

Although partnerships were employed successfully in all parts of the West during the late Middle Ages, they proved inadequate for permanent and far-reaching enterprises of a complex nature. A partnership, even though renewed for successive ventures, was usually dissolved at the death of any member. Such uncertain associations discouraged the development of intricate and specialized techniques of business administration. Furthermore they had the serious drawback of unlimited financial liability. Any partner might be held for the entire amount of indebtedness of his associates. Not until modern times was this restriction eliminated.

Toward the end of the Middle Ages an improved type of business association came into being. A group of men would combine their resources and form a company for one commercial venture. Such combinations worked so well that permanent association for long-time enterprises came into being. They might consist merely of a group of *individual* merchants who formed a "regulated company" for trade in the East or the New World. The members cooperated in certain ways—using the same docks, warehouses, or ships —but each conducting his own business by himself.

This eventually gave rise to a more successful kind of association, the joint-stock company, which appeared in Italy late in the Middle Ages but did not achieve importance until the sixteenth and seventeenth centuries. In this form of organization each member contributed a certain amount of money, for which he received a certain share of stock. He assumed risks and received profits in proportion to the amount of his investment and stock. Such a company was permanent and could operate regardless of deaths, withdrawals, and other changes in its membership. A large stock company, composed of wealthy and influential men, could often get governmental protection, trade monopolies in certain commodities or regions, and various other favors by means of which their profits could be increased. This type of organization was a logical evolution from the medieval partnership, and it became the germ of the modern corporation.

In similar fashion, though much earlier in most cases than the regulated company and the joint-stock company, the West made many minor advances in business technique. Most of these changes foreshadowed the economic practices of the modern world. All of them were inspired by the growing volume of commerce throughout the West. The most marked progress occurred in the field of monetary exchange, especially in connection with the standardization of coinage and the improvement of credit transactions. In the westernmost regions of Europe the rising national monarchies contributed much to the enlargement and stabilization of commercial activities, by endeavoring to establish nationwide currencies and by encouraging the free interchange of goods throughout their realms.

ECONOMIC DIFFICULTIES Many of the improvements in business conditions which we have discussed came into being during the age of the crusades, and at least in part as a result of the economic opportunities offered by the crusades. In practically all cases the new developments appeared first in the Mediterranean cities, whence they eventually spread northward along with the gradually expanding trade of the West. Although progress was rapid and continuous in certain favored urban sections such as northern Italy and the Netherlands, there were regions and periods in which economic prosperity suffered disastrous setbacks.

This was particularly true of the fourteenth and early fifteenth centuries, which was an era of recurring economic discontent and political strife. At first glance one is tempted to attribute the unfavorable conditions to such catastrophes as the widespread famines of 1315-1317, the Black Death of 1348-1349, the recurring peasant and proletarian revolts, or to devastating conflicts of which the Hundred Years' War was the most destructive. Although these events had disastrous effects on all types of economic activity, it seems probable that the situation was dependent on underlying factors of greater permanence than these. For example, the peasant revolts were not so much the *cause* of economic distress as the *result* of developments in agriculture that were unfavorable to the peasants.

Broadly speaking, the economic life of this period lacked the prosperity and stability of the previous age. In fact, most aspects of the civilization of the fourteenth and early fifteenth centuries manifest the same unsettled tendencies. Whereas thirteenth-century civilization represented the culmination of an evolution that had been going on since the early Middle Ages, the fourteenth and early fifteenth centuries were an era of constant and often violent political, social, and economic upsets, readjustments, disorders, and revolutions. The relatively constant progress of Western civilization, thus interrupted for about a century and a half, began to move on apace during the late fifteenth and sixteenth centuries. In some respects, it seems that Europe, having girded its loins afresh, now set forth upon the still greater venture of world expansion. During the crusading period all phases of economic life had been speeded up by the opening of the entire Mediterranean to Western commerce. Again, toward the end of the fifteenth century, with the opening of the Atlantic sea routes, Europe entered upon a new expansive movement. In each case, foreign commerce made tremendous advances; then local trade and industry were affected, and eventually all society from the kings to the rural peasantry shared in the increased economic prosperity.

Between these two eras of rapid expansion came the period in question, the fourteenth and early fifteenth centuries. It should be noted, however, that it was not so much a recession or depression as an era of consolidation and readjustment. In many lines of economic activity, the accumulated resources of the preceding age were so successfully exploited that certain classes in certain favored regions enjoyed increased prosperity. Although foreign expansion was for the most part blocked, landlords, artisans, merchants, and kings were solving many of their economic difficulties and working out new techniques that contributed much to future progress.

AGRICULTURAL DEVELOPMENTS In order to understand the nature of this strange break in the development of Western institutions, it will be necessary to survey the conditions prevailing in commerce, industry, and agriculture. Agricultural conditions before the fourteenth century were unusually prosperous. It has been said that the peasantry were better off during the twelfth and thirteenth centuries than at any time during the entire Middle Ages. It was during this period that serfdom gave way to tenancy in most regions, that many peasant obligations were changed to money payments, and that expanding town life and rising prices of agricultural products brought wealth to the peasantry.

The fourteenth century brought distinctly less favorable conditions. The change can be traced, at least in a general way, to one major factor: in most regions of the West agricultural expansion had come to a standstill. German migration into the Slavic lands on the eastern frontiers was stopped. In many parts of the West there was a similar cessation of migration. The path of external expansion for most agriculturalists seems to have been definitely closed. Meanwhile, by the end of the thirteenth century the manorial system had been extended throughout the West to practically all of the tillable lands. For centuries kings and nobles had been founding villages and offering inducements for agricultural workers to settle on their lands. There was a marked slackening of such opportunities in the fourteenth century. In certain regions, conditions were so difficult that villages were deserted.

Few of the peasantry, even those who had risen from serfdom to free tenancy, were able to obtain farms of their own. Much of their hardships can be attributed to the increasing financial burdens laid upon them by the landlord class. Everywhere, it seems, the upper classes, pressed by the need for ready money in a world of steadily rising costs of living, became more and more exacting. To make matters worse, wealthy townsmen invested their surplus funds in agricultural estates and exploited both the land and the peasantry to the highest possible degree. In the course of these readjustments the financial burdens of the peasants were increased and their ancient customary rights were often reduced. Enterprising or grasping landlords enclosed woodland, wasteland, and common pastureland, formerly available to the peasantry. Great expanses were devoted to sheep raising in order to provide wool for the textile industries.

With the frontiers of opportunity closed both at home and abroad, the peasants were severely repressed. They were even denied the occasional relief of chance opportunity. When the Black Death produced widespread labor shortage, which in turn led to increased wages and other inducements for agricultural workers, the governments interfered in the interests of the hard-pressed landlords. Rigid regulations, such as the English Statutes of Laborers, put a strait jacket on peasant ambitions. Such harsh conditions culminated in the disastrous peasant revolt of 1381 in England.[10] In other regions, notably war-ridden France, the peasantry had even worse grievances. They found, however, to their sorrow that rebellion brought only brutal measures of repression and worse conditions than ever.

10 See below, p. 601, concerning the peasant conditions in England.

Everywhere, the discontented agriculturalists were forced to content themselves with any measures the ruling class saw fit to impose. Whatever improvement there was came by reason of the general increase of prosperity. Some few peasants grew wealthy, but many more sank to the status of landless agricultural laborers, subjected to rigid governmental regulations. Often idle laborers were forced to work, and in some regions there was a revival of serfdom.

Although the lot of the majority of peasants was hard, there were some who prospered. Those who had lands in the vicinity of populous cities could turn to the production of foodstuffs for the town markets. Even here however, the gains were slight, for the townsfolk controlled the markets, and imposed various regulations, fees, and the like, which left little opportunity for profit. Furthermore, enterprising landlords and wealthy burghers were likely to exploit such situations for their own benefit. Capitalist landowners, with their financial advantages, absorbed most of the favored opportunities. The peasantry was destined to have little more than the crumbs that fell from the banquet tables of the landlords and wealthy townsmen.

COMMERCIAL
READJUSTMENTS
As in the case of agriculture, during the fourteenth century commercial expansion was checked in many regions. Western religious, diplomatic, and commercial contacts with the Far East were seriously upset by the disintegration of the Mongolian Empire of Genghis Khan and his successors. The many warring states that took the place of this friendly empire created such difficulties for traders that it was impossible to use the overland routes to China. It was to be centuries before the Far East would be as accessible as it had been in the days of Marco Polo. In the Mediterranean area, likewise, foreign trade was seriously hampered. During the twelfth and thirteenth centuries, thanks to the Christian victories over the Moslems and over the Byzantine Empire (in 1204), the merchants of the West had gained control of the trade of the entire Mediterranean. But their domination was ended by the loss of the last Christian ports in the Holy Land late in the thirteenth century. Henceforth Western trade relations with the Near and the Far East were increasingly uncertain. Even though the Italian merchants made terms with the advancing Turks and continued their commercial activities in the eastern Mediterranean, the ensuing period was marked by constant re-

adjustments. Slowly but surely Western merchants were impelled to turn elsewhere for more profitable fields of exploitation. Venice, for instance, opened a water route to Northern Europe by way of the Strait of Gibraltar and the English Channel, early in the fourteenth century. The Genoese attempted to make direct contact with the resources of the interior of Africa. They also pushed their maritime interests westward, carrying on explorations along the Atlantic coasts of Africa.

Meanwhile, Pisa, Marseilles, Barcelona, and other towns formerly active in Mediterranean commerce, dropped behind in the race. Florence, on the other hand, unhampered by the problems of maritime commerce, concentrated her resources on industry and banking, and enjoyed increasing prosperity. In general the Italian merchants, by dint of intelligent readjustments, maintained their dominance over Western commerce until the fifteenth century.

Commercial developments in the North also illustrate the characteristic instability of European economic life during the fourteenth and early fifteenth centuries. During this period French and English commerce, and that of the Netherlands also to a certain degree, was much upset as a result of the Hundred Years' War. Meanwhile the Hanseatic League enjoyed its greatest period of commercial prosperity, and certain south German cities, such as Augsburg and Nuremberg, began to expand their trading activities.

Contrasts such as these illustrate the fact that European commerce was carrying on, in spite of necessary readjustments in foreign trade and disasters in certain regions. The fairs of Champagne found it impossible to thrive under the increasing burden of taxation laid upon them by King Philip IV, and his policies in Flanders made conditions difficult for the textile centers. A century later, however, Bourges was noted for its wealthy merchants. In Italy, numerous banking firms failed under the pressure of uncollectible loans to bankrupt kings, but the Medici developed an international business in finance. Throughout the period the technique of business, banking, and navigation made progress, and the foundations were laid for the remarkable expansion of commerce that began late in the fifteenth century. By that time, however, it was evident that the future of European business life lay with the enterprising national states of the Atlantic coasts.

INDUSTRIAL
DEVELOPMENTS

The industrial developments of this age followed the same general trends as commerce. The northern towns in the Netherlands, Germany, and England began to compete with Italian industry during the fourteenth and fifteenth centuries. The period also brought readjustments in industrial labor that foreshadow the modern age. The guild system, which had attained a relatively stable form of organization in the thirteenth century, was to face conditions in the ensuing age which forced drastic changes in the relations of employers and employees.

CAPITAL VERSUS
LABOR

The industrial laborers found themselves in a situation somewhat similar to that of the peasantry. Both suffered great hardships as a result of the consolidation of power and profits in the hands of the upper classes. In the towns, the wealthy burghers used the machinery of guild and town government to consolidate their own gains, letting the workers take the losses caused by unsettled business conditions. Within the guilds the journeymen and apprentices found it almost impossible to become masters. As a consequence a rift developed in every craft guild between the masters (capital) and the journeymen and apprentices (labor). Eventually the journeymen formed their own associations; these were organizations somewhat comparable to modern labor unions.

In the Flemish textile region journeymen were sometimes forced to become migratory workers. The stoppage of imports of raw wool from England might close down the shops in a certain region, forcing masses of unemployed journeymen to move on to some other city seeking work. In the market place of a textile town on a Monday morning there might be found crowds of weavers or fullers waiting to be hired for the day or week. On pay day (usually Saturday evening), if re-employed for another week, the worker went to his cheap rented room in the tenement district. If not, he moved on to another town. Here we have the origins of a growing proletariat of rough, uncouth, industrial laborers. They formed a propertyless class, whose labor was a commodity which they were forced to sell like goods in a market. Employers treated them with little consideration—there was usually plenty of unemployed to take the places of disabled or discontented workers. Municipal authorities, unless they were forced to take temporary measures because of a possible revolt, paid no attention to their needs.

Such were the conditions which bred the bloody conflicts between the fourteenth-century working man and the wealthy burghers. Western Europe was already facing one of the most serious problems of modern industrial society—unemployed proletarian labor.

REVOLTS AND
REPRESSION
The increasing rift between capital and labor did not affect to the same degree the small shop-owners and the skilled workers. Town society in the fourteenth century was not so much a clear-cut division into two camps —capital and labor—as it was a complex of various industrial groups. The wealthy vested interests, represented by the guilds of merchants and professional men—notaries, physicians, and the like—had been in control of most towns from their beginnings. Now they were confronted by two major elements of discontent, the unorganized proletarian workers, and the lesser guilds, or "crafts," composed of small shopkeepers and skilled artisans.

When threatened with the overthrow of their power by the workers, the vested interests could usually win by granting concessions to the middle group of craftsmen. In Florence, for instance, in the second half of the fourteenth century, a series of textile strikes and a proletarian revolt frightened the "fat" guilds (comprising the bankers and professional men) into granting additional rights to the "lean" guilds of craft artisans.[11] Two years later (1384), at Liége in Flanders, after a century of resistance to the craftsmen's demands, the upper class granted the lesser guilds such an increase in political representation that they came to dominate municipal policies. This was preferable to revolts and a possible dictatorship of the proletariat. In other towns, the propertied classes sometimes called on the royal government for aid in preserving the balance of power in their favor.

In this medieval struggle between the "haves" and the "have nots" the lesser guilds made steady progress because their support was needed by the ruling class. As for the proletariat, their one ultimate recourse, revolution, was usually unsuccessful. Inasmuch as the general public was conscious of the fact that its prosperity depended on flourishing business life, kings, nobles, skilled artisans, and peasants usually supported the forces of law, order, and financial well-being when these were threatened by proletarian radicalism. Therefore the only gains made by the proletariat were chance favors granted by the wealthy *bourgeoisie*.

[11] See below, p. 636, concerning the Ciompi revolt, and p. 595, concerning other revolts.

GUILD
CONSERVATISM

By the opening of the fifteenth century the major threat of proletarian revolt was over, and the destinies of the towns were safely in the hands of the capitalistic merchant and crafts guilds, who sought to preserve their favored position by regulatory legislation. The guild policies of the fifteenth century were comparable to the mercantilistic policies of our modern age, except that then they operated by *municipal* units. This was a period of narrowly conservative guild regulations. Guild membership and town citizenship were rigidly restricted to preserve the economic privileges of the inner circle of burghers. By means of tariffs, fees, and other regulations, "foreign" goods were excluded. Rival industries in neighboring villages or towns were eliminated; sometimes violence was employed to crush a new industry that threatened the local monopoly.

INDEPENDENT
CAPITALISTIC
INDUSTRY

It was impossible to "freeze" the economic life of the period, however, and new elements were forcing their way into the field. As the guilds tightened their ranks and narrowed their membership, a more progressive type of business developed. We have already mentioned the associations of journeymen composed of craftsmen who were excluded from guild membership. In similar fashion, renegade merchants operated independently outside the ranks and regulations of the guilds. These industrial free lances (called "entrepreneurs," or adventurers) were often self-made businessmen whose ambition was to make money as fast as possible. Some of them had gained experience and wealth as the financial agents of kings. Others had amassed fortunes and had learned the tricks of the financial game in the service of banking or commercial companies. Their chief characteristics were a willingness to take risks and a faculty for handling commercial affairs on a large scale. Such a man might invest his fortune in raw wool at bargain prices, hire unemployed journeymen to make it up into cloth, export it to a promising market, and make a big profit. Fortunes were made by this method of manufacturing. It was called the "putting-out" system because the capitalist put out or distributed his supply of raw material to the artisans to be worked up at home. This was similar to the "sweat-shop" system of modern industry in that it was piece work, and involved the labor of the entire family at very low wages. On the other hand, the workers lived in rural villages and usually had a fair subsistence from their lands; consequently their industrial labor was a welcome opportunity to earn some ready money without the responsibility of securing the raw material or marketing the finished product. By reason of such developments made in this fashion, the guild system of monopolistic trade and industry slowly gave way to individual competitive business.

Under the spur of capitalistic profits improvements were also made in industrial technique. Factory methods, the forerunners of the Industrial Revolution, were introduced. As early as the fourteenth century, an Italian textile manufacturer used water power to run his spinning machines. From guild-controlled economic life, by city units, the West was gradually moving on to a less secure but more progressive type of business—that of individual capitalists and corporations operating within national spheres of influence.

VOYAGES OF
DISCOVERY
By the end of the fifteenth century Western Europe, with its improved capitalistic methods and aggressive national spirit, was prepared for a renewed era of expansion. It was at this time that the patient efforts of certain Portuguese navigators came to a glorious triumph which started Western commerce on a career of world expansion. The fifteenth-century voyages of discovery mark a renewal of European enthusiasm for exploration and commercial exploitation of distant lands. This expansive movement had first begun centuries earlier, during the pre-crusading and crusading eras when Italian merchants began to frequent all parts of the Mediterranean in search of foreign trade. The thirteenth century saw the climax of this early period of expansion. Westerners were to be found not only in the Near East, but merchants such as the Polos carried their commercial ventures as far as the Orient. The fourteenth century marks a break in Europe's commercial development. With the loss of the crusading states and the rise of the Ottoman Turks, trade in the eastern Mediterranean was hampered. Meanwhile, in Northeastern Europe, strong Slavic states had checked the eastward expansion of the Germans and Scandinavians. All along the eastern frontiers of Europe, economic expansion was checked.

Obviously there were fields of commercial opportunity to the West, but until the second quarter of the fifteenth century, exploration, along with other phases of economic expansion, lagged. To be sure, there were occasional Genoese voyagers in the Atlantic. In the Atlantic certain islands were discovered, but nothing of commercial importance came of it. Not until the nations of the Atlantic seaboard were ready for large-scale commercial activities was Western Europe to continue her interrupted expansion. Before Europe could extend her commercial frontiers westward, it was also necessary to solve the problem of navigating the stormy Atlantic. Better types of ships, with higher prows and sturdier hulls, must be developed. There was need for more accurate maps, instruments of navigation, and courageous experienced navigators.

ECONOMIC AC-
TIVITIES IN THE
ATLANTIC

The renewal of Western expansion and the beginning of active exploration in the new region (the Atlantic) came during the fifteenth century. This movement was accompanied by a westward shift in European trading interests, so marked that Italy and the Mediterranean states were threatened with the loss of their commercial leadership to Portugal and the other Atlantic states. Eventually it seemed as if a Europe with its face to the east had turned about to face westward. All of this was a part of the general development in which the nations of the Atlantic seaboard gradually replaced the city-states of the Mediterranean as the leaders of Western economic life.

Although certain aspects of this movement, notably the voyages of discovery, came with dramatic suddenness, they were part and parcel of medieval Europe's economic evolution. Northern Europe, which had for centuries been stirring with commercial activity, had long been jealous of the Italian monopoly of trade with the Near East and the Orient. The states of the Atlantic had developed strong national monarchies, naval resources, and improved mercantile organizations, all of which were ready for action on a large scale. Even before the voyages of discovery of the late fifteenth century, the Spanish, Portuguese, and English had developed merchant marines that were beginning to rival those of the Italian cities in the carrying trade of the West. Portugal and Castile were the first of the Atlantic states to take an active interest in exploration. This was doubtless due to the fact that for centuries they had been in constant contact with the Moslems, a people who had far-reaching trade relations with Africa and the Orient. From them they had learned much concerning the riches of Africa and were eager for direct access to this land of gold, slaves, and fabulous wealth of all kinds. This interest was combined with a zeal for the conquest and conversion of the infidel peoples of foreign lands. Centuries of crusading against the Spanish Moslems had transformed the Portuguese and Castilians into nations of warrior-missionaries who were easily stirred to action against non-Christian peoples.

PRINCE HENRY
THE NAVIGATOR
It was the Portuguese prince, Henry the Navigator, whose patient and intelligent policies, from 1415 to 1460, seriously turned Europe's attention to the continent of Africa and to the possibility of successfully navigating the Atlantic Ocean. Prince Henry was, among other things, a Portuguese crusader, interested in conquering and converting the Moslems of Africa. Throughout his career the religious motive is evident, but he also had a lively appreciation of the importance of the economic resources of central Africa, especially the gold, ivory, and slaves which came to Western Europe by way of Moslem middlemen. In order to advance Portuguese religious and economic domination in Africa Prince Henry set out to improve navigation. Seagoing fleets on the Atlantic coasts would enable the Portuguese to flank the Moslems of Northern Africa and to make direct contact with the center of that fabulously wealthy continent. Here was a field for Christian missions and for the acquisition of untold riches. The results were momentous for all Western Europe.

It was as governor of Ceuta in Northern Africa that Henry first learned the importance of Portuguese maritime activities and the opportunity of obtaining a rich income from Africa. He devoted the rest of his life to the extension of Portuguese interests in this region.

Prince Henry first sent ships to explore the coast of Africa. Their acquisition of unlimited quantities of ivory, gold, and slaves fired the enthusiasm of the nation, and by the second quarter of the century Portuguese navigators were pressing southward each year. By 1450 they had occupied the Madeira and Azores islands and had passed the dangerous Cape Bojador to explore the Gold Coast. After Prince Henry's death in 1460, the mouth of the Congo River was reached. In 1486 Diaz rounded the "Cape of Storms," later renamed Cape of Good Hope.

Then in 1497, spurred on by the news of Columbus' discovery of a westward route to the "Indies," the Portuguese sent Vasco da Gama with four ships to round the Cape and reach the riches of the Orient. Over two years later he returned with two ships and less than half of his men. But their cargo of goods brought from India yielded a profit of 6,000 per cent. For half a century thereafter, Lisbon was the spice market of the West. The all-water route to the Orient gave the Portuguese a virtual monopoly by putting them in direct touch with the producers and by thus eliminating the Italian and Turkish middleman. Soon Portugal had wealth-producing colonies in the Orient.

Meanwhile Spain was exploiting the West Indies and the amassed wealth of Mexico and Peru. Later France, England, Holland, and Sweden were to dispute her possession of the New World, while Holland rivaled Portugal in the Orient. The race was on for colonial possessions, and Western Europe's commercial conquest of the Americas, Asia, and Africa had begun.

THE EVOLUTION
OF MODERN
CAPITALISM

The sum total of economic changes that took place during the late Middle Ages has been referred to by various modern historians as the economic renascence, the age of discoveries, the commercial revolution, and so on. Obviously this was no actual *rebirth* or *revolution*. The word *evolution* best describes the long chain of events which gave rise to modern capitalistic economy. This involves (1) the revival of commerce and of town life in the tenth and eleventh centuries; (2) the enhanced activity of the crusading age; (3) the improvements in capitalistic technique that accompanied and followed the crusades; and (4) the fifteenth-century voyages of discovery that opened new worlds to Western commerce and civilization. As expressed by a modern economist, this great economic evolution "was more important than any later revolution, even than that of the nineteenth century and all the revolution of industry that flowed from it." All of these developments are consequences of the great economic and social transformation that accompanied the rise of towns in Western Europe.

This movement not only affected commerce, industry, and agriculture, it influenced government, religion, and culture. The realization of the worldly comforts, luxuries, and power that wealth gives modified the customs and habits of men in all walks of life. The merchant's ambition and his technique of profit making were transmitted to his fellow townsfolk, to the local tradesmen and artisans. Middle-class society moved into the full sweep of its onward march to wealth and power. The capitalistic spirit spread fast into other circles. The kings, especially in the nationalistic states, came to realize the power of money, and governmental administration was geared to the problem of finding new and increasing sources of revenue. The English and French administrative services were filled with keen-eyed businessmen and clerks who were experts in finance. Even the church and the feudality caught the capitalistic spirit.

In order to keep up with the new financial tempo of a world of money economy, of increasingly high costs of living, and of expanding governmental functions, both clerical and feudal adminstrators were forced into the business of revenue seeking. The church's ability (particularly that of the papacy) to cope with the new trends brought political and financial triumphs but spiritual bankruptcy. In the succeeding chapters we shall find that the financial success of the papacy was accompanied by an increase in worldliness which finally led to religious catastrophe. Meanwhile the kings of the national states were using money power to crush the remnants of feudalism and to unify their people under the standard of despotic and efficient monarchy.

THE PAPACY IN THE LATE MIDDLE AGES

THE three centuries from 1000 to 1300 saw the revival of town life, the rise of the empire and papacy, the rapid growth of nations and a remarkable expansion of European economic life. These developments mark a very distinct change in Western civilization. During the ensuing period, the evolution was even more rapid. In all phases of life there were appearing those characteristics which we tend to think of as modern. The most noticeable change was the increase of interest in the more practical and materialistic aspects of human existence. This was evident not only in political, economic and social life, but even in the activities of the church. In the following chapters we shall survey briefly the new developments of the fourteenth and fifteenth centuries, first tracing the history of the papacy and the manner in which the church reflected the ideals of an increasingly worldly society.

THE DOWNFALL OF THE PAPACY

THE DECLINE OF PAPAL POWER
In contrast to the age of Innocent III, the latter part of the thirteenth century was a disastrous period for the papacy. While nations such as England and France were expanding territorially and centralizing their governmental institutions, the medieval empire and the papacy were suffering unprecedented setbacks. The fall of Frederick II and the Hohenstaufen empire in 1250[1] was prophetic of the passing of the medieval papacy. Although at this time the popes triumphed over their imperial opponents, the victory drew them into a political struggle which eventually destroyed the papacy's spiritual influence in the Christian world.

The era of papal tribulation began when the French pope, Urban IV (1261-1264) and his successor, Clement IV (1265-1268), employed

[1] See above, p. 405.

a French prince, Charles of Anjou, to conduct a "crusade" against the heirs of Frederick II. Thus French influences were brought into Italian affairs. To be sure, this was a temporary advantage to the popes in that it destroyed a dangerous German power in southern Italy. But, on the other hand, for two and a half centuries thereafter, French interference was a constant problem to the papacy. For a time the French ruler, Charles of Anjou, maintained friendly relations with his papal overlord, but he was of little direct assistance because he busied himself with ambitious plans for the expansion of his southern kingdom.

The popes, meanwhile, had become so deeply entangled in the toils of local politics that, even had they been so disposed, they could not have exerted any effective influence in the south. During the twenty-six years from 1268 to 1294 there were nine popes, intervals of two and three years without any pope, and constant strife between the local factions that sought to control the papacy. The church regulations provided for honest elections with no delays,[2] but these regulations were disregarded and political bargaining usually determined the choice. Celestine V (1294), the last of an unimpressive line of popes, was selected more than two years after the death of his predecessor after a political scramble that had involved both local and foreign factions. After a five-month pontificate, characterized by uncertainty and misguided idealism, he resigned in despair. Thus within a quarter of a century after its victory over Frederick II, the papacy drifted into a condition of spiritual impotence and political corruption.

BONIFACE VIII   The career of Boniface VIII (1294-1303) vividly illustrates the depths to which papal ideals had sunk since the days of Innocent III. Cardinal Benedetto Gaetani, as he was called before his election, was a master politician. A trained lawyer, he was well versed in the trickery as well as in the administration of ecclesiastical affairs. Before his election as pope he had made skillful use of his position to advance himself and his family. It was even rumored that he had resorted to underhanded methods in order to bring about the resignation of the disillusioned hermit-pope, Celestine V. At any rate, the cardinal had left no stone unturned to assure his possession of the coveted office.

Shortly after his election the seventy-seven-year-old pope began to

---

[2] See above, p. 383, note 8.

exercise his authority to the fullest extent. In his claims of papal supremacy he was another Innocent III, but unfortunately he proceeded
tactlessly and without restraint. In the Papal States he appropriated the
fruits of his political victory with reckless abandon, advancing his
relatives to lucrative ecclesiastical positions. The powerful Colonna
family was ruthlessly crushed because it dared to oppose his will. A
papal army stormed the Colonna stronghold at Palestrina, leveled
it to the ground, and with ropes about their necks dragged the leading members of the family to ask forgiveness of the lord pope. In
like manner, the irascible old pope rode roughshod over all opponents in and about Rome.

BONIFACE AND THE MONARCHS Outside the Papal States, Boniface was unable to
play the role of dictator. Since his commands went
unheeded even in Lombardy and Sicily, he might
have known that faraway England and France would no longer
tremble at the papal thunders as they had in the days of Innocent III.
But Boniface was to learn by bitter experience that the papacy of his
day was not held in the same high esteem as in the earlier decades
of the thirteenth century. England and France had changed much
in the course of the thirteenth century. In both regions there was
now a strong national spirit that expressed itself in increased loyalty
to the king. This enabled both Edward I of England and Philip IV
of France to defy Boniface VIII's orders and to wage a victorious
war against the papacy.

In England it was the king who took the initiative in this new
struggle between church and state. Even before the accession of Boniface in 1294, Edward had taken steps to exert his royal authority
in financial and judicial affairs. In the very year of the accession of
Boniface he seized all the property of certain English monasteries
and demanded from the clergy 50 per cent of all their incomes, ostensibly as a measure of preparedness for his warfare in Wales and in
France. The clergy protested, but in vain. Two years later (1296)
Boniface, whose efforts to prevent international hostilities had been
rejected by both Edward and Philip, forbade the clergy to pay taxes.
As a result of this rift in relations between church and state, the
English clergy refused to join the barons, knights, and townsfolk in
voting funds for Edward's French war. The king's response was decisive. The clerics were immediately deprived of the protection of the
royal courts, a measure that was equivalent to an invitation for anyone
to plunder the church with impunity. Within a short time the horses

of the archbishop of Canterbury were disappearing, and other bishops were being robbed of their flocks and herds. Soon the English clerics submitted, paying to the royal treasury what they chose to call a "gift." Although this action saved the pope's face, it was evident that England and the English church were no longer subject to papal orders. The days of John's vassalage to Innocent III had passed away.

"CLERICIS LAICOS"

Although Boniface met with a severe check in his skirmish with Edward I, it was the clash with Philip IV of France that brought about his downfall. In 1294 the French clergy were included in the wartime tax program of their king. It is therefore little wonder that Boniface, on learning of the clerical protests against royal taxation, decided to rebuke the rulers of both England and France for their overbearing conduct. This he did in a famous decree, the bull *Clericis laicos*.[3] This was a declaration of the principle of clerical independence from lay control, particularly in the matter of taxation. But the pope's injudicious statement of the case stirred the smoldering resentment of the English and French nations and played into the hands of the two clever and self-seeking monarchs. The bull opened with the tactless assertion that "the laity have been from ancient times hostile to the clergy." It ended with threats of excommunication against all clerics who paid, and all laymen who received, taxes without the pope's permission.

We have already considered Edward's answer to the challenge. Philip's was quite as decisive. Ostensibly as a war measure, he placed an embargo on the exportation of gold, silver, and jewels, and prohibited foreigners from entering or leaving the kingdom. By thus cutting off all papal revenues and officials from France, he dealt the pope a severe blow. Due to the fact that England and Italy were also in open rebellion against him, Boniface was forced to compromise. He did this in three papal bulls wherein he explained that his tax prohibition did not apply to certain classes of clergymen nor to *gifts* made in time of crisis. In effect, the provisions of *Clericis laicos* were nullified.

THE JUBILEE OF 1300

For several years all was peaceful, so far as Philip and Boniface were concerned. It was, however, merely a truce intervening between the preliminary skirmish and the real battle. Boniface's courage was completely restored by the success of the jubilee of 1300. During that centennial year the city of

---

[3] Papal bulls, so called because of the *bulla,* or official seals attached to them, were named according to their opening words; in this case, *Clericis laicos.*

Rome was thronged with eager pilgrims from all parts of Western Christendom. At St. Peter's Church the attendants are said to have used rakes to gather the coins that were dropped about the apostle's statue by pious visitors. Little wonder that the pope, having received such tokens of loyalty, felt impelled to take up the cudgels once more against the two overbearing monarchs. Meanwhile, his protests against Edward I's efforts to conquer Scotland, on the ground that this realm was a papal fief, were disregarded. Parliament sided with the king in rejecting the pope's claim.

PHILIP IV
VERSUS
BONIFACE

In France, King Philip was once more the aggressor. He suddenly arrested, tried, and imprisoned a troublesome French bishop on the charge that, while serving as a papal legate, he had been "disrespectful, blasphemous, and seditious" in his attitude toward his king. Boniface immediately insisted that it was illegal to try a clergyman in a secular court, and ordered Philip to release the bishop and send him to Rome for trial. He also summoned the French clergy to Rome for a council to condemn Philip's actions. Again the issue concerning the control of the clergy was clearly drawn between church and state. This and the conflict between Edward and Boniface are but new episodes in the series of struggles between medieval popes and monarchs. In earlier centuries the popes had been successful.[4] Gregory VII and his successors had checked emperors Henry IV and V; Alexander III had humiliated Frederick Barbarossa; Innocent III had dominated kings, and his successors had brought about the complete destruction of Frederick II's power. The succession of victories that had been won by his predecessors gave Boniface VIII some reason to be confident and aggressive. He was, however, more vigorous than tactful, and his sweeping assertion of the supremacy of the papacy over all monarchs and his extravagant claims and violent language drove the nobles, burghers, and even the clergy of France to Philip's side.

"UNAM
SANCTAM"

To win the support of his people in this critical situation Philip summoned the Estates-General of 1302.[5] To the assembled representatives of the nation the royal lawyers presented a prejudiced and garbled account of the papal position. All classes—including the town representatives, who were in attendance for the first time—joined in protesting against papal

[4] See above, Chapters XIX-XX.
[5] See above, p. 486.

encroachments. Philip's officials also spread antipapal propaganda throughout the realm, thus mobilizing French public opinion. Boniface, little suspecting the storm that was brewing, persisted in his program. In the famous bull, *Unam Sanctam,* he proclaimed that "there is but One Holy and Apostolic Church . . . of which there is one body and head . . . namely Christ and His Vicar. . . . Submission to the Roman Pontiff is absolutely necessary for salvation." Never before nor since have papal claims been asserted in such tactless language and scarcely ever has pride been so closely followed by a disastrous fall.

BONIFACE'S
DOWNFALL

Philip struck quickly and effectively. Nogaret, one of his legal advisers, was sent to Italy with a small force to deal with the pope. If Boniface refused to yield, he was to be seized and brought to France for trial before a church council. Meanwhile, he had been charged with all sorts of false and outlandish crimes, including his "wicked opposition to the Catholic Faith and to Philip, its splendid exemplar." Nogaret, on arriving in Italy, found willing allies among the Colonna and other enemies of Boniface. The conspirators went from Rome to Anagni, where he was spending the summer. Here occurred one of the most spectacular tragedies of papal history. Since Boniface refused to negotiate, the invaders broke into the papal residence and captured him. One of the attacking party is supposed to have struck the courageous old pontiff squarely in the face with his mailed fist. However that may be, Sciarra Colonna, Boniface's bitterest enemy, sought to have him killed, but wiser counsels prevailed, and the invaders withdrew. Never recovering from the mental or physical shock he suffered, Boniface died a month later at Rome. No other pope save, perhaps, Gregory VII ever passed away so tragically. But whereas Gregory's death had left the papacy strong and vigorous, Boniface's downfall saw the papacy mortally stricken.

FRANCE CAP-
TURES THE
PAPACY

The surprising thing about the overthrow of Boniface was the fact that even in the face of a shocked public opinion the aggressors were allowed to reap the fruits of their victory. The new pope, Benedict XI (1303-1304) merely excommunicated Nogaret, Sciarra Colonna, and a few of their accomplices. Philip IV was exonerated from all blame, and when Benedict died, Philip's favored candidate was elected pope after an eleven-month deadlock in the college of cardinals. At the desire

of the French king the new pontiff, Clement V (1305-1314), formerly
the archbishop of Bordeaux, continued to reside in France. He summoned the Italian cardinals to join him there, and most of his new
appointees were Frenchmen. Thus the papal electoral college was
packed with Philip's friends, and the papacy was brought under a
French domination that continued for almost seventy years.

The actions of Clement V illustrate clearly the subservience of
the new papacy to Philip's interests. At the king's request, the pope
conducted an investigation of the acts of Boniface, which completely
exonerated not only Philip but his agents in the affair of Anagni. It
was agreed that they had acted with the best of intentions in defense
of the honor of the church and nation. Boniface's decrees concerning
royal subservience to papal authority were condemned with a declaration to the effect that the kingdoms of the earth—and France in particular—were divinely established. Meanwhile Philip and Clement
helped themselves to the rewards of victory by plundering the French
church. The crowning act was that by which the order of Knights
Templars was despoiled.

PHILIP AND
THE TEMPLARS

The Templars, one of the oldest of the crusading
orders,[6] had by 1300 become wealthy and corrupt.
Philip, who had borrowed large sums from them, was
more interested in appropriating the wealth than in reforming the
lives of the Templars. The pope was first prevailed upon to appoint
a committee to investigate a series of outlandish charges that had
been preferred against them. When the papal commissioners proved
too slow and judicious in their investigation, Philip took matters
into his own hands and had all French members of the order arrested.

Under pressure of inquisitorial methods, some of the victims pled
guilty to unbelievable crimes. Some died under torture; others expired
in prison while awaiting trial. Philip finally had over fifty Templars
burned at the stake in Paris. Among them was the Grand Master
of the Order, De Molay, who had come from the East of his own free
will to defend himself and the order against the false accusations. The
Estates-General, to which the king's lawyers presented their version
of the affair, gave its approval to the royal procedure. The pope objected, however, and it was not until 1312 at the Council of Vienne
that he agreed to abolish the order. Philip then presented huge claims

[6] See above, p. 515.

for the expenses of trial, imprisonment, and for alleged sums owed to his treasury. As a result, little of the confiscated property ever passed out of his hands.

THE "BABY-LONIAN CAP-TIVITY"

From Clement V's accession (1305) it was evident that the head of the church had become a tool of the French king. This situation continued practically unchanged for about seventy years, and to those who resented such domination this period of papal history came to be known as the "Babylonian Captivity." The term, which is still in common use, is a misnomer, for the papacy was not actually captured and carried away to France to be held a prisoner against its will, like the captive Jews in Babylon.[7] What actually happened was that the pro-French faction which triumphed over Boniface VIII at Anagni clinched its victory by putting a Frenchman—Clement V—on the papal throne. For almost seventy years thereafter the papacy was French. Naturally the French popes, cardinals, and lesser officials preferred to live in France. While the papacy was not held in enforced captivity, it is equally true that the French king exerted a great deal of political pressure in order to keep the papacy in safe hands. The election of Clement V's successor, John XXII (1316-1334), was marked by more than two years of unconcealed political manipulation on the part of the interested groups. The new pope made clear his intentions when he filled all vacancies in the college of cardinals with Frenchmen, and began the luxurious papal palace at Avignon. Throughout the greater part of the fourteenth century, Avignon was the headquarters of a French-controlled papacy.[8]

PAPAL FINANCES

Many troublesome responsibilities and problems weighed upon the popes during their residence at Avignon. A pope and his courtiers must live, and, even though the French king seemed at times to own the papacy, he did not pay its bills. This was an age of rising costs of living and governing, and papal expenses at Avignon, with its new palaces, spendthrift ways, and rapacious office seekers, were much higher than they had been in former days at Rome. To make matters worse, while expenses were increasing, income was decreasing. This was because there was less

---

[7] See the Biblical account in II Chronicles, especially 36:6-7; 17-23.

[8] Avignon, on the Rhone River south of Lyons, was not then a part of France but was under French influence. The restored ruins of the papal palace are still to be seen.

revenue from Italy, Germany, and England, whose people resented the fact that the Avignon popes were Frenchmen.

Necessity, therefore, impelled the popes to utilize many new and old methods of replenishing their treasuries. For instance, every person appointed (or "commended") to office by the pope paid some sort of fees or taxes. Furthermore, a fee, called *annates* (or "first-fruits"), was paid by appointees to important offices; this usually amounted to approximately 10 per cent of the first year's income. By a system called *reservations,* the pope "reserved" to himself various appointments, and also fees. All offices that were made vacant by death while the incumbent was on papal business or at Rome, or by papal transfers of officials, paid fees. *Expectatives* were paid by those whom the pope favored with the "expectation" of being appointed to an office not yet vacant. *Provisors* were those whom the pope "provided" as substitutes for regularly elected local candidates. *Vacancies* were the revenues which the pope received from offices as long as they were vacant. In addition to this commercialization of papal patronage, there were innumerable fees for dispensations, indulgences, visitations, and the like, to say nothing of the gratuities and bribes by means of which one was expected to forward his cause in the papal court. In times of special need, *tithes* and "gifts" were sometimes collected.

LUXURIOUS
AVIGNON

Suffice it to say, the Avignon popes lived well. In fact, they made such a record as financiers that contemporaries referred to them and their officials as "money changers," "brokers," "treasurers who steal the Lord's wealth," and "traffickers in souls." Petrarch, himself a former officeholder of the papal court, wrote:

Now I am living in France, in the Babylon of the West [i.e., Avignon]. The sun in its travels sees nothing more hideous than this place. . . . Here reign the successors of the poor fishermen of Galilee; they have strangely forgotten their origin. I am astounded, as I recall their predecessors, to see these men loaded with gold and clad in purple, boasting of the spoils of princes and nations; to see luxurious palaces and heights crowned with fortifications, instead of a boat turned downwards for shelter. We no longer find the simple nets which were once used to gain a frugal sustenance from the lake of Galilee . . . One is stupefied nowadays to hear the lying tongues, and to see worthless parchments turned by a leaden seal [of the pope] into nets which are used in Christ's name, . . . to catch hordes of unwary Christians. . . . Instead of holy solitude we find a criminal host and crowds of infamous satellites; instead of soberness, licentious banquets; instead of pious pilgrimages, preternatural and foul sloth; instead of the bare feet of the apostles, the snowy coursers of brigands fly past us, the horses decked in gold and fed on gold, soon to be shod with gold, if the Lord does not check this slavish luxury.[9]

It can be said in explanation, if not in defense, of the Avignon papacy that it was merely following the trend of the times, and that its practices were no worse than those of many clerical and lay princes. The core of the problem lay in the fact that the popes had ceased to be the spiritual leaders of Christendom and had become the political tools of an ambitious secular monarch. Even though they were efficient in clerical administration and church law, and unceasing in their efforts to end European wars and promote crusades, at the same time they were bitterly criticized for their worldliness by sincere Christians.

Even in France there were those who pointed out the dangers of clerical wealth and corruption. In a book *Concerning the Recovery of the Holy Land* a French lawyer named Peter Dubois suggested that the king ought to reform the church and use its wealth for public purposes such as education and crusades.

PROFESSORIAL
CRITICS OF
THE PAPACY

Naturally, the chief criticism of the papacy came from regions beyond the borders of France. Many of the harshest charges, however, were made by scholastic clergymen who had studied or taught at the University of Paris. Outstanding among them were Marsilius of Padua, William Ockham, and John of Jandon. He who believes that nothing practical or liberal ever came out of medieval scholasticism may well ponder over the reform programs and radical protestant ideas of the fourteenth-century professors of logic. Some of the sternest critics—and also some of the staunchest defenders—of the church were professors who had been trained at this great scholastic center. One of the chancellors of the university in the early fifteenth century, John Gerson, was the leader of the professors and legalists who sought to solve the problems of the church by means of conciliar action. Usually when a Parisian professor made an attack on the clerical organization which controlled the university, he was forced to leave. Consequently, in the fourteenth century, exiled professors and students from the University of Paris could be found teaching and writing in many European lands.

[9] See Robinson, *Readings in European History,* I, 491-504, for the entire account, and for similar criticisms by Wiclif, Marsilius, and others. The quotation is by permission of Ginn and Company.

GERMAN HOS-
TILITY TO THE
AVIGNON POPES
In Germany, at this time, the rulers looked with special favor upon anyone who opposed the papal system. Emperor Louis the Bavarian (1314-1347), for
example, was in constant conflict with Pope John
XXII,[10] and therefore welcomed to his court all antipapalists. Among
these was William Ockham (d. 1349), an English Franciscan, formerly
a professor at the University of Paris, and one of the most brilliant of
the scholastic theologians. He had incurred the wrath of the pope
and all clerical conservatives by his criticism of corrupt and wealthy
monks, and by his *Dialogue,* in which he asserted that the church
was a man-made institution, that the popes and councils had made
mistakes, and that therefore they should be subject to correction and
control by Christian laymen. These teachings blazed the trail for such
later religious radicals as John Wiclif and Martin Luther.

Little did Emperor Louis dream of the far-reaching effects of his
invitation to Ockham to come to his court and continue his attacks on
the pope. The ranks of Louis's antipapal propagandists were also
swelled by the arrival of Marsilius of Padua (d. 1342). Like Ockham,
Marsilius was convinced that the papacy was a man-made institution,
but he also contended that it was the chief cause of the disorders of
the Christian world, past and present. In his *Defender of the Peace* he
insisted that it was the duty of the state to reform the church and thus
to restore peace. He also set forth an ideal—taken from Aristotle—
that is startlingly similar to the popular-sovereignty theory of Rous-
seau. In church as well as state, he considered the people as the ultimate controlling authority.

Ockham, Marsilius, and the other professorial theorists were for
the most part "voices crying in the wilderness." Their advanced ideas
were universally disregarded and condemned. Two centuries passed
before the church was subjected to a reformation at the hands of the
state. Not for five centuries was modern democracy to make even a
pretense of subjecting government to the will of the people. Only one
of the assertions of the professors met with general approval—the
clergy was a corrupt worldly lot, and the "root of the evil" was the
church's wealth.

ITALY AND THE
AVIGNON POPES
In Italy the resentment against the Avignon popes
was perhaps more intense and far reaching than in
Germany. The Romans, in particular, had a double
economic grievance. Like all Europeans, they suffered from the in-

[10] See above, p. 562.

creases in papal taxes, fees, and the like. In addition to this, they had lost all the advantages which were theirs as long as Rome was the capital of the papacy and of Western Christendom. This loss was a blow not only to Roman pride but also to Roman economic prosperity. Lucrative offices in the papal *curia* were now almost completely monopolized by Frenchmen. The incomes formerly derived by Romans from pilgrims, from plaintiffs appealing to the papal court, and from visitors of all kinds were now reduced if not entirely eliminated. Economic as well as spiritual interest made the Italians resentful and critical of their absentee popes. Dante, in his *Divine Comedy,* bitterly condemned the first French pope and elsewhere referred to Rome as a widow, bereft of both imperial and papal defenders. Even more bitter was the criticism that was launched by Petrarch against the "brigand" court at Avignon.

JOHN WICLIF   In England also there was bitter feeling against the papacy. Here the opposition was patriotic as well as economic. At this time the English, at war with France, resented the fact that the French-controlled papacy constantly interfered in the conflict. It was claimed that the treaties and truces proposed by the popes were invariably to the advantage of the enemy. Time and again the pope suggested peace at the very moment when the English were sweeping on to certain victory. Like most Europeans, the English also had financial grievances against the papacy. The entire papal income from England was paid to French popes, and for the support of the luxurious French-controlled papal court at Avignon. Little wonder that English parliaments passed laws such as the Statute of Provisors (1351), prohibiting papal appointments in English churches; and the Statute of Praemunire (1353), which forbade appeals to the papal court. Little wonder that John Wiclif (1320-1384) and his violent attacks on the abuses in the church were tolerated and even encouraged by the English government.

This famous Oxford professor, who had himself held a papal appointment, is often considered as the first outstanding critic of the papacy. But most of his ideas had already been propounded by such men as Ockham, and had been entertained for some time by liberal thinkers throughout Europe. Wiclif's exaggerated reputation rests on the fact that the situation in England made it possible for him to express himself more vigorously than could be done elsewhere. He went beyond the commonplace condemnations of clerical wealth and corruption, and worked out a convincing argument for withholding the annual tribute which King John had bound England to pay into the papal treasury. This made Wiclif popular with both the rulers and the people. For a while they paid little attention to the fact that he was becoming dangerously heretical in his religious views. For instance, he called the pope "antichrist," and denied certain fundamental church doctrines, such as transubstantiation. Even when condemned by the pope and by an English clerical council, he was protected by governmental officials. His supposed encouragement of the peasant revolt of 1381 [11] caused him to lose some of his popularity, but he was allowed to retire unharmed from his church offices and his professorship. He spent his last years in making an English translation of the Bible and in bringing to the attention of the common folk those radical ideas which have given him the title "The Morning Star of the Protestant Reformation." Like Martin Luther, his importance rests not in the originality of his ideas, but in the fact that he popularized the reforms advocated by the most radical thinkers of that day.

PAPAL DEGRADATION AND RECOVERY

HOW THE
SCHISM BEGAN

As time passed, sincere Christians became more and more convinced that the salvation of both the papacy and the church depended upon the return of the popes to Rome. Pressure was brought to bear upon the Avignon popes to bring about this move. In 1367 Urban V actually went to Rome but found conditions so unsatisfactory that he soon returned to Avignon. Ten years later, Gregory XI crossed the Alps to escape the troubled conditions in war-ridden France, but he found the situation in the Papal States little better. It is probable that he would have given in to the desires of his cardinals and returned to Avignon had he not died suddenly in Rome in 1378.

For seventy years Rome had been unable to exert any influence on the papacy, and she now grasped the opportunity. The populace insisted, even with threats of violence, that the new pope must be an Italian, and as a result the archbishop of Bari was elected as Pope Urban VI (1378-1389). But the French cardinals were already resentful over the forced election, and when the pope showed a disposition to rule them with the iron rod of reform, they deserted him, annulled the election on the grounds of mob influence, and elected Cardinal Robert of Geneva. Under the name of Clement VII (1378-1394), he,

---

[11] As a matter of fact, Wiclif did not favor the revolt.

with his twelve French cardinals, returned to Avignon, where they once more set up a pro-French papal court. Meanwhile at Rome, Urban insisted that he was the rightful pope, excommunicated his rival and the renegade cardinals, and appointed Italians in their places.

The nations of Europe, compelled to make their choice between the rival popes, split along strictly political lines. France recognized Clement of Avignon as the true pope, and the same stand was taken by her allies, Scotland, Naples-Sicily, and the Spanish states. Anti-French Europe, including England and the Germanies, supported the Italian pope, Urban VI.

EFFORTS TO
REUNITE THE
PAPACY
Naturally Western Christendom could not permanently support two popes, with duplicate sets of cardinals, lesser officials, and most pernicious revenue collectors. With neither side willing to yield, it took some time to work out a method of eliminating the rivals. After numerous attempts at arbitration and endless discussion among the cardinals, legal experts, and university professors, it was agreed that a general council of representative princes and clerics should be called together to end the deadlock. Accordingly at Pisa, in 1409, a great assembly of cardinals, clerics, and laymen from both sides met, deposed both rivals, and selected a new pope, Alexander V. There were technical irregularities in the procedure, however, and both of the deposed popes held on stubbornly. Instead of two popes, the church now had three, and one of them, Alexander's successor, John XXIII, whose early career had been marked by a series of scandalous adventures with women, was a far better soldier than clergyman.

THE CHURCH'S
PREDICAMENT
The council of Pisa not only failed to end the schism,[12] it did nothing to solve the ever-increasing problems of clerical corruption and heresy. Meanwhile, throughout Europe, public opinion ran high against the clerical leaders who were apparently willing to let the church go to ruin rather than risk the loss of any of their official privileges. In England, Wiclif's teachings had become more radical and were being spread among the lower classes by a group of heretical preachers called Lollards. On the Continent, not only heretics but also radical university men were outspoken in condemning the entire papal system.

Among the common folk, particularly in the Germanies, the old Waldensian heresy had revived and was spreading rapidly. In Bo-

[12] Schism means a division; the term is used especially in connection with divisions in the church.

hemia, popular heresies became closely allied with the ideas of certain intellectual radicals at the University of Prague. One of the most notable of them, Jerome of Prague, was a young scholastic wanderer of noble birth whose advanced ideas and independent personality had led to his expulsion from the University of Paris. Jerome went to the University of Oxford, where he became enthusiastic over the teachings of Wiclif. His return to Bohemia, where Wiclif's works were already known, helped make the University of Prague a hotbed of social and religious radicalism. The principal leader in this radical movement at Prague was Professor John Hus (1370-1415), the "Bohemian Wiclif." As a poor boy Hus had worked his way through the university, making an enviable record in theology and debating. After having won fame as a popular preacher, he became rector of the university. His own peasant background, his position in the university, and an unusually forceful personality combined to make him the outstanding exponent of three revolutionary movements: (1) anti-German nationalism in Bohemia, (2) Wicliffite doctrines on the Continent, and (3) drastic reformation of the clerical system. Like Wiclif before him, and like Luther a century later, Hus was a popularizer of the current professorial ideas of reform.

THE COUNCIL OF CONSTANCE (1414-1418) Hussite radicalism and papal degradation soon brought matters to a head. Disgust with the existing church government was universal. The only question seemed to be when, by whom, and how far the reformation was to be carried out. Matters were brought to a climax by the university professors and the German emperor. The University of Paris had been called upon to solve the legal technicalities of the situation, and two scholastic professors (Peter of Ailly and John Gerson) took the lead in demanding an international conference of laymen and clergymen to consider the situation.

In 1411 Emperor Sigismund joined the ranks of the reformers, and soon became the leader of the movement. By recognizing John XXIII of the Pisa line of popes as the rightful head of the church, Sigismund persuaded him to issue the formal call for a council. This gave the council a legal status. The emperor also won an important advantage by having the council meet on neutral ground, outside of Italy at the imperial city of Constance in the Swiss Alps. Here none of the three popes could exercise undue influence. In order to forestall any possible effort to pack the council it was also proposed that the lay representatives be allowed to vote, and that their votes be grouped by "nations" (Italian, French, German, English, and Spanish). The council convened in November, 1414. For almost four years the little mountain city held the attention of Christendom. Filled to overflowing with bishops, abbots, princes, university professors, diplomats, and curiosity seekers of all descriptions, Constance, at one and the same time, was a religious peace congress and a political convention.

THE COUNCIL CRUSHES HERESY
The first outstanding problem to be considered was settled on strictly conservative grounds, with almost no dissension. It involved the question of three suspected heretics; John Wiclif, Jerome of Prague, and John Hus. The case of John Wiclif was relatively simple. Even before his death in 1384 a number of his ideas had been condemned by the pope, and the University of Oxford had expelled him from its faculty. But he had been allowed to retire to private life and to die undisturbed. Now, thirty years after his death, the Council of Constance revived his case, condemned forty-five points in his writings, and pronounced him a heretic. His remains were disinterred from the holy ground of a quiet English churchyard and burned, and the ashes were scattered.

Jerome of Prague and John Hus offered more serious problems. They had been condemned for Wicliffite opinions and for their criticism of ecclesiastical abuses such as the selling of indulgences; but now Hus, with Luther-like boldness, had publicly burned a papal bull of excommunication. Both he and Jerome were popular and influential, not only among the students and professors at the University of Prague, but also throughout Bohemia, which was at this time a hotbed of anticlericalism and Bohemian national spirit. This put Emperor Sigismund in a predicament. As heir to the crown of Bohemia, he hesitated to risk antagonizing the people by taking action against a national hero; on the other hand, he did not wish to encourage the anti-German nationalism of Hus's followers. Furthermore, as leader of the reform party, Sigismund sympathized with these bold critics of ecclesiastical corruption, but he could neither associate with nor protect them if they were heretics.

THE TRIAL OF HUS
Sigismund's handling of the difficult situation was more politic than courageous. He persuaded the two Bohemian leaders to appear at Constance in order to clear themselves of heresy charges and remove the sentence of excommunication. Hus, it seems, never doubted his ability to prove, by Scriptural authority, the orthodoxy of his beliefs. Like many a heretic he was to learn that the church insisted on implicit obedience from

her followers and was not interested in their personal interpretations of the Bible. In defiance of the emperor's guarantees of safe conduct to and from Constance, Jerome and Hus were thrown into prison shortly after their arrival. Sigismund's protest was overruled on the ground that "promises prejudicial to the Catholic faith" need not be kept. Rather than break up the council, he submitted. The examiners gave Hus every opportunity to prove his orthodoxy and fidelity to the church by making either a general or specific denial of his errors. He stubbornly asserted the right of drawing his own conclusions as to the teachings of Divine Scripture. Even the emperor became bitterly hostile when Hus insisted that Wiclif's doctrines were orthodox. At length the council ceased its efforts. Hus was divested of his priestly garments, condemned as an unrepentant heretic, and burned at the stake. A year later Jerome of Prague suffered the same fate.

The modern mind, admiring the courage of the two Bohemian martyrs, usually condemns the action of the council. From the clerical viewpoint, however, it is apparent that the judges had no alternative: they were compelled to enforce the laws of the church. If the sovereign authority of Christendom was not enforced, religious anarchy might endanger organized Christian civilization. Events were to prove, however, that the burning of one dead heretic and two live 'ones was no solution for the problem of heresy. A century later, under similar conditions, Emperor Charles V kept his promise of safe conduct and Martin Luther not only escaped John Hus's fate, but lived to see his "heresy" triumphant.

THE COUNCIL ENDS THE SCHISM A second and even more difficult problem taken up by the Council of Constance was that of ending the schism. The three existing popes must be eliminated. John XXIII, at his first glimpse of the walled city of Constance amid its encircling mountains, is said to have cried: "A trap for foxes!" He spoke more truly than he thought, for at Constance he, the other two popes, and their clerical dependents were indeed brought to judgment by the emperor, the legal experts, and the long-suffering reformers who were determined to restore the unity of Christendom. Ever since the days of Marsilius of Padua, liberal-minded scholars had been urging that papal actions and clerical conduct should be subject to the authority of Christian laymen and clergymen in general councils. The failure of the Council of Pisa had shown how difficult it was to make such action legal and to enforce it. At Constance this was done by a decree (entitled *Sacrosancta*) to the effect that this "Sacrosanct council" had been lawfully assembled by the emperor, as was the custom since the time of Constantine and Charles the Great, and that "its authority, coming directly from our Lord Jesus Christ, must be obeyed by all persons, even the pope."

Thus the church proclaimed its Great Charter. No longer were popes to be absolute monarchs; henceforth they must submit to the will of Christendom as expressed in great international parliaments. Before the council adjourned it decreed that future popes were to be held in check by councils to be called at fixed periods. Truly a new day of enlightened parliamentary government seemed to be dawning for the Roman Catholic Church.

THE END OF THE SCHISM
It was not without a struggle that the three rival popes succumbed. Pope John XXIII had mobilized a strong following of Italian prelates at Constance, and it was only by insisting on voting as "nations" rather than as individuals that the reformers gained control of the council. John and his faction then sought to have the other two popes deposed so that he would be left supreme pontiff. The reformers checked this move by bringing up seventy charges that had been preferred against John, with the result that he was finally forced to resign. With considerably less difficulty the Avignon and Roman popes were forced out of office, and in 1417, three years after the opening of the council, a new pope, Martin V, was elected. The selection was made by a joint electoral committee consisting of the college of cardinals and thirty members of the council, six from each nation represented. This procedure was a triumph of international unity, even though the candidate chosen was somewhat lacking in spiritual leadership and enthusiasm for reform. Nevertheless, he was a reputable cardinal and a member of the Colonna family whose clerical politicians had long been active in papal affairs. In the selection of the pope, as in the treatment of heresy, the council showed its conservatism. But it reunited the church once more under a recognized leader.

THE FAILURE OF THE REFORM PROGRAM
When the Council of Constance first assembled one might have prophesied that a great reformation was about to sweep over Western Europe. The council opened in a flurry of optimism. Four years later, after forty-five laborious sessions, its efforts seemed to have been in vain, so far as real reform of the universally recognized evils of the

church was concerned. At the opening of the council each nation had been invited to draw up a list of proposals, which were then considered by the various reform commissions. Heated debates took place. In theory all factions favored reform, but there were honest differences of opinion as to the best methods of attaining it. Moreover, the clerical officials, whose interests were threatened by reforms, used every possible means to prevent changes. As time passed and practical difficulties multiplied, the reformers grew weary. Why should they endanger the progress made in other lines and the unity and harmony of the church by insisting on drastic reforms? After two years of discussion, the council agreed upon a set of resolutions condemning some of the worst financial and political abuses of the papal administration, and decreed that the new pope call another council within five years. After making this gesture of reform, they turned to the more immediate problem of selecting a pope.

It was not to be expected that Martin V, once he was recognized as pope, would make any drastic effort at carrying out reforms that threatened to weaken his own political organization. In short, immediately after his election, he adopted in its entirety the corrupt and burdensome financial system of his predecessor. Furthermore, he reaffirmed the doctrine of papal supremacy in a decree formally condemning all who disregarded papal authority in matters of faith or who appealed from his judgment. In order to allay the fears of the various nations, he entered into separate negotiations with their representatives. This resulted in a number of concessions which were better than no reform at all. This system of private arrangements, however, sounded the death knell of real reform and of parliamentary government in the church.

It has been said that if the Council of Constance had only "reformed the church in head and members" as it had promised to do in its early proceedings, the Protestant Revolt of the succeeding century would never have occurred. Whatever the truth of this conjecture, it is obvious that, under the circumstances, such action was impossible. In a spirit of practical conservatism the council compromised on almost every issue. Political expediency rather than spiritual leadership ruled in the selection of a pope; the conciliar reforms were unenforced, a mere "paper program"; and in a spirit of rigid traditionalism earnest radicals were punished as heretics. A century later the church was to reap the bitter fruits of this shortsighted policy.

A REVIVED BUT
UNREFORMED
PAPACY

After the adjournment of the Council of Constance, the papacy resumed its old ways. Pope Martin V, who was busying himself with the tasks of recovering the Papal States and putting his own family (the Colonnas) in control of the city of Rome, manifested no serious intention of carrying out the reforms voted by the council. Meanwhile, the powerful monarchs took it upon themselves to protect their nations from the most burdensome papal abuses. Emperor Sigismund and the pope signed a treaty (called a *concordat*) which limited German contributions and appeals to the papal court. The French king followed suit, and in England laws were passed for the regulation of papal dispensations and indulgences. By such agreements, Martin pacified the important monarchs and made his own position temporarily secure against possible reforms. His success in dividing the opposition was a masterpiece of political strategy, but it had the disadvantage of failing to touch the ever-increasing problem of heresies.

THE BOHEMIAN
HERESY

Heresy was causing both pope and emperor endless trouble in Bohemia, where the burning of Jerome of Prague and John Hus had stirred up a hornet's nest. Hus was considered a martyr not only to the corrupt clergy but also to the faithlessness of the German emperor. King Wenceslaus, who was favorable to the cause for a time, joined in the popular condemnation of his brother Sigismund and of the Council of Constance for having violated the safe-conduct granted to John Hus. When Wenceslaus died, the Bohemians vehemently rejected Sigismund's claim to the crown. Accordingly he prepared to take possession of his inheritance by force, and his ally, Pope Martin V, called upon all Christians to join the emperor in a "crusade" against the heretical nation. In the face of this common danger all factions in Bohemia temporarily forgot their rivalries in the defense of their country. Most notable was the cessation of the bitter feud between the conservative, aristocratic, and burgher sect of Utraquist-Calixtines, and the lower-class radicals, called Taborites.[13] The Taborites, in particular, under their one-eyed general, John Ziska, outgeneraled and outfought the loosely

---

[13] The Utraquist-Calixtines had four main tenets: (1) that in the communion the people should receive, as during the early Christian centuries, *both* the *chalice* of wine and the bread (hence the names Utraquist, from *utraque* meaning *both,* and Calixtines, from *calix* meaning *chalice*); (2) that the lower clergy, and even laymen, might preach; (3) that the members of the clergy should be deprived of all civil power; and (4) that they should be tried in the state courts for all serious crimes. The Taborites (from *Tabor,* the Biblical name of a mountain village which was one

organized hordes of invaders. Time after time the German "crusaders" were defeated by Ziska's peasant armies with their well-organized infantry, cavalry, artillery, and ironclad wagon trains. Later, under a commander named Prokop, the Bohemians took the offensive, invading Austria and Hungary. In one battle a small Bohemian army routed almost three times as many Saxons. On another occasion a "crusading" army of 200,000 was said to have fled in a panic at the mere sight of the terrible Bohemians. After ten years of failure and defeat, both emperor and pope were willing to negotiate. Fortunately there was a newly convened church council to assist in the peaceful solution of the Hussite heresy.

THE COUNCIL OF BASEL — Throughout most of his pontificate, Martin V (1417-1431) skillfully avoided calling councils. He had no desire to convene an assembly of potential reformers who might criticize his administration. But inasmuch as the Council of Constance had provided for periodic councils, he reluctantly sent out the summons for a council at Pavia in 1423. A plague and various international difficulties, however, prevented any important deliberations. But the popes could not permanently postpone action. In the seven years (1424-1431) between the adjournment of the Council of Pavia and the date set for the next council, the Bohemian situation had focused Europe's attention once more on the affairs of the church. Because this was the last thing that the popes desired, the new pope, Eugenius IV (1431-1447), paid no attention to the council and did his best to nullify its work. The council met at Basel in Switzerland in 1431. After a slow start affairs were carried on with laudable seriousness of purpose and remarkable efficiency. At the opening sessions each member was assigned to one of four *deputations,* or committees, to which were allocated (respectively) matters of "faith and doctrine," "the restoration of peace," "reforms," and "miscellaneous business." In each deputation there was unlimited discussion, and even minority reports were considered in the open sessions of the council.

Meanwhile, in taking up the critical Bohemian problem, the coun-

of their important centers) approved these four doctrines, but went much further in their democratic and socialistic tendencies. Their beliefs were much like those of the Waldensians and the Lollards (see above, p. 568). They abolished formal ritual and vestments in church services, addressed one another as "brother" or "sister," and advocated complete social equality among Christians. Of this same primitive peasant type are many of the minor religious sects that still exist in European and American rural districts.

cil began to negotiate directly with the heretics. But the jealous pope, in order to maintain his prerogatives and prevent the council from scoring a diplomatic triumph, dissolved it. Thereupon, the members, refusing to disperse, asserted their independence by reaffirming the principle of conciliar supremacy over the popes. Eugenius was summoned to appear and answer for his actions. Henceforth the actions of both pope and council took the form of a life-and-death struggle.

THE COUNCIL AND THE HUSSITES — In spite of difficulties, the council made remarkable progress. The handling of the difficult Bohemian situation illustrates clearly the enlightened, though rather unwieldy, methods used by the council. For months the Hussite ambassadors debated with the members of the council concerning their divergencies in belief. Embassies passed back and forth from Basel to Prague with proposals and counterproposals. Finally a compromise was arrived at which granted the Bohemians political autonomy (under Emperor Sigismund's control) and two of the moderate demands of the Utraquists (free preaching and double communion). One radical peasant sect of Taborites refused to compromise and was crushed by force of arms. Their leader, Prokop, and with him their cause, perished at the hands of the nobility in the Battle of Lipan in 1434. This was a triumph for economic as well as religious conservatism. Until the outbreak of the Protestant Revolt, Bohemia remained tranquil, her peasantry ground down by baronial landlords, her more moderate heretics given the stamp of conciliar approval, and the Taborites barely surviving in a sect that still exists under the name "Moravian Brethren."

THE COUNCIL AND REFORM — The successful outcome of the Bohemian affair gave proof of the council's ability to handle matters of "faith" and "peace." In "reforming the church in head and members" the outcome, like that at Constance, was disappointing. At Constance too little was done; at Basel, too much. Their success in Bohemia, achieved in spite of the pope's opposition, spurred the Baselites to radical reforms. But most of the proposals were aimed at the papacy, and this alarmed the conservative members of the council. In the unavoidable rift that developed between the radical reformers and their papal opponents, public opinion tended to side with the latter. Furthermore, the pope was able to outplay the council in matters of diplomacy. Like Pope Martin, he won the leading monarchs away from the cause of reform by financial and political concessions. Meanwhile, clever statesmen seized the opportunity to drive sharp bargains with both the council and the pope, selling their support to the highest bidder. These agreements took the form of "pragmatic sanctions" and "concordats."[14] Charles VII of France, for instance, arranged the Pragmatic Sanction of Bourges (1438) which "sanctioned" the right of the French clergy to manage its own ecclesiastical revenues and appointments under the supervision of the king instead of the pope. In return, France recognized the authority of council. At Mayence in 1439 and Vienna in 1448 the pope consented to similar pragmatic sanctions for the Germanies. Ferdinand and Isabella of Spain also made arrangements by which they gained complete control over their national churches. It is clear that sincere church reform by councils had given way to political bargains which allowed the national monarchs to strengthen their own powers by appropriating the ecclesiastical privileges once monopolized by the papacy. It is equally evident that the clergy and people of various regions were becoming more conscious of national bonds of unity. Nationalism influenced the organization of the conciliar representatives according to "nations." Through the actions of both kings and councils, nationalism was rapidly undermining the papal authority.

THE COUNCIL AND CHRISTIAN UNITY   In one respect the Council of Basel promoted a most promising diplomatic mission, the merger of the Greek and Roman Catholic churches. Ever since the early Christian centuries, it had been the papacy's ideal to bring the Eastern and Western churches under one head. During the fifteenth century, as the rising menace of Turkish invasion threatened the Eastern Empire and the Eastern Church, the papacy once more saw an opportunity of realizing its agelong ambition. It seemed likely that the hard-pressed Easterners might recognize the headship of the Roman pope in return for Western assistance against the Turks. This was the situation at the opening of the Council of Basel. As in the case of the Bohemian heresy, the council began its own negotiations with the Easterners. But the ambassadors were at Ferrara, to which place the pope had summoned all of the members of the council. The council refused to be removed to Italy in this summary fashion, and countered by suspending Eugenius IV from office. In so doing the council overstepped itself. Many delegates who approved of sweeping reforms of the papacy were by no means willing to destroy the traditional powers of the popes.

---

[14] Pragmatic (i.e., practical) sanction is a name used for a certain type of decree. A concordat is a treaty between the papacy and a secular power.

It seems probable that the council's drastic action in this case strengthened Eugenius. He not only carried to completion the Eastern diplomatic mission, but undermined the influence of the council by setting up a rival council, first at Ferrara, and later at Florence. When the Greek emperor and his patriarch came from Constantinople to negotiate, they were promised Western assistance against the Turks in return for their acceptance of several details of Roman Catholic doctrine and the recognition of the pope as "the ruler of the Church of God, saving the privileges and rights of the patriarchs of the East." When the Greek envoys returned to Constantinople, however, the outraged populace denounced them as traitors to their religion, and the agreement was never carried out.

THE POPE TRIUMPHS OVER THE COUNCIL
This event marks the turning point of the struggle between the council and the pope. Henceforth the Council of Basel dwindled in numbers, influence, and in everything except radicalism. A modern historian has remarked that their work was done, "in fact, was overdone." The remaining members still clung grimly to their self-imposed task of crushing the papacy. They deposed Eugenius IV for heresy, and elected as pope the Duke of Savoy, a widower with a family of children. This threatened Europe once more with a schism, and it is not strange that the council, the apparent perpetrator of the trouble, lost favor. Papal concessions soon won the European monarchs from their rather lukewarm support of the Baselites. Under Eugenius IV's successor, Nicholas V (1447-1455), the Baselite pope was persuaded to abdicate. He was granted the position of cardinal with a life pension and other equally attractive honors and privileges. In order to save its face, the Council of Basel accepted Felix's resignation, elected Nicholas V to succeed him, and, with a final assertion of the supreme authority of councils, adjourned.

At Rome the following year (1450) a magnificent semicentennial jubilee was celebrated by the triumphant pope. The age of conciliar control was ended. The great councils have to their credit (1) a remarkable democratic experiment in church government; (2) several questionably successful victories over heretics; and (3) several vain efforts at reforming the papacy. As for the papacy, it drifted into a regime of worldliness and political power.[15] It was obvious that neither popes nor councils were capable of assuming the spiritual leadership

[15] For details concerning the popes of this period, see below, pp. 623 ff.

of Christendom. Conciliar radicals were no more successful than papal reactionaries. In the new age of practical economics and politics, kings and national assemblies were destined to assume more and more control over church affairs. Meanwhile, amid the prevailing spiritual uncertainty and political confusion, the ominous rumblings of religious revolt were heard. The roots of Christendom's great civil war, the Protestant Revolt, lie in the century of papal history between Martin V and Martin Luther.

═ XXIX ═

ENGLAND AND FRANCE IN THE LATE MIDDLE AGES

IN our survey of the papacy during the fourteenth and fifteenth centuries we have noted that both France and England were displaying a unity of spirit and an efficiency of royal government that indicates the rapid advance of nationalism. By the opening of the fourteenth century in both countries national solidarity was sufficiently established to administer a decisive setback to the papal ambitions of Boniface VIII. During the ensuing period England and France assumed to a greater degree the characteristics of modern national states. In territorial unity and in centralized governmental finance and administration, noteworthy advances were made. But most noticeable of all was the development of the *spirit* of nationalism among the rank and file of the people. This was accompanied by a rapid increase of despotic royal power. Both of these trends were very closely tied up with the expansion of economic life and with another characteristically modern institution: prolonged and devastating warfare.

THE HUNDRED YEARS' WAR

By the end of the thirteenth century France and England were drifting into renewed warfare. The fact that both states were nationally unified, increasingly prosperous, and centralized in their governmental institutions made for a struggle more devastating than their earlier conflicts. Both Edward I and Philip IV [1] had made extensive financial and diplomatic preparations for the war which they knew was inevitable, but it was left to their successors, a quarter of a century later, to precipitate Europe's first great international conflict.

[1] See above, p. 558.

ROOTS OF
THE CONFLICT
The causes of the Hundred Years' War are complex. Edward III's claim to the French throne by right of inheritance from his mother, Philip IV's daughter,[2] is usually regarded as the immediate cause, but the roots of the Hundred Years' War go much deeper than this. Warfare was made inevitable by the increasing national rivalry and by the bitter hostilities arising from the clash of economic interests. The chief underlying motives for the war were territorial and economic and the outstanding points of friction were Flanders, with its rich textile industries, and Aquitaine, a marvelously fertile land which produced choice wines. Bordeaux was as important a port for the wine trade of Europe as Bruges was for textiles. For needy or ambitious monarchs, both of these regions offered sources of unlimited income.

From the beginnings of their territorial expansion France and England had clashed over territories in western France.[3] When William the Conqueror acquired England in addition to Normandy and thus established an Anglo-Norman empire, trouble began. Thereafter, for four centuries, England and France waged an intermittent warfare which can be divided roughly into three periods. During the first, from William the Conqueror to Henry II, the Anglo-Normans took the offensive, and by the end of the reign of Henry II, England ruled over the western half of France. The French king had not even a window overlooking the Atlantic.

Soon, however, the tide turned, and there was a period of French expansion. By clever intrigues Philip II won most of northwestern France from John of England, and for a century France had the advantage. During the weak reign of John's son, Henry III, the English might have been ousted from Aquitaine in the southwest as well, but for the conscientious scruples of Louis IX. Instead, English rule in Aquitaine was recognized, and for two centuries longer the richest wine-raising region of France was held by foreigners. Philip IV likewise acknowledged the English rights in Aquitaine, but only after Edward I had given him a free reign in Flanders. Thus the solution of the Aquitainian problem was once more postponed, finally to become the chief territorial factor in the third period of hostilities—the Hundred Years' War—when the English once more took the offensive.

The conflicts before 1300 may be regarded as the earlier periods of

---

2 In settling one of their numerous quarrels, Edward I and Philip IV had arranged the marriage of Prince Edward (II) to Philip's daughter.

3 See above, Chapters XXIII-XXIV, for the conflicts referred to on this page.

a *Four Hundred* Years' War over English possessions in France, and also as the underlying causes of the Hundred Years' War. By the end of Philip IV's reign there were several danger points, at any one of which the irrepressible conflict might break forth again.

FLANDERS AND THE WOOL TRADE

In addition to Aquitaine, there was tension along the English Channel, where hostilities were constantly recurring between the fishing fleets of the two na-tions. In 1293 an unauthorized naval battle took place off the Breton coast, in which thousands of men were killed. Meanwhile French fleets were raiding the English seaports. A series of minor engagements followed, and things drifted on thus for years. The region in which England and France were first to clash in formal combat was Flanders, which Philip IV had annexed in accordance with an agreement made with Edward I. Flanders was the greatest textile region of Northern Europe and was its most important trading center. Bruges, "the Venice of the North," at the delta of the Rhine, with its brisk import and export trade, was also a center for industry and banking. At its wharves Italian fleets bringing the spices of the Orient anchored alongside German ships of the Hanseatic League, loaded with raw products from Baltic and Russian lands (timber, tar, wheat, honey, and fish). The chief interest of both France and England in Flanders centered in wool. Both nations, but particularly England, had raw wool to sell to the textile manufacturers of Flanders. Both nations imported fine manufactured cloth from the Flemish factories. And both the French and English kings longed for the tolls and taxes from this thriving industrial and commercial region.

Philip IV, after acquiring control of Flanders, began at once to reap a rich financial harvest. But he went too far. After two years of tyrannical exploitation at the hands of greedy royal officials, the Flem-ish townsfolk revolted. In Bruges, alone, 3,000 Frenchmen were mas-sacred. The French feudal army which Philip sent to quell the revolt underestimated the fighting qualities of the lowly burghers, and at Courtrai, in 1302, it suffered a disgraceful defeat at the hands of the Flemish pikemen. So many French knights were killed and so many golden spurs were carried off as trophies that the victory came to be known as the "Battle of the Spurs." Like Bouvines in 1214,[4] the Battle of Crécy,[5] and the Swiss victories against invading armies,[6] Courtrai is famous in military annals as an example of the fighting ability of de-

---

[4] See above, p. 479.   [6] See below, p. 613.
[5] See below, p. 585.

termined plebeian troops, even when pitted against expert soldiery. It also marks the rising importance of the towns. France, however, failed to learn the lesson that feudal armies were out of date. Army after army sent into Flanders was checked and Philip is said to have remarked: "It rains Flemings." Philip eventually offered terms which were accepted, and for a generation Flanders was troubled less by French intervention than by domestic turmoil.

FLEMISH WOOL   Meanwhile Philip's three sons, Louis X, Philip V, and Charles IV, had passed from the royal stage without leaving any heirs. Consequently Philip's nephew, Philip VI (1328-1350), came to the throne. During the same period in England, Edward I's son, Edward II (1307-1327), defeated by the Scots at Bannockburn, flouted by his parliaments, and finally deposed and murdered by rebellious barons, had been succeeded by Edward III (1327-1377). Edward disputed Philip's claim to the French throne on the ground that he himself was Philip IV's *direct* heir through a daughter, whereas Philip VI was only an indirect heir. The French lawyers, in turn, insisted that, according to ancient custom, the royal succession passed only through male heirs, and that Philip IV's daughter, therefore, could not transmit the crown to her son. Edward III (as we shall see) did not press his claim until actuated by an economic motive.

Philip VI began his reign with a notable victory which led indirectly to the Hundred Years' War. The count of Flanders had appealed to him for assistance in putting down his rebellious Flemish townsfolk and peasants. At Cassel, in 1328, the joint armies of the king and count won a decisive victory over the rebels. Thenceforth events moved rapidly toward an international crisis. The count was pro-French, whereas most of his subjects were pro-English. This was to be expected because they had suffered severely from the financial exploitation of the French king, and because much of the wool used in their textile industries came from England. At the invitation of the English, many Flemish weavers had migrated across the Channel.

In retaliation, Philip persuaded the count to seize all Englishmen in Flanders and to confiscate their goods. Edward III, in turn, cut off the export of raw wool to Flanders. As a result the textile shops were forced to shut down, men were thrown out of work, and starving mobs of artisans began to assail the pro-French government of Flanders. Jacob van Artevelde, a weaver and an influential citizen of Ghent, put himself at the head of the malcontents and opened negotiations with the English king. Edward gladly made an alliance with the rebels and reopened the wool trade with them. It was at this time that an exiled French nobleman persuaded Edward to assert his claim to the French throne. This was, of course, a mere pretext, but it was important in that it gave the Flemish rebels an excuse to shift their allegiance from their count and his overlord, Philip VI, to Edward III.

In this manner Flemish textile interests brought England into undisguised warfare with France, and the *Four Hundred* Years' War was reopened with the beginning of the so-called Hundred Years' War. It might be said that the war was brought on by the clash of economic interests in a textile region (Flanders), a wine-growing region (Aquitaine), and a fishing region (the English Channel).

WAR IN FLANDERS: SLUYS

Actual hostilities between England and France commenced in 1338. In that year Edward III, with funds borrowed from Florentine bankers, equipped an expeditionary force which went to Flanders and began to ravage the French frontier. When the project failed, Edward was unable to meet his obligations, and the Florentines went unpaid. Two years later his seamen won a decisive victory over the French fleet off the port of Sluys near Bruges. This battle is significant in that it marked the beginning of English naval supremacy and showed the decided superiority of the English longbow in warfare.

The English ships were manned with bowmen whose arrows had a maximum range of about one-sixth of a mile, and were deadly in their effectiveness at a hundred yards. Loaded with such destruction, the English fleet sailed down upon the French ships, which were chained together in close ranks at the harbor entrance. On the decks were turrets, manned by Genoese crossbowmen and provided with stones and other missiles. But the usefulness of these instruments of short-range fighting was completely nullified by the longbowmen. Their whistling messengers of death, falling like a shower upon the French ships, drove the defenders to cover and enabled the English to win an overwhelming victory. This effectiveness at long-distance enabled the English to win every major battle of the next century.[7]

With the Flemish campaign of 1339-1340, active fighting ceased for a time. Edward III did not follow up his victory, and when the

---

[7] It is sometimes asserted that the Hundred Years' War modernized European methods of fighting by substituting the impact of a missile (the arrow), for that of a man (the knight). It is true that modern warfare emphasizes fighting by means of missile-hurling machinery, but this is an age-old method. Missiles were used by archers and slingers, and in catapults, centuries before the introduction of that improved

fickle Flemings murdered their leader, Jacob van Artevelde (1345), the English king signed a truce and withdrew his forces. Thus ended the first of the series of wars that comprise the Hundred Years' War. But hostilities soon broke out elsewhere for the conflict could not be stifled.

WAR IN NORTH-
ERN FRANCE:
CRÉCY

In a dispute over the succession in Brittany, France and England took opposite sides, each hoping to get control of that region. Meanwhile French encroachments along the borders of Aquitaine gave Edward an excuse for attacking the southern frontiers of France. In 1346 he set sail for Bordeaux with a small but effective mercenary army. When contrary winds interfered with his original plans, the expedition landed in Normandy, near Cherbourg. So unprepared were the French for an attack in this region that the invaders raided the countryside, sacked Caen, the Norman capital, and marched unopposed along the south bank of the Seine, plundering and ravaging up to the very walls of Paris.

When King Philip finally approached with an immense feudal array, Edward retreated northward toward Flanders. Burning with revenge, Philip hurried after him and at Crécy, near the Somme River, the English were brought to bay. Here was fought one of the most famous battles of the war. The English knights dismounted and arranged themselves in three divisions, each protected by bowmen and "bombardiers" with small cannon. When Philip and his disordered host approached they were astonished to find the small English army awaiting them apparently unafraid. The bowmen were reclining on the ground, many of them chewing grass, farmer fashion. In a blind fury Philip ordered an immediate attack, sending forward first his Genoese crossbowman. They advanced directly into the slanting rays of the afternoon sun, and also into a storm of arrows from the English longbows. The conflict was largely a repetition of Sluys. The long-bowmen picked off the enemy before they could make use of their short-range weapons. Next the French men-at-arms dashed pell-mell across the valley, eager to inflict vengeance upon the hated English. But the feathered shafts continued to spread death and destruction. To add to the confusion the English cannon hurled lighted balls of

missile-hurling weapon, the longbow. Furthermore, for ultimate victory modern generals still rely on the impact of men (the bayonet charge of infantry). The Hundred Years' War marked important changes in warfare, but they were only steps in a long evolution.

fire into the disordered mass, so that it "seemed as if God was thundering."

The French knights fought bravely, but to no effect. When nightfall ended the slaughter, the mighty French army was completely routed; the king and his attendants in full flight. Never had French arms suffered so disgraceful a defeat, and seldom have military commanders learned less from a disaster. The French continued to employ the old-fashioned feudal array against the modernized English forces of efficiently armed infantry.

THE CAPTURE
OF CALAIS

Fortunately for the French, Edward took little real advantage of his victory. He merely continued his northward march, plundering as he went. Then he spent over a year besieging and finally capturing Calais, the French port on the Channel opposite Dover. The inhabitants of the city were deported and replaced by English colonists. Calais, the only permanent acquisition made by the English during the entire war, remained in their hands for almost three centuries. It served as an important point of entry on the Continent for English goods. The French chronicler Froissart wrote that "the English love Calais more than any town in the world, for they say that as long as they are masters of it they hold the keys of France at their girdle."

THE BLACK
DEATH

Shortly after the capture of Calais another truce was concluded, and for almost ten years (1347-1356) there were no important battles. Meanwhile both realms, and most of Europe, were ravaged by a calamity worse than war. From the Orient, where it was said to have taken millions of lives, the Black Death descended upon Europe. Like later ravages of the bubonic plague, it came by sea, probably carried by ship rats. Some ships that had sailed from east Mediterranean ports with complete crews were found drifting weeks later without a living soul on board. The dread plague struck Genoa in 1348, and soon all Italy was in terror. From Marseilles it spread northward through France. English soldiers, returning from France, carried the Death across the Channel. By the end of the year 1348, so it was said, the greater portion of the inhabitants of many cities had been carried off. As a matter of fact, the total of deaths is now thought to have been about one-third of the population—a catastrophe that kept not only business and government but even warfare at a standstill. The Black Death recurred at frequent intervals later in the century and had devastating effects on every phase of human activity.

WAR IN AQUI-
TAINE: POITIERS
Scarcely had France begun to recover from the worst ravages of the Black Death when she was visited with two more calamities—warfare, and a worse than useless king. Philip VI had been succeeded by his son, John the Good (1350-1364). John was called "the Good" because he was considered a "good knight"; that is, he was rash and courageous in battle and a spendthrift. As a king he was a total loss. His financial policies were so disastrous that in 1355 the Estates-General appointed commissioners to supervise the national revenues. But worse things were in store for the hapless nation. The very next year Prince Edward of England, the "Black Prince," starting from Bordeaux with a small army, ravaged the southern French frontier.

As in the Crécy campaign, an immense French array, under King John, finally brought the English to bay and once more the longbowmen poured their merciless fire upon the charging French knights. The disaster at Poitiers, however, was even worse than that of Crécy, for many of the French knights, including the king, were captured and held for immense ransoms. If the king and his useless comrades had been left to their fate, France might have been much better off. But ransoms must be paid, and every French merchant and peasant felt the additional financial burden.

After a portion of his ransom had been paid, King John returned from captivity, leaving a son as surety for the payment of the balance. Within four years he had practically ruined the French government. Fortunately for all concerned, his son broke parole, and John, good knight that he was, insisted on maintaining his untarnished record as a chevalier by returning to captivity. After a pleasant sojourn in London, John died, having enjoyed all of the comforts of royal warfare without any of its burdens. Characteristically enough, one of his last acts was to grant the recently acquired Duchy of Burgundy to a younger son, Philip, thus establishing an independent dynasty which, within the next century, nearly destroyed France. This event had worse consequences for France than the Battle of Poitiers.

STEPHEN MARCEL
AND THE ESTATES-
GENERAL
The political and military disasters of John's reign led to a revolution that threatened to make France a limited monarchy. Stirred to drastic action by the disgraceful defeat at Poitiers, the Estates-General attempted to reform the incompetent royal administration in a manner somewhat similar to that employed by Simon de Montfort and the

nobility of England a century earlier.[8] In 1357 the Estates-General refused to vote funds until their reform program (called "the Great Or-
dinance") had been accepted. Accordingly several of the most no-
torious courtiers were dismissed and a commission of deputies from
the three estates [9] was appointed to supervise the royal government.
Reforms of the military and judicial systems were also voted, and it
was decreed that the Estates-General should meet twice a year.

The leader of this movement was Stephen Marcel, head of the
Parisian merchant guilds. His program, however, failed. Opposition developed and the tide turned when Marcel and a group of radicals
broke into the royal palace, murdered two of the royal ministers, and
insulted the prince regent. The clergy, nobility, and even the populace
in the provinces resented such domination by the Parisian burghers.
Soon a civil war was raging between the royalists and the radicals of
Paris, to be followed by worse catastrophes.

MARCEL'S
DOWNFALL
In 1358 the long-suffering peasants rose against their
masters. Goaded to desperation by the effects of the
Black Death, wartime pillage, peacetime taxes, and
ransom levies for luxury-loving nobles, the "Jacques," as the peasants
were called, burst into a furious revolt. Wild mobs looted, plundered,
tortured, and outraged the nobility at whose hands they had suffered
for centuries. The atrocities perpetrated by the peasants were matched
by the vengeance exacted by the terrified nobles. As a result the suppressed peasantry, more despised than ever, were subjected to still
harsher bondage and the reform movement of the Estates-General was
discredited.

Marcel's position was weakened by the peasant uprising. He had also
hurt his cause by allying himself with Charles "the Bad" of Navarre,
a grandson of Philip IV and a claimant of the French throne. Suspicious of his motives, Marcel's fellow Parisians conspired to murder
him. With his death under such circumstances the reform movement
died. Although the prince regent reformed a few of the most glaring
governmental evils, France sank back into an apathy of indifference,
her once absolute royal government hopelessly disorganized.

Meanwhile, without funds, without a king, and without internal
unity, France was forced to make peace with England. In 1360, by
the Treaty of Brétigny-Calais, Edward III was recognized as ruler of

---

[8] See above, p. 466.

[9] The three estates were the clergy, nobility, and commoners. See above, p. 559,
for the first Estates-General, or meeting of all three estates.

Calais and Aquitaine without feudal obligations to the king of France. At the same time, however, he surrendered his claims to the French throne.

CHARLES V, THE WISE

With the death of his father, John, the prince regent, Charles V (1364-1380), became king. Charles was the very antithesis of his father. Of a thoughtful scholarly nature, he had, through his difficult experiences as regent, become an able administrator. Undertaking many much-needed reforms, he chose honest advisers, expended revenues wisely, and reorganized the old feudal army along more efficient lines. Among his military aides was Bertrand du Guesclin, France's ugliest man but Europe's greatest warrior. His chief service to France was his success in handling the adventuresome mercenaries with whom the country was overrun. These "free companies" of ruffianly soldiers who fought the enemy in wartime, pillaged the countryside, captured cities, and blackmailed the upper classes during times of peace. In some regions, formerly prosperous, it was said that "no longer could one hear a cock crowing or a hen clucking."

After the Treaty of 1360, Charles the Wise sent Bertrand du Guesclin to Spain with all the "companies" he could mobilize. Here they fought for Henry of Trastamara, a claimant of the throne of Castile, against King Pedro II the Cruel, who was supported by the "Black Prince" of England. Thus Charles very cleverly shifted the Hundred Years' War to Spain, and France enjoyed a short period of peace.

Meanwhile Charles had begun the slow process of recovering lost territories. Having won the friendship of the Bretons by careful diplomacy, he began an offensive against the English. Unlike his knightly predecessors, he adopted the Fabian policy of winning a war by avoiding pitched battles. No longer were French armies sent to certain destruction at the hands of the English bowmen. The invaders were allowed to march at will, ravaging and plundering the countryside. Sometimes they starved as a result of their own devastations. The only resistance they met was that of well-defended castles and walled towns. "Let them alone," said Charles, "like a tempest they will disperse themselves." All the English gained was the ill will of the French populace. Meanwhile by land and by sea the French surprised and captured so many strategic points that when a truce was concluded in 1375 little was left of the English possessions on the Continent save the coastal regions.

MISRULE AND
DISUNITY
Unfortunately, when Charles and his great general, du Guesclin, died, the destinies of France were left for forty years in the hands of Charles VI, "the Simple" (1380-1422). Charles was not only "simple"; during part of his reign he was insane. Consequently all of the good work of his father was undone. The government was left to ambitious courtiers, and, as in former days, France suffered from every form of misgovernment. Discontent flared up everywhere. In Flanders, Philip van Artevelde followed his father's example and led a revolt of certain of the townsfolk, which was crushed at Roosebeke in 1382. In Paris, likewise, the lower classes rose in violent but ineffective protest.

More destructive was the civil war that developed between two factions of royal courtiers. For a time the king's brother, Louis of Orleans, controlled affairs. Gradually, however, an ambitious uncle, that same Philip to whom King John had granted Burgundy, became the dominant influence at the court. When Philip's son, John the Fearless, went so far as to have his rival, Louis, assassinated, the Orleanists vowed vengeance. Before long they had won most of southern France to their cause and open warfare was on between the Orleanist South and the Burgundian North. Finally the suffering populace was driven to make one more vain attempt at reform. As in the days of Stephen Marcel, the Estates-General furnished the reform program, and the Parisians—this time under a skinner named Caboche—staged a revolt. Their violence having alienated public sympathy, the "Butcher Revolt" was easily suppressed. Shortly afterwards France was afflicted with another English invasion.

RENEWED WAR-
FARE: AGINCOURT
England, like France, for a time had been too busy with domestic troubles to carry on a successful foreign war. The Black Death had been followed by industrial and agrarian disturbances, and in 1381 the peasantry rose in such numbers that for a time the government seemed about to crumble.[10] After the peasant revolt had been quelled there still remained a stubborn parliament which showed more interest in quizzing royal ministers than in voting money for expeditions to France. Evidence of the discontent of this age is to be found in Langland's *Vision of Piers Plowman* and in the career of John Wiclif.

At the end of the century there came a change of royal dynasty. When Edward III's successor, Richard II, attempted to rule auto-

[10] See below, p. 601.

cratically he became so unpopular that his cousin, Henry of Lancaster, was able to usurp the throne. But as king, Henry IV (1399-1413) was himself troubled by rebellions and also by the knowledge of his uncertain right to the throne. It was the hope of ending this uncertainty and of allaying domestic discord that led his son, Henry V (1413-1422), to renew the war with France. A successful war would win English approval for his Lancastrian dynasty, and the disturbed condition of France at this time seemed to offer a favorable opportunity.

Accordingly, in 1415, Henry revived the old Edwardian claim to the French crown and invaded Normandy. The campaign was almost an exact duplication of that which culminated in Crécy. Henry marched through Normandy, across the Seine, and northward until forced to turn and fight. At Agincourt, English steadiness, the longbow, and a muddy field combined to destroy still another French army.

THE TREATY OF TROYES   Even worse experiences were in store for the French, because of their own lack of unity. Inasmuch as the Orleanist faction was now in control of the French government, their rivals, the Burgundians, allied themselves with the English. The victorious Henry occupied Normandy while John of Burgundy took possession of Paris, including the French king and his court. With hostile forces holding most of northern France, French hopes sank to a new low ebb. A few Orleanists, however, had escaped from Paris with the dauphin, the weak son of the insane king. At Bourges, south of Orleans, these fugitives set up royal court, which tried in vain to carry on the government of France. Among other things they endeavored to win the Burgundians over to the national cause. At the conference however a misunderstanding arose, and in the melee that followed Duke John of Burgundy was killed. This drove his son into a permanent alliance with the English, and together they forced the French king at Paris to accept the humiliating Treaty of Troyes (1420). By this treaty the dauphin was disinherited and the English king, having betrothed a French princess, was recognized as heir to the throne of France. Henry died before Charles VI (1422), but the baby born of the marriage became Henry VI, king of both France and England.

JOAN OF ARC   The French cause seemed lost. In Paris there was an English king supported by Burgundian forces. At Bourges, the dauphin still reigned as Charles VII, king of France. He was so weak, however, that the enemy called him the "King of Bourges." Eventually the English advanced to Orleans, which was the last strategic point between them and the conquest of Bourges and southern France. It was in the defense of Orleans that the tide turned for France. First, the Burgundians deserted their English allies. It seems that the citizens of Orleans had offered to surrender the city, but only to the Burgundians, and when the English commander objected to these terms, the Burgundians withdrew in disgust. Then Joan of Arc appeared with a small royal force to relieve the city. After losing a few skirmishes the English withdrew and southern France was saved.

The career of Joan is well known. Her peasant origin, her visions and voices, her appearance at the dauphin's court, her exploits at Orleans, and her tragic death need no detailed consideration. It is well, however, to examine the part she played in the French recovery. Whatever the mystery of her personality, there is nothing miraculous about the manner in which she saved Orleans and started France on the road to victory. As we have seen, the Burgundians had already fallen out with their English allies. With this preliminary setback it needed only active leadership and a vigorous offensive to drive back the English. Joan's simple confidence in her cause supplied the necessary encouragement for an already rising national spirit. The French had always shown courage; what they needed was effective leaders. For proof of this one need only recollect what Charles the Wise and du Guesclin had accomplished. Joan's exploits shine forth more brightly because of the dark background of misrule and disunity that had intervened.

JOAN'S FAILURE   Burgundy's part in bringing victory to the French was perhaps even more decisive than the exploits of Joan, as the later events of her career indicate. After the relief of Orleans the French began a vigorous offensive in which the new non-feudal military tactics were employed. Soon the English forces fell back to Normandy, which they were determined to hold. But instead of concentrating against them, Joan insisted on an expedition toward the northeast, in order to have the dauphin crowned king at Rheims. From the standpoint of military strategy this was unwise in that it precipitated hostilities with the Burgundians, who controlled this region. After the coronation, Joan insisted on attacking Paris, which was also in the hands of the Burgundians. This attack failed, and at

Compiègne, in the course of another skirmish with the Burgundians, she was captured.

Whatever her military and diplomatic blunders, Joan's personality shines forth with surpassing brightness to the very end. With equanimity and marvelous fortitude she endured a long imprisonment and a heartbreaking trial. Jailers, inquisitors, and executioners could not, or would not, understand the simple, pious, peasant girl. Her king, the dauphin, made no effort to save her, and she was burned for witchcraft by the English authorities. In the light of the evidence and the attitude of professors, priests, statesmen, and public opinion in that day, the outcome was not exceptional, nor particularly unreasonable. When one of the English guards at the execution exclaimed in awestruck tones, "We have burned a *saint*," he expressed the opinion of later ages. The modern world, including the Catholic Church, has done its best to atone for the action of Joan's judges, and in the twentieth century the "Maid of Orleans" was canonized.

THE TREATY
OF ARRAS

It was Burgundy, however, that brought the war to an end. Already disgusted with his English alliance, Duke Philip the Good was willing to desert to the French cause as soon as the dauphin, King Charles VII, paid the price. The alliance was made at Arras in 1435, after England had refused reasonable terms of peace. The Treaty of Arras between France and Burgundy put an end temporarily to their enmities, granted extensive territories to the duke, and recognized the virtual independence of the duchy. Once Burgundy, which held the balance of power, had shifted her alliance from England to France, the war was practically over. It was merely a matter of time for the remodeled French army to conquer Normandy and the remnants of Aquitaine. Bordeaux fell in 1453, and now England had only Calais to show for her hundred years of victories in France.

Although England signed no peace treaty, and stubbornly kept the French fleur-de-lis on her royal coat of arms,[11] the war was over. After having won every major engagement and having ridden roughshod over most of France for a century, England had lost her Continental possessions. France was in possession of Aquitaine, with its fertile grain fields and vineyards. French interests were dominant in Brittany, and a French duke was consolidating the wealthy industrial and agricultural regions of Flanders and Alsace-Lorraine into a new

---

[11] The fleur-de-lis is still a part of the royal coat of arms.

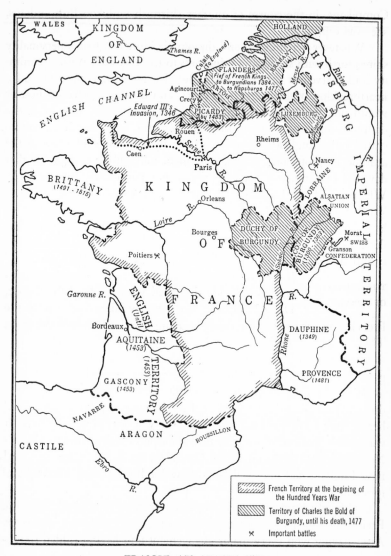

FRANCE AT ABOUT 1500

Showing approximate dates of acquisitions made during and after the
Hundred Years' War

political unit. Meanwhile, throughout a century and a half of almost constant warfare and devastation, both France and England had grown to national stature. The end of the conflict found them far along the road to modern nationalism and royal absolutism.

NATIONALISM AND ABSOLUTE MONARCHY IN FRANCE

Internal developments in France and England during the period of the Hundred Years' War show striking similarities. Both countries emerged from the conflict with a disorganized but vigorous economic life and with stronger national unity than ever before. This came about in spite of unparalleled destruction of life and property. In addition to the wars in France both nations had been torn by devastating civil wars: the Orleanist-Burgundian feud in France, the Wars of the Roses in England. Both had also suffered the periodic visitations of the Black Death, from 1348 on. Meanwhile, on the heels of the plague all Western Europe seemed to be swept by recurring epidemics of social, economic, and political discontent. To mention only a few outstanding examples, from 1355 to 1358 France was disturbed by upheavals of the Parisian townsfolk and the rural "Jacquerie." The years from 1378 to 1382 saw revolts of urban working men or rural peasants in Florence (the Ciompi), in Paris (the Maillotins), in Ghent (Philip van Artevelde), and in England (the peasant revolt of John Ball and Wat Tyler). During the fifteenth century, however, England and France experienced a social, economic, and political reconstruction which eventually culminated in a decided increase of middle-class prosperity and royal absolutism.

In both France and England, during the late fourteenth and early fifteenth centuries, there had been strong evidences of *political* discontent—notably a tendency on the part of certain discontented classes to interfere in the government. The French Estates-General, as has been seen, on several occasions took over the control of royal finances. In England, likewise, the parliamentary representatives insisted on having some check on the expenditure of the money which they voted their monarch. In the end, however, the institutions of centralized royal government triumphed, and, with national spirit and the middle class solidly behind them, the English and French monarchs became more powerful than ever.

The revival of the royal power was one of the most noteworthy developments in France after the Hundred Years' War. In spite of an almost uninterrupted succession of royal blunders, not only in military strategy, but also in financial administration, the French monarchy emerged from the war with more territory and authority than before. Within twenty years (1430-1450) after the appearance of Joan of Arc, Charles VII had recovered from the English all the non-French sections of northern France and Aquitaine. During the same period his powers also increased. The Estates-General granted him a permanent royal land tax (the *taille*), with which to support a permanent royal army. Thus the shiftless son of an insane king, whose government in its first years had been so inefficient that it had almost ruined France, was now voted royal powers which made him virtually absolute. When the Estates-General gave the king money and men with which to crush all opponents, it practically committed suicide: the grant of a royal income and army at one stroke freed the king from dependence on the people's representatives. Herein lies the secret of the rapid rise of French royal power after the war.

One may well ask why the representatives of the French nation so suddenly abdicated in favor of a royal dynasty that had been notoriously inefficient. For one thing, the radical reformers of the late fourteenth century were even less efficient than the kings in maintaining law and order. Then, as now, most nations preferred the certainty of unreformed conservatism to the uncertainty of experimental reforms or rebellions. In a period of turbulence and suffering such as that of the Hundred Years' War, the kingship, unsatisfactory though it was, still served as a symbol of unity. The efficient rule of Charles the Wise had shown France what a strong monarchical power could accomplish. Joan of Arc's implicit trust in the kingship also helped to revive popular faith in it. Therefore, when monarchical leadership brought the war to an unbelievably successful end—even though this may have been due more to good fortune than to good sense— the future of French royalty was safe.

Businessmen, peasants, clerics, and even some of the nobles rallied to the support of a government that seemed to have brought France in triumph through her most terrible ordeal. Furthermore, a strong monarchy meant good business conditions for the burghers, and peace and order for the peasants. The more powerful the kingship, the less feudal disorder, and the more opportunities for the lower classes to prosper. By 1450, in spite of the ravages of warfare and the Black Death, France was not without some signs of prosperity. Peasants and artisans who had taken advantage of the labor shortage and high wages which prevailed during the period of the Black Death were able to live comfortably and to acquire property.

Royal favor also brought commercial prosperity to the faithful burghers of the "Good Towns." Jacques Coeur, merchant of Bourges, made his millions by reason of the king's favors during the early fifteenth century. He was only the wealthiest of many men who combined business with governmental positions to the rapid increase of their private fortunes. Expanding business and expanding royal power were inseparably linked together in a mutually profitable partnership.

THE NOBILITY At the same time, the foes of royalty were relatively weak, for the nobility, medieval monarchy's most formidable opponent, had suffered great losses at the hands of the English bowmen. It is apparent, therefore, that weak as the French monarchy was, its enemies were even weaker. Charles VII played the leading role in French government, not because of his own efficiency, but because of the absence of a strong opposition.

When Charles VII died in 1461 the royal power had fully recovered and was well on the road to absolutism. But the ambitions of its traditional foe, the nobility, had also revived. Under the leadership of the powerful duke of Burgundy, the French nobles were prepared to defend their privileges against further royal encroachments. During the reign of Charles's son, Louis XI (1461-1483), a bitter struggle was waged between the king and the feudal aristocracy.

LOUIS XI, "THE From the start King Louis showed a cleverness and SPIDER KING" determination that promised well for the kingship. History has branded Louis as "the Spider King" and has compared his meanness of personality with that of King John of England. It is true that Louis was physically repulsive: spindle-shanked, knock-kneed, and probably epileptic. He lived simply, even penuriously. He dressed in ill-fitting, coarse clothing. His battered hat, encircled with images of saints and other amulets, indicated not only his carelessness as to personal appearance but also his superstitious obsessions. Suspicious of friends and foes alike, he constantly used religious charms, as well as royal spies, for protection against dangers real and imaginary. Louis was also low-minded, and obscene in his conversation. He had, however, a positive genius for diplomacy, and he won the support of the business classes by his economic policies. More clever than honest, absolutely unhampered by moral scruples, this master of intrigue merited well his epithet, "the Spider."

When Louis showed a disposition to assert his royal powers, the nobles formed a coalition which they called "The League of the Public Welfare," actually a conspiracy on the part of the great feudal barons for the defense of their own vested interests. The populace, however, refused to be misled by a selfish aristocracy which suddenly pretended to be interested in the welfare of the public. The king, even though his motives were not always of the purest, was to be preferred to the people's traditional enemy, the nobility. Since the "Leaguers" were powerful, Louis bought off some of the leading members in order to break the solid front of the opposition. His own brother deserted the league in return for Normandy and Aquitaine. The price was high, but by paying it Louis was able to prevent the duke of Burgundy from realizing his chief ambition, the disintegration of France. Throughout this diplomatic struggle the church, the lesser nobles, and the financially powerful townsfolk remained true to the king. Some of the phases of this popular enthusiasm for monarchy are portrayed in François Villon's writings.

The gradual dissolution of the league proved that Duke Charles the Bold of Burgundy and the league were no match for Louis and his loyal subjects. Even though Louis was defeated in battle and was at one time captured by his opponents, he managed to extricate himself from his difficulties. With time and the French nation on his side, he was bound to triumph.

THE FALL OF
CHARLES OF
BURGUNDY

Louis's success against Duke Charles was due in part to the rash mistakes of the latter. In temperament and methods Charles "the Bold" was the very opposite of Louis. Having acquired by inheritance most of the Netherlands, Charles was determined to obtain Champagne, Alsace, and Lorraine, the regions which separated the Netherlands from his own Burgundian realms.

In Alsace and Lorraine Charles's activities promised success. By furnishing money to the German duke of these regions, he got possession of Alsace as security for the loan. Next he assumed a protectorate over Lorraine, thus completing an almost unbroken sweep of possessions along the west bank of the Rhine, from Switzerland to the North Sea. He then proposed to have the Hapsburg emperor crown him king of this realm. Had this been accomplished, the several duchies between Germany and France would have been welded into a Burgundian kingdom of the Rhinelands, and the whole trend of modern history, with its unending Franco-German rivalry over Alsace-Lorraine, might have been changed.

Having enjoyed success thus far, Charles now began to encounter obstacles. The emperor, after vaguely promising him assistance, changed his mind. It is probable that Louis XI's diplomacy had something to do with this decision. To hamper Charles's cause still further, the townsfolk of Alsace and Lorraine leagued together against his burdensome taxation, and the Swiss cantons began to look with alarm on the ambitious activities of their Burgundian neighbor. Here was a perfect setting for Louis XI's intrigues. He persuaded the duke of Lorraine to break with Charles, and encouraged the Swiss to resist Burgundian encroachments. Charles quickly re-established his power in Alsace and Lorraine, but he was decisively defeated by the Swiss when he invaded the border cantons. Still set on realizing his ambitions, Charles attacked the rebellious city of Nancy in northern Lorraine. It was midwinter, his forces were insufficient, and the city was defended by a strong army, including Swiss troops. Charles the Bold suffered defeat and death, and with him disappeared the Burgundian dream of a great "Middle Kingdom."

FRANCE GAINS
MORE TERRITORY

But the struggle was not over. Charles the Bold left as his successor a daughter Mary, for whose hand and lands there was a scramble. Here for once Louis overreached himself. The *Duchy* of Burgundy reverted to him, since the rules of inheritance prevented its passing to a woman. He was, however, not satisfied. Seizing the neighboring *County* of Burgundy, he then invaded Flanders and insisted that Mary of Burgundy marry his son. This action was opposed by the Flemish towns and by the German emperor, who claimed Mary for his own son, to whom she had been promised. Mary quickly decided in favor of the German prince, Maximilian. Louis then refused to give up the bride's inheritance until Maximilian agreed to a compromise which gave Louis virtual control of the two Burgundies and of Artois (on the French frontier of Flanders).

Thus Louis left in Hapsburg hands most of the Rhineland districts of the Burgundian realm, including the wealthy industrial cities of the Netherlands. He gained for France the two Burgundies, a predominantly agricultural region comprising the upper basins of the Seine and Saône rivers. The prize industrial region of Northern Europe, the Netherlands (with the exception of Artois), went to the Hapsburgs. This was a serious economic loss to France inasmuch as it prevented expansion into a remarkably wealthy district of manufacturing and trading centers. Along the northern, or Flemish, frontier during Louis's reign French boundaries had receded, but to the west they were extended toward the Swiss Alps. The next century was to see new French advances in the direction of Alsace and Lorraine, a region over which, even to the present day, France and Germany have fought.

At home Louis had better territorial successes. The deaths, without heirs, of French nobles gave him complete control of Provence in the southeast, and of Anjou-Maine in the Loire basin. Of all France, only Brittany now remained outside the royal domain. National territorial unity was practically complete.[12]

FRENCH
ABSOLUTISM

During his later years Louis ruled autocratically, without interference from the great nobles, the Estates-General, or the local assemblies. His government was harsh and tyrannical but efficient. Taxes were heavy, but the townsfolk and peasants prospered. Commerce, both foreign and domestic, industry, and mining were encouraged. To all classes, except the rebellious nobility, Louis's despotism was benevolent.

He died in 1483, having feared and fought against death by every possible means. Louis left a young son, Charles VIII (1483-1498), who reaped the fruits of his regime of intrigue. The consolidation of France was complete. The government was centralized, all classes were prosperous and reasonably contented, finances were in good condition and the army was one of the best in Europe. Little wonder that Charles looked about for other worlds to conquer. As we shall see, he found them in Italy.[13] Here the modernized financial, military, and diplomatic machine of the triumphant French nation was put to a severe test.

---

[12] Brittany was acquired by means of the marriage of Louis's son, Charles VIII to Anne of Brittany.

[13] See below, p. 650.

CIVIL WAR, NATIONALISM, AND THE ROYAL POWER IN ENGLAND

In an earlier chapter [14] we have seen that the trend of English government after the Norman Conquest was in the direction of absolutism. At first glance the Hundred Years' War seems to have been a reversal of this line of development. The England of Edward I, just before the war, was a well-unified nation with a strong but limited monarchy. Even though Edward's successors won victory after victory in France, they did not advance the royal authority. On the contrary, the period of the war was marked by vigorous domestic resistance to the king's will and by a distinct increase in parliamentary power. Paradoxically enough, not until the late fifteenth century, after the disastrous close of the war, were the English kings able to regain the lost ground and to attain absolute royal power.

In this respect, England seems to have followed the same general course of the Continental countries during this age. Throughout the fourteenth and fifteenth centuries, England's development was strikingly similar to that of her neighbor across the Channel. The latter half of the fourteenth century, as we have seen, was an age of economic, social, and political disorder in England and elsewhere.

The Black Death increased—even though it did not start—the difficulties of the English landowners with their agricultural laborers. Already the expansion of towns and money economy had broken up the old servile system of tenures. Moreover, the ravages of the plague had put so great a premium on farm labor that wages soared and the government was compelled to set maximum wage scales. The attempt to enforce this policy in the face of rising prices and unsettled conditions led to increased discontent, culminating in the famous Peasants' Revolt of 1381, which threatened to overthrow the government. Although the revolt was quelled, the movement for increased freedom of economic opportunity continued until all of the English peasants had become freemen.

Politically, likewise, this was a period of discontent. The king's constant need for funds with which to carry on the war in France forced him to call parliament with increasing frequency. During the reigns of Edward III and Richard II, parliament averaged one meet-

[14] See above, Chapter XXIII.

ing per year. Parliament also formed the habit of presenting grievances
before voting funds. This procedure was so successful that soon parliamentary representatives were calling the king's ministers to account. In 1376 the "Good Parliament," after forcing an audit of the
royal finances, convicted and removed two high royal officials by
process of impeachment (i.e., by parliamentary trial). This is the first
known example of impeachment in English history. Later, as a result of Richard II's resistance to parliament, he was deposed and the
crown given to the Lancastrian, Henry IV, who agreed to most of
the conditions set by parliament. Again after the death of Henry V
(1413-1422), parliament and the royal council disregarded the royal
will in the choice of a regent.

It is evident that the machinery of representative government in
their local shires gave the English people good training for effective
action in checking arbitrary royal government. The English estates
(clergy, nobility, and commons) had developed a remarkable spirit
of co-operation in resisting royal tyranny. Seldom could the English
kings count on playing the townsfolk or the clergy against the nobility.

LANCASTRIAN-
YORKIST CIVIL
WARS

Toward the end of the fifteenth century, however,
the English parliamentary system suffered a disastrous
setback, caused by disunity and civil warfare. Unable
to cope with the factional strife of the nobility and
the general disregard for law and order, in the end the parliamentary
monarchy gave way to a centralized royal despotism similar to that
in France.

Just about a half century after the outbreak of the civil war between the Orleanists and the Burgundians in France, the English
realm was torn by the strife of two noble factions. England's civil
war followed on the heels of the disastrous outcome of the Hundred
Years' War. The loss of Normandy in 1450 led to violent criticism
of the king's counselors, and eventually to a popular revolt, known
as Cade's Rebellion. Scarcely had this expression of public disapproval been crushed when Richard of York, a descendant of Edward III, set himself up as the rightful heir to the throne. In 1454,
after England lost her last possessions in Aquitaine, and when King
Henry VI went temporarily insane, parliament made Richard "Protector of the Realm." A fight between Richard's and the king's fol-

lowers at St. Albans opened the Lancastrian-Yorkist civil war, often called the "Wars of the Roses." [15]

Henceforth England was in a turmoil. Henry VI (1422-1461), who had begun his royal career as the child-king of both England and France, dragged out his weary life, hopelessly insane. He was deposed and re-enthroned several times by various of the contending leaders. One of them, the Earl of Warwick, earned the epithet, "The King Maker."

Meanwhile outside nations had been drawn into the struggle. Henry's French queen, an energetic and courageous woman, enlisted French and Scotch troops in his service. Louis XI of France gladly supported Henry and Warwick. Since Louis supported the Lancastrians, his enemy, Charles the Bold of Burgundy, naturally allied himself with the Yorkists. Thus the Lancastrian-Yorkist war had a bearing on the Continental struggle between Louis XI and the Burgundians. At one time Edward of York even attempted to revive the war with France.

THE END OF THE CIVIL WAR   With the final deposition of Henry VI and the recognition of Edward IV (1461-1483), England slowly drifted from Lancastrian limited monarchy to Yorkist absolutism. The later years of Edward's reign were quiet, orderly, and relatively prosperous. Due to the success of his financial policies he was practically independent of parliament. Already the government was moving inevitably toward absolutism. Unfortunately for the Yorkists, however, Edward died at a time when his two sons were children. Immediately his relatives began to intrigue for the possession of the little princes in order to control the government. Within a year an uncle of the princes, Richard of Gloucester, managed to get himself proclaimed "Protector of the Realm." As "Protector," he made himself king and exiled or executed all possible rivals, including the two little princes. Legend has it that they were smothered to death as they lay asleep in the Tower of London. Such treachery and despotism rapidly alienated the affections of Richard's subjects, and he was soon overthrown. Two years after Richard's usurpation of the crown, Henry Tudor led an army from France against "the unnatural tyrant." From all sides discontented

[15] The Yorkist symbol was a white rose, and it is sometimes said that the red rose represented the Lancastrian cause. This, and the legend of the rival leaders having picked roses of their respective colors at the outbreak of the war, is legendary.

Englishmen flocked to Henry's banners, and at Bosworth Field, in 1485, Richard was defeated and killed.

HENRY VII AND TUDOR ABSOLUTISM

With Henry VII (1485-1509) the Lancastrian and Yorkist dynasties were united, for he was related to the former, and was married to a daughter of the Yorkist king, Edward IV. His reign marks the end of almost half a century of civil war, and the establishment of absolute monarchy.

His absolutism seems to have been universally welcome. England was equally weary of the weak monarchy of the Lancastrians and the ruthless autocracy of the Yorkists. In Henry they found a strong-minded monarch who was also tactful and economical. He favored and was supported by the powerful middle classes. Since he gave England peace and prosperity, few worried because of his increasingly autocratic rule. The King's Council and the "Court of the Star Chamber" took care of administrative and judicial affairs in such an efficient manner that there was little need for parliaments. The feudal nobility, already weakened by the Wars of the Roses, was subjected to the royal system of taxation and justice. Those who resisted were brought before royal courts where judgment was speedy and punishment harsh for enemies of the king. The upper classes found it expedient to contribute generously to the royal treasury, and eventually many of them learned to profit by the new regime. Although many nobles continued to be active in parliament and in the governmental service, the royal administration was manned chiefly by members of the middle class. This fact is significant of the commercial interests of the government. Treaties were made providing for trading privileges on the Continent, and the Cabots were encouraged to explore and lay claim to lands in the New World. Throughout the ensuing period the aspirations of the middle classes were advanced by the Tudor autocrats. In fact, all England seems to have preferred efficiency and prosperity under despotic rulers to the disorder and factionalism of limited monarchy.

The modern world of dictatorships can perhaps understand how it was that not only England, but also France, the Spains, and most of the formerly republican city-states of Italy went over to absolutism during the fifteenth century. Through most of the modern era, the European world was to remain under autocratic rule. With all its faults autocracy has provided governmental conditions under which expanding town life, industry, and commerce have advanced.

In spite of the success and permanence of the autocratic forms of government that took shape in fifteenth-century England, this period also contributed much to the democratic traditions and institutions of the modern world. The Lancastrian parliamentary system of the first half of the century established ideals and methods that were revived after centuries of autocratic rule. They became vital factors in the development of representative government, not only in England, but also on the Continent and in America.

By the beginning of the fifteenth century the English parliament had assumed an unusually important role in governmental affairs. During the first half of the century its authority increased, attaining an ascendancy more marked than it had ever had before, and than it was to enjoy until late in the seventeenth century. Richard II had tried in vain to check the rising tide, but his deposition marks a great triumph of parliamentary government and the beginning of a period of limited monarchy. Thanks to the fact that the Lancastrian kings (Henry IV and Henry V) were indebted to parliament for the royal crown, and also that they were in constant need of money, they were in no position to challenge the will of that body. Parliament indirectly controlled the appointment of royal officials, called them to account, and constantly held over them the threat of impeachment. The royal council was, in fact, a body of parliament's choosing.

Parliamentary control of finances was equally marked: grants of funds were initiated in the House of Commons, were often made with specific limitations as to their use, and their expenditure checked by a parliamentary audit. Grievances were usually presented in definite form as separate bills, and their acceptance by the king assured, before parliament voted any funds. Freedom of speech, and freedom of members of parliament from arrest during sessions and en route to and from session, were established. In short, the Lancastrian parliament enjoyed rights and privileges which set a standard for modern self-governing bodies.

═ XXX ═

THE GERMANIES AND THE ITALIES

BY the year 1500 the westernmost regions of Europe had attained national territorial unity under strong monarchical governments. Portugal, Castile, and Aragon in the Spanish peninsula, and France and England, further north, were now nations whose populations were bound by strong ties of unity. In each nation, the king was the chief rallying point for the forces of political, economic, religious, and cultural unity.

Turning eastward to the regions of central Europe, we find strikingly different conditions. There was practically no national spirit. The terms "Germanies" and Italies," in contrast to France and England, vividly illustrate the lack of national unity in central Europe. There still lingered in the Germanies and Italies the Roman, Carolingian, and Hohenstaufen theory of a European-wide empire. It was impossible, however, to apply the imperial ideal effectively, and government in these regions actually rested in the hands of innumerable local powers. These were, for the most part, of two types, feudal and municipal. Most of the rural regions of the Germanies and the extreme northern and southern sections of the Italies were controlled by the feudality. The more industrialized regions of the Germanies (along the Danube, Rhine, and Baltic waterways) contained many flourishing city-states. The same was true of most of the Italian peninsula.

The combination of an unattainable imperial *ideal* with the *reality* of small feudal or municipal states prevented the development of nationalism in either of these regions. It is for this reason that we shall refer to them in the plural, the Germanies and the Italies. In theory they were parts of the Holy Roman Empire; in reality they consisted of hundreds of large and small warring units, a conglomeration of disunited states of the Germanies and the Italies. Not until the nineteenth century did the modern national states of Germany and Italy assume their present form.

IMPERIAL DY-
NASTIES IN THE
GERMANIES
During the centuries in which the national monarchies of the West were attaining their early development the Holy Roman Empire was experiencing a precarious existence. Only in the late fifteenth century did it display a renewed vigor which made it, for a short time, the seat of a great new world dominion.

THE RISE OF THE
HAPSBURGS
The fall of Frederick II and of the Hohenstaufen dynasty [1] was followed by a twenty-year interregnum (1254-1273), during which imperial elections degenerated into an undignified scramble for an empty title by political adventurers, both native and foreign. So great were the anarchy and internal confusion that this era has been called the "age of fist law." At length, the pope and the German leaders selected as emperor Count Rudolph of Hapsburg (1273-1292), a south German prince who was sufficiently popular to win the support of, but not so ambitious as to be dangerous to, the feudality or the papacy. Rudolph proved to be an unexpectedly able emperor. He defeated the powerful prince of Bohemia and despoiled him of most of his Austrian conquests. Consequently, the Hapsburg domains were expanded eastward down the Danube to Vienna, and eventually southward to the Adriatic Sea. Thus were laid the foundations of a Hapsburg realm that was destined eventually to become the Austrian Empire, comprising most of southern Germany, including Bohemia and Hungary.

Rudolph's conquests, however, displeased the liberty-loving German baronage. Their resentment is well illustrated by the saying that was current among the opponents of the Hapsburgs: "Sit still on thy throne, O Lord, or the Count of Hapsburg will shove Thee off." At the death of Rudolph the German electors selected a less ambitious emperor, Adolph of the House of Nassau (1292-1298). Within six years, however, Adolph was completely discredited and another Hapsburg named Albert became emperor (1298-1308). He seemed about to consolidate the German realm into a centralized Hapsburg monarchy, when he was struck down by an assassin.

THE LUXEM-
BURG-BOHEMIAN
DYNASTY
For over a century after Albert's death, the onward march of the Hapsburgs was checked. The crown was held by emperors chosen for the most part from the rival house of Luxemburg-Bohemia. Meanwhile, the empire became once again a mere federation of independent

[1] See above, p. 405.

principalities. Henry VII (1308-1313), who renewed the custom of
going down into Italy to receive the imperial crown from the pope,
died in Italy (so it was said) after drinking communion wine into
which a priest-assassin had dropped poison from beneath his finger-
nail. Since the wine had been consecrated, the pious emperor refused
to save himself by taking an emetic. To certain high-minded Italians,
his passing was a tragedy. The poet-politician Dante had hoped in
vain that Henry might save Italy from the disunity and strife into
which she had been brought by the Avignon papacy and the rivalries
of warring city-states. Henry's only real accomplishment was the winning of Bohemia for his family. This of itself was enough to make
the German electors turn elsewhere for their next emperor. For thirty
years after the death of Henry (1313) imperial affairs were in hopeless
confusion.

CHARLES IV:
THE GOLDEN
BULL

In 1347 Henry's grandson, Charles IV, won the imperial election and consolidated his position so successfully that for a century thereafter the crown remained in the possession of the Luxemburg-Bohe-
mian dynasty. Throughout his reign, Charles devoted himself chiefly
to the affairs of his own Bohemian domain. So far as the rest of the
empire was concerned, his policy was one of *laissez faire,* and he came
to be known as "the empire's stepfather." In Bohemia he encouraged
trade and industry, established at Prague the first university within the
empire, and added Brandenburg to his family's domains. Elsewhere
in the Germanies the princes were left to their own resources. A
written constitution (called the "Golden Bull," because of its golden
bulla, or seal) was granted in 1356. This proved to be a veritable charter of rights for the higher nobility. The seven great princes—the
rulers of Brandenburg, Saxe-Wittenberg, the Palatinate, and Bohemia, and the archbishops of Cologne, Mainz, and Treves—were
given sovereign powers within their own territories, and the right
of selecting emperors.

It has been said that in the Golden Bull Charles "legalized
anarchy and called it a constitution." It is perhaps fairer to say that
he recognized the fact that the Germanies were destined to be a
loose confederation of feudal domains instead of a centralized empire
or nation.

DECLINE OF THE
LUXEMBURG
DYNASTY
Charles's worthless son, Wenceslaus (1378-1400) won the imperial election simply because of the fact that he controlled two of the necessary four votes in the electoral body (those of Bohemia and Brandenburg).[2] His long reign was a hopeless failure. He was an inveterate drunkard, so that his councilors are said to have found it necessary to transact all official business early in the morning before the emperor had fallen completely under the influence of strong drink. Eventually he was deposed by his own subjects. After an interregnum during which Germany was plagued by three rival emperors, Sigismund (1410-1437), Wenceslaus' brother, came to the throne. He devoted himself chiefly to religious affairs: notably the elimination of the three claimants to the papacy, and the disastrous wars against the Bohemian Hussites.

By the end of his reign, the Luxemburg-Bohemian dynasty had clearly demonstrated its inability to handle imperial affairs. Since Sigismund died without heirs, the electors turned elsewhere for an emperor and selected Albert of Hapsburg (1438-1439). Thus, once more, after a lapse of more than a century, the Hapsburgs returned to power. Before long they were to bring themselves and the empire to new heights of power and fame.

THE
TRIUMPHANT
HAPSBURG
The Hapsburg recovery was slow and halting. Albert was soon followed by Frederick III (1440-1486), a ruler whose career presents strange contrasts of success and failure. In imperial affairs he had an uninterrupted succession of losses. France, Denmark, Poland, and the Turks appropriated important territories from the empire. Meanwhile, Frederick was not only unable to punish foreign aggressors, but scarcely dared set foot outside his own duchy for fear of hostile German princes. None the less, his confidence in the future of the Hapsburg dynasty was unshaken. Wherever he went he displayed his dynastic emblem with its five-vowel monogram, AEIOU, signifying A[ustriae] E[st] I[mperare] O[rbi] U[niverso]—"Austria is to rule the entire world."

The reign of his remarkable son Maximilian (1486-1519) gave promise of at least partial realization of this grand ideal. Although Maximilian let imperial matters run their own course, he used the prestige and powers of the empire for the territorial aggrandizement

---

[2] Four out of the seven electoral votes constituted a majority.

of the Hapsburg family. By exceptionally fortunate—and also clever
—marriage alliances, he obtained for his grandson Charles an empire of world-wide proportions. The inheritance of Maximilian's wife,
Mary of Burgundy, comprised the Netherlands, Luxemburg, and
Franche-Comté—a realm stretching from the North Sea to the Alps.
His son, Philip, by a profitable marriage with Joanna "the Insane,"
daughter of Ferdinand and Isabella of Spain, eventually brought into
Hapsburg hands Aragon and Castile, with their distant possessions
in Italy and the Americas. These brilliant successes were not, however,
permanent.

The eventual failures of Maximilian, and also of Charles V, were
due in part to the very size of their domains. Like earlier emperors,
they set their hearts on foreign dominion and failed to consolidate
Germany. As in the days of the Saxon Ottos, the Franconian Henrys,
and the Hohenstaufen Fredericks,[3] German unity was neglected for
the mirage of distant crowns and realms. As a consequence, the
empire had no solid foundation, and Germany continued to be an
unwieldy mass of some three hundred separate units presided over
by Hapsburg emperors. Not until the final destruction of this fatal
imperial ideal by Napoleon in the nineteenth century was Germany
able to work toward the national unity which England, France, and
the Spains had realized during the Middle Ages. Meanwhile, throughout the sixteenth century the Hapsburgs were so wealthy and powerful that they played the leading role in European affairs. Until
comparatively recent times their Austrian realm was classed among
the great world powers. Even after Napoleon deprived them of the
crown of the Holy Roman Empire, the Hapsburgs reigned as emperors of Austria, Hungary, and Bohemia for more than a century.
Finally, the World War brought to an inglorious close this long-lived
dynasty.

THE HAPSBURG
DOMINIONS
Before leaving the Hapsburgs, we shall survey the
European realms that were under their sway at the
end of the Middle Ages. During this period the Hapsburg Empire composed three general blocks of territories: (1) the
south German (Austrian) states which were actually owned by the
family; (2) the realms which were acquired by the marriage alliances
of Maximilian and Charles; and (3) the German states of the Holy
Roman Empire, over which they exercised only nominal authority.

[3] See above, Chapters XIX-XX.

We have already considered the south German family domains in connection with the careers of Rudolph of Hapsburg and his successors.
The non-Hapsburg states of the Holy Roman Empire will be described later. We turn now to the Burgundian and Spanish territories
which Maximilian and Charles gained through a series of marriage
alliances.

THE
BURGUNDIAN
INHERITANCE

The first of these acquisitions, the inheritance of
Maximilian's wife, Mary of Burgundy, was a conglomeration of wealthy cities and fertile agricultural
districts lying in the region between Germany and
France. Mary's father, Charles the Bold (1467-1477), had attempted in
vain to weld these valuable, but scattered, territories into a kingdom.[4] Among the fragments were (1) the rich farming and seafaring districts of Holland; (2) Flanders, with its busy commercial
and textile centers—Bruges, Antwerp, Ghent, and Liége; (3) Luxemburg, and certain neighboring regions in France and Lorraine; and
(4) the County of Burgundy. A glance at a map will show the
importance of this inheritance to the Hapsburgs. It expanded their
domains northwestward to the Atlantic, so that from the Adriatic
coasts of Italy to the North Sea there was now an almost unbroken
chain of Hapsburg states. The only breaks in this "territorial string of
beads" were the Swiss Federation and Alsace and Lorraine, which the
Hapsburgs struggled in vain to control.

THE SPANISH
INHERITANCE

Of even greater extent and importance than the Burgundian realm was the Spanish inheritance. It consisted of scattered territories, two of which—Castile
and Aragon—we have already described in some detail.[5] These kingdoms came under Hapsburg control by a curious series of marriages.
In 1469 Queen Isabella of Castile married King Ferdinand of Aragon.
Their daughter married Maximilian's son, Philip of Hapsburg. The
child of this marriage, Charles, inherited not only Castile and Aragon, but Castile's rich American colonies (the result of Columbus'
voyages) and the Aragonese realms in Sardinia, Sicily, and southern Italy as well. These Spanish realms were only a part of the
immense domains which Charles inherited from four grandparents:
Maximilian of Hapsburg Austria, Mary of Burgundy and the Netherlands, Ferdinand of Aragon, Naples, and Sicily, and Isabella of Castile.

[4] See above, pp. 598 f.
[5] See above, pp. 490 ff.

This inheritance was of tremendous consequence for both medieval and modern history. It marks (1) the most remarkable of all the revivals of imperial power in the West, and (2) the concentration (in Hapsburg hands) of expanses of German, French, Spanish, Italian, and American territory so extensive that the dynasty became the chief factor in the economic, political, military, and religious history of the sixteenth century. In the non-Hapsburg regions of Germany, Charles was to meet with serious opposition. To this portion of the empire we now turn our attention.

BEGINNINGS OF THE SWISS CON- FEDERATION

While the Hapsburgs were devoting themselves to the expansion of their family domains, other regions of Germany, unhampered by imperial interference, were developing their own political institutions. Of these practically independent states, Switzerland is the most interesting because it was itself a federation within the imperial federation, and because it was one of the first democratic states in Europe. Very early the Swiss came to believe in the right of peasants as well as of city folk to exercise self-government. Another unique factor in Swiss history is the success with which their democratic institutions resisted the almost universal trend toward absolutism during the late Middle Ages.

The beginnings of the Swiss federation of republics came in the early thirteenth century when the emperor, in order to take the control of an Alpine route from the neighboring overlords, granted local privileges to the peasants of Uri and Schwyz, near the St. Gothard Pass. In spite of the opposition of their clerical and lay lords, the two independent cantons (or counties) flourished. In 1291, just after the death of Rudolph of Hapsburg, the peasants of Unterwalden united with those of Uri and Schwyz in a "Perpetual Pact" which provided for joint action against aggressors. For two centuries thereafter these sturdy mountaineers were compelled to fight for their rights, particularly against the neighboring Hapsburgs. In 1309, however, an anti-Hapsburg emperor, Henry VII, recognized the Swiss Federation. When the Hapsburg duke refused to acknowledge this grant and attacked the Swiss, his feudal army was decisively defeated by the "embattled farmers" at Morgarten (1315), the "Lexington and Concord of Swiss history." Seven years later, at Ampfing, the experience was repeated, and for a time the cantons enjoyed the blessings of peace.

DEFENSIVE WARS Soon the three cantons were joined by other peasant communities such as Glarus and Zug, and by towns such as Lucerne, Zurich, and Berne. In 1361 Emperor Charles IV of the Luxemburg-Bohemian house recognized the enlarged federation, which now comprised eight cantons. Soon the hostile Hapsburgs gathered their forces to crush the little republics. Once more at Sempach, in 1386, the Swiss made good their reputation as fighting men. The legendary hero of this battle, Arnold von Winkelried, was said to have broken through the ranks of the enemy by hurling himself upon the points of their lances, thus opening the way for the charge of the Swiss pikemen. According to the legend,

> "Make way for liberty," he cried,
> "Make way for liberty," and died.

There is probably no more actual truth in this heroic tale than there is in that concerning William Tell, whose exploits with the bow and arrow enliven the history of the earlier struggles between the Swiss and their Hapsburg oppressors.[6]

The story of Arnold does, however, suggest one of the noteworthy factors in the military successes of the Swiss. This was their expert handling of the pike, an eighteen-foot lance which was their favorite weapon. A hollow square of pikemen, with auxiliary crossbowmen and swordsmen, was practically irresistible. Neither armored knights nor infantry could successfully charge upon them. On the offensive, a squad of pikemen could shift into a wedge formation and easily break through an opposing line. Thus the pike was an important factor in the winning of Swiss independence. It gave Swiss armies a superiority similar to that which the longbow gave to the English in the Hundred Years' War. Until the development of effective muskets, Swiss pikemen were invincible, and were in great demand as mercenary soldiers.

EXPANSION AND INDEPENDENCE During the fifteenth and early sixteenth centuries the Swiss Federation expanded in every direction. To the south, territories were gained on the Italian side of the St. Gothard Pass. To the north, additional regions were admitted,

---

[6] The story of William Tell's shooting an apple off his son's head made its first appearance in historical accounts over three centuries after the event was supposed to have occurred. There are similar stories in English, Rhenish, north German, and Scandinavian literature. The earliest example is from the twelfth century.

bringing the federation to its final membership of thirteen cantons. During the same period, other regions were acquired and held as associated districts. Several times during the fifteenth century the Swiss were compelled to fight to preserve their independence. In 1444 an invading French army is said to have been defeated in the Western Alps by a force of 1,300 heroic Swiss warriors, only six of whom survived. Thirty years later, Duke Charles the Bold of Burgundy, in the course of his efforts to extend his Rhineland domains, attempted to occupy the western cantons. Two decisive victories by the Swiss infantry at Granson and Morat (1476) put an end to this danger.

The last major conflict was with the Hapsburg emperor Maximilian, who endeavored to assert his authority over the cantons. After three defeats in 1499 he confirmed the former Swiss rights of self-government. Henceforth, to all intents and purposes, the Swiss Federation was independent, although it was not formally separated from the empire until the Treaty of Westphalia (1648). In reality, therefore, the early Hapsburg period of German history (1273-1500) saw the rise of a group of republics which was destined to be one of the most successful self-governing federations of all time. Even to the present day Switzerland has preserved intact its democratic institutions.[7]

GERMANIC LEAGUES

There were other German leagues that were less permanent than the Swiss Federation. During the early Hapsburg era, when the imperial government was unable to preserve order, the prosperous towns of the Rhineland were constantly threatened by brigands and lawless barons. Consequently they were forced to unite in common defense of their commercial interests. In 1254, Cologne, Mayence, Worms, Speyer, Strassburg, and other neighboring towns formed a league to combat disturbers of law and order. Fleets were provided to patrol the Rhine, and each city contributed forces for offensive warfare against the castles of robber barons. A century later, a similar league was formed by the towns of Alsace, Swabia, and certain parts of Switzerland. Although these leagues of cities continued to exist, they had no permanent political organization such as the Swiss Federation or the great Hanseatic League of northern Germany.

[7] Until the nineteenth century the Swiss government was a loose federation of towns and rural communities. In each region the peasants and townsmen took an active part in government. Since then there has been a trend toward centralized control.

THE HANSEATIC
LEAGUE
The Hanseatic League, which was the largest and most successful of all the German city federations, developed a governmental organization that exercised tremendous economic and political influence. It was originally merely a merger of the merchant guilds along the Rhine and Baltic with groups of German merchants in such foreign centers as London, Bruges, and Wisby. Eventually this became a league of city-states which held regular congresses, called "diets," sent out ambassadors, negotiated treaties, and had naval and military forces. There were four administrative provinces or "circles," comprising Mecklenburg and Pomerania, the Rhinelands and Netherlands, Prussia and Livonia, and Saxony.

At its prime (about 1400), the league boasted a membership of about eighty cities. At one time it proved its military strength by waging a war with Denmark, in the course of which the Danish capital was captured and destroyed. The treaty of peace dictated by the League, at Stralsund in 1370, went so far as to provide that no Danish king should be crowned without the league's approval. Glorious though it was, Hanseatic domination of the political affairs of the Baltic was brief. Within a century after the Danish war its commercial prosperity suffered from the loss of most of the English and Flemish trade. Nature herself turned against the league (about 1425) when the herring shifted their habitat from the Baltic to the Dutch coasts of the North Sea, thus ruining the Hanseatic trade in fish. Later, the rise of national monarchies in Sweden and Denmark threatened the Baltic possessions of the league, which then dwindled to a handful of declining mercantile cities.

THE OTHER
GERMAN STATES
Compared to the Hapsburg states and the various leagues the other German states in the late Middle Ages were relatively unimportant so far as Western Europe was concerned. The history of Brandenburg, Saxony, the Palatinate, Bavaria, Bohemia, and the great ecclesiastical states is for the most part of local interest. When, in 1415, however, Mayor Frederick of Nuremberg was appointed margrave of Brandenburg, his family, the Hohenzollerns, was started on its eventful career as rulers of Brandenburg, Prussia, and eventually of modern Germany. In the same period, the problem of lawlessness in north Germany led to the rise and spread of a curious system of unofficial local government called *Vehmgericht* or Vehmic courts. The procedure was similar to that employed in ancient Germanic trials, except

for its speedy and strict enforcement. The movement spread informally into many regions in somewhat the same fashion as the early American "vigilance committee." In their best days the Vehmic courts served as an effective check on flagrant lawlessness in outlying sections.

THE EASTERN
FRONTIER
On the eastern frontier of Germany, serious dangers threatened, as in the early Middle Ages,[8] because of the constant pressure of Slavic peoples. In the northeast, the Teutonic Knights, a crusading order which had transferred its activities from the Holy Land to the conquest of the heathen Slavs and Prussians along the Baltic coasts, now began to give way before hostile forces. When their most dangerous enemy, the Slavic king of Lithuania, became king of Poland as well, the Knights were doomed. Their military power was shattered by the combined forces of the two kingdoms in 1410. Soon they held nothing but East Prussia, and that only as a fief of Slavic Poland. To the south also, in the course of the Hussite Wars, the Germans were driven back by the Slavs of Bohemia.

Meanwhile, further south the Hungarians, under the leadership of the brave John Hunyadi and his son Mathias (1458-1490), were struggling to check the rising tide of Turkish expansion along the Danube. German Christendom owes much to the Hungarians for their brilliant defensive campaigns against the forces of Mohammed II, who had conquered Constantinople in 1453. Eventually Hungary succumbed to superior forces, and during the early decades of the sixteenth century the Turks were a constant threat to the Hapsburg realms of south Germany. More than once, Vienna was besieged by Moslem hosts. Meanwhile, far to the northeast, beyond the German frontier, Ivan the Great (1462-1505) of Muscovy was freeing his people from the sway of the Mongols and laying the foundations for the kingdom of Russia.

THE ITALIES
In startling contrast to the Germanies, the Italies during the late medieval period of political disunity gave birth to a remarkable civilization. This development began at a time when the dominating influence of both the empire and the papacy had passed away, and the Italies were subject to foreign invasion as well as to devastating local warfare.

Various writers have attributed the greatness of late medieval

[8] See above, pp. 204 f.

THE ITALIES IN THE FIFTEENTH CENTURY

Italy to climate, to the beauties of nature, to the classical heritage, to freedom from imperial rule, to democratic government, and to innumerable other racial, religious, and economic influences. It seems, however, that there was no single influence which can be held responsible. Under all sorts of governments—papal or imperial, despotic or democratic—and during periods of warfare as well as of peace, Italian civilization flourished. There is one marked exception: the feudal regions which lacked prosperous cities had little or no part in the progress of Italian civilization. This cultural lag was most noticeable in the extreme northwestern and southern sections of the peninsula, where there was little town life or economic prosperity. Elsewhere, whatever the types of rulers or governments, there was vibrant activity in warfare, government, business, and in all phases of culture during the last centuries of the Middle Ages.

If there is any one conclusion to be drawn from our study of Western civilization (whether in Roman or medieval times), it would seem to be that flourishing town life is the prerequisite for a rich and progressive civilization. Any type of government that permitted or fostered the growth of towns and business life seems to have contributed to the advancing civilization of the Italies during the late Middle Ages.

POLITICAL CONDITIONS The later centuries of Italian political history are distinguished from the earlier by the absence of a strong imperial or papal power. The downfall of Frederick II and the Hohenstaufen empire (in 1250) put an end to effective German intervention in Italy for two centuries. Fifty years later, the fall of Boniface VIII and the transfer of the papacy to Avignon removed from Italy the dominating influence of the popes. With these two unifying forces removed, Italy fell into the innumerable local units which dominated its history until the nineteenth century.

Politically speaking, there was no *Italy* during the late Middle Ages, but instead, hundreds of Italies. Feudal principalities flourished in the mountainous regions at both ends of the peninsula. In central Italy the papal states disintegrated into a mass of city-states and baronial domains. The Po Valley became, as never before, a region of independent and thriving city-states. Starting in the south, we shall survey in turn the most important states of the "Italies" and their development during this period.

SOUTHERN ITALY AND ITS FRENCH RULERS

NAPLES-SICILY   Few European states have had more changes of masters than southern Italy. The passing of Frederick II in 1250 brought to the Kingdom of Naples and Sicily its fifth change of masters during the Middle Ages. (1) In the sixth century, Emperor Justinian defeated the Ostrogoths and took possession of the entire peninsula in the name of the *Byzantine Empire*. (2) About three centuries later, the *Moslem* tide swept northward from Africa to dominate the region until the eleventh century. These three centuries of Moslem occupation left an impress that has never been entirely removed. This highly civilized influence was followed by (3) a hundred and fifty years of *Norman* rule (1030-1189). Then (4) Frederick II of *Hohenstaufen* inherited Naples-Sicily from his Norman mother.

Already a well-governed and lucrative domain of prosperous towns, during the half-century of Frederick's enlightened control (1200-1250) it became "the first modern state" of Western Europe. After the downfall of Frederick and (5) the triumph of the *Angevin-French* forces, called in by the pope, Naples and Sicily moved toward the disunity and anarchy which has characterized southern Italy during most of the modern era. The most disastrous effect of this change of masters was the decline of economic prosperity and town life.

ANGEVIN RULE   In 1268 Charles of Anjou and his "crusading" army overcame the last of the Hohenstaufen successors of Frederick II. Although the French "crusaders" had been called in by a French pope to save the papacy from German imperial domination, the rescuers soon proved to be as unwelcome as their predecessors. For one thing, Charles was too successful and too ambitious in his foreign policy. He pushed forward vigorously his plan for a crusade against the Eastern emperors who had recently recovered Constantinople from the French and Venetian crusaders of 1204. He even proposed to rescue the Holy Land from the Turks. Such projects, if successful, would have made him master of the Mediterranean and might have revived the prosperity of the kingdom.

Meanwhile, Charles was extending his power into northern Italy, where the defeated Hohenstaufen emperors had formerly held sway over many prosperous cities. This move the popes bitterly opposed.

They had brought the Angevins into Italian politics for the purpose of weakening the Hohenstaufen and strengthening the papacy. But once more the papacy found itself in a dangerous predicament: a strong power was closing in on the papal states from both the north and the south. Had Charles been successful, the papacy would have lost its political power, and Italy might have become a united state in the thirteenth instead of the nineteenth century. Charles of Anjou, however, had even less success in welding the Italies into a political unity than the Lombard kings, Charles the Great, Otto the Great, or the Hohenstaufen Fredericks had had in earlier centuries.

THE SICILIAN SECESSION
Unfortunately for the cause of Italian unity, but fortunately for the popes, Charles of Anjou and his ambitions met with sudden disaster. In 1282 the Sicilians violently revolted against the hated French invaders, at the outset massacring three thousand Frenchmen. Because of the religious service at which the outbreak began, it has been called the "Sicilian Vespers." This revolt, which came just as Charles was about to launch his eastern crusade, soon became an international conflict. The king of Spanish Aragon, who had interests in Sicily, diverted his crusading fleet to aid the Sicilian rebels. Charles in turn used his crusading forces against the Sicilians and Spaniards. He also persuaded the pope (who was French) to preach a crusade against the Spaniards and to appoint Charles's brother, the king of France, as leader. Thus a Sicilian revolt and an eastern crusade became a French-Spanish war for the possession of the south Italian realms which, only a few years earlier, had been wrested from the Hohenstaufen.

Although Charles and the other leaders of this new crusading fiasco died in 1285, war continued. The Sicilians elected a prince from Aragon as their ruler, and eventually succeeded in their war of secession. Henceforth Sicily was ruled by Spanish princes, and recovered a semblance of her former prosperity.

FEUDAL AN-ARCHY IN NAPLES
Angevin rule, which continued in Naples, degenerated into a disorderly baron-controlled government. By the "Constitutions of Salerno," Charles II (1285-1309) recognized the rights of the clergy and the feudality in judicial and financial affairs. This Neapolitan "Great Charter" marked the passing of the efficient centralized government of Norman-Hohenstaufen days and the beginning of a long period of devastating anarchy. Thus, even in Naples, the outcome of the

Angevin conquest was disastrous. Commerce, and with it the prosperity of the seaport towns, declined.

Under the later Angevins, government in Naples went from bad to worse, even though Robert I (1309-1343) ruled with a relatively firm hand and struggled to recover control of Sicily. Under his successors a veritable anarchy ensued. The details of the career of one of the monarchs will suffice as an illustration of conditions. Robert's granddaughter, Joanna I (1343-1382), married an unmanageable young relative from Hungary who brought into southern Italy a flock of his parasitical courtiers. The Hungarians made no end of trouble. The jealous Neapolitan nobility had the young husband murdered, thus precipitating a war of revenge between the Hungarian favorites and the native feudality. After three more marriages, Joanna was herself murdered by the Hungarian courtiers. Their leader then became king and now the "Joannites" sought revenge. Chaotic conditions prevailed until finally the reign of a second Joanna (1414-1435) brought the Angevin dynasty to a well-deserved end. After contracting several marriages, she adopted two heirs, and then found herself unable to decide between them. In the end Alfonso of Aragon conquered Naples and reunited it with Sicily, and the first French intervention in Italian affairs ingloriously ended.

NAPLES-SICILY REUNITED With the accession of Alfonso, called "The Magnanimous" (1442-1458), economic, political, and cultural conditions improved. He was a remarkably efficient ruler of the "enlightened despot" type. Unfortunately he divided his realm between two heirs, John of Sicily (1458-1479) and Ferdinand of Naples (1458-1494). Ferdinand, like his father, was an able ruler, but could not cope with the internal and external forces of disruption. Hostile factions of the nobility intrigued with the Angevins, who were eager to recover their lost kingdom. The popes also supported those who sought to overthrow the existing Spanish regime. Finally in 1494, Charles VIII of France invaded southern Italy for the purpose of recovering the realm of his Angevin relatives.

As we shall see,[9] the French were once more unsuccessful in Italy. Moreover, the devastations of warfare left the hapless kingdom in a sad state of demoralization, and the later Spanish monarchs were unable to build up a centralized and prosperous domain. The feudal anarchy that had begun in Angevin times continued for centuries. In

[9] See below, pp. 649 ff.

only one other part of Italy—the Alpine Piedmont—was the power of the feudality as dominant and persistent as in the south. Between these extremities, by contrast, lay the nonfeudal city-states which during this same period were bringing Italian civilization to marvelous heights of prosperity and cultural achievement.

THE PAPAL STATES

RIENZI'S
REPUBLIC
The Papal States went through stranger vicissitudes than any other part of Italy during the late Middle Ages. During the absence of the popes at Avignon (1305-1378) [10] there was a complete disintegration of law and order in central Italy. Petty despots, city-states, and feudal barons flouted the governmental authority of their absentee papal lords. Civil war was constant. The most interesting and important example of political chaos occurred in Rome, where there was a violent outbreak of republicanism—a chronic ailment of that city.

In the tenth and twelfth centuries, radical leaders had overthrown papal rule and vainly attempted to revive the ancient republican regime of the *Senatus Populusque Romanus.* In the fourteenth century it was Rienzi who raised the standard of liberty. He first appeared as the leader of an embassy which begged the popes to deliver the Roman people from the misrule of the local nobility. Later a popular assembly elected him *tribune* and forced from the pope at Avignon a grudging approval of their selection. For a short time Rienzi's republic functioned with considerable success. Peace, order, and economic reforms were decreed. It was planned that all Italian cities should send representatives to a parliament at Rome, and white-clad "Messengers of Peace" were sent throughout the peninsula to announce the new regime. Unfortunately a conspiracy led by the aristocratic Colonna faction overthrew the republic. After years of exile, Rienzi returned to Rome as an assistant of the new papal governor, Cardinal Albornoz.

With the arrival of Albornoz in 1353, papal authority was restored first in Rome and eventually throughout central Italy. The cardinal was an able diplomat who regained control of most of the Papal States by playing one local faction against another. It is said that he returned to Avignon with wagonloads of keys, each representing a surrendered town or castle. Consequently when the popes

[10] See above, p. 562.

once more took up their residence in Rome (in 1377) they found their ancient domains relatively submissive and orderly. There was, of course, little increase in the power of the popes or in prosperity in central Italy during the ensuing period of the Great Schism.[11] Later, however, the papacy made an astonishing recovery of political authority, accompanied by an equally great loss of spiritual leadership. But the Papal States prospered.

THE RENAS-
CENCE POPES
The century following the Council of Constance (1414-1418) saw the rise of the new papal monarchy. Politically it was so powerful that it played the leading role in freeing Italy from new foreign invaders. Spiritually it became so corrupt that Christendom began to lose faith in the papacy as the head of the church. Inasmuch as the popes claimed to be the spiritual leaders of the Christian world it was to be expected that they would set a high standard of moral righteousness. Failure to do so brought justly merited condemnation from the churchmen and people over whom they claimed to exercise divine authority. A glimpse into the lives of a few of the popes of the fifteenth century shows the manner in which the papacy was losing its moral and spiritual leadership.

Martin V and Eugenius IV [12] were models of virtue compared with most of their successors. The next pope, Nicholas V (1447-1455), was respected for his sincere religiousness, but it was his ambition to be a patron of humanistic culture rather than the moral leader of Christendom. His *curia* was filled with learned men, and he is remembered chiefly for his collection of classical manuscripts which later formed the nucleus of the famous Vatican Library. He fortified the Castle of Sant' Angelo, made over the Vatican into a luxurious palace, and in the year 1450 held a papal jubilee that was as notable a financial success as that of Boniface VIII in 1300.[13]

Calixtus III (1455-1458) was the first of the Spanish Borgia popes and his reign was prophetic of that of Alexander VI. Next came Pius II (1458-1464) better known by his secular name, Aeneas Sylvius Piccolomini. After his election this polished young diplomat, courtier, and humanist, who had written (along with other literary works) a risqué novel became a sincerely pious reformer. He died eleven years after the fall of Constantinople amid energetic plans for a great crusade against the steadily advancing hosts of the Turks. His successor,

[11] See above, p. 567.
[12] See above, p. 574.
[13] See above, p. 578.

Paul II (1464-1471), remained true to type and to his age: he was a vain and handsome Venetian merchant who loved more than anything else his collection of gems. He died, it is said, after having gorged two whole watermelons.

With the last three popes of the century, the Roman *curia* reached even lower depths of degradation. Not even the scandalous popes of the tenth and eleventh centuries,[14] could match them for misdeeds. Autocratic power made their degrading influence all the more dangerous. Sixtus IV (1471-1484), a former Franciscan official, was accused of unnatural vice with his nephews, and is known to have provided lucrative positions for his relatives either at the papal court or in neighboring city-states. His financial regime was characterized by the worst of abuses. He did not hesitate to assist his favorite banking firm, the Pazzi of Florence, in a conspiracy to overthrow the Medici government of that city. About the only accomplishments to his credit are the building of the Sistine Chapel in the papal palace, and his organization of Nicholas V's collections into the famous Vatican Library.

Innocent VIII (1484-1492) filled the papal palace not only with office-seeking relatives but with people of questionable reputation. His financial needs were satisfied by selling papal bulls and indulgences. Contributors of funds for crusades or church buildings were given the pope's written promise of "a part forever in the prayers of the church" and "absolution from sins repented, forgiven, and forgotten." Innocent's diplomacy was equally sordid. After gaining possession of the Turkish prince Jem, brother and rival of the ruling sultan at Constantinople, he used his valuable captive for blackmail and proceeded to extort money from the sultan. Among the treasures he received for keeping the prince in captivity was the Sacred Lance with which the Savior's side was said to have been pierced.

Innocent's successor, Alexander VI (1492-1503), of the house of Borgia, continued this sacrilegious blackmail and succeeded, before the death of Jem, in acquiring the "seamless robe" of Christ. Alexander VI was the most frankly immoral and worldly of the popes of this era. It should be noted, however, that the immoralities and crimes attributed to Alexander and his two children, the infamous Cesare Borgia and the lovely Lucrezia, have been much exaggerated in popular histories and fiction. But, even at its best, the Borgia pontificate shows that the papacy had descended to the prevailingly low moral level of Italian secular life.

[14] See above, pp. 377 f.

The papacy of Alexander, like that of his immediate predecessors and successors, was a despiritualized and corrupt despotism that operated as heartlessly as most of the lay governments of Europe. Naturally under such a regime, church revenues and offices were bartered for political patronage. The prevalence of graft as an accepted factor in the papal and lay politics of this age is well illustrated by the explanation of a contemporary as to the reason why Alexander sold clerical privileges and positions freely: "He had the right, for he had *bought* them." When he created forty-three new cardinals, twelve in one day, and one of these his young son Cesare, he was merely breaking the unenviable records established by preceding popes. His papal jubilee of 1500 was a religious carnival by means of which pious tourists replenished the pope's depleted treasury.

PAPAL POLITI-
CAL SUCCESSES
It is easy to condemn such popes as examples of a hopelessly corrupt clergy. But it is the historian's task to explain rather than to blame. At the outset, it should be noted that for every selfish and worldly pope, there were many sincere clergymen who worked faithfully for the betterment of society. Furthermore the fifteenth-century popes and their corrupt companions were but the products of the age. It was a materialistic era of unparalleled prosperity and luxury. Political and economic achievements were more important than religion. The papacy, having been deprived of its international leadership in church affairs by ambitious national monarchs and church councils, turned to the recovery of its Italian political domains. Here in a world of thriving city-states the popes found little opportunity for religious leadership. The crying need of fifteenth-century Italy was political unity, and it was in this realm that the popes made their mark.

Starting with the Papal States of Rome and vicinity, they restored order, extended their political sway and welded the scattered communities of central Italy into a centralized monarchy which ranked with the leading European powers. Little wonder that the men who achieved success and reaped rewards in such secular activities had little time or appreciation for the spiritual welfare of the church.

The governmental policies of the popes were in keeping with the European-wide drift from feudal limited monarchy to absolutism. Unfortunately papal absolutism was attained by ruthless methods which were in startling contrast with the spiritual ideals of the church. Already, under Pope Martin V, the papacy had turned from idealistic religious reform to worldly achievements. Martin made his own family,

the Colonnas, supreme in Rome. Forty years later Pope Paul II mercilessly crushed the independent baronage of the Papal States. Twenty
years after Paul's death, Pope Alexander VI and his even more infamous son, Cesare Borgia, with brutal forcefulness welded the Papal
States into a Borgia kingdom.

CESARE BORGIA The motives and methods that characterized the
rapid growth of the papal monarchy are most vividly
set forth in the career of the pope's son, Cesare. Popular tradition has
given to the modern world a melodramatic picture of his character.
He is represented as a demon of iniquity, murderer of his own brother,
ravisher of his own sister (the famous Lucrezia), and companion of
his infamous father, Alexander VI, in vice, duplicity, and cruelty.

A more accurate picture of Cesare is that given by the contemporary historian Machiavelli, in whose writings Cesare is pictured as a
ruthless but rather benevolent despot who mercilessly crushed all opponents in order to restore and maintain the unity and security of the
Papal States. He removed political and personal enemies by trickery,
treachery, and ruthless violence because it was the most effective way
of attaining his objective. On one occasion, for instance, he invited a
number of opposing leaders to a conference, only to have them over-
powered and assassinated. On the slightest suspicion of treason his followers were removed by means of the dagger or the poison cup. He
had no scruples whatsoever at breaking treaties, deserting allies, or
deceiving rivals. Such were the so-called "Machiavellian" methods employed by Cesare.

According to Machiavelli, Cesare's merit lay in the fact that he
surpassed his contemporaries in the effectiveness with which he
applied the accepted political tactics of the day. In an Italian world of
ruthless and ambitious men, drastic measures were necessary in order
to preserve the state. Cesare played the game according to accepted
rules and, judged solely on the basis of political results, his policy was
remarkably successful. He was one of the great dictators of history
who have placed expediency above morality. There is no doubt that,
under his rule and that of similar despots, Rome and the Papal States
attained great power and prosperity.

"THE PRINCE" It was from such an unidealistic and practical viewpoint that Machiavelli viewed Cesare and wrote the
little handbook for rulers which he called *The Prince*. In this, one of
the earliest modern analyses of the science of government,[15] Machia-

---

[15] See below, p. 682.

velli endeavored to describe the methods that work best in statecraft.

His approach to politics was purely secular. Ethical ideals such as honesty, morality, and kindliness to him had no importance in themselves; they were significant only from the standpoint of their effectiveness in maintaining a ruler's power. In Machiavelli's eyes the primary law of politics was success. In fact, he judged Italian rulers solely on the basis of the political success or failure of their policies. Since Machiavelli completely divorced means from ends, it followed that all was fair in politics. The successful prince played fair when possible; foul, if necessary, in order to win.

Machiavelli's age held that every way that is necessary is just for necessity knows no law. In civil wars Machiavelli observed that the wise prince "commits all the cruelties which his safety renders necessary *at one time,* in order that he may never have cause to repeat them." He went on to remind his readers that "there is a prince now alive (whose name it may not be proper to mention) who ever *preaches* the doctrines of peace and good faith; but if he observed either the one or the other he would long ago have lost his reputation and dominions."

"Pope Alexander VI [he wrote] played during his whole life a game of deception; and notwithstanding the fact that his faithless conduct was extremely well known, his artifices always proved successful." Mentioning Cesare by name, Machiavelli went on to explain that it was necessary for him to wage cruel warfare in order to unite Romagna to his other dominions and to establish peace and tranquillity. Machiavelli's conclusion was that, from the standpoint of the prince, the state, and the security of the people, the Borgia methods of statecraft were eminently successful, and therefore, justified.

It should be noted that Machiavelli did not give *moral* approval to those "Borgian" methods which are often referred to as "Machiavellian." He merely concluded, on the basis of the evidence of his own day, that they worked. He also insisted on certain obligations that a prince owed his people. In a section of *The Prince* entitled "Whether it is better to be loved or feared," he suggested that

one should wish to be *both,* but it is safer to be feared than loved. . . . A prince ought, however, to make himself feared in such a manner that if he cannot gain the love, he may at least avoid the hatred of his subjects.

In other passages Machiavelli emphasized the gentler virtues of his "Prince":

A prince has little to fear from conspiracies when he possesses the affections of the people. . . . Content the people and manage the nobles and you have the maxim of wise governors. . . . Princes ought to honor talent and protect the arts, particularly commerce and agriculture . . . to entertain the people at certain periods of the year with festivals, to honor with their presence the different trading companies and corporations, and to display on such occasions the greatest affability and facility of access, always remembering to support their station with becoming dignity . . . [Machiavelli also paid high tribute to the importance of public opinion in his suggestion that] if the prince governs with wisdom, his merit will conciliate the esteem and affection of his subjects . . . and he need never fear the lack of defenders. . . . Those who have lost their thrones . . . neglected to institute a national militia . . . and to gain the affection of the people and the friendship of the nobles.[16]

Such passages raise questions concerning the validity of attributing to Machiavelli the less praiseworthy methods of past or present-day politics. He was a keen-eyed and astute reporter who gave a remarkably clear description of fifteenth-century government in Italy. But Machiavelli was also more than this; he was also a penetratingly analytical thinker who treated the business of government from an objective materialistic viewpoint, without reference to religion or morals. In his secular approach to the subject, he was a successor of Plato and Aristotle, and the first outstanding political scientist of modern times.

POPE JULIUS II, SUPER-MACHIAVELLIAN   The passing of the Borgias and the intervention of French kings in Italy [17] threw papal affairs once more into confusion, and Pope Julius II (1503-1513) was called upon to defend the domains of the Roman Church. Although "of a fiery and violent disposition" (according to Machiavelli), the materialistic old pope was admirably suited to the needs of his day. He was known more for "statecraft and military prowess than for religious fervor," and it was these characteristics which enabled him to restore the political power of the papacy. By craft, force, and favorable alliances he gained possession of new territories. To cite merely one instance, he joined the French, Spanish, and German monarchs in an attack upon his fellow countrymen, the Venetians. After gaining ample reward for his part in the plot, he

[16] This and the excerpts in the preceding paragraphs are from Machiavelli, *The Prince*, Chapters XVII, XVIII, XXI in particular.

[17] See below, pp. 650 ff.

turned against his foreign allies and formed a "Holy League" of Italians to drive them out of Italy.

Thus by applying methods as daring as those of Machiavelli's "Prince," the spiritual leader of Christendom added extensive lands to the Papal States and outwitted the cleverest monarchs of Europe in the game of cutthroat diplomacy. To many of his grateful subjects he was the savior of Italy from barbaric northern invaders. At the same time, however, sincere Christians were becoming more and more critical of the secular activities of the papacy. In the end the entire church suffered the penalty for the political successes of the popes. The storm of Protestant Revolution broke upon Julius II's successor, Leo X (1513-1521). While this scion of the Medici banking family of Florence was enjoying his Vatican palace and gardens, far to the north in Saxony a professor of theology at the University of Wittenberg, Martin Luther, was wrestling with the problem of personal salvation.[18]

[18] The third volume in this historical series, treating of the modern era, deals with the Protestant Revolt in detail.

⸗ XXXI ⸗

THE ITALIAN CITY-STATES

THE most productive, and perhaps most confused, region of the Italies, and of all Europe during the late Middle Ages, was that of the wealthy, warlike city-states in the upper half of the peninsula. From Rome northward, Italy was dotted with independent states, similar in many respects to the city-states of ancient Greece. There were hundreds of these self-governing communities, each comprising an industrial or commercial town with surrounding agricultural territory. Although there was infinite variation in the political, economic, and cultural institutions of these city-states, all of them manifested a vigorous activity and a stimulating competition in their internal and external relationships.

We shall consider in some detail three outstanding cities which illustrate the general character of Italian urban life. One of them, Florence, is an outstanding example of the industrial and financial developments of the late Middle Ages. Another of the inland towns, Milan, illustrates more vividly Italian political and diplomatic achievements. The third, Venice, was predominantly commercial, but its prosperity rested on sea power. It is worth noting that Florence and Venice, in both of which business activities were dominant, maintained the republican form of government. Milan drifted rapidly into the despotism that is characteristic of early modern governments. All three cities (and their smaller neighbors likewise) were notable centers of art and literature.

FLORENCE

Florence, an inland city on the Arno River, about a hundred and fifty miles north of Rome, was one of the most important cities of Italy during the late Middle Ages. During this period it became the center of the most brilliant civilization of Italy, and of all Western Europe. Florentine writers and artists of the late Middle Ages attained a fame that is comparable to that of the Athenians in the age of

Pericles, two thousand years earlier. Today, after five centuries of modern progress, the genius of Dante, Petrarch, Boccaccio, Machiavelli, Giotto, Botticelli, Ghiberti, and Donatello [1] is undimmed.

The superior civilization which produced such poets, prose writers, and artists presents a perplexing historical problem. What was it that made the Florentines of this period outstanding leaders in so many types of cultural achievement? It cannot be attributed to geographical environment or cultural inheritance; in these respects the city was no better endowed than its neighbors. Was it economic prosperity, which is considered by many scholars as the fundamental factor which makes it possible for artists and writers to thrive? But there were wealthier cities than Florence: Venice, with the riches of the Orient at her disposal, failed to equal Florence in variety and quantity of cultural achievement. Those who insist that wealth is not as important as its intelligent use argue that the wealthy Florentine burghers and the despots of the Medici family were unusually generous in their patronage of artists and writers. This enlightened use of wealth undoubtedly helped make Florence a great cultural center by attracting geniuses from other parts of Italy. One might consider endlessly the political, religious, and economic influences which have been held responsible for the superior cultural achievements of the Florentines. All of them have a certain validity, but economic factors seem to have been unusually important.

FLORENTINE ECONOMIC PROSPERITY
Florentine civilization rested upon a well-balanced economic life, notably certain highly developed industries and a banking system that gave the city a tremendous financial advantage. Furthermore, unlike many other wealthy cities, the income of the Florentines was fairly well distributed among the various classes of society. Feudal nobles who had gone into business, bankers, merchants, and skilled artisans —all had a share in the economic prosperity. Thanks to this flourishing economic life and the widespread prosperity which it provided, the Florentines were a people of strong secular interests. Man's earthly life and its material pleasures were accepted and enjoyed, even by religious folk. An ascetic monk like Savonarola might persuade the Florentines to burn their "vanities," but soon they returned to their old ways and they eventually permitted his enemies to burn him as a heretic.[2]

[1] For descriptions of the works of these men, see below, Chapters XXXIII, XXXV.
[2] See below, p. 651.

INDIVIDUALISM
AND POLITICAL
TURMOIL
One of the outstanding characteristics of the people of Florence was their spirit of individual initiative. The Florentines seem to have lived in an atmosphere of more vibrant and energetic individualism than could be found anywhere else in Italy or Europe. Unfortunately, this irrepressible individualism is also related to the political turmoil that went on unceasingly in Florence. It was a city of constant and often bitter civil strife. Competition was so keen in economic, political, and social life that men were compelled to exert themselves to the utmost. Perhaps it was this chaotic but active state of society that made the Florentines more progressive than their neighbors who lived under better organized governments but in a less stimulating setting.

Florentine government was never so completely regimented that the citizens lost their sense of individuality. All classes of society were politically active, whether it was under the conservative burgher republic of the thirteenth and fourteenth centuries, or under the enlightened despots who controlled the republic in the fifteenth century. Whatever type of government was in force, the rulers were sensitive to a public opinion which was insistent upon two things, both important factors in cultural advancement: the government must keep out of wars which threatened the prosperity of the people, and the city must be beautiful. Of the two, the Florentines gave more attention and financial support to their buildings, porticoes, and churches than to their military forces.

Another of the essential characteristics of Florentine civilization was its conservative middle-class spirit. As we trace the history of the city, we shall find that its economic, social, and political institutions were predominantly those of prosperous middle-class townspeople. Whether the trend of government was democratic or despotic, Florence had burgher wealth, a cosmopolitan atmosphere that stimulated the exchange of ideas, and, above all, a passion for individual expression. Whatever it is that produces surpassing genius, Florentine civic life, without excessive extremes of wealth and poverty, or democracy and absolutism, provided a fertile soil in which cultural activities flourished. Few civilizations have had so little repression and so much individual freedom.

THE BURGHER
REPUBLIC
Florentine institutions showed the first signs of rapid development in the twelfth and thirteenth centuries. The breakdown of imperial power in northern Italy during this period provided an unusual opportunity for the rise of free-

dom-loving cities such as Florence. The defeat of Frederick the Red-Bearded by the Lombard League (in 1176) had temporarily freed the north Italian cities from foreign domination. The downfall of his grandson, Frederick II (in 1250) removed the last possibility of imperial interference. Of even greater local importance was the fact that this event weakened the feudal aristocracy whom the emperors had supported as the dominant element in city politics. Thus the way was paved for burgher republics.

As a consequence during the last half of the thirteenth century Florence changed from an aristocratic to a moderately democratic system of self-government. In 1250 when the Guelf, or anti-imperialist faction, gained control, the Florentine government was reorganized. The result was a very complicated system of checks and balances. There were two separate sets of executives and civic assemblies. One of these, a survival of the old aristocratic government, consisted of a supreme executive, called the *podesta,* and two advisory councils (of ninety and three hundred, respectively). As a counterbalance to this there was a more democratic executive, called the *capitano* of the people, with two advisory councils and a commission of twelve financial supervisors. When experience proved that this system was too unwieldy, the two existing sets of officials were co-ordinated and controlled by means of a third governing body. This was a central executive council, the *signory,* which consisted of twelve representatives, two from each ward of the city. As the burgher element increased in power, they instituted (in 1282) as the supreme executive power of the city, a commission of six *priors,* one from each of the six wards of the city. Ten years later, burgher control of the government was strengthened by the addition of a supreme military and judicial official, the *gonfalonier* of justice. It was his duty to proceed against enemies of the state at the command of the executives. At the same time (1293), by means of the "Ordinances of Justice," all nobles were disqualified from holding office and were practically forced either to join with the middle class or go into exile.

By the end of the thirteenth century, Florence had become a burgher republic with various sets of officials and councils controlled by a commission of businessmen, the *priors.* Representative institutions were preserved without sacrificing the efficiency of centralized authority. In spite of the bewildering complexity of governmental bodies, public policies were guided by a small group of intelligent and successful guildsmen who represented the city's business leaders.

The century which brought political independence to Florence also brought great economic prosperity. The thirteenth was a century of unusual opportunity for Italian cities. Not only the crusades but also the struggle between the popes and the emperors played into their hands. By allying with the papacy against Emperor Frederick II, Florence gained the double advantage of both political and economic leadership in the neighboring region of Tuscany. She was the head of a league of Tuscan cities which defied Frederick II as successfully as the Lombard League had defied his grandfather, Frederick the Red-Bearded. Eventually most of the cities of the Arno Valley were subjected to Florentine rule. The seaport town of Pisa, at the mouth of the river, accepted Florentine overlordship in order to escape conquest at the hands of the Genoese. Thus Florence obtained a much-needed outlet to the sea. With the assistance of the pope, Siena, a rival city to the south which had an alliance with the emperor, was crushed. This brought to Florence much of the industry and banking of the Sienese territory.

Meanwhile the Florentines and their allies were seizing the castles and estates of the rural nobles who had supported the imperial cause. Throughout the thirteenth century, the success of the papal cause enabled Florence to extend her political sway and financial influence. The bankers of Florence financed the papacy and its allies, and, as a reward, they were allowed to handle the papal revenues in foreign lands. Such transactions brought prestige as well as profits, and by the end of the century Florence was one of the great financial centers of Europe. She had banks of deposit, a dependable gold currency (based on the florin), and taxes on incomes. Her banking and commercial investments extended from Sicily to England and France.

At home prosperity rested upon a solid industrial foundation. The wealth of Florence depended chiefly on wool. The neighboring hills were better suited to sheep raising than to agriculture, and even before the thirteenth century, Florentine textile workers were turning out fine grades of woolen cloth. By the year 1300, two hundred shops, employing a third of the population of Florence, were engaged in the various processes of making cloth. There were guilds of wool carders, cleaners, weavers, and dyers. Raw wool was imported from Spain, France, and England, and the finished product of beautifully dyed cloth was exported to all parts of Europe.[3] Among the other industries

---

[3] So skillful were the Florentine textile workers that rough woolen cloth was imported from Flanders to be finished and re-exported.

which made Florence the greatest textile center of Italy were the manufacture of silk, linen, and other types of cloth. Although textiles were the basis of Florentine commerce, there were also guilds of metal workers, leather workers, and other artisans such as might be found in any city.

FLORENTINE
GUILDS
The political, economic, and social life of Florence was dominated by the guilds, of which there were normally twenty-one. The feudal aristocracy and the proletariat of unskilled laborers were not members of the guilds and therefore had no direct influence in the government. The virtual exclusion of these two classes from public affairs marks a grave defect in Florentine political life. They were discontented and, as we shall see, occasionally resorted to violent revolts.

There were also differences, though not as sharp, among the guildsmen. Seven of the more important guilds, known as the "fat people," dominated governmental affairs. They represented the wealthy burghers: the bankers, notaries, physicians, furriers, cloth makers, and weavers of woolens and silks. The other guilds, called the "little people," were made up of skilled craftsmen.[4] At times when the issue between capital and labor was critical, the lesser guildsmen joined with the proletariat in attempts to force the wealthy burghers to liberalize the government.

In general, the ruling class showed great wisdom and restraint in dealing with such problems. They maintained a conservatively republican government without excessive acts of repression against proletarian leaders. Moderation in governmental policies, based on the universal desire that economic prosperity should endure, is one of the factors that contributed to the welfare of the city.

FACTIONAL
STRIFE
During the fourteenth century Florentine prosperity continued, in spite of unsettled political conditions. Her woolen industries and merchant-banking activities expanded rapidly. Only in the textile centers of Flanders[5] was there anything to compare or to compete with Florentine woolen goods. In finance the bankers of Florence were supreme not only in Italy but also in the North, where they loaned huge sums to the kings

[4] They comprised linenworkers, shoemakers, armorers, ironmakers, masons, carpenters, leather workers, harness makers, saltworkers, butchers, wine makers, innkeepers, bakers, and other minor groups.

[5] See above, p. 582.

of England and France. The prosperity of this era was reflected in innumerable public works such as bridges, town walls, and civic palaces. New churches and ecclesiastical edifices such as Giotto's graceful campanile also indicate the extent of cultural and financial progress.[6]

The period was not, however, one of peace and order. Class conflict was so prevalent that several times the state was threatened with disaster at the hands of exiled nobles or proletarian mobs. The "Blacks," one party of wealthy propertied interests fought against the rising power of the "Whites," who represented another faction of the ruling burgher element. Dante, an enthusiastic supporter of the "Whites," was exiled along with the leaders of that party in 1302. Several times when the bitterness of civil strife threatened disaster, the burgher executives of Florence called in military leaders from outside and gave them temporary dictatorial powers. But even though the shadow of despotism fell upon this stronghold of republican institutions, the vigorous burgher government was able to control or eliminate its dictators when they became dangerous.

PROLETARIAN
REVOLTS
During the fourteenth century, Florence survived not only the peril of feudal exiles and foreign dictators but also of proletarian uprisings. The artisans who belonged to the lesser guilds, and the unrepresented proletarians steadily grew more resentful of the prosperity of the "fat" guilds and their monopoly of governmental power. In 1345 certain textile workers made an unsuccessful demonstration. During the ensuing years, the repeated ravages of the Black Death accentuated the misery of the lower classes. In 1378 they broke forth in a violent revolt. It was instigated by the leaders of the "lean" guilds and actually carried out by the Ciompi, the wool workers. Mobs of riotous textile workers paraded the streets pillaging shops and monasteries. But the violence of the proletariat alienated the "lean" guildsmen, who deserted their lower-class allies, gained control of the government, and continued in power for some time. Eventually, however, in 1382, the conservative element regained its ascendancy and eliminated all radical influences. Among those who went into exile was a certain Salvestro, of the wealthy Medici family, who had taken part in the revolt.

The Ciompi revolt is one of the many episodes in the class war-

[6] See below, p. 727.

fare that prevailed in industrial centers during the fourteenth century. Discontent seems to have been accentuated by the rapid growth of industry and the extremes of wealth and poverty. In Italy, and elsewhere, there was violent popular resentment against conservative burgher government. The people of Rome overthrew their ecclesiastical ruler and revived ancient republican institutions in the twelfth century under the leadership of Arnold of Brescia, and again in the fourteenth under Rienzi, the "tribune of the people."

At about the time when Florence was putting down the Ciompi similarly violent movements were being suppressed elsewhere in Europe. In Ghent, also a textile center, the popular forces led by Philip van Artevelde went down to defeat before the armies of the Count of Flanders at Roosebeke in 1382. In France, rebellious artisans and burghers were ruthlessly suppressed in 1358 when, under the leadership of Stephen Marcel of Paris, they demanded more popular control in government. There were also revolts in 1381-1382 on both sides of the Channel. In England the peasantry and their proletarian allies under John Ball learned the tragic lesson of the impossibility of overthrowing the government and institutions of their "betters." In Florence, as elsewhere, the conservatives retained control. Fortunately, Florentine conservatism was moderate and the city was spared the bloody scenes of revenge that occurred elsewhere. Throughout the history of the city the practical policies of businessmen seem to have prevailed, and without extremes of radicalism or reaction, her civilization made steady progress.

THE RISE OF
THE MEDICI

After the suppression of the Ciompi, the drift from burgher democracy to dictatorship was rapid. For about fifty years, the powerful Albizzi family dominated governmental affairs while the Medici devoted themselves to the development of their banking interests and the winning of a popular following. In 1393 Vieri de' Medici was urged by malcontents to seize the power and make himself tyrant. He refused; the time was not ripe. It was Cosimo de' Medici (1434-1464) who paved the way for permanent Medici control when he led the popular demand for external peace and internal order. He was a popular "boss" whose democratic ways and public charities so endeared him to the people that he came to control many of the governmental commissions. His domination of government was benevolent, but the opposing factions objected nevertheless.

At Cosimo's death his fellow citizens hailed him as "Father of His Country." His grandson Lorenzo, who reaped much of the good fruits of his wise policy, carried on the Medici tradition of efficient, if not democratic, government. Lorenzo was the dominant personality of his day in Italy. Though unbelievably homely in appearance, he was highly cultured, a remarkable poet, an athlete, and a political genius. In 1478 he narrowly escaped death at the hands of assassins. This crystallized public opinion in favor of the Medici. The leading conspirators were lynched by mobs of the citizenry, and Lorenzo was granted dictatorial powers.

Thereafter, like Augustus, the Roman successor of Julius Caesar, Lorenzo *ruled* the city without *reigning*. Although the governmental machinery of the republic remained, Lorenzo's control over domestic and foreign affairs was absolute. He was the unrecognized despot and the uncrowned king of the leading city-state of Italy. Under his efficient and enlightened rule, Florence attained unparalleled artistic and literary fame. Lorenzo's court not only dominated Italian diplomacy, it was also the greatest European center of cultural life.[7]

After Lorenzo's death, decline set in. There was a brief period of reaction, both political and cultural, under the restored republic in which the Dominican reformer, Savonarola, played an important role. Soon Florence reverted to the Medici and their enlightened despotism. Florentine government, like that in most Italian and European states of this period, moved in the direction of absolutism. At the same time in their civic life the Florentines preserved the forms of republicanism, and steered a middle course between the extremes of autocracy and proletarian revolution.

MILAN

In Lombardy, across the Apennines from Florence, was Milan, a city as aggressive in politics as Florence was in commerce and finance. The evolution of government in Milan illustrates the rapid rise of despotism in the same degree to which Florence shows the persistence of republicanism. A glance at Milanese geography indicates that the city was destined to be the political leader of Lombardy. Located in an open plain, without natural defenses, and amid the network of streams that form the Po River system, the city was forced to domi-

[7] See below, pp. 701 f.

nate north central Italy in order to exist. Its domination was facilitated by the fact that the highways leading to and from several of the most important Alpine passes converged at or near Milan. As its ancient name, "Mediolanum," signifies it was the "middle city" of the Po Valley. From early medieval times Milan was a strategic military and political center. During the late Roman Empire it rivaled Rome as the headquarters of Western emperors such as Constantine and Theodosius. Its ecclesiastical organization, established by the famous Bishop Ambrose, rivaled that of the popes of Rome for a time. After the invasions of the Lombards, Milan declined, but in the eleventh century it began once more to assert its political supremacy.

Milan was the leader of the Lombard League which administered a decisive defeat to Frederick the Red-Bearded in 1176. In 1237 Milan led in the defensive against Frederick II. In spite of terrible losses suffered in a disastrous battle (at Cortenuova) the city kept up a vigorous resistance, and after Frederick's downfall (in 1250) Milan began to reap the fruits of its long struggle against German imperial domination in Italy. Eventually it became the ruler of most of the Po Valley. At a time when Florence was assuming the financial leadership in Italy, Milan was launching upon a successful career of political expansion. Meanwhile, with the era of aggressive conquest, there were changes in the city's republican institutions.

FROM REPUBLIC TO DICTATORSHIP During the eleventh and twelfth centuries, the inhabitants of Milan had worked out a republican system of self-government which was well suited to the needs of a peaceful independent town. An executive board consisting of annually elected consuls, twenty in number,[8] was chosen from the aristocratic or wealthy class by a committee of guildsmen. Two councils composed of representative burghers advised and checked the consuls. The entire body of citizens met occasionally in a mass meeting, or *parlemento,* held in the public square or in the cathedral, to give their assent on important matters. This machinery of government was under the control of the nobles and guildsmen. The masses had little influence in government save for a short time during the eleventh century when Milan was dominated by a proletarian organization called "Patarines." [9]

Like the plebeians of ancient Rome, however, and like the *populo* of Florence, the Milanese populace had assemblies which met under

[8] Later the number was reduced to twelve.
[9] See above, p. 440.

the presidency of an elected leader called a *podesta,* or captain of the people. As Milanese territory increased and the need for an efficient centralized administration became more and more apparent, the *podesta* increased in importance. With the support of the populace, he eventually became a dictator. It was by such means that the government of Milan came under the control of the Torre family during the period from 1258-1278. From their ranks the people elected their *podestas,* and two of the Torre held this office for life. From 1278 to 1302, the family of Archbishop Otto Visconti played a similar role, and by the middle of the fourteenth century, Archbishop Giovanni Visconti was recognized as hereditary lord of Milan.

By this time veiled dictatorship had changed to an acknowledged and permanent despotism. For a century thereafter the members of the Visconti family were virtual monarchs of Milan. Under their able autocratic rule the city acquired a land empire that included all of the important Lombard towns from (and including) Genoa, eastward to Padua near the Adriatic Sea. So extensive was the Milanese realm that it seemed as though all Italy might eventually be united under the rule of the Visconti, who had, moreover, powerful foreign connections: Valentina Visconti was married to Louis of Orleans, brother of the king of France. In 1395 the German emperor, who had already recognized the Visconti as "imperial vicars," granted to Gian Galeazzo Visconti the title of duke.

Milan's rapid expansion, however, was her undoing. Other Italian cities, such as Florence and Venice, formed a league to check the encroachments of the Visconti. This resulted in almost constant warfare. Even so, by the end of the fourteenth century, Duke Gian Galeazzo's achievements in diplomacy, conquest, and internal public works had brought great fame to the Visconti and to the Milanese state. Among their architectural accomplishments were the Certosa at Pavia, and the snowy white Gothic cathedral of Milan.[10] Not until the fifteenth century, under Gian's cruel and inefficient sons, did his north Italian realm disintegrate. Foreign intrigues and civic discontent finally culminated in a vain effort on the part of certain malcontents to restore republican government.

THE SFORZA DESPOTS   The ill-starred republic (1447-1450) soon gave way to a dictatorship. General Francesco Sforza, a professional soldier, who possessed both military resources and political sagacity, was able to profit by the weakness of the re-

[10] See below, pp. 718 f.

public and to come into power. Having saved the republic from its foreign enemies, he appropriated the fruits of victory and made himself absolute ruler. Francesco is an excellent example of the self-made Italian despot. Of plebeian birth, he had risen to fame by virtue of his unusual military and diplomatic talents.[11] As the leader (*condotterre*) of a band of mercenaries, he had played a clever game of intrigue between the Milanese and the Venetians. After becoming duke of Milan, he ruled so wisely that the city continued to be the dominant political power in northern Italy. His son, Galeazzo Maria (1466-1478), however, was a heartless despot of the worst possible type, the very antithesis of his father. He was succeeded by the able but unscrupulous Ludovico il Moro, who served first as regent for an infant nephew, then in his own name.

Following the traditional aims and methods of Italian diplomacy, Ludovico cleverly played for every possible advantage. In order to build up his own power he made alliances with both the French and German monarchs. It was he who encouraged Charles VIII of France to attempt the conquest of Naples-Sicily,[12] thus precipitating a series of French invasions of the peninsula, plunging Italy into an era of devastating civil strife, and eventually bringing about his own downfall.

VENICE

If Florence typifies the best in Italian industrial and cultural life, and Milan Italy's most vigorous political leadership, Venice was her outstanding maritime city. Furthermore, Venice, more than any other city, illustrates the persistence of that solidly conservative merchant spirit which was characteristic of the early Italian republics. In Florence the Medici took control out of the hands of the citizens; in Milan the Visconti and the Sforzas transformed a burgher republic into an out-and-out despotism. In Venice, however, governmental institutions remained in the hands of the merchant oligarchy by whose activities the city had grown from a fishing village to a metropolis of Mediterranean commerce. Stability in both government and commerce was characteristic of the Venetians.

Tradition has it that Attila's invasion of northeastern Italy in the fifth century forced many people to take refuge on the sandy islets off the coast which became the site of Venice. Soon what had

---

[11] See below, p. 648, for Machiavelli's description of Francesco.
[12] See below, p. 650.

been a mere fishermen's settlement became a group of towns with a
thriving sea commerce in the Adriatic. As early as the sixth century,
Venetian ships were used by the Eastern Emperor, Justinian, for the
transport of troops to Italy to fight the Ostrogoths. By the end
of the seventh century the twelve island settlements had formed a
civic federation with an elective executive, called the *doge* (i.e., duke).

A MERCHANT-
CONTROLLED
GOVERNMENT

Through the centuries Venetian governmental institutions came more and more under the control of the
merchant class. The doge, for instance, was selected
by a committeee from the Great Council (or assem-
bly), which was controlled by the businessmen. Once elected, the doge
was held in check by an advisory council of six men, appointed by the
same Great Council. He might not even have an interview except in
the presence of the six advisers; on the other hand, they might take action without his consent. Doges who attempted to evade supervision
and to rule in an independent manner were executed. All in all, the
doge, although he held office for life, had less power than many a
president of a modern republic.

All governing bodies in Venice were merchant-controlled. There
was, in addition to the Advisory Council, a Cabinet of Sages, or ministers, who devoted themselves to city affairs, to maritime business,
and to Venetian possessions on the mainland. A Senate, composed of
a hundred and sixty leading citizens (including all ex-officials),
passed laws and directed foreign affairs. Judicial matters were under
the special control of a supreme court called "The Forty." Thus, the
administration of Venetian government was in the hands of a number of councils or commissions, all of which were subject to the will
of the Great Council, which consisted of about five hundred of the
leading merchants. In the twelfth century its membership was expanded to one thousand, but this rather democratic tendency received
a definite setback in the late thirteenth century when membership
was restricted to about five hundred members of the great merchant
families. Later, a list of active citizens was drawn up in what came to
be known as the "Golden Book." The Great Council selected all officers and determined all important policies; rarely were governmental
affairs presented to the entire body of citizens for their approval.

So satisfactory was this merchant-controlled government that
Venice had very few political changes after the thirteenth century. In
1310, during a critical period of external wars and internal revolts,
a temporary committee of public safety was set up for the purpose

of trying and executing any citizens who were dangerous to the republic. In spite of its arbitrary powers and ruthless attitude toward suspects, this Council of Ten worked so effectively that it was continued from year to year, and eventually became the controlling body of the government. It seems likely that the Council of Ten saved the Venetian state from falling into the hands of a military despot.

VENETIAN STABILITY AND PROSPERITY Venice was one of the few city-states of Italy that maintained republican institutions during the age of despots. This was probably due to the fact that the merchant oligarchy gave the city a remarkably efficient government. The courts functioned with satisfaction, taxes were reasonable, and, above all, the citizens enjoyed prosperity. Venetian commerce and industry were pre-eminent in northeastern Italy, on the Adriatic, and throughout much of the Mediterranean. Venetian banks, coinage, and navigation laws influenced the European world for centuries. Her seafaring commerce was carefully regulated, even to such matters as marking the hulls of ships with a line beyond which it was unsafe and illegal to load them. In foreign countries, the state maintained diplomatic representatives for the purpose of safeguarding the interests of the citizenry. Their efficiency, especially the detailed reports which they sent to the home government concerning political and economic conditions abroad, made them the model diplomats of Western Europe. In short, Venetian affairs were handled with the efficiency of a great business concern.

Venice seldom suffered from the violent revolts of a desperate citizenry. The citizens resembled the contented stockholders of a prosperous corporation rather than the subjects of a ruling oligarchy. Their fidelity and the resourcefulness of their leaders were clearly shown when the city was at one time threatened with capture and destruction by Venice's worst enemy, Genoa.

VENICE VERSUS GENOA For centuries these two port towns, located at opposite extremes of the Lombard plain, had waged a bitter warfare for control of the commerce of the eastern Mediterranean.[13] In 1379, during the absence of the main Venetian fleet, the Genoese made a successful attack, captured strategic defensive outposts, and were in a position to starve the city into submission. But the indomitable Venetian officials rallied the citizens, mobilized additional naval squadrons, and by a remark-

[13] See above, p. 535.

able series of successful engagements, captured the besieging fleet. This victory proved to be the turning point of the long struggle. Soon Genoese sea power languished, her home government was torn by dissension and civil war, and she became a minor factor in Italian commercial and political life—a sad contrast to her earlier expansion during the crusading era,[14] and also to Venice, the "Serene Republic," which continued to prosper during the late Middle Ages.

Throughout most of this period Venice was the undisturbed mistress of Mediterranean commerce, and the chief distributor of Oriental goods to the countries of Northern Europe. Her galleys brought spices, silks, and raw goods from Egypt, Syria, the Black Sea ports, and Constantinople. Her merchants penetrated far distant lands in search of commercial concessions. The famous Marco Polo was a member of a Venetian merchant family engaged in trade in the Black Sea region during the thirteenth century.

VENETIAN TRADE   In addition to the imported products of the East, the Venetians sold their own manufactured specialties, particularly fine glassware, such as is still made by expert glassblowers in Venetian shops. The export of such goods furnished the lifeblood of the city, bringing a steady stream of wealth that spelled prosperity to her sailors, shipbuilders, manufacturers, shopkeepers, and great merchant families. From Northern Europe, across the Brenner and other Alpine passes, came German and French merchants to buy Venetian goods for their own local trade. Other Italian cities also patronized the Venetian marts, and businessmen flocked to "the Rialto"; this island, lagoon, and bridge had become the city's "Wall Street." Most of the trade of Venice came and went by sea. Her galleys even passed the Strait of Gibraltar and ventured onto the stormy Atlantic to make regular voyages to England and Flanders.[15] It was fitting that one of the greatest of Venetian festivals was a splendid marriage ceremony in which the doge was symbolically wedded to the sea, the mother by whom the city and citizens were nourished.

One of the most noteworthy tributes to the effectiveness of Venetian government is the success with which the city's political and economic institutions withstood the shock of external attack. In the fourteenth century, as we have seen, a threatened disaster at the hands of the Genoese was turned into a brilliant victory. Toward the mid-

[14] Due to the fact that Genoa sank to an inferior position in Italian life, we omit detailed treatment of her history.

[15] See above, p. 536.

dle of the fifteenth century, the rising power of the Turks in the eastern Mediterranean began to menace the Venetian commercial monopoly. By diplomacy, as well as by warfare, this threatening situation was kept well in hand so that the Venetians and Turks jointly profited by the trade in Oriental goods. The still more dangerous rivalry of the Portuguese, after Vasco da Gama's voyage around Africa to India (1497), was counterbalanced by economic adjustments which partially restored Venetian mercantile prosperity. To be sure, in the opening years of the sixteenth century the *spice* trade of Venice declined, due to Portuguese competition, and later a war with the Turks, combined with a disastrous plague, dealt her a severe blow. But the Venetian merchant marine employed in international commerce appears not to have declined, but actually to have grown in cargo-carrying capacity. The eventual passing of the maritime glory of Venice was primarily due to her failure to keep up with other seagoing peoples. A basic reason for this failure was the exhaustion of one of her vital natural resources, ship timber.[16]

Throughout the critical period in which economic leadership was slowly shifting from the Mediterranean Sea to the Atlantic coasts of Europe, the Venetian government continued to function with remarkable intelligence and with a high degree of success. To be sure, Venice was fighting a losing battle, but the indomitable spirit of the Venetian merchant oligarchy fought off disaster during the later centuries of inevitable decline. Not until the coming of Napoleon, with his invincible military forces, was the proud republic of the Adriatic brought low. Even today, her lovely palazzos, sumptuous churches, and palatial civic structures,[17] are a colorful and inspiring reminder of the great days of one of the greatest cities of all times.

THE TRIUMPH
OF DESPOTISM
In general the smaller city-states manifested political tendencies that were similar to those that we have noted in Florence, Milan, and Venice. During the thirteenth century, most Italian towns were self-governing republics controlled by either the aristocratic or burgher element, or an alliance of the two. Under this type of conservative government the towns and townsfolk acquired prosperity and influence. Even Frederick II, autocratic ruler of Naples-Sicily, recognized the importance of the towns

16 F. C. Lane, "Venetian Shipping during the Commercial Revolution" (*Am. Hist. Rev.*, XXXVIII, 1933). Professor Lane feels that the effects of the Portuguese discovery upon Venetian trade have been exaggerated.
17 See below, pp. 738 f.

and gave them a place in his government. At times he summoned deputies from the towns as well as from the clerical and noble centers, for informal consultation. Furthermore, twice a year, representatives of the towns met to consider complaints against the royal officials. Further north, in cities such as Florence, Siena, Genoa, and Venice, the mechanism of burgher democracy functioned with greater independence. But most thirteenth-century Italian republics were conservative. Their burgher-controlled governments maintained a sort of equilibrium between aristocratic conspirators on the one hand and proletarian radicals on the other.

By the opening of the fourteenth century, the burgher republics had begun to give way to more autocratic forms of government. This was in part due to their inability to handle the increasingly complex problems of expanding city life. If the state was to prosper, commerce must be protected, encroachments of dangerous neighbors must be stopped, and the internal disturbances caused by rebellious nobles or proletarians must be crushed. Usually the passing of the burgher republic was heralded by a temporary dictatorship set up for the purpose of handling a desperate crisis. Inevitably temporary dictatorships became permanent.

In some places a civic official, such as the *podesta,* became the despot by securing an extended term of office and additional powers. Often it was the descendant of a former imperial official who gained permanent control of the city. Occasionally the hired commanders of mercenary armies (*condottieri*) turned upon their employers and made themselves despots by force of arms. By such methods, either before or during the fifteenth century, despots came to power everywhere in the Italian world, some by violence, some by legal means. No important city, save Venice, escaped the trend toward one-man government.

THE RUTHLESS-NESS OF DESPOTISM It was with much violence and brutality that the despots rode into power in many Italian city-states. Ezzelin of Verona, vicar of Frederick II, was one of the earliest of north-Italian despots and perhaps as has been said, "the very worst sort of tyrant known to human history." At the end of the same century (the thirteenth), one of the Visconti of Milan, on being exiled, told his successful rival that he would return to power when the crimes of the victor exceeded his own. He did return, and some of his descendants in the fifteenth century were said to have lived up to the worst of his expectations. They were accustomed to turn loose their boar hounds upon unfortunate people who were energetic in presenting grievances or petitions. On one occasion, during a terrible siege, two hundred starving citizens were massacred for marching to the palace to demand peace.

To many Italian despots, duplicity and physical violence were the sole means of retaining a throne. Assassinations of rivals and suspected traitors were common. Even papal despots, such as the Borgias, made unenviable reputations by their use of the dagger and the poison cup. The more ruthless type of despot trusted no one: not only relatives, but allies were constantly watched, and the breaking of agreements, when advantageous, was to be expected.

"CONDOTTIERI"   Most despots relied heavily on military force. Mercenary troops under the leadership of professional generals (*condottieri*) were their mainstay. Sometimes these military men seized the power for themselves. Such, for instance, was the case with Francesco Sforza at Milan, and with the English adventurer, John Hawkwood, who became ruler of several towns in central Italy. The equestrian statues of Gattamelata and Colleoni, by the Italian sculptors, Donatello and Verrocchio,[18] are striking likenesses of typical *condottieri*. The stern faces of these leaders of a brutalized soldiery suggest the terrorism and suffering that the wars of rival despots brought to the Italian countryside. Whatever the despot lacked in the kindlier virtues, he and his men seldom lacked courage. Many stories are told of the heroism of these medieval soldiers of fortune. An eighteen-year-old boy of the fighting Baglioni family of Perugia, when driven to take cover in the cathedral, with a handful of retainers courageously held off overwhelming forces of the enemy.

Of all despots the Carraras of Padua were doubtless the most spectacular. During the late fourteenth century, Francesco and his son were a constant terror to their Venetian and Milanese neighbors until at last, after a hundred daring escapades and narrow escapes, they were captured and condemned to death. The final picture of this adventurous couple, as given by a contemporary writer, shows old Francesco in his prison cell fighting off the executioners. Hopelessly outnumbered, he seized his prison stool and laid about him right and left in a final outburst of fury, calling on the devil to come and carry his soul off to hell.

18 See below, p. 731.

THE BENEVO-
LENCE OF
DESPOTISM
At their worst, despots were a terrible bane. For the most part, however, their atrocities were perpetrated upon public enemies such as conspiring nobles or rival despots, and not upon their own faithful subjects or upon noncombatants. Most of them were no better, and no worse, than other rulers. The average Italian despot, like the ancient Greek tyrant, seems to have been popular with all classes except for certain vested interests or rival rulers whom he had overthrown. Many of them were benevolent despots in every sense of the word, generous in public works and charity. "Be not the master," Petrarch advised the Scala despot of Verona, "but the father of thy subjects. . . . Soldiers thou mayest employ against the enemy, but with thy subjects good will is sufficient." Giovanni de' Medici, on his deathbed, exhorted his son, Cosimo, "never to give counsel against the people's wishes unless they are bent on ignoble or impolitic actions." Machiavelli, as we have seen, emphasized the necessity of the prince's keeping his loyal subjects happy and prosperous. Italian despotism rested to a great degree upon the good will of the people.

Under the enlightened despotism of the Medici and of Alfonso of Naples, the burden of taxation was lessened. Gian Galeazzo of Milan built canals, drained swamps, and erected magnificent buildings. The Este rulers of Ferrara made their capital one of the first modernized cities of Europe. Merely as good business policy, despots sought to make their subjects prosperous. In the practical handling of government they usually proved their worth. A despot must make his city prosperous in order to maintain his position. Unlike a hereditary monarch, he could not take his position for granted. Therefore, most despots, in order to maintain their power, exerted themselves to the utmost. In the Italian world of rival city-states, this competitive spirit brought about great achievements in political, economic, and cultural life.

THE IDEAL DESPOT
A despot might be a man of charming personality and culture. Francesco Sforza of Milan, born of plebeian stock, was universally popular. It was said that he learned from his soldier-father the wisdom of treating "not only his bankers, but also his people" with kindness and consideration. He is said to have had four rules of conduct: protect the citizens and peasants from ravages, never strike your soldiers, let other men's wives alone, and never ride a hard-mouthed horse or one that drops a shoe. This self-made despot seems to have met with an approval that was almost

universal. His contemporaries were struck with the fact that at sixty years of age he looked like a young man as he rode along on his war-horse. "He was calm and affable in conversation, princely in bearing, with a combination of physical and intellectual gifts that were un-rivalled."

Other despots were more notable than Francesco Sforza for their culture and patronage of learning. Gianlucido Gonzaga of Mantua at eleven years of age knew Greek well enough to write it, and in later years he employed learned scholars to teach that language to the young nobles of his court. He read Livy in the original Latin and was an able art critic. The well-ordered trend of his life is illustrated by the typical morning schedule of his activities: up at dawn, an eight-mile horseback ride, religious service, court, and then a frugal lunch, with gifts of food for the needy.

The famous Federigo of Urbino saw to it that there were no beggars in his land. He was accustomed to walk about unattended, meeting and talking with his subjects. Among the books in his magnificent library were Greek, Latin, and Hebrew classics. Even some of the most ruthless of despots were patrons of culture. A contemporary relates that a certain despot, who murdered three wives and corrupted his own children, "had a mighty love for men of learning."

DESPOTISM AND FOREIGN INVADERS

Toward the end of the fifteenth century, Italian despotism was subjected to a severe diplomatic and military crisis, the test of foreign invasion. It may be said that the despot-controlled cities gave a good account of themselves. Throughout her long history, Italy had often been afflicted with invasion. At this time, as always, the Italians were forced to play their wits against the superior military force of the invaders. In the game of cutthroat diplomacy, the despots played the leading parts, and, on the whole, proved themselves superior to the foreigners. The struggle with the foreign invader involved not only the Italian despots but also the kings of most of the great powers of the West. During the closing years of the fifteenth century, the Italies were the arena for diplomatic and military maneuvers by practically every monarch of Western Europe.

CHARLES VIII OF FRANCE IN ITALY

In the very year in which Columbus sailed westward on his epoch-making voyage, young Charles VIII of France was planning an important expedition. The international situation in the Italies had been completely upset in the year 1492 by the death of Lorenzo de' Medici. For half a century the diplomacy of the Medici had preserved the balance of power among the leading Italian states and had discouraged foreign aggressions. Furthermore, during this same period, the great European powers (England, France, Aragon-Castile, and the empire) were occupied either at home or with wars elsewhere. By 1492, however, Ferdinand and Isabella, having gained the upper hand in the Spains, were looking abroad as was also Emperor Maximilian. As for the French, Charles VIII, thanks to the effective work of his father, had an unrivaled financial, military, and political machine at his disposal.[19]

Charles's youthful ambitions led him into Italy. He had inherited the longstanding claims of the French house of Anjou in Naples-Sicily, and his cousin, Louis of Orleans, had similar interests in Milan, due to the fact that his grandmother had been a member of the Visconti family which had ruled that city until 1447. In addition to these hereditary rights in northern and southern Italy, Charles was enthusiastic over the idea of leading an expedition against the Turks, whose capture of Constantinople in 1453 had revived crusading fervor throughout Western Europe. A French campaign into southern Italy might pave the way for the recovery of the Holy Sepulcher and bring crusading glory to France. Accordingly, in 1493 Charles assumed the title "King of Jerusalem and Sicily," and began his preparations.

THE INTRIGUES
OF LUDOVICO
OF MILAN

Charles VIII's expedition was not motivated solely by his own political ambitions. He came on the invitation of Italians. It had ever been the habit of ambitious Italian rulers to call on foreign powers for aid against their own rivals in the peninsula. Charles, like his father before him, had received such requests from Italian cities, but not, however, until the death of the master diplomat, Lorenzo de' Medici, did Italy seriously invite the intervention of the French. It was then that Ludovico Sforza (il Moro) of Milan allied himself with Charles. This, to all appearances, assured the success of the French expedition. Ludovico, however, was playing a clever diplomatic game. By joining forces with Charles he gave up his former role as Italy's protector against foreign aggressors and actually agreed to assist the French in seizing Italian territory. He concealed his duplicity by claiming that his ally, Charles, was the "Pacificator" of Italy. As a matter of fact, Ludovico hoped that the French alliance would prevent Charles from

[19] See above, p. 600.

claiming Milan as the rightful inheritance of his cousin, Louis of Orleans. At the same time, he was secretly obtaining his own recognition as duke of Milan from Emperor Maximilian, Charles's bitter rival. Ludovico's duplicity succeeded remarkably well. Charles promised him adequate territorial rewards in return for his aid; and by September, 1494, the French armies had crossed the Alps.

Without serious opposition, the French army and fleet proceeded southward. At Milan, Ludovico put his capital's resources at the disposal of the French. The invaders crossed the Apennines unopposed. In Florence confusion reigned supreme. Within two years after the death of Lorenzo de' Medici, his sons had proved their incapacity, and the exponents of republican government had set about to resume control. They were aided by the firebrand monk, Savonarola, who dedicated his unrivaled oratorical powers to the reform of religious and political conditions. His influence with the populace was tremendous, due to the apparently miraculous manner in which he foretold the various episodes of the French invasion. Machiavelli remarked that Savonarola was "coloring his lies to suit the times," but most Florentines were awe-struck at his prophetic utterances. He quickly became the leading figure of the anti-Medici faction. As the French armies approached the city, the Medici were driven out. They appealed to Charles for aid at the same time that Savonarola, with a Florentine embassy, reached the French camp. By the threat of an alliance with the Medici, Charles forced the envoys of the republic to make military concessions. But so much trouble developed during the brief stay of the French in the city that Charles left, on the advice of his generals and with Savonarola's warning that God was calling him onward to reform the papacy.

In Rome, the Borgia pope, Alexander VI, who was overlord of Naples, was inclined to oppose the French, but he agreed to grant them safe passage across papal territory. In return, Charles renounced all intention of either reforming or deposing the pope. One of the indirect results of this agreement was the pope's triumph over Savonarola. Condemned as a heretic and hounded by local enemies, he was eventually burned to death in the same market place in which he had recently persuaded the conscience-stricken Florentines to burn their "vanities."

From Rome the French forces went southward. The chief Neapolitan strongholds were occupied without serious opposition, and for a while all went well. But within a short time, disquieting news was received from the north. Genoa had revolted. Ludovico's secret agreement with Emperor Maximilian leaked out, and it was reported that these two had joined with the Venetians and the pope in an anti-French coalition. To make matters worse, a fleet from Aragon appeared off the coast of Sicily. Charles's decision to withdraw was none too timely. All Italy, save the faithful Florentines, was openly leagued against him, and even in that city anti-French feeling ran high. After an indecisive battle at Fornova near the Po River, Charles made peace with his enemies and returned to France.

LOUIS XII
INVADES ITALY

It might have been expected that the French, having had their fingers burned in Neapolitan affairs in the thirteenth century[20] and again in 1494, would have kept out of Italy. But within six years of Charles's unfortunate venture, his successor, Louis XII, followed the same course. Assuming the title "Duke of Milan" in addition to that of "King of Sicily," he proceeded to win most of the Italians by means of his diplomacy, and then to capture Milan. This success was followed by an agreement with Ferdinand of Aragon for a joint expedition against Naples. But difficulties arose, and eventually the allies signed a treaty according to which Naples was ceded to Ferdinand V and his new French bride. Thus southern Italy came under Spanish control once more, while French influence prevailed in the North.

Although Louis gained possession of Milan and restored the French protectorate in Genoa, his ambitions were not yet satisfied. In 1508 he joined with Ferdinand of Aragon, Emperor Maximilian, and Pope Julius II in a league against Venice. It was understood that he was to receive a goodly portion of the Venetian possessions in Lombardy. All went well until the pope deserted the alliance, made peace with the Venetians, and turned against the French. Within three years, however (in 1515), Louis's successor, Francis I, took the Italians completely by surprise and restored French control in the North. By a rapid march across the Alps and a hard-won victory at Marignano, he recaptured Milan and forced a favorable treaty upon the pope and his allies. France held Milan until the coming of Emperor Charles V and the dynastic wars of the Protestant Revolution.

[20] See above, pp. 620 f.

EFFECTS OF THE
FRENCH
INVASIONS To Italy the French and Spanish invasions brought—
and not for the first time—devastation and subjection to the yoke of foreigners. From the invasions of
the Germans in the fifth century until the nineteenth
century, when nationalism put an end to both internal warfare and
foreign intervention, Italy had a constant history of foreign interference. Dante, Petrarch, and Machiavelli were forerunners of Maz-
zini and Garibaldi in that they hoped that Italy might find a savior
who would rescue her from her sad plight. So far as the foreign
powers were concerned, the outcome of their Italian ventures had no
decisive results. Emperors, French kings, Spanish kings, and even
English kings continued to interfere in Italian affairs, usually to the
misfortune of all concerned. Italy was like the lion's den of Aesop's
fable: into it many tracks led, but from it came only a few—the tracks
of sadly crippled victims.

Many students of art and literature have found compensation for
these misfortunes in the profitable contacts which the French made
with Italian culture during the period of the invasions. It is true that
the French kings were inspired to import Italian artists such as Cellini and da Vinci,[21] and that the members of the French expeditionary forces learned much of Italian culture during their stay in the
peninsula; but it is incorrect to make this the starting point of modern French art and literature, or to attribute to it a "Revival of Learning" in France. As we shall see, the art, literature, and learning of
France were deeply rooted in her own past and had been highly
developed for centuries before the invasions of Italy. France was not
dependent on Italian influences for the genius of writers such as the
historians Joinville, Villehardouin, Froissart, and Commines; nor for
the poetry of the *Song of Roland, Aucassin and Nicolette, Tristram
and Isolde,* and the songs of the troubadours and of the vagabond,
François Villon; nor for the art of the sculptor, Sluter, and that of the
architects who built the Gothic cathedrals.[22] In every line of cultural
endeavor, France had for centuries been developing her own peculiar
arts and literatures. The expeditions to Italy, like the twelfth-century
crusades to the East, brought Frenchmen into contact with other
types of civilization. Experience added new elements and helped to
fertilize a cultural life which was already deeply rooted and well
developed.

[21] See below, p. 721.
[22] These writers and works of art are treated in the succeeding chapters.

═══ XXXII ═══

LEARNING IN THE LATE MIDDLE AGES

THE CULTURAL LIFE OF THE LATE MIDDLE AGES

IN the preceding chapters of our survey of late medieval life we have dealt with religious, political, and economic developments. Only passing notice has been given to the arts, schools, literature, and music, in which fields we find some of the most vital of medieval contributions to our modern civilization. In the remaining chapters we shall concentrate our attention on these topics, tracing their development through the late Middle Ages, from the beginning of the eleventh century to the beginning of the sixteenth. During this period of approximately five hundred years the continuity of cultural development (like that of political, religious, and economic life) was unbroken.[1] We shall also note the beginnings of many influences which have carried on into modern times and which often seem to be as much a part of the history of modern as of medieval civilization. The late Middle Ages were an age of rapid transition in which the rise of new institutions was quite as evident as the decline of the old. In them can be found the beginnings of many of the characteristics of modern literature, learning, and art.

CLERICAL DOMINATION IN CATHEDRAL AND MONASTIC SCHOOLS

LEARNING AND LITERATURE   There is no such thing as a *typically* medieval learning or literature. Like everything in the Middle Ages they show infinite variation of spirit, influence, and technique. There were religious and secular, learned and frivolous, and

---

[1] This is in keeping with present-day trends in historical scholarship. The once-popular contrasts between medieval culture (before the age of Petrarch) and that of the "Renaissance" are now out of favor. One reads of renascences in the Carolingian age, the eleventh century, and the twelfth century. For this reason, and also because of the misleading and inaccurate inferences that are associated with the term *renaissance,* or *renascence* (i.e., revival or rebirth of learning, etc.), we have abandoned it as a designation for this, or any other period of history.

classical and clerical writings in both prose and poetry. There was literature in Latin, in English, German, French, Provençal, Spanish, and Italian. There were men like St. Bernard whose lives and writings were enveloped in a mist of piety; there were learned scholars like Abelard who reveled in rationalistic theology; enthusiasts like Petrarch who were enthralled by the classics; and city-bred laymen of Dante's type who wrote inspired religious poems. A man such as Adelard of Bath devoted his life to science, while other clergymen and lay troubadours lived solely for the worldly pleasures of wine, women, and song.

Until late in the Middle Ages the dominant literature of the West was religious and was written in Latin. There were also the pagan classics and other secular writings, and there was non-Latin literature in the vernacular, notably in England. It was during the later centuries that nonreligious literature in the vernacular languages came into its own. During this period even the Latin writings of the churchmen took on a secular and sometimes profane tone. Until late in the Middle Ages, however, the church was first and foremost in the lives of educated men, and its hold on learning and literature was loosened very slowly and with great difficulty. So long as the clergy were the leaders in education, they controlled literature; this meant that most writing was in Latin and concerned with religious or learned subjects.

EDUCATION But, it may be asked, how is it that the clergy dominated learning and education? In the early Middle Ages the decline of city life and pagan classical schools, and the coming of the Germanic tribes left education in the hands of the church.[2] There was little opportunity for education outside of the local parish schools and the larger monastic or cathedral schools. At the end of the Middle Ages, education was still very largely in the hands of the clergy. Most educated men, and therefore most teachers, were clergymen, and the relatively small numbers of educated laymen were themselves deeply influenced by clerical ideals. The church had a virtual monopoly on learning and literature. Throughout the Middle Ages it was taken for granted that an educated man was a clergyman. A prisoner who could read and write Latin was *ipso facto* taken for a clergyman and turned over to the church courts for trial. The modern term "clerk" (i.e., one who keeps records) is derived from "cleric," the medieval word for a clergyman.

_____
[2] See above, Chapters XIII-XIV, for educational and literary conditions before 1000.

Not only were the teachers "clerics," but most students were supposed to be candidates for some sort of a clerical career. There were, of course, exceptions. The parish schools were open to the general public, and young noblemen, after being trained at home in courtesy, hunting, riding, and warlike exercises, sometimes attended church schools. If they were physically weak or showed intellectual talents, they might be sent to a monastic or cathedral school to be trained for a clerical career. The clergy controlled the primary schools in which the parish priests taught children reading, writing, and the fundamentals of religion, including singing. As they grew older, those who had religious leanings might enter the inner training school of a cathedral or monastery; the others, if intelligent, could attend the outer, or day school. It seems probable that even in the earlier centuries a few of the larger towns had laymen's schools in which burghers' sons studied practical subjects of a secular nature. In the later Middle Ages, as town life became more prevalent, these municipal schools began to recover the position of importance that they had held in late imperial times.

THE LIBERAL ARTS CURRICULUM Until the late Middle Ages, however, the monastic and cathedral schools were the dominant centers of educational life. Although clerically controlled, they taught much more than religion. The curriculum comprised the seven liberal arts that had been taught in the time of Cicero, later in the time of Jerome, Augustine, and Cassiodorus, and still later at the court of Charles the Great. Even during the early Middle Ages these subjects had retained something of their classical and secular aspects. In *grammar,* the fourth- and fifth-century textbooks of Donatus, Priscian, and Martianus Capella were used, along with various works of earlier Roman writers. In *rhetoric* there were readings from classical as well as religious books, and exercises in writing poetry and prose. In *logic,* briefs of arguments were drawn up, and disputations held.[3]

Turning from the literary subjects of the trivium to the more scientific topics of the quadrivium, one is impressed by the narrow range of knowledge. In medieval *arithmetic* much was made of the mysterious significance of numbers, a tendency which medieval scholars seem to have inherited from the ancients. The Roman numerals were used exclusively until the introduction of Hindu-Arabic notation, somewhere about the tenth century. The complete decimal sys-

[3] See below, pp. 658 f.

tem, based on the use of the zero, was not common until much later.[4]
Students were taught various arithmetical formulas, and also the use
of the abacus, or counting board, for complicated calculations.[5] *Geometry,* which concerned itself chiefly with the measurement of land, followed in a crude way the ancient principles of Euclid.[6]

Astronomy was more highly developed. The problem of figuring the church calendar with its constantly shifting dates for Easter and the Lenten holy days necessitated careful training in the positions of the heavenly bodies. Like the ancients, from whom they got their information, teachers, even in the early Middle Ages, had some idea of eclipses, planets, fixed stars, and comets, and they believed that the earth was round.[7] An Anglo-Saxon manual of about the year 1000 reads as follows:

The heaven incloses in its bosom all the world, and it ever turns about us, swifter than any mill wheel, . . . It is all round and entire and studded with stars. . . . The sun is typical of our Savior, Christ, who is the sun of righteousness, as the bright stars are typical of the believers in God's congregation. . . . We speak of the new moon according to the custom of men, but the moon is always the same, though its light often varies. . . . It happens sometimes when the moon runs on the same track that the sun runs, that its orb intercepts the sun's so that the sun is all darkened.[8]

These quotations reveal a surprisingly accurate conception of certain facts, but they also indicate that medieval scholars had adopted the mistaken classical conception (formulated by Ptolemy in the second century) that the earth was the center of the universe. Medieval instructors also taught their students that somewhere inside the earth were the fires of hell and purgatory. Around the earth (so they thought, and so Dante pictured it later in his *Divine Comedy*) were the seven planetary spheres: the moon, Mercury, Venus, the sun,

---

[4] See above, p. 299. A thirteenth-century Italian wrote a treatise on the abacus in which the decimal system of numbering was described. Thenceforth Arabic numerals made headway, but very slowly.

[5] The Chinese still use a counting board that is based on the same principle.

[6] Our own fathers and grandfathers still studied Euclid, whose name was synonymous with geometry.

[7] Bede, in his encyclopedia *Concerning the Nature of Things,* shows a remarkably accurate knowledge of the irregularly convex surface of the earth. He wrote as follows: "We speak of the globe of the earth, not that it is perfectly round, owing to the inequalities of mountains and plains, but because if all its lines be considered it has the perfect form of a sphere."—Robinson, *Readings in European History,* I, 441.

[8] *Ibid.*

Mars, Jupiter, and finally Saturn. These seven spheres, each succeeding one larger than the last, revolved around the earth. The planet that happened to be in sight when one was born was supposed to exert an influence on his life.[9] According to medieval astronomy, beyond the seventh sphere were the fixed stars, classified in twelve sections according to the signs of the zodiac, which were also thought to have an influence on the human body.[10] Beyond the fixed stars was the abode of God.

Music, the fourth of the liberal arts of the quadrivium, was taught in two ways: as philosophical theory (after the fashion of Boethius), and as the practical science of chanting the church services.[11]

METHODS OF INSTRUCTION

Medieval methods of instruction seem to have been for the most part effective, though stern and often brutal. The manner in which the literary subjects of the trivium were presented, and also the amount of nonreligious material that was taught, can be gathered from the following description by a twelfth-century writer, John of Salisbury, who wrote of the methods used at Chartres by a famous master:

By citations from the [classical] authors he showed [his pupils] what was simple and fell under the ordinary rules: grammatical figures, rhetorical effects, and sophistic quibbles. He also pointed out the relationship of his subject to other studies. He did not teach everything in a single session, but in proportion to the capacity of his audience. . . . And realizing that memory is strengthened and the wits sharpened by practice, he urged the pupils, some by warnings, some by floggings, to imitate what they had heard. Everyone was required on the following day to recite some part of what he had heard the day preceding. The evening drill, which was called *declension,* was packed with grammar. . . . To certain of the boys . . . he assigned the [classical] poets or orators and bade them imitate their example. . . . But if anyone, in order to make his own work better, borrowed the [literary] cloak of another, he was reproved for the theft, but usually was not punished. Bernard gently pointed out to the awkward borrowers that anyone who imitated the ancients would himself become worthy of imitation. . . . He admonished them to go through the histories and poems diligently, and to memorize passages daily. . . . He advised them to confine themselves to the works of distinguished

---

[9] The study of such influences, still called astrology, has never died out. Many intelligent people of our day rely on private horoscopic readings or on printed astrological horoscopes such as are sold by the thousands in American five-and-ten-cent stores.

[10] Modern almanacs still show these same zodiacal signs, along with the portions of the body which they are supposed to control.

[11] See above, p. 314, concerning Boethius, and pp. 306 f., concerning chanting.

authors. . . . Daily his pupils wrote both prose and poetry, and tested themselves in discussions.[12]

Apparently at Chartres, which was one of the best liberal arts schools of the time, literary subjects were presented much as they are in modern universities, by lectures, review quizzes, written exercises, and outside reading. It is interesting to note that the lecture system—which was an absolute necessity in the Middle Ages, due to the lack of printed textbooks—was supplemented by individual exercises of various kinds on the part of the student. As in the earlier Middle Ages,[13] it seems that flogging was common. Many contemporary illustrations of medieval school life show the teacher brandishing a bundle of switches, or actually beating a wayward or backward pupil.

Most of the descriptions that have come down to us from medieval times suggest that students, whether from the fear of punishment, or from the love of learning, applied themselves to their studies. The variety of their activities, particularly in the nonliterary subjects, is illustrated in the following description of the things a visitor might see in a typical twelfth-century schoolroom:

There is a great crowd, of all ages, boys and youths, men both young and old. They are studying various subjects. Some are exercising their untrained tongues on the alphabet and on words that are new to them. Others listen to the inflection, composition, and derivation of words; then by reciting and repeating them, they try to memorize. Others furrow [i.e., write on] waxen tablets with the *stylus*. Others, guiding the pen with practiced hand, draw figures of various shapes and colors on parchment. Still others dispute zealously on grave matters, endeavoring to trip one another by mental gymnastics. I see some students making calculations, and others producing various sounds on a cord stretched on a frame. Others explain and demonstrate geometrical figures. Others, with various instruments, show the positions and courses of the stars and the movements of the heavens. Others consider the nature of the planets, the constitution of human beings, and the properties of things.[14]

The diligence with which some students attacked their tasks is illustrated by the following account from the same century:

I practiced memorizing the names of everything I saw or heard of. . . . Daily I examined my notes on topics so that I might retain every proposition, with the questions, objections, and solutions. I informed myself

---

[12] Adapted from translation in Taylor, *The Medieval Mind*, II, 157 f. This and the succeeding quotations from this work are by permission of The Macmillan Company.

[13] See above, p. 298.

[14] Adapted from translation in Taylor, *op. cit.*, II, 137 f.

as to the arguments on both sides of discussions, carefully differentiating the functions of Rhetoric, Oratory, and Sophistry. I set problems in arithmetic. I drew [geometrical] figures on the pavement with charcoal, and with the figure before me demonstrated the different aspects of the obtuse, acute, and right angle, and also of the square. Often I watched out the nocturnal horoscope [i.e., movements of the stars] through the winter nights. Often I strung my harp so as to detect the different sounds and also to delight my mind with the sweet notes.[15]

CLASSICAL
INFLUENCES
Among the texts and reference books used in teaching these subjects, the ancient Roman classics were outstanding. They were used in spite of the opposition of pious conservatives to the writings of non-Christians. A learned clergyman of the twelfth century, writing of the books that he had used as a student, said:

> Our youth was spent in studying rules of grammar, analogies, barbarisms, solecisms, and tropes by means of [the writings of] Donatus, Priscian, and Bede. . . . Quintilian, Caesar, and Cicero urged youths to study grammar. Why condemn the writings of the ancients? It is written that "in the ancients is learning": Jerome gloried in having read Origen; Horace boasted of reading Homer over and over. As a little fellow when I was studying how to write poetry, I profited much from my teacher's advice and read from truthful histories rather than from fables. . . . Besides other well-known books [of history], I kept company with Trogus Pompeius, Josephus, Suetonius, Hegesippus, Quintus Curtius, Tacitus, and Livy, all of whom put into their histories much that makes for moral edification and the advancement of liberal science. And I read many other books which had nothing to do with history. . . .[16]

Thus it seems that, in the process of studying the literary and scientific subjects of the trivium and quadrivium, medieval students often acquired a knowledge of many of the Latin classics. Early in the eleventh century, Bishop Fulbert of Chartres, following in the footsteps of his former master, Gerbert of Rheims, trained young clergymen not only in theology but also in the classical theories of mathematics, music, and medicine. By the end of the twelfth century, Chartres, and also near-by Orleans, had become famous for their emphasis on the classics in the study of the liberal arts. Their libraries were well stocked with the works of most of the famous Roman writers. Professors and students read, cited, and quoted the classics as constantly

[15] Adapted from translation in *ibid.*, II, 89.
[16] Adapted from translation in *ibid.*, II, 160.

and easily as the Scriptures. Thus, in the opinion of some of their contemporaries, they risked the salvation of their souls. As one of the more conservative educators expressed it: How was the soul to profit from the reading of Homer concerning the strife of Hector, or the philosophy of Plato, or the poems of Vergil and Ovid? "All of these are now gnashing their teeth in Hell." The answer to this question was given by a classicist of the same period who asserted that "although dogs may bark and pigs may grunt, I shall always follow the writings of the ancients." The study of the classics flourished, particularly in humanistic centers such as Chartres.

Our best example of the classically trained student of this period is John of Salisbury (d. 1180), English-born, a student at many a Continental school (he attended Abelard's classes at Paris), and finally teacher and bishop at Chartres. He was by all odds the best educated man of his day. So far as the classics are concerned, it has been said that his writings "would have done credit to a humanist of the days of Cosimo and Lorenzo de' Medici." [17] Like the famous Petrarch in Italy over a century later, John believed that "the [classical] poets, historians, orators, and mathematicians should be read, for without them men cannot be literate." Furthermore, like Gerbert of Rheims two centuries earlier, John knew "the consolation of the classics." "They banish the irksomeness of time and place," he wrote. "They provide solace in grief, recreation in labor, cheer amidst poverty, and modesty amidst riches. . . . [By them] the soul is redeemed from its vices, and even in adversity, is refreshed. . . . In human life one finds no more pleasing or useful employment, unless perchance it be the devotion inspired by prayer." [18]

Men such as John, and schools such as Chartres and Orleans, set a high ideal of broad-minded humanistic education in the twelfth century. In the educational centers directed by them, the great Latin writers were known, and most of their works were appreciatively read. Of the poets, Vergil was the most popular; then Ovid (even his *Art of Love*), Horace, and Lucan, in the order named. The prose writings of Cicero, Seneca, Sallust, and Juvenal were also read, quoted, and extensively imitated. If the professors of these medieval schools had had their way, Western Europe would have had a system of education like that of the humanist successors of Petrarch.[19] As it

[17] See below, pp. 696 ff.
[18] Adapted from translation in Taylor, *op. cit.*, II, 140 f.
[19] See below, pp. 700 f.

was, they laid on a broad cultural background of classical as well as
of Christian literature and learning.

THE RISE OF
PROFESSIONAL
SCHOOLS

But then, as now, liberal arts courses and the "humanities" were pushed into the background.[20] Unfortunately for the humanistic schools, their educational aims were less appreciated than those of the
Parisian schools of Abelard's day where logic and rationalistic theology reigned supreme, or of professional schools of law and medicine,
such as Bologna and Salerno. Outside of Orleans, Chartres, and a few
other such centers, most educators specialized in more practical subjects such as logic, theology, law, medicine, and business rhetoric. As
a result, the classics were soon left far behind in the school curriculums.

The trend toward specialized studies was accompanied by such a
great increase in student attendance that, by the end of the twelfth
century, the larger cathedral schools had outgrown their earlier organization and curriculums. The outcome was the rise of universities.

THE RISE OF UNIVERSITIES

THE MEANING
OF "UNIVERSITY"

What we refer to as the medieval university was
usually merely (1) an enlarged cathedral school,
with (2) specialized faculties and (3) a corporate organization. The word *university* comes from *universitas,* which meant
an incorporated organization. Even a craft guild might be referred
to as a *universitas.* The three changes mentioned came about simultaneously during the late twelfth and early thirteenth centuries, along
with the rapid increase in students and teachers. This occurred at
many old educational centers such as Bologna and Salerno in Italy,
Montpellier and Paris in France, and at a few new foundations such
as Oxford and Cambridge in England. For a typical case we turn to
the University of Paris.

THE UNIVERSITY
OF PARIS

During the twelfth century the increase in students
and teachers at Paris led to the establishment of a
studium generale (the common medieval term for
university). This was an enlarged school to which students came from
any country to study not only the liberal arts but also special professional subjects, such as theology and logic. In reality the University of
Paris was a *studium generale* that came into being as a result of

---

[20] "Humanities" and "humanism" are terms used of the study of the ancient
classics, because of their "humanizing" influences. See below, pp. 696 ff.

the growth of the cathedral school of Notre Dame. This school expanded so rapidly that before the end of the twelfth century the masters (i.e., the teachers or professors) formed a teachers' guild for the protection of their interests and the regulation of educational affairs. This organization gained control of the licensing of new teachers (which eventually became the granting of degrees), the disciplining of students, the admission of new masters, and other administrative duties usually handled by the cathedral officials. Thus an educational corporation came into being. The dates usually given for the beginning of the University (1200 and 1215) are merely the dates of the earliest known documents in which King Philip II and Pope Innocent III gave formal recognition to an already existing organization.

DEANS, DEGREES, AND LECTURES — The thirteenth century saw the rise of administrative machinery similar to that of most modern universities. There were, at Paris, a chancellor (president), deacons (deans), separate faculties (for the liberal arts, theology, and so on), examinations, degrees, caps and gowns. A young man, after a few years of study, might become a bachelor of arts. This gave him the privilege of part-time teaching while he continued to study for the master's degree, which made him a full-fledged member of the teaching guild and entitled to be called master or doctor (i.e., teacher).

Buildings were much less important than in modern universities. The student merely registered with the master under whom he wished to study, and attended lectures. Lectures were given wherever the master could find a place to give them, and in much the same manner as in the earlier cathedral or monastic schools. From a high lectern, or reading pulpit, he read and commented on the textbook, of which often he had the only copy available. The students, seated on benches, or perhaps on piles of straw, listened and scribbled notes on wax tablets. Later, if they could afford parchment, these notes were written down in ink; by this means one could acquire a valuable annotated text of his own to use when he set himself up as a teacher. There were also discussions or disputations similar to the quiz section in a modern university course, except for the fact that it was a livelier affair. Concerning disputations, a medieval professor said: "It is more advantageous than reading because it clears up doubts. Nothing is known perfectly which has not been masticated by the teeth of disputation."

COLLEGES AND
STUDENT LIFE
Students lived wherever they could find lodgings, for there were no dormitories. In the thirteenth century wealthy men and monastic orders began to provide rooming houses for worthy students. One of these, established at Paris by Robert Sorbon, became the famous Sorbonne College of the University of Paris. Students also associated themselves into "nations," but they had no organized social or athletic life. They boarded and roomed in all sorts of places, they complained about prices of lodgings, they drank, fought, and quarreled with one another and with the town hoodlums. They might stage a student strike or leave town en masse in protest against the arrest or wounding of a fellow student or the high cost of living. It was a student migration from Oxford that led to the foundation of Cambridge University in 1209. In general students seem to have been a rather rough lot. One writer said of them: "They seek theology at Paris, law at Bologna, and medicine at Montpellier, but nowhere a life that is pleasing to God."

ABELARD AT
PARIS: ELOISE
The rise of the University of Paris, the subjects taught, and the methods of instruction are excellently illustrated in the career of Peter Abelard (d. 1142), a young Breton noble who was attracted to Paris by the fame of her teachers. His brilliantly clever mind and restless personality soon tired of the dull lectures of the Paris logicians. Since he studied under teachers who were bitter rivals, he developed an unusually critical attitude. He openly criticized one of them, and when challenged to prove his case, started classes of his own to which students flocked in large numbers. When driven out by the jealous professors he went elsewhere, took up the study of theology, and eventually returned to Paris to teach. At this time, since there was no university organization, anyone who could get accommodations and students might set himself up as a teacher. Abelard's lectures were so keen and penetrating that he soon had a large following.

Then he fell in love with Eloise, a beautiful and intelligent young girl, niece of a prominent Parisian clergyman. While employed as her private tutor Abelard seduced her, as a result of which the revengeful uncle had him captured and mutilated. Thus the famous love affair of Eloise and Abelard ended in tragedy. She retired to a nunnery and he to a monastery, where he continued to teach and write. Their love life can be traced in Abelard's autobiography and in the letters in which Eloise years later poured forth the yearnings and pent-up bitterness of her soul.

Abelard's intellectual qualities are illustrated by his *Sic et Non,* a book in which he set forth various theological problems with quoted arguments, both pro and con, taken from the Bible and the clerical authorities. Its purpose was to encourage the student to put his beliefs to the test and by sincere doubts to work out a firm rational basis for religious faith. For this reason it was as popular with Abelard's students as it was hated by conservative theologians. Fundamentally, Abelard was an orthodox churchman; he specifically exempted the Bible from criticism. But his tactlessness led him into a violent controversy with the great monastic preacher, St. Bernard, and after being tried for heresy he was forced to retire from active teaching.

From the standpoint of university life, Abelard exemplifies the drawing power of the Parisian schools, the unorganized educational institutions of the earlier days, and the tendency toward specialization in logic and theology. To Paris, the queen city of theology, masters and students flocked from all regions. This hastened the development of the more highly organized form of education which we have described under the name university.

SCHOLASTICISM During the period in which the University of Paris and other theological schools were developing their administrative organizations, the subjects of study underwent great changes. The rational approach to religious problems, which was popularized by Abelard, tended to revolutionize the study of theology. Eventually the rules of ancient Greek logic, as expounded by Aristotle, reigned supreme and under their influence theology became a profound and intricate subject.

Meanwhile many churchmen felt that religion was losing itself in a morass of rationalistic philosophy. Aristotelian logic seems to have had an influence on medieval theology that is comparable to that of Darwinian evolution on religious thought in modern America. At any rate the varying views and the keen logical subtlety with which intricate points were argued speak well for the mental training given at schools such as Paris.

The conservatives (who were called "realists" in the Middle Ages) took the Platonic or Neoplatonic point of view and insisted on the *reality* of all general ideas (they called them "universals"). In their opinion redness, goodness, and other such qualities really existed by themselves. Their rationalistic opponents, who asserted that general ideas were merely *names,* were called "nominalists." They tended to the more factual Aristotelian philosophy which stressed the importance of individual tangible things. For instance, they insisted that redness or goodness could exist only as a characteristic of some individual person or thing.

Trouble developed when the nominalists insisted that the Trinity, the Church, right, wrong, and other such eternal verities, were merely names and had no actual reality in themselves. In desperation many conservatives sought to avoid all discussion on topics of this kind which threatened to upset the theological ideas of the past. Their solution was to reject anything which conflicted with the beliefs of the Fathers. To them, faith was the solution for all religious problems. Of this opinion were the energetic mystic, St. Bernard, Anselm of Canterbury, whose motto was "I believe in order that I may understand," and Hugh of St. Victor, who preferred to rely on divine revelation rather than on human reason.

But most university men were not satisfied by this solution. They followed the lines that had been laid down by Boethius, John the Scot, and Abelard. In temperament and mental approach, most of the men of the universities were anxious to probe their doubts, to put theological dogmas to the test of reason, and to re-establish their beliefs, if necessary, on solid logical foundations. They insisted on examining contradictions in the Scriptures and the writings of the Church Fathers [21] in order to reconcile them. In the mobilization and analysis of opinions they developed remarkable patience, keenness, and ingenuity. The inspiration and method for much of this procedure came from Aristotle's works on logic. His writings, some of which had been known in the West since the time of Boethius, now became so popular that they were quoted and praised almost as much as the Bible, and for a time the church authorities prohibited their use in the universities. But the tide could not be stopped. This application of Aristotelian logic to theological problems, which became the common "method of the university—or school-men," was called scholasticism.

[21] The leading Church Fathers were Augustine, Ambrose, Jerome, and Pope Gregory I.

PETER LOM-
BARD'S SEN-
TENCES

Since intelligent men could not be compelled to turn their backs on Aristotelian reason and to accept theological dogma in blind faith, the church, as in so many crises, took a middle-ground position. It made the decision, which was in keeping with the opinions of John the Scot, Abelard, and other liberal theologians, that faith and reason, piety and intelligence, religion and logic were allies and not enemies. As time went on the rationalistic attitude came into general favor. This was due in part to Peter Lombard's *Sentences,* which has been called one of the most successful textbooks the world has ever seen. Following in Abelard's footsteps, he published a book of apparently contradictory opinions on theological problems. But it was so well organized and had such diplomatically worded solutions that it satisfied all types of educators and became the favorite medieval textbook of theology.

ALBERTUS
MAGNUS

Meanwhile the appearance in the West of Aristotle's complete works (translated from the Arabic) gave the theologians additional material to reconcile with Christian doctrine. In the thirteenth century Albertus Magnus and Thomas Aquinas completed this difficult task to the satisfaction of the most exacting clerical minds. Each of them compiled an immense *summa,* or summary of theology, in which the new Aristotelian science was harmonized with Christianity, and the old Christian faith harmonized with Aristotelian logic. The fundamental beliefs of orthodox Christianity were presented in such a detailed and convincing manner that reason was reconciled with faith.

At the same time the newly acquired information from Aristotle on other subjects was introduced. Albertus Magnus wrote commentaries on Aristotle's treatises concerning physics, the universe, heaven and earth, the elements and the planets, the soul, and meteors. He also compiled works on geography, botany, and zoology, incorporating therein much of the new scientific knowledge of the Moslems. More impressive than the array of subjects concerning which Albertus wrote, is his scientific attitude. He held that God ruled the universe but by natural means. As for himself, he constantly tested what he read by observation and reason, rejecting many statements of classical authorities because they failed to tally with his own experience. He refused to believe that ostriches ate iron, because they would not eat it when he offered it to them. No less interesting is the fact that this same scholastic professor who harmonized religion and science, succeeded in his own life in combining surpassing scholarship with the official activities of the church. He was an officer of the Dominican order and bishop of the great German diocese of Regensburg.

THOMAS
AQUINAS

Albertus' pupil, Thomas Aquinas, brought into a grand synthesis much of the material that his master had worked out in detail. His *Summa Theologica* was a tremendous work of painstaking research and penetrating analysis. In a recent English translation it comprises some twenty stout volumes which deal with every conceivable aspect, not only of God, but also of man and the universe. It was a marvelous combination of Greek science and medieval religion, of profound reasoning and orthodoxy. So satisfying was this great theological and scientific encyclopedia to Roman Catholic thinkers that the learned author was canonized, and is now ranked even above St. Augustine as the greatest of all theologians. By his intellectual labors the Christian faith, badly shaken by Abelardian doubt and Aristotelian rationalism, was re-established on a firm logical foundation.

Thus scholasticism, as exemplified particularly by the logicians and theologians of the University of Paris, gave to the Roman Catholic world an intelligent religious interpretation of knowledge. Its major weakness lay in its attempt to handle all questions by abstract reasoning, in total disregard of observation as a means of arriving at truth. This put a premium on discussion, which tended to run to minutely detailed arguments on points that seem absurd to moderns. To that age, however, such methods promised a reasonable solution for the fundamental problems of church, state, and of all human society. It is not strange, then, that by the end of the thirteenth century, Paris, with its special faculty of theology, was the largest and most influential university in Western Europe. It drew students and masters from all countries and in turn sent its graduates to all parts of the West. Due largely to its influence, logic and theology—the twin sisters of scholasticism—dominated thirteenth-century intellectual life. Even under the assaults of professors, scientists, and humanists during the fourteenth century,[22] scholasticism continued until well into the modern era.

22 See below, pp. 674 ff.

THE UNIVERSITY
OF BOLOGNA

The University of Bologna was as influential in the study of law as Paris was in theology. Early in the twelfth century, law students had begun to flock to this city to study with Irnerius, a famous teacher of the Justinian Code and other aspects of Roman law.[23] The increased interest in Roman law seems to have been due to several influences. By the beginning of the twelfth century commercial and industrial life was flourishing in Italy as nowhere else in the West. This was particularly true of the northern part of the peninsula. Naturally civil law was of great importance to the secularly minded people of this region. Another factor that contributed to the study of civil law was the demand, at the courts of ambitious monarchs such as Frederick Barbarossa, for trained lawyers who were familiar with the legal ideas of imperial Rome. These ideas suited their programs of strong royal government. Twelfth-century Bologna became a center as popular for law students as Paris was for theologians.

Like most of the Italian universities, Bologna was much freer from the domination of the church than were the northern schools. This is exemplified in its unusual type of administrative organization. The law students of Bologna, being mature and energetic men, formed effective associations by means of which they were able to control the prices of food and lodgings and reduce other educational expenses to a minimum. Eventually they evolved a student government association which controlled even the professors. At Bologna, the student guild was the university. The students determined the hours of lectures, fees, professorial absences, and the like. The following excerpt from the regulations illustrates the extent to which this was carried.

We have decreed also that all teachers actually lecturing must read the comments immediately after reading the text of the law, unless the continuity of the laws requires otherwise. . . . They must not yield to the clamor of the students for those portions that are not to be read. . . . If any teacher fails to reach any section [of the material to be covered] on the date specified, he shall be fined 3 pounds; for a second offense 5, and for each succeeding violation, 10 pounds. . . . No teacher shall do more than one section per lecture . . . on penalty of 3 pounds fine for perjury. . . . At the end of each section they must announce what section they will take up next. . . . If it seems wise to transfer a part of a lecture to an-

---

[23] See above, p. 148, concerning the formation of the Justinian Code. For five centuries (600-1100) it had been little used in the West.

other section it must be announced to the students in the preceding lecture so that those who wish may make provision beforehand [penalty, 5 shilling fine]. . . . No teacher shall omit any chapter, paragraph, or law in a section [of the text]. . . . No law or difficult paragraph shall be reserved to the end of the lecture if this is likely to prevent a prompt exit at the sound of the bell.[24]

At Bologna, as at other law schools, there were two divisions of study. Canon or church law was usually taught from Gratian's *Decretum,* a twelfth-century codification of the regulations of the church. More important was the Roman civil law, which was taught from the Justinian Code. During the twelfth and thirteenth centuries there was a great demand for lawyers in both church and state, and legal studies expanded rapidly. Some students took both kinds of law and were given the degree of LL.D. (Doctor of Laws) or J.U.D., *Juris Utriusque Doctor* (Doctor of Both Laws).

SALERNO, PADUA, MONTPELLIER

The third of the professions which gave rise to specialized university study was medicine. Salerno in southern Italy, known since Roman times for its healing waters and learned doctors, became a famous center of study in the late eleventh century when one of its professors, Constantine the African, translated from Arabic into Latin many hitherto unknown medical works. As a result, the twelfth century saw a great expansion of this school. In the thirteenth century it was rivaled by the University of Naples, founded by Frederick II, and also by the University of Padua in Lombardy. Meanwhile, in southern France, Montpellier had become famous.

In these schools the classical works of Hippocrates, Dioscorides, and Galen were still fundamental. To them, however, had been added some of the medical science of the Arabs and of other medieval physicians. But, like law and theology, medicine relied almost entirely on the classical and religious authorities of the past, and for a long time observation and experimentation were neglected. It was left for the nonuniversity men of later centuries to furnish the progressive impulses that led to modern scientific medicine.

UNIVERSITY CONSERVATISM

During the fourteenth and fifteenth centuries, most of the universities stubbornly withstood the efforts of those who advocated progressive ideas. Lectures from antiquated authorities and the endless quibblings of logical

[24] Adapted from Norton, *Readings in the History of Education: Mediaeval Universities,* pp. 112 ff., by permission of the Harvard University Press.

discussions tended to check efforts at the discovery of new truths. Like its descendant, the modern interscholastic debate, the medieval disputation tended to become a contest in mental gymnastics which often obscured rather than clarified the truth. A Spanish scholar of the early sixteenth century asserted that

disputations have blinded judgment. They were originally instituted, but only for the young, to stimulate mental vigor and to make youths keener in their studies. . . . But . . . a base desire for distinction took possession of the minds of the disputants, and, just as in a battle, victory came to be the chief consideration, rather than the elucidation of the truth. . . . Boys began disputing as soon as they were born and ceased only at death.[25]

Antischolastic theologians, experimental scientists, and humanistic classicists found it impossible to effect much improvement in the old-fashioned curriculum and educational methods. In only a few of the new universities were such tendencies encouraged. The humanistic spirit found readier acceptance in some of the lower schools: notably those established by the remarkable Italian teacher, Vittorino de Feltre at Mantua, by the Brethren of the Common Life at Deventer in the Netherlands, and by John Colet at St. Paul's in London. In a few universities there were professorships of Greek and even of Hebrew. The University of Florence actually established a professorship in the literature of Dante in 1373. For the most part, however, the humanists and creative scientists were compelled to work and teach outside the cloistered halls of the universities.

SCIENCE DURING THE LATE MIDDLE AGES

RELIANCE ON PAST KNOWLEDGE

Medieval progress in science seems to have been slower and more bitterly opposed than any other phase of nonreligious learning. The scientific knowledge of medieval scholars seems to us moderns very scanty and inaccurate. In the earlier centuries it consisted merely of the condensed scraps of classical information, magic, and religious mysticism that were taught in the subjects of the quadrivium (arithmetic, geometry, astronomy, and music). Even the most learned teachers relied almost entirely on the information given in encyclopedias which were little more than outlines of science. These were

[25] Adapted from a passage by Juan Vives, quoted in Norton, *Readings,* p. 121 ff.

compiled by churchmen such as Cassiodorus, Isidore of Seville, and
Bede. Of such works, Professor Haskins has said:

their science, thin and barren, and often fantastic, carried on a bare
modicum of ancient learning to the mediaeval world. Based upon the
briefer manuals of the later Empire, this knowledge was by them further
condensed . . . and it was desiccated and often predigested in the
process.[26]

In the later Middle Ages better handbooks appeared. The thirteenth century had the great encyclopedia of Vincent of Beauvais,
and the *Summas* of Albertus Magnus and Thomas Aquinas, all of
which contained sections on science. Then there was an increasing
number of special handbooks devoted entirely to science. The Englishmen Adelard of Bath, Alexander Neckham, and Bartholomew
compiled popular books on natural science. Meanwhile Brunetto Latini
of Florence wrote *The Treasure House* (Trésor), a handbook of
miscellaneous information, in French [27] so that it could be read by
the average citizen. The chief drawback to science was not the lack
of books, but the reliance on books to the exclusion of all else.

SCIENTIFIC
INACCURACIES

The medieval encyclopedias were inaccurate and unprogressive. Due to the excessive reverence of the compilers for classical and religious authorities, they
tended to perpetuate many errors. From the Bible and the works
of Aristotle, Hippocrates, Galen, and Pliny, scholars had for centuries handed down without questions the most ludicrous statements.
Until the thirteenth century, for example, no one seems to have
thought of doubting the opinions of the great Aristotle. One Arabic
commentator said that no one since Aristotle's time had been able
to add to his information or to find any important errors in his
works. Such a credulous attitude encouraged the repetition from
century to century of old misconceptions. For instance, Aristotle had
written that "the weasel when it fights with a snake, first eats
wild rue, the smell of which is noxious to the snake." Fifteen centuries later, Bartholomew the Englishman was repeating this curious
information, as follows: "The weasel eateth rue and balmeth herself
with the juice thereof, and rages then on the cockatrice . . ." [28]

[26] Haskins, *The Renaissance of the Twelfth Century,* p. 279.
[27] It was written in French because the author was living in France at the
time; almost immediately an Italian version was published.
[28] For additional examples, including the myth of the salamander quench-
ing fire, see Barnes, *An Intellectual and Cultural History of the Western World,*
p. 431.

Many another superstition which is considered as typically medieval came originally from Aristotle, Pliny, or some other classical writer. Like their classical predecessors, most medieval scholars believed in magic, the mysterious influence of numbers, of dreams, witches, and the weird concoctions of alchemists.

But medieval science was more plagued by Christian theology than by classical errors. The clerical tendency to allegorize or moralize continually beclouded scientific fact. An extreme example of this influence is found in the encyclopedia compiled by Bishop Rabanus Maurus in the ninth century, who copied entire sections from Isidore, adding to each the moral that he thought proper. For instance, after quoting Isidore's excerpts from certain classical authors on the various kinds of leprosy, he added the pious warning that red leprosy is like a virulent heresy. The same sort of thing crops out constantly in one of the later scientific handbooks called *Physiologus*. One section reads as follows:

> The Lion has three characteristics; as he walks or runs he brushes his footprints with his tail, so that hunters may not track him. This signifies the secrecy of the Incarnation. . . . Secondly, the Lion sleeps with his eyes open; so slept the body of Christ upon the Cross. . . . Thirdly, the lioness brings forth her cub dead; on the third day the father comes and roars in its face, and wakes it to life. This signifies our Lord's resurrection on the third day.[29]

Even great thinkers such as the theologian Thomas Aquinas and the poet Dante accepted without question the antiquated scientific ideas of bygone times. Long after the end of the Middle Ages, science continued to be dominated by the inaccuracies and dogmatism of people who clung to the old religious and classical interpretations of science. Worse than this was the direct opposition of the clergy to new scientific ideas. Faith healing at saints' shrines by means of relics, holy oil, and the like impeded medical science. Magical incantations and soothsaying were prevalent among all classes. For centuries conservatives retarded anatomical experimentation by opposing the dissection of human bodies. As late as the thirteenth century, at the University of Toulouse, one corpse a year was allowed for dissection. So far as astronomy was concerned, even as late as the seventeenth century the clergy, Protestant as well as Catholic, bitterly opposed the Copernican theory of the universe as propounded by Galileo. Less hostile but equally fatal to scientific progress was the profes-

[29] Translation from Taylor, *The Medieval Mind*, I, 76.

sorial emphasis on logic. Aristotelian reasoning was such a fascinating activity that it tended to discourage scientific investigation and the drudgery of fact finding.

SCIENTIFIC PROGRESS

There were, however, some progressive influences, even in the early Middle Ages. Arabian science seems everywhere to have stirred independent thinkers to action. Gerbert of Rheims in the tenth century learned much in the Moslem schools of Spain. He and his contemporaries knew of Hindu-Arabic numerals and taught the West the use of the abacus or counting board. He also had "geometrical diagrams," "star-gazing tubes" for astronomical observations,[30] and a mechanical apparatus to show the positions and movements of the heavenly bodies.[31] Above all else, Gerbert had that inquisitive spirit that is characteristic of advanced science whatever the time or place. A century later, in southern Italy, Constantine the African of Salerno was translating Greek and Arabic medical works into Latin. By the twelfth century, Salerno and other medical schools were using the Arabic medical works of Rasis, Averroes, and Avicenna. In Norman Sicily, too, the scholars of King Roger II's court [32] were making available to Westerners the accumulated classical knowledge of the East and the scientific information of the Arabs.

OBSERVATION AND EXPERIMENT

The West acquired something more valuable than books from the Arabs. The contact with new ideas and people stirred the curiosity of Christian scholars in a way that led to that most important of scientific qualities—observation and experiment. The most remarkable instance is that of Adelard of Bath, a twelfth-century Englishman who revolutionized scientific ideas even more completely than his contemporary, Abelard of Paris, upset the ideas of the theologians. Adelard traveled in Moslem lands, interviewing great scholars, translating mathematical works, and investigating all sorts of natural phenomena.

Migration of this sort soon became common among scholars. Converted Jews from Spain came north, and Christian scholars went south to study the new sciences in Moslem universities. One of the most important of these wanderers was Gerard of Cremona, who settled in Spain and translated ninety or more classical and Arabic works on mathematics, astronomy, and medicine. Soon Western Europe had

[30] These were *not* telescopes with lenses.
[31] See above, p. 299.
[32] See above, p. 397.

acquired not only many hitherto unknown works of classical writers but also a mass of Arabic science. The entire geometry of Euclid, algebra as perfected by such men as Omar Khayyám,[33] trigonometry (a study which seems to have been invented by the Arabs), and such practical instruments as the compass and astrolabe became available.

THIRTEENTH-CENTURY SCIENCE
The thirteenth century marks a high point in the progress of Western science. By this time Europe had assimilated much of classical, Christian, and Arabic science. Furthermore the advancing intellectual life of cities and universities was stimulating a spirit of critical inquiry. In southern Italy and Sicily, at the court of Frederick II, a cosmopolitan center of cultural life, the new science of observation and experimentation was encouraged. Here—so it was said—at the young emperor's command, the eyes of vultures were covered up to determine whether they found their food by smell or sight. Barnacles were imported from the north to test the legend that barnacled geese could be hatched from them. At one time two criminals were killed and cut open to see whether one (who had exercised violently after eating) had digested his food better than the other (who had rested). Questionnaires were sent out in order to get information from scholars in distant lands. Frederick himself set a remarkable example by writing a book on falconry, compiled by careful investigation of all phases of bird lore, and beautifully illustrated. Still more important was his critically scientific attitude toward older authorities. He dared to criticize and correct even the ideas of the great Aristotle. Frederick is thought to have been the first king to restrict the unintelligent practice of medicine by licensing trained physicians.

ROGER BACON
The thirteenth century is also the century of the English monk, Roger Bacon, much-heralded exponent of the modern scientific method of inductive thinking. Bacon's reputation as a scientist, however, rests on his zeal and appreciation for what others were doing, or for what might be done, rather than on his own actual accomplishments. It was, for instance, his teacher, Bishop Robert Grosseteste, who was responsible for the chief arguments he used against the reliance of the scholastics on logic, Aristotle, and other past authorities. Bacon's real contribution was the elucidation and emphasis of the values of the experimental or in-

---

[33] Omar Khayyám was a Moslem scholar and poet of the Persian court, author of the famous *Rubáiyát*.

ductive method. He was a vigorous propagandist of much-needed reforms in educational methods. But he was neither the originator
of the idea nor did he succeed in carrying it out. Like many other
men of his day he criticized hidebound conservatism and loudly
applauded the new science of observation and experiment which only
a few men were actually practicing. Aside from compiling a Greek
grammar, Bacon himself did little scientific work, for his major interest was theology. He did, however, make a startlingly accurate
prophecy of the wonderful things that could be accomplished by real
scientists when he wrote the following lines:

I will now enumerate the marvelous results of art [science] and
nature which will make all kinds of magic appear trivial and unworthy.
. . . Great vessels, both in rivers and on the sea, shall be borne about with
only a single man to guide them and with greater speed than if they were
full of men [rowers]. And carriages can be constructed to move without
animals to draw them . . . machines for flying . . . [and] bridges can be
constructed ingeniously so as to span rivers without any supports. . . .[34]

Bacon also gave generous praise to scientists such as Robert
Grosseteste, and especially to one whom he considered an ideal scientist. This unknown and unheralded scholar was the quiet, hard-working Peter of Maricourt, who seems to have investigated every sort of
phenomena. According to Bacon:

Through experiment he gains knowledge of natural things, medical,
chemical, indeed of everything in the heavens and on earth. . . . For the
last three years he has been working at the invention of a mirror which
should produce combustion at a fixed distance, and he will, with God's
aid, soon reach his end.[35]

SCIENTIFIC
PROGRESS

Although Bacon's hopes for science were not fully
realized, the ensuing period (the fourteenth and fifteenth centuries) made considerable progress. There
were noteworthy advances in scientific theory, especially at the universities of Paris and Oxford, where nominalist philosophers were
emphasizing the importance of the external world of tangible things.
In physics and mathematics progress was made by such men as Albert
of Saxony, Nicholas of Cusa, Nicholas of Oresme, John Buridan, and
Richard Suiseth. Ideas were propounded which anticipated the laws

[34] Translation from Robinson, *Readings,* I, 461, by permission of Ginn and Company.
[35] *Ibid.*

of falling bodies, the heliocentric theory, and various other scientific discoveries of early modern times. Late in the fifteenth century a German experimenter, Regiomontanus, worked out a scientific method of mathematical computation that paved the way for the development of trigonometry and higher mathematics.

In the more practical fields of science, improvements were made in surgery, map making, methods and instruments of navigation, and the manufacture of clocks, gunpowder, and chemicals. There were, however, formidable obstacles to true science. Instruments of scientific accuracy and precise workmanship were lacking. Furthermore, theological dogma and the humanistic emphasis on the writings of classical antiquity diverted many able intellects from the rough path of scientific investigation. The Western world was not yet scientifically minded.

PAINTERS AND SCIENCE: DA VINCI

It has been asserted, and with considerable justice, that one of the real scientists of this period was the artist, Leonardo da Vinci. Like Gerbert of Rheims, Adelard of Bath, and Peter of Maricourt, he was a man possessed of an overpowering curiosity concerning the everyday things of the world about him. Furthermore, he was so versatile that, to quote a modern writer's opinion, "beside him Aristotle's was a single-track mind." Not content merely to work at painting, sculpture, and architecture, he planned innumerable engineering projects, and improved types of artillery, submarines, and flying machines. He experimented in mathematics, chemistry, and physics; and he expressed doubts as to the time-honored theory of the earth as the center of the universe. He understood the nature of fossils, and not only classified plants but made accurate sketches of leaves, stalks, and veins. Like other artists of the fifteenth century, da Vinci is thought to have understood human anatomy better than most professional physicians. His sketchbooks contain marvelously exact studies of muscles, tissues, bones, and even the structure of the human eye.

PRACTICAL SCIENTISTS

It was the practical lay mind that did most for fifteenth- and sixteenth-century science. Medieval alchemy was started on the road to becoming modern chemistry by men such as da Vinci and Paracelsus, a nonprofessional physician. Similarly it was the patient studies of a Polish priest, Copernicus (d. 1543), and his lay successors, Brahe, Kepler, and Galileo, that finally demolished the antiquated geocentric (earth-centered) theory and gave to the modern world the first of its new views of the universe. Another independent spirit, Giordano Bruno, who was burned at the stake by clerical authorities in 1600 for his "free thinking," at least hinted at the idea that the new heliocentric (sun-centered) view of the universe involved the concept of the relativity of motion, time, and space. Such men were the forerunners of our modern physicists.

It is also significant that the first great progress made in medicine was made by practical men of the sixteenth century who had turned their backs on the tomes of formal medical knowledge from the past, and who worked out the problems of medicine from their own observation and experience. Paré, for instance, said with pride, "I learned to treat gunshot wounds, but not from books." Paracelsus, physician and chemist, once made a public bonfire of the works of Galen and other classical writers that were still being taught in the medical schools. By such drastic means progressive scientists indicated their hatred of dogmatic scholarship and their determination to throw off the weight of both classical and theological tradition. Not until well into modern times was the victory won for progressive science.

THE SOCIAL SCIENCES   Like the *natural* sciences, the *social* sciences had no place in the curriculums of medieval universities. Nevertheless, men were greatly concerned over the nature, functions, and regulation of human society, and much was written on these subjects. As in other areas of thought, their ideas concerning government, economics, and history were much influenced by religious and classical authorities and by scholastic methods of reasoning. Thus what they wrote was not so much social *science* based on observation of the actualities of human life as it was social *theory* or *philosophy* of a rather abstract character. Nevertheless the opinions and conclusions of writers were colored to some extent by the existing conditions of life. Much of their writing was propaganda, produced by and for the controversies between conflicting authorities.

PAPAL THEOCRACY   During the early Middle Ages, while the Roman Empire and the Carolingian imperial tradition continued to be the supreme ideal of Westerners, theorists emphasized the unity of human society under one government. In this period, too, the clergy enjoyed a monopoly on learning. It is not surprising, therefore, that a theory of a united Christendom in which the church was the dominant power prevailed. Until late in the Middle Ages, political theorists held to the "City of God" ideal of Augustine, which pictured a human society dependent on the Christian Church and its clerical officials for salvation. This was the central theme of the histories written by Orosius, Gregory of Tours, Bede, and the other clergymen who monopolized the writing of history during the early centuries. Even as late as the time of Emperor Frederick the Red-Bearded, Bishop Otto of Freising compiled a world history (*The Two Cities*) in which he followed the pattern laid down by Augustine and contrasted the superiority of the "City of God" with the defects of the temporal "City of Man."

Political theory followed the same concept of dualistic unity. The ideal government was a unified Christendom in which church and state, led by pope and emperor, were supposed to co-operate in working out the destinies of mankind. The papacy and the Roman Catholic Church were divinely established for the control of *religious* life; the emperor and the Holy Roman Empire controlled temporal, or civil, affairs. But according to the clerical theorists, the church was the superior power because it had been divinely established for the purpose of redeeming man from the evil into which he had fallen by reason of Adam's original sin. The state, with its laws, judges, armies, and rulers, was a necessary evil which had been established to control the actions of sinful men. As such, it was inferior, and subordinate to the church, the clergy, and their official head the pope, who was God's representative on earth. Often the church was compared to the sun, and the state to the moon, which shines only by reason of the light reflected from the sun.

THE PAPALISTS VS. THE IMPE- RIALISTS
The Augustinian ideal might satisfy the popes and the clerical scholars, but it did not fit existing conditions. As a matter of fact, during the early Middle Ages the popes were seldom strong enough to control the emperors, kings, and feudal rulers. More often than not the popes and the clergy were the ruled rather than the rulers. This situation gave rise to new and conflicting theories of government. For one thing, there was no real unity in the West after Charles the Great and the rise of feudalism. During this period the chief controversy was over the relative powers of the popes and emperors. As we have seen,[36] their differences of opinion culminated in the "Investiture Struggle" and a series of conflicts between church

[36] See above, Chapters XIX-XX.

and state. Their constant rivalries gave rise to two schools of historical and political thought: the papalists, and the imperialists. Papalist propaganda, from Gregory VII and the *Dictatus* to the *Policraticus* of John of Salisbury, upheld the Augustinian ideal of the superiority of religion, the church, the clergy, and the papacy over all civil powers. In arguing for limitations on imperial authority, the papalists upheld *limited* monarchy. The kingship, they insisted, was the result of a compact by which the people as a whole delegated certain powers and duties to one of their number. Royal power was a trust, and if misused it might be revoked. They even went so far as to justify the assassination of oppressive or despotic kings.

The imperialists, on the other hand, emphasized the divine right of kings. From the Biblical accounts of the anointing of Saul and David, and from Christ's command to "render unto Caesar the things that are Caesar's," they argued that royal power was derived directly from God and was subject to no human limitations either from the clergy or the laity. On historical grounds, certain imperial theorists claimed that great emperors such as Constantine, Justinian, and Charles the Great had never been subject to the popes; in fact they had controlled the church and had considered themselves responsible to God for its welfare.

As time passed the imperialists gained strength. Frederick the Red-Bearded employed legalists trained in Roman imperial law to find additional arguments in favor of absolute royal power, unlimited by clergy or feudality. Frederick II of Naples and Sicily, in the course of his struggle with the popes, became a vigorous propagandist. He pictured the papacy as a huge octopus which threatened to strangle all types of civil government. He called on the national monarchs and lesser lay princes to join him and crush the papacy before it crushed them. But Frederick was ahead of his time; his warnings were unheeded, and with him the empire fell.

NEW POLITICAL
THEORIES

The next half century saw the rise of a new and more formidable opponent of the papal theocrats.[37] By the year 1300 the national monarchies of France and England had become strong enough to resist papal control. In the course of the struggle between Philip IV and Boniface VIII, the king employed able legalists and political theorists to defend his cause. William of Nogaret and Peter Dubois are the best known of those who asserted the right of kings to check papal encroachments and to control the church in their realms for the welfare of

[37] See above, Chapter XXVIII, for the details of this conflict.

Christian society. Dubois, in particular, suggested many reforms, all to be carried out by the civil power. Among these was a plan for international arbitration of disputes. Such ideas of government are but a hint of the strong undercurrent of nationalism in the West. As nationalism became prominent in religion it started a train of events which was destined to lead to the Protestant Revolt.

It is evident that, by the beginning of the fourteenth century, the church was not only losing its control over the laity, it was unable to maintain its authority over the clergy in distant lands. The decline of clerical influence was due to the disastrous results of the later crusades, the increasing worldliness of the clergy, the rise of national monarchies, and the rapid development of burgher ideals in the towns. Eventually the theorists were forced to adjust their concepts to the new conditions. During the thirteenth century, scholastic theologians such as Albertus Magnus and Thomas Aquinas had used Aristotelian materials and logic to prove the superiority of the church over the state. But, as time passed, their arguments had less and less effect. Dante, a layman but none the less a firm supporter of the scholastic system, came to the conclusion that the Italians must rely on the empire rather than the papacy to establish political unity and save the peninsula from anarchy. In his *De Monarchia,* he upheld the equal rights of church and state in Christian society, but supported the imperial claim of a divine origin of its power.

By the middle of the fourteenth century, radical thinkers had advanced a step further. Professors such as William of Ockham, Marsilius of Padua, and John Wiclif asserted the supremacy of the state. We have already discussed their assertions concerning the right and duty of the state to reform the church.[38] Some of them went so far as to justify the confiscation of clerical wealth.[39] In time, some of these theories found practical application. Marsilius' plan for the correction of wayward popes by means of church councils was put into practice early in the next century.[40] Led by Emperor Sigismund, the lay and clerical representatives of the various "nations" met in

[38] See above, Chapter XXVIII.

[39] In the twelfth century, when Arnold of Brescia advocated such reforms, he was branded as a dangerous heretic. Two centuries later, Peter Dubois in France and John Wiclif in England won the favor of rulers and people when they proposed similar measures.

[40] Marsilius' plan was a part of the democratic ideal (derived from Aristotle) to the effect that the royal power is delegated by the people to their ruler. If misused, it can be withdrawn. The theory was applied in the case of the papal rulers, because of the grave abuses they had committed. It was never seriously considered in civil government.

councils to solve the problems of a church which was unable to regulate itself, to say nothing of controlling the state. The age of the councils saw the complete discrediting of the Augustinian ideal of a church-controlled society.

Although the councils were ultimately vanquished by the papacy, they contributed an important advance in political theory. Organized after the fashion of the representative assemblies in most Western states, the councils attempted (with some temporary success) to apply the ideal of representative government in church affairs. The representative assemblies of England, France, and Spain were an outgrowth of the feudal practice of government based on contractual relations between lord and vassal. No lord, prince, king, or pope had a right to make changes in government without consultation and the consent of all concerned. From this there arose the custom of holding assemblies of representatives of the various classes of people. Such assemblies became permanent institutions in Spain in the twelfth century, in England in the thirteenth, and in France in the fourteenth century.[41] The fifteenth-century councils at Constance and Basel introduced this procedure into church administration. Lay and clerical representatives, organized by "nations" and employing the committee system for working out legislation, took control of church affairs.

For a time, it seemed that the church might become a constitutional monarchy and the pope a limited monarch. Unfortunately for the cause of representative government, the conciliar movement failed, and by the middle of the century the papacy was once more in complete control of the clerical administration. Meanwhile the trend of political development elsewhere was leading toward absolutism. By the year 1500, in England, France, the Spains, and throughout the Italies, despotism was well entrenched, and historians, legalists, and political theorists were glorifying it as the most practical and benevolent type of government.

This was the age in which keen materialistic historians and political scientists viewed government as an institution entirely divorced from the church, religion, and ethics. Machiavelli and Guicciardini analyzed the governments and rulers of their day in a coldly impartial manner. They had one major interest: the expounding of those methods of politics that brought success. With them the Augustinian ideal began to give way to the modern science of govern-

[41] See above, pp. 467 f., 486, 492.

ment. By the end of the Middle Ages many advanced ideas had been set forth: the social compact, the political contract, popular sovereignty in both church and state, the delegation of powers by the people to their monarchs, representative government, and materialistic doctrines such as the justification of self-interest in human affairs.

SOCIAL THEORIES Social and economic theory, no less than political science and history, followed the trend of actual conditions. As long as the rural economy and religious faith of the early Middle Ages were predominant, theorists conceived of Christendom as a simple organization, operated primarily in the interests of the salvation of man's soul. So far as material things were concerned mere subsistence was sufficient. Human society was often compared to the bodily organism: head, arms, and feet corresponded to the three classes of society—the clergy, the nobility, and the peasantry.[42] Not until the twelfth century was there any place for the townsfolk and business classes in the clerical scheme of society. By the thirteenth century, society was commonly thought of as fourfold: the clergy, kings and nobles, townsfolk, and peasants.

ECONOMIC THEORIES The rise of the burghers in the social system was accompanied by a serious clerical problem, the adjustment of religious theory to economic practices. The rural economy of the early centuries had little place for money making. Life was simple and men had few worldly ambitions. Did not the church teach that earth was but a desert drear, a stopping place en route to heaven? But town life and the expansion of business brought opportunities for the improvement of material conditions through the accumulation of money. Thence arose the problem of the morality of financial profit. Although the church took the position that work (even industry and commerce) was necessary for subsistence, it held that riches for riches' sake were sinful. They endangered the salvation of the possessor and they represented an unjust exploitation of his fellow Christians. Thus it was that the church upheld the doctrine of the "just price," and condemned all speculation, excessive profits, and the taking of any interest (usury) for the loan of money.

In economics, as in politics, realities were stronger than theories. The rise of capitalistic methods of business, and especially of banking, offered such attractive opportunities for financial profit that the clerical prohibitions became a dead letter. Never obeyed by Jews and

[42] See above, p. 239.

other non-Christians, they were soon evaded by Italian and south French townsfolk. Interest was taken under the guise of compensation for delayed repayment of a loan. There were similar evasions of the rules concerning "just price," speculation, and the like. By the end of the fifteenth century, the old prohibitions were unenforceable, and even clerical theorists began to give way to the inevitable march of events.

As early as the thirteenth century, Thomas Aquinas had shifted the basis of the clerical position from Christian morals to social duty. A businessman might make money with impunity if his excess profits were to be given to the needy. Thus it was that the church joined hands with capitalism through the medium of the wealthy philanthropist. By the end of the Middle Ages banking and capitalism had become respectable by reason of their humanitarian services. In 1526 Jacob Fugger II, founder of charitable institutions and contributor to the church, died in the odor of sanctity and respectability, his firm having made profits of 54.5 per cent for the preceding seventeen years. With the breakdown of clerical opposition to capitalistic riches, a new social theory began to develop: the humanitarian obligations that go with wealth. This was destined to become the secular ethics of modern civilization.

LITERATURE IN THE LATE MIDDLE AGES

THERE are three outstanding developments in the nonclerical literature of the late Middle Ages: (1) clergymen were writing on secular subjects and in a secular vein; (2) more and more literature was written in the vernacular languages—English, French, Provençal, Italian, and German; and (3) during the twelfth and the fourteenth centuries in particular, a strong humanistic movement glorified the classical Latin and Greek literatures of antiquity. These developments illustrate the increasing secular spirit which accompanied the growth of towns, business, and prosperity during the later Middle Ages.

SECULAR LATIN CLERICAL LITERATURE We turn first to the nonreligious or secular literature written by clergymen. In their Latin writings medieval clergymen frequently gave vent to normal human feelings and worldly desires. Long before the so-called humanistic or classical revival of Petrarch's day, medieval clergymen were manifesting a *humanness* of spirit that was neither classical nor new. Despite popular modern notions concerning the piety of medieval people, the churchmen did not spend most of their waking hours in formal religious activities. Many of them lived in a frankly worldly environment.

PROFESSORIAL SECULARISM Even the learned scholastic professors at the great universities gave literary expression to their natural human instinct. The brilliant Abelard admitted that there was no woman whom he could not captivate with his love lyrics. Unfortunately none of these poems have come down to us, but it was said that in his day the streets of Paris resounded with the fascinating rhythms and emotional themes of his verses to Eloise.

Much less egotistical and more charming in personality was John of Salisbury, in later years bishop of Chartres. He was a close friend of Thomas à Becket, and author of a learned study on political theory, the *Policraticus*. Scholar, bishop, and theologian that he was,

John could write that it was good to "lie still and listen to the lyre
and open all the gates of the senses to pleasure." Apparently the
bishop of Chartres often "opened the gates of his own senses" to the
pleasures of drink, for he once wrote to remind an abbot friend that
"wine, I know, is readier to your hand than *coelia,* which the vulgar
among us here call beer. Nevertheless I am myself a drinker of both,
nor do I abhor anything that can make one drunk." He went on to
ask the abbot to send him some of a certain kind of French wine
which was better than "Falernian or Sicilian, or that Greek wine
which the Chancellor of Sicily used to make me drink, to the grave
detriment of my constitution."[1] Such passages lead one to wonder
whether the medieval university men were any less *human* in actual
life than many of their modern successors.

THE POETRY OF
WINE, WOMEN,
AND SONG

Naturally the clerical students were far more ex-
uberant in their lives and more outspoken in their
writings than were the professors. Although technically classed as a clergyman, the average student
seems to have had a pagan attitude in morals and poetry. He could
laud Bacchus as the god of drunkenness[2] and admire the man who
"carried his liquor best."

> If there's here a fellow lurking Who his proper share is shirking,
> Let the door to him be shown. . . .
> When your heart is set on drinking, Drink on without stay or thinking,
> Till you cannot stand up straight, Nor one word articulate![3]

In the twelfth century one of these students wrote "The Contest between Wine and Water," in which he related how water accused
wine of being a curse to mankind.

> All thy life is foul and sordid, Sunk in misery, steeped in vice;
> Those who drink thee lose their morals, Waste their time in sloth and
>   quarrels,
> Rolling down sin's precipice.
> Thou dost teach man's tongue to stutter; He goes reeling in the gutter
> Who hath deigned to kiss thy lips; Hears men speak without discerning,
> Sees a hundred tapers burning When there are but two poor dips.

But wine finally wins the debate by expatiating as follows on the
danger of drinking infected water.

---

[1] Waddell, "John of Salisbury," in *Essays and Studies by Members of the English Association,* XIII, 34.

[2] See above, p. 286.

[3] Symonds, *Wine Women and Song,* Chatto and Windus, p. 174.

Thou of things the scum and rotten, Sewer, where odures best forgotten
And unmentioned still descend!
Filth and garbage, Stench and poison, Thou dost bear in fetid foison!
Here I stop lest words offend. . . .
Many a man and oft who swallowed Thine infected potion, followed
After death in one day's time.[4]

THE POETRY
OF WOMEN
Toward women the student attitude was frankly sensual, and student poetry reveals none of the romantic chivalry of troubadour literature. From as early a period as the tenth century comes a poem in which a young roué is represented as inviting his mistress to his room for dinner. He promises her cushions, "flowers of sweetest scent," "meats and drinks of rare delight"; there too "wine flows sparkling, free"; there she shall have servants to wait on her, a flutist and a lyre player to entertain her; and love. From the twelfth century comes an interesting poem which opens with prayers to the Virgin Mary, continues with references to Venus, and closes with a passionate love scene:

What more? Around the maiden's neck My arms I flung with yearning;
Upon her lips I gave and took A thousand kisses burning . . .
Who is the man that does not know The sweets that followed after? [5]

There were also many other love lyrics dedicated to Phyllis, or Flora, some of them written in the most sensually descriptive detail. All of this, it should be remembered, was by clerical students.

THE POETRY
OF NATURE
Turning from this type of literature to the student verse in praise of the beauties of nature, one finds descriptions of red roses, village May dances, nightingales singing in the moonlight, and the other attractions of springtime. These have a lighter and finer touch; they suggest the wholesome beauties of spring.

All in all, medieval student poetry opens a bright vista into the supposed solemnity of medieval clerical life, revealing a humanness of spirit that is much like that of city life in all ages. Interestingly enough, this daring pleasure-loving sensousness preceded the classical "renascence" of the humanistic era. Like the Petrarchians, these young medieval pagans of the twelfth century were familiar with classical literature, but, as it has been aptly expressed, theirs was "the universal paganism of youth which needs no instruction from antiquity to learn that the sky is very blue, that the grass is very green

4 *Ibid.,* pp. 167 ff.
5 *Ibid.,* pp. 122 f.

. . . and that wine and love are both intoxicating."[6] In general the student poems present all types of youthful personality, with the exception of the pious. Their attitude toward religion was cynical. Priests, monks, abbots, and bishops were flayed unmercifully for their prosperous respectability, worldliness, and hypocrisy. Even the most sacred of sacraments might be ridiculed in a poem such as the "Gamblers' Mass." The prevailing characteristics of student literature are carefree joyousness and irresponsibility. Their ideal was Golias, the legendary head of the order of wandering clerics who traveled about seeking excitement and worldly enjoyment. His importance in the poetry of the students gave it the name goliardic literature.

THE NATIONAL VERNACULAR LITERATURES
In turning from the Latin literature of the clergy to the vernacular writings of the medieval laity, one might expect to find far more of exuberance and pagan sensuality. There is, however, nothing in all medieval literature until Boccaccio's *Decameron* to match the goliardic poetry which we have just discussed.

The fabliaux, or short stories, enjoyed by the middle and lower classes, come closest. These tales were often coarse, cynical, and sensual, but always humorous and entertaining. They pictured women as lacking in virtue, and men as either dishonest schemers or innocent fools; the clergy were invariably represented as grasping hypocrites, and were made the butt of every joke. It was from this type of popular story that Boccaccio got many of his *Decameron* tales. Of a higher moral tone were the allegorical stories, notably the animal fables, similar to those of Aesop. In these the lion symbolized the king, the wolf the noble, the ass the clergyman, and Reynard the Fox, the clever burgher who got the best of them all by means of his quick wit. Still another type of popular allegory is exemplified by the morality plays and the *Romance of the Rose*,[7] in which the various vices and virtues were personified. All of these types of popular story are the counterpart, in literature, of the rising *burgher* class in society.

"CHANSONS DE GESTE"
The literature of the noble classes was quite different: it emphasized valor in battle, chivalric love for woman, and the special function of the nobility in defending religion and justice. In all lands, in all of the vernacular languages, and in all sorts of variations of lyric, epic, and romantic prose, these ideals were expressed. During the earlier feudal period

---

[6] Stephenson, *Medieval Europe*, p. 447.
[7] See below, p. 690.

the more warlike type of stories and poems were in demand. The
Anglo-Saxons had their *Beowulf;* the Norsemen, their sagas and eddas;
the Germans, the songs of the *Niebelungs* and of *Walthari;* the
Spaniards, the *Cid;* and the French, the *Song of Roland.* The French
called such songs *chansons de geste* (songs of deeds) and the title is descriptive of the general character of all such poems. The heroes were
reckless warriors—Beowulf, Roland, Walthari, the Niebelungs, and
the Arthur and Lancelot of the earlier cycles of poems.

The ideals of the writers and readers (or listeners) of these stories
were those of a primitive feudal society. Men were hardy and bold, and
paid little attention to women. When the hero's wife appears in the
story, it is not uncommon for him to give her a most unchivalrous
beating. Toward women of the lower class, medieval knights were
pictured as overbearing and brutal. Fidelity to one's lord and honor
among *men* were the paramount virtues. Even religion was predominantly masculine in these early centuries, and the most popular saint
was the fighting archangel Michael. But these crude feudal ideals,
and with them the literature of the nobility, were destined to change.
Later, in the twelfth century, as castle life became more peaceful and
as expanding commerce provided a more luxurious type of life, the
literature of the nobility followed the trend of the times: it had less
of warfare and more of the gay court life of beautiful ladies and gallant knights. Thus the songs of deeds gave way to the chivalric songs
of love.

"CHANSONS   In many of the later cycles of literature, warriors such
D'AMOUR"   as Arthur, Roland, Lancelot, and Parsifal were represented as sophisticated lovers. In fact, there is scarcely
a knight of the late medieval tales of the Round Table who does
not dedicate his services to at least one fair lady. The very titles of the
tales tended to combine the names of the hero and heroine: *Lancelot
and Guinevere, Gareth and Lynette,* and so on. Elsewhere the same
trend was apparent, as, for instance, in the prose romances *Aucassin
and Nicolette* and *Tristan and Isolde.* By the end of the twelfth
century the Song of Deeds had become the Song of Love. Even
Roland was refashioned in the late Middle Ages according to the new
mode, and in one poem he is represented as becoming insane for the
love of a girl.[8] Throughout such late medieval literature a man's
fidelity to his ladylove rates equally with his fidelity to his feudal

[8] The *Orlando Furioso* of Ariosto.

lord. Often, as for instance in *Tristan and Isolde,* love for the lady triumphs over feudal honor. This literary trend was contemporaneous with the decline of feudalism. Eventually the gentleman replaced the knight in literature as well as in real life.[9]

TROUBADOURS, TROUVÈRES, AND MINNESINGERS
Similar trends are noticeable in lyric poetry. The troubadours of southern France and Spain, the trouvères of north France, the minnesingers (love singers) of Germany,[10] and the minstrels of various other lands composed and recited songs in praise of their "ladies fair." Many of these gentlemen poets were wandering nobles, like Duke William of Aquitaine, father of the famous Eleanor, and Walther von der Vogelweide. Much of the poetry of the south French (Provençal) troubadours has been preserved, and it shows not only a fine appreciation of the beauties of nature and of womankind, but also a rare zest for living. One of them wrote:

Fair to me is April, bearing Winds that o'er me softly blow,—
Nightingales their music airing While the stars serenely glow;
All the birds as they have power, While the dews of morning wait,
Sing of joy in sky or bower, Each consorting with his mate.
And as all the world is wearing New delight while new leaves grow,
'Twould be vain to try forswearing Love which makes my joys o'erflow;
Both by habit and by dower Gladness is my rightful state,
And when clouds no longer lower Quick my heart throws off its weight.[11]

More prosaic—and bitter—was the violent criticism which the troubadours leveled at the corrupt and wealthy clergy. Like the authors of the fabliaux, they were clergy-haters; and their attacks upon them were always popular with the laity. The anticlerical theme motivated Jean de Meung's *Romance of the Rose,* a thirteenth-century poetical satire on all classes of society, and particularly virulent in its condemnation of the clergy. In this poem, the troubadour spirit joined hands with that of the fabliaux to produce one of the most popular books of the late Middle Ages.

[9] An excellent example of the gentleman and gentlewoman in late medieval literature is found in *The Book of the Courtier* written by Baldassare Castiglione (d. 1529), himself a fine type of Italian gentleman.

[10] Meistersingers were a later (fourteenth- and fifteenth-century) type of singer, principally from the middle and lower classes. They formed guilds and put their members through a rigid course of training in the rules of composition and the execution of music. Wagner's famous opera, *Die Meistersinger von Nurnberg,* portrays the type of life of the "mastersingers."

[11] Translation from Robinson, *Readings,* I, 435.

FRENCH
SECULAR
LITERATURE

By the end of the thirteenth century the national states with their distinctive languages and literatures had become so prominent that they demand separate regional treatment. France, already famous for her troubadour songs, chansons, and romances, produced little of outstanding merit in poetry during the fourteenth and early fifteenth centuries. In history, however, the French developed an interesting type of personal reminiscence, usually called memoirs. Early in the thirteenth century, Villehardouin, one of the barons who participated in the crusade of 1204, wrote his own personal account in French of *The Conquest of Constantinople*. It was a simple tale, told with an unaffectedness that is charming—historical literature of the sort that Gregory of Tours wrote, uncritical yet convincing, because of its frankness. This was the first history written in the French language. Later in the same century, Joinville wrote an equally interesting historical work, *The Life of Louis IX,* the beloved monarch whom he had accompanied on his expedition. Like Villehardouin, Joinville wrote a straightforward account of what he himself saw, did, and felt—a history full of personal anecdotes and possessing the charm of simple sincerity. Both writers, it will be noted, were noble fighting men and reflected the aristocratic viewpoint. Theirs are the first outstanding nonclerical histories since Einhard's *Life of Charles the Great.*

FROISSART

Froissart (d. ca. 1410), who lived about a century after Joinville, was still dominated by the aristocratic concept. A burgher by birth, a cleric by choice, he wrote a set of memoirs that are merely tales of the military and aristocratic events of the period of the Hundred Years' War. He was oblivious to the economic causes or effects of the conflict. Without critical analysis or historical selectivity, he simply endeavored to entertain his highborn readers with accounts of chivalric deeds suited to a bygone day. It is as a teller of such tales as the famous account of the English longbowmen at Crécy, or the Black Prince's exploits, that Froissart has made his place in historical annals.

COMMINES

Commines, a noble officeholder, first under the duke of Burgundy and later under his enemy Louis XI of France, introduced into French historical writing the critical spirit of a Machiavelli a generation before that statesman's time. In his *Memoirs* he did for Louis XI what Machiavelli was to do for Cesare Borgia: he analyzed the characteristics and influences that made for success or failure in international relations. This he was able to do with great success because of his accurate personal knowledge of both the Burgundian and the French courts. With him French memoirs became something more than mere collections of gossipy stories; they became a combination of historical philosophy and biographical character analysis. Furthermore they illustrate the triumph of the new burgher concept of realism in politics, which was already displacing the aristocratic feudal idea of military glory and personal fidelity.

FRENCH POETRY: Resembling Commines in his realistic city-dweller's FRANÇOIS outlook on life was François Villon (d. 1463), a man VILLON who brought new glories to French poetry. Although well educated, and destined for a clerical position, Villon deliberately turned to a wild roving life, somewhat like that of the twelfth-century students. The taverns, criminals, and street women of the large towns were his interest and companions; so much so, in fact, that he narrowly escaped the gallows for his criminal escapades. His poems reflect human life at the opposite extreme from that portrayed by Commines and Froissart. The genius of Villon was his poignant understanding of lower-class life. In his "Little Will" (*Petit Testament*), he bequeathed his fame to a well-to-do relative, his heart to a faithless sweetheart, and his sword (which he had pawned) to the friend who was to redeem it. In his "Great Will," he waxed somewhat cynical as he commented on the infidelity of women and the useless wealth of the rich. "Better [he wrote] to live and rags to wear than to have been a lord and, dead, to rot in a splendid sepulchre." Finally he willed his worldly effects to various friends. All of this was expressed in verse of penetrating understanding and poetic artistry. Villon's greatness is that of the writer who presents in perfect literary form a cause which he sincerely feels. In his case it was that of the "underdogs" of human society with whom he had lived. His daredevil spirit made him the leader of the Paris rabble during the Burgundian period of the Hundred Years' War.[12] Villon might well be called the first poet of the city proletariat.

ENGLISH In England, vernacular literature began earlier, but SECULAR reached its full development later than in France. LITERATURE The Anglo-Saxon language and literature of Alfred's day was soon eclipsed by the French influences that came in with the Norman Conquest, and also by the Latin of the

---

[12] One of these episodes furnished the plot for "The Rogue Song," of moving picture fame.

university men. Late in the Middle Ages, English literature was revived in the writings of Wiclif, "Langland," and Chaucer. Wiclif's translation of the Bible and his antipapal reform pamphlets were so widely read that they set a new standard for English prose. During the same period (the fourteenth century), the so-called Langland's *Vision of Piers Plowman* did a similar service for English poetry. Although simple in style and medieval in its allegorical tendencies, this poem gave such a vivid picture of the corrupt clergy, the selfish nobles, the prosperous merchants, and—above all—the sturdy, hard-working peasants that it is considered a masterpiece of descriptive literature. Furthermore it served as powerful propaganda for social and economic reforms. Along with Wiclif's religious tracts, it is thought to have been both a cause and an expression of the peasant discontent. Although lacking in polish, both of these works had the sincerity and power that make great literature.

CHAUCER
(D. 1400)

The author of the famous *Canterbury Tales* was of a more worldly type, in fact an "English Boccaccio," who combined the viewpoint of a middle-class townsman (risen to become a man of the world) with the art of a poet. Both his literary style and his philosophy of life were more sophisticated than Langland's. Like Boccaccio, he retold current stories to suit the fancy of the worldly-wise, middle-class layman. His satire is urbane, and his portrayals of the various types of English folk are masterpieces of description. Thus he takes a high place among literary geniuses famous for their analyses of human character and their artistic literary expression. In all of his writings he reflects the increasingly prosperous town life of the late Middle Ages.

We have not the space to discuss the rising secular tendencies in the literature of other regions of Europe. Suffice to say that the Spains and Germanies had poetry and prose in which the same trends were present. *The Book of Good Love,* written in the fourteenth century by the Spaniard, Juan Ruiz, has the zestful artistic touch of a student-poet, of a Chaucer, of a Boccaccio. In Germany Walther von der Vogelweide and Wolfram von Eschenbach, the author of *Parsifal,* upheld the more chivalric ideals of early times. But, on the other hand, there were middle-class and peasant poems such as *Meier Helmbrecht* by Wernher the Gardener. In all lands the practical-mindedness of the townsfolk and even of the peasants was reflected in the increase of secularism in literature.

Until the thirteenth century Italy was backward in vernacular literature. But with the rapid increase of towns and prosperity during the crusading age, the secular spirit flourished as never before, and by the year 1300 Italy had produced notable works in the language of the people. One of the most beautiful examples of early Italian literature is the "Canticle of the Sun," written by St. Francis of Assisi. The mingled religiousness and fine appreciation of nature shown in this short poem are as remarkable as the simple humanness of the author's life. It seems that the poverty, disease, and filth of the Italian proletariat among whom he labored could not crush the poetical soul of the saintly friar who called himself and his fellow workers "God's troubadours." He loved the birds, even as he did the destitute and the lepers. And in the "Canticle," he thanked the Lord for all of his creatures: for "Brother Sun who gives the day and lightens us therewith," for "Sister Moon and the stars . . . so clear, precious, and comely," and for "Brother Fire by which the night is lightened."

Later in the same century a wandering friar of very different character from St. Francis composed a chronicle that reveals in vivid detail the secular aspects of Italian town life. Salimbene (d. 1288) in his *Chronicle* presented a gossipy picture of the bustling life of the peasants, merchants, priests, and princes: their clothes, their food, and the everyday occurrences in the public square of a large town.

At the turn of the century Giovanni Villani (d. 1348), a Florentine businessman, was writing a chronicle of a very different sort. Inspired, so he said, by a visit to the ancient ruins of Rome, and "taking style and manner" from the classical historians, he decided to relate "all the origins and doings of the towns of Florence." As a matter of fact, his chronicle turned out to be a social-economic history of thirteenth- and fourteenth-century Florence, full of statistical details concerning income and expenditures, population, schools, churches, dress, banks, industries, and imports. He even mentioned, for example, the fact that in July, 1280, 40,000 loads of melons were brought into the city. Such was the businesslike mind of the Italian historian who, with Dante, brought the Italian language into literary prominence.

DANTE
(D. 1321)

Dante, like Villani, was a layman, born and brought up in a large town. He was a prominent citizen of Florence, member of the druggist and spicers' guild, and for a time one of the six city commissioners (priors). He belonged to the defeated antipapalist faction, and he lost his property and suffered permanent exile. His world-famous works were produced, therefore, while he lived in exile. All of his writings, in both prose and poetry, are piously and conservatively medieval. In a political treatise (written in Latin) *Concerning Monarchy,* he accepted in principle the medieval doctrine of mutual co-operation between papacy and empire. Dante's only other work in Latin, *Concerning Vulgar Eloquence,* was a medievally logical argument in support of the use of Italian as a literary language. He wrote it in Latin in order that it might be read more easily by learned men.

DANTE: DE-
FENDER OF
MEDIEVALISM

Dante's *Banquet* (*Convivio*), written in Italian, was equally conservative. It was an allegory concerning a feast; the intellectual food was philosophy and science. In this work he showed his sincere belief in the entire medieval system of Aristotelian and Christian science, as set forth by Aquinas and the other scholastic theologians. His *New Life,* however, is quite different in spirit. Here Dante told of his love for Beatrice, the lady of his dreams, interweaving with the narrative a series of poems concerning her. In strong contrast to the learned scholastic of the *Banquet,* the Dante of the *New Life* was a timid troubadour who followed the etiquette of chivalric love in singing the praises of his womanly ideal whom he dared to worship only from afar. Here we have an important example of French troubadour influences in Italian literature.

THE DIVINE
COMEDY

Beatrice was also the inspiration of his masterpiece, the *Divine Comedy.* This work is not a comedy in the modern sense of the word, but rather an allegorical epic that sets forth all aspects of human experience from the depths of sin to the heights of divine destiny. In presenting this drama, Dante pictured himself as being guided through the underworld of hell (inferno) and purgatory by Vergil, "the supreme poet," and by Beatrice through the heavenly realms. He described in vivid detail his conversations with the great heroes of antiquity who peopled his underworld. Here Dante revealed a wide knowledge and appreciation of classical learning. But in his portrayals of the fires of hell and the tortures of the damned, he also showed the supreme influence of medieval religiousness. Of the two characteristic influences that dominated medieval thinking (the classics and Christian theology), Christian theology was the more powerful. In the *Divine Comedy* Dante vividly illustrates the supremacy of religion. As he approaches the heavenly realms, his classical guide, Vergil, is replaced by Beatrice, who symbolizes Christian theology. She guides him through the circles of heaven where he sees and talks with saints, martyrs, pious Christians, and learned scholars.

Thus the *Divine Comedy* served as a sort of "Pilgrim's Progress," a detailed picture of man's life in terms of future rewards and punishments. The allegorical treatment, the emphasis on the future world, the lengthy disquisitions on learned topics, and the subordination of classical learning to Christian piety are typical of the church-controlled thought of the Middle Ages.

The characteristics that made the *Divine Comedy* a masterpiece were its sincerity and seriousness of purpose, the vivid and kaleidoscopic descriptions of personalities, and a literary style that glows with life. The princes, kings, popes, thieves, and writers whom Dante pictured in the future world were the same kind of human beings that he saw walking the crowded streets of Italian towns. Thus Dante's poem reflects the bustling town life of the later Middle Ages, and it is chiefly because of its human interest that the *Divine Comedy* makes its great appeal to the average reader. From the standpoint of literary history also, it marks a great development. In this and his other vernacular works, Dante, almost singlehanded, made Italian a literary language. Unfortunately Petrarch and the subsequent humanistic interest in classical Latin undid much of Dante's work, and the permanent development of literature in Italian was held back for over a century.

HUMANISM: THE "RENASCENCE" OF THE CLASSICS IN ITALY

PETRARCH
(D. 1374)

Petrarch represents the late medieval shift of emphasis from logic and theology to the Latin and Greek classics. This shift was a gradual one rather than a sudden "renascence," "rebirth," or "revival." As we have seen, there was a high appreciation of classical literature in the schools of the

eleventh and twelfth centuries. Therefore Petrarch's humanism [13] was
not so much a rediscovery of the classics as it was the discovery in the
already available classics of secular ideas that satisfied the rising spirit
of independence and worldliness of prosperous townsfolk.

Petrarch, like Dante, was a Florentine who spent most of his life
in foreign lands. His parents being exiles, he was born in Arezzo, grew
up at Pisa, and lived near Avignon, the papal residence. There
were two outstanding influences in Petrarch's life and literature:
classical literature, and Laura, a married woman whom he loved
desperately, but in vain. This romantic love inspired his Italian lyrics,
which the modern world hails (with Dante's poems) as examples of
the brilliant dawn of Italian literature. A few lines from one of them
dealing with the death of Laura, will indicate Petrarch's delicacy of
literary expression, and his love of nature.

> Ye limpid brooks by whose clear streams
> My goddess laid her tender limbs!
> Ye gentle boughs whose friendly shade
> Gave shelter to the lovely maid.[14]

The unaffected emotional appeal of these lines contrasts strangely
with Dante's allegorical style, and also with Petrarch's own later poems
written in stilted classical Latin.

PETRARCH
AND THE
CLASSICS

During his later career Petrarch was consumed with
a burning enthusiasm for the ancient Latin classics.
After Laura had passed from his life he turned to his
youthful hobby of collecting classical manuscripts,
and by his activity in this work he started a veritable fad for antique
literature. Soon he made the classics, and with them himself, popular,
not only in Italy but elsewhere as well. In his own rather egotistical
letters he admitted that he was responsible for this classical popularity,
and related with pride the enthusiasm with which scholars and prominent laymen greeted him as he traveled from place to place.

Petrarch was more successful as a propagandist than as a scholar.
His major work, the *Africa,* a long and wearisome epic poem modeled after Vergil's *Aeneid,* was a weak imitation of a great classic;
and his attempt to master the Greek language met with no success.
Thereafter he devoted himself joyfully to the task of publicizing the

---

[13] Medieval humanism is not to be confused with *humanness,* nor with the *religious* humanism of our own day. It can best be defined as a heightened interest in
classical literature and culture.

[14] *The Sonnets, Triumphs and Other Poems of Petrarch,* p. 116.

classics—and himself. Decrying as worthless his earlier poems because
they were written in Italian rather than Latin, he convinced himself,
and many others too, by his enthusiastic and sometimes flowery writings, that the only literature worthy of the attention of intelligent
men was the classics. Like Roger Bacon's blasts against Aristotelian
logic, Petrarch's enthusiasm helped to destroy the already outworn
methods of medieval scholastic thinking. This had a double consequence. Italy, and eventually most of Western Europe, came to
appreciate as never before classical language and literature and the
humanistic ideal of life. At the same time superficial classicism and
sophisticated pagan morals became fastened on the West and were
carried to ludicrous extremes by many of Petrarch's followers. In
literature the result was the passing of medieval logical hairsplitting
and the adoption of the affected literary styles of a bygone age. This
set a premium on pedantic antiquarianism and discouraged scientific
research and straightforward thinking. It also inadvertently saddled
upon future generations an antiquated form of the Latin language
and in so doing probably prevented the living and growing Latin of
the Middle Ages from becoming the universal language of European
scholarship. Many of these results, however, were unintended and were
opposed by Petrarch himself.

"THE FIRST ARDENT CLASSICIST" Much has been written about Petrarch's being "the
first modern man." The phrase is not well chosen
and is misleading. He was a member of the clergy,
as a youth he wrote romantic poems, and in later life
he devoted himself to the ancient classics. Such traits are not particularly modern. On the other hand, the fact that he was very individualistic, that he opposed the narrowly scholastic ideas of the medieval theologians, and that he sought to broaden and humanize life
makes it possible to ascribe a certain modernness to Petrarch. But the
same progressive individualism had appeared long before Petrarch,
and if this is the mark of modernity, then one might consider Abelard of Paris, Adelard of Bath, Roger of Salisbury, Frederick II of
Naples-Sicily, and Roger Bacon as more worthy of the designation, "the
first modern man." Petrarch was, however, an unusually enthusiastic
and expressive man of an age that had already begun to shake off
medieval restrictions. This tendency was due to no one individual,
but rather to the increase of town life and the consequent speeding up
of progress in human thought. Petrarch might better be labeled "the

first ardent classicist of medieval Italy," for he definitely diverted the stream of thought into the channel of classical antiquity.

BOCCACCIO
Petrarch's protégé, Boccaccio (d. 1375), was infinitely more modern in his thinking and literary expression than either Petrarch or Dante. He was a typical product of town life, a thoroughgoing man of the world; unmedieval, irreligious, and sophisticated in both his life and writings. Although born (probably out of wedlock) in Paris, brought up in France, and a resident of various regions, he considered himself a Florentine. His father was a merchant of Florence, and it was as the representative of a Florentine bank that Boccaccio was sent to Naples where, at the Angevin court, he again came in contact with French influences. As with Dante and Petrarch, Boccaccio's greatest literary creations were inspired by a woman, Maria, an illegitimate daughter of King Robert of Naples. But, unlike the ethereal or fictitious women whom many writers of that day claimed as their inspiration, his Maria ("Fiametta," or "Little Flame," as he called her) was a real person, intensely human and sensual in character. It was the sincerity of his all-absorbing passion for Maria that made Boccaccio's writings so readable. In several works he took his own experiences with "Fiametta" as themes for passionate love stories concerning mythical heroes and heroines. The last of this series, written after he realized that "Fiametta" was untrue to him, was a bitterly cynical story written by a Boccaccio who had become a disillusioned womanhater.

BOCCACCIO'S "DECAMERON"
The *Decameron,* his masterpiece, is an artistic arrangement of a hundred short stories, most of them either well-known medieval fabliaux or classical romances. These Boccaccio retold with such amusing realism and human interest that they have won for him the reputation of being one of the cleverest storytellers of all time and also the most immoral of all medieval writers. The latter characterization is hardly justified, for most of the material was merely a revamping of stories that most people already knew. Boccaccio did, however, give to them a human touch and a brilliancy of style that was unique. The *Decameron* has been called the *Human Comedy* in comparison with Dante's *Divine Comedy.*

BOCCACCIO AND THE CLASSICS
With the passing of "Fiametta" from Boccaccio's life, his worldliness, and with it his genius, faded. For a while he was much interested in Dante's work, but he soon became subject to fits of melancholy, and it was during one

of these that he threatened to burn all of his early writings and enter
a monastery. But instead of carrying out his threat he fell under the
spell of Petrarch and classicism, and spent his later days in scholarly
research. He studied Greek and wrote learned works in Latin, including dictionaries of classical biography and geography. Perhaps classical humanism decided Boccaccio against a monastic career, but it made
a pedantic scholar of Italy's most human literary genius. Humanism
did not always make men more human.

HUMANISM
IN ITALY
For a century after Petrarch and Boccaccio had deserted the Italian language for classical Latin, literary
Italy "went classical." Ancient manuscripts were
hunted, copied, translated and studied by learned folk with an enthusiasm that became almost a religion. Princes, popes, and men of
wealth vied in collecting libraries of classical writings and in hiring
Latin and Greek scholars. Experts, such as the Florentine bookseller
Vespasiano and the papal secretary Poggio, traveled about, even to
other lands, seeking classical manuscripts. Aldus Manutius, the Venetian printer, published small cheap editions of the more popular classics.
The Greek language also became popular with intellectuals. In the late
fourteenth century, Greeks had begun to migrate from Constantinople
to the West, where some of them made their fortunes by teaching
Greek and selling antique Greek manuscripts. As early as 1396 an
Easterner named Chrysoloras was lecturing on Greek at the University of Florence. In the year 1420, over thirty years before the Turks
captured Constantinople, hundreds of Greek manuscripts were brought
to Italy from that city. With the Italian interest in Greek came an increased attention to Platonic and Neoplatonic philosophy. Clubs, called
by the ancient Greek name of "Academy," were formed so that learned
men might meet to discuss the ideas of the ancient Greek thinkers.
One effect of this movement was to bring additional discredit to
Aristotelian scholasticism.

HISTORICAL
CRITICISM
Although this classical-minded age developed many
able critics, literary stylists, and cultural dilettantes, it
did little to encourage original scholarship or real
literary genius. Most of the scholars of the age were pedantic. There
were, however, during the fifteenth century, two outstanding humanistic historians who wrote (of course) in classical Latin. Leonardo
Bruni's *History of Florence* and Flavius Blondus's histories of Rome
and Italy set a new standard of accuracy in history. Blondus's work,
it may be noted, contained the first serious history of the Middle

Ages. Most of the other humanist historians were too much interested in attaining a perfect classical style to write accurate history.

In literary and historical criticism, however, a Roman scholar named Laurentius Valla did a truly remarkable work. By keen analysis and careful reasoning he proved conclusively that the old document purporting to be Constantine's donation of the entire western half of the empire to the papacy was a clerical forgery. He also wrote drastic criticisms of the accepted church doctrines of predestination, the sinfulness of worldly pleasure, and the desirability of the monastic and priestly life. Without excuses or apologies, he argued that the human will is free, that man should live for pleasure, and that secular careers were preferable to the clerical life. But in such opinions Valla, like Abelard and the student poets of *Wine Women and Song,* was an ultramodern voice, lost in a babel of medievalism and classicism.

THE DECLINE OF HUMANISM AND THE DEVELOP-
MENT OF ITALIAN LITERATURE

Toward the year 1500, Italian writers descended from the rarified atmosphere of humanism, in which they had been living for over a century, and developed a more progressive literature that was human in spirit and Italian in form. Lorenzo de' Medici and his Florentine court were the center of the renewed interest in Italian. He revived the long-neglected Italian tongue of Dante, of sonnet-writing Petrarch, and of the young Boccaccio. Lorenzo's poems on popular subjects set a high standard of literary excellence, and in them he brought classical ideals down to earth and made literature human. For instance, he composed (in Italian) gay lyrics for the annual carnival parades. In one of them is found the recurring refrain: "Youths and maids, enjoy today, naught ye know of tomorrow"—an indication of the frankly secular spirit of his day.

THE NEW ITALIAN POETRY
Of greater importance than his own compositions was Lorenzo's encouragement of the work of Italian lyric, epic, and dramatic poets. For example, he persuaded Politian, professor of the classics at the University of Florence, a man famous for his translation of Homer, to write a picturesque Italian lyric describing in detail the festivities of a court tournament. The same professor produced the first nonreligious drama in the Italian language. The Florentines, it seems, had begun to lose interest in the medieval type of morality and mystery play. Lorenzo

himself had written a religious play, to be performed under lay (rather than clerical) auspices. Politian, in his *Orfeo,* went a step further: he used the classical theme of the love of Orpheus and Eurydice and gave it a completely secular treatment. Through such works drama was gradually emancipated from religion. It was not long before Italy had popular comedies and secular playhouses. Machiavelli's risqué play, *Mandragola,* indicates the manner in which Italian drama within a half century had drifted from clerical dominance to secular freedom. Late in the sixteenth century appeared the first modern operas, Peri's *Dafne* and *Euridice.*

THE ITALIAN
EPIC
The Medici court also revived epic poetry in Italian. Pulci, a poor writer whom Lorenzo had befriended, transformed the Roland theme of the early French *chansons de geste* into a popular Italian epic, *Il Morgante.* It is a far cry from the hero of the *Song of Roland* to the Orlando of rough pranks and peasant humor that appears in this story. Here the tales of chivalry were burlesqued for the entertainment of the court. Later Italian poets developed the same themes in more artistic and sophisticated forms. Boiardo's *Orlando* presented a more aristocratic and refined Roland, with the love element predominant. Ariosto's *Orlando* told the same story, but in classically Vergilian style. Tasso (d. 1595), however, the last great Italian poet, reverted to medieval religious influences. Living as he did amidst the religious controversies of the Protestant and Catholic reformations, and the renewed fears of Turkish invasions, he composed a strange poem of mingled wars, love, and crusades, the famous epic *Jerusalem Liberated.* In this manner, classically pagan Italy returned to the fold of medieval Catholic piety.

THE NEW
HISTORY
In prose, also, the Italian tongue regained its former leadership, as a result of the works of two famous political historians, Machiavelli (d. 1527) and Guicciardini (d. 1540). Being Florentine administrators they wrote detailed political histories of the Florence of their own day. Keenly critical and analytical in their treatment, both also produced works on the science of government—notably *The Prince* (by Machiavelli), and *Counsels and Reflections* (by Guicciardini). They may be called the "fathers of Italian political science." [15] Furthermore, with them, Italian historiography shook off the dead weight not only of medieval theology, but also of "renascence" classicism, and became the modern science of history and government.

[15] See above, p. 682.

With the opening of the sixteenth century, it is evident that literature, both prose and poetry, in Italy and elsewhere, had shed much of the classical and religious influence that had held it in check during the earlier centuries, and had adopted in large measure those secular characteristics that mark the modern age.

THE DEMOCRATIZATION OF LITERATURE: PRINTING

Far more important and effective in the expansion of thought than university professors, student songsters, or classical humanists, was the work of certain German mechanics of the fifteenth century who developed the science of printing. Tradition has it that Gutenberg of Mainz on the Rhine River was the inventor of European printing. As a matter of fact, the practice of printing an entire page from a carved wooden block had been in use in China for centuries, and in Western Europe for a hundred years before Gutenberg. Some one, or perhaps several ingenious Germans of the fifteenth century, began to use separate metal types for each letter. Thus a page of type could be set up, printed, and disassembled, to be reset later for another page. This, in brief, is the story of the "invention of printing," or—to be more accurate—the development of movable type. Meanwhile there were also marked improvements in presses, ink, and paper.

Although it is not known who actually invented movable type, by about the year 1450 Bibles and other books were being printed at Mayence and at Haarlem in the Netherlands. Within the next half century, presses had been set up in hundreds of other places. Meanwhile various kinds of type (roman, Carolingian, italic, and black letter) had been introduced, and books were being turned out in great quantities. Thus reading was popularized among the middle-class townsfolk. Strange to say, most scholars and booklovers ridiculed the new machine-made manuscripts. The progress of the science was slow and expensive; coloring, ornamented capitals, and illustrations still had to be done separately and by hand. Not until later centuries, with the expansion of education, did printing have any great effect upon the intelligence of the masses. But among the rising middle classes, the new learning and machine-made books exerted a tremendous influence.

≡ XXXIV ≡

THE ARTS IN WESTERN EUROPE IN THE LATE MIDDLE AGES

ROMANESQUE AND GOTHIC ART

THE arts of medieval Europe were as much an expression of its changing life as was its literature. Inasmuch as religion was a dominant force, the building and decoration of churches were among the most important arts. In the changing trends of cathedral architecture, we also find important evidence of the changing life of the Middle Ages. In the earlier period, Roman influences were predominant. As we have already seen,[1] the churches in both the East and the West were built according to the principles of ancient Roman architecture. These principles can be traced in two outstanding types of church, the rectangular basilica, and the domed church.

ROTUNDAS AND DOMES

Domed churches fall into two divisions: those called rotundas in which the dome covers a circular or nearly circular structure, and those in which it covers the square intersection of a cross-shaped church, such as St. Sophia at Constantinople. St. Sophia exemplifies the Byzantine, or East-Roman, style of architecture, sometimes called Romaic. It is an immense church built in the shape of a Greek cross. The ground plan is distinctly Eastern, but the dome is a modification of the low type of Roman dome found, for example, in the Pantheon. Although this same Byzantine ground plan was the model for St. Mark's in Venice and a few domed churches in southern France, in general the Greek-cross style had little direct influence in the West. The circular or octagonal rotunda was more popular, especially for the smaller type of Western church. The dome, as a separate architectural feature, became prominent in Italian church building during the late Middle Ages.

[1] See above, Chapter XVI.

704

BASILICAN
CHURCHES

The history of Western architecture is more closely bound with the development of the rectangular, or basilican church. As we have seen in another section, most of the early Christian churches of the West followed the structural form of the ancient Roman basilica. Thus the pagan basilica was the model for the Christian basilican church. But, as time passed, the form of the basilican church was modified to suit new needs. For instance, the churches of the tenth century were very different structures from the basilican churches of the fifth century. Most of the latter were smaller and cruder in construction.

In northern lands the differences were more marked than in Italy. Many of the later churches in the North had additions, called transepts, built at right angles to the nave. Some English churches had huge square towers at the entrance-end of the edifice. Around the sides and rear of the choir there was often a semicircular aisle, called an *ambulatory*. Sometimes on the outer side of the ambulatory small chapels were built to accommodate the sacred relics and altars presented by wealthy patrons of the church. Such architectural features were employed in France, at Orléans, Tours, Clermont-Ferrand, and Nantes, in the tenth century. Churches of this type are usually spoken of as Romanesque in order to distinguish them from the basilican churches of late Roman times.

EARLY ROMAN-
ESQUE CHURCHES

The term Romanesque (meaning "Roman-like") is particularly applicable to these modified basilican churches whose low-pitched roofs, heavy walls, round arches, and rows of pillars bear witness to their Roman architectural heritage. But inasmuch as the modern world has come to think of Romanesque architecture as restricted to the larger structures of the eleventh and twelfth centuries, we have referred to the churches of the early Middle Ages (500-1000) as *early* Romanesque.

Although all types of rectangular churches have marked similarities, certain differentiations may be noted. In the light of the structural variations that appeared in the course of the centuries, it is possible to distinguish the following stages of development from the age of the Roman basilica to the era of Gothic cathedrals. The Roman buildings of the first four centuries, which furnished the chief models for the rectangular type of church in the West, are called *pagan basilicas*. The Christian edifices which developed during the fourth and fifth centuries were so similar to the basilicas that they are usually referred to as *basilican churches*. As has been indicated, we shall

use the term early Romanesque for the modified basilican churches
of the early Middle Ages (500-1000), and the term Romanesque for
the more highly developed architecture of the eleventh and twelfth
centuries. As the Romanesque cathedral was enlarged and transformed, it evolved into the Gothic cathedral of the later Middle Ages.

MONASTIC
ROMANESQUE
CHURCHES
During the eleventh and twelfth centuries, the
Romanesque style developed rapidly, particularly in
northern France. A monk of this period wrote that
during the early eleventh century "all Gaul was
building more wonderful churches than ever," and that "the world
seemed to be putting off its old garments and was everywhere putting on a white vestment of new churches." The real reason for this
architectural progress seems to have been the rapid economic development of the period. The increase of trade, population, city life, and
wealth made it possible for flourishing communities to rebuild their
churches on a grand scale. Due to the popularity of saints' cults and
pilgrimages, there was a demand for large churches. The number of
visitors to a church on its greatest feast day determined the size of
building needed. Thus a monastery in a sparsely populated place
might have an immense church. In most regions the leaders in architectural activity were the monastic orders whose increasing membership and incomes called for larger churches. For this reason the eleventh and twelfth centuries are sometimes called the age of monastic
architecture.

THE BUILDING
OF A CHURCH
The monks may have been the initiators and even
the architects of most of the churches of this period,
but the laity, both great and small, played their part.
The process of erecting a church involved something more than mere
building operations. Let us suppose that the abbot of a French monastery has decided that his community needs a new church. First he
must mobilize funds, and for this purpose he urges kings, princes,
and nobles far and near to make donations.[2] The members of the
clergy likewise are expected to contribute. For years a large portion of
the revenues of the monastery may have been set aside for the building fund. People who attend the church services and pilgrims who
come to the relic shrine are also encouraged to give their mite. Once
the plans have been drawn up by the monastic architects, masons,

[2] In the year 1020, when Bishop Fulbert of Chartres set about to rebuild his
cathedral recently destroyed by fire, he asked for contributions from nobles in all
parts of France. Among the foreign contributors was King Canute of England.

laborers, and building materials are assembled. At Ramsey, England, in the year 970, the following preparations were made for a new church:

All through the following winter they are getting ready all that the forethought of the masons demanded, whether in tools of iron or tools of wood, and everything else that seemed needful for the future building. At length when the winter is past, the storehouses are thrown open, the most skilled workmen available are brought together, and the length and width of the church . . . are measured out. The foundations are dug deep on account of the marshy character of the site, and the earth is beaten with many strokes of the rammer to solidify it. . . . The laborers, inspired as much by the warmth of their pious devotion as by the desire for pay, are instant in their toil; while some bring the stones, others are mixing mortar, and a third party raises both stones and mortar aloft by the aid of pulleys, and so with the help of the Lord the structure rises daily higher and higher.[3]

Thus year after year the work of construction goes on. Sometimes when materials ran low, members of the local clergy might be sent out with the church's sacred relics to travel about stirring pious folk to action. This might lead to mass pilgrimages in which enthusiastic people brought cartloads of offerings. Timbers and building stone were sometimes hauled long distances by crowds of pious pilgrims intent on expiating their sins or obtaining healing for themselves and their loved ones. A Norman abbot remarked of the zeal of certain of his neighbors in 1115:

Who has ever seen or heard the like? Princes, powerful and wealthy men, men of noble birth, proud and beautiful women, bent their necks to the yoke of the carts which carried the stones, wood, wine, corn, oil, lime, everything necessary for the building of the church and the support of those working at it. One saw as many as a thousand people, men and women, attached to the reins drawing a wagon so heavy was its burden, and a profound silence reigned among the crowd pressing forward with difficulty, in the emotion which filled their hearts. At the head of the long procession, minstrels of the highest sounded their brazen trumpets, and the sacred banners in their brilliant colours swayed in the wind.[4]

Finally, when the church was finished, perhaps a generation or more after it had been started, a great dedication ceremony was held

[3] From the "Chronicle of the Abbey of Ramsey," translated in G. Brown, *The Arts in Early England,* II, 241 f. By permission of John Murray, publisher.

[4] Translation from Funck-Brentano, *The Middle Ages,* pp. 218 f. By permission of G. P. Putnam's Sons.

at which, perchance, the pope might be present if he happened to be in the region at the time. Such ceremonies, attended by prominent clergymen and laymen from distant regions, inspired others to rebuild their churches. Thus it was that the building of churches spread, like an epidemic, during the eleventh and twelfth centuries.

CLUNY   One of the best examples of the new style of monastic architecture was the abbey church built at about the year 1100 at Cluny, the headquarters of the wealthy Cluniac order. This church, which was planned by monastic architects, was at that time the largest in the West. In general plan it was similar to the early basilican churches, but it had important modifications. For instance, there was an immense choir surrounded by a series of semicircular chapels and flanked by transepts, two on each side. Over the double crossing of the nave and transepts were two towers. At the opposite end of the main church, with its immense nave and four side aisles, was a vestibule (or narthex) which was itself a small church. The entrance to this vestibule chapel was surmounted by two square towers, one of which served as the monastic prison.

A noteworthy feature, not only of the church of Cluny, but also of most monastic Romanesque edifices, was the solid stone roof. The roof had always created serious problems for church builders. The early Lombard architects of Como had used a simple type of "groined" vaulting over the side aisles, but it had never been applied on a large scale in Italy. At Cluny the immense nave and the side aisles were covered with stone vaulting. Eventually in the north, most churches came to be roofed with stone, and in later times the builders of the Gothic cathedrals developed intricately beautiful and effective types of ribbed vaulting.

CHURCHES IN NORTH FRANCE AND NORMANDY   In northern France also the monastic builders of this period were improving their architectural technique. Just outside of Paris, at the king's own abbey of St. Denis, a magnificent new church was erected in the early twelfth century. Abbot Suger wrote that "its plans had been outlined with the greatest of care by means of arithmetical and geometrical instruments," and that it had "one beautiful and noteworthy innovation," a circle of chapels around the choir.

Meanwhile, in the Anglo-Norman realms on both sides of the Channel, monastic builders were erecting stone-vaulted churches of grand proportions. William the Conqueror and his wife Matilda, in expiation for their violation of a clerical marriage regulation, built twin monastic churches (St. Trinity and St. Stephen's) in the Norman city of Caen. So widespread was the adoption of the improved architectural style that its influence was soon noticeable in nonmonastic churches. Everywhere, it was said, bishops hastened to replace their old cathedrals with new structures which might perchance rival those of the monastic orders, and attract worshipers. Among the important Romanesque cathedrals built during this period are Notre Dame at Poitiers, St. Saturnin at Toulouse, Westminster Abbey, St. Ambrose at Milan, and the churches of Pisa, Monreale in Sicily, Compostella in Spain, and Mayence, Speyer, and Worms along the Rhine.

THE CISTERCIAN ROMANESQUE
So far as the monks themselves were concerned, a reaction set in against the ornate splendor of the new-style churches. St. Bernard (d. 1153) and his Cistercians objected strenuously to elaborate architecture and sculpturing. Such things, they said, "distract the mind of the monk from his piety and turn him from the evangelical poverty enjoined by St. Benedict." In keeping with their puritanical ideas, the Cistercian leaders decreed that their churches should be simple structures with towers only of wood "and not too high"; furthermore "there shall be neither sculptures nor paintings, only simple wooden crosses; . . . the doors of the churches shall be painted white . . . the legends on the walls, . . . in but one color and the letters without ornamentation." In spite of such restrictions, the Cistercians made real progress in architectural design. Because they used a true ribbed vaulting very much like that of the later structures their churches mark a transition from the heavy Romanesque barrel vaulting to the ribbed vaulting of the Gothic cathedral.

GOTHIC ARCHITECTURE
It is customary to refer to the first phase of medieval architectural development as Romanesque, and to the later phase (from about 1200 on) as Gothic in the North, and Renascence in Italy. Although hallowed by centuries of use, two of these terms are misleading. The Italian "Renascence" churches (as we shall see later) were not so much the result of a renascence of classical styles as of ten centuries of medieval evolution of Roman domed structures. As for "Gothic" architecture, the name was applied by late Italian artists who believed that their Italy had rediscovered the true classical architecture; therefore they rejected the Northern styles as barbarically "Gothic." As a matter of fact, "Gothic" architecture was merely a modification of the Northern Romanesque style. It might better be called French architecture, for it originated in

the Île de France, where are to be found its finest examples. In reality it was the Romanesque church, enlarged, heightened, and glorified by the efforts of French architects.

RIBBED VAULTING The evolution of Gothic architecture took place in Northern Europe. Doubtless this was due to the fact that the heavy-walled Romanesque style, with its small window spaces, was less suited to the North than to the sunny Mediterranean lands. Northern builders found that by strengthening the arches and buttresses at points where the pressure was greatest they could reduce them at other points. Thus by degrees thick walls and heavy vaults gave way to a lighter form of construction. Already, as we have seen, the Cistercian builders had developed a crude sort of ribbed vaulting. Eventually lay architects following the same lines of construction developed a light stone roof reinforced with ribs of masonry. By using reinforcing ribs of various widths, heights, and shapes (also the pointed or broken arch, in place of the semicircle), they were able to concentrate the weight of the roof at a relatively few important points. The contrast between this type of ceiling and the older Roman type of vault or dome has been described by a modern architect as follows: "It was as if people who had worn chopping bowls over their heads exchanged them for light umbrellas supported by steel ribs; in fact the Gothic vault was like reinforced steel construction, but in stone."

PRESSURES AND FLYING BUTTRESSES A stone ceiling, even though its weight was lightened and distributed at various points along the upper walls of the church, exerted a tremendous pressure both downward and outward. Here was a serious problem: How could the walls be kept from buckling under the weight? It was solved as follows. The *downward* pressure was concentrated at the outer and lower ends of the ribs; these were extended downward and merged into great piers, which in turn rested on the solid pavement below. This made possible another improvement: the spaces between the upper portions of the piers could be pierced for stained glass windows.

The handling of the *outward* pressure was also a difficult problem. The Romanesque builders had prevented their church walls from buckling outward by using narrow low ceilings, and by buttressing them with heavy aisle vaults and massive side walls. The genius of the Gothic architects showed itself in their artistic, yet effective, solution of this problem. Substantial and graceful reinforcements for the side walls were provided by means of flying buttresses. These

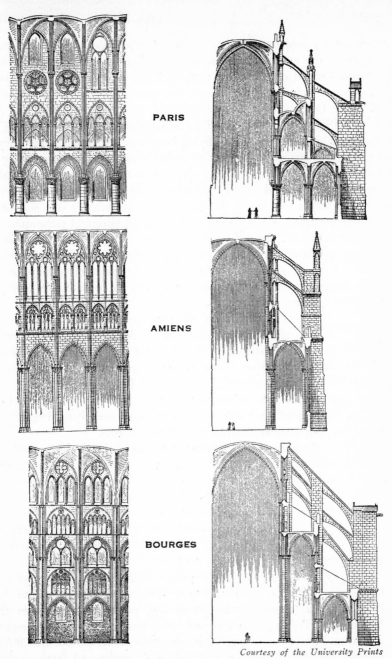

PARIS

AMIENS

BOURGES

LONGITUDINAL AND TRANSVERSE SECTIONS OF
FRENCH CATHEDRALS

were arched supports which strengthened the upper walls from the outside at the points where the outward thrust was strongest. These buttresses rested on the outer walls of the side aisles or of the choir chapels. An unappreciative tourist, on viewing the flying buttresses of Notre Dame in Paris, remarked that the cathedral looked like a lot of scaffolding that would fall down if it were not for the "crutches" along the sides. In reality the flying buttresses are crutches, but they appear to be graceful segments of arches which bridge the space between the eaves of the roof and the tops of the lower walls. To the architect, they were the chief means by which the structure was made not only secure, but also a thing of beauty. Historically they are the chief contribution of the Gothic builders to architectural technique.

It was this principle of concentrating, checking, and balancing the various weights and thrusts of the building that has given the Gothic cathedral its reputation of being one of the finest of architectural types. It made possible a structure that had height, breadth, and beauty without sacrificing stability.

"THE GOTHIC MIRACLE"   The Gothic cathedral has been aptly described as a glorious threefold unity: walls of stained glass, a pinnacled roof of ribbed masonry, and a façade of lacelike sculpture. In contrast to the Romanesque type of church, it was, in truth, "the Gothic miracle." The typical Romanesque church has been compared to "a crawling monster whose heavy spine bears down on its thick paws"; whereas the Gothic nave and flying buttresses seem like "an ancient trireme with banks of oars."

All of the internal and external structure of the Gothic cathedral was worked out with a graceful lightness and refined beauty that evokes enthusiastic praise from those who view it. The interiors of Notre Dame at Paris and of the cathedrals at Amiens, Rheims, and Chartres have a solemn grandeur and spaciousness that stirs the soul.

STAINED GLASS   The inspiring effect of the soaring vault of a Gothic nave is further enhanced by an important nonarchitectural feature which was also developed with remarkable success in northern France. This was the use of stained glass windows in place of mosaic or frescoed murals. During the Romanesque age, France, like Italy, had developed the art of wall painting. In churches at Vienne and Poitiers, one can still see examples of the excellently drawn and exquisitely colored frescoes of the earlier period. In Christian Spain and Italy also, the apses, side walls, vaults, and domes of the churches were decorated with Biblical scenes in brilliant gold and

CHARTRES

RHEIMS

STE. CHAPELLE, PARIS

AMIENS

GOTHIC CATHEDRALS OF FRANCE (XII-XIV C)
(See p. 712.)

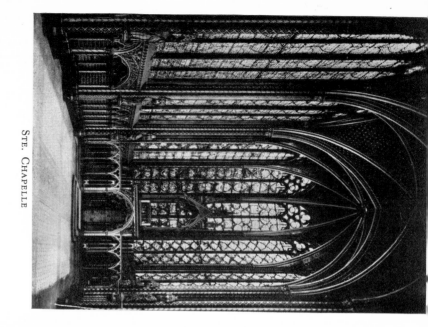

STE. CHAPELLE

Courtesy of the University Prints
CHARTRES

INTERIORS OF GOTHIC CATHEDRALS

(See p. 713.)

bright colors. But, as time went on, the Northern builders turned to stained glass for their decorative effects. As early as the tenth and eleventh centuries, windows in some of the Romanesque churches had been made out of bits of colored glass fastened together with strips of lead so as to form a picture. This art was used with great success in the twelfth-century Gothic cathedrals of Chartres, Angers, and Poitiers. By the thirteenth century most Gothic cathedrals had great stretches of stained glass windows containing vividly colored pictures of Biblical scenes, saints, heroes, demons, and even the every-day events of civic life. The chief object of stained glass windows, so it has been said,

was not to darken the nave but to glorify the light, whose glow scintil-lated with the richness of powdered jewels. . . . Its azures, its dark blues, its saffron and golden yellows, its oranges . . . reds, and its dark greens streaked the nave with the blood of Christ and the sapphire of the sky, with the russet of the autumn grapevines, and with the emerald of the distant seas and of the meadows round about. . . . When, on one of those gray days of the Ile-de-France, one enters Notre Dame to wait for the sun, one knows when it has come out by the blond inundation that suddenly invades the nave, rendering it aerial and golden. . . . At evening when the darkness is almost nocturnal in the vast interior whose vaults one sees hovering high up like the wings of a great bird of the night, one thing alone remains luminous—the glass of the windows. . . . The rose windows gather up the last reflections of the sun.[5]

One who has seen the afternoon sunlight streaming through the win-dows of Notre Dame, or Chartres, or Sainte Chapelle can scarcely un-derstand how it was that a famous modern scholar once characterized the Gothic cathedral as "an ideal gloom in which to worship a tor-tured Christ." More accurate, and also more truly characteristic of the Gothic age, is the assertion of an artist who wrote that "the church was the common house . . . the labor exchange, the popular theater . . . [it was] filled with tumult on market days, with dances on feast days . . . with singing on church days, and with the voice of the people on all days."

"SCULPTURED EMBROIDERY IN STONE" Impressive as is a Gothic interior, the exterior has even greater glories. Here the architectural effect was enhanced by the sculptor's art. The entire façade, from the carved figures of the portals to the topmost pinnacles of the towers, is often a mass of sculptured stone.

[5] Faure, *History of Art*, Harper & Brothers, II, 294.

On the façades there were pictured in stone the same sort of themes that were portrayed in the windows of the interior. Over each entrance is to be seen a relief symbolical of God the Father, or the Virgin Mary, or Joseph, or the saint to whom the portal is dedicated. Above and below and all around are figures by the thousand: historical and Biblical, real and symbolical, or prophets, saints, heroes, heroines, demons, and tortured souls. The façade of a cathedral was the medieval citizen's Bible and Sacred History in stone. On some of them are rows of life-sized kings or Biblical heroes extending from one side of the façade to the other. High up along the cornices and eaves are the gargoyles, queer dragonlike figures that serve as waterspouts. And somewhere on the cathedral there is likely to be at least one irreligious, immoral, or even obscene carving, secretly inserted by some discontented or mischievous workman.

ROMANESQUE AND GOTHIC SCULPTURE

It was on the outside of the Gothic cathedral that medieval sculpture found its most complete expression, just as it was on the interior walls of the Italian churches that the mural painters lavished their art. On the façades and porches of the cathedrals one can trace the evolution of Northern sculpture. The carving on the monastic Romanesque churches was heavy and ascetic, like the monks who built them. Over the entrances were crude symbolical plaques that reflected the sternness of a primitive monastic piety. The reliefs from the twelfth-century church of St. Peter of Moissac in southern France represent Romanesque sculpture at its best. Here is to be seen the severely just God of the Revelation [6] surrounded by the four beasts and the four and twenty elders; here also is the story of Lazarus, and scenes from the life of Christ. There were other churches that had such a profusion of ornament as to shock the puritanical soul of a St. Bernard.[7] A modern artist has spoken of the "opulent embroidery" of the façade of Notre Dame at Poitiers. Most important of all is the fact that Romanesque sculpture had in it the germ that evolved within one short century into the Gothic, a matchless type of sculpture which has ranked thirteenth-century France with Periclean Athens in the annals of artistic achievement. *Romanesque* sculpture had the sturdy realism and vertical lines of *early* Greek art, whereas the best *Gothic* sculpture has the calm grace and maturity of a statue by Phidias.

This new spirit in medieval church sculpture was the product, not

[6] Revelation 4.
[7] See above, p. 432.

A BISHOP,
AMIENS CATHEDRAL

GARGOYLES, NOTRE DAME, PARIS

FRENCH GOTHIC SCULPTURE (XIII C)

(See p. 714.)

Rheims Cathedral   Rheims Cathedral   Notre Dame, Paris

THE VIRGIN MARY

All Courtesy of the University Prints
SAINTS, CHARTRES CATHEDRAL

FRENCH GOTHIC SCULPTURE (XII-XIII C)

(See p. 715.)

of cloistered monks, but of townspeople. By the thirteenth century sculpturing had left the monastery. Laymen rather than monks carved the Christs, the Virgin Marys, and the saints on the façades of Chartres, Rheims, and Amiens cathedrals. These smiling Virgins may have been actual copies of the faces of the women who brought the stone carvers their midday meals of soup and bread. It was contact with the life of busy townsfolk that gave Gothic sculpture its human appeal. The cathedral, sculpture and all, was the product of the town in an age which had emerged from the monastic ruralism of the early Middle Ages.

CHRISTS, SAINTS, AND MADONNAS

The progress made by the French sculptors of the thirteenth century can be seen from a comparison of their Christs and madonnas with those of the previous century. By the thirteenth century, the stern-faced Christ of earlier times had changed into the gracious serene master seen in the statue of the "Beau Dieu" at Amiens. The figures of saints and prophets also took on a more human aspect. Their garments no longer hung in still vertical lines but were skillfully draped in a manner that reminds one of the ancient Greek masterpieces. Many of the faces were done with such feeling that they seem to be actual portraits.

In the figures of the Virgin Mary the genius of thirteenth-century sculpture is perhaps most evident. Amidst majestic figures of God Almighty, of gentle Christs, and animated apostles or saints, the Virgin mother is often the most arresting of them all. And this was no mere chance, for by the thirteenth century Mary had been taken into the hearts of the populace. That is why her title, "Our Lady" (Notre Dame), was given to hundreds of churches. The citizen sculptors of the French communes brought the madonna out of the background of Romanesque sculpture, gave her the place of honor on the façades of the Gothic cathedrals, and also humanized her. On the twelfth-century porch of the north side of Chartres Cathedral she appears in restrained dignity, holding stiffly in her left arm a puppetlike Christ child. On the opposite porch of the south side is a statue from the next century depicting a madonna and child that are full of life and human appeal. Here Mary is a dainty feminine creature, who looks fondly at the animated baby cuddled in the curve of her arm. On the portal of Amiens Cathedral is another thirteenth-century madonna who has a gracious charm not to be found in the earlier statues. Thirteenth-century Rheims has similarly appealing figures in a statue of the angel of the Annunciation and in a slender pensive Mary, portrayed with the simplicity of perfect art. Some of these Rheims statues are so classical in spirit that it is thought that they may have been copied from antique statues of vestal virgins. Whatever their origin, they illustrate the genius of Gothic sculpture, and the supreme position of Mary, the serene and gracious "Queen of Heaven," in late medieval religion.

TYPES OF GOTHIC CATHEDRALS   By the opening of the fourteenth century almost every city within a radius of fifty miles of Paris had erected or had begun the construction of a Gothic cathedral. The larger cities vied with one another to create more expansive naves, more lacelike façades, or taller spires than those of their neighbors. Five of these cathedrals are outstanding architectural achievements and an eternal inspiration to those who love beautiful works of art. At Paris there is Notre Dame, with its rather simple sculptured façade, surmounted by two sturdy towers. The slender central spire, graceful flying buttresses, and three gigantic rose windows are well known to cathedral lovers. A short distance away is Sainte Chapelle, example of delicate small-scale Gothic architecture at its very best. This little relic-chapel, built by St. Louis IX as a shrine for the crown of thorns which he had brought from the Holy Land, is an architectural gem which has received universal acclaim. Above the lower chapel, which serves as a base for the structure, is what many experts consider the most perfect example of a Gothic interior in existence. It is simply a vaulted ceiling supported by walls that are an almost unbroken expanse of magnificent stained windows. Through these the light of day is transformed, shedding a magnificent pattern of color over the entire chapel.

North of Paris is the Cathedral of Amiens, said to have the most perfect nave in all France, and noted for its beautiful statuary. The cathedral at Rheims (a few miles to the east) also has a structural grandeur and richness of sculpturing that has made it world-famous. South of Paris, at Chartres, are the most remarkable examples of medieval stained glass, the greatest profusion of sculpture, and two noteworthy spires.

Elsewhere there were Gothic triumphs that are second only to those already mentioned. Laon has a cathedral that is the twin sister of Notre Dame at Paris, save for its slightly bolder and less refined style. At Beauvais one can still see the magnificent choir of a cathedral that was to have been the greatest church in Christendom. Its unfinished vault, over 150 feet in height, is said to have been, like the tower of Babel, an example of God's unwillingness to let proud human builders attain their ambition. The rather imposing but inconsistent cathedral at Rouen, a mixture of several styles, is overly decorated with flamboyant sculpture and is sometimes cited as an example of the "death struggle of Gothic art, smothered under a profusion of detail." Bourges, Orléans, Le Mans, and hundreds of other cities have their own masterpieces. Unique among them for its picturesque location is the Abbey of Mont St. Michel, perched on a rocklike island off the coast of Normandy. It was begun in the early centuries as a shrine to St. Michael, and was built and rebuilt into a fortress-monastery. Its battlemented lower walls, vaulted halls and chapels, and pinnacled roofs, all surmounted by a graceful spire, make an unforgettable impression.

REGIONAL VARIATIONS IN ARCHITECTURE

ENGLISH
ROMANESQUE

During the eleventh century, England, like France, rebuilt her old churches in the new Romanesque style. Before the Norman Conquest, Edward the Confessor called in French architects to build Westminster Abbey. After the Conquest, English architecture took on even more of the French Romanesque characteristics. Canterbury Cathedral was rebuilt by its new Norman archbishop in the style of St. Stephen's at Caen, of which he had been abbot. Early in the twelfth century, Durham Cathedral, the best preserved of all the Norman Romanesque churches of England, was completed. A grand example of the square-towered, heavy-pillared, Anglo-Norman style, it exemplifies the manner in which the rugged Germanic spirit of the Anglo-Saxons and the Norsemen was tempered and refined by Continental influence.

ENGLISH GOTHIC

As time went on England evolved her own peculiar style of Gothic architecture. The truly English cathedrals have several distinctive traits, the square towers and the simple unsculptured façades, to mention but two. Salisbury Cathedral, built in the thirteenth century, is an excellent illustration of the typical English cathedral, which appears to be much longer and lower than those of France. The sprawling structure of English cathedrals of this type is due to the fact that they were built in the open where there was plenty of space. Continental cathedrals, planted in the midst of crowded cities, were forced upward, like a modern skyscraper.

The *late* Gothic churches of England were more complex and or-

nate in detail. Elaborate ribbed vaulting was developed in intricate patterns. In parish churches, as well, the late Gothic continued the square-
towered lines of Anglo-Saxon and Norman times, but in decorative
detail and in ribbed "fan" vaulting, ultrarefinement predominated.
The same tendency is noticeable in the late French (or flamboyant)
Gothic. With superficial intricacy of decoration, came decline, for
having lost its structural simplicity, Gothic architecture and sculpture
died. Never before nor since has either France or England created
architectural beauty equal to that of the twelfth- and thirteenth-century
cathedrals.

GERMAN
CHURCHES
Germany, once thought to have been the original
home of Gothic architecture, was less influenced by
it than any other part of the West save Italy. Until
the late thirteenth century, most German churches (like those of Italy)
were either circular-domed rotundas or rectangular Romanesque
structures. The best existing example of the circular type is the Church
of St. Gereon at Cologne. There are numerous examples of Romanesque churches, especially along the Rhine. Spires, Mainz, and Worms
have impressive, fortresslike cathedrals. Worms Cathedral, for instance,
has five towers: an octagonal one over the central crossing and two
round towers at each end. The general effect is that of massive and
bewildering complexity. German churches were usually lacking in
sculptured decoration; their builders seem to have aimed at complicated monumental effects.

When Gothic architecture finally came to Germany, it was a
finished product, imported direct from France. Its best example is
Cologne Cathedral, which has been called "a turgid thin and dry
amplification of the cathedral of Amiens. . . . It remains quite by itself in the pedantic stiffness of its lines." Nevertheless Cologne is the
grandest of German Gothic cathedrals and one of the most impressive
in all Europe. Though it lacks the detailed refinements and harmonious lines of the French Gothic, its tremendous pinnacled mass, dominated by twin towers 500 feet in height, makes a spectacular and inspiring landmark.

ITALIAN GOTHIC
The Gothic churches of Italy were also very largely
a foreign importation. In the thirteenth century, Cistercian monks introduced semi-Gothic effects, and pure Gothic designs
were used somewhat in Naples-Sicily and at Assisi. The finest example of Italian Gothic is the Cathedral of Milan, built during the
late Middle Ages under the supervision of French as well as German

CANTERBURY (XIII-XV C)

BURGOS (XIII-XV C)

COLOGNE (XIII-XIX C)

MILAN (XIV-XIX C)

GOTHIC CATHEDRALS

(See pp. 717 ff.)

SAN MINIATO, FLORENCE

PISA, WITH LEANING BELL TOWER

ROMANESQUE CHURCHES OF ITALY (XI and XII C)

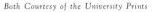(See pp. 726 ff.)

and Italian architects. Like Cologne Cathedral, it exemplifies massiveness rather than purity and refinement of style. Built entirely of marble and characterized by a profusion of statuary and pinnacles, from a distance it gives the impression of a glorious white mountain of sculpture. It covers more ground space than any other church in Europe and, from the spectacular standpoint, vies with Cologne Cathedral and St. Peter's at Rome.

SPANISH CATHEDRALS The Gothic architecture of Spain, like that of Germany and Italy, was imported from France and was superimposed on an already well-developed Romanesque style. During the early Middle Ages, Spanish architecture had been dominated first by Visigothic and then by Arabic influences. Later, during the period of the Spanish "crusades" of the eleventh and twelfth centuries, Provençal and Lombard influences came in. The church at the famous shrine of St. James of Compostella was a copy of a south French church (St. Saturnin at Toulouse) and may have been sculptured by some of the French artists who were at that time commencing to migrate to northern Spain.

In the thirteenth century Spain took over the French Gothic style with such enthusiasm that soon the country had cathedrals comparable to those of Chartres, Amiens, and Rheims. During these centuries, Aragon, Navarre, Castile, and Leon seem in many ways to have been frontier outposts of French civilization. Spanish monarchs married French princesses. Cistercian monks founded monasteries in Spain, using their own Burgundian styles of architecture. Burgos, one of the finest Gothic cathedrals in Spain, was built by a bishop who had traveled in France. Similarly, the cathedrals of Leon and Toledo so closely resemble the churches of France that they are thought to have been planned by French architects.

GOTHIC ARCHITECTURE AND FRENCH GENIUS Spanish Gothic architecture is merely one aspect of the marvelous expansion of French civilization during the age of faith, crusades, towns, and cathedrals.

For two centuries, France had been the great hearth of the Occident. Through the Normans it had conquered Sicily and England. . . . French barons were wearing the crowns of Athens, of Constantinople, of Cyprus, and of Jerusalem. There emanated from the French soul that energy . . . which permitted it each year, at a hundred points in France, to dig canals, to build bridges, aqueducts, and fountains, to open hospitals and schools, and to hang pointed vaults. . . . French romances sped all over the world.

Almost all the heads of the foreign universities had passed through the University of Paris, where the nations maintained permanent colleges. . . . After the great [architect] Guillaume de Sens had broken his legs by a fall from the scaffolding in the nave of Canterbury, a hundred others had answered the call from foreign communes or vestry boards. . . . Spanish cities, in the fourteenth century, called in French architects. Others went as far as Poland, and even Finland. . . . Almost everywhere, at least in the beginning, the master builders would bring a first plan inspired by Amiens, or Rheims, or Chartres, or Notre Dame, or Beauvais.[8]

And thus it was that France for a time led the architectural world. Although Milan boasted the most spacious Gothic cathedral in Europe, and Cologne the tallest spire, France was the creator of this inspired art. Fittingly enough, France is still the repository of the most precious treasures of Gothic architecture and sculpture.

RESIDENCES So far as nonreligious buildings are concerned, the trend during the Middle Ages was somewhat like that in church architecture—from heavy fortresslike structures to a less massive and more habitable type. In this process there were three general stages of evolution comparable to the Romanesque, Gothic, and late Italian types of churches. The feudal castle, which we have already described,[9] was a heavy-walled structure so similar to the Romanesque church that it might be called the Romanesque type of residence. It was suited to an age of feudal warfare. The palaces and châteaux of the ensuing period showed the influence of town life and the increasing demand for material comforts. Like the Gothic cathedrals of that period, secular buildings manifested a lighter and airier type of construction, some of them showing definite traces of Gothic architectural influences. This stage of castle building is exemplified in the Tower of London, Edward I's castle at Carnarvon, and many of the older castles still standing in Continental Europe. Even in Italy, in the famous Doge's Palace at Venice, there are many elements of Gothic architecture.

Late in the Middle Ages, as wealth increased, there was introduced, chiefly from Italy, a much more ornate and splendid type of residential architecture in what is often called the "Renascence" style because of its classical characteristics. Eventually, through the double influence of classical architecture and town life, the medieval castle evolved into the modern palace. The Vatican at Rome and many of

[8] Faure, *op. cit.*, II, 344 ff.
[9] See above, pp. 232 ff.

the splendidly decorated palaces in Florence illustrate the manner in which Italy developed this form of residence. In France the new trend can be seen in the royal châteaux of the Loire Valley (Chenonceaux, Chinon, Chambord, Azay-le-Rideau, and Blois) and of Paris (Fontainebleau, St. Germain-en-Laye, and the new Louvre). Italian artists such as da Vinci and Benvenuto Cellini were among those who were brought to France "to build and work at the king's command, in the Italian style." Usually they merely rebuilt older Gothic structures in the new style. The result was in many cases a hybrid form of structure, such as is still to be seen at Blois on the Loire River. In Germany and England also, many Gothic palaces were given a veneer of classical Italian decoration. This was done at Heidelberg and at Kennilworth. Fortunately along the Rhine most of the castles were left relatively unreconstructed so that we still have in Rheinstein and the "Mouse Tower" splendid examples of the late medieval castle.

During the late Middle Ages wealthy burghers built town houses that were veritable palaces. Such was the Gothic residence of the rich French merchant, Jacques Coeur, at Bourges. The Fuggers of Augsburg also lived in houses of regal splendor. Most of the members of the burgher class, however, lived in rather small, and to us picturesque, town homes of the types already described.[10]

CIVIC CASTLES AND TOWN HALLS   The evolution of the civic or municipal building was somewhat similar to that of the private castle. In the Romanesque period most towns, in addition to their walled defenses, had fortified citadels. Among the rare examples of fortress-towns still in existence are Carcassone in France, Avilla in Spain, and Nuremberg and Rothenburg in Germany. In such towns, one can still see not only the quaint city gates and outer walls, but also the fortified citadels of a grim warlike age. Equally picturesque are the unfortified Gothic structures of the later period of prosperous commercial towns. Among these are the municipal bell tower of Bruges, the ornate city hall at Brussels, and the Cloth (Guild) Hall at Ypres. In Florence, Siena, and most of the larger Italian cities there were sturdy rectangular "public palaces," often with graceful bell towers. That of Siena rises in slender grace 300 feet above the pavement. Interestingly enough, the Gothic style was never supplanted in civic architecture by the classical forms of the Italian "Renascence."

[10] See above, p. 366.

SCULPTURE AND
INDEPENDENT
ENGRAVING

As we have noted in our survey of Romanesque and Gothic churches, the arts of sculpture, glazing, and painting were subordinate to architecture and had little expression apart from the cathedrals. This is further exemplified by the fact that the tombs and statues of great personages were usually placed in churches. Like many other cathedrals, Notre Dame in Paris has high up on its façade a row of portrait statues of monarchs. The cathedral interiors likewise were filled with works of sculpture, mostly tombs on which were depicted the recumbent or praying figures of the notables whose ashes they contained. The crypt and choir chapels of St. Denis near Paris are crowded with sarcophagi and funeral statues of kings and princes from Dagobert, a successor of Clovis, to the many Louis' of modern times.

Most church treasuries contain little gems of the medieval engraver's art: statuettes of religious personages, and madonnas in gold, silver, ivory, or wood. Among the innumerable works of art made and treasured by the church were carved stone vases, gold and silver crosses, bronze standards, chests, and doors, and varied types of metal work or ivory, beautifully carved and set with gems. Perhaps the most carefully and lavishly engraved of all were the relic caskets. Made in all sorts of curious shapes, usually they took the form of a church, but often they were in the shape of the relic they contained. The skull of a saint, for instance, might be encased in a jeweled golden head. Although craftsmen (like works of art) were often imported from the East, the Westerners soon learned foreign techniques for themselves and in time made noteworthy improvements. Venetian glass and Limoges enamels are outstanding examples of Western Europe's achievements in the minor arts.

The same is true of the textile arts. The best silken and cloth-of-gold embroidery came from Constantinople, but Spain produced fine leather work, rugs, and tapestries. As for tapestries, northern France achieved distinction by the famous Bayeux tapestry, a strip of needlework 20 inches wide and 231 feet long, supposedly made by Queen Matilda and her ladies in commemoration of the Norman Conquest, many incidents of which it depicts.

MANUSCRIPT
MAKING

There is one other type of medieval art, bookmaking, of which many beautiful examples are still to be seen in the manuscripts that are treasured in European and American libraries and museums. Medieval bookmaking was an art, a science, and a handicraft which involved the services

BOWL SET WITH GEMS

RELIC CASKET (XII C)

SCENE FROM THE BAYEUX TAPESTRY (XI C)

THE MINOR ARTS

(See p. 722.)

Courtesy of the University Prints

BREVIARY (XIV C)

MANUSCRIPT ILLUMINATION

(See pp. 722 ff.)

of leather workers, scribes, rubricators, illuminators and miniaturists, and binders. Until the development of papermaking in the fifteenth century, most books were written on parchment, which was made from the skins of sheep, goats, or other domestic animals. The preparation of parchment was important. Choice skins without breaks or blemishes were used for the finest and most expensive manuscripts and were carefully cured and polished to a smooth thin texture and color, often as beautiful as old ivory. The membrane of the uterus was sometimes used for especially fine manuscripts or for sheets for illustrations.

The work of copying, done by scribes, demanded accuracy, uniformity, and an experimental knowledge of inks that were not likely to fade. Paragraph and chapter headings were left to a special scribe who used colored ink. Because of the fact that red (*rubra*) was most commonly employed, he was called the *rubricator*.

More artistic in character was the work of the illustrators. Not satisfied with enlarged and colored capital letters, the bookmakers employed skillful draftsmen and artists who decorated the capitals, headings and endings of chapters, and the borders of the pages in intricate designs. Margins were filled with flowers, leaves, animals, humans, and grotesque figures of all kinds, interlaced with curved lines, flourishes, and brackets. A capital "O" might be represented by the yawning mouth of a dragon, with the rest of its body sprawling into the upper and lower margins of the page. Small pictures, called miniatures, were sometimes inserted. Frontispieces and entire pages might contain larger illustrations of men, Biblical scenes, or representations of the activities of the various months of the year. Much of the work of the illustrators was crude and awkward, but some of their masterpieces are marvels of imaginative composition and intricate color work. Although the art of illustration was somewhat influenced by stained-glass work and by mural painting, in the later centuries it contributed much to the art of panel painting in the Netherlands and to fresco painting in Italy.

Until the fourteenth and fifteenth centuries, gilt and bright colors predominated. In the more expensive works gold and silver leaf were used for the illustrations. Small portions of leaf were applied to parts of a picture on a base of plaster or sizing. After careful polishing, these parts shone with mirrorlike brilliancy. Most work, however, was done with fluids. Powdered gold, silver, and color pigments were mixed with sizing or egg white and applied with a brush. The favorite color, red, was made from any one of several materials: from *rubrica,* a reddish clay tinged with iron oxides; from vegetable juices; or from metallic compounds. The expensive vermilion red was obtained from a mercury sulphate; the cheaper and deeper reds came from red lead, *minium,* from which word the name *miniature* was derived. Blue pigments, which were also popular, were made from the very rare lapis lazuli imported from the East, or from copper or indigo compounds. Lapis lazuli blue was so expensive that it was sometimes made from the powdered scrapings taken from older manuscripts. Whatever the colors—red, blue, green, scarlet, or yellow—they were usually made with powdered pigments (derived from metals, colored earths, or vegetables). These were mixed with a fluid medium of egg white, gum arabic, or a sizing composed of boiled parchment, fish bones, or other gluelike substances. The result, a thick, creamy mixture, was applied with a brush.

Once a book had been copied and illustrated, it was turned over to the binders, who sewed the leaves together and enclosed them in stout covers of parchment or wood. The binding of religious books and especially of psalm books (psalters) and prayer books (books of hours) for prominent or wealthy people was a real work of art. The volumes were covered with leather, embossed with metal, fitted with ornate clasps, and often decorated with insets of enamel work, gems, or finely carved ivory.

BURGUNDIAN-NETHERLANDS SCULPTURE

We conclude our survey of the arts of the North with a brief account of Burgundian-Flemish art. Along the northeastern frontier of France, during the late fourteenth century, there arose a school of sculpture and painting that was comparable to that of the so-called Italian Renascence. In most respects and in most regions of the North, the late Middle Ages, when France, England, and Germany were torn by both foreign and civil wars, was a period of artistic decline. But there was an exception. Along the west bank of the Rhine, from Ghent in Flanders to Dijon in Burgundy, a remarkably progressive civilization came into being in the fifteenth century. It seemed to draw the best from all surrounding regions. The dukes of this Burgundian state were bold warriors, clever statesmen, and zealous patrons of culture. Being Frenchmen, they had close contacts with the Île de France. The wealth and civic spirit of the Netherlands were combined with the artistic traditions of France to produce an unusual art, for many of their artists were Netherlanders who had studied in France.

One of the most noteworthy of the sculptors was a Dutchman named Claus Sluter (ca. 1400). At Dijon he decorated the Carthusian monastery in which the tombs of the dukes were to be placed. Of his work there, one astounding piece remains—the "Well of Moses," comprising a six-sided base for a large statue. It consists of statues of six prophets above whom weeping angels hover with outspread wings. The most impressive of the prophets is Moses, a majestic robed figure with a flowing beard, holding the scroll of the law. It is noteworthy that this Moses was executed a century before the time of Michelangelo, whose "Moses" and "David" mark the high point of medieval Italian sculpture.

NETHERLANDS PAINTING

Of equal importance, but much better known than Sluter's statues, are the paintings of John van Eyck (d. 1440). His most famous work is the "Altar Piece of the Lamb" at Ghent. This set of painted panels contains beautifully colored figures of God the Father, the Virgin, Adam and Eve, John the Baptist, angels singing and playing musical instruments, and below these a pageant of marvelously realistic soldiers, learned men, clergymen, pilgrims, saints, martyrs, and angels. All are adoring the Lamb of God, which is depicted as a lamb standing on a platform with blood spurting from its throat into a chalice. This complex and strangely allegorical picture represents the scene in paradise [11] where "a great multitude . . . stood before the Lamb, clothed with white robes, and palms in their hands." It ranks high in artistic importance because of its group composition, magnificent color, and natural facial expression in the individual figures. Van Eyck painted other religious works as well as many quaintly realistic portraits which are much more appealing to the modern mind.

From the standpoint of medieval art all of this is a remarkable example of the increasing secularism of life, as well as of the dawning artistic genius of the Netherlands. Here, amid the busy city life of the North, was a cultural evolution quite as noteworthy in some respects as that which was beginning at this very time in the cities of northern Italy. In both cases, town life, with its vibrant competitive spirit, seems to have furnished the environment and the chief impetus for truly great development in art. And likewise it is such influences, rather than revived classical antiquity, that provided the background for Gothic art, for ancient Athenian culture, and—we believe—for every great productive era in human culture.

[11] Revelation 7:9.

$$\equiv XXXV \equiv$$

THE ARTS IN ITALY IN THE LATE MIDDLE AGES

ITALIAN church building during the early Middle Ages, as we have seen, followed two main lines of development: (1) the rectangular basilica, which evolved into the Romanesque cathedral, and (2) the domed rotunda, which was continued in the circular or octagonal baptistries of later times.

ROMANESQUE CHURCHES

Throughout the Middle Ages most Italian churches were of the rectangular basilican or Romanesque type. Usually there was a central nave flanked by rows of classical columns, two (and often four) side aisles, and sometimes transepts. The façades were simple, with little decorative variation from the traditional style, which tended to rather monotonous lines of round arched doorways with intervening columns or pilasters.[1] In some regions it was the custom to use ornamental strips of colored stone and colonnaded upper galleries to decorate the façades. The twelfth-century cathedral of Pisa is an excellent example of the manner in which the more progressive builders employed arches and rows of columns or pilasters to relieve the monotony of a Romanesque exterior. The classic simplicity of this Pisan style has been compared with that of the ancient Greek Parthenon, in contrast to the lavishly sculptured façades of the Gothic cathedrals of Northern Europe.

The interiors of these churches revealed their basilican ancestry. The nave was separated from the side aisles by rows of classical columns surmounted by the semicircular arches, which supported the upper gallery and clerestory. The windows were narrow and the wide expanse of wall space at the sides of the church and in the curved apse were decorated with mural paintings or mosaics. The flat ceilings were invariably of wood, sometimes in coffered panels. Very few Italian churches had stone roofs. The beautiful cathedral of Pisa exemplifies the unusually large type of church. It has four side aisles roofed with

---

[1] Pilasters are strips of decoration resembling a rectangular pillar set into a wall.

stone vaults, also double rows of monolith columns, and brilliant mosaics.

GOTHIC
INFLUENCES
IN ITALY

In the later Middle Ages two changes took place in Italian church architecture. One was the introduction of the Gothic style; the other the development of the dome. The introduction of Gothic architecture in Lombardy, Assisi, and Naples-Sicily, and the Gothic cathedral of Milan have already been discussed. There is, however, another example of Gothic art in Italy which has been called "one of the most exquisite works of art that mankind ever produced." It is the graceful square bell tower, alongside the cathedral of Florence.[2] Planned by the painter Giotto, its pure simple lines are an ever-present reminder that central Italy was strongly influenced by Gothic tendencies. As a whole, however, Italy never really accepted the Northern style, and later, during the age of classicism, Italian artists gave to it the name "Gothic." To them it was simply another example of barbaric Germanic culture.

THE ROMAN
DOME

The more noteworthy of the two changes in Italian architecture was the continued evolution of the Roman dome, and its use as the crowning feature of the late Romanesque church. As we have already seen,[3] during the early Middle Ages the flat Roman dome assumed higher and more spectacular proportions. During the later Middle Ages it came into its own. At Pisa in the twelfth century a circular baptistry was built, entirely separate from the main church, with a high conical dome somewhat like those of St. Mark's in Venice. Florence likewise had a domed baptistry, but of octagonal form.

The dome was also used to embellish the rectangular churches of these two cities. At Pisa, the classically severe cathedral was adorned with a small but high dome or cupola. At Florence, about two centuries later, Brunelleschi (d. 1446) added to the already existing church a great octagonal dome which was the wonder of the Italian world. Instead of merely placing a cupola over the crossing (as had been

[2] The bell tower illustrates an interesting trait of Italian architecture: the tower was usually placed alongside, rather than on top of, the church. In like manner, the baptistries also were separated from the churches and housed in circular domed buildings. In the later Middle Ages, many Italian churches came to be triple-unit structures, with a rectangular basilica, a circular domed baptistry, and a campanile. Pisa furnishes one of the most picturesque examples of this architectural characteristic.

[3] See above, p. 326.

done at Pisa and on other Romanesque churches), he built the entire choir end of the church in the form of an immense octagonal chapel almost 150 feet in diameter, surmounted by the largest and most spectacular dome ever erected in the West. Contemporaries wrote that the structure "seemed like a new hill rising among the houses, and the graceful Tuscan hills round about recognized it as a sister." The result was a sort of combination church, a nave joined with a rotunda. So important was Brunelleschi's dome that the cathedral at Florence has ever since been called the *Duomo*.

ST. PETER'S   Stupendous as was Brunelleschi's *Duomo,* it was surpassed less than a century later by the new church of St. Peter's at Rome. This was begun by Bramante during the pontificate of Julius II, and completed late in the sixteenth century by Michelangelo and one of his pupils. Bramante is said to have planned a low-lying central dome, like that of the Roman Pantheon, with smaller domes on the transepts, somewhat after the fashion of St. Mark's in Venice and many of the Eastern churches. But Michelangelo decided on a more unified plan in which the entire structure would center in one gigantic dome. He was much criticized for his stubborn insistence, and it is said that he once told certain of the papal underlings: "Your duty is to see that the donations come in and that they are not stolen by grafters; the plan and drawings of the church shall be my affair." Fortunately the pope supported him and after Michelangelo's death employed one of his pupils, who made the dome still lighter and more impressive in appearance.

The result was a tremendous dome of magnificent proportions. It rises to a height of 400 feet, supported by a circle of columns and other structural work, which in turn rests upon the intersecting vaults of the four transepts. Like the immense dome of St. Sophia, constructed just ten centuries earlier, and like many modern domes that have been modeled after it, the airy interior of St. Peter's carries man's gaze to the very skies. But the supreme genius of the builders of St. Peter's showed in its external appearance. Unlike the depressingly low vault of the Roman Pantheon, and the heavily buttressed dome of St. Sophia, St. Peter's has a soaring height that has made it one of the most magnificent landmarks of Rome. Among medieval structures only the Florentine *Duomo* and the Cologne Cathedral can compare with it. Its one defect is that the builders sacrificed security for appearance; later architects were forced to use internal braces to keep the great dome intact. Nevertheless, for spectacular splendor, the modern world has not surpassed this structure.

INFLUENCES ON MODERN ARCHI- TECTURE
The best evidence of the architectural merit of St. Peter's is the fact that for five centuries it has been the supreme model for domed buildings. In the realm of public edifices its triumph has been unchallenged. To mention only a few examples: the Hôtel des Invalides and the Pantheon in Paris, the national capitols of several South American republics, innumerable State capitols in the United States, and our national capitol at Washington bear witness to the lasting popularity of this style. Even in ecclesiastical architecture the dome has played an important role. St. Paul's in London and many of the modern churches of Europe and of America are of the domed style of St. Peter's.

The Roman dome, modified by Eastern and Western builders during ten medieval centuries, became a world-famous architectural type. To Bramante, the Florentine, and later to Michelangelo and his pupils, is due the chief credit for this triumph. It is also noteworthy that St. Peter's marks the triumph of Rome and its sixteenth-century artists over the Florentines, who had reigned supreme throughout the fifteenth century. For centuries thereafter, Michelangelo's Roman school of architects dominated Italian church building.

SCULPTURE IN ITALY: A REVIVAL OF CLASSICAL INFLUENCES [4]

Italy produced little sculpture of importance during the early Middle Ages although there was a certain amount of small-scale engraving, carving on pillars and candlesticks, and reliefs on sarcophagi and walls. Unlike the Northern cathedral builders, the Italians did not cover the façades of their churches with statuary. There are, however, twelfth-century altar and pulpit carvings at Salerno which indicated at least the beginnings of a sculptural art that was decidedly classical in form. It was from this southern region that Nicholas of Pisa (or Apulia) came, bringing to central Italy its first classical impulses and the beginnings of a revived sculpture. Eventually the Gothic sculp-

---

[4] We use the term *classical* with reference to the works of Greek-Roman antiquity. We use the term *revival* instead of renascence or renaissance (a modern French word for *rebirth*), because there are serious objections to using a *French* expression of such implications to designate a development *in Italy* which was an *evolution* as well as a revival.

tural traditions of Italy were to give way almost completely to this new influence.

NICHOLAS OF
PISA (d. 1278)

The first marked change in Italian sculpture came when Nicholas of Pisa and his followers decorated several pulpits with reliefs in a distinctly classical Roman style. The important factor in Nicholas's work was his direct and deliberate imitation of ancient art. He is thought to have copied many of his figures from ancient Roman vases and sarcophagi, remnants of which were to be found in all parts of Italy. On one of his pulpits the Virgin Mary appears reclining on a divan, exactly like a Roman lady in an antique relief. The hair and garment draperies are unmistakably classical. Nicholas's emphasis and dependence on the ancient sculptural styles was as marked as Petrarch's was on classical literary forms and for a time his classical sculpturing was as popular with the Italians as were Petrarch's classical writings. He, his son, and their followers were called to erect pulpits and other sculptured monuments in neighboring Siena, Florence, Rome, Naples, and even across the Apennines in Lombardy.

Fortunately Italian sculpture did not become merely a slavish imitation of classical works. For a century or more the older Romanesque and Gothic influences persisted, and artists continued to picture religious subjects in the pious and primitively realistic attitudes that had long been prevalent in church decoration. Eventually both the old and new styles gave way to a more natural development.

NATURALISM IN
SCULPTURE

During the fourteenth and early fifteenth centuries, certain sculptors attempted to blend the Gothic with the revived classical styles. But neither Gothic nor revived classical influences were responsible for the masterpieces of this period. Progress was made by the study of real life rather than by slavish imitation of old forms. This progressive element is best illustrated by the career of Donatello (d. 1466), a Florentine who gave to Italian sculpture a character all its own. As a young man he and a friend spent every penny of their savings to go to Rome and study art. While there Donatello imbibed the spirit of classical art but he also learned about human beings. His later work reveals an intimate knowledge not only of the human body, but also of the human spirit. In addition to some unusually natural figures on reliefs, pulpits, and choir lofts, he sculptured many remarkable statues. His "St. George" was so convincingly natural in pose and facial ex-

WELL OF MOSES, MONASTERY AT DIJON, BY SLUTER

Both Courtesy of the University Prints

AMBOISE CHAPEL

FRENCH GOTHIC SCULPTURE (XIV-XV C)

(See pp. 724 ff.)

ST. GEORGE BY DONATELLO

DAVID BY MICHELANGELO

MOSES BY MICHELANGELO

All Courtesy of the University Prints
PIETÀ BY MICHELANGELO

ITALIAN SCULPTURE (XV·XVI C)

(See pp. 730 ff.)

pression that when Michelangelo saw it he is said to have given the command: "March." Donatello also did a youthful David, said to have been the first nude statue *in bronze* since Roman times. More impressive is his huge statue of "Gattamelata," a famous military commander, mounted on a sturdy horse. This was the first of a number of famous equestrian statues of which the well-known "Colleoni" by Donatello's successor, Verrocchio, is also highly praised.

DELLA ROBBIA
AND GHIBERTI

Only two other fifteenth-century sculptors can be compared with Donatello in artistic achievements— Luca della Robbia and Ghiberti. The former is well known for his enameled terra cotta plaques, but his marble reliefs on the "Singing Gallery" at Florence are of infinitely greater merit. For graceful naturalness, his figures of choirboys surpass even those by Donatello on the opposite gallery of the same church.

Ghiberti (d. 1455), an artist of equal merit, worked with a different type of material, bronze. His most outstanding achievement was two sets of doors for the baptistry at Florence. This structure, like many Italian churches, already had one set of bronze doors, made by a Pisan artist. Early in the fifteenth century a competition was held for the selection of a sculptor to do the two remaining portals. Out of seven contestants, Ghiberti, then only twenty years of age, won the commission. After twenty years of work, he produced his first set of doors—twenty-four panels depicting scenes from the Old Testament. These were followed by another set, with ten beautifully molded scenes from the New Testament. The scientific care with which they were constructed is indicated in Ghiberti's own description of the manner in which he attained perspective, a feat never before accomplished in bronze. On some of them, he said, "I introduced more than a hundred figures. . . . Observing the laws of vision, I succeeded in giving them an appearance of such reality that if seen from a distance, the figures seemed to be in the full round. In the different planes, the nearer figures are the greater, those further away diminish in size just as occurs in nature." [5]

Along the borders of the doors were designs of leaves, flowers, animals, and nude figures, classical in character but realistically carved. Michelangelo, a century later, said of these doors: "They are so beautiful that they might be the gates of Paradise." They mark the climax of the bronze worker's art in medieval Italy.

[5] Pijoan, *History of Art,* III, 80.

MICHELANGELO   The greatest of Italian sculptors was yet to come—
Michelangelo (d. 1564). His fiery genius, though no-
table in painting and architecture, was most brilliantly displayed in the
handling of marble. His "David," an immense statue of a nude shepherd boy, far surpasses those by Donatello and his immediate successors. It reminds one of the Greek masterpieces of the Periclean
Age, and it well typifies Michelangelo's ability to portray the human
body in marble. He is said to have cared for nothing in art quite
so much as the picturing of the nude masculine form. Equally effective, though very different in spirit, is his "Pietà," a study of the
sorrowing Mary holding the limp body of her crucified Son. Another of his famous Biblical figures is a huge, stern-faced Moses
which he is said to have hewn out of a great block of marble that
another sculptor had discarded. It was to have been a part of a tomb
for Pope Julius II, which was never finished. Michelangelo completed
two other tombs, both for the Medici family. They are famous, not
only for the life-size portrait statues of two young princes, but also
for the symbolical reclining figures of "Night" and "Day" and "Dawn"
and "Twilight," which comprise the lower sections. In these two
works, done during his later days, Michelangelo's earlier energy seems
to have given way to somber pessimism. It was during this period that
he wrote the following melancholy lines concerning the increasing
corruption and violence of the times:

> Ah! glad am I to sleep in stone, while woe
> And dire disgrace rage unreproved near;
> A happy chance to neither see nor hear,
> So wake me not! When passing, whisper low.[6]

His pessimistic forebodings were prophetic: Italian sculpture, along
with almost all phases of civilization, was soon to decline.

DECLINE OF   Between Michelangelo and the slavish and overdone
ITALIAN SCULP-   sculpture of the flamboyant "barocco" period is one
TURE   great name—Benvenuto Cellini (d. 1571). Though
perhaps better known for his racy and egotistical
memoirs, Cellini was a remarkable sculptor, particularly of small objects of the engraver's art. He did one large statue, "Perseus with the
Head of Medusa," but his contemporaries thought more of his smaller
works. He was employed by popes and princes to design and make
cups, candlesticks, the mountings for gems, and other such luxury

[6] Pijoan, *op. cit.*, III, 214.

articles. For the king of France, to whose court he eventually migrated, he carved an exquisite salt cellar, ornamented with classical figures, among them a graceful nude nymph and a stag. Cellini's career and work are indicative of the fact that sixteenth-century society was demanding lavish, overdecorated articles rather than the simpler more sincere works that are the expression of superior art.

PAINTING IN ITALY

EARLY ITALIAN PAINTING

In the early Middle Ages, as we have seen,[7] the walls of the basilican churches, especially those in Italy, were decorated with mosaics. Later, this art gave way to wall paintings, or murals. The Romanesque type of church, with its vast stretches of wall space, called for extensive mural decoration; and painting, being more practicable than mosaic, became the universal form of decoration. It was usually done on the wet plaster (*al fresco*), hence Italian murals are usually called frescoes. The artist painted his picture while the plaster was still moist. As it dried, the color became an integral part of the wall. Such painting called for rapidity of execution, which accounts for the simple and undetailed work of most murals.

Until the time of Giotto (d. 1337), artists followed the stately Byzantine style of the mosaic makers. The figures had a formal beauty and a mosaiclike stiffness. The halos, crowns, crosses, and poses were definitely established according to religious custom. For instance, in portraying the Virgin Mary, artists dared not exercise their own individual tastes; to do so would have been sacrilegious. Likewise, in pictures of the Holy Family, the positions of the Christ child and the mother were fixed by tradition: the baby was held stiffly in the curve of her left arm. Thus, the same stately figures, resplendent in gilt and deep colors, were repeated century after century. Painting—somewhat like music—had become a part of the religious ritualism of the church.

This formal static type of art gave way gradually before two influences which came into prominence in Italy during the thirteenth century. One of these was the rising secular spirit of the towns which we have noted in so many aspects of late medieval life. The expansion of Italian commerce brought prosperity to innumerable towns. And this was reflected in new churches whose spacious walls

[7] See above, pp. 319 f.

had to be decorated. Wealthy merchants and princes often gave huge sums for memorial frescoes and chapels. Thus Italian commercial expansion had a direct influence on the development of art. The other influence was the increased interest in classical culture as an expression of the new secular spirit of the towns. We have already considered the classical influence in Italian literature. It was just as effective in the arts, due to the fact that Italy had on every hand remnants of Roman buildings, statues, mosaics, and other forms of ornamentation. These were studied and imitated by architects and sculptors such as Nicholas of Pisa, in practically the same fashion in which Petrarch and his successors used classical manuscripts. The art of painting profited, though to a lesser degree, from classical influences.

GIOTTO
A major step toward naturalness, or realism, in painting was taken by Giotto, a friend of Dante's, whose portrait he actually painted into one of his Florentine frescoes. Giotto (d. 1337) introduced action and variations of pose into his work. This innovation can readily be seen by comparing the frescoes of earlier painters [8] with Giotto's natural scenes from the life of Christ and of St. Francis. The series of frescoes which he painted in the newly built church of St. Francis at Assisi marks an epoch in the history of Italian painting. For the first time an Italian artist painted pictures that presented human action in an effective manner. In the scene portraying St. Francis preaching to the birds, although the individual figures may seem crudely executed, the group as a whole shows remarkable life, action, and unity.

This tendency to follow nature rather than past tradition was carried on by Giotto's successors—by Gaddi and Orcagna in Florence, and by Duccio, Martini, and the Lorenzetti brothers in Siena. Gradually, during the fourteenth century, Italian fresco painting became more and more realistic. Interestingly enough, the greatest progress was made in Florence, one of the most prosperous of Italian business centers.

FIFTEENTH-
CENTURY
REALISM
The first outstanding advance was made by Masaccio (d. ca. 1428). He was one of three remarkable Florentine artists, the other two being the sculptor Donatello, and Brunelleschi, builder of the *Duomo* of Florence. Masaccio learned—perhaps by studying classical reliefs and

---

[8] Cimabue best illustrates the continued influence of the stiff mosaic types in thirteenth-century painting.

murals—how to paint figures with a convincing realism and how to put depth and perspective into landscapes. A glance at his "Expulsion from Eden" or his "The Tribute Money" in the Church of S. Maria del Carmine at Florence, reveals an art that is as superior to Giotto's as Giotto's was to that of the early thirteenth-century painters. The dramatic realism of Masaccio's work had a great influence on his successors.

Throughout the fifteenth century progress was slow but steady. Technique improved as painters studied real life and followed it in their work. Religious subjects still predominated, for most paintings were still done on the walls of churches. But even the figures of the Virgin Mary and the Christ child took on a remarkable humanness of form and expression. For instance, the madonnas painted by Fra Angelico (d. 1455), though sweet, gentle, and pious, are real women such as one might see on the streets of any busy Italian town. Fra Angelico combined with unusual success three characteristics— the religiousness of the earlier artists, the realism of town life, and the graceful simplicity of the new school of classic imitators.

The work of Fra Lippi (d. 1469), a Franciscan friar who is said to have eloped with a beautiful nun, is another example of the naturalness that was coming into Italian painting. Some of his figures of the Christ child are—as one writer puts it—"chubby, lusty infants who seem about to overpower the mother." As for the madonnas, they are "always pale colorless little girls with a transparent skin. They fold their soft hands as they gaze in surprise upon the newborn Child; indeed, they seem unable to comprehend the fact of their maternity." [9] Lippi's figures are so appealingly human that one can almost believe the story that he had a wife and children who posed as his models.

SECULARISM AND CLASSICISM: BOTTICELLI — The continued influence of economic, social, and political conditions on artistic trends is fully illustrated by Florentine painting of the late fifteenth century. This was the age of the Medici. We have already noted their political influence, and the manner in which their court set the standards of Florentine literature. The distinctly nonreligious atmosphere of the Medici court, its classical interests and refined tastes, and the democratic attitude toward men of genius are well exemplified in the career of Botticelli (d. 1510). He was a cooper's son whose artistic ability made him the leading painter of the Medici

[9] Pijoan, *op. cit.*, III, 117.

court. Like many practical townsmen, he experimented in improving his artistic technique, often painting on wood rather than on wet plaster. He also tended to classical rather than religious subjects. The sinuous graceful lines of his figures are—like his subjects—distinctly nonreligious. His "Birth of Venus" is a purely classical portrayal in which a slender willowy Venus, absolutely nude, stands on an immense shell which is being propelled by the breath of two Zephyrs toward the shore where Spring awaits her, holding a mantle. Botticelli's "Primavera," or "Early Spring," is similarly classical in theme: there are Venus, the three Graces, Spring, Flora, a puffing Zephyr, and a chubby cupid, all in a background of trees, flowers, and plants painted in delicate colors and with remarkably accurate detail. It is interesting to note that certain of the apparently classical figures of this painting are portraits of prominent members of the Medici court.

Botticelli was a painter who combined naturalism with classicism. He observed Nature and the people about him and deliberately introduced them into his portrayals of ancient scenes and people. He was only one of the many Italian artists of the fifteenth century who were depicting real life in the spirit of the secular world of townsfolk and painting with a steadily improving technique.

THE GREAT ITALIAN "MASTERS" — By the year 1500, Italian art, like Italian life, had thrown off much of the piousness and stiff formalism of earlier days. Humanness and realism were apparent in subject matter as well as in treatment. In the masterpieces of three of the greatest painters of all time can be seen the climax of this slowly developing Italian art and civilization. They were Leonardo da Vinci, Michelangelo, and Raphael of Urbino.

LEONARDO DA VINCI (D. 1519) — Leonardo, "jack of all trades" and master of most of them,[10] is best known today for his paintings, particularly "The Last Supper," and "Mona Lisa." "The Last Supper," a fresco covering an entire wall of the dining hall of a monastery in Milan, is the best illustration of his marvelous technique. He was, above all, an inventor whose restless temperament constantly drove him to search for new and better ways of doing things. In fresco painting he experimented with new types of color base.[11] The fading and cracking of the surface of his "Last Supper" is attributed to his experimentation with color media. Much

---

[10] See above, p. 677, for his scientific work.

[11] Color bases, or *media*, are the fluids with which the color pigments are mixed. Leonardo used albumen or sizing bases instead of water, which was commonly em-

of the present picture is a retouched restoration. Da Vinci had greater success in his treatment of backgrounds than with his colors; in fact, here he made notable improvements. In "The Last Supper" he achieved a depth of background that gives one the impression of looking, not at a wall, but into an adjoining room in which Christ and the disciples are eating. Da Vinci's arrangement of the figures in this painting is also effective. By skillful handling of light and shadow, attention is focused on the Christ, who is portrayed against the bright background of three windows, while by a triple or tri-angular method of composition, in addition to the three windows (possibly a symbol of the Holy Trinity), the twelve disciples are grouped in threes.

Da Vinci's "Mona Lisa" is the world's most famous picture, due —according to some critics—to its mysterious disappearance from the Louvre and its subsequent recovery, rather than to any superlative artistic merit. This portrait of a Florentine woman with a serene yet enigmatic smile (similar to that in some of his other paintings) does, however, illustrate da Vinci's skill in giving depth to backgrounds, and his use of light and shadow, as also his intense psychological interest in facial expressions. In later life da Vinci left Italy to become court painter of Francis I of France.

MICHELANGELO
(D. 1564)

Like da Vinci, Michelangelo was a versatile artist —a sculptor, architect, and poet, as well as a famous fresco painter. Compelled by the pope to leave other projects in order to decorate the ceiling and walls of the Sistine Chapel in the Vatican Palace, he performed a tremendous task in the face of great odds. Pope Julius II was an impatient and dictatorial pontiff. On one occasion, when he insisted that more gilt be used, Michelangelo refused, asserting that the prophets he was portraying had become holy men because they despised gold. Then too, the Roman type of plaster was difficult to color, and the long hours of work on a high scaffolding, often while flat on his back, were physically wearisome. As the artist himself expressed it in one of his poems,

My beard turns up to Heaven; my nape falls in,
Fixed on my spine; my breast bone visibly
Grows like a harp; a rich embroidery
Bedews my face from brush drops thick and thin.

ployed in frescoes. The miniaturists and Flemish painters of the late Middle Ages made greater progress than the Italians in the use of sizing, albumen, and oils as bases for color. Out of these experiments came modern *oil* paints.

Not until four long weary years was the work completed, and to this day the nine immense ceiling panels, representing scenes of the Creation and of early Biblical history, are among the finest paintings in the world. Michelangelo was noted for his forcefully energetic figures, and in these scenes he portrayed a Jehovah of tremendous power, prophets, classical sibyls, slaves, athletes, and other decorative figures, and painted with vigor, decisiveness, and marvelous technical skill.

On the front wall of the chapel Michelangelo painted an immense scene of "The Last Judgment," 66 feet in height and 33 feet in width. In this complex and somewhat confused picture, the attention is focused on a powerful and forceful Christ who, with upraised arm, parts the sinners from the saints, consigning the former to hell's fires. About him are shown hundreds of figures in various attitudes of celestial joy or dark despair.

Most of Michelangelo's frescoes reflect the restless untiring activity of a brilliant artist. He is an excellent example of the vibrant energy that made this period of Italian history so productive of artistic and literary geniuses.

RAPHAEL OF URBINO (D. 1520)

In strange contrast to the vigor of Michelangelo's work is the calmness of Raphael of Urbino's painting. He depicted scenes and figures of quiet repose, using a smooth technique and pleasing color effects. His many madonnas, and particularly the well-known "Sistine Madonna," have a sweet gracefulness that to some borders on the insipid. Although Raphael marks the perfect combination of pious subject matter and flawless artistic technique, not all of his work was religious. He decorated the Vatican Palace with scenes from classical mythology as well as from church history, and he painted many portraits. The number of paintings turned out by Raphael and his assistants was unbelievably large. This reflects the widespread prosperity of an age in which there was a tremendous demand for portraits and other works of art by which men of wealth might aggrandize themselves and their native towns.

SPLENDOR AND DECADENCE

After da Vinci, Michelangelo, and Raphael, Italian painting suffered a decline which seems to have been accentuated by the wars that devastated the peninsula, and by the reactionary tendencies of the Catholic Reformation. Only in Venice, still relatively prosperous and secure on her secluded isles and lagoons, did art continue to thrive during the sixteenth century.

Giotto (XIII-XIV C)

Cimabue (XIII C)

Botticelli (XV C)

Raphael (XVI C)

ITALIAN PAINTING — RELIGIOUS SUBJECTS: Madonnas

(See pp. 734 ff.)

BOTTICELLI — THE BIRTH OF VENUS (XV C)

MICHELANGELO — THE CREATION OF MAN (XVI C)

ITALIAN PAINTING — SECULAR SUBJECTS

(See pp. 735 ff.)

Here Titian (d. 1576) and his less famous contemporaries (Bellini, Tintoretto, and Veronese) continued to decorate the walls of public buildings, churches, and the palaces of the merchant princes with their masterpieces. The works of the Venetian painters reflect, above everything else, prosperity. Here, painted in deep rich colors, are well-fed merchants, buxom matrons, and everywhere garments of luxurious texture. The madonnas and religious scenes painted by these artists are also in the same rich manner. Titian's "Assumption of the Virgin" has been called a glorious portrait of a beautiful Venetian girl clad in a luxurious mantle. And, finally, the historic scenes with which these artists covered the extensive walls of the great public buildings were gorgeous pageants, which, like their other artistic works, exemplify "the wealth and splendor that was medieval Venice."

MEDIEVAL MUSIC

Music touched the lives of medieval men at many points. It was one of the four subjects of the quadrivium, the scientific course which all students studied in the schools. But one who reads Boethius's treatise on music is impressed by the fact that the study of music in the medieval schools was mostly philosophical and had little connection with music as we think of it. There was, however, another type of music in the Middle Ages which was more practical and human. It was religious, and it contributed a great deal to the ritualistic beauty of the church service. It is this aspect of medieval music which has exerted the greatest influence on the modern age and which therefore has the chief place in our survey. In the development of the music of the medieval church we find the beginnings of modern music.

For the first thousand years of the Christian era, the music of Western Europe was predominantly religious and was usually simple one-part singing called *monophony*. During the later Middle Ages, from about 1000 to 1500, marked changes occurred. The development of music during this period can be pictured as a twofold conflict between religious and secular songs, and between one-part music (monophony) and many-part music (polyphony). In the rivalry between religious and secular music the former fared well, and by the sixteenth century it had proved its permanence and greatness as a factor in Western cultural life. Leaving the details of this development for later consideration, we now turn our attention to the manner in which, during the eleventh, twelfth, and thirteenth centuries, polyphony won a decisive victory over monophony in both sacred and secular music.

The church music of the tenth century doubtless sounded much as it had during most of the early Christian centuries. It was chanted monophony; that is, the voices sang in unison save for the fact that the boys' voices were in a higher register than those of the men. Even this simple one-part singing was at times so effective that a man like Augustine in the fourth century was overcome by the "dangerous pleasure" of listening to it.[12] Out of this chanting came modern polyphonic music.

Some of the unrecorded *secular* songs of the early Middle Ages may have been polyphonic, but so far as is known the first noteworthy advance in this direction came in church music during the ninth and tenth centuries. Then it became customary to chant double; that is, the principal voice, which was called the tenor (from the Latin *tenere,* "to hold"), was accompanied by another voice which sang the same tune and words in parallel, four or five tones above or below. This sort of parallel singing was called *organum;* that is, it was "organized." This is somewhat similar to the manner in which singers today, on a festive occasion, organize their voices to sing "Sweet Adeline" in two parts, one voice singing the air and another paralleling it. Two-part, or double, organum was also expanded into triple or quadruple organum by having additional voices sing the same melody an octave above or below the two chief voices.

This music was, of course, far more discordant than the sugary harmonies of modern popular songs, but it was such a pleasing contrast to the simple unison of plain chant that further improvements were made. The accompanying voices came to move, not rigidly in parallel, but freely and with variations; that is, as the principal voice ascended, the second voice might descend, and vice versa, thus producing an interweaving of melodies. Sometimes the voices sang different words and entirely different melodies.[13] This flexible type of part singing was called free organum, or discant. In the musical notation accompanying a thirteenth-century treatise, we find an illustration of the freedom with

---

[12] See above, p. 304.

[13] The effect was somewhat like that which would be produced if "Way Down Upon the Swanee River" and "Humoresque" were sung simultaneously. At times there was true harmony.

which the voices proceeded. In a passage in which the tenor sang three prolonged notes, the upper voice sang almost fifty notes which ran up and down the scale.

In one type of free organum (called *conductus*) melodies from popular tunes were introduced. In another type (the *motet*) the tenor might sing a rather formal theme (perhaps a plain chant) set to one or two words while the accompanying voices sang separate words and tunes of much more complicated form. In one musical composition the tenor sang a long-drawn-out "allelujah," while each of the other two voices sang eight words set to an entirely different tune. This merely hints at some of the complications of late medieval singing.

NOTATION AND THE MUSICAL STAFF

The evolution of complex melodies with variations of tone and time for the different voices led to the development of notation. The early singers of plain chant followed the ancient Roman custom of using letters above the words to indicate the tone. According to a tenth-century historian, it was not until the time of Charles the Great that certain papal musicians "superseded the use of alphabetical characters by certain notations (*notuli*) placed over the words that were to be sung." These *notuli,* or neumes, as they were more commonly known, were not like modern musical notes. They were merely the ancient Greek accent marks; for example, the accent (′) over a word indicated a higher tone; the period (.) a lower tone. But since these marks did not indicate *how much higher* or lower it was to be sung, further improvements were introduced. Sometime in the eleventh century (at the suggestion of an Italian monk, Guido of Arezzo), a horizontal line was drawn above the words and the neumes were placed at certain intervals above or below this line. The next step was to add other lines, and soon a four-line staff had been developed.

Such simple directions were satisfactory for plain song in which all sang the same melody. But the complications of free organum, in which the various voices sang notes of different tone and length, demanded more explicit directions. Squares, rectangles, and diamonds (with or without stems) came to be used instead of neumes to indicate tones of different lengths. By the thirteenth century a five- and sometimes six-line staff was being used, and each voice had its own notation. Not until the sixteenth century were round dotted notes employed. Rests, or pauses, were indicated by vertical lines, the length of the rest being shown by the length of the line.

SECULAR AND
INSTRUMENTAL
MUSIC
Meanwhile popular secular music was making a place for itself, in spite of the bitter opposition of the clergy. Very little is known of the exact nature of the music of the people, since the clerical writers of the time made little mention of nonreligious singing save to condemn it. Nevertheless, it is clear that there was much popular song, for, as in all ages, the populace danced and sang. A Belgian chronicler of the eleventh century mentioned "the *evil songs*" sung concerning a new emperor, and from almost every medieval century there are brief records of some sort of popular music; drinking, dancing, love, boating, reaping, and hunting songs. This music was very different from that of the church. Like all popular music, including modern jazz, it had a pronounced rhythm. Many of the secular tunes were dance rhythms.

There was also much instrumental music. In addition to pipe organs,[14] there were harpers and bards in the halls of the great nobles, and in the market places jongleurs and wandering minstrels amused the populace. The multiplicity of instruments in the twelfth and thirteenth centuries can be imagined from the boast of a jongleur who claimed that he could play the lute, the violin, the bag pipe, the syrinx, the harp, the gigue, the gittern, the symphony, the psaltery, the organistrum, the regals, the tabor, and the rote.

The lute, violin, syrinx, harp, gigue, gittern, psaltery, regals, tabor, and rote were all stringed instruments, played by plucking with the fingers or with a bow. The symphony and the organistrum (hurdy-gurdy) were played by means of a revolving wheel, so as to give a continuous tone. There were also other instruments: horns, trumpets, cymbals, drums, tambourines, and the dulcimer which was played with little hammers like a xylophone. In addition to playing such instruments, the accomplished jongleur could recite "tales and fables plenty, satires, pastorals full of sport," and do all sorts of sleight-of-hand tricks and acrobatics, including "play at quarter staff," "stool feats," and knife balancing.[15]

TROUBADOURS
AND TROUVÈRES
Of higher social ranking than the jongleurs, though certainly not as varied in their accomplishments, were the Provençal troubadours and the northern French trouvères of the twelfth and thirteenth centuries.[16] These gay singers

[14] See above, pp. 313 f.
[15] A detailed description is given in an old French poem which describes the counterclaims of two rival jongleurs. See Burney, *A General History of Music*, I, 593 f.
[16] See above, p. 690.

of lighthearted songs about love, spring, and wine composed and sang both poems and music. Often, however, they hired jongleurs to play their accompaniments. One of the thirteenth-century trouvères, Adam de la Hale, composed what is sometimes called the first comic opera, *Robin et Marion*. Similar to the troubadours and trouvères in their influence were the Spanish troubadours, the minnesingers (love singers) and meistersingers of Germany, the minstrels of England, and the Italian "canzonettists." A thirteenth-century Italian friar described with unusually sympathetic interest the manner in which the young folk of his day sang and played. With violas and cithara and other musical instruments they "made sweet melodies, accompanying them with gestures"; and their singing "was so new and lovely in words and melody that it gladdened the heart exceedingly." In the various regions of the West, secular singing was monophonic, like the plain chant of the church. But often the accompanying instrument added an additional element which tended to produce polyphonic music.

ROUNDS: "SU-MER IS ICUMEN IN" Late in the Middle Ages a new type of interwoven polyphonic music became popular. It was called the cantilena, or rondel, and was similar to modern rounds such as "Three Blind Mice." The earliest, and also one of the most famous rounds, called "Sumer is icumen in," came from thirteenth-century England, where part singing was well developed. The original manuscript of this round was written on a six-line staff, with square and diamond-shaped notes; there are also rest marks, and a cross to indicate the interval at which the second and third voices take up the melody. The first line appears as follows:

Su - mer is i - cum - en in,   Lhu - de sing cuc - cu,
Per - spi - ce Chris - ti - co - la,   que - dig - na - ti - o,[17]

An inset of instructions at the end of the song reads as follows:

[17] In modern English the words are "Summer is come, Loudly sings the cuckoo." *The Oxford History of Music*, vol. I, contains facsimiles of the notation and the Latin text of the instructions.

Four companions can sing this round. It ought not to be done by fewer than three or two in addition to those who do the refrain.[18] It is sung thus: one begins, along with those who sing the refrain, the rest remaining silent; when he comes to the first note after the cross, another begins, and so on. Each group stops at the end for the space of one long note.

The important thing about this round is that in it a simple tune was made to produce polyphonic harmony simply by having the different voices pick up the tune at various times and follow the first voice to the end. It marks a distinct step in the development of modern harmony. It should also be noted that it was popular enough to be set to religious as well as to secular words.

Some of the later rounds were more complicated, as is apparent from the following description "Concerning Rounds":

Let a melody . . . be devised and let each voice sing this in turn. And at the same time let other melodies be devised to accompany it in the second and (if there be three voices) in the third voice; let them proceed in consonances, and so that when one voice ascends another descends, and let the third not follow too closely the movement of either of the others, except perhaps for the sake of greater beauty. And let all these melodies be sung by each voice in turn.[19]

It is apparent from this description that secular music was taking on the same complicated variations that were characteristic of church music.

COMPLICATED
PART SINGING
Meanwhile church music, having freed itself from the simplicity of plain chant, developed more and more variations. Four- and even five-part songs, with intricate interweaving of the various voices, became common in the later Middle Ages. An English writer of the fourteenth century gave the following description of the complications of part singing:

Let there be brought together four or five men expert in singing, and let the first begin the plain song in the tenor; let the second settle his voice in the fifth above; the third in the octave; the fourth, if there be a fourth, in the twelfth. Then . . . all except the tenor should break and flower the notes. . . . But let him who is to discant . . . [keep] in thirds, sixths, and tenths above the tenor . . . ascending and descending according as it may

---

[18] The refrain, sung constantly throughout, is merely the repetition of "sing cuc-cu nu, sing cuc-cu."

[19] *The Oxford History of Music,* I, 171. By courtesy of the Clarendon Press I have used several quotations from this work.

seem to him expedient and most agreeable to the hearer. Thus [they] make great melody.[20]

It will be noted that this writer mentioned as an important factor "him who is to discant." By this time discant—"singing apart" or in separate melodies—had become universal. From this came counterpoint, or "note against note," in which real musical compositions were created by balancing the notes or phrases sung by one voice with those of the others. Eventually composers began to build up pleasing combinations of tones. Thus, having emancipated themselves from traditional melodies, they became real masters of musical construction, and in both sacred and secular music true harmony came into being.

THE OPPOSITION TO COMPLICATED SINGING But during the later Middle Ages there were singers who took such liberties that they shocked their listeners. A fourteenth-century musician wrote scornfully of singers whose voices wander about "trusting wholly to providence" for co-ordination with the other voices. "They throw sounds about at random, like awkward people throwing stones at a mark, without hitting it once in a hundred times." Another writer condemned singers for "discanting too wantonly and multiplying superfluous notes." In their "vocal antics," he said, "they bark and bay in the manner of dogs and like lunatics delight in disorderly and aimless hurryings to and fro." Still another ridiculed the spectacular antics of those singers who "imitate the agonies of a dying man." [21]

There were also puritanical souls to whom the newer types of church music seemed to be dangerously irreligious. Late in the twelfth century St. Bernard of Clairvaux warned Christians against the "loss of spiritual grace when one is distracted by the quick and airy movements of a song." John of Salisbury, who lived at about the same time, was even more bitter. He wrote as follows:

Music defiles the service of religion. For the admiring simple souls of the congregation are of necessity depraved in the very presence of the Lord, in the sacred recesses of the sanctuary by the riot of the wantoning voice, by its eager ostentation, and by its womanish affectations in the mincing of notes and sentences.[22]

[20] *Ibid.*, I, 317.
[21] See *ibid.*, I, 290 ff., for the Latin text and English translations of these and other criticisms of the new styles of singing.
[22] *Ibid.*, I, 290.

Early in the fourteenth century a papal decree asserted that the music of the mass was being ruined by the insertion of "notes of small value," and "portions of secular songs." These were sung in a manner that was "intoxicating to the ear," with the voices "incessantly running to and fro," and with unseemly gestures; thus devotion, the true aim of worship, was sacrificed and "wantonness increases."

CHOIR MASTERS OF THE NETHER-LANDS Nothing could stop the tendency toward more and more ornate music. With the increase of wealth and luxury, all types of art became more sophisticated. Many musical compositions were intricate webs of interwoven themes of all sorts, secular as well as sacred. In a manner similar to that in which the late Gothic cathedrals were embellished with innumerable pinnacles, so the music sung in the cathedrals became more and more intricate. One fifteenth-century "note juggler" is said to have worked out a composition that called for forty-eight parts. Kings, princes, and wealthy merchants vied with one another in getting fine organs, large choirs, and famous directors for their private chapels and town churches. The leaders in this age of flamboyant church music were mostly men from the Netherlands. From Dufay (d. 1474) to Lassus (d. 1594), Flemish choirmasters were found in all parts of Europe. Many of their compositions are still sung in Protestant and Catholic churches and by modern musical organizations.

There were also famous choirmasters from other lands, notably William Byrd, director of music at Queen Elizabeth's chapel, and Fink, a German who directed the choirs of the royal Polish chapel at Cracow. Some of these musicians used chromatic scales and true harmonic forms in their compositions.

THE MUSICAL REFORMATION It was sixteenth-century Italy that made the greatest contribution to medieval church music. Here Palestrina, organist and director of the Sistine Chapel choir at Rome, restored to the music of the mass something of its earlier simplicity and grandeur. He abandoned the ornate styles and secular themes of his immediate predecessors and developed a music that had the solemnity of simple yet dignified harmony. His masses combined plain song with a sustained and flowing harmony that is distinctly modern in its appeal. One of the greatest works of all religious music is his "Mass for Pope Marcellus." Palestrina has been called "the savior of church music," and truly it seems that he and his successors saved church music from becoming a complex of mere musical ornament. Thanks to them, the modern world still has and uses that inspiring medieval music which is so in keeping with the ritualistic and architectural atmosphere of the cathedral.

EPILOGUE

W E have surveyed in this volume the changing civilization
of Western Europe through a period of almost fifteen hundred years. For reasons of convenience we began our story
with the Age of Augustus and end it with the opening of the sixteenth century—the era of Henry VII of England, Charles VIII of
France, Emperor Charles V, Machiavelli, Raphael, and Vasco da
Gama and Columbus. There is, of course, no definite date at which
the civilization that is called medieval succeeded that of the ancient
world or gave way to that of modern times. Nevertheless, within
the centuries we have considered, what is known as the civilization
of the Middle Ages came into being, achieved great triumphs, and
evolved into the civilization that is called modern.

It is difficult to summarize any extended period of human history. This is particularly true of the Middle Ages, and any characterization of the civilization of that era must be marked by numerous
qualifications and exceptions, and accompanied by the danger of
unwarranted oversimplification. The early Middle Ages were so different from the later Middle Ages that it may seem incorrect to regard their varying institutions as different expressions of the same
civilization. The people of the West in the early Middle Ages lived
under much the same conditions as those of the late Roman Empire,
while the customs of the fifteenth century resembled those of the
early modern period more closely than those of the early Middle
Ages. It is for this reason that we have constantly differentiated
between the early and late Middle Ages. The whole period might
well be divided into three rather distinct epochs, each comprising
approximately five centuries: (1) the transition from ancient to medieval civilization, (2) the early Middle Ages, and (3) the late Middle
Ages, which was itself a period of transition from medieval to modern
times.

The institutions of the early Middle Ages were a continuation
of those of the late Roman Empire, though with constant modifications. Within the five centuries following the Age of Augustus, the

749

Roman civilization of the West gave way to a regime of Germanic rulers such as Theodoric and Clovis. By the end of the fifth century Western civilization had lost its predominantly Roman character and had assumed the modes of life that are usually thought of as medieval. This period contrasted sharply with the Augustan Age, especially in the decentralization and ruralism of its government and economic and social life. There was no longer any one central administration. For protection, justice, and other forms of social control, men looked to the local landholding nobility—Roman, clerical, or Germanic. While a Theodoric or a Charles the Great might hold temporary sway over extensive regions in a manner that was reminiscent of imperial times, the majority of human beings lived under local regimes that were in marked contrast to the integrated life of the Roman world. Most medieval folk were born, lived, and died on rural estates without ever seeing a great city and with infrequent visits to neighboring cathedrals, shrines, manorial villages, or markets. The nobility and the higher clergy, of course, did see much more of the outside world. Measured by modern standards and in terms of material comforts, life, on the whole, was primitive. War, invasion, flood, and famine, which took terrible toll of life and property, were not constant, but they were nevertheless the common experience of medieval people.

The picture of life in the West during the early medieval centuries is sometimes so forbidding that many people take it for granted that the entire Middle Ages was an era of political anarchy, subsistence economy, rural community life, and primitive culture dominated by ignorance and superstition, and relieved only by the feeble comforts of a priest-ridden religion. If this was perhaps the case in many sections for extended periods, it is nevertheless an inaccurate view not only of the whole medieval period, but of the entire early Middle Ages. Our survey of the political, economic, social, and cultural life of this period has indicated that in every century there were centers in which progress was made in most lines of human endeavor. Even at best, however, early medieval civilization was backward as compared with that of earlier and later ages.

So superior were conditions during the late medieval centuries (1000-1500) that we have made a definite distinction between them and the early Middle Ages. By the eleventh century the earlier localized regime, dominated by noble landlords, was beginning to give way to larger-scale units under kings who were destined to become the leaders of nations. In certain regions self-governing towns were winning a place for the burgher class in the world of kings and feudal barons. Most important of all, from the standpoint of the future, was the increase of economic exchange, with the consequent expansion of industry, commerce, and town life. Eventually the ideals of the townsfolk affected the thought and actions of the feudality, the royalty, and the clergy. For one thing, the profit motive tended to transform the primitive and rural institutions of the earlier centuries.

The baron-controlled manorial estate was rivaled and eventually eclipsed by the flourishing industrial town. The warring feudal noble tended to become an administrator with a keen appreciation for financial advantages. Royal courts relied more and more on burgher advisers, experts in taxation, and legalists who could make judicial procedure effective and also financially profitable. Even the church was forced to adapt its administration to a world in which money power was increasingly important. From the religious standpoint, however, the increasingly secular interests of the clergy were accompanied by a decline in spiritual influence. This had momentous consequences for the church and Western Christendom.

By the end of the fifteenth century the West had been transformed from a rural feudal society into one in which towns, industry and commerce were vital, dynamic factors. In some respects the earlier centuries may have been a true Age of Faith and Feudalism, but it is evident that from the eleventh century onward Western civilization was motivated more by business ideals than by Christian faith or feudal chivalry. Economic profits and the materialistic interests emanating from them were the chief motivating factors of late medieval society, and they most clearly distinguish this period from the early Middle Ages. From the economic and social viewpoint—the fundamental importance of which our own day is inclined to emphasize—the entire period from the eleventh to the sixteenth century was an era of transition from medieval ruralism to the modern type of burgher-controlled society and capitalistic economy.

In cultural activities, also, the late Middle Ages manifests progressive trends that are closely associated with the expanding life of the townsfolk. In literature, education, and the arts, fields hitherto practically monopolized by the monastic clergy, the secular clergy and eventually the townsmen began to take an active part. Cathedral schools rivaled monastic schools, and finally both were eclipsed in importance by the universities. Meanwhile the educational curriculum became less theological, and in many towns secular schools flourished. The same general tendencies are also apparent in medieval literature. The roll of honor of late medieval literature reveals the name of many a genius who was the product of town life and the exponent of its secular spirit. Dante, Petrarch, Boccaccio, Chaucer, Villon, Commines, and Machiavelli are but a few of those whose writings have the unmistakably human touch that comes to men who have known the close contacts and invigorating influences of an urban environment.

In the history of the arts, too, we find evidence of a rapidly expanding town civilization. To accommodate the teeming city populations, larger churches were built. The Gothic cathedral was more than an expression of medieval religiousness: it also reflected the wealth and pride of the city, of the burghers who contributed funds, the masons who handled the blocks of stone, and of the guildsmen who dedicated stained glass windows. Towered town halls, guild halls, and burgher residences also indicate the increase of economic prosperity. Even in the ornately decorated prayerbooks and tombs of the wealthy or highborn, and in the frescoed walls of churches, there was manifest the rising standard of living and the secular interests of the age. Religious paintings in many cathedrals were gifts of prosperous citizens whose likenesses appear somewhere in the picture, kneeling in proud adoration before the Holy Virgin and Child. The rapid advance of the arts in Italy and the Netherlands during the late Middle Ages synchronizes with the flourishing of business life in the cities of these regions. The rapidly advancing art of the Italian and Flemish-Dutch "masters" was more closely associated with the rise of towns than with the revival of interest in classical antiquity. Even in the realm of church music, it will be noted that the most marked developments were made by music masters from the prosperous towns of the Netherlands and Italy.

Without unduly stressing the influence of town life on culture, and with regard for other contributing factors such as religious inspiration, individual genius, and wealthy patrons, it is, nevertheless, safe to say that the highest cultural achievements of the Middle Ages were the outgrowth of a flourishing city life. We recollect that it was townsmen, in the bustling industrial centers of Mayence on the Rhine River and Haarlem in the Netherlands, who gave to the Western world its first practicable system of printing. To be sure, literary and artistic genius existed in the less invigorating atmosphere of monastic, rural, and feudal communities, but it was the development of business activities and burgher society that brought the culture of the Middle Ages to full bloom.

The economic and social forces of town life carried Western civilization onward at accelerated pace during the last centuries of the Middle Ages. As we approach the year 1500, the process of development suggests not so much the passing of medievalism as the rapid evolution of modern culture. We therefore hesitate to concern ourselves with the question, when and why did the Middle Ages end? Those who, for purposes of convenience, are insistent on a division of history into precisely dated epochs, may take note of Columbus' discovery of America in 1492, or Vasco da Gama's return from India in 1499, as events that mark the shift from medieval life to the world-wide scope of the modern age. We prefer to leave with the reader a less definite but more dynamic image: that of the stream of human civilization in the West, flowing more and more deeply and strongly during the late medieval centuries, and then, at about the year 1500, beginning to broaden out in flood tide.

It is perhaps difficult to realize that this enlarged stream had its source in the ancient Roman world and was fed by the Christian Church and the deluge of Germanic invasion, and that during the early Middle Ages its current was narrow, restricted, and sluggish. It is also difficult to explain fully why its movement quickened during the late Middle Ages and expanded with such force in the sixteenth century. In fact, when viewed as merely a section of the great stream of Western civilization, it may seem that the Middle Ages is a meaningless concept. Why call a portion of human history, that is nowhere near the middle point of the stream, the *Middle* Ages? Are not the first fifteen centuries of the Christian era in reality the earlier stages of development of *modern* Occidental civilization?

From certain points of view, such queries are justifiable, and the designations ancient, medieval, and modern might well be abandoned were it not for their convenience as universally recognized terms of general reference. Even were we inclined to eliminate the Middle Ages as a distinct epoch, custom and usage dictate some such historical divisions. Thus the year 1500 has come to be recognized as an important turning point in history. It is here, therefore, that we turn over to another the task of tracing the later developments of Western Civilization.[1]

[1] The expansion of Western civilization during the past five centuries will be presented in the third volume of this series, *The Modern World*, by Professor Alice F. Tyler.

It is obvious, however, that the flow of civilization does not cease at the point where one historian lays down the pen and another takes it up. Like a great river, the stream of human life moves onward with increasing volume before, as well as after, the year 1500. The history of the fifteenth and sixteenth centuries, whatever it be called, sweeps forward irresistibly into the disturbed yet vibrant era that we recognize as unmistakably modern.

CHRONOLOGICAL TABLES

TABLE I

The Roman Empire, Christianity, the Germans
(1-500 A.D.)

TABLE II

The West and the East
(500-1000)

TABLE III

The West
(1000-1500)

TABLE I

THE ROMAN EMPIRE, CHRISTIANITY, THE GERMANS
(1-500 A.D.)

The Empire		*Cultural History*
27 B.C.-14 A.D.	Augustus Caesar	d. 55 B.C. Lucretius
ca. 4 B.C.	Birth of Christ	d. 54 Catullus
		d. 44 Julius Caesar
9 A.D.	Arminius defeats Varus	d. 43 Cicero
		d. 27 Varro
		d. 19 Vergil
		d. 8 Horace
		d. 18 A.D. Ovid
		d. 17 Livy
54-68 A.D.	Nero	d. 65 Seneca
64	Burning of Rome	
70	Destruction of Jerusalem	
79	Destruction of Pompeii and	d. 79 Pliny the Elder
	Herculaneum	80 Colosseum
98-117	Trajan	d. 95 Quintilian
117-138	Hadrian	d. 102 Martial
		d. 120 Tacitus
		d. 120 Epictetus
		d. 125 Plutarch
161-180	Marcus Aurelius	Pantheon
		Temple of Baal-
193-211	Septimius Severus	bek
211-217	Caracalla	d. ca. 200 Galen
		ca. 211 Baths of Cara-
222-235	Alexander Severus	calla
235-249	Barracks emperors	d. 212 Papinian
249-251	Decius	d. 228 Ulpian
250	Persecution of Christians	d. 230 Tertullian
251	Gothic victory over Decius	d. 240 Dio Cassius
	Germanic invasions	d. 258 Cyprian
268-270	Claudius "Gothicus"	d. 270 Plotinus
270-275	Aurelian "Restorer of the	
	World"	
284-305	Diocletian	

The West	*The East*	
284-305 Maximian	284-305 Diocletian	d. 304 Porphyry
305-312 Civil War	305-311 Galerius	
306- Constantine	311 Edict of Toleration	
312 x Milvian	312-323 Licinius	
Bridge		
313 Edicts of Toleration, Nicomedia-Milan		
323-337 CONSTANTINE, SOLE EMPEROR		330- Constantinople
		built
325 Council of Nicæa		
		ca. 350 Donatus
361-363 Julian the Apostate, sole emperor		
364-375 Valentinian I 364-378 Valens		
375-383 Gratian 378 x Adrianople		
383-392 Valentinian II 379- Theodosius pacifies		
the East		

The West	The East	Cultural History
	381 Council of Constantinople	d. 393 Ausonius
392-395 THEODOSIUS, SOLE EMPEROR		d. ca. 395 Ammianus Marcellinus
395-423 Honorius	395-408 Arcadius Visigoths revolt, Alaric	d. 397 Ambrose of Milan
d. 408 Stilicho, Visigoths in Italy	408-450 Theodosius II Huns along the	ca. 400 Claudian
410 Rome plundered by Visigoths	Danube River	d. ca. 410 Prudentius
415-711 Visigothic kingdom, Spain		d. 420 Jerome
		d. 430 Augustine of Hippo
		d. 431 Paulinus of Nola
425-455 Valentinian III	438 Theodosian Code	ca. 439 Martianus Capella
429-534 Vandal kingdom in Africa		
ca. 449 Angles, Saxons, Jutes enter England		
ca. 450 Burgundians in Rhone Valley	450-457 Marcian	
451 Attila and Huns x Chalons- Troyes		
440-461 Pope Leo I	457-474 Leo I	
452 Huns in Italy		
455 Vandals plunder Rome		
455-476 "Puppet" emperors, Ricimer	474-491 Zeno	
476 Odoacer deposes Romulus Augustulus, last of Western emperors		
481-511 CLOVIS, king of Franks	491-518 Anastasius	d. ca. 484 Salvian d. ca. 484 Apollinaris Sidonius
493-526 THEODORIC, king of Ostrogothic Italy		ca. 500 Priscian

TABLE II

THE WEST AND THE EAST

(500-1000)

The West		The East	Cultural History
		518-527 Justin I	
			d. 524 Boethius
535-552	Justinian's war vs. Ostrogoths	527-565 JUSTINIAN	529-533 Justinian Code
			532-537 St. Sophia
			d. ca. 550 Benedict of Nursia or Monte Cassino
568	Lombards invade Italy		d. ca. 575-ca. 585 Cassiodorus
			d. 584 Chilperic of Neustria
590-604	POPE GREGORY I		
597	Conversion of Anglo-Saxons		d. 594 Gregory of Tours
575-613	Brunhild of Austrasia		
			d. 604 Augustine of Kent
		610-641 Heraclius	
			d. ca. 609 Venantius Fortunatus
613-629	Chlotar, king of Franks	622 Mohammed's "flight"	d. 615 Columban
			d. 636 Isidore of Seville
639-751	"Do-nothing" kings	638- Moslem conquests: Syria, Egypt, etc.	
687	x Tertry Pepin of Heristal		d. 690 Theodore of Tarsus
			d. 690 Benedict Biscop
697	Moslem conquest of Carthage		
711	Moslems enter Spain		
714-741	Charles Martel	717-741 Leo III, iconoclasm	
732	x Tours-Poitiers, defeat of Moslems		d. 735 The Venerable Bede
741-768	Pepin the Short		
751	Pepin crowned king		d. 754 Boniface
768-814	CHARLES THE GREAT		
772-804	Charles's Saxon wars		
774	Charles's invasion of Lombardy		

The West	The East	Cultural History
787 First Norse raids in England		
		d. ca. 799 Peter of Pisa
800 Charles crowned emperor	797-802 Irene	d. ca. 800 Paul the Deacon
802-839 Egbert of Wessex		d. 804 Alcuin
814-840 Louis the Pious		d. 821 Theodulf
ca. 831 Moslem conquest of Sicily		
840-855 Lothaire I		d. 840 Einhard
840-876 Louis the German		
840-877 Charles the Bald		
841 x Fontenoy		842 Strassburg Oaths
843 Treaty of Verdun		
846 Moslems raid Rome		
849 Defeat of Moslems near Ostia		d. 849 Walafrid Strabo
858-867 Pope Nicholas I		d. 856 Rabanus Maurus
		d. ca. 862 Lupus of Ferrières
	867-886 Basil I	d. 868 Ratramnus
870 Treaty of Mersen		d. ca. 869 Gottschalk
871-899 ALFRED THE GREAT		
ca. 870 Norsemen in Iceland		
878 Alfred defeats Danes at Edington Peace of Wedmore		d. ca. 880 John the Scot (Erigena)
		d. 882 Hincmar of Rheims
885 Alfred's Treaty of London with Danes		
885-887 Paris besieged by Norsemen		
888-898 Odo, king of France		
891 Emperor Arnulf defeats Norsemen at Dyle, near Louvain		
898 Hungarians in Germany		
910 Monastery of Cluny founded		

The West	The East	Cultural History
911 Normandy granted to Rollo		
911-918 Conrad I of Germany		
912-961 Abd-er-Rahman III of Moslem Spain		d. 912 Notker, the Stammerer, of St. Gall
		d. 915 Regino of Prum
919-936 Henry I, the Fowler, of Germany		
924-940 Ethelstan of England		
928-929 Brandenburg captured by Henry I		
933 Hungarians defeated on the Unstrutt		
936-973 Emperor OTTO I, THE GREAT		d. 948 Abbot Odo of Cluny
955 Hungarians defeated on the Lech near Augsburg		
962 Otto I crowned emperor		d. 966 Flodoard of Rheims
ca. 962 Novgorod established by Rurik	976-1025 Basil II	
978-1002 Almansor, climax of Moslem power in Spain		d. ca. 985 Roswitha
983-1002 Emperor Otto III		d. 988 Dunstan
987-996 Hugh Capet, king of France		d. ca. 997 Richer of Rheims
1000-1035 Sancho the Great of Navarre		

TABLE III

THE WEST

(1000-1500)

General History		Cultural History
ca. 1000	Norsemen in America	
ca. 1000	Hungary Christianized under King Stephen	d. 1003 Gerbert (Sylvester II)
1016	Canute the Dane conquers England	d. 1004 Abbo of Fleury
		d. 1028 Fulbert of Chartres
1037-1065	Ferdinand I of Leon-Castile	d. 1036 Avicenna
1039-1056	Emperor Henry III	
1042-1066	Edward the Confessor of England	
1046	Council at Sutri, deposition of three rival popes	
1048-1054	Pope Leo IX	d. 1048 Odilo of Cluny
		ca. 1050 Guido of Arezzo
1056-1106	EMPEROR HENRY IV	
1059	Lateran council; reform of papal elections; cardinals	
1061-1091	Normans conquer Sicily from Moslems	
1065-1109	Alfonso VI of Castile	
1066	x Senlac-Hastings, Norman conquest	
1066-1087	WILLIAM THE CONQUEROR, king of England	
1071	Turks defeat Byzantine army at Manzikert	
1073-1085	POPE GREGORY VII (Hildebrand)	
1075	Decrees against lay investiture	
1076	Emperor Henry IV deposed	
1078	Nicæa captured by Turks	
1081-1118	Emperor Alexius I at Constantinople	
1081-1084	Norman invasions of Balkan regions	
1084	Rome sacked by Normans	
1085	Toledo captured by Christians	
1086	Moslem victory at Zalaca (Spain)	
1086	Domesday survey and Salisbury oaths	ca. 1090 Irnerius at Bologna
1088-1099	Pope Urban II	Constantine the African at Salerno
1095	Councils of Piacenza and Clermont	
1099	Crusaders capture Jerusalem	
1103-1154	Roger II; count of Sicily, 1103; king of Naples-Sicily, 1130	
1108-1137	Louis VI of France	d. 1109 Anselm of Canterbury
1122	Concordat at Worms ends investiture struggle	
		ca. 1140 Gratian's *Decretum*
		d. 1142 Abelard
1144	Edessa captured by Moslems	
1147-1149	Crusade of Conrad III and Louis VII	
1147	Lisbon captured from Moslems	
1152-1190	EMPEROR FREDERICK I, the Red-Bearded	
		d. 1153 Bernard of Clairvaux

General History	*Cultural History*
1154-1189 HENRY II of England and Normandy	
	d. 1158 Otto of Freising
1159-1181 Pope Alexander III	
1162 Milan destroyed by Frederick I	d. 1164 Peter Lombard
1174-1193 Saladin	
1176 x Legnano, Frederick I defeated by Lombard League	
1180-1223 PHILIP II of France	d. 1180 John of Salisbury
1183 Peace of Constance, Frederick I recognizes the Lombard cities	
1187 Jerusalem captured by Saladin	Gothic cathedrals at Chartres, Notre Dame, Lincoln, etc.
1189-1192 Crusade of Frederick I, Philip II, and Richard I, the Lion-Hearted	
1189-1199 Richard I, the Lion-Hearted	Universities at Paris, Oxford, Bologna, etc.
1190-1197 Emperor Henry VI	
1198-1216 POPE INNOCENT III	d. 1198 Averroës
1199-1216 John of England	1200 Philip II's charter to the University of Paris
1204 John of England loses Normandy to Philip II	
1204 Constantinople captured by Venetian and French crusaders	
1204-1261 Latin Empire of Constantinople	
1208-1229 Albigensian crusades	1209 University of Cambridge
1210 Franciscan order approved by Innocent III	
1212 Children's Crusade	
1212 Spanish victory over Moslems at Navas de Tolosa	d. 1213 Villehardouin
1212-1250 EMPEROR FREDERICK II	
1214 x Bouvines	
1215 Great Charter	
1215 Fourth Lateran Council	
1216 Dominican order approved by Honorius III	
1220 Frederick II crowned emperor	
	Aristotle's writings popular at Paris
1226-1270 LOUIS IX, "the Saint," of France	d. 1226 St. Francis of Assisi
1228 Crusade of Frederick II	
1236 Cordova captured by Castilians	
1243-1254 Pope Innocent IV	
1244 Seville captured by Castilians	
1248-1254 Crusade of Louis IX to Egypt	
1252-1284 Alfonse X, the Wise, of Castile	d. 1253 Robert Grosseteste
1254-1273 Interregnum, no emperors	
1261 Byzantine Empire restored in Constantinople	
1266-1285 Charles of Anjou, king of Naples-Sicily	
1268 Charles of Anjou completes conquest of Naples	
1270 Crusade of Louis IX to Tunis	
1272-1307 EDWARD I of England	d. 1274 Thomas Aquinas

General History	Cultural History
1273-1292 Emperor Rudolph of Hapsburg	d. 1278 Nicholas of Pisa
	d. 1280 Albertus Magnus
1282 Sicilian Vespers	
1285-1314 PHILIP IV of France	
1291 Swiss confederation of three cantons	
1291 Acre captured by Moslems	
1291-1327 James II of Aragon	
1294-1303 POPE BONIFACE VIII	d. 1294 Roger Bacon
1295 The "Model" Parliament in England	
1300 Papal jubilee of Boniface VIII	
1302 First Estates-General in France	
1302 x Courtrai, triumph of Flemish	
1305-1378 Avignon papacy, or "Babylonian Captivity"	
1309 Enlarged Swiss confederation recognized	
1310 Council of Ten in Venice	
1314 x Bannockburn	
1314-1347 Emperor Louis IV, the Bavarian	
1315 Swiss victory at Morgarten	
	d. ca. 1319 Joinville
	d. 1321 Dante
1327-1377 Edward III of England	
1328-1350 Philip VI of France	
1328 x Cassel, defeat of Flemish	
	d. 1337 Giotto
1339 Beginning of Hundred Years' War	
1340 English victory at Sluy	
	d. 1342 Marsilius of Padua
1346 English victory at Crècy	
1343 Revolt of Florentine workers	
1348-1349 Black Death appears in Europe	d. 1348 Giovanni Villani
	d. 1349 William of Ockham
1351 English Statute of Provisors	
1353 English Statute of Praemunire	
1353 Cardinal Albornoz in Rome	
1356 The Golden Bull in Germany	
1356-1358 Revolts in Paris, Stephen Marcel, the Jacquerie	
1364-1380 Charles V of France	
	d. 1374 Petrarch
1377-1399 Richard II of England	d. 1375 Boccaccio
1378-1382 Ciompi revolt in Florence	
1378 End of Avignon papacy, beginning of the Great Schism	
1378-1381 Chioggia war of Venice and Genoa	
1378-1402 Gian Galeazzo Visconti of Milan	
1381 Peasant revolt in England	
1382 Flemish defeat at Roosebeke	
	d. 1384 John Wiclif
1386 Swiss victory at Sempach	
	1396 Chrysoloras at Florence
1399-1413 Henry IV of Lancaster in England	
	d. ca. 1400 Claus Sluter
	d. 1400 Chaucer
1409 Council of Pisa	

General History	Cultural History
1410-1437 Emperor Sigismund	d. ca. 1410 Froissart
1414-1418 Council of Constance	
1415-1460 Prince Henry the Navigator of Portugal	d. 1415 John Hus
1415 English victory at Agincourt	
1417 End of Great Schism; Pope Martin V	
1419-1436 Hussite Wars	
1420 Treaty of Troyes between England and France	
1422 Henry VI recognized as king of both realms	
1422-1461 Charles VII, "the Dauphin," of France	
	d. ca. 1428 Masaccio
1429 Joan of Arc at Orlèans	d. 1429 John Gerson
1431-1449 Council of Basel	
1434-1464 Cosimo de' Medici in Florence	
1435 Treaty of Arras virtually ends Hundred Years' War	
1438-1439 Pragmatic Sanctions of Bourges and Mayence	
	d. 1440 John Van Eyck
	d. 1446 Brunelleschi
	d. 1446 Vittorino da Feltre
1447-1455 Pope Nicholas V	
1448 Concordat of Vienna	
1450 Papal Jubilee of Pope Nicholas V	ca. 1450 Printing in Germany
1450-1466 Francesco Sforza of Milan	
1453 Turks capture Constantinople	
1454-1485 Wars of the Roses in England	d. 1455 Fra Angelico
	d. 1455 Ghiberti
	d. 1457 Laurentius Valla
1461-1483 Louis XI of France	d. ca. 1463 François Villon
1462-1505 Ivan the Great of Muscovy	d. 1464 Nicholas of Cusa
	d. 1466 Donatello
1467-1477 Charles the Bold of Burgundy	
1469 Marriage of Ferdinand and Isabella	d. 1469 Fra Filippo Lippi
1469-1492 Lorenzo de' Medici in Florence	
1474-1504 Isabella of Castile	
1476 Swiss victories at Granson and Morat	
1478-1500 Ludovico il Moro of Milan	
1479-1516 Ferdinand II of Aragon	d. 1482 Lucca della Robbia
1483-1498 Charles VIII of France	
1485-1509 Henry VII of England	
1486-1519 Emperor Maximilian	d. 1488 Verrocchio
1492 First voyage of Columbus	
1492-1503 Pope Alexander VI	
1494 French invasion of Italy	d. 1494 Politian
1497-1498 Voyage of Vasco da Gama	
1499 Savonarola burned at Florence	

BIBLIOGRAPHY

GENERAL WORKS ON VARIOUS PERIODS AND TOPICS

Textbooks:

Adams, G. B., *Civilization During the Middle Ages,* Scribner's, 1914

Ault, W. O., *Europe in the Middle Ages,* Heath, 1937

Barnes, H. E., *The History of Western Civilization,* Harcourt, Brace, 1935

Boak, A. E. R., *A History of Rome to 565 A.D.,* Macmillan, 1930

Brown, S. M., *Medieval Europe,* Harcourt, Brace, 1935

Caldwell, W. E., *The Ancient World,* Farrar & Rinehart, 1937

Collins, R. W., *A History of Medieval Civilization in Europe,* Ginn, 1936

Davis, H. W. C., *Medieval Europe,* Holt, 1911

Ferrero, G., and Barbagallo, C., *A Short History of Rome,* Putnam's, 1918-19, Vol. II

Frank, T., *A History of Rome,* Holt, 1923

Hulme, E. M., *The Middle Ages,* Holt, 1929

Moore, F. G., *The Roman's World,* Columbia, 1936

Moss, H., *The Birth of the Middle Ages,* Oxford, 1935

Munro, D. C., and Sontag, R. J., *The Middle Ages,* Appleton-Century, 1928

Previté-Orton, C. W., *Outlines of Medieval History,* Cambridge, 1929

Robinson, C. E., *A History of Rome from 753 B.C. to A.D. 410,* Crowell, 1935

Robinson, J. H., *An Introduction to the History of Western Europe,* Ginn, 1929, Vol. I

Rostovtzeff, M. I., *A History of the Ancient World,* Oxford, 1926-28, Vol. II

Sandys, J. E., *A Companion to Latin Studies,* Cambridge, 1925

Sellery, G. C., and Krey, A. C., *Medieval Foundations of Western Civilization,* Harper, 1929

Stephenson, C., *Mediæval History,* Harper, 1935

Thatcher, O. J., and McNeal, E. H., *Europe in the Middle Age,* Scribner's, 1920

Thompson, J. W., and Johnson, E. N., *An Introduction to Medieval Europe,* Norton, 1937

Thorndike, L., *The History of Medieval Europe,* Houghton Mifflin, 1928

Trever, A. A., *History of Ancient Civilization,* Harcourt, Brace, 1937, Vol. II

Histories of Special Subjects:

Barnes, H. E., *An Intellectual and Cultural History of the Western World,* Cordon, 1937

Boissonade, P., *Life and Work in Medieval Europe,* Knopf, 1927

Bryce, J., *The Holy Roman Empire,* Burt, 1904

Chase, G. H., and Post, C. R., *History of Sculpture,* Harper, 1924

Cambridge Medieval History, Macmillan, 1911-36, 8 vols.

Cheney, S., *A World History of Art,* Viking, 1937

Cheyney, E. P., *Dawn of a New Era,* Harper, 1936

Crump, G. C., and Jacob, E. F., *The Legacy of the Middle Ages,* Oxford, 1926

Day, C., *A History of Commerce,* Longmans, 1922

Encyclopedia of the Social Sciences, Macmillan, 1930-5

Flick, A. C., *The Rise of the Medieval Church,* Putnam's, 1909

Gibbon, E., *The History of the Decline and Fall of the Roman Empire,* Bury edition, 7 vols., 1896-1900

Gras, N. S., *A History of Agriculture,* Crofts, 1925

Guignebert, C., *Christianity, Past and Present,* Macmillan, 1927

Hearnshaw, F. J. C., *Medieval Contributions to Modern Civilization,* Holt, 1922

Heaton, H., *Economic History of Europe,* Harper, 1936

Knight, M. M., *Economic History of Europe to the End of the Middle Ages,* Houghton Mifflin, 1926

Lodge, R., *The Close of the Middle Ages,* Macmillan, 1901

Milman, H. H., *History of Latin Christianity,* Murray, 1883, 9 vols.

Munro, D. C., and Sellery, G. C., *Medieval Civilization,* Appleton-Century, 1907

Oman, C. W. C., *The Dark Ages,* 476-918, Macmillan, 1894

Paetow, L. J., *A Guide to the Study of Medieval History,* Crofts, 1931

Pijoan, J., *A History of Art,* Harper, 1933, Vols. I-II

Pirenne, H., *Economic and Social History of Medieval Europe,* Harcourt, Brace, 1937

Poole, R. L., *Illustrations of the History of Medieval Thought and Learning,* Macmillan, 1920

Previté-Orton, C. W., *A History of Europe, 1198-1378,* Putnam's, 1937

Randall, J. H., *The Making of the Modern Mind,* Houghton Mifflin, 1927

Robinson, J. H., *The Mind in the Making,* Harper, 1921

———, *The New History,* Macmillan, 1912

Reinach, S., *Apollo: An Illustrated Manual of the History of Art,* Scribner's, 1917

Sarton, G., *Introduction to the History of Science,* Carnegie Institution, 1927–

Schaff, P., *History of the Christian Church,* Scribner's, 1882-1910, 7 vols.

Shepherd, W. R., *Historical Atlas*, Holt, 1929

Singer, C. H., *From Magic to Science*, Liveright, 1928

Taylor, H. O., *The Mediæval Mind*, Macmillan, 1927, 2 vols.

Tout, T. F., *The Empire and Papacy*, Macmillan, 1898

Thompson, J. W., *An Economic and Social History of the Middle Ages* (300-1300), Appleton-Century, 1928

————, *An Economic and Social History of Europe in the Later Middle Ages*, Appleton-Century, 1931

Thorndike, L., *A History of Magic and Experimental Science*, Macmillan, 1929-34, Vols. I-IV

Troeltsch, E., *The Social Teaching of the Christian Churches*, Macmillan, 1931, 2 vols.

Waugh, W. T., *A History of Europe from 1376 to 1494*, Putnam's, 1932

Source Books, containing excerpts from first-hand source material:

Ayer, J. C., *Source Book of Church History for the First Six Centuries*, Scribner's, 1913-26

Cave, R. C., and Coulson, H. H., *A Source Book for Medieval Economic History*, Bruce, 1936

Coulton, G. G., *Life in the Middle Ages*, Cambridge, 1928-30, 4 vols.

Cunliffe, J. W., *Century Readings in European History*, Appleton-Century, 1925

Davies, R. T., *Documents Illustrating the History of Civilization in Medieval England, 1066-1500*, Dutton, 1926

Henderson, E. F., *Select Historical Documents of the Middle Ages*, Bell, 1892-1905

Lindsay, J., *Medieval Latin Poets*, Elkin Mathews and Marrot, 1934

McKeon, R., *Selections from Medieval Philosophers*, Scribner's, 1929-30, 2 vols.

Ogg, F. A., *A Source Book of Medieval History*, American Book, 1908

Records of Civilization: Sources and Studies. Ed. by A. P. Evans, Columbia, 1915

Robinson, J. H., *Readings in European History*, Ginn, 1906, Vol. I

Showerman, G., *Century Readings in Ancient Classical Literature*, Appleton-Century, 1925

Scott, J. H., Hyma, A., and Noyes, A. H., *Readings in Medieval History*, Crofts, 1933

Thatcher, O. J., and McNeal, E. H., *A Source Book of Mediæval History*, Scribner's, 1905

Translations and Reprints from Original Sources in European History, Pennsylvania, 1894-1906

Webster, H., *Historical Selections*, Heath, 1929

Special Readings on Specific Topics and Periods:

Briefer and more general accounts are to be found in the textbooks listed above; see tables of contents and indices. Many of the specific *topics* are treated in detail in the histories of special subjects listed above. Likewise, the *source books* listed above contain translated excerpts concerning most of the periods and topics. The following lists are therefore supplementary.

CHAPTERS I-II: ROME

Abbott, F. F., and Johnson, A. C., *Municipal Administration in the Roman Empire,* Princeton, 1926

Arnold, W. T., *The Roman System of Provincial Administration to the Accession of Constantine the Great,* Blackwell, 1914

Arragon, R. F., *The Transition from the Ancient to the Medieval World,* Holt, 1936

Brewster, E. H., *Roman Craftsmen and Tradesmen of the Early Empire,* Banta, 1918

Bailey, C., *The Legacy of Rome,* Oxford, 1923

Buckland, W. W., *Roman Law from Augustus to Justinian,* Cambridge, 1932

Cambridge Medieval History, Vol. I

Chapot, V., *The Roman World,* Knopf, 1928

Charlesworth, M. P., *Trade Routes and Commerce of the Roman Empire,* Cambridge, 1924

Davis, W. S., *The Influence of Wealth in Imperial Rome,* Macmillan, 1910

Dill, S., *Roman Society from Nero to Marcus Aurelius,* Macmillan, 1904

———, *Roman Society in the Last Century of the Western Empire,* Macmillan, 1899

Duff, J. W., *A Literary History of Rome in the Silver Age,* Scribner's, 1927

Friedlander, L., *Roman Life and Manners under the Early Empire,* Dutton, 1928-36, 4 vols.

Frank, T., *An Economic History of Rome,* Johns Hopkins, 1927

——— (ed.), *An Economic Survey of Ancient Rome,* Johns Hopkins, Vols. I-III, 1933-7. In progress

Glover, T. R., *Life and Letters in the Fourth Century,* Cambridge, 1901

Heitland, W. E., *Agricola, A Study of Agriculture and Rustic Life in the Greco-Roman World from the Point of View of Labour,* Cambridge, 1921

———, *The Roman Fate,* Cambridge, 1925

Hodgkin, T., *The Dynasty of Theodosius,* Oxford, 1889

Homo, L., *Roman Political Institutions,* Knopf, 1929

Jolowicz, H. F., *Historical Introduction to the Study of Roman Law,* Cambridge, 1932

Jones, A. H. M., *The Cities of the Eastern Roman Provinces,* Oxford, 1937

Lot, F., *The End of the Ancient World and the Beginning of the Middle Ages,* Knopf, 1931

Mackail, J. W., *Latin Literature,* Scribner's, 1895

Mommsen, T., *The Provinces of the Roman Empire from Cæsar to Diocletian,* Scribner's, 1909, 2 vols.

Nilsson, M. P., *Imperial Rome,* Bell, 1926

Parker, H. M., *A History of the Roman World from A.D. 138 to 337,* Methuen, 1935

Pijoan, J., *A History of Art,* Harper, 1933, Vol. I

Reid, J. S., *The Municipalities of the Roman Empire,* Cambridge, 1913

Rostovtzeff, M. I., *The Social and Economic History of the Roman Empire,* Oxford, 1926

Simkovitch, V., "Rome's Fall Reconsidered," *Political Science Quarterly,* Vol. XXXI

Strong, E. S., *Roman Sculpture, from Augustus to Constantine,* Scribner's, 1907

Taylor, H. O., *The Classical Heritage of the Middle Ages,* Macmillan, 1911

Thorndike, L., *A History of Magic and Experimental Science,* Macmillan, 1923, Vol. I

Tucker, T. G., *Life in the Roman World of Nero and St. Paul,* Macmillan, 1910

Westermann, W. L., "The Economic Basis of the Decline of Ancient Culture," *American Historical Review,* Vol. XXX

Zulueta, F. de, *De patrociniis vicorum,* Oxford, 1909

Sources (in addition to the material in the *source books* listed above):

Howe, G., and Harrer, G. A., *Roman Literature in Translation,* Harper, 1924

Ammianus Marcellinus, *Roman History,* Yonge (trans.), Bell, 1894

Salvian, *On the Government of God,* E. M. Sanford (trans.), Columbia, 1930

Apollinaris Sidonius, *Letters,* O. M. Dalton (trans.), Oxford, 1915

The Loeb Classical Library contains complete translations of many Roman writings, with the original texts.

CHAPTERS III-IV: THE RISE OF CHRISTIANITY, THE PAPACY, MONASTICISM

Angus, S., *The Environment of Early Christianity,* Scribner's, 1931

———, *The Mystery Religions and Christianity,* Murray, 1925

Baldwin, S., *The Organization of Medieval Christianity,* Holt, 1929

Baynes, N., *Constantine the Great and the Christian Church,* British Academy, 1930

Blatchford, A., *Church Councils and Their Decrees,* Green, 1909

Butler, E., *Benedictine Monasticism*, Longmans, 1924
Cadoux, C. J., *The Early Church and the World*, Clark, 1925
Case, S., *The Social Origins of Christianity*, Chicago, 1923
Canfield, L., *Early Persecutions of the Christians*, Longmans, 1913
Chapman, J., *St. Benedict and the Sixth Century*, Longmans, 1929
Coleman, C., *Constantine the Great and Christianity*, Longmans, 1914
Cumont, F., *The Oriental Religions in Roman Paganism*, Open Court, 1911
Duchesne, L., *The Early History of the Christian Church*, Murray, 1909-24, 3 vols.
Dudden, H., *The Life and Times of St. Ambrose*, Oxford, 1935, 2 vols.
————, *Gregory the Great*, Longmans, 1905, 2 vols.
Eisler, R., *The Messiah Jesus*, MacVeagh, 1931
Flick, A., *The Rise of the Medieval Church*, Putnam's, 1909
Foakes-Jackson, F., *The Rise of Gentile Christianity*, Doubleday-Doran, 1927
Glover, T., *The Conflict of Religions in the Early Roman Empire*, Methuen, 1909
Goodenough, E., *The Church in the Roman Empire*, Holt, 1931
Guignebert, C., *Christianity, Past and Present*, Macmillan, 1927
Halliday, W., *The Pagan Background of Early Christianity*, University of Liverpool, 1925
Hardy, E., *Christianity and the Roman Government*, Macmillan, 1925
Harnack, A., *The Mission and Expansion of Christianity*, Putnam's, 1908, 2 vols.
Hatch, E., *The Organization of the Early Christian Churches*, Longmans, 1918
Huttman, M. A., *The Establishment of Christianity and the Proscription of Paganism*, Columbia, 1914
Kidd, B., *A History of the Church to A.D. 461*, Clarendon, 1922, 3 vols.
Kruger, G., *The Papacy*, Unwin, 1909
Labriolle, P., *The History and Literature of Christianity*, Knopf, 1925
Lowrie, W., *Monuments of the Early Church*, Macmillan, 1901
McCabe, J., *St. Augustine and His Age*, Putnam's, 1903
Marett, R., *The Sacraments of Simple Folk*, Oxford, 1933
Merril, E., *Essays in Early Church History*, Macmillan, 1924
Palmer, F., *Heretics, Saints, and Martyrs*, Harvard, 1925
Rand, E., *Founders of the Middle Ages*, Harvard, 1928
Sohm, R., *Outlines of Church History*, Macmillan, 1909
The History of Christianity in the Light of Modern Knowledge, Harcourt, Brace, 1929
Whitaker, T., *The Neo-Platonists*, Cambridge, 1928
Wishart, A., *Monks and Monasteries*, Brandt, 1900

Woodward, E. L., *Christianity and Nationalism in the Later Roman Empire*, Longmans, 1916
Workman, H., *The Evolution of the Monastic Ideal*, Kelly, 1913
——, *Persecution in the Early Church*, Kelly, 1906

Sources:

A select *Library of Nicene and Post-Nicene Fathers*, Scribner's, 1903-9, contains selected works of Augustine, Ambrose, Jerome, etc.
Augustine, *The City of God*, Grant, 1909
——, *Confessions*, Macmillan, 1912
Jerome, *Select Letters*, Putnam's, 1933
Gregory the Great, *Dialogues*, Warner, 1911
——, *The Pastoral Rule*, Oxford, 1874
——, *Select Letters*, in the *Library of Nicene and Post-Nicene Fathers*
New Testament, especially the book of Acts
Orosius, *Seven Books of History Against the Pagans*, Columbia, 1936
Salvian, *On the Government of God*, Columbia, 1930
The Book of the Popes, Columbia, 1916
The See of Peter, Columbia, 1927
The Rule of St. Benedict, Chatto and Windus, 1925
Translations and Reprints, Vol. IV, No. 1 (Persecutions)

Chapters V-VI: The Germans

Brogan, O., "Trade between the Roman Empire and the Free Germans," *Journal of Roman Studies*, Vol. XXVI, Pt. 2, 1936
Bury, J. B., *The Invasion of Europe by the Barbarians*, Macmillan, 1928
Cambridge Medieval History, Vols. I-II
de Coulanges, Fustel, *The Origin of Property in Land*, Swan Sonnenschein, 1891
Dill, S., *Roman Society in the Last Century of the Western Empire*, Macmillan, 1899
——, *Roman Society in Gaul in the Merovingian Age*, Macmillan, 1926
Dopsch, A., *The Economic and Social Foundations of European Civilization*, Harcourt, Brace, 1937
East, G., *An Historical Geography of Europe*, Methuen, 1935
Gummere, F. B., *Germanic Origins*, Scribner's, 1892
Haddon, A. C., *Wanderings of Peoples*, Macmillan, 1911
Hodgkin, T., *Italy and Her Invaders*, Oxford, 1916, 8 vols.
——, *Theodoric the Goth*, London, 1923
——, *The Dynasty of Theodosius*, Oxford, 1889
Holmes, T. S., *The Origin and Development of the Church in Gaul*, Macmillan, 1911

Jenks, E., *Law and Politics in the Middle Ages*, Macmillan, 1898
Lot, F., *The End of the Ancient World and the Beginning of the Middle Ages*, Knopf, 1931
MacBridge, J. H., *The Barbarian Invasions of the Roman Empire*, Stratford, 1926
Moss, H., *The Birth of the Middle Ages*, Oxford, 1935
———, "The Economic Consequences of the Barbarian Invasions," *Economic History Review*, May, 1937
Parker, H. M. D., *The Roman Legions*, Oxford, 1928
Villari, P., *The Barbarian Invasions of Italy*, London, 1902

Sources:

Ammianus Marcellinus, *Roman History*, Yonge (trans.), Bell, 1894
Gregory of Tours, *The History of the Franks*, O. M. Dalton (trans.), Oxford, 1927
Hayes, C. J., *Introduction to the Sources Relating to the Germanic Invasions*, Columbia, 1909
Translations and Reprints, Vol. IV, No. 4; Vol. VI, No. 3

CHAPTER VII: BYZANTINE CIVILIZATION

Ashburner, W., *The Rhodian Sea Law*, Oxford, 1909
———, "The Farmer's Law," *Journal of Hellenic Studies*, Vol. XXX (1910), XXXII (1912)
Baynes, N. H., *The Byzantine Empire*, Holt, 1925
Boak, A. E., "The Book of the Prefect," *Journal of Economic and Business History*, I, 4, August, 1929
Bury, J. B., *History of the Later Roman Empire*, Macmillan, 1923, Vol. II
———, *A History of the Eastern Roman Empire*, Macmillan, 1912
Cambridge Medieval History, Vols. II and IV
Dalton, O. M., *Byzantine Art and Archæology*, Oxford, 1911
Diehl, C., *Byzantine Portraits*, Knopf, 1927
———, *History of the Byzantine Empire*, Princeton, 1925
Hardy, E. R., *Large Estates in Byzantine Egypt*, Columbia
Holmes, W. G., *The Age of Justinian and Theodora*, Macmillan, 1905-7, 2 vols.
Hussey, J., *Church and Learning in the Byzantine Empire, 867-1185*, London, 1937
Jackson, T. G., *Byzantine and Romanesque Architecture*, Chicago, 1920, 2 vols.
Lot, F., *The End of the Ancient World and the Beginning of the Middle Ages*, Knopf, 1931
Millingen, A. Van, *Byzantine Churches in Constantinople*, Macmillan, 1912
Runciman, S., *Byzantine Civilization*, Longmans, 1933

Vasiliev, A. A., *History of the Byzantine Empire,* Wisconsin, 1928-30, 2 vols.
Walton, F. P., *Historical Introduction to the Roman Law,* Green, 1912

Sources:
Procopius, *History of the Wars,* H. B. Dewing (trans.), Putnam's, 1914-28, 5 vols.
————, *Secret History,* H. B. Dewing (trans.), Harvard, 1935
Wright, F. A., *The Works of Liudprand of Cremona,* Dutton, 1930

Chapter VIII: Moslem Civilization

Amir Ali, M. S., *Short History of the Saracens,* Macmillan, 1924
————, *The Spirit of Islam,* Doubleday, Doran, 1923
Arnold, T. W., *The Preaching of Islam,* Scribner's, 1913
————, *The Caliphate,* Oxford, 1924
————, and Guillaume, Alfred (eds.), *The Legacy of Islam,* Oxford, 1931
Brown, E. G., *Arabian Medicine,* Macmillan, 1921
Cambridge Medieval History, Vol. III
Dozy, R. P., *Spanish Islam,* Duffield, 1913
Fischel, W. J., *Jews in the Economic and Political Life of Mediæval Islam,* Royal Asiatic Society, 1937
Goldziher, I., *Mohammed and Islam,* Yale, 1917
Hell, J., *Arab Civilization,* Heffer, 1926
Hitti, P. K., *History of the Arabs,* Macmillan, 1937
Hogarth, D. G., *Arabia,* Oxford, 1922
Levy, R., *Introduction to the Sociology of Islam,* Williams & Norgate, 1931-3, 2 vols.
Lewis, B., "The Islamic Guilds," *Economic History Review,* VIII, 1 (Nov., 1937)
Margoliouth, D. S., *Mohammed and the Rise of Islam,* Putnam's, 1927
————, *Mohammedanism,* Home University, 1911
Muir, W., *The Caliphate: Its Rise, Decline, and Fall,* Grant, 1924
O'Leary, D. E., *Arabia before Mohammed,* Dutton, 1927
Saladin, H., and Migeon, G., *Manuel d'Art Musulman,* Picard, 1907, 2 vols.

Sources:
Arabian Nights, translated by Burton, Kamashastra, 1885, 17 vols.
The Koran, translated by Palmer, Oxford, 1880, 2 vols.; and also by Sale, Warne, 1929
The Meaning of the Glorious Koran, by Pickthall, Knopf, 1930
Speeches and Table Talk of the Prophet Mohammed, edited by Lane Poole, Macmillan, 1882

CHAPTERS IX-X: THE FRANKISH EMPIRE AND ITS DISRUPTION

Cambridge Medieval History, Vols. II, III
Craigie, W. A., *The Icelandic Sagas,* Cambridge, 1913
Davis, H. W. C., *Charlemagne,* Putnam's, 1900
Haskins, C. H., *The Normans in European History,* Houghton Mifflin, 1915
Hodgkin, T., *Charles the Great,* Macmillan, 1903
Joranson, E., *The Danegeld in France,* Augustana, 1923
Kendrick, T. D., *History of the Vikings,* Scribner's, 1930
Kitchin, G. W., *History of France,* Oxford, 1899, Vol. I
Mawer, A., *The Vikings,* Macmillan, 1913
Olrik, A., *Viking Civilization,* Norton, 1930
Robinson, C. H., *The Conversion of Europe,* Longmans, 1917
Thompson, J. W., *The Dissolution of the Carolingian Fisc in the Ninth Century,* California, 1935
———, "The Commerce of France in the Ninth Century," *Journal of Political Economy,* XXIII (1915), 857-887
Williams, M. W., *Social Scandinavia in the Viking Age,* Macmillan, 1920

CHAPTERS XI-XII: FEUDALISM AND THE MANOR

Ashley, W. J., *Introduction to English Economic History and Theory,* Longmans, 1909, Vol. I
Bateson, M., *Medieval England,* Putnam's, 1904
Bell, C. H., *Peasant Life in Old German Epics,* Columbia, 1931
Boissonade, *Life and Work in Medieval Europe,* Knopf, 1927
Cambridge Medieval History, Vol. III, Chap. XVIII; Vol. VII, Chap. XXIV
Coulton, G. G., *The Medieval Village,* Cambridge, 1926
Cutts, E. L., *Scenes and Characters of the Middle Ages,* O'Connor, 1922
Davis, W. S., *Life on a Medieval Barony,* Harper, 1923
Denholm-Young, N., *Seigneurial Administration in England,* Oxford, 1937
Encyclopedia of the Social Sciences, see "Feudalism," "Manorial System"
Evans, J., *Life in Medieval France,* Oxford, 1925
Fedden, K. W. D., *Manor Life in Old France,* Columbia, 1933
Gras, N. S. B., *A History of Agriculture,* Crofts, 1925
Jenks, E., *Law and Politics in the Middle Ages,* Holt, 1898
Lipson, E., *Economic History of England,* Macmillan, 1929-31, Vol. I
Luchaire, A., *Social France in the Time of Philip Augustus,* Holt, 1912
Neilson, N., *Medieval Agrarian Economy,* Holt, 1936
Oman, C. W. C., *History of the Art of War in the Middle Ages,* Houghton Mifflin, 1924, 2 vols.
Power, E. E., *Medieval People,* Houghton Mifflin, 1924
Prestage, E., *Chivalry,* Knopf, 1928

Prothero, R. E., *English Farming, Past and Present*, Longmans, 1922
Salzman, L. F., *English Life in the Middle Ages*, Oxford, 1926
Seignobos, C., *The Feudal Régime*, Holt, 1902
Stenton, F. M., *The First Century of English Feudalism, 1066-1166*, Oxford, 1932
Thompson, A. H., *Military Architecture in England during the Middle Ages*, Frowde, 1912
Vinogradoff, P., *English Society in the Eleventh Century*, Oxford, 1908
——, *Growth of the Manor*, Oxford, 1908

Sources:

Coulton, G. G., *Life in the Middle Ages*, Macmillan, 1930, Vol. III
Translations and Reprints, Vol. III, No. 5; Vol. IV, No. 3

Chapters XIII-XVII: Learning, Literature, and the Arts in the Early Middle Ages

General Accounts:

Barnes, H. E., *An Intellectual and Cultural History of the Western World*, Cordon, 1937
Cambridge Medieval History, Vols. III, V
Crump, C. G., and Jacobs, E. T., *The Legacy of the Middle Ages*, Oxford, 1926
Foligno, C., *Latin Thought During the Middle Ages*, Oxford, 1929
Hearnshaw, F. J. C., *Medieval Contributions to Modern Civilization*, Holt, 1922
Taylor, H. O., *The Medieval Mind*, Macmillan, 1919, Vol. I, Chaps. IV-XIII
——, *The Classical Heritage of the Middle Ages*, Macmillan, 1925

Learning and Literature:

Allen, P. S., and Jones, H. M., *The Romanesque Lyric*, North Carolina, 1928
Beeson, C. H., *Lupus of Ferriéres*, Medieval Academy, 1930
Brehaut, E., *An Encyclopedist of the Dark Ages: Isidore of Seville*, Columbia, 1912
Cambridge History of English Literature, Cambridge, 1907, Vol. I
Dalton, O. M., *The History of the Franks by Gregory of Tours*, Oxford, 1927, Vol. I (Introduction)
De Labriolle, P., *The History and Literature of Christianity*, Knopf, 1925
Dudden, F., *Gregory the Great*, Longmans, 1905
Gaskoin, C. J. B., *Alcuin: His Life and Works*. Columbia, 1904
Ker, W. P., *The Dark Ages*, Scribner's, 1904
Laistner, M. L. W., *Thought and Letters in Western Europe*, Dial, 1931

McGiffert, A. C., *History of Christian Thought*, Scribner's, 1932, 2 vols.

MacKinney, L. C., *Early Medieval Medicine*, Johns Hopkins, 1937

Patch, H. R., *The Tradition of Boethius*, Oxford, 1935

Poole, R. L., *Illustrations of the History of Medieval Thought and Learning*, Macmillan, 1926

Rand, E. K., *Founders of the Middle Ages*, Harvard, 1928

Symonds, J. A., *Wine, Women, and Song*, Chatto and Windus, 1925

Thorndike, L., *A History of Magic and Experimental Science*, Macmillan, 1923, Vol. I

Waddell, H., *The Wandering Scholars*, Houghton Mifflin, 1927

West, A. F., *Alcuin and the Rise of Christian Schools*, Scribner's, 1892

Music:

Dickinson, E., *Music in the History of the Western Church*, Scribner's, 1925

Duncan, E., *The Story of Minstrelsy*, Scribner's, 1907

Gray, C., *History of Music*, Knopf, 1928

Oxford History of Music, Oxford, 1929, introductory vol., and Vol. I

The Arts:

Chase, G. H., and Post, C. R., *History of Sculpture*, Harper, 1924

Cheney, S., *A World History of Art*, Viking, 1937

Gardner, H., *Art through the Ages*, Harcourt, Brace, 1936

Jameson, A. B., *Sacred and Legendary Art*, Houghton Mifflin, 1911, 2 vols.

Lethaby, W. R., *Medieval Art*, Scribner's, 1913

Lowrie, W., *Monuments of the Early Church*, Macmillan, 1923

Middleton, J. H., *Illuminated Manuscripts in Classical and Medieval Times*, Cambridge, 1892

Morey, C. R., *Christian Art*, Longmans, 1935

Pijoan, *History of Art*, Harper, 1933, Vol. II

Strzygowski, J., *Origin of Christian Church Art*, Oxford, 1923

Sources:

Allen, P. S., *Medieval Latin Lyrics*, Chicago, 1931

Bede, *Ecclesiastical History of England*, King (trans.), Putnam's, 1930, 3 vols.; also Sellar (trans.), Bell, 1912

Beowulf, Gummere (trans.), Macmillan, 1909

Cubberley, E. P., *Readings in the History of Education*, Houghton Mifflin, 1934

Kuhnmuench, O. J., *Early Christian Latin Poets*, Loyola University (Chicago), 1929

Liudprand of Cremona, *Works*, Wright (trans.), Dutton, 1930

Roswitha, *Plays*, St. John (trans.), Chatto and Windus, 1924

Translations and Reprints, Vol. II, No. 7, *Life of Columban by the Monk Konas*
Waddell, H., *Medieval Latin Lyrics,* Constable, 1933
Willibald, *Life of St. Boniface,* Robinson (trans.), Harvard, 1916

CHAPTER XVIII: THE RISE OF TOWNS

Ashley, W. J., *The Economic Organization of England,* Longmans, 1935
Benson, E., *Life in a Medieval City,* Macmillan, 1920
Boissonade, P., *Life and Work in Medieval Europe,* Knopf, 1927
Cambridge Medieval History, Vol. V (especially Chap. XIX), and Vol. VI (especially Chaps. XIV-XV)
Cunningham, W., *The Growth of English Industry and Commerce in Modern Times,* Macmillan, 1917, Vol. I
Evans, J., *Life in Mediæval France,* Milford, 1925, Chap. VII
Gibbins, H. D. B., *Industry in England,* Scribner's
Gras, N. S. B., *An Introduction to Economic History,* Harper, 1922
Guilford, E. L., *Travellers and Travelling in the Middle Ages,* Macmillan, 1924
Lipson, E., *Economic History of England,* Macmillan, 1937, 7th ed., Vol. I
Newton, A. P., *Travel and Travellers in the Middle Ages,* Knopf, 1926
Pirenne, H., *Medieval Cities,* Princeton, 1925
———, *Belgian Democracy,* Longmans, 1915
———, *Economic and Social History of Medieval Europe,* Paul, Trench, Trubner, 1936
Power, E. E., *Medieval People,* Houghton Mifflin, 1924
Renard, G. F., *Guilds in the Middle Ages,* Harcourt, Brace, 1919
Salzman, L. F., *English Industries of the Middle Ages,* Oxford, 1924
———, *English Trade in the Middle Ages,* Oxford, 1931
———, *English Life in the Middle Ages,* Oxford, 1926
Stephenson, C., *Borough and Town,* Medieval Academy, 1933
Tilley, A. A., *Mediæval France,* Cambridge, 1922
Unwin, G., *Studies in Economic History,* Macmillan, 1927
———, *The Gilds and Companies of London,* Scribner's, 1909
Usher, A. P., *Introduction to the Industrial History of England,* Harrap, 1921

Sources:

Bland, A., Brown, P., and Tawney, R., *English Economic History: Select Documents,* Bell, 1915
Compani, Dino, *The Chronicle of* . . . , Temple Classics, 1906
Translations and Reprints, Vol. II, No. 1, Guibert of Nogert, *Autobiography*
Villani, G., Selections from the First Nine Books of *The Chronicle Florentine* . . . , Constable, 1896

CHAPTERS XIX-XX: EMPIRE AND PAPACY

Balzani, U., *The Popes and the Hohenstaufen*, Longmans, 1901
Bryce, James, *The Holy Roman Empire*, Macmillan, Rev. Ed., 1923
Butler, F. W., *The Lombard Communes*, Unwin, 1906
Cambridge Medieval History, Vols. III, V, VI
Evans, J., *Monastic Life at Cluny*, Milford, 1931
Fisher, H., *The Medieval Empire*, Macmillan, 1898, Vol. I
Haskins, C. H., *The Normans in European History*, Houghton Mifflin, 1915
Henderson, E. F., *A Short History of Germany*, Macmillan, 1927, Vol. I
Johnson, E. N., *The Secular Activities of the German Episcopate*, Nebraska, 1932
Kantorowicz, E., *Frederick II*, Constable, 1931
MacDonald, A. J., *Hildebrand, Pope Gregory VII*, Methuen, 1932
Packard, S. R., *Europe and the Church under Innocent III*, Holt, 1927
Smith, L. M., *The Early Monastery of Cluny*, Oxford, 1920
Thompson, J. W., *Feudal Germany*, Chicago, 1928
Tout, T. F., *The Empire and the Papacy*, Rivington, 1914
Villari, P., *Medieval Italy*, Unwin, 1910

Sources:

The Correspondence of Pope Gregory VII, E. Emerton (trans.), Columbia, 1932

CHAPTERS XXI-XXII: THE MEDIEVAL CHURCH

Cambridge Medieval History, Vols. V and VI
Coulton, G. G., *Five Centuries of Religion*, Cambridge, 1927-36, 3 vols.
Cutts, E. L., *Parish Priests and Their People in the Middle Ages*, Gorham, 1914
Davison, E., *Forerunners of St. Francis*, Houghton Mifflin, 1927
Evans, A. P., "Social Aspects of Medieval Heresy." In *Persecution and Liberty*. Essays in Honor of G. L. Burr, Appleton-Century, 1931
Flick, A. C., *The Rise of the Medieval Church*, Knopf, 1930
Foakes-Jackson, F. J., *Introduction to the History of Christianity, A.D. 500-1314*, Macmillan, 1921
Fortescue, A., *The Mass*, Longmans, 1937
Gasquet, A., *Parish Life in Medieval England*, Benziger, 1902
Guignebert, C., *Christianity, Past and Present*, Macmillan, 1927
Heath, S. H., *Pilgrim Life in the Middle Ages*, Houghton Mifflin, 1911
History of Christianity in the Light of Modern Knowledge, The, Harcourt, 1929
Jarrett, B., *Life of St. Dominic*, Benziger, 1924
Jorgenson, J., *St. Francis of Assisi*, Longmans, 1912

Krehbiel, E. B., *The Interdict*, American Historical Association, 1909

Lagarde, A., *The Latin Church in the Middle Ages*, Scribner's, 1915

Lea, H. C., *Studies in Church History*, Lea, 1883

——, *An History of Sacerdotal Celibacy in the Christian Church*, Macmillan, 1907, 2 vols.

——, *A History of the Inquisition of the Middle Ages*, Harper, 1888, 3 vols.

Luchaire, A., *Social France at the Time of Philip Augustus*, Holt, 1912

Lunt, W. E., *Papal Revenues in the Middle Ages*, Columbia, 1934, 2 vols.

Owst, G. R., *Preaching in Medieval England*, Macmillan, 1926

Poole, R. L., *Illustrations of the History of Medieval Thought and Learning*, Macmillan, 1926

Sabatier, P., *Life of St. Francis of Assisi*, Scribner's, 1894

Salvatorelli, *Life of St. Francis of Assisi*, Knopf, 1928

Smith, L. M., *The Early Monastery of Cluny*, Oxford, 1920

Taylor, H. O., *The Medieval Mind*, Macmillan, Vol. I, Chaps. XVI-XXII; Vol. II, Chap. XXX

Wood, Mary, *The Spirit of Protest in Old French Literature*, Columbia, 1916

Vacandard, E., *The Inquisition*, Longmans, 1908

Warner, H., *The Albigensian Heresy*, Macmillan, 1922

Sources:

Coulton, G. G., *Life in the Middle Ages*, Macmillan, 1930, Vols. I, IV

——, *From St. Francis to Dante*, Nutt, 1907

St. Francis of Assisi, *The Writings of St. Francis of Assisi*, Paschal Robinson (trans.), Dent, 1906

The Little Flowers, and the Life of St. Francis, with the Mirror of Perfection, Dent, 1910

The Lives of St. Francis of Assisi by Brother Thomas of Celano, A. G. F. Howell (trans.), Methuen, 1908

Translations and Reprints, Vol. II, No. 4; Vol. III, No. 6

CHAPTERS XXIII-XXIV: THE BIRTH OF MODERN NATIONS—ENGLAND, FRANCE, SPAIN

England:

Adams, G. B., *Constitutional History of England*, Holt, 1921

Baldwin, J. F., *The King's Council in England during the Middle Ages*, Oxford, 1913

Ballard, A., *The Domesday Inquest*, Methuen, 1906

Cambridge Medieval History, Vols. III, V, VI

Green, A. S., *Henry II*, Macmillan, 1888

Hunt, W., and Poole, R. L., *The Political History of England*, Longmans, 1906-   , Vols. I-IV

Lunt, W. E., *History of England*, Harper, 1928.

Larson, L. M., *Canute the Great*, Putnam's, 1912

McKechnie, W. S., *Magna Carta*, Macmillan, 1914

Morris, W. A., *The Medieval Sheriff to 1300*, Manchester, 1925

————, *The Constitutional History of England to 1216*, Macmillan, 1930

Pollard, A. F., *The Evolution of Parliament*, Longmans, 1920

Pollock, F., and Maitland, F. W., *The History of English Law before the Time of Edward I*, Cambridge, 1923, 2 vols.

Poole, R. L., *The Exchequer in the Twelfth Century*, Oxford, 1912

Powicke, F. M., *The Loss of Normandy*, Manchester, 1913

Stenton, F. M., *The First Century of English Feudalism, 1066-1166*, Oxford, 1932

————, *William the Conqueror*, Putnam's, 1908

Trevelyan, G. M., *History of England*, Longmans, 1926

White, A. B., *The Making of the English Constitution*, Putnam's, 1925

France:

Cambridge Medieval History, Vols. III, V, VI

Haskins, C. H., *Normans in European History*, Houghton Mifflin, 1915

————, *Norman Institutions*, Harvard, 1918

Hutton, W. H., *Philip Augustus*, Macmillan, 1896

Kitchin, G. W., *History of France*, Oxford, Vol. I

Luchaire, A., *Social France at the Time of Philip Augustus*, Holt, 1929

MacDonald, J. R. M., *History of France*, Methuen, 1915, Vol. I

Perry, F., *St. Louis*, Putnam's, 1901

Tilley, A. A., *Mediæval France*, Cambridge, 1922

Spain:

Burke, U. R., *A History of Spain from the Earliest Times to the Death of Ferdinand the Catholic*, Longmans, 1894-5, 2 vols.

Cambridge Medieval History, Vols. III, VI

Chapman, C. E., *A History of Spain*, Macmillan, 1922

Hume, M. A. S., *The Spanish People*, Heineman, 1901

Merriman, R. B., *The Rise of the Spanish Empire in the Old World and the New*, Macmillan, 1918-   , Vols. I-II

Scott, S. P., *History of the Moorish Empire in Europe*, Lippincott, 1904, 3 vols.

Whishaw, B. and E., *Arabic Spain*, Murray, 1912

CHAPTERS XXV-XXVI: THE CRUSADES AND THE EXPANSION OF EUROPE

Archer, T. A., and Kingsford, C. L., *The Crusades,* Putnam's, 1895

Cambridge Medieval History, Vols. IV-V

Guilford, E. L., *Travellers and Travelling in the Middle Ages,* Macmillan, 1924

Heath, S., *Pilgrim Life in the Middle Ages,* Unwin, 1912

La Monte, J., *Feudal Monarchy in the Latin Kingdom of Jerusalem,* Medieval Academy, 1932

Lamb, H., *The Crusades,* Doubleday, Doran, 1931

Newhall, R. A., *The Crusades,* Holt, 1927

Oman, C. W. C., *The Art of War in the Middle Ages,* Houghton Mifflin, 1924

Paetow, L. J. (ed.), *The Crusades and Other Historical Essays Presented to Dana C. Munro,* Crofts, 1928

Pears, E., *The Fall of Constantinople: Being the Story of the Fourth Crusade,* Longmans, 1885

Stevenson, W. B., *The Crusaders in the East,* Cambridge, 1907

Woodhouse, F. C., *The Military Religious Orders,* Pott, Young, 1879

Yewdale, R. B., *Bohemond I, Prince of Antioch,* Princeton, 1924

Sources:

An Arab-Syrian Gentleman and Warrior in the Period of the Crusades, P. K. Hitti (trans.), Columbia, 1929

Archer, T. A., *The Crusade of Richard I,* Putnam's, 1889

David, C. W., *De Expugnatione Lyxbonensi (The Conquest of Lisbon),* in *Records of Civilization,* Columbia, 1936

Dawes, E. A. S., *The Alexiad,* Paul, Trench, Trubner, 1928

Duncalf, F., and Krey, A. C., *Parallel Source Problems in Medieval History* (The Capture of Jerusalem in 1099), Harper, 1912

Joinville, *Chronicle of the Crusade of St. Louis,* in *Memoirs of the Crusades,* Dutton, 1908

Krey, A. C., *The First Crusade: The Accounts of Eyewitnesses and Participants,* Princeton, 1921

MacNeal, E. H., *The Conquest of Constantinople, from the Old French of Robert of Clari,* in *Records of Civilization,* Columbia, 1936

Richard of Devizes and Geoffrey de Vinsauf, *Chronicles of the Crusades . . . of Richard Cœur de Lion,* Bohn, 1848

Translations and Reprints, Vol. I, Nos. 2 and 4; Vol. III, No. 1

Villehardouin, *Chronicle of the Fourth Crusade and the Conquest of Constantinople,* in *Memoirs of the Crusades,* Dutton, 1908

CHAPTER XXVII: THE ECONOMIC EXPANSION OF WESTERN EUROPE

Abrahams, I., "Jewish Life in the Middle Ages," *Jewish Publication Society,*
    1896
Ashley, W. J., *The Economic Organization of England,* Longmans, 1914,
    Chaps. III-IV
Beazley, C. R., *The Dawn of Modern Geography,* Oxford, 1905-6, 3 vols.
Byrne, E. H., *Genoese Shipping,* Medieval Academy, 1930
Cambridge Medieval History, Vol. VI, Chaps. XIV-XV; Vol. VII, Chap.
    XXIV
Cambridge Modern History, Cambridge, 1902, Vol. I, Chaps. I, XV
Carlile, W. W., *The Evolution of Modern Money,* Macmillan, 1901
Cheyney, E. P., *The European Background of American History, 1300-
    1600,* Harper, 1904, Chap. I ff.
————, *Introduction to the Industrial and Social History of England,* Mac-
    millan, 1920
Cunningham, W., *The Growth of English Industry and Commerce in
    Modern Times,* Cambridge, 1917
Day, C., *History of Commerce,* Longmans, 1907
Ehrenberg, R., *Capital and Finance in the Age of the Renaissance,* Cape,
    1928
Gillespie, J. E., *A History of Geographical Discovery, 1400-1800,* Holt, 1933
Gras, N. S. B., *An Introduction to Economic History,* Harper, 1922
Grayzel, S., *The Church and the Jews in the XIIIth Century,* Dropsie Col-
    lege, 1933
Grosclose, E., *Money: The Human Conflict,* Oklahoma, 1934
Gudde, E. F., *Social Conflicts in Medieval German Poetry,* California, 1933
Jacobs, J., "Jewish Contributions to Civilization," *Jewish Publication So-
    ciety,* 1919
Lane, F. C., *Venetian Ships and Shipbuilders,* Johns Hopkins, 1934
Meigs, J. F., *The Story of the Seaman,* Lippincott, 1924, 2 vols.
Mohl, R., *The Three Estates in Medieval and Renaissance Literature,* Co-
    lumbia, 1933
Newton, A. P., *The Great Age of Discovery,* University of London, 1932
Nussbaum, F. L., *History of the Economic Institutions of Modern Europe,*
    Crofts, 1933
Packard, L. B., *The Commercial Revolution, 1400-1776,* Holt, 1927
Petit-Dutaillis, C. E., *Studies and Notes Supplementary to Stubbs' Consti-
    tutional History,* W. E. Rhodes (trans.), Longmans, 1914
Piotrowski, R., *Cartels and Trusts,* Unwin, 1933
Pirenne, H., *Economic and Social History of Medieval Europe,* Harcourt,
    Brace, 1937
Power, E. E., *Medieval People,* Houghton Mifflin, 1924

Sanborn, F. R., *Origins of the Early English Maritime and Commercial Law*, Appleton-Century, 1930

Thompson, J. W., *Economic and Social History of the Middle Ages*, Appleton-Century, 1928, Chaps. XVII ff., especially XX, XXIII, XXVIII

———, *An Economic and Social History of Europe in the Later Middle Ages*, Appleton-Century, 1931

Sources:

Bland, A. E., Brown, P. A., and Tawney, R. H., *English Economic History: Select Documents*, Harcourt, Brace, 1915

Cheyney, E. P., *Readings in English History*, Ginn, 1922

Marco Polo, *Travels*, Liveright, 1926

Yule, H., *The Book of Ser Marco Polo*, Murray, 1903

CHAPTER XXVIII: THE PAPACY IN THE LATE MIDDLE AGES

Boase, T. S., *Boniface VIII*, Constable, 1933

Cambridge Medieval History, Vols. VI-VIII

Coulton, G. G., *Five Centuries of Religion*, Cambridge, 1929, 3 vols.

Carlyle, R. W. and A. J., *A History of Medieval Political Theory in the West*, Blackwood, 1903-6

Deanesly, M., *History of the Medieval Church*, Methuen, 1925

Dunning, W., *History of Political Theories*, Macmillan, 1928

Figgis, J. N., *Studies of Political Thought from Gerson to Grotius*, Cambridge, 1907

Flick, A., *The Decline of the Medieval Church*, Paul, Trench, Trubner, 1930

Hearnshaw, F. J., *Social and Political Ideas of Some Great Medieval Thinkers*, Harrap, 1923

Kitts, E. J., *Pope John XXIII and Master John Hus of Bohemia*, Constable, 1910

———, *In the Days of the Councils*, Constable, 1908

Lucas, H. S., *The Renaissance and the Reformation*, Harper, 1934

Lunt, W., *Papal Revenues in the Middle Ages*, Columbia, 1934, 2 vols.

Lutzow, Count, *The Life and Times of Master John Hus*, Dent, 1909

Mann, H. K., *The Lives of the Popes in the Early Middle Ages*, Paul, Trench, Trubner, 1932

McIlwain, C. H., *The Growth of Political Thought in the West*, Macmillan, 1932

Poole, R. L., *Wycliffe and the Movements for Reform*, Randolph, 1889

Salembier, L., *The Great Schism of the West*, Paul, Trench, Trubner, 1907

Schaff, D. S., *John Huss*, Scribner's, 1915

Smith, A. L., *Church and State in the Middle Ages,* Oxford, 1913
Trevelyan, G. M., *England in the Age of Wycliffe,* Longmans, 1904
Waugh, W. T., *A History of Europe from 1378-1494,* Methuen, 1932
Wylie, J. H., *The Council of Constance,* Longmans, 1900

Sources:

See the source references on Learning and Literature, listed below.

CHAPTER XXIX: ENGLAND AND FRANCE IN THE LATE MIDDLE AGES

Bridge, J. S., *A History of France from the Death of Louis XI,* Oxford,
    1921
Cambridge Medieval History, Vols. VII-VIII
Cambridge Modern History, Vol. I
Cheyney, E. P., *The Dawn of a New Era,* Harper, 1936
Coulton, G. G., *Chaucer and His England,* Methuen, 1908
Gray, H. L., *The Influence of the Commons on Early Legislation,* Har-
    vard, 1932
Kitchin, G. W., *History of France,* Oxford, Vol. I
Lucas, H., *The Low Countries and the Hundred Years' War,* Michigan,
    1929
Lunt, W., *History of England,* Harper, 1928
MacDonald, J. R. M., *History of France,* Methuen, 1915, Vol. I
McIlwain, C. H., *The Growth of Political Thought in the West,* Macmil-
    lan, 1932
Mowat, R. B., *The Later Middle Ages* (1254-1494), Oxford, 1917
Paine, A. B., *Joan of Arc,* Macmillan, 1925
Pasquet, D., *The Origins of the House of Commons,* Cambridge, 1925
Pickthorn, K., *Early Tudor Governments, Henry VII,* Cambridge, 1934
Pollard, A. F., *The Evolution of Parliament,* Longmans, 1926
Ramsay, J. R., *The Revenues of the Kings of England,* Oxford, 1925, 2
    vols.
Trevelyan, G. M., *History of England,* Longmans, 1926
——, *England in the Age of Wycliffe,* Longmans, 1904
Vickers, K., *England in the Later Middle Ages,* Methuen, 1913
Waugh, W. T., *A History of Europe from 1378 to 1494,* Putnam, 1932

Sources:

See the source references on Learning and Literature, listed below.

CHAPTERS XXX-XXXI: THE GERMANIES AND ITALIES IN THE LATE MIDDLE AGES

General Accounts:

Cambridge Medieval History, Vols. VI-VIII
Cambridge Modern History, Vol. I
Cheyney, E. P., *The Dawn of a New Era,* Harper, 1936
Lodge, R., *The Close of the Middle Ages,* Macmillan, 1906
Lucas, H. S., *The Renaissance and the Reformation,* Harper, 1934
Waugh, W. T., *A History of Europe from 1378-1494,* Putnam's, 1932

Germany:

Bryce, James, *The Holy Roman Empire,* Macmillan, Rev. Ed., 1923
Henderson, E. F., *A Short History of Germany,* Vol. I, Macmillan, 1920
King, W., *Chronicles of Three Free Cities: Hamburg, Bremen, and Lübeck,* Dutton, 1914
McCrackan, W. D., *The Rise of the Swiss Republic,* Holt, 1901
Nowack, F., *Medieval Slavdom and the Rise of Russia,* Holt, 1930
Schevill, F., *History of the Balkan Peninsula,* Harcourt, Brace, 1922
Zimmern, H., *The Hansa Towns,* Putnam's, 1889

Italy:

Ady, C. M., *A History of Milan under the Sforzas,* Methuen, 1907
Armstrong, E., *Lorenzo de' Medici,* Putnam's, 1927
Brinton, S., *The Golden Age of the Medici,* Methuen, 1925
Browning, O., *Guelfs and Ghibellines (1250-1409),* Methuen, 1893
———, *The Age of the Condottieri (1409-1530),* Methuen, 1895
Butler, W. F., *The Lombard Communes,* Unwin, 1906
Duffy, B., *The Tuscan Republics, Florence, Pisa, Lucca,* Putnam's, 1893
Ewart, K. D., *Cosimo de' Medici,* Macmillan, 1899
Hazlitt, W. C., *The Venetian Republic,* Smith and Elder, 1860
Heywood, W., *A History of Pisa,* Cambridge, 1921
Miller, W., *Medieval Rome (1073-1600),* Putnam's, 1902
Muir, D., *A History of Milan under the Visconti,* Methuen, 1924
Portigliotti, G., *The Borgias,* Knopf, 1928
Schevill, F., *The History of Florence,* Harcourt, Brace, 1936
———, *Siena: The Story of a Medieval Commune,* Scribner's, 1909
Villari, P., *The Life and Times of Girolamo Savonarola,* Unwin, 1888
———, *The Life and Times of Niccolo Machiavelli,* Unwin, 1898
Wiel, A. J., *Venice,* Putnam's, 1904
Woodward, W., *Cesare Borgia,* Dutton, 1914
Young, G. F., *The Medici,* Murray, 1909

Sources:

See the source references on Learning and Literature, listed below.

Chapters XXXII-XXXIII: Learning and Literature in the Late Middle Ages (1000-1500)

Adams, H., *Mont-Saint-Michel and Chartres*, Houghton Mifflin, 1913

Allen, P. S., and Jones, H. M., *The Romanesque Lyric*, North Carolina, 1928

Burckhardt, J., *The Civilization of the Renaissance in Italy*, Harrap, 1929

Cambridge Medieval History, Vols. V-VIII

Cambridge Modern History, Vol. I

Carter, T. F., *The Invention of Printing in China and Its Spread Westward*, Columbia, 1925

Chubb, T. C., *The Life of Giovanni Boccaccio*, Liveright, 1930

Dampier, W. C., *A History of Science*, Macmillan, 1930

de Wulf, M., *History of Mediæval Philosophy*, Macmillan, 1926, 2 vols.

——, *Philosophy and Civilization in the Middle Ages*, Princeton, 1922

Dunning, W. A., *History of Political Theories*, Macmillan, 1920

Grabmann, M., *Thomas Aquinas*, Longmans, 1928

Graves, F. P., *History of Education During the Middle Ages*, Macmillan, 1910

Hart, I., *Makers of Science: Mathematics, Physics, Astronomy*, Oxford, 1924

Haskins, C. H., *Studies in the History of Medieval Science*, Harvard, 1924

——, *Studies in Medieval Culture*, Oxford, 1929

——, *The Renaissance of the Twelfth Century*, Harvard, 1927

——, *The Rise of the Universities*, Holt, 1923

Hearnshaw, F. J., *The Social and Political Ideas of Some Great Medieval Thinkers*, Brentano, 1923

Höffding, H., *History of Modern Philosophy*, Macmillan, 1908, Vol. I

Huizinga, J., *The Waning of the Middle Ages*, Arnold, 1924

Hutton, E., *Giovanni Boccaccio*, Lane, 1910

Jusserand, J. J., *Piers Plowman*, Putnam's, 1894

McCabe, J., *Peter Abelard*, Putnam's, 1901

O'Leary, D. E., *Arabic Thought and Its Place in History*, Dutton, 1920

Paetow, L. J., *The Arts Course in the Medieval Universities*, Illinois, 1910

Putnam, G., *Books and Their Makers during the Middle Ages*, Putnam's, 1896-7, 2 vols.

Rashdall, H., *The Universities of Europe in the Middle Ages*, Oxford, 1936, 2 vols.

Riesmann, D., *The Story of Medicine in the Middle Ages*, Hoeber, 1935

Robinson, J. H., and Rolfe, H. W., *Petrarch, the First Modern Man of Letters*, Putnam's, 1914

Rossetti, D. G., *Dante and His Circle*, Little, 1905

Singer, C. (ed.), *Studies in the History and Method of Science*, Oxford, 1917, 2 vols.

Smith, P., *A History of Modern Culture*, Holt, 1930-4, Vol. I

Steele, R. R., *Medieval Lore*, Oxford, 1924

Symonds, J. A., *The Renaissance in Italy*, Murray, 1923, 7 vols.

Tattham, E., *Francesco Petrarca*, Macmillan, 1926, 2 vols.

Thompson, J. W., and others, *The Civilization of the Renaissance*, Chicago, 1929

Thorndike, L., *History of Magic and Experimental Science*, Macmillan, 1923, Vols. II-IV

Usher, A. P., *A History of Mechanical Inventions*, McGraw-Hill, 1929

Vossler, K., *Medieval Culture*, Constable, 1929, 2 vols.

Waddell, *The Wandering Scholars: Peter Abelard*, Holt, 1933

Sources:

Most of the outstanding works of the period are to be found in English translations. Everyman's Library (Dutton) contains the following:

Anglo-Saxon Chronicle; Arthurian Tales; Aucassin and Nicolette; Boccaccio, *The Decameron;* Cellini, *Autobiography;* Chaucer, *Canterbury Tales;* Dante, *The Divine Comedy; The Fall of the Nibelungs;* Froissart, *Chronicles; High History of the Holy Grail;* Langland, *Piers Plowman;* Machiavelli, *History of Florence, The Prince;* Marco Polo, *Travels;* St. Francis, *The Little Flowers;* Villehardouin and Joinville, *Memoirs of the Crusades.* The Riverside Literature Series (Houghton Mifflin) has Beowulf, Chaucer, Malory's *Morte d'Arthur,* the *Nibelungenlied,* and the *Song of Roland.* The Modern Library has Cellini, Boccaccio, and François Villon. Columbia University Records of Civilization has the *Correspondence of Gregory VII,* and Otto of Freising, *Two Cities.* Commines' *Mémoires* are to be found in the Bohn Library. Petrarch's *Love Songs* are published by Oxford (1915), his *Sonnets, Triumphs, and Other Poems* by Bell (1912) and his *Letters to Classical Authors,* by the University of Chicago (1910).

CHAPTERS XXXIV-XXXV: THE ARTS IN THE LATE MIDDLE AGES

Berenson, B., *The Italian Painters of the Renaissance*, Oxford, 1930

Cambridge Medieval History, Vols. VII-VIII

Cambridge Modern History, Vol. I

Chase, G. H., and Post, C. R., *History of Sculpture*, Harper, 1924

Faure, E., *History of Art*, Harper, 1921-30, Vols. II-V

Gardner, A., *Medieval Sculpture in France*, Cambridge, 1931

Jackson, T. G., *Gothic Architecture in France, England, and Italy*, Chicago, 1915

Jackson, T. G., *The Renaissance of Roman Architecture,* Cambridge, 1921
Kimball, F., and Edgell, G., *A History of Architecture,* Harper, 1918
Mather, F. J., *A History of Italian Painting,* Holt, 1923
Porter, A. K., *Medieval Architecture,* Baker and Taylor, 1909
Rooses, M., *Art in Flanders,* Scribner's, 1927
Symonds, J. A., *The Renaissance in Italy: The Fine Arts,* Scribner's
Vasari, G., *Lives of the Painters, Sculptors, and Architects,* Dutton, 1927,
    4 vols.
Waugh, W. T., *A History of Europe from 1378 to 1494,* Methuen, 1932
Wölfflin, H., *The Art of the Italian Renaissance,* Putnam's, 1913

Music:
Dickinson, Edward, *Music in the History of the Western Church,* Scrib-
    ner's, 1925
Gray, C., *History of Music,* Knopf, 1928
Oxford History of Music, Vols. I-II

INDEX